SEVENTH EDITION

Financial Institutions and Markets

Jeff Madura

Florida Atlantic University

THOMSON
™
SOUTH-WESTERN

Australia · Canada · Mexico · Singapore · Spain · United Kingdom · United States

THOMSON
SOUTH-WESTERN

Financial Institutions and Markets, 7e
Jeff Madura

VP/Editorial Director
Jack W. Calhoun

VP/Editor-in-Chief
Dave Shaut

Executive Editor
Michael R. Reynolds

Senior Developmental Editor
Trish Taylor

Marketing Manager
Heather MacMaster

Production Editor
Amy McGuire

Manager of Technology, Editorial
Vicky True

Technology Project Editor
John Barans

Web Coordinator
Karen Schaffer

Sr. Manufacturing Coordinator
Sandee Milewski

Production House
G&S Book Services

Printer
China Translation & Printing
Services, Ltd.

Art Director
Chris Miller

Internal Designer
Ramsdell Design

Cover Designer
Ramsdell Design

Cover Image
© Getty Images

ASIA (including India)
Thomson Learning
5 Shenton Way
#01-01 UIC Building
Singapore 068808

CANADA
Thomson Nelson
1120 Birchmount Road
Toronto, Ontario
Canada M1K 5G4

AUSTRALIA/NEW ZEALAND
Thomson Learning Australia
102 Dodds Street
Southbank, Victoria 3006
Australia

UK/EUROPE/MIDDLE
EAST/AFRICA
Thomson Learning
High Holborn House
50-51 Bedford Road
London WC1R 4LR
United Kingdom

LATIN AMERICA
Thomson Learning
Seneca, 53
Colonia Polanco
11560 Mexico
D.F.Mexico

SPAIN (includes Portugal)
Thomson Paraninfo
Calle Magallanes, 25
28015 Madrid, Spain

Dedication

This text is dedicated to Best Friends Animal Sanctuary in Kanab, Utah, for its commitment to, compassion for, and care of more than 1,500 animals, many of which were previously homeless. Most of the royalties the author receives from this text will be invested in an estate that will ultimately be donated to Best Friends.

Brief Contents

Contents

Part III
Equity Markets   129

CHAPTER 6

Offering Stocks and Monitoring Investors   130

CHAPTER 7

Valuing Stocks and Assessing Risk   168

CHAPTER 16

Foreign Exchange Derivative Markets   461

APPENDIX 16A
Impact of the Asian Crisis on Foreign Exchange Markets and Other Financial Markets   489

APPENDIX 16B
Currency Option Pricing   499

Part VI
Commercial Banking   505

CHAPTER 17

Commercial Bank Operations   506

Part VII
Nonbank Operations   615

CHAPTER 21

Thrift Operations   616

CHAPTER 22

Consumer Finance Operations   643

CHAPTER 23

Mutual Fund Operations   655

Preface

Financial markets facilitate the flow of funds from individuals to finance investments by corporations, governments, and individuals. Financial institutions are the key players in financial markets because they serve as intermediaries that determine the flow of funds. *Financial Institutions and Markets* describes financial markets and the financial institutions that serve those investors and firms. It provides a conceptual framework that can be used to understand why markets exist. Each type of financial market is described, with a focus on the securities that are traded in that market and the participation by financial institutions.

Today, many financial institutions offer all types of financial services, such as banking, securities services, mutual fund services, and insurance services. Although financial institutions overlap in the services they offer, the services that can be offered are distinctly different. Therefore, the discussion of financial services in this book is organized by type of service rather than institution type.

Intended Market

This text is suitable for both undergraduate- and master's-level courses in financial markets, financial institutions, or both. To maximize students' comprehension, more difficult questions and problems should be assigned, along with the special applications at the end of each chapter and the Comprehensive Project.

Organization of the Text

This text is organized as follows: Part I (Chapters 1 through 3) introduces the key financial markets and financial institutions, describes interest rate movements in the financial markets, and explains why yields vary among securities. Part II (Chapters 4 and 5) describes the functions of the Federal Reserve System (the Fed) and explains how its monetary policy influences interest rates and other economic conditions. Part III (Chapters 6 through 8) describes equity securities markets, Part IV (Chapters 9 through 12) covers the major debt security markets, and Part V (Chapters 13 through 16) covers the derivative security markets. Each chapter in Parts III through V focuses on a particular market. The integration of each market with other markets is stressed throughout these chapters. Part VI (Chapters 17 through 20) concentrates on commercial banking, and Part VII (Chapters 21 through 25) covers all other types of financial services.

Courses that emphasize financial markets should focus on the first five parts (Chapters 1 through 16); however, some chapters in the section on commercial banking are

also relevant. Courses that emphasize financial institutions and financial services should focus on Parts I, II, VI, and VII, although some background on securities markets (Parts III, IV, and V) may be helpful.

Finally, instructors of courses that emphasize financial markets and institutions may wish to focus on certain chapters of this book and skip others, depending on other courses available to their students. For example, if a course on derivative securities is commonly offered, Part V of this text may be ignored. Alternatively, if an available investments course provides a thorough background on types of securities, Parts III and IV can be given limited attention. Or, instructors may prefer to use most of their class time on chapters that contain the most difficult concepts and allow students to read the more descriptive chapters on their own.

Chapters can be rearranged without a loss in continuity. Regardless of the order in which chapters are studied, it is highly recommended that the special exercises and selected questions in each chapter be assigned. These exercises may serve as a focal point for class discussion.

Coverage of Major Concepts and Events

Numerous concepts relating to recent events and current trends in financial markets are discussed throughout the chapters, including the following:

- Governance in financial markets
- Impact of the Sarbanes-Oxley Act on financial markets
- Role of specialists
- The Fed's impact on financial markets
- Online investment in securities
- Role of analysts
- Value-at-risk measurements
- Asymmetric information
- Emerging stock markets
- Option pricing
- Valuation of financial institutions
- Regulatory reform in financial services
- Mutual fund trading scandals
- Modified duration
- Interest rate swaps and currency swaps
- Collateralized mortgage obligations (CMOs)
- Portfolio insurance strategies

Because each chapter is self-contained, instructors can use classroom time to focus on the more complex concepts and rely on the text to cover the other concepts.

Major Organization Changes

Three chapters have been eliminated, as the main material from these chapters was incorporated into other related chapters. The chapter on international banking has been incorporated into the commercial banking chapters where appropriate. The chapter on pension fund operations has been integrated with the chapter on insurance company operations. The chapter on credit unions has been combined with the chapter on thrift operations.

Major Content Changes

New coverage on asymmetric information and the link between financial reporting and security values has been added. The impact of the Sarbanes-Oxley Act on market transparency and the pricing of securities is given heavy emphasis. Information on electronic trading in various financial markets has been expanded. New coverage has been added on trading halts, spreads, extended trading sessions, bank structure, and single stock futures. Revisions to the Basel Accord and to regulations that have an impact on securities firms have also been updated. Expanded coverage explains how the yield curve structure applies to various types of securities. The concept of modified duration is given more attention. Updates are provided on scandals involving analysts, specialists, and mutual funds.

More illustrations have been added throughout the text to provide examples and applications of concepts.

Features of the Text

The features of the text are as follows:

- *Part-Opening Diagram.* A diagram is provided at the beginning of each part to illustrate generally how the key concepts in that part are related. This offers information about the organization of chapters in that part.
- *Objectives.* A bulleted list at the beginning of each chapter identifies the key concepts in that chapter.
- *Illustrations.* Illustrations are provided to reinforce key concepts.
- *Global Aspects.* Global Aspects icons in the margins throughout the text indicate international coverage of the chapter topics being discussed.
- *Summary.* A bulleted list at the end of each chapter summarizes the key concepts. This list corresponds to the list of objectives at the beginning of the chapter.
- *Point/Counter-Point.* A controversial issue is introduced, along with opposing arguments, and students are asked to determine which argument is correct and explain why.
- *Questions and Applications.* The questions and applications section at the end of each chapter tests students' understanding of the key concepts and may serve as homework assignments or study aids in preparation for exams.
- *Flow of Funds Exercise.* A running exercise is provided at the end of each chapter to illustrate how a manufacturing company relies on all types of financial markets and financial services provided by financial institutions.
- *Interpreting Financial News.* At the end of each chapter, students are challenged to interpret comments made in the media about the chapter's key concepts. This gives students practice in interpreting announcements by the financial media.
- *Internet Exercises.* At the end of each chapter, students are challenged to use the Internet to access financial information and resolve issues related to the chapter discussion.
- *Problems.* Selected chapters include problems to test students' computational skills.
- *WSJ Exercise.* At the end of selected chapters, this end-of-chapter exercise allows students to apply information provided in *The Wall Street Journal* to specific concepts explained in that chapter.
- *Integrative Problem.* An integrative problem at the end of each part integrates the key concepts of chapters within that part.

■ *Comprehensive Project.* This project, found in Appendix A, requires students to apply real data to several key concepts described throughout the book.

The concepts in each chapter can be reinforced using one or more of the preceding features. Each instructor will have his or her own method for helping students get the most out of the text. Each instructor's use of the features will vary depending on the students' level and the focus of the course. A course that focuses mostly on financial markets may emphasize tools such as the WSJ exercises and Part I of the Comprehensive Project (on taking positions in securities and derivative instruments). Conversely, a course that focuses on financial institutions may emphasize, for example, an exercise in which students have to review recent annual reports (see Part II of the Comprehensive Project) to fully understand how a particular financial institution's performance is affected by its policies, industry regulations, and economic conditions.

Supplements to the Text

The following supplements are available:

■ A **PowerPoint** presentation package of lecture slides, revised and expanded by Oliver Schnusenberg of the University of North Florida, is available at http://aise.swlearning.com.

■ An **Instructor's Manual** contains the chapter outline and a summary of key concepts for discussion as well as answers to the end-of-chapter Questions and Problems. The instructor's manual is also available to instructors at http://aise.swlearning.com.

■ The **Test Bank** has been revised and expanded with new multiple-choice questions and is available at http://aise.swlearning.com.

■ The **ExamView**™ computerized testing program, also available at http://aise.swlearning.com, contains all of the questions in the printed test bank. It is an easy-to-use test creation software package compatible with Microsoft Windows. Instructors can add or edit questions, instructions, and answers, and select questions at random or by number after previewing them on the screen. Instructors can also create and administer quizzes online, whether over a LAN, a WAN, or the Internet.

Acknowledgments

The motivation to write this textbook came primarily from the encouragement of E. Joe Nosari (Florida State University). Several professors helped develop the text outline and offered suggestions on which of the concepts from earlier editions of this book should be covered in this edition. They are acknowledged in alphabetical order: Ibrihim Affaneh, Indiana University of Pennsylvania; Henry C. F. Arnold, Seton Hall University; James C. Baker, Kent State University; Gerald Bierwag, Florida International University; Carol Billingham, Central Michigan University; Randy Billingsley, Virginia Tech University; Rita M. Biswas, State University of New York at Albany; Howard W. Bohnen, St. Cloud State University; Paul J. Bolster, Northeastern University; M. E. Bond, University of Memphis; Stephen Borde, University of Central Florida; Emile J. Brinkman, University of Houston–University Park; Sarah Bryant, George Washington University; James B. Burnham, Duquesne University; William Carner, University of Missouri–Columbia; Joseph Cheng, Ithaca College; William T. Chittenden, Northern Illinois University;

C. Steven Cole, University of North Texas; M. Cary Collins, University of Tennessee; Mark Correll, University of Colorado; Wayne C. Curtis, Troy State University; Steven Dobson, California Polytechnic State University; Robert M. Donchez, University of Colorado–Boulder; Richard J. Dowen, Northern Illinois University; James Felton, Central Michigan University; Stuart Fletcher, Appalachian State University; Clifford L. Fry, University of Houston; Edward K. Gill, California State University–Chico; Claire G. Gilmore, St. Joseph's University; Owen Gregory, University of Illinois–Chicago; Paul Grier, SUNY–Binghamton; Ann Hackert, Idaho State University; John Halloran, University of Notre Dame; Gerald A. Hanweck, George Mason University; Joel Harper, Oklahoma State University; Hildegard R. Hendrickson, Seattle University; Jerry M. Hood, Loyola University–New Orleans; Ronald M. Horowitz, Oakland University; Paul Hsueh, University of Central Florida; Carl D. Hudson, Auburn University; John S. Jahera Jr., Auburn University; Mel Jameson, University of Nevada; Ken Johnson, Auburn University at Montgomery; Shane Johnson, Bowling Green State University; Jarrod Johnston, University of Minnesota–Duluth; Victor Kalafa, Cross Country Staffing; Richard H. Keehn, University of Wisconsin–Parkside; James B. Kehr, Miami University of Ohio; James W. Kolari, Texas A&M University; George Kutner, Marquette University; Robert Lamy, Wake Forest University; Stephen Larson, Eastern Illinois University; David J. Leahigh, King's College; David N. Leggett, Bentley College; Morgan Lynge Jr., University of Illinois; Judy E. Maese, New Mexico State University; Timothy A. Manuel, University of Montana; Joseph S. Mascia, Adelphi University; Robert W. McLeod, University of Alabama; Kathleen S. McNichol, LaSalle University; James McNulty, Florida Atlantic University; Charles Meiburg, University of Virginia; Jose Mercado-Mendez, Central Missouri State University; Neil Murphy, Virginia Commonwealth University; Dale Osborne, University of Texas–Dallas; Coleen Pantalone, Northeastern University; Thomas H. Payne, University of Tennessee–Chattanooga; Sarah Peck, University of Iowa; D. Anthony Plath, University of North Carolina–Charlotte; Rose Prasad, Central Michigan University; Alan Reichert, Cleveland State University; Kenneth L. Rhoda, LaSalle University; Lawrence C. Rose, Massey University; Jack Rubens, Bryant College; Oliver Schnusenberg, University of North Florida; Robert Schweitzer, University of Delaware; Ahmad Sorhabian, California State Polytechnic University–Pomona; S. R. Stansell, East Carolina University; Michael Suerth; Richard S. Swasey, Northeastern University; Olaf J. Thorp, Babson College; James D. Tripp, University of Tennessee–Martin; K. C. Tseng, California State University–Fresno; Alan Tucker, Pace University; Harry J. Turtle, University of Manitoba; Geraldo M. Vasconcellos, Lehigh University; Michael C. Walker, University of Cincinnati; David A. Whidbee, Washington State University; Colin Young, Bentley College; and Stephen Zera, California State University–San Marcos.

Other colleagues who offered new suggestions for clarification include Kevin Ahlgrim, Illinois State University; Mike Bond, Cleveland State University; Zane Dennick-Ream, Robert Morris University; Osman Kilic, Quinnipiac University; Kartono Liano, Mississippi State University; Cheryl McGaughey, Angelo State University; Robert McLeod, University of Alabama; and John Thornton, Kent State University.

This text also benefited from the research departments of several Federal Reserve district banks, the Federal National Mortgage Association, the National Credit Union Administration, the U.S. League of Savings Institutions, the American Council of Life Insurance, the Investment Company Institute, and the Chicago Mercantile Exchange.

I acknowledge the help and support from the people at South-Western, including Mike Reynolds (Executive Editor) and Trish Taylor (Senior Developmental Editor). Special thanks are due to Amy McGuire (Production Editor) and Pat Lewis (Copyeditor) for their efforts to ensure a quality final product.

Finally, I wish to thank my parents, Arthur and Irene Madura, and my wife, Mary, for their moral support.

About the Author

Jeff Madura is the SunTrust Bank Professor of Finance at Florida Atlantic University. He has written several textbooks, including *International Financial Management*. His research on banking and financial markets has been published in numerous journals, including *Journal of Financial and Quantitative Analysis; Journal of Money, Credit and Banking; Journal of Banking and Finance; Financial Review; Journal of Risk and Insurance; Journal of Financial Research;* and *Journal of Financial Services Research*. He has received awards for excellence in teaching and research and has served as a consultant for commercial banks, securities firms, and other corporations. He has served as a director for the Southern Finance Association and Eastern Finance Association and has been president of the Southern Finance Association.

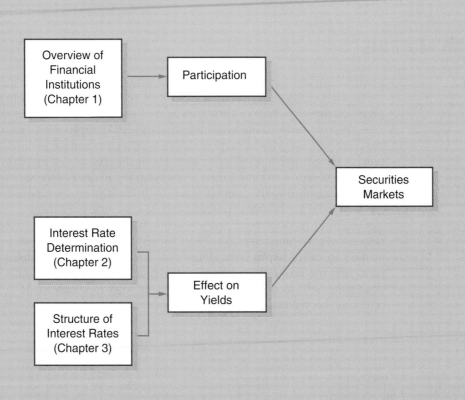

PART I

The U.S. Financial Environment

Part I focuses on the flow of funds across financial markets, interest rates, and security prices. Chapter 1 introduces the key financial markets and the financial institutions that participate in those markets. Chapter 2 explains how various factors influence interest rates and how interest rate movements in turn affect the values of securities purchased by financial institutions. Chapter 3 identifies factors other than interest rates that influence security prices. Participants in financial markets use this information to value securities and make investment decisions within financial markets.

Overview of Financial Institutions (Chapter 1) → Participation

Interest Rate Determination (Chapter 2)

Structure of Interest Rates (Chapter 3)

Effect on Yields

Securities Markets

Financial Markets and Institutions

A **financial market** is a market in which financial assets (securities) such as stocks and bonds can be purchased or sold. Funds are transferred in financial markets when one party purchases financial assets previously held by another party. Financial markets facilitate the flow of funds and thereby allow financing and investing by households, firms, and government agencies. This chapter provides a background on financial markets and the financial institutions that participate in them.

The specific objectives of this chapter are to:

- describe the types of financial markets that accommodate various transactions,

- introduce the concept of security valuation within financial markets,

- describe the role of financial institutions within financial markets, and

- identify the types of financial institutions that facilitate transactions in financial markets.

Financial Markets

Financial markets transfer funds from those who have excess funds to those who need funds. They enable college students to obtain student loans, families to obtain mortgages, businesses to finance their growth, and governments to finance their expenditures. Without financial markets, many students could not go to college, many families could not purchase a home, corporations could not grow, and the government could not provide as many public services. Households and businesses that supply funds to financial markets earn a return on their investment; the return is necessary to ensure that funds are supplied to the financial markets. If funds were not supplied, the financial markets would not be able to transfer funds to those who need them.

The main participants in financial markets can be classified as households, businesses, and government agencies. Those participants who provide funds to the financial markets are called **surplus units.** Households are the main type of surplus unit. Participants who use financial markets to obtain funds are called **deficit units.** Many deficit units issue (sell) securities to surplus units in order to obtain funds. A security is a certificate that represents a claim on the issuer.

ILLUSTRATION
The U.S. Treasury relies heavily on the financial markets to obtain funds and thus serves as a major deficit unit. It issues Treasury securities in the financial markets, which are purchased by households and other surplus units. These securities are a form of debt. They specify a maturity date when the Treasury will repay the surplus units who are holding the securities. Some businesses also issue debt securities. Other businesses issue stocks, which allow investors to become part owners of the business.

Types of Financial Markets

Each financial market is created to satisfy particular preferences of market participants. For example, some participants may want to invest funds for a short-term period, whereas others want to invest for a long-term period. Some participants are willing to tolerate a high level of risk when investing, whereas others need to avoid risk. Some participants that need funds prefer to borrow, whereas others prefer to issue stock. There are many different types of financial markets, and each market can be distinguished by the maturity structure and trading structure of its securities.

Money versus Capital Markets The financial markets that facilitate the transfer of debt securities are commonly classified by the maturity of the securities. Those financial markets that facilitate the flow of short-term funds (with maturities of less than one year) are known as **money markets,** while those that facilitate the flow of long-term funds are known as **capital markets.**

Primary versus Secondary Markets Whether referring to money market securities or capital market securities, it is necessary to distinguish between transactions in the primary market and transactions in the secondary market. **Primary markets** facilitate the issuance of new securities, while **secondary markets** facilitate the trading of existing securities. Primary market transactions provide funds to the initial issuer of securities; secondary market transactions do not. The issuance of new corporate stock or new Treasury securities is a primary market transaction, while the sale of existing corporate stock or Treasury security holdings by any business or individual is a secondary market transaction.

An important characteristic of securities that are traded in secondary markets is **liquidity,** which is the degree to which securities can easily be liquidated (sold) without a loss of value. Some securities have an active secondary market, meaning that there are many willing buyers and sellers of the security at a given point in time. Investors prefer liquid securities so that they can easily sell the securities whenever they want (without a loss in value). If a security is illiquid, investors may not be able to find a willing buyer for it in the secondary market and may have to sell the security at a large discount just to attract a buyer.

Organized versus Over-the-Counter Markets Some secondary stock market transactions occur at an **organized exchange,** or a visible marketplace for secondary market transactions. The New York Stock Exchange and American Stock Exchange are organized exchanges for secondary stock market transactions. Other financial market transactions occur in the **over-the-counter (OTC) market,** which is a telecommunications network.

Knowledge of Financial Markets Is Power Knowledge of financial markets can enhance financial decisions. Financial market participants must decide which financial markets to use to achieve their investment goals or obtain needed financing.

http://

http://www.nyse.com
New York Stock Exchange market summary, quotes, financial statistics, and more.

http://www.nasdaq.com
Comprehensive historic and current data on all Nasdaq transactions.

Securities Traded in Financial Markets

Securities can be classified as money market securities, capital market securities, or derivative securities. Each type of security tends to have specific return and risk characteristics, as described in detail in the chapters covering financial markets. The term *risk* is used here to represent the uncertainty surrounding the expected return.

Money Market Securities

Money market securities are debt securities that have a maturity of one year or less. They generally have a relatively high degree of liquidity. Money market securities tend to have a low expected return but also a low degree of risk. Various types of money market securities are listed in the top section of Exhibit 1.1, and capital market securities are listed in the bottom section.

EXHIBIT 1.1 Summary of Popular Securities

Money Market Securities	Issued by	Common Investors	Common Maturities	Secondary Market Activity
Treasury bills	Federal government	Households, firms, and financial institutions	13 weeks, 26 weeks, 1 year	High
Retail certificates of deposit (CDs)	Banks and savings institutions	Households	7 days to 5 years or longer	Nonexistent
Negotiable certificates of deposit (NCDs)	Large banks and savings institutions	Firms	2 weeks to 1 year	Moderate
Commercial paper	Bank holding companies, finance companies, and other companies	Firms	1 day to 270 days	Low
Eurodollar deposits	Banks located outside the U.S.	Firms and governments	1 day to 1 year	Nonexistent
Banker's acceptances	Banks (exporting firms can sell the acceptances at a discount to obtain funds)	Firms	30 days to 270 days	High
Federal funds	Depository institutions	Depository institutions	1 day to 7 days	Nonexistent
Repurchase agreements	Firms and financial institutions	Firms and financial institutions	1 day to 15 days	Nonexistent
Capital Market Securities				
Treasury notes and bonds	Federal government	Households, firms, and financial institutions	3 to 30 years	High
Municipal bonds	State and local governments	Households and firms	10 to 30 years	Moderate
Corporate bonds	Firms	Households and firms	10 to 30 years	Moderate
Mortgages	Individuals and firms	Financial institutions	15 to 30 years	Moderate
Equity securities	Firms	Households and firms	No maturity	High (for stocks of large firms)

Capital Market Securities

Securities with a maturity of more than one year are called **capital market securities.** Three common types of capital market securities are bonds, mortgages, and stocks.

Bonds and Mortgages Bonds are long-term debt obligations issued by corporations and government agencies to support their operations. Mortgages are long-term debt obligations created to finance the purchase of real estate.

Bonds provide a return to investors in the form of interest income (coupon payments) every six months. Since bonds and mortgages represent debt, they specify the amount and timing of interest and principal payments to investors who purchase them. At maturity, investors holding the debt securities are paid the principal. Debt securities can be sold in the secondary market if investors do not want to hold them until maturity. Since the prices of debt securities can change over time, investors may be able to enhance their return by selling the securities for a higher price than they paid for them.

Some debt securities are risky because the issuer could default on its obligation to repay the debt. Under these circumstances, the debt security will not provide the entire amount of coupon payments and principal that was promised. Long-term debt securities tend to have a higher expected return than money market securities, but they have more risk as well.

Stocks Stocks (also referred to as equity securities) are certificates representing partial ownership in the corporations that issued them. They are classified as capital market securities because they have no maturity and therefore serve as a long-term source of funds. Some corporations provide income to their stockholders by distributing a portion of their quarterly earnings in the form of dividends. Other corporations retain and reinvest all of their earnings, which allows them more potential for growth.

Equity securities differ from debt securities in that they represent partial ownership. As corporations grow and increase in value, the value of the stock increases, and investors can earn a capital gain from selling the stock for a higher price than they paid for it. Thus, investors can earn a return from stocks in the form of periodic dividends (if there are any) and a capital gain when they sell the stock. However, investors can experience a negative return if the corporation performs poorly and its stock price declines over time as a result. Equity securities have a higher expected return than most long-term debt securities, but they also exhibit a higher degree of risk.

Derivative Securities

http://
http://www.cboe.com
Information about
derivative securities.

In addition to money market and capital market securities, derivative securities are also traded in financial markets. **Derivative securities** are financial contracts whose values are derived from the values of underlying assets (such as debt securities or equity securities). Many derivative securities enable investors to engage in speculation and risk management.

Speculation Derivative securities allow an investor to speculate on movements in the underlying assets without having to purchase those assets. Some derivative securities allow investors to benefit from an increase in the value of debt securities, while others allow investors to benefit from a decrease in the value of debt securities. Similarly,

investors can use different types of derivative securities to benefit from an increase or a decline in the value of equity securities. Since derivative securities allow investors to speculate on movements in underlying assets without purchasing the assets, they enable investors to take a large investment position without a large initial outlay and therefore to have a high degree of financial leverage. As a result of this financial leverage, the returns from investing in derivative securities are more pronounced than from simply investing in the underlying assets themselves. Investors who speculate in derivative contracts can achieve higher returns than if they had speculated in the underlying assets, but they are also exposed to higher risk.

Risk Management Derivative securities can be used in a manner that will generate gains if the value of the underlying assets declines. Consequently, financial institutions and other firms can use derivative securities to adjust the risk of their existing investments in securities. If a firm maintains investments in bonds, for example, it can take specific positions in derivative securities that will generate gains if bond values decline. In this way, derivative securities can be used to reduce a firm's risk. The loss on the bonds is offset by the gains on these derivative securities.

ILLUSTRATION   Exhibit 1.2 shows how derivative securities can be combined with an investment in securities to change the investor's return and risk characteristics. Weber Inc. invests in securities that reflect the particular return and risk levels represented by Point A. If Weber desires to increase its potential return, it can take a specific position in derivative securities that will enhance its returns if the securities it has invested in perform well. If those securities perform poorly, however, the position in derivative securities will magnify any losses that occur. Thus, this derivative position pushes the firm's return-risk characteristics to Point B on the exhibit. Alternatively, Weber can take the opposite position in derivative securities; if Weber's investment securities perform poorly, this derivative position will generate a gain, offsetting the losses on the securities. However, this derivative position will likely generate a loss if the securities experience a gain. Consequently, this derivative position limits Weber's losses or gains, so the firm's return-risk characteristics resulting from this position are represented by Point C in the exhibit.

EXHIBIT 1.2

How Derivatives Can Be Used to Alter an Investor's Return and Risk Characteristics

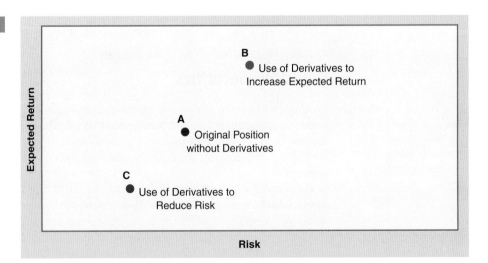

Valuing Securities in Financial Markets

Each type of security generates a unique stream of expected cash flows to investors. As mentioned earlier, investors holding securities may receive periodic (coupon or dividend) payments and also receive a payment when they sell the securities. In addition, each security has a unique level of uncertainty surrounding the expected cash flows that it will provide to investors and therefore surrounding its return. The valuation of a security is measured as the present value of its expected cash flows, discounted at a rate that reflects the uncertainty. Since the cash flows and the uncertainty surrounding the cash flows for each security are unique, the value of each security is unique.

Market Pricing of Securities

Securities are priced in the market according to how they are valued by market participants.

ILLUSTRATION Nike stock provides cash flows to investors in the form of quarterly dividends and its stock price at the time investors sell the stock. Both the future dividends and the future stock price are uncertain. Thus, the cash flows that Nike stock will provide to investors in the future are also uncertain. Investors can attempt to estimate the future cash flows that they will receive by obtaining information that may indicate Nike's future performance, such as reports about the athletic shoe industry, announcements by Nike about its recent sales, and published opinions about Nike's management ability. The valuation process is illustrated in Exhibit 1.3.

Impact of Information on Valuations Although all investors rely on valuation to make investment decisions, different investors may derive different valuations of a security based on the existing set of information. That is, investors interpret and use information in different ways. Some investors may rely mostly on economic or industry

EXHIBIT 1.3
Use of Information to Make Investment Decisions

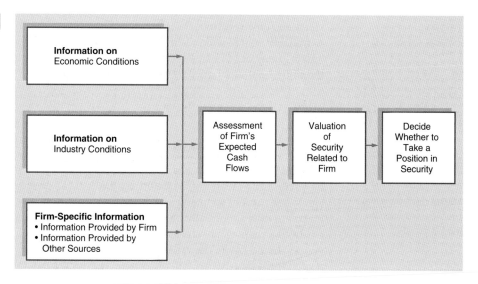

information to value a security, while others may rely on published opinions about the firm's management. Each security has an equilibrium market price at which the demand for that security is equal to the supply of that security for sale. Yet, because investors derive different values for a particular security, they do not necessarily agree that the market price is appropriate. Investors commonly take a position in a security when their assessment of its value differs from the market valuation. Thus, as shown in Exhibit 1.3, investors determine whether to take a position in a security by first using information to estimate expected cash flows, and then develop their own valuation.

Impact of Valuations on Pricing When investors receive new information that clearly indicates the likelihood of higher cash flows or less uncertainty, they revise all of their valuations of that security upward. Consequently, the prevailing price is no longer in equilibrium, as most investors now view the security as undervalued at that price. The demand for the security increases at that price, and the supply of that security for sale decreases. As a result, the market price rises to a new equilibrium level.

Conversely, when investors receive unfavorable information, they reduce the expected cash flows or increase the discount rate used in valuation. All of the valuations of the security are revised downward, which results in shifts in the demand and supply conditions and a decline in the equilibrium price.

As time passes, new information about economic conditions and corporate performance becomes available. Investors quickly attempt to assess how this information will influence the values of securities. As investors buy or sell in response to this information, security prices reach a new equilibrium. Some information has an immediate impact on security prices because market participants take positions in securities as soon as the information is released.

Announcements that do not contain any new valuable information will not elicit a market response. In some cases, market participants take their position in anticipation of a particular announcement. If the announcement was fully anticipated, there will be no market response to the announcement.

Impact of the Internet on the Valuation Process The Internet has improved the valuation of securities in several ways. Prices of securities are quoted online and can be obtained at any given moment by investors. The actual sequence of transactions is provided for some securities. Much more information about the firms that issue securities is available online, which allows securities to be priced more accurately. Furthermore, orders to buy or sell many types of securities can be submitted online, which expedites the adjustment in security prices to new information.

Market Efficiency

http://

http://finance.yahoo.com
Market quotations and
overview of financial
market activity.

Because securities have market-determined prices, their favorable or unfavorable characteristics as perceived by the market are reflected in their prices. When security prices fully reflect all available information, the markets for these securities are said to be efficient. When markets are inefficient, investors can use available information ignored by the market to earn abnormally high returns on their investments.

Even if markets are efficient, this does not imply that individual or institutional investors should ignore the various investment instruments available. Investors differ with respect to the risk they are willing to incur, the desired liquidity of securities, and their tax status, making some types of securities more desirable to some investors than to others.

Some securities that are not as safe and liquid as desired may still be considered if the potential return is sufficiently high. Investors normally attempt to balance the objective of high return with their particular preference for low risk and adequate liquidity. When financial markets are efficient, any relevant information pertaining to risk will be reflected in the prices of securities.

Asymmetric Information

Much of the information used to value securities issued by firms is provided by the managers of those firms. A firm's managers possess information about its financial condition that is not necessarily available to investors. This situation is referred to as asymmetric information. The gap between the information known by managers and the information available to investors can be reduced if managers frequently disclose financial data and information to the public. Firms that have publicly traded stock are required to disclose financial information. Investors commonly rely on financial statements provided by the managers. Alternatively, they may rely on opinions by financial experts, but these opinions may be based on financial statements that were created by the firm's managers. The accounting process plays a key role in the valuation process because investors use accounting reports of a firm's revenue and expenses as a base for estimating its future cash flows. Since investors commonly use a firm's cash flows to estimate its value, the valuation process is influenced by the financial statements that are used to derive cash flow estimates.

Even when information is disclosed, however, an asymmetric information problem may still exist if some of the information provided by the firm's managers cannot be trusted. Accounting guidelines contain some flexibility that may allow unscrupulous managers to manipulate a firm's financial statements. The financial statements of firms with publicly traded stock must be audited once a year by certified public accountants. Nevertheless, there have been many cases in which a firm's earnings were overestimated, but this was not detected until the following year. Under conditions of asymmetric information, securities may be mispriced simply because the investors are using incomplete information provided by the firm's managers. Although the Internet makes information more accessible, it cannot correct misleading information provided by a firm's managers. A possible solution to the asymmetric information problem is more stringent regulations that penalize any parties who are responsible for disclosing misleading financial information, as discussed in the following section.

Financial Market Regulation

In general, securities markets are regulated to ensure that the participants are treated fairly. Many regulations were enacted in response to fraudulent practices before the Great Depression.

Disclosure

Since the use of incorrect information can result in poor investment decisions, many regulations attempt to ensure that businesses disclose accurate information. The Securities Act of 1933 was intended to ensure complete disclosure of relevant financial information on publicly offered securities and to prevent fraudulent practices in selling these

securities. The Securities Exchange Act of 1934 extended the disclosure requirements to secondary market issues. It also declared illegal a variety of deceptive practices, such as misleading financial statements and trading strategies designed to manipulate the market price. In addition, it established the Securities and Exchange Commission (SEC) to oversee the securities markets, and the SEC has implemented additional laws over time. Securities laws do not prevent investors from making poor investment decisions but only attempt to ensure full disclosure of information and thus protect against fraud.

As explained earlier, a security's market price is driven by new information that affects its valuation. When information is disclosed to only a small set of investors, those investors have a major advantage over other investors. Even with regulatory oversight, cases continue to occur in which some investors had an unfair advantage because they had better access to information. Regulations are frequently refined to ensure equal access to disclosure by firms that have issued securities.

Regulatory Response to Financial Scandals

The Enron, WorldCom, and other financial scandals in the 2001–2002 period proved that the existing regulations were not sufficient to prevent fraud. Enron misled investors by exaggerating its earnings. It also failed to disclose relevant information that would have adversely affected its stock price. By the time the information became public, many of Enron's executives had sold off their holdings of Enron stock. They were able to sell the stock at a relatively high price because the negative information was withheld from the public. WorldCom also misled its investors by exaggerating its earnings. Participants in the financial markets were shocked by the degree to which these firms were able to distort their financial statements before the adverse information became public.

Many financial market participants had presumed that financial statements were accurate. In some cases, the auditors who were hired to ensure that a firm's financial statements were accurate were not meeting their responsibility. As a result, executives were able to sell their stock before most financial market participants were aware of the firm's real financial condition.

In response to the financial scandals, various regulators imposed new rules requiring firms to provide more complete and accurate financial information. They also imposed more restrictions to ensure proper auditing by auditors and proper oversight by the firm's board of directors. These rules were intended to regain the trust of investors who supply the funds to the financial markets. Through these measures, regulators tried to eliminate or reduce the asymmetric information problem and alleviate suspicions that surplus units (investors) have about the information provided by deficit units (firms). Consequently, surplus units may be more willing to supply funds in the future.

Other Regulations

In addition to the markets themselves, financial institutions participating in these markets are also regulated. Some regulations apply to all financial institutions, while others are applicable only to a specific type. Historically, regulations limited the types of financial services that any financial firm could offer. In recent years, however, many of these regulations have been removed. Details on regulations are provided throughout the text.

The performance of various financial institutions is linked to regulation. In regulating any type of financial institution, regulators face a tradeoff: they must try to impose enough regulation to ensure safety without imposing so many rules that they reduce competition and efficiency.

Global Financial Markets

Financial markets are continuously being developed throughout the world to improve the transfer of funds from surplus units to deficit units. In some countries, the financial markets are just starting to be developed. In others, such as the United States, the financial markets are being transformed to remove inefficiencies. Because the financial markets are much more developed in some countries than in others, they vary among countries in terms of the volumes of funds that are transferred from surplus units to deficit units and the types of funding that are available.

How Financial Markets Influence Economic Development

Many foreign countries have recently converted to market-oriented economies, in which businesses are created to accommodate the needs or preferences of consumers. A market economy requires the development of financial markets, where businesses can obtain the financing they need to produce products and consumers can obtain the financing they need to purchase specific products.

ILLUSTRATION Before 1990, many countries in Eastern Europe had very limited opportunities for surplus units and deficit units. Consequently, private businesses did not have access to funds and could not expand. In addition, households did not have access to funds and could not purchase homes. Businesses were mostly owned by the government and had to rely on government funding. Since 1990, the governments of these countries have allowed for **privatization,** or the sale of government-owned firms to individuals. In addition, some businesses have issued stock, which allows many other investors who do not work in the business to participate in the ownership. Financial markets have been established in these countries to ensure that these businesses can obtain funding from surplus units. With these changes, private businesses are now able to obtain funds by borrowing or by issuing stock to investors. Surplus units have the opportunity to provide credit (loans) to some businesses or become stockholders of other businesses.

Global Integration

Many financial markets are globally integrated, allowing participants to move funds out of one country's markets and into another's. Foreign investors serve as key surplus units in the United States by purchasing U.S. Treasury securities and other types of securities issued by businesses. Conversely, some investors based in the United States serve as key surplus units for foreign countries by purchasing securities issued by foreign corporations and government agencies. In addition, investors assess the potential return and the risk of securities in financial markets across countries and invest in the market that satisfies their return and risk preferences.

With these more integrated financial markets, U.S. market movements may have a greater impact on foreign market movements, and vice versa. Because interest rates are influenced by the supply of and demand for available funds, they are now more susceptible to foreign lending or borrowing activities.

Barriers to Global Integration Although the global integration of financial markets has increased, various barriers still exist. Some barriers may restrict the transfer of funds to a foreign financial market. One barrier is the lack of information about foreign

companies in which investors would like to invest. The Internet has made this type of information much more accessible in recent years, but the information that is available may not be standardized across countries. For example, each country imposes its own accounting regulations regarding how businesses report their financial condition. Consequently, investors may have difficulty interpreting the financial statements provided by businesses in other countries.

Another barrier is the excessive cost of executing international transactions in financial markets. These transactions tend to require more effort by the intermediaries and therefore are more costly to the surplus or deficit units that wish to invest or obtain funds internationally. The transaction costs have declined substantially with the use of electronic communications, but are still higher than for domestic transactions.

Financial Market Integration within Europe The most pronounced progress in global financial market integration has occurred in Europe. Historically, the financial markets in each country in Western Europe were well developed but isolated from those of other countries. Even when no laws prohibited transactions outside the country, differences in tax laws and other regulations complicated international transactions. In the 1980s and 1990s, however, numerous regulations were eliminated so that surplus and deficit units in one European country could use financial markets throughout Europe. Some stock exchanges in different European countries merged, making it easier for investors to conduct all of their stock transactions on one exchange. Since 1999, the adoption of the euro as the currency by 12 European countries (the so-called eurozone) has encouraged more financial market integration within Europe because all securities issued within these countries are now denominated in the euro. Thus, investors in any of these countries do not have to convert their currency.

Foreign Exchange Market

International financial transactions (except for those within the eurozone) normally require the exchange of currencies. The **foreign exchange market** facilitates the exchange of currencies. Many commercial banks and other financial institutions serve as intermediaries in the foreign exchange market. They serve as brokers by matching up participants who want to exchange one currency for another. Some of these financial institutions also serve as dealers by taking positions in currencies to accommodate foreign exchange requests.

ILLUSTRATION   O'Hara Bank of Chicago receives requests by corporations to exchange dollars for Japanese yen (the Japanese currency). It also receives requests by other corporations to exchange yen for dollars. At a given point in time, the bank's ask quote for yen (the price at which it is willing to sell yen) is slightly higher than its bid quote (the price at which it is willing to purchase yen). Thus, the bank earns a profit when it accepts yen from one corporation and provides them to another corporation. It also provides this service for several other currencies.

The bank may also serve as a dealer when a corporation requests a currency exchange that cannot be offset by requests by other corporations. For instance, a Mexican company wants to exchange its pesos for U.S. dollars to purchase supplies from a U.S. firm. O'Hara Bank currently has no customers that need pesos. It accommodates the Mexican company's request and now has pesos. The bank could benefit from this position if the market value of the Mexican peso rises over time. Conversely, it could incur a loss from this position if the market value of the peso declines.

Foreign Exchange Rates Like securities, most currencies have a market-determined price (exchange rate) that changes in response to supply and demand conditions. If there is a sudden shift in the aggregate demand by corporations, government agencies, and individuals for a given currency, or a shift in the aggregate supply of that currency for sale (to be exchanged), the price will change.

ILLUSTRATION Yesterday, several banks that accommodate the exchange between Mexican pesos and U.S. dollars experienced more requests from customers wanting to exchange pesos for dollars than from customers wanting to exchange dollars for pesos. Consequently, many of the banks are now holding larger inventories of pesos than they desire. They decide to reduce their price for pesos in an attempt to discourage future customer requests to exchange pesos for dollars. At the lower price, the customers would now receive fewer dollars for a given amount of pesos.

Role of Financial Institutions in Financial Markets

If financial markets were **perfect,** all information about any securities for sale in primary and secondary markets (including the creditworthiness of the security issuer) would be continuously and freely available to investors. In addition, all information identifying investors interested in purchasing securities as well as investors planning to sell securities would be freely available. Furthermore, all securities for sale could be broken down (or unbundled) into any size desired by investors, and security transaction costs would be nonexistent. Under these conditions, financial intermediaries would not be necessary.

Because markets are **imperfect,** securities buyers and sellers do not have full access to information and cannot always break down securities to the precise size they desire. Financial institutions are needed to resolve the problems caused by market imperfections. They receive requests from surplus and deficit units on what securities are to be purchased or sold, and they use this information to match up buyers and sellers of securities. Because the amount of a specific security to be sold does not always equal the amount desired by investors, financial institutions sometimes unbundle the securities by spreading them across several investors until the entire amount is sold. Without financial institutions, the information and transaction costs of financial market transactions would be excessive.

Role of Depository Institutions

A major type of financial intermediary is the depository institution, which accepts deposits from surplus units and provides credit to deficit units through loans and purchases of securities. Depository institutions are popular financial institutions for the following reasons:

- They offer deposit accounts that can accommodate the amount and liquidity characteristics desired by most surplus units.
- They repackage funds received from deposits to provide loans of the size and maturity desired by deficit units.
- They accept the risk on loans provided.
- They have more expertise than individual surplus units in evaluating the creditworthiness of deficit units.
- They diversify their loans among numerous deficit units and therefore can absorb defaulted loans better than individual surplus units could.

To appreciate these advantages, consider the flow of funds from surplus units to deficit units if depository institutions did not exist. Each surplus unit would have to identify a deficit unit desiring to borrow the precise amount of funds available for the precise time period in which funds would be available. Furthermore, each surplus unit would have to perform the credit evaluation and incur the risk of default. Under these conditions, many surplus units would likely hold their funds rather than channel them to deficit units. Thus, the flow of funds from surplus units to deficit units would be disrupted.

When a depository institution offers a loan, it is acting as a creditor, just as if it had purchased a debt security. Yet, the more personalized loan agreement is less marketable in the secondary market than a debt security, because detailed provisions on a loan can differ significantly among loans. Any potential investors would need to review all provisions before purchasing loans in the secondary market.

A more specific description of each depository institution's role in the financial markets follows.

Commercial Banks In aggregate, commercial banks are the most dominant depository institution. They serve surplus units by offering a wide variety of deposit accounts, and they transfer deposited funds to deficit units by providing direct loans or purchasing debt securities. Commercial banks serve both the private and public sectors, as their deposit and lending services are utilized by households, businesses, and government agencies.

Savings Institutions Savings institutions, which are sometimes referred to as thrift institutions, are another type of depository institution. Savings institutions include savings and loan associations (S&Ls) and savings banks. Like commercial banks, S&Ls offer deposit accounts to surplus units and then channel these deposits to deficit units. However, S&Ls have concentrated on residential mortgage loans, whereas commercial banks have concentrated on commercial loans. This difference in the allocation of funds has caused the performance of commercial banks and S&Ls to differ significantly over time. In recent decades, however, deregulation has permitted S&Ls more flexibility in allocating their funds, causing their functions to become more similar to those of commercial banks. Although S&Ls can be owned by shareholders, most are mutual (depositor owned).

Savings banks are similar to S&Ls, except that they have more diversified uses of funds. However, this difference has narrowed over time. Like S&Ls, most savings banks are mutual.

Credit Unions Credit unions differ from commercial banks and savings institutions in that they (1) are nonprofit and (2) restrict their business to the credit union members, who share a common bond (such as a common employer or union). Because of the common bond characteristic, credit unions tend to be much smaller than other depository institutions. They use most of their funds to provide loans to their members.

Role of Nondepository Financial Institutions

Nondepository institutions generate funds from sources other than deposits but also play a major role in financial intermediation. These institutions are briefly described here.

Finance Companies Most finance companies obtain funds by issuing securities, then lend the funds to individuals and small businesses. The functions of finance companies overlap the functions of depository institutions, yet each type of institution concentrates

on a particular segment of the financial markets (explained in the chapters devoted to these institutions).

Mutual Funds Mutual funds sell shares to surplus units and use the funds received to purchase a portfolio of securities. They are the dominant nondepository financial institution when measured in total assets. Some mutual funds concentrate their investment in capital market securities, such as stocks or bonds. Others, known as **money market mutual funds,** concentrate in money market securities. The minimum denomination of the types of securities purchased by mutual funds is typically greater than the savings of an individual surplus unit. By purchasing shares of mutual funds and money market mutual funds, small savers are able to invest in a diversified portfolio of securities with a relatively small amount of funds.

Securities Firms Securities firms provide a wide variety of functions in financial markets. Some securities firms use their information resources to act as a **broker,** executing securities transactions between two parties. Many financial transactions are standardized to a degree. For example, stock transactions are normally in multiples of 100 shares. To expedite the securities trading process, the delivery procedure for each security transaction is also somewhat standard.

Brokers charge a fee for executing transactions. The fee is reflected in the difference (or **spread**) between their **bid** and **ask** quotes. The markup as a percentage of the transaction amount will likely be greater for less common transactions, as more time is needed to match up buyers and sellers. It will also likely be greater for transactions of relatively small amounts in order to provide adequate compensation for the time involved in executing the transaction.

In addition to brokerage services, securities firms also provide investment banking services. Some securities firms place newly issued securities for corporations and government agencies; this task differs from traditional brokerage activities because it involves the primary market. When securities firms **underwrite** newly issued securities, they may sell the securities for a client at a guaranteed price, or they may simply sell the securities at the best price they can get for their client.

Furthermore, securities firms often act as **dealers,** making a market in specific securities by adjusting their inventory of securities. Although a broker's income is mostly based on the markup, the dealer's income is influenced by the performance of the security portfolio maintained. Some dealers also provide brokerage services and therefore earn income from both types of activities.

Another investment banking activity offered by securities firms is advisory services on mergers and other forms of corporate restructuring. Securities firms may not only help a firm plan its restructuring but also execute the change in the firm's capital structure by placing the securities issued by the firm.

Insurance Companies Insurance companies provide insurance policies to individuals and firms that reduce the financial burden associated with death, illness, and damage to property. They charge premiums in exchange for the insurance that they provide. They invest the funds that they receive in the form of premiums until the funds are needed to cover insurance claims. Insurance companies commonly invest the funds in stocks or bonds issued by corporations or in bonds issued by the government. In this way, they finance the needs of deficit units and thus serve as important financial intermediaries. Their overall performance is linked to the performance of the stocks and bonds in which they invest.

Pension Funds Many corporations and government agencies offer pension plans to their employees. The employees, their employers, or both periodically contribute funds to the plan. Pension funds provide an efficient way for individuals to save for their retirement. The pension funds manage the money until the individuals withdraw the funds from their retirement accounts. The money that is contributed to individual retirement accounts is commonly invested by the pension funds in stocks or bonds issued by corporations or in bonds issued by the government. In this way, pension funds finance the needs of deficit units and thus serve as important financial intermediaries.

Comparison of Roles among Financial Institutions

The role of financial institutions in facilitating the flow of funds from individual surplus units to deficit units is illustrated in Exhibit 1.4. Surplus units are shown on the left side of the exhibit, and deficit units are shown on the right side. Three different flows of funds from surplus units to deficit units are shown in the exhibit. One set of flows represents deposits from surplus units that are transformed by depository institutions into loans for deficit units. A second set of flows represents purchases of securities (commercial paper) issued by finance companies that are transformed into finance company loans for deficit units. A third set of flows reflects the purchases of shares issued by mutual funds, which are used by the mutual funds to purchase debt and equity securities of deficit units.

The deficit units also receive funding from insurance companies and pension funds. Because insurance companies and pension funds purchase massive amounts of stocks

EXHIBIT 1.4 Comparison of Roles among Financial Institutions

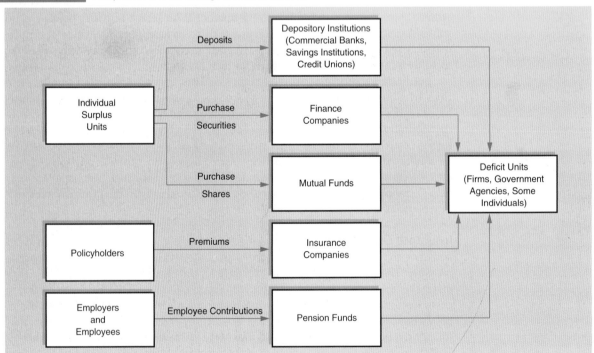

and bonds, they finance much of the expenditures made by large deficit units, such as corporations and government agencies.

Securities firms are not shown in Exhibit 1.4, but they play a very important role in facilitating the flow of funds. Many of the transactions between the financial institutions and deficit units are executed by securities firms. Furthermore, some funds flow directly from surplus units to deficit units as a result of security transactions, with securities firms serving as brokers.

Role as a Monitor of Publicly Traded Firms In addition to the roles just described, financial institutions also serve as monitors of publicly traded firms. Because insurance companies, pension funds, and some mutual funds are major investors in stocks, they can have some influence over the management of publicly traded firms. In recent years, many large institutional investors have publicly criticized the management of specific firms, which has resulted in corporate restructuring or even the firing of executives in some cases. Thus, institutional investors not only provide financial support to companies but exercise some degree of corporate control over them. By serving as activist shareholders, they can help ensure that managers of publicly held corporations are making decisions that are in the best interests of the shareholders.

Financial Institutions

Exhibit 1.5 summarizes the main sources and uses of funds for each type of financial institution. Households with savings are served by the depository institutions. Households with deficient funds are served by depository institutions and finance companies. Large corporations and governments that issue securities obtain financing from all types of financial institutions.

EXHIBIT 1.5

Summary of Institutional Sources and Uses of Funds

Financial Institutions	Main Sources of Funds	Main Uses of Funds
Commercial banks	Deposits from households, businesses, and government agencies	Purchases of government and corporate securities; loans to businesses and households
Savings institutions	Deposits from households, businesses, and government agencies	Purchases of government and corporate securities; mortgages and other loans to households; some loans to businesses
Credit unions	Deposits from credit union members	Loans to credit union members
Finance companies	Securities sold to households and businesses	Loans to households and businesses
Mutual funds	Shares sold to households, businesses, and government agencies	Purchases of long-term government and corporate securities
Money market funds	Shares sold to households, businesses, and government agencies	Purchases of short-term government and corporate securities
Insurance companies	Insurance premiums and earnings from investments	Purchases of long-term government and corporate securities
Pension funds	Employer/employee contributions	Purchases of long-term government and corporate securities

Competition between Financial Institutions

A financial institution is expected to operate in a manner that will maximize the value of its owners. The value of a financial institution is the present value of its future cash flows. Thus, its value is closely tied to its growth and profitability. In addition, its value is influenced by its degree of risk, since the required rate of return by investors in it is positively related to its risk. Managers serve as agents for the owners and should make decisions with the intention to maximize firm value. In the 1960s and 1970s, managerial decision making was limited because financial institution operations were highly specialized and constrained. There was limited competition across different types of financial institutions. Commercial banks served as the key lenders of short-term corporate funds, while securities firms helped corporations obtain long-term funds. Savings institutions specialized in mortgages, while insurance companies focused their investment in bonds.

There was also very little competition in obtaining funds during those decades. Deposits provided by surplus units to commercial banks and savings institutions were heavily regulated to prevent competition. Then, in the 1970s, the development of mutual funds created competition for funds held by surplus units. Deregulation of deposit rates in the early 1980s provided additional competition for these funds. Furthermore, in the 1980s, regulators allowed savings institutions, insurance companies, and other financial institutions to be more flexible in their use of funds. The momentum for additional flexibility continued in the 1990s. Today, many financial institutions are offering a greater variety of products and services to diversify their business. As a consequence, their services overlap more and competition has increased. Because there are different regulatory agencies for different types of financial institutions, coordination among these regulators is difficult to maintain. Differential regulations can cause some financial institutions to have a comparative advantage over others.

Impact of the Internet on Competition The Internet has promoted more intense competition among financial institutions. Some commercial banks have been created solely as online entities. Because they have lower costs, they can offer higher interest rates on deposits and lower rates on loans. Other banks also offer online services, which can reduce costs, increase efficiency, and intensify banking competition. Some insurance companies conduct much of their business online, which reduces their operating costs and forces other insurance companies to price their services competitively. Some brokerage firms conduct much of their business online, which reduces their operating costs; because these firms can lower the fees they charge, they force other brokerage firms to price their services competitively. The Internet has also made it possible for corporations and municipal governments to circumvent securities firms by conducting security offerings online and selling directly to investors. This capability forces securities firms to be more competitive in the services they offer to issuers of securities.

Consolidation of Financial Institutions

As regulations have been reduced, managers of financial institutions have more flexibility to offer services that could increase their cash flows and value. The reduction in regulations has allowed financial institutions more opportunities to capitalize on economies of scale. Commercial banks have acquired other commercial banks so that they can generate a higher volume of business supported by a given infrastructure. By increasing

the volume of services produced, the average cost of provid
loans) can be reduced. Savings institutions have consolidate[...]
scale for their mortgage lending business. Insurance compa[...]
that they can reduce the average cost of providing insurance

The reduction in regulations has also allowed different ty[...]
to capitalize on economies of scope. Commercial banks have
tutions, securities firms, finance companies, mutual funds,
Although the operations of each type of financial institutic.. .
separately, a financial conglomerate offers advantages to customers who prefer to obtain
all of their financial services from a single financial institution.

ILLUSTRATION Consider the merger of Citicorp and Travelers Group to form Citigroup. Citicorp's business in the United States was focused on commercial banking, consumer finance, credit cards, and small business finance. Travelers Group had historically focused on life insurance and property and casualty insurance. Before the merger with Citicorp, however, it had acquired Salomon Brothers, a securities firm that provided investment banking services such as underwriting new securities issued by corporations, and Smith Barney, another securities firm that provided brokerage services.

The merger between Citicorp and Travelers resulted in a financial conglomerate worth $72 billion that offers commercial loans, advisory services for corporations planning to restructure, consumer loans, credit cards, insurance, underwriting services, brokerage services, and mutual funds. Although each type of operation within Citigroup is unique, it can benefit from its relationship with the other operations in the same financial conglomerate. For example, since the underwriting of securities normally utilizes some brokerage operations to help place newly issued securities for firms, the underwriting unit may pass some business off to the brokerage operating unit. The mutual fund unit can pass on some business to the brokerage unit to execute its security transactions. Furthermore, each unit can link its customers with the other units to provide additional services.

Several other recent mergers have also resulted in financial conglomerates. Morgan Stanley, an investment bank, acquired Dean Witter in order to expand its brokerage business. Wachovia, a commercial bank, acquired CoreStates Financial in order to expand its financial services. J.P. Morgan Chase, a commercial bank, acquired Bank One in order to expand its retail banking and credit card businesses. The combined assets of these two financial institutions exceed $1 trillion. Overall, such acquisitions have allowed financial institutions to expand their services.

Wells Fargo is a classic example of the evolution in financial services. It originally focused on commercial banking, but has expanded its nonbank services to include mortgages, small business loans, consumer loans, real estate, brokerage, investment banking, online financial services, and insurance. In a recent annual report, Wells Fargo stated:

> **❝Our diversity in businesses makes us much more than a bank. We're a diversified financial services company. We're competing in a highly fragmented and fast growing industry: Financial Services. This helps us weather downturns that inevitably affect any one segment of our industry.❞**

1.6 Organizational Structure of a Financial Conglomerate

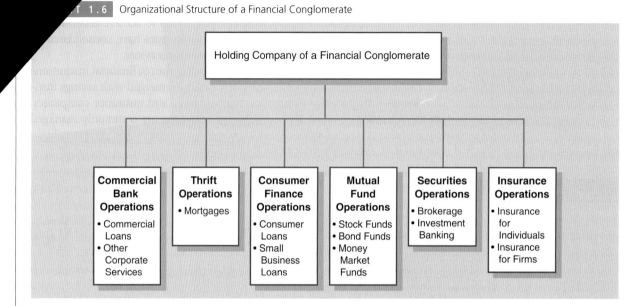

Impact of Consolidation on Valuation When managers of financial institutions pursue consolidation to achieve economies of scale or scope, they may be able to increase their firm's value by increasing cash flows (increasing revenue or reducing expenses). Alternatively, consolidation may be intended to diversify the institution's services and reduce risk. A lower level of risk allows for a reduction in the required rate of return by investors and can increase value.

Typical Structure of a Financial Conglomerate A typical organizational structure of a financial conglomerate is shown in Exhibit 1.6. Historically, each of the financial services (such as banking, mortgages, brokerage, and insurance) had significant barriers to entry, so only a limited number of firms competed in that industry. The barriers prevented most firms from offering a wide variety of these services. In recent years, the barriers to entry have been reduced, allowing firms that had specialized in one service to more easily expand into other financial services. Many firms expanded by acquiring other financial service firms. Thus, many financial conglomerates are composed of various financial institutions that were originally independent, but are now units (or subsidiaries) of the conglomerate.

An individual customer can rely on the financial conglomerate for convenient access to life and health insurance, brokerage, mutual funds, investment advice and financial planning, bank deposits, and personal loans. A corporate customer can turn to the financial conglomerate for property and casualty insurance, health insurance plans for employees, business loans, advice on restructuring its businesses, issuing new debt or equity securities, and management of its pension plan. Many financial conglomerates expect to grow by providing additional financial services to their existing customers. For example, Wells Fargo provides its 15 million customers with about one-fourth of the financial services they need (on average). Thus, it plans to pursue its existing customer base to try to provide the other three-fourths of services that are currently provided by other financial services companies.

Global Expansion by Financial Institutions

 **GL BALASPECTS**   Many financial institutions have expanded internationally to capitalize on their expertise. Commercial banks, insurance companies, and securities firms have expanded through international mergers. An international merger between financial institutions enables the merged company to offer the services of both entities to its entire customer base. For example, a U.S. commercial bank may have specialized in lending while a European securities firm specialized in services such as underwriting securities. A merger between the two entities allows the U.S. bank to provide its services to the European customer base (clients of the European securities firm), while the European securities firm can offer its services to the U.S. customer base. By combining specialized skills and customer bases, the merged financial institutions can offer more services to clients and have an international customer base.

The adoption of the euro by 12 European countries has increased business between European countries and created a more competitive environment in Europe. European financial institutions, which had primarily competed with other financial institutions based in their own country, recognized that they would now face more competition from financial institutions in other countries. Consequently, many financial institutions have engaged in international mergers so that they can serve clients throughout Europe and provide a wider variety of services. By offering their services to a larger customer base, they can increase efficiency (reduce the cost) and therefore price their services more competitively.

Many financial institutions have attempted to benefit from opportunities in emerging markets. For example, Merrill Lynch and other large securities firms have expanded into many countries to offer underwriting services for firms and government agencies. The need for this service has increased most dramatically in countries where businesses have been privatized. In addition, commercial banks have expanded into emerging markets to provide loans. Although lending in emerging markets can produce high returns, it is also subject to a high level of risk. The Asian crisis that began in 1997 resulted in numerous defaults on international business loans provided by financial institutions from the United States and Europe. Some financial institutions continue to offer loans in emerging markets, although not as aggressively as before the crisis.

SUMMARY

- Financial markets facilitate the transfer of funds from surplus units to deficit units. Because funding needs vary among deficit units, various financial markets have been established. The primary market allows for the issuance of new securities, while the secondary market allows for the sale of existing securities. Money markets facilitate the sale of short-term securities, while capital markets facilitate the sale of long-term securities.

- The valuation of a security represents the present value of future cash flows that it is expected to gener-

ate. New information that indicates a change in expected cash flows or the degree of uncertainty affects the prices of securities in financial markets. Investors monitor economic conditions and firm-specific conditions that may have an impact on expected cash flows or the degree of uncertainty surrounding securities issued by that firm.

- Depository and nondepository institutions help to finance the needs of deficit units. Depository institutions can serve as effective intermediaries within financial markets because they have greater

information on possible sources and uses of funds, they are capable of assessing the creditworthiness of borrowers, and they can repackage deposited funds in sizes and maturities desired by borrowers.

Nondepository institutions are major purchasers of securities and therefore provide funding to deficit units.

■ The main depository institutions are commercial banks, savings institutions, and credit unions. The main nondepository institutions are finance companies, mutual funds, pension funds, and insurance companies. Many financial institutions have been consolidated (due to mergers) into financial conglomerates, where they serve as subsidiaries of the conglomerate while conducting their specialized services. Thus, some financial conglomerates are able to provide all types of financial services. Consolidation allows for economies of scale and scope, which can enhance cash flows and increase the financial institution's value. In addition, consolidation can diversify the institution's services and increase value through the reduction in risk.

POINT COUNTER-POINT

Will Computer Technology Cause Financial Intermediaries to Become Extinct?

Point Yes. Financial intermediaries benefit from access to information. As information becomes more accessible, individuals will have the information they need before investing or borrowing funds. They will not need financial intermediaries to make their decisions.

Counter-Point No. Individuals rely not only on information, but also on expertise. Some financial intermediaries specialize in credit analysis so that they can make loans. Surplus units will continue to provide funds to financial intermediaries rather than make direct loans, because they are not capable of credit analysis, even if more information about prospective borrowers is available. Some financial intermediaries no longer have physical buildings for customer service, but they still require people who have the expertise to assess the creditworthiness of prospective borrowers.

Who Is Correct? Use your favorite search engine to learn more about this issue. Offer your own opinion on this issue.

QUESTIONS AND APPLICATIONS

1. **Interpreting Financial News** "Interpreting Financial News" tests your ability to comprehend common statements made by Wall Street analysts and portfolio managers who participate in the financial markets. Interpret the following statements made by Wall Street analysts and portfolio managers:
   a. "The price of IBM will not be affected by the announcement that its earnings have increased as expected."
   b. "The lending operations at Bank of America should benefit from strong economic growth."
   c. "The brokerage and underwriting performance at Merrill Lynch should benefit from strong economic growth."
2. **Securities Laws** What was the purpose of the Securities Act of 1933? What was the purpose of the Securities Exchange Act of 1934? Do these laws prevent investors from making poor investment decisions? Explain.
3. **Marketability** Commercial banks use some funds to purchase securities and other funds to make loans. Why are the securities more marketable than loans in the secondary market?
4. **Types of Markets** Distinguish between primary and secondary markets. Distinguish between money and capital markets.
5. **Mutual Funds** What is the function of a mutual fund? Why are mutual funds popular among investors? How does a money market mutual fund differ from a stock or bond mutual fund?
6. **Managing in Financial Markets: Utilizing Financial Markets** As a financial manager of a large firm, you plan to borrow $70 million over the next year.

a. What are the more likely alternatives for you to borrow $70 million?
b. Assuming that you decide to issue debt securities, describe the types of financial institutions that may purchase these securities.
c. How do individuals indirectly provide the financing for your firm when they maintain deposits at depository institutions, invest in mutual funds, purchase insurance policies, or invest in pensions?

7. **Role of Accounting in Financial Markets** Integrate the roles of accounting, regulations, and financial market participation. That is, explain how financial market participants rely on accounting, and why regulatory oversight of the accounting process is necessary.

8. **Surplus and Deficit Units** Explain the meaning of surplus units and deficit units. Provide an example of each. Which types of financial institutions do you deal with? Explain whether you are acting as a surplus unit or a deficit unit in your relationship with each financial institution.

9. **Comparing Financial Institutions** Classify the types of financial institutions mentioned in this chapter as either depository or nondepository. Explain the general difference between depository and nondepository institution sources of funds. It is often stated that all types of financial institutions have begun to offer services that were previously offered only by certain types. Consequently, many financial institutions are becoming more similar in terms of their operations. Yet, the performance levels still differ significantly among types of financial institutions. Why?

10. **Financial Intermediation** Look in a recent business periodical for news about a recent financial transaction that involves two financial institutions. For this transaction, determine the following:
a. How will each institution's balance sheet be affected?
b. Will either institution receive immediate income from the transaction?
c. Who is the ultimate user of funds?
d. Who is the ultimate source of funds?

11. **International Barriers** If barriers to international securities markets are reduced, will a country's interest rate be more or less susceptible to foreign lending or borrowing activities? Explain.

12. **Internet Exercise** Assess the current price of the common stock of IBM, using the website http://www.nyse.com. Insert the ticker symbol "IBM" within the box called "Quick quotes."

What was the closing price on IBM's stock yesterday? From the volume graph, estimate the number of shares traded yesterday. What are the 52-week high and low prices for IBM?

13. **International Flow of Funds** In what way could the international flow of funds cause a decline in interest rates?

14. **Impact of Privatization on Financial Markets** Explain how the privatization of companies in Europe can lead to the development of new securities markets.

15. **Efficient Markets** Explain the meaning of efficient markets. Why might we expect markets to be efficient most of the time? In recent years, several securities firms have been guilty of using inside information when purchasing securities, thereby achieving returns well above the norm (even when accounting for risk). Does this suggest that the security markets are not efficient? Explain.

16. **Credit Unions** With regard to the profit motive, how are credit unions different from other financial institutions?

17. **Securities Firms** What are the functions of securities firms? Many securities firms employ brokers and dealers. Distinguish between the functions of a broker and those of a dealer, and explain how each is compensated.

18. **Imperfect Markets** Distinguish between perfect and imperfect security markets. Explain why the existence of imperfect markets creates a need for financial intermediaries.

19. **Depository Institutions** How have the asset compositions of savings and loan associations differed from those of commercial banks? Explain why and how this distinction may change over time.

20. **Standardized Securities** Why is it necessary for securities to be somewhat standardized? Explain why some financial flows of funds cannot occur through the sale of standardized securities. If securities were not standardized, how would this affect the volume of financial transactions conducted by brokers?

21. **Nondepository Institutions** Compare the main sources and uses of funds for finance companies, insurance companies, and pension funds.

FLOW OF FUNDS EXERCISE

Roles of Financial Markets and Institutions

This continuing exercise focuses on the interactions of a single manufacturing firm (Carson Company) in the financial markets. It illustrates how financial markets and institutions are integrated and facilitate the flow of funds in the business and financial environment. At the end of every chapter, this exercise provides a list of questions about Carson Company that require the application of concepts learned within the chapter, as related to the flow of funds.

Carson Company is a large manufacturing firm in California that was created 20 years ago by the Carson family. It was initially financed with an equity investment by the Carson family and 10 other individuals. Over time, Carson Company has obtained substantial loans from finance companies and commercial banks. The interest rate on the loans is tied to market interest rates and is adjusted every six months. Thus, Carson's cost of obtaining funds is sensitive to interest rate movements. It has a credit line with a bank in case it suddenly needs to obtain funds for a temporary period. It has purchased Treasury securities that it could sell if it experiences any liquidity problems.

Carson Company has assets valued at about $50 million and generates sales of about $100 million per year. Some of its growth is attributed to its acquisitions of other firms. Because of its expectations of a strong U.S. economy, Carson plans to grow in the future by expanding its business and through acquisitions. It expects that it will need substantial long-term financing and plans to borrow additional funds either through loans or by issuing bonds. It is also considering the issuance of stock to raise funds in the next year. Carson closely monitors conditions in financial markets that could affect its cash inflows and cash outflows and therefore affect its value.

a. In what way is Carson a surplus unit?

b. In what way is Carson a deficit unit?

c. How might finance companies facilitate Carson's expansion?

d. How might commercial banks facilitate Carson's expansion?

e. Why might Carson have limited access to additional debt financing during its growth phase?

f. How might investment banks facilitate Carson's expansion?

g. How might Carson use the primary market to facilitate its expansion?

h. How might it use the secondary market?

i. If financial markets were perfect, how might this have allowed Carson to avoid financial institutions?

j. The loans provided by commercial banks to Carson required that Carson receive approval from them before pursuing any large projects. What is the purpose of this condition? Does this condition benefit the owners of the company?

WSJ EXERCISE

Differentiating between Primary and Secondary Markets

Review the different tables relating to stock markets and bond markets that appear in Section C of *The Wall Street Journal*. Explain whether each of these tables is focused on the primary or secondary markets.

CHAPTER 2

Interest Rates Determination

nterest rate movements have a direct influence on the market values of debt securities, such as money market securities, bonds, and mortgages, and have an indirect influence on equity security values. Thus, participants in financial markets attempt to anticipate interest rate movements when restructuring their positions. Interest rate movements also affect the value of most financial institutions. The cost of funds to depository institutions and the interest received on some loans by financial institutions are affected by interest rate movements. In addition, the market values of securities (such as bonds) held by depository institutions or nondepository institutions are affected as well. Thus, managers of financial institutions attempt to anticipate interest rate movements so that they can capitalize on favorable movements or reduce their institution's exposure to unfavorable movements.

The specific objectives of this chapter are to:

■ apply the loanable funds theory to explain why interest rates change,

■ identify the most relevant factors that affect interest rate movements, and

■ explain how to forecast interest rates.

Loanable Funds Theory

http://

http://www.bloomberg.com
Information on interest
rates in recent months.

The **loanable funds theory,** commonly used to explain interest rate movements, suggests that the market interest rate is determined by the factors that control the supply of and demand for loanable funds. The theory is especially useful for explaining movements in the general level of interest rates for a particular country. Furthermore, it can be used along with other concepts to explain why interest rates among some debt securities of a given country vary, which is the focus of the next chapter. The phrase "demand for loanable funds" is widely used in financial markets to refer to the borrowing activities of households, businesses, and governments. The common sectors that demand loanable funds are identified and described here. Then the sectors that supply loanable funds to the markets are described. Finally, the demand and supply concepts are integrated to explain interest rate movements.

Household Demand for Loanable Funds

Households commonly demand loanable funds to finance housing expenditures. In addition, they finance the purchases of automobiles and household items, which results in

installment debt. As the aggregate level of household income rises over time, so does installment debt. The level of installment debt as a percentage of disposable income has been increasing since 1983. It is generally lower in recessionary periods.

If households could be surveyed at any given point in time to indicate the quantity of loanable funds they would demand at various interest rate levels, there would be an inverse relationship between the interest rate and the quantity of loanable funds demanded. This simply means that at any point in time, households would demand a greater quantity of loanable funds at lower rates of interest.

ILLUSTRATION   Consider the household demand-for-loanable-funds schedule shown in Exhibit 2.1. This schedule depicts the amount of funds that would be demanded at various possible interest rates at a given point in time. Various events can cause household borrowing preferences to change and thereby shift the demand schedule. For example, if tax rates on household income are expected to significantly decrease in the future, households might believe that they can more easily afford future loan repayments and thus be willing to borrow more funds. For any interest rate, the quantity of loanable funds demanded by households would be greater as a result of the tax law adjustment. This represents an outward shift (to the right) in the demand schedule.

Business Demand for Loanable Funds

Businesses demand loanable funds to invest in long-term (fixed) and short-term assets. The quantity of funds demanded by businesses depends on the number of business projects to be implemented. Businesses evaluate a project by comparing the present value of its cash flows to its initial investment, as follows:

$$NPV = -INV + \sum_{t=1}^{n} \frac{CF_t}{(1+k)^t}$$

where

NPV = net present value of project

INV = initial investment

CF_t = flow in period t

k = required rate of return on project

EXHIBIT 2.1

Relationship between Interest Rates and Household Demand (D_h) for Loanable Funds at a Given Point in Time

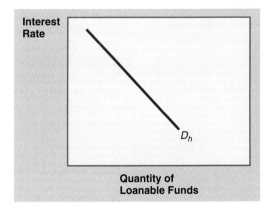

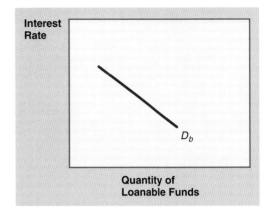

EXHIBIT 2.2

Relationship between Interest Rates and Business Demand (D_b) for Loanable Funds at a Given Point in Time

Projects with a positive net present value (NPV) are accepted because the present value of their benefits outweighs the costs. The required return to implement a given project will be lower if interest rates are lower because the cost of borrowing funds to support the project will be lower. Consequently, more projects will have positive NPVs, and businesses will need a greater amount of financing. This implies that businesses will demand a greater quantity of loanable funds when interest rates are lower, as illustrated in Exhibit 2.2.

In addition to long-term assets, businesses also invest in short-term assets (such as accounts receivable and inventory) in order to support ongoing operations. Any demand for funds resulting from this type of investment is positively related to the number of projects implemented and thus is inversely related to the interest rate. The opportunity cost of investing in short-term assets is higher when interest rates are higher. Therefore, firms generally attempt to support ongoing operations with fewer funds during periods of high interest rates. This is another reason that a firm's total demand for loanable funds is inversely related to interest rates at any point in time. Although the demand for loanable funds by some businesses may be more sensitive than others to interest rates, all businesses are likely to demand more funds if interest rates are lower at a given point in time.

Shifts in the Demand for Loanable Funds The business demand-for-loanable-funds schedule can shift in reaction to any events that affect business borrowing preferences. If economic conditions become more favorable, the expected cash flows on various proposed projects will increase. More proposed projects will have expected returns that exceed a particular required rate of return (sometimes called the hurdle rate). Additional projects will be acceptable as a result of more favorable economic forecasts, causing an increased demand for loanable funds. The increase in demand will result in an outward shift in the demand curve (to the right).

Government Demand for Loanable Funds

http://

http://www.publicdebt.treas
.gov Information on the
U.S. government budget
deficit.

Whenever a government's planned expenditures cannot be completely covered by its incoming revenues from taxes and other sources, it demands loanable funds. Municipal (state and local) governments issue municipal bonds to obtain funds, while the federal government and its agencies issue Treasury securities and federal agency securities. These securities represent government debt.

Federal government expenditure and tax policies are generally thought to be independent of interest rates. Thus, the federal government demand for funds is said to be

EXHIBIT 2.3

EXHIBIT 2.3

Impact of Increased Government Budget Deficit on the Government Demand for Loanable Funds

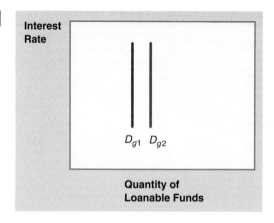

interest-inelastic, or insensitive to interest rates. In contrast, municipal governments sometimes postpone proposed expenditures if the cost of financing is too high, implying that their demand for loanable funds is somewhat sensitive to interest rates.

Like the household and business demand, the government demand for loanable funds can shift in response to various events.

ILLUSTRATION   The federal government demand-for-loanable-funds schedule is D_{g1} in Exhibit 2.3. If new bills are passed that cause a net increase of $20 billion in the deficit, the federal government demand for loanable funds will increase by that amount. The new demand schedule is D_{g2} in the exhibit.

Foreign Demand for Loanable Funds

GLBALASPECTS   The demand for loanable funds in a given market also includes foreign demand by foreign governments or corporations. For example, the British government may obtain financing by issuing British Treasury securities to U.S. investors, representing a British demand for U.S. funds. Because foreign financial transactions are becoming so common, they can have a significant impact on the demand for loanable funds in any given country. A foreign country's demand for U.S. funds is influenced by the differential between its interest rates and U.S. rates (along with other factors). Other things being equal, a larger quantity of U.S. funds will be demanded by foreign governments and corporations if their domestic interest rates are high relative to U.S. rates. Therefore, for a given set of foreign interest rates, the quantity of U.S. loanable funds demanded by foreign governments or firms will be inversely related to U.S. interest rates.

http://www.bloomberg
.com/markets Interest rate
information.

The foreign demand schedule can shift in response to economic conditions. For example, assume the original foreign demand schedule is D_{f1} in Exhibit 2.4. If foreign interest rates rise, foreign firms and governments will likely increase their demand for U.S. funds, as represented by a shift from D_{f1} to D_{f2}.

Aggregate Demand for Loanable Funds

The aggregate demand for loanable funds is the sum of the quantities demanded by the separate sectors at any given interest rate, as shown in Exhibit 2.5. Because most of these

Impact of Increased Foreign Interest Rates on the Foreign Demand for U.S. Loanable Funds

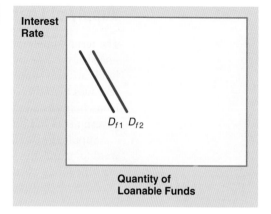

sectors are likely to demand a larger quantity of funds at lower interest rates (other things being equal), the aggregate demand for loanable funds is inversely related to interest rates at any point in time. If the demand schedule of any sector changes, the aggregate demand schedule will be affected as well.

Determination of the Aggregate Demand Schedule for Loanable Funds

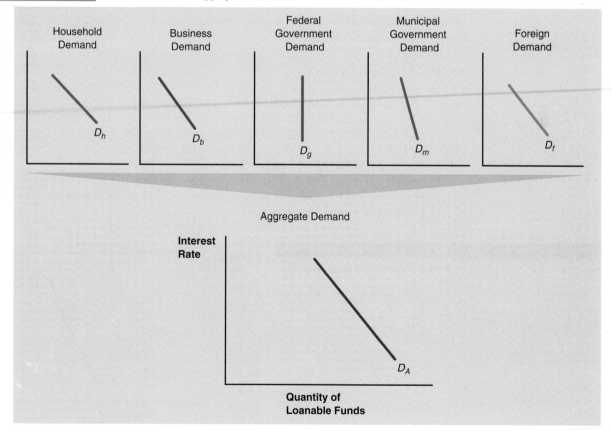

Supply of Loanable Funds

The term "supply of loanable funds" is commonly used to refer to funds provided to financial markets by savers. The household sector is the largest supplier, but loanable funds are also supplied by some government units that temporarily generate more tax revenues than they spend or by some businesses whose cash inflows exceed outflows. Households as a group, however, represent a net supplier of loanable funds, whereas governments and businesses are net demanders of loanable funds.

Suppliers of loanable funds are willing to supply more funds if the interest rate (reward for supplying funds) is higher, other things being equal (Exhibit 2.6). A supply of loanable funds exists at even a very low interest rate because some households choose to postpone consumption until later years, even when the reward (interest rate) for saving is low.

Foreign households, governments, and corporations commonly supply funds to their domestic markets by purchasing domestic securities. In addition, they have been a major creditor to the U.S. government by purchasing large amounts of Treasury securities. The large foreign supply of funds to the U.S. market is partially attributed to the high saving rates of foreign households.

The supply of loanable funds in the United States is also influenced by the monetary policy implemented by the Federal Reserve System. The Fed controls the amount of reserves held by depository institutions and can influence the amount of savings that can be converted into loanable funds.

Note that minimal attention has been given to financial institutions in this section. Although financial institutions play a critical intermediary role in channeling funds, they are not the ultimate suppliers of funds. Any change in a financial institution's supply of funds results only from a change in habits by the households, businesses, or governments that supply the funds.

The aggregate supply schedule of loanable funds represents the combination of all sector supply schedules along with the supply of funds provided by the Fed's monetary policy. The steep slope of the aggregate supply schedule in Exhibit 2.6 indicates that it is interest-inelastic, or somewhat insensitive to interest rates. The quantity of loanable funds demanded is normally expected to be more elastic, meaning more sensitive to interest rates, than the quantity of loanable funds supplied.

The supply curve can shift in or out in response to various conditions. For example, if the tax rate on interest income is reduced, the supply curve will shift outward, as

EXHIBIT 2.6

Aggregate Supply Schedule for Loanable Funds

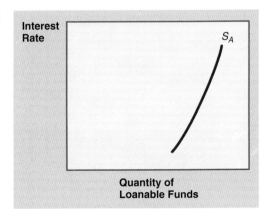

households save more funds at each possible interest rate level. Conversely, if the tax rate on interest income is increased, the supply curve will shift inward, as households save fewer funds at each possible interest rate level.

Equilibrium Interest Rate

An understanding of equilibrium interest rates is necessary to assess how various events can affect interest rates. In reality, there are several different interest rates because some borrowers pay a higher rate than others. At this point, however, the focus is on the forces that cause the general level of interest rates to change, as interest rates across borrowers tend to change in the same direction. The determination of an equilibrium interest rate is presented first from an algebraic perspective and then from a graphic perspective. Following this presentation, several examples are offered to reinforce the concept.

Algebraic Presentation The equilibrium interest rate is the rate that equates the aggregate demand for funds with the aggregate supply of loanable funds. The aggregate demand for funds (D_A) can be written as

$$D_A = D_h + D_b + D_g + D_m + D_f$$

where D_h = household demand for loanable funds

D_b = business demand for loanable funds

D_g = federal government demand for loanable funds

D_m = municipal government demand for loanable funds

D_f = foreign demand for loanable funds

The aggregate supply of funds (S_A) can be written as

$$S_A = S_h + S_b + S_g + S_m + S_f$$

where S_h = household supply of loanable funds

S_b = business supply of loanable funds

S_g = federal government supply of loanable funds

S_m = municipal government supply of loanable funds

S_f = foreign supply of loanable funds

In equilibrium, $D_A = S_A$. If the aggregate demand for loanable funds increases without a corresponding increase in aggregate supply, there will be a shortage of loanable funds. Interest rates will rise until an additional supply of loanable funds is available to accommodate the excess demand. If the aggregate supply of loanable funds increases without a corresponding increase in aggregate demand, there will be a surplus of loanable funds. Interest rates will fall until the quantity of funds supplied no longer exceeds the quantity of funds demanded.

In many cases, both supply and demand for loanable funds are changing. Given an initial equilibrium situation, the equilibrium interest rate should rise when $D_A > S_A$ and fall when $D_A < S_A$.

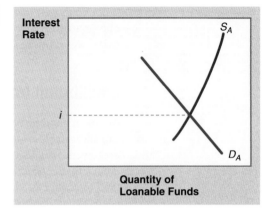

Graphic Presentation By combining the aggregate demand and aggregate supply schedules of loanable funds (refer to Exhibits 2.5 and 2.6), it is possible to compare the total amount of funds that would be demanded to the total amount of funds that would be supplied at any particular interest rate. Exhibit 2.7 illustrates the combined demand and supply schedules. At the equilibrium interest rate of i, the supply of loanable funds is equal to the demand for loanable funds.

At any interest rate above i, there is a surplus of loanable funds. Some potential suppliers of funds would be unable to successfully supply their funds at the prevailing interest rate. Once the market interest rate is lowered to i, the quantity of funds supplied is sufficiently reduced and the quantity of funds demanded is sufficiently increased such that there is no longer a surplus of funds. When a disequilibrium situation exists, market forces should cause an adjustment in interest rates until equilibrium is achieved.

If the prevailing interest rate is below i, there will be a shortage of loanable funds. Borrowers will not be able to obtain all the funds that they desire at that rate. Because of the shortage of funds, the interest rate will increase, causing two reactions. First, more savers will enter the market to supply loanable funds now that the reward (interest rate) is higher. Second, some potential borrowers will decide not to demand loanable funds at the higher interest rate. Once the interest rate rises to i, the quantity of loanable funds supplied has increased and the quantity of loanable funds demanded has decreased to the extent that a shortage no longer exists. An equilibrium position is achieved once again.

Economic Forces That Affect Interest Rates

Although it is useful to identify those who supply or demand loanable funds, it is also necessary to recognize the underlying economic forces that cause a change in the supply of or the demand for loanable funds. The following economic factors influence the demand for or supply of loanable funds and therefore influence interest rates.

Impact of Economic Growth on Interest Rates

Assume that as a result of more optimistic economic projections, most businesses increase their planned expenditures for expansion, which translates into additional borrowing. The aggregate demand schedule will shift outward (to the right). The supply-of-loanable-funds schedule may also shift, but it is more difficult to know how it will shift. It is possible that the increased expansion by businesses will lead to more income

EXHIBIT 2.8

Impact of Increased Expansion by Firms

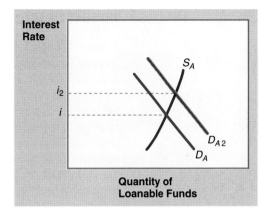

for construction crews and others who service the expansion. In this case, the quantity of savings, and therefore of loanable funds supplied at any possible interest rate, could increase, causing an outward shift in the supply schedule. Yet, there is no assurance that the volume of savings will actually increase. Even if a shift occurs, it will likely be of a smaller magnitude than the shift in the demand schedule.

Overall, the expected impact of the increased expansion by businesses is an outward shift in the demand schedule and no obvious change in the supply schedule (Exhibit 2.8). The shift in the aggregate demand schedule to D_{A2} in the exhibit causes an increase in the equilibrium interest rate to i_2.

Just as economic growth puts upward pressure on interest rates, an economic slowdown puts downward pressure on the equilibrium interest rate.

ILLUSTRATION Consider how a slowdown in the economy would affect the demand and supply schedules of loanable funds and the equilibrium interest rate. The demand schedule would shift inward (to the left), reflecting less demand for loanable funds at any possible interest rate. The supply schedule might possibly shift a little, but the direction of its shift is questionable. One could argue that a slowdown should cause increased saving at any possible interest rate as households prepare for the possibility of being laid off. At the same time, the gradual reduction in labor income that occurs during an economic slowdown could reduce households' ability to save. Historical data support this latter expectation. Any shift that does occur would likely be minor relative to the shift in the demand schedule. Therefore, the equilibrium interest rate is expected to decrease, as illustrated in Exhibit 2.9.

EXHIBIT 2.9

Impact of an Economic Slowdown

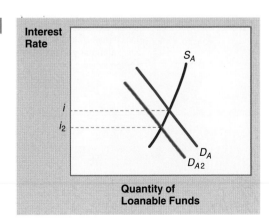

Impact of Inflation on Interest Rates

Inflation can affect interest rates because of its effect on the supply of savings and the demand for loanable funds. Consider a situation in which the U.S. inflation rate is expected to increase. Households that supply funds may reduce their savings at any interest rate level so that they can make more purchases now before prices rise. This shift in behavior is reflected by an inward shift (to the left) in the supply curve of loanable funds. In addition, households and businesses may be willing to borrow more funds at any interest rate level so that they can purchase products now before prices increase. This is reflected by an outward shift (to the right) in the demand curve for loanable funds. These shifts are illustrated in Exhibit 2.10. The new equilibrium interest rate is higher because of the shifts in saving and borrowing behavior.

Fisher Effect More than 50 years ago, Irving Fisher proposed a theory of interest rate determination that is still widely used today. It does not contradict the loanable funds theory but simply offers an additional explanation for interest rate movements. Fisher proposed that nominal interest payments compensate savers in two ways. First, they compensate for a saver's reduced purchasing power. Second, they provide an additional premium to savers for forgoing present consumption. Savers are willing to forgo consumption only if they receive a premium on their savings above the anticipated rate of inflation, as shown in the following equation:

$$i = E(INF) + i_R$$

where
$$i = \text{nominal or quoted rate of interest}$$
$$E(INF) = \text{expected inflation rate}$$
$$i_R = \text{real interest rate}$$

This relationship between interest rates and expected inflation is often referred to as the **Fisher effect.** The difference between the nominal interest rate and the expected inflation rate is the real return to a saver after adjusting for the reduced purchasing power over the time period of concern. It is referred to as the **real interest rate** because, unlike the nominal rate of interest, it adjusts for the expected rate of inflation. The preceding equation can be rearranged to express the real interest rate as

$$i_R = i - E(INF)$$

EXHIBIT 2.10

Impact of an Increase in Inflationary Expectations on Interest Rates

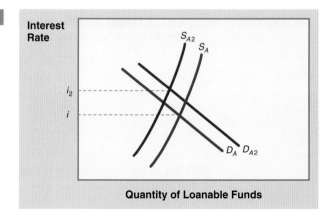

If the nominal interest rate was equal to the expected inflation rate, the real interest rate would be zero. Savings would accumulate interest at the same rate that prices were expected to increase, so the purchasing power of savings would remain stable.

There is a positive (though not perfect) relationship between nominal annual interest rates and inflation rates over time. When nominal interest rates in the United States were relatively high in the 1970s, so was the inflation rate. In recent years, nominal interest rates have been very low, and inflation has been low as well.

The real interest rate over an upcoming period can be forecasted by subtracting the expected inflation rate over that period from the nominal interest rate quoted for that period. Because the expected inflation rate is difficult to estimate, the real interest rate is difficult to forecast.

When the inflation rate is higher than anticipated, the real interest rate is relatively low. Borrowers benefit because they were able to borrow at a lower nominal interest rate than would have been offered if inflation had been accurately forecasted. When the inflation rate is lower than anticipated, the real interest rate is relatively high and borrowers are adversely affected.

Throughout the text, the term *interest rate* will be used to represent the nominal, or quoted, rate of interest. Keep in mind, however, that because of inflation, purchasing power is not necessarily increasing during periods of rising interest rates.

Impact of the Money Supply on Interest Rates

The Federal Reserve can affect the supply of loanable funds by increasing or reducing the total amount of deposits held at commercial banks or other depository institutions. The process by which the Fed adjusts the money supply is described in Chapter 4. When the Fed increases the money supply, it increases the supply of loanable funds, which places downward pressure on interest rates. If the Fed's actions affect inflationary expectations (as explained in Chapter 5), however, this will also increase the demand for loanable funds, which could offset the effect of the increase in the supply of funds.

If the Fed reduces the money supply, it reduces the supply of loanable funds. Assuming no change in demand, this action places upward pressure on interest rates.

Impact of September 11 The September 11, 2001 attack on the United States had a pronounced impact on U.S. interest rates. The attack disrupted travel and other forms of spending and aroused concerns that the economy might weaken further. Firms cut back on their expansion plans because some plans were no longer feasible, given the likelihood of a weaker economy. Several firms announced layoffs within a week of the attack. Households reduced their plans to borrow because of uncertainty about their jobs. The reduction in borrowing by firms and households caused a decline in the demand for loanable funds. One offsetting factor was the U.S. response to clean up the damage and to increase military spending, which increased the government demand for loanable funds. Nevertheless, this pressure did not fully offset the decline in the demand for loanable funds by firms and households. Furthermore, the Fed increased the supply of loanable funds in the banking system, which also placed downward pressure on interest rates.

Impact of the Weak Economy in 2001–2002 In the 2001–2002 period, economic conditions in the United States weakened. The economic slowdown tended to reduce the demand for loanable funds and therefore placed downward pressure on interest rates. Also, during this period, the Fed increased the money supply growth, which placed additional downward pressure on interest rates. Consequently, interest rates

reached very low levels. In 2003–2004, economic conditions improved, but the Fed maintained a large enough money supply to keep interest rates low.

Impact of Budget Deficits on Interest Rates

When the federal government enacts fiscal policies that result in more expenditures than tax revenue, the budget deficit is increased. Consider how an increase in the federal government deficit would affect interest rates, assuming no other changes in habits by consumers and firms occur. A higher federal government deficit increases the quantity of loanable funds demanded at any prevailing interest rate, causing an outward shift in the demand schedule. Assuming no offsetting increase in the supply schedule, interest rates will rise. Given a certain amount of loanable funds supplied to the market (through savings), excessive government demand for these funds tends to "crowd out" the private demand (by consumers and corporations) for funds. The federal government may be willing to pay whatever is necessary to borrow these funds, but the private sector may not. This impact is known as the **crowding-out effect.** Exhibit 2.11 illustrates the flow of funds between the federal government and the private sector.

There is a counterargument that the supply schedule might shift outward if the government creates more jobs by spending more funds than it collects from the public (this is what causes the deficit in the first place). If this were to occur, the deficit might not necessarily place upward pressure on interest rates. Much research has investigated this issue and, in general, has shown that higher deficits place upward pressure on interest rates.

The U.S. government is a frequent participant in the market for loanable funds. In 2003, the annual budget deficit exceeded $400 billion. Since a large budget deficit results in a large demand for borrowed funds, it may be surprising that U.S. interest rates were so low in 2003. The large government demand for funds was offset by a weak demand for funds by firms and individuals, a large supply of savings provided by individuals, and an increase in the money supply provided by the Fed.

Impact of Foreign Flows of Funds on Interest Rates

 GL BALASPECTS   The interest rate for a specific currency is determined by the demand for funds denominated in that currency and the supply of funds available in that currency.

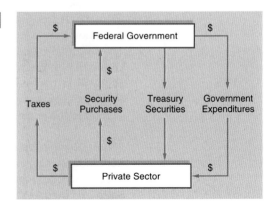

EXHIBIT 2.11

Flow of Funds between the Federal Government and the Private Sector

EXHIBIT 2.12

Demand and Supply Schedules for Loanable Funds Denominated in U.S. Dollars and Brazilian Real

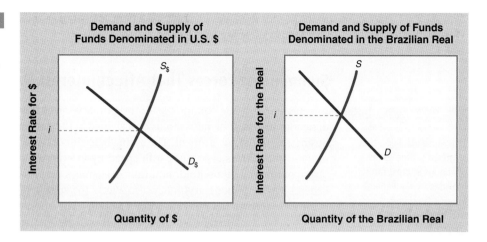

ILLUSTRATION

The supply and demand schedules for the U.S. dollar and for Brazil's currency (the real) are compared for a given point in time in Exhibit 2.12. Although the demand schedule for loanable funds should be downward sloping for every currency and the supply schedule should be upward sloping, the actual positions of these schedules vary among currencies. First, notice that the demand and supply curves are farther to the right for the dollar than for the Brazilian real. The amount of dollar-denominated loanable funds supplied and demanded is much greater than the amount of Brazilian real–denominated loanable funds because the U.S. economy is much larger than Brazil's economy.

Also notice that the positions of the demand and supply schedules for loanable funds are much higher for the Brazilian real than for the dollar. The supply schedule for loanable funds denominated in the Brazilian real shows that hardly any amount of savings would be supplied at low interest rate levels because the high inflation in Brazil encourages households to spend all of their disposable income before prices increase more. It discourages households from saving unless the interest rate is sufficiently high. In addition, the demand for loanable funds in the Brazilian real shows that borrowers are willing to borrow even at very high rates of interest because they want to make purchases now before prices increase. Firms are willing to pay 70 percent interest on a loan to purchase machines whose prices will have increased by 90 percent by next year.

Because of the different positions of the demand and supply schedules for the two currencies shown in Exhibit 2.12, the equilibrium interest rate is much higher for the Brazilian real than for the dollar. As the demand and supply schedules change over time for a specific currency, so will the equilibrium interest rate. For example, if Brazil's government could substantially reduce the local inflation, the supply schedule of loanable funds denominated in real would shift out (to the right) while the demand schedule of loanable funds would shift in (to the left), which would result in a lower equilibrium interest rate. Investors from other countries commonly invest in savings accounts in countries such as Brazil where the interest rates are high. However, the currencies of these countries usually weaken over time, which may more than offset the interest rate advantage.

In recent years, massive flows of funds have shifted between countries, causing abrupt adjustments in the supply of funds available in each country and therefore affecting interest rates. In general, the shifts are driven by large institutional investors seeking a high return on their investments. These investors commonly attempt to invest

funds in debt securities in countries where interest rates are high and where the currency is not expected to weaken.

Summary of Forces That Affect Interest Rates

http://research.stlouisfed.org/fred2 Time series of various interest rates provided by the Federal Reserve Economic Databank.

In general, economic conditions are the primary forces behind a change in the supply of savings provided by households or a change in the demand for funds by households, businesses, or the government. The saving behavior of the households that supply funds in the United States is partially influenced by U.S. fiscal policy, which determines the taxes paid by U.S. households and thus determines the level of disposable income. The Federal Reserve's monetary policy also affects the supply of funds in the United States because it determines the U.S. money supply. The supply of funds provided to the United States by foreign investors is influenced by foreign economic conditions, including foreign interest rates.

The demand for funds in the United States is indirectly affected by U.S. monetary and fiscal policies because these policies influence economic conditions such as economic growth and inflation, which affect business demand for funds. Fiscal policy determines the budget deficit and therefore determines the federal government demand for funds.

ILLUSTRATION A brief survey of U.S. interest rates over recent decades illustrates how these forces can interact to affect interest rates. In the late 1970s, interest rates were high as a result of a strong economy and inflationary expectations. A recession in the early 1980s caused a weak economy, which led to a decline in interest rates. In the late 1980s, interest rates drifted upward in response to a strong economy but then declined in the early 1990s as the economy weakened. In 1994, when economic growth resumed, interest rates increased. For the next several years, however, they drifted lower. Even though economic growth was strong in the late 1990s, the government demand for funds was unusually low as the U.S. fiscal budget had a surplus at that time. From 2000 to the beginning of 2003, the U.S. economy was very weak, which reduced the demand for loanable funds and caused interest rates to reach their lowest level in more than 30 years. Exhibit 2.13 shows nominal interest rates since 1980.

This summary does not cover every possible interaction among the forces that can affect interest rate movements, but it is sufficient for understanding why interest rates change over time. In fact, it will be used as the base to explain why prices of various securities change over time in other chapters, because many security prices are affected by interest rate movements.

Forecasting Interest Rates

http://research.stlouisfed.org/fred2 Quotations of existing interest rates and trends of historical interest rates for various debt securities.

Although there are no published comprehensive schedules that measure the quantity of funds to be supplied or demanded at every possible interest rate, the expected impact of a particular event can be assessed without even knowing the specific numbers that correspond to these schedules. Any event that causes an outward shift in the demand schedule should force interest rates up (as long as the supply schedule is not forced out to an equal or greater degree). Though it is difficult to predict the precise change in the interest rate due to a particular event, being able to assess the direction of supply or de-

EXHIBIT 2.13 Interest Rates over Time (One-Year Treasury Bill Rate Used as a Proxy)

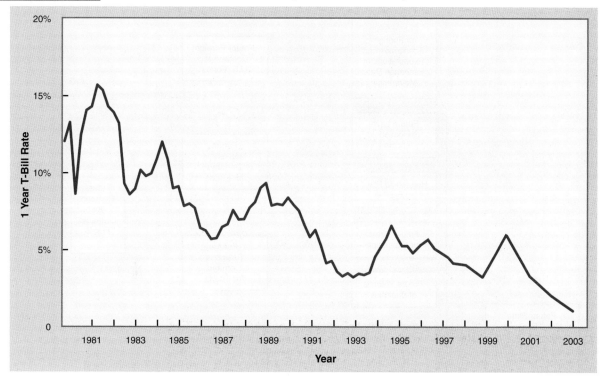

mand schedule shifts can at least help in understanding why interest rates changed in a specific direction.

Exhibit 2.14 summarizes the key factors that are evaluated when forecasting interest rates. With an understanding of how each factor affects interest rates, it is possible to forecast how interest rates may change in the future. When forecasting household demand for loanable funds, it may be necessary to assess consumer credit data to determine the borrowing capacity of households. Seasonal factors (such as Christmas or summer vacations) can also be important, as can the expected unemployment rate and a host of other factors that affect the earning power of households. The potential supply of loanable funds provided by households may be determined in the same manner.

Business demand for loanable funds can be forecasted by assessing future plans for corporate expansion and the future state of the economy. Federal government demand for loanable funds could be influenced by the future state of the economy because it affects tax revenues to be received and the amount of unemployment compensation to be paid out, factors that affect the size of the government deficit. The Federal Reserve System's money supply targets may be assessed by reviewing public statements about the Fed's future objectives, although those statements are somewhat vague.

To forecast future interest rates, the net demand for funds (ND) should be forecast:

$$ND = D_A - S_A$$
$$= (D_h + D_b + D_g + D_m + D_f) - (S_h + S_b + S_g + S_m + S_f)$$

If the forecasted level of ND is positive or negative, a disequilibrium will exist temporarily. If positive, it will be corrected by an upward adjustment in interest rates. If

EXHIBIT 2.14   Framework for Forecasting Interest Rates

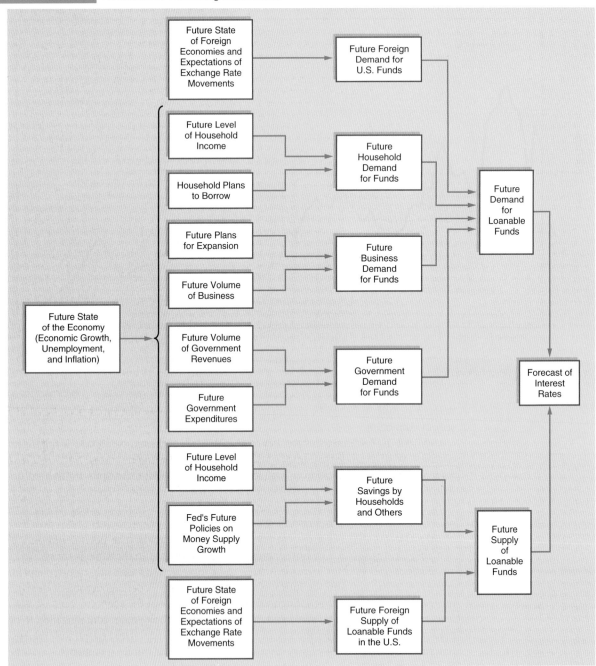

negative, it will be corrected by a downward adjustment. The larger the forecasted magnitude of *ND*, the larger the adjustment in interest rates.

Some analysts focus more on changes in D_A and S_A than on estimating the aggregate level of D_A and S_A. For example, assume that today the equilibrium interest rate is 7 percent. This interest rate will change only if D_A and S_A change to create a temporary disequilibrium. If the government demand for funds (D_g) is expected to increase substan-

tially, and no other components are expected to change, D_A will exceed S_A, placing upward pressure on interest rates. Thus, the forecast of future interest rates can be derived without estimating every component comprising D_A and S_A.

Forecasts of interest rates are wrong when forecasts of the components comprising D_A or S_A are wrong. For example, if government demand for loanable funds (D_g) is overestimated, while all the components are properly estimated, D_A will be overestimated. Consequently, interest rates will probably be lower than forecast.

Numerous statistical models have been applied to forecast interest rates. Many of these models attempt to account for a wide variety of factors that can affect the demand for funds or the supply of funds available. Even the most sophisticated models have not been able to accurately forecast interest rates, however. In fact, it is even difficult to accurately determine the future direction of interest rates. The use of a statistical model to forecast interest rates is explained in Appendix B.

To illustrate the difficulty in forecasting interest rates, consider how U.S. interest rates will be affected by the simultaneous existence of a higher government deficit, increased growth in the money supply, and increased foreign funds coming into the United States. There is no clear-cut answer. One can, however, make an educated guess by estimating the individual impact of each event on interest rates and then combining the expected impacts of all these events. Because some events may have a greater impact than others, it is necessary to measure not only the direction but also the magnitude of each impact.

SUMMARY

- The loanable funds framework shows how the equilibrium interest rate is dependent on the aggregate supply of available funds and the aggregate demand for funds. As conditions cause the aggregate supply or demand schedules to change, interest rates gravitate toward a new equilibrium.

- The relevant factors that affect interest rate movements include changes in economic growth, inflation, the budget deficit, foreign interest rates, and the money supply. These factors can have a strong impact on the aggregate supply of funds or on the aggregate demand for funds and therefore can affect

the equilibrium interest rate. In particular, economic growth has a strong influence on the demand for loanable funds, and changes in the money supply have a strong impact on the supply of loanable funds.

- Given that the equilibrium interest rate is determined by supply and demand conditions, changes in the interest rate can be forecasted by forecasting changes in the supply of or the demand for loanable funds. Thus, the factors that influence the supply of and the demand for funds must be forecasted in order to forecast interest rates.

POINT COUNTER-POINT

Does a Large Fiscal Budget Deficit Result in Higher Interest Rates?

Point No. In some years (such as 2003), the fiscal budget deficit was large and interest rates were very low.

Counter-Point Yes. When the federal government borrows large amounts of funds, it can crowd out other potential borrowers, and the interest rates are bid up by the deficit units.

Who Is Correct? Use your favorite search engine to learn more about this issue. Offer your own opinion on this issue.

QUESTIONS AND APPLICATIONS

1. **Managing in Financial Markets: Forecasting Interest Rates** As the treasurer of a manufacturing company, your task is to forecast the direction of interest rates. You plan to borrow funds and may use the forecast of interest rates to determine whether you should obtain a loan with a fixed interest rate or a floating interest rate. The following information can be considered when assessing the future direction of interest rates:

   ■ Economic growth has been high over the last two years, but you expect that it will be stagnant over the next year.

   ■ Inflation has been 3 percent over each of the last few years, and you expect that it will be about the same over the next year.

   ■ The federal government has announced major cuts in its spending, which should have a major impact on the budget deficit.

   ■ The Federal Reserve is not expected to affect the existing supply of loanable funds over the next year.

   ■ The overall level of savings by households is not expected to change.

   a. Given the preceding information, determine how the demand for and the supply of loanable funds would be affected (if at all), and determine the future direction of interest rates.

   b. You can obtain a one-year loan at a fixed rate of 8 percent or a floating-rate loan that is currently at 8 percent but would be revised every month in accordance with general interest rate movements. Which type of loan is more appropriate based on the information provided?

   c. Assume that Canadian interest rates have abruptly risen just as you have completed your forecast of future U.S. interest rates. Consequently, Canadian interest rates are now 2 percentage points above U.S. interest rates. How might this specific situation place pressure on U.S. interest rates? Considering this situation along with the other information provided, would you change your forecast of the future direction of U.S. interest rates?

2. **Impact of Government Spending** Jayhawk Forecasting Services analyzed several factors that could affect interest rates in the future. Most factors were expected to place downward pressure on interest rates. Jayhawk also felt that although the annual budget deficit was to be cut by 40 percent from the previous year, it would still be very large. Thus, Jayhawk believed that the deficit's impact would more than offset the other effects and therefore forecast interest rates to increase by 2 percent. Comment on Jayhawk's logic.

3. **Interest Rate Movements** Explain why interest rates changed as they did over the past year.

4. **Real Interest Rate** Estimate the real interest rate over the last year. If financial market participants overestimate inflation in a particular period, will real interest rates be relatively high or low? Explain.

5. **Impact of Expected Inflation** How might expectations of higher oil prices affect the demand for loanable funds, the supply of loanable funds, and interest rates in the United States? Will this affect the interest rates of other countries in the same way? Explain.

6. **Interest Elasticity** Explain what is meant by interest elasticity. Would you expect federal government demand for loanable funds to be more or less interest-elastic than household demand for loanable funds? Why?

7. **Interpreting Financial News** Interpret the following comments made by Wall Street analysts and portfolio managers:
   a. "The flight of funds from bank deposits to U.S. stocks will pressure interest rates."
   b. "Since Japanese interest rates have recently declined to very low levels, expect a reduction in U.S. interest rates."
   c. "The cost of borrowing by U.S. firms is dictated by the degree to which the federal government spends more than it taxes."

8. **Impact of a Recession** Explain why interest rates tend to decrease during recessionary periods. Review historical interest rates to determine how they react to recessionary periods. Explain this reaction.

9. **Global Interaction of Interest Rates** Why might you expect interest rate movements of various industrialized countries to be more highly correlated in recent years than in earlier years?

10. **Impact of Government Spending** If the federal government planned to expand the space program, how might this affect interest rates?

11. **Decomposing Interest Rate Movements** The interest rate on a one-year loan can be decomposed into a one-year risk-free (free from default risk) component and a risk premium that reflects the potential for default on the loan in that year. A change in economic conditions can affect the risk-free rate and the risk premium. The risk-free rate is normally affected by changing economic conditions to a greater degree than the risk premium. Explain how a weaker economy will likely affect the risk-free component, the risk premium, and the overall cost of a one-year loan obtained by (a) the Treasury, and (b) a corporation. Will the change in the cost of borrowing be more pronounced for the Treasury or for the corporation? Why?

12. **Internet Exercise** Go to http://research.stlouisfed.org/fred2. Under "Categories," select "Interest rates" and then select the three-month Treasury bill series (secondary market). Describe how this rate has changed in recent months. Using the information in this chapter, explain why the interest rate changed as it did.

13. **Impact of Exchange Rates on Interest Rates** Assume that if the U.S. dollar strengthens, it can place downward pressure on U.S. inflation. Based on this information, how might expectations of a strong dollar affect the demand for loanable funds in the United States and U.S. interest rates? Is there any reason to think that expectations of a strong dollar could also affect the supply of loanable funds? Explain.

14. **Impact of the Economy** Obtain or develop forecasts of economic growth and inflation. Use this information to forecast interest rates one year from now.

15. **Impact of War** A war tends to cause significant reactions in financial markets. Why would a war in Iraq place upward pressure on U.S. interest rates? Why might some investors expect a war like this to place downward pressure on U.S. interest rates?

16. **Impact of Stock Market Crises** During periods in which investors suddenly become fearful that stocks are overvalued, they dump their stocks, and the stock market experiences a major decline. During these periods, interest rates tend to decline. Use the loanable funds framework discussed in this chapter to explain how the massive selling of stocks leads to lower interest rates.

17. **Nominal versus Real Interest Rate** What is the difference between the nominal interest rate and the real interest rate? What is the logic behind the Fisher effect's implied positive relationship between expected inflation and nominal interest rates?

18. **Impact of September 11** Offer an argument for why the terrorist attack on the United States on September 11, 2001, could have placed downward pressure on U.S. interest rates. Offer an argument for why the terrorist attack could have placed upward pressure on U.S. interest rates.

19. **Impact of the Money Supply** Should increasing money supply growth place upward or downward pressure on interest rates?

20. **Forecasting Interest Rates** Why do forecasts of interest rates differ among experts?

PROBLEMS

1. **Real Interest Rate** Suppose that Treasury bills are currently paying 9 percent and the expected inflation is 3 percent. What is the real interest rate?

2. **Nominal Rate of Interest** Suppose the real interest rate is 6 percent and the expected inflation is 2 percent. What would you expect the nominal rate of interest to be?

FLOW OF FUNDS EXERCISE

How the Flow of Funds Affects Interest Rates

Recall that Carson Company has obtained substantial loans from finance companies and commercial banks. The interest rate on the loans is tied to market interest rates and is adjusted every six months. Thus, its cost of

obtaining funds is sensitive to interest rate movements. Because of its expectations that the U.S. economy will strengthen, Carson plans to grow in the future by expanding its business and through acquisitions. Carson expects that it will need substantial long-term financing to finance its growth and plans to borrow additional funds either through loans or by issuing bonds. It is also considering the issuance of stock to raise funds in the next year.

a. Explain why Carson should be very interested in future interest rate movements.

b. Given Carson's expectations, do you think that Carson expects interest rates to increase or decrease in the future? Explain.

c. If Carson's expectations of future interest rates are correct, how would this affect its cost of borrowing on its existing loans and on future loans?

d. Explain why Carson's expectations about future interest rates may affect its decision about when to borrow funds and whether to obtain floating-rate or fixed-rate loans.

WSJ EXERCISE

Forecasting Interest Rates

Review the "Credit Markets" section in a recent issue of *The Wall Street Journal* (listed in the index on the front page). Use this section to determine the factors likely to have the largest impact on future interest rate movements. Then create your own forecasts as to whether interest rates will increase or decrease from now until the end of this school term, based on your assessment of any factors that affect interest rates. Explain your forecast.

CHAPTER 3

Interest Rates Structure

The annual interest rate offered by debt securities at a given point in time varies among debt securities. Consequently, the yields offered by debt securities at a given point in time have a particular structure. Some types of debt securities always offer a higher yield than others. Individual and institutional investors must understand why quoted yields vary so that they can determine whether the extra yield on a given security outweighs any unfavorable characteristics. Financial managers of corporations or government agencies in need of funds must understand why quoted yields of debt securities vary so that they can estimate the yield they would have to offer in order to sell new debt securities.

The specific objectives of this chapter are to:

■ describe how characteristics of debt securities cause their yields to vary,

■ demonstrate how to estimate the appropriate yield for any particular debt security, and

■ explain the theories behind the term structure of interest rates (relationship between the term to maturity and the yield of securities).

Why Debt Security Yields Vary

Debt securities offer different yields because they exhibit different characteristics that influence the yield to be offered. In general, securities with unfavorable characteristics will offer higher yields to entice investors. Yet, some debt securities have favorable features as well. The yields on debt securities are affected by the following characteristics:

■ Credit (default) risk
■ Liquidity
■ Tax status
■ Term to maturity
■ Special provisions

Credit (Default) Risk

Because most securities are subject to the risk of default, investors must consider the creditworthiness of the security issuer. Although investors always have the option of

purchasing risk-free Treasury securities, they may prefer some other securities if the yield compensates them for the risk. Thus, if all other characteristics besides credit (default) risk are equal, securities with a higher degree of risk would have to offer higher yields to be chosen. Credit risk is especially relevant for longer-term securities that expose creditors to the possibility of default for a longer time.

Credit risk premiums of 1 percent, 2 percent, or more may not seem significant. But for a corporation borrowing $30 million through the issuance of bonds, an extra percentage point as a premium reflects $300,000 in additional interest expenses per year.

Investors who do not necessarily desire to assess the creditworthiness of corporations that issue bonds can benefit from bond ratings provided by rating agencies. These ratings are based on a financial assessment of the issuing corporation. The higher the rating, the lower the perceived credit risk. As time passes, economic conditions can change, and the perceived credit risk of a corporation can change as well. Thus, bonds previously issued by a firm could be rated at one level, while a subsequent issue from the same firm could be rated at a different level. The ratings could also differ if the collateral provisions differ among the bonds.

Rating Agencies The most popular rating agencies are Moody's Investor Service and Standard & Poor's Corporation. A summary of their rating classification schedules is provided in Exhibit 3.1. Moody's ratings range from Aaa for highest quality to C for lowest quality, and Standard & Poor's range from AAA to D. Because these rating agencies use different methods to assess the creditworthiness of firms and state governments, a particular bond could be assigned a different rating by each agency; however, differences are usually small.

Some financial institutions such as commercial banks are required by law to invest only in **investment-grade bonds,** that is, bonds that are rated as Baa or better by Moody's and BBB or better by Standard & Poor's. This requirement is intended to limit the portfolio risk of the financial institutions.

Accuracy of Credit Ratings In general, credit ratings have served as reasonable indicators of the likelihood of default. Bonds assigned a low credit rating experience default more frequently than bonds assigned a high credit rating. Nevertheless, credit rating

EXHIBIT 3.1

Rating Classification by Rating Agencies

Description of Security	Ratings Assigned by: Moody's	Ratings Assigned by: Standard & Poor's
Highest quality	Aaa	AAA
High quality	Aa	AA
High-medium quality	A	A
Medium quality	Baa	BBB
Medium-low quality	Ba	BB
Low quality (speculative)	B	B
Poor quality	Caa	CCC
Very poor quality	Ca	CC
Lowest quality (in default)	C	DDD, D

Yields across Securities

Yield quotations of different types of securities are listed each day in *The Wall Street Journal,* as shown here. The yields can be compared to reinforce how premiums are required to compensate for various characteristics. For example, the difference in yields between the long-term ("10+yr") Treasury bonds and high-quality ("High Qlty") corporate bonds is attributed to the safety, liquidity, and relative tax advantage of Treasury securities. The difference in yields between the long-term high-quality and medium-quality corporate bonds is primarily attributed to default risk differentials. The difference between the municipal (tax-exempt) and corporate bond yields is mainly attributed to the tax advantage of municipal bonds.

Yield Comparisons

Based on Merrill Lynch Bond Indexes, priced as of midafternoon Eastern time.

	8/10	8/9	52-WEEK HIGH	52-WEEK LOW
Corp. Govt. Master	3.96%	3.89%	4.47%	3.16%
Treasury				
1-10 yr	2.98	2.90	3.45	2.07
10+ yr	4.89	4.86	5.43	4.36
Agencies				
1-10 yr	3.31	3.23	3.86	2.25
10+ yr	5.28	5.25	5.93	4.66
Corporate				
1-10 yr High Quality	3.76	3.69	4.26	2.84
Medium Quality	4.36	4.29	4.86	3.48
10+ yr High Quality	5.76	5.74	6.26	5.23
Medium Quality	6.19	6.16	6.86	5.60
Yankee bonds (1)	4.34	4.28	4.81	3.53
Current-coupon mortgages (2)				
GNMA 5.48% (3)	5.16	5.08	5.82	4.53
FNMA 5.48%	5.24	5.18	5.95	4.58
FHLMC 5.48%	5.25	5.19	6.01	4.61
High-yield corporates	7.72	7.70	9.58	6.88
Tax-Exempt Bonds				
7-12 yr G.O. (AA)	3.70	3.65	4.33	3.08
12-22 yr G.O. (AA)	4.20	4.16	4.93	3.85
22+ yr revenue (A)	4.89	4.88	5.42	4.31

Note: High quality rated AAA-AA; medium quality A-BBB/Baa; high yield, BB/Ba-C.
(1) Dollar-denominated, SEC-registered bonds of foreign issuers sold in the U.S. (2) Reflects the 52-week high and low of mortgage-backed securities indexes rather than the individual securities shown. (3) Government guaranteed.

agencies do not always detect firms' financial problems. For example, they did not recognize Enron's financial problems until shortly before Enron filed for bankruptcy. Their inability to detect Enron's problems may be partially attributed to Enron's fraudulent financial statements that the credit agencies presumed were accurate.

Shifts in Credit Risk Premiums The risk premium corresponding to a particular bond rating can change over time.

ILLUSTRATION During the stock market crash on October 19, 1987, there was a shift in the risk perception of bonds, as shown in Exhibit 3.2. The risk perception can be measured by a bond's risk premium (the difference between the bond's yield and a risk-free Treasury bond with the same maturity). Notice from the exhibit how the default risk premium on both Baa and Aaa bonds increased after the crash. The significant jump in the risk premium suggests that investors changed their risk perception of these bonds.

Liquidity

Investors prefer securities that are *liquid,* meaning that they could be easily converted to cash without a loss in value. Thus, if all other characteristics are equal, securities with

EXHIBIT 3.2

Impact of the Stock Market Crash of October 1987 on Default Risk Premiums

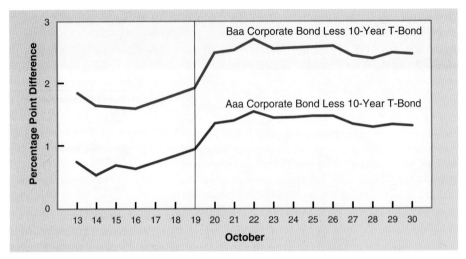

Source: *Chicago Fed Letter,* December 1987.

lower liquidity will have to offer a higher yield to be preferred. Securities with a short-term maturity or an active secondary market have higher liquidity. For investors who will not need their funds until the securities mature, lower liquidity is tolerable. Other investors, however, are willing to accept a lower return in exchange for a high degree of liquidity.

Tax Status

Investors are more concerned with after-tax income than before-tax income earned on securities. If all other characteristics are similar, taxable securities will have to offer a higher before-tax yield to investors than tax-exempt securities to be preferred. The extra compensation required on such taxable securities depends on the tax rates of individual and institutional investors. Investors in high tax brackets benefit most from tax-exempt securities.

When assessing the expected yields of various securities with similar risk and maturity, it is common to convert them into an after-tax form, as follows:

$$Y_{at} = Y_{bt}(1 - T)$$

where
$$Y_{at} = \text{after-tax yield}$$

$$Y_{bt} = \text{before-tax yield}$$

$$T = \text{investor's marginal tax rate}$$

Investors retain only a percentage $(1 - T)$ of the before-tax yield once taxes are paid.

ILLUSTRATION Consider a taxable security that offers a before-tax yield of 14 percent. When converted into after-tax terms, the yield will be reduced by the tax percentage. The precise after-tax yield is dependent on the tax rate (T). If the tax rate of the investor is 20 percent, the after-tax yield will be

EXHIBIT 3.3

After-Tax Yields Based on
Various Tax Rates and
Before-Tax Yields

Tax Rate	Before-Tax Yield							
	6%	8%	10%	12%	14%	16%	18%	20%
10%	5.40%	7.20%	9.00%	10.80%	12.60%	14.40%	16.20%	18.00%
15	5.10	6.80	8.50	10.20	11.90	13.60	15.30	17.00
20	4.80	6.40	8.00	9.60	11.20	12.80	14.40	16.00
28	4.32	5.76	7.20	8.64	10.08	11.52	12.96	14.40
34	3.96	5.28	6.60	7.92	9.24	10.56	11.88	13.20

$$Y_{at} = Y_{bt}(1 - T)$$
$$Y_{at} = 14\%(1 - .2)$$
$$= 11.2\%$$

Exhibit 3.3 presents after-tax yields based on a variety of tax rates and before-tax yields. For example, a taxable security with a before-tax yield of 6 percent will generate an after-tax yield of 5.4 percent to an investor in the 10 percent tax bracket, 4.8 percent to an investor in the 20 percent tax bracket, and so on. This exhibit shows why investors in high tax brackets are attracted to tax-exempt securities.

Computing the Equivalent Before-Tax Yield In some cases, investors wish to determine the before-tax yield necessary to match the after-tax yield of a tax-exempt security that has a similar risk and maturity. This can be done by rearranging the terms of the previous equation:

$$Y_{bt} = \frac{Y_{at}}{(1 - T)}$$

Suppose that a firm in the 20 percent tax bracket is aware of a tax-exempt security that is paying a yield of 8 percent. To match this after-tax yield, taxable securities must offer a before-tax yield of

$$Y_{bt} = \frac{Y_{at}}{(1 - T)} = \frac{8\%}{(1 - .2)} = 10\%$$

State taxes should be considered along with federal taxes in determining the after-tax yield. Treasury securities are exempt from state income tax, and municipal securities are sometimes exempt as well. Because states impose different income tax rates, a particular security's after-tax yield may vary with the location of the investor.

Term to Maturity

Maturity differs among securities and is another reason that security yields differ. The **term structure of interest rates** defines the relationship between maturity and annualized yield, holding other factors such as risk constant.

Any available business periodical can be used to determine the annualized yields of Treasury securities with different terms to maturity.

Example of Relationship between Maturity and Yield of Treasury Securities (as of February 25, 2004)

Time to Maturity	Yield
3 months	1.0%
6 months	1.2
1 year	1.6
2 years	1.8
3 years	2.0
4 years	2.5
5 years	3.0
10 years	4.0
20 years	4.5
30 years	4.9

ILLUSTRATION

The annualized yields for federal government securities of varied maturities are listed in Exhibit 3.4. A graphic comparison of these maturities and annualized yields is provided in Exhibit 3.5. The curve created by connecting the points plotted in that exhibit is commonly referred to as a yield curve. Because this yield curve is upward sloping, it indicates that the Treasury securities with longer maturities offered higher annualized yields. A downward-sloping curve implies the opposite, and a horizontal yield curve implies that annualized yields are similar for securities with different maturities.

The term structure of interest rates shown in Exhibit 3.5 shows that securities that are similar in all ways except their term to maturity may offer different yields. Because

Development of Yield Curve Based on the Data in Exhibit 3.4

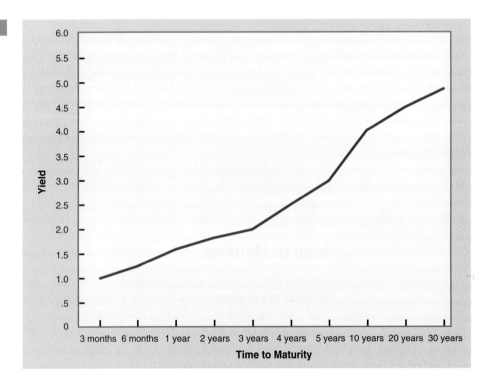

the demand and supply conditions for securities may vary among maturities, so may the price (and therefore the yield) of securities. A comprehensive explanation of the term structure of interest rates is provided later in this chapter.

Special Provisions

If a security offers any special provision to investors, its yield may be influenced. One type of provision, called a **call feature,** allows the issuer of the bonds to buy the bonds back before maturity at a specified price.

ILLUSTRATION   Any firm that issued callable bonds in the early 1980s when interest rates were very high can provide a classic example of the use of call feature. Florida Power & Light had issued bonds offering a 16 percent yield in 1981. By 1986, interest rates had dropped substantially, so the call feature was used to retire the 1981 bonds and new bonds were issued at a yield of about 9.9 percent. The result was an interest savings of about 6.1 percent, or $61,000 per $1 million borrowed on an annual basis.

Because a call feature could force investors to sell their bonds sooner than they would like, investors may require extra compensation to purchase the bonds. This is especially true during those periods when interest rates are expected to decrease, making it more likely that the bonds will be called. Thus, the yield on callable bonds should be higher than on noncallable bonds, other things being equal.

Another special provision of bonds that can affect the yield is a **convertibility clause,** which allows investors to convert the bond into a specified number of common stock shares. If the market price of the bonds declines, investors who wish to dispose of the bonds have an alternative to selling them in the market. For this reason, investors will accept a lower yield on securities that contain the convertibility feature, other things being equal.

Explaining Actual Yield Differentials

http://
http://www.bloomberg.com
Assess the most recent yield curve.

Even small differentials in yield can be relevant to the financial institutions that are borrowing or investing millions of dollars. Yield differentials are sometimes measured in basis points; a basis point equals .01 percent, and 100 basis points equals 1 percent. If security Q offers a yield of 5.4 percent while security R offers a yield of 5.1 percent, the yield differential is .30 percent or 30 basis points. Yield differentials are measured for money market securities next, followed by capital market securities.

Yield Differentials of Money Market Securities

Commercial paper rates are typically just slightly higher than T-bill (Treasury bill) rates, as investors require a slightly higher return to compensate for default risk and less liquidity. Negotiable certificates of deposit rates are higher than yields on Treasury bills with the same maturity because of their lower degree of liquidity and higher degree of default risk during that period.

Exhibit 3.6 illustrates the annualized yields of T-bills and commercial paper (with a three-month maturity). Although these yields are quite volatile from year to year, their respective differences normally do not change much over time. The difference between

EXHIBIT 3.6 Yield Comparison of Securities with Identical (Three-Month) Maturities over Time

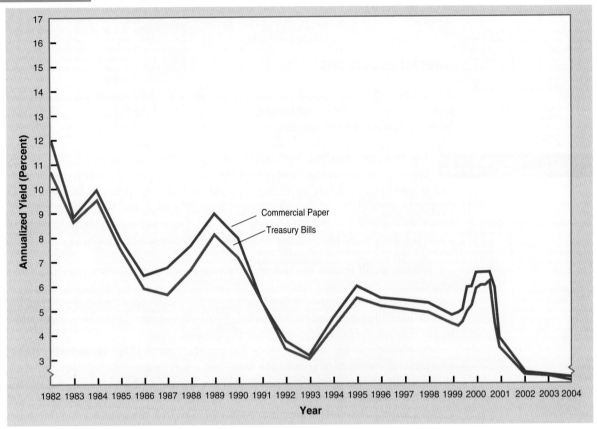

yields on T-bills and other commercial paper is higher during recessionary periods because the default risk is higher then.

Market forces cause the yields of all securities to move in the same direction. To illustrate, assume the budget deficit increases substantially and the Treasury issues a large number of T-bills to finance the increased deficit. This action creates a large supply of T-bills in the market, placing downward pressure on the price and upward pressure on the T-bill yield. As the yield begins to rise, it approaches the yield of other short-term securities. Businesses and individual investors are now encouraged to purchase T-bills rather than these risky securities because they can achieve about the same yield while avoiding default risk. The switch to T-bills lowers demand for risky securities, thereby placing downward pressure on their price and upward pressure on their yields. Thus, the risk premium on risky securities would not disappear completely.

Yield Differentials of Capital Market Securities

With regard to capital market securities, municipal bonds have the lowest before-tax yield, yet their after-tax yield is typically above that of Treasury bonds from the perspective of investors in high tax brackets. Treasury bonds are expected to offer the lowest yield because they are free from default risk and can easily be liquidated in the sec-

EXHIBIT 3.7 Yield Differentials of Corporate Bonds

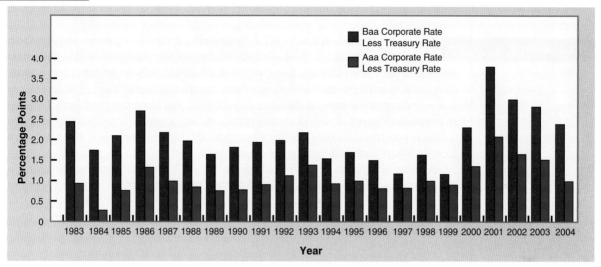

Note: Chart shows yield to maturity on seasoned corporate and Treasury debt with 10 years to maturity.

ondary market. Investors prefer municipal or corporate bonds over Treasury bonds only if the after-tax yield is sufficiently higher to compensate for default risk and a lower degree of liquidity.

To assess how capital market security yields can vary because of default risk, Exhibit 3.7 illustrates yields of corporate bonds in two different risk classes. The yield differentials among capital market securities can change over time as perceptions of risk change.

Estimating the Appropriate Yield

The discussion up to this point suggests that the appropriate yield to be offered on a debt security is based on the risk-free rate for the corresponding maturity, with adjustments to capture various characteristics. This model is specified below:

$$Y_n = R_{f,n} + DP + LP + TA + CALLP + COND$$

where

Y_n = yield of an n-day debt security

$R_{f,n}$ = yield of an n-day Treasury (risk-free) security

DP = default premium to compensate for credit risk

LP = liquidity premium to compensate for less liquidity

TA = adjustment due to the difference in tax status

$CALLP$ = call feature premium to compensate for the possibility that the security will be called

$COND$ = convertibility discount

These are the characteristics identified earlier that explain yield differentials among securities. Although maturity is another characteristic that can affect the yield, it is not

included here because it is controlled for by matching the maturity of the risk-free security to that of the security of concern.

Suppose that the three-month T-bill's annualized rate is 8 percent and Elizabeth Company plans to issue 90-day commercial paper. Elizabeth will need to determine the default premium (DP) and liquidity premium (LP) to offer on its commercial paper to make it as attractive to investors as a three-month (13-week) T-bill. The federal tax status of commercial paper is the same as for T-bills. Yet, income earned from investing in commercial paper is subject to state taxes, whereas income earned from investing in T-bills is not. Investors may require a premium for this reason alone if they reside in a location where state and local income taxes apply.

Assume that Elizabeth Company believes that a 0.7 percent default risk premium, a 0.2 percent liquidity premium, and a 0.3 percent tax adjustment are necessary to sell its commercial paper to investors. Because call and convertibility features are applicable only to bonds, they can be ignored here. The appropriate yield to be offered on the commercial paper (called Y_{cp}) is

$$
\begin{aligned}
Y_{cp,n} &= R_{f,n} + DP + LP + TA \\
&= 8\% + .7\% + .2\% + .3\% \\
&= 9.2\%
\end{aligned}
$$

As time passes, the appropriate commercial paper rate will change, perhaps because of changes in the risk-free rate, default premium, liquidity premium, and tax adjustment.

Some corporations may postpone plans to issue commercial paper until the economy improves and the required premium for credit risk is reduced. Yet even then, the market rate of commercial paper may increase if interest rates increase. For example, if over time the default risk premium decreases from 0.7 percent to 0.5 percent but $R_{f,n}$ increases from 8 percent to 8.7 percent, the appropriate yield to be offered on commercial paper (assuming no change in the previously assumed liquidity and tax adjustment premiums) would be

$$
\begin{aligned}
Y_{cp} &= R_{f,n} + DP + LP + TA \\
&= 8.7\% + .5\% + .2\% + .3\% \\
&= 9.7\%
\end{aligned}
$$

The strategy to postpone issuing commercial paper would backfire in this example. Even though the default premium decreased by 0.2 percent, the general level of interest rates rose by 0.7 percent, so the net change in the commercial paper rate is +0.5 percent. As this example shows, the increase in a security's yield over time does not necessarily mean the default premium has increased.

The assessment of yields as described here could also be applied to long-term securities. If, for example, a firm desires to issue a 20-year corporate bond, it will use the yield of a new 20-year Treasury bond as the 20-year risk-free rate and add on the premiums for credit risk, liquidity risk, and so on, to determine the yield at which it can sell corporate bonds.

A simpler and more general relationship is that the yield offered on a debt security is positively related to the prevailing risk-free rate and the security's risk premium (RP). This risk premium captures any risk characteristics of the security, including credit risk and liquidity risk.

USING THE WALL STREET JOURNAL

WSJ Yield Curve

A graph illustrating the yield curve is typically shown in the "Credit Markets" section of *The Wall Street Journal*. Annualized yields of Treasury securities are shown for terms to maturity ranging from one month to 30 years. Yield curves are shown for three different points in time, but the curves overlap if the yield curve has not changed.

Treasury Yield Curve
Yield to maturity of current bills, notes and bonds.

Source: Reuters

A Closer Look at Term Structure

Of all the factors that affect the yields offered on debt securities, the factor that is most difficult to understand is the term to maturity. For this reason, a more comprehensive explanation of the relationship between term to maturity and annualized yield (referred to as the term structure of interest rates) is necessary.

Various theories have been used to explain the relationship between maturity and annualized yield of securities, including the pure expectations theory, liquidity premium theory, and segmented markets theory. Each of these theories is explained here.

Pure Expectations Theory

According to the **pure expectations theory,** the term structure of interest rates (as reflected in the shape of the yield curve) is determined solely by expectations of future interest rates.

Impact of an Expected Increase in Interest Rates To understand how interest rate expectations may influence the yield curve, assume that the annualized yields of short-term and long-term securities are similar; that is, the yield curve is flat. Then assume that investors begin to believe that interest rates will rise. They will respond by investing their funds mostly in the short term so that they can soon reinvest their funds at higher yields after interest rates increase. When investors flood the short-term market

EXHIBIT 3.8   How Interest Rate Expectations Affect the Yield Curve

Panel A: Impact of a Sudden Expectation of Higher Interest Rates

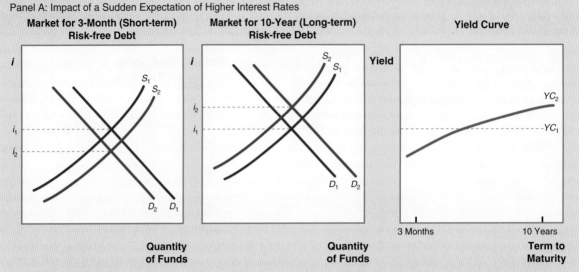

E($\uparrow i$) → Supply of funds provided by investors $\uparrow$ in short-term (such as 3-month) markets, and $\downarrow$ in long-term (such as 10-year) markets. Demand for funds by borrowers $\uparrow$ in long-term markets and $\downarrow$ in short-term markets. Therefore, the yield curve becomes upward sloping as shown here.

Panel B: Impact of a Sudden Expectation of Lower Interest Rates

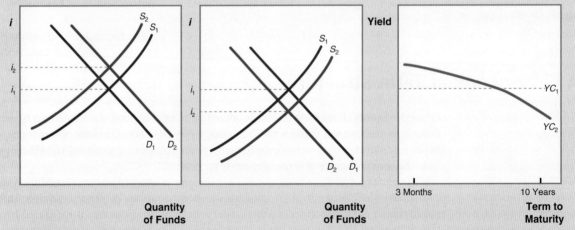

E($\downarrow i$) → Supply of funds provided by investors $\uparrow$ in long-term (such as 10-year) markets, and $\downarrow$ in short-term (such as 3-month) markets. Demand for funds by borrowers $\uparrow$ in short-term markets and $\downarrow$ in long-term markets. Therefore, the yield curve becomes downward sloping as shown here.

and avoid the long-term market, they may cause the yield curve to adjust as shown in Panel A of Exhibit 3.8. The large supply of funds in short-term markets will force annualized yields down. Meanwhile, the reduced supply of long-term funds forces long-term yields up.

Even though the annualized short-term yields become lower than annualized long-term yields, investors in short-term funds are satisfied because they expect interest rates to rise. They will make up for the lower short-term yield when the short-term securities mature, and they reinvest at a higher rate (if interest rates rise) at maturity.

	Impact of Expected Increase in Interest Rates	Impact of Expected Decrease in Interest Rates
Supply of short-term funds provided by investors	Upward pressure	Downward pressure
Demand for short-term funds by borrowers	Downward pressure	Upward pressure
Yield on new short-term securities	Downward pressure	Upward pressure
Supply of long-term funds provided by investors	Downward pressure	Upward pressure
Demand for long-term funds issued by borrowers	Upward pressure	Downward pressure
Yield on long-term securities	Upward pressure	Downward pressure
Shape of yield curve	Upward slope	Downward slope

Assuming that the borrowers who plan to issue securities also expect interest rates to increase, they will prefer to lock in the present interest rate over a long period of time. Thus, borrowers will generally prefer to issue long-term securities rather than short-term securities. This results in a relatively small demand for short-term funds. Consequently, there is downward pressure on the yield of short-term funds. There is also an increase in the demand for long-term funds by borrowers, which places upward pressure on long-term funds. Overall, the expectation of higher interest rates changes the demand for funds and the supply of funds in different maturity markets, which forces the original flat yield curve (labeled YC_1) to pivot upward (counterclockwise) and become upward sloping (YC_2).

Impact of an Expected Decline in Interest Rates If investors expect interest rates to decrease in the future, they will prefer to invest in long-term funds rather than short-term funds, because they could lock in today's interest rate before interest rates fall. Borrowers will prefer to borrow short-term funds so that they can reborrow at a lower interest rate once interest rates decline.

Based on the expectation of lower interest rates in the future, the supply of funds provided by investors will be low for short-term funds and high for long-term funds. This will place upward pressure on short-term yields and downward pressure on long-term yields as shown in Panel B of Exhibit 3.8. Overall, the expectation of lower interest rates causes the shape of the yield curve to pivot downward (clockwise). The impact of interest rate expectations on the slope of the yield curve is summarized in Exhibit 3.9.

Algebraic Presentation Investors monitor the yield curve to determine the rates that exist for securities with various maturities. They can purchase either a security with a maturity that matches their investment horizon or a security with a shorter term and reinvest the proceeds at maturity. If a particular investment strategy is expected to generate a higher return over the investment horizon, investors may use that strategy. This could affect the prices and yields of securities with different maturities, realigning the rates so that the expected return over the entire investment horizon would be similar, regardless of the strategy used. If investors were indifferent to security maturities, they would want the return of any security to equal the compounded yield of consecutive investments in shorter-term securities. That is, a two-year security should offer a return that is similar to the anticipated return from investing in two consecutive one-year securities. A four-year security should offer a return that is competitive with the expected return from investing in two consecutive two-year securities or four consecutive one-year securities, and so on.

To illustrate these equalities, consider the relationship between interest rates on a two-year security and a one-year security as follows:

$$(1 + {}_{t}i_2)^2 = (1 + {}_{t}i_1)(1 + {}_{t+1}r_1)$$

where

${}_{t}i_2$ = known annualized interest rate of a two-year security as of time t

${}_{t}i_1$ = known annualized interest rate of a one-year security as of time t

${}_{t+1}r_1$ = one-year interest rate that is anticipated as of time $t + 1$ (one year ahead)

The term i represents a quoted rate, which is therefore known, whereas r represents a rate to be quoted at some point in the future, which is therefore uncertain. The left side of the equation represents the compounded yield to investors who purchase a two-year security, while the right side of the equation represents the anticipated compounded yield from purchasing a one-year security and reinvesting the proceeds in a new one-year security at the end of one year. If time t is today, ${}_{t+1}r_1$ can be estimated by rearranging terms:

$$1 + {}_{t+1}r_1 = \frac{(1 + {}_{t}i_2)^2}{(1 + {}_{t}i_1)}$$

$${}_{t+1}r_1 = \frac{(1 + {}_{t}i_2)^2}{(1 + {}_{t}i_1)} - 1$$

The term ${}_{t+1}r_1$, referred to as the **forward rate,** is commonly estimated in order to represent the market's forecast of the future interest rate. As a numerical example, assume that as of today (time t) the annualized two-year interest rate is 10 percent, while the one-year interest rate is 8 percent. The forward rate is estimated as follows:

$${}_{t+1}r_1 = \frac{(1 + .10)^2}{(1 + .08)} - 1$$

$$= .1203704$$

Conceptually, this rate implies that one year from now, a one-year interest rate must equal about 12.037 percent in order for consecutive investments in two one-year securities to generate a return similar to that of a two-year investment. If the actual one-year rate beginning one year from now (at period $t + 1$) is above (below) 12.037 percent, the return from two consecutive one-year investments will exceed (be less than) the return on a two-year investment.

The forward rate is sometimes used as an approximation of the market's consensus interest rate forecast, because if the market had a different perception, demand and supply of today's existing two-year and one-year securities would adjust to capitalize on this information. Of course, there is no guarantee that the forward rate will forecast the future interest rate with perfect accuracy.

The greater the difference between the implied one-year forward rate and today's one-year interest rate, the greater the expected change in the one-year interest rate. If the term structure of interest rates is solely influenced by expectations of future interest rates, the following relationships hold:

Scenario	Structure of Yield Curve	Expectations about the Future Interest Rate
1. $_{t+1}r_1 > {}_t i_1$	**Upward slope**	**Higher than today's rate**
2. $_{t+1}r_1 = {}_t i_1$	**Flat**	**Same as today's rate**
3. $_{t+1}r_1 < {}_t i_1$	**Downward slope**	**Lower than today's rate**

Forward rates can be determined for various maturities. The relationships described here can be applied when assessing the change in the interest rate of a security with any particular maturity.

The previous example can be expanded to solve for other forward rates. The equality specified by the pure expectations theory for a three-year horizon is

$$(1 + {}_t i_3)^3 = (1 + {}_t i_1)(1 + {}_{t+1}r_1)(1 + {}_{t+2}r_1)$$

where

$_t i_3 =$ annualized rate on a three-year security as of time t

$_{t+2}r_1 =$ one-year interest rate that is anticipated as of time $t + 2$ (two years)

All other terms were already defined. By rearranging terms, we can isolate the forward rate of a one-year security beginning two years from now:

$$1 + {}_{t+2}r_1 = \frac{(1 + {}_t i_3)^3}{(1 + {}_t i_1)(1 + {}_{t+1}r_1)}$$

$$_{t+2}r_1 = \frac{(1 + {}_t i_3)^3}{(1 + {}_t i_1)(1 + {}_{t+1}r_1)} - 1$$

If the one-year forward rate beginning one year from now ($_{t+1}r_1$) has already been estimated, this estimate along with actual one-year and three-year interest rates can be used to estimate the one-year forward rate two years from now. Recall that our previous example assumed $_t i_1 = 8$ percent and estimated $_{t+1}r_1$ to be about 12.037 percent.

ILLUSTRATION Assume that a three-year security has an annualized interest rate of 11 percent ($_t i_3 = 11$ percent). Given this information, the one-year forward rate two years from now is

$$_{t+2}r_1 = \frac{(1 + {}_t i_3)^3}{(1 + {}_t i_1)(1 + {}_{t+1}r_1)} - 1$$

$$= \frac{(1 + .11)^3}{(1 + .08)(1 + .12037)} - 1$$

$$= \frac{1.367631}{1.21} - 1$$

$$= 13.02736\%$$

Thus, the market anticipates a one-year interest rate of 13.02736 percent as of two years from now.

The yield curve can also be used to forecast annualized interest rates for periods other than one year. For example, the information provided in the last example could be used to determine the two-year forward rate beginning one year from now.

According to the pure expectations theory, a one-year investment followed by a two-year investment should offer the same annualized yield over the three-year horizon as a three-year security that could be purchased today. This equality is shown as follows:

$$(1 + {}_{t+1}r_3)^3 = (1 + {}_t i_1)(1 + {}_{t+1}r_2)^2$$

where
$$\quad {}_{t+1}r_2 = \text{annual interest rate of a two-year security} $$
$$\text{anticipated as of time } t + 1$$

By rearranging terms, ${}_{t+1}r_2$ can be isolated:

$$(1 + {}_{t+1}r_2)^2 = \frac{(1 + {}_t i_3)^3}{(1 + {}_t i_1)}$$

Recall that today's annualized yields for one-year and three-year securities are 8 percent and 11 percent, respectively. With this information, ${}_{t+1}r_2$ is estimated as follows:

$$(1 + {}_{t+1}r_2)^2 = \frac{(1 + {}_t i_3)^3}{(1 + {}_t i_1)}$$
$$= \frac{(1 + .11)^3}{(1 + .08)}$$
$$= 1.266325$$
$$(1 + {}_{t+1}r_2) = \sqrt{1.266325}$$
$$= 1.1253$$
$${}_{t+1}r_2 = .1253$$

Thus, the market anticipates an annualized interest rate of about 12.53 percent for two-year securities beginning one year from now.

Pure expectations theory is based on the premise that the forward rates are unbiased estimators of future interest rates. If forward rates are biased, investors could attempt to capitalize on the bias.

In the previous numerical example, the one-year forward rate beginning one year ahead was estimated to be about 12.037 percent. If the forward rate was thought to contain an upward bias, the expected one-year interest rate beginning one year ahead would be less than 12.037 percent. Therefore, investors with funds available for two years would earn a higher yield by purchasing two-year securities rather than purchasing one-year securities for two consecutive years. Their actions would cause an increase in the price of two-year securities and a decrease in that of one-year securities. The yields of the securities would move inversely with the price movements. The attempt by investors to capitalize on the forward rate bias would essentially eliminate the bias.

If forward rates are unbiased estimators of future interest rates, financial market efficiency is supported, and the information implied by market rates about the forward rate cannot be used to generate abnormal returns. As new information develops, investor preferences would change, yields would adjust, and the implied forward rate would adjust as well.

If a long-term rate is expected to equal a geometric average of consecutive short-term rates covering the same time horizon (as is suggested by pure expectations theory), long-term rates would likely be more stable than short-term rates. As expectations about consecutive short-term rates change over time, the average of these rates is less volatile than the individual short-term rates. Thus, long-term rates are much more stable than short-term rates.

Liquidity Premium Theory

Some investors may prefer to own short-term rather than long-term securities because a shorter maturity represents greater liquidity. In this case, they may be willing to hold long-term securities only if compensated with a premium for the lower degree of liquidity. Although long-term securities can be liquidated prior to maturity, their prices are more sensitive to interest rate movements. Short-term securities are normally considered to be more liquid because they are more likely to be converted to cash without a loss in value.

The preference for the more liquid short-term securities places upward pressure on the slope of a yield curve. Liquidity may be a more critical factor to investors at particular points in time, and the liquidity premium will change over time accordingly. As it does, so will the yield curve. This is the **liquidity premium theory.**

Exhibit 3.10 combines the simultaneous existence of expectations theory and a liquidity premium. Each graph shows different interest rate expectations by the market. Regardless of the interest rate forecast, the yield curve is affected in a somewhat similar manner by the liquidity premium.

Estimation of the Forward Rate Based on a Liquidity Premium
When expectations theory is combined with the liquidity theory, the yield on a security will not necessarily be equal to the yield from consecutive investments in shorter-term securities

---

EXHIBIT 3.10 Impact of Liquidity Premium on the Yield Curve under Three Different Scenarios

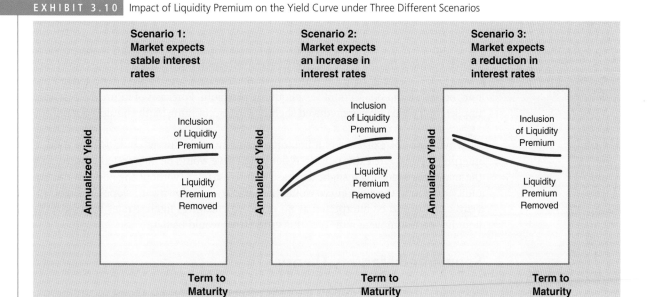

over the same investment horizon. For example, the yield on a two-year security can be determined as

$$(1 + {}_ti_2)^2 = (1 + {}_ti_1)(1 + {}_{t+1}r_1) + LP_2$$

where LP_2 represents the liquidity premium on a two-year security. The yield generated from the two-year security should exceed the yield from consecutive investments in one-year securities by a premium that compensates the investor for less liquidity. The relationship between the liquidity premium and term to maturity can be expressed as follows:

$$0 < LP_1 < LP_2 < LP_3 < \cdots < LP_{20}$$

where the subscripts represent years to maturity. This implies that the liquidity premium would be more influential on the difference between annualized interest rates on one-year and 20-year securities than on the difference between one-year and two-year securities.

If liquidity influences the yield curve, the forward rate overestimates the market's expectation of the future interest rate. A more appropriate formula for the forward rate would account for the liquidity premium. By rearranging the terms of the previous equation, the one-year forward rate can be derived as follows:

$$_{t+1}r_1 = \frac{(1 + {}_ti_2)^2}{(1 + {}_ti_1)} - 1 - [LP_2/(1 + {}_ti_1)]$$

ILLUSTRATION Reconsider the example where $i_1 = 8$ percent and $i_2 = 10$ percent. Assume that the liquidity premium on a two-year security is 0.5 percent. The one-year forward rate can be derived from this information:

$$_{t+1}r_1 = \frac{(1 + {}_ti_2)^2}{(1 + {}_ti_1)} - 1 - [LP_2/(1 + {}_ti_1)]$$

$$_{t+1}r_1 = \frac{(1.10)^2}{1.08} - 1 - [.005/(1 + .08)]$$

$$= .11574$$

This estimate of the one-year forward rate is below the estimate derived in the previous related example in which the liquidity premium was not considered. The previous estimate (12.037 percent) of the forward rate should overstate the market's expected interest rate, because it did not account for a liquidity premium. Forecasts of future interest rates implied by a yield curve are reduced slightly when accounting for the liquidity premium.

Even with the existence of a liquidity premium, yield curves could still be used to interpret interest rate expectations. A flat yield curve would be interpreted to mean that the market is expecting a slight decrease in interest rates (without the effect of the liquidity premium, the yield curve would have had a slight downward slope). A slight upward slope would be interpreted as no expected change in interest rates because if the liquidity premium were removed, this yield curve would be flat.

Segmented Markets Theory

According to **segmented markets theory,** investors and borrowers choose securities with maturities that satisfy their forecasted cash needs. Pension funds and life insurance com-

panies may generally prefer long-term investments that coincide with their long-term liabilities. Commercial banks may prefer more short-term investments to coincide with their short-term liabilities. If investors and borrowers participate only in the maturity market that satisfies their particular needs, markets are segmented. That is, investors (or borrowers) will shift from the long-term market to the short-term market or vice versa only if the timing of their cash needs changes. According to segmented markets theory, the choice of long-term versus short-term maturities is predetermined according to need rather than expectations of future interest rates.

ILLUSTRATION Assume that most investors have funds available to invest for only a short period of time and therefore desire to invest primarily in short-term securities. Also assume that most borrowers need funds for a long period of time and therefore desire to issue mostly long-term securities. The result will be downward pressure on the yield of short-term securities and upward pressure on the yield of long-term securities. Overall, the scenario described would create an upward-sloping yield curve.

Now consider the opposite scenario in which most investors wish to invest their funds for a long period of time, while most borrowers need funds for only a short period of time. According to segmented markets theory, there will be upward pressure on the yield of short-term securities and downward pressure on the yield of long-term securities. Exhibit 3.11 illustrates how the segmented markets theory can explain the shape of the yield curve at any point in time. If the supply of funds provided by investors and the demand for funds by borrowers were better balanced between the short-term and long-term markets, the yields of short- and long-term securities would be more similar.

The example separated the maturity markets into just short term and long term. In reality, several maturity markets may exist. Within the short-term market, some investors may prefer maturities of one month or less, while others prefer maturities of one to three months. Regardless of how many maturity markets exist, the yields of securities with various maturities should be somewhat influenced by the desires of investors and borrowers to participate in the maturity market that best satisfies their needs. A corporation that needs additional funds for 30 days would not consider issuing long-term bonds for such a purpose. Savers with short-term funds are restricted from some long-term investments, such as 10-year certificates of deposit, that cannot be easily liquidated.

EXHIBIT 3.11 Impact of Different Scenarios on the Yield Curve According to Segmented Markets Theory

	Impact of Scenario 1: (Investors Have Mostly Short-Term Funds Available; Borrowers Want Long-Term Funds)	Impact of Scenario 2: (Investors Have Mostly Long-Term Funds Available; Borrowers Want Short-Term Funds)
Supply of short-term funds provided by investors	Upward pressure	Downward pressure
Demand for short-term funds by borrowers	Downward pressure	Upward pressure
Yield on new short-term securities	Downward pressure	Upward pressure
Supply of long-term funds provided by investors	Downward pressure	Upward pressure
Demand for long-term funds issued by borrowers	Upward pressure	Downward pressure
Yield on long-term securities	Upward pressure	Downward pressure
Shape of yield curve	Upward slope	Downward slope

Limitation of the Theory A limitation of the segmented markets theory is that some borrowers and savers have the flexibility to choose among various maturity markets. Corporations that need long-term funds may initially obtain short-term financing if they expect interest rates to decline. Investors with long-term funds may make short-term investments if they expect interest rates to rise. Some investors with short-term funds available may be willing to purchase long-term securities that have an active secondary market.

Some financial institutions focus on a particular maturity market, but others are more flexible. Commercial banks obtain most of their funds in short-term markets but spread their investments into short-, medium-, and long-term markets. Savings institutions have historically focused on attracting short-term funds and lending funds for long-term periods. If maturity markets were completely segmented, an adjustment in the interest rate in one market would have no impact on other markets. Yet, there is clear evidence that interest rates among maturity markets move closely in tandem over time, proving there is some interaction among markets, which implies that funds are being transferred across markets. Note that this theory of segmented markets conflicts with the general presumption of the pure expectations theory that maturity markets are perfect substitutes for one another.

Implications Although markets are not completely segmented, the preference for particular maturities can affect the prices and yields of securities with different maturities and therefore affect the yield curve's shape. Therefore, the segmented markets theory appears to be a partial explanation for the yield curve's shape, but not the sole explanation.

A more flexible perspective of the segmented markets theory, called the **preferred habitat theory,** offers a compromise explanation for the term structure of interest rates. This theory suggests that although investors and borrowers may normally concentrate on a particular natural maturity market, certain events may cause them to wander from it. For example, commercial banks that obtain mostly short-term funds may select investments with short-term maturities as a natural habitat. However, if they wish to benefit from an anticipated decline in interest rates, they may select medium- and long-term maturities instead. Preferred habitat theory acknowledges that natural maturity markets may influence the yield curve but recognizes that interest rate expectations could entice market participants to stray from preferred maturities.

Research on Term Structure Theories

An abundance of research has been conducted on the term structure of interest rates, offering insight into the various theories. Researchers have found that interest rate expectations have a strong influence on the term structure of interest rates. However, the forward rate derived from a yield curve does not accurately predict future interest rates. This may suggest that other factors are relevant. The liquidity premium, for example, could cause consistent positive forecasting errors, meaning that forward rates tend to overestimate future interest rates. Studies have documented variation in the yield-maturity relationship that cannot be explained by interest rate expectations or liquidity. Thus, the variation could be attributed to different supply and demand conditions for particular maturity segments.

General Research Implications Although the results of research differ, there is some evidence that expectations theory, liquidity premium theory, and segmented markets

theory all have some validity. Thus, if the term structure is used to assess the market's expectations of future interest rates, investors should first net out the liquidity premium and any unique market conditions for various maturity segments.

Integrating Theories of the Term Structure

To illustrate how all three theories can simultaneously affect the yield curve, assume the following conditions:

1. Investors and borrowers who select security maturities based on anticipated interest rate movements currently expect interest rates to rise.
2. Most borrowers are in need of long-term funds, while most investors have only short-term funds to invest.
3. Investors prefer more liquidity to less.

The first condition, related to expectations theory, suggests the existence of an upward-sloping yield curve, other things being equal. This is shown in Exhibit 3.12 as Curve E. The segmented markets information (condition 2) also favors the upward-sloping yield curve. When conditions 1 and 2 are considered simultaneously, the appropriate yield curve may look like Curve E + S. The third condition relating to liquidity would then place a higher premium on the longer-term securities because of their lower degree of liquidity. When this condition is included with the first two, the yield curve may look like Curve E + S + L.

In this example, all conditions placed upward pressure on long-term yields relative to short-term yields. In reality, there will sometimes be offsetting conditions, as one condition places downward pressure on the slope of the yield curve while the others place upward pressure on the slope. If condition 1 were revised to suggest the expectation of lower interest rates in the future, this condition by itself would result in a downward-sloping yield curve. When combined with the other conditions that favor an upward-sloping curve, it would create a partial offsetting effect. This yield curve would exhibit a downward slope if the effect of the interest rate expectations dominated the combined liquidity premium and segmented markets effects. Conversely, an upward slope would exist if the liquidity premium and segmented markets effects dominated the effects of interest rate expectations.

Effect of Conditions in Example of Yield Curve

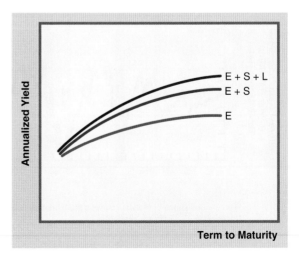

Using Term Structure

The term structure of interest rates is used to forecast interest rates, forecast recessions, and make investment and financing decisions, as explained next.

Forecast Interest Rates At any point in time, the shape of the yield curve can be used to assess the general expectations of investors and borrowers about future interest rates. Recall from expectations theory that an upward-sloping yield curve generally results from the expectation of higher interest rates, while a downward-sloping yield curve generally results from the expectation of lower interest rates. The expectations about future interest rates must be interpreted cautiously, however, because liquidity and specific maturity preferences could influence the yield curve's shape. It is generally believed, though, that interest rate expectations are a major contributing factor to the yield curve's shape, and the curve's shape should provide a reasonable indication (especially if the liquidity premium effect is accounted for) of the market's expectations about future interest rates.

Although investors can use the yield curve to interpret the market's consensus expectation of future interest rates, they may have their own interest rate projections. By comparing their projections to those implied by the yield curve, they can attempt to capitalize on the difference. For example, if an upward-sloping yield curve exists, suggesting a market expectation of increasing rates, investors expecting stable interest rates could benefit from investing in long-term securities. From their perspective, long-term securities are undervalued because they reflect the market's expectation of higher interest rates. Strategies such as this are effective only if the investor can consistently forecast better than the market.

Forecast Recessions Some analysts believe that flat or inverted yield curves indicate a recession in the near future. The rationale is that given a positive liquidity premium, such yield curves reflect the expectation of lower interest rates. This is commonly associated with expectations of a reduced demand for loanable funds, which could result in a recession. Exhibit 3.13 shows the differential between 10-year and three-month Trea-

EXHIBIT 3.13 • The Yield Curve* as a Signal for Recessions

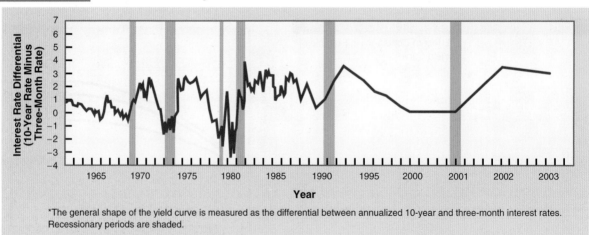

*The general shape of the yield curve is measured as the differential between annualized 10-year and three-month interest rates. Recessionary periods are shaded.

Source: *FRBSF Weekly Letter*, March 10, 1989, updated by author.

sury securities over time. A differential close to zero reflects a flat yield curve, while a negative differential reflects an inverted yield curve. Each time the yield curve became flat or inverted, a recession occurred shortly thereafter.

Most recently, the yield curve became flat or slightly inverted in 2000. At that time, the shape of the curve indicated expectations of a slower economy, which would result in lower interest rates. In 2001, the economy weakened substantially.

Investment Decisions If the yield curve is upward sloping, some investors may attempt to benefit from the higher yields on longer-term securities, even though they have funds to invest for only a short period of time. The secondary market allows investors the opportunity to attempt this strategy, referred to as *riding the yield curve.* Consider an upward-sloping yield curve such that some one-year securities offer an annualized yield of 7 percent while 10-year bonds can be purchased at par value and offer a coupon rate of 10 percent. An investor with funds available for one year may decide to purchase the bonds and sell them in the secondary market after one year. The investor earns 3 percent more than was possible on the one-year securities, if the bonds can be sold after one year at the price at which they were purchased. The risk of this strategy is the uncertainty of the price at which the security can be sold in the near future. If the upward-sloping yield is interpreted as the market's consensus of higher interest rates in the future, the price of a security would be expected to decrease in the future. In this case, investors are justified in purchasing a long-term security for a short-term period only if they believe the consensus forecast interpreted from the yield curve is incorrect. Although the market's forecast implied by the yield curve often differs from the interest rate that actually occurs, it is difficult to know in advance whether the market will overestimate or underestimate the future interest rate.

The yield curve is commonly monitored by financial institutions whose liability maturities are distinctly different from their asset maturities. Consider a bank that obtains much of its funds through short-term deposits and uses the funds to provide long-term loans or purchase long-term securities. An upward-sloping yield curve is favorable to the bank because annualized short-term deposit rates are significantly lower than annualized long-term investment rates. The bank's spread is higher than it would be if the yield curve were flat. Some commercial banks may attempt to capitalize on an upward-sloping yield curve by pursuing a greater proportion of short-term deposits and long-term investments. Yet, if the bank believes that the upward slope of the yield curve indicates higher interest rates in the future (as reflected in the expectations theory), it will expect its cost of liabilities to increase over time, as future deposits would be obtained at higher interest rates. Any long-term loans previously provided at a fixed rate would represent a relatively low return in the future if interest rates increase.

Financing Decisions The yield curve is also useful for firms that plan to issue bonds. By assessing the prevailing rates on securities for various maturities, firms can estimate the rates to be paid on bonds with different maturities. This may enable them to decide the maturity for the bonds they issue.

Impact of Debt Management on Term Structure

Debt management involves the Treasury's decisions about how to finance the deficit. These decisions can have a significant influence on economic variables monitored by financial market participants. The Treasury must determine the composition of

short-term versus long-term debt, which can affect the term structure of interest rates and therefore the relative desirability of various securities. The composition can also affect the level of investment and therefore aggregate demand. If the Treasury uses a relatively large proportion of long-term debt, this will place upward pressure on long-term yields. Because long-term investment is sensitive to long-term financing rates, corporations may reduce their investment in fixed assets. Conversely, if the Treasury uses mostly short-term securities to finance its deficit, long-term interest rates may be relatively low, thereby stimulating corporate investment in fixed assets.

ILLUSTRATION

In May 1993, the U.S. Treasury established a policy of reducing its offering of 30-year bonds, while increasing its offering of short-term securities. At the time of the decision, the yield curve exhibited a steep upward slope, as annualized interest rates on short-term Treasury securities were 3 to 4 percentage points lower than annualized interest rates on long-term Treasury securities. A shift to borrowing more short-term funds and fewer long-term funds places upward pressure on short-term interest rates and downward pressure on the long-term interest rates, as shown in Exhibit 3.14. The top left graph represents the market for short-term funds while the top right graph represents the market for long-term funds. Although there are numerous maturity markets, the focus on only two markets is sufficient to make a point here. In the short-term market, the equilibrium short-term interest rate is determined by the supply and demand

EXHIBIT 3.14   Potential Impact of Treasury Shift from Long-Term to Short-Term Financing

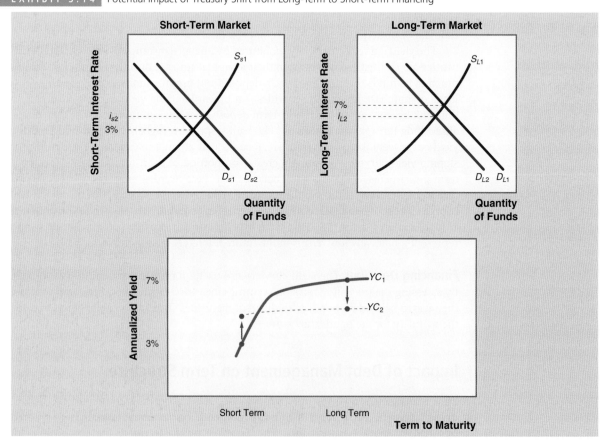

schedules for short-term funds, which were initially S_{s1} and D_{s1}, respectively. In the long-term market, the equilibrium long-term interest rate is determined by the supply and demand schedule for long-term funds, which were initially S_{L1} and D_{L1}, respectively. The shift in government policy causes the demand schedule for short-term funds to shift outward to D_{s2} and the demand schedule for long-term funds to shift inward from D_{L1} to D_{L2}. Consequently, the short-term interest rate rises from 3 percent to i_{s2}, while the long-term interest rate declines from 7 percent to i_{L2}. This effect may result in a flatter yield curve (from yield curve YC_1 in the lower graph of Exhibit 3.14 to yield curve YC_2).

Historical Review of the Term Structure

Changes in the shape of the yield curve over time are illustrated in Exhibit 3.15. Notice that the slope of each yield curve is more pronounced for maturities up to five years and then levels off somewhat for longer maturities. Yield curves are not always upward sloping. In the early 1980s, securities with shorter maturities commonly offered higher annualized yields because of the very high interest rates of that period combined with the expectation that rates would decrease. Although the upward slope has generally persisted since 1982, the degree of slope has changed.

Impact of September 11 on the Term Structure The terrorist attack on September 11, 2001, caused investors to shift into short-term Treasury securities as a source of safety and liquidity. In addition, the Federal Reserve increased the amount of funds available in the banking system. Although there was an abrupt decline in short-term

EXHIBIT 3.15

Yield Curves at Various Points in Time

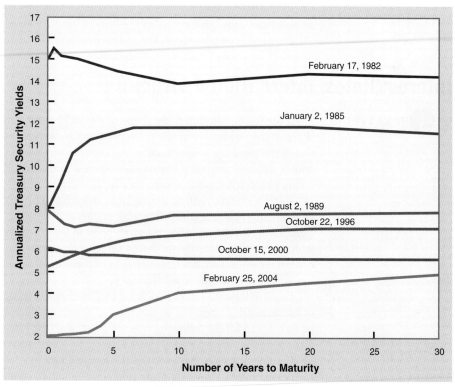

Source: *FRBNY Quarterly Review,* various issues.

EXHIBIT 3.16

Impact of the September 11
Attack on the Term
Structure

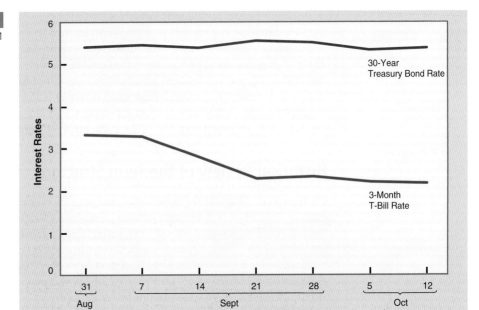

interest rates, the attack did not have a major effect on long-term rates, as shown in Exhibit 3.16. The difference between the long-term and short-term rate for any date shown in Exhibit 3.16 indicates the steepness of the yield curve at that time. Thus, the exhibit shows that the yield curve became steeper after September 11. The shift illustrates how an event can cause an increase in the flow of funds to liquid safe securities (short-term Treasury bills), which reduces short-term interest rates and creates a steeper yield curve.

Interest Rates: International Structure

 GL BALASPECTS Since the factors that affect the shape of the yield curve can vary among countries, the shape of the yield curve at any given point in time varies among countries. Exhibit 3.17 shows the yield curve for six different countries at a given point in time. Each country with a different currency has its own interest rate levels for various maturities. Each country's interest rates are based on supply and demand conditions.

Interest rate movements across countries tend to be positively correlated as a result of internationally integrated financial markets. Yet, the actual interest rates may vary significantly across countries at a given point in time. This implies that the differential in interest rates is primarily attributed to general supply and demand conditions across countries rather than differences in default premiums, liquidity premiums, or other factors unique to the individual securities.

Because forward rates (as defined in this chapter) reflect the market's expectations of future interest rates, the term structure of interest rates for various countries should be monitored for the following reasons. First, with the integration of financial markets, movements in one country's interest rate can affect interest rates in other countries. Thus, some investors may estimate the forward rate in a foreign country to predict the foreign interest rate, which in turn may affect domestic interest rates. Second, foreign securities and some domestic securities are influenced by foreign economies, which are dependent on foreign interest rates. If the foreign forward rates can be used to forecast

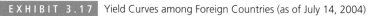

EXHIBIT 3.17   Yield Curves among Foreign Countries (as of July 14, 2004)

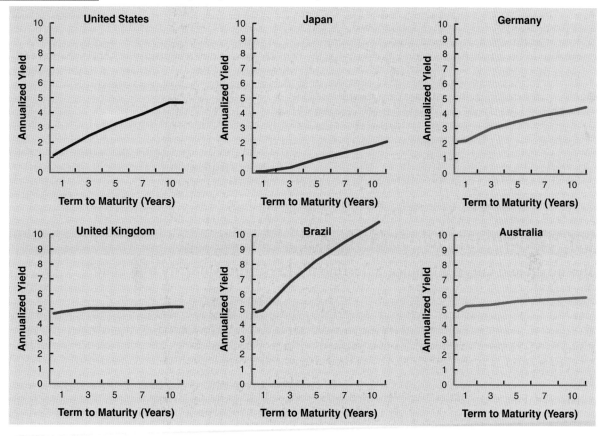

foreign interest rates, they can enhance forecasts of foreign economies. Because exchange rates are also influenced by foreign interest rates, exchange rate projections may be more accurate when using foreign forward rates to forecast foreign interest rates.

If the real interest rate was fixed, inflation rates for future periods could be predicted for any country in which the forward rate could be estimated. Recall that the nominal interest rate consists of an expected inflation rate plus a real interest rate. Because the forward rate represents an expected nominal interest rate for a future period, it also represents an expected inflation rate plus a real interest rate in that period. The expected inflation in that period is estimated as the difference between the forward rate and the real interest rate.

SUMMARY

■ Quoted yields of debt securities at a given point vary for the following reasons. First, securities with higher credit (default) risk must offer a higher yield. Second, securities that are less liquid must offer a higher yield. Third, taxable securities must offer a higher before-tax yield than tax-exempt securities.

Fourth, securities with longer maturities offer a different yield (not consistently higher or lower) than securities with shorter maturities. Fifth, securities with a call provision offer a higher yield, while securities with a convertibility clause offer a lower yield.

- The appropriate yield for any particular debt security can be estimated by first determining the risk-free Treasury security rate on a debt security with a similar maturity. Then, adjustments can be made according to the credit risk, liquidity, tax status, and other provisions.

- The term structure of interest rates can be explained by three theories. Pure expectations theory suggests that the shape of the yield curve is dictated by interest rate expectations. The liquidity premium theory suggests that securities with shorter maturities have greater liquidity and therefore should not have to offer as high a yield as securities with longer terms to maturity. The segmented markets theory suggests that investors and borrowers have different needs, which cause the demand and supply conditions to vary across different maturities; that is, there is a segmented market for each term to maturity, which causes yields to vary among these maturity markets. When consolidating the theories, the term structure of interest rates is dependent on interest rate expectations, investor preferences for liquidity, and unique needs of investors and borrowers in each maturity market.

POINT COUNTER-POINT

Should a Yield Curve Influence a Borrower's Preferred Maturity of a Loan?

Point Yes. If there is an upward-sloping yield curve, a borrower should pursue a short-term loan to capitalize on the lower annualized rate charged for a short-term period. The borrower can obtain a series of short-term loans rather than one loan to match the desired maturity.

Counter-Point No. The borrower will face uncertainty regarding the interest rate charged on subsequent loans that are needed. An upward-sloping yield curve would suggest that interest rates will rise in the future, which will cause the cost of borrowing to increase. Overall, the cost of borrowing may be higher when using a series of loans than when matching the debt maturity to the time period in which funds are needed.

Who Is Correct? Use your favorite search engine to learn more about this issue. Offer your own opinion on this issue.

QUESTIONS AND APPLICATIONS

1. **Segmented Markets Theory** Suppose that the Treasury decided to finance its deficit with mostly long-term funds. How could this decision affect the term structure of interest rates? If short-term and long-term markets are segmented, would the Treasury's decision have a more or less pronounced impact on the term structure? Explain.

2. **Managing in Financial Markets: Monitoring Yield Curve Adjustments** As an analyst of a bond rating agency, you have been asked to interpret the implications of the recent shift in the yield curve. Six months ago, the yield curve exhibited a slight downward slope. Over the last six months, long-term yields declined, while short-term yields remained the same. Analysts said that the shift was due to revised expectations of interest rates.

a. Given the shift in the yield curve, does it appear that firms increased or decreased their demand for long-term funds over the last six months?
b. Interpret what the shift in the yield curve suggests about the market's changing expectations of future interest rates.
c. Recently, an analyst argued that the underlying reason for the yield curve shift is that many large U.S. firms anticipate a recession. Explain why an anticipated recession could force the yield curve to shift as it has.
d. What could the specific shift in the yield curve signal about the ratings of existing corporate bonds? What types of corporations would be most likely to experience a change in their bond

ratings as a result of the specific shift in the yield curve?

3. **Characteristics That Affect Security Yields** Identify the relevant characteristics of any security that can affect the security's yield.

4. **Forward Rate** What is the meaning of the forward rate in the context of the term structure of interest rates? Why might forward rates consistently overestimate future interest rates? How could such a bias be avoided?

5. **Impact of Call Feature** Would yields be higher for callable bonds or noncallable bonds that are similar in all other respects? Why?

6. **Interpreting Financial News** Interpret the following comments made by Wall Street analysts and portfolio managers:
   a. "An upward-sloping yield curve persists because many investors stand ready to jump into the stock market."
   b. "Low-rated bond yields rose as recession fears caused a flight to quality."
   c. "The shift from an upward-sloping yield curve to a downward-sloping yield curve is sending a warning about a possible recession."

7. **Tax Effects on Yields** Do investors in high tax brackets or those in low tax brackets benefit more from tax-exempt securities? Why? Do municipal bonds or corporate bonds offer a higher before-tax yield at a given point in time? Why? Which has the higher after-tax yield? If taxes did not exist, would Treasury bonds offer a higher or lower yield than municipal bonds with the same maturity? Why?

8. **Global Interaction among Yield Curves** Assume that the yield curves in the United States, France, and Japan are flat. If the U.S. yield curve then suddenly becomes positively sloped, do you think the yield curves in France and Japan would be affected? If so, how?

9. **Liquidity Premium Theory** Explain the liquidity premium theory.

10. **Impact of Credit Risk on Yield** What effect does a high credit risk have on securities?

11. **Internet Exercise** Assess the shape of the yield curve, using the website http://www.bloomberg.com. Click on "Market data," then on "Rates and bonds."

    Is the Treasury yield curve upward or downward sloping? What is the yield of a 90-day Treasury bill? What is the yield of a 30-year Treasury bond? Based on the various theories attempting to explain the shape of the yield curve, what could explain the difference between these two yields? Which theory, in your opinion, is the most reasonable? Why?

12. **Segmented Markets Theory** If a downward-sloping yield curve is mainly attributed to segmented markets theory, what does that suggest about the demand for and supply of funds in the short-term and long-term maturity markets?

13. **Effect of Crises on the Yield Curve** During some crises, investors shift their funds out of the stock market and into money market securities for safety, even if they do not fear rising interest rates. Explain how and why these actions by investors affect the yield curve. Is the shift due to the expectations theory, liquidity premium theory, or segmented markets theory?

14. **Pure Expectations Theory** Explain how a yield curve would shift in response to a sudden expectation of rising interest rates, according to the pure expectations theory.

15. **Preferred Habitat Theory** Explain the preferred habitat theory.

16. **Multiple Effects on the Yield Curve** Assume that (1) investors and borrowers expect that the economy will weaken and that inflation will decline, (2) investors require a small liquidity premium, and (3) markets are partially segmented and the Treasury currently has a preference for borrowing in short-term markets. Explain how each of these forces would affect the term structure, holding other factors constant. Then explain the effect on the term structure overall.

17. **Pure Expectations Theory** Assume there is a sudden expectation of lower interest rates in the future. What would be the effect on the shape of the yield curve? Explain.

18. **Segmented Markets Theory** If the segmented markets theory causes an upward-sloping yield curve, what does this imply? If markets are not completely segmented, should we dismiss the segmented markets theory as even a partial explanation for the term structure of interest rates? Explain.

19. **Impact of Liquidity on Yield** Discuss the relationship between the yield and liquidity of securities.

20. **Yield Curve** If liquidity and interest rate expectations are both important for explaining the shape of

a yield curve, what does a flat yield curve indicate about the market's perception of future interest rates?

21. **Yield Curve** What factors influence the shape of the yield curve? Describe how financial market participants use the yield curve.

PROBLEMS

1. **Forward Rate**
   a. Use the Forward Interest Rate Template on the CD to determine the forward rate for various one-year interest rate scenarios if the two-year interest rate is 8 percent, assuming no liquidity premium. Explain the relationship between the one-year interest rate and the one-year forward rate, holding the two-year interest rate constant.
   b. Use the Forward Interest Rate Template on the CD to determine the one-year forward rate for the same one-year interest rate scenarios as in question (a), assuming a liquidity premium of .4 percent. Does the relationship between the one-year interest rate and the forward rate change when considering a liquidity premium?
   c. At the beginning of 2001, the yield curve in the United States exhibited a slight upward slope. When economic conditions weakened substantially in 2001, the one-year interest rate declined substantially, but the two-year and longer-term interest rates declined only slightly. Use the Forward Interest Rate Template to simulate such changes in the one-year and two-year interest rates, and explain how the one-year forward rate was affected by these changes. Based on your estimated changes in the forward rate, how would the expected interest rate be affected? Would your general answer about the expected interest rate vary with the liquidity premium that you might assume throughout this example?
   d. Use the Forward Interest Rate Template to determine how the one-year forward rate would be affected if the quoted two-year interest rate rises, holding the quoted one-year interest rate and the liquidity premium constant. Explain the logic of this relationship.
   e. Use the Forward Interest Rate Template to determine how the one-year forward rate would be affected if the liquidity premium rises, holding the quoted one-year and two-year interest rates constant. Explain the logic of this relationship.

2. **Forward Rate** If $_t i_1 > _t i_2$, what is the market consensus forecast about the one-year forward rate one year from now? Is this rate above or below today's one-year interest rate? Explain.

3. **Commercial Paper Yield**
   a. A corporation is planning to sell its 90-day commercial paper to investors offering an 8.4 percent yield. If the three-month T-bill's annualized rate is 7 percent, the default risk premium is estimated to be 0.6 percent, and there is a 0.4 percent tax adjustment, what is the appropriate liquidity premium?
   b. If due to unexpected changes in the economy the default risk premium increases to 0.8 percent, what is the appropriate yield to be offered on the commercial paper (assuming no other changes occur)?

4. **Debt Security Yield**
   a. Use the Debt Security Yield template to determine how the appropriate yield to be offered on a security is affected by a higher risk-free rate. Explain the logic of this relationship.
   b. Use the Debt Security Yield Template to determine how the appropriate yield to be offered on a security is affected by a higher default risk premium. Explain the logic of this relationship.
   c. Use the Debt Security Yield Template to determine how the appropriate yield to be offered on a security is affected by a higher call premium. Explain the logic of this relationship.
   d. Use the Debt Security Yield Template to determine how the appropriate yield to be offered on a security is affected by the existence of a convertibility discount. Explain the logic of this relationship.

5. **Forward Rate**
   a. Assume that as of today, the annualized two-year interest rate is 13 percent, while the one-year interest rate is 12 percent. Use only this information to estimate the one-year forward rate.

b. Assume that the liquidity premium on a two-year security is 0.3 percent. Use this information to reestimate the one-year forward rate.

6. **After-Tax Yield** Use the Tax-Adjusted Yield Template to determine how the after-tax yield is affected by higher tax rates, holding the before-tax yield constant. Explain the logic of this relationship.

7. **Deriving Current Interest Rates** Assume that interest rates for one-year securities are expected to be 2 percent today, 4 percent one year from now, and 6 percent two years from now. Using only the pure expectations theory, what are the current interest rates on two-year and three-year securities?

8. **Forward Rate** Assume that as of today, the annualized interest rate on a three-year security is 10 percent, while the annualized interest rate on a two-year security is 7 percent. Use only this information to estimate the one-year forward rate two years from now.

9. **After-Tax Yield** You need to choose between investing in a one-year municipal bond with a 7 percent yield and a one-year corporate bond with an 11 percent yield. If your marginal federal income tax rate is 30 percent and no other differences exist between these two securities, which one would you invest in?

FLOW OF FUNDS EXERCISE

Influence of the Structure of Interest Rates

Recall that Carson Company has obtained substantial loans from finance companies and commercial banks. The interest rate on the loans is tied to the six-month Treasury bill rate (and includes a risk premium) and is adjusted every six months. Thus, Carson's cost of obtaining funds is sensitive to interest rate movements. Because of its expectations that the U.S. economy will strengthen, Carson plans to grow in the future by expanding its business and through acquisitions. Carson expects that it will need substantial long-term financing to finance its growth and plans to borrow additional funds either through loans or by issuing bonds. It is also considering the issuance of stock to raise funds in the next year.

a. Assume that the market's expectations of the economy are similar to those of Carson. Also assume that the yield curve is primarily influenced by interest rate expectations. Would the yield curve be upward sloping or downward sloping? Why?

b. If Carson could obtain more debt financing for 10-year projects, would it prefer to obtain credit at a long-term fixed interest rate or at a floating rate? Why?

c. If Carson attempts to obtain funds by issuing 10-year bonds, explain what information would help to estimate the yield it would have to pay on 10-year bonds. That is, what are the key factors that would influence the rate it would pay on the 10-year bonds?

d. If Carson attempts to obtain funds by issuing loans with floating interest rates every six months, explain what information would help to estimate the yield it would have to pay over the next 10 years. That is, what are the key factors that would influence the rate it would pay over the 10-year period?

e. An upward-sloping yield curve suggests that the initial rate that financial institutions could charge on a long-term loan to Carson would be higher than the initial rate that they could charge on a loan that floats in accordance with short-term interest rates. Does this imply that creditors should prefer to provide a fixed-rate loan rather than a floating-rate loan to Carson? Explain why Carson's expectations of future interest rates are not necessarily the same as those of some financial institutions.

EXERCISE

Interpreting the Structure of Interest Rates

a. **Explaining Yield Differentials** Using the most recent issue of *The Wall Street Journal*, review the "Yield Comparison Table" (sometimes listed in the section entitled "Credit Markets"). Use the table to report the following yields.

Type	Maturity	Yield
Treasury	10-year	_____
Corporate: high-quality	10-year	_____
Corporate: medium-quality	10-year	_____
Municipal: (tax-exempt)	10-year	_____

If credit (default) risk is the only reason for the yield differentials, what is the default risk premium on the corporate high-quality bonds? On the medium-quality bonds?

During a recent recession, high-quality corporate bonds offered a yield of 0.8 percent above Treasury bonds, and medium-quality bonds offered a yield of about 3.1 percent above Treasury bonds. How do these yield differentials compare to the differentials today? Explain the reason for the change in yield differentials.

Using the information in the previous table, complete the table below.

b. **Examining Recent Adjustments in Credit Risk** Using the most recent issue of *The Wall Street Journal*, review the section called "Credit Ratings." Report any changes in credit ratings, and for each change, explain the following:

■ What was the reason given for the change in credit ratings? How does this reason relate to credit risk?

■ How will the change in ratings influence the market price of these securities?

■ How will the change in ratings influence the yield to be earned by investors who previously invested in these securities and are about to sell them?

■ How will the change in ratings influence the expected yield to be earned by investors who now invest in these securities?

Marginal tax bracket of investors	Before-tax yield necessary to achieve existing after-tax yield of tax-exempt bonds	If the tax-exempt bonds have the same risk and other features as high-quality corporate bonds, which type of bond is preferable for investors in each tax bracket?
10%	_____	_____
15%	_____	_____
20%	_____	_____
28%	_____	_____
34%	_____	_____

c. **Determining and Interpreting Today's Term Structure** Using the most recent issue of *The Wall Street Journal*, review the table called "Treasury Bonds, Notes & Bills" (listed in the index on the front page as "Treasury Issues"). Use the table to determine the yields for the following maturities:

Term to Maturity	Annualized Yield
1 year	_____
2 years	_____
3 years	_____

Assuming that the differences in these yields are solely because of interest rate expectations, determine the one-year forward rate as of one year from now and the one-year forward rate as of two years from now.

d. *The Wall Street Journal* provides a "Treasury Yield Curve." Use this curve to describe the market's expectations about future interest rates. If a liquidity premium exists, how would this affect your perception of the market's expectations?

Part I Integrative Problem

Interest Rate Forecasts and Investment Decisions

This problem requires an understanding of how economic conditions affect interest rates and bond yields (Chapters 1, 2, and 3).

Your task is to use information about existing economic conditions to forecast U.S. and Canadian interest rates. The following information is available to you:

1   Over the past six months, U.S. interest rates have declined, and Canadian interest rates have increased.

2   The U.S. economy has weakened over the past year, and the Canadian economy has improved.

3   The U.S. savings rate (proportion of income saved) is expected to decrease slightly over the next year, while the Canadian savings rate will remain stable.

4   The U.S. and Canadian central banks are not expected to implement any policy changes that would have a significant impact on interest rates.

5   You expect the U.S. economy to strengthen considerably over the next year but still be weaker than it was two years ago. You expect the Canadian economy to remain stable.

6   You expect the U.S. annual budget deficit to increase slightly from last year but be significantly less than the average annual budget deficit over the past five years. You expect the Canadian budget deficit to be about the same as last year.

7   You expect the U.S. inflation rate to rise slightly, but still remain below the relatively high levels of two years ago. You expect the Canadian inflation rate to decline.

8   Based on some events last week, most economists and investors around the world (including yourself) expect the dollar to weaken against the Canadian dollar and other foreign currencies over the next year. This expectation was already accounted for in your forecasts of inflation and economic growth.

9   The yield curve in the United States currently exhibits a consistent downward slope. The yield curve in Canada currently exhibits an upward slope. You believe that the liquidity premium on securities is quite small.

Questions

1   Using the information available to you, forecast the direction of U.S. interest rates.

2   Using the information available to you, forecast the direction of Canadian interest rates.

3   Assume that the perceived risk of corporations in the United States is expected to increase. Explain how the yield of newly issued U.S. corporate bonds will change to a different degree than the yield of newly issued U.S. Treasury bonds.

PART II

The Fed and Monetary Policy

The chapters in Part II explain how the Federal Reserve System (the Fed) affects economic conditions. Because the policies implemented by the Fed can influence securities prices, they are closely monitored by financial market participants. By assessing the Fed's policies, market participants can more accurately value securities and make more effective investment and financing decisions.

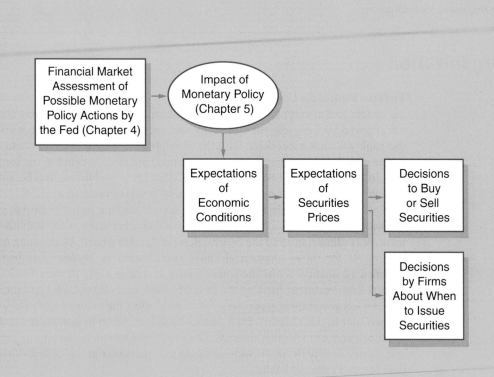

CHAPTER 4

U.S Federal Reserve Bank Functions

The Federal Reserve System (the Fed), as the central bank of the United States, has the responsibility for conducting national monetary policy. Such policy influences interest rates and other economic variables that determine the prices of securities. Participants in the financial markets therefore closely monitor the Fed's monetary policy. It is important that they understand how the Fed's actions may influence security prices so that they can manage their security portfolios in response to the Fed's policies.

The specific objectives of this chapter are to:

■ identify the key components of the Fed that dictate monetary policy,

■ describe the tools used by the Fed to influence monetary policy,

■ explain how bank regulation in the early 1980s affected monetary policy, and

■ explain how monetary policy is used in other countries.

Fed Organization

The First Bank of the United States was created in 1791 to oversee the commercial banking system and attempt to maintain a stable economy. Because its 20-year charter was not renewed by Congress, the First Bank was terminated in 1811. A major criticism of the bank was that it interfered with the development of the banking system and economic growth. Its termination, however, reduced public confidence in the banking system. In 1816 the Second Bank of the United States was established, and because its 20-year charter also was not renewed by Congress, it was terminated in 1836.

During the late 1800s and early 1900s, several banking panics occurred, culminating with a major crisis in 1907. This motivated another attempt to establish a central bank. Accordingly, in 1913 the Federal Reserve Act was passed, establishing reserve requirements for those commercial banks that desired to become members. It also specified 12 districts across the United States as well as a city in each district where a Federal Reserve district bank was to be established. Each district bank had the ability to buy and sell government securities, which could affect the money supply (as will be explained later in this chapter). Each district bank focused on its particular district, without much concern for other districts. Over time, the system became more centralized, and money supply decisions were assigned to a particular group of individuals rather than across 12 district banks.

http://
http://www.clevelandfed.org
Features economic and
banking topics.

The Fed earns most of its income in the form of interest on its holdings of U.S. government securities (to be discussed shortly). It also earns some income from providing services to financial institutions. Most of its income is transferred to the Treasury.

The Fed is involved (along with other agencies) in regulating commercial banks. It also conducts monetary policy, adjusting the money supply in an attempt to achieve full employment and price stability (low or zero inflation) in the United States.

- The Fed as it exists today has five major components:
- Federal Reserve district banks
- Member banks
- Board of Governors
- Federal Open Market Committee (FOMC)
- Advisory committees

Federal Reserve District Banks

The 12 Federal Reserve districts are identified in Exhibit 4.1, along with the city where each district bank is located and the district branches. The New York district bank is considered the most important because many large banks are located in this district. Commercial banks that become members of the Fed are required to purchase stock in their **Federal Reserve district bank.** This stock, which is not traded in a secondary market, pays a maximum dividend of 6 percent annually.

Each Fed district bank has nine directors. Six are elected by member banks in that district. Of these six directors, three are professional bankers and three are businesspeople. The other three directors are appointed by the Board of Governors (to be discussed shortly). The nine directors appoint the president of their Fed district bank.

Fed district banks facilitate operations within the banking system by clearing checks, replacing old currency, and providing loans (through the discount window) to depository institutions in need of funds. They also collect economic data and conduct research projects on commercial banking and economic trends.

Fed Member Banks

Commercial banks can elect to become member banks if they meet specific requirements of the Board of Governors. All national banks (chartered by the Comptroller of the Currency) are required to be members of the Fed, but other banks (chartered by their respective states) are not. Currently, about 35 percent of all banks are members; these banks account for about 70 percent of all bank deposits.

Fed Board of Governors

http://
http://www.federalreserve
.gov Background on the
Board of Governors, board
meetings, board members,
and the structure of the
Fed.

The **Board of Governors** (sometimes called the Federal Reserve Board) is made up of seven individual members with offices in Washington, D.C. Each member is appointed by the president of the United States (and confirmed by the Senate) and serves a nonrenewable 14-year term. This long term is thought to reduce political pressure on the governors and thus encourage the development of policies that will benefit the U.S. economy over the long run. The terms are staggered so that one term expires in every even-numbered year.

Locations of Federal Reserve District Banks and Branches

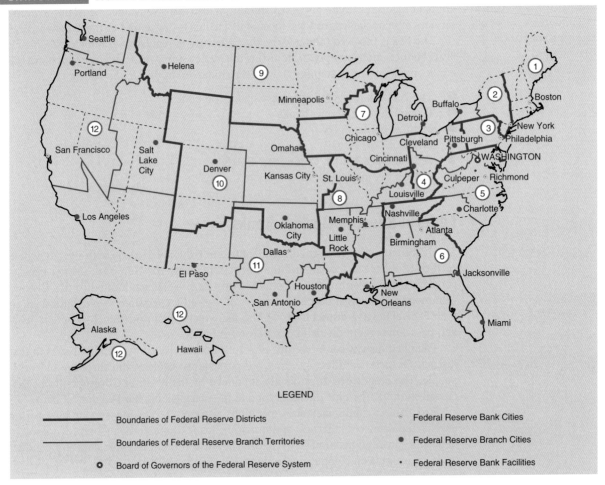

LEGEND

—————— Boundaries of Federal Reserve Districts   ∘ Federal Reserve Bank Cities

—————— Boundaries of Federal Reserve Branch Territories   • Federal Reserve Branch Cities

⊙ Board of Governors of the Federal Reserve System   · Federal Reserve Bank Facilities

Source: *Federal Reserve Bulletin.*

One of the seven board members is selected by the president to be Federal Reserve chairman for a four-year term, which may be renewed. The chairman has no more voting power than any other member, but may have more influence. For example, both Paul Volcker, who served as chairman from 1979 to 1987, and Alan Greenspan, who succeeded him in 1987, are regarded as very persuasive.

The board has two main roles: (1) regulating commercial banks and (2) controlling monetary policy. It supervises and regulates commercial banks that are members of the Fed and bank holding companies. It oversees the operation of the 12 Federal Reserve district banks as they provide services to depository institutions and supervise specific commercial banks. It also establishes regulations on consumer finance. Previously, the board was responsible for determining ceiling interest rates on bank deposits, but those ceilings were completely phased out by 1986 as a result of the Depository Institutions Deregulation and Monetary Control Act of 1980. The board continues to participate in the supervision of member banks and in setting credit controls, such as margin requirements (percentage of a purchase of securities that must be paid with nonborrowed funds).

With regard to monetary policy, the board has direct control over two monetary policy tools and participates in the control of a third tool. First, it has the power to revise reserve requirements imposed on depository institutions. Second, it authorizes changes in the **discount rate,** or the interest rate charged on Fed district bank loans to depository institutions. Any changes in the discount rate or reserve requirements can affect the money supply level, as explained later in the chapter. The board can also control the money supply by participating in the decisions of the Federal Open Market Committee, discussed next.

Federal Open Market Committee (FOMC)

http://www.federalreserve.gov Obtain the minutes of the most recent Federal Open Market Committee (FOMC).

The **Federal Open Market Committee (FOMC)** is made up of the seven members of the Board of Governors plus the presidents of five Fed district banks (the New York district bank plus four of the other 11 Fed district banks as determined on a rotating basis). Presidents of the seven remaining Fed district banks typically participate in the FOMC meetings but are not allowed to vote on policy decisions. The chairman of the Board of Governors serves as chairman of the FOMC.

The main goals of the FOMC are to promote high employment, economic growth, and price stability. Achievement of these goals would stabilize financial markets, interest rates, foreign exchange values, and so on. Because the FOMC may not be able to achieve all of its main goals simultaneously, it may concentrate on resolving a particular economic problem.

The FOMC attempts to achieve its goals through control of the money supply. It meets about every six weeks to review economic conditions and determine appropriate monetary policy to improve economic conditions and prevent potential adverse conditions from erupting.

In order to make monetary policy decisions, FOMC members assess the current economic situation, using statistics on recent economic growth, inflation, and the unemployment rate. They also review global economic conditions and their relationship with U.S. conditions. Then, the members discuss their main concerns about the U.S. economy. For example, when the unemployment rate is high and the inflation rate is low, they focus on correcting unemployment by using a stimulative monetary policy. Conversely, when inflation is high and unemployment is low, the focus is on reducing inflation by using a restrictive monetary policy (designed to slow economic growth and thereby reduce inflation). When both the unemployment rate and the inflation rate are high, the FOMC faces a more challenging dilemma, as it is difficult to achieve a monetary policy that can reduce both problems simultaneously.

Advisory Committees

The Federal Advisory Council consists of one member from each Federal Reserve district. Each district's member is elected each year by the board of directors of the respective district bank. The council meets with the Board of Governors in Washington, D.C., at least four times a year and makes recommendations about economic and banking issues.

The Consumer Advisory Council is made up of 30 members, representing the financial institutions industry and its consumers. This committee normally meets with the Board of Governors four times a year to discuss consumer issues.

The Thrift Institutions Advisory Council is made up of 12 members, representing savings banks, savings and loan associations, and credit unions. Its purpose is to offer views on issues specifically related to these institutions. It meets with the Board of Governors three times a year.

Integration of Federal Reserve Components

Exhibit 4.2 shows the relationships among the various components of the Federal Reserve System. The advisory committees advise the board, while the board oversees operations of the district banks. The board and representatives of the district banks make up the FOMC.

Monetary Policy Tools

Changes in the money supply can have a major impact on economic conditions. Financial market participants closely monitor the Fed's actions so that they can anticipate how the money supply will be affected. They then use this information to forecast economic conditions and securities prices. The relationship between the money supply and economic conditions is discussed in detail in the following chapter. First, it is important to understand *how* the Fed controls the money supply.

The Fed can use three monetary policy tools to either increase or decrease the money supply:

- Open market operations
- Adjustments in the discount rate
- Adjustments in the reserve requirement ratio

Open Market Operations

http://www.federalreserve.gov/policy.htm Provides minutes of FOMC meetings. Notice from the minutes how much attention is given to any economic indicators that can be used to anticipate future economic growth or inflation.

The FOMC meets eight times a year. At each meeting, the target money supply growth level and interest rate level are determined, and actions are taken to implement the monetary policy dictated by the FOMC. If the Fed wants to consider changing the money growth or interest rate targets before its next scheduled meeting because of unusual circumstances, it may engage in a conference call meeting.

FOMC Meeting Agenda About two weeks before the FOMC meeting, FOMC members are sent the **Beige Book,** which is a consolidated report of regional economic conditions in each of the 12 districts. Each Federal Reserve district bank is responsible for reporting its regional conditions, and all of these reports are consolidated to compose the Beige Book.

The FOMC meeting is conducted in the Board room of the building where the Board of Governors is located in Washington, D.C. The meeting is attended by the seven members of the Board of Governors, the 12 presidents of the Fed district banks, and staff members (typically economists) of the Board of Governors. The meeting begins with presentations by the staff members about current economic conditions and recent economic trends. They provide data and trends for wages, consumer prices, unemployment, gross domestic product, business inventories, foreign exchange rates, interest rates, and financial market conditions.

EXHIBIT 4.2
Integration of Federal
Reserve Components

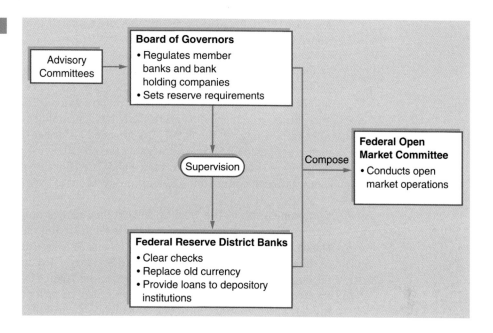

The staff members also assess production levels, business investment, residential construction, international trade, and international economic growth. This assessment is conducted to predict economic growth and inflation in the United States, assuming that the Fed does not adjust its monetary policy. For example, a reduction in business inventories may lead to an expectation of stronger economic growth, as firms will need to boost production in order to replenish inventories. Conversely, an increase in inventories may indicate that firms will reduce their production and possibly their work force as well. An increase in business investment indicates that businesses are expanding their production capacity and are likely to increase their production in the future. An increase in economic growth in foreign countries is important because a portion of the increased incomes in those countries will be spent on U.S. products or services. The Fed uses this information to determine whether U.S. economic growth is adequate.

Much attention is also given to any factors that can affect inflation. For example, oil prices are closely monitored because they affect the cost of producing and transporting many products. A decline in business inventories when production is near full capacity may indicate an excessive demand for products that will pull prices up. This condition indicates higher inflation because firms may raise the prices of their products when they are producing near full capacity and experience shortages. If firms attempt to expand capacity under these conditions, they will have to raise wages to obtain additional qualified employees. They will incur higher costs from raising wages and therefore raise the prices of their products. The Fed becomes concerned when several indicators suggest that higher inflation is likely.

The staff members typically base their forecasts for economic conditions on the assumption that the prevailing monetary growth level will still be applied in the future. When it is highly likely that the monetary growth level will be changed, they provide forecasts for economic conditions under different monetary growth scenarios. Their goal is to provide facts and economic forecasts, but not to make judgments about the appropriate monetary policy. The members normally receive some economic information a

few days before the meeting so that they are prepared when listening to the presentations by staff members.

Once the presentations are completed, each FOMC member has a chance to offer recommendations about whether the prevailing monetary growth and interest rate target levels should be changed and, if so, how they should be changed. Even the nonvoting members are given time to offer recommendations. The chairman of the Fed may also offer a recommendation and usually has some influence over the other members. After each member of the FOMC has provided his or her recommendation, the voting members of the FOMC vote on whether the prevailing money supply and interest rate target levels should be revised. Most FOMC decisions on monetary policy are unanimous, although it is not unusual for some decisions to have one or two dissenting votes.

Communication to the Trading Desk If the Fed determines that a change in its monetary policy is appropriate, its decision is forwarded to the **Trading Desk** (or the **Open Market Desk**) at the New York Fed district bank. It is here that open market operations, or the Fed's trading of government securities, are carried out. The FOMC's decision on the target money supply level is forwarded to the Trading Desk at the New York Federal Reserve district bank through a statement called the **policy directive.** The FOMC objectives are specified in the form of a target range, such as an annualized growth rate of 3 to 5 percent in the money supply over the next few months, rather than one specific money supply level.

The FOMC also specifies a desired target range for the federal funds rate, the rate charged by banks on short-term loans to each other. Even though this rate is determined by the banks that participate in the federal funds market, it is subject to the supply and demand for funds in the banking system. Thus, the Fed can influence the federal funds rate by revising the amount of funds in the banking system. In recent years, the Fed has specified a single federal funds target rate when it has engaged in open market operations. Since all short-term interest rates are affected by the supply of and demand for funds, they tend to move together. Thus, the Fed's actions affect all short-term interest rates that are market determined and may even affect long-term interest rates as well.

http://

http://www.publicdebt.treas
.gov Treasury note and
bond auction results.

Role of the Trading Desk After receiving the policy directive from the FOMC, the manager of the Trading Desk instructs traders who work at that desk on the amount of government securities to buy or sell in the secondary market based on the directive. The buying and selling of government securities (through the Trading Desk) is referred to as **open market operations;** this is the most common means by which the Fed controls the money supply. Even though the Trading Desk at the Federal Reserve Bank of New York receives a policy directive from the FOMC only eight times a year, it continuously uses open market operations in response to ongoing changes in bank deposit levels to maintain the money supply within the specified target range.

Fed Purchase of Securities When traders at the Trading Desk at the Federal Reserve Bank of New York are instructed to purchase a specified dollar amount of securities, they call government securities dealers. The dealers provide a list of securities for sale that gives the denomination and maturity of each security as well as the dealer's ask quote (the price at which the dealer is willing to sell the security). From this list, the traders attempt to purchase those that are most attractive (lowest prices for whatever maturities are desired) until they have purchased the amount requested by the manager of the Trading Desk. The accounting department of the New York district bank then notifies the government bond department to receive and pay for those securities.

When the Fed purchases securities through the government securities dealers, the account balances of the dealers are credited with this amount. Thus, the total amount of funds at the dealers' banks increases. The total funds of commercial banks increase by the dollar amount of securities purchased by the Fed. This activity initiated by the Fed's policy directive represents a loosening of money supply growth.

The Trading Desk is sometimes directed to buy a sufficient amount of Treasury securities to force a decline in the federal funds rate to a new targeted level set by the FOMC. The Trading Desk then buys Treasury securities until it has reduced the federal funds rate to the new targeted level. As the supply of funds in the banking system increases, the federal funds rate declines along with other interest rates.

The Fed's purchase of government securities has a different impact than a purchase by another investor would have because the Fed's purchase results in additional bank funds and increases the ability of banks to make loans and create new deposits. An increase in funds can allow for a net increase in deposit balances and therefore an increase in the money supply. Conversely, the purchase of government securities by someone other than the Fed (such as an investor) results in offsetting account balance positions at commercial banks.

Fed Sale of Securities If the Trading Desk at the Federal Reserve Bank of New York is instructed to decrease the money supply, its traders sell government securities (obtained from previous purchases) to government securities dealers. The securities are sold to the dealers that submit the highest bids. As the dealers pay for the securities, their account balances are reduced. Thus, the total amount of funds at commercial banks is reduced by the market value of the securities sold by the Fed. This activity initiated by the FOMC's policy directive is referred to as a tightening of money supply growth.

The Trading Desk is sometimes directed to sell a sufficient amount of Treasury securities to increase the federal funds rate to a new targeted level set by the FOMC. When the Trading Desk sells a sufficient amount of Treasury securities, it creates a shortage of funds in the banking system. Consequently, the federal funds rate increases along with other interest rates.

Fed Use of Repurchase Agreements In some cases, the Fed may desire to increase the aggregate level of bank funds for only a few days to ensure adequate liquidity in the banking system on those days. Under these conditions, the Trading Desk may trade **repurchase agreements** rather than government securities. It purchases Treasury securities from government securities dealers with an agreement to sell back the securities at a specified date in the near future. Initially, the level of funds rises as the securities are sold; it is then reduced when the dealers repurchase the securities. The Trading Desk uses repurchase agreements during holidays and other such periods to correct temporary imbalances in the level of bank funds. To correct a temporary excess of funds, the Trading Desk sells some of its Treasury securities holdings to securities dealers and agrees to repurchase them at a specified future date.

How Open Market Operations Affect Interest Rates Even though most interest rates are market determined, the Fed can have a strong influence on these rates by controlling the supply of loanable funds. When the Fed uses open market operations to increase bank funds, banks have more funds that can be loaned out. This can influence various market-determined interest rates. First, the federal funds rate may decline because some banks have a larger supply of excess funds to lend out in the federal funds market. Second, banks with excess funds may offer new loans at a lower interest rate in

order to make use of these funds. Third, these banks may also lower interest rates offered on deposits because they have more than adequate funds to conduct existing operations.

Since open market operations commonly involve the buying or selling of Treasury bills, the yields on Treasury securities are influenced along with the yields (interest rates) offered on bank deposits. For example, when the Fed buys Treasury bills as a means of increasing the money supply, it places upward pressure on their prices. Since these securities offer a fixed value to investors at maturity, a higher price translates into a lower yield for investors who buy them and hold them until maturity. While Treasury yields are affected directly by open market operations, bank rates are also affected because of the change in the money supply that open market operations bring about.

As the yields on Treasury bills and bank deposits decline, investors search for alternative investments such as other debt securities. As more funds are invested in these securities, the yields will decline. Thus, open market operations used to increase bank funds influence not only bank deposit and loan rates but also the yields on other debt securities. The reduction in yields on debt securities lowers the cost of borrowing for the issuers of new debt securities. This can encourage potential borrowers (including corporations and individuals) to borrow and make expenditures that they might not have made if interest rates were higher.

If open market operations are used to reduce bank funds, the opposite effects occur. More banks have deficient funds, and fewer banks have any excess funds. Thus, there is upward pressure on the federal funds rate, on the loan rates charged to individuals and firms, and on the rates offered to bank depositors. As bank deposit rates rise, some investors may be encouraged to create bank deposits rather than invest in other debt securities. This activity reduces the amount of funds available for these debt instruments, thereby increasing the yield offered on the instruments. More specific details about how money supply adjustments can affect interest rates and economic conditions are provided in the following chapter.

Dynamic versus Defensive Open Market Operations Depending on the intent, open market operations can be classified as either **dynamic** or **defensive.** Dynamic operations are implemented to increase or decrease the level of funds; defensive operations offset the impact of other conditions that affect the level of funds. For example, if the Fed expects a large inflow of cash into commercial banks, it could offset this inflow by selling some of its Treasury security holdings.

Open Market Operations in Response to the Crash On October 19, 1987, stock prices declined by more than 22 percent on average, the largest decline in history. The Federal Reserve System took action to prevent further adverse effects. On the morning after the crash, the Fed issued a statement that it was prepared to provide liquidity to the financial markets. It became actively involved in open market operations to ensure adequate liquidity. Because it was concerned that economic growth would be adversely affected by the crash, the Fed loosened the money supply.

The Fed also monitored bank deposit balances to ensure that the crash did not cause runs on bank deposits. It also monitored credit relationships between commercial banks and securities firms, which can change abruptly during a financial crisis. In general, the financial fears that caused the crash did not escalate, and financial markets stabilized shortly after the crash. The Fed's efforts to ensure adequate liquidity and restore confidence in the financial system may have been partially responsible for calming the markets.

Open Market Operations in Response to the Weak U.S. Economy When the U.S. economy weakened in 2001, the Fed attempted to stimulate the economy by using open

market operations to increase money supply growth. As a result of these open market operations, the federal funds rate and other short-term interest rates declined. Although the lower rates reduced the cost of borrowing, businesses did not respond to the lower interest rates; that is, they did not decide to borrow just because interest rates were lower. This lack of response led to continued efforts by the Fed to stimulate the economy. During 2001, the Fed made 11 attempts to reduce interest rates. Each effort was associated with an adjustment of either .25 percent or .50 percent in the federal funds target rate. The economy remained weak in 2002, but improved in 2003. The rebound in the economy was partially attributed to the low interest rates.

Open Market Operations in Response to the September 11 Attack on the United States The terrorist attack on September 11, 2001, directly affected the U.S. financial center in New York City. Stock markets were closed for the remainder of the week. The FOMC held a telephone conference call on the day of the attack. It decided to use open market operations so that it could add liquidity to the banking system in case individuals began to withdraw funds from cash machines out of fear of a banking crisis. The FOMC recognized that the attack might slow the economy even further, but decided not to reduce the federal funds target rate at that time.

The stock markets remained closed until September 17. Early on the morning of September 17, the FOMC held another telephone conference call and decided to use open market operations to reduce the federal funds target rate by .50 percent just before the stock markets reopened. Although stocks declined substantially on that day, the effects would likely have been worse if the Fed had not intervened.

Adjusting the Discount Rate

The discount window of the Fed offers loans to depository institutions to correct liquidity problems. The loans are normally for very short-term periods such as one day or a week. Credit extended by the Fed represents an increase in funds at depository institutions. If depository institutions borrow from one another instead, funds are simply transferred among institutions, and the total level of funds is not increased.

To increase the money supply, the Fed (specifically, the Board of Governors) used to authorize a reduction in the discount rate. This encouraged depository institutions that are short on funds to borrow from the Fed rather than from other sources such as the federal funds market. To decrease the money supply, the Fed discouraged use of the discount window by increasing the discount rate. Depository institutions in need of short-term funds obtained funding from alternative sources. As existing discount window loans were repaid to the Fed and new loans were obtained from sources other than the discount window, the level of funds decreased.

In January 2003, the Fed changed the structure of its discount rate. It classified its loans as primary credit or secondary credit. Primary credit may be used for any purpose and is available only to depository institutions that meet specific requirements for financial soundness (such as sufficient capital). Secondary credit is provided to banks that do not qualify for primary credit. A premium above the discount rate is charged for secondary credit. That is, depository institutions that do not meet the requirements for financial soundness pay a higher rate on Fed loans, which reflects a risk premium.

In addition to changing the structure of the discount rate in January 2003, the Fed also established a policy in which the discount rate (now also referred to as the primary credit lending rate) would be set at a level above the federal funds rate. Thus, loans from the Fed should serve only as a backup source of funds for depository institutions.

Before the 2003 policy, adjustments to the discount rate were sometimes viewed as signals about the Fed's future monetary policy. An increase in the discount rate was sometimes interpreted as a signal that the Fed may implement a loose money policy, and reduce the federal funds rate in the near future. Conversely, a reduction in the discount rate was sometimes interpreted as a signal that the Fed may implement a tight money policy, and increase the federal funds rate in the near future. As a result of the 2003 policy, the discount rate is adjusted in response to changes in the federal funds rate. Thus, the discount rate is no longer an effective monetary policy tool, and no longer serves as a possible signal of changes in other interest rates.

Adjusting the Reserve Requirement Ratio

Depository institutions are subject to a **reserve requirement ratio,** which is the proportion of their deposit accounts that must be held as reserves. This ratio is set by the Board of Governors. Depository institutions have historically been forced to maintain between 8 and 12 percent of their transactions accounts (such as checking accounts) and a smaller proportion of their other savings accounts as required reserves, which cannot be used to earn interest.

Because the reserve requirement ratio affects the degree to which the money supply can change, it is sometimes modified by the Board of Governors to adjust the money supply. When the board reduces the reserve requirement ratio, it increases the proportion of a bank's deposits that can be lent out by depository institutions. As the funds loaned out are spent, a portion of them will return to the depository institutions in the form of new deposits. The lower the reserve requirement ratio, the greater the lending capacity of depository institutions, so any initial change in bank reserves can cause a larger change in the money supply.

During the 1980s, the Board of Governors removed the reserve requirement ratio on some types of time deposits. In December 1990, the reserve requirement ratio on negotiable certificates of deposit was removed. In 1992, the reserve requirement ratio on transactions accounts was reduced from 12 percent to 10 percent, where it has remained.

How Reserve Requirement Adjustments Affect Money Growth To illustrate how adjustments in the reserve requirement ratio can affect money supply growth, a simplified example follows. Assume the following information:

Assumption 1. Banks obtain all their funds from demand deposits and use all funds except required reserves to make loans.

Assumption 2. The public does not store any cash; any funds withdrawn from banks are spent; and any funds received are deposited in banks.

Assumption 3. The reserve requirement ratio on demand deposits is 10 percent.

Based on these assumptions, 10 percent of all bank deposits are maintained as required reserves, and the other 90 percent are loaned out (zero excess reserves). Now assume that the Fed initially uses open market operations by purchasing $100 million worth of Treasury securities.

As the Treasury securities dealers sell securities to the Fed, their deposit balances at commercial banks increase by $100 million. Banks maintain 10 percent of the $100 million, or $10 million, as required reserves and lend out the rest. As the $90 million lent out is spent, it returns to banks as new demand deposit accounts (by whoever receives the funds that were spent). Banks maintain 10 percent, or $9 million, of these new deposits as required reserves and lend out the remainder ($81 million). Because of this cycle, the initial increase in demand deposits (money) multiplies into a much larger

EXHIBIT 4.3

Illustration of Multiplier Effect

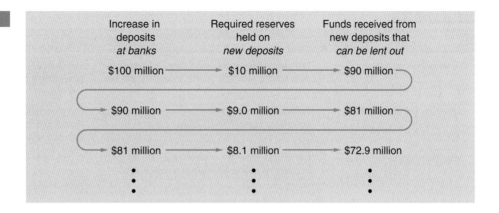

amount. Exhibit 4.3 summarizes this cycle. This cycle will not continue forever. Every time the funds lent out return to a bank, a portion (10 percent) is retained as required reserves. Thus, the amount of new deposits created is less for each round. Under the previous assumptions, the initial money supply injection of $100 million would multiply by 1/(reserve requirement ratio), or 1/.10, to equal 10, so the total change in the money supply once the cycle is complete is $100 million × 10 = $1 billion.

As this simplified example demonstrates, an initial injection of funds will multiply into a larger amount. The reserve requirement controls the amount of loanable funds that can be created from new deposits. A higher reserve requirement ratio causes an initial injection of funds to multiply by a smaller amount. Conversely, a lower reserve requirement ratio causes it to multiply by a greater amount. In this way, the Fed can adjust money supply growth by adjusting the reserve requirement ratio.

Our example exaggerates the amount by which money multiplies. Consumers sometimes hold cash, and banks sometimes hold excess reserves, contradicting the assumptions of banks holding only demand deposits and zero excess reserves. Consequently, major leakages occur, and money does not multiply to the extent shown in the example. The money multiplier can change over time because of changes in the excess reserve level and in consumer preferences for demand deposits versus time deposits (which are not included in the most narrow definition of money). This complicates the task of forecasting how an initial adjustment in bank reserves will ultimately affect the money supply level.

Comparison of Monetary Policy Tools

Exhibit 4.4 compares the ways that monetary policy tools increase or decrease money supply growth. The Fed most frequently uses open market operations as a monetary policy tool because they are convenient and because the other tools have certain disadvantages.

An adjustment in the discount rate affected the money supply only if depository institutions responded (borrow more or less from the Fed than normal) to the adjustment. In addition, borrowings through the discount window are for a very short term, so any adjustment in funds resulting from an increase or decrease in loans from the Fed is only temporary. Now that changes in the discount rate are dictated by changes in the federal funds rate, the discount rate is not a useful monetary policy tool.

An adjustment in the reserve requirement ratio can cause erratic shifts in the money supply. Thus, the probability of missing the target money supply level is higher when using the reserve requirement ratio.

EXHIBIT 4.4 Comparison of Monetary Policy Tools

Monetary Policy Tool	To Increase Money Supply Growth	To Decrease Money Supply Growth
Open market operations	Fed should (through the Trading Desk) purchase government securities in the secondary market.	Fed should (through the Trading Desk) sell government securities in the secondary market.
Adjusting the discount rate	Fed used to lower the discount rate to encourage borrowing through the discount window.	Fed used to raise the discount rate to discourage borrowing through the discount window.
Adjusting reserve requirements	Fed should lower the reserve requirement ratio to cause money to multiply at a higher rate.	Fed should raise the reserve requirement ratio to cause money to multiply at a lower rate.

Open market operations do not suffer from these limitations. In addition, open market operations can be used without signaling the Fed's intentions and can easily be reversed without the public's knowing. A reverse adjustment in the reserve requirement ratio could arouse more concern among the public, reduce the Fed's credibility, and create paranoia in financial markets.

Because the rate by which injected funds will multiply is uncertain (even when leaving the reserve requirement ratio unchanged), there is no guarantee that open market operations will accomplish the money growth target. Even so, they can be used continuously over time to manipulate the money supply toward the desired target.

How Technical Factors Affect Funds

Even if the Fed does not intervene, the volume of funds can change as a result of so-called technical factors, such as currency in circulation and Federal Reserve float. When the amount of currency in circulation increases (such as during the holiday season), the corresponding increase in net deposit withdrawals reduces funds. When it decreases, the net addition to deposits increases funds. Federal Reserve float is the amount of checks credited to bank funds that have not yet been collected. A rise in float causes an increase in bank funds, and a decrease in float causes a reduction in bank funds.

Staff at the Federal Reserve Bank of New York along with those at the Board of Governors in Washington, D.C., provide daily forecasts of how technical factors such as these will affect the level of funds. The Fed must account for such influences when implementing monetary policy. The manager of the Trading Desk incorporates the expected impact of technical factors on funds into the instructions to traders. If the policy directive calls for growth in funds but technical factors are expected to increase funds, the instructions will call for a smaller injection of funds than if the technical factors did not exist. Conversely, if technical factors are expected to reduce funds, the instructions will call for a larger injection of funds to offset the impact of the technical factors.

Fed Control of the Money Supply

When the Fed manipulates the money supply to influence economic variables, it must decide what form of money to manipulate. The optimal form of money should (1) be controllable by the Fed and (2) have a predictable impact on economic variables when

EXHIBIT 4.5

Comparison of Money
Supply Measures

Money Supply Measures
M1 = currency + checking deposits
M2 = M1 + savings deposits, MMDAs, overnight repurchase agreements, Eurodollars, noninstitutional money market mutual funds, and small time deposits
M3 = M2 + institutional money market mutual funds, large time deposits, and repurchase agreements and Eurodollars lasting more than one day

http://

http://www.federalreserve
.gov/releases Features
various Federal Reserve
statistical releases.

adjusted by the Fed. The most narrow form of money, known as **M1,** includes currency held by the public and checking deposits (such as demand deposits, NOW accounts, and automatic transfer balances) at depository institutions. Although M1 has received the most attention in recent years, it does not include all funds that can be used for transactions purposes. For example, checks can be written against a **money market deposit account (MMDA)** offered by depository institutions or against a money market mutual fund. In addition, funds can easily be withdrawn from savings accounts to make transactions. For this reason, a broader measure of money, called **M2,** also deserves consideration. It includes everything in M1 as well as savings accounts and small time deposits, MMDAs, and some other items. Another measure of money, called **M3,** includes everything in M2 as well as large time deposits and other items. Although there are even a few broader measures of money, M1, M2, and M3 receive the most attention. A comparison of M1, M2, and M3 is provided in Exhibit 4.5.

The Fed first introduced the M1, M2, and M3 monetary aggregates in 1971. In 1978, the Full Employment and Balanced Growth Act (more commonly known as the Humphrey-Hawkins Act) required the Fed to set one-year target ranges for money supply growth twice a year. Particularly during the 1980s, M1 target ranges were closely watched by market participants to anticipate interest rate changes by the Fed.

During the deregulation phase (early 1980s) in the depository institutions industry, various new deposit accounts were created, and households began to switch among accounts. When funds were transferred from demand deposit accounts to MMDAs, M1 was reduced even though the Fed had taken no action to reduce it. When funds were transferred from savings into NOW accounts, M1 increased simply because of a change in household saving habits rather than monetary policy actions. Consequently, the M1 measure became quite volatile over this period and was difficult for the Fed to control. The Fed stopped announcing growth ranges for M1 in 1987.

Since the broader M2 measure includes most deposit accounts, it was not as sensitive to changes in consumer habits. Even though individual components of M2 (such as MMDAs and NOW accounts) were affected by deregulation, the overall level of M2 was not.

The money measurement M1 is more volatile than M2 or M3. Since M1 can change simply because of changes in the types of deposits maintained by households, M2 and M3 are more reliable measures for monitoring and controlling the money supply.

Limitations of Controlling Money Supply

In the 1970s, the Fed attempted to simultaneously control the money supply and interest rates within specified target ranges. It used the federal funds rate as its representative interest rate to control, which in turn can influence other interest rates. Simultaneous control of the money supply and federal funds rate is not always possible. Assume that the Fed sets hypothetical target ranges for money supply growth and the federal funds rate. Assume that both variables are near the upper boundary of their respective

ranges. If the Fed desires to maintain the federal funds rate within its range, it would likely inject more funds into the economy (increase money supply growth). However, this will force the money supply growth above its upper boundary. If instead the Fed maintains money supply growth within its range, it may be unable to prevent the federal funds rate from rising above its upper boundary.

The Fed recognized that it could not simultaneously control both variables and as of October 1979 chose to focus primarily on the money supply. Over the next decades, the Fed hit its long-term money supply targets with some success. From time to time, however, various factors distorted the relationship between the money supply and economic conditions.

In the early 1990s, when interest rates were at a low point, many savers moved funds out of savings accounts and time deposits into stock and bond mutual funds, which are not included in any of the money supply measures. Consequently, in July 1993, Alan Greenspan announced in congressional testimony that the measures of money are not always reliable indicators of financial conditions in the economy.

For the next several years, the Fed focused on maintaining the federal funds rate within a narrow target range. When the Humphrey-Hawkins legislation requiring the Fed to set target ranges for money supply growth expired in 2000, the Fed announced that it would no longer set such targets. Nevertheless, the Fed also stated that the behavior of money and credit would continue to have value for gauging economic and financial conditions. In addition, M2 still remains a component of the Index of Leading Economic Indicators.

Monetary Control Act of 1980

In 1980 Congress passed the **Depository Institutions Deregulation and Monetary Control Act (DIDMCA).** Commonly referred to as the Monetary Control Act, it had two key objectives. First, it was intended to deregulate some aspects of the depository institutions industry (discussed in the chapters on depository institutions). Second, it was intended to enhance the Fed's ability to control the money supply.

Before DIDMCA, member banks of the Federal Reserve were subject to its reserve requirements, and nonmember banks were subject to the reserve requirements of their respective states. Nonmember banks often had an advantage in that they could typically maintain their required reserves in some interest-bearing form (such as Treasury securities). A member bank's required reserves could be held only as balances at the Fed or as vault cash and therefore could not earn interest. This disadvantage to member banks became more pronounced in the 1970s, when interest rates were generally higher than in previous years. The opportunity cost of tying up funds in a non-interest-bearing form increased. As a result, some member banks dropped their membership.

As Fed memberships decreased, so did the Fed's ability to control the money supply through reserve requirement adjustments, because it could adjust reserve requirements only of *member* banks. The Monetary Control Act mandates that all depository institutions be subject to the same reserve requirements imposed by the Fed. The reserve requirements were reduced relative to what the Fed previously required, but all required reserves were still to be held in a non-interest-bearing form. The revised reserve requirements were phased in over an eight-year period.

A related provision of the Monetary Control Act is that all depository institutions must report their deposit levels promptly to the Fed. This improves the Fed's knowledge of the current level of deposits in the banking system at any point in time. In the past, the Fed may have underestimated the prevailing money supply at times and thus increased

the money supply above the level desired. With the improved reporting system, it has a better feel for the prevailing money supply level and therefore makes better adjustments.

In addition to its reserve requirement and reporting provisions, the Monetary Control Act allowed all depository institutions that offer transaction accounts (such as demand deposits or NOW accounts) to have access to the discount window. Previously, only member banks were allowed access. This provision provided the Fed additional control over the money supply because more institutions have access to the discount window. As noted earlier, however, the Fed no longer uses discount rate adjustments to control the money supply.

Global Monetary Policy

GL BALASPECTS

Each country has its own central bank that conducts monetary policy. The central banks of industrialized countries tend to have somewhat similar goals, which essentially reflect price stability (low inflation) and economic growth (low unemployment). Resources and conditions vary among countries, however, so a given central bank may focus more on a particular economic goal.

Like the Fed, central banks of other industrialized countries use open market operations, reserve requirement adjustments, and adjustments in the interest rate they charge on loans to banks as monetary policy tools. The monetary policy tools are generally used as a means of affecting local market interest rates in order to influence economic conditions.

Because country economies are integrated, the Fed must consider economic conditions in other major countries when assessing the U.S. economy. The Fed may be most effective when it coordinates its activities with those of central banks of other countries. Central banks commonly work together when they intervene in the foreign exchange market, but coordinating monetary policies can be difficult because of conflicts of interest.

A Single Eurozone Monetary Policy

The national currencies of the following 12 European countries were recently withdrawn from the financial system and replaced by the euro: Austria, Belgium, Finland, France, Germany, Greece, Ireland, Italy, Luxembourg, the Netherlands, Portugal, and Spain. The three other members of the European Union (Denmark, Sweden, United Kingdom) at that time decided not to participate in the euro initially but may join later. In 2004, 10 emerging countries in Europe, including the Czech Republic and Hungary, joined the European Union and may participate in the euro later if they satisfy the limitations imposed on government deficits.

The European Central Bank (ECB), based in Frankfurt, is responsible for setting monetary policy for all participating European countries. Its objective is to control inflation in the participating countries and to stabilize (within reasonable boundaries) the value of the euro with respect to other major currencies. Thus, the ECB's monetary goals of price stability and currency stability are somewhat similar to those of individual countries around the world, but differ in that they are focused on a group of countries rather than a single country. Because participating countries are subject to the monetary policy imposed by the ECB, a given country will no longer have full control over the monetary policy imposed within its borders at any given time. The implementation

of a common monetary policy may lead to more political unification among partici-pating countries and encourage them to develop similar national defense and foreign policies.

Impact of the Euro on Monetary Policy As just described, the use of a common cur-rency forces countries to abide by a common monetary policy. Any changes in the money supply affect all European countries using the euro as their form of money. Hav-ing a single currency also means that the interest rate offered on government securities must be similar across the participating European countries. Any discrepancy in rates would encourage investors within these countries to invest in the country with the high-est rate, which would realign the interest rates among the countries.

Although having a single monetary policy may allow for more consistent economic conditions across the eurozone countries, it prevents any participating country from solving local economic problems with its own unique monetary policy. Eurozone gov-ernments may disagree on the ideal monetary policy to enhance their local economies, but they must agree on a single monetary policy. Yet any given policy used in a particu-lar period may enhance some countries and adversely affect others. Each participating country is still able to apply its own fiscal policy (tax and government expenditure de-cisions), however.

One concern about the euro is that each of the participating countries has its own agenda, which may prevent unified decisions about the future direction of the eurozone economies. Each country was supposed to show restraint on fiscal policy spending so that it could improve its budget deficit situation. Nevertheless, some countries have ig-nored restraint in favor of resolving domestic unemployment problems. The euro's ini-tial instability was partially attributed to political maneuvering as individual countries tried to serve their own interests at the expense of the other participating countries. This lack of solidarity is exactly the reason why there was some concern about using a single currency (and therefore monetary policy) among several European countries.

Variations in the Value of the Euro Since the euro was introduced in 1999, it has ex-perienced a bumpy ride. Its value initially declined substantially against the British pound, the dollar, and many other currencies. By October 2001, its value was $.90, or about 25 percent less than its value when it was introduced. The weakness was partially attributed to capital outflows from Europe. More money was flowing out of Europe and into U.S. and other financial markets than was flowing from these countries to Europe. The net outflows from Europe were partially caused by lack of confidence in the euro. Investors preferred to hold assets denominated in dollars than in euros.

During the 2002–2003 period, however, the euro appreciated substantially. One reason for its strength in this period was that the interest rate on the euro was higher than that of the dollar. Thus, capital flowed to the eurozone to take advantage of the higher interest rate on euro-denominated debt securities.

Global Central Bank Coordination

In some cases, the central banks of various countries coordinate their efforts for a com-mon cause. Shortly after the terrorist attack on the United States on September 11, 2001, central banks of several countries injected money denominated in their respec-tive currencies into the banking system to provide more liquidity. This strategy was in-

tended to ensure that sufficient money would be available in case customers began to withdraw funds from banks or cash machines. On September 17, 2001, the Fed's move to reduce interest rates before the U.S. stock market reopened was immediately followed by similar decisions by the Bank of Canada (Canada's central bank) and the European Central Bank.

Sometimes, however, central banks have conflicting objectives. For example, it is not unusual for two countries to simultaneously experience weak economies. In this situation, each central bank may consider intervening to weaken its home currency, which could increase foreign demand for exports denominated in that currency. If both central banks attempt this type of intervention simultaneously, however, the exchange rate between the two currencies will be subject to conflicting forces.

ILLUSTRATION Today, the Fed plans to intervene directly in the foreign exchange market by selling dollars for yen in an attempt to weaken the dollar. Meanwhile, the Bank of Japan plans to sell yen for dollars in the foreign exchange market in an attempt to weaken the yen. The effects are offsetting. One central bank can attempt to have a more powerful impact by selling more of its home currency in the foreign exchange market, but the other central bank may respond to offset that force.

SUMMARY

■ The key components of the Federal Reserve System are the Board of Governors and the Federal Open Market Committee. The Board of Governors determines the reserve requirements on account balances at depository institutions. It also represents an important subset of the Federal Open Market Committee (FOMC), which determines the monetary policy of the United States. The FOMC's monetary policy has a major influence on interest rates and other economic conditions.

■ The three main tools used by the Fed to conduct monetary policy are open market operations, the discount rate, and the reserve requirement ratio. In its open market operations, the Fed buys and sells securities as a means of adjusting the money supply. The Fed purchases securities as a means of increasing the money supply and sells them as a means of reducing the money supply.

The Fed used to raise the discount rate as a restrictive monetary policy to discourage bank borrowing from the Fed. Conversely, the Fed used to reduce the discount rate as an expansionary policy to encourage more bank borrowing from the Fed.

The Fed can raise the reserve requirement ratio as a restrictive monetary policy to reduce the degree to which money multiplies. Conversely, the Fed can reduce the ratio as an expansionary monetary policy to increase the degree to which money multiplies.

■ In 1980, Congress passed DIDMCA, which imposed uniform reserve requirements across all depository institutions. Thus, the reserve requirement became a more powerful monetary policy tool because it affected more depository institutions. DIDMCA also allowed all depository institutions with transaction accounts access to the discount window. However, the discount rate is no longer an effective monetary policy tool.

■ Each country has its own central bank, which is responsible for conducting monetary policy to achieve economic goals such as low inflation and low unemployment. Twelve countries in Europe recently adopted a single currency, which causes all of these countries to be subject to the same monetary policy.

POINT COUNTER-POINT

Should There Be One Global Central Bank?

Point Yes. One global central bank could serve all countries in the manner that the European Central Bank now serves several European countries. If there was a single central bank, there could be a single monetary policy across all countries.

Counter-Point No. A global central bank could create a global monetary policy only if a single currency was used throughout the world. Moreover, all countries would not agree on the monetary policy that is appropriate.

Who Is Correct? Use your favorite search engine to learn more about this issue. Offer your own opinion on this issue.

QUESTIONS AND APPLICATIONS

1. **Internet Exercise** Assess the current structure of the Federal Reserve System, using the website http://www.federalreserve.gov.

    Who is the current chairman of the Board of Governors? Who is the current vice chairman? Who are the other members of the Board of Governors? How often does the Board meet? When is the next scheduled meeting, and what items are scheduled to be discussed at this meeting?

2. **Control of Money Supply** Describe the characteristics that would be desirable for a measure of money to be manipulated by the Fed. Explain why it is difficult to simultaneously control the money supply and the federal funds rate.

3. **Tools Used by the Fed** Which tool used by the Fed is the most important on a weekly basis from the perspective of financial market participants?

4. **Interpreting Financial News** Interpret the following statements made by Wall Street analysts and portfolio managers:
    a. "The Fed's future monetary policy will be dependent on the economic indicators to be reported this week."
    b. "The Fed's role is to take the punch bowl away just as the party is coming alive."
    c. "Inflation will likely increase because real short-term interest rates currently are negative."

5. **The Fed** Briefly describe the origin of the Federal Reserve System. Describe the functions of the Fed district banks.

6. **Policy Directive** What is the policy directive, and who carries it out?

7. **Impact of Monetary Control Act** Have the reserve requirement provisions of the Monetary Control Act improved the Fed's ability to manipulate the money supply? Explain.

8. **Managing in Financial Markets: Anticipating the Fed's Actions** As a manager of a large U.S. firm, one of your assignments is to monitor U.S. economic conditions so that you can forecast the demand for products sold by your firm. You recognize that the Federal Reserve attempts to implement monetary policy to affect economic growth and inflation. In addition, you recognize that the federal government implements spending and tax policies (fiscal policy) to affect economic growth and inflation. Yet, it is difficult to achieve high economic growth without igniting inflation. It is often said that the Federal Reserve is independent of the administration in Washington, D.C., yet there is much interaction between monetary and fiscal policies.

    Assume that the economy is currently stagnant, and some economists are concerned about the possibility of a recession. Some industries, however, are experiencing high growth, and inflation is higher this year than in the previous five years. Assume that the Federal Reserve chairman's term will expire in four months and that the president of the United States will have to appoint a new chairman (or reappoint the existing chairman). It is widely known that the existing chairman would like to be reappointed. Also assume that next year is an election year for the administration.
    a. Given the circumstances, do you expect that the administration will be more concerned

about increasing economic growth or reducing inflation?

b. Given the circumstances, do you expect that the Fed will be more concerned about increasing economic growth or reducing inflation?

c. Your firm is relying on you for some insight on how the government will influence economic conditions and therefore the demand for your firm's products. Given the circumstances, what is your forecast of how the government will affect economic conditions?

9. **FOMC** What are the main goals of the Federal Open Market Committee? How does it attempt to achieve these goals?

10. **Monetary Control Act** What are the two key objectives of the Monetary Control Act? How does the Monetary Control Act help the Fed avoid improper adjustments in the money supply?

11. **Reserve Requirements** How is money supply growth affected by an increase in the reserve requirement ratio?

12. **Open Market Operations** Explain how the Fed increases the money supply through open market operations.

13. **Discount Window** How is the money supply adjusted through the discount window? What policy change occurred in 2003 that caused the discount rate to be an ineffective monetary policy tool?

FLOW OF FUNDS EXERCISE

Monitoring the Fed

Recall that Carson Company has obtained substantial loans from finance companies and commercial banks. The interest rate on the loans is tied to market interest rates and is adjusted every six months. Because of its expectations of a strong U.S. economy, Carson plans to grow in the future by expanding its business and through acquisitions. It expects that it will need substantial long-term financing and plans to borrow additional funds either through loans or by issuing bonds. It is also considering the issuance of stock to raise funds in the next year.

Given its large exposure to interest rates charged on its debt, Carson closely monitors Fed actions. It subscribes to a special service that attempts to monitor the Fed's actions in the Treasury security markets. It recently received an alert from the service that suggested the Fed has been selling large holdings of its Treasury securities in the secondary Treasury securities market.

a. How should Carson interpret the actions by the Fed? That is, will these actions place upward or downward pressure on Treasury securities prices? Explain.

b. Will these actions place upward or downward pressure on Treasury yields? Explain.

c. Will these actions place upward or downward pressure on interest rates? Explain.

 # EXERCISE

Reviewing Fed Policies

Review the "Credit Markets" section in recent issues of *The Wall Street Journal* and search for any comments that relate to the Fed's money supply targets or the federal funds target rate. Does it appear that the Fed may attempt to revise its money supply growth target or its federal funds target rate? If so, why?

CHAPTER 5

Monetary Theory and Policy

The previous chapter discussed the Fed and how it controls the money supply, information essential to financial market participants. It is just as important for participants to know how changes in the money supply affect the economy, which is the subject of this chapter.

The specific objectives of this chapter are to:

■ describe the well-known theories about monetary policy,

■ explain the tradeoffs involved in monetary policy,

■ describe how financial market participants monitor and forecast the Fed's policies, and

■ explain how monetary and fiscal policies are related.

Monetary Theory

The type of monetary policy implemented by the Fed depends on the economic philosophies of the FOMC members. Some of the more well-known theories that can influence the Fed's policies are described here.

Pure Keynesian Theory

One of the most popular theories that can influence Fed policy is the **Keynesian theory,** which was developed by John Maynard Keynes, a British economist. To do justice to this theory would require an entire text. The Keynesian theory suggests how the Fed can affect the interaction between the demand for money and the supply of money to influence interest rates, the aggregate level of spending, and therefore economic growth.

The general points of Keynesian theory can be explained by using the loanable funds framework described in Chapter 2. Recall that the interaction of the supply of loanable funds available and the demand for loanable funds determines the interest rate charged on loanable funds. Much of the demand for loanable funds is by households, corporations, and government agencies that need to borrow money. Recall that the demand schedule indicates the quantity of funds that would be demanded (at that time) at various possible interest rates. This schedule is downward sloping because many potential borrowers would borrow a larger quantity of funds at lower interest rates.

The supply schedule of loanable funds indicates the quantity of funds that would be supplied (at that time) at various possible interest rates. This schedule is upward sloping because suppliers of funds tend to supply a larger amount of funds when the interest rate is higher. Assume that as of today, the demand and supply schedules for loan-

EXHIBIT 5.1   Keynesian View on the Effects of an Increased Money Supply

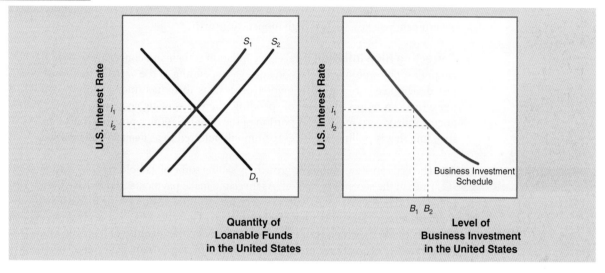

able funds are represented by D_1 and S_1 in the left graph of Exhibit 5.1. Based on these schedules, the equilibrium interest rate would be i_1. The right graph of Exhibit 5.1 represents the typical relationship between the interest rate on loanable funds and the level of business investment as of today. The relation is inverse because corporations are more willing to expand when interest rates are relatively low. Given today's equilibrium interest rate of i_1, the level of business investment is B_1.

Correcting a Weak Economy   If the economy is weak, the Fed can increase the level of spending as a means of stimulating the economy. It uses open market operations to increase the money supply, a move that is intended to reduce interest rates and encourage more borrowing and spending.

ILLUSTRATION   The Fed can attempt to stimulate the economy by purchasing Treasury securities in the secondary market. As the investors who sell their Treasury securities receive payment from the Fed, their account balances at financial institutions increase, without any offsetting decrease in the account balances of any other financial institutions. Thus, there is a net increase in the supply of loanable funds. If the Fed's action results in an increase of $5 billion in loanable funds, the quantity of loanable funds supplied will now be $5 billion higher at any possible interest rate level. This means that the supply schedule for loanable funds shifts outward to S_2 in Exhibit 5.1. The difference between S_2 and S_1 is that S_2 incorporates the $5 billion of loanable funds added as a result of the Fed's actions.

Given the shift in the supply schedule for loanable funds, the quantity of loanable funds supplied exceeds the quantity of loanable funds demanded at the interest rate level i_1. Thus, the interest rate will decline to i_2, the level at which the quantities of loanable funds supplied and demanded are equal.

The lower interest rate level causes an increase in the level of business investment from B_1 to B_2. The increase in business investment represents new business spending that was triggered by lower interest rates, which reduced the corporate cost of financing new projects.

The Keynesian philosophy advocates an active role for the federal government in correcting economic problems. The theory conflicts with the classical theory that production (supply) creates its own demand and gained support during the Great Depression when

the existing level of production had clearly exceeded demand, causing massive layoffs. Under such conditions, the Keynesian theory would have prescribed stimulative federal government policies, such as high monetary growth.

Correcting High Inflation If excessive inflation is the main concern, the pure Keynesian philosophy would still focus on aggregate spending as the variable that must be adjusted. The Fed can use open market operations to reduce money supply growth, a move that can reduce the level of spending, thereby slowing economic growth and reducing inflationary pressure. A portion of the high inflation is possibly due to excessive spending that is pulling up prices, commonly referred to as **demand-pull inflation.**

ILLUSTRATION The Fed can slow economic growth by selling some of its holdings of Treasury securities in the secondary market. As investors make payments to purchase these Treasury securities, their account balances decrease, without any offsetting increase in the account balances of any other financial institutions. Thus, there is a net decrease in deposit accounts (money), which results in a net decrease in the quantity of loanable funds. Assume that the Fed's action causes a decrease of $5 billion in loanable funds. The quantity of loanable funds supplied will now be $5 billion lower at any possible interest rate level. This reflects an inward shift in the supply schedule from S_1 to S_2, as shown in Exhibit 5.2.

Given the inward shift in the supply schedule for loanable funds, the quantity of loanable funds demanded exceeds the quantity of loanable funds supplied at the original interest rate level (i_1). Thus, the interest rate will increase to i_2, the level at which the quantities of loanable funds supplied and demanded are equal.

The higher interest rate level increases the corporate cost of financing new projects and therefore causes a decrease in the level of business investment from B_1 to B_2. As economic growth is slowed by the reduction in business investment, inflationary pressure may be reduced. Thus, reducing the money supply is an indirect means by which the Fed may reduce inflation.

Summary of Keynesian View Exhibit 5.3 summarizes the Keynesian view of how the Fed (as the central bank of the United States) can affect economic conditions through its

EXHIBIT 5.2   Keynesian View of the Effects of a Reduced Money Supply

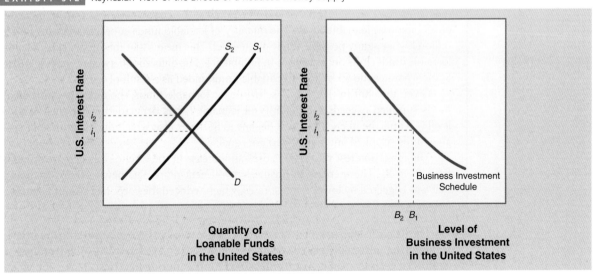

EXHIBIT 5.3

Summary of the Keynesian View of How Monetary Policy Affects Economic Conditions

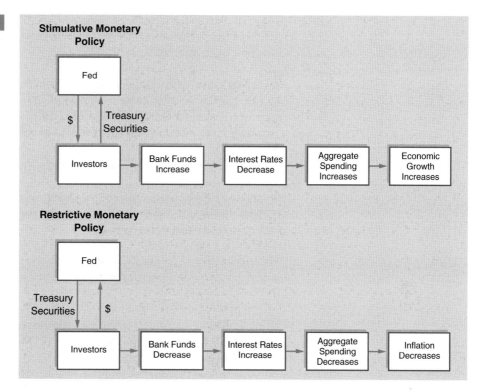

influence on the level of bank funds. The top part of the exhibit illustrates a stimulative monetary policy intended to boost economic growth, and the bottom part illustrates a restrictive monetary policy intended to reduce inflation.

Effects of a Credit Crunch on a Stimulative Policy

The economic impact of monetary policy (as explained by the Keynesian view) may depend on the willingness of banks to lend funds. Even if the Fed increases the level of bank funds during a weak economy, banks may be unwilling to extend credit to some potential borrowers, and the result is a *credit crunch*. It could be argued that if banks do not lend out the newly created funds, the economy will not be stimulated. Yet the perception that banks will not lend out sufficient funds is caused by the effects of a weak economy on loan repayment probability. Banks provide loans only after confirming that the borrower's future cash flows will be adequate to make loan repayments. In a weak economy, the future cash flows of many potential borrowers are more uncertain, causing a reduction in loan applications (demand for loans) and in the number of qualified loan applicants.

Banks and other lending institutions have a responsibility to their depositors, shareholders, and regulators to avoid loans that are likely to default. Because default risk rises during a weak economy, some potential borrowers will be unable to obtain loans. Others may qualify only if they pay high-risk premiums to cover their default risk. Thus, it is possible that the effects of monetary policy can be limited if potential borrowers do not qualify or are unwilling to incur the high-risk premiums. Nevertheless, the credit crunch should not affect borrowers with very low risk. A stimulative monetary policy will be more effective if there are sufficient qualified borrowers that will borrow more funds once interest rates are reduced.

A credit crunch could even occur during a period when a restrictive monetary policy is implemented. As the money supply is reduced, and interest rates rise, some potential

borrowers may be unable to obtain loans because the interest payments would be too high. Thus, the effects of the restrictive monetary policy are magnified because the higher interest rates not only discourage some potential borrowers but also prevent others from obtaining loans.

Overall, a credit crunch may partially offset the desired effects of a stimulative monetary policy and magnify the effects of a restrictive monetary policy. Yet, assuming the Fed recognizes the possible influence of the credit crunch, it could modify its specific money supply targets to offset any distortions caused by the crunch.

Quantity Theory and the Monetarist Approach

The quantity theory is applicable to monetary policy because it suggests a particular relationship between the money supply and the degree of economic activity. It is based on the so-called equation of exchange, as follows:

$$MV = P_G Q$$

where
- M = amount of money in the economy
- V = velocity of money
- P_G = weighted price level of goods and services in the economy
- Q = quantity of goods and services sold

Velocity is the average number of times each dollar changes hands per year. The right side of the equation of exchange represents the total value of goods and services produced. If velocity is constant, a given adjustment in the money supply will produce a predictable change in the total value of goods and services. Thus, a direct relationship between money supply and gross domestic product is evident.

An early form of the theory assumed Q is constant in the short run, which would imply a direct relationship between the money supply and prices. If the money supply is increased, the average price level will increase. However, the assumption of a stable quantity is not realistic today. The original quantity theory has been revised by the **Monetarists** into what is referred to as the **modern quantity theory of money.** Milton Friedman and others relaxed the stable-quantity assumption to suggest that a given increase in the money supply leads to a predictable increase in the value of goods and services produced.

Because velocity represents the ratio of money stock to nominal output, it is affected by any factor that influences this ratio. Income patterns can affect velocity because they influence the amount of money held by households. Factors that increase the ratio of households' money holdings to income reduce velocity, while factors that reduce this ratio increase velocity. Households maintain more money if they receive their income less frequently, whereas credit cards can reduce the need to hold money balances. Expectations of high inflation encourage households to hold smaller money balances, thereby increasing velocity. Nevertheless, Friedman has found that velocity changes in a predictable manner and is not related to fluctuations in the money supply. Therefore, the equation of exchange can be applied to assess how money can affect aggregate spending.

Comparison of the Monetarist and Keynesian Theories The Monetarist approach advocates stable, low growth in the money supply. It may be criticized for being too passive, but its supporters contend that it allows economic problems to resolve themselves without causing additional problems. Suppose the United States experiences a recession. Whereas the typical Keynesian monetary policy prescription would be high money growth, Monetarists would avoid a loose money policy on the grounds that it tends to

ignite inflationary expectations, which can increase the demand for money and place upward pressure on interest rates. The Monetarist cure for the recession would not call for any revision in the existing monetary policy. Instead, Monetarists would expect the stagnant economy to reduce corporate and household borrowing and thus result in lower interest rates. Once interest rates are reduced to a low enough level, they will encourage borrowing and therefore stimulate economic growth. Because the Monetarist approach to achieve lower interest rates does not require an increase in money supply growth, inflationary expectations should not be ignited as they might be under the Keynesian approach.

A major limitation of the Monetarist approach is the time required to improve the economy. Is the public willing to suffer while the recession cures itself, or would it prefer a more active (Keynesian) approach to quickly resolve the recession, even though other economic problems might arise as a result?

While recognizing the strong impact of money supply fluctuations on the economy, Monetarists do not believe money growth should be actively adjusted. Instead, they believe in accepting a natural rate of unemployment, and they criticize the government for trying to achieve a rate lower than the natural rate at the price of inflation, especially because the lower rate is unlikely to prevail in the long run. Friedman has found that the impact of money supply growth on economic growth has a long lag time and is uncertain, which is why he advocates a constant rate of monetary growth.

Keynesians and Monetarists also differ in the relative importance they assign to inflation and unemployment. Keynesians tend to focus on maintaining low unemployment and are therefore more willing to tolerate any inflation that results from stimulative monetary policies. Monetarists are more concerned about maintaining low inflation and are therefore more willing to tolerate what they refer to as a natural rate of unemployment.

Theory of Rational Expectations

The **theory of rational expectations** holds that the public accounts for all existing information when forming its expectations. As applied to monetary policy, this theory suggests that households and business, having witnessed historical effects of monetary policy actions, will use this information to forecast the impact of an existing policy and act accordingly.

If the Fed uses a loose monetary policy to stimulate the economy, households will respond by increasing their spending as they anticipate that higher inflation will result from the policy. In addition, businesses will increase their investment in machinery and equipment in an attempt to beat impending higher costs of borrowing. Further, participants in the labor market will negotiate for higher wages to compensate for higher anticipated inflation, and the level of savings will be reduced while the level of borrowing will increase. These forces will offset the impact of an increase in the money supply. Therefore, the policy will not affect interest rates or economic growth. In general, the rational expectations theory supports the contention of Friedman and some other Monetarists that changes in monetary policy are unlikely to have any sustained positive impact on the economy.

ILLUSTRATION Exhibit 5.4 illustrates the criticism of the Keynesian theory by the Monetarist approach and rational expectations theory. The D_1, S_1, and S_2 curves reflect the Keynesian view on how a stimulative monetary policy (increased money supply) can place downward pressure on interest rates. In fact, these curves are the same as those shown in Exhibit 5.1. A key criticism of the Keynesian view is that it assumes that the quantity of loanable funds demanded is not changed by the adjustment in the money supply. Proponents of the Monetarist approach and rational expectations theory suggest that the

EXHIBIT 5.4

Effects of an Increased Money Supply According to the Monetarist Approach and the Rational Expectations Theory

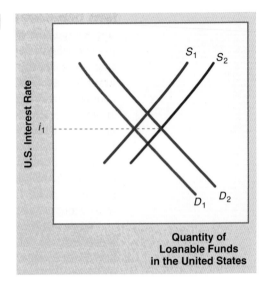

Quantity of
Loanable Funds
in the United States

increased money supply will increase inflationary expectations, which will cause a higher demand for loanable funds at any possible interest rate. This is reflected by an outward shift in the demand schedule for loanable funds, as illustrated by the D_2 curve in Exhibit 5.4. The outward shift in the demand schedule can completely offset the outward shift in the supply schedule, so the interest rate is not reduced at all. Thus, the level of business investment will not be affected by the Fed's adjustment in the money supply, and the general level of spending in the economy will remain as it was. Under these conditions, the adjustment in the money supply is not effective at stimulating economic growth.

Which Theory Is Correct?

Most economists who serve on the Federal Open Market Committee (FOMC) recognize the virtues and the limitations of each theory. They tend to believe that monetary policy can be an effective tool for controlling economic growth, inflation, and unemployment. Therefore, they adjust monetary growth targets when they see fit, in line with the Keynesian philosophy. However, they are aware of the potential adverse consequence of excessive money supply growth (as suggested by Monetarists), especially when the prevailing inflation level is high. If a stimulative boost in the economy is needed and if severe inflation does not appear to be a potential consequence, a loose-money policy may be implemented. If inflation is a major concern, the Fed is more concerned about the potential adverse effects on inflation that could result from a loose-money policy.

The decisions by the FOMC members may also be influenced by the political party of the president who appointed them. It is important for financial market participants to keep track of the FOMC members over time. As they are replaced, the overall philosophy of the FOMC may shift, resulting in a different monetary policy.

Fed Tradeoffs

The Fed monitors economic variables, such as inflation, unemployment, and gross domestic product (GDP), over time. Although it does not have direct control over these variables, it can attempt to influence them by manipulating the money supply.

Ideally, the Fed would like to maintain low inflation, steady GDP growth, and low unemployment. Because GDP growth can lead to low unemployment, these two goals may be achieved simultaneously. Consistently maintaining both low inflation and low unemployment is more difficult. For more than 200 years, economists have recognized a possible tradeoff between the two. In 1958, in an article that became famous, Professor A. W. Phillips compared the annual percentage change in the average unemployment rate and wages in the United Kingdom from 1861 to 1913. His research confirmed a negative relationship between the two variables. This relationship suggested that government policies designed to cure unemployment may place upward pressure on wages. In addition, government policies designed to cure inflation may cause more unemployment. This negative relationship came to be known as the **Phillips curve.** The concept provided a new framework for the central bank and the administration to use in determining government policies.

When economists applied the Phillips curve concept to U.S. inflation and unemployment data, they found that the relationship frequently changed. Shifts in the Phillips curve were attributed to unionization, changing productivity, and, more recently, changing expectations about inflation.

When inflation is higher than the Fed deems acceptable, the Fed may consider implementing a tight-money policy to reduce economic growth. As economic growth slows, producers cannot as easily raise their prices and still maintain sales volume. Similarly, workers are not in demand and do not have much bargaining power on wages. Thus, the use of tight money to slow economic growth can reduce the inflation rate. A possible cost of the lower inflation rate is higher unemployment. If the economy becomes stagnant because of the tight-money policy, sales decrease, inventories accumulate, and firms may reduce their workforce to reduce production.

Given that a loose-money policy can reduce unemployment whereas a tight-money policy can reduce inflation, the Fed must determine whether unemployment or inflation is the more serious problem. It may not be able to cure both problems simultaneously. In fact, it may not be able to fully eliminate either problem. Although a loose-money policy can stimulate the economy, it does not guarantee that unskilled workers will be hired. Although a tight-money policy can reduce inflation caused by excessive spending, it cannot reduce inflation caused by such factors as an agreement by the members of the oil cartel to keep oil prices high.

Other Forces Effect on the Tradeoff

Other forces may also affect the tradeoff faced by the Fed. Consider a situation where because of specific cost factors (higher energy and insurance costs, etc.), inflation will be at least 3 percent. This amount of inflation will exist no matter what type of monetary policy the Fed implements. Also assume that because of the number of unskilled workers and people between jobs, the unemployment rate will be at least 4 percent. A loose-money policy sufficiently stimulates the economy to maintain unemployment at that minimum level of 4 percent. However, such a stimulative policy may also cause additional inflation beyond the 3 percent level. A tight-money policy could maintain inflation at the 3 percent minimum, but unemployment would likely rise above the 4 percent minimum.

This tradeoff is illustrated in Exhibit 5.5. Here the Fed can use a very stimulative (loose-money) policy that is expected to result in Point A (9 percent inflation and 4 percent unemployment). Alternatively, it can use a very restrictive (tight-money) policy that is expected to result in Point B (3 percent inflation and 8 percent unemployment). Or it

Tradeoff between Reducing Inflation and
Unemployment

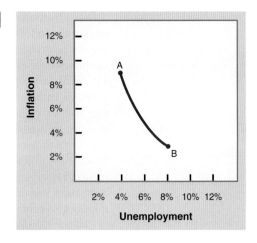

can implement a compromise policy that will result in some point along the curve between A and B.

Historical data on annual inflation and unemployment rates show that when one of
these problems worsens, the other does not automatically improve. Both variables can
rise or fall over time. Yet this does not refute the tradeoff faced by the Fed. It simply
means that some outside factors have affected inflation or unemployment or both.

ILLUSTRATION Recall that the Fed could have achieved Point A, Point B, or somewhere along the
curve connecting these points during a particular time period. Now assume that oil
prices have substantially increased and several product liability lawsuits have occurred.
These events will affect consumer prices such that the minimum inflation rate will be,
say, 6 percent. In addition, assume that various training centers for unskilled workers
have been closed, leaving a higher number of unskilled workers. This forces the minimum unemployment rate to 6 percent. Now the Fed's tradeoff position has changed. The
Fed's new set of possibilities is shown as Curve CD in Exhibit 5.6. Note that the points
reflected on Curve CD are not as desirable as the points along Curve AB that were previously attainable. No matter what type of monetary policy the Fed uses, both the inflation rate and the unemployment rate will be higher than in the previous time period. This is not the fault of the Fed. In fact, the Fed is still faced with a tradeoff between

Adjustment in the Tradeoff between
Unemployment and Inflation over Time

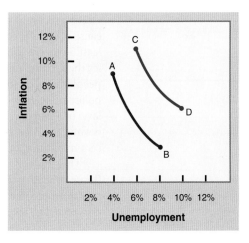

Point C (11 percent inflation, 6 percent unemployment), Point D (6 percent inflation, 10 percent unemployment), or somewhere within those points along Curve CD.

When FOMC members are primarily concerned with either inflation or unemployment, they tend to agree on the type of monetary policy that should be implemented. When both inflation and unemployment are relatively high, however, there is more disagreement among the members about the proper monetary policy to implement. All members would agree that a loose-money policy may stimulate the economy and reduce unemployment, at least in the short run, but would also agree that this policy could ignite inflation. Therefore, some members would likely argue for a tight-money policy to prevent inflation from rising, while other members would suggest that a loose-money policy should be implemented to reduce unemployment even if it results in higher inflation.

How the Fed's Focus Shifted during the Persian Gulf War A classic example of the tradeoff confronting the Fed was the crisis in the Persian Gulf during the summer of 1990. There were numerous indications of a possible recession in the United States, encouraging the Fed to implement a loose-money policy. However, the abrupt increase in oil prices at that time placed upward pressure on U.S. inflation. Consequently, the Fed was less willing to use a loose-money policy because of the additional inflationary pressure that would result.

How the Fed's Emphasis Shifted during 2001–2004 The tradeoffs involved in monetary policy can be understood by considering the Fed's decisions during the 2001–2004 period, as shown in Exhibit 5.7, which summarizes the Fed's main concern at the time of each FOMC meeting. In 2001 when economic conditions were weak, the Fed not only decided to reduce the federal funds target rate at several meetings, but also announced that it was maintaining a bias toward loosening in case the economy remained sluggish. This meant that the Fed was ready to reduce the federal funds rate even further if necessary to stimulate the economy.

From January to December 2001, the FOMC reduced the targeted federal funds rate 10 times, resulting in a cumulative decline of 4.25 percent in the targeted federal funds rate. As the federal funds rate was reduced, other market interest rates declined as well. Each reduction in the targeted federal funds rate reflected an effort by the Fed to encourage more borrowing and spending by consumers and businesses. The large cumulative reduction in interest rates was unusual for a one-year period.

During this period, the economy did not respond to the Fed's interest rate reductions, which is why the Fed continued to reduce rates. One reason for the limited effect on the economy may be that the Fed was focusing on influencing short-term interest rates rather than long-term interest rates. Exhibit 5.8 shows the impact on the targeted federal funds rate over this period along with the Treasury bill (T-bill) rate and a 10-year Treasury bond rate. Notice that in November 2000, short-term interest rates exceeded the 10-year Treasury bond rate, reflecting a downward-sloping yield curve. As the Fed reduced the targeted federal funds rate, the T-bill rate declined along with it, but the Treasury bond rate was less responsive. Consequently, the short-term rates declined below the 10-year Treasury bond rate by 2001, as the bond rate was hardly affected. Other long-term interest rates also remained stable over this period. To the extent that corporations rely on long-term funding to support most of their projects, their cost of borrowing was not significantly reduced over this period. The Fed's effects on the economy might have been stronger had it been able to reduce long-term interest rates during this period.

After the economy failed to respond as hoped in 2001, the Fed reduced the federal funds target rate twice more in 2002 and 2003. Finally, the economy began to show

http://www.federalreserve.gov Click on "federal funds rate." Shows recent changes in the federal funds target rate.

EXHIBIT 5.7   Sample of Conclusions of FOMC Meetings

Meeting	Signs of Economic Growth or Inflation	Action Taken on Federal Funds Target Rate (FFTR)
Early January 2001 (Conference Call Meeting)	Retail sales were weak through the holiday season. The major concern was the weak economy.	Decreased FFTR by .5%
Late January 2001	The high-technology sector continued to show weakness. The overall economy showed more signs of weakness. The major concern was the weak economy.	Decreased FFTR by .5%
March 2001	Consumer spending increased slightly, but manufacturing orders declined as firms tried to reduce the inventories that had accumulated in recent months. The major concern was the weak economy.	Decreased FFTR by .5%
April 2001 (Conference Call Meeting)	Consumer spending leveled off. The major concern was the weak economy.	Decreased FFTR by .5%
May 2001	The economy weakened further, but inflation increased slightly. The major concern was the weak economy.	Decreased FFTR by .5%
June 2001	There were some signs of improvement, but consumer spending was still low. The major concern was the weak economy.	Decreased FFTR by .25%
August 2001	The economy remained sluggish, and there were mixed signals about consumer spending.	Decreased FFRR by .25%
September 2001	On September 11, the terrorist attack on the U.S. caused concern that economic conditions would deteriorate. The Fed decided on September 17 (before stock markets reopened) to reduce interest rates.	Decreased FFTR by .5%
October 2001	The economy weakened further, as businesses and consumers reduced their travel and spending.	Decreased FFTR by .5%
December 2001	Productivity was still low; inflation was also low.	Reduced FFTR by .25%
November 2002	The economy was still not showing strong signs of recovery; the threat of inflation remained low.	Reduced FFTR by .5%
June 2003	The economy had improved but did not show sustainable growth; inflationary expectations were low.	Reduced FFTR by .25%
January 2004	The economy was improving, but since inflation was low, there was no need to raise interest rates.	No change
March 2004	The economy continued to improve while inflation remained low.	No change
May 2004	The economy continued to improve while inflation remained low.	No change
June 2004	The economy continued to improve, but there was concern that inflation could increase in the future.	Increased FFTR by .25%
August 2004	There were signs of higher inflation, partially due to an increase in oil prices. The economy was stable.	Increased FFTR by .25%

some signs of improvement, and by 2004, economic growth was strong, the Fed's focus began to shift from concern about the economy to concern about the potential for higher inflation. In June 2004, the Fed increased the targeted federal funds rate.

Fed-Monitored Economic Indicators

The Fed monitors various economic indicators. The most important are economic growth indicators and inflation indicators, both of which are discussed next.

EXHIBIT 5.8
Impact of the Fed on Short-Term versus Long-Term Rates

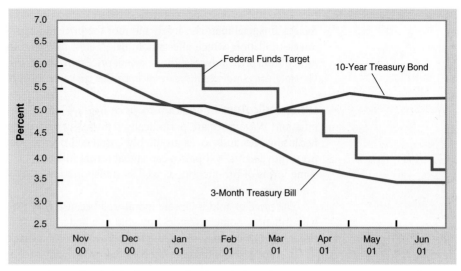

Source: *Monetary Trends,* Federal Reserve Bank of St. Louis, September 2001.

Economic Growth Indicators

The Fed monitors various indicators of economic growth because high economic growth creates a more prosperous economy and can result in lower unemployment. GDP, which measures the total value of goods and services produced during a specific period, is measured each month. It serves as the most direct indicator of economic growth in the United States. The level of production adjusts in response to changes in consumers' demand for goods and services. A high production level indicates strong economic growth and can result in an increased demand for labor (lower unemployment).

The Fed also monitors national income, which is the total income earned by firms and individual employees during a specific period. A strong demand for U.S. goods and services results in a large amount of income to firms and employees.

The unemployment rate is monitored as well, because one of the Fed's primary goals is to maintain a low rate of unemployment in the United States. The unemployment rate does not necessarily indicate the degree of economic growth, however, because it measures only the number and not the types of jobs that are being filled. It is possible to have a substantial reduction in unemployment during a period of weak economic growth if new low-paying jobs are created during that period.

Several other indexes serve as indicators of growth in specific sectors of the U.S. economy, including an industrial production index, a retail sales index, and a home sales index. A composite index combines various indexes to indicate economic growth across sectors. In addition to the many indicators reflecting recent conditions, the Fed may also desire to use forward-looking indicators, such as consumer confidence surveys, to forecast future economic growth.

Inflation Indicators

Producer and Consumer Price Indexes The Fed closely monitors price indexes and other indicators to assess the U.S. inflation rate. The producer price index represents prices at the wholesale level, and the consumer price index represents prices paid by consumers (retail level). There is a lag time of about one month after the period being

measured due to the time required to compile price information for the indexes. Nevertheless, financial markets closely monitor the price indexes because they may be used to forecast inflation, which affects nominal interest rates and the prices of some securities. Agricultural price indexes indicate recent price movements in grains, fruits, and vegetables. Housing price indexes indicate recent price movements in homes and rental properties.

Other Indicators In addition to price indexes, there are several other indicators of inflation. Wage rates are periodically reported in various regions of the United States. Because wages and prices are highly correlated over the long run, wages can indicate price movements. Oil prices can signal future inflation because they affect the costs of some forms of production, as well as transportation costs and the prices paid by consumers for gasoline.

The price of gold is closely monitored because gold prices tend to move in tandem with inflation. Some investors buy gold as a hedge against future inflation. Therefore, a rise in gold prices may signal the market's expectation that inflation will increase.

In some cases, indicators of economic growth are also used to indicate inflation. For example, the release of several favorable employment reports may arouse concern that the economy will overheat and cause demand-pull inflation. Although these reports offer favorable information about economic growth, their information about inflation is unfavorable. The financial markets can be adversely affected by such reports, as investors anticipate that the Fed will have to increase interest rates to reduce the inflationary momentum.

How the Fed Uses Indicators

When the Fed meets to decide on its monetary policy, it assesses the most recent reports of all economic growth indicators and inflation indicators. The Fed uses the indicators to anticipate how economic conditions will change and then determines what monetary policy would be appropriate under these conditions. When economic indicators suggest that economic conditions are weak and getting weaker, the Fed is more willing to use an expansionary monetary policy (especially if inflation is low). When economic indicators suggest that productivity and employment are near full capacity, the Fed tends to reduce money supply growth. If the Fed notices that agricultural prices have risen because of adverse weather conditions, it may expect this form of inflation to be temporary and will not adjust its monetary policy. If numerous indicators suggest a large increase in the prices of all goods and services, however, the Fed may implement a monetary policy that is designed to reduce inflation.

Index of Leading Economic Indicators

In addition to the economic indicators monitored by the Fed, the Conference Board publishes indexes of leading, coincident, and lagging economic indicators, which are widely followed by market participants. **Leading economic indicators** are used to predict future economic activity. Usually, three consecutive monthly changes in the same direction in these indicators suggest a turning point in the economy. **Coincident economic indicators** tend to reach their peaks and troughs at the same time as business cycles. **Lagging economic indicators** tend to rise or fall a few months after business-cycle expansions and contractions.

The Conference Board is an independent, not-for-profit membership organization whose stated goal is to create and disseminate knowledge about management and the

EXHIBIT 5.9

The Conference Board's Indexes of Leading, Coincident, and Lagging Indicators

Leading Index

1. Average weekly hours, manufacturing
2. Average weekly initial claims for unemployment insurance
3. Manufacturers' new orders, consumer goods and materials
4. Vendor performance, slower deliveries diffusion index
5. Manufacturers' new orders, nondefense capital goods
6. Building permits, new private housing units
7. Stock prices, 500 common stocks
8. Money supply, M2
9. Interest rate spread, 10-year Treasury bonds less federal funds
10. Index of consumer expectations

Coincident Index

1. Employees on nonagricultural payrolls
2. Personal income less transfer payments
3. Industrial production
4. Manufacturing and trade sales

Lagging Index

1. Average duration of unemployment
2. Inventories to sales ratio, manufacturing and trade
3. Labor cost per unit of output, manufacturing
4. Average prime rate
5. Commercial and industrial loans
6. Consumer installment credit to personal income ratio
7. Consumer price index for services

marketplace to help businesses strengthen their performance and better serve society. The Conference Board conducts research, convenes conferences, makes forecasts, assesses trends, and publishes information and analyses. A summary of the Conference Board's leading, coincident, and lagging indexes is provided in Exhibit 5.9.

Monetary Policy Lags

One of the main reasons that monetary policy is so complex is the lag between the time an economic problem arises and the time it will take for an adjustment in money supply growth to solve it. Three specific lags are involved. First, there is a **recognition lag,** or the lag between the time a problem arises and the time it is recognized. Most economic problems are initially revealed by statistics, not actual observation. Because economic statistics are reported only periodically, they will not immediately signal a problem. For example, the unemployment rate is reported monthly. A sudden increase in unemployment may not be detected until the end of the month when statistics reveal the problem. And

even though most economic variables are updated monthly, the recognition lag could still be longer than one month. For example, if unemployment increases slightly each month for two straight months, the Fed may not necessarily act on this information, because the information may not appear to be significant. Only after a few more months of steadily increasing unemployment might the Fed recognize that a serious problem exists. In such a case, the recognition lag may be four months or longer.

The lag from the time a serious problem is recognized until the time the Fed implements a policy to resolve it is known as the **implementation lag.** Then, even after the Fed implements a policy, there will be an **impact lag** until the policy has its full impact on the economy. For example, an adjustment in money supply growth may have an immediate impact on the economy to some degree, but its full impact may not be manifested until a year or so after the adjustment.

These lags hinder the Fed's control of the economy. Suppose the Fed uses a loose-money policy to stimulate the economy and reduce unemployment. By the time the implemented monetary policy begins to take effect, the unemployment rate may have already reversed itself as a result of some other outside factors (such as a weakened dollar that increased foreign demand for U.S. goods and created U.S. jobs). Thus, the more serious problem may now be inflation (because the economy is heating up again), which may be further ignited by the loose-money policy. Without monetary policy lags, implemented policies would have a higher rate of success.

Assessing Monetary Policy Impact

Financial market participants will not all necessarily react to monetary policy in the same manner because they trade different securities. Monetary policy may have a different expected or actual impact on long-term mortgage rates than on corporate and municipal bond rates, money market rates, and stock prices. Exhibit 5.10 shows the various components of the financial environment that are affected by monetary policy. As this exhibit suggests, interest rates are the most influential economic variable on the performance of many financial markets.

Even financial market participants that trade the same securities may react differently to monetary policy because they may have different expectations about the policy's impact on economic variables. They have only limited success in forecasting economic variables because of the difficulty in forecasting (1) money supply movements and (2) how future money supply movements will affect interest rates. Each of these forecasting aspects is discussed in the following subsections.

Forecasting Money Supply Movements

Business periodicals from time to time specify the weekly ranges of M1 and M2 based on the Fed's most recent disclosure of its target range. The Fed is less concerned about meeting its targets on a weekly basis than about meeting its long-term targets. Nevertheless, some financial participants compare the actual money supply levels with weekly ranges that can be estimated from the Fed's longer-term target ranges. Weekly ranges represent the path that the Fed would follow over time if it were to move toward its targets at a constant rate. For example, if the target growth range is specified as 4 to 6 percent annually, the money supply should grow at a weekly rate of between 4%/52 and 6%/52 (given 52 weeks per year). If the Fed consistently over- or undershoots these weekly ranges, it may desire to offset the deviations at some point in the future.

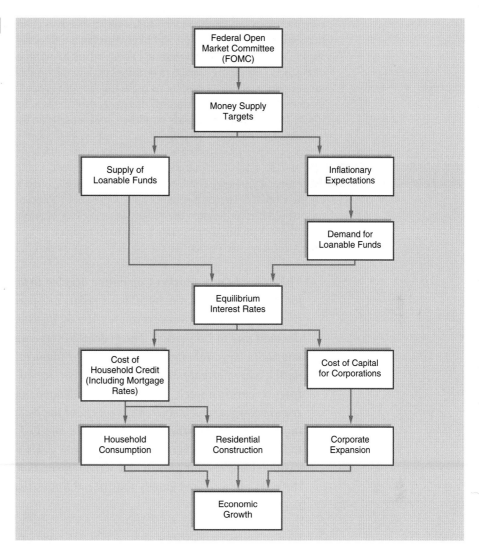

When the actual money supply falls outside the target range, it could be because of a change in the Fed's range that has not yet been publicly announced. The Fed may be meeting its new targets, while financial market participants believe it plans to adjust the money supply to meet its previously announced range. Normally, the Fed attempts to avoid revising target ranges because if it changes them too often, it may lose some credibility. Persistent changes might suggest that it is unsure of how money supply fluctuations affect the economy.

Improved Communication from the Fed Before 1999, the Fed did not disclose what happened at an FOMC meeting until several weeks after the meeting. It was hoping to stabilize financial markets by concealing its change in monetary policy. However, market participants took positions based on their speculation about the Fed's monetary policy. The uncertainty and speculation caused volatile price movements in the securities markets just after an FOMC meeting.

Since 1999, the Fed has been more willing to disclose its conclusions. It now immediately communicates the results of its FOMC meetings. Specifically, it announces

the amount by which the federal funds target rate was changed (if at all) and also mentions whether its next action will likely involve a tightening or loosening of the money supply. If the Fed is more concerned about future inflation, it says its position is a "tightening bias," implying that it may raise the federal funds target rate and tighten the money supply if inflation remains high. If it is more concerned about future unemployment (weak economic conditions), it says its position is a "loosening bias," implying that it may lower the federal funds target rate and loosen the money supply if the economy weakens further.

ILLUSTRATION At 7:30 A.M. on September 17, 2001, the FOMC determined that it should adjust monetary policy. The U.S. stock markets, which had been closed since the attack on the United States on September 11, were about to reopen. Anticipating that the attack would further weaken the already faltering U.S. economy, the FOMC decided to reduce the federal funds target rate by 50 basis points (.50 percent). A portion of the Fed's information release on September 17, 2001, is provided here:

> *The Federal Open Market Committee decided today to lower its target for the federal funds rate by 50 basis points to 3 percent. In a related action, the Board of Governors approved a 50 basis point reduction in the discount rate to 2.5 percent. The Federal Reserve will continue to supply unusually large volumes of liquidity to the financial markets as needed, until a more normal functioning market is restored. . . . Even before the tragic events last week, employment, production, and business spending remained weak, and last week's events have the potential to damp spending further. . . . For the forseeable future, the Fed continues to believe that against the background of its long-run goals of price stability and sustainable economic growth and of the information currently available, the risks are weighted mainly toward conditions that may generate economic weakness.*

The Fed issues such a release after each FOMC meeting, not just under unusual circumstances as in this example. Notice that the Fed not only immediately announced its intentions, but indicated that it anticipated continued economic weakness (see the last sentence). It was implying that it was positioned to loosen money supply growth further if the economy continued to weaken.

http://www.federalreserve.gov Schedule of FOMC meetings and minutes of previous FOMC meetings.

Because of the quick and clear communication following FOMC meetings, financial market participants do not have to guess at the FOMC's decision. Before the meetings, however, they still speculate about what the FOMC will do. Moreover, after the meeting they still have to assess the impact of the Fed's actions on security valuations. When the Fed releases information about a future tightening or loosening bias, market participants attempt to assess the probability that the Fed will implement that policy in the future.

Forecasting the Impact of Monetary Policy

Even if financial market participants correctly anticipate changes in money supply movements, they may not be able to predict future economic conditions. The historical relationship between the money supply and economic variables has not remained per-

fectly stable over time. Some adjustments in the money supply caused by the behavior of depositors can distort the relationship between money supply levels and economic growth. For example, when interest rates decline, some individuals may withdraw their deposits to invest in stocks. Consequently, the money supply level (as measured by M2) decreases even though the funds are still invested in the United States. This type of reduction in the money supply may not have the same effect on the economy as when funds are pulled out of the economy by the Fed. Thus, the relationship between the money supply and economic growth is affected.

Impact of Monetary Policy across Financial Markets Because monetary policy can have a strong influence on interest rates and economic growth, it affects the securities traded in all financial markets. The type of influence monetary policy can have on each financial market is summarized in Exhibit 5.11. Some institutions hire economists to focus on assessing monetary policy so that they can determine how their various securities portfolios will be affected.

EXHIBIT 5.11   Impact of Monetary Policy across Financial Markets

Type of Financial Market	Relevant Factors Influenced by Monetary Policy	Key Institutional Participants
Money market	Interest rates: • Affect the secondary market values of existing money market securities. • Affect yields on newly issued money market securities. Economic growth: • Affects the risk premium on money market securities.	Commercial banks, savings institutions, credit unions, money market funds, insurance companies, finance companies, pension funds.
Bond market	Interest rates: • Affect the secondary market values of existing bonds. • Affect the yields offered on newly issued bonds. Economic growth: • Affects the risk premium on corporate and municipal bonds.	Commercial banks, savings institutions, bond mutual funds, insurance companies, finance companies, pension funds.
Mortgage market	Interest rates: • Affect the demand for housing and therefore the demand for mortgages. • Affect the secondary market values of existing mortgages. • Affect the interest rates on new mortgages. Economic growth: • Affects the demand for housing and therefore the demand for mortgages. • Affects the risk premium on mortgages.	Commercial banks, savings institutions, credit unions, insurance companies, pension funds.
Stock market	Interest rates: • Affect the required return on stocks and therefore the market values of stocks. Economic growth: • Affects projections for corporate earnings and therefore stock values.	Stock mutual funds, insurance companies, pension funds.
Foreign exchange	Interest rates: • Affect the demand for currencies and therefore the values of currencies, which in turn affect currency option prices.	Institutions that are exposed to exchange rate risks.

Integrating Monetary and Fiscal Policies

Although the Fed has the power to make decisions without the approval of the presidential administration, the Fed's monetary policy is commonly influenced by the administration's fiscal policies. In some situations, the Fed and the administration have used complementary policies to resolve economic problems. In other situations, they have used conflicting policies. A framework for explaining how monetary policy and fiscal policy affect interest rates is shown in Exhibit 5.12. As this framework shows, monetary policy not only has a direct effect on the supply of funds, but can have an indirect effect on the supply of funds and on the demand for funds. Although fiscal policy typically influences the demand for loanable funds, monetary policy normally has a larger impact on the supply of loanable funds.

History

The presidential administration has historically been most concerned with maintaining strong economic growth and low unemployment. The Fed generally shared the same

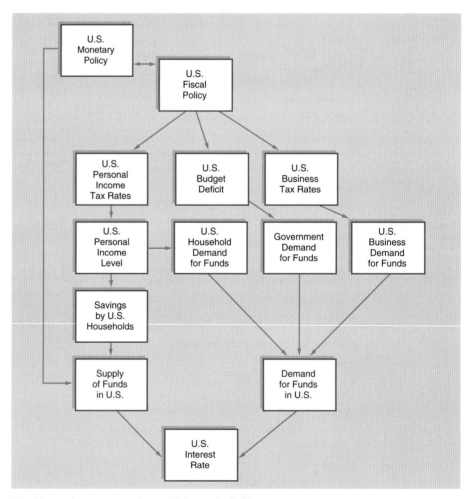

Note: Diagram does not account for possible international effects.

concern in the early 1970s. A year before President Nixon's reelection in 1972, the economy was somewhat stagnant, and inflation was higher than in previous years. The Nixon administration and the Fed combined their power to resolve these problems. The administration enforced wage-price controls (although many exceptions were allowed) to limit inflation, while the Fed used a stimulative monetary policy to reduce unemployment. Although such a stimulative policy can normally lead to higher inflation, the wage-price controls temporarily prevented inflationary consequences. By the 1972 presidential election, economic conditions had improved, which was a primary reason for Nixon's victory. When the wage-price controls were lifted in 1973, however, inflation increased.

By 1980, inflation was close to 10 percent annually, and unemployment was also high. At that time, the administration attempted to stimulate the economy by reducing tax rates. In contrast, the Fed used a relatively tight monetary policy to reduce inflation. As expected, the tight-money policy slowed economic growth and effectively reduced inflation. Although the Fed was given partial credit for lowering inflation, it was also criticized for causing the recession and for not resolving the recession as quickly as it could have. Had the Fed used a stimulative policy to eliminate the recession, however, inflation could have reignited.

The Fed's increased concern for inflation during the early 1980s relative to the 1970s was partially attributed to the appointment of Paul Volcker as chairman in 1979. Volcker was a strong believer in reducing the inflationary spiral that had persisted throughout the 1970s. Financial market participants who understood Volcker's beliefs may have been able to forecast the Fed's anti-inflationary monetary policy during the early 1980s.

The Fed and the administration sometimes differ on whether economic growth (and unemployment) or inflation deserves the most attention. Some of their most intense arguments occurred during the 1982 recession. The administration was being criticized for the high unemployment rate and blamed the Fed's tight monetary policy for keeping interest rates high and reducing the level of borrowing and spending. The Fed argued that the high interest rates were due to the large budget deficit resulting from the administration's fiscal policy. It also argued that the administration was putting too much emphasis on satisfying short-term goals for political (election) reasons and not enough emphasis on reducing inflation.

The Fed ultimately loosened the money supply in 1983, which reduced interest rates, increased economic growth, and pulled the United States out of the recession. In recent years, there has been less disagreement between the Fed and the administration, as the inflation rate and unemployment rate have been maintained at relatively low levels.

Monetizing the Debt

An ongoing dilemma faced by the Fed is whether to help finance the federal budget deficit that has been created by fiscal policy.

ILLUSTRATION   Consider a situation in which the administration decides to implement a new fiscal policy that will result in a larger federal deficit than was originally expected. The Fed must first assess the potential impact that this new fiscal policy will have on the economy. A likely concern of the Fed is the possibility of a crowding-out effect, in which excessive borrowing by the Treasury crowds out other potential borrowers (such as households or corporations) in competing for whatever loanable funds are available. This can cause higher interest rates and therefore may restrict economic growth. The Fed may counter by loosening the money supply, which might offset the increased demand for loanable funds by the federal government. This action is known as **monetizing the**

Fed's Process of Monetizing the Debt

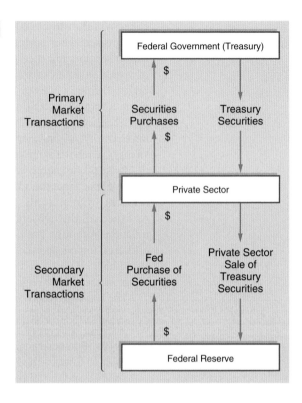

debt, as the Fed is partially financing the federal deficit. Exhibit 5.13 illustrates how this works. As the Treasury issues new securities in the primary market to finance the deficit, there may be upward pressure on interest rates. The Fed could offset this pressure by using open market operations to purchase Treasury securities (from government securities dealers) in the secondary market. Before the Fed monetizes the debt, it may first monitor how the additional borrowing by the Treasury is affecting interest rates. If there is no significant change in interest rates, the Fed may decide not to intervene.

When the Fed purchases Treasury securities, the Treasury must repurchase the securities at maturity just as if an individual or a firm owned them. Thus, Treasury securities held by the Fed still reflect debt from the Treasury's perspective. The Treasury may sometimes prefer that the Fed monetize the debt, however, because if it does not, interest rates could rise and reduce economic growth.

The Fed may prefer not to monetize the debt because this strategy requires higher money supply growth, which could ignite inflation. If the Fed does not monetize the debt, however, a weak economy may be more likely.

Market Assessment of Integrated Policies

Financial market participants must consider the potential policies of both the administration (fiscal) and the Fed (monetary) when assessing future economic conditions. Exhibit 5.14 provides a broad overview of how the participants monitor monetary and fiscal policy actions. The participants forecast the type of monetary and fiscal policies that will be implemented and then determine how these anticipated policies will affect future economic conditions. For example, they must forecast shifts in the supply of and

Simultaneous Assessment of Fiscal and Monetary Policies

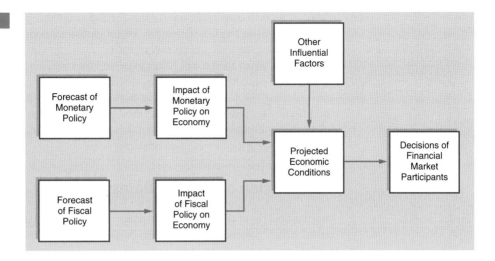

demand for loanable funds, which requires a forecast of the factors that affect such funds. The supply of loanable funds can be affected by the Fed's adjustment of the money supply or any changes in tax policies by the administration. The demand for loanable funds is affected by any change in inflationary expectations, which can be influenced by fluctuations in the money supply or aggregate spending. In addition, the demand for loanable funds is affected by government expenditures. Tax rate changes could also affect the demand for loanable funds if they affect the incentive for firms or individuals to borrow.

Once forecasts of the supply of and demand for loanable funds are completed, interest rate movements can be forecast. Interest rate projections are necessary to forecast the aggregate demand for goods and services, which will influence the level of economic growth, the unemployment rate, and the inflation rate. Other factors not directly related to government policies, such as oil prices and labor contract situations, also have an impact on the economic variables, and these, too, have to be considered.

Global Effects of Monetary Policy

 GL BAL ASPECTS   Financial market participants must recognize that the type of monetary policy implemented by the Fed is somewhat dependent on various international factors, as explained next.

Impact of the Dollar

A weak dollar can stimulate U.S. exports, discourage U.S. imports, and therefore stimulate the U.S. economy. In addition, it tends to exert inflationary pressure in the United States. Thus, the Fed is less likely to use a stimulative monetary policy when the dollar is weak. A strong dollar tends to reduce inflationary pressure but also dampens the U.S. economy. Therefore, the Fed is more likely to use a stimulative policy during a strong-dollar period.

Impact of Global Economic Conditions

The Fed recognizes that economic conditions are integrated across countries, so it considers prevailing global economic conditions when conducting monetary policy. When

global economic conditions are strong, foreign countries purchase more U.S. imports and can stimulate the U.S. economy. When global economic conditions are weak, the foreign demand for U.S. imports weakens.

In 2001, when the United States experienced a very weak economy, the economies of many other countries were also weak. The Fed's decision to lower U.S. interest rates and stimulate the U.S. economy was partially driven by these weak global economic conditions. The Fed recognized that the United States would not receive any stimulus from other countries (such as a strong demand for U.S. imports) where income and aggregate spending levels were also relatively low.

Transmission of Interest Rates

International flows of funds can also affect the Fed's monetary policy. If there is upward pressure on U.S. interest rates that can be offset by foreign inflows of funds, the Fed may not feel compelled to use a loose-money policy. However, if foreign investors reduce their investment in U.S. securities, the Fed may be forced to intervene to prevent interest rates from rising.

Given the international integration in money and capital markets, a government's budget deficit can affect interest rates of various countries. This concept, referred to as **global crowding out,** is illustrated in Exhibit 5.15. An increase in the U.S. budget deficit causes an outward shift in the federal government demand for U.S. funds and therefore in the aggregate demand for U.S. funds (from D_1 to D_2). This crowding-out effect forces the U.S. interest rate to increase from i_1 to i_2 if the supply curve (S) is unchanged. As U.S. rates rise, they attract funds from investors in other countries, such as Germany and Japan. As foreign investors use more of their funds to invest in U.S. securities, the supply of available funds in their respective countries declines. Consequently, there is upward pressure on non-U.S. interest rates as well. The impact will be most pronounced on those countries whose investors are most likely to be attracted to the higher U.S. interest rates. The possibility of global crowding out has caused national governments to criticize one another for large budget deficits.

Fed Policy during the Asian Crisis

Although the Fed's objectives normally focus on the United States, it recognizes that the economic growth of foreign countries can influence U.S. economic growth, and vice versa. This complicates the determination of the proper monetary policy to impose. For

EXHIBIT 5.15 Illustration of Global Crowding Out

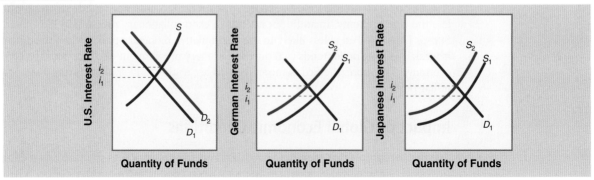

example, during the Asian crisis in the late 1990s, the Fed may have lowered U.S. interest rates more than it would have without the crisis. Although there was some concern that the lower rates would lead to higher U.S. inflation, a greater concern was that if rates were not lowered, the United States would experience a weak economy, which would be transmitted to other countries. The lower U.S. interest rates provided some stimulus to the U.S. economy, offsetting the reduction in U.S. economic growth due to lower demand for U.S. exports during the crisis, and also helped to sustain the U.S. demand for foreign exports. Thus, the Fed's monetary policy was not only influenced by international conditions, but also had an influence on those conditions.

SUMMARY

- The Keynesian theory suggests how the Fed can affect the interaction between the demand for money and the supply of money, which affects interest rates, aggregate spending, and economic growth. As the Fed increases the money supply, interest rates should decline, which results in more aggregate spending (because of cheaper financing rates) and higher economic growth. As the Fed decreases the money supply, interest rates should increase, which results in less aggregate spending (because of higher financing rates), lower economic growth, and lower inflation.

- The Monetarist approach suggests that excess growth in the money supply can cause inflationary expectations. Therefore, expansionary monetary policy by the Fed may have limited effects because increasing the money supply may also result in an increased demand for money (in response to higher inflationary expectations). Thus, interest rates may not necessarily be controlled by the Fed's adjustment in the money supply, and the impact of monetary policy on aggregate spending is questionable.

- A stimulative monetary policy is likely to increase economic growth, but may also cause higher inflation. A restrictive monetary policy is likely to reduce inflation, but may also reduce economic growth. Thus, the Fed faces a tradeoff when implementing monetary policy. Given a possible tradeoff, the Fed tends to assess whether the potential benefits of any proposed monetary policy outweigh the potential adverse effects.

- Financial market participants attempt to forecast the Fed's future monetary policies and the effects of these policies on economic conditions. Using this information, they can determine how their security holdings would be affected and can adjust their security portfolios accordingly.

- The proper monetary policy may be dependent on the prevailing fiscal policy. If the fiscal policy involves excessive government borrowing, there is upward pressure on interest rates, and a loose monetary policy may be necessary to offset that pressure on interest rates. However, such a strategy could cause higher inflation in the long run.

POINT COUNTER-POINT

Can the Fed Prevent U.S. Recessions?

Point Yes. The Fed has the power to reduce market interest rates and can therefore encourage more borrowing and spending. In this way, it stimulates the economy.

Counter-Point No. When the economy is weak, individuals and firms are unwilling to borrow regardless of the interest rate. Thus, the borrowing (by those who are

qualified) and spending will not be influenced by the Fed's actions. The Fed should not intervene, but should let the economy work itself out of a recession.

Who Is Correct? Use your favorite search engine to learn more about this issue. Offer your own opinion on this issue.

QUESTIONS AND APPLICATIONS

1. **Monetary Policy during the War in Iraq** Consider the likely discussion that was occurring in the FOMC meetings during the war in Iraq in 2003. The U.S. economy was weak at that time. Do you think the FOMC should have proposed a loose-money policy or a tight-money policy once the war began? This war could have resulted in major damage to oil wells. Explain why this possible effect would have received much attention at the FOMC meetings. If this possibility was perceived to be highly likely at the time of the meetings, explain how it may have complicated the decision about monetary policy at that time. Given the conditions stated in this question, would you have suggested that the Fed use a tight-money policy, a loose-money policy, or a stable-money policy? Support your decision with logic, and acknowledge any adverse effects of your decision.

2. **Interpreting Financial News** Interpret the following statements made by Wall Street analysts and portfolio managers:
   a. "Lately, the Fed's policies are driven by gold prices and other indicators of the future rather than by recent economic data."
   b. "The Fed cannot boost money growth at this time because of the weak dollar."
   c. "The Fed's fine-tuning may distort the economic picture."

3. **Monitoring Money Supply** Why do financial market participants closely monitor money supply movements? Why do financial market participants who monitor monetary policy have only limited success in forecasting economic variables?

4. **Monetizing the Debt** Explain what monetizing the debt means. How can this action improve economic conditions? What is the risk involved?

5. **Impact of Monetary Policy** How does the Fed's monetary policy affect economic conditions?

6. **Managing in Financial Markets: Forecasting Monetary Policy** As a manager of a firm, you are concerned about a potential increase in interest rates, which would reduce the demand for your firm's products. The Fed is scheduled to meet in one week to assess economic conditions and set monetary policy. Economic growth has been high, but inflation has also increased from 3 percent to 5 percent (annualized) over the last four months. The level of unemploy-

ment is very low and cannot possibly go much lower.
   a. Given the situation, is the Fed likely to adjust monetary policy? If so, how?
   b. Recently, the Fed has allowed the money supply to expand beyond its long-term target range. Does this affect your expectation of what the Fed will decide at its upcoming meeting?
   c. Assume that the Fed has just learned that the Treasury will need to borrow a larger amount of funds than originally expected. Explain how this information may affect the degree to which the Fed changes the monetary policy.

7. **Interpreting the Fed's Monetary Policy** When the Fed increases money supply to lower the federal funds rate, will the cost of capital of U.S. companies be reduced? Explain how the segmented markets theory regarding the term structure of interest rates could influence the degree of which the Fed's monetary policy affects long-term interest rates.

8. **Tradeoffs of Monetary Policy** Describe the economic tradeoff faced by the Fed in achieving its economic goals.

9. **Economic Indicators** Stock market conditions serve as a leading economic indicator. Assuming the U.S. economy is currently in a recession, discuss the implications of this indicator. Why might this indicator possibly be inaccurate?

10. **Monetarist Approach** Briefly summarize the Monetarist approach.

11. **Confounding Effects** What factors might be considered by financial market participants who are assessing whether an increase in money supply growth will affect inflation?

12. **Monetary Policy Today** Assess the economic situation today. Is the administration more concerned with reducing unemployment or inflation? Does the Fed have a similar opinion? If not, is the administration publicly criticizing the Fed? Is the Fed publicly criticizing the administration? Explain.

13. **Internet Exercise** Review the website http://www.federalreserve.gov/fomc with a focus on the activities of the FOMC.
   When is the FOMC scheduled to meet next? How many more times will the FOMC meet this

year? Succinctly summarize the minutes of the last meeting. What did the FOMC discuss at the last meeting? Did the FOMC make any changes in the current monetary policy? What is the FOMC's current monetary policy?

14. **Choice of Monetary Policy** When does the Fed use a loose-money policy, and when does it use a tight-money policy? What is a criticism of a loose-money policy? What is the risk of using a monetary policy that is too tight?

15. **Fed's Monetary Policy** Why would the Fed try to avoid frequent changes in the money supply?

16. **Lagged Effects of Monetary Policy** Compare the recognition lag and the implementation lag.

17. **Keynesian Approach** Briefly summarize the pure Keynesian philosophy and identify the key variable considered.

18. **Impact of Foreign Policies** Why might a foreign government's policies be closely monitored by investors in other countries, even if the investors plan no investments in that country? Explain how monetary policy in one country can affect interest rates in other countries.

19. **Impact of Money Supply Growth** Explain why an increase in the money supply can affect interest rates in different ways. Include the potential impact of the money supply on the supply of and the demand for loanable funds when answering this question.

20. **Fed Control** Why may the Fed have difficulty in controlling the economy in the manner desired? Be specific.

21. **Fed's Control of Inflation** Assume that the Fed's primary goal is to cure inflation. How can it use open market operations to achieve its goal? What is a possible adverse effect of this action by the Fed (even if it achieves its goal)?

FLOW OF FUNDS EXERCISE

Anticipating Fed Actions

Recall that Carson Company has obtained substantial loans from finance companies and commercial banks. The interest rate on the loans is tied to market interest rates and is adjusted every six months. Because of its expectations of a strong U.S. economy, Carson plans to grow in the future by expanding its business and through acquisitions. It expects that it will need substantial long-term financing and plans to borrow additional funds either through loans or by issuing bonds. It is also considering the issuance of stock to raise funds in the next year.

An economic report just noted the strong growth in the economy, which has caused the economy to be close to full employment. In addition, the report estimated that the annualized inflation rate increased to 5 percent, up from 2 percent last month. The factors that caused the higher inflation (shortages of products and shortages of labor) are expected to continue.

a. How will the Fed's monetary policy change based on the report?

b. How will the likely change in the Fed's monetary policy affect Carson's future performance? Could it affect Carson's plans for future expansion?

c. Explain how a tight monetary policy could affect the amount of funds borrowed at financial institutions by deficit units such as Carson Company. How might it affect the credit risk of deficit units such as Carson Company? How might it affect the performance of financial institutions that provide credit to deficit units such as Carson Company?

WSJ EXERCISE

Market Assessment of Fed Policy

Review the "Credit Markets" section in a recent issue of *The Wall Street Journal* (listed in the index on the first page). Summarize the market assessments of the Fed.

Also summarize the market's expectations about future interest rates. Are these expectations based primarily on the Fed's monetary policy or on other factors?

Part II Integrative Problem

Fed Watching

This problem requires an understanding of the Fed (Chapter 4) and monetary policy (Chapter 5). It also requires an understanding of how economic conditions affect interest rates and securities prices (Chapters 2 and 3).

Like many other investors, you are a "Fed watcher," who constantly monitors any actions taken by the Fed to revise monetary policy. You believe that three key factors affect interest rates. Assume that the most important factor is the Fed's monetary policy. The second most important factor is the state of the economy, which influences the demand for loanable funds. The third factor is the level of inflation, which also influences the demand for loanable funds. Because monetary policy can affect interest rates, it affects economic growth as well. By controlling monetary policy, the Fed influences the prices of all types of securities.

The following information is available:

- Economic growth has been consistently strong over the past few years but is beginning to slow down.
- Unemployment is as low as it has been in the past decade but has risen slightly over the past two quarters.
- Inflation has been about 5 percent per year for the past few years.
- The dollar has been strong.
- Oil prices have been very low.

Yesterday, an event occurred that you believe will cause much higher oil prices in the United States and a weaker U.S. economy in the near future. You plan to determine whether the Fed will respond to the economic problems that are likely to develop.

You have reviewed previous economic slowdowns caused by a decline in the aggregate demand for goods and services and found that each slowdown precipitated a loose-money policy by the Fed. Inflation was 3 percent or less in each of the previous economic slowdowns. Interest rates generally declined in response to these policies, and the U.S. economy improved.

Assume that the Fed's philosophy regarding monetary policy is to maintain economic growth and low inflation. There does not appear to be any major fiscal policy forthcoming that will have a major effect on the economy. Thus, the future economy is up to the Fed. The Fed's present policy is to maintain a 2 percent annual growth rate in the money supply. You believe that the economy is headed toward a recession unless the Fed uses a very stimulative monetary policy, such as a 10 percent annual growth rate in the money supply.

The general consensus of economists is that the Fed will revise its monetary policy to stimulate the economy for three reasons: (1) it recognizes the potential costs of higher unemployment if a recession occurs, (2) it has consistently used a stimulative policy in the past to prevent recessions, and (3) the administration has been pressuring the Fed to use a stimulative monetary policy. Although you consider the opinions of the economists, you plan to make your own assessment of the Fed's future policy. Two quarters

ago, GDP declined by 1 percent. Last quarter, GDP declined again by 1 percent. Thus, there is clear evidence that the economy has recently slowed down.

Questions

1   Do you think that the Fed will use a stimulative monetary policy at this point? Explain.

2   You maintain a large portfolio of U.S. bonds. You believe that if the Fed does not revise its monetary policy, the U.S. economy will continue to decline. If the Fed stimulates the economy at this point, you believe that you would be better off with stocks than with bonds. Based on this information, do you think you should switch to stocks? Explain.

PART III

Equity Markets

Equity markets facilitate the flow of funds from individual or institutional investors to corporations. Thus, they enable corporations to finance their investments in new or expanded business ventures. They also facilitate the flow of funds between investors. Chapter 6 describes stock offerings and explains how participants in the stock market monitor firms that have publicly traded stock. Chapter 7 explains the valuation of stocks, describes investment strategies involving stocks, and indicates how a stock's performance is measured. Chapter 8 describes the stock market microstructure and explains how orders are placed and executed on stock exchanges.

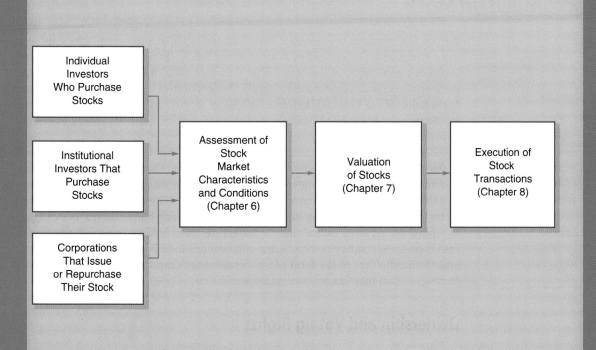

CHAPTER 6

Offering Stocks and Monitoring Investors

S tock markets facilitate equity investment into firms and the transfer of equity investments between investors.

The specific objectives of this chapter are to:

■ describe the process of initial public offerings,

■ describe the process of secondary offerings,

■ explain how stock markets facilitate secondary market trading,

■ describe investor participation in the stock markets,

■ explain how the stock market is used to monitor and control firms, and

■ describe the globalization of stock markets.

Background on Stock

A stock is a certificate representing partial ownership in a corporation. Like debt securities, common stock is issued by firms to obtain funds. However, the purchaser of stock becomes a part owner of the firm, rather than a creditor. Individuals and financial institutions are common purchasers of stock. Owners of stock can benefit from the growth in the value of the firm and therefore have more to gain than creditors. However, they are also susceptible to large losses, as the values of even the most respected corporations have declined substantially in some periods.

Stocks are issued by corporations that need long-term funds. The primary market enables corporations to issue new stock to investors, and the secondary market enables investors to sell stocks that they had previously purchased. Thus, the primary market facilitates new financing for corporations, whereas the secondary market creates liquidity for investors who invest in stocks. Although the issuing corporation is not obligated to repurchase its stock at any time in the future, shareholders can sell it to other investors in the secondary market. Some corporations distribute a portion of their earnings to shareholders in the form of dividends; other corporations reinvest all of their earnings so that they can achieve greater expansion.

Ownership and Voting Rights

The ownership of common stock entitles shareholders to a number of rights not available to other individuals. Normally, only the owners of common stock are permitted to

vote on certain key matters concerning the firm, such as the election of the board of directors, authorization to issue new shares of common stock, approval of amendments to the corporate charter, and adoption of bylaws. Many investors assign their vote to management through the use of a proxy. Many other shareholders simply fail to vote at all. As a result, management normally receives the majority of the votes and can elect its own candidates as directors.

Preferred Stock

Preferred stock represents an equity interest in a firm that usually does not allow for significant voting rights. Preferred shareholders technically share the ownership of the firm with common shareholders and are therefore compensated only when earnings have been generated. Thus, if the firm does not have sufficient earnings from which to pay the preferred stock dividends, it may omit the dividend without fear of being forced into bankruptcy. A cumulative provision on most preferred stock prevents dividends from being paid on common stock until all preferred stock dividends (both current and those previously omitted) have been paid. Normally, the owners of preferred stock do not participate in the profits of the firm beyond the stated fixed annual dividend. All profits above those needed to pay dividends on preferred stock belong to the owners of common stock.

Because the dividends on preferred stock can be omitted, a firm assumes less risk when issuing it than when issuing bonds. If a firm omits preferred stock dividends, however, it may be unable to raise new capital until the omitted dividends have been paid, because investors will be reluctant to make new investments in a firm unable to compensate its existing sources of capital.

From a cost perspective, preferred stock is a less desirable source of capital for a firm than bonds. Because a firm is not legally required to pay preferred stock dividends, it must entice investors to assume the risk involved by offering higher dividends. In addition, preferred stock dividends are technically compensation to owners of the firm. Therefore, the dividends paid are not a tax-deductible expense to the firm, whereas interest on bonds is tax deductible. Because preferred stock normally has no maturity, it represents a permanent source of financing.

Issuers Participating in Stock Markets

The stock market is like other financial markets in that it links the surplus units (that have excess funds) with deficit units (that need funds). Corporations that need funds can issue stock to investors. The sale of stock to obtain funds differs from the issuance of debt securities in that stock allows investors to have ownership rights in the deficit unit. This ownership feature attracts many investors who want to have an equity interest in a firm, but do not necessarily want to manage their own firm. The massive growth in the stock market has enabled many corporations to expand to a much greater degree and has allowed investors to share in the profitability of corporations.

When a corporation first decides to issue stock to the public, usually to raise funds, it engages in an initial public offering. Even after a firm has gone public, it may need to raise additional equity to support its growth. In that case, it can engage in a secondary offering by issuing additional shares of stock to the public. Some firms have had several secondary offerings to support their expansion. The next section describes initial public offerings, and the following section describes secondary offerings.

Initial Public Offerings

An initial public offering (IPO) is a first-time offering of shares by a specific firm to the public. As a privately held firm expands, it may need more funds than it can obtain through borrowing and therefore will consider an IPO. A common first step for a growing firm is to obtain private equity funding from venture capitalist (VC) firms, which seek to invest in firms that offer high potential for growth over time. These VC firms typically prefer an investment period of two to five years. Therefore, an IPO is commonly used not only to obtain new funding but also to offer VC firms a way to cash in their investment. Many VC firms sell their shares in the secondary market between 6 and 24 months after the IPO.

Going Public

Since firms that engage in an IPO are not well known to investors, they must provide detailed information about their operations and their financial condition. A firm planning on going public normally hires a securities firm (or investment bank) that serves as the lead underwriter for the IPO. The lead underwriter is involved in the development of the prospectus and the pricing and placement of the shares.

Developing a Prospectus A few months before the IPO, the issuing firm (with the help of the lead underwriter) develops a prospectus and files it with the Securities and Exchange Commission (SEC). The prospectus contains detailed information about the firm and includes financial statements and a discussion of the risks involved. It is intended to provide potential investors with the information they need to decide whether to invest in the firm. Within about 30 days, the SEC will assess the prospectus and determine whether it contains all the necessary information. In many cases, before approving the prospectus, the SEC recommends some changes that provide more information about the firm's financial condition.

Once the SEC approves the prospectus, it is sent to institutional investors who may want to invest in the IPO. In addition, the firm's management and the underwriters of the IPO meet with institutional investors. In many cases, the meetings occur in the form of a road show; the firm's managers travel to various cities and put on a presentation for large institutional investors in each city. The institutional investors are informed of the road show in advance so that they can attend if they may be interested in purchasing shares of the IPO. Some institutional investors may even receive separate individual presentations. Institutional investors are targeted because they may be willing to buy large blocks of shares at the time of the IPO. For this reason, they typically have priority over individual investors in purchasing shares during an IPO.

Pricing The lead underwriter must determine the so-called offer price at which the shares will be offered at the time of the IPO. The price that investors are willing to pay per share is influenced by prevailing market and industry conditions. If other publicly traded firms in the same industry are priced high relative to their earnings or sales, then the price assigned to shares in the IPO will be relatively high.

Before a firm goes public, it attempts to gauge the price that will be paid for its shares. During the road show, the lead underwriter solicits indications of interest in the IPO by institutional investors as to the number of shares that they may demand at various possible offer prices. This process is referred to as bookbuilding. The survey is then

Possible Offer Price	Total Shares Demanded	Total Proceeds to Issuer
$13	3,000,000	$39,000,000
$12	3,500,000	$42,000,000
$11	4,000,000	$44,000,000
$10	4,300,000	$43,000,000

summarized as shown in Exhibit 6.1. Based on the feedback received, the underwriter determines the offer price at which it expects to be able to issue all the shares. Assuming that the underwriter in this example wants to issue at least 4 million shares, it will use $11 as the offer price. As a result, many institutional investors pay a lower price than they would have been willing to pay for the shares. Some institutional investors, for example, would have paid $13, but the underwriter used an offer price of $11 for all investors to ensure that at least 4 million shares would be sold. Some critics suggest that this process provides institutional investors with special favors and may be a way for the investment bank that is underwriting the IPO to attract other business from institutional investors. To the extent that the shares were essentially discounted from their appropriate price, the proceeds that the issuing firm receives from the IPO are lower than it deserves.

In some other countries, an auction process is used for IPOs, and investors pay whatever they bid for the shares. The top bidder's order is accommodated first, followed by the next highest bidder, and so on, until all shares are issued. The issuer can set a minimum price at which the bidding must occur for shares to be issued. This process prevents the underwriter from setting the offer price at a level that is intended to please specific institutional investors.

Transaction Costs The transaction cost to the issuing firm is usually 7 percent of the funds raised. For example, an IPO of $50 million would result in a transaction cost of $3.5 million (7% × $50 million). The lead underwriter commonly allows other securities firms to participate in the offering by placing shares with various institutional investors. These participating securities firms form a so-called syndicate and receive a portion of the transaction cost incurred by the issuing firm.

Underwriter Efforts to Ensure Price Stability

The lead underwriter's performance can be partially measured by the movement in the IPO firm's share price following the IPO. If investors quickly sell an IPO stock in the secondary market, there will be downward pressure on the stock's price. If most stocks placed by a particular underwriter perform poorly after the IPO, institutional investors may no longer want to purchase shares underwritten by that underwriter.

The lead underwriter attempts to ensure stability in the stock's price after the offering by requiring a lockup provision, which prevents the original owners of the firm and the VC firms from selling their shares for a specified period (usually six months from the date of the IPO). The purpose of the lockup provision is to prevent downward pressure that could occur if the original owners or VC firms sold their shares in the secondary market. In reality, however, the provision simply defers the possible excess supply of shares sold in the secondary market. When the lockup period expires, the number of shares for sale in the secondary market may increase abruptly, and the share price commonly declines significantly. In fact, some investors who are allowed to sell their shares

before the lockup expiration date now recognize this effect and sell their IPO shares just before the expiration date. Consequently, the stock price begins to decline shortly before that date.

ILLUSTRATION

When Click Commerce Inc. engaged in an IPO, it placed 5 million shares with investors. An additional 32 million shares were held by insiders (the original owners before the IPO). Thus, the 5 million shares placed in the market at the time of the IPO represented only about 13 percent of the total shares of the firm. The remaining 87 percent of the shares were locked up. Thus, to the extent that Click Commerce insiders wanted to cash out of their investment when the lockup expired, there was potential for the supply of shares for sale to increase abruptly, possibly causing a large decline in the price of the stock.

Exhibit 6.2 shows Click Commerce's share price on the four days before and after its lockup expiration date. As the exhibit shows, the share price began to decline before the lockup expiration, indicating that some investors anticipated downward price pressure and dumped their shares just before the lockup expired. The share price continued to slide at the time of the expiration and for a few days afterward—probably due to selling pressure from insiders who were no longer subject to the lockup. From four days before the lockup expiration to four days after it, the share price of Click Commerce declined by about 26 percent. The percentage decline in this case was larger than normal, but many stocks experience a decline of at least 10 percent over the short period surrounding the lockup expiration date.

As a second example, ICG engaged in an IPO on August 4, 1999. The stock price rose from $10 to about $200 per share over the next five months. The price declined to $120 on February 4, 2000, when the lockup expired. Just after the lockup expired, insiders sold about 3.6 million shares, and the price declined to about $100 per share. Over the following months, insiders sold more than 20 million shares, and by August 2001, ICG's price was less than $1 per share. Thus, although the lockup period may have prevented downward pressure on the price, that pressure was simply deferred un-

EXHIBIT 6.2

Share Price of Click Commerce on the Days Surrounding Its Lockup Expiration Date

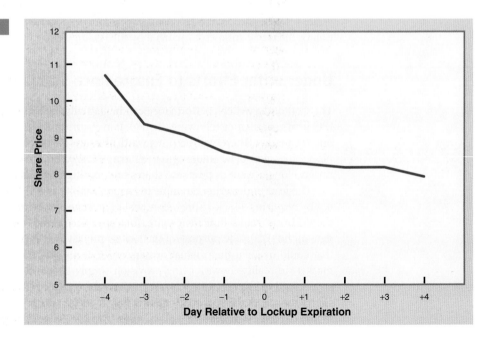

til the lockup expired. The downward pressure can be especially strong when the stock price rises because of excessive demand by investors during the lockup period. When the lockup period expires, insiders commonly sell their shares if they believe that the stock is priced higher than it should be.

IPO Timing

IPOs tend to occur more frequently during bullish stock markets, when potential investors are more interested in purchasing new stocks. Prices of stocks tend to be higher in these periods, and issuing firms attempt to capitalize on such prices.

ILLUSTRATION In the late 1990s, stocks of most firms were priced high relative to their respective earnings or revenues. Investor demand for new stocks was strong. Firms were more willing to engage in IPOs because they were confident that they could sell all of their shares at relatively high prices.

In the 2000–2001 period, the stock market weakened, reducing the valuation of stocks relative to earnings or revenues. For this reason, many firms withdrew their plans to engage in IPOs. They recognized that their shares would have to be sold for a lower price than they desired. In addition, as economic conditions weakened, some firms cut back on their expansion plans and therefore reduced their need for additional funds. These firms recognized that they should defer their offering until economic conditions were more favorable and stock prices were higher.

IPO Initial Returns

The initial (first-day) return of IPOs in the United States has averaged about 20 percent over the last 30 years. Such a return is unusual for a single day and exceeds the typical return earned on stocks over an entire year. The initial return on IPOs was especially high for Internet firms during the 1996–1999 period. During 1998, for example, the mean increase in price on the first trading day following the IPO was 84 percent for Internet stocks. Thus, a $1 million investment in each of the Internet IPOs in 1998 would have resulted in a one-day gain of $840,000. Such a high initial return may indicate that the IPO was underpriced, implying that the offer price was lower than it should have been. In that case, the issuer received less than it should have from issuing the shares. The beneficiaries were the institutional investors that were able to purchase the shares at the low offer price.

ILLUSTRATION On January 15, 1999, an IPO by an Internet stock called MarketWatch.com jumped from the initial offer price of $17 per share to $130 per share within the first two hours of trading (a return of about 665 percent at that point) and then declined to $97.50 per share by the end of the day. The one-day return for investors who purchased shares at the offer price was about 474 percent. On December 9, 1999, the IPO for VA Linux had an offer price of $30 per share. By the end of the first day, the price was $239, providing for an initial return of 697 percent for investors who purchased shares at the offer price and sold their shares after one day.

Such unusually high performance has attracted individual investors to the IPO market. Brokerage firms such as E*Trade, Fidelity, and Schwab have asked for allotments of IPO shares from the securities firms underwriting the IPOs so that they can offer IPO

shares online to their individual investors. The brokerage firms have been able to obtain only about 2 percent of the total share allotment on average, however. When they do receive allotments, they typically make the shares available to their bigger clients. Underwriters still prefer to allocate most of the IPO shares to large institutional investors with whom they may do other business. In addition, it is easier to allocate large chunks of shares to institutional investors than to break the issue up into smaller pieces for individual investors.

Flipping Shares Some investors who know about the unusually high initial returns on IPOs attempt to purchase the stock at its offer price and sell the stock shortly afterward. This strategy is referred to as flipping. Investors who engage in flipping have no intention of investing in the firm over the long run and are simply interested in capitalizing on the initial return that occurs for many IPOs. If many institutional investors flip their shares, they may cause the market price of the stock to decline shortly after the IPO. Thus, underwriters are concerned that flipping may place excessive downward pressure on the stock's price. To discourage flipping, some securities firms make more shares of future IPOs available to institutional investors that retain shares for a relatively long period of time. The securities firms may also prevent institutional investors that engage in flipping from participating in any subsequent IPOs that they underwrite.

Google's IPO

On August 18, 2004, Google engaged in an IPO that attracted massive media attention because of Google's name recognition. Google generated $1.6 billion from the offering—more than four times the value of the combined IPOs by Amazon.com, America Online, Microsoft, Netscape, and Priceline.com. The two co-founders, Larry Page and Sergey Brin, sold a portion of their shares within the IPO for about $40 million each, but retained shares valued at $3 billion each. The Google IPO offers interesting insight into the process by which firms obtain equity funding from investors.

Estimating the Stock's Value Investors attempt to determine the value of the stock that is to be issued so that they can decide whether to invest in the IPO. In the case of Google, some investors used Yahoo! as a benchmark because Yahoo! stock has been publicly traded since 1996. To determine the appropriate price of Google's stock, investors multiplied Google's earnings per share by Yahoo!'s price-earnings ratio. This method has some major limitations, however. First, Google and Yahoo! are not exactly the same type of business. Some investors might argue that Microsoft would be a better benchmark than Yahoo! for Google. If Google has more growth potential than Yahoo!, it may deserve a higher multiple. In addition, Yahoo! and Google use different accounting methods, so estimating a value by comparing the earnings of the two firms is subject to error. These limitations of valuation are discussed in more detail in Chapter 12, but the main point here is that stock valuations are subject to error, especially for IPOs, because their prices were not market determined in the past.

Even the firm issuing stock in an IPO is unsure of its market value, because it is difficult to judge what investors will be willing to pay for the newly issued stock. Google initially expected that its stock would sell for between $118 and $135 per share, but then revised its estimate to below $100 before the IPO.

Google's Communication to Investors before the IPO Like any firm that is about to engage in an IPO, Google provided substantial financial information about its opera-

tions and recent performance. However, Google was unique in that it communicated in terms that most investors could easily understand. In addition, it emphasized that it would concentrate on long-term growth rather than on short-term goals such as meeting quarterly earnings targets. Many firms focus on meeting short-term earnings targets, because they know that investors obsess over quarterly earnings and that their stock valuations are influenced by earnings. Google maintained that it could make better decisions if it was not subject to the continual strain of having to satisfy a particular short-term earnings target.

The Auction Process Google's IPO was unique in that it used a Dutch auction process instead of relying almost exclusively on institutional investors. Specifically, it allowed all investors to submit a bid for its stock by a specific deadline. It then ranked the bid prices and determined the minimum price at which it would be able to sell all of the shares that it wished to issue. All bids that were equal to or above that minimum price were accepted, and all bids below the minimum price were rejected.

More than 30 investment banks were involved in the IPO and served as intermediaries between Google and the investors. In a traditional IPO, the investment banks have more responsibility to place the shares, and they tend to focus on placing the shares with institutional investors. Thus, individual investors rarely have access to an IPO. They commonly obtain shares later on the day of the IPO when some of the institutional investors flip their shares. Typically, the individual investors pay a higher price than the offer price paid by institutional investors.

By using a Dutch auction process, Google allowed individual investors to participate directly in the IPO and therefore to obtain shares at the initial offer price. Nevertheless, some interested individual investors decided not to submit a bid during Google's Dutch auction because of the complicated registration process required to purchase the shares. To participate in the auction, they had to complete forms to prove to their respective investment bank that they were financially qualified. Also, some individual investors preferred to wait until after an initial equilibrium price of the stock was established. Consequently, some of these investors decided to buy shares after the auction was completed.

From Google's perspective, the benefit of the auction process was lower costs (as a percentage of proceeds) than with a traditional IPO. The auction process may have saved Google about $20 million in fees. In addition, the auction process allowed Google to attract a diversified investor base, including many individual investors. However, such an auction process is unlikely to be as successful for firms that are not as well known to individual investors as Google.

Results of Google's Dutch Auction Google's auction process resulted in a price of $85 per share, meaning that all investors whose bids were accepted paid $85 per share. Google was able to sell all of its 19.6 million shares at this price, which generated proceeds of $1.67 billion. Recall that Google initially hoped to sell the shares for between $118 and $135 per share. If it could have sold its shares for $120 per share instead of $85 per share, it would have generated an additional $686,000,000 in proceeds from the IPO.

Trading after the Auction Any transactions that occurred after the auction was completed took place in the secondary market, meaning that investors were buying shares that were previously purchased by other investors. Some investors who obtained shares at the time of the IPO sold (flipped) their shares in the secondary market shortly after the auction was completed. The share price increased by 18 percent to $100.34 by the end of the first day, so investors who obtained shares through the auction process and sold their shares at the end of the first day earned an 18 percent return. This also means

IPO Scorecard

The Wall Street Journal identifies recent firms that have engaged in IPOs. It provides the ticker symbol in the second column, the offer price the day of the IPO in the third column, and the recent closing price in the fourth column. The return relative to the offer price is disclosed in the fifth column, and the return relative to the first-day close is disclosed in the sixth column. The return relative to the offer price is higher than the return relative to the first-day close whenever the price rises over the first day.

IPO Scorecard/*Update on New Stock Issues*

IPOs continue to struggle, with several postponements and withdrawals ahead of the Google IPO next week. Still, some deals, like the offering from electronic stock market Archipelago Holdings Inc., are expected to make it to market later this week.

COMPANY	SYMBOL	OFFER PRICE	YESTERDAY'S CLOSE	% CHANGE FROM OFFER PRICE	% CHANGE FROM FIRST-DAY CLOSE	IPO DATE*
Kite Realty Group Trust	KRG	$13.00	$13.00	unch.	—*	Aug. 11
Placer Sierra Bancshares	PLSB	20.00	19.50	-2.5%	—*	Aug. 11
Westlake Chemical	WLK	14.50	14.65	+1.0	—*	Aug. 11
WPT Enterprises Inc	WPTE	8.00	7.19	-10.1	+4.8%	Aug. 10
Biomed Realty Trust	BMR	15.00	16.20	+8.0	+1.9	Aug. 6
Navteq Corp	NVT	22.00	27.00	+22.7	+6.7	Aug. 6
Syneron Medical Ltd	ELOS	12.00	9.33	-22.3	-13.2	Aug. 6
Commercial Vehicle Group	CVGI	13.00	13.45	+3.5	+2.7	Aug. 5
New River Pharmaceuticals	NRPH	8.00	7.05	-11.9	+0.7	Aug. 5
RightNow Technologies	RNOW	7.00	7.05	+0.7	-6.0	Aug. 5
EnerSys	ENS	12.50	11.99	-4.1	-4.1	July 30
MortgageIT Holdings	MHL	12.00	11.51	-4.1	-4.1	July 30
Volterra Semiconductor	VLTR	8.00	7.76	-3.0	-5.9	July 29
Gramercy Capital Group	GKK	15.00	14.10	-6.0	-6.0	July 28

*First trading day   Sources: WSJ Market Data Group; Dow Jones Newswires

that investors who purchased their shares at the end of the first day paid 18 percent more than if they had purchased the shares through the auction process.

During the first two days of trading, the trading volume in the secondary market was about 1.7 times the shares issued in the IPO. Clearly, many investors were flipping their shares to benefit from the increased market price after the auction.

IPO Market Abuses

IPOs have received negative publicity because of several abuses. In 2003, regulators issued new guidelines in an effort to prevent such abuses in the future. Some of the more common abuses are described here.

Spinning Spinning occurs when an investment bank allocates shares from an IPO to corporate executives who may be considering an IPO or other business that will require the help of an investment bank. The bankers hope that the executives will remember the favor and hire the investment bank in the future.

Laddering When there is substantial demand for an IPO, some brokers engage in laddering; that is, they encourage investors to place bids for the shares on the first day that are above the offer price. This helps to build upward price momentum. Some investors may be willing to participate to ensure that the broker will reserve some shares of the next hot IPO for them.

Excessive Commissions Some brokers have also charged excessive commissions when demand was high for an IPO. Investors were willing to pay the price because they could normally recover the cost from the return on the first day. Since the investment bank set an offer price significantly below the market price that would occur by the end of the first day of trading, investors were willing to accommodate brokers. The gain to the broker was a loss to the issuing firm, however, because its proceeds were less than they would have been if the offer price had been set higher.

IPOs: Long-Term Performance

There is strong evidence that IPOs of firms perform poorly on average over a period of a year or longer. Thus, from a long-term perspective, many IPOs are overpriced at the time of the issue. Investors may be overly optimistic about firms that go public. To the extent that the investors base their expectations on the firm's performance before the IPO, they should be aware that firms do not perform as well after going public as they did before.

ILLUSTRATION Consider the case of MarketWatch.com, whose stock price jumped from the offer price of $17 to $97.50 at the close of the first day. The stock price consistently declined to less than $3 per share or by more than 90 percent within a few years. The price trend shown in Exhibit 6.3 suggests that investors were irrational when they paid close to $100 per share at the time of the IPO. The stock price rebounded to about $15 by 2004, but never came close to the price level of the close of the IPO date.

Although the long-term performance of this stock since its IPO is poor, its performance for particular investors varies. Those institutional investors that purchased shares at the offer price ($17 per share) and flipped the shares a day or two after the IPO (for close to $100 per share) earned a return of more than 400 percent in just a few days. Those institutional investors that purchased shares at the offer price and held on to them for a long period of time experienced a loss. But the biggest losers were the individual investors who purchased shares just after the IPO. They were unable to buy shares at the offer price because all the shares were initially purchased by institutional investors. Over the next few days after the IPO, individuals were able to purchase shares (at the market price of close to $100 per share) that were sold (flipped) by some institutional investors that had been able to obtain shares at the offer price. These individual investors lost more than 90 percent of their original investment.

The example of MarketWatch.com is not intended to suggest that every IPO that had a large initial return experienced poor long-term performance. Nevertheless, there is evidence of poor long-term performance on average even when considering all IPOs over

Stock Price Performance
of MarketWatch.com
Following Its IPO

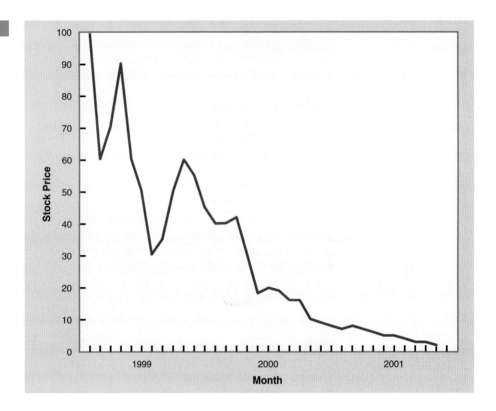

various time periods. The weak performance of IPOs may be partially attributed to irrational valuations at the time of the IPO, which were corrected over time. In addition, it may be partially attributed to the firm's managers, who may spend excessively and are less efficient with the firm's funds than they were before the IPO.

Secondary Stock Offerings

A secondary stock offering is a new stock offering by a specific firm whose stock is already publicly traded. Firms engage in secondary stock offerings to raise more equity so that they can more easily expand their operations. A firm that wants to engage in a secondary stock offering must file the offering with the SEC. It will likely hire a securities firm to advise on the number of shares it can sell, to help develop the prospectus submitted to the SEC, and to place the new shares with investors.

A firm will attempt to sell shares from a secondary offering at its prevailing market price. If the firm floods the market with more shares than investors are willing to purchase, however, it can cause a decline in the equilibrium price of all of its shares. Therefore, firms tend to monitor stock market movements when deciding the best time to engage in a secondary stock offering. They are more willing to issue new stock when the market price of their outstanding shares is relatively high and the general outlook for the firm is favorable. Under these conditions, they can issue new shares at a relatively high price, which allows them to generate more funds for a given amount of shares issued.

In the late 1990s, the volume of publicly placed stock increased substantially in response to the high market valuations of stock. From 2000 to 2002, however, the volume of publicly placed stock declined as a result of the weak economy and low stock

valuations. In the 2003–2004 period, the IPO volume increased, but not to the degree of the late 1990s.

Corporations sometimes direct their sales of stock toward a particular group, such as their existing shareholders, by giving them preemptive rights (first priority) to purchase the new stock. By placing newly issued stock with existing shareholders, the firm avoids diluting ownership. Preemptive rights are exercised by purchasing new shares during the subscription period (which normally lasts a month or less) at the price specified by the rights. Alternatively, the rights can be sold to someone else.

Shelf-Registration

Corporations can publicly place securities without the time lag often caused by registering with the SEC. With this so-called shelf-registration, a corporation can fulfill SEC requirements up to two years before issuing new securities. The registration statement contains financing plans over the upcoming two years. The securities are, in a sense, shelved until the firm needs to issue them. Shelf-registrations allow firms quick access to funds without repeatedly being slowed by the registration process. Thus, corporations anticipating unfavorable conditions can quickly lock in their financing costs. Although this is beneficial to the issuing corporation, potential purchasers must realize that the information disclosed in the registration is not continually updated and therefore may not accurately reflect the firm's status over the shelf-registration period.

Stock Exchanges

Any shares of stock that have been issued as a result of an initial public offering or a secondary offering can be traded by investors in the secondary market. In the United States, stock trading between investors occurs on the organized stock exchanges and the over-the-counter (OTC) market.

Organized Exchanges

http://
http://www.nyse.com
New York Stock Exchange market summary, quotes, financial statistics, etc.

Each organized exchange has a trading floor where floor traders execute transactions in the secondary market for their clients. Among the most popular organized stock exchanges are the New York Stock Exchange, the American Stock Exchange, the Midwest Stock Exchange, and the Pacific Stock Exchange. The New York Stock Exchange (NYSE) is by far the largest, controlling 80 percent of the value of all organized exchange transactions in the United States. Exhibit 6.4 shows the average volume of trading per day at the NYSE measured on an annual basis. Notice how the volume has increased over time, especially during the strong market conditions in the late 1990s. The firms listed on the NYSE are typically much larger than those listed on the other exchanges. For some firms, more than 5 million shares are traded on a daily basis.

Individuals or firms that purchase a seat on a stock exchange become members of the exchange and obtain the right to trade securities there. The term *seat* is somewhat misleading because all trading is carried out by individuals standing in groups. There are 1,366 seats on the NYSE. The price of a seat on the NYSE has exceeded $1 million since 1995. In 2004, the price of a seat was $1.8 million.

The NYSE has two broad types of members: floor brokers and specialists. Floor brokers are either commission brokers or independent brokers. Commission brokers are employed by brokerage houses and executes orders for clients on the floor of the NYSE.

EXHIBIT 6.4   Trends in Trading Volume at the New York Stock Exchange

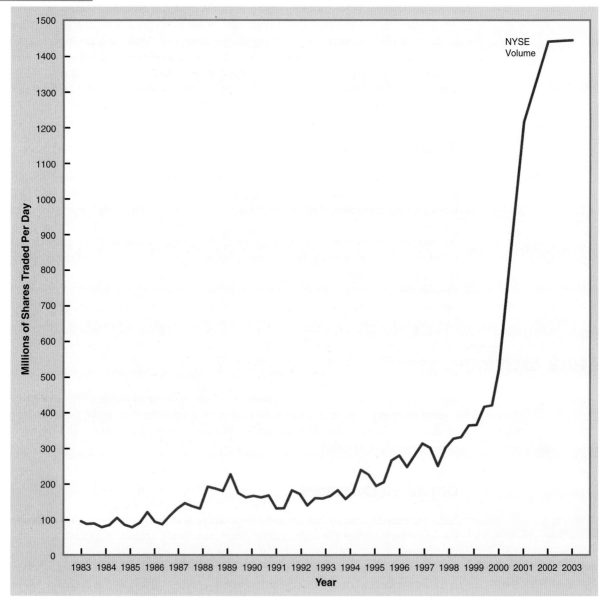

Independent brokers trade for their own account and are not employed by any particular brokerage house. However, they sometimes handle the overflow for brokerage houses and handle orders for brokerage houses that do not employ full-time brokers. The fee independent brokers receive depends on the size and liquidity of the order they trade.

Specialists can match orders of buyers and sellers. In addition, they can buy or sell stock for their own account and therefore create more liquidity for the stock.

The Trading Floor Each organized exchange has a trading floor where the buying and selling of securities take place. The trading floor at the NYSE consists of trading posts and trading booths. The specialists and their clerks maintain 20 trading posts. Above

each post, computer monitors display the stocks traded there and the last price for each stock traded at that post. Along the perimeter of the trading floor are about 1,500 trading booths where brokers obtain orders. Once an order is received, the broker will represent that order as an agent at the appropriate trading post. Member firms can also send orders directly to the trading posts through the SuperDot system, which is an electronic system for matching up buy and sell orders for small trades.

The trading that takes place on the floor of an exchange resembles an auction. Any member of the exchange can act as both a seller and a buyer. Those members of the exchange attempting to sell a client's stock strive to obtain the highest price possible, while members purchasing stock for their clients aim for the lowest price possible. When members of the exchange announce the sale of a certain number of shares of a certain stock, they receive bids for that stock by other members. The sellers either accept the highest bid immediately or wait until an acceptable bid is offered.

ILLUSTRATION Maria contacts her brokerage firm (which is a member of the NYSE) and states her desire to sell 100 shares of IBM. The broker stores the order and transmits it to the NYSE trading floor either directly through a computer or by telephone. On the floor of the NYSE, the order is initially stored in the SuperDot system. Then, depending on the order details, the order is either routed directly to the specialist's trading post or to the broker's trading booth.

If the order is transmitted directly to the trading post from the SuperDot system, the order will appear on the specialist's display book screen. The specialist can use his own funds to purchase the stock at the prevailing market price if he desires. If the order is transmitted to the broker's trading booth, the brokerage firm's clerk receiving the order will inform its floor broker on the NYSE that a new order has arrived. The floor broker takes the order to the appropriate trading post and can execute the sale of 100 shares of IBM.

Listing Requirements The NYSE imposes listing requirements for corporations whose stock is listed there, such as a minimum number of shares outstanding and a minimum level of earnings, cash flow, and revenue over a recent period. Once a stock is listed, the exchange also requires that the share price of the stock be at least $1 per share.

The requirement of a minimum number of shares outstanding is intended to ensure adequate liquidity. For a stock to be liquid, there should be many willing buyers and sellers at any time so that an investor can easily buy or sell the stock at the prevailing market price. In a liquid market, the bid price that brokers are willing to pay for a stock should be just slightly less than the ask price at which they would sell the stock.

The organized stock exchanges charge an initial fee to firms that wish to have their stock listed and meet the requirements. The fee is dependent on the size of the firm. The American Stock Exchange (Amex) also has listing requirements, but they are not as stringent as the NYSE requirements.

As time passes, some new listings occur, along with some delistings. The Amex was about as large as the NYSE in 1970, when about 1,200 firms were listed on each exchange. Since then, listings on the NYSE have increased to more than 3,000, while listings on the Amex have declined to about 800.

Over-the-Counter Market

Stocks not listed on the organized exchanges are traded in the over-the-counter (OTC) market. Like the organized exchanges, the OTC market also facilitates secondary market transactions. Unlike the organized exchanges, the OTC market does not have a trading

floor. Instead, the buy and sell orders are completed through a telecommunications network. Because there is no trading floor, it is not necessary to buy a seat to trade on this exchange, but it is necessary to register with the SEC.

http://

http://www.nasdaq.com
Trends and other statistical
information on various
Nasdaq indexes.

Nasdaq Many stocks in the OTC market are served by the **National Association of Securities Dealers Automatic Quotations (Nasdaq),** which is an electronic quotation system that provides immediate price quotations. Firms that wish to have their prices quoted by the Nasdaq must meet specific requirements on minimum assets, capital, and number of shareholders. About 5,000 stocks trade on the Nasdaq. Although most stocks listed in the Nasdaq market are relatively small firms, stocks of some very large firms such as Apple Computer and Intel are also traded there. Transaction costs as a percentage of the investment tend to be higher on the Nasdaq than on the NYSE or the Amex.

The Nasdaq market is composed of two segments, the Nasdaq National Market and the Nasdaq Small Cap Market. The Nasdaq National Market facilitates the trading of large stocks such as Apple Computer and Intel.

Although more stocks are listed on the Nasdaq than on the NYSE, the market value of these stocks is typically much lower than that of stocks listed on the NYSE. The aggregate market value of stocks traded on the Nasdaq is less than one-fourth the aggregate market value of all stocks listed on the NYSE.

In March 1998, the Nasdaq and Amex merged, and the Philadelphia Stock Exchange plans to merge with them in the future. The Amex is an auction market like the NYSE, while the Nasdaq uses a computerized system. Small companies that are less liquid may benefit from an auction market because the orders are channeled to a trader who stands ready to make a market in that stock. Other stocks may be most easily traded on Nasdaq's computerized telecommunications system. The merger of the Amex and Nasdaq allows investors to have some trades executed automatically on this exchange. For example, an electronic order to purchase 100 shares of a specific firm's stock will be matched with an electronic offer to sell 100 shares of that stock.

OTC Bulletin Board The OTC Bulletin Board lists stocks that have a price below $1 per share. These stocks are sometimes referred to as penny stocks. More than 3,500 stocks are listed here. Many of these stocks were traded in the Nasdaq market but no longer meet Nasdaq requirements. These stocks are less liquid than those traded on exchanges, as there is a very limited amount of trading. They are typically traded by individual investors only. Institutional investors tend to focus on more liquid stocks that can be easily sold in the secondary market at any time.

Pink Sheets In addition, the OTC market has another segment known as the "pink sheets" where even smaller stocks are traded. Like the stocks on the OTC Bulletin Board, these stocks typically do not satisfy the Nasdaq's listing requirements. About 20,000 stocks are available in this segment, but financial data on them are very limited, if available at all. Even brokers may not be able to obtain information on many of these firms. Families and officers of these firms commonly control much of the stock.

Extended Trading Sessions

The NYSE, Amex, and Nasdaq market offer extended trading sessions beyond normal trading hours. A late trading session enables investors to buy or sell stocks after the market closes, and an early morning session (sometimes referred to as a pre-market session) enables them to buy or sell stocks just before the market opens on the following day. Be-

WSJ USING THE WALL STREET JOURNAL
After-Hours Trading

The Wall Street Journal provides information on after-hours trading activity each day. The number of stocks that advanced and declined in price is disclosed, along with volume information, the most actively traded stocks during the after-hours session, and the biggest winners (price-gainers) and losers during the session.

Late-Trading Snapshot   08/10/04 4 p.m. - 6:30 p.m. ET

Late Price Percentage Gainers   ...And Losers

ISSUE (EXCH)	VOL (000s)	LAST	CHG	% CHG	ISSUE (EXCH)	VOL (000s)	LAST	CHG	% CHG
Essex (Nq)	6.9	8.60	+0.42	+5.1	NtlSemi (N)	982.9	14.20	-1.50	-9.6
YakComm (SC)	10.0	8.26	+0.25	+3.1	Abercrombie A (N)	208.2	30.88	-2.58	-7.7
VCA Antech (Nq)	57.7	39.48	+0.95	+2.5	UTStarcom (Nq)	143.9	16.70	-1.25	-7.0
Activision (Nq)	6.7	13.70	+0.31	+2.3	PMC Sierra (Nq)	341.6	10.25	-0.70	-6.4
RdtnTheraSvcs (Nq)	5.0	12.23	+0.23	+1.9	Broadcom A (Nq)	426.2	31.08	-1.80	-5.5
PlanarSys (Nq)	9.1	12.10	+0.23	+1.9	AT&T Wrls (N)	33.8	13.54	-0.78	-5.4
MasTec (N)	5.6	5.80	+0.10	+1.8	AlteraCp (Nq)	172.5	19.30	-1.10	-5.4
BridgeBnkNtl (SC)	13.6	12.61	+0.21	+1.7	Xilinx (Nq)	365.3	27.18	-1.51	-5.3
Mannkind (Nq)	10.0	12.11	+0.15	+1.2	CiscoSys (Nq)	15,107.7	19.39	-1.07	-5.2
TomOnline ADS (Nq)	7.5	10.14	+0.12	+1.2	IntgtDvc (Nq)	76.9	10.51	-0.49	-4.5

Late Most Active Issues

ISSUE (EXCH)	VOL (000s)	LAST	CHG	% CHG	ISSUE (EXCH)	VOL (000s)	LAST	CHG	% CHG
CiscoSys (Nq)	15,107.7	19.39	-1.07	-5.2	Microsoft (Nq)	885.6	27.46	-0.26	-0.9
Nasdaq 100 (A)	10,107.6	33.00	-0.21	-0.6	JDS Uniphs (Nq)	735.3	3.13	-0.07	-2.2
SPDR (A)	5,018.1	107.93	-0.45	-0.4	DeltaAir (N)	724.7	3.75	+0.03	+0.8
BestBuy (N)	1,473.0	45.15	...	...	AppleCptr (Nq)	595.8	30.75	-0.77	-2.4
SemiConHldrs (A)	1,407.3	30.15	-0.71	-2.3	SonusNetwks (Nq)	588.8	4.26	-0.12	-2.7
Dynegy A (N)	1,032.5	4.17	+0.01	+0.2	Compuware (Nq)	583.2	4.88	+0.02	+0.4
NtlSemi (N)	982.9	14.20	-1.50	-9.6	CptrAssoc (N)	543.7	23.66	...	...
Amgen (Nq)	952.7	54.10	+0.06	+0.1	Disney (N)	510.6	22.36	-0.08	-0.4
SunMicrsys (Nq)	901.9	3.54	-0.05	-1.4	iShrRu2000 (A)	474.4	104.53	-0.49	-0.5
Intel (Nq)	899.4	22.40	-0.14	-0.6	Atmel (Nq)	465.0	3.62	-0.02	-0.5

Late-Trading Activity

	TUESDAY	MONDAY	FRIDAY	THURSDAY	WEDNESDAY
Issues Traded	2,735	3,206	2,477	2,774	2,572
Advances	423	665	552	619	570
Declines	642	569	474	500	532
Unchanged	1,670	1,972	1,451	1,655	1,470
Advancing Volume	8,760,289	15,904,505	20,203,293	26,285,188	13,724,107
Declining Volume	56,545,834	12,866,239	9,997,784	23,522,281	14,336,900
Total Volume	82,478,192	44,445,811	44,601,859	72,521,776	39,598,337

The Late-Trading Snapshot reflects trading activity in NYSE and Amex issues reported by electronic trading services, securities dealers and regional exchanges between 4 p.m. and 6:30 p.m. Eastern time, and in Nasdaq NMS issues between 4 p.m. and 6:30 p.m., with a minimum price of $3 and volume of 5,000. The primary market is indicated for each issue. N-NYSE A-Amex Nq-Nasdaq SC-Nasdaq SmallCap

yond the sessions offered by the exchanges, some electronic computer networks (ECNs) allow for trading at any time. Since many announcements about firms are made after normal trading hours, investors can attempt to take advantage of this information before the market opens the next day. However, the market liquidity during the extended trading sessions is limited. For example, the total trading volume of a widely traded stock may typically be about 5 percent (or less) of its trading volume during the day. Some stocks are rarely traded at all during the night. Thus, a large trade is more likely to jolt the stock price during an extended trading session because a large price adjustment may be necessary to entice other investors to take the opposite position. Some investors attempt to take

EXHIBIT 6.5   Example of Stock Price Quotations

YTD % change	Hi	Lo	Stock	Sym	DIV	Yld%	PE	Vol 100s	Last	Net Chg
+10.3	121.88	80.06	IBM	IBM	.56	.6	20	71979	93.77	+1.06
Year-to-date percentage change in stock price	Highest price of the stock in this year	Lowest price of the stock in this year	Name of stock	Stock symbol	Annual dividend paid per year	Dividend yield, which represents the annual dividend as a percentage of the prevailing stock price	Price-earnings ratio based on the prevailing stock price	Trading volume during the previous trading day	Closing stock price	Change in the stock price on the previous trading day from the close on the day before

advantage of unusual stock price movements during extended trading sessions, but are exposed to the risk that the market price will not adjust in the manner that they anticipated.

Stock Quotations Provided by Exchanges

http://www.nasdaq.com
U.S. stock quotes and charts.

The trading of stocks between investors in the secondary market can cause any stock's price to change. Investors can monitor stock price quotations in financial newspapers such as *The Wall Street Journal, Barron's,* and *Investor's Business Daily,* or even local newspapers. Although the format varies among newspapers, most quotations provide similar information. Stock prices are always quoted on a per share basis, as in the example in Exhibit 6.5. Use the exhibit to supplement the following discussion of other information in stock quotations.

52-Week Price Range The stock's highest price and lowest price over the previous 52 weeks are commonly listed just to the left of the stock's name. The high and low prices indicate the range for the stock's price over the last year. Some investors use this range as an indicator of how much the stock price fluctuates. Other investors compare this range to the prevailing stock price because they wish to purchase a stock only when its prevailing price is below its 52-week high.

Notice that IBM's 52-week high price was $121.88 and its low price was $80.06 per share. The low price is about 34 percent below the high price, which suggests a wide difference over the last year. When IBM's stock price hit its 52-week low, the company's market value was more than one-third less than it was when the price reached its 52-week high.

Symbol Each stock has a specific symbol that is used to identify the firm. This symbol may be used to communicate trade orders to brokers. Ticker tapes at brokerage firms or on financial news television shows use the symbol to identify each firm. If included in the stock quotations, the symbol normally appears just to the right of the firm's name. Each symbol is usually composed of two to four letters. IBM's ticker symbol is the same as its name. Nike's symbol is NKE, the symbol for Home Depot is HD, and the symbol for Motorola is MOT.

Dividend The annual dividend (DIV) is commonly listed to the right of the firm's name and symbol. It shows the dividends distributed to stockholders over the last year on a

per share basis. IBM's dividend is $.56 per share, which indicates an average of $.19 per share for each quarter. The annual dollar amount of dividends paid can be determined by multiplying the dividends per share times the number of shares outstanding.

Dividend Yield Next to the annual dividend, some stock quotation tables also show the dividend yield (Yld), which is the annual dividend per share as a percentage of the stock's prevailing price. Since IBM's annual dividend is $.56 per share and its prevailing stock price is $93.77, its stock's dividend yield is

$$
\begin{aligned}
\text{Dividend yield} &= \frac{\text{Dividends paid per share}}{\text{Prevailing stock price}} \\
&= \frac{\$.56}{\$93.77} \\
&= .60\%
\end{aligned}
$$

Some firms attempt to provide a somewhat stable dividend yield over time, but other firms do not.

Price-Earnings Ratio Most stock quotations include the stock's price-earnings (PE) ratio, which represents its prevailing stock price per share divided by the firm's earnings per share (earnings divided by number of existing shares of stock) generated over the last year. IBM's PE ratio of 20 in Exhibit 6.5 is derived by dividing its stock price of $93.77 by the previous year's earnings. PE ratios are closely monitored by some investors who believe that a low PE ratio (relative to other firms in the same industry) signals that the stock is undervalued based on the company's earnings.

Volume Stock quotations also usually include the volume (referred to as "Vol" or "Sales") of shares traded on the previous day. The volume is normally quoted in hundreds of shares. It is not unusual for 1 million shares of a large firm's stock to be traded on a single day. Exhibit 6.5 shows that more than 7 million shares of IBM were traded. Some newspapers also show the percentage change in the volume of trading from the previous day.

Previous Day's Price Quotations Stock quotations show the closing price ("Last") on the previous day. In addition, the change in the price ("Net Chg") is typically provided and indicates the increase or decrease in the stock price from the closing price on the day before.

Stock Index Quotations

http://
http://finance.yahoo.com/?u
Quotations on various U.S.
stock market indexes.

Stock indexes serve as performance indicators of specific stock exchanges or of particular subsets of the market. The indexes allow investors to compare the performance of individual stocks with more general market indicators. Some of the more closely monitored indexes are identified next.

Dow Jones Industrial Average The Dow Jones Industrial Average (DJIA) is a price-weighted average of stock prices of 30 large U.S. firms. ExxonMobil, IBM, and the Coca-Cola Company are among the stocks included in the index. Although this index is commonly monitored, it has some limitations as a market indicator. First, because the index is price weighted, it assigns a higher weight over time to those stocks that experience

USING THE WALL STREET JOURNAL

WSJ Stock Information

The Wall Street Journal provides the following information related to this chapter on a daily basis:

■ Price quotations on stocks traded on various exchanges.

■ Share price information for foreign stocks of many different countries (in a section called "Foreign Markets").

■ Rumors or expectations about particular stocks (in "Heard on the Street").

■ Stock index prices of global markets (in "World Markets").

■ Recent trends in the market, forecasts by economists, and trends in economic activity (in "Abreast of the Market").

■ Summary information on stock market trading, including most active issues, number of issues traded, number of advances and declines, biggest percentage gainers and losers, and a breakdown of the trading volume on the NYSE every half-hour.

■ Firms that issued new stocks or debt securities (in "New Securities").

■ Summaries of general market movements (in "Stock Market Data Bank"), as shown here. The change in the index is measured relative to the previous trading day and to the year-end price.

Major Stock Indexes

	DAILY					52-WEEK			YTD
Dow Jones Averages	HIGH	LOW	CLOSE	NET CHG	% CHG	HIGH	LOW	% CHG	% CHG
30 Industrials	9944.67	9815.47	9944.67	+130.01	+1.32	10737.70	9271.76	+ 6.82	– 4.87
20 Transportations	3044.91	2971.10	3044.87	+ 74.79	+2.52	3204.31	2598.88	+16.77	+ 1.26
15 Utilities	284.00	282.09	283.98	+ 1.55	+0.55	284.51	236.03	+18.98	+ 6.40
65 Composite	2961.79	2917.96	2961.79	+ 43.96	+1.51	3072.25	2646.22	+11.51	– 1.30
Dow Jones Indexes									
Wilshire 5000	10452.75	10311.81	10452.74	+140.94	+1.37	11314.42	9481.27	+ 9.68	– 3.21
US Total Market	254.29	250.91	254.29	+ 3.38	+1.35	274.54	230.99	+ 9.48	– 3.19
US Large-Cap	232.98	230.06	232.98	+ 2.93	+1.27	250.84	215.24	+ 7.47	– 3.49
US Mid-Cap	307.40	303.10	307.40	+ 4.30	+1.42	334.64	266.28	+15.19	– 1.76
US Small-Cap	343.45	337.13	343.45	+ 6.32	+1.87	386.09	298.59	+15.02	– 3.98
US Growth	962.44	948.70	962.44	+ 13.74	+1.45	1069.37	900.78	+ 6.23	– 5.79
US Value	1343.75	1328.01	1343.75	+ 15.81	+1.19	1422.20	1191.28	+11.86	– 0.43
Global Titans 50	178.66	176.80	178.66	+ 1.81	+1.02	191.85	162.46	+ 9.05	– 3.32
Asian Titans 50	104.27	103.11	103.68	– 0.43	–0.41	118.74	88.09	+17.70	– 1.81
DJ STOXX 50	2576.82	2557.60	2576.82	+ 15.47	+0.60	2804.06	2386.92	+ 4.92	– 3.14
Nasdaq Stock Market									
Nasdaq Comp	1808.70	1782.26	1808.70	+ 34.06	+1.92	2153.83	1686.61	+ 7.21	– 9.72
Nasdaq 100	1346.71	1324.38	1346.71	+ 27.88	+2.11	1553.66	1240.37	+ 8.54	– 8.26
Biotech	636.20	622.97	636.18	+ 13.99	+2.25	845.11	622.19	– 7.85	–12.15
Computer	811.23	798.82	811.23	+ 15.27	+1.92	1012.13	772.20	+ 4.83	–13.23
Standard & Poor's Indexes									
500 Index	1079.04	1065.22	1079.04	+ 13.82	+1.30	1157.76	984.03	+ 8.96	– 2.96
MidCap 400	561.34	552.42	561.34	+ 8.92	+1.61	616.70	492.26	+13.82	– 2.55
SmallCap 600	269.48	264.70	269.48	+ 4.78	+1.81	296.35	230.17	+17.08	– 0.35
SuperComp 1500	240.35	237.16	240.35	+ 3.19	+1.35	258.20	217.97	+ 9.65	– 2.81
New York Stock Exchange and Others									
NYSE Comp	6295.13	6227.44	6295.11	+ 67.56	+1.08	6780.03	5569.62	+12.52	– 2.25
NYSE Financial	6486.80	6408.03	6486.68	+ 78.41	+1.22	7109.18	5729.79	+11.15	– 2.84
Russell 2000	529.84	518.38	529.83	+ 11.45	+2.21	606.39	466.95	+13.47	– 4.86
Value Line	340.87	335.02	340.87	+ 5.85	+1.75	386.84	307.77	+10.75	– 6.01
Amex Comp	1223.57	1214.60	1218.17	+ 0.23	+0.02	1275.96	956.98	+26.25	+ 3.80

Source: Reuters

WSJ USING THE WALL STREET JOURNAL
Stock Market Conditions

The Wall Street Journal provides detailed information on stock market conditions during the previous day, under the following headings:

- Dow Jones Averages Hour by Hour. This table provides hour-by-hour data for:
  - The DJIA (30 stocks).
  - The index of 20 transportation stocks.
  - The index of 15 utility stocks.
  - The composite of the DJIA, transportation, and utility indexes.
- The Dow Jones Averages. This table provides charts of stock index movements over the last six months for:
  - The DJIA.
  - The transportation index.
  - The utility index.

- Dow Jones U.S. Industry Groups. This table lists:
  - Leading industries during the previous trading day, including a few firms within those industries.
  - Lagging industries during the previous trading day, including a few firms within those industries.
- NYSE Highs/Lows. This table lists:
  - Stocks that reached their highest price on the previous trading day based on prices over the last year.
  - Stocks that reached their lowest price on the previous trading day based on prices over the last year.

higher prices. Therefore, the index tends to have an upward bias in its estimate of the market's overall performance. Second, because the DJIA is based on only 30 large stocks, it does not necessarily serve as an adequate indicator of the overall market or especially of smaller stocks.

Standard & Poor's (S&P) 500 The Standard & Poor's (S&P) 500 index is a value-weighted index of stock prices of 500 large U.S. firms. Because this index contains such a large number of stocks, it is more representative of the U.S. stock market than the DJIA. However, because the S&P 500 index focuses on large stocks, it does not serve as a useful indicator for stock prices of smaller firms.

Wilshire 5000 Total Market Index The Wilshire 5000 Total Market Index was created in 1974 to reflect the values of 5,000 U.S. stocks. Since more stocks have been added over time, the index now contains more than 5,000 stocks. It represents the broadest index of the U.S. stock market. It is widely quoted in financial media and closely monitored by the Federal Reserve and many financial institutions.

New York Stock Exchange Indexes The NYSE provides quotations on indexes that it created. The Composite Index represents the average of all stocks traded on the NYSE. This is an excellent indicator of the general performance of stocks traded on the NYSE, but because these stocks represent mostly large firms, the Composite Index is not an appropriate measure of small stock performance. In addition to the Composite Index, the NYSE also provides indexes for four sectors:

1. Industrial
2. Transportation
3. Utility
4. Financial

EXHIBIT 6.6   Trends of Stock Market Sectors

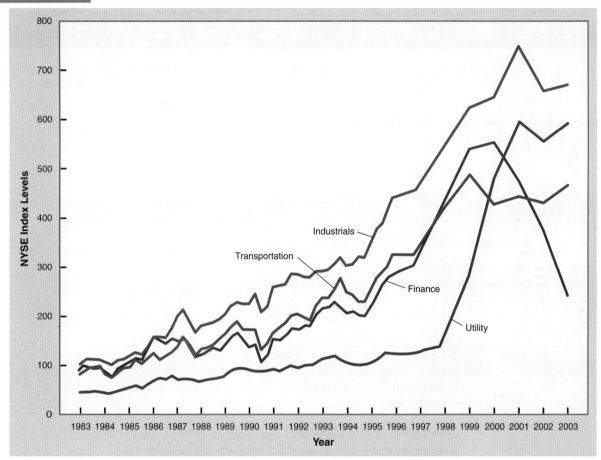

These indexes are commonly used as benchmarks for comparison to an individual firm or portfolio in that respective sector. Exhibit 6.6 shows the movements in the NYSE indexes. All of these indexes had a value of 50 as of 1966. Notice that although the indexes are positively correlated, there are substantial differences in their movements during some periods.

Other Stock Indexes The Amex provides quotations on several indexes of stocks traded on its exchange, including several sectors. The National Association of Security Dealers provides quotations on indexes of stocks traded on the Nasdaq. These indexes are useful indicators of small stock performance because many small stocks are traded on the Nasdaq.

Investor Participation in the Secondary Market

The market price of a stock is determined by investor trading on stock exchanges or in the over-the-counter market. The price of a firm's stock represents the market value of the firm per share of stock.

| ILLUSTRATION | Assume that Vector Company has a market value of $600 million. If it has 20 million shares of stock, it should have a stock price of |

$$\text{Stock price} = \frac{\text{Value of firm}}{\text{Number of shares}}$$

$$= \frac{\$600,000,000}{20,000,000 \text{ shares}}$$

$$= \$30 \text{ per share}$$

A stock price by itself does not clearly indicate the firm's value. Two firms could have the same share price, and yet one could be twice the value of the other if it has twice as many shares of stock.

Investors attempt to invest in the stocks of firms that will provide them with a high return on their investment and that exhibit a tolerable level of risk. The return on the investment to investors is determined by the dividends received and the price of the stock from the time when they purchased the shares until the time when they sell the shares.

How Investor Decisions Affect Stock Prices

Investors consider buying shares of a particular stock when their valuation of the stock exceeds the prevailing market price. Investors who are currently holding shares of a stock consider selling those shares when their valuation of the stock is below the prevailing market price. Investors agree that the firm's valuation should reflect its future performance. However, they do not always agree on how to estimate the firm's future performance, and they use different valuation models (as explained in Chapter 7). The difference in valuations among investors causes some investors to believe a stock is undervalued while others believe it is overvalued. This difference in opinions allows for market trading, because it means that there will be buyers and sellers of the same stock at a given point in time.

As investors change their valuations of a stock, there is a shift in the demand for shares or the supply of shares for sale, and the equilibrium price changes. When investors revise their expectations of a firm's performance upward, they revise their valuations upward. If the consensus among investors is a favorable revision of expected performance, there are more buy orders for the stock. Demand for shares exceeds the supply of shares for sale, placing upward pressure on the market price. Conversely, if the consensus among investors is lowered expectations of the firm's future performance, there are more sell orders for the stock. The supply of shares for sale exceeds the demand for shares, placing downward pressure on the market price. Overall, the prevailing market price is determined by the participation of investors in aggregate. Stock transactions between investors in the secondary market do not affect the capital structure of the issuer, but merely transfer shares from one investor to another.

Investor Reliance on Information Investors respond to the release of new information that affects their opinions about the firm's future performance. In general, favorable news about the performance of a firm will make investors believe that the firm's stock is undervalued at its prevailing price. The demand for shares of that stock will increase, placing upward pressure on the stock's price. Unfavorable news about the performance

EXHIBIT 6.7

How New Information
Affects the Equilibrium
Price of a Stock

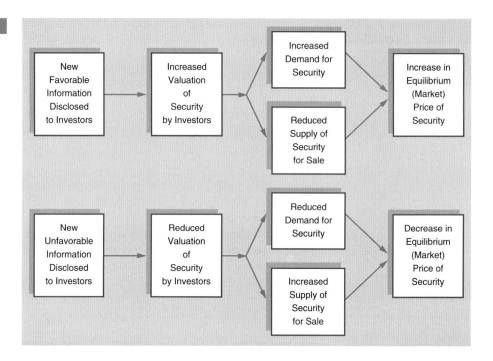

of a firm will make investors believe that the firm's stock is overvalued at its prevailing price. Some investors will sell their holdings of that stock, placing downward pressure on the stock's price.

Exhibit 6.7 illustrates how information is related to a firm's valuation and the equilibrium price of each stock. Information is incorporated into stock prices through its impact on investors' demand for shares and the supply of shares for sale by investors.

Each stock has its own demand and supply conditions and therefore has a unique market price. Nevertheless, new information about macroeconomic conditions commonly causes expectations for many firms to be revised in the same direction and therefore cause stock prices to move in the same direction.

Investors continually respond to new information in their attempt to purchase stocks that are undervalued or sell any of their stock holdings that are overvalued. When investors properly determine which stocks are undervalued, they can achieve abnormally high returns from investing in those stocks. Thus, the valuation process used by an investor can have a strong influence on the investor's investment performance.

Investor Types

As noted earlier, investors can be classified as individual or institutional. The investment by individuals in a large corporation commonly exceeds 50 percent of the total equity. Each individual's investment is typically small, however, causing the ownership to be scattered among numerous individual shareholders. Consequently, individual investors are unable to effectively monitor corporations or have substantial influence on management.

Institutional investors include all the financial institutions such as mutual funds, insurance companies, and pension funds. Since a financial institution typically takes a much larger equity position in a corporation, it has more voting power and is more ca-

Type of Financial Institution	Participation in Stock Markets
Commercial banks	• Issue stock to boost their capital base. • Manage trust funds that usually contain stocks.
Stock-owned savings institutions	• Issue stock to boost their capital base.
Savings banks	• Invest in stocks for their investment portfolios.
Finance companies	• Issue stock to boost their capital base.
Stock mutual funds	• Use the proceeds from selling shares to invest in stocks.
Securities firms	• Issue stock to boost their capital base. • Place new issues of stock. • Offer advice to corporations that consider acquiring the stock of other companies. • Execute buy and sell orders of investors.
Insurance companies	• Issue stock to boost their capital base. • Invest a large proportion of their premiums in the stock market.
Pension funds	• Invest a large proportion of pension fund contributions in the stock market.

pable of enacting changes in the management of a corporation. Institutional investors sometimes hold a large proportion of a corporation's stock and can influence corporate policies through proxy contests. In recent years, several firms have made significant concessions to their institutional investors, including adding major shareholders to their boards of directors. Pension funds, stock mutual funds, and insurance companies hold more than 40 percent of the value of all stocks.

Exhibit 6.8 summarizes the participation of various types of financial institutions in the stock market. Insurance companies, pension funds, and stock mutual funds are common purchasers of newly issued stock in the primary markets on a daily basis. These institutions also invest in stock that is being traded in the secondary market. The high volume of trading in the secondary stock market is attributed to institutional buying and selling. Thus, financial institutions increase the marketability of stocks by creating such an active secondary market.

Financial institutions not only participate in stock markets by investing funds, but sometimes issue their own stock as a means of raising funds. Many stock market transactions involve two financial institutions. For example, an insurance company may purchase the newly issued stock of a commercial bank. If the insurance company someday sells this stock in the secondary market, a mutual fund or pension fund may act as the purchaser.

Because some financial institutions hold large amounts of stock, their collective sales or purchases of stocks can significantly affect stock market prices. Institutional investors also have more resources to monitor a corporation, so corporations recognize that they must respond to advice or complaints by institutional investors in order to keep them as investors. Many institutional investors own millions of shares of a single firm and therefore are willing to spend time to ensure that managers serve the shareholders' interests. In addition, institutional investors are accustomed to assessing firms on a daily basis and have expertise in monitoring firms. Thus, they have more experience and resources than individual investors to monitor firms.

Investor Monitoring

Since the stock price is normally related to the firm's performance, the return to investors is dependent on how well the firm is managed. A firm's managers serve as agents for shareholders by making decisions that are supposed to maximize the stock's price. The separation of ownership (by shareholders) and control (by managers) can result in agency problems because of conflicting interests. Managers may be tempted to serve their own interests rather than those of the investors who own the firm's stock. Investors rely on the board of directors of each firm to ensure that its managers make decisions that enhance the firm's performance and maximize the stock price. Shareholders monitor their stock's price movements to assess whether the managers are achieving the goal of share price maximization. If the stock price is lower than expected, shareholders may attempt to take action to improve the management of the firm.

The easiest way for shareholders to monitor the firm is to monitor changes in its value (as measured by its share price) over time. Since the share price is continuously available, shareholders can quickly detect any abrupt changes in the value of the firm. The return to shareholders is directly influenced by changes in the stock's price over time. When the stock price declines or does not rise as high as shareholders expected, shareholders may blame the weak performance on the firm's managers.

Accounting Irregularities

Investors commonly rely on financial statements reported by a firm as a means of monitoring the firm. Yet, to the extent that firms can manipulate the financial statements, they may be able to hide information from investors. In recent years, many firms (including Enron, Tyco, and WorldCom) used unusual accounting methods to create their financial statements. As a result, it was very difficult for investors to ascertain the true financial condition of these firms and therefore to monitor them. The problem was compounded because the auditors hired to audit the financial statements of some firms allowed them to use these irregular accounting methods. A subset of a firm's board members serve on an audit committee, which is supposed to ensure that the audit is done properly, but in some firms, the committee failed to monitor the auditors. Overall, investors' monitoring of some firms was limited because the accountants distorted the financial statements, the auditors did not properly audit, and the audit committees of those firms did not oversee the audit properly.

Sarbanes-Oxley Act

The Sarbanes-Oxley Act was enacted in 2002 to ensure more accurate disclosure of financial information to investors. The act attempts to force accountants to conform to regular accounting standards in preparing a firm's financial statements and to force auditors to take their auditing role seriously. In particular, the act does the following:

- Prevents a public accounting firm from auditing a client firm whose chief executive officer (CEO), chief financial officer (CFO), or other employees with similar job descriptions were employed by the accounting firm within one year prior to the audit. This provision maintains some distance between the audit firm and the client.
- Requires that only outside board members of a firm be on the firm's audit committee, which is responsible for making sure that the audit is conducted in an unbiased

manner. Outside board members are more likely to serve the interests of existing and prospective shareholders than inside board members who are part of the firm's management.

- Prevents the members of a firm's audit committee from receiving consulting or advising fees or other compensation from the firm beyond that earned from serving on the board. This provision prevents a firm from providing excessive compensation to the members of an audit committee as a means of paying them off so that they do not closely oversee the audit.

- Requires that the CEO and CFO of firms that are of at least a specified size certify that the audited financial statements are accurate. This provision forces the CFO and CEO to be accountable.

- Specifies major fines or imprisonment for employees who mislead investors or hide evidence. This provision attempts to ensure that a firm's employees will be penalized for their role in distorting the accounting statements.

- Allows public accounting firms to offer nonaudit consulting services to an audit client only if the client's audit committee pre-approves the nonaudit services to be rendered before the audit begins. This provision attempts to ensure that a firm does not pay off an auditor with extra fees for consulting services in return for the auditor's certification that the firm's financial statements are accurate.

The act prevents some forms of accounting abuses by publicly traded firms and should improve the ability of existing and prospective shareholders to monitor these firms. For many firms, however, the cost of adhering to the guidelines of the Sarbanes-Oxley Act will exceed $1 million per year. Consequently, many small publicly traded firms decided to revert back to private ownership as a result of the act. These firms perceived that they would have a higher value if they were private rather than publicly held because they could avoid the substantial reporting costs that are required of publicly traded firms.

Shareholder Activism

If shareholders are displeased with the way managers are managing a firm, they have three general choices. The first is to do nothing and retain the shares in the hope that management's actions will ultimately lead to strong stock price performance. A second choice is to sell the stock. This choice is common among shareholders who do not believe that they can change the firm's management or do not wish to spend the time and money needed to bring about change. A third choice is to engage in shareholder activism. Some of the more common types of shareholder activism are examined here.

Communication with the Firm Shareholders can communicate their concerns to other investors in an effort to place more pressure on the firm's managers or its board members. For example, shareholders may voice concerns about a firm that expands outside its core businesses, attempts to acquire other companies at excessive prices, or defends against a takeover that the shareholders believe would be beneficial.

Institutional investors commonly communicate with high-level corporate managers and have opportunities to offer their concerns about the firm's operations. The managers may be willing to consider the changes suggested by large institutional investors because they do not want those investors to sell their holdings of the firm's stock.

Some institutional investors have become much more involved in monitoring management, as they have realized that they can enhance the value of their security portfolios

by ensuring that the firms in which they invest are properly managed. An institutional investor such as a pension fund, a life insurance company, or a mutual fund that holds a substantial amount of a corporation's stock may request a seat on the corporation's board of directors. Alternatively, the investor may request that the corporation at least replace one of the executives on the board with an outside investor to ensure that the board makes decisions to satisfy shareholders. The hope is that any changes suggested by shareholders result in stronger performance and a higher stock price for the firm.

ILLUSTRATION   The California Public Employees' Retirement System (CALPERS) manages the pensions for employees of the state of California. It manages more than $80 billion of securities and commonly maintains large stock positions in some firms. When CALPERS believes that these firms are not being managed properly, it communicates its concerns and sometimes proposes solutions. Some of the firms adjust their management to accommodate CALPERS.

CALPERS periodically announces a list of firms that it believes have serious agency problems. These firms may have been unwilling to respond to CALPERS's concerns about their management style.

Firms are especially responsive when institutional investors communicate as a team. Institutional Shareholder Services (ISS) Inc. is a firm that organizes institutional shareholders to push for a common cause. After receiving feedback from institutional investors about a particular firm, ISS organizes a conference call with high-ranking executives of the firm so that it can obtain information from the firm. It then announces the time of the conference call to investors and allows them to listen in on the call. The questions focus on institutional shareholders' concerns about the firm's management. Unlike earnings conference calls, which are controlled by firms, ISS runs the conference call. Common questions asked by ISS include:

- Why is your CEO also the chair of the board?
- Why is your executive compensation much higher than the industry norm?
- What is your process for nominating new board members?

Transcripts of the conference calls are available within 48 hours after the call.

Proxy Contest Shareholders may also engage in proxy contests in an attempt to change the composition of the board. This is a more formal effort than communicating with the firm and is normally considered only if an informal request for a change in the board (through communication with the board) is ignored. A change in the board may be beneficial if it forces the board to make decisions that are more focused on maximizing the stock price. If the dissident shareholders gain enough votes, they can elect one or more directors who share their views. In this case, shareholders are truly exercising their control.

ILLUSTRATION   As a classic example of the influence of a proxy, the directors of UAL were forced to sell the parent company of United Airlines to its employees. If they had not agreed to this, they could have been replaced through a proxy campaign led by Coniston Partners of New York, which owned about 12 percent of UAL. Even when managers win a proxy contest, they usually leave a company within three years after the contest.

The ISS may recommend that shareholders vote a certain way on specific proxy issues. As a result of these more organized efforts, institutional shareholders are becom-

ing more influential on management decisions. At some firms, they have succeeded in implementing changes that can enhance shareholder value, such as:

- Limiting severance pay for executives who are fired.
- Revising the voting guidelines on the firm's executive compensation policy.
- Requiring more transparent reporting of financial information.
- Imposing ceilings on the CEO's salary and bonus.
- Removing bylaws that prevented takeovers by other firms.
- Allowing for an annual election of all directors so that ineffective directors can be quickly removed from the board.

Shareholder Lawsuits Investors may sue the board if they believe that the directors are not fulfilling their responsibilities to shareholders. This action is intended to force the board to make decisions that are aligned with shareholders' interests. Many lawsuits have been filed when corporations prevent takeovers, pursue acquisitions, or make other restructuring decisions that some shareholders believe will reduce the stock's value.

A firm's board of directors is responsible for supervising the business and affairs of a corporation. The board attempts to ensure that the business is managed in a way that serves the shareholders. Directors also have the responsibility of monitoring operations and ensuring that the firm complies with the laws. They cannot oversee every workplace decision, but they can ensure that the firm has a process that can guide some decisions about moral and ethical conduct. They can also ensure that the firm has a system for internal control and reporting. At some firms, the boards have been negligent in representing the shareholders. Nevertheless, since business performance is subject to uncertainty, directors cannot be held responsible every time a key business decision has an unsatisfactory outcome. When directors are sued, the court system typically focuses on whether the directors' decisions were reasonable, rather than on whether they increased the firm's profitability. Thus, from the court's perspective, the directors' decision-making process is more relevant than the outcome.

The Corporate Monitoring Role

The firm's managers frequently compare the prevailing market valuation (as measured by the price) of their firm's stock to their own valuation of that stock. If they believe that stock is undervalued in the market, they may take actions to capitalize on this discrepancy.

Stock Repurchases

The notion of asymmetric information means that a firm's managers have information about the firm's future prospects that is not known by the firm's investors. When corporate managers believe that their firm is undervalued, they can use the firm's excess cash to purchase a portion of their shares in the market at a relatively low price based on their valuation of what the shares are really worth. For example, several firms repurchased shares just after the October 1987 stock market crash, apparently believing that the postcrash prices were too low. Several firms also repurchased some of their shares in the 2001–2002 period, when share prices were at very low levels.

Stock repurchases are common even when the stock market is performing well, as long as firms believe that their stock is undervalued. In 2004 (when stock prices were already high), many U.S. firms announced plans to repurchase stock.

In general, studies have found that stock prices respond favorably to stock repurchase announcements, which implies that the announcement signals management's perception that the share price is undervalued. The market responds favorably to this signal.

Reebok International Ltd. announced that it would repurchase one-third of its stock (24 million shares) at an expected cost of about $864 million. Consequently, Reebok would use a higher proportion of debt to finance its business operations. Reebok's stock price immediately increased by 11 percent in response to the stock repurchase announcement.

Although many stock repurchase plans are viewed as a favorable signal, investors may question why the firm does not use its funds to expand its business instead of buying back its stock. Thus, investors' response to a stock repurchase plan varies with the firm's characteristics.

Market for Corporate Control

When corporate managers notice that another firm in the same industry has a low stock price as a result of poor management, they may attempt to acquire that firm. They hope to purchase the business at a low price and improve its management so that they can increase the value of the business. In addition, the combination of the two firms may reduce redundancy in some operations and allow for synergistic benefits. In this way, the managers of the acquiring firm may earn a higher return than if they used their funds for some other type of expansion. In essence, weak businesses are subject to a takeover by more efficient corporations and are therefore subject to the "market for corporate control." Thus, if a firm's stock price is relatively low because of poor performance, it may become an attractive target for other corporations.

A firm may especially benefit from acquisitions when its own stock price has risen. It can use its stock as currency to acquire the shares of a target by exchanging some of its own shares for the target's shares. Some critics claim that acquisitions of inefficient firms typically lead to layoffs and are unfair to employees. The counter to this argument is that without the market for corporate control, firms would be allowed to be inefficient, which is unfair to the shareholders who invested in them. Managers recognize that if their poorly performing business is taken over, they may lose their jobs. Thus, the market for corporate control can encourage managers to make decisions that maximize the stock's value so that they can discourage takeovers.

In general, studies have found that the share prices of target firms react very positively, but that the share prices of acquiring firms are not favorably affected. Investors may not expect the acquiring firm to achieve its objectives. For example, there is some evidence that firms engaging in acquisitions do not eliminate inefficient operations after the acquisitions, perhaps because of the potential low morale that results from layoffs.

Leveraged Buyouts The market for corporate control is enhanced by the use of leveraged buyouts (LBOs), which are acquisitions that require substantial amounts of borrowed funds. That is, the acquisition requires a substantial amount of financial leverage. Some so-called buyout firms identify poorly managed firms, acquire them (mostly with the use of borrowed funds), improve their management, and then sell them at a higher price than they paid. Alternatively, a group of managers who work for the firm may believe that they can restructure the firm's operations to improve cash flows. The managers may attempt an LBO in the hope that they can improve the firm's performance.

The use of debt to retire a company's stock creates a very highly leveraged capital structure. One favorable aspect of such a revised capital structure is that the ownership of the firm is normally reduced to a small group of people, who may be managers of the firm. Thus, agency costs should be reduced when managers act in their own interests instead of the firm's. A major concern about LBOs, however, is that the firm will experience cash flow problems over time because of the high periodic debt payments that result from the high degree of financial leverage. A firm financed in this way has a high potential return but is risky.

Some firms that engage in LBOs issue new stock after improving the firm's performance. This process is referred to as a reverse leveraged buyout (reverse LBO). Whereas an LBO may be used to purchase all the stock of a firm that has not achieved its potential performance (causing its stock to be priced low), a reverse LBO is normally desirable when the stock can be sold at a high price. In essence, the owners hope to issue new stock at a much higher price than they paid when enacting the LBO. The volume of reverse LBOs was relatively low in the late 1980s, when stock prices were low shortly after the 1987 stock market crash. The volume increased during the bullish stock market in the late 1990s, however.

Barriers to Corporate Control

The power of corporate control to eliminate agency problems is limited due to barriers that can make it more costly for a potential acquiring firm to acquire another firm whose managers are not serving the firm's shareholders. Some of the more common barriers to corporate control are identified next.

Antitakeover Amendments Some firms have added **antitakeover amendments** to their corporate charter. There are various types of antitakeover amendments. For example, an amendment may require that at least two-thirds of the shareholder votes approve a takeover before the firm can be acquired. Antitakeover amendments are supposed to be enacted to protect shareholders against an acquisition that will ultimately reduce the value of their investment in the firm. However, it may be argued that shareholders are adversely affected by antitakeover amendments.

Poison Pills **Poison pills** are special rights awarded to shareholders or specific managers upon specified events. They can be enacted by a firm's board of directors without the approval of shareholders. Sometimes a target enacts a poison pill to defend against takeover attempts. For example, a poison pill might give all shareholders the right to be allocated an additional 30 percent of shares (based on their existing share holdings) without cost whenever a potential acquirer attempts to acquire the firm. The poison pill makes it more expensive and more difficult for a potential acquiring firm to acquire the target.

Golden Parachutes A **golden parachute** specifies compensation to managers in the event that they lose their jobs or there is a change in the control of the firm. For example, all managers might have the right to receive 100,000 shares of the firm's stock whenever the firm is acquired. It can be argued that a golden parachute provides managers with security so that they can make decisions that will improve the long-term performance of the firm. That is, managers protected by a golden parachute may be more willing to make decisions that enhance shareholder wealth over the long run even though the decisions adversely affect the stock price in the short run. The counterargument, however, is that a golden parachute allows managers to serve their own interests, rather than shareholder interests, because they receive large compensation even if they are fired.

Golden parachutes can discourage takeover attempts by increasing the cost of the acquisition. A potential acquiring firm recognizes that it will incur the expense associated with the golden parachutes if it acquires a particular target that has enacted golden parachutes prior to the takeover attempt. To the extent that this (or any) defense against takeovers is effective, it disrupts the market for corporate control by allowing managers of some firms to be protected while serving their own interests rather than shareholder interests.

Stock Market Globalization

 GL BALASPECTS   Stock markets are becoming globalized in the sense that barriers between countries have been removed or reduced. Thus, firms in need of funds can tap foreign markets, and investors can purchase foreign stocks. In recent years, many firms have obtained funds from foreign markets through international stock offerings. This strategy may represent an effort by a firm to enhance its global image. Alternatively, because the issuing firm is tapping a larger pool of potential investors, it may more easily place the entire issue of new stock.

Foreign Stock Offerings in the United States

Many of the recent stock offerings in the United States by non-U.S. firms have resulted from privatization programs in Latin America and Europe, whereby businesses that were previously government owned are sold to U.S. shareholders. Some of these businesses are so large that the local stock markets cannot digest the stock offerings. Consequently, U.S. investors are financing many privatized businesses based in foreign countries.

When a non-U.S. firm issues stock in its own country, its shareholder base is quite limited because a few large institutional investors may own most of the shares. By issuing stock in the United States, the firm diversifies its shareholder base; such diversification can reduce share price volatility when large investors sell shares.

Although some large non-U.S. firms have developed a market for their stock in the United States, others are unwilling to do so because of SEC regulations. The SEC requires that any firms desiring to list their stock on a U.S. stock exchange must provide financial statements that satisfy U.S. accounting standards and are compatible with the financial statements of U.S. firms. Non-U.S. firms can avoid the expense of providing these statements if they choose not to list on U.S. exchanges.

Some non-U.S. firms obtain equity financing by using American depository receipts (ADRs), which are certificates representing bundles of stock. The use of ADRs circumvents some disclosure requirements imposed on stock offerings in the United States, yet enables non-U.S. firms to tap the U.S. market for funds. The ADR market grew after businesses were privatized in the early 1990s because some of them issued ADRs to obtain financing.

International Placement Process

Investment banks facilitate the international placement of new stock through one or more syndicates across countries. Many investment banks and commercial banks based in the United States provide underwriting and other investment banking services in foreign countries.

The ability of investment banks to place new shares in foreign markets is somewhat dependent on the stock's perceived liquidity in those markets. A secondary market for the stock must be established in foreign markets to enhance liquidity and make newly issued stocks more attractive. Listing stock on a foreign stock exchange not only enhances the stock's liquidity but may also increase the firm's perceived financial standing when the exchange approves the listing application. Listing on foreign stock exchanges can also protect a firm against hostile takeovers because it disperses ownership and makes it more difficult for other firms to gain a controlling interest. Listing on a foreign stock exchange entails some costs, such as expenses for converting financial data in an annual report into a foreign currency and making financial statements compatible with the accounting standards used in that country.

Global Stock Exchanges

A summary of the world's major stock markets is provided in Exhibit 6.9. Numerous other exchanges also exist. In the past, the growth of many foreign stock markets was limited because their firms relied more on debt financing than equity financing. Recently, however, firms outside the United States have been issuing stock more frequently, which has allowed for substantial growth of non-U.S. stock markets. The percentage of individual versus institutional ownership of shares varies across stock markets. Financial institutions and other firms own a large proportion of the shares outside the United States, and individual investors own a relatively small proportion.

Euronext In 2000, the Amsterdam, Brussels, and Paris stock exchanges merged to create the Euronext market. Since then, the Lisbon stock exchange has joined Euronext as well. The Euronext market has about 1,500 firms listed, and about 300 of those firms

EXHIBIT 6.9 Stock Exchanges Around the World

Country	Stock Market Capitalization (in millions of $)	Country	Stock Market Capitalization (in millions of $)	Country	Stock Market Capitalization (in millions of $)
Argentina	$ 192,499	Ireland	$ 81,882	Philippines	$ 41,523
Australia	372,974	Israel	55,964	Poland	26,017
Austria	29,935	Italy	768,364	Portugal	60,681
Belgium	182,481	Japan	3,157,222	South Africa	139,750
Brazil	186,238	Luxembourg	34,016	Spain	504,219
Chile	56,310	Malaysia	120,007	Sweden	328,339
Finland	293,635	Mexico	121,403	Switzerland	792,316
France	1,146,634	Netherlands	640,456	Thailand	36,340
Germany	1,270,243	New Zealand	18,613	Turkey	47,150
Greece	86,538	Nigeria	5,404	United Kingdom	2,576,992
Hungary	10,637	Norway	65,034	United States	15,104,037
India	110,396	Pakistan	4,944	Yugoslavia	10,817
Indonesia	23,006	Peru	11,134	Zimbabwe	7,972

Source: World Development Indicators, 2002, International Bank for Reconstruction and Development.

Biggest Movers

The Wall Street Journal provides a summary of world-wide industry performance under the heading "DJ Global Groups Biggest Movers." It lists the leading industries that performed very well in stock markets around the world during the previous trading day, along with a summary of the performance of some firms in each industry. It also identifies the lagging global industries that performed very poorly during the previous trading day, along with a summary of the performance of some key firms in each industry. Another section, "Dow Jones Global Sectors," provides a summary of the performance of key global sectors, such as automobiles, banks, energy, and technology.

are from other countries. Most of the largest firms based in Europe have listed their stock on the Euronext market. This market is likely to grow over time as other stock exchanges may join this market as well. A single European stock market would make it easier for investors who may want to do all of their trading in one market, which has similar guidelines for all stocks regardless of their home country. At this point, the guidelines have not been completely standardized across the stocks listed.

Emerging Stock Markets

Emerging markets enable foreign firms to raise large amounts of capital by issuing stock. These markets also provide a means for investors from the United States and other countries to invest their funds.

Some emerging stock markets are relatively new and small and may not be as efficient as the U.S. stock market. Thus, some stocks may be undervalued, a possibility that has attracted investors to these markets. Because some of these markets are small, however, they may be susceptible to manipulation by large traders. Furthermore, insider trading is more prevalent in many foreign markets because rules against it are not enforced. In general, large institutional investors and insiders based in the foreign markets may have some advantages.

Although international stocks can generate high returns, they also may exhibit high risk. Some of the emerging stock markets are often referred to as casinos because of the wild gyrations in gains and losses the panic trading that occurs.

The emerging markets experience large price swings because of two characteristics. First, the small number of shares for some firms allows large trades to jolt the equilibrium price. Second, valid financial information about firms is sometimes lacking, causing investors to trade according to rumors. Trading patterns based on continual rumors are more volatile than trading patterns based on factual data.

Methods Used to Invest in Foreign Stocks

Investors can obtain foreign stocks by purchasing shares directly, purchasing American depository receipts (ADRs), investing in international mutual funds, and purchasing world equity benchmark shares (WEBS). Each of these methods is explained in turn.

Direct Purchases Investors can easily invest in stocks of foreign companies that are listed on the local stock exchanges. However, this set of stocks is quite limited. Foreign

stocks not listed on local stock exchanges can be purchased through some full-service brokerage firms that have offices in foreign countries, but the transaction costs incurred from purchasing foreign stocks in this manner are high.

American Depository Receipts An alternative means of investing in foreign stocks is by purchasing ADRs, which are attractive to U.S. investors for the following reasons. First, they are closely followed by U.S. investment analysts. Second, companies represented by ADRs are required by the SEC to file financial statements consistent with the generally accepted accounting principles in the United States. These statements may not be available for other non-U.S. companies. Third, reliable quotes on ADR prices are consistently available, with existing currency values factored in to translate the price into dollars. A disadvantage, however, is that the selection of ADRs is limited. Also, the ADR market is less active than other stock markets, so ADRs are less liquid than most listed U.S. stocks.

International Mutual Funds Another way to invest in foreign stocks is to purchase shares of international mutual funds (IMFs), which are portfolios of international stocks created and managed by various financial institutions. Thus, individuals can diversify across international stocks by investing in a single IMF. Some IMFs focus on a specific foreign country, while others contain stocks across several countries or even several continents.

http://

http://finance.yahoo.com/?u
Quotations on various stock market indexes around the world.

World Equity Benchmark Shares Although investors have closely monitored international stock indexes for years, they were typically unable to invest directly in these indexes. The index was not traded, but was simply a measure of performance for a set of stocks. World equity benchmark shares (WEBS) represent indexes that reflect composites of stocks for particular countries. They are also commonly referred to as iShares. The shares of the index can be purchased or sold, thereby allowing investors to invest directly in a stock index representing any one of several countries. For example, investors who wish to invest in an index representing Mexico's stock market can purchase WEBS.

SUMMARY

- An initial public offering (IPO) is a first-time offering of shares by a specific firm to the public. Many firms engage in an IPO when they have feasible business expansion plans, but are already near their debt capacity. A firm that engages in an IPO must develop a prospectus that is filed with the SEC and does a road show to promote its offering. It hires an underwriter to help with the prospectus and road show and to place the shares with investors.

- A secondary stock offering is an offering of shares by a firm that already has publicly traded stock. Firms engage in secondary offerings when they need more equity funding to support additional expansion.

- Stock markets facilitate the transfer of stock ownership between investors. The trading of a stock in the stock market determines its equilibrium price.

- Investors are commonly classified as individual or institutional. The proportion of a firm's shares held by any individual investor tends to be small, which limits the ability of an individual investor to influence the firm's management. Institutional investors have larger equity positions and therefore are more capable of influencing the firm's management. Stock mutual funds, pension funds, and insurance companies are the major institutional investors in the stock market. Securities firms serve as brokers by matching up buyers and sellers in the stock market.

- Corporations sometimes serve as investors when they believe that their own business or another business is undervalued. If they believe their own business is undervalued, they can repurchase shares of stock in the secondary market at a relatively low

price. If they believe that another poorly performing business is undervalued, they may consider acquiring the shares of that business and then reorganizing the business (replacing managers) to improve its value. This makes poorly performing businesses subject to the market for corporate control.

■ Many U.S. firms issue shares in foreign countries, as well as in the United States, so that they can spread their shares among a larger set of investors. In a similar manner, many non-U.S. firms not only issue shares in their own markets but also tap the U.S. market for funds. This strategy not only enlarges the investor base, but also may enhance the global name recognition of a firm.

Global stock exchanges exist to facilitate the trading of stocks around the world. U.S. investors invest in foreign stocks by direct purchases on foreign stock exchanges, by purchasing ADRs, by investing in mutual funds, and by investing in world equity benchmark shares.

POINT COUNTER-POINT

Should a Stock Exchange Enforce Some Governance Standards on the Firms Listed on the Exchange?

Point No. Governance is the responsibility of the firms, and not the stock exchange. The stock exchange should simply ensure that the trading rules of the exchange are enforced and should not intervene in the firms' governance issues.

Counter-Point Yes. When a stock exchange enforces governance standards such as requiring a firm to have a majority of outside members on its board of directors, it can enhance the credibility of the exchange.

Who Is Correct? Use your favorite search engine to learn more about this issue. Offer your own opinion on this issue.

QUESTIONS AND APPLICATIONS

1. **ADRs** Explain how ADRs enable U.S. investors to become part owners of foreign companies.

2. **Shareholder Rights** Explain the rights of common stockholders that are not available to other individuals.

3. **Managing in Financial Markets: Investing in an IPO**
   a. As a portfolio manager of a financial institution, you are invited to numerous road shows in which firms that are going public promote themselves and the lead underwriter invites you to invest in the IPO. Beyond any specific information about the firm, what other information would you need to decide whether to invest in the upcoming IPO?

4. **Lockups** Describe a lockup provision and explain why it is required by the lead underwriter.

5. **Impact of Accounting Irregularities** How do you think accounting irregularities affect the pricing of corpo-

rate stock in general? From an investor's viewpoint, how do you think the information used to price stocks changes given that accounting irregularities exist?

6. **Stock Offerings** What is the danger of issuing too much stock? What is the role of the investment bank that serves as the underwriter, and how can it ensure that the firm does not issue too much stock?

7. **Interpreting Financial News** Interpret the following statements made by Wall Street analysts and portfolio managers:
   a. "The recent wave of IPOs is an attempt by many small firms to capitalize on the recent runup in stock prices."
   b. "IPOs transfer wealth from unsophisticated investors to large institutional investors who get in at the offer price and get out quickly."

c. "Firms must be more accountable to the market when making decisions because they are subject to indirect control by institutional investors."

8. **Stock Repurchases** Explain why the stock price of a firm may rise when the firm announces that it is repurchasing its shares.

9. **IPOs** Why do firms engage in IPOs? What is the amount of fees that the lead underwriter and its syndicate charge a firm that is going public? Why are there many IPOs in some periods and few IPOs in other periods?

10. **Role of Organized Exchanges** Are organized stock exchanges used to place newly issued stock? Explain.

11. **Venture Capital** Explain the difference between obtaining funds from a venture capital firm and engaging in an IPO. Explain how the IPO may serve as a means by which the venture capital firm can cash out.

12. **Internet Exercise** Go to http://ipoportal.edgar-online.com/ipo/home.asp. Review an IPO that is scheduled for the near future. Review the deal information about this IPO.
a. What is the offer amount? How much are total expenses? How much are total expenses as a percentage of the deal amount? How many shares are issued? How long is the lockup period? Review some additional IPOs that are scheduled. What is the range for the offer amount? What is the range for the lockup period length?

13. **Impact of Sarbanes-Oxley Act** Briefly describe the provisions of the Sarbanes-Oxley Act. Discuss how this act will affect monitoring by shareholders.

14. **Prospectus and Road Show** Explain the use of a prospectus developed before an IPO. Why does a firm do a road show before its IPO? What factors influence the offer price of stock at the time of the IPO?

15. **Corporate Control** Describe how the interaction between buyers and sellers affects the market value of a firm, and explain how that can subject a firm to the market for corporate control.

16. **Bookbuilding** Describe the process of bookbuilding. Why is bookbuilding sometimes criticized as a means of setting the offer price?

17. **Asymmetric Information** Discuss the concept of asymmetric information and explain how it may cause corporate managers to serve as investors.

18. **Initial Return** What is the meaning of an initial return for an IPO? Were initial returns of Internet IPOs in the late 1990s higher or lower than normal? Why?

19. **NYSE** Explain why stocks traded on the NYSE exhibit lower risk than stocks that are traded on other exchanges.

20. **Flipping** What is the meaning of "flipping" shares? Why would investors want to flip shares?

21. **Role of IMFs** How have international mutual funds (IMFs) increased the international integration of capital markets among countries?

22. **Performance of IPOs** How do IPOs perform over the long run?

23. **Spinning and Laddering** Describe spinning and laddering in the IPO market. How do you think these actions influence the price of a newly issued stock? Who is adversely affected as a result of these actions?

PROBLEM

1. **Dividend Yield** Over the last year, Calzone Corporation paid a quarterly dividend of $0.10 in each of the four quarters. The current stock price of Calzone Corporation is $39.78. What is the dividend yield for Calzone stock?

FLOW OF FUNDS EXERCISE

Contemplating an Initial Public Offering (IPO)

Recall that if the economy continues to be strong, Carson Company may need to increase its production capacity by about 50 percent over the next few years to satisfy demand. It would need financing to expand and accommodate the increase in production. Recall that the yield curve is currently upward sloping. Also recall that Carson is concerned about a possible slowing of the economy because of potential Fed actions to reduce inflation. It is also considering the issuance of stock or bonds to raise funds in the next year.

a. If Carson issued stock now, it would have the flexibility to obtain more debt and would also be able to reduce its cost of financing with debt. Why?

b. Why would an IPO result in heightened concerns in financial markets about Carson Company's potential agency problems?

c. Explain why institutional investors such as mutual funds and pension funds that invest in stock for long-term periods (at least a year or two) may be more interested in investing in some IPOs than they are in purchasing other stocks that have been publicly traded for several years.

d. Given that institutional investors such as insurance companies, pension funds, and mutual funds are the major investors in IPOs, explain the flow of funds that results from an IPO. That is, what is the original source of the money that is channeled through the institutional investors and provided to the firm going public?

WSJ EXERCISE

Assessing Stock Market Movements

Review the section "Abreast of the Market" in a recent issue of *The Wall Street Journal.* Indicate whether the market prices increased or decreased, and explain what caused the market's movement.

CHAPTER 7

Valuing Stocks and Assessing Risk

S ince the values of stocks change continuously, so do stock prices. Institutional and individual investors constantly value stocks so that they can capitalize on expected changes in stock prices.

The specific objectives of this chapter are to:

■ explain methods of valuing stocks and determining the required rate of return on stocks,

■ identify the factors that affect stock prices,

■ explain how analysts affect stock prices,

■ explain how to measure the risk of stocks, and

■ explain the concept of stock market efficiency.

Stock Valuation Methods

Investors conduct valuations of stocks when making their investment decisions. They consider investing in undervalued stocks and selling their holdings of stocks that they consider to be overvalued. Common methods for valuing stocks include the price-earnings (PE) method and the dividend discount model, which are described next.

http://
http://www.bloomberg.com
Click on "Earnings Center."
Earnings forecasts for
various firms.

Price-Earnings (PE) Method

A relatively simple method of valuing a stock is to apply the mean price-earnings (PE) ratio (based on expected rather than recent earnings) of all publicly traded competitors in the respective industry to the firm's expected earnings for the next year.

ILLUSTRATION Consider a firm that is expected to generate earnings of $3 per share next year. If the mean ratio of share price to expected earnings of competitors in the same industry is 15, then the valuation of the firm's shares is:

$$\text{Valuation per share} = (\text{Expected earnings of firm per share}) \times (\text{Mean industry PE ratio})$$

$$= \$3 \times 15$$

$$= \$45$$

The logic of this method is that future earnings are an important determinant of a firm's value. Although earnings beyond the next year are also relevant, this method im-

plicitly assumes that the growth in earnings in future years will be similar to that of the industry.

Reasons for Different Valuations This method has several variations, which can result in different valuations. For example, investors may use different forecasts for the firm's earnings or the mean industry earnings over the next year. The previous year's earnings are often used as a base for forecasting future earnings, but the recent year's earnings do not always provide an accurate forecast of the future.

A second reason for different valuations when using the PE method is that investors disagree on the proper measure of earnings. Some investors prefer to use operating earnings or exclude some unusually high expenses that result from onetime events. A third reason is that investors may disagree on which firms represent the industry norm. Some investors use a narrow industry composite composed of firms that are very similar (in terms of size, lines of business, etc.) to the firm being valued; other investors prefer a broad industry composite. Consequently, even if investors agree on a firm's forecasted earnings, they may still derive different values for that firm as a result of applying different PE ratios. Furthermore, even if investors agree on the firms to include in the industry composite, they may disagree on how to weight each firm.

Limitations of the PE Method The PE method may result in an inaccurate valuation for a firm if errors are made in forecasting the firm's future earnings or in choosing the industry composite used to derive the PE ratio. In addition, some question whether an investor should trust a PE ratio, regardless of how it is derived. In 1994, the mean PE ratio for a composite of 500 large firms was 14. By 1998, the mean PE ratio for this same group of firms was 28, which implies that the valuation for a given level of earnings had doubled. Some investors may interpret such increases in PE ratios as a sign of irrational optimism in the stock market.

Dividend Discount Model

One of the first models used for pricing stocks was developed by John B. Williams in 1931. This model is still applicable today. Williams stated that the price of a stock should reflect the present value of the stock's future dividends, or

$$\text{Price} = \sum_{t=1}^{\infty} \frac{D_t}{(1 + k)^t}$$

where

$$t = \text{period}$$

$$D_t = \text{dividend in period } t$$

$$k = \text{discount rate}$$

The model can account for uncertainty by allowing D_t to be revised in response to revised expectations about a firm's cash flows, or by allowing k to be revised in response to changes in the required rate of return by investors.

ILLUSTRATION   To illustrate how the dividend discount model can be used to value a stock, consider a stock that is expected to pay a dividend of $7 per share per year forever. This constant dividend represents a perpetuity, or an annuity that lasts forever. The present value of the cash flows (dividend payments) to investors in this example is the present

value of a perpetuity. Assuming that the required rate of return (k) on the stock of concern is 14 percent, the present value (PV) of the future dividends is

$$PV \text{ of stock} = D/k$$
$$= \$7/.14$$
$$= \$50 \text{ per share}$$

Unfortunately, the valuation of most stocks is not this simple because their dividends are not expected to remain constant forever. If the dividend is expected to grow at a constant rate, however, the stock can be valued by applying the constant-growth dividend discount model:

$$PV \text{ of stock} = D_1/(k - g)$$

where D_1 is the expected dividend per share to be paid over the next year, k is the required rate of return by investors, and g is the rate at which dividends are expected to grow. For example, if a stock is expected to provide a dividend of $7 per share next year, the dividend is expected to increase by 4 percent per year, and the required rate of return is 14 percent, the stock can be valued as

$$PV \text{ of stock} = \$7/(.14 - .04)$$
$$= \$70 \text{ per share}$$

Relationship between Dividend Discount Model and PE Ratio for Valuing Firms

The dividend discount model and the PE ratio may seem to be unrelated, since the dividend discount model is highly dependent on the required rate of return and the growth rate, whereas the PE ratio is driven by the mean multiple of competitors' stock prices relative to their earnings expectations, along with the earnings expectations of the firm being valued. Yet, the PE multiple is influenced by the required rate of return on stocks of competitors and the expected growth rate of competitor firms. When using the PE ratio for valuation, the investor implicitly assumes that the required rate of return and the growth rate for the firm being valued are similar to those of its competitors. When the required rate of return on competitor firms is relatively high, the PE multiple will be relatively low, which results in a relatively low valuation of the firm for its level of expected earnings. When the competitors' growth rate is relatively high, the PE multiple will be relatively high, which results in a relatively high valuation of the firm for its level of expected earnings. Thus, the inverse relationship between required rate of return and value exists when applying either the PE ratio or the dividend discount model. In addition, there is a positive relationship between a firm's growth rate and its value when applying either method.

Limitations of the Dividend Discount Model

The dividend discount model may result in an inaccurate valuation of a firm if errors are made in determining the dividend to be paid over the next year, or the growth rate, or the required rate of return by investors. The limitations of this model are more pronounced when valuing firms that retain most of their earnings, rather than distribute them as dividends, because the model relies on the dividend as the base for applying the growth rate. For example, many Internet-related stocks retain any earnings to support growth and thus are not expected to pay any dividends.

Adjusted Dividend Discount Model

The dividend discount model can be adapted to assess the value of any firm, even those that retain most or all of their earnings. From the investor's perspective, the value of the stock is (1) the present value of the future dividends to be received over the investment horizon, plus (2) the present value of the forecasted price at which the stock will be sold at the end of the investment horizon. To forecast the price at which the stock can be sold, investors must estimate the firm's earnings per share (after removing any nonrecurring effects) in the year that they plan to sell the stock. This estimate is derived by applying an annual growth rate to the prevailing annual earnings per share. Then, the estimate can be used to derive the expected price per share at which the stock can be sold.

ILLUSTRATION   Assume that a firm currently has earnings of $12 per share. Future earnings can be forecasted by applying the expected annual growth rate to the firm's existing earnings (E):

$$\text{Forecasted earnings in } n \text{ years} = E(1 + G)^n$$

where G is the expected growth rate of earnings and n is the number of years until the stock is to be sold.

If investors expect that the earnings per share will grow by 2 percent per year and expect to sell the firm's stock in three years, the earnings per share in three years are forecasted to be

$$\text{Earnings in three years} = \$12 \times (1 + .02)^3$$
$$= \$12 \times 1.0612$$
$$= \$12.73$$

The forecasted earnings per share can be multiplied by the PE ratio of the firm's industry to forecast the future stock price. If the mean PE ratio of all other firms in the same industry is 6, the stock price in three years can be forecasted as follows

$$\text{Stock price in three years} = (\text{Earnings in three years}) \times (\text{PE ratio of industry})$$
$$= \$12.73 \times 6$$
$$= \$76.38$$

This forecasted stock price can be used along with expected dividends and the investor's required rate of return to value the stock today. If the firm is expected to pay a dividend of $4 per share over the next three years, and if the investor's required rate of return is 14 percent, the present value of expected cash flows to be received by the investor is

$$PV = \$4/(1.14)^1 + \$4/(1.14)^2 + \$4/(1.14)^3 + \$76.38/(1.14)^3$$
$$= \$3.51 + \$3.08 + \$2.70 + \$51.55$$
$$= \$60.84$$

In this example, the present value of the cash flows is based on (1) the present value of dividends to be received over the three-year investment horizon, which is $9.29 per share ($3.51 + $3.08 + $2.70), and (2) the present value of the forecasted price at

which the stock can be sold at the end of the three-year investment horizon, which is $51.55 per share.

Limitations of the Adjusted Dividend Discount Model This model may result in an inaccurate valuation if errors are made in deriving the present value of dividends over the investment horizon or the present value of the forecasted price at which the stock can be sold at the end of the investment horizon. Since the required rate of return affects both of these factors, the use of an improper required rate of return will lead to inaccurate valuations. Possible methods for determining the required rate of return are discussed next.

Determining the Required Rate of Return to Value Stocks

When investors attempt to value a firm based on discounted cash flows, they must determine the required rate of return by investors who invest in that stock. Investors require a return that reflects the risk-free interest rate plus a risk premium. Although investors generally require a higher return on firms that exhibit more risk, there is not complete agreement on the ideal measure of risk or the way risk should be used to derive the required rate of return. Two commonly used models for deriving the required rate of return are the capital asset pricing model and the arbitrage pricing model.

Capital Asset Pricing Model

The capital asset pricing model (CAPM) is sometimes used to estimate the required rate of return for any firm with publicly traded stock. The CAPM is based on the premise that the only important risk of a firm is systematic risk, or the risk that results from exposure to general stock market movements. The CAPM is not concerned with so-called unsystematic risk, which is specific to an individual firm, because investors can avoid that type of risk by holding diversified portfolios. That is, any particular adverse condition (such as a labor strike) affecting one particular firm in an investor's stock portfolio should be offset in a given period by some favorable condition affecting another firm in the portfolio. In contrast, the systematic impact of general stock market movements on stocks in the portfolio cannot be diversified away because most of the stocks would be adversely affected by a general market decline.

The CAPM suggests that the return of an asset (R_j) is influenced by the prevailing risk-free rate (R_f), the market return (R_m), and the covariance between the R_j and R_m as follows:

$$R_j = R_f + B_j(R_m - R_f)$$

where B_j represents the beta and is measured as $COV(R_j, R_m)/VAR(R_m)$. This model implies that given a specific R_f and R_m, investors will require a higher return on an asset that has a higher beta. A higher beta reflects a higher covariance between the asset's returns and market returns, which contributes more risk to the portfolio of assets held by the investor.

Estimating the Risk-Free Rate and the Market Risk Premium The yield on newly issued Treasury bonds is commonly used as a proxy for the risk-free rate. The terms within the parentheses measure the market risk premium, or the excess return of the market above the risk-free rate. Historical data over 30 or more years can be used to determine the average market risk premium over time, which serves as an estimate of the market risk premium that will exist in the future.

Estimating the Firm's Beta A firm's beta is a measure of its systematic risk, as it reflects the sensitivity of the stock's return to the market's overall return. For example, a stock with a beta of 1.2 means that for every 1 percent change in the market overall, the stock tends to change by 1.2 percent in the same direction. The beta is typically measured with monthly or quarterly data over the last four years or so. It is reported in investment services such as *Value Line,* or it can be computed by the individual investor who understands how to apply regression analysis. A stock's sensitivity to market conditions may change over time in response to changes in the firm's operating characteristics. Thus, the beta may adjust as time passes, and the stock's value should also adjust in response.

Investors can measure their exposure to systematic risk by determining how the value of their present stock portfolio has been affected by market movements. They can apply regression analysis by specifying the stock portfolio's periodic (monthly or quarterly) return over the last 20 or so periods as the dependent variable and the market's return (as measured by the S&P 500 index or some other suitable proxy) as the independent variable over those same periods. After inputting these data, a computer spreadsheet package such as Excel can be used to run the regression analysis. Specifically, the focus is on the estimation of the slope coefficient by the regression analysis, which represents the estimate of each stock's beta (for more details, see the discussion under "Beta of a Stock" later in the chapter). Additional results of the analysis can also be assessed, such as the strength of the relationship between the firm's returns and market returns. (See Appendix B for more information on using regression analysis.)

ILLUSTRATION To illustrate how the CAPM can be used to estimate the required rate of return on a firm's stock, consider a firm that has a beta of 1.2 (based on the application of regression analysis to determine the sensitivity of the firm's return to the market return). Also, assume that the prevailing risk-free rate is 6 percent and that the market risk premium is 7 percent (based on historical data that show that the annual market return has exhibited a premium of 7 percent above the annual risk-free rate). Using this information, the risk premium (above the risk-free rate) is 8.4 percent (computed as the market risk premium of 7 percent times the beta of 1.2). Thus, the required rate of return on the firm is

$$R_j = 6\% + 1.2(7\%)$$
$$= 14.4\%$$

The firm's required rate of return is 14.4 percent, so its estimated future cash flows would be discounted using a discount rate of 14.4 percent to derive the firm's present value. At this same point in time, the required rates of return for other firms could also be determined. Although the risk-free rate and the market risk premium are the same regardless of the firm being assessed, the beta varies across firms. Therefore, at a given point in time, the required rates of return estimated by the CAPM will vary across firms because of differences in their risk premiums, which are attributed to differences in their systematic risk (as measured by beta).

Limitations of the CAPM The CAPM suggests that the return of a particular stock is positively related to its beta. However, a study by Fama and French[1] found that beta was unrelated to the return on stocks over the period 1963–1990.

[1] Eugene F. Fama and Kenneth R. French, "The Cross-Section of Expected Stock Returns," *Journal of Finance* (June 1992): 427–465.

Subsequently, Chan and Lakonishok[2] reassessed the relation between stock returns and beta. They found that the relation varied with the time period used, which implies that it is difficult to make projections about the future based on the findings in any specific period. Thus, they concluded that although it is appropriate to question whether beta is the driving force behind stock returns, it may be premature to pronounce beta dead.

Furthermore, if beta is a stable measure of the firm's sensitivity to market movements, it would still be useful for determining which stocks are more feasible investments when the stock market is expected to perform well. Thus, investors should still monitor a firm's beta.

Chan and Lakonishok assessed the 10 worst months for the U.S. stock market in order to compare the returns of firms with relatively high betas versus firms with relatively low betas. They found that firms with the highest betas performed much worse than firms with low betas in those periods. They also found that high-beta firms outperformed low-beta firms during market upswings. These results support the measurement of beta as an indicator of the firm's response to market upswings or downswings.

Arbitrage Pricing Model

An alternative pricing model is based on the arbitrage pricing theory (APT). The APT differs from the CAPM in that it suggests that a stock's price can be influenced by a set of factors in addition to the market. The factors may possibly reflect economic growth, inflation, and other variables that could systematically influence asset prices. The following model is based on the APT:

$$E(R) = B_0 + \sum_{i=1}^{m} B_i F_i$$

where

$E(R)$ = expected return of asset

B_0 = a constant

$F_i \ldots F_m$ = values of factors 1 to m

B_i = sensitivity of the asset return to particular force

The model suggests that in equilibrium, expected returns on assets are linearly related to the covariance between asset returns and the factors. This is distinctly different from the CAPM, where expected returns are linearly related to the covariance between asset returns and the market. The appeal of the APT is that it allows for factors (such as industry effects) other than the market to influence the expected returns of assets. Thus, the required rate of return may be based not only on the firm's sensitivity to market conditions but also on its sensitivity to industry conditions. A possible disadvantage of the APT is that it is not as well defined as the CAPM. This characteristic could be perceived as an advantage, however, since it allows investors to include whatever factors they believe are relevant in deriving the required rate of return for a particular firm.

Factors That Affect Stock Prices

Stock prices are driven by three types of factors: (1) economic factors, (2) market-related factors, and (3) firm-specific factors.

---

[2] Louis K. C. Chan and Josef Lakonishok, "Are the Reports of Beta's Death Premature?" *Journal of Portfolio Management* (Summer 1993): 51–62.

Economic Factors

A firm's value should reflect the present value of its future cash flows. Investors consider various economic factors that affect a firm's cash flows when valuing a firm to determine whether a firm's stock is over- or undervalued.

http://biz.yahoo.com/ c/e.html Calendar of upcoming announcements of economic conditions that may affect stock prices.

Impact of Economic Growth An increase in economic growth is expected to increase the demand for products and services produced by firms and therefore increase a firm's cash flows and valuation. Participants in the stock markets monitor economic indicators such as employment, gross domestic product, retail sales, and personal income because these indicators may signal information about economic growth and therefore affect cash flows. In general, unexpected favorable information about the economy tends to cause a favorable revision of a firm's expected cash flows and therefore places upward pressure on the firm's value. Because the government's fiscal and monetary policies affect economic growth, they are also continually monitored by investors.

Exhibit 7.1 shows the U.S. stock market performance, based on the S&P 500 index, an index of 500 large U.S. stocks. The stock market's strong performance in the late

EXHIBIT 7.1 Stock Market Trend Based on the S&P 500 Index

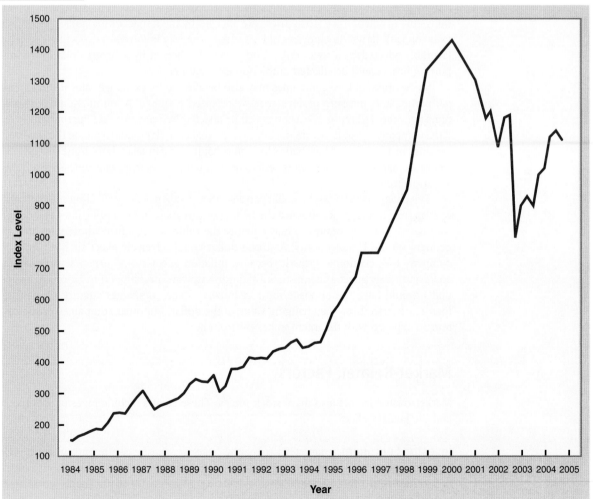

http://

http://research.stlouisfed.org
Economic information
that can be used to value
securities, including money
supply information, gross
domestic product, interest
rates, and exchange rates.

1990s was partially due to the strong economic conditions in the United States at that time. Conversely, the stock market's weak performance in 2000 and in 2001 was primarily due to the weak economic conditions at that time. The rise in stock prices in 2003 was influenced by indicators that the economy would improve in the near future.

Impact of Interest Rates   One of the most prominent economic forces driving stock market prices is the risk-free interest rate. Investors should consider purchasing a risky asset only if they expect to be compensated with a risk premium for the risk incurred. Given a choice of risk-free Treasury securities or stocks, investors should purchase stocks only if they are appropriately priced to reflect a sufficiently high expected return above the risk-free rate. The relation between interest rates and stock prices is not constant over time. However, most of the largest stock market declines have occurred in periods when interest rates increased substantially. Furthermore, the stock market's rise in the late 1990s is partially attributed to the low interest rates during that period, which encouraged investors to shift from debt securities (with low rates) to equity securities.

Impact of the Dollar's Exchange Rate Value   The value of the dollar can affect U.S. stock prices for a variety of reasons. First, foreign investors tend to purchase U.S. stocks when the dollar is weak and sell them when it is near its peak. Thus, the foreign demand for any given U.S. stock may be higher when the dollar is expected to strengthen, other things being equal. Also, stock prices are affected by the impact of the dollar's changing value on cash flows. Stock prices of U.S. firms primarily involved in exporting could be favorably affected by a weak dollar and adversely affected by a strong dollar. U.S. importing firms could be affected in the opposite manner.

Stock prices of U.S. companies may also be affected by exchange rates if stock market participants measure performance by reported earnings. A multinational corporation's consolidated reported earnings will be affected by exchange rate fluctuations even if the company's cash flows are not affected. A weaker dollar tends to inflate the reported earnings of a U.S.-based company's foreign subsidiaries. Some analysts argue that any effect of exchange rate movements on financial statements is irrelevant unless cash flows are also affected.

The changing value of the dollar can also affect stock prices by affecting expectations of economic factors that influence the firm's performance. For example, if a weak dollar stimulates the U.S. economy, it may enhance the value of a U.S. firm whose sales are dependent on the U.S. economy. A strong dollar could adversely affect such a firm if it dampens U.S. economic growth. Because inflation affects some firms, a weak dollar could indirectly affect a firm's stock by putting upward pressure on inflation. A strong dollar would have the opposite indirect impact. Some companies attempt to insulate their stock price from the changing value of the dollar, but other companies purposely remain exposed with the intent to benefit from it.

Market-Related Factors

Market-related factors also drive stock prices. These factors include investor sentiment and the January effect.

Investor Sentiment   A key market-related factor is investor sentiment, which represents the general mood of investors in the stock market. Since stock valuations reflect expectations, in some periods the stock market performance is not highly correlated

with existing economic conditions. For example, even though the economy is weak, stock prices may rise if most investors expect that the economy will improve in the near future. That is, there is a positive sentiment because of optimistic expectations.

Stocks can exhibit excessive volatility because their prices are partially driven by fads and fashions, which may be unrelated to the present value of future dividends. During the late 1990s, stock prices increased beyond what might be attributed to strong economic conditions. At that time, investor sentiment was unusually optimistic about Internet firms. In 2000 and 2001, investor sentiment shifted, causing a substantial decline in stock prices.

A study by Roll[3] confirmed that stock prices are driven by other forces besides fundamental factors. Roll found that only about one-third of the variation in stock returns can be explained by systematic economic forces. A related study by Cutler, Poterba, and Summers[4] reassessed this issue by considering the influence of major news announcements not accounted for in Roll's study. Even after accounting for this information, most of the variation in stock returns could not be explained. The study suggested that movements in stock prices may be partially attributed to investors' reliance on other investors for stock market valuation. Rather than making their own assessment of a firm's value, many investors appear to focus on the general investor sentiment. This can result in irrational exuberance, whereby stock prices increase without reason.

Given the potential changes in valuation caused by market sentiment, some investors attempt to anticipate future momentum of stock prices based on the trend of recent stock prices (referred to as technical analysis). The rationale behind technical analysis is that if trends are repetitive, investors can take positions in stocks as they recognize the particular trend occurring. Technical analysis is most commonly used to anticipate short-term movements in stock prices.

January Effect Because many portfolio managers are evaluated over the calendar year, they tend to invest in riskier small stocks at the beginning of the year and shift to larger (more stable) companies near the end of the year to lock in their gains. This tendency places upward pressure on small stocks in January of every year, causing the so-called January effect. Some studies have found that most of the annual stock market gains occur in January. Once investors discovered the January effect, they attempted to take more positions in stocks in the prior month. This has placed upward pressure on stocks in mid-December, causing the January effect to begin in December.

Firm-Specific Factors

A firm's stock price is affected not only by macroeconomic and market conditions but also by firm-specific conditions. Some firms are more exposed to conditions within their own industry than to general economic conditions, so participants monitor industry sales forecasts, entry into the industry by new competitors, and price movements of the industry's products. Stock market participants may focus on announcements by specific firms that signal information about a firm's sales growth, earnings, or other characteristics that may cause a revision in the expected cash flows to be generated by that firm.

---

[3] Richard Roll, "The International Crash of 1987," *Financial Analysts Journal* (October 1988): 19–35.
[4] David M. Cutler, James M. Poterba, and Lawrence H. Summers, "What Moves Stock Prices?" *Journal of Portfolio Management* (Spring 1989): 4–12.

Dividend Policy Changes An increase in dividends may reflect the firm's expectation that it can more easily afford to pay dividends. A decrease in dividends may reflect the firm's expectation that it will not have sufficient cash flow.

Earnings Surprises Recent earnings are used to forecast future earnings and therefore to forecast a firm's future cash flows. When a firm's announced earnings are higher than expected, some investors raise their estimates of the firm's future cash flows and therefore revalue its stock upward. Conversely, an announcement of lower than expected earnings can cause investors to reduce their valuation of a firm's future cash flows and its stock.

Acquisitions and Divestitures The expected acquisition of a firm typically results in an increased demand for the target's stock and therefore raises the stock price. Investors recognize that the target's stock price will be bid up once the acquiring firm attempts to acquire the target's stock. The effect on the acquiring firm's stock is less clear, as it depends on the perceived synergies that could result from the acquisition. Divestitures tend to be regarded as a favorable signal about a firm if the divested assets are unrelated to the firm's core business. The typical interpretation by the market in this case is that the firm intends to focus on its core business.

Expectations Investors do not necessarily wait for a firm to announce a new policy before they revalue the firm's stock. Instead, they attempt to anticipate new policies so that they can make their move in the market before other investors. In this way, they may be able to pay a lower price for a specific stock or sell the stock at a higher price. For example, they may use the firm's financial reports or recent statements by the firm's executives to speculate on whether the firm will adjust its dividend policy. The disadvantage of trading based on incomplete information is that the investors may not properly anticipate the firm's future policies.

Integration of Factors Affecting Stock Prices

http://screen.yahoo.com/
stocks.html Screens stocks
based on various possible
valuation indicators.

Exhibit 7.2 illustrates the underlying forces that cause a stock's price to change over time. As with the pricing of debt securities, the required rate of return is relevant, as are the economic factors that affect the risk-free interest rate. Stock market participants also monitor indicators that can affect the risk-free interest rate, which affects the required return by investors who invest in stocks. Indicators of inflation (such as the consumer price index and producer price index) and of government borrowing (such as the budget deficit and the volume of funds borrowed at upcoming Treasury bond auctions) also affect the risk-free rate and therefore affect the required return of investors. In general, whenever these indicators signal the expectation of higher interest rates, there is upward pressure on the required rate of return by investors and downward pressure on a firm's value.

In addition, the firm's expected future cash flows are commonly estimated to derive its value, and these cash flows are influenced by economic conditions, industry conditions, and firm-specific conditions. This exhibit provides an overview of what stock market participants monitor when attempting to anticipate future stock price movements.

EXHIBIT 7.2 Framework for Explaining Changes in a Firm's Stock Price over Time

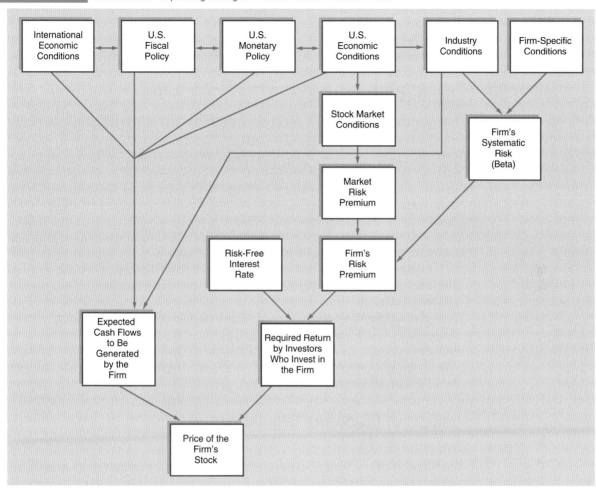

Role of Analysts in Valuing Stocks

http://
http://finance.yahoo.com/
mru?u List of stocks
that were upgraded or
downgraded by analysts.

Most investors agree that the factors just identified affect stock prices. However, they tend to disagree on how any particular stock's price will be affected by changes in those factors. Given the difficulty in valuing stocks, many investors rely on opinions of stock analysts who are employed by securities firms or other financial firms. Analysts play an important role in the market valuation of stocks. Through their recommendations, they influence the buying or selling decisions of some investors and therefore can influence the price of stocks. Many analysts are assigned to specific stocks and issue ratings that can indicate whether investors should buy the stock or sell the stock. The ratings have historically been confusing, however, because they use recommendations such as strong buy, buy, accumulate buy, hold, and sell. In 2001, research by Thomson Financial determined that the analysts at the largest brokerage firms typically recommended "sell" for less than 1 percent of all the stocks for which they provided ratings. Some analysts respond (anonymously) that investors simply are interpreting the ratings wrongly. Ratings such as "accumulate

buy" or "hold" may really mean sell. As a result of the media attention to this issue, some analysts are changing their ratings to make them clearer to investors.

Ratings for a particular stock are provided along with stock quotes and other information at http://finance.yahoo.com/?u. This website provides summaries of ratings by well-known analysts and recent changes in analyst ratings for any stock.

Conflicts of Interest

Analysts face some obvious conflicts of interest. First, many analysts are employed by securities firms that have other investment banking relationships with the firms that they rate, such as facilitating mergers or secondary offerings of stock. A firm normally will not seek the services of an investment bank whose analysts rate it as a "sell." The firm would prefer to hire an investment bank that has a more favorable valuation of it. For example, an investment bank may be more likely to find an acquirer for a firm if it believes that the firm is currently undervalued. Investment banks recognize the possible loss in income if they rate a firm poorly. This may explain why an investment bank's analysts are typically unwilling to rate any firm as a "sell."

Another conflict of interest occurs when analysts own the stock of some of the firms that they rate. If they own a specific stock, they may refrain from making any negative comments about the firm while they own its stock in the hope that the stock's price will rise even higher. Alternatively, they could provide somewhat neutral recommendations for stocks that they wish to buy, hoping to purchase the stocks at a relatively low price in the near future. As these examples illustrate, analysts may make recommendations that are in their own best interests or those of their respective employers, but not necessarily in the best interests of investors.

Impact of Disclosure Regulations

Historically, analysts were able to obtain valuable information by communicating with executives of a firm. In many cases, this gave them an advantage over other investors because the analysts might be the first to learn that the firm was revising its revenue or earnings forecast downward. The analysts could use this information to revise their own estimates of the firm's quarterly earnings or to revise their rating of the firm. Their actions affected investor demand for the firm's shares or the amount of shares that investors wanted to sell and therefore affected the share price. Thus, the information provided to the analysts was ultimately accounted for in the market, but the analysts had the information before the other market participants.

In the late 1990s, some firms began to announce significant changes in their expected revenue or earnings through the media, rather than provide the information to the analysts first. In October 2000, the Securities and Exchange Commission (SEC) enacted Regulation FD ("Fair Disclosure"), which requires that firms disclose any significant information that could affect share price simultaneously to all market participants. Consequently, analysts no longer have an information advantage over other market participants.

Unbiased Analyst Rating Services

Some analyst rating services are considered to be unbiased because they are not attempting to provide other services for the firms that they rate. Some of the more popu-

lar analyst rating services include Morningstar, *Value Line*, and *Investor's Business Daily*. Morningstar relies on traditional valuation methods (such as revenue and cost estimates) to determine whether a firm is undervalued. *Value Line* rates each stock from 1 (highest) to 5 (lowest). *Investor's Business Daily* rates a stock from 1 to 99, with scores over 80 representing recommended buys and scores under 70 recommended sells. Morningstar rates stocks from 5-star (highest) to 1-star. *Investor's Business Daily* covers more than 10,000 stocks, *Value Line* covers 1,700, and Morningstar covers 500.

Analyst rating services typically charge their subscribers between $100 and $600 per year. There are also some online rating services. For example, the website http://www.msn.com not only provides stock quotes but also has stock ratings (provided by StockScouter) for 6,500 stocks.

Stock Risk

A stock's risk reflects the uncertainty about future returns, such that the actual return may be less than expected. The return from investing in stock over a particular period is measured as

$$R = \frac{(SP - INV) + D}{INV}$$

where
$$INV = \text{initial investment}$$
$$D = \text{dividend}$$
$$SP = \text{selling price of the stock}$$

The main source of uncertainty is the price at which the stock will be sold. Dividends tend to be much more stable than stock prices. Dividends contribute to the immediate return received by investors, but reduce the amount of earnings reinvested by the firm, which limits its potential growth.

Risk Measures

The risk of a stock can be measured by its price volatility, its beta, and by the value-at-risk method.

Volatility of a Stock A stock's volatility serves as a measure of risk because it may indicate the degree of uncertainty surrounding the stock's future returns. The volatility is often referred to as total risk because it reflects movements in stock prices for any reason, not just movements attributable to stock market movements. A stock's returns over a historical period such as the last 12 quarters may be compiled to estimate future volatility. If the standard deviation of the stock's returns over the last 12 quarters is 3 percent, and if there is no perceived change in volatility, there is a 68 percent probability that the stock's returns will be within 3 percentage points (one standard deviation) of the expected outcome and a 95 percent probability that the stock's returns will be within 6 percentage points (2 standard deviations) of the expected outcome.

Volatility of a Stock Portfolio A portfolio's volatility is dependent on the volatility of the individual stocks in the portfolio, the correlations between returns of the stocks in

the portfolio, and the proportion of total funds invested in each stock. The portfolio's volatility can be measured by the standard deviation:

$$\sigma_p = \sqrt{w_i^2\sigma_i^2 + w_j^2\sigma_j^2 + 2w_iw_j\sigma_i\sigma_j\text{CORR}_{ij}}$$

where
σ_i = standard deviation of returns of the ith stock

σ_j = standard deviation of returns of the jth stock

CORR_{ij} = correlation coefficient between the ith and jth stocks

w_i = proportion of funds invested in the ith stock

w_j = proportion of funds invested in the jth stock

For portfolios containing more securities, the formula for the standard deviation would contain the standard deviation of each stock and the correlation coefficients between all pairs of stocks in the portfolio, weighted by the proportion of funds invested in each stock. The equation for a two-stock portfolio is sufficient to demonstrate that a stock portfolio has more volatility when its individual stock volatilities are high, other factors held constant. In addition, a stock portfolio has more volatility when its individual stock returns are highly correlated, other factors held constant. As an extreme example, if the returns of the stocks are all perfectly positively correlated (correlation coefficients = 1.0), the portfolio will have a relatively high degree of volatility because all stocks will experience peaks or troughs simultaneously. Conversely, a stock portfolio containing some stocks with low or negative correlation will exhibit less volatility because the stocks will not experience peaks and troughs simultaneously. Some offsetting effects will occur, smoothing the returns of the portfolio over time.

Beta of a Stock As explained earlier, a stock's beta measures the sensitivity of its returns to market returns. This measure of risk is used by many investors who have a diversified portfolio of stocks and believe that the unsystematic risk of the portfolio is diversified away (because favorable firm-specific characteristics will offset unfavorable firm-specific characteristics). The beta of a stock can be estimated by obtaining returns of the firm and the stock market over the last 12 quarters and applying regression analysis to derive the slope coefficient as in this model:

$$R_{jt} = B_0 + B_1R_{mt} + \mu_t$$

where
R_{jt} = return of stock j during period t

R_{mt} = market return during period t

B_0 = intercept

B_1 = regression coefficient that serves as an estimate of beta

μ_t = error term

Some investors or analysts prefer to use monthly returns rather than quarterly returns to estimate the beta. The choice is dependent on the holding period for which one wants to assess sensitivity. If the goal is to assess sensitivity to monthly returns, then monthly data would be more appropriate.

The regression analysis estimates the intercept (B_0) and the slope coefficient (B_1), which serves as the estimate of beta. If the slope coefficient of an individual stock is estimated to be 1.4, this means that for a given return in the market, the stock's expected

return is 1.4 times that amount. Such sensitivity is favorable when the stock market is performing well, but unfavorable when the stock market is performing poorly. This implies that the probability distribution of returns is very dispersed, reflecting a wide range of possible outcomes for the individual stock.

Beta serves as a measure of risk because it can be used to derive a probability distribution of returns based on a set of market returns. As explained earlier, beta is useful for investors who are primarily concerned with systematic risk because it captures the movement in a stock's price that is attributable to movements in the stock market. It ignores stock price movements attributable to firm-specific conditions because such unsystematic risk can be avoided by maintaining a diversified portfolio.

ILLUSTRATION Exhibit 7.3 shows how the probability distribution of a stock's returns is dependent on its beta. At one extreme, Stock A with a very low beta is less responsive to market movements in either direction, so its possible returns range only from −4.8 percent under poor market conditions to 6 percent under the most favorable market conditions. Stock D with a very high beta has possible returns that range from −11.2 percent under poor market conditions to 14 percent under the most favorable market conditions.

Beta of a Stock Portfolio Participants in the stock market tend to invest in a portfolio of stocks rather than a single stock and therefore are more concerned with the risk of a portfolio than with the risk of an individual stock. The risk of individual stocks is necessary to derive portfolio risk. Portfolio risk is commonly measured by beta or volatility (standard deviation), just as the risk of individual stocks is.

The beta of a stock portfolio can be measured as

$$B_p = \sum w_i B_i$$

That is, the portfolio beta is a weighted average of the betas of stocks that comprise the portfolio, where the weights reflect the proportion of funds invested in each stock. The equation is intuitive as it simply suggests that a portfolio consisting of high-beta stocks will have a relatively high beta. This type of portfolio normally performs poorly relative to other stock portfolios in a period when the market return is negative. The risk of such a portfolio could be reduced by replacing some of the high-beta stocks with low-beta stocks. Of course, the expected return for the portfolio would be lower as a result.

The beta of a stock and its volatility are typically related. High-beta stocks are expected to be very volatile because they are more sensitive to market returns over time. Conversely, low-beta stocks are expected to be less volatile because they are less responsive to market returns.

Value at Risk Value at risk is a risk measurement that estimates the largest expected loss to a particular investment position for a specified confidence level. This method became very popular in the late 1990s after some mutual funds and pension funds experienced abrupt large losses. The value-at-risk method is intended to warn investors about the potential maximum loss that could occur. If the investors are uncomfortable with the potential loss that could occur in a day or a week, they can revise their investment portfolio to make it less risky.

The value-at-risk measurement focuses on the pessimistic portion of the probability distribution of returns from the investment of concern. For example, a portfolio manager might use a confidence level of 90 percent, which estimates the maximum daily

EXHIBIT 7.3 How Beta Influences Probability Distributions

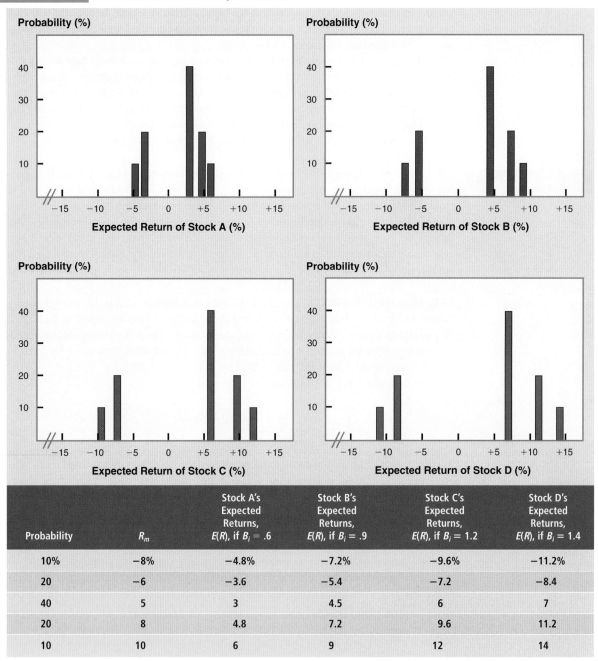

Probability	R_m	Stock A's Expected Returns, E(R), if $B_i = .6$	Stock B's Expected Returns, E(R), if $B_i = .9$	Stock C's Expected Returns, E(R), if $B_i = 1.2$	Stock D's Expected Returns, E(R), if $B_i = 1.4$
10%	−8%	−4.8%	−7.2%	−9.6%	−11.2%
20	−6	−3.6	−5.4	−7.2	−8.4
40	5	3	4.5	6	7
20	8	4.8	7.2	9.6	11.2
10	10	6	9	12	14

expected loss for a stock in 90 percent of the trading days over an upcoming period. The higher the level of confidence desired, the larger the maximum expected loss that could occur for a given type of investment. That is, one may expect that the daily loss from holding a particular stock will be no worse than −5 percent when using a 90 percent confidence level, but no worse than −8 percent when using a 99 percent confidence level. In essence, the more confidence investors have that the actual loss will be no

greater than the expected maximum loss, the further they move into the left tail of the probability distribution.

The value at risk is also commonly used to measure the risk of a portfolio. Some stocks may be perceived to have high risk when assessed individually, but low risk when assessed as part of a portfolio. This is because the likelihood of a large loss in the portfolio is influenced by the probabilities of simultaneous losses in all of the component stocks for the period of concern.

Applying Value at Risk

Value at risk can be applied to measure the maximum loss for a specific stock based on a specified confidence level.

Methods of Determining the Maximum Expected Loss

Numerous methods can be used when applying value at risk. Three basic methods are discussed next.

Use of Historical Returns to Derive the Maximum Expected Loss An obvious way to use value at risk is to assess historical data. For example, an investor may determine that out of the last 100 trading days, a stock experienced a decline of greater than 7 percent on 5 different days, or 5 percent of the days assessed. This information could be used to infer a maximum daily loss of no more than 7 percent for that stock, based on a 95 percent confidence level for an upcoming period.

Use of Standard Deviation to Derive the Maximum Expected Loss An alternative approach is to measure the standard deviation of daily returns over the previous period and apply it to derive boundaries for a specific confidence level.

ILLUSTRATION Assume that the standard deviation of daily returns for a particular stock in a recent historical period is 2 percent. Also assume that the 95 percent confidence level is desired for the maximum loss. If the daily returns are normally distributed, the lower boundary (the left tail of the probability distribution) is about 1.65 standard deviations away from the expected outcome. Assuming an expected daily return of .1 percent, the lower boundary is

$$.1\% - [1.65 \times (2\%)] = -3.2\%$$

The expected daily return of .1 percent may have been derived from the use of subjective information, or it could be the average daily return from the recent historical period assessed. The lower boundary for a given confidence level can be easily derived for any expected daily return. For example, if the expected daily return is .14 percent, the lower boundary is

$$.14\% - [1.65 \times (2\%)] = -3.16\%$$

Use of Beta to Derive the Maximum Expected Loss A third method of estimating the maximum expected loss for a given confidence level is to apply the stock's beta.

ILLUSTRATION Assume that the stock's beta over the last 100 days is 1.2. Also assume that the stock market is expected to perform no worse than −2.5 percent on a daily basis based on a 95 percent confidence level. Given the stock's beta of 1.2 and a maximum

market loss of −2.5 percent, the maximum loss to the stock over a given day is estimated to be

$$1.2 \times (-2.5\%) = -3.0\%$$

The maximum expected loss for the 95 percent confidence level can be derived subjectively or by assessing the last 100 days or so (in the same manner described for the two previous methods to derive a maximum expected loss for an individual stock).

Deriving the Maximum Dollar Loss

Once the maximum percentage loss for a given confidence level is determined, it can be applied to derive the maximum dollar loss of a particular investment.

ILLUSTRATION Assume that an investor has a $20 million investment in a stock. The maximum dollar loss is determined by applying the maximum percentage loss to the value of the investment. If the investor used beta to measure the maximum expected loss as explained above, the maximum percentage loss over one day would be −3 percent, so the maximum daily loss in dollars is

$$(-3\%) \times \$20,000,000 = \$600,000$$

Since many institutional and individual investors manage stock portfolios, value at risk is commonly applied to assess the maximum possible loss of the entire portfolio. The same three methods used to derive the maximum expected loss of one stock can be applied to derive the maximum expected loss of a stock portfolio for a given confidence level. For instance, the returns of the stock portfolio over the last 100 days or so can be assessed to derive the maximum expected loss. Alternatively, the standard deviation of the portfolio's returns can be estimated over the last 100 days to derive a lower boundary at a specified confidence level. As another alternative, the beta of the portfolio's returns can be estimated over the last 100 days and then applied to a maximum expected daily loss in the stock market to derive a maximum expected loss in the stock portfolio over a given day.

Common Adjustments to the Value-at-Risk Applications

The basic methods of applying value at risk can be adjusted to improve the assessment of risk in particular situations, as explained next.

Investment Horizon Desired An investor who wants to assess the maximum loss over a week or a month can apply the same methods, but should use a historical series that matches the investment horizon. For example, to assess the maximum loss over a given week in the near future, a historical series of weekly returns of that stock (or stock portfolio) can be used.

Length of Historical Period Used The previous examples used a historical series of 100 trading days, but if, for example, conditions have changed such that only the most recent 70 days reflect the general state of market conditions, then those 70 days could be used. However, a subperiod of weak market performance should not be discarded because it could occur again.

Time-Varying Risk The risk of a stock can vary over time for the following reasons. First, market conditions can change, such that the particular line of business reflected

by the stock is subject to more competition or other industry conditions. For example, an abrupt increase in competition will increase the probability that the firm will fail and will normally result in a higher response to poor market conditions and a higher degree of volatility. Second, the firm's operations may change, causing a change in the response of its stock price to market returns and a change in the volatility of the stock's returns. Consequently, the assessment of a maximum expected loss based on historical risk characteristics may not be accurate. It is important for investors to recognize how the stock's risk varies over time so that they can properly assess its risk in the future.

Restructuring the Investment Portfolio Portfolio managers may apply value at risk to potential investments. For example, if they are considering the sale of Stock X and the purchase of Stock Y, they should apply value at risk to their potential new portfolio. Then, they can compare the risk of this portfolio to their existing portfolio to decide whether they should make these changes. Even if they plan to increase their investment in some stocks without selling others, they should reapply value at risk to reflect the new proportions of their stock portfolio allocated to each security that result from the restructured portfolio.

Forecasting Stock Price Volatility and Beta

Since the operations of a particular firm and its competitive environment can change over time, its risk can change as well. Investors are most concerned with the risk of their investments over the future horizon in which they hold those investments so that they can anticipate the range of possible returns that may result.

Methods of Forecasting Stock Price Volatility

Some of the more common methods of forecasting stock price volatility are the historical method, the time-series method, and the implied standard deviation method, which are described next.

Historical Method With the historical method, a historical period is used to derive a stock's standard deviation of returns, and then that estimate is used as the forecast over the future. Although the stock price volatility level may change over time, this method can be useful if there is no obvious trend in volatility, so the best forecast may be the volatility in the most recent period.

Time-Series Method A second method for forecasting stock price volatility is to use a time series of volatility patterns in previous periods.

ILLUSTRATION The standard deviation of daily stock returns is determined for each of the last several months. Then, a time-series trend of these standard deviation levels is used to form an estimate for the standard deviation of daily stock returns over the next month. This method differs from the first in that it uses information beyond that contained in the previous month. The forecast may be based on a weighting scheme such as 50 percent times the standard deviation in the last month (month 4), plus 25 percent times the standard deviation in the month before that (month 3), plus 15 percent times the standard deviation in month 2, plus 10 percent times the standard deviation in month 1.

This scheme places more weight on the most recent data, but allows data from the last four months to influence the forecast. Normally, the weights and the number of previous periods (lags) that were most accurate (lowest forecast error) in previous periods are used. Various economic and political factors can cause stock price volatility to change abruptly, however, so even sophisticated time-series models do not necessarily generate accurate forecasts of stock price volatility.

Implied Standard Deviation A third method for forecasting stock price volatility is to derive the stock's implied standard deviation (ISD) from the stock option pricing model. The premium on a call option for a stock is dependent on factors such as the relationship between the current stock price and the exercise (strike) price of the option, the number of days until the expiration date of the option, and the anticipated volatility of the stock price movements. There is a formula for estimating the call option premium based on various factors. The actual values of these factors are known, except for the anticipated volatility. However, by plugging in the actual option premium paid by investors for that specific stock, it is possible to derive the anticipated volatility level. Market participants who wish to forecast volatility over a 30-day period will consider a call option on the stock that has 30 days to expiration. This measurement represents the anticipated volatility of the stock over a 30-day period by investors who are trading stocks. Participants may use this measurement as their own forecast of that specific stock's volatility.

Forecasting a Stock Portfolio's Volatility

Portfolio managers who monitor total risk rather than systematic risk are more concerned about stock volatility than about beta. Recall that a stock portfolio's volatility is dependent on the volatility of the individual stocks in the portfolio, as well as their correlations. Since the volatilities and correlations of the individual stocks can change over time, so can the volatility of the portfolio. One method of forecasting portfolio volatility is to first derive forecasts of individual volatility levels as described earlier. Then, the correlation coefficient for each pair of stocks in the portfolio is forecasted by estimating the correlation in recent periods and determining whether there was a trend in the change in correlations. The forecasted volatilities of individual stocks and the correlation coefficients are then used to estimate the future portfolio volatility. This approach explicitly captures the recent trends in individual volatilities and correlations.

Forecasting a Stock Portfolio's Beta

Given that the beta of any stock can change over time and that a stock portfolio's beta is dependent on the betas of its individual stocks, the portfolio's beta is subject to change. One way to forecast a portfolio's beta is to first forecast the betas of the individual stocks in the portfolio and then sum the individual forecasted betas, weighted by the proportion of investment in each stock.

The beta of each individual stock may be forecasted in a subjective manner; for example, a portfolio manager may forecast a stock's beta to increase from its existing level of .8 to .9 because the firm has initiated a more aggressive growth strategy. Alternatively, the manager can assess a set of historical periods to determine whether there is a trend in the beta over those periods and then apply the trend. For example, a portfolio manager who is attempting to forecast the beta of stocks based on a daily horizon may estimate the betas in each of the previous four 100-day periods. Assume that the beta was estimated to be .6 four periods ago, .62 three periods ago, .7 two periods ago, and .8 last

period. This firm's beta appears to have an upward trend, which may support a forecast of a slightly higher beta in the next period. However, the stock's beta will not continually change in one direction.

The same procedure can be used to forecast betas based on a different horizon. For example, a portfolio manager who wants to forecast the beta based on monthly stock returns can attempt to determine the trend by assessing recent 12-month periods.

Stock Performance Measurement

The performance of a stock or a stock portfolio over a particular period can be measured by its excess return (return above the risk-free rate) over that period divided by its risk. Two common methods of measuring performance are the Sharpe index and the Treynor index.

Sharpe Index

If total variability is thought to be the appropriate measure of risk, a stock's risk-adjusted returns can be determined by the reward-to-variability ratio (also called the Sharpe index), computed as

$$\text{Sharpe index} = \frac{\overline{R} - \overline{R}_f}{\sigma}$$

where

$\overline{R} = $ average return on the stock

$\overline{R}_f = $ average risk-free rate

$\sigma = $ standard deviation of the stock's returns

The higher the stock's mean return relative to the mean risk-free rate and the lower the standard deviation, the higher the Sharpe index. This index measures the excess return above the risk-free rate per unit of risk.

ILLUSTRATION   Assume the following information for two stocks:

- Average return for Sooner stock = 16%
- Average return for Longhorn stock = 14%
- Average risk-free rate = 10%
- Standard deviation of Sooner stock returns = 15%
- Standard deviation of Longhorn stock returns = 8%

$$\text{Sharpe index for Sooner stock} = \frac{16\% - 10\%}{15\%}$$

$$= .40$$

$$\text{Sharpe index for Longhorn stock} = \frac{14\% - 10\%}{8\%}$$

$$= .50$$

Even though Sooner stock had a higher average percentage return, Longhorn stock had a higher performance because of its lower risk. If a stock's average return is less than the average risk-free rate, the Sharpe index for that stock will be negative.

Treynor Index

If beta is thought to be the most appropriate type of risk, a stock's risk-adjusted returns can be determined by the Treynor index, computed as

$$\text{Treynor index} = \frac{\overline{R} - \overline{R}_f}{B}$$

where B is the stock's beta. The Treynor index is similar to the Sharpe index, except that it uses beta rather than standard deviation to measure the stock's risk. The higher the Treynor index, the higher the return relative to the risk-free rate, per unit of risk.

ILLUSTRATION Using the information provided earlier on Sooner and Longhorn stock and assuming that Sooner's stock beta is 1.2 and Longhorn's beta is 1.0, the Treynor index is computed for each stock as follows:

$$\text{Treynor index for Sooner stock} = \frac{16\% - 10\%}{1.2}$$

$$= .05$$

$$\text{Treynor index for Longhorn stock} = \frac{14\% - 10\%}{1.0}$$

$$= .04$$

Based on the Treynor index, Sooner stock had the higher performance.

A comparison of this and the previous illustration shows that the stock determined to have the higher performance is dependent on the measure of risk and therefore on the index used. In some cases, the indexes will lead to the same results. Like the Sharpe index, the Treynor index is negative for a stock whose average return is less than the average risk-free rate.

Stock Market Efficiency

If stock markets are efficient, the prices of stocks at any point in time should fully reflect all available information. As investors attempt to capitalize on new information that is not already accounted for, stock prices should adjust immediately. Investors commonly over- or underreact to information. This does not mean markets are inefficient unless the reaction is biased (consistently over- or underreacting). In this case, investors who recognize the bias will be able to earn abnormally high risk-adjusted returns.

Forms of Efficiency

Efficient markets can be classified into three forms: weak, semistrong, and strong.

Weak-Form Efficiency Weak-form efficiency suggests that security prices reflect all trade-related information, such as historical security price movements and volume of securities trades. Thus, investors will not be able to earn abnormal returns on a trading strategy that is based solely on past price movements.

Semistrong-Form Efficiency Semistrong-form efficiency suggests that security prices fully reflect all public information. The difference between public information and market-

WSJ Insider Trading Spotlight

Large insider trading transactions are disclosed in *The Wall Street Journal*. The insiders are identified, along with their titles, and the value of the transactions.

INSIDER TRADING SPOTLIGHT

Biggest Individual Trades
(Based on reports filed with regulators last week)

COMPANY NAME	SYMBOL	INSIDER'S NAME	TITLE	$ VALUE (000)	NO. OF SHRS IN TRANS (000)	RANGE OF SHR VALUES	TRANS DATES
Buyers							
Chesapeake Energy	CHK	A. McClendon	CEO	**5,000**	339	14.75	8/02/04
Chesapeake Energy	CHK	T. Ward	P	**5,000**	339	14.75	8/02/04
Midway Games	MWY	S. Redstone	B	**3,858**	337	11.35-11.53	7/30/04
Midway Games	MWY	S. Redstone	B	**3,292**	281	11.55-11.81	8/03/04
Midway Games	MWY	S. Redstone	B	**3,276**	287	11.01-11.80	7/28/04
Valence Technology	VLNC	C. Berg	DOI	**2,000**	728	2.75	7/27/04
Praecis Pharmaceuticals	PRCS	G. Baker	DI	**1,902**	776	2.45	8/03/04
Brooke	BXX	M. Hess	DI	**1,635**	103	15.86	7/22/04
Brooke	BXX	R. Orr	CEOI	**1,635**	103	15.86	7/22/04
Auxilium Pharmaceuticals	AUXL	P. Chambon	DOI	**1,494**	199	7.50	7/28/04
Sellers							
Dex Media	DEX	S. Traynor	BI	**206,963**	10,893	19.00	7/27/04
Dex Media	DEX	R. Minicucci	BI	**206,963**	10,893	19.00	7/27/04
Dex Media	DEX	A. Denicola	DOI	**206,963**	10,893	19.00	7/27/04
Dex Media	DEX	D. Mackesy	BI	**206,963**	10,893	19.00	7/27/04
Dex Media	DEX	R. Carson	BI	**206,963**	10,893	19.00	7/27/04
Dex Media	DEX	P. Queally	BI	**206,963**	10,893	19.00	7/27/04
Dex Media	DEX	J. Matthews	BI	**206,963**	10,893	19.00	7/27/04
Dex Media	DEX	P. Welsh	BI	**206,963**	10,893	19.00	7/27/04
Dex Media	DEX	J. Almeida	DOI	**206,963**	10,893	19.00	7/27/04

related information is that public information also includes announcements by firms, economic news or events, and political news or events. Market-related information is a subset of public information. Thus, if semistrong-form efficiency holds, weak-form efficiency must hold as well. It is possible, however, for weak-form efficiency to hold, while semistrong-form efficiency does not. In this case, investors could earn abnormal returns by using the relevant information that was not immediately accounted for by the market.

Strong-Form Efficiency Strong-form efficiency suggests that security prices fully reflect all information, including private or insider information. If strong-form efficiency holds, semistrong-form efficiency must hold as well. If insider information leads to abnormal returns, however, semistrong-form efficiency could hold, while strong-form efficiency does not.

Inside information allows insiders (such as some employees or board members) an unfair advantage over other investors. For example, if employees of a firm are aware of

favorable news about the firm that is not yet disclosed to the public, they may consider purchasing shares or advising their friends to purchase the firm's shares. Though such actions are illegal, they still happen and can create market inefficiencies.

Even if insiders do not act on inside information, a particular group of investors may receive information before others and therefore have an unfair advantage.

ILLUSTRATION Consider the Bank of New York's announcement that it was experiencing loan defaults on its credit card business. The bank first announced this information through a conference call to about 90 securities analysts and institutional investors at about 2:00 P.M. on June 19, 1996. After the announcement, its stock price declined by about 2.6 percent that afternoon. The bank then issued a news release to the public at about 4:30 P.M. on the same afternoon—30 minutes after the stock market closed. Small investors were upset that they received the information later than many institutional investors and therefore could not respond as quickly to the news. They argued that this allowed institutional investors a head start on selling the stock in response to negative information. Regulation FD has been enacted to ensure that firms fully disclose their information at the same time to all investors, which should prevent some market inefficiencies.

Tests of the Efficient Market Hypothesis

Tests of market efficiency are segmented into three categories, as discussed next.

Test of Weak-Form Efficiency Weak-form efficiency has been tested by searching for a nonrandom pattern in security prices. If the future change in price is related to recent changes, historical price movements could be used to earn abnormal returns. In general, studies have found that historical price changes are independent over time. Therefore, historical information is already reflected by today's price and cannot be used to earn abnormal profits. Even when some dependence was detected, the transaction costs would offset any excess return earned.

There is some evidence that stocks have performed better in specific time periods. For example, as mentioned earlier, small stocks have performed unusually well in the month of January ("January effect"). Second, stocks have historically performed better on Fridays than on Mondays ("weekend effect"). Third, stocks have historically performed well on the trading days just before holidays ("holiday effect"). To the extent that a given pattern continues and can be used by investors to earn abnormal returns, market inefficiencies exist. In most cases, there is no clear evidence that such patterns persist once they are recognized by the investment community.

One could argue that the stock market is inefficient based on the number of so-called corrections that occur. During the twentieth century, there were more than 100 specific days when the market (as measured by the Dow Jones Industrial Average) declined by 10 percent or more. On more than 300 specific days during the century, the market declined by more than 5 percent. These abrupt declines frequently followed a market runup, which implies that the runup may have been excessive. Thus, a market correction was necessary to remove the excessive runup.

Test of Semistrong-Form Efficiency Semistrong-form efficiency has been tested by assessing how security returns adjust to particular announcements. Some announcements are specific to a firm, such as an announced dividend increase, an acquisition, or a stock split. Other announcements are economy related, such as an announced decline in the federal funds rate. In general, security prices immediately reflected the informa-

tion from the announcements. That is, the securities were not consistently over- or undervalued. Consequently, abnormal returns could not consistently be achieved. This is especially true when considering transaction costs.

There is evidence of unusual profits when investing in initial public offerings (IPOs). In particular, the return over the first day following the IPO tends to be abnormally high. One reason for this underpricing is that the investment banking firms underwriting an IPO intentionally underprice to ensure that the entire issue can be placed. In addition, underwriters are required to exercise due diligence in ensuring the accuracy of the information that they provide to investors about the corporation. Thus, underwriters are encouraged to err on the low side when setting a price for IPOs.

Some analysts might contend that given imperfect information about IPOs, investors will participate only if prices are low. Thus, the potential return must be high enough to compensate for the lack of information about these corporations and the risk incurred. Using this argument, the underpricing does not imply market inefficiencies but rather reflects the high degree of uncertainty.

Test of Strong-Form Efficiency Tests of strong-form efficiency are difficult, because the inside information used is not publicly available and cannot be properly tested. Nevertheless, many forms of insider trading could easily result in abnormally high returns. For example, there is clear evidence that share prices of target firms rise substantially when the acquisition is announced. If insiders purchased stock of targets prior to others, they would normally achieve abnormally high returns. Insiders are discouraged from using this information because it is illegal, not because markets are strong-form efficient.

Foreign Stock Valuation, Performance, and Efficiency

 Some of the key concepts in this chapter can be adjusted so that they apply on a global basis, as explained next.

Valuing Foreign Stocks

Foreign stocks can be valued by using the price-earnings method or the dividend discount model with an adjustment to reflect international conditions.

Price-Earnings (PE) Method The expected earnings per share of the foreign firm are multiplied by the appropriate PE ratio (based on the firm's risk and local industry) to determine the appropriate price of the firm's stock. Though easy to use, this method is subject to some limitations when valuing foreign stocks. The PE ratio for a given industry may change continuously in some foreign markets, especially when the industry is composed of just a few firms. Thus, it is difficult to determine the proper ratio that should be applied to a specific foreign firm. In addition, the PE ratio for any particular industry may need to be adjusted for the firm's country because reported earnings can be influenced by the country's accounting guidelines and tax laws.

Furthermore, even if U.S. investors are comfortable with their estimate of the proper PE ratio, the value derived by this method is denominated in the local foreign currency (since the estimated earnings are denominated in that currency). Therefore, U.S. investors still need to consider exchange rate effects. Even if the stock is undervalued in the foreign country, it may not necessarily generate a reasonable return for U.S. investors if the foreign currency depreciates against the dollar.

Dividend Discount Model The dividend discount model can be applied to value foreign stocks by discounting the stream of expected dividends, but with an adjustment to account for expected exchange rate movements. Foreign stocks pay dividends in the currency in which they are denominated. Thus, the cash flow per period to U.S. investors is the dividend (denominated in the foreign currency) multiplied by the value of that foreign currency in dollars. An expected appreciation of the currency denominating the foreign stocks will result in higher expected dollar cash flows and a higher present value. The dividend can normally be forecasted with more accuracy than the value of the foreign currency. Because of exchange rate uncertainty, the value of the foreign stock from a U.S. investor's perspective is subject to more uncertainty than the value of the stock from a local investor's perspective.

Measuring Performance from Investing in Foreign Stocks

An investor's performance from investing in foreign stocks is most properly measured by considering the objective of the investor. For example, if portfolio managers are assigned to select stocks in Europe, their performance should be compared to the performance of a European index, measured in U.S. dollars. In this way, the performance measurement controls for general market movements and exchange rate movements in the region where the portfolio manager has been assigned to invest funds. Thus, if the entire European market experiences poor performance over a particular quarter, or if the main European currency (the euro) depreciates against the dollar over the period, the portfolio managers assigned to Europe are not automatically penalized. Conversely, if the entire European market experiences strong performance over a particular quarter, or the euro appreciates against the dollar, the managers are not automatically rewarded. Instead, the performance of portfolio managers will be measured relative to the general market conditions of the region to which they are assigned.

Performance from Global Diversification

A substantial amount of research has demonstrated that investors in stocks can benefit by diversifying internationally. Most stocks are highly influenced by the country where their firms are located (although some firms are more vulnerable to economic conditions than others).

Since a given stock market partially reflects the current and/or forecasted state of its country's economy, and economies do not move in tandem, particular stocks of the various markets are not expected to be highly correlated. This contrasts with a purely domestic portfolio (such as all U.S. stocks), in which most stocks are often moving in the same direction and by a somewhat similar magnitude.

Nevertheless, stock price movements among international stock markets are integrated to a degree because some underlying economic factors reflecting the world's general financial condition may systematically affect all markets. Since one country's economy can influence the economies of other countries, expectations about economies across countries may be somewhat similar. Thus, stock markets across countries may respond to some of the same expectations. Integration is an important concept because of its implications about benefits from international diversification. A high degree of integration implies that stock returns of different countries would be affected by common factors. Therefore, the returns of stocks from various countries would move in tandem, allowing only modest benefits from international diversification.

WSJ Global Stock Market Quotations

The recent performance of various stock markets is summarized each day in *The Wall Street Journal,* as shown here. For each stock market, the summary table provides the percentage change from the previous trading day, from one year ago, and from the beginning of the year. This table can be used to confirm that stock markets generally move in the same direction, but by different degrees. Much of the information in the indexes is from the U.S. perspective, meaning that the data account for exchange rate adjustments over the period of concern. Notice that the table also summarizes the performance of a world stock index, which represents a weighted composite of various stock markets.

International Stock Market Indexes

COUNTRY	INDEX	8/10/04 CLOSE	NET CHG	% CHG	YTD NET CHG	YTD % CHG	P/E
World	DJ World Index	183.22	+1.83	+1.01	-3.73	-2.00	16
Argentina	Merval	967.62	+3.92	+0.41	-104.33	-9.73	...
Australia	S&P/ASX 200	3499.60	-9.60	-0.27	+199.80	+6.05	16
Belgium	Bel-20	2475.27	+23.11	+0.94	+231.09	+10.30	10
Brazil	Sao Paulo Bovespa	21736.72	+475.81	+2.24	-499.67	-2.25	10
Canada	S&P/TSX Composite	8231.26	+47.82	+0.58	+10.37	+0.13	16
Chile	Santiago IPSA	1532.27	-0.12	-0.01	+47.47	+3.20	19
China	Dow Jones China 88	120.43	+0.53	+0.44	-15.30	-11.27	...
China	Dow Jones Shanghai	155.10	+0.71	+0.46	-14.31	-8.45	21
China	Dow Jones Shenzhen	141.82	+0.37	+0.26	-13.92	-8.94	23
Europe	DJ STOXX 600	229.40	+1.39	+0.61	+0.09	+0.04	20
Europe	DJ STOXX 50	2576.82	+15.47	+0.60	-83.55	-3.14	18
Euro Zone	DJ Euro STOXX	236.34	+1.82	+0.78	-6.87	-2.82	20
Euro Zone	DJ Euro STOXX 50	2619.42	+22.90	+0.88	-141.24	-5.12	16
France	Paris CAC 40	3533.06	+35.76	+1.02	-24.84	-0.70	14
Germany	Frankfurt Xetra DAX	3720.64	+30.31	+0.82	-244.52	-6.17	15
Hong Kong	Hang Seng	12408.04	-59.37	-0.48	-167.90	-1.34	16
India	Bombay Sensex	5252.05	+18.84	+0.36	-586.91	-10.05	14
Israel	Tel Aviv 25	524.22	-1.55	-0.29	+20.07	+3.98	...
Italy	Milan MIBtel	20071.00	+106.00	+0.53	+149.00	+0.75	13
Japan	Tokyo Nikkei 225	10953.55	+44.85	+0.41	+276.91	+2.59	...
Japan	Tokyo Nikkei 300	212.45	+0.20	+0.09	+8.91	+4.38	...
Japan	Tokyo Topix Index	1105.02	+3.45	+0.31	+61.33	+5.88	115
Mexico	I.P.C. All-Share	9910.84	+96.78	+0.99	+1115.56	+12.68	14
Netherlands	Amsterdam AEX	316.24	+3.16	+1.01	-21.41	-6.34	10
Russia	DJ Russia Titans 10	2065.66	-40.77	-1.94	-109.47	-5.03	31
Singapore	Straits Times	1901.41	-21.34	-1.11	+136.89	+7.76	13
South Africa	Johannesburg All Share	10180.41	-47.10	-0.46	-206.81	-1.99	12
South Korea	KOSPI	748.62	+6.49	+0.87	-62.09	-7.66	13
Spain	IBEX 35	7654.70	+21.10	+0.28	-82.50	-1.07	15
Sweden	SX All Share	202.96	+2.05	+1.02	+8.79	+4.53	20
Switzerland	Zurich Swiss Market	5383.00	+24.40	+0.46	-104.80	-1.91	15
Taiwan	Weighted	5393.73	-5.72	-0.11	-496.96	-8.44	11
Turkey	Istanbul National 100	19392.64	+144.54	+0.75	+767.62	+4.12	18
U.K.	London FTSE 100-share	4350.90	+36.50	+0.85	-126.00	-2.81	12
U.K.	London FTSE 250-share	5875.00	+40.60	+0.70	+72.70	+1.25	16

Source: Republished with permission of Dow Jones & Company, Inc., from *The Wall Street Journal,* August 11, 2004; permission conveyed through the Copyright Clearance Center, Inc.

In general, correlations between stock indexes have been higher in recent years than they were several years ago. One reason for the increased correlations is the increased integration of business between countries, which results in more intercountry trade flows and capital flows, causing each country to have more influence on other countries. In particular, many European countries have become more integrated because of a movement to standardize regulations throughout Europe and the use of a single currency (the euro) to facilitate trade between countries.

Integration of Markets during the 1987 Crash Exhibit 7.4 compares the U.S. stock market to three foreign stock markets during October 1987. Not only did the U.S. market suffer a major decline, but the other three markets were severely affected as well. The high correlation among country stock markets during the crash suggests that the underlying cause of the crash systematically affected all markets. Many institutional investors buy and sell stocks on numerous stock exchanges. Because they anticipated a worldwide decline in stock prices, they liquidated some stocks from all markets, not just from the U.S. market.

EXHIBIT 7.4   Impact of the Crash on Four Stock Markets

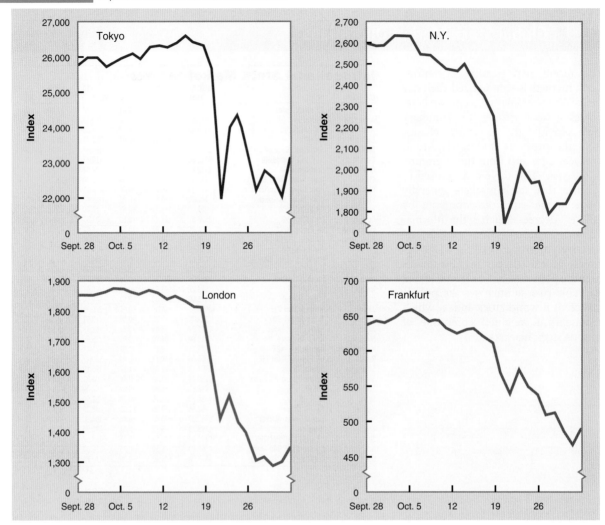

Source: *Economic Trends,* Federal Reserve Bank of Cleveland (November 1987):17.

Integration of Markets during Mini-Crashes   Although there has not been another world stock market crash since 1987, there have been several mini-crashes. For example, on August 27, 1998 (referred to as "Bloody Thursday"), Russian stock and currency values declined abruptly in response to severe financial problems in Russia, and most stock markets around the world experienced losses on that day. U.S. stocks declined by more than 4 percent. Such mini-crashes that adversely affect most stock markets illustrate that even a well-diversified international stock portfolio is not insulated from some events that have adverse consequences for stocks in every country. In the case of Bloody Thursday, the adverse effects extended beyond stocks that would be directly affected by financial problems in Russia, as paranoia caused investors to sell stocks across all markets due to fears that stocks might be overvalued.

Diversification among Emerging Stock Markets   Emerging markets provide an alternative outlet for investors from the United States and other countries to invest their funds. The potential economic growth rate is relatively high. In addition, investors may

achieve extra diversification benefits from investing in emerging markets because their respective economies may not necessarily move in tandem with those of the more developed countries. Thus, the correlation between these stocks and those of other countries is low, and investors can reduce risk by including some stocks from these markets within their portfolio. However, emerging market stocks tend to exhibit a high degree of volatility, which partially offsets the advantage of their low correlations with stocks of other countries.

International Market Efficiency

Some foreign markets are likely to be inefficient because of the relatively small number of analysts and portfolio managers who monitor stocks in those markets. It is easier to find undervalued stocks when a smaller number of market participants monitor the market. Research has documented that some foreign markets are inefficient, based on slow price responses to new information about specific firms (such as earnings announcements). The inefficiencies are more common in smaller foreign stock markets. Some emerging stock markets are relatively new and small and may not be as efficient as the U.S. stock market. Thus, some stocks may be undervalued, a possibility that has attracted investors to these markets. Because some of these markets are small, however, they may be susceptible to manipulation by large traders. Furthermore, insider trading is more prevalent in many foreign markets because rules against it are not enforced. In general, large institutional investors and insiders based in the foreign markets may have some advantages.

Although these markets may appeal to investors seeking abnormal returns, they also tend to have more volatile price movements than the larger markets. They are more exposed to major government turnover and other forms of political risk. They also expose U.S. investors to a high degree of exchange rate risk because their local currencies are typically very volatile. From 1990 to 1996 (before the Asian crisis), emerging stock markets such as Argentina, Brazil, Indonesia, and the Philippines experienced at least one year when stocks declined in value by at least 40 percent (after accounting for exchange rate effects on U.S. investors). During the Asian crisis of 1997–1998, these markets and other Asian markets experienced major declines. Thus, stock market inefficiencies in emerging markets may sometimes result in excessive optimism and overvalued stocks, resulting in periodic corrections.

SUMMARY

- Stocks are commonly valued using the price-earnings (PE) method or the dividend discount model. The PE method applies the industry PE ratio to the firm's earnings to derive its value. The dividend discount model estimates the value as the present value of expected future dividends.

- Stock prices are affected by those factors that affect future cash flows or the required rate of return by investors. Economic conditions, market conditions, and firm-specific conditions can affect a firm's cash flows or the required rate of return.

- Many investors rely on analyst recommendations when making investment decisions. Analysts can have a major impact on the value of a stock because of their influence on the demand for a stock by investors. Recently, analysts have come under scrutiny, as their recommendations tend to be overly optimistic.

- The risk of a stock is measured by its volatility, its beta, or its value-at-risk estimate. Investors are giving more attention to risk measurement in light of abrupt downturns in the prices of some stocks in recent years.

■ Stock market efficiency implies that stock prices reflect all available information. Weak-form efficiency suggests that security prices reflect all trade-related information, such as historical security price movements and volume of securities trades. Semistrong-form efficiency suggests that security prices fully reflect all public information. Strong-form efficiency suggests that security prices fully reflect all information, including private or insider information. Evidence supports weak-form efficiency to a degree, but there is less support for semistrong or strong-form efficiency.

POINT COUNTER-POINT

Should the Market Rely on Analysts' Opinions?

Point Yes. Analysts specialize in recognizing when a stock is under- or overvalued. They are more skilled than most investors. They also have better access to information than investors.

Counter-Point No. Even if analysts have better skills and information, they tend to offer overly optimistic projections. They are subject to major conflicts of interest and are unwilling to provide negative reports of stocks.

Who Is Correct? Use your favorite search engine to learn more about this issue. Offer your own opinion on this issue.

QUESTIONS AND APPLICATIONS

1. **Internet Exercise** Go to http://finance.yahoo.com/?u.
   a. Compare the performance of the Dow, Nasdaq, and S&P 500 indexes. Click on each of these indexes and describe the trend for that index since January. Which index has had the best performance?
2. **Wall Street** In the movie *Wall Street,* Bud Fox is a broker who conducts trades for Gordon Gekko's firm. Gekko purchases shares of firms he believes are undervalued. Various scenes in the movie offer excellent examples of concepts discussed in this chapter.
   a. Bud Fox makes the comment to Gordon Gekko that a firm's breakup value is twice its market price. What is Bud suggesting in this statement? How would employees of the firm respond to Bud's statement?
   b. Once Bud informs Gekko that another investor, Mr. Wildman, is secretly planning to acquire a target firm in Pennsylvania, Gekko tells Bud to buy a large amount of this stock. Why?
   c. Gekko states "Wonder why fund managers can't beat the S&P 500? Because they are sheep." What is Gekko's point? How does it relate to market efficiency?

3. **Market Efficiency** Explain the difference between weak-form, semistrong-form, and strong-form efficiency. Which of these forms of efficiency is most difficult to test? Which is most likely to be refuted? Explain how to test weak-form efficiency in the stock market.
4. **Price-Earnings Model** Explain the use of the price-earnings ratio for valuing a stock. Why might investors derive different valuations for a stock when using the price-earnings method? Why might investors derive an inaccurate valuation of a firm when using the price-earnings method?
5. **Impact of Interest Rates** How are the interest rate, the required rate of return on a stock, and the valuation of a stock related?
6. **Investor Sentiment** Explain why investor sentiment can affect stock prices.
7. **Impact of Takeover Rumors** Why can expectations of an acquisition affect the value of the target's stock?
8. **Interpreting Financial News** Interpret the following statements made by Wall Street analysts and portfolio managers:

a. "The stock market's recent climb has been driven by falling interest rates."

b. "Future stock prices are dependent on the Fed's policy meeting next week."

c. "Given a recent climb in stocks that cannot be explained by fundamentals, a correction is inevitable."

9. **Value-at-Risk** Describe the value-at-risk method for measuring risk.

10. **Dividend Discount Model** Describe the dividend discount valuation model. What are some limitations of the dividend discount model?

11. **Stock Portfolio Volatility** Identify the factors that affect a stock portfolio's volatility and explain their effects.

12. **Managing in Financial Markets: Stock Portfolio Dilemma** As an investment manager, you frequently make decisions about investing in stocks versus other types of investments and about types of stocks to purchase.

a. You have noticed that investors tend to invest more heavily in stocks after interest rates have declined. You are considering this strategy as well. Is it rational to invest more heavily in stocks once interest rates have declined?

b. Assume that you are about to select a specific stock that will perform well in resonse to an expected runup in the stock market. You are very confident that the stock market will perform well in the near future. Recently, a friend recommended that you consider purchasing stock of a specific firm because it had decent earnings over the last few years, it has a low beta (reflecting a low degree of systematic risk), and its beta is expected to remain low. You normally rely on beta as a measurement of a firm's systematic risk. Should you seriously consider buying that stock? Explain.

c. You are considering an investment in an initial public offering (IPO) by Marx Company, which has performed very well recently, according to its financial statements. The firm will use some of the proceeds from selling stock to pay off some of its bank loans. How can you apply stock valuation models to estimate this firm's value, when its stock was not publicly traded? Once you estimate the value of the firm, how can you use this information to determine whether to invest in it? What are some limitations in estimating the value of this firm?

d. In the past, your boss assessed your performance based on the actual return on the portfolio of U.S. stocks that you manage. For each quarter in which your portfolio generated an annualized return of at least 20 percent, you received a bonus. Now your boss wants you to develop a method for measuring your performance from managing the portfolio. Offer a method that accurately measures your performance.

e. Assume that you were also asked to manage a portfolio of European stocks. How would your method for measuring your performance in managing this portfolio differ from the method you devised for the U.S. stock portfolio in the previous question?

13. **Market Efficiency** A consulting firm was hired to determine whether a particular trading strategy could generate abnormal returns. The strategy involved taking positions based on recent historical movements in stock prices. The strategy did not achieve abnormal returns. Consequently, the consulting firm concluded that the stock market is weak-form efficient. Do you agree? Explain.

14. **Leveraged Buyout** At the time a management group of RJR Nabisco initially considered engaging in a leveraged buyout, RJR's stock price was less than $70 per share. Ultimately, RJR was acquired by the firm Kohlberg, Kravis, and Roberts (KKR) for about $108 per share. Does the large discrepancy between the stock price before an acquisition was considered versus after the acquisition mean that RJR's price was initially undervalued? If so, does this imply that the market was inefficient?

15. **Analyst Conflicts of Interest** What conflicts of interest are faced by many analysts who rate stocks?

16. **Impact of Inflation** Assume that the expected inflation rate has just been revised upward by the market. Would the required return by investors who invest in stocks be affected? Explain.

17. **January Effect** Describe the January effect.

18. **Impact of Economic Growth** Explain how economic growth affects the valuation of a stock.

19. **Beta** Explain how to estimate the beta of a stock. Explain the logic regarding how beta serves as a measure of the stock's risk.

20. **Earnings Surprises** How do earnings surprises affect valuations of stocks?

21. **Impact of Exchange Rates** Explain how the value of the dollar affects stock valuations.

22. **Analyst Recommendations** How do analyst recommendations affect stock valuations?

23. **Implied Volatility** Explain the meaning and use of implied volatility.

PROBLEMS

1. **Measuring the Portfolio Beta** Assume the following information:

   ■ Beta of IBM = 1.31
   ■ Beta of LUV = 0.85
   ■ Beta of ODP = 0.94

   If you invest 40 percent of your money in IBM, 30 percent in LUV, and 30 percent in ODP, what is your portfolio's beta?

2. **Measuring the Portfolio Beta** Using the information from Problem 1, suppose that you instead decide to invest $20,000 in IBM, $30,000 in LUV, and $50,000 in ODP. What is the beta of your portfolio now?

3. **Value at Risk**
   a. Determine how the lower boundary of a stock would be affected by an increase in the volatility (standard deviation), based on a 95 percent confidence interval.
   b. Determine how the upper boundary of a stock would be affected by an increase in the volatility (standard deviation), based on a 95 percent confidence interval.

4. **Risk-Adjusted Return Measurements** Assume the following information over a five-year period:

   ■ Average risk-free rate = 6%
   ■ Average return for Crane stock = 11%
   ■ Average return for Load stock = 14%
   ■ Standard deviation of Crane stock returns = 2%
   ■ Standard deviation of Load stock returns = 4%
   ■ Beta of Crane stock = 0.8
   ■ Beta of Load stock = 1.1

   Determine which stock has higher risk-adjusted returns when using the Sharpe index. Which stock has higher risk-adjusted returns when using the Treynor index? Show your work.

5. **Deriving the Required Rate of Return** A stock has a beta of 2.2, the risk-free rate is 6 percent, and the expected return on the market is 12 percent. Using the CAPM, what would you expect the required

rate of return on this stock to be? What is the market risk premium?

6. **Using the Dividend Discount Model** Suppose that you are interested in buying the stock of a company that has a policy of paying a $6 per share dividend every year. Assuming no changes in the firm's policies, what is the value of a share of stock if the required rate of return is 11 percent?

7. **Measuring Stock Returns** Suppose you bought a stock at the beginning of the year for $76.50. During the year, the stock paid a dividend of $0.70 per share and had an ending share price of $99.25. What is the total percentage return from investing in that stock over the year?

8. **Measuring Expected Return** Assume Mess stock has a beta of 1.2. If the risk-free rate is 7 percent and the market return is 10 percent, what is the expected return of Mess stock?

9. **Using the Dividend Discount Model** Suppose you know that a company *just paid* a dividend of $1.75 per share on its stock and that the dividend will continue to grow at a rate of 8 percent per year. If the required return on this stock is 10 percent, what is the current share price?

10. **Using the PE Method** You found that IBM is expected to generate earnings of $4.38 per share this year and that the mean PE ratio for its industry is 27.195. Using the PE valuation method, what should be the value of IBM shares?

11. **CAPM Relationships**
    a. When using the CAPM, determine how the required rate of return on a stock would be affected if the risk-free rate is lower.
    b. When using the CAPM, determine how the required rate of return on a stock would be affected if the market return is lower.
    c. When using the CAPM, determine how the required rate of return on a stock would be affected if the beta is higher.

12. **Deriving the Required Rate of Return** The next expected dividend for Sun Inc. will be $1.20 per share and analysts expect the dividend to grow at a rate of 7 percent indefinitely. If Sun stock currently sells for $22 per share, what is the required rate of return?

13. **Value at Risk** If your portfolio beta was calculated to be 0.89 and the stock market has a maximum expected loss of -2.5 percent on a daily basis, what is the maximum daily loss to your portfolio?

14. **Stock Portfolio Volatility Template** Use the Stock Portfolio Volatility Template to determine how the stock volatility would be affected if the correlation between two stocks is higher.

15. **Deriving the Required Rate of Return** A share of common stock currently sells for $110. Current dividends are $8 per share and are expected to grow at 6 percent per year indefinitely. What is the rate of return required by investors in the stock?

16. **Using the Dividend Discount Model** Micro Inc. will pay a dividend of $2.30 per share next year. If the company plans to increase its dividend by 9 percent per year indefinitely, and you require a 12 percent return on your investment, what should you pay for the company's stock?

17. **Value at Risk** IBM has a beta of 1.31.
    a. If you assume that the stock market has a maximum expected loss of -3.2 percent on a daily basis (based on a 95 percent confidence level), what is the maximum daily loss for the IBM stock?
    b. If you have $19,000 invested in IBM stock, what is your maximum daily dollar loss?

18. **Dividend Model Relationships**
    a. When computing the price of a stock with a dividend discount model, determine how the price of a stock would be affected if the required rate of return is increased. Explain the logic of this relationship.
    b. When computing the price of a stock using the constant growth dividend discount model, determine how the price of a stock would be affected if the growth rate is reduced. Explain the logic of this relationship.

19. **Deriving the Stock's Beta** You are considering investing in a stock that has an expected return of 13 percent. If the risk-free rate is 5 percent and the market risk premium is 7 percent, what must the beta of this stock be?

FLOW OF FUNDS EXERCISE

Valuing Stocks

Recall that if the economy continues to be strong, Carson Company may need to increase its production capacity by about 50 percent over the next few years to satisfy demand. It would need financing to expand and accommodate the increase in production. Recall that the yield curve is currently upward sloping. Also recall that Carson is concerned about a possible slowing of the economy because of potential Fed actions to reduce inflation. It is also considering the issuance of stock or bonds to raise funds in the next year. If Carson goes public, it might even consider using its stock as a means of acquiring some target firms. It would also consider engaging in a secondary offering at a future point in time if the IPO is successful and if its growth continues over time. It would also change its compensation system to compensate most of its managers with shares of its stock that would represent about 30 percent of their compensation and would pay the remainder of the compensation as salary.

a. At the present time, the price-earnings (PE) ratio (stock price per share divided by earnings per share) of other firms in Carson's industry is relatively low but should rise in the future. Why might this information affect the time at which Carson issues its stock?

b. Assume that Carson Company believes that issuing stock is an efficient means of circumventing the potential for high interest rates. Even if long-term interest rates have increased by the time it issues stock, Carson thinks that it would be insulated by issuing stock instead of bonds. Is this view correct?

c. Carson Company recognizes the importance of a high stock price at the time it engages in an IPO (if it goes public). But why would its stock price be important to Carson Company even after the IPO?

d. If Carson Company goes public, it may be able to motivate its managers by granting them stock as

part of their compensation. Explain why the stock may motivate them to perform well. Then explain why the use of stock as compensation may motivate them to use a very short-term focus, even though they are supposed to focus on maximizing shareholder wealth over the long run. How can a firm provide stock as motivation but prevent the managers from using a very short-term focus?

WSJ EXERCISE

Reviewing Abrupt Shifts in Stock Valuation

Review the "Price Percentage Gainers and Losers" in the "Stock Market Data Bank" in Section C of a recent issue of *The Wall Street Journal*. Notice that the largest one-day gainers and losers are shown for the New York Stock Exchange, American Stock Exchange, and Nasdaq market. Which has the biggest gainers? Which has the biggest losers? Offer an explanation as to why one market has bigger gainers and bigger losers than the others.

The Link between Accounting and Stock Valuation

In a publicly traded firm, the managers who run the firm are separate from the investors who own it. Managers are hired to serve as agents of the corporation and are expected to serve the interests of the firm's shareholders by making decisions that maximize the value of the firm. The firm's management is required to provide substantial information about the firm's financial condition and performance. Shareholders and other investors use this information to monitor management and to value the firm. For example, if investors use the price-earnings method to derive a valuation, they rely on the reported earnings. If they use the dividend discount model, they may derive an expected growth rate from recently reported earnings or revenue figures. If they use the adjusted dividend discount model, they may rely on financial statements to estimate future cash flows.

If firms provide inaccurate financial information, investors will derive inaccurate valuations, and money will flow to the wrong sources in the stock markets. In addition, inaccurate financial information creates more risk for stocks because investors must worry about the uncertainty surrounding the reported financial statement numbers. If financial statement data are questionable, stock values may decline whenever investors recognize that the earnings or some other proxy used to estimate cash flows is overstated. Investors will require a higher rate of return to hold stocks subject to downside risk because of distorted accounting. Thus, deceptive accounting practices disrupt the stock market and increase the cost of capital raised by issuing of stock.

To ensure that managers serve shareholder interests, firms commonly tie managerial compensation to the stock price. For example, managers may be granted stock options that allow them to buy the firm's stock at a specified price over a specified time period (such as the next five years). In this way, the managers benefit directly from a high stock price just like other shareholders and thus should make decisions that result in a high stock price for the shareholders.

Unfortunately, some managers recognize that it may be easier to increase their stock's price by manipulating the financial statements than by improving the firm's operations. When the firm's reported earnings are inflated, investors will likely overestimate the value of its stock, regardless of the method they use to value stocks.

Managers may be tempted to temporarily inflate reported earnings because doing so may temporarily inflate the stock's price. If no limits are imposed on the stock options granted, managers may be able to exercise their options (buying the stock at the price

specified in the option contracts) during this period of a temporarily inflated price and immediately sell the stock in the secondary market. They can capitalize on the inflated stock price before other investors realize that the earnings and stock price are inflated.

Problems with Creative Accounting

Managers would not be able to manipulate a firm's financial information if accounting rules did not allow them to be creative. The accounting for a firm's financial statement items is guided by generally accepted accounting principles (GAAP) set by the Financial Standards Accounting Board (FASB). However, these guidelines allow for substantial flexibility in accounting, which means that there is no standard formula for converting accounting numbers into cash flows. The accounting confusion is compounded by the desire of some managers to inflate their firm's earnings in particular periods when they wish to sell their holdings of the firm's stock. Specifically, the accounting can inflate revenue in a particular period without inflating expenses or defer the reporting of some expenses until a future quarter. Investors who do not recognize that some of the accounting numbers are distorted may overestimate the value of the firm.

Creative Classification of Expenses

When a firm discontinues one of its business projects, it commonly records this as a write-off, or a one-time charge against earnings. Investors tend to ignore writeoffs when estimating future expenses because they do not expect them to occur again. Some firms, however, shift a portion of their normal operating expenses into the writeoff, even though those expenses will occur again in the future. Investors who do not recognize this accounting gimmick will underestimate the future expenses.

As a classic example of shifting expenses, WorldCom attempted to write off more than $7 billion following the acquisition of MCI in 1998. When the Securities and Exchange Commission (SEC) questioned this accounting, WorldCom changed the amount to about $3 billion. If it had succeeded in including the extra $4 billion in the writeoff, it could have reduced its reported operating expenses by $4 billion. Thus, investors who trusted WorldCom's income statement would have underestimated its future expenses by about $4 billion per year and therefore would have grossly overestimated the value of the stock.

Earnings Restatements: After the Damage Is Done

When firms go beyond the loose accounting guidelines, the SEC may require them to restate their earnings and provide a corrected set of financial statements. In recent years, the SEC has forced hundreds of firms to restate their earnings, but the investors who lost money because they trusted a firm's distorted accounting were not reimbursed.

Governance Applied to Prevent Distorted Accounting

Several types of governance can be used to attempt to prevent firms from using distorted accounting, as explained next.

Auditing

Firms are required to hire auditors to audit their financial statements and verify that the statements are within the accounting guidelines. The auditors, however, rely on these firms for their future business. Many large firms pay auditors more than $1 million per year for their auditing services and also for nonauditing services. Thus, the auditors may be tempted to sign off on distorted accounting so that they will be rehired by their clients in the future. If the auditors uphold proper standards that force their clients to revise their reported earnings, they may not be hired again. The temptation to sign off on creative accounting used by client firms is especially strong given the subjectivity allowed by the accounting rules. Auditors may be more willing to sign off on financial statements that are somewhat confusing but do not a directly violate accounting rules.

Board of Directors

A firm's board of directors is expected to represent the firm's shareholders. The directors oversee the firm's financial reporting process and should attempt to ensure that the financial information provided by the firm is accurate. However, some boards have not forced managers to accurately disclose their financial condition. A board can be ineffective if it is run by insiders who are the same managers that the board is supposed to monitor. Board members who are managers of the firm (insiders) are less likely to scrutinize the firm's management. In recent years, many firms have increased the proportion of independent board members (outsiders), who are not subject to pressure from the firm's executives. Yet, even some independent board members have strong ties to the firm's employees or receive substantial consulting income beyond their compensation for serving on the board. Thus, they may be willing to overlook distorted accounting or other unethical behavior in order to maintain their existing income stream from the firm.

Recently, several proposals have been made to try to increase the independence of board members. For example, on January 9, 2003, the Commission on Public Trust and Private Enterprise released its recommendations to improve corporate governance. The Commission is a panel of the Conference Board, and its purpose is to address the widespread abuses that led to corporate scandals and declining public trust in companies, their leaders, and U.S. capital markets. The Commission issues best-practices guidelines.

Among its recommendations was that each corporation should consider separating the offices of chair of the board and CEO. Furthermore, the board chair should be an independent director. The Commission also recommended that a Lead Independent Director position should be established in cases where the chair is not an independent director. In addition, the Commission recommended that a Presiding Director position be established in cases where a corporation does not separate the functions of chair of the board and CEO.

Compensation of Board Members Some boards are ineffective because of the way the board members are compensated. If board members receive stock options from the firm as compensation, the options' value is tied to the firm's stock price. Consequently, some board members may be tempted to ignore their oversight duties, as they may benefit from selling their shares of the stock (received as compensation) while the price is temporarily inflated. Meanwhile, shareholders who hold their stock for a longer time period will be adversely affected once the market recognizes that the financial statements are distorted.

Board members are more likely to serve the long-term interests of shareholders if they are compensated in a manner that encourages them to maximize the long-term value of the firm. If they are provided stock that they cannot sell for a long-term period, they are more likely to focus on maximizing the long-term value of the firm.

Recent regulations address the issue of potential abuses resulting from granting stock options to managers and board members. On July 1, 2003, the SEC ruled that corporations listed on the New York Stock Exchange (NYSE) or the Nasdaq market must have shareholder approval before giving executives company stock or options. The rules were drafted and approved by the NYSE and Nasdaq. In addition, the FASB recently proposed that corporations be required to expense executive stock options on their income statements. If adopted, this measure would increase transparency in financial reporting and might improve corporate governance. As a result of these measures, several companies, including American Express, Bank of America, and General Electric, stopped granting stock options to nonemployee directors in favor of long-term stock awards.

Board's Independent Audit Committee Some board members may serve on an independent audit committee, which is responsible for monitoring the firm's auditor. The committee is expected to ensure that the audit is completed without conflicts of interest so that the auditors will provide an unbiased audit. Some boards have not prevented distorted audits, however, either because they did not recognize the conflicts of interest or because they were unwilling to acknowledge them.

Role of Credit Rating Agencies

Investors may also rely on credit rating agencies such as Standard & Poor's or Moody's to assess a firm's risk level. However, these agencies do not always detect a firm's financial problems in advance. They normally focus on assessing a firm's risk level based on the financial statements provided, rather than on determining whether the financial statements are accurate. The agencies may assume that the financial statements are accurate because they were verified by an auditor and the audit was conducted ethically.

Role of the Market for Corporate Control

In the market for corporate control, firms that perform poorly should be acquired and reorganized by other more efficient firms (called raiders). The raiders have an incentive to seek out inefficient firms because they can buy them at a low price (reflecting their poor performance) and remove their inefficient management. Nevertheless, the market for corporate control does not necessarily prevent faulty accounting. First, raiders may not be able to identify firms that inflated their earnings. Second, firms that have inflated their earnings are probably overvalued, and raiders will not want to acquire them at their inflated price. Third, an acquisition involves substantial costs of integrating businesses, and there is the risk that these costs will offset any potential benefits.

The Enron Scandal

The most famous recent example of the use of creative accounting occurred at Enron Corporation. Enron was formed in 1985 from the merger of two natural gas pipeline companies. It grew relatively slowly until the 1990s when the deregulation of the utili-

ties industry presented new opportunities. Enron began to expand in several directions. It acquired power plants in the United States and also expanded internationally, acquiring a power distributor in Brazil, a power plant in India, and a water company in the United Kingdom, among others. Perhaps most importantly, it took advantage of the new deregulated environment to pioneer the trading of natural gas and electricity. Soon it had branched out beyond simple energy trading to trade such instruments as weather derivatives. In 1999, it introduced Enron Online, an Internet-based trading platform that gave the company the appeal of an "Internet stock" at a time when such stocks were highly desired. The company introduced online trading of metals, wood products, and even broadband capacity, as well as energy. All of this enabled Enron to grow to become the seventh largest firm in the United States in terms of gross revenues by 2000.

Most investors were caught by surprise when Enron began to experience financial problems in October 2001 and then filed for bankruptcy on December 2, 2001. At the time, it was the largest U.S. firm to go bankrupt. In retrospect, Enron's stock may have been overvalued for many years, but some investors and creditors were fooled by its financial statements. The Enron fiasco received much publicity because it demonstrated how a firm could manipulate its financial statements, and therefore manipulate its valuation, in spite of various controls designed to prevent that type of behavior. This section offers some insight into why investor valuations and risk assessments of Enron were so poor.

Enron's Letter to Its Shareholders

If investors trusted the claims made by Enron in its annual report, it is understandable that they would value the stock highly. The letter to shareholders in Enron's 2000 annual report included the following statements:

- "Enron's performance in 2000 was a success by any measure, as we continued to outdistance the competition and solidify our leadership in each of our businesses.
- Enron has built unique and strong businesses that have limitless opportunities for growth.
- At a minimum, we see our market opportunities company-wide tripling over the next five years.
- Enron is laser-focused on earnings per share, and we expect to continue strong performance.
- Enron is increasing earnings per share and continuing our strong return to shareholders.
- The company's total return to shareholders was 89% in 2000, compared with a −9% returned by the S&P 500.
- The 10-year return to Enron shareholders was 1,415%, compared with 383% for the S&P 500.
- We plan to . . . create significant shareholder value for our shareholders."

Enron's Stock Valuation

Normally, the valuation of a firm is obtained by using the firm's financial statements to derive cash flows and to derive a required rate of return that is used to discount the cash flows. Enron's valuation was excessive because of various irregularities in its financial statements.

Estimating Cash Flows Since Enron's earnings were distorted, the estimates of its cash flows derived from those earnings were also distorted. Moreover, Enron's earnings were manipulated to create the perception of consistent earnings growth, which tempted investors to apply a high growth rate when estimating future cash flows.

Estimating the Required Rate of Return Investors can derive a required rate of return as the prevailing long-term risk-free interest rate plus the firm's risk premium. The risk premium can be measured by the firm's existing degree of financial leverage, its ability to cover interest payments with operating earnings, and its sensitivity to market movements.

Until the accounting distortions were publicized, Enron's risk was underestimated. The company concealed much of its debt by keeping it off its consolidated financial statements, as will be explained shortly. Consequently, investors who estimated Enron's sensitivity to market movements using historical data were unable to detect Enron's potential for failure. As a result, they used a lower risk premium than was appropriate. Thus, the financial statements caused investors both to overestimate Enron's future cash flows and to underestimate its risk. Both effects led to a superficially high stock price.

Applying Market Multiples Given the difficulty of estimating cash flows and the required rate of return, some investors may have tried to value Enron's stock by using market multiples. Determining the appropriate PE multiple for Enron was also difficult, however, because its reported earnings did not represent its real earnings.

Another problem with applying the industry PE method to Enron was the difficulty of identifying the proper industry. One of the company's main businesses was trading various types of energy derivative contracts. Enron did not want to be known as a trading company, however, because the valuations of companies such as investment banks that engage in trading are generally lower for a given level of earnings per share.

Enron's Managerial Motives

One of the main reasons for Enron's problems was its management. Managers are expected to maximize the value of the firm's stock. Like many firms, Enron granted stock options to some of its managers as a means of motivating them to make decisions that would maximize the value of its stock. However, Enron's management seemed to focus more on manipulating the financial statements to create a perception of strong business performance than on improving the actual performance. By manipulating the financial statements, Enron consistently met its earnings forecasts and increased its earnings over 20 consecutive quarters leading up to 2001. In this way, it created a false sense of security about its performance, thereby increasing the demand for its stock. This resulted in a superficially high stock price over a period in which some managers sold their stock holdings. Twenty-nine Enron executives or board members sold their holdings of Enron stock for more than $1 billion in total before the stock price plummeted.

Internal Monitoring Some firms use internal monitoring to ensure some degree of control over managers and encourage them to make decisions that benefit shareholders. Unfortunately, Enron's internal monitoring was also susceptible to manipulation. For example, managers were periodically required to measure the market value of various energy contracts that the company held. Since there was not an active market for some of

these contracts, the prevailing valuations of the contracts were arbitrary. Managers used estimates that resulted in very favorable valuations, which in turn led to a higher level of reported performance and higher managerial compensation.

Monitoring by the Board of Directors The board members serve as representatives of the firm's shareholders and are responsible for ensuring that the managers serve shareholder interests. In fact, board members are commonly compensated with stock so that they have an incentive to ensure that the stock price is maximized. In the case of Enron, some board members followed executives in selling their shares while the stock price was superficially high.

Enron's Financial Statement Manipulation

Some of the methods Enron used to report its financial conditions were inconsistent with accounting guidelines. Other methods were within the rules, but were misleading. Consequently, many investors invested in Enron without recognizing financial problems that were hidden from the financial statements. Some of these investors lost most or all of their investment.

Accounting for Partnerships One of the most common methods used by Enron to manipulate its financial statements involved the transfer of assets to partnerships that it owned called special-purpose entities (SPEs). It found outside investors to invest at least 3 percent of each partnership's capital. Under accounting guidelines, a partnership with this minimum level of investment from an outside investor does not have to be classified as a subsidiary. Since Enron did not have to classify its SPEs as subsidiaries, it did not have to include the financial information for them in its consolidated financial statements. Thus, the debt related to the SPEs was removed from Enron's consolidated financial statements. Since most investors focused on the consolidated financial statements, they did not detect Enron's financial problems.

In addition, whenever Enron created a partnership that would buy one of its business segments, it would book a gain on its consolidated financial statements from the sale of the asset to the partnership. Losses from a partnership would be booked on the partnership's financial statements. Thus, Enron was booking gains from its partnerships on its consolidated financial statements while hiding their losses. On November 8, 2001, Enron announced that it was restating its earnings for the previous five years because three of its partnerships should have been included in the consolidated financial statements. This announcement confirmed the suspicion of some investors that previous earnings figures were exaggerated. Enron's previously reported earnings were reduced by about $600 million over the previous five years, but the correction came too late for many investors who had purchased Enron stock when the reported earnings (and share price) were much higher.

Financing of Partnerships Enron's partnerships were financed by various creditors such as banks. The loans were to be paid off either from the cash flow generated by the assets transferred to the partnership or from the ultimate sale of the assets. When the partnerships performed poorly, they could not cover their debt payments. In some cases, Enron backed the debt with its stock, but as its stock price plummeted, this collateral no longer covered the debt, setting in motion the downward spiral that ultimately led to the company's bankruptcy.

Arthur Andersen's Audit

Investors and creditors commonly presume that financial statements used to value a firm are accurate when they have been audited by an independent accounting firm. In reality, however, the auditor and the firm do not always have an arm's length relationship. The accounting firm that conducts an audit is paid for the audit and recognizes the potential annuity from repeating this audit every year. In addition, accounting firms that provide auditing services also provide consulting services. Enron hired Arthur Andersen both to serve as its auditor and to provide substantial consulting services. In 2000, Arthur Andersen received $25 million in auditing fees from Enron and an additional $27 million in consulting fees.

Although Arthur Andersen was supposed to be completely independent, it recognized that if it did not sign off on the audit, it would lose this lucrative audit and consulting business. Furthermore, the annual bonus an accounting firm pays to its employees assigned to audit a client may be partially based on their billable hours, which would have been reduced if the firm's relationship with such a large client was severed.

Oversight by Investment Analysts

Even if financial statements are contrived, some investors may presume that investment analysts will detect discrepancies. If analysts simply accept the financial statements, however, rather than questioning their accuracy, the analysts will not necessarily serve as a control mechanism. The difficulties analysts faced in interpreting Enron's financial statements are highlighted by a humorous list created by some Enron employees of why the company restructured its operations so frequently. Reason number 7 was "Because the basic business model is to keep the outside investment analysts so confused that they will not be able to figure out that we do not know what we are doing." The humor now escapes some analysts, as well as some creditors and investors.

Another problem, though, is that like the supposedly independent auditors who hope to generate more business for their accounting firm, investment analysts may encounter a conflict of interest when they attempt to rate firms. As explained earlier, analysts employed by securities firms have been criticized for assigning very high ratings to firms they cover so that their employer may someday receive some consulting business from those firms.

As an example of what can happen to analysts who are "too critical," consider the experience of an analyst at BNP Paribus who downgraded Enron in August 2001, a few months before the company's financial problems became public. At the time, BNP Paribus was providing some consulting services for Enron. The analyst was demoted and then fired shortly after his downgrade of Enron. To the extent that many other analysts were subjected to a similar conflict of interest, it may explain why they did not downgrade Enron until after its financial problems were publicized. Even if analysts had detected financial problems at Enron, they might have been reluctant to lower their rating.

Market for Corporate Control

As explained earlier, if a firm's managers are running a firm into the ground, a raider has an incentive to purchase that firm at a low price and improve it so that it can be sold someday for a much higher price. However, this theory presumes that the stock price of the firm properly reflects its actual business performance. If the firm's financial state-

ments reflect strong performance, a raider will not necessarily realize that the firm is experiencing financial problems. Moreover, even if the raider is able to detect the problems, it will not be willing to pursue a firm whose value is overpriced by the market because of its contrived financial statements.

When Enron's stock price was high, few raiders could have afforded to acquire it. Once the stock price plummeted, Dynegy considered an acquisition of Enron. Dynegy quickly backed off, however, even though the stock price had fallen 90 percent from its high. Dynegy said it was concerned about problems it found when trying to reconcile Enron's cash position with what its financial statements suggested (among other reasons).

Monitoring by Creditors

Enron relied heavily on creditors for its financing. Since Enron's consolidated financial statements showed a superficially high level of earnings and a low level of debt, it had easy access to credit from a wide variety of creditors. Enron maintained a low cost of capital by using contrived statements that concealed its risk. Its balance sheet showed debt of $13 billion, but by some accounts, the actual amount of its debt was $20 billion. The hidden debt concealed Enron's true degree of financial leverage.

Bank of America and J.P. Morgan Chase each had exposure estimated at $500 million. Many other banks had exposure estimated at more than $100 million. They would not have provided so much credit if they had fully understood Enron's financial situation.

Even the debt rating agencies had difficulty understanding Enron's financial situation. On October 16, 2001, Enron announced $2 billion in writeoffs that would reduce its earnings. At this time, Standard & Poor's, the debt rating agency, affirmed Enron's rating at BBB+, along with its opinion that Enron's balance sheet should improve in the future. Over the next 45 days, S&P became more aware of Enron's financial condition and lowered its rating to junk status.

Many of Enron's creditors attempted to sue Enron once it became clear that the financial statements were misrepresented. By this time, however, Enron's value was depleted, as its price had already fallen to less than $1 per share.

Oversight by Regulators

The Enron fiasco prompted questions about whether additional regulations should be implemented to ensure proper disclosure of financial information. In particular, the accounting guidelines for the SPE partnerships and the potential conflict of interest between the audit and consulting segments of accounting firms are currently receiving much attention.

SPE Partnerships The FASB had discussed possible changes in reporting standards for SPE partnerships over the 20 years prior to the Enron fiasco. Nevertheless, it never took any action to correct this obvious means of hiding debt from consolidated financial statements. Perhaps this event will prompt the FASB to take some initiative.

Conflict between Audit and Consulting Duties In 2000, the SEC proposed a rule to prevent the potential conflict of interest for accounting firms that provide auditing and consulting services to a given client. It proposed that an accounting firm should provide either auditing or consulting services, but not both types of services. This proposal met strong resistance. Several accounting firms and the American Institute of Certified Public

Accountants (AICPA) lobbied members of Congress to discourage the SEC from pushing this proposal. At least 50 members of Congress wrote to the SEC, objecting to the proposal. Most of the letters came from members who had received donations from the accounting lobby. Of the 14 senators who wrote to the SEC, 11 were on the Banking Committee, which could influence the future funding for the SEC. The chairman of that committee received about $200,000 in contributions from the accounting lobby over the 1995–2000 period. His wife was on the board of directors at Enron. Twenty of the House members who wrote to the SEC were on the Energy and Commerce Committee. The chairman of this committee received about $143,000 in donations from the accounting lobby. Overall, the members of Congress who wrote letters to the SEC objecting to the accounting proposal received more than $3.5 million from the accounting lobby.

Prevention of Accounting Fraud

In response to the accounting fraud at Enron and other firms, regulators are attempting to ensure more accurate financial disclosure by firms. Stock exchanges have instituted new regulations for listed firms. The SEC has been given more resources and power to monitor financial reporting. Perhaps the most important regulatory changes have occurred as a result of the Sarbanes-Oxley Act of 2002. Some of the act's more important provisions were summarized in Chapter 6.

DISCUSSION QUESTIONS

The following discussion questions focus on the use of financial statements in the valuation of firms. They should generate much discussion, especially when accounting and finance students are present. These questions can be used in several ways. They may serve as an assignment on a day that the professor is unable to attend class. They are also useful for small group exercises. For each issue, one group could be randomly selected and asked to present their solution. Then, other students not in that group may suggest alternative answers if they feel that the solution can be improved. Each issue does not necessarily have a perfect solution, so students should be able to present different points of view.

1. Should an accounting firm be required to provide only auditing services or consulting services? Explain your answer. If an accounting firm is allowed to offer only one service, might there be any conflicts of interest due to referrals (and finder's fees)?

2. Should members of Congress be allowed to set regulations on accounting and financial matters while receiving donations from related lobbying groups?

3. What alternative sources of information about a firm should investors rely on if they cannot rely on financial statements?

4. Should investors have confidence in ratings by analysts who are affiliated with securities firms that provide consulting services to firms? Explain.

5. Does an analyst who is employed by a securities firm and is assigned to rate firms face a conflict of interest? What is a solution to this potential conflict?

6. How might a firm's board of directors discourage its managers from attempting to manipulate financial statements to create a temporarily high stock price?

7. How can the compensation of a firm's board of directors be structured so that the board members will not be tempted to allow accounting or other managerial decisions that could cause a superficially high price over a short period?

CHAPTER 8

Market Strategies and Microstructure

R ecently, much attention has been given to **market microstructure,** which is the process by which securities such as stocks are traded. For a stock market to function properly, a structure is needed to facilitate the placing of orders, speed the execution of the trades ordered, and provide equal access to information for all investors.

The specific objectives of this chapter are to:

- describe the common types of stock transactions,
- explain how stock transactions are executed,
- explain the role of electronic communications networks (ECNs) in executing transactions,
- describe the regulation of stock transactions, and
- explain how barriers to international stock transactions have been reduced.

Stock Market Transactions

Some of the more common stock market transactions desired by investors are market and limit orders, margin trades, short sales, and orders to trade stock indexes. Each of these types of transactions is discussed next.

Placing an Order

http://
http://finance.yahoo.com/
b?u Overview of stock
market performance.

To place an order to buy or sell a specific stock, an investor contacts a brokerage firm. Brokerage firms serve as financial intermediaries between buyers and sellers of stock in the secondary market. They receive orders from customers and pass the orders on to the exchange through a telecommunications network. The orders are frequently executed a few seconds later. Full-service brokers offer advice to customers on stocks to buy or sell; discount brokers only execute the transactions desired by customers. For a transaction involving 100 shares, a full-service broker may charge a fee of about 4 percent of the transaction amount versus about 1 percent or less for a discount broker. The larger the transaction amount, the lower the percentage charged by many brokers. Some discount brokers charge a fixed price per trade, such as $30 for any trade that is less than 500 shares.

Investors can contact their brokers to determine the prevailing price of a stock. The broker may provide a bid quote if the investor wants to sell a stock or an ask quote if the

investor wants to buy a stock. Investors communicate their order to brokers by specifying (1) the name of the stock, (2) whether to buy or sell that stock, (3) the number of shares to be bought or sold, and (4) whether the order is a market or a limit order. A **market order** to buy or sell a stock means to execute the transaction at the best possible price. A **limit order** differs from a market order in that a limit is placed on the price at which a stock can be purchased or sold.

ILLUSTRATION Stock Z is currently selling for $55 per share. If an investor places a market order to purchase (or sell) the stock, the transaction will be executed at the prevailing price at the time the transaction takes place. For example, the price may have risen to $55.25 per share or declined to $54.75 by the time the transaction occurs.

Alternatively, the investor could place a limit order to purchase Stock Z only at a price of $54.50 or less. The limit order can be placed for the day only or for a longer period. Other investors who wish to sell Stock Z may place limit orders to sell the stock only if it can be sold for $55.25 or more. The advantage of a limit order is that it may enable an investor to obtain the stock at a lower price. The disadvantage is that there is no guarantee the market price will ever reach the limit price established by the investor.

Stop-Loss Order A **stop-loss order** is a particular type of limit order. The investor specifies a selling price that is below the current market price of the stock. When the stock price drops to the specified level, the stop-loss order becomes a market order. If the stock price does not reach the specified minimum, the stop-loss order will not be executed. Investors generally place stop-loss orders to either protect gains or limit losses.

ILLUSTRATION Paul bought 100 shares of Bostner Corporation one year ago at a price of $50 per share. Today, Bostner stock trades for $60 per share. Paul believes that Bostner stock has additional upside potential and does not want to liquidate his position. Nonetheless, he would like to make sure that he realizes at least a 10 percent gain from the stock transaction. Consequently, he places a stop-loss order with a price of $55. If the stock price drops to $55, the stop-loss order will convert to a market order, and Paul will receive the prevailing market price at that time, which will be about $55. If Paul receives exactly $55, his gain from the transaction would be 100 shares × ($55 − $50) = $500. If the price of Bostner stock keeps increasing, the stop-loss order will never be executed.

Stop-Buy Order A stop-buy order is another type of limit order. In this case, the investor specifies a purchase price that is above the current market price. When the stock price rises to the specified level, the stop-buy order becomes a market order. If the stock price does not reach the specified maximum, the stop-buy order will not be executed.

ILLUSTRATION Karen would like to invest in the stock of Quan Company, but only if there is some evidence that stock market participants are demanding that stock. The stock is currently priced at $12. She places a stop-buy order at $14 per share, so if demand for Quan stock is sufficient to push the price to $14, she will purchase the stock. If the price remains below $14, her order will not be executed.

Placing an Order Online The mechanics of placing an order have changed substantially in recent years. Now at least 70 Internet brokers accept orders online, provide real-time

quotes, and provide access to information about firms. This trend is likely to continue. Individual investors currently maintain at least 5 million online brokerage accounts; about one of every seven stock transactions is now initiated online. The online brokerage business has taken some business away from the full-service and even discount brokerages, but the traditional brokerage firms are responding by offering some online services. Many firms that previously required investors to phone in their orders now allow investors to transmit their orders online for a lower commission per trade. Some full-service brokers allow their larger investors online access to information about any firm of interest.

Some of the more popular online brokerage firms include Ameritrade (http://www.ameritrade.com), Charles Schwab (http://www.schwab.com), Datek (http://www.datek.com), and E*Trade (http://www.etrade.com). The typical commission per trade conducted by online brokerage firms is between $8 and $25. Usually, a minimum balance of between $1,000 and $5,000 is required to open an account. The more popular online brokerage firms execute market order trades in about 8 seconds on average.

Margin Trading

When investors place an order, they may consider purchasing the stock on margin; in that case, they use cash along with funds borrowed from their broker to make the purchase. The Federal Reserve imposes **margin requirements,** which limit the amount of credit brokers can extend to their customers by specifying the proportion of invested funds that can be borrowed versus paid in cash. Margin requirements were first imposed in 1934, following a period of volatile market swings, to discourage excessive speculation and ensure greater stability. Currently, at least 50 percent of an investor's invested funds must be paid in cash. Margin requirements are intended to ensure that investors can cover their position if the value of their investment declines over time. Thus, with margin requirements, a major decline in stock prices is less likely to cause defaults on loans from brokers and therefore will be less damaging to the financial system.

The ability of higher margin requirements to stabilize stock price movements depends on whether the requirements discourage excessive speculation. Although margin requirements have been changed only 22 times in the United States, they have been changed about 100 times in Japan over the past 35 years. A study by Hardouvelis and Peristiani[1] found that the volatility of the Japanese stock market was higher when investors were allowed to borrow a higher percentage of their investment. The authors' findings suggest that the Federal Reserve might be able to control U.S. stock market volatility by adjusting margin requirements.

To purchase stock on margin, investors must establish an account (called a **margin account**) with their broker and put up some cash as collateral. They are required to satisfy a **maintenance margin,** which is the minimum amount of the margin (their own equity) that they must maintain as a percentage of the stock's value. Investors initially satisfy the maintenance margin by depositing cash when they request the purchase of a stock. This initial deposit is referred to as the **initial margin.** Brokerage firms may have more stringent maintenance margin requirements than the minimum set by the Federal Reserve.

[1]Gikas Hardouvelis and Steve Peristiani, "Do Margin Requirements Matter? Evidence from U.S. and Japanese Stock Markets," *FRBNY Quarterly Review* (Winter 1989–90): 16–34.

Impact on Returns The return on a stock is affected by the proportion of the investment that is from borrowed funds. Over short-term periods, the return on stocks (R) purchased on margin can be estimated as follows:

$$R = \frac{SP - INV - LOAN + D}{INV}$$

where

SP = selling price of stock

INV = initial investment by investor, not including borrowed funds

$LOAN$ = loan payments on borrowed funds, including both principal and interest

D = dividend payments

ILLUSTRATION Consider a stock priced at $40 that pays an annual dividend of $1 per share. An investor purchases the stock on margin, paying $20 per share and borrowing the remainder from the brokerage firm at 10 percent annual interest. If, after one year, the stock is sold at a price of $60 per share, the return on the stock is

$$R = \frac{\$60 - \$20 - \$22 + \$1}{\$20}$$

$$= \frac{\$19}{\$20}$$

$$= 95\%$$

In this example, the stock return (including the dividend) would have been 52.5 percent if the investor had used only personal funds rather than borrowing funds. This illustrates how the use of borrowed funds can magnify the returns on an investment.

Any losses are also magnified, however, when borrowed funds are used to invest in stocks. Reconsider the previous example and assume that the stock is sold at a price of $30 per share (instead of $60) at the end of the year. If the investor did not use any borrowed funds when purchasing the stock for $40 per share at the beginning of the year, the return on this investment would be

$$R = \frac{\$30 - \$40 - \$0 + \$1}{\$40}$$

$$= -22.5\%$$

However, if the investor had purchased the stock on margin at the beginning of the year, paying $20 per share and borrowing the remainder from the brokerage firm at 10 percent annual interest, the return over the year would be

$$R = \frac{\$30 - \$20 - \$22 + \$1}{\$20}$$

$$= -55\%$$

As these examples illustrate, purchasing stock on margin not only increases the potential return from investing in stock but may magnify the potential losses as well.

Margin Calls If a stock's value declines, so does the investor's equity value. Thus, the investor's equity may no longer represent the minimum percentage of the stock's value required by the broker. In this case, the investor receives a **margin call** from the broker, which means that the investor is required to provide more collateral (more cash or stocks) or sell the stock. Because of the potential for margin calls, a large volume of margin lending exposes the stock markets to a potential crisis. A major downturn in the market could result in many margin calls, some of which may force investors to sell their stock holdings if they do not have the cash to build their maintenance margin. Such a response results in more sales of stocks, additional downward pressure on stock prices, and additional margin calls. During the stock market crash in October 1987, for example, investors who did not have cash available to respond to margin calls sold their stock, putting additional downward pressure on stock prices.

The volume of margin lending reported by New York Stock Exchange (NYSE) firms reached a peak of $278 billion in March 2000 when market conditions were very favorable. As stock market conditions weakened, the volume of margin lending declined. By August 2001, margin lending reported by NYSE member firms had declined to $165 billion. Nevertheless, the attack on the United States on September 11, 2001, caused an abrupt decline in stock prices, and once again, many investors had to sell their stock because they could not back up their account with additional cash. These sales placed additional downward pressure on stock prices.

Short Selling

In a **short sale,** investors place an order to sell a stock that they do not own. They sell a stock short (or "short the stock") when they anticipate that its price will decline. When they sell short, they are essentially borrowing the stock from another investor and will ultimately have to provide that stock back to the investor from whom they borrowed it. If the price of the stock declines by the time investors purchase it in the market (to return to the investor from whom they borrowed), the short-sellers earn the difference between what they initially sold the stock for versus what they paid to obtain the stock. Short-sellers must make payments to the investor from whom the stock was borrowed to cover the dividend payments that the investor would have received if the stock had not been borrowed. The short-seller's profit is the difference between the original selling price and the price paid for the stock, after subtracting any dividend payments made. The risk of a short sale is that the stock price may increase over time, forcing the short-seller to pay a higher price for the stock than the price at which it was initially sold.

ILLUSTRATION On May 5, the market value of Vizer Company stock was $70 per share. Ed conducted an analysis of Vizer stock and concluded that the price should be much lower. He called his broker and placed an order to sell 100 shares of Vizer stock. Since he did not have shares of Vizer to sell, this transaction was a short sale. Vizer stock does not pay dividends, so Ed did not have to cover dividend payments for the stock that his brokerage firm borrowed and sold for him. The sale of the stock resulted in proceeds of $7,000, which he placed in his account at the brokerage firm. During the next two months, the price of Vizer stock declined. On July 18, Ed placed an order through his brokerage firm to purchase 100 shares of Vizer stock and offset his short position. The market value at the time was $60, so he paid $6,000 for the shares. Thus, Ed earned $1,000 from his short position. This example ignores transaction costs associated with the short sale.

The risk from taking a short position is that the stock's price may rise instead of decline as expected. If the price had increased after Ed created the short position, his purchase price would have been higher than his selling price. In this case, Ed would have incurred a loss on the short position.

Measuring the Short Position of a Stock One measure of the degree of short positions is the ratio of the number of shares sold short divided by the total number of shares outstanding. For many stocks, this measure is between .5 and 2 percent. A relatively high percentage (such as 3 percent) suggests a large amount of short positions in the market, which implies that a relatively large number of investors expect the stock's price to decline.

Some financial publications disclose the level of short sales for stocks with the short interest ratio, which is the shares sold short divided by the average daily trading volume over a recent period. The higher the ratio, the higher the level of short sales. A short interest ratio of 2.0 for a particular stock indicates that the number of shares currently sold short is two times the number of shares traded per day, on average. A short interest ratio of 20 or more reflects an unusually high level of short sales, indicating that many investors believe that the stock price is currently overvalued. Some stocks have had short interest ratios exceeding 100 at a particular point in time.

The short interest ratio is also measured for the market to determine the level of short sales for the market overall. A high short interest ratio for the market indicates a high level of short selling activity in the market. The largest short positions are periodically disclosed in *The Wall Street Journal*. For each firm for which there is a large short position, the number of shares sold short is disclosed and compared to the corresponding number a month earlier. The change in the overall short position by investors from the previous month is also shown.

Using a Stop-Buy Order to Offset Short Selling Investors who have established a short position commonly request a stop-buy order to limit their losses.

ILLUSTRATION A year ago, Mary sold short 200 shares of Patronum Corporation stock for $70 per share. Patronum's stock currently trades for $80 a share. Consequently, Mary currently has an unrealized loss on the short sale, but she believes that Patronum stock will drop below $70 in the near future. She is unwilling to accept a loss of more than $15 per share on the transaction. Consequently, she places a stop-buy order for 200 shares with a specified purchase price of $85 per share. If Patronum stock increases to $85 per share, the stop-buy order becomes a market order, and Mary will pay approximately $85 per share. If Patronum stock does not increase to $85 per share, the stop-buy order will never be executed.

Investing in Stock Indexes

In addition to trading individual stocks, investors can trade stock indexes. A recent study by Greenwich Associates found that indexing may represent as much as 30 percent of all stock investments. Indexing has become very popular because purchasing an index entails lower transaction costs than does purchasing specific stocks. Second, several studies have found that actively managed stock portfolios do not outperform stock indexes and may even underperform the indexes on average.

In response to investors' desire to trade stock indexes, the American Stock Exchange (Amex) created **exchange traded funds (ETFs),** which are funds that are designed to mimic

particular stock indexes and are traded on a stock exchange. ETFs have become very popular. By 2004, the value of existing ETFs was about $150 billion.

Comparison of ETFs with Mutual Funds ETFs resemble some index mutual funds (discussed in Chapter 23) in several ways. First, for both ETFs and index mutual funds, the share price adjusts over time in response to the change in the index level. Second, both pay dividends in the form of additional shares to investors. Third, since both ETFs and index mutual funds are intended to track an index, their portfolio management is relatively simple, which results in lower management fees than for actively managed mutual funds.

Because ETFs are traded on an exchange, however, they exhibit some unique features. Unlike mutual funds, they can be traded throughout the day. They can be purchased on margin. They can also be sold short by investors who expect a decline in the underlying index, whereas mutual funds cannot be sold short.

One of the most important features of ETFs is the tax advantage. If stocks within an ETF are sold (perhaps because the index is revised), there is no tax effect on investors as there would be with a mutual fund. Since the ETF behaves like a stock, investors are subject to capital gains taxes only when they sell their shares. Thus, they can defer the capital gains for as long as they hold the ETFs.

A disadvantage of ETFs, however, is that there is a transaction cost every time shares are purchased just as there is when more shares of a stock are purchased. Investors do not incur a transaction fee when making periodic investments in some mutual funds.

Some mutual funds known as closed-end funds behave more like stocks, but the prices of their shares commonly differ from the underlying value of the stocks they represent. In contrast, the price of ETF shares typically equals the underlying value. Investors in a closed-end fund are subject to the risk that the price of the shares may decline even if the prices of stocks within the fund do not decline.

Types of ETFs The most popular ETF is the so-called Cube (its trading symbol is QQQ) created by the Bank of New York. Cubes are traded on the Amex and represent the Nasdaq 100 index, which consists of many technology firms. Thus, Cubes are ideal for investors who believe that technology stocks will perform well but do not want to select individual technology stocks. Cubes are also commonly sold short by investors who expect that technology stocks will decline in value. The high degree of uncertainty surrounding technology stocks resulted in substantial price movements during the 2000–2001 period, which allowed for large returns from positions in Cubes. The potential loss from a position in Cubes was also large, but not as large as for a position consisting of a single technology stock.

Another example of an ETF is the Standard & Poor's Depository Receipt (also called Spider), which is a basket of stocks matched to the S&P 500 index. Spiders enable investors to take positions in the index by purchasing shares. Thus, investors who anticipate that the stock market as represented by the S&P 500 will perform well may purchase shares of Spiders, especially when their expectations reflect the composite as a whole rather than any individual stock within the composite. Spiders trade at one-tenth the S&P 500 value, so if the S&P 500 is valued at 1400, a Spider is valued at $140. Thus, the percentage change in the price of the shares over time is equivalent to the percentage change in the value of the S&P 500 index.

Several other ETFs have also been created. For example, Diamonds are shares of the Dow Jones Industrial Average (DJIA) and are measured as one one-hundredth of the DJIA value. Mid-cap Spiders are shares that represent the S&P 400 Midcap Index. There

WSJ · USING THE WALL STREET JOURNAL

Exchange Traded Portfolios

The Wall Street Journal summarizes the performance of exchange traded funds. To the left of the name of the fund is the year-to-date (YTD) percentage change in the price, and the price range over the last 52 weeks. To the right of the name of the fund is the dividend per share (5th column), dividend yield (6th column), trading volume (7th column), closing price (8th column), and the net change in the share price from the previous day (9th column).

EXCHANGE TRADED PORTFOLIOS

Tuesday, August 10, 2004
Includes Exchange-Traded Funds and HOLDRs

AMEX

YTD %CHG	52 WEEKS HI	LO	STOCK (SYM)	DIV	YLD %	VOL 100s	CLOSE	NET CHG
-4.8	107.92	91.45	Diamond DIA	2.02e	2.0	72377	99.57	1.15
-8.8	89.82	71.70	PharmaHldrs PPH	1.62e	2.2	2595	72.54	0.74
-5.1	96.15	83.80	RetailHldrs RTH	.86e	1.0	17219	85.68	1.15
-27.4	3.65	2	B2BHldrs BHH	.09e	4.5	164	2.01	0.01
-2.8	160.25	122.80	BiotchHldrs BBH	.03e	...	8199	131.51	3.06
4.8	17.40	9.25	BrdBndHldrs BDH	.06e	.4	557	14.09	0.25
-12.5	66.08	48.27	Europe01Hldrs EKH	2.01e	3.8	11	53.40	-0.13
-10.7	40.16	30.26	IntArchHldrs IAH	.18e	.6	118	32.14	0.34
1.7	64.65	37.39	IntrntHldrs HHH		...	7262	51.03	1.88
-21.4	4.61	2.88	IntInfrHldrs IIH	.08e	2.7	328	2.97	0.06
-5.9	56.60	47.84	Mkt2000Hldrs MKH	1.05e	2.1	90	50.94	-0.01
-3.3	140.26	112.30	RegBkHldrs RKH	3.98e	3.1	4116	128.18	1.63
14.5	76.39	53.67	OilSvcHldrs OIH	.42e	.6	20153	71	-0.36
-25.6	45.78	30.18	SemiConHldrs SMH	.11e	.4	154648	30.86	0.32
-13.9	40.20	30.80	SftwreHldrs SWH	.13e	.4	1901	32.73	0.59
1.3	29.48	24.01	TelecomHldrs TTH	1.00e	3.6	3777	27.85	0.30
6.3	83.96	69.05	UtilHldrs UTH	3.11e	3.7	7262	83.32	0.26
9.4	59.81	37.93	WirlsHldrs WMH	.65e	1.2	26	52.80	0.63
12.8	58.57	42.11	iShrDJUSEn IYE	.92e	1.6	1288	55.79	-0.31
1.8	57.90	49.16	iShrDJTA IYT	.55e	1.0	135	54.81	1.26
-5.3	46.50	36.96	iShrDJUSBM IYM	.90e	2.1	341	43.18	0.65
-6.5	58.20	49.22	iShrDJUSCCy IYC	.14e	.3	129	51.80	0.84
0.3	52.85	42.28	iShrDJUSCNC IYK	.93e	1.9	173	48.45	0.54
-3.1	110.79	89.91	iShrDJUSFin IYG	2.50e	2.5	26	99.99	1.17
-5.2	60.90	51.60	iShrDJUSHlth IYH	.50e	.9	1063	54	0.77

YTD %CHG	52 WEEKS HI	LO	STOCK (SYM)	DIV	YLD %	VOL 100s	CLOSE	NET CHG
-3.4	66.38	54.80	iShrRu3000 IWV	1.13e	1.9	999	60.80	0.65
-5.2	121.15	90.14	iShrRu2000 IWM	1.27e	1.2	86126	105.02	1.62
-0.4	96.59	66.13	iShrSP/Tpx ITF	.24e	.3	42	83.30	0.18
-2.4	124	96.53	iShrSP400 IJH	1.33e	1.2	905	112.32	1.48
-5.4	102.45	93.36	iShrSP1500 ISI	.62e	.7	231	94.52	0.88
-5.1	58.01	48.72	iShrSP500G IVW	.77e	1.5	1038	52.75	0.58
-0.3	58.88	48.07	iShrSP500V IVE	1.16e	2.1	2553	55.18	0.61
-3.2	49.59	38.95	iShrSPGblTele IXP	.65e	1.5	21	44.08	0.60
-5.3	50.99	41.73	iShrSPHlthcr IXJ	.30e	.7	142	45.14	0.55
-11.8	55.97	40.80	iShrSPGbl IT IXN		...	9	44.71	0.80
-2.5	62.74	50.09	iShrSPGblFnl IXG	1.31e	2.3	11	56.91	0.36
-2.8	117	97.92	iShrSP500 IVV	2.10e	1.9	3376	108.15	1.10
8.7	66.84	49.31	iShrSPGbl GE IXC	.62e	1.0	8066	63.98	-0.27
-4.0	128.95	103.32	iShrSP400G IJK	.61e	.5	1640	114	1.94
-0.5	147.30	111.10	iShrSP600 IJR	1.19e	.9	3289	133.38	2.21
-0.2	64.90	45.01	iShrTr40 ILF	.74e	1.3	66	58.74	0.40
6.3	119.85	93.45	iShrCohenSt ICF	6.79e	6.0	1165	112.78	0.23
-8.9	39	29.93	Nasdaq 100 QQQ	.01e	...	962390	33.21	0.41
0.8	37.22	29.20	PwrShsDynMkt PWC	.37e	1.1	141	34.59	0.53
-11.1	43.85	30.80	PwrShsDynOTC PWO		...	7	35.51	0.61
-2.0	144.16	113.42	RydexSP500 ETF RSP	1.69e	1.3	401	132.76	1.50
-2.6	116.97	97.76	SPDR SPY	1.72e	1.6	510836	108.38	1.38
-6.1	32.58	27.36	SPDR ConsDiscr XLY	.24e	.8	464	29.57	0.43
0.3	23.67	20.04	SPDR ConStpl XLP	.42e	1.9	2300	21.85	0.17
13.6	32.85	23.63	SPDR Engy XLE	.61e	1.9	22789	31.31	-0.12
-1.6	30.61	24.86	SPDR Fncl XLF	.70e	2.5	33640	27.69	0.38
-6.6	31.98	27.31	SPDR Hlthcare XLV	.44e	1.6	778	28.16	0.41
1.7	28.78	22.61	SPDR Indu XLI	.42e	1.5	9137	27.22	0.45
-3.9	27.34	21.70	SPDR Materials XLB	.60e	2.3	15421	25.66	0.41
-7.9	22.24	16.90	SPDR Tch XLK	.14e	.7	7810	18.78	0.32

http://

http://www.ishares.com
Information on the trading of iShares.

are also Sector Spiders, which are intended to match a specific sector index. For example, a Technology Spider is a fund representing 79 technology stocks from the S&P 500 composite. Another type of ETF is the world equity benchmark shares (WEBS), which are designed to track stock indexes of specific countries. Barclays Bank has created several different ETFs (which it calls iShares) that represent specific countries.

By 2001, 94 different ETFs with an aggregate value of $80 billion were trading on the Amex. The New York Stock Exchange (NYSE) pursued ETFs because of their popularity. In 2001, the creators of some ETFs that were listed on the Amex decided to also list them on the NYSE.

On May 31, 2001, Vanguard announced the creation of its own ETFs, called Vanguard Index Participation Equity Receipts (VIPERs). An example is Vanguard Total Stock Market VIPER, which tracks the Wilshire 5000 index. Unlike the mutual funds Vanguard manages, VIPERs are traded on the Amex, and the price per share changes throughout the day.

How Trades Are Executed

Transactions on the stock exchanges and the Nasdaq are facilitated by floor brokers, specialists, and market-makers.

http://

http://www.nyse.com
Information about how trading is conducted on the NYSE.

Floor Brokers

Floor brokers are situated on the floor of a stock exchange. There are hundreds of computer booths along the perimeter of the trading floor, where floor brokers receive orders from brokerage firms. The floor brokers then fulfill and execute those orders.

ILLUSTRATION Bryan Adams calls his broker at Zepellin Securities, where he has a brokerage account, and requests the purchase of 1,000 shares of Clapton Inc. stock, which is traded on the NYSE. The broker at Zepellin communicates this information to the NYSE trading floor. A floor broker who may be an employee of Zepellin or some other brokerage firm receives the order at a booth and goes to a specific trading post where Clapton stock is traded. There are 20 trading posts on the NYSE, and a different set of stocks is traded at each trading post. The floor broker communicates the desire to purchase 1,000 shares of Clapton stock at a specific price. Other floor brokers who have orders to sell Clapton stock either communicate their willingness to accept the bid or signal the "ask" price at which they would be willing to sell the shares. If the floor brokers can agree on a price, a transaction is executed. The transaction is recorded and transmitted to the tape display. Bryan will likely receive a message from the broker, indicating that the trade was executed, and will receive confirmation in the mail within three days. Bryan provides payment to his brokerage firm within three days.

Specialists

http://

http://www.bloomberg.com
Click on "Stocks on the Move." Identifies stocks that experienced large price changes for the day, with an explanation.

Specialists can serve a broker function on stock exchanges by matching up buy and sell orders. They gain from accommodating these orders because their bid and ask prices differ. In addition, they also take positions in specific stocks to which they are assigned.

There are 443 specialists on the NYSE, and each one is typically assigned five to eight stocks. Most of them are employed by one of seven specialist firms. The specialists are required to signal to floor brokers if they have unfilled orders.

Specialists have access to the book (list) of market and limit orders. At the beginning of each day, they set their bid and ask prices to reflect a balance between buy and sell orders. The bid price is the price at which the specialist would purchase the stock; the ask price is the price at which the specialist would sell the stock.

ILLUSTRATION The price of Mackin Company stock closed at $32 last night. After the market closed, Mackin announced that it had been awarded a patent on a new invention. Many investors placed orders to buy the stock after hearing this news. Before the market opened on the following morning, the specialist assessed the buy and sell orders for Mackin stock. At a price of $32, there was an imbalance because the demand for the shares was much larger than the supply of shares for sale. The specialist decided that a proper equilibrium price would be about $33 per share. At that price, the quantity of Mackin shares for sale would be equal to the quantity of shares demanded. That is, the higher price would eliminate a portion of the demand (because some investors would be

unwilling to pay that price), thereby allowing supply and demand to be equal. He established a bid price of $33.00 and an ask price of $33.02.

Making a Market Specialists are required to "make a market" in the stocks that they are assigned. This role is commonly misunderstood. Making a market implies that the specialists stand ready to buy or sell the stocks that they are assigned if no other investors are willing to participate. Making a market does not mean that specialists are offsetting all orders by taking the opposite side of every transaction. In fact, many transactions occur without a specialist's involvement. Specialists participate in about 10 percent of the value of all shares traded; the other transactions are completed on the exchange without their participation.

Making a market does not mean that specialists must prevent a stock price from falling. A large amount of sell orders and a small amount of buy orders for a particular stock will naturally result in a decline in the stock price. Specialists may buy some shares to partially offset this imbalance between supply and demand, but they are buying the shares at the discounted price that resulted from the imbalance. They may sell some shares to partially offset an imbalance when demand exceeds supply, but they are selling the shares at the higher price that resulted from the imbalance. Thus, although specialists incur risk when they take positions on any given day, they commonly earn substantial profits from their positions on average. Since they have access to the book of limit orders on the buy side and sell side, they are sometimes said to be involved in a poker game in which only they can see everyone's cards.

Furthermore, specialists can set the spread to reflect their preferences. If they wish to avoid investing in a stock they are assigned at a particular point in time, they can widen the spread so that their bid price is substantially below the ask price. Under these circumstances, there will be a more favorable bid price for the stock than their bid price, and they can simply serve the broker function by matching buy and sell orders.

ILLUSTRATION Suppose that a stock is currently priced at $40, and there are numerous large limit orders to sell at various prices slightly less than $40 and only a few limit orders to buy. Clearly, the sentiment is on the sell side, and the equilibrium price will likely decline. Specialists can use this inside information when they decide whether to accommodate orders.

ILLUSTRATION The specialist for the stock of Closet Inc. is aware that the equilibrium price is currently $39.99 per share. She notices many limit orders by institutional investors to sell shares of Closet stock at $40 per share. Since she has a large inventory of Closet stock and is concerned because the limit orders suggest possible downward pressure on the price, she decides to sell a large block of her own shares of Closet stock at $39.99. This trade will take priority over the other orders because it is at a slightly lower price. Consequently, the specialist is able to sell her shares ahead of other investors who want to sell their shares. This act, which is referred to as "front-running" (or "penny-jumping"), may even prevent the orders of other investors from being executed if the price reverses as a result. In this example, the specialist who sold a block of shares at $39.99 could cause downward price momentum. Some of the institutional investors who placed limit orders to sell at $40 may have to revise their orders to specify a new lower price in order to sell their shares. They might have been able to sell their shares at $40 if the specialist had not traded in front of them.

Specialists may counter that the example shows how they "provide price improvement." In the example, the specialist sold shares at a penny per share less than other in-

vestors who were willing to sell their shares. However, the specialist's trade jumped in front of other potential sellers. Although the specialists may argue that they "make a market" for the security, a counterargument is that the investors make the market and specialists only use it to their advantage. The special priority of the specialists is enforced by a "trade-through rule" established by the Securities and Exchange Commission (SEC) in 1975, which requires that an order for NYSE-listed stocks must be executed on the exchange that offers the best price for the investor. The intention of the rule was to benefit investors, but it has allowed specialists to have priority in trading, which can place investors at a disadvantage.

Many institutional investors would prefer to use automated trading to circumvent the specialists because they believe their orders would be handled faster and more fairly. The NYSE's Superdot system uses automated trading, but it accounts for less than 10 percent of the trading on the NYSE. The "trade-through rule" allows specialists to intervene in place of the Superdot system or other automated systems (discussed shortly). In the past, the NYSE was slow to respond to the concerns of institutional investors. Given that the specialists own about one-third of the seats on the NYSE and that the NYSE is self-regulated, this is not surprising.

In the 2001–2003 period, the NYSE's regulatory division frequently ignored specialists' violations. Finally, the NYSE's weak self-regulatory efforts and the trading violations prompted the SEC to intervene. In 2004, the SEC investigated several specialist firms for various illegal activities. In addition, the SEC allowed investors to circumvent the trade-through rule. Consequently, trades should occur more quickly, and investors may have a better chance of having their trades executed before the price moves outside the range at which they are willing to buy or sell. They are also more likely to complete their trade without being subjected to front-running by specialists.

Market-Makers on the Nasdaq Transactions in the Nasdaq market are facilitated by so-called market-makers, who stand ready to buy specific stocks in response to customer orders made through a telecommunications network. They benefit from the difference (spread) between the bid and ask prices. They also can take positions in stocks. Thus, market-makers serve the Nasdaq market in a manner similar to the specialists on the NYSE and Amex. Some market-makers make a market in a few stocks, while others make a market for many stocks. For each stock that is traded in the Nasdaq market, there are 12 market-makers on average.

Market-makers take positions to capitalize on the discrepancy between the prevailing stock price and their own valuation of the stock. When many uninformed investors take buy or sell positions that push a stock's price away from its fundamental value, the stock price is distorted as a result of the "noise" caused by the uninformed investors (called "noise traders"). Market-makers may take the opposite position of the uninformed investors and therefore stand to benefit if their expectations are correct.

Brokers make the decision on the route by which an order is executed, meaning that they determine whether the order will be filled by a specific market-maker. The spread quoted for a given stock may vary among market-makers. Therefore, the manner by which the trade is routed by the broker can affect the size of the spread. Some market-makers compensate brokers for orders routed to them. So, while a brokerage firm may charge a customer only $10 for a trade, it may also receive a payment from the market-maker. The market-maker may use a wider spread so that it can offer such a payment to the broker. The point is that some customers may pay only $10 for a buy order to be executed, but the order is executed at a price that is relatively high because the market-maker charged a large spread. Customers should attempt to compare not only the fee brokers charge for a trade, but also the spread quoted by the market-maker selected by

the brokerage firm. They do not have direct control over the routing process, but can at least select a broker that uses the type of routing process that they prefer. The market is not sufficiently transparent to monitor the routing process, but technology may soon allow customers to more easily monitor the routing and the quoted spreads.

Some brokers own market-maker firms; for example, Charles Schwab & Co. owns Mayer & Schweitzer. In this case, investors who are told that they will be charged a very small commission may also incur a transaction fee through the market-maker.

Effect of the Spread on Transaction Costs

When investors place an order, they are quoted an ask price, or the price that the broker is asking for that stock. There is also a bid price, or the price at which the broker would purchase the stock. The spread is the difference between the ask price and the bid price and is commonly measured as a percentage of the ask price.

ILLUSTRATION Boletto Company stock is quoted by a broker as bid $39.80, ask $40.00. The bid-ask spread is

$$\text{Spread} = \frac{\$40.00 - \$39.80}{\$40.00}$$

$$= .5\%$$

This spread of .5 percent implies that if investors purchased the stock and then immediately sold it back before market prices changed, they would incur a cost of .5 percent of their investment for the round-trip transaction.

The transaction cost due to the spread is separate from the commission charged by the broker. The spread has declined substantially over time due to more efficient methods of executing orders and increased competition from electronic communication networks.

The spread is influenced by the following factors:

$$\text{Spread} = f(\text{Order Costs}, \text{Inventory Costs}, \text{Competition}, \text{Volume}, \text{Risk})$$
$$\qquad\qquad\quad + \qquad\qquad + \qquad\qquad - \qquad\quad - \qquad +$$

Order Costs Order costs are the costs of processing orders, including clearing costs and the costs of recording transactions.

Inventory Costs Inventory costs include the cost of maintaining an inventory of a particular stock. There is an opportunity cost because the funds could have been used for some other purpose. If interest rates are relatively high, the opportunity cost of holding an inventory should be relatively high. The higher the inventory costs, the larger the spread that will be established to cover these costs.

Competition The specialist for a particular stock on the NYSE faces competition from other electronic markets where the stock can be traded. For stocks traded in the Nasdaq market, having multiple market-makers promotes competition. If there are only a few market-makers for a particular stock, there is a greater chance of collusion among them. When there is collusion, the spread will be wider than it would be if the market-makers

were competing. Conversely, when more market-makers are competing to sell a particular stock, the spread is likely to be smaller.

Volume Stocks that are more liquid have less chance of experiencing an abrupt change in price. Those stocks that have a large trading volume are more liquid because there is a sufficient number of buyers and sellers at any time. This liquidity makes it easier to sell a stock at any point in time and therefore reduces the risk of a sudden decline in the stock's price.

Risk If the firm represented by a stock has relatively risky operations, its stock price is normally more volatile over time. Thus, the specialist or market-maker is subject to more risk from holding an inventory in this type of stock and will set a higher spread as a result.

At a given point in time, the spread can vary among stocks. The specialists or market-makers who make a market for a particular stock are exposed to the risk that the stock's price could change abruptly in the secondary market and reduce the value of their position in that stock. Thus, any factors that affect this type of risk to a specialist or a market-maker of a stock can affect the spread of that stock at a given point in time.

Electronic Communication Networks (ECNs)

Electronic communication networks (ECNs) are automated systems for disclosing and sometimes executing stock trades. They were created in the mid-1990s to publicly display buy and sell orders of stock. They were adapted to facilitate the execution of orders and normally service institutional rather than individual investors. In 1997, the SEC allowed ECNs complete access to orders placed in the Nasdaq market. The SEC requires that any quote provided by a market-maker be made available to all market participants. This eliminated the practice of providing more favorable quotes exclusively to proprietary clients. It also resulted in significantly lower spreads between the bid and ask prices quoted on the Nasdaq. ECNs are appealing to investors because they may allow for more efficient execution of trades. ECNs in aggregate now account for about 30 percent of the total trading volume on the Nasdaq. They also execute a small proportion of all transactions on the NYSE.

Some ECNs focus on market orders. They receive orders and route them through various networks searching for the best price. Other ECNs receive limit orders and electronically match them up with other orders that are still not fulfilled. Exhibit 8.1 shows an example of an ECN book at a given point in time. The book lists the limit buy orders and limit sell orders that are currently not fulfilled. When a new limit order matches an existing order, the transaction is immediately executed, and the matching order is removed from the book. If the new limit order cannot immediately be matched to an existing order on the ECN book, it is added to the book. An ECN can execute a transaction in an average time of about 2 seconds.

ILLUSTRATION Assume that the ECN book shown in Exhibit 8.1 is the book for a particular stock and that a new limit order is placed to sell 300 shares of that stock at a price of no less than $32.68. This order can be matched by the order to buy 300 shares at a bid price of $32.68. Upon the execution of this trade, the order on the ECN book to buy 300 shares at a bid price of $32.68 is removed. Assume now that a new limit order is placed to purchase 1,400 shares at a price of no more than $32.80. This order is matched up with the order to sell 400 shares at an ask price of $32.78 and the order to sell 1,000

EXHIBIT 8.1

Example of an ECN Book at a Given
Point in Time

Bid or Ask?	Shares	Price
Bid	500	$32.50
Bid	300	$32.50
Bid	400	$32.56
Bid	1,000	$32.60
Bid	400	$32.64
Bid	1,200	$32.64
Bid	300	$32.68
Ask	400	$32.78
Ask	1,000	$32.80
Ask	300	$32.84
Ask	500	$32.84
Ask	600	$32.88

shares at $32.80. Then those orders are removed from the ECN book because they have been fulfilled.

Several ECNs have become well known. Archipelago serves as an ECN for many online buyers and sellers. It provides low-cost, fast, and anonymous access to the market and facilitates the trades of more than 100 million shares a day. Island is a well-known firm (owned by Datek Holdings Corporation, an Internet brokerage firm) that serves as an ECN by facilitating the trading of about 100 million shares per day on the Nasdaq, or about 10 percent of the total Nasdaq trading volume. It executes many of the trades of technology stocks such as Dell and Yahoo!. Instinet, a subsidiary of the Reuters Group (of the United Kingdom), is another ECN that commonly facilitates daily stock transactions requested by U.S. financial institutions after the U.S. exchanges are closed. Instinet now executes many transactions for Nasdaq stocks.

ECNs have historically been subjected to regulation by the National Association of Securities Dealers, which includes the market-makers with which the ECNs compete. Consequently, some ECNs have applied to establish their own stock exchanges so that they will not be regulated by their competitors. Archipelago established the first fully electronic stock exchange through an alliance with the Pacific Stock Exchange, the fourth largest U.S. exchange, which trades more than 2,500 securities issued by firms. The alliance resulted in the creation of the Archipelago Exchange, which allows complete electronic trading of stocks listed on the NYSE, on the Amex, and in the Nasdaq market. This new exchange allows all buyers and sellers, including individual investors, brokers, and market-makers, to interact electronically.

Interaction between Direct Access Brokers and ECNs A **direct access broker** is a trading platform on a computer website that allows investors to trade stocks without the use of a broker. The website itself serves as the broker and interacts with ECNs that can execute the trade. Some of the more popular direct access brokers include Charles Schwab's CyberTrader (http://www.cybertrader.com), Touch Trade (http://www.touchtrade.net), Fire Fly

Trading (http://www.fireflytrading.com), and NobleTrading (http://www.nobletrading.com). Each of these websites offers a variety of trading platforms, which range from those that are easier to use and offer less information to those that are more complex but provide more information. A monthly fee is usually charged for access to a trading platform; the fee is higher for platforms that offer more information. To use a direct access broker, investors must meet certain requirements, such as maintaining liquid securities valued at more than $50,000. The advantage of a direct access broker is that investors interested in trading a particular stock can monitor the supply of shares for sale at various prices and the demand for shares at various prices on various ECNs. Thus, the market becomes more transparent because investors can visualize the overall supply and demand conditions at various possible prices. Investors can use this information to determine how stock prices may change in the near future.

The use of direct access brokers and ECNs allows computers to match buyers and sellers without relying on the floor brokers or traders on stock exchanges. The trend is toward a floorless exchange where all trades will be executed in cyberspace, and orders will be submitted and confirmed through automated systems. As this technology is implemented across countries, it may ultimately create a single global floorless exchange where investors can easily trade any security in any country by submitting requests from a personal computer.

Program Trading

A common form of computerized trading is program trading, which the NYSE defines as the simultaneous buying and selling of a portfolio of at least 15 different stocks that are in the S&P 500 index and have an aggregate value of more than $1 million. This is a narrow definition, as the term is sometimes used in other contexts. The most common program traders are large securities firms. They conduct the trades for their own accounts or for other institutional investors such as pension funds, mutual funds, and insurance companies. The term *program* refers to the use of computers in what is known as the Designated Order Turnaround (DOT) system at the NYSE, which allows traders to send orders to many trading posts at the exchange.

More than 20 million shares per day are traded as a result of program trading. About 75 percent of these shares are traded on the NYSE, 5 percent are traded on other U.S. markets, and 20 percent are traded on non-U.S. markets. During a typical week, a securities firm may trade hundreds of millions of shares through program trading.

Program trading is commonly used to reduce the susceptibility of a stock portfolio to stock market movements. For example, in one form of program trading, numerous stocks that have become "overpriced" (based on a particular model used to value those stocks) are sold. Program trading can also involve the purchase of numerous stocks that have become "underpriced."

Program trading can be combined with the trading of stock index futures to create portfolio insurance. With this strategy, the investor uses futures or options contracts on a stock index. Thus, a decline in the market would result in a gain on the futures or options position, which can offset the reduced market value of the stock portfolio.

Impact of Program Trading on Stock Volatility Program trading is often cited as the reason for a decline or rise in the stock market. The underlying reason for a large amount of program trading, however, is that institutional investors believe that numerous stocks

are over- or undervalued. Although program trading can cause share prices to reach a new equilibrium more rapidly, that does not necessarily imply that it causes more volatility in the stock market. A study by Furbush[2] examined the relationship between the intensity of program trading and stock price volatility. Furbush assessed five-minute intervals of stock index prices and stock index futures prices during the week of the October 1987 crash. He found that greater declines in stock prices were not systematically associated with more intense program trading.

A study by Roll[3] compared the magnitude of the October 1987 crash for markets using program trading versus markets in other countries. Roll found that the average share price decline of markets using program trading averaged 21 percent versus a 28 percent decline for other countries. Thus, it does not appear that program trading caused more pronounced losses during the crash.

Some critics have also suggested that program trading instigated the crash. Roll found, however, that many Asian stock markets where program trading did not exist plunged several hours before the opening of the U.S. market on Black Monday (October 19, 1987).

Collars Applied to Program Trading Since there is some concern that program trading can cause abrupt stock price movements and therefore cause more market volatility, the NYSE has implemented collars (sometimes referred to as "curbs"), which restrict program trading when the Dow Jones Industrial Average changes by 2 percent from the closing index on the previous trading day. Specifically, when the collars are imposed, program trading that reflects a sell order is allowed only when the last movement in the stock's price was up (an "uptick"). Program trading that reflects a buy order is allowed only when the last movement in the stock's price was down (a "downtick"). These restrictions are intended to prevent program trading from adding momentum to the prevailing direction of stock price movements on a day when stock prices have already moved substantially from the previous closing level. The collars allow program trading on days when it will exert price pressure in the opposite direction of the last price movement so that it may have a stabilizing effect on the market.

Regulation of Stock Trading

http://
http://www.nyse.com
Regulations imposed on firms that are listed on the NYSE.

Regulation of stock markets is necessary to ensure that investors are treated fairly. Without regulation, there would be more trading abuses that would discourage many investors from participating in the market. Stock trading is regulated by the individual exchanges and by the SEC. The Securities Act of 1933 and the Securities Exchange Act of 1934 were enacted to prevent unfair or unethical trading practices on the security exchanges. As a result of the 1934 act, stock exchanges were empowered and expected to discipline individuals or firms that violate regulations imposed by the exchange. The NYSE states that every transaction made at the exchange is under surveillance. The NYSE uses a computerized system to detect unusual trading of any particular stock that is traded on the exchange. It also employs personnel who investigate any abnormal price or trading volume of a particular stock or unusual trading practices of individuals.

[2]Dean Furbush, "Program Trading and Price Movement: Evidence from the October 1987 Market Crash," *Financial Management* (Autumn 1989): 68–83.
[3]Richard Roll, "The International Crash of October 1987," *Financial Analysts Journal* (October 1988): 19–35.

In 2002, the NYSE issued a regulation requiring its listed firms to have a majority of independent directors (not employees of the firm) on their respective boards of directors. This requirement was intended to reduce directors' potential conflicts of interests so that they will concentrate on ensuring that the firm's management is focused on maximizing the stock's value for its shareholders.

Ironically, the NYSE was criticized in 2003 for not abiding by some of the governance guidelines that it was imposing on other firms. In August 2003, the financial media reported that Richard Grasso, chairman of the NYSE, would receive $140 million in deferred compensation. The board members involved in determining Grasso's compensation were criticized for setting a bad example for the firms listed on the exchange. Grasso's annual salary and bonus were much higher than the chief executive officers of other firms in the financial services industry were receiving. Many institutional investors were outraged and called for a complete overhaul of the NYSE's governance guidelines for itself. Grasso resigned in September 2003. One lesson from this incident is that although there is a movement in financial markets to improve corporate governance, some conflicts of interest that adversely affect shareholders are still present.

Circuit Breakers

Stock exchanges can impose circuit breakers, which are restrictions on trading when stock prices or a stock index reaches a specified threshold level. The NYSE has experimented with different types of circuit breakers since the stock market crash of October 1987. The prevailing circuit breakers have three threshold levels for a daily change in the Dow Jones Industrial Average from its previous closing price: Level 1 (10 percent), Level 2 (20 percent), and Level 3 (30 percent). If the Level 1 threshold is reached, there is a brief (30- or 60-minute) halt in trading. If the Level 2 threshold is reached, there is a slightly longer (1- to 2-hour) halt in trading. If the Level 3 threshold is reached, the market will close for the day. The Nasdaq market and other regional exchanges impose similar circuit breakers. More information on circuit breakers is available at http://www.nasdaqtrader.com/trader/help/circuitbreaker.stm.

Trading Halts

Stock exchanges may impose trading halts on particular stocks when they believe market participants need more time to receive and absorb material information that could affect the value of a stock. They have imposed trading halts on stocks that are associated with mergers, earnings reports, lawsuits, and other news. A trading halt does not prevent a stock from experiencing a loss in response to news. Instead, the purpose of the halt is to ensure that the market has complete information before trading on the news. A trading halt may last for just a few minutes, or for several hours, or even for several days. Once the stock exchange believes that the market has complete information, it will allow trading to resume. At that time, the dealers at the stock exchange will quote bid and ask prices, based on their view of what the market demand and supply conditions for the stock will be.

Trading halts are intended to reduce stock price volatility, as the market price is adjusted by market forces in response to news. Thus, the halts can prevent excessive optimism or pessimism about a stock by restricting trading until the news about the firm is completely and widely disseminated to the market. However, some critics believe that the trading halts slow the inevitable adjustment in the stock's price to the news. In gen-

eral, research has found that the stock volatility is relatively high after a halt is lifted, but that the volatility subsides over the next few days.

Securities and Exchange Commission (SEC)

http://www.sec.gov
Information about the SEC's role and its regulatory actions.

The Securities Act of 1933 and the Securities Exchange Act of 1934 gave the Securities and Exchange Commission authority to monitor the exchanges and required listed companies to file a registration statement and financial reports with the SEC and the exchanges. In general, the SEC attempts to protect investors by ensuring full disclosure of pertinent information that could affect the values of securities. In particular, some of the more relevant SEC regulations require the following:

- Firms must publicly disclose all information about themselves that could affect the value of their securities.
- Employees of firms may take positions in their own firm's securities only during periods when they do not know of inside information that will affect the value of the firm once the information becomes public.
- Participants in security markets who facilitate trades must work in a fair and orderly manner.

The regulations prevent abuses that would give someone an unfair advantage over other investors and therefore could reduce the willingness of investors to invest in security markets. SEC regulations allow all investors to have the same access to public information. The SEC's focus is on sufficient disclosure rather than on accuracy, as it relies on auditors to certify that the financial statements are accurate.

Structure of the SEC The SEC is composed of five commissioners appointed by the president of the United States and confirmed by the Senate. Each commissioner serves a five-year term. The terms are staggered so that each year one commissioner's term ends and a new appointee is added. The president also selects one of the five commissioners to chair the commission.

The commissioners meet to assess whether existing regulations are successfully preventing abuses and to revise the regulations as needed. Specific staff members of the SEC may be assigned to develop a proposal for a new regulation to prevent a particular abuse that is occurring. When the commission adopts new regulations, they are distributed to the public for feedback before final approval. Some of the more critical proposals are subject to congressional review before final approval.

Key Divisions of the SEC The SEC has several important divisions that attempt to ensure a fair and orderly stock market. The Division of Corporate Finance reviews the registration statement filed when a firm goes public, corporate filings for annual and quarterly reports, and proxy statements that involve voting for board members or other corporate issues. The Division of Market Regulation requires the orderly disclosure of securities trades by various organizations that facilitate the trading of securities. The Division of Enforcement assesses possible violations of the SEC's regulations and can take action against individuals or firms. An investigation can involve the examination of securities data or transactions; the SEC has the power to obtain information from specific individuals by subpoena. When the SEC finds that action is warranted, it may negotiate a settlement with the individuals or firms that are cited for violations, file a case against

them in federal court, or even work with law enforcement agencies if the violations involve criminal activity. Such actions are normally intended to prevent the violations from continuing and to discourage other individuals or firms from engaging in illegal securities activities.

ILLUSTRATION Near the end of 1991, most stock prices were quoted in eighths, such as $32⅛ to represent $32.125. Yet, the bid and ask prices for stocks (even the most liquid stocks) in the Nasdaq market at that time were rarely quoted in "odd-eighths," such as 1/8, 3/8, 5/8, or 7/8. Instead, Nasdaq market-makers typically structured bid and ask prices in even-eighths, such as a bid price of $32²⁄₈ and an ask price of $32⁴⁄₈. In this way, the spread on each transaction was always at least $.25. This structure was peculiar, especially considering that odd-eighths were sometimes used earlier in the year, allowing a spread on those same stocks of $.125. Within a few months, the spread had doubled. This aroused suspicion that the market-makers had implicitly colluded by agreeing to set wider spreads.

This activity continued until it was publicized in 1996. At that time, the SEC charged that the National Association of Securities Dealers (NASD), which regulates the Nasdaq, had failed to prevent some activities by Nasdaq market-makers that reduced competition. In August 1996, the NASD settled the case by offering to spend $100 million to improve its monitoring of Nasdaq market-makers.

SEC Oversight of Corporate Disclosure In October 2000, the SEC issued Regulation Fair Disclosure (FD), which requires firms to disclose relevant information broadly to investors at the same time. As mentioned in Chapter 7, one of the most important results of Regulation FD is that a firm may no longer provide analysts with information that they could use before the market was aware of the information. Before Regulation FD, some firms would commonly hint to analysts that their earnings would be higher than initially anticipated. Thus, the analysts could advise their preferred clients to purchase the stocks before the price was pushed up by the increased demand for shares by other investors who received the information later.

Since Regulation FD, a firm must announce a change in expected earnings to all investors and other interested parties (such as analysts) at the same time. The firm may disclose the information on its website, through a filing of a document (8-K form) with the SEC, and through a news release. The firm may hold a conference call with analysts after the news is announced, but is expected to include all material information in the announcement. Thus, the conference call will not give analysts an unfair advantage because the key information has already been disclosed. In addition, most firms have now opened up their conference calls to investors, who can listen in by phone or online through a website. Analysts who always relied on their own analytical abilities to develop their recommendations are continuing business as usual, but analysts who relied on what might be considered inside information from firms have had to modify their methods of forming insightful opinions about the firms they cover.

Some analysts suggest that the regulation has caused firms to disclose less information to them and to the public than before. To ensure that they do not violate Regulation FD, some firms may offer less information so that no parties have an unfair advantage. In particular, smaller firms find it expensive to issue a press release every time they have relevant information. The SEC is reviewing Regulation FD and may alter it so that it still allows for a flow of information from firms, while ensuring that investors receive the information at the same time as analysts.

SEC Oversight of Analyst Recommendations As explained in earlier chapters, many investors rely on analysts for analyses and recommendations on whether to buy or sell particular stocks. In recent years, the SEC has become concerned about analyst recommendations that appear to be excessively optimistic and can ultimately lead to major losses for investors who rely on these recommendations when deciding whether to purchase the stock.

ILLUSTRATION

One widely publicized abuse occurs when an analyst at the security firm that underwrites an IPO for a firm continuously issues a buy recommendation for the IPO firm, even after there are clear signals that the firm is experiencing financial problems. This behavior was especially obvious during the 2000–2001 period when many analysts maintained their "buy" recommendations on Internet stocks that their firm had underwritten, even after there was substantial evidence that these firms had financial problems. Considering the conflict of interest that analysts face when their employer serves as their client's investment bank such "strong buy" ratings may be misleading.

An SEC investigation in 2001 determined that many research analysts of securities firms took positions in stocks contrary to their recommendations. Some analysts would issue a "buy" recommendation for a firm whose IPO had recently been underwritten by their employer but then sell their personal holdings of that stock during this same period. In one case, an analyst even sold the stock short while issuing a buy recommendation—confirmation that his personal view differed from the publicized opinion he issued to satisfy his employer.

How Barriers to International Stock Trading Have Decreased

 **GL BALASPECTS**

Although the international trading of stocks has grown over time, until recently it was limited by three barriers: transaction costs, information costs, and exchange rate risk. Now, however, these barriers have been reduced, as explained next.

Reduction in Transaction Costs

Most countries have their own stock exchanges, where the stocks of local, publicly held companies are traded. In recent years, countries have consolidated their exchanges, increasing efficiency and reducing transaction costs. Some European stock exchanges use an extensive cross-listing system (called Eurolist) so that investors in a given European country can easily purchase stocks of companies based in other European countries.

In particular, the stock exchange of Switzerland may serve as a model that will be applied by many other stock exchanges around the world because of its efficiency. The Swiss stock exchange is now fully computerized, so a trading floor is not needed. Orders by investors to buy or sell flow to financial institutions that are certified members of the exchange. These institutions are not necessarily based in Switzerland. The details of the orders, such as the stock's name, the number of shares to be bought or sold, and the price at which the investor is willing to buy or sell, are fed into a computer system. The system matches buyers and sellers and then sends information confirming the transaction to the financial institution, which then informs the investor that the transaction has been completed.

When there are many more buy orders than sell orders for a given stock, the computer will not be able to accommodate all orders. Some buyers will then increase the price they are willing to pay for the stock. Thus, the price adjusts in response to the demand (buy orders) for the stock and the supply (sell orders) of the stock for sale, as recorded by the computer system. Similar dynamics occur on a trading floor, but the computerized system has documented criteria by which it prioritizes the execution of orders, whereas traders on a trading floor may execute some trades in ways that favor themselves at the expense of investors.

Over time, it is likely that other stock exchanges will adopt similar systems, which resemble the electronic communication networks (ECNs) decribed earlier. The Brussels stock exchange already has conformed to the computerized system. Furthermore, the Internet will allow investors to use their computers to place orders (through the website of a member of the stock exchange) that will then be executed and confirmed by the computer system back through the Internet to the investor. Thus, all parts of the trading process from the placement of orders to the confirmations that transactions have been executed will be conducted by computers. The ease of placing such orders regardless of the location of the investor and the stock exchange is sure to increase the volume of international stock transactions in the future.

Reduction in Information Costs

Information about foreign stocks is now available on the Internet, enabling investors to make more informed decisions without having to purchase information about these stocks. Consequently, investors should be more comfortable assessing foreign stocks. Differences in accounting rules may still limit the degree to which financial data about foreign companies can be interpreted or compared to data about firms in other countries, but there has been some progress in making accounting standards uniform across countries.

Reduction in Exchange Rate Risk

When investing in a foreign stock denominated in a foreign currency, investors are subject to the possibility that the currency denominating the stock will depreciate against the investor's currency over time. The potential for a major decline in a stock's value simply because of a large degree of depreciation is greater for emerging markets, such as Indonesia or Russia, where the local currency can change by 10 percent or more on a single day.

The conversion of many European countries to a single currency (the euro) in 1999 should lead to more stock offerings in Europe by U.S. and European-based firms. Before 1999, a European firm needed a different currency in every European country in which it conducted business; therefore, the firm would borrow currency from local banks in each country. Now, the firm can use the euro to finance its operations across several European countries and may be able to obtain all the financing it needs with one stock offering denominated in euros. The firm can then use a portion of the revenue (in euros) to pay dividends to shareholders who have purchased the stock. In addition, European investors based in countries where the euro serves as the local currency can now invest in stocks in other European countries that are denominated in euros without being exposed to exchange rate risk.

SUMMARY

- Investors engage in various types of stock transactions. They can place an order by phone or online. They can request that a transaction be executed at the prevailing price or only if the stock price reaches a specified level. They can finance a portion of their stock purchase with borrowed funds as a means of increasing the potential return on their investment. They can sell stocks short, and they can also invest in stock indexes.

- Organized stock exchanges are used to facilitate secondary market transactions. Members of the exchanges trade stock for their own accounts or for their clients. The exchanges are served by floor brokers and specialists, who execute transactions. An over-the-counter exchange also exists, where stock transactions are executed through a telecommunications network.

- Electronic communication networks (ECNs) are automated systems for disclosing and sometimes exe-

cuting stock trades. They facilitate the execution of orders and normally service institutional rather than individual investors. The ECNs can interact with a trading platform on a website (called a direct access broker) that allows investors to trade stocks without the use of a broker.

- Regulations are imposed in stock markets to ensure that investors are treated fairly. Stock trading is regulated by the individual exchanges and by the SEC. Many of the regulations are imposed to prevent unfair or unethical trading practices on the security exchanges. The stock exchanges and the SEC attempt to prevent the use of inside information by investors.

- As various stock markets have removed their barriers to foreign investors, they have become more globally integrated. Transaction costs, information costs, and exchange rate risk have all been reduced, making it easier for investors to engage in international stock trading.

POINT COUNTER-POINT

Is a Specialist or a Market-Maker Needed?

Point Yes. A specialist or a market-maker can make a market by serving as the counterparty on a transaction. Without specialists or market-makers, stock orders might be heavily weighted toward buys or sells, and price movements would be more volatile.

Counter-Point No. Specialists and market-makers do not prevent stock prices from declining. A stock that

has more selling pressure than buying pressure will experience a decline in price, as it should. The electronic communication networks can serve as the intermediary between buyer and seller.

Who Is Correct? Use your favorite search engine to learn more about this issue. Offer your own opinion on this issue.

QUESTIONS AND APPLICATIONS

1. **Internet Exercise** Go to http://finance.yahoo.com/?u. Insert a ticker symbol for a stock that interests you and then click on "Get." Then click on the various links (such as Chart, Profile, News, Research, and Insider).

    a. Describe the information that is provided by each of these links.

2. **Stock Trading** Describe the role of a floor broker and a specialist. Explain how specialists or market-

makers may attempt to capitalize on stock price discrepancies.

3. **Orders** Explain the difference between a market order and a limit order.

4. **Bid-Ask Spread** Explain the bid-ask spread situation in the NASDAQ market in 1991. How was it changed as a result of the SEC?

5. **Bid-Ask Spread of Penny Stocks** Your friend just told you about a penny stock he purchased, which increased in price from $0.10 to $0.50 per share. You start investigating penny stocks, and after conducting a large amount of research, you find a stock with a quoted price of $0.05. Upon further investigation, you notice that the ask price for the stock is $0.08 and that the bid price is $0.01. Discuss the possible reasons for this wide bid-ask spread.

6. **Managing in Financial Markets: Taking a Position in Exchange Traded Funds** As a U.S. portfolio manager, you have invested in numerous stocks in Japan. These stocks tend to move in tandem with the Japanese stock market. You are concerned that the Japanese stocks will decline in price over the next week, although you expect that the stock prices will begin to turn back up at the end of the week. You do not want to sell all your Japanese stocks because you would have to pay taxes on the capital gains earned over the last year. In addition, you would have to pay the brokerage commissions from selling them all and buying them all back in a week.

   a. Explain how you could take a position in an exchange traded fund representing the Japanese stock index that could offset the effects on your Japanese stocks over the next week.

   b. Some ETFs are valued according to the value of the stock index. For example, if the stock index in Japan changes by 4 percent, the value of the ETF would change by the same amount. How does this differ from your investment in the Japanese stocks? Explain why your position in this type of ETF may not necessarily offset the effects on your Japanese stocks, even if the stocks tend to move in tandem with the Japanese market.

   c. In a week or so, you would like to increase your investment in Japan. You have $20,000 available to invest at this time, but would like to purchase more than $20,000 of Japanese stocks. How can you achieve your goal without selling any of the existing stocks in your portfolio?

What is the risk of this strategy relative to the risk of purchasing stocks worth $20,000?

7. **Short Selling** Under what conditions might investors consider short selling a specific stock? Describe the short selling process. Explain the short interest ratio.

8. **ECNs** What are electronic communication networks (ECNs)?

9. **Interpreting Financial News** Interpret the following statements made by Wall Street analysts and portfolio managers:

   a. "Individual investors who purchase stock on margin might as well go to Vegas."

   b. "Exchange traded funds allow you to bet on a market without supporting portfolio managers."

   c. "The trading floor may become extinct due to ECNs."

10. **Reg FD** What are the implications of Regulation FD?

11. **Program Trading** What is program trading? Briefly describe the conclusions reached by Furbush and by Roll from their studies of the relationship between the intensity of program trading and the magnitude of the declines in stock prices during the stock market crash of 1987.

12. **ETFs** What are some advantages of purchasing exchange traded funds (ETFs) as compared to mutual funds? What is a disadvantage?

13. **Implications of NYSE Compensation** The former chairman of the NYSE, Richard Grasso, resigned in 2003 as a result of institutional outrage over his excessive compensation package. Besides setting a bad example for the firms listed on the NYSE, discuss why institutional investors would be outraged.

14. **Circuit Breakers** Explain how circuit breakers are used to reduce the likelihood of a large stock market crash.

15. **Margins** Explain how margin requirements can affect the potential return and risk from investing in a stock. What is the maintenance margin?

16. **Front-Running** Describe "front-running." Explain how front-running may prevent limit orders from investors from being executed.

17. **SEC** Briefly describe the structure and role of the Securities and Exchange Commission (SEC).

18. **Stock Exchange Transaction Costs** Explain how foreign stock exchanges such as the Swiss stock exchange have reduced transactions costs.

PROBLEMS

1. **Buying on Margin** Suppose that you buy a stock for $48 by paying $25 and borrowing the remaining $23 from a brokerage firm at 8 percent annualized interest. The stock pays an annual dividend of $0.80 per share, and after one year, you are able to sell it for $65. Calculate your return on the stock. Then, calculate the return on the stock if you had used only personal funds to make the purchase. Repeat the problem assuming that only personal funds are used and that at the end of one year you are able to sell the stock at $40.

2. **Margin** How would the return on a stock be affected by a lower initial investment (and higher loan amount)? Explain the relationship between the proportion of funds borrowed and the return.

3. **Buying on Margin** Assume that Vogl stock is priced at $50 per share and pays a dividend of $1 per share. An investor purchases the stock on margin, paying $30 per share and borrowing the remainder from the brokerage firm at 10 percent annualized interest. If, after one year, the stock is sold at a price of $60 per share, what is the return to the investor?

4. **Buying on Margin** Assume that Duever stock is priced at $80 per share and pays a dividend of $2 per share. An investor purchases the stock on margin, paying $50 per share and borrowing the remainder from the brokerage firm at 12 percent annualized interest. If, after one year, the stock is sold at a price of $90 per share, what is the return to the investor?

FLOW OF FUNDS EXERCISE

Shorting Stocks

Recall that if the economy continues to be strong, Carson Company may need to increase its production capacity by about 50 percent over the next few years to satisfy demand. It would need financing to expand and accommodate the increase in production. Recall that the yield curve is currently upward sloping. Also recall that Carson is concerned about a possible slowing of the economy because of potential Fed actions to reduce inflation. It is also considering the issuance of stock or bonds to raise funds in the next year.

a. In some cases, a stock's price is too high or too low because of asymmetric information—information known by the firm but not by investors. How can Carson attempt to minimize asymmetric information?

b. Carson Company is concerned that if it issues stock, its stock price over time could be adversely affected by certain institutional investors that take large short positions in a stock. When this happens, the stock's price may be undervalued because of the pressure on the price caused by the large short positions. What can Carson do to counter major short positions taken by institutional investors if it really believes that its stock price should be higher? What is the potential risk involved in this strategy?

Part III Integrative Problem

Stock Market Analysis

This problem requires an understanding of the different methods for valuing stocks.

As a stock portfolio manager, you spend most of your day searching for stocks that appear to be undervalued. In the last few days, you have received information about two stocks that you are assessing—Olympic stock and Kenner stock. Many stock analysts believe that Olympic stock and Kenner stock are undervalued because their price-earnings ratios are lower than the industry average. Olympic Inc. has a PE ratio of 6, versus an industry PE ratio of 8. Its stock price declined recently in response to an announcement that its quarterly earnings would be lower than expected due to expenses from recent restructuring. The restructuring is expected to improve Olympic's future performance, but its earnings will take a large onetime hit this quarter.

Kenner Company has a PE ratio of 9, versus a PE ratio of 11 in its industry. Its earnings have been decent in recent years, but it has not kept up with new technology and may lose market share to competitors in the future.

Questions

1   Should you still consider purchasing Olympic stock in light of the analysts' arguments about why it may be undervalued?

2   Should you still consider purchasing Kenner stock in light of the analysts' arguments about why it may be undervalued?

3   Some stock analysts have just predicted that the prices of most stocks will fall because interest rates are expected to rise, which would cause investors to use higher required rates of return when valuing stocks. The analysts used this logic to suggest that the present value of future cash flows would decline if interest rates rise. The expected increase in interest rates is due to expectations of a stronger economy, which will result in an increased demand for loanable funds by corporations and individuals. Do you believe that stock prices will decline if the economy strengthens and interest rates rise?

PART IV

Debt Markets

Part IV focuses on how debt security markets facilitate the flow of funds from surplus units to deficit units. Chapter 9 focuses on money markets for investors and borrowers trading short-term securities. Chapters 10 and 11 focus on the bond markets, and Chapter 12 focuses on the mortgage markets. Because some financial market participants trade securities in all of these markets, there is much interaction among these markets, as emphasized throughout the chapters.

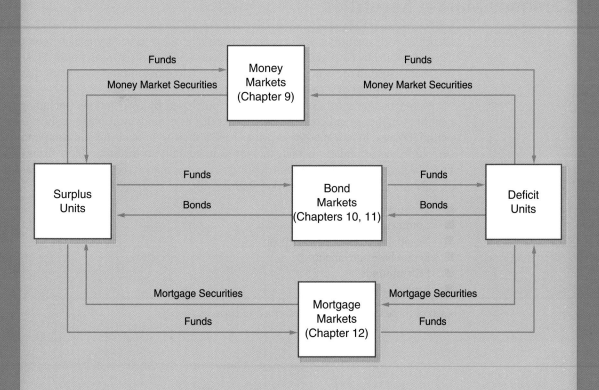

CHAPTER 9

U.S. Money Markets

Money markets are used to facilitate the transfer of short-term funds from individuals, corporations, or governments with excess funds to those with deficient funds. Even investors who focus on long-term securities tend to hold some money market securities. Money markets enable financial market participants to maintain liquidity.

The specific objectives of this chapter are to:

■ provide a background on the most popular money market securities,

■ explain how money markets are used by institutional investors,

■ explain the valuation and risk of money market securities, and

■ explain how money markets have become globally integrated.

U.S. Money Market Securities

Securities with maturities within one year are referred to as **money market securities.** They are issued by corporations and governments to obtain short-term funds. They are originally issued in the primary market through a telecommunications network that informs investors that new securities are for sale.

Money market securities are commonly purchased by corporations (including financial institutions) and government agencies that have funds available for a short-term period. Because money market securities have a short-term maturity and can typically be sold in the secondary market, they provide liquidity to investors. Most firms and financial institutions maintain some holdings of money market securities for this reason.

The more popular money market securities are:

■ Treasury bills
■ Commercial paper
■ Negotiable certificates of deposit
■ Repurchase agreements
■ Federal funds
■ Banker's acceptances

Each of these instruments is described in turn.

Treasury Bills

When the U.S. government needs to borrow funds, the U.S. Treasury frequently issues short-term securities known as Treasury bills (or T-bills). These are sold weekly through an auction. One-year T-bills are issued on a monthly basis. The par value (amount received by investors at maturity) of T-bills was historically a minimum of $10,000, but is now $1,000 and in multiples of $1,000 thereafter. T-bills are sold at a discount from par value, and the gain to an investor holding a T-bill until maturity is the difference between par value and the price paid.

    T-bills are attractive to investors because they are backed by the federal government and therefore are virtually free of credit (default) risk. Another attractive feature of T-bills is their liquidity, which is due to their short maturity and strong secondary market. Existing T-bills can be sold in the secondary market through government securities dealers, who profit by purchasing the bills at a slightly lower price than the price at which they sell them.

Investors in Treasury Bills Depository institutions commonly invest in T-bills so that they can retain a portion of their funds in assets that can easily be liquidated if they suddenly need to accommodate deposit withdrawals. Other financial institutions also invest in T-bills in the event that they need cash because cash outflows exceed cash inflows. Individuals with substantial savings invest in T-bills for liquidity purposes. Many individuals invest in T-bills indirectly by investing in money market funds, which in turn purchase large amounts of T-bills. Corporations invest in T-bills so that they have easy access to funding if they incur sudden unanticipated expenses.

Pricing Treasury Bills The price that an investor will pay for a T-bill with a particular maturity is dependent on the investor's required rate of return on that T-bill. That price is determined as the present value of the future cash flows to be received. Since the T-bill does not generate interest payments, the value of a T-bill is the present value of the par value.

ILLUSTRATION If investors require a 7 percent annualized return on a one-year T-bill, the price that they will be willing to pay is

$$P = \$10,000/1.07$$
$$= \$9,345.79$$

Since T-bills do not pay interest, the investors should pay this price so that the $10,000 they receive a year later will have to generate a 7 percent return.

To price a T-bill with a maturity shorter than one year, the annualized return can be reduced by the fraction of the year in which funds will be invested.

ILLUSTRATION If investors require a 6 percent annualized return on a six-month T-bill, this reflects a 3 percent unannualized return over six months. The price that they would be willing to pay is

$$P = \$10,000/1.03$$
$$= \$9,708.74$$

EXHIBIT 9.1

Example of a Treasury Bill Application

PD F 5176-2

OMB NO. 1535-0069

TREASURY DIRECT

TENDER FOR 26-WEEK TREASURY BILL

TENDER INFORMATION AMOUNT OF TENDER: $ ______

TERM ______

BID TYPE (Check One) ☐ NONCOMPETITIVE ☐ COMPETITIVE AT ___ . ___ %

TREASURY DIRECT ACCOUNT NUMBER ___ - ___ - ___

INVESTOR INFORMATION

ACCOUNT NAME

ADDRESS (FOR NEW ACCOUNT ONLY)

CITY STATE ZIP CODE

TAXPAYER IDENTIFICATION NUMBER

1ST NAMED OWNER ___ - ___ - ___ SOCIAL SECURITY NUMBER OR ___ - ___ EMPLOYER IDENTIFICATION NUMBER

TELEPHONE NUMBERS (FOR NEW ACCOUNT ONLY)

WORK (___) ___ - ___ HOME (___) ___ - ___

PAYMENT ATTACHED TOTAL PAYMENT: $ ______

CASH (01): $ ______ CHECKS (02/03): $ ______

SECURITIES (05/06): $ ______ $ ______

OTHER (07): $ ______ $ ______

DIRECT DEPOSIT INFORMATION (FOR NEW ACCOUNT ONLY)

ROUTING NUMBER

FINANCIAL INSTITUTION NAME

ACCOUNT NUMBER ACCOUNT TYPE (Check One) ☐ CHECKING

ACCOUNT NAME ☐ SAVINGS

AUTOMATIC REINVESTMENT

1 2 3 4 Circle the number of sequential 26-week reinvestments you want to schedule at this time

AUTHORIZATION

I submit this tender pursuant to the provisions of Department of the Treasury Circulars, Public Debt Series Nos. 2-86 (31 CFR Part 357) and 1-93 (31 CFR Part 356), and the applicable offering announcement.

Under penalties of perjury, I certify that the number shown on this form is my correct taxpayer identification number and that I am not subject to backup withholding because (1) I have not been notified that I am subject to backup withholding as a result of a failure to report all interest or dividends, or (2) the Internal Revenue Service has notified me that I am no longer subject to backup withholding. I further certify that all other information provided on this form is true, correct and complete.

SIGNATURE DATE

*U.S. GPO: 1994-376-760/00319 SEE INSTRUCTIONS FOR PRIVACY ACT AND PAPERWORK REDUCTION ACT NOTICE

FOR DEPARTMENT USE

TENDER NUMBER 912794

CUSIP

ISSUE DATE

RECEIVED BY

DATE RECEIVED

EXT REG ☐

FOREIGN ☐

BACKUP ☐

REVIEW ☐

CLASS

NUMBERS

Treasury Bill Auction The primary T-bill market is an auction by mail. Investors submit bids on T-bill applications for the maturity of their choice. Exhibit 9.1 shows an example of a 26-week T-bill application. Applications can be obtained at no charge from a Federal Reserve district or branch bank. Alternatively, investors can ask a broker or a commercial bank to obtain and send in the application for them. The fee charged for this service normally ranges from $25 to $75.

Financial institutions can arrange to submit their bid for T-bills (and other Treasury securities) online using the Treasury Automated Auction Processing System (TAAPS-*Link*). Financial institutions using this arrangement set up an account with the Treasury. Then they can select the specific maturity and face value that they desire and submit their bids electronically. Payments to the Treasury are withdrawn electronically from the

account, and payments received from the Treasury when the securities mature are deposited electronically into the account.

At the weekly auctions, the Treasury offers 13-week (three-month) and 26-week (six-month) T-bills. As of July 2001, the Treasury began to include 4-week T-bills in some of the weekly auctions. The 4-week T-bills are offered when the Treasury anticipates a short-term cash deficiency over a given month. The Treasury also periodically offers some other T-bills with shorter-term maturities, called cash management bills.

At the auctions, investors have the option of bidding competitively or noncompetitively. The Treasury has a specified amount of funds that it plans to borrow during the 13- or 26-week period, and this dictates the amount of T-bill bids that it will accept for that maturity. Investors who wish to ensure that their bids will be accepted can use noncompetitive bids. Noncompetitive bidders are limited to purchasing T-bills with a maximum par value of $1 million per auction, however. Consequently, large corporations typically make competitive bids so they can purchase larger amounts.

After accounting for noncompetitive bids, the Treasury accepts the highest competitive bids first and works it way down until it has generated the amount of funds from competitive bids that it needs. Any bids below that cutoff point are not accepted. Since 1998, the Treasury applies the lowest accepted bid price to all competitive bids that are accepted and to all noncompetitive bids. Thus, the price paid by competitive and noncompetitive bidders reflects the lowest price of the competitive bids. Competitive bids are still submitted because, as noted above, many bidders want to purchase more T-bills than the maximum that can be purchased on a noncompetitive basis.

The results of the weekly auction of 13-week and 26-week T-bills are summarized in major daily newspapers each Tuesday and are also provided online at the Treasury's Public Debt website. Some of the more commonly reported statistics are the dollar amount of applications and Treasury securities sold, the average price of the accepted competitive bids, and the coupon equivalent (annualized yield) for investors who paid the average price.

The results of a recent T-bill auction are shown in Exhibit 9.2. At each auction, the prices paid for six-month T-bills are significantly lower than the prices paid for three-month T-bills because the investment term is longer. The lower price results in a higher unannualized yield that compensates investors for their longer-term investment.

Estimating the Yield As explained earlier, T-bills do not offer coupon payments but are sold at a discount from par value. Their yield is influenced by the difference between the selling price and the purchase price. If an investor purchases a newly issued T-bill and holds it until maturity, the return is based on the difference between the par value and the purchase price. If the T-bill is sold prior to maturity, the return is based on the difference between the price for which the bill was sold in the secondary market and the purchase price.

http://www.ny.frb.org
Click on "Treasury Direct."
Results of recent Treasury bill auctions.

http://www.federalreserve.gov/releases
Links to a database of Treasury bill rates over time

EXHIBIT 9.2
Example of Treasury Bill Auction Results

	13-Week Treasury Bill Auction	26-Week Treasury Bill Auction
Applications	$22,685,977,000	$23,991,246,000
Accepted bids	$9,022,977,000	$8,005,496,000
Average price of accepted bids (per $100 par value)	$98.792	$97.508
Coupon equivalent (yield)	4.918%	5.139%

Source: The Wall Street Journal. See The Wall Street Journal on any Tuesday for the information pertaining to Monday's Treasury bill auction.

http://

http://research.stlouisfed.org
Obtain yields offered on
T-bills and various other
money market securities.

The annualized yield from investing in a T-bill (Y_T) can be determined as

$$Y_T = \frac{SP - PP}{PP} \times \frac{365}{n}$$

where

SP = selling price

PP = purchase price

n = number of days of the investment (holding period)

ILLUSTRATION

An investor purchases a T-bill with a six-month (182-day) maturity and $10,000 par value for $9,600. If this T-bill is held to maturity, its yield is

$$Y_T = \frac{\$10,000 - \$9,600}{\$9,600} \times \frac{365}{182} = 8.36\%$$

If the T-bill is sold prior to maturity, the selling price and therefore the yield are dependent on market conditions at the time of the sale.

Suppose the investor plans to sell the T-bill after 120 days and forecasts a selling price of $9,820 at that time. The expected annualized yield based on this forecast is

$$Y_T = \frac{\$9,820 - \$9,600}{\$9,600} \times \frac{365}{120} = 6.97\%$$

The higher the forecasted selling price, the higher the expected annualized yield.

Estimating the Treasury Bill Discount Business periodicals frequently quote the T-bill discount (or T-bill rate) along with the T-bill yield. The T-bill discount represents the percent discount of the purchase price from par value (Par) for newly issued T-bills and is computed as

$$\text{T-bill discount} = \frac{\text{Par} - PP}{\text{Par}} \times \frac{360}{n}$$

A 360-day year is used to compute the T-bill discount.

ILLUSTRATION

Using the information from the previous example, the T-bill discount is

$$\text{T-bill discount} = \frac{\$10,000 - \$9,600}{\$10,000} \times \frac{360}{182} = 7.91\%$$

For a newly issued T-bill that is held to maturity, the T-bill yield will always be higher than the discount. The difference occurs because the purchase price is the denominator of the yield equation, while the par value is the denominator of the T-bill discount equation, and the par value will always exceed the purchase price of a newly issued T-bill. In addition, the yield formula uses a 365-day year versus a 360-day year for the discount computation.

Commercial Paper

Commercial paper is a short-term debt instrument issued only by well-known, credit-worthy firms and is typically unsecured. It is normally issued to provide liquidity or finance a firm's investment in inventory and accounts receivable. The issuance of com-

http://

http://beginnersinvest.about
.com/od/commercialpaper
Provides valuable
information and related
articles about commerical
paper.

mercial paper is an alternative to short-term bank loans. Financial institutions such as finance companies and bank holding companies are major issuers of commercial paper.

The minimum denomination of commercial paper is usually $100,000. The typical denominations are in multiples of $1 million. Maturities are normally between 20 and 45 days but can be as short as one day or as long as 270 days. The 270-day maximum is due to a Securities and Exchange Commission (SEC) ruling that paper with a maturity exceeding 270 days must be registered.

Because of the high minimum denomination, individual investors rarely purchase commercial paper directly although they may invest in it indirectly by investing in money market funds that have pooled the funds of many individuals. Money market funds are major investors in commercial paper. An active secondary market for commercial paper does not exist. However, it is sometimes possible to sell the paper back to the dealer who initially helped to place it. In most cases, investors hold commercial paper until maturity.

Ratings Since commercial paper is issued by corporations that are susceptible to business failure, the commercial paper could possibly default. The risk of default is influenced by the issuer's financial condition and cash flow. Investors can attempt to assess the probability that commercial paper will default by monitoring the issuer's financial condition. The focus is on the issuer's ability to repay its debt over the short term because the payments will be completed within a short-term period. The rating serves as an indicator of the potential risk of default. Money market funds can invest only in commercial paper that has a top-tier or second-tier rating, and second-tier paper cannot represent more than 5 percent of their assets. Thus, corporations can more easily place commercial paper that is assigned a top-tier rating. The ratings are assigned by rating agencies such as Moody's Investor Service, Standard & Poor's Corporation, and Fitch Investor Service.

A higher-risk classification can increase a corporation's commercial paper rate by as much as 150 basis points (1.5 percent). The difference has reached 150 basis points during some recessions but has been less than 50 basis points over other periods.

From 1970 to 1988, there were only a few major defaults on commercial paper. In 1989, however, several major issuers defaulted, including Wang Labs, Lomas Financial, and Drexel Burnham Lambert. All of these issues were rated highly until the default. These defaults led to a growing number of commercial paper issues (called **junk commercial paper**) that were rated low or not rated at all. In the last decade, the number of defaults on commercial paper has been very low.

Volume of Commercial Paper The volume of commercial paper issued over time is shown in Exhibit 9.3. In general, the volume of commercial paper issued has increased substantially over time. The tendency of firms to use commercial paper for short-term financing is influenced by their ability to obtain funds in the commercial paper market at a relatively low cost. The volume of commercial paper commonly declines during recessions when corporations tend to borrow less. In addition, some corporations are viewed as having higher default risk on their debt during recessions, so any new commercial paper they issued would be assigned a low rating. This would raise the cost of financing with commercial paper or perhaps even prevent the corporations from obtaining funds in the commercial paper market. Notice in Exhibit 6.3 how the volume of commercial paper declined substantially in 2001 and 2002, when economic conditions were very weak.

Placement Some firms place commercial paper directly with investors. Ford Motor Credit and other firms have recently sold their commercial paper online to investors.

EXHIBIT 9.3   Volume of Commercial Paper over Time

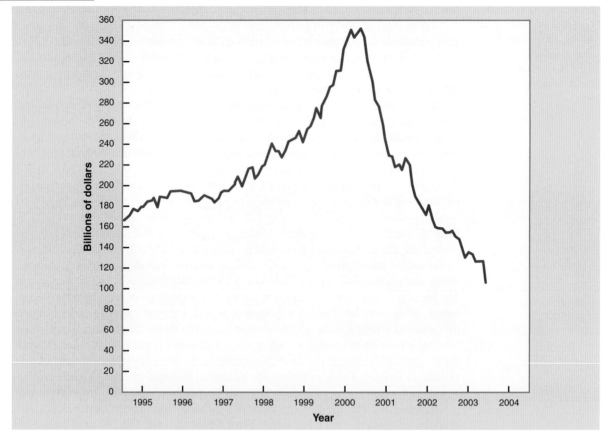

Source: Federal Reserve.

Other firms rely on commercial paper dealers to sell their commercial paper, at a cost of usually one-eighth of 1 percent of the face value. This transaction cost is generally less than it would cost to establish a department within the firm to place commercial paper directly. Companies that frequently issue commercial paper may reduce expenses by creating such a department, however. Most nonfinancial companies prefer to use commercial paper dealers rather than in-house resources to place their commercial paper. Their liquidity needs, and therefore their commercial paper issues, are cyclical, so they would use an in-house direct-placement department only a few times during the year. Finance companies typically maintain an in-house department because they frequently borrow in this manner.

Backing Commercial Paper Issuers of commercial paper typically maintain backup lines of credit in case they cannot roll over (reissue) commercial paper at a reasonable rate because, for example, their assigned rating was lowered. A backup line of credit provided by a commercial bank allows the company the right (but not the obligation) to borrow a specified maximum amount of funds over a specified period of time. The fee for the line can either be a direct percentage of the total accessible credit (such as 0.5 percent) or be in the form of required compensating balances (such as 10 percent of the line).

Estimating the Yield At a given point in time, the yield on commercial paper is slightly higher than the yield on a T-bill with the same maturity because commercial paper car-

ries some credit risk and is less liquid. Like T-bills, commercial paper is sold at a discount from par value. The nominal return to investors who retain the paper until maturity is the difference between the price paid for the paper and the par value. Thus, the yield received by a commercial paper investor can be determined in a manner similar to the T-bill yield, although a 360-day year is usually used.

ILLUSTRATION   If an investor purchases 30-day commercial paper with a par value of $1,000,000 for a price of $990,000, the yield ($Y_{cp}$) is

$$Y_{cp} = \frac{\$1,000,000 - \$990,000}{\$990,000} \times \frac{360}{30}$$

$$= 12.12\%$$

When a firm plans to issue commercial paper, the price (and therefore yield) to investors is uncertain. Thus, the cost of borrowing funds is uncertain until the paper is issued. Consider the case of a firm that plans to issue 90-day commercial paper with a par value of $5,000,000. It expects to sell the commercial paper for $4,850,000. The yield it expects to pay investors (its cost of borrowing) is estimated to be

$$Y_{cp} = \frac{Par - PP}{PP} \times \frac{360}{n}$$

$$= \frac{\$5,000,000 - \$4,850,000}{\$4,850,000} \times \frac{360}{90}$$

$$= 12.37\%$$

http://www.federalreserve
.gov/releases Links to a
database of commercial
paper rates over time.

When firms sell their commercial paper at a lower (higher) price than projected, their cost of raising funds will be higher (lower) than they initially anticipated. For example, if the firm initially sold the commercial paper for $4,865,000, the cost of borrowing would have been about 11.1 percent. (Check the math as an exercise.)

Ignoring transaction costs, the cost of borrowing with commercial paper is equal to the yield earned by investors holding the paper until maturity. The cost of borrowing can be adjusted for transaction costs (charged by the commercial paper dealers) by subtracting the nominal transaction fees from the price received.

Some corporations prefer to issue commercial paper rather than borrow from a bank because it is usually a cheaper source of funds. Yet, even the large creditworthy corporations that are able to issue commercial paper normally obtain some short-term loans from commercial banks in order to maintain a business relationship with them.

Commercial Paper Yield Curve   The commercial paper yield curve represents the yield offered on commercial paper at various maturities. The curve is typically established for a maturity range from 0 to 90 days because most commercial paper has a maturity within that range. This yield curve is important because it may influence the maturity that is used by firms that issue commercial paper and by the institutional investors that purchase commercial paper. The shape of this yield curve could be roughly drawn from the short-term range of the traditional Treasury yield curve. However, that curve is graphed over a long time period, so it is difficult to derive the precise shape of a yield curve over a three-month range from that graph.

The same factors that affect the Treasury yield curve from 0 to 10 years affect the commercial paper yield curve, but are applied to very short-term horizons. In particular,

expectations of interest over the next few months can influence the commercial paper yield curve.

ILLUSTRATION Assume that many firms that issue paper and institutional investors expect that the one-month interest rate as of one month from now will be much higher than the prevailing one-month interest rate. Firms that want to issue commercial paper would likely prefer to issue two-month or three-month commercial paper so that they can lock in the yield that they will pay and avoid having to refinance in one month. Conversely, institutional investors would likely prefer to invest in one-month commercial paper so that they can reinvest their funds at the higher yields (if interest rates rise as expected) when the commercial paper matures. Thus, there will be a surplus of funds in the one-month commercial market, but stronger demand and a smaller supply of funds in the two-month market. The result is an upward-sloping commercial paper yield curve, as shown in the top panel of Exhibit 9.4. A downward-sloping commercial paper yield curve could exist if firms and investors expected that short-term interest rates would decrease. In this case, firms would prefer to issue commercial paper with shorter term maturities, which would result in a higher annualized yield for these maturities.

EXHIBIT 9.4

Commercial Paper Yield Curve

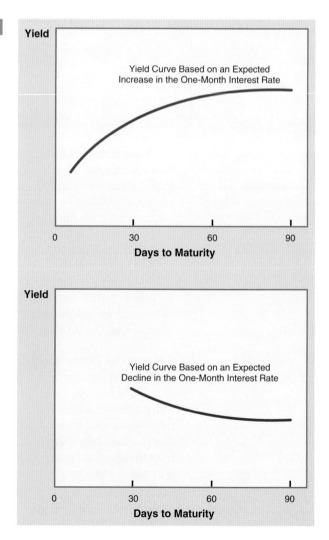

The shapes of the yield curves of other money market securities will be similar to the shape of the yield curve for commercial paper because the financial institutions that participate in the commercial paper market tend to participate in all of these markets.

Negotiable Certificates of Deposit (NCDs)

Negotiable certificates of deposit (NCDs) are certificates that are issued by large commercial banks and other depository institutions as a short-term source of funds. The minimum denomination is $100,000, although a $1 million denomination is more common. Nonfinancial corporations often purchase NCDs. Although NCD denominations are typically too large for individual investors, they are sometimes purchased by money market funds that have pooled individual investors' funds. Thus, money market funds allow individuals to be indirect investors in NCDs, creating a more active NCD market.

Maturities on NCDs normally range from two weeks to one year. A secondary market for NCDs exists, providing investors with some liquidity. However, institutions prefer not to have their newly issued NCDs compete with their previously issued NCDs that are being resold in the secondary market. An oversupply of NCDs for sale can force them to sell their newly issued NCDs at a lower price.

Placement Some issuers place their NCDs directly; others use a correspondent institution that specializes in placing NCDs. Another alternative is to sell NCDs to securities dealers, who in turn resell them. A portion of unusually large issues is commonly sold to NCD dealers. Normally, however, NCDs can be sold to investors directly at a higher price.

Premium NCDs must offer a premium above the T-bill yield to compensate for less liquidity and safety. The premiums are generally higher during recessionary periods. The premiums also reflect the market's perception about the safety of the financial system.

Yield NCDs provide a return in the form of interest along with the difference between the price at which the NCD is redeemed (or sold in the secondary market) and the purchase price. Given that an institution issues an NCD at par value, the annualized yield that it will pay is the annualized interest rate on the NCD. If investors purchase this NCD and hold it until maturity, their annualized yield is the interest rate. However, the annualized yield can differ from the annualized interest rate for investors who either purchase or sell the NCD in the secondary market instead of holding it from inception until maturity.

ILLUSTRATION An investor purchased an NCD a year ago in the secondary market for $970,000. He redeems it today upon maturity and receives $1,000,000. He also receives interest of $40,000. His annualized yield (Y_{NCD}) on this investment is

$$Y_{NCD} = \frac{SP - PP + \text{interest}}{PP}$$

$$= \frac{\$1,000,000 - \$970,000 + \$40,000}{\$970,000}$$

$$= 7.22\%$$

Repurchase Agreements

With a repurchase agreement (or repo), one party sells securities to another with an agreement to repurchase the securities at a specified date and price. In essence, the repo transaction represents a loan backed by the securities. If the borrower defaults on the loan, the lender has claim to the securities. Most repo transactions use government securities, although some involve other securities such as commercial paper or NCDs. A **reverse repo** refers to the purchase of securities by one party from another with an agreement to sell them. Thus, a repo and a reverse repo can refer to the same transaction but from different perspectives. These two terms are sometimes used interchangeably, so a transaction described as a repo may actually be a reverse repo.

Financial institutions such as banks, savings and loan associations, and money market funds often participate in repurchase agreements. Many nonfinancial institutions are active participants as well. Transaction amounts are usually for $10 million or more. The most common maturities are from one day to 15 days and for one, three, and six months. A secondary market for repos does not exist. Some firms in need of funds will set the maturity on a repo to be the minimum time period for which they need temporary financing. If they still need funds when the repo is about to mature, they will borrow additional funds through new repos and use these funds to fulfill their obligation on maturing repos.

Placement Repo transactions are negotiated through a telecommunications network. Dealers and repo brokers act as financial intermediaries to create repos for firms with deficient and excess funds, receiving a commission for their services.

When the borrowing firm can find a counterparty to the repo transaction, it avoids the transaction fee involved in having a government securities dealer find the counterparty. Some companies that commonly engage in repo transactions have an in-house department for finding counterparties and executing the transactions. These same companies that borrow through repos may, from time to time, serve as the lender. That is, they purchase the government securities and agree to sell them back in the near future. Because the cash flow of any large company changes on a daily basis, it is not unusual for a firm to act as an investor one day (when it has excess funds) and a borrower the next (when it has a cash shortage).

Estimating the Yield The repo rate is determined by the difference between the initial selling price of the securities and the agreed-upon repurchase price, annualized with a 360-day year.

ILLUSTRATION An investor initially purchased securities at a price (PP) of $9,852,217, with an agreement to sell them back at a price (SP) of $10,000,000 at the end of a 60-day period. The yield (or repo rate) on this repurchase agreement is

$$\text{Repo rate} = \frac{SP - PP}{PP} \times \frac{360}{n}$$

$$= \frac{\$10,000,000 - \$9,852,217}{\$9,852,217} \times \frac{360}{60}$$

$$= 9\%$$

Federal Funds

The federal funds market allows depository institutions to effectively lend or borrow short-term funds from each other at the so-called **federal funds rate.** The federal funds

http://

http://www.federalreserve
.gov/fomc Provides an
excellent summary of the
Fed's adjustment in the
federal funds rate over
time.

rate is the rate charged on federal funds transactions. It is influenced by the supply and demand for funds in the federal funds market. The Federal Reserve adjusts the amount of funds in depository institutions in order to influence the federal funds rate (as explained in Chapter 4) and several other short-term interest rates. All types of firms closely monitor the federal funds rate because the Federal Reserve manipulates it to affect general economic conditions. Many market participants view changes in the federal funds rate as an indicator of potential changes in other money market rates.

The federal funds rate is normally slightly higher than the T-bill rate at any point in time. The negotiations between two depository institutions may take place directly over a communications network or may occur through a federal funds broker. Once a loan transaction is agreed upon, the lending institution can instruct its Federal Reserve district bank to debit its reserve account and to credit the borrowing institution's reserve account by the amount of the loan. If the loan is for just one day, it will likely be based on an oral agreement between the parties, especially if the institutions commonly do business with each other.

Commercial banks are the most active participants in the federal funds market. Federal funds brokers serve as financial intermediaries in the market, matching up institutions that wish to sell (lend) funds with those that wish to purchase (borrow) them. The brokers receive a commission for their service. The transactions are negotiated through a telecommunications network that links federal funds brokers with the participating institutions. Most loan transactions are for $5 million or more and usually have a one- to seven-day maturity (although the loans may often be extended by the lender if the borrower desires more time).

The volume of interbank loans on commercial bank balance sheets over time is an indication of the importance of lending between depository institutions. The interbank loan volume outstanding now exceeds $200 billion.

Banker's Acceptances

A **banker's acceptance** indicates that a bank accepts responsibility for a future payment. Banker's acceptances are commonly used for international trade transactions. An exporter that is sending goods to an importer whose credit rating is not known will often prefer that a bank act as a guarantor. The bank therefore facilitates the transaction by stamping ACCEPTED on a draft, which obligates payment at a specified point in time. In turn, the importer will pay the bank what is owed to the exporter along with a fee to the bank for guaranteeing the payment.

Exporters can hold a banker's acceptance until the date at which payment is to be made, but they frequently sell the acceptance before then at a discount to obtain cash immediately. The investor who purchases the acceptance then receives the payment guaranteed by the bank in the future. The investor's return on a banker's acceptance, like that on commercial paper, is derived from the difference between the discounted price paid for the acceptance and the amount to be received in the future. Maturities on banker's acceptances often range from 30 to 270 days. Because there is a possibility that a bank will default on payment, investors are exposed to a slight degree of credit risk. Thus, they deserve a return above the T-bill yield as compensation.

Because acceptances are often discounted and sold by the exporting firm prior to maturity, an active secondary market exists. Dealers match up companies that wish to sell acceptances with other companies that wish to purchase them. The bid price of dealers is less than their ask price, which creates their spread, or their reward for doing business. The spread is normally between one-eighth and seven-eighths of 1 percent.

EXHIBIT 9.5
Sequence of Steps in the
Creation of a Banker's
Acceptance

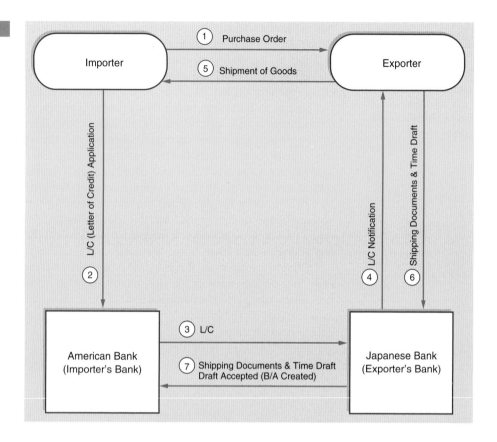

Steps Involved in Banker's Acceptances The sequence of steps involved in a banker's acceptance is illustrated in Exhibit 9.5. To understand these steps, consider the example of a U.S. importer of Japanese goods. First, the importer places a purchase order for the goods (Step 1). If the Japanese exporter is unfamiliar with the U.S. importer, it may demand payment before delivery of goods, which the U.S. importer may be unwilling to make. A compromise may be reached through the creation of a banker's acceptance. The importer asks its bank to issue a **letter of credit (L/C)** on its behalf (Step 2). The L/C represents a commitment by that bank to back the payment owed to the Japanese exporter. Then the L/C is presented to the exporter's bank (Step 3), which informs the exporter that the L/C has been received (Step 4). The exporter then sends the goods to the importer (Step 5) and sends the shipping documents to its bank (Step 6), which passes them along to the importer's bank (Step 7). At this point, the banker's acceptance is created, which obligates the importer's bank to make payment to the holder of the banker's acceptance at a specified future date. The banker's acceptance may be sold to a money market investor at a discount. Potential purchasers of acceptances are short-term investors. When the acceptance matures, the importer pays its bank, which in turn pays the money market investor who presents the acceptance.

The creation of a banker's acceptance allows the importer to receive goods from an exporter without sending immediate payment. The selling of the acceptance creates financing for the exporter. Even though banker's acceptances are often created to facilitate international transactions, they are not limited to money market investors with international experience. Investors who purchase acceptances are more concerned with

the credit of the bank that guarantees payment than with the credit of the exporter or importer. For this reason, the credit risk on a banker's acceptance is somewhat similar to that of NCDs issued by commercial banks. Yet, because acceptances have the backing of the bank as well as the importing firm, they may be perceived as having slightly less credit risk than NCDs.

Institutional Use of Money Markets

The institutional use of money market securities is summarized in Exhibit 9.6. Financial institutions purchase money market securities in order to simultaneously earn a return and maintain adequate liquidity. They issue money market securities when experiencing a temporary shortage of cash. Because money markets serve businesses, the average transaction size is very large and is typically executed through a telecommunications network.

Money market securities can be used to enhance liquidity in two ways. First, newly issued securities generate cash. The institutions that issue new securities have created a short-term liability in order to boost their cash balance. Second, institutions that previously purchased money market securities will generate cash upon liquidation of the securities. In this case, one type of asset (the security) is replaced by another (cash).

Most financial institutions maintain sufficient liquidity by holding either securities that have very active secondary markets or securities with short-term maturities. T-bills are the most popular money market instrument because of their marketability, safety, and short-term maturity. Although T-bills are purchased through an auction, other money market instruments are commonly purchased through dealers or specialized brokers. For example, commercial paper is purchased through commercial paper dealers or directly from the issuer, NCDs are usually purchased through brokers specializing in NCDs, federal funds are purchased (borrowed) through federal funds brokers, and repurchase agreements are purchased through repo dealers.

Financial institutions whose future cash inflows and outflows are more uncertain will generally maintain additional money market instruments for liquidity. For this reason,

EXHIBIT 9.6   Institutional Use of Money Markets

Type of Financial Institution	Participation in the Money Markets
Commercial banks and savings institutions	• Bank holding companies issue commercial paper. • Some banks and savings institutions issue NCDs, borrow or lend funds in the federal funds market, engage in repurchase agreements, and purchase T-bills. • Commercial banks create banker's acceptances. • Commercial banks provide backup lines of credit to corporations that issue commercial paper.
Finance companies	• Issue large amounts of commercial paper.
Money market mutual funds	• Use proceeds from shares sold to invest in T-bills, commercial paper, NCDs, repurchase agreements, and banker's acceptances.
Insurance companies	• May maintain a portion of their investment portfolio as money market securities for liquidity.
Pension funds	• May maintain a portion of their investment portfolio as money market securities that may be liquidated when portfolio managers desire to increase their investment in bonds or stocks.

depository institutions such as commercial banks allocate a greater portion of their asset portfolio to money market instruments than pension funds usually do.

Financial institutions that purchase money market securities are acting as a creditor to the initial issuer of the securities. For example, when they hold T-bills, they are creditors to the Treasury. The T-bill transactions in the secondary market commonly reflect a flow of funds between two nongovernment institutions. T-bills represent a source of funds for those financial institutions that liquidate some of their T-bill holdings. In fact, this is the main reason that financial institutions hold T-bills. Liquidity is also the reason financial institutions purchase other money market instruments, including federal funds (purchased by depository institutions), repurchase agreements (purchased by depository institutions and money market funds), banker's acceptances, and NCDs (purchased by money market funds).

Some financial institutions issue their own money market instruments to obtain cash. For example, depository institutions issue NCDs, and bank holding companies and finance companies issue commercial paper. Depository institutions also obtain funds through the use of repurchase agreements or in the federal funds market.

Many money market transactions involve two financial institutions. For example, a federal funds transaction involves two depository institutions. Money market funds commonly purchase NCDs from banks and savings institutions. Repurchase agreements are frequently negotiated between two commercial banks.

Valuation of Money Market Securities

Many types of money market securities make no interest payments but do provide principal at maturity. The value of these money market securities is measured as the present value of the principal payment to be paid at maturity. The discount rate used to discount the money market security is the required rate of return by investors. Thus, the value reflects the present value of a future lump-sum payment.

ILLUSTRATION Assume that a money market security has a par value of $10,000 and a maturity of one year, and that investors require a return of 7 percent on this security. The present value (*PV*) of this security is

$$PV = \$10,000/(1.07)^1$$
$$= \$9,345.79$$

If investors require a 9 percent return on that security instead of 7 percent, its present value will be

$$PV = \$10,000/(1.09)^1$$
$$= \$9,174.31$$

This value is lower than in the previous example because if investors require a higher return, they will be willing to purchase the security only if its price is lower.

If short-term interest rates decline, the required rate of return on money market securities will decline, and the values of money market securities will increase. Although money market security values are sensitive to interest rate movements in the same di-

rection as bonds, they are not as sensitive as bond values to interest rate movements. The lower degree of sensitivity is primarily attributed to the shorter term to maturity. With money market securities, the principal payment will occur in the next year, whereas the principal payment on bonds may be 10 or 20 years away. In other words, an increase in interest rates is not as harmful to a money market security because it will mature soon anyway, and the investor can reinvest the proceeds at the prevailing rate at that time. An increase in interest rates is more harmful to a bond with 20 years until maturity because the investor will be earning a low rate on the bond for the next 20 years.

Explaining Money Market Price Movements

The market price of money market securities (P_m) should equal the present value of their future cash flows. Since money market securities normally do not make periodic interest payments, their cash flows are in the form of one lump-sum payment of principal. Therefore, the market price of a money market security can be determined as

$$P_m = \text{Par}/(1 + k)^n$$

where
Par = par value or principal amount to be provided at maturity

k = required rate of return by investors

n = time to maturity

Since money market securities have maturities of one year or less, n is measured as a fraction of one year.

A change in P_m can be modeled as

$$\Delta P_m = f(\Delta k) \text{ and } \Delta k = f(\Delta R_f, \Delta RP)$$

where
R_f = risk-free interest rate

RP = risk premium

Therefore,

$$\Delta P_m = f(\Delta R_f, \Delta RP)$$

Exhibit 9.7 identifies the underlying forces that can affect the short-term risk-free interest rate (the T-bill rate) and the risk premium and can therefore cause the price of a money market security to change over time. When pricing T-bills, the focus is on the factors that affect the risk-free interest rate, as the risk premium is not needed. Thus, the difference in the required return of a risky money market security (such as commercial paper) versus the T-bill (for a given maturity) is the risk premium, which is influenced by economic, industry, and firm-specific conditions.

Impact of September 11 To understand how the valuations and therefore the yields offered on money market securities can change, consider the effect of the terrorist attack on the United States on September 11, 2001. The economy was weak at the time, and investors anticipated that the event would cause additional weakness. They sold stocks and transferred funds into money market securities such as T-bills and commercial paper. This created an unusually strong demand for money market securities, which placed upward pressure on their price and downward pressure on their yields. At the

EXHIBIT 9.7 Framework for Pricing Money Market Securities

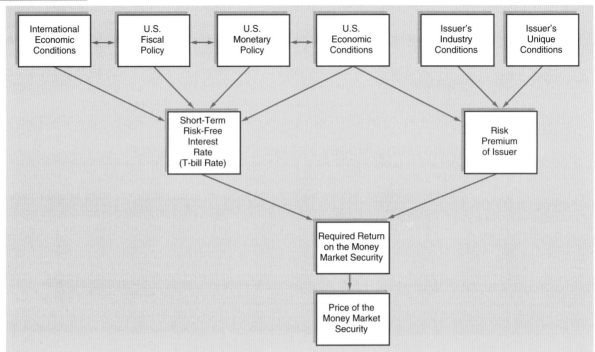

same time investors were taking these actions, the Federal Reserve was acting to add liquidity to the banking system and to reduce the federal funds rate. Consequently, all money market security yields declined to their lowest level in more than 30 years.

Efficiency of Money Market Securities

The money markets are referred to as efficient if the prices of the securities reflect all available information. In general, the money markets are widely perceived to be efficient, in that the prices reflect all available public information. Most money market securities are subject to large trading volume and therefore are monitored by many investors. The price of a money market security such as commercial paper can decline quickly if the issuer suddenly announces financial problems. However, this type of adjustment in price does not reflect a violation of market efficiency. In fact, it is because of market efficiency that the price adjusts so quickly to new information. Most investors buy money market securities because they need liquidity, not because they think they can capitalize on mispricing of the securities. They are more likely to think that they could earn larger gains in other financial markets, but rely on the money markets for liquidity.

Indicators of Future Money Market Security Prices

Money market participants closely monitor economic indicators that may signal future changes in the strength of the economy, which can signal changes in short-term interest rates and in the required return from investing in money market securities. Some of the

more closely monitored indicators of economic growth include employment, gross domestic product, retail sales, industrial production, and consumer confidence. An unexpected favorable movement in these indicators tends to create expectations of increased economic growth and higher interest rates, which place downward pressure on prices of money market securities.

Money market participants also closely monitor indicators of inflation, such as the consumer price index and the producer price index. In general, an unexpected increase in these indexes tends to create expectations of higher interest rates and places downward pressure on money market prices. Whenever indicators signal a potential increase in interest rates, money market participants tend to shift their investments into securities with relatively short terms to maturity so that they can receive a higher yield by reinvesting in newly issued securities once interest rates rise.

Risk of Money Market Securities

When corporate treasurers, institutional investors, and individual investors invest in money market securities, they are subject to the risk that the return on their investment will be less than anticipated. The forces that influence price movements of money market securities cannot be perfectly anticipated, so future money market prices (and therefore yields) cannot be perfectly anticipated either. If the money market securities will not be held until maturity, the prices at which they can be sold in the future (and therefore the return on the investment) will depend primarily on the risk-free interest rate and the perceived credit risk at the time the securities are sold. Because the investment horizon for money market securities is short term, the investment is not subject to a major loss in value as a result of an increase in interest rates, but it still faces a potential loss of value if the issuer of the money market security defaults.

At one extreme, if corporate treasurers, institutional investors, and individual investors want to avoid risk, they can purchase T-bills and hold them to maturity, but investors who choose T-bills forgo a higher expected return because T-bills do not need to offer a risk premium. Consequently, investors must weigh the higher potential return of investing in other money market securities against the exposure to risk (that the actual return could be lower than the expected return). Since the risk of a large loss is primarily attributed to the possibility of default, investors commonly invest in money market securities (such as commercial paper) that offer a slightly higher yield than T-bills and are very unlikely to default. Although investors can assess economic and firm-specific conditions to determine the credit risk of an issuer of a money market security, information about the issuer's financial condition is limited.

Measuring Risk

Participants in the money markets can use sensitivity analysis to determine how the value of money market securities may change in response to a change in interest rates.

ILLUSTRATION   Assume that Long Island Bank has money market securities with a par value of $100 million that will mature in nine months. Since the bank will need a substantial amount of funds in three months, it wants to know how much cash it will receive from selling these securities three months from now. Assume that it expects the unannualized required rate of return on those securities for the remaining six months to be

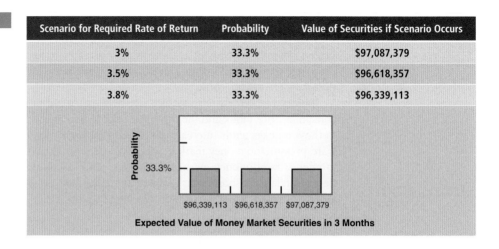

Probability Distribution
of Proceeds from Selling
Money Market Securities

Scenario for Required Rate of Return	Probability	Value of Securities if Scenario Occurs
3%	33.3%	$97,087,379
3.5%	33.3%	$96,618,357
3.8%	33.3%	$96,339,113

3 percent, or 3.5 percent, or 3.8 percent with a 33.3 percent chance for each of these three scenarios.

Exhibit 9.8 shows the probability distribution of the proceeds that Long Island Bank will receive from selling the money market securities in three months, based on the possible scenarios for the required rate of return at that time. Based on this exhibit, the bank expects that it will receive at least $96,339,113, but it could receive more if interest rates (and therefore the required rate of return) are relatively low in three months. By deriving a probability distribution of outcomes, the bank can anticipate whether the proceeds to be received will be sufficient to cover the amount of funds that it needs in three months.

Interaction among Money Market Yields

Companies investing in money markets closely monitor the yields on the various instruments. Because the instruments serve as reasonable substitutes for each other, the investing companies may exchange instruments to achieve a more attractive yield. This causes yields among these instruments to be somewhat similar. If a disparity in yields arises, companies will avoid the low-yield instruments in favor of the high-yield instruments. This places upward pressure on the yields of the low-yield securities and downward pressure on the high-yield securities, causing realignment.

During periods of heightened uncertainty about the economy, investors tend to shift from risky money market securities to Treasury securities. This so-called flight to quality creates a greater differential between yields, as risky money market securities must provide a larger premium to attract investors.

Exhibit 9.9 shows the yields of money market securities over time. The high degree of correlation among security yields is obvious. T-bills consistently offer slightly lower yields than the other securities because they are very liquid and free from credit risk.

Globalization of Money Markets

 GL BALASPECTS Market interest rates vary among countries, as shown in Exhibit 9.10. The interest rate differentials occur because geographic markets are somewhat segmented. The interest rates of 12 European countries, however, have converged and are now the same as a result of

EXHIBIT 9.9   Money Market Yields (Averages, Annualized)

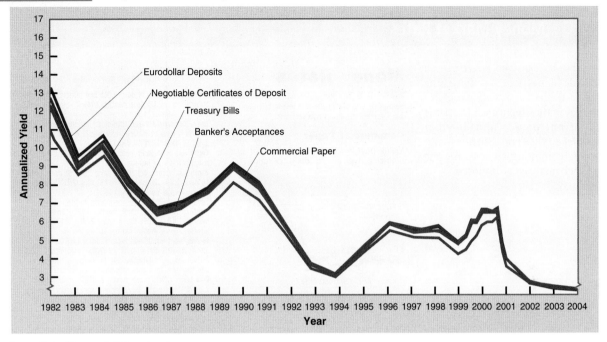

Source: *Federal Reserve Bulletin*, various issues.

the conversion of their currencies to the euro in January 1999. In addition, the interest rates of some other countries have become more highly correlated over time, as the flow of funds between countries has increased. The increase in the flow of funds is attributed to tax differences among countries, speculation on exchange rate movements, and a reduction in government barriers that were previously imposed on foreign investment in securities. U.S. T-bills and commercial paper are very accessible to foreign investors. In addition, securities such as Eurodollar deposits, Euronotes, and Euro-commercial paper are

EXHIBIT 9.10   International Money Market Rates over Time

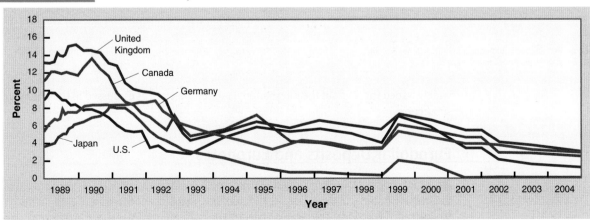

Source: Federal Reserve.

USING THE WALL STREET JOURNAL

WSJ   Money Market Rates

A table in *The Wall Street Journal* called "Money Rates" provides the interest rates on a wide variety of money market securities. The name of the rate or security is listed in boldface type. For securities with several common maturities, the rate on each maturity is disclosed.

Money Rates

Monday, September 27, 2004

The key U. S. and foreign annual interest rates below are a guide to general levels but don't always represent actual transactions.

Commercial Paper

Yields paid by corporations for short-term financing, typically for daily operation

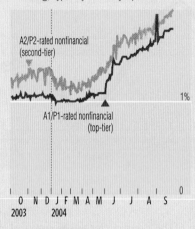

A2/P2-rated nonfinancial (second-tier)

A1/P1-rated nonfinancial (top-tier)

1%

```
 I  I  I I I I I I I  I   I  I  0
 O  N D J F M A M J  J  A  S
 2003      2004
```

Source: Federal Reserve

Prime Rate: 4.75% (effective 09/22/04). The base rate on corporate loans posted by at least 75% of the nation's 30 largest banks.
Discount Rate (Primary): 2.75% (effective 09/21/04).
Federal Funds: 1.813% high, 1.625% low, 1.375% near closing bid, 1.875% offered. Effective rate: 1.76%. Source: Prebon Yamane (USA) Inc. Federal-funds target rate: 1.750% (effective 09/21/04).
Call Money: 3.50% (effective 09/22/04).
Commercial Paper: Placed directly by General Electric Capital Corp.: 1.76% 30 to 59 days; 1.80% 60 to 89 days; 1.86% 90 to 119 days; 1.93% 120 to 149 days; 1.98% 150 to 174 days; 2.04% 175 to 209 days; 2.08% 210 to 239 days; 2.12% 240 to 263 days; 2.15% 264 to 270 days.
Euro Commercial Paper: Placed directly by General Electric

Capital Corp.: 2.04% 30 days; 2.06% two months; 2.09% three months; 2.12% four months; 2.14% five months; 2.17% six months.
Dealer Commercial Paper: High-grade unsecured notes sold through dealers by major corporations: 1.77% 30 days; 1.84% 60 days; 1.89% 90 days.
Certificates of Deposit: 1.80% one month; 1.92% three months; 2.10% six months.
Bankers Acceptances: 1.78% 30 days; 1.84% 60 days; 1.91% 90 days; 1.99% 120 days; 2.05% 150 days; 2.11% 180 days. Source: Prebon Yamane (USA) Inc.
Eurodollars: 1.80% - 1.78% one month; 1.87% - 1.84% two months; 1.93% - 1.91% three months; 2.02% - 1.98% four months; 2.07% - 2.05% five months; 2.14% - 2.10% six months. Source: Prebon Yamane (USA) Inc.
London Interbank Offered Rates (Libor): 1.8400% one month; 1.9700% three months; 2.1700% six months; 2.4500% one year. Effective rate for contracts entered into two days from date appearing at top of this column.
Euro Libor: 2.08013% one month; 2.11575% three months; 2.20425% six months; 2.37738% one year. Effective rate for contracts entered into two days from date appearing at top of this column.
Euro Interbank Offered Rates (Euribor): 2.081% one month; 2.116% three months; 2.204% six months; 2.379% one year. Source: Reuters.
Foreign Prime Rates: Canada 4.00%; European Central Bank 2.00%; Japan 1.375%; Switzerland 2.47%; Britain 4.75%.
Treasury Bills: Results of the Monday, September 27, 2004, auction of short-term U.S. government bills, sold at a discount from face value in units of $1,000 to $1 million: 1.710% 13 weeks; 1.950% 26 weeks. Tuesday, September 21, 2004 auction: 1.605% 4 weeks.
Overnight Repurchase Rate: 1.69%. Source: Garban Intercapital.
Freddie Mac: Posted yields on 30-year mortgage commitments. Delivery within 30 days 5.38%, 60 days 5.44%, standard conventional fixed-rate mortgages: 2.875%, 2% rate capped one-year adjustable rate mortgages.
Fannie Mae: Posted yields on 30 year mortgage commitments (priced at par) for delivery within 30 days 5.44%, 60 days 5.50%, standard conventional fixed-rate mortgages; 3.30%, 6/2 rate capped one-year adjustable rate mortgages. Constant Maturity Debt Index: 1.941% three months; 2.120% six months; 2.387% one year.
Merrill Lynch Ready Assets Trust: 1.00%.
Consumer Price Index: August, 189.5, up 2.7% from a year ago. Bureau of Labor Statistics.

widely traded throughout the international money markets, as discussed in the following subsections.

Eurodollar Deposits and Euronotes

As corporations outside the United States (especially in Europe) increasingly engaged in international trade transactions in U.S. dollars, the U.S. dollar deposits in non-U.S. banks (called **Eurodollar certificates of deposit** or Eurodollar CDs) grew. Furthermore, because interest rate ceilings were historically imposed on dollar deposits in U.S. banks,

corporations with large dollar balances often deposited their funds overseas to receive a higher yield.

Eurodollar CD volume has grown substantially over time, as the U.S. dollar is used as a medium of exchange in a significant portion of international trade and investment transactions. Some firms overseas receive U.S. dollars as payment for exports and invest in Eurodollar CDs. Because these firms may need dollars to pay for future imports, they retain dollar-denominated deposits rather than convert dollars to their home currency.

In the so-called **Eurodollar market,** banks channel the deposited funds to other firms that need to borrow them in the form of Eurodollar loans. The deposit and loan transactions in Eurodollars are typically $1 million or more per transaction, so only governments and large corporations participate in this market. Because transaction amounts are large, investors in the market avoid some costs associated with the continuous small transactions that occur in retail-oriented markets. In addition, Eurodollar CDs are not subject to reserve requirements, which means that banks can lend out 100 percent of the deposits that arrive. For these reasons, the spread between the rate banks pay on large Eurodollar deposits and what they charge on Eurodollar loans is relatively small. Consequently, interest rates in the Eurodollar market are attractive for both depositors and borrowers. The rates offered on Eurodollar deposits are slightly higher than the rates offered on NCDs.

A secondary market for Eurodollar CDs exists, allowing the initial investors to liquidate their investment if necessary. The growth in Eurodollar volume has made the secondary market more active.

Investors in fixed-rate Eurodollar CDs are adversely affected by rising market interest rates, while issuers of these CDs are adversely affected by declining rates. To deal with this interest rate risk, **Eurodollar floating-rate CDs** (called **FRCDs**) have been used in recent years. The rate adjusts periodically to the London Interbank Offer Rate (LIBOR), which is the interest rate charged on interbank dollar loans. As with other floating-rate instruments, the rate on FRCDs ensures that the borrower's cost and the investor's return reflect prevailing market interest rates.

Over time, the volume of deposits and loans denominated in other foreign currencies has also grown because of increased international trade, increased flows of funds among subsidiaries of multinational corporations, and existing differences among country regulations on bank deposit rates. Consequently, the so-called **Eurocurrency market** was developed; it is made up of several banks (called **Eurobanks**) that accept large deposits and provide large loans in foreign currencies. These same banks also make up the **Eurocredit market,** which is distinguished from the Eurocurrency market mainly by the longer maturities on loans.

The Eurobanks participating in the Eurocurrency market are located not only in Europe but also in the Bahamas, Canada, Japan, Hong Kong, and some other countries. Since 1978, Eurocurrency deposits at commercial banks have more than quadrupled. Over this time period, the value of dollar deposits has represented between 70 percent and 80 percent of the market value of all Eurocurrency deposits. In recent years, the percentage has declined slightly because of the growth in nondollar Eurocurrency deposits.

Short-term **Euronotes** are issued in bearer form, with common maturities of one, three, and six months. Typical investors in Euronotes often include the Eurobanks that are hired to place the paper. These Euronotes are sometimes underwritten in a manner that guarantees the issuer a specific price. In addition, the underwriters may even guarantee a price at which the notes can be rolled over (reissued at maturity). The Euronotes described here differ from the traditional meaning of medium-term loans provided by Eurobanks.

Euro-Commercial Paper

Euro-commercial paper (Euro-CP) is issued without the backing of a banking syndicate. Maturities can be tailored to satisfy investors. Dealers that place commercial paper have created a secondary market by being willing to purchase existing Euro-CP before maturity.

The Euro-CP rate is typically between 50 and 100 basis points above LIBOR. Euro-CP is sold by dealers, at a transaction cost ranging between 5 and 10 basis points of the face value. This market is tiny compared to the U.S. commercial paper market. Nevertheless, some non-U.S. companies can more easily place their paper here, where they have a household name.

Performance of Foreign Money Market Securities

The performance of an investment in a foreign money market security is measured by the **effective yield** (yield adjusted for the exchange rate), which is dependent on the (1) yield earned on the money market security in the foreign currency and (2) the exchange rate effect. The yield earned on the money market security (Y_f) is

$$Y_f = \frac{SP_f - PP_f}{PP_f}$$

where SP_f = selling price of the foreign money market security in the foreign currency

PP_f = purchase price of the foreign money market security in the foreign currency

The exchange rate effect (denoted as %ΔS) measures the percentage change in the spot exchange rate (in dollars) from the time the foreign currency was obtained to invest in the foreign money market security until the time the security was sold and the foreign currency was converted into the investor's home currency. Thus, the effective yield is

$$Y_e = (1 + Y_f) \times (1 + \%\Delta S) - 1$$

ILLUSTRATION A U.S. investor obtains Mexican pesos when the peso is worth $.12 and invests in a one-year money market security that provides a yield (in pesos) of 22 percent. At the end of one year, the investor converts the proceeds from the investment back to dollars at the prevailing spot rate of $.13 per peso. In this example, the peso increased in value by 8.33 percent, or .0833. The effective yield earned by the investor is

$$Y_e = (1 + Y_f) \times (1 + \%\Delta S) - 1$$
$$= (1.22) \times (1.0833) - 1$$
$$= 32.16\%$$

The effective yield exceeds the yield quoted on the foreign currency whenever the currency denominating the foreign investment increases in value over the investment horizon.

To illustrate the potential effects of exchange rate movements, the effective yield for a U.S. investor that invests in British money market securities is shown in Exhibit 9.11.

EXHIBIT 9.11 Comparison of Effective Yields between U.S. and British Money Market Yields for a U.S. Investor

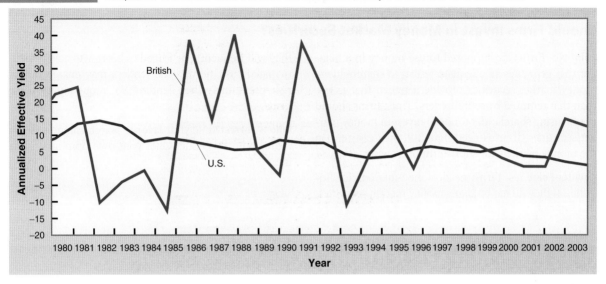

The effective yield was higher than the alternative domestic yields during certain periods as a result of the strengthened pound. Conversely, the effective yield on British money market securities was negative in periods when the pound depreciated. Most investors would not invest in foreign money market securities in every period but would choose to do so only when the foreign currency is expected to appreciate. The results displayed in Exhibit 9.11 show both the high potential yields and the risk from investing in foreign money market securities. The risk could be reduced somewhat by spreading the investment across securities denominated in several currencies.

SUMMARY

- The main money market securities are Treasury bills, commercial paper, NCDs, repurchase agreements, federal funds, and banker's acceptances. These securities vary according to the issuer. Consequently, their perceived degree of credit risk can vary. They also have different degrees of liquidity. Therefore, the quoted yields at any given point in time vary among money market securities.

- Financial institutions manage their liquidity by participating in money markets. They may issue money market securities when they experience cash shortages and need to boost liquidity. They can also sell holdings of money market securities to obtain cash.

- The value of a money market security represents the present value of future cash flows generated by that

security. Since money market securities represent debt, their expected cash flows are typically known. However, the pricing of money market securities changes in response to a shift in the required rate of return by investors. The required rate of return changes in response to interest rate movements or to a shift in the security's credit risk.

- Interest rates vary among countries. Some investors are attracted to high interest rates in foreign countries, which cause funds to flow to those countries. Consequently, money markets have become globally integrated. Investments in foreign money market securities are subject to exchange rate risk because the foreign currency denominating the securities could depreciate over time.

POINT COUNTER-POINT

Should Firms Invest in Money Market Securities?

Point No. Firms are supposed to use money in a manner that generates an adequate return to shareholders. Money market securities provide a return that is less than that required by shareholders. Thus, firms should not be using shareholder funds to invest in money market securities. If firms need liquidity, they can rely on the money markets for short-term borrowing.

Counter-Point Yes. Firms need money markets for liquidity. If they do not hold any money market securities,

they will frequently be forced to borrow to cover unanticipated cash needs. The lenders may charge higher risk premiums when lending so frequently to these firms.

Who Is Correct? Use your favorite search engine to learn more about this issue. Offer your own opinion on this issue.

QUESTIONS AND APPLICATIONS

1. **Influence of Money Market Activity on Working Capital** Assume that interest rates for most maturities are unusually high. Also, assume that the net working capital (defined as current assets minus current liabilities) levels of many corporations are relatively low in this period. Explain how the money markets play a role in the relationship between the interest rates and the level of net working capital.

2. **Managing in Financial Markets: Money Market Portfolio Dilemma** As the treasurer of a corporation, one of your jobs is to maintain investments in liquid securities such as Treasury securities and commercial paper. Your goal is to earn as high a return as possible but without taking much of a risk.
   a. The yield curve is currently upward sloping, such that 10-year Treasury bonds have an annualized yield 3 percentage points above the annualized yield of three-month T-bills. Should you consider using some of your funds to invest in 10-year Treasury securities?
   b. Assume that you have substantially more cash than you would possibly need for any liquidity problems. Your boss suggests that you consider investing the excess funds in some money market securities that have a higher return than short-term Treasury securities, such as negotiable certificates of deposit (NCDs). Even though NCDs are less liquid, this would not cause a problem if you have more funds than you need. Given the situation, what use of the excess funds would benefit the firm the most?

   c. Assume that commercial paper is currently offering an annualized yield of 7.5 percent, while Treasury securities are offering an annualized yield of 7 percent. Economic conditions have been stable, and you expect conditions to be very favorable over the next six months. Given this situation, would you prefer to hold a diversified portfolio of commercial paper issued by various corporations or T-bills?
   d. Assume that commercial paper typically offers a premium of 0.5 percent above the T-bill rate. Given that your firm typically maintains about $10 million in liquid funds, how much extra will you generate per year by investing in commercial paper versus T-bills? Is this extra return worth the risk that the commercial paper could default?

3. **Commercial Paper Ratings** Why do ratings agencies assign ratings to commercial paper?

4. **Primary Market** Explain how the Treasury uses the primary market to obtain adequate funding.

5. **Motive to Issue Commercial Paper** The maximum maturity of commercial paper is 270 days. Why would a firm issue commercial paper instead of longer-term securities, even if it needs funds for a long period of time?

6. **Interpreting Financial News** Interpret the following statements made by Wall Street analysts and portfolio managers.

a. "Money markets are not used to get rich, but to avoid being poor."

b. "Until conditions are more favorable, investors are staying on the sidelines."

c. "My portfolio is overinvested in stocks because of the low money market rates."

7. **Secondary Market for T-bills** Describe the activity in the secondary T-bill market. How can this degree of activity benefit investors in T-bills? Why might a financial institution sometimes consider T-bills as a potential source of funds?

8. **Risk and Return of Commercial Paper** You have the choice of investing in top-rated commercial paper or commercial paper that has a lower risk rating. How do you think the risk and return performances of the two investments differ?

9. **Internet Exercise** Go to http://research.stlouisfed.org/fred2. Under "Categories," select "Interest rates." Compare the yield offered on a T-bill to the yield offered by another money market security with a similar maturity. What is the difference in yields? Why do you think the yields differ?

10. **T-bill Auction** How can investors using the primary T-bill market be assured that their bid will be accepted? Why do large corporations typically make competitive bids rather than noncompetitive bids for T-bills?

11. **Negotiable CDs** How can small investors participate in investments in negotiable certificates of deposits (NCDs)?

12. **Commercial Paper Yield Curve** How do you think the shape of the yield curve for commercial paper and other money market instruments compares to the yield curve for Treasury securities? Explain your logic.

13. **Applying Term Structure Theories to Commercial Paper** Apply the term structure of interest rate theories that were discussed in Chapter 3 to explain the shape of the existing commercial paper yield curve.

14. **Repurchase Agreements** Based on what you know about repurchase agreements, would you expect them to have a lower or higher annualized yield than commercial paper? Why?

15. **Banker's Acceptances** Explain how each of the following would use banker's acceptances: (a) exporting firms, (b) importing firms, (c) commercial banks, and (d) investors.

16. **Commercial Paper** Who issues commercial paper? What types of financial institutions issue commercial paper? Why do some firms create a department that can directly place commercial paper? What criteria affect the decision to create such a department?

17. **Foreign Money Market Yield** Explain how the yield on a foreign money market security would be affected if the foreign currency denominating that security declines to a greater degree.

18. **Commercial Paper Rates** Explain how investors' preferences for commercial paper change during a recession. How should this reaction affect the difference between commercial paper rates and T-bill rates during recessionary periods?

PROBLEMS

1. **T-bill Yield**
   a. Determine how the annualized yield of a T-bill would be affected if the purchase price is lower. Explain the logic of this relationship.
   b. Determine how the annualized yield of a T-bill would be affected if the selling price is lower. Explain the logic of this relationship.
   c. Determine how the annualized yield of a T-bill would be affected if the number of days is shorter, holding the purchase price and selling price constant. Explain the logic of this relationship.

2. **T-bill Yield** The Treasury is selling 91-day T-bills with a face value of $10,000 for $8,800. If the investor holds them until maturity, calculate the yield.

3. **Return on NCDs** Phil purchased an NCD a year ago in the secondary market for $980,000. The NCD matures today at a price of $1,000,000, and Phil received $45,000 in interest. What is Phil's return on the NCD?

4. **Commercial Paper Yield** Assume an investor purchased six-month commercial paper with a face value of $1 million for $940,000. What is the yield?

5. **Effective Yield** A U.S. investor obtains British pounds when the pound is worth $1.50 and invests in a one-year money market security that provides a yield of 5 percent (in pounds). At the end of one year, the investor converts the proceeds from the investment back to dollars at the prevailing spot rate of $1.52 per pound. Calculate the effective yield.

6. **Required Rate of Return** A money market security that has a par value of $10,000 sells for $8,816.60. Given that the security has a maturity of two years, what is the investor's required rate of return?

7. **Return on T-bills** Current T-bill yields are approximately 2 percent. Assume an investor considering the purchase of a newly issued three-month T-bill expects interest rates to increase within the next three months and has a required rate of return of 2.5 percent. Based on this information, how much is this investor willing to pay for a three-month T-bill?

8. **T-bill Yield** Assume an investor purchased a six-month T-bill with a $10,000 par value for $9,000 and sold it 90 days later for $9,100. What is the yield?

9. **T-bill Yield** You paid $98,000 for a $100,000 T-bill maturing in 120 days. If you hold it until maturity, what is the T-bill yield? What is the T-bill discount?

10. **Repurchase Agreement** Stanford Corporation arranged a repurchase agreement in which it purchased securities for $4.9 million and will sell the securities back for $5 million in 40 days. What is the yield (or repo rate) to Stanford Corporation?

11. **T-bill Discount** Newly issued three-month T-bills with a par value of $10,000 sold for $9,700. Compute the T-bill discount.

FLOW OF FUNDS EXERCISE

Financing in the Money Markets

Recall that Carson Company has obtained substantial loans from finance companies and commercial banks. The interest rate on the loans is tied to market interest rates and is adjusted every six months. It has a credit line with a bank in case it suddenly needs to obtain funds for a temporary period. It previously purchased Treasury securities that it could sell if it experiences any liquidity problems.

If the economy continues to be strong, Carson may need to increase its production capacity by about 50 percent over the next few years to satisfy demand. It is concerned about a possible slowing of the economy because of potential Fed actions to reduce inflation. It needs funding to cover payments for supplies. It is also considering the issuance of stock or bonds to raise funds in the next year.

a. The prevailing commercial paper rate on paper issued by large publicly traded firms is lower than the rate Carson would pay when using a line of credit. Do you think that Carson could issue commercial paper at this prevailing market rate?

b. Should Carson obtain funds to cover payments for supplies by selling its holdings of Treasury securities or by using its credit line? Which alternative has a lower cost? Explain.

WSJ EXERCISE

Assessing Yield Differentials of Money Market Securities

Use the "Money Rates" section of The Wall Street Journal to determine the 30-day yield (annualized) of commercial paper, certificates of deposit, banker's acceptances, and T-bills. Which of these securities has the highest yield? Why? Which of these securities has the lowest yield? Why?

Bond Markets

B ond markets facilitate the flow of long-term debt from surplus units to deficit units.

The specific objectives of this chapter are to:

■ provide a background on bonds,

■ explain how bond markets are used by institutional investors, and

■ explain how bond markets have become globally integrated.

Bond Background

Bonds represent long-term debt securities that are issued by government agencies or corporations. The issuer of a bond is obligated to pay interest (or coupon) payments periodically (such as annually or semiannually) and the par value (principal) at maturity. Bonds are often classified according to the type of issuer. Treasury bonds are issued by the Treasury, federal agency bonds are issued by federal agencies, municipal bonds are issued by state and local governments, and corporate bonds are issued by corporations.

Most bonds have maturities of between 10 and 30 years. Bonds are classified by the ownership structure as either bearer bonds or registered bonds. **Bearer bonds** require the owner to clip coupons attached to the bonds and send them to the issuer to receive coupon payments. **Registered bonds** require the issuer to maintain records of who owns the bond and automatically send coupon payments to the owners.

Bond Yields

The issuer's cost of financing with bonds is commonly measured by the so-called **yield to maturity,** which reflects the annualized yield that is paid by the issuer over the life of the bond. The yield to maturity is the annualized discount rate that equates the future coupon and principal payments to the initial proceeds received from the bond offering.

ILLUSTRATION Consider an investor who can purchase bonds with 10 years until maturity, a par value of $1,000, and an 8 percent annualized coupon rate for $936. The yield to maturity on this bond can be determined by using a financial calculator as follows:

Input	10	−936	80	1000		
Function Key	N	PV	PMT	FV	CPT	I
Answer						9%

The yield to maturity does not include transaction costs associated with issuing the bond.

An investor who invests in a bond when it is issued and holds it until maturity will earn the yield to maturity. Many investors, however, do not hold a bond to maturity and therefore focus on their holding period return, or the return from their investment over a particular holding period. If they hold the bond for a very short time period (such as less than one year), they may estimate their holding period return as the sum of the coupon payments plus the difference between the selling price and the purchase price of the bond, as a percentage of the purchase price. For relatively long holding periods, a better approximation of the holding period yield is the annualized discount rate that equates the payments received to the initial investment. Since the selling price to be received by investors is uncertain if they do not hold the bond to maturity, their holding period yield is uncertain at the time they purchase the bond. Consequently, an investment in bonds is subject to the risk that the holding period return will be less than expected. The valuation and return of bonds from the investor's perspective are discussed more thoroughly in the following chapter.

http://money.cnn.com/ markets/bondcenter Yields and information on all types of bonds for various maturities.

Treasury and Federal Agency Bonds

The U.S. Treasury commonly issues Treasury notes or Treasury bonds to finance federal government expenditures. The minimum denomination for Treasury notes or bonds is $1,000. The key difference between a note and a bond is that note maturities are usually less than 10 years, whereas bond maturities are 10 years or more. An active over-the-counter secondary market allows investors to sell Treasury notes or bonds prior to maturity.

The yield from holding a Treasury bond, as with other bonds, depends on the coupon rate and on the difference between the purchase price and the selling price. Investors in Treasury notes and bonds receive semiannual interest payments from the Treasury. Although the interest is taxed by the federal government as ordinary income, it is exempt from state and local taxes, if any exist. Domestic and foreign firms and individuals are common investors in Treasury notes and bonds.

Since October 2001, the Treasury has relied on 10-year Treasury bonds to finance the U.S. budget deficit instead of also issuing 30-year Treasury bonds, as it had done previously. Consequently, the Treasury's influence on yields offered on other types of bonds with maturities of 30 years has been reduced.

Treasury Bond Auction

The Treasury obtains long-term funding through Treasury bond offerings, which are conducted through periodic auctions. Treasury bond auctions are normally held in the middle of each quarter. The Treasury announces its plans for an auction, including the date, the amount of funding that it needs, and the maturity of the bonds to be issued. At the time of the auction, financial institutions submit bids for their own accounts or for their clients.

Bids can be submitted on a competitive or a noncompetitive basis. Competitive bids specify a price that the bidder is willing to pay and a dollar amount of securities to be purchased. Noncompetitive bids specify only a dollar amount of securities to be purchased (subject to a maximum limit). The Treasury ranks the competitive bids in descending order according to the price bid per $100 of par value. All competitive bids are accepted until the point at which the desired amount of funding is achieved. Since November 1998, the Treasury has used the lowest accepted bid price as the price applied to all accepted competitive bids and all noncompetitive bids. Competitive bids are commonly used because many bidders want to purchase more Treasury bonds than the maximum that can be purchased on a noncompetitive basis.

The Salomon Brothers Scandal During each Treasury bond offering, bond dealers purchase Treasury bonds and then redistribute them to clients (other financial institutions) that wish to purchase them. During a 1990 Treasury bond auction, Salomon Brothers (now Salomon Smith Barney, a division of Citigroup) purchased 65 percent of the bonds issued, exceeding the 35 percent maximum allowed for any single bond dealer. Some other bond dealers had made commitments to sell Treasury bonds to their clients (financial institutions), but were unable to obtain a sufficient amount because Salomon Brothers had dominated the auction. The other dealers had to obtain the Treasury bonds from Salomon in order to fulfill their commitments. Because Salomon controlled most of the auction, it was able to charge high prices for the bonds desired by the other dealers.

The episode aroused concern that investors might lose faith in the auction process and be discouraged from obtaining Treasury bonds. If the market came to perceive that bond prices were being manipulated, the demand for Treasury bonds would decline, raising the yields that the Treasury would have to offer to sell the bonds and ultimately increasing the cost to taxpayers.

In the summer of 1991, the Securities and Exchange Commission (SEC) and the Justice Department reviewed Salomon Brothers' involvement in the Treasury auction process. On August 18, 1991, the Treasury Department temporarily barred Salomon Brothers from bidding on Treasury securities for clients. In May 1992, Salomon paid fines of $190 million to the SEC and Justice Department. It also created a reserve fund of $100 million to cover claims from civil lawsuits.

Trading Treasury Bonds

Bond dealers serve as intermediaries in the secondary market by matching up buyers and sellers of Treasury bonds, and they also take positions in these bonds. About 2,000 brokers and dealers are registered to trade Treasury securities, but about 30 so-called primary dealers dominate the trading. These dealers make the secondary market for the Treasury bonds. They quote a bid price for customers who want to sell existing Treasury bonds to the dealers and an ask price for customers who want to buy existing Treasury bonds from them. The dealers profit from the spread between the bid and ask prices. Because of the large volume of secondary market transactions and intense competition among bond dealers, the spread is very narrow. When the Federal Reserve engages in open market operations, it normally conducts trading with the primary dealers of government securities. The primary dealers also trade Treasury bonds among themselves.

Treasury bonds are registered at the New York Stock Exchange, but the secondary market trading occurs over-the-counter (through a telecommunications network). The typical daily transaction volume in government securities (including money market securities) for the primary dealers is about $200 billion. Most of this trading volume

occurs in the United States, but Treasury bonds are traded worldwide. They are traded in Tokyo from 7:30 P.M. to 3:00 A.M. New York time. The Tokyo and London markets overlap for part of the time, and the London market remains open until 7:30 A.M., when trading begins in New York.

Investors can contact their broker to buy or sell Treasury bonds. The brokerage firms serve as an intermediary between the investors and the bond dealers. Discount brokers usually charge a fee between $40 and $70 for Treasury bond transactions valued at $10,000. Institutional investors tend to contact the bond dealers directly.

Online Trading Investors can also buy bonds through the Treasury-Direct program (http://www.publicdebt.treas.gov). They can have the Treasury deduct their purchase from their bank account. They can also reinvest proceeds received when Treasury bonds mature into newly issued Treasury bonds.

Treasury Bond Quotations

Quotations for Treasury bond prices are published in financial newspapers such as *The Wall Street Journal, Barron's,* and *Investor's Business Daily.* They are also provided in *USA Today* and local newspapers. A typical format for Treasury bond quotations is shown in Exhibit 10.1. Each row represents a specific bond. The coupon rate, shown in the first column, will vary substantially among bonds because bonds issued when interest rates were high (such as in the early 1980s) will have higher coupon rates than those issued when interest rates were low (such as in the 2002–2004 period).

The Treasury bonds are organized in the table according to their maturity (shown in the second column), with those closest to maturity listed first. This allows investors to easily find Treasury bonds that have a specific maturity. If the bond contains a call feature allowing the issuer to repurchase the bonds prior to maturity, it is specified beside the maturity date in the second column. For example, the second and third bonds in Exhibit 10.1 mature in the year 2018 but can be called from the year 2013 on.

The bid price (what a bond dealer is willing to pay) and the ask price (what a bond dealer is willing to sell the bond for) are quoted per hundreds of dollars of par value, with fractions (to the right of the colon) expressed as thirty-seconds of a dollar. For example, if the first bond has a face value of $100,000, its ask price will be $120,719. This bond has a much higher price than the other two bonds shown, primarily because it offers a higher coupon rate. However, its yield to maturity is similar to the other yields (see the last column in Exhibit 10.1). From an investor's point of view, the coupon rate advantage over the other two bonds is essentially offset by the high price to be paid for that bond.

Online Quotations Treasury bond prices are accessible online at http://www.investingin bonds.com. This website provides the spread between the bid and the ask (offer) prices for various maturities. Treasury bond yields are accessible online at http://www.federalre serve.gov/releases/H15/. The yields are updated on a daily basis and are disclosed for several different maturities.

<table>
<tr><td colspan="5">**EXHIBIT 10.1**
Example of Bond Price Quotations</td></tr>
<tr><th>Rate</th><th>Maturity Date</th><th>Bid</th><th>Ask</th><th>Yield</th></tr>
<tr><td>10.75</td><td>Aug. 2005</td><td>120:17</td><td>120:23</td><td>8.37%</td></tr>
<tr><td>8.38</td><td>Aug. 2013–18</td><td>100:09</td><td>100:15</td><td>8.32%</td></tr>
<tr><td>8.75</td><td>Nov. 2013–18</td><td>103:05</td><td>103:11</td><td>8.34%</td></tr>
</table>

Government Bond Price Quotations

Government bond price quotations in the secondary market are reported in *The Wall Street Journal*, as shown here. The table is organized by term to maturity; bonds that have the shortest term to maturity are listed first. For each bond, the coupon rate is shown in the first column, the maturity date in the second column, the bid price (per $100 of par value) in the third column, and the ask price (per $100 of par value) in the fourth column. The bid and ask price quotations after the colon are in thirty-seconds, so a quote of 100:03 reflects a price of $100.09 per $100 of par value. The change in the bond's price from the previous day in thirty-seconds is shown in the fifth column, so a change of 1 reflects an increase of $\frac{1}{32}$, or $.03125 per $100 of par value. Notice that the changes in prices are much larger for bonds with longer terms to maturity. The yield to maturity is listed in the last column for investors who plan to purchase bonds today and hold them to maturity. The yield curve can be derived by plotting the yield to maturity for various maturities shown in the last column.

TREASURY BONDS, NOTES & BILLS

Explanatory Notes

Representative Over-the-Counter quotation based on transactions of $1 million or more. Treasury bond, note and bill quotes are as of mid-afternoon. Colons in bid-and-asked quotes represent 32nds; 101:01 means 101 1/32. Net changes in 32nds. n-Treasury note. i-Inflation-Indexed issue. Treasury bill quotes in hundredths, quoted on terms of a rate of discount. Days to maturity calculated from settlement date. All yields to maturity and based on the asked quote. Latest 13-week and 26-week bills are boldfaced. For bonds callable prior to maturity, yields are computed to the earliest call date for issues quoted above par and to the maturity date for issues below par. *When issued.
Source: eSpeed/Cantor Fitzgerald

U.S. Treasury strips as of 3 p.m. Eastern time, also based on transactions of $1 million or more. Colons in bid and asked quotes represent 32nds; 99:01 means 99 1/32. Net changes in 32nds. Yields calculated on the asked quotation. ci-stripped coupon interest. bp-Treasury bond, stripped principal. np-Treasury note, stripped principal. For bonds callable prior to maturity, yields are computed to the earliest call date for issues quoted above par and to the maturity date for issues below par.
Source: Bear, Stearns & Co. via Street Software Technology Inc.

RATE	MATURITY MO/YR	BID	ASKED	CHG	ASK YLD
3.500	Jan 11i	112:29	112:30	-6	1.39
5.000	Feb 11n	107:00	107:00	-6	3.78
13.875	May 11	120:01	120:02	...	2.20
5.000	Aug 11n	106:27	106:28	-7	3.87
14.000	Nov 11	125:11	125:12	-2	2.41
3.375	Jan 12i	112:24	112:25	-6	1.55
4.875	Feb 12n	105:26	105:27	-7	3.97
3.000	Jul 12i	110:00	110:01	-6	1.65
4.375	Aug 12n	102:07	102:08	-7	4.04
4.000	Nov 12n	99:17	99:18	-7	4.06
10.375	Nov 12	122:24	122:25	-5	2.99
3.875	Feb 13n	98:11	98:12	-7	4.10
3.625	May 13n	96:12	96:13	-6	4.11
1.875	Jul 13i	100:27	100:28	-7	1.77
4.250	Aug 13n	100:13	100:14	-8	4.19
12.000	Aug 13	133:01	133:02	-2	3.16
4.250	Nov 13n	100:07	100:08	-7	4.22
2.000	Jan 14i	101:20	101:21	-7	1.81
4.000	Feb 14n	98:04	98:05	-8	4.24
4.750	May 14n	103:30	103:31	-8	4.25
13.250	May 14	143:00	143:01	-5	3.39
2.000	Jul 14i	101:12	101:13	-7	1.84
12.500	Aug 14	141:06	141:07	-7	3.47
11.750	Nov 14	139:02	139:03	-6	3.54
11.250	Feb 15	158:03	158:04	-12	4.31
10.625	Aug 15	154:04	154:04	-11	4.38
9.875	Nov 15	147:28	147:29	-11	4.42
9.250	Feb 16	142:20	142:21	-11	4.47
7.250	May 16	124:16	124:17	-10	4.54
7.500	Nov 16	127:01	127:02	-10	4.59
8.750	May 17	139:19	139:20	-11	4.61
8.875	Aug 17	141:04	141:05	-11	4.63
9.125	May 18	144:18	144:19	-11	4.69
9.000	Nov 18	143:25	143:26	-13	4.74
8.875	Feb 19	142:20	142:21	-13	4.77
8.125	Aug 19	135:02	135:03	-11	4.81
8.500	Feb 20	139:19	139:20	-9	4.84
8.750	May 20	142:22	142:23	-9	4.84
8.750	Aug 20	142:28	142:29	-9	4.86
7.875	Feb 21	133:07	133:08	-8	4.91
8.125	May 21	136:10	136:11	-8	4.91
8.125	Aug 21	136:16	136:17	-9	4.93
8.000	Nov 21	135:07	135:08	-9	4.94
7.250	Aug 22	126:17	126:18	-8	5.00
7.625	Nov 22	131:09	131:10	-8	4.99
7.125	Feb 23	125:07	125:08	-8	5.02
6.250	Aug 23	114:16	114:17	-8	5.05
7.500	Nov 24	130:29	130:30	-8	5.04
2.375	Jan 25i	102:07	102:08	-5	2.24
7.625	Feb 25	132:19	132:20	-9	5.05
6.875	Aug 25	123:01	123:02	-8	5.08
6.000	Feb 26	111:19	111:20	-7	5.10
6.750	Aug 26	121:20	121:21	-8	5.10
6.500	Nov 26	118:11	118:12	-9	5.11
6.625	Feb 27	120:02	120:03	-8	5.11
6.375	Aug 27	116:27	116:28	-7	5.12
6.125	Nov 27	113:16	113:17	-7	5.12
3.625	Apr 28i	124:10	124:11	-4	2.29
5.500	Aug 28	105:00	105:01	-7	5.13
5.250	Nov 28	101:19	101:20	-7	5.13

RATE	MATURITY MO/YR	BID	ASKED	CHG	ASK YLD	RATE	MATURITY MO/YR	BID	ASKED	CHG	ASK YLD
Government Bonds & Notes						7.000	Jul 06n	108:19	108:20	-3	2.40
6.000	Aug 04n	100:02	100:03	...	1.13	2.750	Jul 06n	100:18	100:19	-4	2.43
7.250	Aug 04n	100:02	100:03	...	1.51	2.375	Aug 06n	99:27	99:28	-3	2.43
13.750	Aug 04	100:05	100:06	-1	0.63	6.500	Oct 06n	108:11	108:12	-4	2.53
2.125	Aug 04n	100:01	100:02	...	1.02	2.625	Nov 06n	100:04	100:05	-3	2.55
1.875	Sep 04n	100:02	100:03	...	1.19	3.500	Nov 06n	102:01	102:02	-3	2.55
2.125	Oct 04n	100:04	100:05	...	1.41	3.375	Jan 07i	107:15	107:16	-2	0.28
5.875	Nov 04n	101:04	101:05	...	1.39	2.250	Feb 07n	99:00	99:01	-4	2.64
7.875	Nov 04n	101:21	101:22	...	1.42	6.250	Feb 07n	108:22	108:23	-3	2.64
11.625	Nov 04	102:20	102:21	-1	1.41	6.625	May 07n	110:06	110:07	-4	2.75
2.000	Nov 04n	100:04	100:05	...	1.48	4.375	May 07n	104:08	104:09	-4	2.75
1.750	Dec 04n	100:01	100:02	-1	1.54	3.125	May 07n	100:30	100:31	-4	2.75
1.625	Jan 05n	100:00	100:00	...	1.62	3.250	Aug 07n	101:05	101:06	-4	2.83
7.500	Feb 05n	102:29	102:30	-2	1.70	6.125	Aug 07n	109:11	109:12	-5	2.85
1.500	Feb 05n	99:28	99:29	-1	1.64	3.000	Nov 07n	100:08	100:09	-4	2.91
1.625	Mar 05n	99:29	99:30	-1	1.72	3.625	Jan 08i	110:01	110:02	-4	0.65
1.625	Apr 05n	99:28	99:29	-1	1.75	3.000	Feb 08n	100:00	100:00	-5	3.00
6.500	May 05n	103:16	103:17	-2	1.80	5.500	Feb 08n	108:08	108:09	-5	2.99
6.750	May 05n	103:22	103:23	-2	1.82	2.625	May 08n	98:11	98:12	-4	3.08
12.000	May 05	107:23	107:24	-1	1.73	5.625	May 08n	108:29	108:30	-5	3.09
1.250	May 05n	99:17	99:18	-2	1.80	3.125	Aug 08n	100:08	100:09	-5	3.17
1.125	Jun 05n	99:11	99:12	-1	1.84	3.125	Sep 08n	99:22	99:23	-5	3.19
1.500	Jul 05n	99:19	99:20	-1	1.89	3.125	Oct 08n	99:19	99:20	-5	3.22
6.500	Aug 05n	104:18	104:19	-3	1.89	3.375	Nov 08n	100:16	100:17	-5	3.24
10.750	Aug 05	108:26	108:27	-2	1.90	4.750	Nov 08n	106:00	106:00	-5	3.23
2.000	Aug 05n	100:02	100:03	-2	1.91	3.375	Dec 08n	100:13	100:14	-5	3.27
1.625	Sep 05n	99:19	99:20	-2	1.94	3.250	Jan 09n	99:25	99:26	-5	3.30
1.625	Oct 05n	99:16	99:17	-2	2.00	3.875	Jan 09i	112:20	112:21	-5	0.95
5.750	Nov 05n	104:18	104:19	-3	2.03	3.000	Feb 09n	98:20	98:21	-5	3.32
5.875	Nov 05n	104:23	104:24	-3	2.03	2.625	Mar 09n	96:30	96:31	-5	3.34
1.875	Nov 05n	99:23	99:24	-3	2.06	4.125	Apr 09n	98:29	98:30	-6	3.37
1.875	Dec 05n	99:20	99:21	-3	2.12	3.875	May 09n	102:03	102:04	-6	3.38
1.875	Jan 06n	99:18	99:19	-3	2.16	5.500	May 09n	109:12	109:13	-6	3.34
5.625	Feb 06n	105:05	105:06	-3	2.11	4.000	Jun 09n	102:19	102:20	-6	3.40
9.375	Feb 06	110:22	110:23	-3	2.13	3.625	Jul 09n	100:28	100:29	-6	3.42
1.625	Feb 06n	99:03	99:04	-3	2.19	6.000	Aug 09n	111:21	111:22	-7	3.44
1.500	Mar 06n	98:25	98:26	-3	2.23	10.375	Nov 09	102:13	102:14	...	1.02
2.250	Apr 06n	99:28	99:29	-4	2.30	4.250	Jan 10i	116:01	116:02	-6	1.19
2.000	May 06n	99:15	99:16	-2	2.29	6.500	Feb 10n	114:19	114:20	-6	3.56
4.625	May 06n	103:30	103:31	-3	2.30	11.750	Feb 10	105:06	105:07	1	1.51
6.875	May 06n	107:26	107:27	-3	2.30	10.000	May 10	106:08	106:09	1	1.66
2.500	May 06n	100:08	100:09	-3	2.34	5.750	Aug 10n	111:04	111:05	-6	3.67
2.750	Jun 06n	100:21	100:22	-3	2.37	12.750	Nov 10	113:08	113:09	1	2.03

Stripped Treasury Bonds

The cash flows of bonds are commonly transformed (stripped) by securities firms so that one security represents the principal payment only while a second security represents the interest payments. For example, consider a 10-year Treasury bond with a par value of $100,000 that has a 12 percent coupon rate and semiannual coupon payments. This bond could be stripped into a principal-only (PO) security that will provide $100,000 upon maturity and an interest-only (IO) security that will provide 20 semiannual payments of $6,000 each.

Investors who desire a lump-sum payment in the distant future can choose the PO part, and investors desiring periodic cash inflows can select the IO part. Because the cash flows of the underlying securities are different, so are the degrees of interest rate sensitivity.

A market for Treasury strips was originally created by securities firms in the early 1980s. Merrill Lynch created the Treasury Investment Growth Receipts (TIGRs) by purchasing Treasury securities and then stripping them to create PO and IO securities. Other securities firms also began to create their own versions of these **stripped securities.** In 1985, the Treasury created the STRIPS program, which exchanges stripped securities for underlying Treasury securities. STRIPS are not issued by the Treasury, but are created and sold by various financial institutions. They can be created for any Treasury security. Since they are components of Treasury securities, they are backed by the U.S. government. They do not have to be held until maturity, as there is an active secondary market. STRIPS have become very popular. More than $11 billion of securites are being stripped every month.

Inflation-Indexed Treasury Bonds

In 1996, the Treasury announced that it would periodically issue inflation-indexed bonds that provide returns tied to the inflation rate. These bonds, commonly referred to as TIPS (Treasury inflation-protected securities), are intended for investors who wish to ensure that the returns on their investments keep up with the increase in prices over time. The coupon rate offered on TIPS is lower than the rate on typical Treasury bonds, but the principal value is increased by the amount of the U.S. inflation rate (as measured by the percentage increase in the consumer price index) every six months.

ILLUSTRATION Consider a 10-year inflation-indexed bond that has a par value of $10,000 and a coupon rate of 4 percent. Assume that during the first six months since the bond was issued, the inflation rate (as measured by the consumer price index) was 1 percent. The principal of the bond is increased by $100 (1% × $10,000). Thus, the coupon payment after six months will be 2 percent (half of the yearly coupon rate) of the new par value, or 2% × $10,100 = $202. Assume that the inflation rate over the next six months is 3 percent. The principal of the bond is increased by $303 (3% × $10,100), which results in a new par value of $10,403. The coupon payment at the end of the year is based on the coupon rate and the new par value, or 2% × $10,403 = $208.06. This process is applied every six months over the life of the bond. If prices double over the 10-year period in which the bond exists, the par value of the bond will also double and thus will be equal to $20,000 at maturity.

Inflation-indexed government bonds have become very popular in some other countries where inflation tends to be high, including Australia, Turkey, Brazil, and the United Kingdom. They are also becoming popular in the United States.

Savings Bonds

Savings bonds are issued by the Treasury, but can be purchased from many financial institutions. They are attractive to small investors because they can be purchased with as little as $25. Larger denominations are available as well. The Series EE savings bond provides a market-based rate of interest, while the I savings bond provides a rate of interest that is tied to inflation. The interest accumulates monthly and adds value to the amount received at the time of redemption.

Savings bonds have a 30-year maturity and do not have a secondary market. The Treasury does allow savings bonds issued after February 2003 to be redeemed anytime after a 12-month period, but there is a penalty equal to the last three months of interest.

The interest income on savings bonds is not subject to state and local taxes, but is subject to federal taxes. For federal tax purposes, investors holding savings bonds can report the accumulated interest on an annual basis or only at the time they redeem the bonds or at maturity.

Federal Agency Bonds

Federal agency bonds are issued by federal agencies. The **Government National Mortgage Association (Ginnie Mae)** issues bonds and uses the proceeds to purchase mortgages that are insured by the Federal Housing Administration (FHA) and by the Veteran's Administration (VA). The bonds are backed both by the mortgages that are purchased with the proceeds and by the federal government.

The Federal Home Loan Mortgage Association (called Freddie Mac) issues bonds and uses the proceeds to purchase conventional mortgages. These bonds are not backed by the federal government, but have a very low degree of credit risk.

The **Federal National Mortgage Association (Fannie Mae)** is a federally chartered corporation owned by individual investors. It issues bonds and uses the proceeds to purchase residential mortgages. These bonds are not backed by the federal government, but have a very low degree of credit risk.

Municipal Bonds

Like the federal government, state and local governments frequently spend more than the revenues they receive. To finance the difference, they issue **municipal bonds,** most of which can be classified as either **general obligation bonds** or **revenue bonds.** Payments on general obligation bonds are supported by the municipal government's ability to tax, whereas payments on revenue bonds must be generated by revenues of the project (tollway, toll bridge, state college dormitory, etc.) for which the bonds were issued.

The volume of state and local government bonds issued is displayed in Exhibit 10.2. Revenue bonds have generally dominated since 1975. The total amount of bond financing by state and local governments has generally increased over time.

Credit Risk

Both types of municipal bonds are subject to some degree of credit (default) risk. If a municipality is unable to increase taxes, it could default on general obligation bonds. If it issues revenue bonds and does not generate sufficient revenue, it could default on these bonds.

USING THE WALL STREET JOURNAL

Government Agency & Similar Issues

Bond price quotations provided for bonds issued by Fannie Mae, Freddie Mac, and other government agencies are disclosed in *The Wall Street Journal*. The coupon rate is provided in the first column, while the maturity date is in the second column. The bid and ask prices are quoted in the third and fourth columns, while the yield to maturity is disclosed in the fifth column.

Government Agency & Similar Issues

Over-the-Counter mid-afternoon quotations based on large transactions, usually $1 million or more. Colons in bid and asked quotes represent 32nds; 101:01 means 101 1/32.

All yields are calculated to maturity, and based on the asked quote.

*Callable issue, maturity date shown. For issues callable prior to maturity, yields are computed to the earliest call date for issues quoted above par, or 100, and to the maturity date for issues below par.

Source: Bear, Stearns & Co. via Street Software Technology Inc.

Fannie Mae Issues

RATE	MAT	BID	ASKED	YLD
6.50	8-04	100:02	100:04	...
3.50	9-04	100:06	100:08	0.98
1.88	12-04	100:00	100:02	1.71
7.13	2-05	102:20	102:22	1.82
3.88	3-05	101:03	101:05	1.89
5.75	6-05	103:00	103:02	2.08
7.00	7-05	104:13	104:15	2.12
1.88	9-05	99:26	99:28	2.00
2.88	10-05	100:29	100:31	2.03
6.00	12-05	105:00	105:02	2.15
2.00	1-06	99:18	99:20	2.26
5.50	2-06	104:20	104:22	2.32
2.13	4-06	99:15	99:17	2.41
5.50	5-06	104:29	104:31	2.54
2.25	5-06	99:17	99:19	2.49
5.25	6-06	104:26	104:28	2.52
2.50	6-06	99:29	99:31	2.52
1.75	6-06	98:11	98:13	2.64
2.75	8-06	99:29	99:31	2.77
4.38	10-06	103:15	103:17	2.70
2.63	11-06	99:21	99:23	2.76
4.75	1-07	104:03	104:05	2.94
5.00	1-07	104:31	105:01	2.84
2.63	1-07*	99:03	99:05	2.98
2.38	2-07	98:22	98:24	2.89
7.13	3-07	109:28	109:30	3.11
5.25	4-07	105:25	105:26	2.97
4.25	7-07	103:07	103:09	3.07
6.63	10-07	110:09	110:11	3.18
3.50	10-07*	101:03	101:05	...
3.25	11-07	100:04	100:06	3.19
3.25	1-08	99:27	99:29	3.28
3.50	1-08*	100:08	100:10	2.83
5.75	2-08	107:31	108:01	3.30
6.00	5-08	109:02	109:04	3.39
2.88	5-08*	97:24	97:26	3.50
2.50	6-08	96:23	96:25	3.40
3.25	8-08	99:01	99:03	3.50
4.00	9-08	101:12	101:14	3.62
3.75	9-08	99:21	99:23	3.83
3.88	11-08*	100:03	100:05	3.74
3.38	12-08	98:30	99:00	3.62
4.00	12-08*	100:15	100:17	3.34
5.25	1-09	106:14	106:16	3.65
3.25	2-09	98:06	98:08	3.67
3.13	3-09*	96:31	97:01	3.84
4.25	5-09	102:03	102:05	3.75
6.38	6-09	111:11	111:13	3.78
6.63	9-09	112:20	112:22	3.85
7.25	1-10	115:30	116:00	3.95
7.13	6-10	115:26	115:28	4.05
6.63	11-10	113:17	113:19	4.14
6.25	2-11	110:03	110:05	4.43
5.50	3-11	107:08	107:10	4.22
6.00	5-11	110:00	110:02	4.27
5.50	10-11*	101:27	101:29	...
5.38	11-11	106:04	106:06	4.37
5.00	11-11*	100:05	100:07	4.17
6.00	12-11*	101:15	101:17	1.72
6.00	1-12*	101:24	101:26	1.80
6.13	3-12	110:23	110:25	4.43
6.25	3-12*	102:15	102:17	2.04
5.50	7-12*	101:26	101:28	3.45
5.25	8-12	103:01	103:03	4.78
4.38	9-12	98:31	99:01	4.52
4.75	2-13*	98:23	98:25	4.93
4.63	5-13	98:06	98:08	4.87
4.38	7-13*	96:12	96:14	4.87
4.63	10-13	99:18	99:20	4.68
5.13	1-14	100:27	100:29	5.00
4.13	4-14	95:08	95:10	4.73
6.25	5-29	109:13	109:17	5.54
7.13	1-30	121:01	121:05	5.56
7.25	5-30	122:28	123:00	5.56
6.63	11-30	114:13	114:17	5.57

Freddie Mac

RATE	MAT	BID	ASKED	YLD
4.50	8-04	100:01	100:03	...
3.25	11-04	100:12	100:14	1.59
6.88	1-05	102:03	102:05	1.76
1.88	1-05	99:31	100:01	1.83
3.88	2-05	100:30	101:00	1.88
1.75	5-05	99:22	99:24	2.00
4.25	6-05	101:23	101:25	2.11
7.00	7-05	104:12	104:14	2.13
1.50	8-05	99:17	99:19	1.90
2.88	9-05	100:28	100:30	2.00
2.13	11-05	99:29	99:31	2.15
5.25	1-06	104:03	104:05	2.26
1.88	2-06	99:09	99:11	2.32
2.38	4-06	99:28	99:30	2.41
5.25	7-06	105:14	105:16	2.55
2.63	12-05	100:17	100:19	2.18
2.50	3-06	100:06	100:08	2.34
2.25	9-06	99:02	99:04	2.69
2.88	12-06	100:04	100:06	2.79
2.38	2-07	98:23	98:25	2.88
4.88	3-07	104:25	104:27	2.92
3.50	9-07	100:31	101:01	3.14
4.00	10-07*	101:17	101:19	...
3.25	2-08*	99:13	99:14	3.41
2.75	3-08	98:03	98:05	3.30
3.50	4-08*	99:18	99:20	3.61
5.75	4-08	108:06	108:09	3.34
3.63	9-08	100:10	100:12	3.53
5.13	10-08	106:03	106:05	3.53
3.88	1-09*	99:25	99:27	3.91
5.75	3-09	108:21	108:23	3.67
3.38	4-09	98:14	98:16	3.72
4.25	7-09	102:00	102:02	3.79
4.75	8-09*	100:02	100:04	...
6.63	9-09	112:22	112:24	3.85
4.38	2-10*	99:30	100:00	4.37
7.00	3-10	114:31	115:01	3.98
6.88	9-10	114:23	114:25	4.11
4.75	12-10*	100:24	100:26	4.11
4.13	2-11*	98:01	98:03	4.46
5.63	3-11	107:31	108:01	4.22
5.88	3-11	108:01	108:03	4.45
6.00	6-11	110:04	110:06	4.27
6.38	8-11*	105:18	105:20	3.40
5.50	9-11	107:00	107:02	4.33
5.75	1-12	108:15	108:17	4.39
6.25	3-12*	105:30	106:00	3.78
5.13	7-12	104:05	104:07	4.49
5.13	8-12*	100:03	100:05	...
4.75	10-12*	99:01	99:03	4.89
5.25	11-12*	101:03	101:05	4.85
4.50	1-13	99:15	99:17	4.57
4.38	3-13	98:16	98:18	4.58
4.75	5-13*	97:19	97:21	5.09
4.00	6-13*	94:09	94:11	4.79
4.50	11-30	90:00	90:04	4.64
5.13	11-13*	100:01	100:03	5.05
4.88	11-13	101:12	101:14	4.68
4.50	1-14	98:12	98:14	4.70
5.00	1-14*	99:15	99:17	5.06
6.75	9-29	115:25	115:29	5.57
6.75	3-31	116:09	116:13	5.56
6.25	7-32	109:24	109:28	5.55

Federal Farm Credit Bank

RATE	MAT	BID	ASKED	YLD
2.38	10-04	100:03	100:05	1.29
3.88	12-04	100:22	100:24	1.70
3.88	2-05	100:28	100:30	1.86
4.38	4-05	101:16	101:18	2.02
2.13	8-05	100:06	100:08	1.89
2.50	11-05	100:13	100:15	2.12
2.63	12-05	100:16	100:18	2.18
2.50	3-06	100:06	100:08	2.34
2.25	9-06	99:02	99:04	2.69

RATE	MAT	BID	ASKED	YLD
2.38	10-06	99:11	99:13	2.66
3.00	4-08*	98:24	98:26	3.35

Federal Home Loan Bank

RATE	MAT	BID	ASKED	YLD
3.63	10-04	100:11	100:13	1.38
4.13	11-04	100:19	100:21	1.59
4.00	2-05	101:00	101:02	1.90
4.38	2-05	101:06	101:08	1.89
1.63	4-05	99:21	99:23	2.02
6.88	8-05	104:27	104:29	1.93
2.25	12-05	100:00	100:02	2.20
2.50	12-05	100:11	100:13	2.20
2.00	2-06	99:14	99:16	2.34
5.13	3-06	103:25	103:27	2.61
2.50	3-06	99:28	99:30	2.53
5.38	5-06	104:27	104:29	2.51
2.25	5-06	99:17	99:19	2.48
1.88	6-06	98:25	98:27	2.51
2.88	9-06	100:12	100:14	2.66
4.88	11-06	104:15	104:17	2.79
1.88	1-07	97:23	97:25	2.83
4.88	2-07	104:20	104:22	2.93
5.38	2-07	105:26	105:28	2.93
2.75	3-08	98:03	98:05	3.30
2.63	7-08	96:29	96:31	3.46
5.80	9-08	108:15	108:17	3.53
3.63	11-08	100:00	100:02	3.61
6.00	5-11	109:17	109:19	4.34
5.63	11-11	107:12	107:14	4.42
5.75	5-12	108:11	108:13	4.46
4.50	11-12	99:19	99:21	4.55
3.88	6-13	94:23	94:25	4.60
4.50	9-13	98:24	98:26	4.66
5.25	6-14	103:26	103:28	4.75

GNMA Mtge. Issues

RATE	MAT	BID	ASKED	YLD
4.00	30Yr	92:14	92:16	5.19
4.50	30Yr	96:07	96:09	5.16
5.00	30Yr	99:05	99:07	5.19
5.50	30Yr	101:17	101:19	5.12
6.00	30Yr	103:16	103:18	4.80
6.50	30Yr	104:31	105:01	4.24
7.00	30Yr	106:14	106:16	3.74
7.50	30Yr	107:20	107:22	3.77
8.00	30Yr	108:25	108:27	3.95
8.50	30Yr	108:31	109:01	4.47

Tennessee Valley Authority

RATE	MAT	BID	ASKED	YLD
6.38	6-05	103:17	103:19	2.04
5.38	11-08	106:15	106:17	3.70
5.63	1-11	107:31	108:02	4.18
6.00	3-13	109:30	110:00	4.58
4.75	8-13	100:29	100:31	4.62
6.25	12-17	111:13	111:16	5.05
6.75	11-25	114:15	114:18	5.07
7.13	5-30	120:28	121:00	5.58

Nevertheless, in general the risk of default on municipal bonds is low. Less than .5 percent of all municipal bonds issued since 1940 have defaulted. Because there is some concern about the risk of default, investors commonly monitor the ratings of municipal bonds. Moody's, Standard & Poor's, and Fitch Investor Service assign ratings to municipal bonds based on the ability of the issuer to repay the debt. The ratings are important to the issuer because a better rating will cause investors to require a smaller risk premium, and the municipal bonds can be issued at a higher price (lower yield).

EXHIBIT 10.2 Dollar Volume of State and Local Government Securities Issued

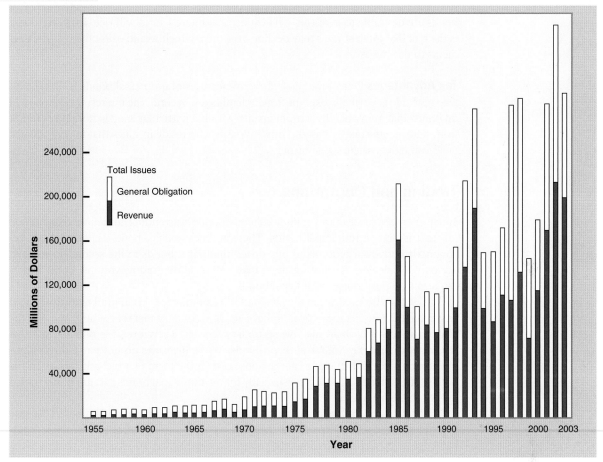

Sources: Bloomberg, L.P.; J. P. Morgan; Salomon Brothers; *Current Issues in Economics and Finance,* FRBNY, June 1995, p. 4, updated by author.

Some municipal bonds are insured to protect against default. The issuer pays for this protection, so that it can issue the bond at a higher price, which translates into a higher price paid by the investor. Thus, investors indirectly bear the cost of the insurance.

Municipal Bond Characteristics

Revenue bonds and general obligation bonds typically promise semiannual interest payments. Common purchasers of these bonds include financial and nonfinancial institutions as well as individuals. The minimum denomination of municipal bonds is typically $5,000. A secondary market exists for them, although it is less active than the one for Treasury bonds.

Most municipal bonds contain a call provision, which allows the issuer to repurchase the bonds at a specified price before the bonds mature. A municipality may exercise its option to repurchase the bonds if interest rates decline substantially because it can reissue bonds at the lower interest rate and reduce its cost of financing.

Variable-Rate Municipal Bonds Variable-rate municipal bonds have a floating interest rate based on a benchmark interest rate. The coupon payment adjusts to movements

in the benchmark interest rate. Some variable-rate municipal bonds are convertible to a fixed rate until maturity under specified conditions. In general, variable-rate municipal bonds are desirable to investors who expect that interest rates will rise. However, there is the risk that interest rates may decline over time, which would cause the coupon payments to decline as well.

Tax Advantages One of the most attractive features of municipal bonds is that the interest income is normally exempt from federal taxes. Second, the interest income earned on bonds that are issued by a municipality within a particular state is normally exempt from state income taxes (if any). Thus, investors who reside in states that impose income taxes can reduce their taxes further.

Trading and Quotations

Today, there are more than 1 million different bonds outstanding, and more than 50,000 different issuers of municipal bonds. There are hundreds of bond dealers that can accommodate investor requests to buy or sell municipal bonds in the secondary market, but only five dealers account for more than half of all the trading volume. Bond dealers can also take positions in municipal bonds.

Investors who expect that they will not hold a municipal bond until maturity should ensure that the bonds they consider have active secondary market trading. Many of the municipal bonds have an inactive secondary market. Therefore, it is difficult to know the prevailing market values of these bonds. While investors do not pay a direct commission on trades, they incur transactions costs in the form of a bid-ask spread on the bonds. This spread can be large, especially for the municipal bonds that are rarely traded in the secondary market.

The electronic trading of municipal bonds is becoming very popular, in part because it enables investors to circumvent the more expensive route of calling brokers. Trading Edge, a broker of fixed-income securities, established an electronic trading website, http://www.tradingedge.com in 1999. Another popular electronic bond website is http://www.eBondTrade.com. Such websites provide access to information on municipal bonds and allow online buying and selling of municipal bonds.

Municipal bond price quotations are accessible online at http://www.munidirect.com and at http://www.investinginbonds.com. Quotations can be obtained for any state and can be sorted by maturity, credit rating, coupon rate, or other characteristics.

Municipal Bond Yields

The yield offered by a municipal bond differs from the yield on a Treasury bond with the same maturity for three reasons. First, the municipal bond must pay a risk premium to compensate for the possibility of default risk. Second, the municipal bond must pay a slight premium to compensate for being less liquid than Treasury bonds with the same maturity. Third, as explained earlier, the income earned from a municipal bond is exempt from federal taxes. This tax advantage of municipal bonds more than offsets their two disadvantages and allows municipal bonds to offer a lower yield than Treasury bonds.

Yield Curve on Municipal Bonds At any given time, there are municipal bonds in the secondary market that have only a short time to maturity and others that have longer terms to maturity. A municipal bond yield curve can be constructed from the municipal bonds that are available. An example of a municipal bond yield curve is shown in

EXHIBIT 10.3
Annualized Yield Offered on
Securities

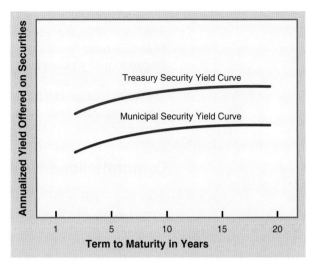

Exhibit 10.3, which also includes a Treasury yield curve for comparison. Notice that the municipal security yield curve is lower than the Treasury yield curve, which is primarily attributed to the tax differential between the two types of securities. The gap due to the tax differential is offset slightly by the default risk and liquidity differential. The yield on municipal securities is commonly 20 to 30 percent less than the yield offered on Treasury securities with similar maturities.

The shape of a municipal security yield curve tends to be similar to the shape of a Treasury security yield curve for two reasons. First, like the Treasury yield curve, the municipal yield curve is influenced by interest rate expectations. If investors expect interest rates to rise, they tend to favor shorter-term securities, which results in high short-term security prices and low short-term yields in both the municipal and Treasury markets. Second, investors require a premium for longer-term securities with lower liquidity in both the municipal and Treasury markets. If supply conditions differ, the shapes could differ.

ILLUSTRATION At a particular point in time, assume that the economy is strong and municipalities experience budget surpluses. Many of them will not have to issue new bonds, so those municipalities that do need long-term funds can more easily find buyers. Meanwhile, the Treasury may still issue new long-term securities to finance the existing federal deficit. In this case, the gap between the Treasury and municipal yields may be larger for new long-term securities than for the securities that were issued in the past and now have a shorter term to maturity.

Corporate Bonds

When corporations need to borrow for long-term periods, they issue **corporate bonds,** which usually promise the owner interest on a semiannual basis. The minimum denomination is $1,000. Larger bond offerings are normally achieved through public offerings, which must first be registered with the SEC. The degree of secondary market activity varies; some big corporations have a large amount of bonds outstanding, which increases secondary market activity and the bonds' liquidity. The bonds issued by smaller corporations tend to be less liquid because their trading volume is relatively low.

Although most corporate bonds have maturities between 10 and 30 years, corporations such as Boeing, Ford, and ChevronTexaco have recently issued 50-year bonds. These bonds can be attractive to insurance companies that are attempting to match their long-term policy obligations. Recently, Bell South, the Coca-Cola Company, and Walt Disney Company issued 100-year bonds.

The interest paid by corporations is tax deductible, which reduces the corporate cost of financing with bonds. Since equity (stock) financing by corporations does not involve interest payments, it does not offer such a tax advantage.

Corporate Bond Yields and Risk

Institutional and individual investors who want an investment that provides stable income may consider purchasing corporate bonds. The interest income earned on corporate bonds represents ordinary income to the bondholders and is therefore subject to federal and state (if any) taxes. Thus, corporate bonds do not provide the same tax benefits to bondholders as municipal bonds.

Yield Curve At a given point in time, the yield curve for corporate bonds will be affected by interest rate expectations, a liquidity premium, and the specific maturity preferences of corporations issuing bonds. Since these are the same factors that affect the yield curve of Treasury bonds, the shape of the yield curve for corporate bonds will also normally be similar to the yield curve for Treasury bonds, except that the curve will be higher to reflect credit risk and less liquidity.

Default Rate The general level of defaults on corporate bonds is dependent on economic conditions. When the economy is strong, firms generate higher revenue and are better able to cover their debt payments. When the economy is weak, some firms may not generate sufficient revenue to cover their operating and debt expenses and therefore default on their bonds. Exhibit 10.4 shows the default rate on corporate bonds over time. Notice that the default rate was less than 1 percent in the late 1990s when U.S. economic conditions were strong, but it exceeded 3 percent in 2002 when economic conditions were weak.

EXHIBIT 10.4 Default Rate on Corporate Bonds over Time

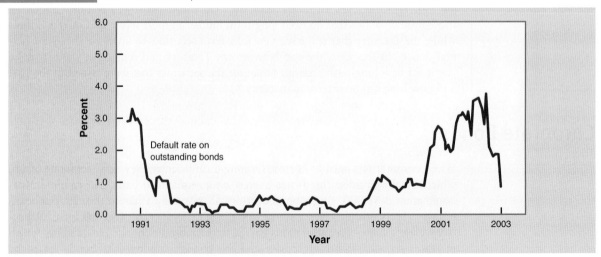

Source: Federal Reserve

Investor Assessment of Risk Since credit risk is associated with corporate bonds, investors may consider purchasing corporate bonds only after assessing the issuing firm's financial condition and ability to cover its debt payments. Thus, investors may rely heavily on financial statements created by the issuing firm. This presents an asymmetric information problem in that the firm knows its true condition, but investors do not. Thus, it can be a challenge for investors to properly assess a firm's ability to cover its debt payments.

ILLUSTRATION Last year, Spectral Insurance Company considered purchasing bonds that were recently issued by Ladron Company. Spectral assessed Ladron's financial statements to determine whether it would have sufficient cash flows in the future to cover its debt payments. In reviewing the revenue and expenses that Ladron reported for the last year, Spectral noticed that Ladron had a large expense categorized as "nonrecurring," which indicates a one-time expense that should not occur again. Spectral ignored those expenses because it wanted to focus only on the typical operating expenses that will occur every year. After estimating Ladron's future cash flows in this manner, Spectral decided that Ladron would be capable of covering its debt payments and purchased bonds issued by Ladron for $20 million.

Last week, Ladron announced that it must file for bankruptcy because it incurred another huge nonrecurring expense this year. Spectral's mistake was that it fully trusted the financial statements reported by Ladron. Like many companies, Ladron classified some operating expenses as "nonrecurring expenses" so that it could reduce its reported operating expenses and increase its reported operating earnings. This is misleading, but may be within accounting guidelines. Nevertheless, Spectral incurred major losses on its investments because of the asymmetric information problem.

Bond Ratings Corporate bonds are rated by rating agencies. Corporate bonds that receive higher ratings can be placed at higher prices (lower yields). Therefore, corporations can achieve a lower cost of financing when their bonds are rated highly. Corporations are especially interested in achieving an investment-grade status on their bonds (medium quality or above) because commercial banks will only invest in bonds that have investment-grade status. A corporate bond's rating may change over time if the issuer's ability to repay the debt changes.

Although bond rating agencies are skilled at assessing ability to repay debt, they are also subject to the asymmetric information problem. They commonly consider the financial statements provided by the issuer of bonds when making their assessment and will not necessarily detect any misleading information contained in the financial statements.

Corporate Bond Private Placements

Some corporate bonds are privately placed rather than sold in a public offering. A private placement does not have to be registered with the SEC. Small firms that borrow relatively small amounts of funds (such as $30 million) may consider private placements rather than public offerings, since they may be able to find an institutional investor that will purchase the entire offering. Although the issuer does not need to register with the SEC, it still needs to disclose financial data to convince any prospective purchasers that the bonds will be repaid in a timely manner. The issuer may hire a securities firm to place the bonds because such firms are normally better able to identify institutional investors that may be interested in purchasing privately placed debt.

The institutional investors that commonly purchase a private placement are insurance companies and pension funds. Since privately placed bonds do not have an active

secondary market, they are more desirable to institutional investors that are willing to invest for long periods of time.

Corporate Bond Characteristics

Corporate bonds can be described according to a variety of characteristics. The bond **indenture** is a legal document specifying the rights and obligations of both the issuing firm and the bondholders. It is very comprehensive (normally several hundred pages) and is designed to address all matters related to the bond issue (collateral, payment dates, default provisions, call provisions, etc.).

Federal law requires that for each bond issue of significant size a **trustee** be appointed to represent the bondholders in all matters concerning the bond issue. The trustee's duties include monitoring the issuing firm's activities to ensure compliance with the terms of the indenture. If the terms are violated, the trustee initiates legal action against the issuing firm and represents the bondholders in that action. Bank trust departments are frequently hired to perform the duties of trustee.

Sinking-Fund Provision Bond indentures frequently include a **sinking-fund provision,** or a requirement that the firm retire a certain amount of the bond issue each year. This provision is considered to be an advantage to the remaining bondholders because it reduces the payments necessary at maturity.

Specific sinking-fund provisions can vary significantly among bond issues. For example, a bond with 20 years until maturity could have a provision to retire 5 percent of the bond issue each year. Or it could have a requirement to retire 5 percent each year beginning in the fifth year, with the remaining amount to be retired at maturity. The actual mechanics of bond retirement are carried out by the trustee.

Protective Covenants Bond indentures normally place restrictions on the issuing firm that are designed to protect the bondholders from being exposed to increasing risk during the investment period. These so-called protective covenants frequently limit the amount of dividends and corporate officers' salaries the firm can pay and also restrict the amount of additional debt the firm can issue. Other financial policies may be restricted as well.

Protective covenants are needed because shareholders and bondholders have different expectations of a firm's management. Shareholders may prefer that managers use a relatively large amount of debt because they can benefit directly from risky managerial decisions that will generate higher returns on investment. In contrast, bondholders simply hope to receive their principal back, with interest. Since they do not share in the excess returns generated by a firm, they would prefer that managerial decisions be conservative. Protective covenants can prevent managers from taking excessive risk and therefore satisfy the preferences of bondholders. If managers are unwilling to accept some protective covenants, they may not be able to obtain debt financing.

Call Provisions Most bonds include a provision allowing the firm to call the bonds. A **call provision** normally requires the firm to pay a price above par value when it calls its bonds. The difference between the bond's call price and par value is the **call premium.** Call provisions have two principal uses. First, if market interest rates decline after a bond issue has been sold, the firm might end up paying a higher rate of interest than the prevailing rate for a long period of time. Under these circumstances, the firm may consider selling a new issue of bonds with a lower interest rate and using the proceeds to retire the previous issue by calling the old bonds.

Second, a call provision may be used to retire bonds as required by a sinking-fund provision. Many bonds have two different call prices: a lower price for calling the bonds to meet sinking-fund requirements and a higher price if the bonds are called for any other reason.

Bondholders normally view a call provision as a disadvantage because it can disrupt their investment plans and reduce their investment returns. As a result, firms must pay slightly higher rates of interest on bonds that are callable, other things being equal.

Bond Collateral Bonds can be classified according to whether they are secured by collateral and by the nature of that collateral. Usually, the collateral is a mortgage on real property (land and buildings). A **first mortgage bond** has first claim on the specified assets. A **chattel mortgage bond** is secured by personal property.

Bonds unsecured by specific property are called **debentures** (backed only by the general credit of the issuing firm). These bonds are normally issued by large, financially sound firms whose ability to service the debt is not in question. **Subordinated debentures** have claims against the firm's assets that are junior to the claims of both mortgage bonds and regular debentures. Owners of subordinated debentures receive nothing until the claims of mortgage bondholders, regular debenture owners, and secured short-term creditors have been satisfied. The main purchasers of subordinated debt are pension funds and insurance companies.

Low- and Zero-Coupon Bonds In the early 1980s, firms began issuing bonds with coupons roughly half the size of the prevailing rate and later issued bonds with zero coupons. These **low-coupon** or **zero-coupon bonds** are therefore issued at a deep discount from par value. Investors are taxed annually on the amount of interest earned, even though much or all of the interest will not be received until maturity. The amount of interest taxed is the amortized discount. (The gain at maturity is prorated over the life of the bond.) Low- and zero-coupon corporate bonds are purchased mainly for tax-exempt investment accounts (pension funds, individual retirement accounts, etc.).

To the issuing firm, these bonds have the advantage of requiring low or no cash outflow during their life. Additionally, the firm is permitted to deduct the amortized discount as interest expense for federal income tax purposes, even though it does not pay interest. This adds to the firm's cash flow. Finally, the demand for low- and zero-coupon bonds has been great enough that firms can, in most cases, issue them at a lower cost than regular bonds.

Variable-Rate Bonds The highly volatile interest rates experienced during the 1970s inspired the development of **variable-rate bonds** (also called floating-rate bonds), which affect the investor and borrower as follows: (1) they allow investors to benefit from rising market interest rates over time, and (2) they allow issuers of bonds to benefit from declining rates over time.

Most issues tie their coupon rate to the London Interbank Offer Rate (LIBOR), the rate at which banks lend funds to each other on an international basis. The rate is typically adjusted every three months.

Variable-rate bonds became very popular in 2004, when interest rates were at low levels. Since most investors presumed that interest rates were likely to rise, they were more willing to purchase variable-rate than fixed-rate bonds. In fact, the volume of variable-rate bonds exceeded that of fixed-rate bonds during this time.

Convertibility Another type of bond, known as a **convertible bond,** allows investors to exchange the bond for a stated number of shares of the firm's common stock. This conversion feature offers investors the potential for high returns if the price of the firm's

common stock rises. Investors are therefore willing to accept a lower rate of interest on these bonds, which allows the firm to obtain financing at a lower cost.

Trading Corporate Bonds

http://bonds.yahoo.com/rates.html Yields on all types of bonds for various maturities.

Corporate bonds can be traded on an exchange or in the over-the-counter market. More than 2,000 corporate bonds with a market value of more than $2 trillion are traded on the New York Stock Exchange (NYSE). Firms that have their stock listed on the NYSE can list their bonds for free. The bonds listed on the NYSE are traded through its Automated Bond System (ABS), which is an electronic system used by investment firms that are members of the NYSE. The ABS displays prices and matches buy and sell orders.

The number of bonds traded on the NYSE has declined substantially in recent years, as many bonds are now traded in an over-the-counter bond market. Information about the trades in the over-the-counter market is provided by the National Association of Securities Dealers' Trade Reporting and Compliance Engine, which is referred to as "Trace." Some bonds also trade on the American Stock Exchange.

Types of Orders Various bond dealers take positions in corporate bonds and accommodate orders. Individual investors buy or sell corporate bonds through brokers, who communicate the orders to bond dealers. Investors who wish to buy or sell bonds can normally place a **market order;** in this case, the desired transaction will occur at the prevailing market price. Alternatively, they can place a **limit order;** in this case, the transaction will occur only if the price reaches the specified limit. When purchasing bonds, investors use a limit order to specify the maximum limit price they are willing to pay for a bond. When selling bonds, investors use a limit order to specify a minimum limit price at which they are willing to sell their bonds.

Trading Online Corporate bonds are increasingly being traded online. One of the most popular online bond brokerage websites is http://www.Tradebonds.com, which provides bond prices for a large sample of brokers. This site is targeted toward investors who buy in large quantities, but other popular online bond brokerage websites, such as http://www.schwab.com and http://www.etrade.com/global.html, are aimed toward small investors. The pricing of bonds is more transparent online because investors can easily compare the bid and ask spreads among brokers. This transparency has encouraged some brokers to narrow their spreads so that they do not lose business to competitors.

Corporate Bond Quotations

http://averages.dowjones.com Links to corporate bond indexes so that you can monitor the general performance of corporate bonds.

The financial press publishes quotations for corporate bonds, just as it does for Treasury bonds, although in a slightly different format (look back at Exhibit 10.1 to review the format for Treasury bonds). In particular, corporate bond prices are reported in eighths, rather than the thirty-seconds used for Treasury bonds. Thus, a quotation of 101 5/8 for a Disney bond means $101.62 per $100 par value. Corporate bond quotations also typically include the volume of trading, which is normally measured as the number of bonds traded for that day. As in Treasury bond quotations, the yield to maturity is included. A review of bond quotations on any given day will reveal significant differences among the yields of some bonds. These differences may be due to different risk levels, different provisions (such as call features), or different maturities. Bond quotations are typically listed according to the exchange where the bonds trade. Thus, *The Wall Street*

Corporate Bond Price Quotations

Corporate bond price quotations are provided in *The Wall Street Journal* as shown here. The bonds are listed alphabetically by the name of the issuing corporation. The coupon rate of the bond is shown in the second column and reflects the annual coupon payment as a percentage of the par value. The latest price of each bond is shown in the third column, and the yield to maturity based on the latest price is shown in the fourth column. The spread is shown in the fifth column, based on the difference between ask and bid prices (measured in basis points, or hundredths of a percent). The trading volume of each bond is provided in the last column.

Corporate Bonds

Monday, August 9, 2004

Forty most active fixed-coupon corporate bonds

COMPANY (TICKER)	COUPON	MATURITY	LAST PRICE	LAST YIELD	*EST SPREAD	UST†	EST $ VOL (000's)
Ford Motor Credit (F)	7.000	Oct 01, 2013	102.880	6.574	232	10	209,079
Ford Motor Credit (F)	7.375	Oct 28, 2009	108.243	5.530	210	5	114,335
Ford Motor Credit (F)	5.625	Oct 01, 2008	102.303	5.000	157	5	97,014
Verizon Wireless Capital LLC (VZW)	5.375	Dec 15, 2006	105.020	3.133	70	2	94,445
Liberty Media (L)	5.700	May 15, 2013	97.767	6.030	177	10	93,005
General Motors (GM)	8.375	Jul 15, 2033	104.250	7.995	294	30	82,367
Comcast Cable Communications Holdings (CMCSA)	8.375	Mar 15, 2013	118.756	5.594	133	10	80,076
DaimlerChrysler North America Holding (DCX)	8.500	Jan 18, 2031	119.753	6.869	182	30	77,200
DaimlerChrysler North America Holding (DCX)	6.500	Nov 15, 2013	106.186	5.632	137	10	76,224
Ford Motor Credit (F)	5.800	Jan 12, 2009	102.439	5.174	175	5	68,607
Wal-Mart Stores (WMT)	6.875	Aug 10, 2009	113.099	3.959	55	5	65,600
Morgan Stanley (MWD)	6.600	Apr 01, 2012	110.506	4.931	68	10	63,297
Ford Motor Credit (F)	7.375	Feb 01, 2011	106.944	6.061	182	10	56,380
Safeway (SWY)	6.500	Mar 01, 2011	108.517	4.961	72	10	54,000
Ford Motor Credit (F)	7.875	Jun 15, 2010	110.167	5.796	238	5	50,613
Walt Disney (DIS)	6.375	Mar 01, 2012	108.756	4.970	72	10	50,366
Associates of North America (C)	6.250	Nov 01, 2008	109.343	3.829	42	5	50,019
Ford Motor (F)	7.450	Jul 16, 2031	96.087	7.799	275	30	49,634
Citigroup (C)	4.250	Jul 29, 2009	101.190	3.983	56	5	48,725
Citigroup (C)	5.125	May 05, 2014	101.023	4.990	74	10	48,470
DaimlerChrysler North America Holding (DCX)	7.750	Jan 18, 2011	114.456	5.086	83	10	42,970
General Electric Capital (GE)	5.450	Jan 15, 2013	104.703	4.765	51	10	42,775
Goldman Sachs Group (GS)	6.875	Jan 15, 2011	112.150	4.664	41	10	42,610
General Motors Acceptance (GM)	6.125	Sep 15, 2006	104.891	3.672	125	2	39,263
General Motors Acceptance (GM)	7.250	Mar 02, 2011	106.171	6.093	186	10	38,713
Merrill Lynch (MER)	4.500	Nov 04, 2010	100.118	4.477	105	5	37,393
Lehman Brothers Holdings (LEH)	7.000	Feb 01, 2008	110.764	3.667	24	5	34,445
J.P. Morgan Chase (JPM)	6.500	Feb 01, 2006	105.647	2.559	13	2	32,742
RBS Capital Trust II (RBS)	6.425	Feb 16, 2034	99.703	6.447	139	30	32,600
Ford Motor Credit (F)	7.600	Aug 01, 2005	104.702	2.654	24	2	32,273
AT&T Wireless Services (AWE)	7.875	Mar 01, 2011	116.260	4.939	70	10	31,510
Target (TGT)	7.000	Jul 15, 2031	116.321	5.795	75	30	31,422
Telus (TCN)	8.000	Jun 01, 2011	115.445	5.267	103	10	30,600
Safeway (SWY)	7.250	Feb 01, 2031	108.810	6.545	150	30	29,800
Goldman Sachs Group (GS)	6.600	Jan 15, 2012	110.437	4.905	66	10	29,797
General Motors (GM)	8.250	Jul 15, 2023	103.758	7.864	281	30	29,713
Halliburton (HAL)-c	3.125	Jul 15, 2023	107.940	1.108	n.a.	n.a.	29,674
Lehman Brothers Holdings (LEH)	6.625	Jan 18, 2012	110.698	4.890	65	10	29,090
Sprint Capital (FON)	8.375	Mar 15, 2012	118.102	5.432	117	10	28,600
Ford Motor (F)	6.625	Oct 01, 2028	88.441	7.684	264	30	28,353
Goldman Sachs Group (GS)	3.875	Jan 15, 2009	99.383	4.028	60	5	28,209

Volume represents total volume for each issue; price/yield data are for trades of $1 million and greater. * Estimated spreads, in basis points (100 basis points is one percentage point), over the 2, 3, 5, 10 or 30-year hot run Treasury note/bond. 2-year: 2.750 07/06; 3-year: 3.125 05/07; 5-year: 3.625 07/09; 10-year: 4.750 05/14; 30-year: 5.375 02/31. †Comparable U.S. Treasury issue. c-Convertible bond.

Source: MarketAxess Corporate BondTicker

Journal lists bonds traded on the NYSE in one section and those traded on the American Stock Exchange in another (although typically on the same page).

Corporate bond price quotations are accessible online at http://www.investinginbonds .com. The quotations can be sorted by maturity, credit rating, coupon rate, or other characteristics.

Junk Bonds

Credit rating agencies assign quality ratings to corporate bonds based on their perceived degree of credit risk. Those bonds that are perceived to have high risk are referred to as **junk bonds.** Junk bonds became popular during the 1980s when firms desired debt financing to finance acquisitions. These firms were attempting to expand without issuing new stock so that profits could ultimately be distributed to existing shareholders. Some of the firms planning to use debt financing were perceived to have high risk, especially given the high proportion of debt in their capital structure. About two-thirds of all junk bond issues are used to finance takeovers (including leveraged buyouts, or LBOs). Some junk bond issues are used by firms to revise their capital structure. The proceeds from issuing bonds are used to repurchase stock, thereby increasing the proportion of debt in the capital structure. Although the newly issued bonds are assigned a low-grade ("junk") quality rating, numerous financial institutions are willing to purchase them because of the relatively high yield offered.

Size of the Junk Bond Market There are currently about 3,700 junk bond offerings in the United States, with a total market value of about $80 billion. This amount represents about 25 percent of the value of all corporate bonds and about 5 percent of the value of all bonds (including Treasury and municipal bonds). About one-third of all junk bonds were once rated higher but have been downgraded to below investment grade. The remaining two-thirds were considered to be below investment-grade quality when they were initially issued.

Participation in the Junk Bond Market There are about 70 large issuers of junk bonds, each with more than $1 billion in debt outstanding. Nextel is the largest issuer, with about $8 billion in debt. The primary investors in junk bonds are mutual funds, life insurance companies, and pension funds. In addition, more than 100 so-called high-yield mutual funds commonly invest in junk bonds. Individuals account for about one-tenth of all investors in the junk bond market. Recently, some issuers of junk bonds have attempted to attract more individual investors by lowering the minimum denomination to $1,000. High-yield mutual funds allow individual investors to invest in a diversified portfolio of junk bonds with a small investment.

The secondary market for junk bonds in the United States is facilitated by about 20 bond traders (or market makers) that make a market for junk bonds. That is, they execute secondary market transactions for customers and also invest in junk bonds for their own account.

Risk Premium of Junk Bonds Junk bonds offer high yields that contain a risk premium to compensate investors for the high risk. Typically, the premium is between 3 percent and 7 percent above Treasury bonds with the same maturity. Exhibit 10.5 compares the yields offered by junk (high-yield) bonds versus BBB- and AA-rated bonds. The difference in yields for the various types of bond is primarily attributed to a difference in risk. First, notice that at any point in time the difference between the yields offered by junk bonds versus BBB-rated bonds is larger than the difference in yields between the BBB- and

EXHIBIT 10.5 Comparison of Yields of Junk Bonds versus Other Bonds

Note. The data are monthly averages through October 2003 provided by the Federal Reserve. The AA and BBB rates are calculated from bonds in the Merrill Lynch AA index and BBB index, respectively, with seven to ten years of maturity remaining. The high-yield rate is the yield on the Merrill Lynch 175 high-yield index.

AA-rated bonds. Second, notice that the difference between the yields of junk bonds versus BBB-rated bonds changes over time. During periods of weak economies, such as 1990–1991 and 2001–2002, the difference is larger. Although investors always require a higher yield on junk bonds than bonds rated BBB or above, they require a higher premium during weak economies when there is a greater likelihood that the issuer will not generate sufficient cash flows to cover the debt payments.

Performance of Junk Bonds Junk bonds are generally perceived to offer high returns with high risk. During the mid-1980s, junk bond defaults were relatively infrequent, which may have renewed public interest in them and encouraged corporations to issue more.

After the stock market crash of October 1987, the market became more concerned about the risk of junk bonds. Issuers had to lower the price to compensate for the higher perceived risk. The junk bond market received another blow in the late 1980s, when insider trading charges were filed against Drexel Burnham Lambert, Inc., the main dealer in the market, for violating various regulations.

In the early 1990s, the popularity of junk bonds declined as a result of three key factors. First, there were allegations of insider trading against some participants in the junk bond market. Second, the financial problems of a few major issuers of junk bonds scared some investors away. Third, the financial problems in the thrift industry caused regulators to regulate investments by thrifts more closely. The Financial Institutions Reform, Recovery, and Enforcement Act (FIRREA) mandated that savings institutions liquidate their investments in junk bonds. Because savings institutions controlled about 7 percent of the junk bond market, there was additional downward pressure on prices. Although these institutions were given five years to liquidate their junk bonds to alleviate this

pressure on prices, many thrifts liquidated their bonds within a few months after the FIRREA was enacted.

During the late-1990s, junk bonds performed very well, and there were few defaults. Consequently, junk bonds became popular once again. However, the defaults increased during the 2001–2002 period when economic conditions were weak.

Contagion Effects in the Junk Bond Market Investors may be systematically discouraged from investment in junk bonds by specific adverse information, which means that the junk bond market is susceptible to **contagion effects.** Many firms that issue junk bonds have excessive debt service payments and may possibly experience cash flow deficiencies if sales are less than anticipated. Thus, they are all susceptible to a single underlying event, such as an economic downturn. Furthermore, media reports about a single well-known firm that may be unable to service its junk bond payments can cause increased concern (whether justified or not) about other highly leveraged firms. Such concern can encourage investors to sell holdings of junk bonds or discourage other investors from purchasing junk bonds.

How Corporate Bonds Facilitate Restructuring

Firms can issue corporate bonds to finance the restructuring of their assets and to restructure their capital structure. Such restructuring can have a major impact on the firm's degree of financial leverage, the potential return to shareholders, the risk to shareholders, and the risk to bondholders.

http://bonds.yahoo.com/glossary1.html Provides a glossary of common terms used in the bond market.

Using Bonds to Finance a Leveraged Buyout A leveraged buyout (LBO) is typically financed with senior debt (such as debentures and collateralized loans) and subordinated debt. The senior debt accounts for 50 to 60 percent of LBO financing on average.

LBO activity increased dramatically in the late 1980s, when it was more than double the level in the early 1960s. In 1988, there were more than 100 LBOs in which a publicly held firm was taken private. The premium paid when repurchasing shares to execute an LBO typically ranged between 30 percent and 40 percent above the prevailing market price. This suggests that the investors conducting the LBO believed that the firm was substantially undervalued when it was publicly held. Their expectation was that by reducing the equity interest of the firm down to a small group of people (possibly management and other employees), managerial efficiency of the firm would increase. The costs of monitoring to ensure that management's decisions are in the best interests of the shareholders are negligible when management owns all of the stock.

Although LBOs may possibly enhance managerial efficiency, they raised concerns about corporate debt levels. During the 1980s, corporate debt of U.S. firms increased substantially. The impact of the recession in the early 1990s on corporate performance may have been more pronounced because of the high degree of financial leverage.

The best-known LBO was the $24.7 billion buyout of RJRNabisco, Inc. by Kohlberg Kravis Roberts, Inc. (KKR) in 1988. KKR's equity investment was only about $1.4 billion, less than 6 percent of the purchase price. The debt financing was primarily composed of long-term bonds and bank loans. Before the acquisition, RJR's long-term debt was less than its shareholders' equity. After the acquisition, RJR's long-term debt was more than 12 times its shareholders' equity. Annual interest expenses were expected to be more than five times what they were before the acquisition. In 1988, RJR's cash flows totaled $1.8 billion, which was not expected to be sufficient to meet interest payments on the debt. Thus, the company needed additional cash flow to accommodate the substantial

CHAPTER 10 • BOND MARKETS   287

USING THE WALL STREET JOURNAL

WSJ Bond Information

The Wall Street Journal provides the following information related to this chapter on a daily basis:

■ Price quotations on corporate bonds traded on the New York Stock Exchange and American Stock Exchange.

■ Price quotations on Treasury bonds and notes, and on bonds issued by other government agencies (see "Treas./ Gov't. Issues").

■ Recent price trends in debt markets (see "Credit Markets"). This section explains major changes in the prices and also provides a yield curve based on Treasury securities with different maturities.

■ Firms that have issued new debt securities (see "New Securities Issues").

■ Price information on bonds of various types of issuers. An example is shown here. Percentage changes in the bond prices are shown since the previous day, since the beginning of the year, and over a 12-month period. This table can be used to compare price changes across different types of bonds.

Major Bond Indexes

| U.S. Treasury Securities | | | | 52-WEEK | | | YTD |
Lehman Brothers	CLOSE	NET CHG	% CHG	HIGH	LOW	% CHG	% CHG
Intermediate	7645.15	+0.08	+0.00	7734.54	7323.99	+4.06	+2.01
Long-term	12353.14	+5.24	+0.04	12758.67	11198.53	+9.11	+3.81
Composite	8696.14	+1.08	+0.01	8852.48	8201.40	+5.58	+2.55

Broad Market Lehman Brothers (preliminary)

	CLOSE	NET CHG	% CHG	HIGH	LOW	% CHG	% CHG
U.S. Aggregate	1082.79	+0.88	+0.07	1094.87	1016.47	+4.76	+2.10
U.S. Gov't/Credit	1252.43	+0.84	+0.06	1275.99	1175.53	+4.77	+1.93

U.S. Corporate Debt Issues Merrill Lynch

	CLOSE	NET CHG	% CHG	HIGH	LOW	% CHG	% CHG
Corporate Master	1469.23	+1.05	+0.07	1494.43	1363.44	+7.63	+2.12
High Yield	673.24	-0.02	-0.00	673.91	583.00	+14.98	+3.10
Yankee Bonds	1071.63	+0.73	+0.07	1088.87	1007.29	+6.29	+2.10

Mortgage-Backed Securities current coupon; Merrill Lynch: Dec. 31, 1986=100

	CLOSE	NET CHG	% CHG	HIGH	LOW	% CHG	% CHG
Ginnie Mae	435.11	+0.53	+0.12	436.04	403.10	+7.91	+3.29
Fannie Mae	434.85	+0.53	+0.12	439.19	406.04	+7.08	+2.35
Freddie Mac	266.16	+0.16	+0.06	268.83	247.66	+7.45	+2.59

Tax-Exempt Securities Merrill Lynch; Dec. 22, 1999

	CLOSE	NET CHG	% CHG	HIGH	LOW	% CHG	% CHG
6% Bond Buyer Muni	110.50	-0.09	-0.08	133.88	104.94	+4.37	-1.56
7-12 Yr G.O.	199.46	-0.12	-0.06	202.96	184.05	+8.03	+1.96
12-22 Yr G.O.	211.02	-0.06	-0.03	216.41	192.36	+9.28	+1.88
22+ Yr Revenue	197.32	-0.11	-0.06	203.97	181.96	+8.33	+0.57

Source: Republished with permission of Dow Jones & Company, Inc., from The Wall Street Journal, August 12, 2004; permission conveyed through the Copyright Clearance Center, Inc.

increase in financial leverage. As a result of the increase in financial leverage, prices of RJR bonds declined by 20 percent when the LBO was announced. After the LBO, RJR attempted to sell various businesses to improve its cash position.

It is of interest to note that RJR issued stock to reduce its degree of financial leverage in 1990 and again in 1991. Nabisco has since been sold by RJR. Many other firms with excessive financial leverage resulting from a previous LBO also reissued stock in the 1990s. They typically used some of the proceeds from the stock issuance to retire some outstanding debt, thereby reducing their periodic interest payments on debt. This process was more feasible for firms that could issue shares of stock for high prices because the proceeds would retire a larger amount of outstanding debt.

Using Bonds to Revise the Capital Structure Corporations commonly issue bonds in order to revise their capital structure. If they believe that they will have sufficient cash flows to cover their debt payments, they may consider using more debt and less equity, which implies a higher degree of financial leverage. Debt is normally perceived to be a cheaper source of capital than equity, as long as the corporation has the ability to meet its debt payments. Furthermore, a high degree of financial leverage allows the earnings of the firm to be distributed to a smaller group of shareholders. In some cases, corporations

EXHIBIT 10.6   Participation of Financial Institutions in Bond Markets

Financial Institution	Participation in Bond Markets
Commercial banks and savings and loan associations (S&Ls)	• Purchase bonds for their asset portfolio. • Sometimes place municipal bonds for municipalities. • Sometimes issue bonds as a source of secondary capital.
Finance companies	• Commonly issue bonds as a source of long-term funds.
Mutual funds	• Use funds received from the sale of shares to purchase bonds. Some bond mutual funds specialize in particular types of bonds, while others invest in all types.
Brokerage firms	• Facilitate bond trading by matching up buyers and sellers of bonds in the secondary market.
Investment banking firms	• Place newly issued bonds for governments and corporations. They may place the bonds and assume the risk of market price uncertainty or place the bonds on a best-efforts basis in which they do not guarantee a price for the issuer.
Insurance companies	• Purchase bonds for their asset portfolio.
Pension funds	• Purchase bonds for their asset portfolio.

issue bonds and use the proceeds to repurchase some of their existing stock. This strategy is referred to as a debt-for-equity swap.

When corporations use an excessive amount of debt, they may be unable to make their debt payments. Consequently, they may revise their capital structure by reducing their level of debt. In an equity-for-debt swap, corporations issue stock and use the proceeds to retire existing debt.

Institutional Use of Bond Markets

http://www.bloomberg.com
Yield curves of major
countries' government
securities.

All financial institutions participate in the bond markets, as summarized in Exhibit 10.6. Commercial banks, bond mutual funds, insurance companies, and pension funds are dominant participants in the bond market activity on any given day. A financial institution's investment decisions will often simultaneously affect bond market and other financial market activity. For example, an institution that anticipates higher interest rates may sell its bond holdings and purchase either money market securities or stocks. Conversely, financial institutions that expect lower interest rates may shift investments from their money market securities and/or stock portfolios to their bond portfolio.

Bond Market Globalization

GL🌐BALASPECTS   In recent years, financial institutions such as pension funds, insurance companies, and commercial banks have commonly purchased foreign bonds. For example, pension funds of General Electric, United Technologies Corporation, and IBM frequently invest in foreign bonds with the intention of achieving higher returns for their employees. Many public pension funds also invest in foreign bonds for the same reason. Because of the frequent cross-border investments in bonds, the bond markets have become increasingly integrated among countries. In addition, mutual funds containing U.S. securities are accessible to foreign investors.

Primary dealers of U.S. Treasury notes and bonds have opened offices in London, Tokyo, and other foreign cities to accommodate the foreign demand for these securities.

http://
http://bonds.yahoo.com
Summary of bond market
activity and analysis of
bond market conditions.

When the U.S. markets close, markets in Hong Kong and Tokyo are opening. As these markets close, European markets are opening. The U.S. market opens as markets in London and other European cities are closing. Thus, the prices of U.S. Treasury bonds at the time the U.S. market opens may differ substantially from the previous day's closing price.

In recent years, low-quality bonds have been issued globally by governments and large corporations. These bonds are referred to as **global junk bonds.** The demand for these bonds has been high as some institutional investors are attracted to their high yields. For example, corporate bonds have been issued by Klabin (Brazil) and Cementos Mexicanos (Mexico), while government bonds have been issued by Brazil, Mexico, Venezuela, the Czech Republic, and Spain.

The global development of the bond market is primarily attributed to the bond offerings by country governments. In general, bonds issued by foreign governments (referred to as sovereign bonds) are attractive to investors because of the government's ability to meet debt obligations. Nevertheless, some country governments have defaulted on their bonds, including Argentina (1982, 1989, 1990, 2001), Brazil (1986, 1989, 1991), Costa Rica (1989), Russia and other former Soviet republics (1993, 1998), and the former Yugoslavia (1992). Given that sovereign bonds are exposed to credit risk, credit ratings are assigned to them by Moody's and Standard & Poor's. Rating agencies tend to disagree more about the credit risk of sovereign bonds than about bonds issued by U.S. corporations. Perhaps this is due to a lack of consistent information available for country governments, which results in more arbitrary ratings. Also, the process of rating specific countries is still relatively new.

Eurobond Market

In 1963, U.S.-based corporations were limited to the amount of funds they could borrow in the United States for overseas operations. Consequently, these corporations began to issue bonds in the so-called Eurobond market, where bonds denominated in various currencies were placed. The U.S. dollar is used the most, denominating 70 to 75 percent of the Eurobonds.

Non-U.S. investors who desire dollar-denominated bonds may use the Eurobond market if they prefer bearer bonds to the registered corporate bonds issued in the United States. Alternatively, they may use the Eurobond market because they are more familiar with bond placements within their own country.

An underwriting syndicate of investment banks participates in the Eurobond market by placing the bonds issued. It normally underwrites the bonds, guaranteeing a particular value to be received by the issuer. Thus, the syndicate is exposed to underwriting risk, or the risk that it will be unable to sell the bonds above the price that it guaranteed the issuer.

The issuer of Eurobonds can choose the currency in which the bonds are denominated. The issuer's periodic coupon payments and repayment of principal will normally be in this currency. Moreover, the financing cost from issuing bonds depends on the currency chosen. In some cases, a firm may denominate the bonds in a currency with a low interest rate and use earnings generated by one of its subsidiaries to cover the payments. For example, the coupon rate on a Eurobond denominated in Swiss francs may be 5 percentage points lower than a dollar-denominated bond. A U.S. firm may consider issuing Swiss franc–denominated bonds and converting the francs to dollars for use in the United States. Then it could instruct a subsidiary in Switzerland to cover the periodic coupon payments with earnings that the subsidiary generates. In this way, a lower financing rate would be achieved without exposure to exchange rate risk.

SUMMARY

- Bonds can be classified in four categories according to the type of issuer: Treasury bonds, federal agency bonds, municipal bonds, and corporate bonds. The issuers are perceived to have different levels of credit risk. In addition, the bonds have different degrees of liquidity and different provisions. Thus, quoted yields at a given point in time vary across bonds.

- Many institutional investors, such as commercial banks, insurance companies, pension funds, and

bond mutual funds, are major investors in bonds. These institutional investors adjust their holdings of bonds in response to expectations of future interest rates.

- Bond yields vary among countries. Investors are attracted to high bond yields in foreign countries, causing funds to flow to those countries. Consequently, bond markets have become globally integrated.

POINT COUNTER-POINT

Should Financial Institutions Invest in Junk Bonds?

Point Yes. Financial institutions have managers who are capable of weighing the risk against the potential return. They can earn a significantly higher return when investing in junk bonds than the return on Treasury bonds. Their shareholders benefit when they increase the return on the portfolio.

Counter-Point No. The financial system is based on trust in financial institutions and confidence that the finan-

cial institutions will survive. If financial institutions take excessive risk, the entire financial system is at risk.

Who Is Correct? Use your favorite search engine to learn more about this issue. Offer your own opinion on this issue.

QUESTIONS AND APPLICATIONS

1. **Internet Exercise** Assess today's risk premiums on industrial bonds, using the website http://www.bondsonline.com. Click on "Corporate bond spreads" and then on "Industrials."

    What is the risk premium on AA-rated bonds with a 30-year maturity? What is the risk premium on BBB-rated bonds with a 30-year maturity? What is the risk premium on CCC-rated bonds with a 30-year maturity? Given the prevailing economic conditions, which of these three categories of bonds would be the best investment (in your opinion)?

2. **Debentures** What are debentures? How do they differ from subordinated debentures?

3. **Bond Indenture** What is a bond indenture? What is the function of a trustee, as related to the bond indenture?

4. **Variable-Rate Bonds** Are variable-rate bonds attractive to investors who expect interest rates to decrease? Explain. Would a firm consider variable-rate bonds if it expected that interest rates will decrease? Explain.

5. **Interpreting Financial News** Interpret the following statements made by Wall Street analysts and portfolio managers:
    a. "The values of some stocks are dependent on the bond market. When investors are not interested in junk bonds, the values of stocks ripe for leveraged buyouts decline."
    b. "The recent trend in which many firms are using debt to repurchase some of their stock is a good strategy as long as they can withstand the stagnant economy."

c. "Although yields among bonds are related, to-day's rumors of a tax cut caused an increase in the yield on municipal bonds, while the yield on corporate bonds declined."

6. **Calling Bonds** As a result of September 11, 2001, economic conditions were expected to decline. How do you think this would have affected the tendency of firms to call bonds?

7. **Convertible Bonds** Why can convertible bonds be issued by firms at a higher price than other bonds?

8. **Sinking-Fund Provision** Explain the use of a sinking-fund provision. How can it reduce the investor's risk?

9. **Managing in Financial Markets: Forecasting Bond Returns** As a portfolio manager for an insurance company, you are about to invest funds in one of three possible investments: (1) 10-year coupon bonds issued by the U.S. Treasury, (2) 20-year zero-coupon bonds issued by the Treasury, or (3) one-year Treasury securities. Each possible investment is perceived to have no risk of default. You plan to maintain this investment for a one-year period. The return of each investment over a one-year horizon will be about the same if interest rates do not change over the next year. However, you anticipate that the U.S. inflation rate will decline substantially over the next year, while most of the other portfolio managers in the United States expect inflation to increase slightly.
   a. If your expectations are correct, how will the return of each investment be affected over the one-year horizon?
   b. If your expectations are correct, which of the three investments should have the highest return over the one-year horizon? Why?
   c. Offer one reason why you might not select the investment that would have the highest expected return over the one-year investment horizon.

10. **Event Risk** An insurance company purchased bonds issued by Hartnett Company two years ago. Today, Hartnett Company has begun to issue junk bonds and is using the funds to repurchase most of its existing stock. Why might the market value of those bonds held by the insurance company be affected by this action?

11. **Zero-Coupon Bonds** What are the advantages and disadvantages to a firm that issues low- or zero-coupon bonds?

12. **Call Provisions** Explain the call provision of bonds. How can it affect the price of a bond?

13. **Impact of FIRREA on the Junk Bond Market** Explain how the Financial Institutions Reform, Recovery and Enforcement Act (FIRREA) could have affected the market value of junk bonds.

14. **Junk Bonds** Merrito Inc. is a large U.S. firm that issued bonds several years ago. Its bond ratings declined over time, and about a year ago, the bonds were rated in the junk bond classification. Nevertheless, investors were buying the bonds in the secondary market because of the attractive yield they offered. Last week, Merrito defaulted on its bonds, and the prices of most other junk bonds declined abruptly on the same day. Explain why news of the financial problems of Merrito Inc. could cause the prices of junk bonds issued by other firms to decrease, even when those firms had no business relationships with Merrito. Explain why the prices of those junk bonds with less liquidity declined more than those with a high degree of liquidity.

15. **Global Interaction of Bond Yields** Assume that bond yields in Japan rise. How might U.S. bond yields be affected? Why?

16. **Bond Downgrade** Explain how the downgrading of bonds for a particular corporation affects the corporation, the investors that currently hold these bonds, and other investors who may invest in the bonds in the near future.

17. **Protective Covenants** What are protective covenants? Why are they needed?

18. **Yield Curve for Municipal Securities** Explain how the shape of the yield curve for municipal securities compares to the Treasury yield curve. Under what conditions do you think the two yield curves could be different?

19. **Bond Collateral** Explain the use of bond collateral, and identify the common types of collateral for bonds.

PROBLEMS

1. **Inflation-Indexed Treasury Bond** Assume that the U.S. economy experienced deflation during the year and that the consumer price index decreased by 1 percent in the first six months of the year and by 2 percent during the second six months of the year. If an investor had purchased inflation-indexed Treasury bonds with a par value of $10,000 and a coupon rate of 5 percent, how much would she have received in interest during the year?

2. **Inflation-Indexed Treasury Bond** An inflation-indexed Treasury bond has a par value of $1,000 and a coupon rate of 6 percent. An investor purchases this bond and holds it for one year. During the year, the consumer price index increases by 1 percent every six months, for a total increase in inflation of 2 percent. What are the total interest payments the investor will receive during the year?

FLOW OF FUNDS EXERCISE

Financing in the Bond Markets

If the economy continues to be strong, Carson may need to increase its production capacity by about 50 percent over the next few years to satisfy demand. It would need financing to expand and accommodate the increase in production. Recall that the yield curve is currently upward sloping. Also recall that Carson is concerned about a possible slowing of the economy because of potential Fed actions to reduce inflation. It needs funding to cover payments for supplies. It is also considering the issuance of stock or bonds to raise funds in the next year.

a. Assume that Carson has two choices to satisfy the increased demand for its products. It could increase production by 10 percent with its existing facilities. In this case, it could obtain short-term financing to cover the extra production expense and then use a portion of the revenue received to finance this level of production in the future. Alternatively, it could issue bonds and use the proceeds to buy a larger facility that would allow for 50 percent more capacity.

b. Carson currently has a large amount of debt, and its assets have already been pledged to back up its existing debt. It does not have additional collateral. At this point in time, the credit risk premium it would pay is similar in the short-term and long-term debt markets. Does this imply that the cost of financing is the same in both markets?

c. Should Carson consider using a call provision if it issues bonds? Why? Why might Carson decide not to include a call provision on the bonds?

d. If Carson issues bonds, it would be a relatively small bond offering. Should Carson consider a private placement of bonds? What type of investor might be interested in participating in a private placement? Do you think Carson could offer the same yield on a private placement as it could on a public placement? Explain.

e. Financial institutions such as insurance companies and pension funds commonly purchase bonds. Explain the flow of funds that runs through these financial institutions and ultimately reaches corporations such as Carson Company that issue bonds.

WSJ EXERCISE

Impact of Treasury Financing on Bond Prices

The Treasury periodically issues new bonds to finance the deficit. Review recent issues of *The Wall Street Journal* or check related online news to find a recent article on such financing. Does the article suggest that financial markets are expecting upward pressure on interest rates as a result of the Treasury financing? What happened to prices of existing bonds when the Treasury announced its intentions to issue new bonds?

CHAPTER 11

Valuing Bonds and Assessing Risk

T he values of bonds can change substantially over time. Hence, financial institutions that consider buying or selling bonds closely monitor their values.

The specific objectives of this chapter are to:

■ explain how bonds (and other debt securities) are priced,

■ identify the factors that affect bond prices,

■ explain how the sensitivity of bond prices to interest rates is dependent on particular bond characteristics, and

■ explain the benefits of diversifying bonds internationally.

Valuing Bonds

Bonds are debt obligations with long-term maturities commonly issued by governments or corporations to obtain long-term funds. They are commonly purchased by financial institutions that wish to invest funds for long-term periods.

Bond valuation is conceptually similar to the valuation of capital budgeting projects, businesses, or even real estate. The appropriate price reflects the present value of the cash flows to be generated by the bond in the form of periodic interest (or coupon) payments and the principal payment to be provided at maturity. Because these expected cash flows are known, the valuation of bonds is generally perceived to be easier than the valuation of equity securities.

The current price of a bond should be the present value (*PV*) of its remaining cash flows:

$$PV \text{ of bond} = \frac{C}{(1 + k)^1} + \frac{C}{(1 + k)^2} + \ldots \frac{C + \text{Par}}{(1 + k)^n}$$

where C = coupon payment provided in each period

Par = par value

k = required rate of return per period used to discount the bond

n = number of periods to maturity

ILLUSTRATION Consider a bond that has a par value of $1,000, pays $100 at the end of each year in coupon payments, and has three years remaining until maturity. Assume that the prevailing annualized yield on other bonds with similar characteristics is 12 percent. In

Valuation of a Three-Year Bond

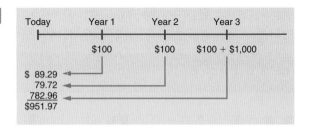

this case, the appropriate price of the bond can be determined as follows. The future cash flows to investors who would purchase this bond are $100 in Year 1, $100 in Year 2, and $1,100 (computed as $100 in coupon payments plus $1,000 par value) in Year 3. The appropriate market price of the bond is its present value:

$$PV \text{ of bond} = \$100/(1 + .12)^1 + \$100/(1 + .12)^2 + \$1,100/(1 + .12)^3$$

$$= \$89.29 + \$79.72 + \$782.96$$

$$= \$951.97$$

This valuation procedure is illustrated in Exhibit 11.1. Because this example assumes that investors require a 12 percent return, k equals 12 percent. At the price of $951.97, the bondholders purchasing this bond will receive a 12 percent annualized return.

Valuing Bonds with a Present Value Table

Bond valuation can be simplified with a present value table, such as the table in Exhibit 11A.3 in the appendix to this chapter. Each **present value interest factor** (PVIF) in this table represents the present value of $1 for a specified period (n) and interest rate. Coupon payments and the par value can be multiplied by their respective PVIFs to determine the present value of the bond.

ILLUSTRATION

The present value of the bond just described can be estimated as follows, using the table in the chapter appendix:

$$PV \text{ of bond} = \$100(\text{PVIF}_{k=12\%, n=1}) + \$100(\text{PVIF}_{k=12\%, n=2}) + \$1,100(\text{PVIF}_{k=12\%, n=3})$$

$$= \$100(.8929) + \$100(.7972) + \$1,100(.7118)$$

$$= \$89.29 + \$79.72 + \$782.98$$

$$= \$951.99$$

The slightly different answer is due to rounding.

When using a financial calculator, the present value of the bond in the previous example can be determined as follows:

Input	3	12	100	1000		
Function Key	N	I	PMT	FV	CPT	PV
Answer						951.97

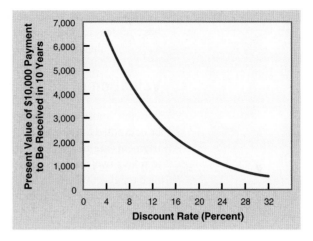

EXHIBIT 11.2

Relationship between Discount Rate and Present Value of $10,000 Payment to Be Received in 10 Years

Impact of the Discount Rate on Bond Valuation

The discount rate selected to compute the present value is critical to accurate valuation. Exhibit 11.2 shows the wide range of present value results at different discount rates, for a $10,000 payment in 10 years. The appropriate discount rate for valuing any asset is the yield that could be earned on alternative investments with similar risk and maturity.

Since investors require higher returns on riskier securities, they use higher discount rates to discount the future cash flows of these securities. Consequently, the value of a high-risk security will be lower than the value of a low-risk security when both securities have the same expected cash flows.

Impact of the Timing of Payments on Bond Valuation

The market price of a bond is also affected by the timing of the payments made to bond-holders. Funds received sooner can be reinvested to earn additional returns. Thus, a dollar to be received soon has a higher present value than one to be received later. The impact of maturity on the present value of a $10,000 payment is shown in Exhibit 11.3, assuming that a return of 10 percent could be earned on available funds. The $10,000 payment has a present value of $8,264 if it is to be paid in two years. This implies that if $8,264 were invested today and earned 10 percent annually, it would be worth $10,000

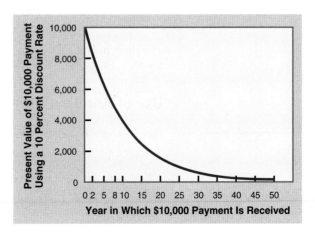

EXHIBIT 11.3

Relationship between Time of Payment and Present Value of Payment

in two years. Exhibit 11.3 also shows that a $10,000 payment made 20 years from now has a present value of only $1,486, and a $10,000 payment made 50 years from now has a present value of only $85 (based on the 10 percent discount rate).

Valuation of Bonds with Semiannual Payments

In reality, most bonds have semiannual payments. The present value of such bonds can be computed as follows. First, the annualized coupon should be split in half because two payments are made per year. Second, the annual discount rate should be divided by 2 to reflect two six-month periods per year. Third, the number of periods should be doubled to reflect two times the number of annual periods. Incorporating these adjustments, the present value is determined as follows:

$$\begin{matrix} PV \text{ of bond with} \\ \text{semiannual payments} \end{matrix} = \frac{C/2}{[1 + (k/2)]^1} + \frac{C/2}{[1 + (k/2)]^2} + \cdots \frac{C/2 + Par}{[1 + (k/2)]^{2n}}$$

where $C/2$ is the semiannual coupon payment (half of what the annual coupon payment would have been) and $k/2$ is the periodic discount rate used to discount the bond. The last part of the equation shows $2n$ in the denominator exponent to reflect the doubling of periods.

ILLUSTRATION As an example of the valuation of a bond with semiannual payments, consider a bond with $1,000 par value, a 10 percent coupon rate paid semiannually, and three years to maturity. Assuming a 12 percent required return, the present value is computed as follows:

$$PV \text{ of bond} = \frac{\$50}{(1.06)^1} + \frac{\$50}{(1.06)^2} + \frac{\$50}{(1.06)^3} + \frac{\$50}{(1.06)^4} + \frac{\$50}{(1.06)^5} + \frac{\$50 + \$1,000}{(1.06)^6}$$

$$= \$47.17 + \$44.50 + \$41.98 + \$39.60 + \$37.36 + \$740.21$$

$$= \$950.82$$

This example could also have been worked using PVIF tables.[1]

When using a financial calculator, the present value of the bond in the previous example can be determined as follows:

Input	6	6	50	1000		
Function Key	N	I	PMT	FV	CPT	PV
Answer						950.82

The remaining examples assume annual coupon payments so that we can focus on the concepts presented without concern about adjusting annual payments.

Use of Annuity Tables for Valuation

Any bond can be valued by separating its payments into two components:

$$PV \text{ of bond} = PV \text{ of coupon payments} + PV \text{ of principal payment}$$

---

[1] Technically, the semiannual rate of 6 percent is overstated. For a required rate of 12 percent per year, the precise six-month rate would be 5.83 percent. With the compounding effect, which would generate interest on interest, this semiannual rate over two periods would achieve a 12 percent return. Because the approximate semiannual rate of 6 percent is higher than the precise rate, the present value of the bond is slightly understated.

A bond's coupon payments represent an **annuity,** or an even stream of payments over a given period of time. The present value of any annuity can be determined by multiplying the annuity amount times the appropriate present value interest factor of an annuity (PVIFA). The table in Exhibit 11A.4 in the chapter appendix can be used to identify the appropriate PVIFA.

ILLUSTRATION Recall the example of the 10 percent coupon bond with annual coupon payments, a $1,000 par value, and three years to maturity. The PVIFA is $PVIFA_{k=12\%,n=3} = 2.4018$, as shown in Exhibit 11A.4. This is used to determine the $PVIFA_{k=12\%,n=3}$ present value of the coupon payments:

$$PV \text{ of coupon payments} = C(PVIFA_{k=12\%,n=3})$$
$$= \$100(2.4018)$$
$$= \$240.18$$

The present value of the principal must also be determined:

$$PV \text{ of principal} = \frac{\$1,000}{(1.12)^3} \text{ or } \$1,000(PVIF_{k=12\%,n=3})$$
$$= \$1,000(.7118)$$
$$= \$711.80$$

When the *PV* of coupon payments is combined with the principal, the bond's present value is about $951.98 (computed as $240.18 + $711.80).

The use of PVIFA tables is especially efficient for valuing long-term bonds.

ILLUSTRATION The present value of bonds with an 8 percent coupon rate, a par value of $100,000, and 20 years to maturity, assuming a 14 percent required rate of return, is

$$PV \text{ of bonds} = PV \text{ of coupon payments} + PV \text{ of principal}$$
$$= \$8,000(PVIFA_{k=14\%,n=20}) + \$100,000(PVIF_{k=14\%,n=20})$$
$$= \$8,000(6.6231) + \$100,000(.0728)$$
$$= \$52,985 + \$7,280$$
$$= \$60,265$$

This implies that investors requiring a 14 percent return would pay no more than $60,265 for these bonds.

Relationships between Coupon Rate, Required Return, and Bond Price

Bonds that sell at a price below their par value are called discount bonds. The larger the investor's required rate of return relative to the coupon rate, the larger the discount of a bond with a particular par value.

Consider a zero-coupon bond (which has no coupon payments) with three years remaining to maturity and $1,000 par value. Assume the investor's required rate of return on the bond is 13 percent. The appropriate price of this bond can be determined by the present value of its future cash flows:

$$PV \text{ of bond} = \$0/(1 + .13)^1 + \$0/(1 + .13)^2 + \$1,000/(1 + .13)^3$$
$$= \$0 + \$0 + \$693.05$$
$$= \$693.05$$

The very low price of this bond is necessary to generate a 13 percent annualized return to investors. If the bond offered coupon payments, the price would have been higher because those coupon payments would provide part of the return required by investors.

Consider another bond with a similar par value and maturity that offers a 13 percent coupon rate. The appropriate price of the bond would now be

$$PV \text{ of bond} = \$130/(1 + .13)^1 + \$130/(1 + .13)^2 + \$1,130/(1 + .13)^3$$
$$= \$115.04 + \$101.81 + \$783.15$$
$$= \$1,000$$

Notice that the price of this bond is exactly equal to its par value. This is because the entire compensation required by investors is provided by the coupon payments.

Finally, consider a bond with a similar par value and term to maturity that offers a coupon rate of 15 percent, which is above the investor's required rate of return. The appropriate price of this bond as determined by its present value is

$$PV \text{ of bond} = \$150/(1 + .13)^1 + \$150/(1 + .13)^2 + \$1,150/(1 + .13)^3$$
$$= \$132.74 + \$117.47 + \$797.01$$
$$= \$1,047.22$$

The price of this bond exceeds its par value because the coupon payments are large enough to offset the high price paid for the bond and still provide a 13 percent annualized return.

From the examples provided, the following relationships should now be clear. First, if the coupon rate of a bond is below the investor's required rate of return, the present value of the bond (and therefore the price of the bond) should be below the par value. Second, if the coupon rate equals the investor's required rate of return, the price of the bond should be the same as the par value. Finally, if the coupon rate of a bond is above the investor's required rate of return, the price of the bond should be above the par value. These relationships are shown in Exhibit 11.4 for a bond with a 10 percent coupon and a par value of $1,000. If investors require a return of 5 percent and desire a 10-year maturity, they will be willing to pay $1,390 for this bond. If they require a return of 10 percent on this same bond, they will be willing to pay $1,000. If they require a 15 percent return, they will be willing to pay only $745. The relationships described here hold for any bond, regardless of its maturity.

Implications for Financial Institutions

The impact of interest rate movements on a financial institution depends on how the institution's asset and liability portfolios are structured, as illustrated in Exhibit 11.5. Fi-

Relationship between Required Return and Present Value for a 10 Percent Coupon Bond with Various Maturities

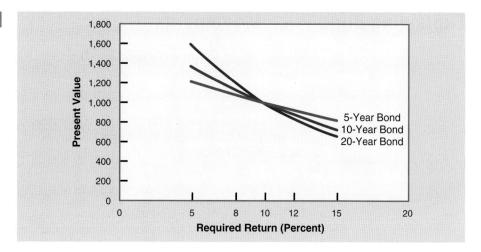

nancial institutions with interest rate–sensitive liabilities that invest heavily in bonds are exposed to interest rate risk. Many financial institutions attempt to adjust the size of their bond portfolio according to their expectations about future interest rates. The expected return is higher when unevenly matched rate sensitivities are used because the mismatch allows an institution to take advantage of the effects of interest rate expectations. When rates are expected to rise, bonds can be sold and the proceeds used to purchase short-term securities, whose market values are less influenced by interest rate movements. When rates are expected to fall, the bond portfolio can be expanded in order to capitalize on the expectations. An aggressive approach offers greater potential for high return but also exposes investors to more risk when their expectations are wrong.

Like bonds, fixed-rate mortgages generate periodic fixed payments. Thus, the preceding comments apply to financial institutions such as savings institutions that hold mortgage portfolios. A primary reason for the financial problems of savings institutions in the late 1980s was the rise in interest rates, which reduced the market value of their mortgage portfolios. This is a classic example of interest rate risk, or the risk that the market value of assets will decline in response to interest rate movements.

Potential Returns to Financial Institutions with Different Investment Strategies

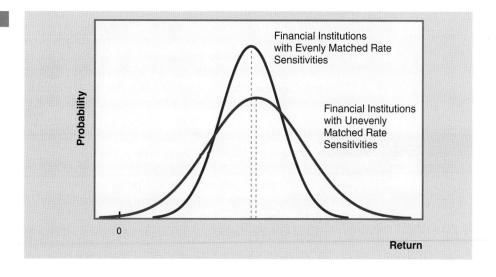

Explaining Bond Price Movements

As explained earlier, the price of a bond should reflect the present value of future cash flows (coupon payments and the par value), based on a required rate of return (k), so that

$$\Delta P = f(\Delta k)$$

Since the required rate of return on a bond is primarily determined by the prevailing risk-free rate (R_f), which is the yield on a Treasury bond with the same maturity, and the risk premium (RP) on the bond, the general price movements of bonds can be modeled as

$$\Delta P_b = f(\Delta R_f, \Delta RP)$$

An increase in either the risk-free rate or the general level of the risk premium on bonds results in a higher required rate of return on bonds and therefore causes bond prices to decrease.

The factors that are commonly monitored by bond market participants because they affect the risk-free rate or default risk premiums, and therefore affect bond prices, are identified next.

Factors That Affect the Risk-Free Rate

http://research.stlouisfed.org/
fred2 Assesses economic
conditions that affect bond
prices.

The long-term risk-free rate is driven by inflationary expectations (INF), economic growth (ECON), the money supply (MS), and the budget deficit (DEF):

$$\Delta R_f = f(\Delta \text{INF}, \Delta \text{ECON}, \Delta \text{MS}, \Delta \text{DEF})$$
$$\qquad\quad +\qquad\ +\qquad ?\qquad +$$

The general relationships are summarized next.

Impact of Inflationary Expectations If the level of inflation is expected to increase, there will be upward pressure on interest rates and, therefore, on the required rate of return on bonds. Conversely, a reduction in the expected level of inflation results in downward pressure on interest rates and, therefore, on the required rate of return on bonds. Bond market participants closely monitor indicators of inflation, such as the consumer price index and the producer price index.

Inflationary expectations are partially dependent on oil prices, which affect the cost of energy and transportation. Bond portfolio managers therefore forecast oil prices and their potential impact on inflation in order to forecast interest rates. A forecast of lower oil prices results in expectations of lower interest rates, causing bond portfolio managers to purchase more bonds. A forecast of higher oil prices results in expectations of higher interest rates, causing bond portfolio managers to sell some of their holdings.

ILLUSTRATION High oil prices in 2004 caused an increase in inflationary expectations. Bond prices plunged in response to these expectations.

Inflationary expectations are also partially dependent on exchange rate movements. Holding other things equal, inflationary expectations are likely to rise when a weaker dollar is expected, because that will increase the prices of imported supplies. A weaker dollar also prices foreign competitors out of the market, allowing U.S. firms to increase their prices. Thus, U.S. interest rates are expected to rise and bond prices are expected

to decrease when the dollar is expected to weaken. Foreign investors anticipating dollar depreciation are less willing to hold U.S. bonds because the coupon payments will convert to less of their home currency in that event. This could cause an immediate net sale of bonds, placing further downward pressure on bond prices.

Expectations of a strong dollar should have the opposite results. A stronger dollar reduces the prices paid for foreign supplies, thus lowering retail prices. In addition, because a stronger dollar makes the prices of foreign products more attractive, domestic firms must maintain low prices in order to compete. Consequently, low inflation and therefore low interest rates are expected, and bond portfolio managers are likely to purchase more bonds.

http://research.stlouisfed.org
Assess the yield of 30-year Treasury bonds over the last 24 months.

Impact of Economic Growth Strong economic growth tends to place upward pressure on interest rates, while weak economic conditions place downward pressure on rates. Any signals about future economic conditions will affect expectations about future interest rate movements and cause bond markets to react immediately. For example, any economic announcements (such as measurements of economic growth or unemployment) that signal stronger than expected economic growth tend to reduce bond prices. Investors anticipate that interest rates will rise, causing a decline in bond prices. Therefore, they sell bonds, which places immediate downward pressure on bond prices. Conversely, any economic announcements that signal a weaker than expected economy tend to increase bond prices, because investors anticipate that interest rates will decrease, causing bond prices to rise. Therefore, investors buy bonds, which places immediate upward pressure on bond prices. This explains why sudden news of a possible economic recession can cause the bond market to rally.

Bond market participants closely monitor economic indicators that may signal future changes in the strength of the economy, which signal changes in the risk-free interest rate and in the required return from investing in bonds. Some of the more closely monitored indicators of economic growth include employment, gross domestic product, retail sales, industrial production, and consumer confidence. An unexpected favorable movement in these indicators tends to arouse expectations of an increase in economic growth and an increase in interest rates, thereby placing downward pressure on bond prices.

Conversely, an unexpected unfavorable movement in these indicators tends to signal a weaker economy, which arouses expectations of lower interest rates and places upward pressure on bond prices. However, a weaker economy can also increase the default risk premium on some risky bonds because the issuers may have more difficulty meeting their payment obligations under weaker economic conditions. The upward pressure on the required return on these bonds due to the higher default risk premium may partially offset the downward pressure due to the expected reduction in the risk-free rate.

Impact of Money Supply Growth When the Federal Reserve increases money supply growth, two reactions are possible. First, the increased money supply may result in an increased supply of loanable funds. If demand for loanable funds is not affected, the increased money supply should place downward pressure on interest rates, causing bond portfolio managers to expect an increase in bond prices and thus to purchase bonds based on such expectations.

In a high-inflation environment, however, bond portfolio managers may expect a large increase in the demand for loanable funds (as a result of inflationary expectations), which would cause an increase in interest rates and lower bond prices. Such forecasts would encourage immediate sales of long-term bonds.

Impact of Budget Deficit As the annual budget deficit changes, so does the federal government's demand for loanable funds. An increase in the annual budget deficit from the previous year results in a higher level of borrowing by the federal government, which can place upward pressure on the risk-free interest rate. In other words, excessive borrowing by the Treasury can result in a higher required return on Treasury bonds. An excessive amount of borrowing by the federal government can indirectly affect the required rate of return and therefore the yield on all types of bonds.

ILLUSTRATION If the Treasury issues an unusually large number of Treasury bonds in the primary market, the result is downward pressure on the market price and upward pressure on the market yield of these bonds. Consequently, holders of corporate bonds with credit risk may then switch to Treasury bonds because by holding such bonds, they can achieve almost the same yield without exposure to credit risk. This tendency places downward pressure on corporate bond prices and upward pressure on corporate bond yields, restoring the yield differential between corporate bonds and Treasury bonds. Since some investors perceive various bonds as substitutes, their buy and sell decisions will stabilize yield differentials among the bonds.

Just as an increased budget deficit can increase the yields offered on all bonds, a reduced budget deficit can reduce the yields offered on all bonds. In the late 1990s, the U.S. government had a budget surplus, which resulted in a lower risk-free interest rate, a lower required rate of return on bonds, and higher bond prices.

Factors That Affect the Credit (Default) Risk Premium

The credit risk premium tends to be larger for corporate or municipal bonds than for money market securities issued by a given corporation because the probability of a corporation experiencing financial distress is higher for a bond with a longer term to maturity. The general level of credit risk on corporate or municipal bonds can change in response to a change in economic growth (ECON):

$$\Delta RP = f(\Delta ECON)$$

Strong economic growth tends to improve a firm's cash flows and reduce the probability that the firm will default on its debt payments. Conversely, weak economic growth may increase the probability of default, especially for firms that are very sensitive to economic conditions.

A firm's managers may make decisions that affect its risk and therefore affect the risk of the bonds that it issues. If the managers invest very conservatively, risk may be reduced. Alternatively, risk may increase if they attempt to expand by acquiring businesses that they are not capable of managing effectively. If they increase their reliance on equity financing, they can more easily cover their existing debt payments. Conversely, if they rely more on borrowed funds, they may have more difficulty covering their debt payments.

ILLUSTRATION Last year Breckenridge Company issued bonds that received a BBB rating, while Vail Company issued bonds that received a BB rating. Last week, the bonds of both firms were downgraded. Breckenridge's bonds were downgraded because it recently borrowed additional funds from banks, which raised concerns about its high debt level. Vail's bonds were downgraded because conditions in its industry have weakened. Thus,

for different reasons, the rating agency perceived that both companies' bonds have a higher likelihood of default than before. Since these firms already obtained their money from issuing the bonds, they are not directly affected by the downgraded rating (although it may restrict their ability to borrow additional funds). In contrast, the investors who are holding those bonds at the time of the downgrade are directly affected because the market value of bonds normally declines in response to a downgrade. If the investors holding the bonds want to sell them in the secondary market, they will have to sell them at a lower price to compensate potential buyers for the higher level of credit risk.

Although the risk of a specific corporate bond can change due to actions of the firm's managers, such as increasing its use of debt, such actions are firm-specific and do not affect the general risk level of all bonds. Conversely, changes in economic conditions can have a systematic effect on the risk of many firms and therefore can affect the valuations of many bonds at the same time.

Changes in the Credit Risk Premium over Time Exhibit 11.6 compares yields on various types of bonds over time. The yields among securities are highly correlated. Notice that the difference between the corporate Baa and corporate Aaa bond yields widened during the weak economic periods of the early 1990s and the 2001–2002 period when investors required a higher credit risk premium.

Exhibit 11.7 focuses on a shorter time period and illustrates more clearly how the credit risk premium changes over time. In 1999, when the economy was strong, the credit risk premium on AAA-rated bonds was about 1 percent. Notice how the premium

EXHIBIT 11.6 Comparison of Bond Yields

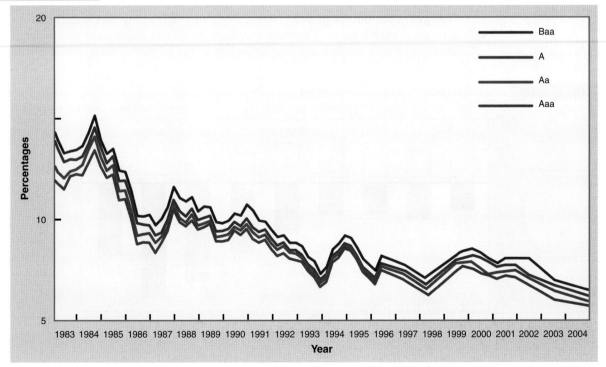

Note: Trends depict quarterly averages of bond yields.
Source: *Federal Reserve Bulletin.*

Bond Credit Risk Premium over Time

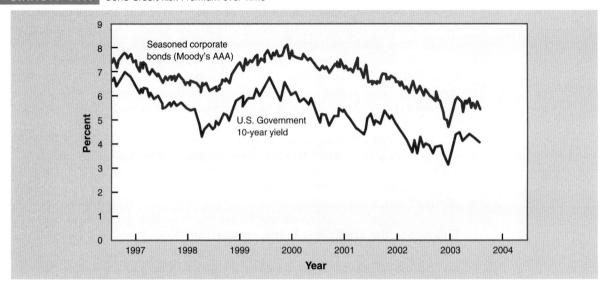

Source: Federal Reserve.

begins to widen in 2000. In the 2001–2002 period, the premium was about 2 percent. Thus, the most highly rated corporations incurred an extra 1 percent cost of financing in that period because of a heightened risk perception in the bond markets resulting from a weak economy.

Changes in Bond Ratings over Time A corporate bond's rating can change over time in response to changes in its financial condition. Exhibit 11.8 shows the percentage of bonds that were upgraded and downgraded each year for several years. Notice that in

Changes in Corporate Bond Ratings over Time

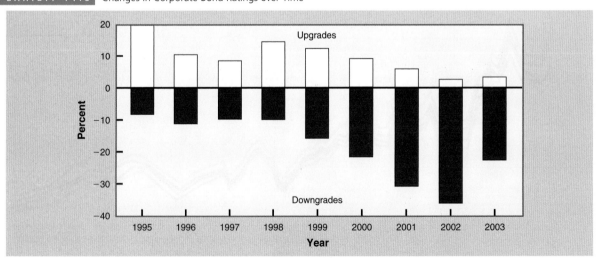

Note: Data are at an annual rate; for 2003, they are the annualized values of monthly data through May. Debt upgrades and downgrades are expressed as a percentage of the par value of all bonds outstanding.
Source: Moody's Investors Service and the Federal Reserve.

the late 1990s, when economic conditions were strong, there were more upgrades than downgrades. In the 2001–2003 period, when economic conditions were weak, there were more downgrades than upgrades.

Summary of Factors Affecting Bond Prices

When considering the factors that affect the risk-free rate and the risk premium, the general price movements in bonds can be modeled as

$$\Delta P_b = f(\Delta R_f, \Delta RP)$$
$$= f(\underset{-}{\Delta INF}, \underset{?}{\Delta ECON}, \underset{+}{\Delta MS}, \underset{-}{\Delta DEF})$$

The relationships suggested here assume that other factors are held constant. In reality, other factors are changing as well, which makes it difficult to disentangle the precise impact of each factor on bond prices. The effect of economic growth is uncertain because a high level of economic growth can adversely affect bond prices by causing a higher risk-free rate, but can favorably affect bond prices by lowering the default risk premium. To the extent that international conditions affect each of the factors, they also influence bond prices.

Exhibit 11.9 summarizes the underlying forces that can affect the long-term risk-free interest rate and the default risk premium and therefore cause the general level of bond prices to change over time. When pricing Treasury bonds, investors focus on the factors that affect the long-term risk-free interest rate, as the default risk premium is not needed. Thus, the primary difference in the required return of a risky bond (such as a corporate bond) versus a Treasury bond for a given maturity is the default risk premium, which is influenced by economic and industry conditions.

http://www.publicdebt.treas.gov Treasury note and bond auction results.

EXHIBIT 11.9

Framework for Explaining Changes in Bond Prices over Time

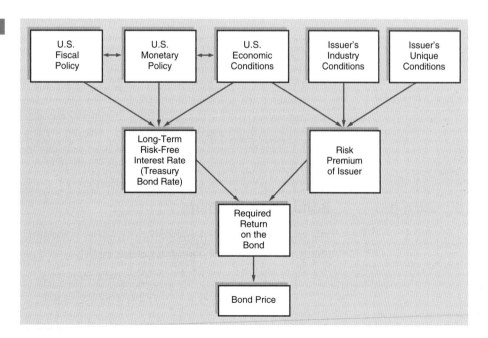

Impact of Bond-Specific Characteristics The preceding discussion is intended simply to identify factors that affect general price movements of bonds. It is important to note that a bond's price can also be affected by factors specific to the bond, such as a change in the capital structure of the firm that issued the bond. Yield differentials among bonds can also change when investors perceive a characteristic of a particular type of bond to be more or less favorable than before. For example, if interest rates suddenly decline, existing bonds that have a call feature are more likely to be called. Thus, bonds containing a call feature will sell only if the price is lowered. This implies that the yield differential adjusts to the changing perception of the factor that caused the differential.

Bond Market Efficiency

If the bond market is efficient, this would suggest that bond prices fully reflect all available information. In general, bond prices should reflect information that is publicly available. However, bond prices may not necessarily reflect information about firms that is known only by the managers of the firms.

ILLUSTRATION Davenport Inc. is experiencing very weak sales this quarter, but those results are not obvious to bondholders. Thus, the prices of Davenport's bonds remain unchanged. One month later, Davenport discloses to the public that its sales were very weak and it will incur a large loss this quarter. This announcement causes bond market participants to be more concerned about the possibility that Davenport could default on its bonds. Consequently, many bondholders attempt to sell their Davenport bonds, and the prices of the bonds decline as a result. The price adjusted quickly once the information was public.

Bond Price to Interest Rate Movements

When institutional and individual investors invest in bonds, they are subject to the risk that the return on their bonds will be less than anticipated. The forces that influence bond price movements cannot be perfectly anticipated, so future bond prices (and therefore returns) cannot be perfectly anticipated. If the bonds are not held until maturity, the prices at which they can be sold in the future (and therefore the return on the investment) are normally most sensitive to changes in the risk-free interest rate.

Investors can at least attempt to determine how sensitive the prices of their bond holdings are to possible changes in any conditions that affect the required rate of return on bonds. Such a measurement of bond price sensitivity can indicate the degree to which the market value of their bond holdings may decline in response to an increase in interest rates (and therefore in the required rate of return).

Bond Price Elasticity

The sensitivity of bond prices (P) to changes in the required rate of return (k) is commonly measured by the bond price elasticity (P^e), which is estimated as

$$P^e = \frac{\text{percent change in } P}{\text{percent change in } k}$$

Exhibit 11.10 compares the price sensitivity of 10-year bonds with $1,000 par value and four different coupon rates: 0 percent, 5 percent, 10 percent, and 15 percent. Ini-

EXHIBIT 11.10 Sensitivity of 10-Year Bonds with Different Coupon Rates to Interest Rate Changes

Effects of a Decline in the Required Rate of Return:					
(1) Bonds with a Coupon Rate of:	(2) Initial Price of Bonds When $k = 10\%$	(3) Price of Bonds When $k = 8\%$	(4) = [(3) − (2)]/(2) Percentage Change in Bond Price	(5) Percentage Change in k	(6) = (4)/(5) Bond Price Elasticity (P^e)
0%	$ 386	$ 463	+19.9%	−20.0%	−.997
5	693	799	+15.3	−20.0	−.765
10	1,000	1,134	+13.4	−20.0	−.670
15	1,307	1,470	+12.5	−20.0	−.624
Effects of an Increase in the Required Rate of Return:					
(1) Bonds with a Coupon Rate of:	(2) Initial Price of Bonds When $k = 10\%$	(3) Price of Bonds When $k = 12\%$	(4) = [(3) − (2)]/(2) Percentage Change in Bond Price	(5) Percentage Change in k	(6) = (4)/(5) Bond Price Elasticity (P^e)
0%	$ 386	$ 322	−16.6%	+20.0%	−.830
5	693	605	−12.7	+20.0	−.635
10	1,000	887	−11.3	+20.0	−.565
15	1,307	1,170	−10.5	+20.0	−.525

tially, the required rate of return (k) on the bonds is assumed to be 10 percent. The price of each bond is therefore the present value of its future cash flows, discounted at 10 percent. The initial price of each bond is shown in Column 2. The top panel shows the effect of a decline in interest rates that reduces the investor's required return to 8 percent. The prices of the bonds based on an 8 percent required return are shown in Column 3. The percentage change in the price of each bond resulting from the interest rate movements is shown in Column 4. The bottom panel shows the effect of an increase in interest rates that increases the investor's required return to 12 percent.

The price elasticity for each bond is estimated in Exhibit 11.10 according to the assumed change in the required rate of return. Notice in the exhibit that the price sensitivity of any particular bond is greater for declining interest rates than rising interest rates. The bond price elasticity is negative in all cases, reflecting the inverse relationship between interest rate movements and bond price movements.

Influence of Coupon Rate on Bond Price Sensitivity A zero-coupon bond, which pays all of its proceeds to the investor at maturity, is most sensitive to changes in the required rate of return because the adjusted discount rate is applied to one lump sum in the distant future. Conversely, the price of a bond that pays all of its yield in the form of coupon payments is less sensitive to changes in the required rate of return because the adjusted discount rate is applied to some payments that occur in the near future. The adjustment in the present value of such payments in the near future due to a change in the required rate of return is not as pronounced as an adjustment in the present value of payments in the distant future.

Exhibit 11.10 confirms that the prices of zero- or low-coupon bonds are more sensitive to changes in the required rate of return than prices of bonds with relatively high

coupon rates. Notice in the exhibit that when the required rate of return declines from 10 percent to 8 percent, the price of the zero-coupon bonds rises from \$386 to \$463. Thus, the bond price elasticity (P^e) is

$$P^e = \frac{\dfrac{\$463 - \$386}{\$386}}{\dfrac{8\% - 10\%}{10\%}}$$

$$= \frac{+19.9\%}{-20\%}$$

$$= -.995$$

This implies that for each 1 percent change in interest rates, zero-coupon bonds change by 0.995 percent in the opposite direction. Column 6 in Exhibit 11.10 shows that the price elasticities of the higher-coupon bonds are considerably lower than the price elasticity of the zero-coupon bond.

Financial institutions commonly restructure their bond portfolios to contain higher-coupon bonds when they are more concerned about a possible increase in interest rates (and therefore an increase in the required rate of return). Conversely, they restructure their portfolios to contain low- or zero-coupon bonds when they expect a decline in interest rates and wish to capitalize on their expectations by holding bonds that will be very price-sensitive.

Influence of Maturity on Bond Price Sensitivity As interest rates (and therefore required rates of return) decrease, long-term bond prices (as measured by their present value) increase by a greater degree than short-term bond prices because the long-term bonds will continue to offer the same coupon rate over a longer period of time than the short-term bonds. Of course, if interest rates increase, prices of the long-term bonds will decline by a greater degree.

Duration

http://
http://invest-faq.com
Contains links to many different concepts about bonds, including duration.

An alternative measure of bond price sensitivity is the bond's duration, which is a measurement of the life of the bond on a present value basis. The longer a bond's duration, the greater its sensitivity to interest rate changes. A commonly used measure of a bond's duration (DUR) is

$$DUR = \frac{\sum_{t=1}^{n} \dfrac{C_t(t)}{(1+k)^t}}{\sum_{t=1}^{n} \dfrac{C_t}{(1+k)^t}}$$

where C_t = coupon or principal payment generated by the bond

t = time at which the payments are provided

k = bond's yield to maturity, which reflects the required rate of return by investors

The numerator of the duration formula represents the present value of future payments, weighted by the time interval until the payments occur. The longer the intervals until payments are made, the larger the numerator, and the larger the duration. The denominator of the duration formula represents the discounted future cash flows resulting from the bond, which is the present value of the bond.

ILLUSTRATION The duration of a bond with $1,000 par value and a 7 percent coupon rate, three years remaining to maturity, and a 9 percent yield to maturity is

$$\text{DUR} = \frac{\dfrac{\$70}{(1.09)^1} + \dfrac{\$70(2)}{(1.09)^2} + \dfrac{\$1,070(3)}{(1.09)^3}}{\dfrac{\$70}{(1.09)^1} + \dfrac{\$70}{(1.09)^2} + \dfrac{\$1,070}{(1.09)^3}}$$

$$= 2.80 \text{ years}$$

By comparison, the duration of a zero-coupon bond with a similar par value and yield to maturity is

$$\text{DUR} = \frac{\dfrac{\$1,000(3)}{(1.09)^3}}{\dfrac{\$1,000}{(1.09)^3}}$$

$$= 3 \text{ years}$$

The duration of a zero-coupon bond is always equal to the bond's term to maturity. The duration of any coupon bond is always less than the bond's term to maturity because some of the payments occur at intervals prior to maturity.

Duration of a Portfolio Bond portfolio managers commonly attempt to immunize their portfolio, that is, insulate it from the effects of interest rate movements. A first step in this process is to determine the sensitivity of their portfolio to interest rate movements. Once the duration of each individual bond is measured, the bond portfolio's duration (DUR_p) can be estimated as

$$\text{DUR}_p = \sum_{j=1}^{m} w_j \text{DUR}_j$$

where m = number of bonds in the portfolio

w_j = bond j's market value as a percentage of the portfolio market value

DUR_j = bond j's duration

In other words, the duration of a bond portfolio is the weighted average of bond durations, weighted according to relative market value. Financial institutions concerned with interest rate risk may compare their asset duration to their liability duration. A positive difference means that the market value of the institution's assets is more rate sensitive than the market value of its liabilities. Thus, during a period of rising interest rates, the market value of the assets would be reduced by a greater degree than that of the liabilities. The institution's real net worth (market value of net worth) would therefore decrease.

Modified Duration The duration measurement of a bond or a bond portfolio can be modified to estimate the impact of a change in the prevailing bond yields on bond prices. The modified duration (denoted as DUR*) is estimated as

$$DUR^* = \frac{DUR}{(1 + k)}$$

where k represents the prevailing yield on bonds.

The modified duration can be used to estimate the percentage change in the bond's price in response to a 1 percentage point change in bond yields. For example, assume that Bond X has a duration of 8 while Bond Y has a duration of 12. Assuming that the prevailing bond yield is 10 percent, the modified duration is estimated for each bond:

Bond X	**Bond Y**
$DUR^* = \dfrac{8}{(1 + .10)}$	$DUR^* = \dfrac{12}{(1 + .10)}$
$= 7.27$	$= 10.9$

Given the inverse relationship between the change in bond yields and the response in bond prices, the estimate of modified duration should be applied such that the bond price moves in the opposite direction from the change in bond yields. According to the modified duration estimates, a 1 percentage point increase in bond yields (from 10 percent to 11 percent) would lead to a 7.27 percent decline in the price of Bond X and a 10.9 percent decline in the price of Bond Y. A .5 percentage point increase in yields (from 10 percent to 10.5 percent) would lead to a 3.635 percent decline in the price of Bond X (computed as 7.27 × .5) and a 5.45 percent decline in the price of Bond Y (computed as 10.9 × .5). The percentage increase in bond prices in response to a decrease in bond yields is estimated in the same manner.

The percentage change in a bond's price in response to a change in yield can be expressed more directly with a simple equation:

$$\%\Delta P = -DUR^* \times \Delta y$$

where
$$\%\Delta P = \text{percentage change in the bond's price}$$
$$\Delta y = \text{change in yield}$$

The equation above simply expresses the relationship discussed in the preceding paragraphs mathematically. For example, the percentage change in price for Bond X for an increase in yield of 0.2 percentage point would be:

$$\%\Delta P = -7.27 \times 0.002$$
$$= -1.45\%$$

Thus, if interest rates rise by 0.2 percentage point, the price of Bond X will drop 1.45 percent. Similarly, if interest rates decrease by 0.2 percentage point, the price of Bond X will increase by 1.45 percent according to the modified duration estimate.

Estimation Errors from Using Modified Duration If investors rely strictly on modified duration to estimate the percentage change in the price of a bond, they will tend to overestimate the price decline associated with an increase in rates and underestimate the price increase associated with a decrease in rates.

ILLUSTRATION Consider a bond with a 10 percent coupon that pays interest annually and has 20 years to maturity. Assuming a required rate of return of 10 percent (the same as the coupon rate), the value of the bond is $1,000. Based on the formula provided earlier, this bond's modified duration is 8.514. If investors anticipate that bond yields will increase by 1 percentage point (to 11 percent), then they can estimate the percentage change in the bond's price to be

$$\% \Delta P = -8.514 \times 0.01$$
$$= -0.08514 \text{ or } -8.514\%$$

If bond yields rise by 1 percentage point as expected, the price (present value) of the bond would now be $920.37. (Verify this new price by using the time value function on your financial calculator.) The new price reflects a decline of 7.96 percent [calculated as ($920.37 − $1,000)/$1,000]. The decline in price is less pronounced than was estimated in the previous equation. The difference between the estimated percentage change in price (8.514 percent) and the actual percentage change in price (7.96 percent) is due to convexity.

Bond Convexity A more complete formula to estimate the percentage change in price in response to a change in yield will incorporate the property of convexity as well as modified duration.

The estimated modified duration suggests a linear relationship in the response of the bond price to a change in bond yields. This is shown by the straight line in Exhibit 11.11. For a given 1 percentage point change in bond yields from our initially assumed bond yield of 10 percent, the modified duration predicts a specific change in bond price. However, the actual response of the bond's price to a change in bond yields is convex and is represented by the curve in Exhibit 11.11. Notice that if the bond yield (horizontal axis) changes slightly from the initial level of 10 percent, the difference between the expected bond price adjustment according to the modified duration estimate (the line on Exhibit 11.11) and the bond's actual price adjustment (the convex curve on Exhibit 11.11) is small. For relatively large changes in the bond yield, however, the bond

EXHIBIT 11.11

Relationship between Bond Yields and Prices

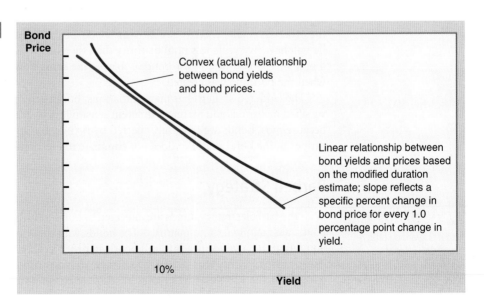

price adjustment as estimated by modified duration is less accurate. The larger the change in the bond yield, the larger the error from estimating the change in bond price in response to the change in yield.

Since a bond's price change in response to a change in yields is positively related to the maturity of the bond, convexity is also more pronounced for bonds with a long maturity. The prices of low- or zero-coupon bonds are more sensitive to changes in yields. Similarly, bond convexity is more pronounced for bonds with low (or no) coupon rates.

Bond Investment Strategies Used by Investors

Many investors value bonds and assess their risk when managing investments. Some investors such as bond portfolio managers of financial institutions commonly follow a specific strategy for investing in bonds. Some of the more common strategies are described here.

Matching Strategy

Some investors create a bond portfolio that will generate periodic income that can match their expected periodic expenses. For example, an individual investor may invest in a bond portfolio that will provide sufficient income to cover periodic expenses after retirement. Alternatively, a pension fund may invest in a bond portfolio that will provide employees with a fixed periodic income after retirement. The matching strategy involves estimating future cash outflows and then developing a bond portfolio that can generate sufficient coupon or principal payments to cover those cash outflows.

Laddered Strategy

With a laddered strategy, funds are evenly allocated to bonds in each of several different maturity classes. For example, an institutional investor might create a bond portfolio with one-fourth of the funds invested in bonds with five years until maturity, one-fourth invested in 10-year bonds, one-fourth in 15-year bonds, and one-fourth in 20-year bonds. In five years, when the bonds that had five years until maturity are redeemed, the proceeds can be used to buy 20-year bonds. Since all the other bonds in the portfolio will have five years less until maturity than they had when the portfolio was created, a new investment in 20-year bonds achieves the same maturity structure that existed when the portfolio was created.

The laddered strategy has many variations, but in general, this strategy achieves diversified maturities and therefore different sensitivities to interest rate risk. Nevertheless, because most bonds are adversely affected by rising interest rates, diversification of maturities in the bond portfolio does not eliminate interest rate risk.

Barbell Strategy

http://

http://biz.yahoo.com/c/e .html Calendar of upcoming announcements of economic conditions that may affect bond prices.

With the barbell strategy, funds are allocated to bonds with a short term to maturity and bonds with a long term to maturity. The bonds with the short term to maturity provide liquidity if the investor needs to sell bonds in order to obtain cash. The bonds with the long term to maturity tend to have a higher yield to maturity than the bonds with shorter terms to maturity. Thus, this strategy allocates some funds to achieving a relatively high return and other funds to covering liquidity needs.

Interest Rate Strategy

With the interest rate strategy, funds are allocated in a manner that capitalizes on interest rate forecasts. This strategy is very active because it requires frequent adjustments in the bond portfolio to reflect the prevailing interest rate forecast.

Consider a bond portfolio with funds initially allocated equally across various bond maturities. If recent economic events result in an expectation of higher interest rates, the bond portfolio will be revised to concentrate on bonds with short terms to maturity. Because these bonds are the least sensitive to interest rate movements, they will limit the potential adverse effects on the bond portfolio's value. The sales of all the intermediate-term and long-term bonds will result in significant commissions.

Now assume that after a few weeks, new economic conditions result in an expectation that interest rates will decline in the future. Again the bond portfolio will be restructured, but now it will concentrate on long-term bonds. If interest rates decline as expected, this type of bond portfolio will be most sensitive to the interest rate movements and will experience the largest increase in value.

Although this type of strategy is rational for investors who believe that they can accurately forecast interest rate movements, it is very difficult for even the most sophisticated investors to consistently forecast future interest rate movements. If investors guess wrong, their portfolio will likely perform worse than if they had used a passive strategy of investing in bonds with a wide variety of maturities.

Return and Risk of International Bonds

GLBALASPECTS
The value of an international bond represents the present value of future cash flows to be received by the bonds' local investors. Thus, the bond's value changes over time in response to changes in the risk-free interest rate of the currency denominating the bond and in response to changes in the perceived credit risk of the bond. Since these two factors affect the market price of the bond, they also affect the return on the bond to investors over a particular holding period. An additional factor that affects the return to investors from another country is exchange rate risk. The influence of each of these factors is described next.

Influence of Foreign Interest Rate Movements

http://www.bloomberg.com/markets Yields of government securities from major countries.

As the risk-free interest rate of a currency changes, the required rate of return by investors in that country changes as well. Thus, the present value of a bond denominated in that currency changes. A reduction in the risk-free interest rate of the foreign currency will result in a lower required rate of return by investors who use that currency to invest, which results in a higher value for bonds denominated in that currency. Conversely, an increase in the risk-free rate of that currency results in a lower value for bonds denominated in that currency. In general, the return on a bond denominated in a specific currency over a particular holding period is enhanced if the corresponding interest rate declines over that period; the return is reduced if the corresponding interest rate increases over that period. U.S. bond prices may be rising (due to a reduction in U.S. interest rates), while the prices of bonds denominated in other currencies are decreasing (due to an increase in the interest rates of these currencies).

Total Rates of Return on International Bonds

The returns on bonds in various international markets are disclosed in *The Wall Street Journal*. The returns are shown for one day, one month, and three months, and since the end of the previous year. The returns are disclosed in local currency terms and in U.S. dollar terms (from a U.S. investor's perspective).

Total Rates of Return on International Bonds

In percent, based on J.P. Morgan Government Bond Index, Dec. 31, 1987=100

		LOCAL CURRENCY TERMS				U.S. DOLLAR TERMS			
	INDEX VALUE	1 DAY	1 MO	3 MOS	SINCE 12/31	INDEX VALUE	1 DAY	1 MO	3 MOS	SINCE 12/31
Japan	217.40	−0.02	+0.71	−0.31	−0.38	237.52	−0.25	−1.62	+2.28	−3.64
Britain	434.33	+0.16	+1.30	+2.71	+2.37	423.52	+0.16	+0.51	+6.33	+5.17
Germany	294.65	+0.11	+1.29	+2.47	+3.82	291.04	+0.58	+0.68	+6.43	+1.36
France	393.08	+0.11	+1.25	+2.46	+3.73	392.39	+0.58	+0.64	+6.43	+1.28
Canada	430.20	−0.31	+0.90	+1.88	+2.82	425.78	−0.02	+1.46	+7.98	+1.18
Netherlands	316.07	+0.10	+1.26	+2.40	+3.68	311.72	+0.58	+0.65	+6.36	+1.23
EMU-d	208.57	+0.11	+1.32	+2.54	+3.86	209.43	+0.58	+0.71	+6.50	+1.40
Global-a	341.03	−0.01	+1.10	+2.00	+2.21	334.62	+0.13	+0.20	+4.84	+0.41
EMBI+-b	300.37	+0.05	+3.58	+11.92	+1.88	300.37	+0.05	+3.58	+11.92	+1.88

a-18 int'l govt. markets. b-external-currency emerging mkt. debt, Dec 31, 1993=100. d-Jan. 2, 1995=100.

Influence of Credit Risk

As the perceived credit (default) risk of an international bond changes, the risk premium within the required rate of return by investors is affected. Consequently, the present value of the bond changes. An increase in risk causes a higher required rate of return on the bond and therefore lowers the present value of the bond. A reduction in risk causes a lower required rate of return on the bond and increases the present value of the bond. Thus, investors who are concerned about a possible increase in the credit risk of an international bond monitor economic and political conditions in the relevant country that could affect the credit risk.

Influence of Exchange Rate Fluctuations

Changes in the value of the foreign currency denominating a bond affect the U.S. dollar cash flows generated from the bond and thereby affect the return to U.S. investors who invested in the bond. Consider a U.S. financial institution's purchase of bonds with a par value of £2 million, a 10 percent coupon rate (payable at the end of each year), currently priced at par value, and with six years remaining until maturity. Exhibit 11.12 shows how the dollar cash flows to be generated from this investment will differ under three scenarios. The cash flows in the last year also account for the principal payment. The sensitivity of dollar cash flows to the pound's value is obvious.

From the perspective of the investing institution, the most attractive foreign bonds offer a high coupon rate and are denominated in a currency that strengthens over the investment horizon. Although the coupon rates of some bonds are fixed, the future value of any foreign currency is uncertain. Thus, there is a risk that the currency will depreciate and more than offset any coupon rate advantage.

EXHIBIT 11.12 Dollar Cash Flows Generated from a Foreign Bond under Three Scenarios

	Year					
Scenario I (Stable Pound)	1	2	3	4	5	6
Forecasted value of pound	$1.50	$1.50	$1.50	$1.50	$1.50	$1.50
Forecasted dollar cash flows	$300,000	$300,000	$300,000	$300,000	$300,000	$3,300,000
Scenario II (Weak Pound)						
Forecasted value of pound	$1.48	$1.46	$1.44	$1.40	$1.36	$1.30
Forecasted dollar cash flows	$296,000	$292,000	$288,000	$280,000	$272,000	$2,860,000
Scenario III (Strong Pound)						
Forecasted value of pound	$1.53	$1.56	$1.60	$1.63	$1.66	$1.70
Forecasted dollar cash flows	$306,000	$312,000	$320,000	$326,000	$332,000	$3,740,000

International Bond Diversification

When investors attempt to capitalize on investments in foreign bonds that have higher interest rates than they can obtain locally, they may diversify their foreign bond holdings among countries to reduce their exposure to different types of risk, as explained next.

Reduction of Interest Rate Risk Institutional investors diversify their bond portfolios internationally to reduce exposure to interest rate risk. If all bonds in a portfolio are from a single country, their values will all be systematically affected by interest rate movements in that country. International diversification of bonds reduces the sensitivity of the overall bond portfolio to any single country's interest rate movements.

Reduction of Credit Risk Another key reason for international diversification is the reduction of credit (default) risk. Investment in bonds issued by corporations from a single country can expose investors to a relatively high degree of credit risk. The credit risk of corporations is highly dependent on economic conditions. Shifts in credit risk will likely be systematically related to the country's economic conditions. Because economic cycles differ across countries, there is less chance of a systematic increase in the credit risk of internationally diversified bonds.

Reduction of Exchange Rate Risk Financial institutions may attempt to reduce their exchange rate risk by diversifying among foreign securities denominated in various foreign currencies. In this way, a smaller proportion of their foreign security holdings will be exposed to the depreciation of any particular foreign currency. Because the movements of many foreign currency values within one continent are highly correlated, U.S. investors may reduce exchange rate risk only slightly when diversifying among securities. For this reason, U.S. financial institutions commonly attempt to purchase securities across continents rather than within a single continent, as a review of the foreign securities purchased by pension funds, life insurance companies, or most international mutual funds will reveal.

The conversion of many European countries to a single currency (the euro) in 1999 has resulted in more bond offerings in Europe by European-based firms. Before 1999, a European firm needed a different currency in every European country in which it

conducted business and therefore borrowed currency from local banks in each country. Now, a firm can use the euro to finance its operations across several European countries and may be able to obtain all the financing it needs with one bond offering in which the bond is denominated in euros. The firm can then use a portion of the revenue (in euros) to pay coupon payments to bondholders who have purchased the bonds. In addition, European investors based in countries where the euro serves as the local currency can now invest in bonds in other European countries that are denominated in euros without being exposed to exchange rate risk.

SUMMARY

- The value of a debt security (such as bonds) is the present value of future cash flows generated by that security, using a discount rate that reflects the investor's required rate of return. As market interest rates rise, the investor's required rate of return increases. The discounted value of bond payments declines when the higher discount rate is applied. Thus, the present value of a bond declines, which forces the bond price to decline.

- Bond prices are affected by the factors that influence interest rate movements, including economic growth, the money supply, oil prices, and the dollar. Bond prices are also affected by a change in credit risk.

- Other things being equal, the longer a bond's time to maturity, the more sensitive its price is to interest rate movements. Prices of bonds with relatively low coupon payments are also more sensitive to interest rate movements.

- Foreign bonds may possibly offer higher returns, but are exposed to exchange rate risk. Investors can reduce their exposure to exchange rate risk by diversifying among various currency denominations.

POINT COUNTER-POINT

Does Governance of Firms Affect the Prices of Their Bonds?

Point No. Bond prices are primarily determined by interest rate movements and therefore are not affected by the governance of the firms that issued bonds.

Counter-Point Yes. Bond prices reflect the risk of default. Firms that impose more effective governance may be able to reduce their default risk and therefore increase the price of the bond.

Who Is Correct? Use your favorite search engine to learn more about this issue. Offer your own opinion on this issue.

QUESTIONS AND APPLICATIONS

1. **Bond Price Elasticity** Explain the concept of bond price elasticity. Would bond price elasticity suggest a higher price sensitivity for zero-coupon bonds or high-coupon bonds that are offering the same yield to maturity? Why? What does this suggest about the market value volatility of mutual funds containing zero-coupon Treasury bonds versus high-coupon Treasury bonds?

2. **Impact of War** When there is major friction (such as a war) in the Middle East, bond prices in many countries tend to decline. What is the link between problems in the Middle East and bond prices? Would you expect bond prices to decline more in Japan or in the United Kingdom as a result of the crisis? [The answer is tied to how interest rates may change in those countries.] Explain.

3. **Managing in Financial Markets: Bond Investment Dilemma** As an investor, you plan to invest your funds in long-term bonds. You have $100,000 to invest. You may purchase highly rated municipal bonds at par with a coupon rate of 6 percent; you have a choice of a maturity of 10 years or 20 years. Alternatively, you could purchase highly rated corporate bonds at par with a coupon rate of 8 percent; these bonds also are offered with maturities of 10 years or 20 years. You do not expect to need the funds for five years. At the end of the fifth year, you will definitely sell the bonds because you will need to make a large purchase at that time.

   a. What is the annual interest you would earn (before taxes) on the municipal bond? On the corporate bond?

   b. Assume that you are in the 20 percent tax bracket. If the level of credit risk and the liquidity for the municipal and corporate bonds are the same, would you invest in the municipal bonds or the corporate bonds? Why?

   c. Assume that you expect all yields paid on newly issued notes and bonds (regardless of maturity) to decrease by a total of 4 percentage points over the next two years and to increase by a total of 2 percentage points over the following three years. Would you select the 10-year maturity or the 20-year maturity for the type of bond you plan to purchase? Why?

4. **Bond Investment Decision** Based on your forecast of interest rates, would you recommend that investors purchase bonds today? Explain.

5. **Source of Bond Price Movements** Determine the direction of bond prices over the last year and explain the reason for it.

6. **Required Return on Bonds** Why does the required rate of return for a particular bond change over time?

7. **International Bonds** A U.S. insurance company purchased British 20-year Treasury bonds instead of U.S. 20-year Treasury bonds because the coupon rate was 2 percent higher on the British bonds. Assume that the insurance company sold the bonds after five years. Its yield over the five-year period was substantially less than the yield it would have received on the U.S. bonds over the same five-year period. Assume that the U.S. insurance company had hedged its exchange rate exposure. Given that the lower yield was not because of default risk or exchange rate risk, explain how the British bonds could possibly generate a lower yield than the U.S. bonds. (Assume that either type of bond could have been purchased at the par value.)

8. **Internet Exercise** Using the website http://www.bondsonline.com, go to the section on corporate bond spreads. The spreads are listed in the form of basis points (100 basis points = 1 percent) above the Treasury security with the same maturity.

   a. First determine the difference between the AAA and CCC spreads. This indicates how much more of a yield is required on CCC-rated bonds versus AAA-rated bonds. Next, determine the difference between AAA and BBB spreads. Then determine the difference between BBB and CCC spreads. Is the difference larger between the AAA and BBB or the BBB and CCC spreads? What does this tell you about the perceived risk of the bonds in these rating categories?

   b. Compare the AAA spread for a short-term maturity (such as 2 years) versus a long-term maturity (such as 10 years). Is the spread larger for the short-term or the long-term maturity? Offer an explanation for this.

   c. Next, compare the CCC spread for a short-term maturity (such as 2 years) versus a long-term maturity (such as 10 years). Is the spread larger for the short-term or the long-term maturity? Offer an explanation for this. Notice that the difference in spreads for a given rating level among maturities varies with the rating level that you assess. Offer an explanation for this.

9. **How Interest Rates Affect Bond Prices** Explain the impact of a decline in interest rates on:

   a. An investor's required rate of return.

   b. The present value of existing bonds.

   c. The prices of existing bonds.

10. **Impact of Economic Conditions** Assume that breaking news causes bond portfolio managers to suddenly expect much higher economic growth. How might bond prices be affected by this expectation? Explain. Now assume that breaking news causes bond portfolio managers to suddenly anticipate a recession. How might bond prices be affected? Explain.

11. **Economic Effects on Bond Prices** An analyst recently suggested that there will be a major economic expansion, which will favorably affect the prices of high-rated fixed-rate bonds, because the credit risk of bonds will decline as corporations experience better performance. Do you agree with the conclusion

of the analyst if the economic expansion occurs? Explain.

12. **Impact of the Fed** Assume that the bond market participants suddenly expect the Fed to substantially increase the money supply.
   a. Assuming no threat of inflation, how would bond prices be affected by this expectation?
   b. Assuming that inflation may result, how would bond prices be affected?
   c. Given your answers to (a) and (b), explain why expectations of the Fed's increase in the money supply may sometimes cause bond market participants to disagree about how bond prices will be affected.

13. **Interpreting Financial News** Interpret the following statements made by Wall Street analysts and portfolio managers:
   a. "Given the recent uncertainty about future interest rates, investors are fleeing from zero-coupon bonds."
   b. "Citigroup's stock price increased as a result of the abrupt decline in interest rates, which caused investors to revalue Citigroup's assets."
   c. "Bond markets declined when the Treasury flooded the market with its new bond offering."

14. **Exposure to Bond Price Movements** How would a financial institution with a large bond portfolio be affected by falling interest rates? Would it be affected more than a financial institution with a greater concentration of bonds (and fewer short-term securities)? Explain.

15. **Impact of the Trade Deficit** Bond portfolio managers closely monitor the trade deficit figures, because the trade deficit can affect exchange rates, which can affect inflationary expectations and therefore interest rates.
   a. When the trade deficit figure is higher than anticipated, bond prices typically decline. Explain why this reaction may occur.
   b. On some occasions, the trade deficit figure has been very large, but the bond markets did not respond to the announcement. Assuming that no other information offset its impact, explain why the bond markets may not have responded to the announcement.

16. **Comparison of Bonds to Mortgages** Since fixed-rate mortgages and bonds have similar payment flows, how is a financial institution with a large portfolio of fixed-rate mortgages affected by rising interest rates? Explain.

17. **Impact of Oil Prices** Assume that oil-producing countries have agreed to reduce their oil production by 30 percent. How would bond prices be affected by this announcement? Explain.

18. **Implications of a Shift in the Yield Curve** Assume that there is a sudden shift in the yield curve, such that the new yield curve is higher and more steeply sloped today than it was yesterday. If a firm issues new bonds today, would its bonds sell for higher or lower prices than if it had issued the bonds yesterday? Explain.

19. **Relevance of Bond Price Movements** Why is the relationship between interest rates and bond prices important to financial institutions?

20. **Inflation Effects** Assume that inflation is expected to decline in the near future. How could this affect future bond prices? Would you recommend that financial institutions increase or decrease their concentration in long-term bonds based on this expectation? Explain.

21. **International Bonds** The pension fund manager of Utterback (a U.S. firm) purchased German 20-year Treasury bonds instead of U.S. 20-year Treasury bonds. The coupon rate was 2 percent lower on the German bonds. Assume that the manager sold the bonds after five years. The yield over the five-year period was substantially more than the yield it would have received on the U.S. bonds over the same five-year period. Explain how the German bonds could possibly generate a higher yield than the U.S. bonds for the manager, even if the exchange rate is stable over this five-year period. (Assume that the price of either bond was initially equal to its respective par value). Be specific.

22. **Coupon Rates** If a bond's coupon rate is above its required rate of return, would its price be above or below its par value? Explain.

23. **Bond Price Sensitivity** Explain how bond prices may be affected by money supply growth, oil prices, and economic growth.

24. **Bond Price Sensitivity** Is the price of a long-term bond more or less sensitive to a change in interest rates than the price of a short-term security? Why?

PROBLEMS

1. **Predicting Bond Values** (Use the chapter appendix to answer this problem.) The portfolio manager of Ludwig Company has excess cash that is to be invested for four years. He can purchase four-year Treasury notes that offer a 9 percent yield. Alternatively, he can purchase new 20-year Treasury bonds for $2.9 million that offer a par value of $3 million and an 11 percent coupon rate with annual payments. The manager expects that the required return on these same 20-year bonds will be 12 percent four years from now.
   a. What is the forecasted market value of the 20-year bonds in four years?
   b. Which investment is expected to provide a higher yield over the four-year period?

2. **Valuing a Zero-Coupon Bond**
   a. A zero-coupon bond with a par value of $1,000 matures in 10 years. At what price would this bond provide a yield to maturity that matches the current market rate of 8 percent?
   b. What happens to the price of this bond if interest rates fall to 6 percent?
   c. Given the above changes in the price of the bond and the interest rate, calculate the bond price elasticity.

3. **Bond Convexity** Describe how bond convexity affects the theoretical linear price-yield relationship of bonds. What are the implications of bond convexity for estimating changes in bond prices?

4. **Bond Valuation** Assume the following information for an existing bond that provides annual coupon payments:

   Par value = $1,000
   Coupon rate = 11%
   Maturity = 4 years
   Required rate of return by investors = 11%

   a. What is the present value of the bond?
   b. If the required rate of return by investors were 14 percent instead of 11 percent, what would be the present value of the bond?
   c. If the required rate of return by investors were 9 percent, what would be the present value of the bond?

5. **Valuing a Zero-Coupon Bond** Assume that you require a 14 percent return on a zero-coupon bond with a par value of $1,000 and six years to maturity. What is the price you should be willing to pay for this bond?

6. **Predicting Bond Values** (Use the chapter appendix to answer this problem.) Spartan Insurance Company plans to purchase bonds today that have four years remaining to maturity, a par value of $60 million, and a coupon rate of 10 percent. Spartan expects that in three years, the required rate of return on these bonds by investors in the market will be 9 percent. It plans to sell the bonds at that time. What is the expected price it will sell the bonds for in three years?

7. **Predicting Bond Values** A bond you are interested in pays an annual coupon of 4 percent, has a yield to maturity of 6 percent and has 13 years to maturity. If interest rates remain unchanged, at what price would you expect this bond to be selling 8 years from now? Ten years from now?

8. **Predicting Bond Portfolio Value** (Use the chapter appendix to answer this problem). Ash Investment Company manages a broad portfolio with this composition:

	Par Value	Present Market Value	Years Remaining to Maturity
Zero-coupon bonds	$200,000,000	$ 63,720,000	12
8% Treasury bonds	300,000,000	290,000,000	8
11% corporate bonds	400,000,000	380,000,000	10
		$733,720,000	

Ash expects that in four years, investors in the market will require an 8 percent return on the zero-coupon bonds, a 7 percent return on the Treasury bonds, and a 9 percent return on corporate bonds. Estimate the market value of the bond portfolio four years from now.

9. **Bond Duration** Determine how the duration of a bond would be affected if the coupons are extended over additional time periods.

10. **Sensitivity of Bond Values**
    a. How would the present value (and therefore the market value) of a bond be affected if the coupon payments are smaller and other factors remain constant?

b. How would the present value (and therefore the market value) of a bond be affected if the required rate of return is smaller and other factors remain constant?

11. **Valuing a Zero-Coupon Bond** Assume the following information for existing zero-coupon bonds:

Par value = $100,000
Maturity = 3 years
Required rate of return by investors = 12%

How much should investors be willing to pay for these bonds?

12. **Predicting Bond Values** (Use the chapter appendix to answer this problem.) Sun Devil Savings has just purchased bonds for $38 million that have a par value of $40 million, five years remaining to maturity, and a coupon rate of 12 percent. It expects the required rate of return on these bonds to be 10 percent two years from now.

a. At what price could Sun Devil Savings sell these bonds for two years from now?

b. What is the expected annualized yield on the bonds over the next two years, assuming they are to be sold in two years?

c. If the anticipated required rate of return of 10 percent in two years is overestimated, how would the actual selling price differ from the forecasted price? How would the actual annualized yield over the next two years differ from the forecasted yield?

13. **Bond Yields** (Use the chapter appendix to answer this problem.) Hankla Company plans to purchase either (1) zero-coupon bonds that have 10 years to maturity, a par value of $100 million, and a purchase price of $40 million, *or* (2) bonds with similar default risk that have five years to maturity, a 9 percent coupon rate, a par value of $40 million, and a purchase price of $40 million.

Hankla can invest $40 million for five years. Assume that the market's required return in five years is forecasted to be 11 percent. Which alternative would offer Hankla a higher expected return (or yield) over the five-year investment horizon?

14. **Bond Elasticity** Determine how the bond elasticity would be affected if the bond price changed by a larger amount, holding the change in the required rate of return constant.

15. **Bond Value Sensitivity to Exchange Rates and Interest Rates** Cardinal Company, a U.S.-based insurance company, considers purchasing bonds denomi-

nated in Canadian dollars, with a maturity of six years, a par value of C$50 million, and a coupon rate of 12 percent. The bonds can be purchased at par by Cardinal and would be sold four years from now. The current exchange rate of the Canadian dollar is $0.80. Cardinal expects that the required return by Canadian investors on these bonds four years from now will be 9 percent. If Cardinal purchases the bonds, it will sell them in the Canadian secondary market four years from now. The exchange rates are forecast as follows:

Year	Exchange Rate of C$	Year	Exchange Rate of C$
1	$0.80	4	0.72
2	0.77	5	0.68
3	0.74	6	0.66

a. Refer to earlier examples in this chapter to determine the expected U.S. dollar cash flows to Cardinal over the next four years. Refer to Chapter 3 to determine the present value of a bond.

b. Does Cardinal expect to be favorably or adversely affected by the interest rate risk? Explain.

c. Does Cardinal expect to be favorably or adversely affected by exchange rate risk? Explain.

16. **Bond Valuation** You are interested in buying a $1,000 par value bond with 10 years to maturity and an 8 percent coupon rate that is paid semiannually. How much should you be willing to pay for the bond if the investor's required rate of return is 10 percent?

17. **Predicting Bond Values** (Use the chapter appendix to answer this problem.) Bulldog Bank has just purchased bonds for $106 million that have a par value of $100 million, three years remaining to maturity, and an annual coupon rate of 14 percent. It expects the required rate of return on these bonds to be 12 percent one year from now.

a. At what price could Bulldog Bank sell these bonds for one year from now?

b. What is the expected annualized yield on the bonds over the next year, assuming they are to be sold in one year?

18. **Bond Duration** A bond has a duration of five years and a yield to maturity of 9 percent. If the yield to maturity changes to 10 percent, what should be the percentage price change of the bond?

FLOW OF FUNDS EXERCISE

Interest Rate Expectations, Economic Growth, and Bond Financing

Recall that if the economy continues to be strong, Carson Company may need to increase its production capacity by about 50 percent over the next few years to satisfy demand. It would need financing to expand and accommodate the increase in production. Recall that the yield curve is currently upward sloping. Also recall that Carson is concerned about a possible slowing of the economy because of potential Fed actions to reduce inflation. It needs funding to cover payments for supplies. It is also considering the issuance of stock or bonds to raise funds in the next year.

a. At a recent meeting, the Chief Executive Officer (CEO) stated his view that the economy will remain strong, as the Fed's monetary policy is not likely to have a major impact on interest rates. So he wants to expand the business to benefit from the expected increase in demand for Carson's products. The next step would be to determine how to finance the expansion. The Chief Financial Officer (CFO) stated that if Car-

son Company needs to obtain long-term funds, the issuance of fixed-rate bonds would be ideal at this point in time because she expects that the Fed's monetary policy to reduce inflation will cause long-term interest rates to rise. If the CFO is correct about future interest rates, what does this suggest about the future economic growth, the future demand for Carson's products, and the need to issue bonds?

b. If you were involved in the meeting described here, what do you think needs to be resolved before deciding to expand the business?

c. At the meeting described here, the CEO stated: "The decision to expand should not be dictated by whether interest rates are going to increase or not. Bonds should be issued only if the potential increase in interest rates is attributed to a strong demand for loanable funds rather than the Fed's reduction in the supply of loanable funds." What does this statement mean?

WSJ EXERCISE

Comparing Bond Price Sensitivity among Bonds

Use *The Wall Street Journal* to determine the prices of Treasury bonds with a 10-year maturity and three different coupon rate characteristics: a relatively high coupon rate, a relatively low coupon rate, and a zero-coupon rate. Determine the percentage change in the price of

each bond that would occur if interest rates rose by 1 percentage point. What if interest rates decreased by 2 percentage points? Based on your results, which type of bond was most sensitive to a change in interest rates? Which type was least sensitive? Explain your results.

Forecasting Bond Prices and Yields

Forecasting Bond Prices

To illustrate how a financial institution can assess the potential impact of interest rate movements on its bond holdings, assume that Longhorn Savings and Loan recently purchased Treasury bonds in the secondary market with a total par value of $40 million. The bonds will mature in five years and have an annual coupon rate of 10 percent. Longhorn is attempting to forecast the market value of these bonds two years from now because it may sell the bonds at that time. Therefore, it must forecast the investor's required rate of return and use that as the discount rate to determine the present value of the bonds' cash flows over the final three years of their life. The computed present value will represent the forecasted price two years from now.

To continue with our example, assume the investor's required rate of return two years from now is expected to be 12 percent. This rate will be used to discount the periodic cash flows over the remaining three years. Given coupon payments of $4 million per year (10% × $40 million) and a par value of $40 million, the predicted present value is determined as follows:

$$
\begin{aligned}
PV \text{ of bonds two years from now} &= \frac{\$4,000,000}{(1.12)^1} + \frac{\$4,000,000}{(1.12)^2} + \frac{\$44,000,000}{(1.12)^3} \\
&= \$3,571,429 + \$3,188,775 + \$31,318,331 \\
&= \$38,078,535
\end{aligned}
$$

An illustration of this exercise is provided in Exhibit 11A.1, using a time line. The market value of the bonds two years ahead is forecasted to be slightly more than $38 million. This is the amount Longhorn expects to receive if it sells the bonds then.

As a second example, assume that Aggie Insurance Company recently purchased corporate bonds in the secondary market with a par value of $20 million, a coupon rate of 14 percent (with annual coupon payments), and three years until maturity. The firm desires to forecast the market value of these bonds in one year because it may sell the bonds at that time. It expects the investor's required rate of return on similar investments to be 11 percent in one year. Using this information, it discounts the bond's cash flows

EXHIBIT 11A.1

Forecasting the Market
Value of Bonds

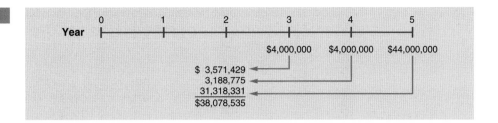

($2.8 million in annual coupon payments and a par value of $20 million) over the final two years at 11 percent to determine their present value (and therefore market value) one year from now:

$$PV \text{ of bonds one year from now} = \frac{\$2,800,000}{(1.11)^1} + \frac{\$22,800,000}{(1.11)^2}$$

$$= \$2,522,522 + \$18,504,991$$

$$= \$21,027,513$$

Thus, the market value of the bonds is expected to be slightly more than $21 million one year from now.

Forecasting Bond Yields

The yield to maturity can be determined by solving for the discount rate at which the present value of future payments (coupon payments and par value) to the bondholder would equal the bond's current price. The trial-and-error method can be used by applying a discount rate and computing the present value of the payments stream. If the computed present value is higher than the current bond price, the computation should be repeated using a higher discount rate. Conversely, if the computed present value is lower than the current bond price, try a lower discount rate. Calculators and bond tables are also available to determine the yield to maturity.

If bonds are held to maturity, the yield is known. However, if they are sold prior to maturity, the yield is not known until the time of sale. Investors can, however, attempt to forecast the yield with the methods just demonstrated, in which the forecasted required rate of return is used to forecast the market value (and therefore selling price) of the bonds. This selling price can then be incorporated into the cash flow estimates to determine the discount rate at which the present value of cash flows equals the investor's initial purchase price. Suppose that Wildcat Bank purchases bonds with the following characteristics:

- Par value = $30 million
- Coupon rate = 15 percent (annual payments)
- Remaining time to maturity = 5 years
- Purchase price of bonds = $29 million

The bank plans to sell the bonds in four years. The investor's required rate of return on similar securities is expected to be 13 percent at that time. Given this information, Wildcat forecasts its annualized bond yield over the four-year period in the following manner.

The first step is to forecast the present value (or market price) of the bonds four years from now. To do this, the remaining cash flows (one final coupon payment of $4.5 mil-

lion plus the par value of $30 million) over the fifth and final year should be discounted (at the forecasted required rate of return of 13 percent) back to the fourth year when the bonds are to be sold:

$$PV \text{ of bond four years from now} = \frac{\$34,500,000}{(1.13)^1}$$

$$= \$30,530,973$$

This predicted present value as of four years from now serves as the predicted selling price in four years.

The next step is to incorporate the forecasted selling price at the end of the bond portfolio's cash flow stream. Then the discount rate that equates the present value of the cash flow stream to the price at which the bonds were purchased will represent the annualized yield. In our example, Wildcat Bank's cash flows are coupon payments of $4.5 million over each of the four years it holds the bonds; the fourth year's cash flows should also include the forecasted selling price of $30,530,973 and therefore sum to $35,030,973. Recall that Wildcat Bank purchased the bonds for $29 million. Given this information, the equation to solve for the discount rate (k) is

$$\$29 \text{ million} = \frac{\$4,500,000}{(1+k)^1} + \frac{\$4,500,000}{(1+k)^2} + \frac{\$4,500,000}{(1+k)^3} + \frac{\$35,030,973}{(1+k)^4}$$

The trial-and-error method can be used to determine the discount rate if a calculator is not available. The use of PVIF and PVIFA tables, such as those in Exhibits 11A.3 and 11A.4 at the end of this appendix, can expedite the process. With a discount rate of 17 percent, the present value would be

$$PV \text{ of bonds using a } 17\% \text{ discount rate} = \frac{\$4,500,000}{(1.17)^1} + \frac{\$4,500,000}{(1.17)^2} + \frac{\$4,500,000}{(1.17)^3} + \frac{\$35,030,973}{(1.17)^4}$$

$$= \$3,846,154 + \$3,287,311 + \$2,809,667 + \$18,694,280$$

$$= \$28,637,412$$

This present value is slightly less than the initial purchase price. Thus, the discount rate at which the present value of expected cash flows equals the purchase price is just slightly less than 17 percent. Consequently, Wildcat Bank's expected return on the bonds is just short of 17 percent.

It should be recognized that the process for determining the yield to maturity assumes that any payments received prior to the end of the holding period can be reinvested at the yield to maturity. If, for example, the payments could be reinvested only at a lower rate, the yield to maturity would overstate the actual return to the investor over the entire holding period.

With a computer program, the financial institution could easily create a distribution of forecasted yields based on various forecasts for the required rate of return four years from now. Without a computer, the process illustrated here must be completed for each forecast of the required rate of return. The computer actually follows the same steps but is much faster.

Financial institutions that forecast bond yields must first forecast interest rates for the point in time when they plan to sell their bonds. These forecasted rates can be used

along with information about the securities to predict the required rate of return that will exist for the securities of concern. The predicted required rate of return is applied to cash flows beyond the time of sale to forecast the present value (or selling price) of the bonds at the time of sale. The forecasted selling price is then incorporated when estimating cash flows over the investment horizon. Finally, the yield to maturity on the bonds is determined by solving for the discount rate that equates these cash flows to the initial purchase price. The accuracy of the forecasted yield depends on the accuracy of the forecasted selling price of the bonds, which in turn depends on the accuracy of the forecasted required rate of return for the time of the sale.

Forecasting Bond Portfolio Values

Financial institutions can quantitatively measure the impact of possible interest rate movements on the market value of their bond portfolio by separately assessing the impact on each type of bond and then consolidating the individual impacts. Assume that Seminole Financial Inc. has a portfolio of bonds with the required return (k) on each type of bond as shown in the upper portion of Exhibit 11A.2. Interest rates are expected to increase, causing an anticipated increase of 1 percent in the required return of each type of bond. Assuming no adjustment in the portfolio, Seminole's anticipated bond portfolio position is displayed in the lower portion of Exhibit 11A.2.

The anticipated market value of each type of bond in the exhibit was determined by discounting the remaining year's cash flows beyond one year by the anticipated required return. The market value of the portfolio is expected to decline by more than $12 million as a result of the anticipated increase in interest rates.

This simplified example assumed a portfolio of only three types of bonds. In reality, a financial institution may have several types of bonds, with several maturities for each

EXHIBIT 11A.2

Forecasts of Bond Portfolio Market Value

Present Bond Portfolio Position of Seminole Financial Inc.:				
Type of Bonds	Present k	Par Value	Years to Maturity	Present Market Value of Bonds
9% coupon Treasury bonds	9%	$ 40,000,000	4	$ 40,000,000
14% coupon corporate bonds	12%	100,000,000	5	107,207,200
10% coupon gov't agency bonds	10%	150,000,000	8	150,000,000
		$290,000,000		$297,207,200

Forecasted Bond Portfolio Position of Seminole Financial Inc.:				
Type of Bonds	Forecasted k	Par Value	Years to Maturity as of One Year from Now	Forecasted Market Value of Bonds in One Year
9% coupon Treasury bonds	10%	$ 40,000,000	3	$ 39,004,840
14% coupon corporate bonds	13%	100,000,000	4	102,973,000
10% coupon gov't agency bonds	11%	150,000,000	7	142,938,000
		$290,000,000		$284,915,840

type. Computer programs are widely available for assessing the market value of portfolios. The financial institution inputs the cash flow trends of all bond holdings and the anticipated required rates of return for each bond at the future time of concern. The computer uses the anticipated rates to estimate the present value of cash flows at that future time. These present values are then consolidated to determine the forecasted value of the bond portfolio.

The key variable in forecasting the bond portfolio's market value is the anticipated required return for each type of bond. The prevailing interest rates on short-term securities are commonly more volatile than rates on longer-term securities, so the required returns on bonds with three or four years to maturity may change to a greater degree than the longer-term bonds. In addition, as economic conditions change, the required returns of some risky securities could change even if the general level of interest rates remains stable.

Forecasting Bond Portfolio Returns

Financial institutions measure their overall bond portfolio returns in various ways. One way is to account not only for coupon payments but also for the change in market value over the holding period of concern. The market value at the beginning of the holding period is perceived as the initial investment. The market value at the end of that period is perceived as the price at which the bonds would have been sold. Even if the bonds are retained, the measurement of return requires an estimated market value at the end of the period. Finally, the coupon payments must be accounted for as well. A bond portfolio's return is measured the same way as an individual bond's return. Mathematically, the bond portfolio return can be determined by solving for k in the following equation:

$$MVP = \sum_{t=1}^{n} \frac{C_t}{(1 + k)^t} + \frac{MVP_n}{(1 + k)^n}$$

where
MVP = today's market value of the bond portfolio

C_t = coupon payments received at the end of period t

MVP_n = market value of the bond portfolio at the end of the investment period of concern

k = discount rate that equates the present value of coupon payments and the future portfolio market value to today's portfolio market value

To illustrate, recall that Seminole Financial Inc. forecasted its bond portfolio value for one year ahead. Its annual coupon payments (C) sum to $32,600,000 (computed by multiplying the coupon rate of each type of bond by the respective par value). Using this information, along with today's MVP and the forecasted MVP (called MVP_n), its annual return is determined by solving for k as follows:

$$MVP = \frac{C_1 + MVP_n}{(1 + k)^1}$$

$$\$297,207,200 = \frac{\$32,600,000 + \$284,915,840}{(1 + k)^1}$$

$$\$297,207,200 = \frac{\$317,515,840}{(1 + k)^1}$$

The discount rate (or k) is estimated to be about 7 percent. (Work this yourself for verification.) Therefore, the bond portfolio is expected to generate an annual return of about 7 percent over the one-year investment horizon. The computations to determine the bond portfolio return can be tedious, but financial institutions use computer programs. If this type of program is linked with another program to forecast future bond prices, a financial institution can input forecasted required returns for each type of bond and let the computer determine projections of the bond portfolio's future market value and its return over a specified investment horizon.

EXHIBIT 11A.3 Present Value Interest Factors (PVIF)

Period n	1%	2%	3%	4%	5%	6%	7%	8%	9%	10%	11%	12%
1	.9901	.9804	.9709	.9615	.9524	.9434	.9346	.9259	.9174	.9091	.9009	.8929
2	.9803	.9612	.9426	.9246	.9070	.8900	.8734	.8573	.8417	.8264	.8116	.7972
3	.9706	.9423	.9151	.8890	.8638	.8396	.8163	.7938	.7722	.7513	.7312	.7118
4	.9610	.9238	.8885	.8548	.8227	.7921	.7629	.7350	.7084	.6830	.6587	.6355
5	.9515	.9057	.8626	.8219	.7835	.7473	.7130	.6806	.6499	.6209	.5935	.5674
6	.9420	.8880	.8375	.7903	.7462	.7050	.6663	.6302	.5963	.5645	.5346	.5066
7	.9327	.8706	.8131	.7599	.7107	.6651	.6227	.5835	.5470	.5132	.4817	.4523
8	.9235	.8535	.7894	.7307	.6768	.6274	.5820	.5403	.5019	.4665	.4339	.4039
9	.9143	.8368	.7664	.7026	.6446	.5919	.5439	.5002	.4604	.4241	.3909	.3606
10	.9053	.8203	.7441	.6756	.6139	.5584	.5083	.4632	.4224	.3856	.3522	.3220
11	.8963	.8043	.7224	.6496	.5847	.5268	.4751	.4289	.3875	.3505	.3173	.2875
12	.8874	.7885	.7014	.6246	.5568	.4970	.4440	.3971	.3555	.3186	.2858	.2567
13	.8787	.7730	.6810	.6006	.5303	.4688	.4150	.3677	.3262	.2897	.2575	.2292
14	.8700	.7579	.6611	.5775	.5051	.4423	.3878	.3405	.2992	.2633	.2320	.2046
15	.8613	.7430	.6419	.5553	.4810	.4173	.3624	.3152	.2745	.2394	.2090	.1827
16	.8528	.7284	.6232	.5339	.4581	.3936	.3387	.2919	.2519	.2176	.1883	.1631
17	.8444	.7142	.6050	.5134	.4363	.3714	.3166	.2703	.2311	.1978	.1696	.1456
18	.8360	.7002	.5874	.4936	.4155	.3503	.2959	.2502	.2120	.1799	.1528	.1300
19	.8277	.6864	.5703	.4746	.3957	.3305	.2765	.2317	.1945	.1635	.1377	.1161
20	.8195	.6730	.5537	.4564	.3769	.3118	.2584	.2145	.1784	.1486	.1240	.1037
21	.8114	.6598	.5375	.4388	.3589	.2942	.2415	.1987	.1637	.1351	.1117	.0926
22	.8034	.6468	.5219	.4220	.3418	.2775	.2257	.1839	.1502	.1228	.1007	.0826
23	.7954	.6342	.5067	.4057	.3256	.2618	.2109	.1700	.1378	.1117	.0907	.0738
24	.7876	.6217	.4919	.3901	.3101	.2470	.1971	.1577	.1264	.1015	.0817	.0659
25	.7798	.6095	.4776	.3751	.2953	.2330	.1842	.1460	.1160	.0923	.0736	.0588
26	.7720	.5976	.4637	.3607	.2812	.2198	.1722	.1352	.1064	.0839	.0663	.0525
27	.7644	.5859	.4502	.3468	.2678	.2074	.1609	.1252	.0976	.0763	.0597	.0469
28	.7568	.5744	.4371	.3335	.2551	.1956	.1504	.1159	.0895	.0693	.0538	.0419
29	.7493	.5631	.4243	.3207	.2429	.1846	.1406	.1073	.0822	.0630	.0485	.0374
30	.7419	.5521	.4120	.3083	.2314	.1741	.1314	.0994	.0754	.0573	.0437	.0334
35	.7059	.5000	.3554	.2534	.1813	.1301	.0937	.0676	.0490	.0356	.0259	.0189
40	.6717	.4529	.3066	.2083	.1420	.0972	.0668	.0460	.0318	.0221	.0154	.0107
45	.6391	.4102	.2644	.1712	.1113	.0727	.0476	.0313	.0207	.0137	.0091	.0061
50	.6080	.3715	.2281	.1407	.0872	.0543	.0339	.0213	.0134	.0085	.0054	.0035

EXHIBIT 11A.3 *(Concluded)*

Period *n*	13%	14%	15%	16%	17%	18%	19%	20%	25%	30%	35%	40%	50%
1	.8850	.8772	.8696	.8621	.8547	.8475	.8403	.8333	.8000	.7692	.7407	.7143	.6667
2	.7831	.7695	.7561	.7432	.7305	.7182	.7062	.6944	.6400	.5917	.5487	.5102	.4444
3	.6931	.6750	.6575	.6407	.6244	.6086	.5934	.5787	.5120	.4552	.4064	.3644	.2963
4	.6133	.5921	.5718	.5523	.5337	.5158	.4987	.4823	.4096	.3501	.3011	.2603	.1975
5	.5428	.5194	.4972	.4761	.4561	.4371	.4190	.4019	.3277	.2693	.2230	.1859	.1317
6	.4803	.4556	.4323	.4104	.3898	.3704	.3521	.3349	.2621	.2072	.1652	.1328	.0878
7	.4251	.3996	.3759	.3538	.3332	.3139	.2959	.2791	.2097	.1594	.1224	.0949	.0585
8	.3762	.3506	.3269	.3050	.2848	.2660	.2487	.2326	.1678	.1226	.0906	.0678	.0390
9	.3329	.3075	.2843	.2630	.2434	.2255	.2090	.1938	.1342	.0943	.0671	.0484	.0260
10	.2946	.2697	.2472	.2267	.2080	.1911	.1756	.1615	.1074	.0725	.0497	.0346	.0173
11	.2607	.2366	.2149	.1954	.1778	.1619	.1476	.1346	.0859	.0558	.0368	.0247	.0116
12	.2307	.2076	.1869	.1685	.1520	.1372	.1240	.1122	.0687	.0429	.0273	.0176	.0077
13	.2042	.1821	.1625	.1452	.1299	.1163	.1042	.0935	.0550	.0330	.0202	.0126	.0051
14	.1807	.1597	.1413	.1252	.1110	.0985	.0876	.0779	.0440	.0254	.0150	.0090	.0034
15	.1599	.1401	.1229	.1079	.0949	.0835	.0736	.0649	.0352	.0195	.0111	.0064	.0023
16	.1415	.1229	.1069	.0930	.0811	.0708	.0618	.0541	.0281	.0150	.0082	.0046	.0015
17	.1252	.1078	.0929	.0802	.0693	.0600	.0520	.0451	.0225	.0116	.0061	.0033	.0010
18	.1108	.0946	.0808	.0691	.0592	.0508	.0437	.0376	.0180	.0089	.0045	.0023	.0007
19	.0981	.0829	.0703	.0596	.0506	.0431	.0367	.0313	.0144	.0068	.0033	.0017	.0005
20	.0868	.0728	.0611	.0514	.0443	.0365	.0308	.0261	.0115	.0053	.0025	.0012	.0003
21	.0768	.0638	.0531	.0443	.0370	.0309	.0259	.0217	.0092	.0040	.0018	.0009	.0002
22	.0680	.0560	.0462	.0382	.0316	.0262	.0218	.0181	.0074	.0031	.0014	.0006	.0001
23	.0601	.0491	.0402	.0329	.0270	.0222	.0183	.0151	.0059	.0024	.0010	.0004	.0001
24	.0532	.0431	.0349	.0284	.0231	.0188	.0154	.0126	.0047	.0018	.0007	.0003	.0001
25	.0471	.0378	.0304	.0245	.0197	.0160	.0129	.0105	.0038	.0014	.0006	.0002	.0000
26	.0417	.0331	.0264	.0211	.0169	.0135	.0109	.0087	.0030	.0011	.0004	.0002	.0000
27	.0369	.0291	.0230	.0182	.0144	.0115	.0091	.0073	.0024	.0008	.0003	.0001	.0000
28	.0326	.0255	.0200	.0157	.0123	.0097	.0077	.0061	.0019	.0006	.7002	.0001	.0000
29	.0289	.0224	.0174	.0135	.0105	.0082	.0064	.0051	.0015	.0005	.0002	.0001	.0000
30	.0256	.0196	.0151	.0116	.0090	.0070	.0054	.0042	.0012	.0004	.0001	.0000	.0000
35	.0139	.0102	.0075	.0055	.0041	.0030	.0023	.0017	.0004	.0001	.0000	.0000	.0000
40	.0075	.0053	.0037	.0026	.0019	.0013	.0010	.0007	.0001	.0000	.0000	.0000	.0000
45	.0041	.0027	.0019	.0013	.0009	.0006	.0004	.0003	.0000	.0000	.0000	.0000	.0000
50	.0022	.0014	.0009	.0006	.0004	.0003	.0002	.0001	.0000	.0000	.0000	.0000	.0000

EXHIBIT 11A.4 Present Value Interest Factors for an Annuity (PVIFA)

Period n	1%	2%	3%	4%	5%	6%	7%	8%	9%	10%	11%	12%
1	0.9901	0.9804	0.9709	0.9615	0.9524	0.9434	0.9346	0.9259	0.9174	0.9091	0.9009	0.8929
2	1.9704	1.9416	1.9135	1.8861	1.8594	1.8334	1.8080	1.7833	1.7591	1.7355	1.7125	1.6901
3	2.9410	2.8839	2.8286	2.7751	2.7232	2.6730	2.6243	2.5771	2.5313	2.4869	2.4437	2.4018
4	3.9020	3.8077	3.7171	3.6299	3.5460	3.4651	3.3872	3.3121	3.2397	3.1899	3.1024	3.0373
5	4.8534	4.7135	4.5797	4.4518	4.3295	4.2124	4.1002	3.9927	3.8897	3.7908	3.6959	3.6048
6	5.7955	5.6014	5.4172	5.2421	5.0757	4.9173	4.7665	4.6229	4.4859	4.3553	4.2305	4.1114
7	6.7282	6.4720	6.2303	6.0021	5.7864	5.5824	5.3893	5.2064	5.0330	4.8684	4.7122	4.5638
8	7.6517	7.3255	7.0197	6.7327	6.4632	6.2098	5.9713	5.7466	5.5348	5.3349	5.1461	4.9676
9	8.5660	8.1622	7.7861	7.4353	7.1078	6.8017	6.5152	6.2469	5.9952	5.7590	5.5370	5.3282
10	9.4713	8.9826	8.5302	8.1109	7.7217	7.3601	7.0236	6.7101	6.4177	6.1466	5.8892	5.6502
11	10.368	9.7868	9.2526	8.7605	8.3064	7.8869	7.4987	7.1390	6.8052	6.4951	6.2065	5.9377
12	11.255	10.575	9.9540	9.3851	8.8633	8.3838	7.9427	7.5361	7.1607	6.8137	6.4924	6.1944
13	12.134	11.348	10.635	9.9856	9.3936	8.8527	8.3577	7.9038	7.4869	7.1034	6.7499	6.4235
14	13.004	12.106	11.296	10.563	9.8986	9.2950	8.7455	8.2442	7.7862	7.3667	6.9819	6.6282
15	13.865	12.849	11.938	11.118	10.380	9.7122	9.1079	8.5595	8.0607	7.6061	7.1909	6.8109
16	14.718	13.578	12.561	11.652	10.838	10.106	9.4466	8.8514	8.3126	7.8237	7.3792	6.9740
17	15.562	14.292	13.166	12.166	11.274	10.477	9.7632	9.1216	8.5436	8.0216	7.5488	7.1196
18	16.398	14.992	13.754	12.659	11.690	10.828	10.059	9.3719	8.7556	8.2014	7.7016	7.2497
19	17.226	15.678	14.324	13.134	12.085	11.158	10.336	9.6036	8.9501	8.3649	7.8393	7.3658
20	18.046	16.351	14.877	13.590	12.462	11.470	10.594	9.8181	9.1285	8.5136	7.9633	7.4694
21	18.857	17.011	15.415	14.029	12.821	11.764	10.836	10.017	9.2922	8.6487	8.0751	7.5620
22	19.660	17.658	15.937	14.451	13.163	12.042	11.061	10.201	9.4424	8.7715	8.1757	7.6446
23	20.456	18.292	16.444	14.857	13.489	12.303	11.272	10.371	9.5802	8.8832	8.2664	7.7184
24	21.243	18.914	16.936	15.247	13.799	12.550	11.469	10.529	9.7066	8.9847	8.3481	7.7843
25	22.023	19.523	17.413	15.622	14.094	12.783	11.654	10.675	9.8226	9.0770	8.4217	7.8431
26	22.795	20.121	17.877	15.983	14.375	13.003	11.826	10.810	9.9290	9.1609	8.4881	7.8957
27	23.560	20.707	18.327	16.330	14.643	13.211	11.987	10.935	10.027	9.2372	8.5478	7.9426
28	24.316	21.281	18.764	16.663	14.898	13.406	12.137	11.051	10.116	9.3066	8.6016	7.9844
29	25.066	21.844	19.188	16.984	15.141	13.591	12.278	11.158	10.198	9.3696	8.6501	8.0218
30	25.808	22.396	19.600	17.292	15.372	13.765	12.408	11.258	10.274	9.4269	8.6938	8.0552
35	29.409	24.999	21.487	18.665	16.374	14.498	12.948	11.655	10.567	9.6442	8.8552	8.1755
40	32.835	27.355	23.115	19.793	17.159	15.046	13.332	11.925	10.757	9.7791	8.9511	8.2438
45	36.095	29.490	24.519	20.720	17.774	15.456	13.606	12.108	10.881	9.8628	9.0079	8.2825
50	39.196	31.424	25.730	21.482	18.256	15.762	13.801	12.233	10.962	9.9148	9.0417	8.3045

EXHIBIT 11A.4 (Concluded)

Period n	13%	14%	15%	16%	17%	18%	19%	20%	25%	30%	35%	40%	50%
1	0.8850	0.8772	0.8696	0.8621	0.8547	0.8475	0.8403	0.8333	0.8000	0.7692	0.7407	0.7143	0.6667
2	1.6681	1.6467	1.6257	1.6052	1.5852	1.5656	1.5465	1.5278	1.4400	1.3609	1.2894	1.2245	1.1111
3	2.3612	2.3216	2.2832	2.2459	2.2096	2.1743	2.1399	2.1065	1.9520	1.8161	1.6959	1.5889	1.4074
4	2.9745	2.9137	2.8550	2.7982	2.7432	2.6901	2.6386	2.5887	2.3616	2.1662	1.9969	1.8492	1.6049
5	3.5172	3.4331	3.3522	3.2743	3.1993	3.1272	3.0576	2.9906	2.6893	2.4356	2.2200	2.0352	1.7366
6	3.9975	3.8887	3.7845	3.6847	3.5892	3.4976	3.4098	3.3255	2.9514	2.6427	2.3852	2.1880	1.8244
7	4.4226	4.2883	4.1604	4.0386	3.9224	3.8115	3.7057	3.6046	3.1611	2.8021	2.5075	2.2628	1.8829
8	4.7988	4.6389	4.4873	4.3436	4.2072	4.0776	3.9544	3.8372	3.3289	2.9247	2.5982	2.3306	1.9220
9	5.1317	4.9464	4.7716	4.6065	4.4506	4.3030	4.1633	4.0310	3.4631	3.0190	2.6653	2.3790	1.9480
10	5.4262	5.2161	5.0188	4.8332	4.6585	4.4941	4.3389	4.1925	3.5705	3.0915	2.7150	2.4136	1.9653
11	5.6869	5.4527	5.2337	5.0286	4.8364	4.6560	4.4865	4.3271	3.6564	3.1473	2.7519	2.4383	1.9769
12	5.9176	5.6603	5.4206	5.1971	4.9884	4.7932	4.6105	4.4392	3.7251	3.1903	2.7792	2.4559	1.9846
13	6.1218	5.8424	5.5831	5.3423	5.1183	4.9095	4.7147	4.5327	3.7801	3.2233	2.7994	2.4685	1.9897
14	6.3025	6.0021	5.7245	5.4675	5.2293	5.0081	4.8023	4.6106	3.8241	3.2487	2.8144	2.4775	1.9931
15	6.4624	6.1422	5.8474	5.5755	5.3242	5.0916	4.8759	4.6755	3.8593	3.2682	2.8255	2.4839	1.9954
16	6.6039	6.2651	5.9542	5.6685	5.4053	5.1624	4.9377	4.7296	3.8874	3.2832	2.8337	2.4885	1.9970
17	6.7291	6.3729	6.0472	5.7487	5.4746	5.2223	4.9897	4.7746	3.9099	3.2948	2.8398	2.4918	1.9980
18	6.8399	6.4674	6.1280	5.8178	5.5339	5.2732	5.0333	4.8122	3.9279	3.3037	2.8443	2.4941	1.9986
19	6.9380	6.5504	6.1982	5.8775	5.5845	5.3162	5.0700	4.8435	3.9424	3.3105	2.8476	2.4958	1.9991
20	7.0248	6.6231	6.2593	5.9288	5.6278	5.3527	5.1009	4.8696	3.9539	3.3158	2.8501	2.4970	1.9994
21	7.1016	6.6870	6.3125	5.9731	5.6648	5.3837	5.1268	4.8913	3.9631	3.3198	2.8519	2.4979	1.9996
22	7.1695	6.7429	6.3587	6.0113	5.6964	5.4099	5.1486	4.9094	3.9705	3.3230	2.8533	2.4985	1.9997
23	7.2297	6.7921	6.3988	6.0442	5.7234	5.4321	5.1668	4.9245	3.9764	3.3254	2.8543	2.2989	1.9998
24	7.2829	6.8351	6.4338	6.0726	5.7465	5.4509	5.1822	4.9371	3.9811	3.3272	2.8550	2.4992	1.9999
25	7.3300	6.8729	6.4641	6.0971	5.7662	5.4669	5.1951	4.9476	3.9849	3.3286	2.8556	2.4994	1.9999
26	7.3717	6.9061	6.4906	6.1182	5.7831	5.4804	5.2060	4.9563	3.9879	3.3297	2.8560	2.4996	1.9999
27	7.4086	6.9352	6.5135	6.1364	5.7975	5.4919	5.2151	4.9636	3.9903	3.3305	2.8563	2.4997	2.0000
28	7.4412	6.9607	6.5335	6.1520	5.8099	5.5016	5.2228	4.9697	3.9923	3.3312	2.8565	2.4998	2.0000
29	7.4701	6.9830	6.5509	6.1656	5.8204	5.5098	5.2292	4.9747	3.9938	3.3317	2.8567	2.4999	2.0000
30	7.4957	7.0027	6.5660	6.1772	5.8294	5.5168	5.2347	4.9789	3.9950	3.3321	2.8568	2.4999	2.0000
35	7.5856	7.0700	6.6166	6.2153	5.8582	5.5386	5.2512	4.9915	3.9984	3.3330	2.8571	2.5000	2.0000
40	7.6344	7.1050	6.6418	6.2335	5.8713	5.5482	5.2582	4.9966	3.9995	3.3332	2.8571	2.5000	2.0000
45	7.6609	7.1232	6.6543	6.2421	5.8773	5.5523	5.2611	4.9986	3.9998	3.3333	2.8571	2.5000	2.0000
50	7.6752	7.1327	6.6605	6.2463	5.8801	5.5541	5.2623	4.9995	3.9999	3.3333	2.8571	2.5000	2.0000

CHAPTER 12

Mortgage Markets

ortgages are securities used to finance real estate purchases; they are originated by various financial institutions, such as savings institutions and mortgage companies. A secondary mortgage market accommodates originators of mortgages that desire to sell their mortgages prior to maturity. Both the origination process and the secondary market activities for mortgages have become much more complex in recent years. The mortgage markets serve individuals or firms that need long-term funds to purchase real estate. They also serve financial institutions that wish to serve as creditors by lending long-term funds for real estate purchases.

The specific objectives of this chapter are to:

■ describe the characteristics of residential mortgages,

■ describe the common types of creative mortgage financing, and

■ explain how mortgage-backed securities are used.

Mortgages: Background

A mortgage is a form of debt that finances investment in property. The debt is secured by the property, so if the property owner does not meet payment obligations, the creditor can seize the property. Financial institutions such as savings institutions and mortgage companies serve as intermediaries by originating mortgages. They accept mortgage applications and assess the creditworthiness of the applicants. They focus on an applicant's monthly income relative to the mortgage payment, but also consider the potential down payment on the property, as well as the applicant's prevailing assets and liabilities. The mortgage represents the difference between the down payment and the value to be paid for the property. The mortgage contract specifies the mortgage rate, the maturity, and the collateral that is backing the loan. The originator charges an origination fee for this process. In addition, if it uses its own funds to finance the property, it will earn profit from the difference between the mortgage rate that it charges and the rate that it paid to obtain the funds.

Mortgage Types

Mortgages are distinguished by type of property. Exhibit 12.1 shows the mortgage debt outstanding over time by type of property. The majority of mortgage debt outstanding is on one- to four-family properties, with commercial properties a distant second. The level

EXHIBIT 12.1   Volume of Mortgage Debt by Type of Property

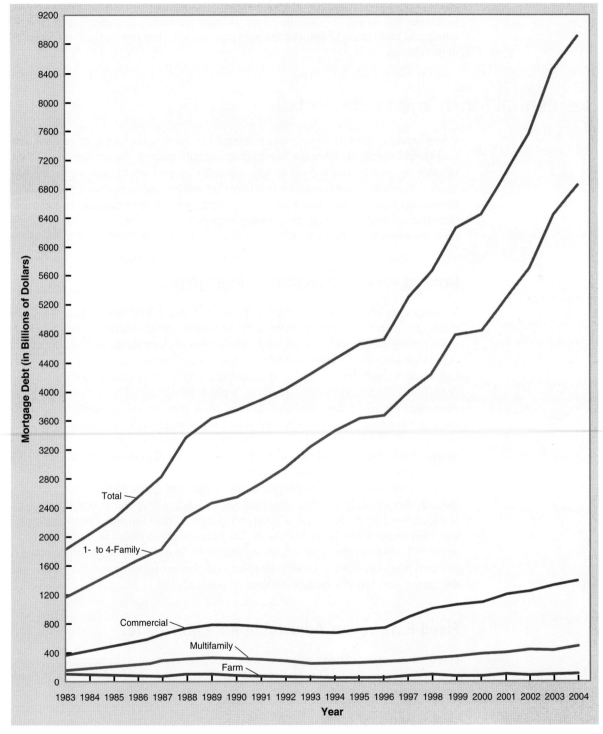

Source: *Federal Reserve Bulletin.*

of mortgage debt has generally risen over time, although not at a constant rate. During recessions, mortgage debt rises at a slower rate because families tend to avoid housing purchases that would increase their debt. Because residential mortgages (one- to four-family and multifamily) dominate the mortgage market, they receive the most attention in this chapter.

Residential Mortgage Characteristics

When financial institutions originate residential mortgages, the mortgage contract created should specify whether the mortgage is federally insured, the amount of the loan, whether the interest rate is fixed or adjustable, the interest rate to be charged, the maturity, and other special provisions that may vary among contracts. Over time, financial institutions have become more aware of the specific borrowing preferences of those who purchase residential housing. Each family requesting a mortgage may have a different preference for the loan structure.

Insured versus Conventional Mortgages

Mortgages are often classified as federally insured or conventional. Federally insured mortgages guarantee loan repayment to the lending financial institution, thereby covering it against the possibility of default by the borrower. An insurance fee of 0.5 percent of the loan amount is applied to cover the cost of insuring the mortgage. The guarantor can be either the Federal Housing Administration (FHA) or the Veterans Administration (VA). To qualify for FHA and VA mortgage loans from a financial institution, borrowers must meet various requirements specified by those government agencies. In addition, the maximum mortgage amount is limited by law (although the limit varies among states to account for differences in the cost of housing). The volume of FHA loans has consistently exceeded that of VA loans since 1960. Both types of mortgages have become increasingly popular over the past 30 years.

Financial institutions also provide conventional mortgages. Although not federally insured, they can be privately insured so that the lending financial institutions can still avoid exposure to credit risk. The insurance premium paid for such private insurance will likely be passed on to the borrowers. They can choose to incur the credit risk themselves and avoid the insurance fee. Most participants in the secondary mortgage market will purchase only those conventional mortgages that are privately insured (unless the mortgage's loan-to-value ratio is less than 80 percent).

Fixed-Rate versus Adjustable-Rate Mortgages

One of the most important provisions in the mortgage contract is the interest rate. It can be specified as a fixed rate or can allow for periodic rate adjustments over time. A **fixed-rate mortgage** locks in the borrower's interest rate over the life of the mortgage. Thus, the periodic interest payment received by the lending financial institution is constant, regardless of how market interest rates change over time. A financial institution that holds fixed-rate mortgages in its asset portfolio is exposed to interest rate risk because it commonly uses funds obtained from short-term customer deposits to make long-term mortgage loans. If interest rates increase over time, the financial institution's cost of obtaining funds (from deposits) will increase. The return on its fixed-rate mortgage loans

http://
http://www.bloomberg.com/
markets/rates/index.html
Provides quotes on
mortgage rates.

will be unaffected, however, causing its profit margin to decrease.

Borrowers with fixed-rate mortgages do not suffer from the effects of rising interest rates, but they also fail to benefit from declining rates. Although they can attempt to refinance (obtain a new mortgage to replace the existing mortgage) at the lower prevailing market interest rate, they will incur transaction costs such as closing costs and an origination fee.

In contrast to a fixed-rate mortgage, an **adjustable-rate mortgage (ARM)** allows the mortgage interest rate to adjust to market conditions. Its contract will specify a precise formula for this adjustment. The formula and the frequency of adjustment can vary among mortgage contracts. A common ARM uses a one-year adjustment, with the interest rate tied to the average Treasury bill rate over the previous year (for example, the average T-bill rate plus 2 percent may be specified).

Some ARMs now contain an option clause that allows mortgage holders to switch to a fixed rate within a specified period, such as one to five years after the mortgage is originated (the specific provisions vary).

A comparison of fixed and adjustable mortgage rates on new 30-year mortgages is provided in Exhibit 12.2. The fixed rate is typically higher than the adjustable rate at any given point in time when a mortgage is originated. Home buyers attempt to assess future interest rate movements at the time a mortgage is originated. If they expect that interest rates will remain somewhat stable or decline during the period they will own

EXHIBIT 12.2 Comparison of Fixed and Adjustable Mortgage Rates over Time

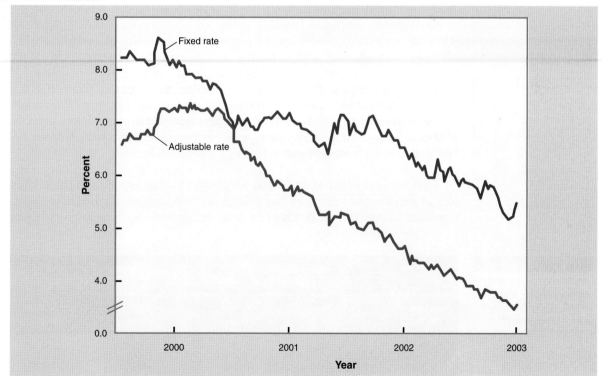

Note: The data, which are weekly and extend through July 9, 2003, are contract rates on 30-year mortgages.
Source: Federal Home Loan Mortgage Corporation, and Federal Reserve.

the property, they will prefer an ARM. Conversely, if they expect that interest rates will increase substantially over time, they will prefer a fixed-rate mortgage.

Financial Institution's Perspective Because the interest rate of an ARM moves with prevailing interest rates, financial institutions can stabilize their profit margin. If their cost of funds rises, so does their return on mortgage loans. For this reason, ARMs have become very popular over time.

Most ARMs specify a maximum allowable fluctuation in the mortgage rate per year and over the mortgage life, regardless of what happens to market interest rates. These so-called caps are commonly 2 percent per year and 5 percent for the mortgage lifetime. To the extent that market interest rates move outside these boundaries, the financial institution's profit margin on ARMs could be affected by interest rate fluctuations. Nevertheless, this interest rate risk is significantly less than that of fixed-rate mortgages.

Although an ARM reduces the uncertainty about the financial institution's profit margin, it creates uncertainty for the borrower, whose future mortgage payments will depend on future interest rates. Because some home purchasers prefer fixed-rate mortgages, lending institutions continue to offer them but, as mentioned, tend to charge a higher rate (at the time of origination) than the initial rate charged on ARMs.

Mortgage Maturities

During the 1970s, mortgages typically were originated with a 30-year maturity. Recently, however, the 15-year mortgage has become very popular because of the potential savings in total interest expenses. Exhibit 12.3 compares the payments for 15- and 30-year mortgages based on various mortgage loan amounts and an 8 percent rate.

ILLUSTRATION A 30-year $100,000 mortgage at 8 percent requires monthly payments (excluding taxes and insurance) of $733.76. The same mortgage for 15 years would require monthly payments of $955.65, for an approximate total of $172,017 versus $264,155 for the 30-year mortgage. Total payments are lower on mortgages with shorter lives due to the more rapid amortization and consequent lower cumulative interest. Nevertheless, the higher monthly payments on shorter mortgages represent an opportunity cost, as the additional funds could have been put to some other use. Many borrowers, however, believe that this disadvantage is outweighed by the favorable features.

From the perspective of the lending financial institution, interest rate risk is lower on a 15-year fixed-rate mortgage than on a 30-year fixed-rate mortgage because the former exists for only half the period of the latter. Accordingly, financial institutions gen-

EXHIBIT 12.3

Comparison of Payments Necessary for 15- and 30-Year Mortgages (Based on an Interest Rate of 8 Percent)

| Amount of Mortgage | Approximate Monthly Payment for a: | | Approximate Total Payments for a: | |
	15-Year Mortgage	30-Year Mortgage	15-Year Mortgage	30-Year Mortgage
$ 50,000	$ 478	$ 367	$ 86,009	$132,077
75,000	717	550	129,013	198,116
100,000	956	734	172,017	264,155
200,000	1,911	1,467	344,035	528,310

erally charge a lower interest rate on 15-year loans than on 30-year loans, other provisions being equal.

As an alternative to a mortgage with a 15- or 30-year maturity, some borowers choose a **balloon-payment mortgage,** which requires interest payments for a three- to five-year period. At the end of this period, the borrower must pay the full amount of the principal (the balloon payment). Because no principal payments are made until maturity, the monthly payments are lower. Realistically, most borrowers have not saved enough funds to pay off the mortgage in three to five years, so the balloon payment in effect forces them to request a new mortgage. Therefore, they are subject to the risk that mortgage rates will be higher at the time they refinance the mortgage.

Amortizing Mortgages Given the maturity and interest rate on a mortgage, an **amortization schedule** can be developed to show the monthly payments broken down into principal and interest. During the early years of a mortgage, most of the payment reflects interest. Over time, as some of the principal is paid off, the interest proportion decreases.

The lending institution that holds a fixed-rate mortgage will receive equal periodic payments over a specified period of time. The amount depends on the principal amount of the mortgage, the interest rate, and the maturity. If insurance and taxes are included in the mortgage payment, then they, too, influence the amount.

ILLUSTRATION

Consider a 30-year (360-month) $100,000 mortgage at an annual interest rate of 8 percent. To focus on the mortgage principal and interest payments, insurance and taxes are not included in this example. A breakdown of the monthly payments into principal versus interest is shown in Exhibit 12.4. In the first month, the interest payment is $666.67, while the principal payment is only $67.10. Note that a larger proportion of interest is paid in the earlier years and a larger portion of principal in the later years. Computer programs are widely available to determine the amortization schedule for any type of mortgage.

EXHIBIT 12.4

Example of Amortization Schedule for Selected Years (Based on a 30-Year $100,000 Mortgage at 8 Percent)

Payment Number	Payment of Interest	Payment of Principal	Total Payment	Remaining Loan Balance
1	$666.66	$ 67.10	$733.76	$99,932.90
2	666.21	67.55	733.76	99,865.35
⋮	⋮	⋮	⋮	⋮
100	604.22	129.54	733.76	90,504.68
101	603.36	130.40	733.76	90,374.28
⋮	⋮	⋮	⋮	⋮
200	482.01	251.75	733.76	72,051.18
201	480.34	253.42	733.76	71,797.76
⋮	⋮	⋮	⋮	⋮
300	244.52	489.24	733.76	36,188.12
301	241.25	492.51	733.76	35,695.61
⋮	⋮	⋮	⋮	⋮
359	9.68	724.08	733.76	728.91
360	4.85	728.91	733.76	0

http://www.bloomberg.com
Click on "Mortgage Calculator." Calculates monthly mortgage payments based on the loan amount, the maturity, and the interest rate.

Creative Mortgage Financing

Various methods of creative financing have been developed to make housing more affordable, including

■ Graduated-payment mortgages
■ Growing-equity mortgages
■ Second mortgages
■ Shared-appreciation mortgages

Although these are the most common methods, several other innovative techniques exist. Moreover, as the needs and preferences of borrowers change over time, additional methods of creative financing are likely to emerge.

Graduated-Payment Mortgage (GPM)

A **graduated-payment mortgage (GPM)** allows the borrower to initially make small payments on the mortgage; the payments increase on a graduated basis over the first 5 to 10 years and then level off. GPMs are tailored for families who anticipate higher income and thus the ability to make larger monthly mortgage payments as time passes. In a sense, they are delaying part of their mortgage payment.

Growing-Equity Mortgage

A **growing-equity mortgage** is similar to a GPM in that the monthly payments are initially low and increase over time. Unlike the GPM, however, the payments never level off but continue to increase (typically by about 4 percent per year) throughout the life of the loan. With such an accelerated payment schedule, the entire mortgage may be paid off in 15 years or less.

Second Mortgage

A second mortgage can be used in conjunction with the primary or first mortgage. Some financial institutions may limit the amount of the first mortgage based on the borrower's income. Other financial institutions may then offer a second mortgage, with a maturity shorter than on the first mortgage. In addition, the interest rate on the second mortgage is higher because its priority claim against the property in the event of default is behind that of the first mortgage. The higher interest rate reflects greater compensation as a result of the higher risk incurred by the provider of the second mortgage.

Sellers of homes sometimes offer buyers a second mortgage. This is especially common if the old mortgage is assumable and the selling price of the home is much higher than the remaining balance on the first mortgage. By offering a second mortgage, the seller can make the house more affordable and therefore more marketable. The seller and the buyer negotiate specific interest rate and maturity terms.

Shared-Appreciation Mortgage

A **shared-appreciation mortgage** allows a home purchaser to obtain a mortgage at a below-market interest rate. In return, the lender providing the attractive loan rate will

share in the price appreciation of the home. The precise percentage of appreciation allocated to the lender is negotiated at the origination of the mortgage.

Institutional Use of Mortgage Markets

Most institutional participation can be broadly classified as either originating and servicing a mortgage (accepting and processing payments) or financing a mortgage. Historically, financial institutions would originate a mortgage, service it, and finance it until it was paid off. The development of an active secondary market has changed the mortgage business in three ways. First, it allows financial institutions that originate mortgages to sell them. Second, the secondary market allows some institutional investors to invest in mortgages even if they have no desire to originate or service them. Third, it allows institutional investors in mortgages to sell them whenever they wish to use their funds for other purposes.

Financial Institutions That Originate Mortgages

Mortgage companies originate mortgages and then quickly sell them. The companies do not maintain large mortgage portfolios. The majority of their earnings are generated from origination and servicing fees. Because mortgage companies typically do not finance mortgages themselves, they are not as exposed to interest rate risk as other financial institutions.

Commercial banks and savings institutions are the primary originators of mortgages. Credit unions also originate mortgages for their members and may finance the mortgages they originate.

Secondary Market Participation

When financial institutions cannot provide the financing for all the mortgages that they originate, they sell the mortgages in the secondary market. The buyers of mortgages in the secondary mortgage market include various savings institutions, pension funds, life insurance companies and mutual funds that want to invest in mortgages. If these financial institutions decide to sell the mortgages they invested in prior to maturity, they can sell them in the same secondary market.

ILLUSTRATION USA Savings and Loan originates mortgages and then sells them in the secondary market to Safety Insurance Company. The borrowers continue to send their monthly mortgage payments to USA Savings and Loan, even though USA no longer holds claim to the mortgages. USA processes the payments and charges the new holder of the mortgages (Safety Insurance Company) a fee for the processing. It deducts this fee from the mortgage payments received and sends the remainder to the holder of the mortgages. Two years later, Safety Insurance Company sells the mortgages it is holding in the secondary market.

Roles of Fannie Mae, Ginnie Mae, and Freddie Mac The Federal National Mortgage Association (Fannie Mae), the Government National Mortgage Association (Ginnie Mae), and the Federal Home Loan Mortgage Association (Freddie Mac) have contributed substantially to the growth of the secondary market for mortgages. Fannie Mae was created by the government in 1938 to develop a more liquid secondary market for mortgages. It

issues debt securities and uses the proceeds to purchase mortgages in the secondary mortgage market. It has more than $800 billion of securities outstanding.

Since 1968 Fannie Mae has been a private company. Although it receives no government funding, it is exempt from state income tax and has credit lines from the U.S. Treasury. Thus, it is commonly perceived to be backed by the government, and this enables Fannie Mae to obtain funds by issuing securities at a low cost (at close to the risk-free rate).

Ginnie Mae was created in 1968 as a corporation that is wholly owned by the federal government. It supplies funds to low- and moderate-income homeowners indirectly by facilitating the flow of funds into the secondary mortgage market. It has more than $600 billion of securities outstanding that it has issued to obtain the funds that it invests in mortgages. Freddie Mac was chartered as a corporation by the federal government in 1970 to ensure that sufficient funds flow into the mortgage market. It went public in 1989. Like Fannie Mae, Freddie Mac is exempt from state income tax and has lines of credit with the Treasury. It now has more than $600 billion in debt securities outstanding, which were issued primarily so that it could invest the proceeds in mortgages.

As a result of Fannie Mae, Ginnie Mae, and Freddie Mac, the secondary mortgage market is very liquid. In addition, there is more funding in the mortgage market than there would be without them. Consequently, mortgage rates are more competitive, and housing is more affordable for some homeowners.

The Freddie Mac Accounting Scandal After 2000, Freddie Mac expanded its role by investing not only in mortgages, but also in corporate bonds, strip malls, and hotels. As a result, its overall business became more risky than the type of business for which it was chartered. It then began to use irregular accounting techniques to stabilize its earnings and hide its risk over time. In 2003, the accounting irregularities were publicized, and Freddie Mac's risk became more transparent. This scandal shook the mortgage markets, as market participants were shocked by the lack of oversight over such a large corporation that enjoyed special benefits from the federal government. Freddie Mac was required to restate its earnings over the 2000–2002 period, and its CEO and other senior managers were replaced.

Securitization The secondary market for mortgages has been enhanced as a result of **securitization,** or the pooling and repackaging of loans into securities. The securities are then sold to investors, who become the owners of the loans represented by those securities. This process allows for the sale of smaller mortgage loans that could not easily be sold in the secondary market on an individual basis. When several small mortgage loans are packaged together, they become more attractive to the large institutional investors that focus on large transactions. Securitization removes the loans from the balance sheet of the financial institution that provided them. Consequently, securitization can reduce a financial institution's exposure to credit (default) risk or interest rate risk.

Institutional Investors in Mortgages

Exhibit 12.5 provides a breakdown of financial institutions that invest in mortgages. The financial institutions identified here hold in aggregate about 37 percent of the entire dollar amount of all mortgages. Ginnie Mae and Freddie Mac hold a large proportion of the mortgages not held by the financial institutions identified in the exhibit.

Exhibit 12.6 classifies the mortgages of financial institutions into four borrower categories. Savings institutions are very active in the one- to four-family and multifamily

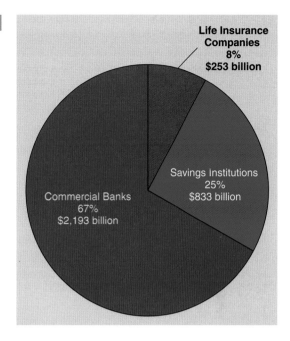

EXHIBIT 12.5

Mortgages by Holder
Source: Federal Reserve, 2004.

markets. They also participate in commercial mortgages but to a lesser degree. They have continually increased their participation in commercial mortgages in recent years, however. Commercial banks dominate the commercial mortgage market, with life insurance companies behind them. Commercial banks also heavily participate in residential mortgages.

Institutional Players in Mortgage Activities

Given the distinct activities by mortgage market participants, financial institutions must select among them. First, an institution can simply play the role of a mortgage originator, originating mortgages for a fee and then selling them in the secondary market and also selling the servicing rights. Second, it can sell the mortgages but maintain the servicing. Third, it can focus on servicing mortgages originated by other financial institutions. Fourth, it can simply focus on investing in mortgages. Fifth, it can invest in mortgages that it is allowed to service.

A financial institution's choice of mortgage activities depends on whether it prefers to invest funds in mortgages for long periods of time or to generate fee income without

EXHIBIT 12.6

Mortgage Holdings among Financial Institutions (in Billions of Dollars)

	Mortgages Allocated to:				
	One- to Four-Family	Multi-family	Commercial	Farm	Total
Savings institutions	$ 676	$ 72	$ 84	$ 1	$ 833
Commercial banks	1,320	100	732	40	2,192
Life insurance companies	5	38	197	13	253

Source: Federal Reserve, 2004.

EXHIBIT 12.7   Institutional Use of Mortgage Markets

Type of Financial Institution	Participation in Mortgage Markets
Commercial banks and savings institutions	• Originate and service commercial and residential mortgages and maintain mortgages within their investment portfolios. • Issue mortgage-backed securities to finance some of their mortgage holdings. • Purchase mortgage-based securities.
Credit unions and finance companies	• Originate mortgages and maintain mortgages within their investment portfolios.
Mortgage companies	• Originate mortgages and sell them in the secondary market.
Mutual funds	• May sell shares and use the proceeds to construct portfolios of mortgage pass-through securities.
Brokerage firms	• Serve as financial intermediaries between sellers and buyers of mortgages in the secondary market.
Investment banking firms	• Offer instruments to help institutional investors in mortgages hedge against interest rate risk.
Insurance companies	• Commonly purchase mortgages in the secondary market.

tying up funds. The origination role and the servicing role can generate fee income and do not tie up funds. Conversely, investing in mortgages requires a large investment, which is subject to risk, but can also provide a reasonable return.

Many financial institutions prefer to participate in all three activities but to different degrees. For example, an institution may have a fixed amount of funds that it plans to invest in mortgages. When it originates a larger amount of mortgages than it wishes to finance, it sells off the residual. It may also relinquish the servicing of the mortgages that are sold.

The institutional use of mortgage markets is summarized in Exhibit 12.7. Some institutional participation involves neither origination nor financing of mortgages. Brokerage firms participate by matching up sellers and buyers of mortgages in the secondary market. Investment banking firms participate by helping institutional investors hedge their mortgage holdings against interest rate risk by using interest rate swaps, which provide a stream of variable-rate payments in exchange for fixed-rate payments.

Valuing Mortgage Pools

Since mortgages are commonly sold in the secondary market, they are continually valued by institutional investors. The market price (P_M) of mortgages should equal the present value of their future cash flows:

USING THE WALL STREET JOURNAL

Mortgage Market Information

The Wall Street Journal provides the following information related to this chapter on a daily basis:

■ Price quotations on mortgage-based securities and on collateralized mortgage obligations.

■ Reports on recent performance and new issuances of mortgage-backed securities, contained in the "Credit Markets" section.

$$P_M = \sum_{t=1}^{n} \frac{C + \text{Prin}}{(1 + k)^t}$$

where C represents the interest payment (similar to a coupon payment on bonds), Prin represents the principal payment made each period, and k represents the required rate of return by investors. Similar to bonds, the market value of a mortgage is the present value of the future cash flows to be received by the investor. Unlike bonds, the periodic cash flows commonly include a payment of principal along with an interest payment.

The required rate of return on a mortgage is primarily determined by the existing risk-free rate for the same maturity. However, other factors such as credit risk and the lack of liquidity will cause the required return on many mortgages to exceed the risk-free rate.

ILLUSTRATION Consider the pricing of a mortgage with 20 years remaining until maturity. Assume that the 20-year risk-free rate is currently 9 percent, which is determined by assessing the yield offered to investors who purchase 20-year Treasury bonds. The required return on 20-year mortgages must be higher than the 20-year risk-free rate to compensate investors for credit risk and the lack of liquidity. Mortgages that have very low credit risk and a high degree of liquidity may require a premium of about 1 or 2 percentage points above the risk-free rate. Thus, they would have a required return of 10 or 11 percent. Mortgages that have more credit risk or less liquidity will require a higher premium beyond the prevailing risk-free rate.

The difference between the 30-year mortgage rate and the 30-year Treasury bond rate is primarily attributed to credit risk and therefore tends to increase during periods when the economy is weak (such as the 2002 recession). The trend in the required rate of return on 30-year fixed-rate mortgages is shown in Exhibit 12.8. The 30-year Treasury bond rate is also shown to illustrate that the mortgage rate is primarily driven by movements in the long-term risk-free rate.

Since the required rate of return on a fixed-rate mortgage is primarily driven by the prevailing risk-free rate (R_f) and the risk premium (RP), the change in the value (and therefore in the market price) of a mortgage (P_M) can be modeled as

$$\Delta P_M = f(\underset{-}{\Delta R_f}, \underset{-}{\Delta RP})$$

An increase in either the risk-free rate or the risk premium on a fixed-rate mortgage results in a higher required rate of return when investing in the mortgage and therefore causes the mortgage price to decrease.

The factors that are commonly monitored by mortgage market participants because they affect the risk-free rate or risk premium, and therefore affect mortgage prices, are identified next.

Factors That Affect the Risk-Free Interest Rate

The risk-free rate of interest is driven by inflationary expectations (INF), economic growth (ECON), the money supply (MS), and the budget deficit (DEF):

$$\Delta k = f(\underset{+}{\Delta \text{INF}}, \underset{+}{\Delta \text{ECON}}, \underset{-}{\Delta \text{MS}}, \underset{+}{\Delta \text{DEF}})$$

EXHIBIT 12.8   Comparison of Mortgage Rates to Treasury Rates over Time

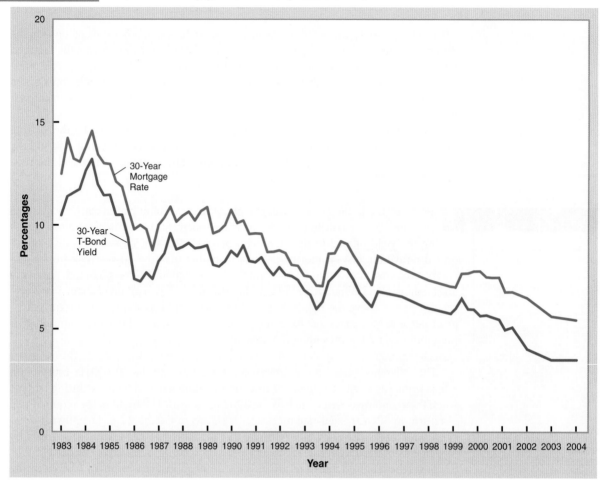

Inflationary Expectations An expectation of higher inflation puts upward pressure on interest rates and therefore on the required return on mortgages. Conversely, an expectation of lower inflation puts downward pressure on interest rates and therefore on the required rate of return on mortgages.

Economic Growth An increase in economic growth can cause an increase in the risk-free interest rate and therefore an increase in the required rate of return on mortgages and a decline in mortgage prices. Conversely, a decrease in economic growth can cause a decrease in the risk-free interest rate and therefore a decrease in the required rate of return on mortgages and an increase in mortgage prices.

Money Supply Growth A relatively high level of money supply growth tends to place downward pressure on the risk-free interest rate (assuming that it does not increase inflation expectations) and therefore places downward pressure on the required rate of return on mortgages and upward pressure on mortgage prices. A relatively low level of money supply growth tends to place upward pressure on the risk-free interest rate and therefore puts upward pressure on the required rate of return on mortgages; the result is lower mortgage prices.

Budget Deficit An increase or decrease in the annual budget deficit changes the federal government's demand for funds and can affect the risk-free interest rate. In 1998, 1999, and 2000, the U.S. government had a budget surplus, which reduced the government's overall demand for loanable funds. This placed downward pressure on the risk-free rate and on the required rate of return on mortgages and increased the price of mortgages.

Factors That Affect the Risk Premium

The average risk premium on all mortgages can change in response to a change in economic growth (ECON):

$$\Delta RP = f(\underset{-}{\Delta \text{ECON}})$$

Strong economic growth tends to improve income or cash flows and reduce the probability that the issuer of a mortgage will default on its debt payments. Conversely, weak economic growth may reduce income or cash flows and therefore increase the probability of default, especially for issuers that are very sensitive to economic conditions.

Summary of Factors Affecting Mortgage Prices

When considering the factors that affect the risk-free rate and the default risk premium, the price movements in a mortgage can be modeled as

$$\Delta P_M = f(\underset{-}{\Delta R_f}, \underset{-}{\Delta RP})$$

or

$$\Delta P_M = f(\underset{-}{\Delta \text{INF}}, \underset{?}{\Delta \text{ECON}}, \underset{+}{\Delta \text{MS}}, \underset{-}{\Delta \text{DEF}})$$

The relationships suggested here assume that other factors are held constant. In reality, other factors are changing as well, which makes it difficult to disentangle the precise impact of each factor on mortgage prices. The effect of economic growth is uncertain because a high level of economic growth can adversely affect mortgage prices by increasing the risk-free rate, but can also favorably affect mortgage prices by lowering the default risk premium.

Exhibit 12.9 summarizes the underlying forces that can affect the long-term risk-free interest rate and the default risk premium and therefore cause the price of a fixed-rate mortgage to change over time. This exhibit provides a broad overview of the factors that must be monitored by mortgage market participants who are attempting to anticipate mortgage prices. International economic conditions can indirectly affect mortgage prices through their effect on the long-term risk-free interest rate.

Impact of the September 11 Attack on Mortgage Rates The terrorist attack on the United States on September 11, 2001, aroused concern that the U.S. economy would weaken further. Short-term interest rates declined by a full percentage point within one month. Long-term interest rates, however, declined only slightly. Consequently, the 30-year conventional mortgage declined by only about .25 percentage point over the next month. Since short-term interest rates declined substantially, many financial institutions

EXHIBIT 12.9

Framework for Explaining
Changes in Mortgage Prices
over Time

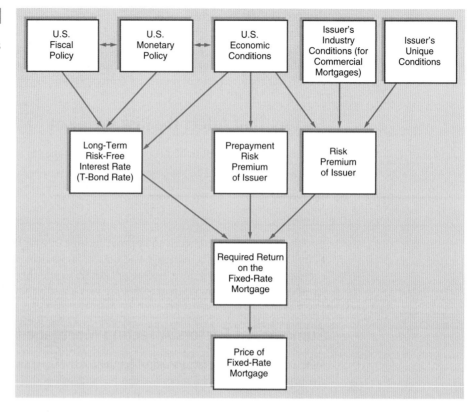

reduced the initial rate they offered on a floating-rate mortgage to a greater degree than
the rate they offered on a fixed-rate mortgage.

Indicators of Changes in Mortgage Prices

Mortgage market participants closely monitor economic indicators that may signal future changes in the strength of the economy, which signal changes in the risk-free interest rate and in the required return from investing in mortgages. For example, they
monitor indicators of inflation, such as the consumer price index and the producer price
index. In general, an unexpected increase in these indexes tends to create expectations
of higher interest rates and places downward pressure on fixed-rate mortgage prices. In
addition, announcements about the government deficit or the amount of money that the
Treasury hopes to borrow in a Treasury bond auction are closely monitored.

Mortgage market participants also closely monitor indicators of economic growth in
the real estate sector, including new sales of single-family homes, construction spending, and office space. An expected increase in housing activity, and therefore in the issuance of mortgages, places downward pressure on mortgage prices.

A decline in indicators such as housing starts can signal a reduction in the issuance
of mortgages, which places downward pressure on mortgage rates and upward pressure
on mortgage prices. However, such signals reflect a weaker economy, which can increase
the default risk premium on some mortgages because the issuers may have more difficulty meeting their payment obligations. The prices of these mortgages are being pressured by opposing forces.

Risk from Mortgage Investing

Given the uncertainty of the factors that influence mortgage prices, future mortgage prices (and therefore returns) are uncertain. The uncertainty financial institutions face from investing in mortgages is due to three types of risk, as explained next.

Interest Rate Risk

Financial institutions that hold mortgages are subject to interest rate risk because the values of mortgages tend to decline in response to an increase in interest rates. Mortgages are long term but are commonly financed by some financial institutions with short-term deposits, so the investment in mortgages may create high exposure to interest rate risk. Such mortgages can also generate high returns when interest rates fall, but the potential gains are limited because borrowers tend to refinance (obtain new mortgages at the lower interest rate and prepay their mortgages) when interest rates decline.

When investors hold fixed-rate mortgages until maturity, they do not experience a loss due to a change in interest rates. However, holding fixed-rate mortgages to maturity can create an opportunity cost of what the investors might have earned if they had invested in other securities. For example, if interest rates rise consistently from the time fixed-rate mortgages are purchased until they mature, investors who hold the mortgages to maturity gave up the potential higher return that they would have earned if they had simply invested in money market securities over the same period.

Limiting Exposure to Interest Rate Risk Financial institutions can limit their exposure to interest rate risk by selling mortgages shortly after originating them. However, even institutions that use this strategy are partially exposed to interest rate risk. As a financial institution originates a pool of mortgages, it may commit to a specific fixed rate on some of the mortgages. The mortgages are stored in what is referred to as a mortgage pipeline, until there is a sufficient pool of mortgages to sell. By the time the complete pool of mortgages is originated and sold, interest rates may have risen. In this case, the value of the mortgages in the pool may have declined by the time the pool is sold.

Another way financial institutions can limit interest rate risk is by maintaining adjustable-rate residential mortgages. Alternatively, they could invest in fixed-rate mortgages that have a short time remaining until maturity. However, this conservative strategy may reduce the potential gains that could have been earned.

Prepayment Risk

Prepayment risk is the risk that a borrower may prepay the mortgage in response to a decline in interest rates. This type of risk is distinguished from interest rate risk to emphasize that even if investors in mortgages do not need to liquidate the mortgages, they are still susceptible to the risk that the mortgages they hold will be paid off. In this case, the investor receives payment to retire the mortgage and has to reinvest at the prevailing (lower) interest rates. Thus, the interest rate on the new investment will not be as high as the rate that would have been received on the retired mortgages.

Exhibit 12.10 shows mortgage refinancing activity over time. During the 1990s, mortgage refinancing activity was low. When economic growth slowed in the 2001–2002 period, however, interest rates declined, and mortgage refinancing increased substantially. As this exhibit illustrates, financial institutions that invest in fixed-rate mortgages may

EXHIBIT 12.10 Mortgage Refinancing Activity over Time

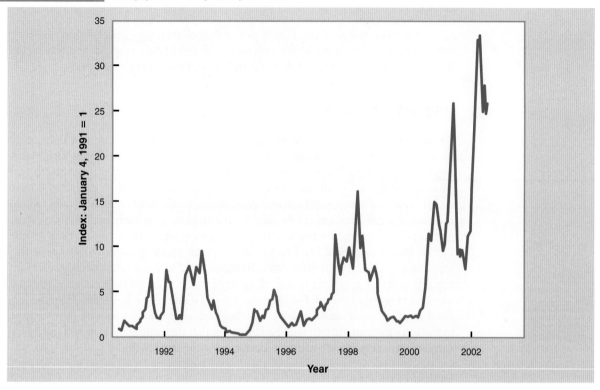

Source: Mortgage Bankers Association and Federal Reserve.

experience only limited benefits in periods when interest rates decline. Although these mortgages offer attractive yields compared to the prevailing low interest rates, they are commonly retired as a result of refinancing.

Limiting Exposure to Prepayment Risk Financial institutions can insulate against prepayment risk in the same manner that they limit exposure to interest rate risk. They can sell loans shortly after originating them or invest in adjustable-rate mortgages.

Credit Risk

The third type of risk is credit (or default) risk, which is the possibility that borrowers will make late payments or even default. Whether investors sell their mortgages prior to maturity or hold them until maturity, they are subject to credit risk. At one extreme, institutional investors and individual investors who want to avoid credit risk can purchase Treasury bonds as a long-term investment instead of mortgages and hold them to maturity. Yet, by doing so, investors would forgo a higher expected return because Treasury bonds do not need to offer a risk premium. Consequently, investors must weigh the higher potential return from investing in mortgages against the exposure to risk (that the actual return could be lower than the expected return).

The probability that a borrower will default is influenced both by economic conditions and by the following characteristics specific to the borrower:

■ *Level of equity invested by borrower.* The lower the level of equity invested by the borrower, the higher the probability that the borrower will default. One proxy for this

factor is the loan-to-value ratio, which indicates the proportion of the property's value that is financed with debt. When borrowers invest a relatively small amount of equity, the loan-to-value ratio is higher, and borrowers have less to lose in the event that they stop making their mortgage payments. For example, mortgages with a loan-to-value ratio of 90 to 95 percent when they originate default much more frequently than mortgages with a loan-to-value ratio of 80 percent. The loan-to-value ratio is an important factor not only at the time of origination but also throughout the life of the mortgage. If the market value of the property suddenly declines, both the loan-to-value ratio and the probability of default will increase.

- *Borrower's income level.* Borrowers who have a lower level of income relative to the periodic loan payments are more likely to default on their mortgages. Income determines the amount of funds that borrowers have available per month to make mortgage payments. Income levels change over time, however, so it is difficult for mortgage lenders to anticipate whether prospective borrowers will continue to earn their monthly income over the life of the mortgage, especially given the high frequency of layoffs.

- *Borrower's credit history.* Other conditions being similar, borrowers with a history of credit problems are more likely to default on their loans than those without credit problems.

Limiting Exposure to Credit Risk Financial institutions can purchase insurance to protect against the possibility of default on mortgages. However, the insurance premium paid may possibly reduce the potential return on the mortgages to the return that could be earned on Treasury bonds with the same maturity. Alternatively, a financial institution can limit its exposure to credit risk by maintaining the mortgages it originates. To the extent that its borrowers are local, the financial institution may have better insight into how they may be affected by economic conditions than if it purchased pools of mortgages from other regions of the country. It may also have more confidence in the creditworthiness of the borrowers it approved for mortgages than it would have buying a pool of mortgages originated by someone else.

http://
http://loan.yahoo.com/m/
Information about home values, mortgage rates, home equity loans, and credit reports.

Measuring Risk

Financial institutions attempt to estimate the future cash flows to be generated from their mortgage portfolios in various future periods so that they can anticipate how much cash will be available to pay off debt or depositors or to invest in other securities. This task may appear easy for a financial institution whose portfolio is composed of fixed-rate mortgages because the interest payments to be received are known. Prepayment risk and credit risk, however, create uncertainty about the future payments. Sensitivity analysis can be used to forecast the cash flows for different scenarios, such as weak economic conditions and therefore a relatively high default rate on mortgage payments. It can also be used to forecast the mortgage payments for a scenario of low interest rates (and therefore a high amount of mortgage prepayments).

ILLUSTRATION Exhibit 12.11 provides three scenarios for the mortgage prepayment level and a probability of each scenario. The results from assessing all scenarios can be consolidated to develop a probability distribution of expected cash flows one year from now. Assume that the fixed-rate mortgage portfolio has a par value of $100 million with interest payments of $9 million per year, and that none of the mortgages will mature this

EXHIBIT 12.11 Prepayment Risk Assessment of Mortgages

Scenario	Probability	Fixed Payments	% of Mortgage Portfolio Prepaid	Prepaid Mortgages	Total Payments Received
Rising interest rates	20%	$9,000,000	3%	$ 3,000,000	$12,000,000
Stable interest rates	50%	9,000,000	7%	7,000,000	16,000,000
Declining interest rates	30%	9,000,000	20%	20,000,000	29,000,000

year. The financial institution can assess the historical relationship between interest rates and the level of prepayments to estimate the percentage of the mortgage portfolio that will be prepaid for a given interest rate scenario.

Notice from the exhibit that the estimate of prepaid principal is very sensitive to the amount of prepayments. If interest rates rise, the level of prepaid principal is low, and the cash flows to be received are relatively low. If interest rates decline, however, the level of prepayments is high, and the estimate of the cash flows to be received is very high. In this scenario, the financial institution has to reinvest a large amount of funds (assuming that it does not need to pay off debt or other obligations) at a time when interest rates are low. A financial institution can benefit from anticipating how much cash flow it may receive under various scenarios so that it can prepare to use the cash flows efficiently, regardless of which scenario occurs.

The illustration implicitly assumed that the cash flows are solely influenced by the level of mortgage prepayment. In reality, other variables may be influential and could also be included. For example, the sensitivity analysis could incorporate possible scenarios for default rates on the mortgage payments, since a fraction of the expected payments will not be received due to default.

Sensitivity analysis could also be used to estimate the market value of the mortgage portfolio in response to various interest rate conditions because market values of fixed-rate mortgages can easily be estimated for a given estimate of the required rate of return. This would require some assumptions about how the fixed payments and prepaid mortgages received by the institution would be reinvested. Nevertheless, the analysis provides the financial institution with a probability distribution for the market value of its portfolio at a specific point in the future. If the risk of the portfolio is too high (the probability distribution of market values of the portfolio for the specific future time is too wide), the financial institution can restructure its portfolio by including mortgages that are less sensitive to interest rate movements.

Limited Disclosure about Mortgage Valuations Financial institutions that hold mortgages report the value of their mortgage holdings in their financial statements. When interest rates rise, however, the institutions do not revise the reported values of their various mortgage holdings because not all of the market values are known. A financial institution recognizes a loss in the value of the mortgages it holds only when it sells them at a loss. Thus, a financial institution may be highly exposed to rising interest rates, but the values of its mortgage holdings remain unchanged until it sells the mortgages. Although some analysts and sophisticated investors are experienced at assessing the risk of a financial institution's assets, they do not necessarily have enough information to assess the risk.

Mortgage-Backed Securities

As an alternative to selling their mortgages outright in the secondary market, financial institutions can issue mortgage-backed securities, which are securities backed by mortgage loans.

Mortgage Pass-Through Securities

Mortgage-backed securities come in various forms; the most common are **mortgage pass-through securities.** A group of mortgages held by a trustee of the issuing institution serves as collateral for these securities. The interest and principal payments on the mortgages are sent to the financial institution, which then transfers (passes through) the payments to the owners of the mortgage-backed securities after deducting fees for servicing and for guaranteeing payments to the owners. This process allows the savings institutions and banks that originate mortgages to adjust their balance sheets. Thus, they can earn fees from servicing the mortgages while avoiding exposure to interest rate risk and credit risk.

Pass-through securities are attractive because they can be purchased in the secondary market without purchasing the servicing of the mortgages that back them. In addition, the holders of pass-throughs are insured in the event of default. Furthermore, pass-throughs are very liquid and can be used as collateral for repurchase agreements.

Interest Rate Risk on Mortgage-Backed Securities A financial institution can reduce its exposure to interest rate risk by issuing pass-through securities because the payments received from mortgages are tied to the payments sent to security owners. To the extent that financial institutions use pass-through securities to finance mortgage holdings, they can insulate their profit margin from interest rate fluctuations. The interest and principal payments to owners of pass-through securities can vary over time. For example, if a higher-than-normal proportion of the mortgages backing the securities are prepaid in a specific period, the payments received by the financial institution will be passed through (after deducting a servicing fee) to the security owners.

Prepayment Risk on Mortgage-Backed Securities Although exposure to interest rate risk is reduced, the owners of pass-through securities are exposed to prepayment risk. The primary source of prepayment risk associated with a mortgage pool obviously arises from a borrower's right to prepay a mortgage in part or in full without penalty, which alters the expected life of mortgages depending upon market rates. Some amount of prepayments may occur naturally. When interest rates decline, however, prepayments are accelerated, and the owners of these securities are adversely affected.

ILLUSTRATION Consider a mortgage pass-through security with a par value of $1 million yielding 10 percent for 30 years. Assume the market rate is 10 percent and that normal prepayments on the mortgage pool are expected to be $500 monthly. The monthly minimum required payment on the security is $8,775. Including the $500 prepayment, the total monthly cash flow from this security is $9,275. The payments to the owner of this pass-through security will be completed after about 23 years. If the market interest rate is expected to remain at 10 percent, the security will still be valued at $1 million even if there are prepayments.

Now reconsider this example but assume that the market interest rate immediately declines from 10 percent to 9 percent. At this lower interest rate, prepayments will increase because borrowers will refinance at the new lower rates and pay off their old mortgages. Assume the expected monthly prepayment amount increases to $800 for a total monthly cash flow of $9,575 on the mortgage pass-through security, or $300 more than in the original example. At this accelerated prepayment rate, the payments to the owner of the mortgage pass-through security will be completed after about 20 years. Thus, the expected life of the security is three years shorter because of the accelerated prepayments. At a market interest rate of 9 percent, the present value of the payments is $1,073,734. The value of the security increased as a result of the decline in market interest rates, but the increase in value is limited because of the prepayments.

Owners of mortgage-backed securities are also subject to the possibility that prepayments will decelerate in response to rising interest rates.

ILLUSTRATION Reconsider the previous example but assume that the market rate increases from 10 percent to 11 percent. The monthly prepayment at this higher interest rate will be smaller because individuals are less likely to prepay their mortgages when their mortgage rate is lower than market interest rates. Assume the expected monthly prepayment is only $200 per month, which means the total monthly payment is equal to $8,975, and the security's expected life is about 26 years. Thus, the expected life of the mortgage pass-through security is extended. This is a disadvantage to the owner because the new market interest rate at which funds could be reinvested is higher than the rate the owner is earning on the security.

Types of Mortgage Pass-Through Securities

Five of the more common types of mortgage pass-through securities are the following:

- Ginnie Mae mortgage-backed securities
- Fannie Mae mortgage-backed securities
- Publicly issued pass-through securities
- Participation certificates
- Collateralized mortgage obligations (CMOs)

Each type is described in turn.

Ginnie Mae Mortgage-Backed Securities Financial institutions issue securities that are backed by FHA and VA mortgages. Ginnie Mae (Government National Mortgage Association, or GNMA) guarantees timely payment of principal and interest to investors who purchase these securities. The funds received from their sale are used to finance the mortgages. All mortgages pooled together to back Ginnie Mae pass-throughs must have the same interest rate. The interest rate received by purchasers of the pass-throughs is slightly less (typically 50 basis points) than that rate. This difference reflects a fee to the financial institution servicing the loan and to Ginnie Mae for guaranteeing full payment of interest and principal to the security purchasers. The outstanding balance of Ginnie Mae pass-throughs has grown substantially in recent years.

Fannie Mae Mortgage-Backed Securities Fannie Mae (Federal National Mortgage Association, or FNMA) issues mortgage-backed securities and uses the funds to purchase mortgages. In essence, Fannie Mae channels funds from investors to financial in-

stitutions that desire to sell their mortgages. These financial institutions may continue to service the mortgages and earn a fee for this service, while Fannie Mae receives a fee for guaranteeing timely payment of principal and interest to the holders of the mortgage-backed securities. The mortgage payments on mortgages backing these securities are sent to the financial institutions that service the mortgages. The payments are channeled through to the purchasers of mortgage-backed securities, which may be collateralized by conventional or federally insured mortgages.

Some mortgage-backed securities issued by Fannie Mae are stripped by separating the principal and interest payments streams and selling them as separate securities. For investors who purchase these securities, the timing of the payments is uncertain because many mortgages are prepaid when interest rates decline, as described earlier.

Publicly Issued Pass-Through Securities (PIPs) Another type of pass-through security, the publicly issued pass-through security (PIP), is similar to Ginnie Mae mortgage-backed securities, except that it is backed by conventional rather than FHA or VA mortgages. The mortgages backing the securities are insured through private insurance companies.

Participation Certificates (PCs) Freddie Mac (Federal Home Loan Mortgage Association) sells **participation certificates (PCs)** and uses the proceeds to finance the origination of conventional mortgages from financial institutions. This provides another outlet (in addition to Fannie Mae) for savings institutions and savings banks that desire to sell their conventional mortgages in the secondary market.

Collateralized Mortgage Obligations (CMOs) **Collateralized mortgage obligations (CMOs)** were developed in 1983. They have semiannual interest payments, unlike other mortgage-backed securities, which have monthly payments. The CMOs that represent a particular mortgage pool are segmented into classes (or tranches). The first class has the quickest payback. Any repaid principal is initially sent to owners of the first-class CMOs until the total principal amount representing that class is fully repaid. Then any further principal payments are sent to owners of the second-class CMOs until the total principal amount representing that class is fully repaid. This process continues until principal payments are made to owners of the last-class CMOs. CMO issues commonly have between 3 and 10 classes. Individual CMOs have a maximum average life of 10 years.

The attractive feature of CMOs is that investors can choose a class that fits their maturity desires. Even though investors are still uncertain as to when the securities will mature, they have a better feel for the maturity structure than with other pass-through securities. Investors who purchase third-class CMOs know that they will not receive any principal payments until the first- and second-class CMO owners are completely paid off.

One concern about CMOs is the speed of payback in response to lower interest rates. When interest rates decline, mortgages are prepaid, which accelerates the payments back to the holders of CMOs. This forces investors to reinvest their funds elsewhere under the prevailing (low interest rate) conditions. In some periods, massive mortgage prepayments caused accelerated payments on CMOs. Given the uncertainty about CMOs' maturity (because of the possible prepayment), determining the market valuation of CMOs is very difficult.

CMOs are sometimes segmented into "interest-only" (IO) and "principal-only" (PO) classes. Investors in interest-only CMOs receive only interest payments that are paid on the underlying mortgages. When mortgages are prepaid, the interest payments on the underlying mortgages are terminated, and so are payments to investors in interest-only CMOs. For example, mortgage prepayments may cut off the interest rate payments on

the CMO after a few years, even though these payments were initially expected to last five years or more. Consequently, investors in these CMOs could lose 50 percent or more of their initial investment. The relatively high yields offered on interest-only CMOs are attributed to their high degree of risk.

Because investors in the principal-only CMO receive principal payments only, they generally receive payments further into the future. Even though the payments to these investors represent principal, the maturity is uncertain because of possible prepayment of the underlying mortgages. For these investors, accelerated prepayment of mortgages is beneficial because they receive their complete payments earlier than expected.

Although CMOs can be a useful investment, their risks must be recognized. Coastal States Life Insurance Company invested much of its available funds in CMOs and failed in 1992 when the market value of its CMOs declined. Insurance regulators are now closely monitoring insurance companies that may have excessive exposure in CMOs. In addition, many mutual funds that invest in CMOs are reassessing their potential risk. Just as loans to less developed countries and high-yield (junk) bonds received more attention after their performance declined, CMOs are now receiving much more attention. Given their popularity in recent years and the difficulty in measuring their market value, regulators are concerned that a pronounced decline in CMO values could have a severe effect on many financial institutions.

Mortgage-Backed Securities for Small Investors

Pass-through securities have been historically restricted to large investors. Ginnie Mae pass-throughs, for example, come in minimum denominations of $25,000, with $5,000 increments above. In recent years, however, unit trusts have been created that allow small investors to participate. For example, a portfolio of Ginnie Mae pass-through securities is sold in $1,000 pieces. Each piece represents a tiny fraction of the overall portfolio of securities. These unit trusts have become very popular in recent years. The composition of the portfolio is not adjusted over time.

Some mutual funds offer Ginnie Mae funds, which, like the unit trusts, represent a portfolio of GNMA pass-through securities. Unlike a unit trust, the composition of a mutual fund's portfolio can be actively managed (adjusted) by the securities firm over time. As would be expected, the market values of Ginnie Mae unit trusts and mutual funds are inversely related to interest rate movements. A Ginnie Mae unit trust is more sensitive to rising interest rates because its composition cannot be adjusted. A mutual fund can modify the composition of its Ginnie Mae portfolio (shift to shorter-term maturities) if it anticipates increasing interest rates. Some mutual funds also invest in Fannie Mae mortgage-backed securities and PCs (participation certificates), allowing the small investor access to them.

Globalization of Mortgage Markets

 GL BAL ASPECTS   Mortgage market activity is not confined within a single country. For example, non-U.S. financial institutions hold mortgages on U.S. property, and vice versa. Large U.S. banks often maintain mortgage-banking subsidiaries in foreign countries. In addition, the use of interest rate swaps to hedge mortgages in the United States often involves a non-U.S. counterpart. Although investment banking firms may serve as the financial intermediary, they commonly search for a non-U.S. financial institution that desires to swap variable-rate payments in exchange for fixed-rate payments.

Participants in mortgage markets closely follow international economic conditions because of the potential impact on interest rates. Bond and mortgage portfolio decisions are highly influenced by announcements related to the value of the dollar. In general, any announcements that imply a potentially weaker dollar tend to cause expectations of higher U.S. inflation and therefore higher U.S. interest rates. The demand for fixed-rate mortgages will likely decline in response to such announcements. Announcements that imply a potentially stronger dollar tend to cause the opposite expectations and effects. It is difficult to show evidence of these relationships, however, because expectations do not always occur and often change from one day to the next.

SUMMARY

■ Residential mortgages can be characterized by whether they are federally insured, the type of interest rate used (fixed or floating), and the maturity. Quoted interest rates on mortgages vary at a given point in time, depending on these characteristics.

■ Popular methods of creative mortgage financing include graduated-payment mortgages, growing-equity mortgages, second mortgages, and shared-appreciation mortgages. These mortgages may enable borrowers to obtain adequate financing.

■ Mortgage pass-through securities represent mortgages that are serviced by the financial institutions that originated them, but are held by other investors. Five of the more popular types of mortgage pass-through securities are Ginnie Mae, Fannie Mae, publicly issued, participation certificates, and collateralized mortgage obligations (CMOs).

POINT COUNTER-POINT

Is the Trading of Mortgages Similar to the Trading of Corporate Bonds?

Point Yes. In both cases, the issuer's ability to repay the debt is based on income. Both types of debt securities are highly influenced by interest rate movements.

Counter-Point No. The assessment of corporate bonds requires an analysis of financial statements representing the firms that issued the bonds. The assessment of mort-

gages requires an understanding of the structure of the mortgage market (CMOs, etc.).

Who Is Correct? Use your favorite search engine to learn more about this issue. Offer your own opinion on this issue.

QUESTIONS AND APPLICATIONS

1. **Internet Exercise** Assess a mortgage payment schedule such as http://realestate.yahoo.com/realestate/calculators/amortization.html.
   a. Assume a loan amount of $120,000, an interest rate of 7.4 percent, and a 30-year maturity. Given this information, what is the monthly payment? In the first month, how much of the monthly payment is interest, and how much is principal? What is the outstanding balance after the first year? In the last month of payment,

   how much of the monthly payment is interest, and how much is principal?

2. **Graduated-Payment Mortgage** Describe the graduated-payment mortgage. What type of homeowners would prefer this type of mortgage?

3. **Exposure to Interest Rate Movements** Mortgage lenders with fixed-rate mortgages should benefit when interest rates decline, yet research has shown that such a favorable impact is dampened. By what?

4. **Financing Mortgages** What type of financial institution finances the majority of one- to four-family mortgages? What type of financial institution finances the majority of commercial mortgages?

5. **FHA Mortgages** Distinguish between FHA and conventional mortgages.

6. **Managing in Financial Markets: CMO Investment Dilemma** As a manager of a savings institution, you must decide whether to invest in collateralized mortgage obligations (CMOs). You can purchase interest-only (IO) or principal-only (PO) classes. You anticipate that economic conditions will weaken in the future and that government spending (and therefore government demand for funds) will decrease.
   a. Given your expectations, would IOs or POs be a better investment?
   b. Given the situation, is there any reason why you might not purchase the class of CMOs that you selected in the previous question?
   c. Your boss suggests that since CMOs typically have semiannual interest payments, their value at any point in time should be the present value of their future payments. Your boss also says that the valuation of CMOs should be simple. Why is your boss wrong?

7. **Mortgage Maturities** Why is the 15-year mortgage attractive to homeowners? Is the interest rate risk to the financial institution higher for a 15-year or a 30-year mortgage? Why?

8. **Maturities of Pass-Through Securities** Explain how the maturity on pass-through securities can be affected by interest rate movements.

9. **Growing-Equity Mortgage** Describe the growing-equity mortgage. How does it differ from a graduated-payment mortgage?

10. **Selling Mortgages** Explain why some financial institutions prefer to sell the mortgages they originate.

11. **CMOs** Describe how collateralized mortgage obligations (CMOs) are used and why they have been popular.

12. **ARMs** How does the initial rate on adjustable-rate mortgages (ARMs) differ from the rate on fixed-rate mortgages? Why? Explain how caps on ARMs can affect a financial institution's exposure to interest rate risk.

13. **Balloon-Payment Mortgage** Explain the use of a balloon-payment mortgage. Why might a financial institution prefer to offer this type of mortgage?

14. **Interpreting Financial News** Interpret the following comments made by Wall Street analysts and portfolio managers:
   a. "If interest rates continue to decline, the interest-only CMOs will take a hit."
   b. "Estimating the proper value of CMOs is like estimating the proper value of a baseball player; the proper value is much easier to assess five years later."
   c. "When purchasing principal-only CMOs, be ready for a bumpy ride."

15. **Second Mortgages** Why are second mortgages offered by some home sellers?

16. **Mortgage Companies** Explain how a mortgage company's degree of exposure to interest rate risk differs from that of other financial institutions.

17. **Mortgage Rates and Risk** What is the general relationship between mortgage rates and long-term government security rates? Explain how mortgage lenders can be affected by interest rate movements. Also explain how they can insulate against interest rate movements.

18. **Mortgage Pass-Through Securities** Describe how mortgage pass-through securities are used. How can the use of pass-through securities reduce a financial institution's interest rate risk?

19. **Secondary Market** Compare the secondary market activity for mortgages to the activity for other capital market instruments (such as stocks and bonds). Provide a general explanation for the difference in the activity level.

20. **Mortgage Valuation** Describe the factors that affect mortgage prices.

21. **Shared-Appreciation Mortgage** Describe the shared-appreciation mortgage.

PROBLEM

1. **Amortization** Use an amortization table that determines the monthly mortgage payment based on a specific interest rate and principal with a 15-year maturity and then for a 30-year maturity. Is the monthly payment for the 15-year maturity twice the amount for the 30-year maturity or less than twice the amount? Explain.

FLOW OF FUNDS EXERCISE

Mortgage Financing

Carson Company currently has a mortgage on its office building through a savings institution. It is attempting to determine whether it should convert its mortgage from a floating rate to a fixed rate. Recall that the yield curve is currently upward sloping. Also recall that Carson is concerned about a possible slowing of the economy because of potential Fed actions to reduce inflation. The fixed rate that it would pay if it refinances is higher than the prevailing short-term rate, but lower than the rate it would pay from issuing bonds.

a. What macroeconomic factors could affect interest rates and therefore affect the mortgage refinancing decision?

b. If Carson refinances its mortgage, it also must decide on the size of a down payment. If it uses more funds for a larger down payment, it will need to borrow more funds to finance its expansion. Should Carson use a minimum down payment or a larger down payment if it refinances the mortgage? Why?

c. Who is indirectly providing the money that is used by companies such as Carson to purchase office buildings? That is, where does the money that the savings institutions channel into mortgages come from?

EXERCISE

Explaining Mortgage Rate Premiums

Review the "Yield Comparisons" table next to the "Credit Markets" section of a recent issue of *The Wall Street Journal* to determine the Ginnie Mae mortgage rate and the Fannie Mae mortgage rate. How do these rates compare to the long-term (10+ year) Treasury bond yield? Why do you think there is a difference between the Ginnie Mae rate and Treasury bond yields?

Part IV Integrative Problem

Asset Allocation

This problem requires an understanding of how economic conditions influence interest rates and security prices (Chapters 9, 10, 11, and 12).

As a personal financial planner, one of your tasks is to prescribe the allocation of available funds across money market securities, bonds, and mortgages. Your philosophy is to take positions in securities that will benefit most from your forecasted changes in economic conditions. As a result of a recent event in Japan, you expect that in the next month Japanese investors will reduce their investment in U.S. Treasury securities and shift most of their funds into Japanese securities. You expect that this shift in funds will persist for at least a few years. You believe this single event will have a major effect on economic factors in the United States, such as interest rates, exchange rates, and economic growth in the next month. Because the prices of securities in the United States are affected by these economic factors, you must determine how to revise your prescribed allocation of funds across securities.

Questions

1 How will U.S. interest rates be directly affected by the event (holding other factors equal)?

2 How will economic growth in the United States be affected by the event? How might this influence the values of securities?

3 Assume that day-to-day exchange rate movements are dictated primarily by the flow of funds between countries, especially international bond and money market transactions. How will exchange rates be affected by possible changes in the international flow of funds that are caused by the event?

4 Using your answer to (1) only, explain how prices of U.S. money market securities, bonds, and mortgages will be affected.

5 Now use your answer to (2) along with your answer to (1) to assess the impact on security prices. Would prices of risky securities be affected more or less than those of risk-free securities with a similar maturity? Why?

6 Assume that for diversification purposes, you prescribe that at least 20 percent of an investor's funds should be allocated to money market securities, to bonds, and to mortgages. That allows you to allocate the remaining 40 percent however you desire across those securities. Based on all the information you have about the event, prescribe the proper allocation of funds across the three types of U.S. securities. (Assume that the entire investment will be concentrated in U.S. securities.) Defend your prescription.

7 Would you recommend high-risk or low-risk money market securities? Would you recommend high-risk or low-risk bonds? Why?

8 Assume that you would consider recommending that as much as 20 percent of the funds be invested in foreign debt securities. Revise your prescription to include foreign securities if you desire (identify the type of security and the country).

9 If the event of concern increased the demand for, instead of reducing the supply of, loanable funds in the United States, would the assessment of future interest rates be different? What about the general assessment of economic conditions? What about the general assessment of bond prices?

PART V

Derivative Security Markets

Derivatives are financial contracts whose values are derived from the values of underlying assets. They are widely used to speculate on future expectations or to reduce a security portfolio's risk. The chapters in Part V focus on derivative security markets. Each chapter explains how institutional portfolio managers and speculators use these markets. Many financial market participants simultaneously use all these markets, as is emphasized throughout the chapters.

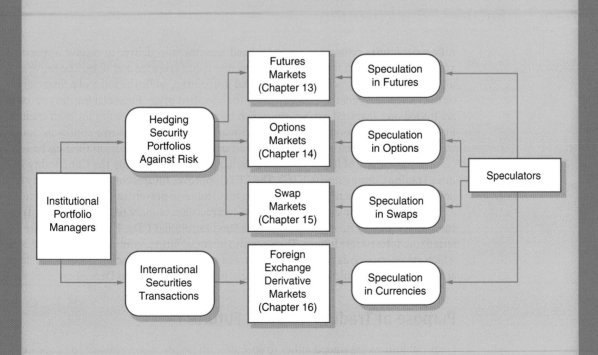

CHAPTER 13

Futures Markets for Financial Assets

In recent years, financial futures markets have received much attention both because they have the potential to generate large returns to speculators and because they entail a high degree of risk. However, these markets can also be used to reduce the risk of financial institutions and other corporations. Financial futures markets facilitate the trading of financial futures contracts.

The specific objectives of this chapter are to:

- explain how financial futures contracts are valued,

- explain how interest rate futures contracts are used to speculate or hedge, based on anticipated interest rate movements,

- explain how stock index futures contracts are used to speculate or hedge, based on anticipated stock price movements, and

- describe how financial institutions participate in the financial futures markets.

Financial Futures: Background

A **financial futures contract** is a standardized agreement to deliver or receive a specified amount of a specified financial instrument at a specified price and date. The buyer of a financial futures contract buys the financial instrument, while the seller of a financial futures contract delivers the instrument for the specified price. Financial futures contracts are traded on organized exchanges, which establish and enforce rules for such trading. Futures exchanges provide an organized marketplace where futures contracts can be traded. They clear, settle, and guarantee all transactions that occur on their exchanges.

The operations of financial futures exchanges are regulated by the Commodity Futures Trading Commission (CFTC). The CFTC approves futures contracts before they can be listed by futures exchanges and imposes regulations to prevent unfair trading practices.

Many of the popular financial futures contracts are on debt securities such as Treasury bills, Treasury notes, Treasury bonds, and Eurodollar CDs. These contracts are referred to as **interest rate futures.** There are also financial futures contracts on stock indexes, which are referred to as **stock index futures.** For each type of contract, the settlement dates at which delivery would occur are in March, June, September, and December.

Purpose of Trading Financial Futures

Financial futures are traded either to speculate on prices of securities or to hedge existing exposure to security price movements. **Speculators** in financial futures markets take

positions to profit from expected changes in the price of futures contracts over time. **Hedgers** take positions to reduce their exposure to future movements in interest rates or stock prices.

Many hedgers who maintain large portfolios of stocks or bonds take a futures position to hedge their risk. Speculators commonly take the opposite position and therefore serve as the counterparty on many futures transactions. Thus, speculators provide liquidity to the futures market.

Speculators in futures can be classified according to their methods. **Day traders** attempt to capitalize on price movements during a single day; normally, they close out their futures positions on the same day the positions were initiated. **Position traders** maintain their futures positions for longer periods of time (for weeks or months) and thus attempt to capitalize on expected price movements over a longer time horizon.

Steps Involved in Trading Futures

Most financial futures contracts in the United States are traded on the Chicago Board of Trade (CBOT) or the Chicago Mercantile Exchange (CME). The trading floor for most futures contracts is open from 8:30 A.M. to 3:15 P.M. Only the members of a futures exchange (or persons to whom members have leased their privileges) can engage in futures transactions on the exchange floor. A person becomes a member by purchasing a seat on the exchange. The price of a seat on any exchange fluctuates over time, in accordance with the demand for seats and supply of seats for sale.

Members of a futures exchange can be classified as either **commission brokers** (also called floor brokers) or **floor traders.** Commission brokers execute orders for their customers. Many of them are employees of brokerage firms, but others work independently. Floor traders (also called **locals**) trade futures contracts for their own account.

Over-the-Counter Trading Many types of futures contracts and other derivative contracts are now being sold over the counter, whereby a financial intermediary (such as a commercial bank or an investment bank) finds a counterparty or serves as the counterparty. These over-the-counter arrangements are more personalized and can be tailored to the specific preferences of the parties involved. Such tailoring is not possible for the more standardized futures contracts sold on the exchanges.

Electronic Trading Some futures contracts are now traded electronically. The Chicago Mercantile Exchange has an electronic trading platform called GLOBEX that complements its floor trading. Some futures contracts are traded both on the trading floor and on GLOBEX, while others are traded only on GLOBEX. Transactions can occur on GLOBEX virtually around the clock (closed about one hour per day for maintenance) and on weekends. In 2004, the Chicago Board of Options Exchange (CBOE) opened a fully electronic futures exchange.

Trading through a Brokerage Firm Customers who desire to buy or sell futures contracts open accounts at brokerage firms that execute futures transactions. Under exchange requirements, a customer must establish a margin deposit with the broker before a transaction can be executed. This so-called **initial margin** is typically between 5 percent and 18 percent of a futures contract's full value. Brokers commonly require margin deposits above those required by the exchanges. As the futures contract price changes on a daily basis, its value is "marked to market," or revised to reflect the prevailing

conditions. When the value of a customer's contract moves in an unfavorable direction, that customer may receive a margin call from the broker, requiring additional funds to be deposited in the margin account. The margin requirements reduce the risk that customers will later default on their obligations.

Type of Orders Customers can place a market order or a limit order. With a market order, the trade will automatically be executed at the prevailing price of the futures contract. With a limit order, the trade will be executed only if the price is within the limit specified by the customer. For example, a customer may place a limit order to buy a particular futures contract if it is priced no higher than a specified price. Similarly, a customer may place an order to sell a futures contract if it is priced no lower than a specified minimum price.

How Orders Are Executed The brokerage firm communicates its customers' orders to telephone stations located near the trading floor of the futures exchange. The floor brokers accommodate these orders. Each type of financial futures contract is traded in a particular location on the trading floor. The floor brokers make their offers to trade by open outcry, specifying the quantity of contracts they wish to buy or sell. Other floor brokers and traders interested in trading the particular type of futures contract can respond to the open outcry. When two traders on the trading floor reach an agreement, each trader documents the specifics of the agreement (including the price), and the information is transmitted to the customers.

Floor brokers receive transaction fees in the form of a bid-ask spread. That is, they purchase a given futures contract for one party at a slightly lower price than the price at which they sell the contract to another party. For every buyer of a futures contract, there must be a corresponding seller.

The futures exchange facilitates the trading process but does not take buy or sell positions on the futures contract. Instead, the exchange acts as a clearinghouse. A clearinghouse facilitates the trading process by recording all transactions and guaranteeing timely payments on the futures contracts. This precludes the need for a purchaser of a futures contract to check the creditworthiness of the contract seller. In fact, purchasers of contracts do not even know who the sellers are, and vice versa. The clearinghouse also supervises the delivery of contracts as of the settlement date.

http://www.cme.com
Explains how investors can use electronic routing, tracking, and execution of orders.

Interpreting Financial Futures Tables

Prices of interest rate futures contracts vary from day to day and are reported in the financial pages of newspapers. *The Wall Street Journal* provides a comprehensive summary of trading activity on various financial futures contracts. Assume the information in Exhibit 13.1 appears on a particular day in May 2005 and refers to the previous trading day. From this exhibit, the futures contract specifying delivery of the Treasury bills for June opened at 94.00 (per $100 par value). The highest trading price for the day was 94.26, the low was 94.00, and the closing price (settle price in Column 5) at the end of the day was 94.20. The change in Column 6 is the difference between the settle price and the quoted settle price on the previous trading day. The reported discount in Column 7 is based on the settle price and represents the percentage difference between the purchase price and par value. The change in the discount in Column 8 is the difference

EXHIBIT 13.1   Example of Treasury Bill Futures Quotations

Treasury Bill Futures								
(1)	(2)	(3)	(4)	(5)	(6)	(7)	(8)	(9)
						Discount		
	Open	High	Low	Settle	Change	Settle	Change	Open Interest
June 2005	94.00	94.26	94.00	94.20	+.30	5.80	−.30	16,000
Sept 2005	93.80	94.05	93.80	94.05	+.28	5.95	−.28	2,519
Dec 2005	93.62	93.79	93.62	93.75	+.24	6.25	−.24	287
Mar 2006	93.45	93.60	93.45	93.60	+.23	6.40	−.23	206

between the quoted discount and the discount on the previous day. The open interest in Column 9 is the number of outstanding futures contracts for the settlement date of concern.

Exhibit 13.1 provides information for T-bill futures contracts with four different settlement months. Once the June settlement date passes, the other months will move up one row in the table, and information on T-bill futures with a settlement date for the following June will appear in the fourth row.

Futures on Treasury bonds and notes are also available and can be used for hedging portfolio positions or for speculation. Specific characteristics of these contracts are shown in Exhibit 13.2. Both Treasury bond and note futures traded on the Chicago Board of Trade represent a face value of $100,000, which is substantially less than the $1 million face value of securities underlying the T-bill futures contracts.

EXHIBIT 13.2

Characteristics of Treasury Bond and Note Futures Traded on the Chicago Board of Trade

Characteristic of Futures Contract	U.S. Treasury Bond Futures	U.S. Treasury Note Futures
Size	$100,000 face value.	$100,000 face value.
Deliverable grade	U.S. Treasury bonds maturing at least 15 years from date of delivery if not callable; coupon is 8%. (The coupon rate on new contracts is periodically adjusted to reflect market interest rate levels.)	U.S. Treasury notes maturing at least 6½ years but not more than 10 years from the first day of the delivery month; coupon rate is 6%. [The coupon rate on new contracts is periodically adjusted to reflect market interest rate levels.]
Price quotation	In points ($1,000) and thirty-seconds of a point.	In points ($1,000) and thirty-seconds of a point.
Minimum price fluctuation	One thirty-second ($\frac{1}{32}$) of a point, or $31.25 per contract.	One thirty-second ($\frac{1}{32}$) of a point, or $31.25 per contract.
Daily trading limits	Three points ($3,000) per contract above or below the previous day's settlement price.	Three points ($3,000) per contract above or below the previous day's settlement price.
Settlement months	March, June, September, December.	March, June, September, December.

Valuing Financial Futures

http://

http://www.cme.com
Quotations for futures
contracts.

If there are more traders with buy offers than sell offers for a particular contract, the futures price will rise until this imbalance is removed. Price changes on financial futures contracts are indicated on quotation tickers. As the market price of the financial asset represented by the financial futures contract changes, so will the value of the contract. For example, if the prices of Treasury bonds rise, the value of an existing Treasury bond futures contract should rise because the contract has locked in the price at which Treasury bonds can be purchased.

The price of any financial futures contract generally reflects the expected price of the underlying security (or index) as of the settlement date. Thus, any factors that influence that expected value should influence the current prices of financial futures. A primary factor is the current price of the underlying security (or index), which normally serves as a somewhat useful indicator of the future price. In addition, some information about economic or market conditions may influence the futures price even though it does not affect the current price. For example, a particular regulatory event anticipated six months from now could possibly affect the futures price even though it does not affect the price of the underlying security. Thus, the futures price is mainly a function of the prevailing price of the underlying security plus an expected adjustment in that price by the settlement date. The futures price should change in response to either changes in the prevailing price or changes in the expected adjustment in that price by the settlement date.

Impact of Opportunity Cost

Another factor that influences the futures price is the opportunity cost (or benefits) involved in holding a futures contract rather than owning the underlying security. An investor who purchases stock index futures rather than the stocks themselves does not receive the dividends. By itself, this factor would cause the stock index futures to be priced lower than the stocks themselves. However, because the investor's initial investment is much smaller when purchasing the stock index futures, the investor may be able to generate interest income on the remaining funds. By itself, this factor would cause the stock index futures to be priced higher than the stocks themselves. When both factors are considered, the effects are somewhat offsetting.

Explaining Price Movements of Bond Futures Contracts

Price movements of bond futures contracts are driven by economic conditions. A framework for explaining movements in bond futures prices is provided in Exhibit 13.3.

Since Treasury bond futures prices tend to move with the prices of Treasury bonds, participants in the Treasury bond futures market closely monitor the same economic indicators monitored by participants in the Treasury bond market. These indicators may signal future changes in the strength of the economy, which signal changes in the risk-free interest rate and in the required return from investing in bonds. Some of the more closely monitored indicators of economic growth include employment, gross domestic product, retail sales, industrial production, and consumer confidence. When indicators signal an increase in economic growth, participants anticipate an increase in interest

EXHIBIT 13.3

Framework for Explaining Changes in Treasury Bond and Treasury Bill Futures Prices over Time

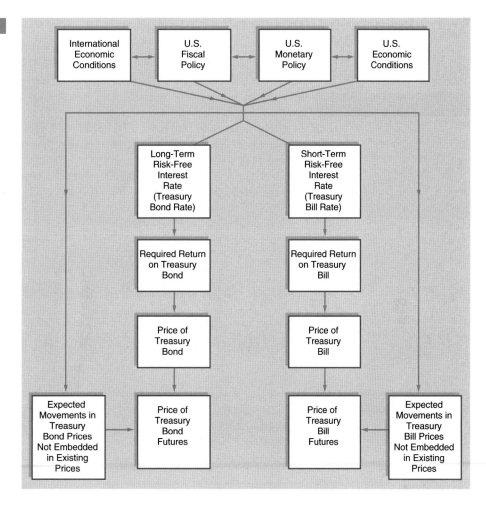

rates, which places downward pressure on bond prices and therefore also on Treasury bond futures prices. Conversely, when indicators signal a decrease in economic growth, participants anticipate lower interest rates, which places upward pressure on bond prices and therefore also on Treasury bond futures.

Participants in the Treasury bond futures market also closely monitor indicators of inflation, such as the consumer price index and the producer price index. In general, an unexpected increase in these indexes tends to create expectations of higher interest rates and places downward pressure on bond prices and therefore also on Treasury bond futures prices.

Indicators that reflect the amount of long-term financing are also monitored. For example, announcements about the government deficit or the amount of money that the Treasury hopes to borrow in a Treasury bond auction are closely monitored. Any information that implies more government borrowing than expected tends to signal upward pressure on the long-term risk-free interest rate (the Treasury bond rate), downward pressure on bond prices, and therefore downward pressure on Treasury bond futures prices.

Speculating with Interest Rate Futures

The following example explains how speculators use interest rate futures.

In February, Jim Sanders forecasts that interest rates will decrease over the next month. If his expectation is correct, the market value of T-bills should increase. Sanders calls a broker and purchases a T-bill futures contract. Assume that the price of the contract was 94.00 (a 6 percent discount) and that the price of T-bills as of the March settlement date is 94.90 (a 5.1 percent discount). Sanders can accept delivery of the T-bills and sell them for more than he paid for them. Because T-bill futures represent $1 million of par value, the nominal profit from this speculative strategy is

Selling price	$949,000	(94.90% of $1,000,000)
− Purchase price	− 940,000	(94.00% of $1,000,000)
= Profit	$9,000	(0.90% of $1,000,000)

In this example, Sanders benefited from his speculative strategy because interest rates declined from the time he took the futures position until the settlement date. If interest rates had risen over this period, the price of T-bills as of the settlement date would have been below 94.00 (reflecting a discount above 6 percent), and Sanders would have incurred a loss.

Assume that the price of T-bills as of the March settlement date is 92.50 (representing a discount of 7.5 percent). In this case, the nominal profit from Sander's speculative strategy is

Selling price	$925,000	(92.50% of $1,000,000)
− Purchase price	− 940,000	(94.00% of $1,000,000)
= Profit	−$15,000	(− 1.50% of $1,000,000)

Now suppose instead that, as of February, Sanders had anticipated that interest rates would rise by March. He therefore sold a T-bill futures contract with a March settlement date, obligating him to provide T-bills to the purchaser as of the delivery date. When T-bill prices declined by March, Sanders was able to obtain T-bills at a lower market price in March than the price at which he was obligated to sell those bills. Again, there is always the risk that interest rates (and therefore T-bill prices) will move contrary to expectations. In that case, Sanders would have paid a higher market price for the T-bills than the price at which he could sell them.

The potential payoffs from trading futures contracts are illustrated in Exhibit 13.4. The left graph represents a purchaser of futures, and the right graph represents a seller of futures. The S on each graph indicates the initial price at which a futures position is created. The horizontal axis represents the market value of the securities represented by a futures contract as of the delivery date. The maximum possible loss when purchasing futures is the amount to be paid for the securities, but this loss will occur only if the market value of the securities falls to zero. The amount of gain (or loss) to a speculator who initially purchased futures will equal the loss (or gain) to a speculator who initially sold futures on the same date (assuming zero transaction costs).

EXHIBIT 13.4

Potential Payoffs from
Speculating in Financial
Futures

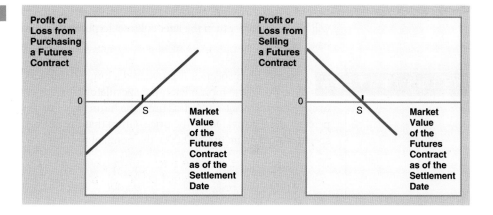

Impact of Leverage

Since investors commonly use a margin account to take futures positions, the return from speculating in interest rate futures should reflect the degree of financial leverage involved. The return is magnified substantially when considering the relatively small margin maintained by many investors.

ILLUSTRATION

In the example where Jim Sanders earned a profit of $9,000 on a futures contract, this profit represents 0.90 percent of the value of the underlying contract par value. Consider that Sanders could have taken the interest rate futures position with an initial margin of perhaps $10,000. Under these conditions, the $9,000 profit represents a return of 90 percent over the period of less than two months in which he maintained the futures position.

Just as financial leverage magnifies positive returns, it also magnifies losses. In the example where Sanders lost $15,000 on a futures contract, he would have lost 100 percent of his initial margin and would have been required to add more funds to his margin account when the value of the futures position began to decline.

Closing Out Futures Positions

Most buyers and sellers of financial futures contracts do not actually make or accept delivery of the financial instrument; instead, they offset their positions by the settlement date. For example, speculators who purchased Treasury bond futures contracts could sell similar futures contracts by the settlement date. Because they now own a contract to receive and a contract to deliver, the obligations net out. The gain or loss from involvement in futures positions depends on the futures price at the time of the purchase versus the futures price at the time of the sale. If the price of the securities represented by the futures contract has risen over the period of concern, speculators who initially purchased interest rate futures will likely have paid a lower futures price than the price at which they can sell the futures contract. Thus, a positive gain will have resulted, and the size of the gain will depend on the degree of movement in the prices of the securities underlying the contract.

Consider the opposite situation (referred to as a "short" position) where the sale of futures is followed by a purchase of futures a few months later to offset the initial short

position. If security prices have risen over this period, the earlier contract to sell futures will be priced lower than the later contract to purchase futures. Thus, the speculator will have a loss.

ILLUSTRATION

Assume that a speculator purchased a futures contract on Treasury bonds at a price of 90–00. One month later, the speculator sells the same futures contract in order to close out the position. At this time, the futures contract specifies 92–10, or 92 and $\frac{10}{32}$ percent of the par value, as the price. Given that the futures contract on Treasury bonds specifies a par value of $100,000, the nominal profit is

Selling price	$92,312	($92^{10}/_{32}$% of $100,000)
− Purchase price	− 90,000	(90.00% of $100,000)
= Profit	$2,312	($2^{10}/_{32}$% of $100,000)

When the initial position is a sale of the futures contract, a purchase of that same type of contract will close out the position. For example, assume a speculator took an initial short position. Using the numbers above, a loss of $2,312 (ignoring transaction costs) will result from closing out the short position one month later. Participants close out a position when they expect that a larger loss will occur if the position is not closed out. If the short position is not closed out before the settlement date, the investor taking that position is obligated to deliver the securities underlying the futures contract at that time.

According to estimates, only 2 percent of all futures contracts actually involve delivery, yet this does not reduce their effectiveness for speculation or hedging. Because the contract prices move with the financial instrument representing the contract, an offsetting position at the settlement date generates the same gain or loss as if the instrument were delivered.

Hedging with Interest Rate Futures

Financial institutions can classify their assets and liabilities by the sensitivity of their market value to interest rate movements. The difference between a financial institution's volume of rate-sensitive assets and rate-sensitive liabilities represents its exposure to interest rate risk. Over the long run, an institution may attempt to restructure its assets or liabilities to balance the degree of rate sensitivity. Yet, restructuring the balance sheet takes time. In the short run, the institution may consider using financial futures to hedge its exposure to interest rate movements. A variety of financial institutions use financial futures to hedge their interest rate risk, including mortgage companies, securities dealers, commercial banks, savings institutions, pension funds, and insurance companies.

Using Interest Rate Futures to Create a Short Hedge

Financial institutions most commonly use interest rate futures to create a **short hedge.** Consider a commercial bank that currently holds a large amount of corporate bonds and long-term fixed-rate commercial loans. Its primary source of funds has been short-term deposits. The bank will be adversely affected if interest rates rise in the near future because its liabilities are more rate-sensitive than its assets. Although the bank believes that

its bonds are a reasonable long-term investment, it anticipates that interest rates will rise temporarily. Therefore, it hedges against the interest rate risk by selling futures on securities that have characteristics similar to the securities it is holding, so the futures prices will change in tandem with these securities. One possible strategy is to sell Treasury bond futures because the price movements of Treasury bonds are highly correlated with movements in corporate bond prices.

If interest rates rise as expected, the market value of existing corporate bonds held by the bank will decline. Yet, this decline could be offset by the favorable impact of the futures position. The bank locked in the price at which it could sell Treasury bonds. It can purchase Treasury bonds at a lower price just prior to settlement of the futures contract (because the value of bonds will have decreased) and profit from fulfilling its futures contract obligation. Alternatively, it could offset its short position by purchasing futures contracts similar to the type that it sold earlier.

ILLUSTRATION

Assume that Charlotte Insurance Company plans to satisfy cash needs in six months by selling its Treasury bond holdings for $5 million at that time. It is concerned that interest rates might increase over the next three months, which would reduce the market value of the bonds by the time they are sold. To hedge against this possibility, Charlotte plans to sell Treasury bond futures. It sells 50 Treasury bond futures contracts with a par value of $5 million ($100,000 per contract) for 98–16 (or 98 and $\frac{16}{32}$ percent of par value).

Suppose that the actual price of the futures contract declines to 94–16 because of an increase in interest rates. Charlotte can close out its short futures position by purchasing contracts identical to those it has sold. If it purchases 50 Treasury bond futures contracts at the prevailing price of 94–16, its profit per futures contract will be

Selling price	$98,500	(98.50% of $100,000)
− Purchase price	− 94,500	(94.50% of $100,000)
= Profit	$4,000	(4.00% of $100,000)

Charlotte had a position in 50 futures contracts, so its total profit from its position will be $200,000 ($4,000 per contract × 50 contracts). This gain on the futures contract position will help offset the reduced market value of Charlotte's bond holdings. Charlotte could also have earned a gain on its position by purchasing an identical futures contract.

If interest rates rise by a greater degree over the six-month period, the market value of Charlotte's Treasury bond holdings will decrease further. However, the price of Treasury bond futures contracts will also decrease by a greater degree, creating a larger gain from the short position in Treasury bond futures. If interest rates decrease, the futures prices will rise, causing a loss on Charlotte's futures position. But this will be offset by a gain in the market value of Charlotte's bond holdings. In this case, the firm would have experienced better overall performance without the hedge. Firms cannot know whether a hedge of interest rate risk will be beneficial in a future period because they cannot always predict the direction of future interest rates.

The preceding example presumes that the **basis,** or the difference between the price of a security and the price of a futures contract, remains the same. In reality, the price of the security may fluctuate more or less than the futures contract used to hedge it. If so, a perfect offset will not result when a given face value amount of securities is hedged with the same face value amount of futures contracts.

EXHIBIT 13.5

Comparison of Probability
Distributions of Returns;
Hedged versus Unhedged
Positions

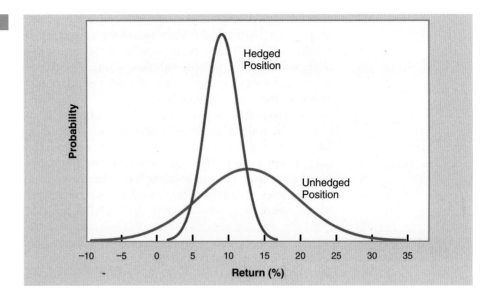

EXHIBIT 13.5

Comparison of Probability
Distributions of Returns;
Hedged versus Unhedged
Positions

Tradeoff from Using a Short Hedge When one considers both the rising and the declining interest rate scenarios, the advantages and disadvantages of interest rate futures
are obvious. Interest rate futures can hedge against both adverse and favorable events.
Exhibit 13.5 compares two probability distributions of returns generated by a financial
institution whose liabilities are more rate-sensitive than its assets. If the institution
hedges its exposure to interest rate risk, its probability distribution of returns is nar-
rower than if it does not hedge. The return from hedging would have been higher than
without hedging if interest rates increased (see the left side of the graph) but lower if interest rates decreased (see the right side of the graph).

A financial institution that hedges with interest rate futures is less sensitive to economic events. Thus, financial institutions that frequently use interest rate futures may be
able to reduce the variability of their earnings over time, which reflects a lower degree
of risk. Nevertheless, it should be recognized that hedging is unlikely to remove all uncertainty because it is virtually impossible to perfectly hedge the sensitivity of all cash
flows to interest rate movements.

Cross-Hedging Financial institutions sometimes want to hedge the interest rate risk of
assets that cannot be perfectly matched by interest rate futures contracts. In this case,
they attempt to identify an asset represented by futures contracts whose market value
moves closely in tandem with that of the assets they want to hedge. The use of a futures
contract on one financial instrument to hedge a position in a different financial instrument is known as **cross-hedging.** The effectiveness of a cross-hedge depends on the degree of correlation between the market values of the two financial instruments. If the
price of the underlying security of the futures contract moves closely in tandem with the
security hedged, the futures contract can provide an effective hedge.

For example, a financial institution may take a short position in Treasury bond futures contracts to hedge the interest rate risk of a portfolio of corporate bonds. The Treasury bonds and corporate bonds may be similarly sensitive to interest rate movements
(assuming their maturities and coupon payment structures are similar). However, shifts
in credit conditions could sever the close relationship between Treasury bond and corporate bond prices because the prices may be affected differently by economic condi-

tions that influence the probability of default. For example, news that signals the possibility of a recession could cause investors to shift from corporate bonds to Treasury bonds. During this transition, the market value of the institution's corporate bond portfolio may decline, while Treasury bond prices are rising. Thus, the sale of Treasury bond futures to hedge against the expected temporary decline in the market value of a corporate bond portfolio would not have been effective.

Even when the futures contract is highly correlated with the portfolio being hedged, the value of the futures contract may change by a higher or lower percentage than the portfolio's market value. If the futures contract value is less volatile than the portfolio value, hedging will require a greater amount of principal represented by the futures contracts. For example, assume that for every percentage movement in the price of the futures contract, the value of the portfolio moves by 1.25 percent. In this case, the value of futures contracts to fully hedge the portfolio would be 1.25 times the principal of the portfolio.

Using Interest Rate Futures to Create a Long Hedge

Some financial institutions use a **long hedge** to reduce exposure to the possibility of declining interest rates. Consider government securities dealers who plan to purchase long-term bonds in a few months. If the dealers are concerned that prices of these securities will rise before the time of their purchases, they may purchase Treasury bond futures contracts. These contracts lock in the price at which Treasury bonds can be purchased, regardless of what happens to market rates prior to the actual purchase of the bonds.

As another example, consider a bank that has obtained a significant portion of its funds from large CDs with a maturity of five years. Also assume that most of its assets represent loans with rates that adjust every six months. This bank would be adversely affected by a decline in interest rates because interest earned on assets would be more sensitive than interest paid on liabilities. To hedge against the possibility of lower interest rates, the bank could purchase T-bill futures to lock in the price on T-bills at a specified future date. If interest rates decline, the gain on the futures position could partially offset any reduction in the bank's earnings due to the reduction in interest rates.

Hedging Net Exposure

Because interest rate futures contracts entail transaction costs, they should be used only to hedge **net exposure,** which reflects the difference between asset and liability positions. Consider a bank that has $300 million in long-term assets and $220 million worth of long-term fixed-rate liabilities. If interest rates rise, the market value of the long-term assets will decline, but the bank will benefit from the fixed rate on the $220 million in long-term liabilities. Thus, the net exposure is only $80 million (assuming that the long-term assets and liabilities are similarly affected by rising interest rates). The financial institution should therefore focus on hedging its net exposure of $80 million by creating a short hedge.

Bond Index Futures

A bond index futures contract allows for the buying and selling of a bond index for a specified price at a specified date. For financial institutions that trade in municipal

Interest Rate Futures Quotations

The Wall Street Journal provides quotations on various interest rate futures contracts, as shown here. The most popular index futures contract is the Treasury bond futures. For each type of contract, there are various settlement dates, one date for each row. For each settlement date, the open, high, low, and settle (closing) prices are quoted across the row. The change in the futures price from the previous day is also shown along with the high and low prices since the futures contract with a specific settlement date was created. The open interest (number of existing contracts that have not been offset) is also shown for each settlement date.

Interest Rate Futures

Treasury Bonds (CBT)-$100,000; pts 32nds of 100%

Sept	110-28	111-02	110-16	110-22	−5	114-30	101-24	541,533
Dec	109-13	109-18	109-09	109-15	−4	113-07	100-24	22,677

Est vol 126,010; vol Fri 420,509; open int 564,513, +14,696.

Treasury Notes (CBT)-$100,000; pts 32nds of 100%

Sept	112-22	12-265	112-11	12-155	−7.5	15-095	106-13	1,381,685
Dec	111-15	111-15	111-08	11-085	−8.0	13-045	105-14	103,420

Est vol 446,246; vol Fri 1,236,553; open int 1,485,407, +45,191.

5 Yr. Treasury Notes (CBT)-$100,000; pts 32nds of 100%

Sept	110-31	111-03	10-235	10-265	−5.0	112-15	106-29	1,195,171

Est vol 305,581; vol Fri 794,239; open int 1,373,393, +21,894.

2 Yr. Treasury Notes (CBT)-$200,000; pts 32nds of 100%

Sept	106-06	06-072	06-027	06-037	−2.5	106-11	04-187	189,058

Est vol 19,307; vol Fri 41,913; open int 189,620, −131.

30 Day Federal Funds (CBT)-$5,000,000; 100 - daily avg.

Aug	98.585	98.585	98.580	98.580	...	98.935	98.365	224,219
Sept	98.47	98.47	98.46	98.46	−.01	98.90	98.14	83,175
Oct	98.38	98.38	98.36	98.37	−.01	98.85	98.24	96,679
Nov	98.23	98.23	98.22	98.23	...	98.96	97.74	69,986
Dec	98.11	98.12	98.10	98.11	−.01	98.93	97.55	37,401
Ja05	98.07	98.07	98.06	98.06	−.01	98.30	97.47	16,753
Feb	97.91	97.91	97.91	97.90	−.02	97.93	97.38	1,984

Est vol 86,894; vol Fri 199,807; open int 530,454, +18,557.

10 Yr. Interest Rate Swaps (CBT)-$100,000; pts 32nds of 100%

Sept	109-22	109-27	109-21	109-22	−7	110-09	103-19	53,384

Est vol 1,047; vol Fri 2,187; open int 53,384, +621.

10 Yr. Muni Note Index (CBT)-$1,000 x index

Sept	103-04	103-05	102-30	102-30	−6	103-30	97-25	2,912

Est vol 84; vol Fri 322; open int 2,912, +121.
Index: Close 103-12; Yield 4.575.

Source: Republished with permission of Dow Jones & Company, Inc., from *The Wall Street Journal,* August 10, 2004; permission conveyed through the Copyright Clearance Center, Inc.

bonds, the Chicago Board of Trade offers **Municipal Bond Index (MBI) futures.** The index is based on the **Bond Buyer Index** of 40 actively traded general obligation and revenue bonds. The specific characteristics of MBI futures are shown in Exhibit 13.6. Because MBI futures are based on an index rather than on the bonds themselves, there is no physical exchange of bonds. Instead, these futures contracts are settled in cash.

EXHIBIT 13.6   Characteristics of Municipal Bond Index Futures

Characteristics of Futures Contract	Municipal Bond Index Futures
Trading unit	1,000 times the Bond Buyer Municipal Bond Index. A price of 90–00 represents a contract size of $90,000.
Price quotation	In points and thirty-seconds of a point.
Minimum price fluctuation	One thirty-second ($\frac{1}{32}$) of a point, or $31.25 per contract.
Daily trading limits	Three points ($3,000) per contract above or below the previous day's settlement price.
Settlement months	March, June, September, December.
Settlement procedure	Municipal Bond Index futures settle in cash on the last day of trading.

ILLUSTRATION

Palm Insurance Company will be receiving large cash flows in the near future. Although it plans to use some of the incoming funds to purchase municipal bonds, Palm is concerned that because of the likely downward trend in interest rates, municipal bond prices may increase before it can purchase them. Thus, it purchases MBI futures. If Palm's expectation is correct, the futures position will generate a gain, which can be used to pay for the higher-priced bonds once it has sufficient funds. Conversely, if bond prices fall, Palm will incur a loss from its futures position, but it will be able to purchase bonds at a lower price.

Meanwhile Evergreen Securities has agreed to underwrite bonds for various municipalities. It expects the market prices of bonds to decline in the near future. Such an event could reduce underwriting profits if the market price falls before these bonds are sold. To hedge this risk, Evergreen sells MBI futures. The futures position will generate a gain and offset the reduced underwriting profits if the firm's expectations are correct.

Stock Index Futures

A stock index futures contract allows for the buying and selling of a stock index for a specified price at a specified date. Futures for various stock indexes are traded on the Chicago Mercantile Exchange. Exhibit 13.7 shows the contracts that are available and their valuation.

ILLUSTRATION

The S&P 500 index futures contract is valued as the index times $250, so if the index is valued at 1600, the contract is valued at $1600 \times \$250 = \$400,000$. Mini S&P 500 index futures contracts are available for small investors. These contracts are valued at $50 times the index, so if the index is valued at 1600, the contract is valued at $1600 \times \$50 = \$80,000$.

A futures contract on the S&P 500 index represents a composite of 500 large corporations. The purchase of an S&P 500 futures contract obligates the purchaser to purchase the S&P 500 index at a specified settlement date for a specified amount. Thus, participants who expect the stock market to perform well before the settlement date may consider purchasing S&P 500 index futures. Conversely, participants who expect the stock market to perform poorly before the settlement date may consider selling S&P 500 index futures.

EXHIBIT 13.7

Stock Index Futures Contracts

Type of Stock Index Futures Contract	Contract Is Valued As
S&P 500 index	$250 times index
Mini S&P 500 index	$50 times index
S&P Midcap 400 index	$500 times index
S&P Small Cap index	$200 times index
Nasdaq 100 index	$100 times index
Mini Nasdaq 100 index	$20 times index
Mini Nasdaq Composite index	$20 times index
Russell 2000 index	$500 times index
Nikkei (Japan) 225 index	$5 times index

Stock index futures contracts have four settlement dates in a given year—the third Friday in March, June, September, and December. The securities underlying the stock index futures contracts are not deliverable; settlement occurs through a cash payment. On the settlement date, the futures contract is valued according to the quoted stock index. The net gain or loss on the stock index futures contract is the difference between the futures price when the initial position was created and the value of the contract as of the settlement date.

Like other financial futures contracts, stock index futures can be closed out before the settlement date by taking an offsetting position. For example, if an S&P 500 futures contract with a December settlement date is purchased in September, this position can be closed out in November by selling a S&P 500 futures contract with the same December settlement date. When a position is closed out prior to the settlement date, the net gain or loss on the stock index futures contract is the difference between the futures price when the position was created and the futures price when the position is closed out.

Some speculators prefer to trade stock index futures rather than actual stocks because of the smaller transaction costs. The commission for a purchase and subsequent sale of S&P 500 futures contracts is substantially less than the commission for purchasing and selling the equivalent stocks in the S&P 500.

Valuing Stock Index Futures Contracts

The value of a stock index futures contract is highly correlated with the value of the underlying stock index. Nevertheless, the value of the stock index futures contract commonly differs from the price of the underlying asset because of unique features of the stock index futures contract.

ILLUSTRATION Consider that an investor can buy either a stock index or a futures contract on the stock index with a settlement date of six months from now. In either case, the investor will own the stock index in six months, but buying the index rather than the index futures offers distinct advantages and disadvantages. On the favorable side, the buyer of the index receives dividends, whereas the buyer of the index futures does not. On the unfavorable side, the buyer of the index must use funds to buy the index, whereas the buyer of index futures can engage in the futures contract simply by establishing a margin deposit with a relatively small amount of assets (such as Treasury securities) that may generate interest while they are used to satisfy margin requirements.

Assume that the index will pay dividends equal to 3 percent over the next six months. Also assume that the purchaser of the index will borrow funds to purchase the index, at an interest rate of 2 percent over the six-month period. In this example, the advantage of holding the index (a 3 percent dividend yield) relative to holding a futures contract on the index more than offsets the 2 percent cost of financing the purchase of the index. The so-called net financing cost (also called cost of carry) to the purchaser of the underlying assets (the index) is the 2 percent cost of financing minus the 3 percent yield earned on the assets, or −1 percent. A negative cost of carry indicates that the cost of financing is less than the yield earned from dividends.

If the spot price of the index is the same as the futures price, the futures price will be more attractive. In fact, given the information in this example, speculators can engage in arbitrage whereby they earn a risk-free profit without tying up their funds. Specifically, they use borrowed funds to purchase the index at the spot price and simultaneously sell index futures. This strategy generates a 3 percent gain due to the dividend yield and in-

curs a 2 percent cost of financing, or a net gain of 1 percent without tying up any funds over the six-month period. Such arbitrage puts upward pressure on the spot price of the index (because of the purchases of the index) and downward pressure on the index futures price. Once the futures price is 1 percent less than the spot price, arbitrage will no longer be possible because the 3 percent gain from dividends is offset by the 2 percent cost of financing and the 1 percent discount on the futures price. That is, the -1 percent cost of carry is offset by selling index futures at 1 percent less than the spot rate at which the index was purchased. As this example illustrates, the price of the index futures contract is driven by the underlying index, along with the cost of carry. Arbitrage ensures that as the index value and the cost of carry change over time, so will the price of the index futures contract. In general, the underlying security (or index) tends to change by a much greater degree than the cost of carry, so changes in financial futures prices are primarily attributed to changes in the values of the underlying securities (or indexes).

Indicators Monitored by Participants in Stock Index Futures Since stock index futures prices are primarily driven by movements in the corresponding stock indexes, participants in stock index futures monitor indicators that may signal changes in the stock indexes. These investors monitor some of the same economic indicators as bond futures participants, but do not necessarily respond to new information in the same way. Furthermore, index futures participants tend to have divergent views on how the new information will affect a stock index. Consequently, although the new information may cause substantial trading of stock index futures, the trades may not be in the same direction. Thus, the impact of new information on the prices of stock index futures cannot be easily anticipated.

Speculating with Stock Index Futures

Stock index futures can be traded to capitalize on expectations about general stock market movements.

ILLUSTRATION Boulder Insurance Company plans to purchase a variety of stocks for its stock portfolio in December, once cash inflows are received. Although the company does not have cash to purchase the stocks immediately, it is anticipating a large jump in stock market prices before December. Given this situation, it decides to purchase S&P 500 index futures. The futures price on the S&P 500 index with a December settlement date is 1500. The value of an S&P 500 futures contract is $250 times the index. Because the S&P 500 futures prices should move with the stock market, it will rise over time if the company's expectations are correct. Assume that the S&P 500 index rises to 1600 on the settlement date.

In this example, the nominal profit on the S&P 500 index futures is

Selling price	$400,000	(Index value of 1600 × $250)
− Purchase price	− 375,000	(Index value of 1500 × $250)
= Profit	$25,000	

Thus, Boulder was able to capitalize on its expectations even though it did not have sufficient cash to purchase stock. If stock prices had declined over the period of concern, the S&P 500 futures price would have decreased, and Boulder would have incurred a loss on its futures position.

378 PART V • DERIVATIVE SECURITY MARKETS

Hedging with Stock Index Futures

Stock index futures are also commonly used to hedge the market risk of an existing stock portfolio.

> **ILLUSTRATION** Glacier Stock Mutual Fund expects the stock market to decline temporarily, causing a temporary decline in its stock portfolio. The fund could sell its stocks with the intent to repurchase them in the near future, but it would incur excessive transaction costs. A more efficient solution is to sell stock index futures. If the fund's stock portfolio is similar to the S&P 500 index, Glacier can sell futures contracts on that index. If the stock market declines as expected, Glacier will generate a gain when closing out the stock index futures position, which will somewhat offset the loss on its stock portfolio.

This hedge is more effective when the investor's portfolio is diversified like the S&P 500 index. The value of a less diversified stock portfolio will correlate less with the S&P 500 index, so a gain from selling index futures may not completely offset the loss in the portfolio during a market downturn. Assuming that the stock portfolio moves in tandem with the S&P 500, a full hedge would involve the sale of the amount of futures contracts whose combined underlying value is equal to the market value of the stock portfolio being hedged.

> **ILLUSTRATION** Assume that a portfolio manager has a stock portfolio valued at $400,000. Also assume that S&P 500 index futures contracts are available for a settlement date one month from now at a level of 1600, which is about equal to today's index value. The manager could sell S&P 500 futures contracts to hedge the stock portfolio. Since the futures contract is valued at $250 times the index level, the contract will result in a payment of $400,000 at settlement date. One index futures contract will be needed to match the existing value of the stock portfolio. Assuming that the stock index moves in tandem with the manager's stock portfolio, any loss on the portfolio should be offset by the gain on the futures contract. For example, if the stock portfolio declines by about 5 percent over one month, this reflects a loss of $20,000 (5% of $400,000 = $20,000). Yet, the S&P 500 index should also have declined by 5 percent (to a level of 1520). Consequently, the S&P 500 index futures contract that was sold by the manager should result in a gain of $20,000 [(1600 −1520) × $250], which offsets the loss on the stock portfolio.

If the stock market experiences higher prices over the month, the S&P 500 index will rise, creating a loss on the futures contract. The value of the manager's stock portfolio will have increased to offset the loss, however.

Test of Suitability of Stock Index Futures The suitability of using stock index futures to hedge can be assessed by measuring the sensitivity of the portfolio's performance to market movements over a period prior to taking a hedge position. The sensitivity of a hypothetical position in futures to those same market movements in that period could also be assessed. A general test of suitability is to determine whether the hypothetical derivative position would have offset adverse market effects on the portfolio's performance. Although it may be extremely difficult to perfectly hedge all of a portfolio's exposure to market risk, for a hedge to be suitable there should be some evidence that such a hypothetical hedge would have been moderately effective for that firm. That is, if the position in financial derivatives would not have provided an effective hedge of market risk over a recent period, a firm should not expect that it will provide an effective hedge

	Proportion of Stock Portfolio Hedged			
Scenario for Market Return	**0%**	**33%**	**67%**	**100%**
−20%	−20%	−13.4%	−6.7%	0%
−10	−10	−6.7	−3.3	0
0	0	0	0	0
10	+10	+6.7	+3.3	0
20	+20	+13.4	+6.7	0

Note: Numbers are based on the assumption that the stock portfolio moves in perfect tandem with the market.

in the future. This test of suitability uses only data that were available at the time the hedge was to be enacted.

Determining the Proportion of the Portfolio to Hedge Portfolio managers do not necessarily hedge their entire stock portfolio, because they may wish to be partially exposed in the event that stock prices rise. For instance, if the portfolio in the preceding example was valued at $1.2 million, the portfolio manager could have hedged one-third of the stock portfolio by selling one stock index futures contract. The short position in one index futures contract would reflect one-third of the value of the stock portfolio. Alternatively, the manager could have hedged two-thirds of the stock portfolio by selling two stock index futures contracts. The higher the proportion of the portfolio that is hedged, the more insulated the manager's performance is from market conditions, whether those conditions are favorable or unfavorable. Exhibit 13.8 illustrates the net gain (including the gain on the futures and the gain on the stock portfolio) to the portfolio manager under five possible scenarios for the market return (shown in the first column). If the stock market declines, any degree of hedging is beneficial, but the benefits are greater if a higher proportion of the portfolio was hedged. If the stock market performs well, any degree of hedging reduces the net gain, but the reduction is greater if a higher proportion of the portfolio was hedged. In essence, hedging with stock index futures reduces the sensitivity to both unfavorable and favorable market conditions.

Dynamic Asset Allocation with Stock Index Futures

Institutional investors are increasingly using **dynamic asset allocation,** in which they switch between risky and low-risk investment positions over time in response to changing expectations. This strategy allows managers to increase the exposure of their portfolios when they expect favorable market conditions, and to reduce their exposure when they expect unfavorable market conditions. When they anticipate favorable market movements, stock portfolio managers can purchase stock index futures, which intensify the effects of market conditions. Conversely, when they anticipate unfavorable market movements, they can sell stock index futures to reduce the effects that market conditions will have on their stock portfolios. As expectations change frequently, portfolio managers commonly alter their degree of exposure. Stock index futures allow portfolio managers to alter their risk-return position without restructuring their existing stock portfolios. Using dynamic asset allocation in this way avoids the substantial transaction costs that would be associated with restructuring the stock portfolios.

Stock Index Futures Quotations

The Wall Street Journal provides quotations on various stock index futures contracts, as shown here. The most popular index futures contract is the S&P 500 index futures. For each type of contract, there are various settlement dates, one date for each row. For each settlement date, the open, high, low, and settle (closing) prices are quoted across the row. The change ("Chg") in the futures price from the previous day is also shown along with the high and low prices since the futures contract with a specific settlement date was created. The open interest (number of existing contracts that have not been offset) is also shown for each settlement date.

Index Futures

DJ Industrial Average (CBT)-$10 x index
Dec	10063	10063	9976	9993	-54	10575	8440	42,899

Est vol 4,296; vol Fri 6,865; open int 42,911, -707.
Idx prl: Hi 10046.65; Lo 9985.37; Close 9988.54, -58.70.

Mini DJ Industrial Average (CBT)-$5 x index
| Dec | 10063 | 10066 | 9977 | 9993 | -54 | 10511 | 9790 | 33,040 |

Vol Mon 3; open int 33,055, -675.

DJ-AIG Commodity Index (CBT)-$100 x index
| Oct | 483.3 | 484.0 | 483.3 | 484.0 | 3.0 | 484.0 | 456.8 | 2,806 |

Est vol 74,221; vol Fri 0; open int 2,896, unch.
Idx prl: Hi 151.426; Lo 149.673; Close 150.340, +1.003.

S&P 500 Index (CME)-$250 x index
| Dec | 111130 | 111390 | 110330 | 110520 | -630 | 116010 | 78100 | 596,066 |
| Mr05 | 110750 | 111000 | 110460 | 110620 | -630 | 116060 | 84380 | 10,644 |

Est vol 31,638; vol Fri 26,835; open int 607,404, -341.
Idx prl: Hi 1110.11; Lo 1103.24; Close 1103.52, -6.59.

Mini S&P 500 (CME)-$50 x index
| Dec | 111125 | 111400 | 110325 | 110525 | -625 | 114675 | 106050 | 557,182 |

Vol Mon 421,754; open int 559,366, -10,782.

S&P Midcap 400 (CME)-$500 x index
| Dec | 588.00 | 588.00 | 582.50 | 584.50 | -5.00 | 616.50 | 549.25 | 12,686 |

Est vol 344; vol Fri 175; open int 12,687, -18.
Idx prl: Hi 588.50; Lo 581.97; Close 582.76, -5.74.

Nasdaq 100 (CME)-$100 x index
| Dec | 140500 | 140900 | 138650 | 139150 | -1300 | 152800 | 131050 | 73,552 |

Est vol 7,271; vol Fri 12,232; open int 73,564, +131.
Idx prl: Hi 1396.42; Lo 1383.24; Close 1385.55, -13.50.

Mini Nasdaq 100 (CME)-$20 x index
| Dec | 1404.5 | 1409.5 | 1386.5 | 1391.5 | -13.0 | 1532.5 | 1308.0 | 230,678 |

Vol Mon 280,676; open int 231,386, -8,147.

GSCI (CME)-$250 x nearby index
| Oct | 332.80 | 333.00 | 330.50 | 332.50 | 3.30 | 333.00 | 293.00 | 17,369 |

Est vol 69; vol Fri 39; open int 17,372, -7.
Idx prl: Hi 332.94; Lo 330.31; Close 332.18, +2.49.

TRAKRS Long-Short Tech (CME)-$1 x index
| July | ... | ... | ... | 35.51 | -.14 | 45.25 | 19.76 | 186,517 |

Est vol 0; vol Fri 0; open int 186,517, unch.
Idx prl: Hi 35.19; Lo 34.89; Close 34.95, -.25.

Russell 2000 (CME)-$500 x index
| Dec | 564.90 | 566.15 | 557.95 | 560.15 | -5.85 | 605.35 | 517.25 | 26,694 |

Est vol 1,078; vol Fri 690; open int 26,694, +160.
Idx prl: Hi 565.97; Lo 558.36; Close 558.36, -7.61.

Russell 1000 (NYBOT)-$500 x index
| Dec | 592.25 | 592.25 | 589.75 | 590.50 | -3.50 | 604.50 | 588.70 | 72,090 |

Est vol 231; vol Fri 227; open int 72,090, -1.
Idx prl: Hi 593.23; Lo 589.41; Close 589.54, -3.69.

Source: Republished with permission of Dow Jones & Company, Inc., from *The Wall Street Journal,* September 28, 2004; permission conveyed through the Copyright Clearance Center, Inc.

Prices of Stock Index Futures versus Prices of Underlying Stocks

The prices of index futures and the prices of the stocks representing the index can differ to some degree. To understand why, consider a situation in which many institutional investors anticipate a temporary decline in stock prices. Because they expect the decline to be only temporary, the investors prefer not to liquidate their stock portfolios. As a form of portfolio insurance, they sell stock index futures so that any decline in the market value of their stock portfolio will be offset by a gain on their futures position. When numerous institutional investors sell index futures instead of selling stocks to prepare for a market decline, their actions can cause the index futures price to be below the prevailing stock prices.

In some cases, index futures prices may exceed the prices of the stocks that the index comprises. As favorable information about the stock market becomes available, investors

can buy either stock index futures or the actual stocks that make up the index. The futures can be purchased immediately with a small up-front payment. Purchasing actual stocks may take longer because of the time needed to select specific stocks. In addition, a larger up-front investment is necessary. This explains why the price of stock index futures may reflect investor expectations about the market more rapidly than stock prices.

Recent studies have found a high degree of correlation between the stock index futures and the index itself. Price movements in the stock index sometimes lag behind movement in the stock index futures by up to 45 minutes. This confirms that the stock index futures more rapidly reflect new information that can influence expectations about the stock market. Even though the index futures price movements frequently precede stock index movements, the relationship is not consistent enough to develop an exploitable trading strategy in which positions in a stock index are taken based on the most recent movement in the futures index.

Arbitrage with Stock Index Futures

The New York Stock Exchange (NYSE) narrowly defines program trading as the simultaneous buying and selling of at least 15 different stocks that in aggregate is valued at more than $1 million. Program trading is commonly used in conjunction with the trading of stock index futures contracts in a strategy known as **index arbitrage.** Securities firms act as **arbitrageurs** by capitalizing on discrepancies between prices of index futures and stocks. Index arbitrage involves the buying or selling of stock index futures with a simultaneous opposite position in the stocks that the index comprises. The index arbitrage is instigated when prices of stock index futures differ significantly from the stocks represented by the index. For example, if the index futures contract is priced high relative to the stocks representing the index, an arbitrageur may consider purchasing the stocks and simultaneously selling stock index futures. Alternatively, if the index futures are priced low relative to the stocks representing the index, an arbitrageur may purchase index futures and simultaneously sell stocks. An arbitrage profit is attainable if the price differential exceeds the costs incurred from trading in both markets.

Index arbitrage does not cause the price discrepancy between the two markets, but rather responds to it. The arbitrageur's ability to detect price discrepancies between stock and futures markets is enhanced by computers. Roughly 50 percent of all program trading activity is for the purpose of index arbitrage.

Some critics suggest that the index arbitrage activity of purchasing index futures while selling stocks adversely affects stock prices. However, if index futures did not exist, institutional investors could not use portfolio insurance. In this case, a general expectation of a temporary market decline would more likely encourage the sales of stocks to prepare for the decline, which would accelerate the drop in prices.

Stock Index Futures Circuit Breakers

Circuit breakers are trading restrictions imposed on specific stocks or stock indexes. The Chicago Mercantile Exchange imposes circuit breakers on the S&P 500 futures contract.

By prohibiting trading for short time periods when prices decline to specific threshold levels, circuit breakers may allow investors to determine whether circulating rumors are true and to work out credit arrangements if they have received a margin call. If prices are still perceived to be too high when the markets reopen, the prices will decline further. Thus, circuit breakers do not guarantee that prices will turn upward. Nevertheless, they may be able to prevent large declines in prices that would be attributed to panic selling rather than to fundamental forces.

EXHIBIT 13.9   Use of Circuit Breakers during the Mini-Crash on October 13, 1989

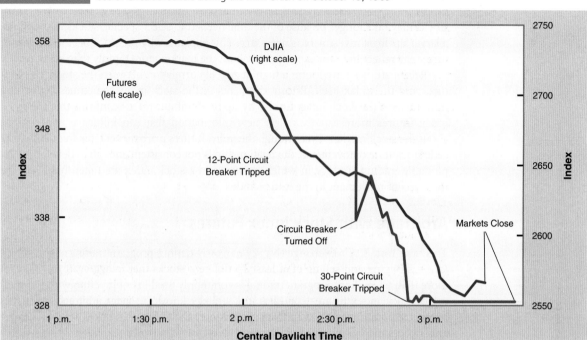

Note: The futures price is the minute-by-minute average of the December 1989 S&P 500 stock index futures contract traded at the Chicago Mercantile Exchange. The stock price is the minute-by-minute average of the Dow Jones Industrial Average.
Source: *Economic Review,* Federal Reserve Bank of Kansas City (March–April 1990): 39.

The first test for the circuit breakers was on October 13, 1989, when stocks declined by about 5 percent on average. Exhibit 13.9 shows the price trends of stocks and index futures on this day. At 2:07 P.M., the first circuit breaker tripped as the S&P futures contract declined by 12 points below the previous day's closing price. Stocks were not subject to that circuit breaker, however, and their prices continued to decline while index futures trading was halted. When the index futures market reopened, the index futures price dropped sharply, then increased for a few minutes, and then declined until 2:45 P.M.; at that time, it was 30 points below the previous day's close. Consequently, the second breaker was imposed. It is unclear whether the circuit breakers reduced panic selling on this day, as it is difficult to determine how futures prices would have changed without the circuit breakers.

On July 23, 1990, the circuit breakers were tested once again. Stock market prices plunged in the morning, causing a circuit breaker to be imposed on stock index futures. Meanwhile, the NYSE asked members to temporarily stop index arbitrage trades. The pessimism subsided shortly thereafter. Some traders acknowledged that the market decline could have been much more pronounced without the use of circuit breakers on this day.

Single Stock Futures

A single stock futures contract is an agreement to buy or sell a specified number of shares of a specified stock on a specified future date. Such contracts have been traded on futures exchanges in Australia and Europe since the 1990s. In 2001, the Nasdaq

market and the London International Financial Futures and Options Exchange (LIFFE) engaged in a joint venture to create a U.S. market for trading single stock futures. The contracts are available for specific stocks that are traded on the Nasdaq market or NYSE. The nominal size of a contract is 100 shares. Investors can buy or sell singles stock futures contracts through their broker. The orders to buy and sell a specific single stock futures contract are matched electronically. Single stock futures have become increasingly popular in the short period of time they have existed. They are regulated by the Commodity Futures Trading Commission (CFTC) and the Securities and Exchange Commission (SEC).

Settlement dates are on the third Friday of the delivery month on a quarterly basis (March, June, September, and December) for the next five quarters, as well as the nearest two months. For example, on January 3, an investor could purchase a stock futures contract for the third Friday in the next two months (January or February), or over the next five quarters (March, June, September, December, and March of the following year). Trading hours are from 9:30 A.M. to 4 P.M. eastern standard time. An investor can buy single stock futures on margin.

Investors who expect a particular stock's price to rise over time may consider buying futures on that stock. To obtain a contract to buy March futures on 100 shares of Zyco stock for $5,000 ($50 per share), an investor must submit the $5,000 payment to the clearinghouse on the third Friday in March and will receive shares of Zyco stock on the settlement date. If Zyco stock is valued at $53 at the time of settlement, the investor can sell the stock in the stock market for a gain of $3 per share or $300 for the contract (ignoring commissions). This gain would likely reflect a substantial return on the investment since the investor had to invest only a small margin (perhaps 20 percent of the contract price) to take a position in futures. If Zyco stock is valued at $46 at the time of settlement, the investor would incur a loss of $4 share, which would reflect a substantial percentage loss on the investment. Thus, single stock futures offer potential high returns but also high risk.

Investors who expect a particular stock's price to decline over time can sell futures contracts on that stock. This activity is somewhat similar to selling a stock short, except that single stock futures can be sold without borrowing the underlying stock from a broker as short-sellers must do. To obtain a contract to sell March futures of Zyco stock, an investor must deliver Zyco stock to the clearinghouse on the third Friday in March and will receive the payment specified in the futures contract.

Investors can close out their position at any time by taking the opposite position. For example, assume that shortly after the investor purchased futures on Zyco stock with a March delivery at $50 per share, the stock price declines. Rather than incur the risk that the price could continue to decline, the investor could sell a Zyco futures contract with a March delivery. If this contract specifies a price of $48 per share, the investor's gain will be the difference between the selling price and the buying price, which is −$2 per share or −$200 for the contract.

The Chicago Board of Options Exchange and the Chicago Board of Trade recently engaged in a joint venture called OneChicago, which serves as another market for trading single stock futures. The contract specifications are similar to those established by Nasdaq and LIFFE. The contracts are traded electronically.

Risk of Trading Futures Contracts

Users of futures contracts must recognize the various types of risk exhibited by such contracts and other derivative instruments.

Market Risk

Market risk refers to fluctuations in the value of the instrument as a result of market conditions. Firms that use futures contracts to speculate should be concerned about market risk. If their expectations about future market conditions are wrong, they may suffer losses on their futures contracts. Firms that use futures contracts to hedge are less concerned about market risk because if market conditions cause a loss on their derivative instruments, they should have a partial offsetting gain on the positions that they were hedging.

Basis Risk

A second type of risk is **basis risk,** or the risk that the position being hedged by the futures contracts is not affected in the same manner as the instrument underlying the futures contract. This type of risk applies only to those firms or individuals who are using futures contracts to hedge. For example, consider a bond portfolio manager who uses Treasury bond futures contracts to hedge a portfolio of Treasury bonds that have, on average, five years remaining until maturity. The value of the Treasury bonds may not necessarily move in perfect tandem with the value of the Treasury bond portfolio, because the maturities (and the duration) of the bond portfolio and the underlying securities in the futures contract are not exactly the same. Therefore, a short position in Treasury bond futures contracts will not perfectly offset the impact of interest rate movements on the Treasury bond portfolio.

Liquidity Risk

A third type of risk is **liquidity risk,** which refers to potential price distortions due to a lack of liquidity. For example, a firm may purchase a particular bond futures contract to speculate on expectations of rising bond prices. However, when it attempts to close out its position by selling an identical futures contract, it may find that there are no willing buyers for this type of futures contract at that time. In this case, the firm will have to sell the futures contract at a lower price. Users of futures contracts may reduce liquidity risk by using only those futures contracts that are widely traded.

Credit Risk

A fourth type of risk is **credit risk,** which is the risk that a loss will occur because a counterparty defaults on the contract. This type of risk exists for over-the-counter transactions, in which a firm or individual relies on the creditworthiness of a counterparty.

The possibility that counterparties will not fulfill their obligations is not a concern when trading futures and other derivatives on exchanges, because the exchanges normally guarantee that the provisions of the contract will be honored. The financial intermediaries that make the arrangements in the over-the-counter market can also take some steps to reduce this type of risk. First, the financial intermediary can require that each party provide some form of collateral to back up its position. Second, the financial intermediary can serve as a guarantor (for a fee) in the event that the counterparty does not fulfill its obligation.

Prepayment Risk

Prepayment risk refers to the possibility that the assets to be hedged may be prepaid earlier than their designated maturity. Suppose a commercial bank sells Treasury bond futures in order to hedge its holdings of corporate bonds, and just after the futures position is created, the bonds are called by the corporation that initially issued them. If interest rates subsequently decline, the bank will incur a loss from its futures position without a corresponding gain from its bond position (because the bonds were called earlier).

As a second example, consider a savings and loan association with large holdings of long-term fixed-rate mortgages that are mostly financed by short-term funds. It sells Treasury bond futures to hedge against the possibility of rising interest rates; then, after the futures position is established, interest rates decline, and many of the existing mortgages are prepaid by homeowners. The savings and loan association will incur a loss from its futures position without a corresponding gain from its fixed-rate mortgage position (because the mortgages were prepaid).

Operational Risk

A sixth type of risk is **operational risk,** which is the risk of losses as a result of inadequate management or controls. For example, firms that use futures contracts to hedge are exposed to the possibility that the employees responsible for their futures positions do not fully understand how values of specific futures contracts will respond to market conditions. Furthermore, those employees may take more speculative positions than the firms desire if the firms do not have adequate controls to monitor their positions.

Futures Markets Regulation

Given recent cases in which firms incurred major losses on futures contracts or other derivative securities, there is more awareness about **systemic risk,** or the risk that a particular event (such as financial problems at one particular firm) could spread adverse effects among several firms or among financial markets. The concern about systemic risk stems from the intertwined relationships among firms that engage in derivative securities trading that obligates them to make future payments to each other.

ILLUSTRATION   Nexus Inc. requests several transactions in derivative securities, in which it buys futures on Treasury bonds in an over-the-counter market. Bangor Bank accommodates Nexus by taking the opposite side of the transactions. The bank's positions in these contracts also serve as a hedge against its existing exposure to interest rate risk. As time passes, Nexus experiences financial problems. As interest rates rise and the value of a Treasury bond futures contract declines, Nexus will take a major loss on the futures transactions. It files for bankruptcy, as it is unable to fulfill its obligation to buy the Treasury bonds from Bangor Bank at the settlement date. Bangor Bank was relying on this payment to hedge its exposure to interest rate risk. Consequently, Bangor Bank experiences financial problems and cannot make the payments on other over-the-counter derivatives contracts that it has with three other financial institutions. These financial institutions were relying on those funds to cover their own obligations on derivative

contracts with several other firms. These firms may then be unable to honor their payment obligations resulting from derivative contract agreements, causing the adverse effects to spread further.

Lengthy delays in payment could also disrupt the financial markets. Systemic risk is more pronounced as a result of the increasing use of over-the-counter markets for the trading of derivative securities.

Various regulators have attempted to reduce systemic risk by ensuring that participants in derivative securities markets have adequate collateral to back their derivative positions and that the participants fully disclose their exposure to risk resulting from derivative positions. For example, the Federal Reserve System monitors the commercial banks that participate in the derivative securities markets to ensure that they have adequate capital.

Furthermore, accounting regulators revised accounting standards in 1994 to require more disclosure about derivative positions. Specifically, firms are now required to report both their objectives in using derivative securities and the means by which they plan to achieve those objectives. The accounting guidelines also encourage firms to measure the impact of various possible economic scenarios on their derivative positions. Some, but not all, types of derivative securities must be reported in the financial statements. Similarly, some, but not all, derivative securities must be valued in financial statements at their market value. There is an ongoing effort to make the accounting rules more consistent among derivative securities in the United States and throughout other countries as well.

Institutional Use of Futures Markets

Exhibit 13.10 summarizes the manner in which various types of financial institutions participate in futures markets. Financial institutions generally use futures contracts to reduce risk, as has already been illustrated by several examples. Some commercial banks and savings institutions use a short hedge to protect against a possible increase in interest rates. Some bond mutual funds, pension funds, and life insurance companies take

EXHIBIT 13.10

Institutional Use of Futures Markets

Type of Financial Institution	Participation in Futures Markets
Commercial banks	• Take positions in futures contracts to hedge against interest rate risk.
Savings institutions	• Take positions in futures contracts to hedge against interest rate risk.
Securities firms	• Execute futures transactions for individuals and firms. • Take positions in futures contracts to hedge their own portfolios against stock market or interest rate movements.
Mutual funds	• Take positions in futures contracts to speculate on future stock market or interest rate movements. • Take positions in futures contracts to hedge their portfolios against stock market or interest rate movements.
Pension funds	• Take positions in futures contracts to hedge their portfolios against stock market or interest rate movements.
Insurance companies	• Take positions in futures contracts to hedge their portfolios against stock market or interest rate movements.

short positions in interest rate futures to insulate their bond portfolios from a possible increase in interest rates. Stock mutual funds, pension funds, and insurance companies take short positions in stock index futures to partially insulate their respective stock portfolios from adverse stock market movements.

Futures Markets Globalization

 GL BALASPECTS   The trading of financial futures also requires the assessment of international financial market conditions. The flow of foreign funds into and out of the United States can affect interest rates and therefore the market value of Treasury bonds, corporate bonds, mortgages, and other long-term debt securities. Portfolio managers assess international flows of funds to forecast changes in interest rate movements, which in turn affect the value of their respective portfolios. Even speculators assess international flows of funds to forecast interest rates so that they can determine whether to take short or long futures positions.

Non-U.S. Participation in U.S. Futures Contracts

Financial futures contracts on U.S. securities are commonly traded by non-U.S. financial institutions that maintain holdings of U.S. securities. These institutions use financial futures to reduce their exposure to U.S. stock market or interest rate movements. The Chicago Board of Trade has allowed more access to non-U.S. customers by expanding its trading hours to cover various time zones.

Foreign Stock Index Futures

Foreign stock index futures have been created to either speculate on or hedge against potential movements in foreign stock markets. Expectations of a strong foreign stock market encourage the purchase of futures contracts on the representative index. Conversely, if firms expect a decline in the foreign market, they will consider selling futures on the representative index. In addition, financial institutions with substantial investment in a particular foreign stock market can hedge against a temporary decline in that market by selling foreign stock index futures.

Some of the more popular foreign stock index futures contracts are identified in Exhibit 13.11. Numerous other foreign stock index futures contracts have been created. In

EXHIBIT 13.11
Popular Foreign Stock Index Futures Contracts

Name of Stock Futures Index	Description
Nikkei 225	225 Japanese stocks
Toronto 35	35 stocks on Toronto stock exchange
Financial Times Stock Exchange 100	100 stocks on London stock exchange
Barclays share price	40 stocks on New Zealand stock exchange
Hang Seng	33 stocks on Hong Kong stock exchange
Osaka	50 Japanese stocks
All Ordinaries share price	307 Australian stocks

fact, futures exchanges have been established in Ireland, France, Spain, and Italy. Financial institutions around the world can use futures contracts to hedge against temporary declines in their asset portfolios. Speculators can take long or short positions to speculate on a particular market with a relatively small initial investment. Financial futures on debt instruments (such as futures on German government bonds) are also offered by numerous exchanges in non-U.S. markets, including the London International Financial Futures Exchange, Singapore International Monetary Exchange (SIMEX), and Sydney Futures Exchange (SFE). In 2001, the LIFFE was acquired by Euronext, an alliance of European stock exchanges.

Electronic trading of futures contracts is creating an internationally integrated futures market. As mentioned earlier, the Chicago Mercantile Exchange has instituted GLOBEX, a round-the-world electronic trading network. It allows financial futures contracts to be traded even when the trading floor is closed.

Currency Futures Contracts

A **currency futures contract** is a standardized agreement to deliver or receive a specified amount of a specified foreign currency at a specified price (exchange rate) and date. The settlement months are March, June, September, and December. Some companies act as hedgers in the currency futures market by purchasing futures on currencies that they will need in the future to cover payables or by selling futures on currencies that they will receive in the future. Speculators in the currency futures market may purchase futures on a foreign currency that they expect to strengthen against the U.S. dollar or sell futures on currencies that they expect to weaken against the U.S. dollar.

Purchasers of currency futures contracts can hold the contract until the settlement date and accept delivery of the foreign currency at that time, or they can close out their long position prior to the settlement date by selling the identical type and number of contracts before then. If they close out their long position, their gain or loss is determined by the futures price when they created the position versus the futures price at the time the position was closed out. Sellers of currency futures contracts either deliver the foreign currency at the settlement date or close out their position by purchasing an identical type and number of contracts prior to the settlement date.

SUMMARY

■ A financial futures contract is a standardized agreement to deliver or receive a specified amount of a specified financial instrument at a specified price and date. As the market value of the underlying instrument changes, so will the value of the financial futures contract. As the market value of the underlying instrument rises, there is a greater demand for the futures contract that has locked in the price of the instrument.

■ An interest rate futures contract locks in the price to be paid for a specified debt instrument. Speculators who expect interest rates to decline can purchase interest rate futures contracts, because the market value of the underlying debt instrument should rise. Speculators who expect interest rates to rise can sell interest rate futures contracts, because the market value of the underlying debt instrument should decrease.

Financial institutions (or other firms) that desire to hedge against rising interest rates can sell interest rate futures contracts. Financial institutions that desire to hedge against declining interest rates can purchase these contracts. If interest rates move in the anticipated direction, the financial institutions will gain from their futures position, which can partially offset any adverse effects of the interest rate movements on their normal operations.

■ Speculators who expect stock prices to increase can purchase stock index futures contracts; speculators who expect stock prices to decrease can sell these contracts. Stock index futures can be sold by financial institutions that expect a temporary decline in stock prices and wish to hedge their stock portfolios.

■ Depository institutions such as commercial banks and savings institutions commonly sell interest rate futures contracts to hedge against a possible increase in interest rates. Bond mutual funds, pension funds, and insurance companies also sell interest rate futures contracts to hedge their bond portfolios against a possible increase in interest rates.

Stock mutual funds, pension funds, and insurance companies frequently sell stock index futures contracts to hedge their stock portfolios against a possible temporary decrease in stock prices.

POINT COUNTER-POINT

Has the Futures Market Created More Uncertainty for Stocks?

Point Yes. Futures contracts encourage speculation on indexes. Thus, an entire market can be influenced by the trading of speculators.

Counter-Point No. Futures contracts are commonly used to hedge portfolios and therefore can reduce the effects of weak market conditions. Moreover, investing in stocks is just as speculative as taking a position in futures markets.

Who Is Correct? Use your favorite search engine to learn more about this issue. Offer your own opinion on this issue.

QUESTIONS AND APPLICATIONS

1. **Hedging with Futures** Elon Savings and Loan Association has a large number of 30-year mortgages with floating interest rates that adjust on an annual basis and obtains most of its funds by issuing five-year certificates of deposit. It uses the yield curve to assess the market's anticipation of future interest rates. It believes that expectations of future interest rates are the major force affecting the yield curve. Assume that a downward-sloping yield curve with a steep slope exists. Based on this information, should Elon consider using financial futures as a hedging technique? Explain.

2. **Internet Exercise** Go to http://legacy.futuresource.com/partners/cme. Review the charts for an equity index product such as the S&P 500. Explain how the price pattern moved recently. Now compare that to the actual trend of the S&P 500, which is provided at http://finance.yahoo.com/?u (just click on S&P 500 there to access the charts). Describe the relationship between the movements in S&P 500 futures and movements in the S&P 500 index.

3. **Gains from Purchasing Futures** Explain how purchasers of financial futures contracts can offset their position. How is their gain or loss determined? What is the maximum loss to a purchaser of a futures contract?

4. **Hedging Decision** Why do some financial institutions remain exposed to interest rate risk, even when they believe that the use of interest rate futures could reduce their exposure?

5. **Managing in Financial Markets: Managing Portfolios with Futures Contracts** As a portfolio manager, you are monitoring previous investments that you made in stocks and bonds of U.S. firms, as well as stocks and bonds of Japanese firms. Though you plan to

keep all of these investments over the long run, you are willing to hedge against adverse effects on your investments that result from economic conditions. You expect that over the next year, U.S. and Japanese interest rates will decline, the U.S. stock market will perform poorly, the Japanese stock market will perform well, and the Japanese yen (the currency) will depreciate against the dollar.

a. Should you consider taking a position in U.S. bond index futures to hedge your investment in U.S. bonds? Explain.

b. Should you consider taking a position in Japanese bond index futures to hedge your investment in Japanese bonds? Explain.

c. Should you consider taking a position in U.S. stock index futures to hedge your investment in U.S. stocks? Explain.

d. Should you consider taking a position in Japanese stock index futures to hedge your investment in Japanese stocks? (Note: The Japanese stock index is denominated in yen and therefore is used to hedge stock movements, not currency movements.)

e. Should you consider taking a position in Japanese yen futures to hedge the exchange rate risk of your investment in Japanese stocks and bonds?

6. **Impact of Futures Hedge** Explain how the probability distribution of a financial institution's returns is affected when it uses interest rate futures to hedge. What does this imply about its risk?

7. **Hedging Decision** Blue Devil Savings and Loan Association has a large number of 10-year fixed-rate mortgages and obtains most of its funds from short-term deposits. It uses the yield curve to assess the market's anticipation of future interest rates. It believes that expectations of future interest rates are the major force affecting the yield curve. Assume that an upward-sloping yield curve with a steep slope exists. Based on this information, should Blue Devil consider using financial futures as a hedging technique? Explain.

8. **Stock Index Futures** Describe stock index futures. How could they be used by a financial institution that is anticipating a jump in stock prices but does not yet have sufficient funds to purchase large amounts of stock? Explain why stock index futures may reflect investor expectations about the market more quickly than stock prices.

9. **Futures Contracts** Describe the general characteristics of a futures contract. How does a clearinghouse facilitate the trading of financial futures contracts?

10. **Gains from Selling Futures** Explain how sellers of financial futures contracts can offset their position. How is their gain or loss determined?

11. **Interpreting Financial News** Interpret the following statements made by Wall Street analysts and portfolio managers:

a. "The existence of financial futures contracts allows our firm to hedge against temporary market declines without liquidating our portfolios."

b. "Given my confidence in the market, I plan to use stock index futures to increase my exposure to market movements."

c. "We used currency futures to hedge the exchange rate exposure of our international mutual fund focused on German stocks."

12. **Long versus Short Hedge** Explain the difference between a long hedge and a short hedge used by financial institutions. When is a long hedge more appropriate than a short hedge?

13. **Futures Pricing** How does the price of a financial futures contract change as the market price of the security it represents changes? Why?

14. **Hedging with Futures** Assume a financial institution has a larger amount of rate-sensitive assets than rate-sensitive liabilities. Would it be more likely to be adversely affected by an increase or a decrease in interest rates? Should it purchase or sell interest rate futures contracts in order to hedge its exposure?

15. **Circuit Breakers** Explain the use of circuit breakers.

16. **Hedging with Futures** Explain why some futures contracts may be more suitable than others for hedging exposure to interest rate risk.

17. **Cross-Hedging** Describe the act of cross-hedging. What determines the effectiveness of a cross-hedge?

18. **Treasury Bond Futures** Will speculators buy or sell Treasury bond futures contracts if they expect interest rates to increase? Explain.

19. **Index Arbitrage** Explain how index arbitrage may be used.

20. **Hedging with Futures** Assume a financial institution has a larger amount of rate-sensitive liabilities than rate-sensitive assets. Would it be more likely to be adversely affected by an increase or a decrease in interest rates? Should it purchase or sell interest rate

futures contracts in order to hedge its exposure?

21. **Selling Stock Index Futures** Why would a pension fund or insurance company even consider selling stock index futures?

22. **Hedging with Bond Futures** How might a savings and loan association use Treasury bond futures to hedge its fixed-rate mortgage portfolio (assuming that its main source of funds is short-term deposits)? Explain how prepayments on mortgages can limit the effectiveness of the hedge.

PROBLEMS

1. **Profit from Stock Index Futures** Marks Insurance Company sold S&P 500 stock index futures that specified an index of 1690. When the position was closed out, the index specified by the futures contract was 1720. Determine the profit or loss, ignoring transaction costs.

2. **Profit from T-bill Futures** Toland Company sold T-bill futures contracts when the quoted price was 94.00. When this position was closed out, the quoted price was 93.20. Determine the profit or loss per contract, ignoring transaction costs.

3. **Profit from T-bill Futures** Spratt Company purchased T-bill futures contracts when the quoted price was 93.50. When this position was closed out, the quoted price was 94.75. Determine the profit or loss per contract, ignoring transaction costs.

4. **Profit from T-bond Futures** Egan Company purchased a futures contract on Treasury bonds that specified a price of 91–00. When the position was closed out, the price of the Treasury bond futures contract was 90–10. Determine the profit or loss, ignoring transaction costs.

5. **Profit from T-bill Futures** Suerth Investments Inc. purchased T-bill futures contracts when the quoted price was 95.00. When this position was closed out, the quoted price was 93.60. Determine the profit or loss per contract, ignoring transaction costs.

6. **Profit from T-bill Futures** Rude Dynamics Inc. sold T-bill futures contracts when the quoted price was 93.26. When this position was closed out, the quoted price was 93.90. Determine the profit or loss per contract, ignoring transaction costs.

7. **Profit from T-bond Futures** R. C. Clark sold a futures contract on Treasury bonds that specified a price of 92–10. When the position was closed out, the price of the Treasury bond futures contract was 93–00. Determine the profit or loss, ignoring transaction costs.

FLOW OF FUNDS EXERCISE

Hedging with Futures Contracts

Recall that if the economy continues to be strong, Carson Company may need to increase its production capacity by about 50 percent over the next few years to satisfy demand. It would need financing to expand and accommodate the increase in production. Recall that the yield curve is currently upward sloping. Also recall that Carson is concerned about a possible slowing of the economy because of potential Fed actions to reduce inflation. Carson currently relies mostly on commercial loans with floating interest rates for its debt financing.

a. How could Carson use futures contracts to reduce the exposure of its cost of debt to interest rate movements? Be specific about whether it would use a short hedge or a long hedge.

b. Will the hedge that you described in the previous question perfectly offset the increase in debt costs if interest rates increase? Explain what drives the profit from the short hedge, versus what drives the higher cost of debt to Carson if interest rates increase.

WSJ EXERCISE

Assessing Changes in Futures Prices

Use *The Wall Street Journal* to determine the recent changes in the futures prices on Treasury bonds and on the S&P 500 index.

	Recent Change in Futures Prices	Your Explanation for the Change in the Futures Price
Treasury bonds		
S&P 500 Index		

CHAPTER 14

Options Markets

S tock options can be used by speculators to benefit from their expectations and by financial institutions to reduce their risk. Options markets facilitate the trading of stock options.

The specific objectives of this chapter are to:

■ describe how stock options are traded,

■ explain how stock options are used to speculate,

■ explain why stock option premiums vary,

■ explain the use of stock index options, and

■ explain the use of options on futures.

Background on Options

http://
http://www.cboe.com
The volume of calls versus the volume of puts—use to assess their respective popularity.

Options are classified as calls or puts. A **call option** grants the owner the right to purchase a specified financial instrument for a specified price (called the **exercise price** or **strike price**) within a specified period of time. There are two major differences between purchasing an option and purchasing a futures contract. First, the option requires that a premium be paid in addition to the price of the financial instrument. Second, owners of options can choose to let the option expire on the so-called expiration date without exercising it. That is, call options grant a right, but not an obligation, to purchase a specified financial instrument. The seller (sometimes called the **writer**) of a call option is obligated to provide the specified financial instrument at the price specified by the option contract if the owner exercises the option. Sellers of call options receive an up-front fee (the premium) from the purchaser as compensation.

A call option is said to be **in the money** when the market price of the underlying security exceeds the exercise price, **at the money** when the market price is equal to the exercise price, and **out of the money** when it is below the exercise price.

The second type of option is known as a **put option.** It grants the owner the right to sell a specified financial instrument for a specified price within a specified period of time. As with call options, owners pay a premium to obtain put options. They can exercise the options at any time up to the expiration date but are not obligated to do so.

A put option is said to be "in the money" when the market price of the underlying security is below the exercise price, "at the money" when the market price is equal to the exercise price, and "out of the money" when it exceeds the exercise price.

Call and put options specify 100 shares for the stocks to which they are assigned. Premiums paid for call and put options are determined on the trading floor of exchanges through competitive open outcry between exchange members. The premium for a particular option changes over time as it becomes more or less desirable to traders.

Participants can close out their option positions by making an offsetting transaction. For example, purchasers of an option can offset their positions at any time by selling an identical option. The gain or loss is determined by the premium paid when purchasing the option versus the premium received when selling an identical option. Sellers of options can close out their positions at any time by purchasing an identical option.

The stock options just described are known as "American-style" stock options. They can be exercised at any time until the expiration date. In contrast, "European-style" stock options can be exercised only just before expiration.

Markets Used to Trade Options

The Chicago Board of Options Exchange (CBOE), which was created in 1973, is the most important exchange for trading options. It serves as a market for options on more than 1,500 different stocks. Before the creation of the CBOE, some stock options were exchanged between financial institutions, but the contracts were customized and exchanged largely through personal agreements. In contrast, the options listed on the CBOE have a standardized format, as will be explained shortly. The standardization of the contracts on the CBOE proved to be a major advantage because it allowed for easy trading of existing contracts (a secondary market). More details about stock options traded on the CBOE are provided at http://www.cboe.com.

With standardization, the popularity of options increased, and the options became more liquid. Since there were numerous buyers and sellers of the standardized contracts, buyers and sellers of a particular option contract could be matched. Various stock exchanges noticed the growing popularity of stock options and began to list options. In particular, the American Stock Exchange, Philadelphia Stock Exchange, and Pacific Stock Exchange list options on many different stocks. Today, about 51 percent of all option trading in the United States is conducted on the CBOE, with most of the remaining trades divided among various stock exchanges.

The International Securities Exchange is the first over-the-counter options exchange. It does not have a visible trading floor; instead, its brokers and market-makers conduct trades from different locations through a computer network in much the same way that stock transactions are conducted on the Nasdaq market. When options contracts were first traded, the exchanges did not compete for the contracts. An option contract for a particular firm would be sold on only one exchange. Today, any particular options contract may be traded on various exchanges, and the competition among the exchanges may result in more favorable prices for customers.

Listing Requirements Each exchange has its own requirements for the stocks for which it creates options. One key requirement is a minimum trading volume of the underlying stock, as the volume of options traded on a particular stock will normally be higher if the stock trading volume is high. The decision to list an option is made by each exchange, not by the firms represented by the options contracts.

Role of the Options Clearing Corporation (OCC) Like a stock transaction, the trading of an option involves a buyer and a seller. The sale of an option imposes specific obligations on the seller under specific conditions. The exchange itself does not take posi-

tions in option contracts, but provides a market where the options can be bought or sold. The Options Clearing Corporation (OCC) serves as a guarantor on option contracts traded in the United States, which means that the buyer of an option contract does not have to be concerned that the seller will back out of the obligation.

Regulation of Options Trading Options trading is regulated by the Securities and Exchange Commission (SEC) and by the various option exchanges. The regulation is intended to ensure fair and orderly trading. For example, it attempts to prevent insider trading (trading based on information that insiders have about their firms and that is not yet disclosed to the public). It also attempts to prevent price fixing among floor brokers that could cause wider bid-ask spreads that would impose higher costs on customers.

How Option Trades Are Executed

The trading of options on an exchange is conducted by floor brokers and market-makers.

Floor Brokers Floor brokers execute transactions desired by investors.

ILLUSTRATION An investor calls her broker to place an order to purchase a specific option on a particular stock. The brokerage firm identifies the exchange where that stock option is listed. It owns a specific "seat" on that exchange, which allows it to have a floor broker at the exchange who can trade various option contracts. The floor broker receives the order and goes to the specific location (a particular spot on the trading pit) at the exchange where the option is traded. He executes the desired purchase of the stock option in the trading pit. The trade reflects an agreement between that floor broker and another floor broker in the pit, who was responsible for selling the same type of option for a different customer.

Some orders are executed electronically at options exchanges instead of through floor brokers. For example, the Philadelphia Stock Exchange has a computerized system that matches up small orders to buy or sell options.

Market-Makers Market-makers can execute stock option transactions for customers, but they also trade stock options for their own account. In some cases, a market-maker may facilitate a buy order for one customer and a sell order for a different customer. The market-maker earns the difference between the bid price and the ask price for this trade. For example, a particular stock option may be quoted at a bid-ask price of bid $5, with an ask price of $5.30 per share. The spread is $.30 per share, which is the amount the market-maker earns from facilitating the trade between two parties. Today, actively traded options have a spread of $.25 or less. The spread has declined significantly in recent years.

Market-makers not only benefit from the spread, but may also earn profits when they take positions in options. Like any investors, they are subject to the risk of losses on their positions.

Order Types

As with stocks, an investor can use either a market order or a limit order for an option transaction. A market order will result in the immediate purchase or sale of an option at the prevailing market price of the option. With a limit order, the transaction will occur

EXHIBIT 14.1
McDonald's Stock Option
Quotations

	Strike	Exp.	Vol.	Call	Vol.	Put
McDonald's	45	Jun	180	4½	60	2¾
	45	Oct	70	5¾	120	3¾
	50	Jun	360	1⅛	40	5⅛
	50	Oct	90	3½	40	6½

only if the market price is no higher or lower than a specified price limit. For example, an investor may request the purchase of a specific option only if it can be purchased at or below some specified price. Conversely, an investor may request to sell an option only if it can be sold for some specified limit or more.

Online Trading Option contracts can also be purchased or sold online. Many online brokerage firms, including E*Trade and Datek, facilitate options orders. Some online option contract orders are routed to computerized networks on options exchanges, where they are executed. For these orders, computers handle the order from the time it is placed until it is executed.

Stock Option Quotations

Financial newspapers and some local newspapers publish quotations for stock options. Exhibit 14.1 provides an example of McDonald's stock options as of May 1, when the stock was priced at about $45.62 per share. There are more options on McDonald's stock than are shown here, with additional exercise prices and expiration dates. Each row represents a specific option on McDonald's stock. The first column lists the exercise (strike) price, and the second column lists the expiration date. (The expiration date for stock options traded on the CBOE is the Saturday following the third Friday of the specified month.) The third and fourth columns show the volume and the most recently quoted premium of the call option with that exercise price and expiration date. The fifth and sixth columns show the volume and the most recently quoted premium of the put option with that exercise price and expiration date. A comparison of the premiums among the four options illustrates how specific factors affect option premiums. First, a comparison of the first and third rows (to control for the same expiration date) reveals that an option with a higher exercise price has a lower call option premium and a higher put option premium. A comparison of the second and fourth rows further confirms this relationship. Second, comparing the first and second rows (to control for the same exercise price) reveals that an option with a longer term to maturity has a higher call option premium and a higher put option premium. A comparison of the third and fourth rows further confirms this relationship.

http://

http://biz.yahoo.com/opt/
Summary of the most
actively traded stock
options.

Speculating with Stock Options

Stock options are frequently traded by investors who are attempting to capitalize on their expectations. Whether call options or put options are traded depends on the speculator's expectations.

Speculating with Call Options

Call options can be used to speculate on the expectation of an increase in the price of the underlying stock.

Pat Jackson expects Steelco stock to increase from its current price of $113 per share but does not want to tie up her available funds by investing in stocks. She purchases a call option on Steelco with an exercise price of $115 for a premium of $4 per share. Before the option's expiration date, Steelco's price rises to $121. At that time, Jackson exercises her option, purchasing shares at $115 per share. She then immediately sells those shares at the market price of $121 per share. Her net gain on this transaction is measured below:

Amount received when selling shares	$121 per share
− Amount paid for shares	−$115 per share
− Amount paid for the call option	−$ 4 per share
= Net gain	$ 2 per share or $200 for one contract

Pat's net gain of $2 per share reflects a return of 50 percent (not annualized).

If the price of Steelco stock had not risen above $115 before the option's expiration date, Jackson would have let the option expire. Her net loss would have been the $4 per share she initially paid for the option, or $400 for one option contract. This example reflects a 100 percent loss, as the entire amount of the investment is lost.

The potential gains or losses from this call option are shown in the left portion of Exhibit 14.2, based on the assumptions that (1) the call option is exercised on the expiration date, if at all, and (2) if the call option is exercised, the shares received are immediately sold. Exhibit 14.2 shows that the maximum loss when purchasing this option is the premium of $4 per share. For stock prices between $115 and $119, the option is exercised, and the purchaser of a call option incurs a net loss of less than $4 per share. The

EXHIBIT 14.2 Potential Gains or Losses on a Call Option: Exercise Price = $115, Premium = $4

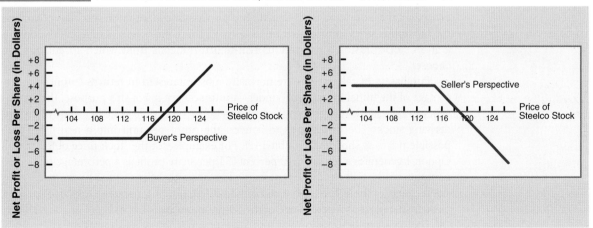

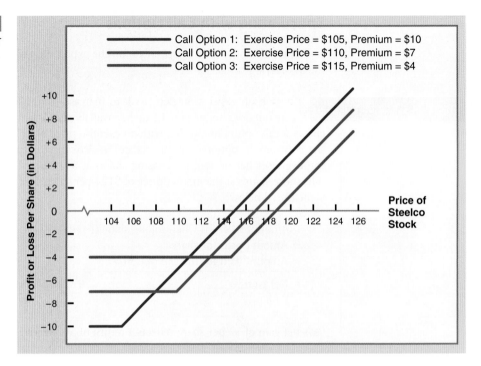

stock price of $119 is a break-even point, because the gain from exercising the option exactly offsets the premium paid for it. At stock prices above $119, a net gain is realized.

The right portion of Exhibit 14.2 shows the net gain or loss to a writer of the same call option, assuming that the writer obtains the stock only when the option is exercised. Under this condition, the call option writer's net gain (loss) is the call option purchaser's net loss (gain), assuming zero transaction costs. The maximum gain to the writer of a call option is the premium received.

Several call options are available for a given stock, and the risk-return potential will vary among them. Assume that three types of call options were available on Steelco stock with a similar expiration date, as described in Exhibit 14.3. The potential gains or losses per unit for each option are also shown in Exhibit 14.3, assuming that the option is exercised on the expiration date, if at all. It is also assumed that if the speculators exercise the call option, they immediately sell the stock. This comparison of different options for a given stock illustrates the various risk-return tradeoffs from which speculators can choose.

Purchasers of call options are normally most interested in returns (profit as a percentage of the initial investment) under various scenarios. For this purpose, the contingency graph can be revised to reflect returns for each possible price per share of the underlying stock. The first step is to convert the profit per unit into a return for each possible price, as shown in Exhibit 14.4. For example, for the stock price of $116, Call Option 1 generates a return of 10 percent ($1 per share profit as a percentage of the $10 premium paid), Call Option 2 generates a loss of about 14 percent ($1 per share loss as a percentage of the $7 premium paid), and Call Option 3 generates a loss of 75 percent ($3 per share loss as a percentage of the $4 premium paid).

The data can be transformed into a contingency graph as shown in Exhibit 14.5. This graph illustrates that for Call Option 1 both the potential losses and the potential

EXHIBIT 14.4

Potential Returns on Three Different Call Options

Price of Steelco	Option 1: Exercise Price = $105 Premium = $10		Option 2: Exercise Price = $110 Premium = $7		Option 3: Exercise Price = $115 Premium = $4	
	Profit Per Unit	Percentage Return	Profit Per Unit	Percentage Return	Profit Per Unit	Percentage Return
$104	−$10	−100%	−$7	−100%	−$4	−100%
106	−9	−90	−7	−100	−4	−100
108	−7	−70	−7	−100	−4	−100
110	−5	−50	−7	−100	−4	−100
112	−3	−30	−5	−71	−4	−100
114	−1	−10	−3	−43	−4	−100
116	1	10	−1	−14	−3	−75
118	3	30	1	14	−1	−25
120	5	50	3	43	1	25
122	7	70	5	71	3	75
124	9	90	7	100	5	125
126	11	110	9	129	7	175

EXHIBIT 14.5

Potential Returns for Three Call Options (Buyer's Perspective)

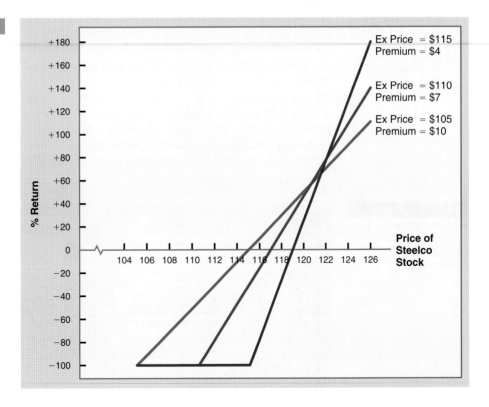

returns in the event of a high stock price are relatively low. Conversely, the potential losses for Call Option 3 are relatively high, but so are the potential returns in the event of a high stock price.

Speculating with Put Options

Put options can be used to speculate on the expectation of a decrease in the price of the underlying stock.

ILLUSTRATION   A put option on Steelco is available with an exercise price of $110 and a premium of $2. If the price of Steelco stock falls below $110, speculators could purchase the stock and then exercise their put options to benefit from the transaction. However, they would need to make at least $2 per share on this transaction to fully recover the premium paid for the option. If the speculators exercise the option when the market price is $104, their net gain is measured as follows:

Amount received when selling shares	$110 per share
− Amount paid for shares	−$104 per share
− Amount paid for the put option	−$ 2 per share
= Net gain	$ 4 per share

The net gain here is 200 percent, or twice as much as the amount paid for the put options.

The potential gains or losses from the put option described here are shown in the left portion of Exhibit 14.6, based on the assumptions that (1) the put option is exercised on the expiration date, if at all, and (2) the shares would be purchased just before the put option is exercised. Exhibit 14.6 shows that the maximum loss when purchasing this option is $2 per share. For stock prices between $108 and $110, the purchaser of a put option incurs a net loss of less than $2 per share. The stock price of $108 is a break-even point, because the gain from exercising the put option would exactly offset the $2 per share premium.

The right portion of Exhibit 14.6 shows the net gain or loss to a writer of the same put option, assuming that the writer sells the stock received as the put option is exercised. Under this condition, the put option writer's net gain (loss) is the put option purchaser's net loss (gain), assuming zero transaction costs. The maximum gain to the writer of a put

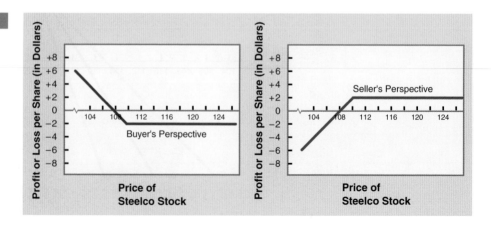

WSJ

Most Active Listed Options

The most actively traded stock options are identified in *The Wall Street Journal*. The name of the firm is listed in the first column, while the expiration month and exercise (strike) price is shown in the second and third columns. A "p" is shown in the fourth column for put options. The trading volume is provided in the fifth column, and the exchange where the option is listed is identified in the sixth column. The last quoted premium is in the seventh column. The closing price of the underlying stock is disclosed in the ninth column.

MOST ACTIVE LISTED OPTIONS

Wednesday, August 11, 2004

Composite volume and close for actively traded equity and LEAPS, or long-term options, with results for the corresponding put or call contract. Volume figures are unofficial. Open interest is total outstanding for all exchanges and reflects previous trading day. Close when possible is shown for the underlying stock or primary market. **XC**-Composite. **p**-Put. **o**-Strike price adjusted for split.

OPTION/STRIKE				VOL	EXCH	LAST	NET CHG	CLOSE	OPEN INT	OPTION/STRIKE				VOL	EXCH	LAST	NET CHG	CLOSE	OPEN INT
Nasd100Tr	Aug	33	p	31,519	XC	0.50	0.10	32.92	261,916	Oracle	Sep	11		10,409	XC	0.20	-0.10	10.19	18,354
Nasd100Tr	Aug	33		30,748	XC	0.45	-0.15	32.92	70,082	CareerEd	Jan 06	50		10,060	XC	2.15	0.05	30.79	3,191
Nasd100Tr	Sep	33	p	25,931	XC	1.10	0.15	32.92	155,686	Nasd100Tr	Sep	34		9,384	XC	0.60	-0.15	32.92	77,617
Nasd100Tr	Sep	35	p	21,497	XC	2.35	-0.25	32.92	182,358	Broadcom	Aug	30		9,323	XC	0.75	-2.55	29.21	1,116
SemiHTr	Aug	30		19,302	XC	0.55	-0.75	29.59	21,930	MicronT	Sep	13		9,210	XC	0.30	-0.25	11.75	6,305
Nasd100Tr	Aug	32		19,068	XC	1.10	-0.30	32.92	28,181	Amazon	Aug	37.50		9,144	XC	0.65	-0.30	36.56	9,611
Cisco	Aug	20	p	18,687	XC	1.65	1.15	18.29	61,270	Citigrp	Sep	42.50	p	8,847	XC	0.55	-0.15	44.35	37,557
Nasd100Tr	Aug	35		17,190	XC	0.35	-0.05	32.92	141,504	Intel	Aug	22.50		8,652	XC	0.35	-0.20	22.16	24,507
Nasd100Tr	Aug	34	p	16,253	XC	1.15	0.20	32.92	209,294	Gen El	Aug	32.50		8,500	XC	0.30	0.05	32.20	46,409
Dell Inc	Aug	32.50	p	14,741	XC	0.45	0.25	33.57	38,162	Corning	Nov	12.50		8,316	XC	0.50	-0.15	10.66	6,494
Nasd100Tr	Sep	33		13,902	XC	1.05	-0.20	32.92	26,363	SemiHTr	Sep	30		8,112	XC	1.25	-0.70	29.59	13,518
Nasd100Tr	Sep	34	p	13,658	XC	1.65	0.20	32.92	114,807	NewsCp A	Jan	35		8,006	XC	0.75	0.05	29.80	28,820
Cisco	Aug	20		13,434	XC	0.05	-0.95	18.29	64,825	Cisco	Jan	20		7,568	XC	1.20	-1.05	18.29	58,509
Yahoo	Oct	25		13,232	XC	4.30	0.60	27.42	26,267	Calpine	Jan 06	5		7,547	XC	0.70	0.05	3.62	48,187
Nasd100Tr	Aug	32	p	12,694	XC	0.20	0.10	32.92	83,756	Broadcom	Aug	32.50		7,458	XC	0.25	-1.15	29.21	10,463
Cisco	Jan	15	p	12,277	XC	0.70	0.30	18.29	29,746	Guidant	Aug	60		7,413	XC	0.30	0.05	54.83	21,173
Agilent	Aug	22.50		11,919	XC	0.70	-0.55	21.77	11,682	Nasd100Tr	Aug	36	p	7,081	XC	3.10	0.40	32.92	96,124
Nasd100Tr	Sep	31	p	10,910	XC	0.45	0.10	32.92	126,819	Elan	Jan	20		6,976	XC	5.10	0.90	20.49	36,599
Nasd100Tr	Aug	34		10,506	XC	0.13	-0.07	32.92	131,960	PMC Srra	Aug	10	p	6,877	XC	0.55	0.35	9.79	9,056
JohnJn	Sep	60		10,471	XC	0.20	0.15	56	1,837	Cisco	Sep	20		6,842	XC	0.30	-1.05	18.29	34,529

Volume & Open Interest Summaries

AMERICAN				**CHICAGO BOARD**			
Call Vol:	338,145	Open Int:	58,194,502	Call Vol:	712,094	Open Int:	77,727,720
Put Vol:	311,680	Open Int:	46,026,955	Put Vol:	631,782	Open Int:	65,838,222
BOSTON				**INTL SECURITIES**			
Call Vol:	41,810	Open Int:		Call Vol:	797,669	Open Int:	68,815,394
Put Vol:	42,054	Open Int:		Put Vol:	668,712	Open Int:	57,186,150

PHILADELPHIA			
Call Vol:	224,187	Open Int:	54,469,486
Put Vol:	174,545	Open Int:	44,104,743
PACIFIC			
Call Vol:	178,409	Open Int:	72,896,026
Put Vol:	100,531	Open Int:	59,083,234
TOTAL			
Call Vol:	2,292,314		
Put Vol:	1,929,304		

option is the premium received. As with call options, normally several put options are available for a given stock, and the potential gains or losses will vary among them.

Excessive Risk from Speculation

In 1995, Barings PLC, an investment bank in the United Kingdom, incurred losses of more than $1 billion as a result of positions in stock options and other derivative instruments. A brief summary of the Barings case identifies the reasons for the substantial losses and indicates measures that other firms can take to ensure that they will not experience such losses.

In 1992, Nicholas Leeson, a clerk in Barings's London office, was sent to manage the accounting at a Singapore subsidiary called Baring Futures. Shortly after he began his new position in Singapore, Leeson took and passed the examinations required to trade on the floor of the Singapore International Monetary Exchange (SIMEX). Baring Futures served as a broker on this exchange for some of its customers. In less than one year after he arrived in Singapore, Leeson was trading derivative contracts on the SIMEX as an employee of Baring Futures. He then began to trade for the firm's own account rather than just as a broker, trading options on the Nikkei (Japanese) stock index. At the same time, he also continued to serve as the accounting manager for Baring Futures. In this role Leeson was able to conceal losses on any derivative positions, so the financial reports to Barings PLC showed massive profits.

In January 1995, an earthquake in Japan led to a major decline in Japanese stock prices, and the Nikkei index declined. This caused a loss exceeding the equivalent of $100 million on Leeson's options positions. Leeson attempted to recover these losses by purchasing Nikkei index futures contracts, but the market declined further over the next two months. Leeson's losses accumulated, exceeding the equivalent of $300 million. Leeson had periodically needed funds to cover margin calls as his positions declined in value. Barings PLC met the funding requests to cover the equivalent of millions of dollars to satisfy the margin calls and did not recognize that the margin calls were signaling a major problem.

In late February 1995, an accounting clerk at Barings who noticed some discrepancies met with Leeson to reconcile the records. During the meeting, when Leeson was asked to explain specific accounting entries, he excused himself and never returned. He left Singapore that night and faxed his resignation to Barings PLC from Kuala Lumpur, Malaysia. The next day, employees of the Singapore office reviewed Leeson's private records and realized that he had accumulated major losses. At this point, Barings PLC asked the Bank of England (the central bank) for assistance in resolving the situation. When Barings PLC and the Bank of England investigated, they found that Leeson had accumulated losses of more than the equivalent of $1 billion—more than double the entire amount of equity of Barings PLC. Barings was insolvent and was acquired by a Dutch firm called Internationale Nederlanden Groep (ING). Later that year, Leeson was extradited to Singapore and pleaded guilty to charges of fraud. He was sentenced to prison for six and one-half years. Until Barings discovered the losses, Leeson was scheduled to earn an annual bonus exceeding the equivalent of $600,000.

Any firms that use futures or other derivative instruments can draw a few obvious lessons from the Barings collapse. First, firms should closely monitor the trading of derivative contracts by their employees to ensure that derivatives are being used within the firm's guidelines. Second, firms should separate the reporting function from the trading function so that traders cannot conceal trading losses. Third, when firms receive margin calls on derivative positions, they should recognize that there may be potential losses on their derivative instruments, and they should closely evaluate those positions. The Barings case provided a wake-up call to many firms, which recognized the need to establish guidelines for their employees who take derivative positions and to more closely monitor the actions of these employees.

Determining Stock Option Premiums

Stock option premiums are determined by market forces. Any characteristic of an option that results in many willing buyers but few willing sellers will place upward pres-

sure on the option premium. Thus, the option premium must be sufficiently high to equalize the demand by buyers and the supply that sellers are willing to sell. This generalization applies to both call options and put options. The specific characteristics that affect the demand and supply conditions, and therefore affect the option premiums, are described below.

Determining Call Option Premiums

Call option premiums are affected primarily by the following factors:

- Market price of the underlying instrument (relative to option's exercise price)
- Volatility of the underlying instrument
- Time to maturity of the call option

Influence of the Market Price The higher the existing market price of the underlying financial instrument relative to the exercise price, the higher the call option premium, other things being equal. A financial instrument's value has a higher probability of increasing well above the exercise price if it is already close to or above the exercise price. Thus, a purchaser would be willing to pay a higher premium for a call option on that instrument.

The influence of the market price of an instrument (relative to the exercise price) on the call option premium can also be understood by comparing options with different exercise prices on the same instrument at a given point in time.

ILLUSTRATION Consider the data shown in Exhibit 14.7 for KSR call options quoted on March 19, 2005, with a similar expiration date. The stock price of KSR was about $140 at that time. The premium for the call option with the $130 exercise price was almost $10 higher than the premium for the option with the $150 exercise price. This example confirms that a higher premium is required to lock in a lower exercise price on call options.

Influence of the Stock's Volatility The greater the volatility of the underlying stock, the higher the call option premium, other things being equal. If a stock is volatile, there is a higher probability that its price will increase well above the exercise price. Thus, a purchaser would be willing to pay a higher premium for a call option on that stock. To illustrate, call options on small stocks normally have higher premiums than call options on large stocks because small stocks are typically more volatile.

Influence of the Call Option's Time to Maturity The longer the call option's time to maturity, the higher the call option premium, other things being equal. A longer time

EXHIBIT 14.7

Relationship between Exercise Price and Call Option Premium on KSR Stock

Exercise Price	Premium for April Expiration Date
$130	11⅝
135	7½
140	5¼
145	3¼
150	1⅞

Long-Term Option Quotations

Quotations for long-term options (called "LEAPS") are published in *The Wall Street Journal,* as shown here. For each stock identified in the left column, one or more exercise ("Strike") prices are listed (see the second column). The expiration date ("Exp.") is in the third column. The next two columns indicate the volume of contracts that have been traded for the call option on that day and the most recent premium paid for the call option. The last two columns indicate the volume of contracts traded on that day for the put option in that stock and the most recent premium paid for the put option.

LEAPS-LONG TERM OPTIONS

OPTION/STRIKE	EXP	CALL VOL	CALL LAST	PUT VOL	PUT LAST	OPTION/STRIKE	EXP	CALL VOL	CALL LAST	PUT VOL	PUT LAST	OPTION/STRIKE	EXP	CALL VOL	CALL LAST	PUT VOL	PUT LAST
ATT Wrls 12.50	Jan 06	2080	2.30	270	0.40	IAC InterA 30	Jan 07	1000	2.55	...	...	Sears 45	Jan 06	1000	3.10	...	...
AMD 5	Jan 06	...	...	520	0.40	Intel 17.50	Jan 06	3	6.70	536	1.45	SemiHTr 25	Jan 07	...	...	8895	3.20
11.52 10	Jan 06	84	3.80	524	2.05	22.54 22.50	Jan 06	1479	3.90	91	3.40	30.86 30	Jan 06	21	5.90	5128	4.30
Altria 50	Jan 06	1647	4.20	...	...	IBM 110	Jan 06	1895	1.75	...	...	Sepracor 30	Jan 06	...	...	900	3.60
AppleC 30	Jan 06	648	7	110	4.70	JDS Uniph 5	Jan 06	119	0.55	3012	2.20	SiriusSat 2.50	Jan 06	527	0.70	...	...
BankAm 80	Jan 06	20	9.70	1686	7.10	Level3 2.50	Jan 06	853	1.20	103	0.85	SP Fncl 30	Jan 06	2075	1.45	...	...
Boeing 45	Jan 06	60	8.70	4750	4.20	Lucent 5	Jan 06	787	0.35	300	2.10	TimeWarn 15	Jan 06	83	2.90	3400	1.45
49.61 55	Jan 06	4750	3.80	...	...	Lyondell 5	Jan 06	...	...	1050	0.25	16.10 15	Jan 07	...	...	2006	1.95
BostSci 35	Jan 06	1004	5.80	10	7.10	Merck 40	Jan 06	...	...	590	3.10	VimpelCm 30	Jan 06	...	...	2440	2.75
Calpine 2.50	Jan 06	295	1.40	737	0.80	44.65 50	Jan 06	1628	2.25	1	8.60	WalMart 60	Jan 06	551	2.65	1	10.20
Cephalon 30	Jan 07	...	...	1000	3.30	Microsft 27.50	Jan 06	79	3.30	1871	2.85	WillmsCos 10	Jan 06	...	...	750	0.95
Cisco 22.50	Jan 06	1610	2.60	7	4.20	Motorola 12.50	Jan 06	30	4.20	8032	1.45						
CocaCola 45	Jan 06	895	3.20	6	5.10	Nasd100Tr 25	Jan 06	1000	10	118	1.21						
43.46 60	Jan 07	722	0.85	...	...	33.19 27	Jan 06	1000	8.50	...	...						
DJIA Diam 84	Jan 06	...	...	17268	3.30	33.19 29	Jan 06	1200	7.20	...	...	**Volume & Open Interest**					
Dell Inc 42.50	Jan 06	850	1.65	...	...	33.19 30	Jan 06	50	6.50	567	2.50	**Summaries**					
34.32 45	Jan 07	654	2.30	10	11.80	33.19 32	Jan 06	...	...	2050	3.30	BOSTON					
DeltaAir 2.50	Jan 06	200	2	1010	1.30	33.19 37	Jan 06	2310	3	23	5.70	Call Vol: 6,521 Open Int: 0					
3.72 5	Jan 06	730	1.35	2236	3.20	33.19 40	Jan 06	1113	1.90	45	7.90	Put Vol: 2,196 Open Int: 0					
3.72 7.50	Jan 06	526	0.80	1533	5.10	33.19 55	Jan 06	10	0.13	602	21.60	CHICAGO BOARD					
ETrade 7.50	Jan 06	1	4.30	540	0.70	Nokia 7.50	Jan 06	2	4.30	2040	0.45	Call Vol: 34,903 Open Int: 13,515,292					
10.96 10	Jan 06	565	2.80	...	...	11.46 15	Jan 06	158	0.90	770	4.50	Put Vol: 43,096 Open Int: 13,873,662					
EKodak 20	Jan 07	...	...	800	2.05	NwstAirl 5	Jan 06	...	...	2836	1.55	INTL SECURITIES					
Elan 30	Jan 06	686	2.80	...	...	Nvidia 10	Jan 06	49	3.50	735	2.45	Call Vol: 30,749 Open Int: 13,013,960					
18.50 40	Jan 06	650	1.10	20	23.70	Oracle 10	Jan 06	5009	2.10	6	1.30	Put Vol: 26,369 Open Int: 13,140,688					
Genentch 45	Jan 06	...	...	1000	6.90	10.60 10	Jan 07	285	2.75	20221	1.70	PACIFIC					
GenMotrs 10	Jan 06	3238	32.20	...	...	10.60 15	Jan 06	15012	0.55	10000	4.70	Call Vol: 12,300 Open Int: 13,239,934					
42.17 15	Jan 06	2349	27.20	3000	0.30	10.60 15	Jan 07	16002	0.90	...	...	Put Vol: 11,442 Open Int: 13,321,560					
42.17 30	Jan 06	...	...	2030	2.30	Peoplesoft 17.50	Jan 06	900	2.60	...	...	TOTAL					
42.17 45	Jan 06	213	3.60	647	8.30	16.08 22.50	Jan 06	900	0.95	...	...	Call Vol: 84,473					
Goodyear 7.50	Jan 06	564	4.80	...	...	QwestCm 5	Jan 06	810	0.25	216	2.45	Put Vol: 83,103					
10.90 10	Jan 06	554	3	3	2.10	RF MicD 5	Jan 06	...	...	529	1.15						

period until expiration allows the owner of the option more time to exercise the option. Thus, there is a higher probability that the instrument's price will move well above the exercise price before the option expires.

The relationship between the time to maturity and the call option premium is illustrated in Exhibit 14.8 for KSR call options quoted on March 19, 2005, with a similar ex-

EXHIBIT 14.8

Relationship between Time to Maturity and Call Option Premium on KSR Stock

Expiration Date	Premium for Option with a $135 Exercise Price
March	4½
April	7½
July	13¼

ercise price of $135. The premium was $4.50 per share for the call option with a March expiration month versus $7.50 per share for the call option with an April expiration month. The difference reflects the additional time in which the April call option can be exercised.

Determining Put Option Premiums

The premium paid on a put option is dependent on the same factors that affect the premium paid on a call option. However, the direction of influence varies for one of the factors, as explained next.

Influence of the Market Price The higher the existing market price of the underlying financial instrument relative to the exercise price, the lower the put option premium, other things being equal. A financial instrument's value has a higher probability of decreasing well below the exercise price if it is already close to or below the exercise price. Thus, a purchaser would be willing to pay a higher premium for a put option on that instrument. This influence on the put option premium differs from the influence on the call option premium, because a lower market price is preferable from the perspective of put option purchasers.

The influence of the market price of an instrument (relative to the exercise price) on the put option premium can also be understood by comparing options with different exercise prices on the same instrument at a given point in time. For example, consider the data shown in Exhibit 14.9 for KSR put options with a similar expiration date quoted on March 19, 2005. The premium for the put option with the $150 exercise price was more than $8 per share higher than the premium for the option with the $135 exercise price. The difference reflects the more favorable price at which the stock can be sold when holding the put option with the higher exercise price.

Influence of the Stock's Volatility The greater the volatility of the underlying stock, the higher the put option premium, other things being equal. This relationship also held for call option premiums. If a stock is volatile, there is a higher probability of its price deviating far from the exercise price. Thus, a purchaser would be willing to pay a higher premium for a put option on that stock, because its market price is more likely to decline well below the option's exercise price.

Influence of the Put Option's Time to Maturity The longer the time to maturity, the higher the put option premium, other things being equal. This relationship also

EXHIBIT 14.9
Relationship between Exercise Price and Put Option Premium on KSR Stock

Exercise Price	Premium for June Expiration Date
$130	$1\frac{7}{8}$
135	$3\frac{1}{8}$
140	$5\frac{3}{8}$
145	$8\frac{1}{2}$
150	$12\frac{1}{4}$

EXHIBIT 14.10

Relationship between Time to Maturity and Put Option Premium on KSR Stock

Expiration Date	Premium for Option with a $135 Exercise Price
March	½
April	3⅛
July	7¼

held for call option premiums. A longer time period until expiration allows the owner of the option more time to exercise the option. Thus, there is a higher probability that the instrument's price will move well below the exercise price before the option expires.

The relationship between the time to maturity and the put option premium is shown in Exhibit 14.10 for KSR put options with a similar exercise price of $135 quoted on March 19, 2005. The premium was $7.25 per share for the put option with a July expiration month versus $.50 per share for the put option with a March expiration month. The difference reflects the additional time in which the put option with the July expiration date can be exercised.

Explaining Changes in Option Premiums

Exhibit 14.11 identifies the underlying forces that cause option prices to change over time. Economic conditions and market conditions can cause abrupt changes in the stock price or in the anticipated volatility of the stock price over the time remaining until option expiration. These changes would have a major impact on the stock option's premium.

Indicators Monitored by Participants in Options Market

Since the premiums paid on stock options are highly influenced by the price movements of the underlying stocks, participants in the stock option market closely monitor the same indicators that are monitored when trading the underlying stocks. Participants who have an options position or are considering taking a position monitor several indicators for the set of underlying stocks, including economic indicators, corresponding industry-specific conditions, and firm-specific conditions. Participants trading stock options may assess a given set of information differently than those who trade stocks, however. For example, an owner of a call option representing a particular stock may not be as concerned about the possibility of a labor strike as an owner of the firm's stock would be, because the call option limits the downside risk.

Traders of options tend to monitor economic indicators because economic conditions affect cash flows of firms and, therefore, can affect expected stock valuations and stock option premiums. Economic conditions can also affect the premiums by affecting the expected stock volatility. Therefore, these traders closely monitor economic indicators such as a change in the Federal Reserve's federal funds rate target, the employment level, and the gross domestic product.

EXHIBIT 14.11 Framework for Explaining Why a Stock Option's Premium Changes over Time

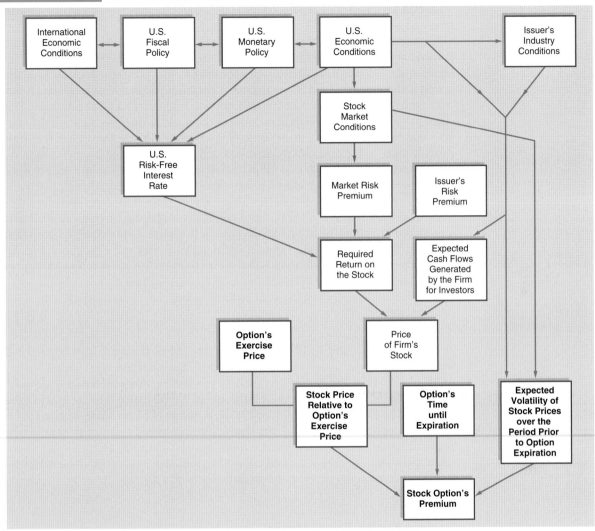

Hedging with Stock Options

Call and put options on selected stocks and stock indexes are commonly used for hedging against possible stock price movements. Financial institutions such as mutual funds, insurance companies, and pension funds manage large stock portfolios and are the most common users of options for hedging.

Hedging with Call Options

Call options on a stock can be used to hedge a position in that stock.

ILLUSTRATION Portland Pension Fund owns a substantial amount of Steelco stock. It expects that the stock will perform well in the long run, but is somewhat concerned that the stock may perform poorly over the next few months because of temporary problems

Steelco is experiencing. The sale of a call option on Steelco stock can hedge against such a potential loss. This is known as a **covered call,** because the option is covered, or backed, by stocks already owned.

If the market price of Steelco stock rises, the call option will likely be exercised, and Portland will fulfill its obligation by selling its Steelco stock to the purchaser of the call option at the exercise price. Conversely, if the market price of Steelco stock declines, the option will not be exercised. Consequently, Portland would not have to sell its Steelco stock, and the premium received from selling the call option would represent a gain that could partially offset the decline in the price of the stock. In this case, although the market value of the institution's stock portfolio is adversely affected, the decline is at least partially offset by the premium received from selling the call option.

Assume that Portland Pension Fund purchased Steelco stock at the market price of $112 per share. To hedge against a temporary decline in Steelco's stock price, Portland sells call options on Steelco stock with an exercise price of $110 per share for a premium of $5 per share. The net profit to Portland when using covered call writing is represented in Exhibit 14.12 for various possible scenarios. For comparison purposes, the profit that Portland would earn if it did not use covered call writing but sold the stock on the option's expiration date is also shown (see the diagonal line) for various possible scenarios. Notice that the results with covered call writing are not as bad as without covered call writing when the stock performs poorly, but not as good when the stock performs well.

The table in Exhibit 14.12 explains the profit or loss per share from covered call writing. At any price above $110 per share as of the expiration date, the call option would be exercised, and Portland would have to sell its holdings of Steelco stock at the exercise price of $110 per share to the purchaser of the call option. The net gain to Portland would be $3 per share, determined as the premium of $5 per share, received when writing the option, minus the $2 per share difference between the price paid for the Steelco stock and the price at which the stock is sold. Comparing the profit or loss per scenario with versus without covered call writing, it is clear that covered call writing limits the upside potential return on stocks but also reduces the risk.

Hedging with Put Options

Put options on stock are also used to hedge stock positions.

ILLUSTRATION   Reconsider the example in which Portland Pension Fund was concerned about a possible temporary decline in the price of Steelco stock. Portland could hedge against a temporary decline in Steelco's stock price by purchasing put options on that stock. In the event that Steelco's stock price declines, Portland would likely generate a gain on its option position, which would help offset the reduction in the stock's price. If Steelco's stock price does not decline, Portland would not exercise its put option.

Put options are typically used to hedge when portfolio managers are mainly concerned about a temporary decline in a stock's value. When portfolio managers are mainly concerned about the long-term performance of a stock, they are likely to sell the stock itself rather than hedge the position.

EXHIBIT 14.12

Risk-Return Tradeoff from
Covered Call Writing

Explanation of Profit Per Share from Covered Call Writing							
Market Price of Steelco as of the Expiration Date	Price at which Portland Pension Fund Sells Steelco Stock		Premium Received from Writing the Call Option		Price Paid for Steelco Stock		Profit or Loss Per Share
$104	$104	+	$5	−	$112	=	−$3
105	105	+	5	−	112	=	−2
106	106	+	5	−	112	=	−1
107	107	+	5	−	112	=	0
108	108	+	5	−	112	=	1
109	109	+	5	−	112	=	2
110	110	+	5	−	112	=	3
111	110	+	5	−	112	=	3
112	110	+	5	−	112	=	3
113	110	+	5	−	112	=	3
114	110	+	5	−	112	=	3
115	110	+	5	−	112	=	3
116	110	+	5	−	112	=	3
117	110	+	5	−	112	=	3
118	110	+	5	−	112	=	3
119	110	+	5	−	112	=	3
120	110	+	5	−	112	=	3

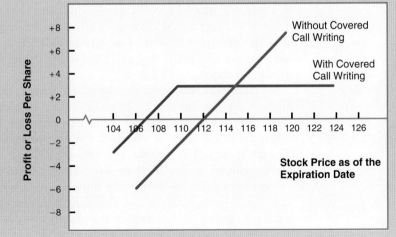

Using Options to Measure a Stock's Risk

Recall that one of the measures of a stock's risk is the standard deviation of its returns. Stock options are commonly used to derive the market's anticipation of a stock's standard deviation over the life of the option. Recall that a stock option's premium is influenced by factors such as the prevailing stock price, the time to expiration, and the volatility of the stock. The price of an option is often determined by using a formula (see the chapter appendix) based on the values of these factors, including a guess at the market's anticipation of the stock's volatility over the remaining life of the option.

Although market participants' anticipated volatility of a stock is not observable, the stock option formula can be used to derive an estimate for a specific stock's volatility. By plugging in values for the factors that affect a particular stock option's premium and for the prevailing premium, it is possible to derive the implied standard deviation of a stock. Thus, the implied standard deviation is derived by determining what its value must be, given the values of other factors that affect the stock option's premium and given the prevailing option premium.

When a firm experiences an event that creates more uncertainty, its implied standard deviation increases. For example, if a firm's CEO suddenly resigns, the implied standard deviation will likely increase. The premium to be paid for a stock option will increase in response, even if the stock price itself does not change. An increase in uncertainty results in a higher implied standard deviation for the stock, which means that the writer of an option requires a higher premium to compensate for the anticipated increase in the stock's volatility.

Options on ETFs and Stock Indexes

Options are also traded on exchange traded funds (ETFs) and stock indexes. Recall from Chapter 8 that ETFs are funds that are designed to mimic particular indexes and are traded on an exchange. Thus, an ETF option provides the right to trade a specified ETF at a specified price by a specified expiration date. Since ETFs are traded like stocks, options on ETFs are traded like options on stocks. Investors who exercise a call option on an ETF will receive delivery of the ETF in their account. Investors who exercise a put option on an ETF will have the ETF transferred from their account to the counterparty on the put option.

A **stock index option** provides the right to trade a specified stock index at a specified price by a specified expiration date. Call options on stock indexes allow the right to purchase the index, and put options on stock indexes allow the right to sell the index. If and when the index option is exercised, the cash payment is equal to a specified dollar amount multiplied by the difference between the index level and the exercise price.

Options on stock indexes are somewhat similar to options on ETFs. However, the values of stock indexes change only at the end of each trading day, whereas ETF values can change throughout the day. Therefore, an investor who wants to capitalize on the expected movement of an index within a particular day will trade options on ETFs. An investor who wants to capitalize on the expected movement of an index over a longer period of time (such as a week or several months) can trade options on either ETFs or indexes.

Options on indexes have become popular for speculating on general movements in the stock market overall. Speculators who anticipate a sharp increase in stock market prices overall may consider purchasing call options on one of the market indexes. Con-

EXHIBIT 14.13

Sampling of ETFs and
Indexes on Which Options
Are Traded

Sampling of ETFs on Which Options Are Traded	
iShares Nasdaq Biotechnology	iShares Russell 1000 Growth Index Fund
iShares Goldman Sachs Technology Index	Energy Select Sector SPDR
iShares Goldman Sachs Software Index	Financial Select Sector SPDR
iShares Russell 1000 Index Fund	Utilities Select Sector SPDR
iShares Russell 1000 Value Index Fund	Health Care Select Sector SPDR
Sampling of Indexes on Which Options Are Traded	
Asia 25 Index	S&P SmallCap 600 Index
Euro 25 Index	Nasdaq 100 Index
Mexico Index	Russell 1000 Index
Dow Jones Industrial Average	Russell 1000 Value Index
Dow Jones Transportation Average	Russell 1000 Growth Index
Dow Jones Utilities Average	Russell Midcap Index
S&P 100 Index	Goldman Sachs Internet Index
S&P 500 Index	Goldman Sachs Software Index
Morgan Stanley Biotechnology Index	

versely, speculators who anticipate a stock market decline may consider purchasing put options on these indexes.

A sampling of options that are traded on ETFs and on stock indexes is provided in Exhibit 14.13. In general, investors can trade options on ETFs or indexes to speculate on expected changes in broad markets or specific sectors.

Hedging with Stock Index Options

Financial institutions and other firms commonly take positions in options on ETFs or indexes to hedge against market or sector conditions that would adversely affect their asset portfolio or cash flows. The following discussion is based on the use of options on stock indexes, but options on ETFs could be used in the same manner.

Financial institutions such as insurance companies and pension funds maintain large stock portfolios whose values are driven by general market movements. If the stock portfolio is broad enough, any changes in its value will likely be highly correlated with the market movements. For this reason, portfolio managers consider purchasing put options on a stock index to protect against stock market declines. The put options should be purchased on the stock index that most closely mirrors the portfolio to be hedged. If the stock market experiences a severe downturn, the market value of the portfolio declines, but the put options on the stock index will generate a gain because the value of the index will be less than the exercise price. The greater the market downturn, the greater the decline in the market value of the portfolio, but the greater the gain from holding put options on a stock index. Thus, this offsetting effect minimizes the overall impact on the firm.

If the stock market rises, the put options on the stock index will not be exercised. Thus, the firm will not recover the cost of purchasing the options. This situation is sim-

USING THE WALL STREET JOURNAL

WSJ Stock Index Option Quotations

Quotations for various stock index options are published in *The Wall Street Journal*, as shown here. Some of the more popular index options are the Dow Jones Industrial Average, the S&P 100 index, and the S&P 500 index (shown here). Options are also available on a Japanese stock index. For each option, the expiration month is shown in the first column. The exercise ("Strike") price appears in the second column, followed by the letter "c" (for call option) or "p" (for put option). The volume of contracts traded on the day ("Vol.") for that specific option is also disclosed, along with the premium that was last quoted ("Last"). The "Net Chg." is the change in the price from the previous trading day; "Open Int." is the open interest, or amount of contracts outstanding on that particular option.

Source: Republished with permission of Dow Jones & Company, Inc., from *The Wall Street Journal*, August 10, 2004; permission conveyed through the Copyright Clearance Center, Inc.

S & P 500(SPX)				
Sep 500 c	1,470	566.30	-2.90	21,371
Sep 500 p	1,336	0.05	...	22,196
Sep 750 p	2	0.25	0.15	7,994
Sep 800 p	500	0.25	...	20,624
Aug 825 p	120	0.05	-0.05	7,322
Sep 850 p	169	0.90	0.10	18,738
Oct 850 c	5	217.20	...	...
Aug 900 p	12	0.40	0.15	20,004
Sep 900 c	5	168.50	3.00	7,072
Sep 900 p	28	1.20	-0.75	20,312
Oct 900 p	332	3.30	-0.80	1,806
Aug 925 p	295	0.25	0.05	16,455
Sep 925 p	272	2	-0.40	13,316
Aug 950 p	752	0.40	-0.20	21,170
Sep 950 c	20	118.70	3.40	1,530
Sep 950 p	90	2.80	-1.10	49,041
Oct 950 p	5	6.50	-1.40	2,992
Aug 965 p	20	0.60	...	1,242
Aug 975 p	304	0.75	-0.95	66,955
Sep 975 p	2,926	4.70	-0.80	11,139
Oct 975 p	40	9.20	-1.40	4,471
Sep 995 p	64	6.30	-1.30	31,371
Oct 995 p	100	11.50	-3.50	273
Nov 995 p	1	18.60	5.60	8
Sep 1005 c	47	69.80	-4.20	1,656
Sep 1005 p	804	7.80	-1.60	28,111
Oct 1005 p	1,030	13.20	-2.50	4,388
Nov 1005 p	105	20.50	...	1,817
Aug 1015 p	21	2	-1.40	4,965
Aug 1020 p	349	2.80	-1.00	2,176
Aug 1025 c	6	45	1.00	5,764
Aug 1025 p	3,826	2.70	-1.30	41,366
Sep 1025 c	22	51.20	1.20	6,904
Sep 1025 p	1,841	11.50	-0.50	52,675
Oct 1025 c	2	58.20	0.20	688
Oct 1025 p	125	18	-2.00	8,900
Sep 1030 p	1,886	11.70	-3.10	1,361
Sep 1035 p	19	13	-2.50	5,729
Aug 1040 p	551	4.80	-1.70	11,165
Oct 1040 p	1	21.70	...	...
Aug 1045 p	19	5.50	-2.50	275
Sep 1045 p	200	15.90	-2.30	1,685
Aug 1050 c	50	22.30	-0.20	4,881
Aug 1050 p	8,796	6.90	-2.30	39,607
Sep 1050 c	130	34	1.50	12,664
Sep 1050 p	2,816	18	-2.40	83,417
Oct 1050 c	5	41	...	90
Oct 1050 p	141	27	1.50	3,695

ilar to purchasing other forms of insurance, but not using them. Some portfolio managers may still believe the options were worthwhile for temporary protection against downside risk.

Hedging with Long-Term Stock Index Options
Long-term equity anticipations (LEAPs) are used by option market participants who want options with longer terms until expiration. For example, LEAPs on the S&P 100 and S&P 500 indexes are available, with expiration dates extending at least two years ahead. Each of these indexes is revised to one-tenth its normal size when applying LEAPs. This results in smaller premiums, which makes the LEAPs more affordable to smaller investors.

The transaction costs for hedging over a long period are lower than the costs of continually repurchasing short-term put options each time the options expire or are exercised. Furthermore, the costs of continually repurchasing put options are uncertain, whereas the costs of purchasing a put option on a long-term index option are known immediately.

Dynamic Asset Allocation with Stock Index Options

Dynamic asset allocation involves switching between risky and low-risk investment positions over time in response to changing expectations. Some portfolio managers use stock index options as a tool for dynamic asset allocation. For example, when portfolio managers anticipate favorable market conditions, they purchase call options on a stock index, which intensify the effects of the market conditions. Essentially, the managers are using stock index options to increase their exposure to stock market conditions. Con-

versely, when they anticipate unfavorable market movements, they can purchase put options on a stock index to reduce the effects that market conditions will have on their stock portfolios.

Because stock options are available with various exercise prices, portfolio managers can select an exercise price that provides the degree of protection desired. For example, assume an existing stock index is quite similar to the managers' stock portfolio and that they want to protect against a loss beyond 5 percent. If the prevailing level of the index is 400, the managers can purchase put options that have an exercise price of 380, because that level is 5 percent lower than 400. If the index declines to a level below 380, the managers will exercise the option, and the gain from doing so will partially offset the reduction in the stock portfolio's market value.

This strategy is essentially a form of insurance, where the premium paid for the put option is similar to an insurance premium. Because the index must decline by 5 percent before the option will possibly be exercised, this is similar to the "deductible" that is common in insurance policies. If portfolio managers desire to protect against even smaller losses, they can purchase a put option that specifies a higher exercise price on the index, such as 390. To obtain the extra protection, however, they would have to pay a higher premium for the option. In other words, the cost of the portfolio insurance would be higher because of the smaller "deductible" desired.

In another form of dynamic asset allocation, portfolio managers sell (write) call options on stock indexes in periods when they expect the stock market to be very stable. This strategy does not create a perfect hedge, but it can enhance the portfolio's performance in periods when stock prices are stagnant or declining.

Portfolio managers can adjust the risk-return profile of their investment position by using stock index options rather than restructuring their existing stock portfolios. This form of dynamic asset allocation avoids the substantial transaction costs associated with restructuring the stock portfolios.

Using Index Options to Measure Market Risk

Just as a stock's implied volatility can be derived from information about options on that stock, a stock index's implied volatility can be derived from information about options on that stock index. The same factors that affect the option premium on a stock affect the option premium on an index. Thus, the premium on an index option is positively related to the expected volatility of the underlying stock index. If investors want to assess the expected volatility of the stock index, they can use software packages to insert values for the prevailing option premium and the other factors (except volatility) that affect an option premium.

Impact of the September 11 Crisis on the Volatility of Indexes Although the uncertainty for each stock varies, the uncertainty surrounding the stock market in general can be measured by changes in the implied volatility in a stock market index. Exhibit 14.14 shows the trend of the implied volatility of the Nasdaq technology index on the days surrounding September 11, 2001. Notice how the implied volatility increased when the markets reopened on September 17. The implied volatility drifted upward over the next few days and then declined toward the levels that existed before the crisis. This trend illustrates how the risk perception in the stock market can be monitored over time. The implied volatilities of other types of stock indexes can also be monitored to

EXHIBIT 14.14

Implied Volatility of the
Nasdaq Technology Index
on the Days Surrounding
September 11, 2001

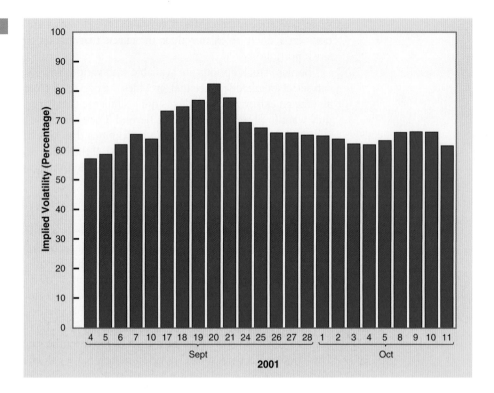

determine shifts in the uncertainty surrounding the underlying stocks represented by those indexes.

Options on Futures Contracts

In recent years, the concept of options has been applied to futures contracts to create options on futures contracts (sometimes referred to as "futures options"). An option on a particular futures contract allows the right (but not an obligation) to purchase or sell that futures contract for a specified price within a specified period of time. Thus, options on futures grant the power to take the futures position if favorable conditions occur but the flexibility to avoid the futures position (by letting the option expire) if unfavorable conditions occur. As with other options, the purchaser of options on futures pays a premium.

Options are available on stock index futures. They are used for speculating on expected stock market movements or hedging against adverse market conditions. Individuals and financial institutions use them in a manner similar to the way stock index options are used.

Options are also available on interest rate futures, such as Treasury note futures or Treasury bond futures. The settlement dates of the underlying futures contracts are usually a few weeks after the expiration date of the corresponding options contracts.

A call option on interest rate futures grants the right to purchase a futures contract at a specified price within a specified period of time. A put option on financial futures grants the right (again, not an obligation) to sell a particular financial futures contract at a specified price within a specified period of time. Because interest rate futures contracts can hedge interest rate risk, options on interest rate futures might be considered by any

financial institution that is exposed to this risk, including savings institutions, commercial banks, life insurance companies, and pension funds.

Speculating with Options on Futures

Speculators who anticipate a change in interest rates should also expect a change in bond prices. They could take a position in options on Treasury bond futures to capitalize on their expectations.

Speculation Based on an Expected Decline in Interest Rates If speculators expect a decline in interest rates, they may consider purchasing a call option on Treasury bond futures. If their expectations are correct, the market value of Treasury bonds will rise, and the price of a Treasury bond futures contract will rise as well. The speculators can exercise their option to purchase futures at the exercise price, which will be lower than the value of the futures contract.

ILLUSTRATION Kelly Warden expects interest rates to decline and purchases a call option on Treasury bond futures. The exercise price on Treasury bond futures is 94–32 (94 and $^{32}/_{64}$ percent of $100,000, or $94,500). The call option is purchased at a premium of 2–00 (or 2 percent of $100,000), which equals $2,000. Assume that interest rates do decline and as a result, the price of the Treasury bond futures contract rises over time and is valued at 99–00 ($99,000) shortly before the option's expiration date. At this time, Kelly decides to exercise the option and closes out the position by selling an identical futures contract (to create an offsetting position) at a higher price than the price at which she purchased the futures. Kelly's net gain from this speculative strategy is

Selling price of T-bond futures	$99,000	(99.00% of $100,000)
− Purchase price of T-bond futures	− $94,500	(94.50% of $100,000)
− Call option premium paid	− $ 2,000	(2.00% of $100,000)
= Net gain to purchaser of call option on futures	$ 2,500	(2.50% of $100,000)

This net gain of $2,500 represents a return on investment of 125 percent.

The seller of the call option will have the opposite position of the buyer. Thus, the gain (or loss) to the buyer will equal the loss (or gain) to the seller of the call option.

ILLUSTRATION Ellen Rose sold the call option purchased by Kelly Warden in the previous example. Ellen is obligated to purchase and provide the futures contract at the time the option is exercised. Her net gain from this speculative strategy is

Selling price of T-bond futures	$94,500	(94.50% of $100,000)
− Purchase price of T-bond futures	− $99,000	(99.00% of $100,000)
+ Call option premium received	+ $ 2,000	(2.00% of $100,000)
= Net gain to seller of call option on futures	− $ 2,500	(−2.50% of $100,000)

In the absence of transaction costs, Ellen's loss is equal to Kelly's gain. If the Treasury bond futures price had remained below the exercise price of 94–32 ($94,500) until the expiration date, the option would not have been exercised; in that case, the net gain from

Options on Futures Quotations

Quotations of options on futures are published in *The Wall Street Journal*. The exercise ("Strike") price of the futures contract is specified in the left column. The premiums for various expiration months of the call options on the futures contracts are shown in the next three columns, and premiums for various expiration months of put options on the futures contracts are shown in the last three columns. The expiration month of each option occurs shortly before the settlement date of the corresponding futures contract.

Interest Rate

T-Bonds (CBT)
$100,000; points and 64ths of 100%

Price	Nov	Dec	Jan	Nov	Dec	Jan
112	2-16	2-50	...	0-28	0-62	...
113	1-36	2-09	...	0-48	1-21	...
114	1-01	1-39	...	1-13	1-51	...
115	0-39	1-12	...	1-51	2-24	...
116	0-22	0-54	0-54	...	3-01	...
117	0-12	0-37	...	...	3-48	...

Est vol 34,426;
Fr vol 19,967 calls 29,169 puts
Op int Fri 186,009 calls 215,894 puts

T-Notes (CBT)
$100,000; points and 64ths of 100%

Price	Nov	Dec	Jan	Nov	Dec	Jan
111	2-35	2-51	...	0-07	0-23	...
112	1-45	2-04	...	0-17	0-40	...
113	1-01	1-27	1-26	0-37	0-63	1-38
114	0-34	0-60	0-63	1-05	1-32	...
115	0-15	0-37	...	...	...	...
116	0-06	0-22	...	...	2-58	...

Est vol 193,857 Fr 58,889 calls 81,290 puts
Op int Fri 1,069,378 calls 1,173,454 puts

5 Yr Treas Notes (CBT)
$100,000; points and 64ths of 100%

Price	Nov	Dec	Mar	Nov	Dec	Mar
11000	1-18	1-32	1-27	0-11	0-25	1-10
11050	0-58	1-10	1-10	0-19	0-35	1-25
11100	0-37	0-55	0-61	0-30	0-48	...
11150	0-23	0-41	0-49	0-48	1-02	...
11200	0-13	0-29	0-39	...	1-22	...
11250	0-06	0-19	...	...	...	...

Est vol 10,858 Fr 16,917 calls 57,672 puts
Op int Fri 232,149 calls 418,455 puts

30 Day Federal Funds (CBT)
$5,000,000; 100 minus daily average

Price	Sep	Oct	Nov	Sep	Oct	Nov
983125	.095	.002	.002	...	...	...
983750	.032	.002	.002	.002	.122	...
984375	.002	...	...	.035	.185	...
985000	.002	.002	...	.097	.247	...

purchasing the call option on Treasury bond futures would have been −$2,000 (the premium paid for the option), and the net gain from selling the call option would have been $2,000.

When interest rates decline, the buyers of call options on Treasury bonds may simply sell their previously purchased options just before expiration. If interest rates rise, the options will not be desirable. In that case, buyers of call options on Treasury bond futures will let their options expire, and their loss will be the premium paid for the call options on futures. Thus, the loss from purchasing options on futures is more limited than the loss from simply purchasing futures contracts.

Some speculators who expect interest rates to remain stable or decline may be willing to sell a put option on Treasury bond futures. If their expectations are correct, the price of a futures contract will likely rise, and the put option will not be exercised. Therefore, sellers of the put option would earn the premium that was paid to them when they sold the option.

Speculation Based on an Expected Increase in Interest Rates If speculators expect interest rates to increase, they can benefit from purchasing a put option on Treasury bond futures. If their expectations are correct, the market value of Treasury bonds will decline, and the price of a Treasury bond futures contract will decline as well. The speculators can exercise their option to sell futures at the exercise price, which will be

higher than the value of the futures contract. They can then purchase futures (to create an offsetting position) at a lower price than the price at which they sold futures. If interest rates decline, the speculators will likely let the options expire, and their loss will be the premium paid for the put options on futures.

ILLUSTRATION John Drummer expects interest rates to increase and purchases a put option on Treasury bond futures. Assume the exercise price on Treasury bond futures is 97–00 ($97,000) and the premium paid for the put option is 3–00 ($3,000). Assume that interest rates do increase and as a result, the price of the Treasury bond futures contract declines over time and is valued at 89–00 ($89,000) shortly before the option's expiration date. At this time, John decides to exercise the option and closes out the position by purchasing an identical futures contract. John's net gain from this speculative strategy is

Selling price of T-bond futures	$97,000	(97.00% of $100,000)
− Purchase price of T-bond futures	− $89,000	(89.00% of $100,000)
− Put option premium received	− $ 3,000	(3.00% of $100,000)
= Net gain to purchaser of put option on futures	$ 5,000	(5.00% of $100,000)

John's net gain of $5,000 represents a return on investment of about 167 percent.

The person who sold the put option on Treasury bond futures to John in this example incurred a loss of $5,000, assuming that the position was closed out (by selling an identical futures contract) on the same date that John's position was closed out. If the Treasury bond futures price had remained above the exercise price of 97–00 until the expiration date, the option would not have been exercised, and John would have lost $3,000 (the premium paid for the put option).

Some speculators who anticipate an increase in interest rates may be willing to sell a call option on Treasury bond futures. If their expectations are correct, the price of the futures contract will likely decline, and the call option will not be exercised.

Hedging with Options on Futures

Options on futures contracts are also used to hedge against risk. Put options on interest rate futures can be purchased to hedge bond portfolios, and put options on stock index futures can be purchased to hedge stock portfolios.

Hedging with Options on Interest Rate Futures

Financial institutions commonly hedge their bond or mortgage portfolios with options on interest rate futures contracts. The position they take on the options contract is designed to create a gain that can offset a loss on their bond or mortgage portfolio, while allowing some upside potential.

ILLUSTRATION Emory Savings and Loan Association has a large number of long-term fixed-rate mortgages that are mainly supported by short-term funds and would therefore be adversely affected by rising interest rates. As the previous chapter showed, sales of Trea-

EXHIBIT 14.15

Results from Hedging with Put Options on Treasury Bond Futures

	Scenario 1: • Interest Rates Rise • T-Bond Futures Price Declines to 91–00	Scenario 2: • Interest Rates Decline • T-Bond Futures Price Increases to 104–00
Effect on Emory's spread	Spread is reduced.	Spread is increased, but mortgage prepayments may occur.
Effect on T-bond futures price	Futures price decreases.	Futures price increases.
Decision on exercising the put option	Exercise put option.	Do not exercise put option.
Selling price of T-bond futures	$98,000	Not sold
− Purchase price of T-bond futures	−$91,000	Not purchased
− Price paid for put option	−$ 2,000	−$2,000
= Net gain per option	$5,000	−$2,000

sury bond futures can partially offset the adverse effect of rising interest rates in such a situation. Recall that if interest rates decline instead, the potential increase in Emory's interest rate spread (difference between interest revenues and expenses) would be partially offset by the loss on the futures contract.

One potential limitation of selling interest rate futures to hedge mortgages is that households may prepay their mortgages. If interest rates decline and most fixed-rate mortgages are prepaid, Emory will incur a loss on the futures position without an offsetting gain on its spread. To protect against this risk, Emory can purchase put options on Treasury bond futures. Assume that Emory purchases put options on Treasury bond futures with an exercise price of 98–00 ($98,000) for a premium of 2–00 ($2,000) per contract. The initial Treasury bond futures price is 99–00 at the time. First, assume that interest rates rise, causing the Treasury bond futures price to decline to 91–00. In this scenario, Emory will exercise its right to sell Treasury bond futures and offset its position by purchasing identical futures contracts, generating a net gain of $5,000 per contract, as shown in Exhibit 14.15. The gain on the futures position helps to offset the reduction in Emory's spread that occurs because of the higher interest rates.

Now consider a second scenario in which interest rates decline, causing the Treasury bond futures price to rise to 104–00. In this scenario, Emory does not exercise the put options on Treasury bond futures because the futures position would result in a loss.

The preceding example shows how a put option on futures offers more flexibility than simply selling futures. However, a premium must be paid for the put option. Financial institutions that wish to hedge against rising interest rate risk should compare the possible outcomes from selling interest rate futures contracts versus purchasing put options on interest rate futures in order to hedge interest rate risk.

Hedging with Options on Stock Index Futures

Financial institutions and other investors commonly hedge their stock portfolios with options on stock index futures contracts. The position they take on the options contract is designed to create a gain that can offset a loss on their stock portfolio, while allowing some upside potential.

ILLUSTRATION You currently manage a stock portfolio that is valued at $400,000 and plan to hold these stocks over a long-term period. However, you are concerned that the stock market may experience a temporary decline over the next three months and that your stock portfolio will probably decline by about the same degree as the market. You want to create a hedge so that your portfolio will decline no more than 3 percent from its present value, but you would like to maintain any upside potential. You can purchase a put option on index futures to hedge your stock portfolio. Put options on S&P 500 index futures are available with an expiration date about three months from now.

Assume that the S&P 500 index level is currently 1600, and that one particular put option on index futures has a strike price of 1552 (which represents a 3 percent decline from the prevailing index level) and a premium of 10. Since the options on S&P 500 index futures are priced at $250 times the quoted premium, the dollar amount to be paid for this option is 10 × $250 = $2,500. If the index level declines below 1552 (reflecting a decline of more than 3 percent), you may exercise the put option on index futures, which gives you the right to sell the index for a price of 1552. At the settlement date of the futures contract, you will receive $250 times the differential between the futures price of 1552 and the prevailing index level. For example, if the market declines by 5 percent, the index will decline from 1600 to 1520. There will be a gain on the index futures contract of (1552 − 1520) × $250 = $8,000. Meanwhile, a 5 percent decline in the value of the portfolio reflects a loss of $20,000 (5 percent of $400,000 = $20,000). The $8,000 gain (excluding the premium paid) from the options contract reduces the overall loss to $12,000, or 3 percent of the portfolio.

Determining the Degree of the Hedge with Options on Stock Index Futures In the previous example, any loss less than 3 percent is not hedged. When using put options to hedge, various strike prices exist for an option on a specific stock index and for a specific expiration date. For example, put options on the S&P 500 index may be available with strike prices of 1760, 1800, 1840, and so on. The higher the strike price relative to the prevailing index value, the higher the price at which the investor can lock in the sale of the index. However, a higher premium must be paid to purchase put options with a higher strike price. From a hedging perspective, this simply illustrates that a higher price must be paid to be "insured" (or protected) against losses resulting from stock market downturns. This concept is analogous to automobile insurance, where a person must pay a higher premium for a policy with a lower deductible.

Selling Call Options to Cover the Cost of Put Options In the previous example, the cost of hedging with a put option on index futures is $2,500. Given your expectations of a weak stock market over the next three months, you could generate some fees by selling call options on S&P 500 index futures to help cover the cost of purchasing put options.

ILLUSTRATION Assume that there is a call option on S&P 500 index futures with a strike price of 1648 (3 percent above the existing index level) and a premium of 10. You can sell a call option on index futures for $2,500 (10 × $250) and use the proceeds to pay the premium on the put option. The obvious disadvantage of selling a call option to finance the purchase of the put option is that it limits your upside potential. For example, if the market rises by 5 percent over the three-month period, the S&P 500 index level will rise to 1680. The difference between this level and the strike price of 1648 on the call option forces you to make a payment of (1680 − 1648) × $250 = $8,000 to the owner of the call option. This partially offsets the gain to your portfolio that resulted from the favorable market conditions.

When attempting to hedge larger portfolios than the one in the previous example, additional put options would be purchased to hedge the entire portfolio against a possible decline in the market. For example, if your stock portfolio was $1,200,000 instead of $400,000 as in the previous example, you would need to purchase three put options on S&P 500 index futures contracts. Since each index futures contract would have a value of $400,000, you would need a short position in three index futures contracts to hedge the entire stock portfolio (assuming that the market and the stock portfolio move in tandem).

Institutional Use of Options Markets

Exhibit 14.16 summarizes the uses of options by various types of financial institutions; some of these were illustrated in the previous examples. Although options positions are sometimes taken by financial institutions for speculative purposes, they are more commonly used for hedging. Savings institutions and bond mutual funds use options on interest rate futures to hedge interest rate risk. Stock mutual funds, insurance companies, and pension funds use stock index options and options on stock index futures to hedge their stock portfolios.

J.P. Morgan Chase, Citigroup, and some other commercial banks have aggressively penetrated the options market by offering options and other derivative securities to various firms. These banks commonly serve as an intermediary between two parties that take derivative positions in an over-the-counter market.

Options as Compensation

Some financial institutions and nonfinancial firms distribute call options on their own stock to their managers as compensation. For example, a manager may receive a salary along with call options on 1,000 shares of stock that have an exercise price above the

EXHIBIT 14.16   Institutional Use of Options Markets

Type of Financial Institution	Participation in Options Markets
Commercial banks	• Sometimes offer options to businesses.
Savings institutions	• Sometimes take positions in options on futures contracts to hedge interest rate risk.
Mutual funds	• Stock mutual funds take positions in stock index options to hedge against a possible decline in prices of stocks in their portfolios. • Stock mutual funds sometimes take speculative positions in stock index options in an attempt to increase their returns. • Bond mutual funds sometimes take positions in options on futures to hedge interest rate risk.
Securities firms	• Serve as brokers by executing stock option transactions for individuals and businesses.
Pension funds	• Take positions in stock index options to hedge against a possible decline in prices of stocks in their portfolio. • Take positions in options on futures contracts to hedge their bond portfolios against interest rate movements.
Insurance companies	• Take positions in stock index options to hedge against a possible decline in prices of stocks in their portfolio. • Take positions in options on futures contracts to hedge their bond portfolios against interest rate movements.

prevailing price and an expiration date of five years from today. The purpose of awarding options as compensation is to increase the managers' incentive to make decisions that increase the value of the firm's stock. With options, their compensation is more directly aligned with the value of the firm's stock.

Distortion between Performance and Option Compensation Many option compensation programs do not account for general market conditions, however. For example, managers who received stock options during the 2001–2002 period may have earned low compensation even though their firm performed relatively well, because the stock prices of most firms were weak in this period. Conversely, the managers who received stock options during 2003 may have earned very high compensation even though their firm performed relatively poorly, because the stock prices of most firms increased substantially at this time. Since compensation from holding options is driven more by general market conditions than by the relative performance of a firm's managers, options are not always effective at rewarding good performance.

How Stock Option Compensation Can Destroy Shareholder Value Another concern with using options as compensation is that managers with substantial options may be tempted to manipulate the stock's price upward in the near future, even though doing so adversely affects the stock price in the future. For example, they might use accounting methods that defer the reporting of some expenses until next year, while accelerating the reporting of some revenue. In this way, short-term earnings will appear favorable, but earnings in the following period will be reduced. When the managers believe that the stock price has peaked, they can exercise their options and then sell their shares in the secondary market. Firms can prevent the wrongful use of options by requiring that managers hold them for several years before exercising them.

Reporting Option Compensation as an Expense While firms readily promote their option compensation programs as a means of rewarding employees for strong performance, they are not always willing to acknowledge that the options are an expense. By awarding stock options, the firm allows managers to buy stock under some conditions at below-market prices. Since the firm could have sold that stock to other investors at the market price, there is clearly an opportunity cost to the firm. Although there has been much discussion about acknowledging this expense, the Financial Accounting Standards Board (FASB) has been unwilling to require firms to report this cost as an expense on the income statement. Consequently, a firm's earnings will appear higher when it uses stock options to compensate its managers and does not report the expense on the income statement. Although some firms have begun to report the options expense on the income statement, other firms will not do so unless it is required. This discrepancy makes it difficult for investors to determine and compare firms' actual earnings.

Options Market Globalization

 GL🌐BALASPECTS

The globalization of stock markets has resulted in the need for a globalized market in stock options. Options on stock indexes representing various countries are now available. Options exchanges have been established in numerous countries, including Australia, Austria, Belgium, France, Germany, and Singapore. U.S. portfolio managers who maintain large holdings of stocks from specific countries are heavily exposed to the conditions of those markets. Rather than liquidate the portfolio of foreign stocks to protect against a possible temporary decline, the managers can purchase put options on the foreign stock

index of concern. Portfolio managers residing in these countries can also use this strategy to hedge their stock portfolios.

Portfolio managers desiring to capitalize on the expectation of temporary favorable movements in foreign markets can purchase call options on the corresponding stock indexes. Thus, the existence of options on foreign stock indexes allows portfolio managers to hedge or speculate based on forecasts of foreign market conditions. The trading of options on foreign stock indexes avoids the transaction costs associated with buying and selling large portfolios of foreign stocks.

Currency Options Contracts

A **currency call option** provides the right to purchase a specified currency for a specified price within a specified period of time. Corporations involved in international business transactions use currency call options to hedge future payables. If the exchange rate at the time payables are due exceeds the exercise price, corporations can exercise their options and purchase the currency at the exercise price. Conversely, if the prevailing exchange rate is lower than the exercise price, corporations can purchase the currency at the prevailing exchange rate and let the options expire.

Speculators purchase call options on currencies that they expect to strengthen against the dollar. If the foreign currency strengthens as expected, they can exercise their call options to purchase the currency at the exercise price and then sell the currency at the prevailing exchange rate.

A **currency put option** provides the right to sell a specified currency for a specified price within a specified period of time. Corporations involved in international business transactions may purchase put options to hedge future receivables. If the exchange rate at the time they receive payment in a foreign currency is less than the exercise price, they can exercise their option by selling the currency at the exercise price. Conversely, if the prevailing exchange rate is higher than the exercise price, they can sell the currency at the prevailing exchange rate and let the options expire.

Speculators purchase put options on currencies they expect to weaken against the dollar. If the foreign currency weakens as expected, the speculators can purchase the currency at the prevailing spot rate and exercise their put options to sell the currency at the exercise price.

For every buyer of a currency call or put option, there must be a seller (or writer). A writer of a call option is obligated to sell the specified currency at the specified strike price if the option is exercised. A writer of a put option is obligated to purchase the specified currency at the specified strike price if the option is exercised. Speculators may be willing to write call options on foreign currencies that they expect to weaken against the dollar or write put options on those they expect to strengthen against the dollar. If a currency option expires without being exercised, the writer earns the up-front premium received.

SUMMARY

■ Stock options are traded on exchanges, just as many stocks are. Orders submitted by a brokerage firm are transmitted to a trading floor, where floor brokers execute the trades. Some trades are executed electronically.

■ Speculators purchase call options on stocks whose prices are expected to rise and purchase put options on those expected to decrease. They purchase call options on interest rate futures contracts when they expect interest rates to decrease. They buy currency

call options when they expect foreign currencies to strengthen and currency put options when they expect foreign currencies to weaken.

■ The premium of a call option is influenced by the characteristics of the option and of the underlying stock that can affect the potential gains. First, the higher the market price of the stock relative to the exercise price, the higher the premium. Second, the higher the stock's volatility, the higher the premium. Third, the longer the term until expiration, the higher the premium.

For put options, the higher the market price of the stock relative to the exercise price, the lower the premium. The volatility of the underlying stock and the term to expiration are related to the put option premium in the same manner as they are to the call option premium.

■ Index options can be used to speculate on movements in stock indexes, with a small investment. Put options on stock indexes can be purchased to hedge a stock portfolio whose movements are somewhat similar to that of the stock index.

■ Options on stock index futures can be used to speculate on movements in the value of the stock index futures contract. Put options on stock index futures can be purchased to hedge portfolios of stocks that move in tandem with the stock index.

POINT COUNTER-POINT

If You Were a Major Shareholder of a Publicly Traded Firm, Would You Prefer That Stock Options Be Traded on That Stock?

Point No. Options can be used by investors to speculate, and excessive trading of the options may push the stock price away from its fundamental price.

Counter-Point Yes. Options can be used by investors to temporarily hedge against adverse movements in the stock, so they may reduce the selling pressure on the stock in some periods.

Who Is Correct? Use your favorite search engine to learn more about this issue. Offer your own opinion on this issue.

QUESTIONS AND APPLICATIONS

1. **Hedging Effectiveness** Three savings and loan institutions (S&Ls) have identical balance sheet compositions: a high concentration of short-term deposits that are used to provide long-term, fixed-rate mortgages. The S&Ls took the following positions one year ago.

Name of S&L	Position
LaCrosse	Sold financial futures
Stevens Point	Purchased put options on interest rate futures
Whitewater	Did not take any position in futures

Assume that interest rates declined consistently over the last year. Which of the three S&Ls would have achieved the best performance based on this information? Explain.

2. **Internet Exercise** Go to http://www.cboe.com. Under "Market Quotes," select "Delayed option quotes." Insert the ticker symbol for a stock option in which you are interested. Assess the results. Did the premium ("Net") on the call options increase or decrease today? Did the premium on the put options increase or decrease today? Based on the changes in the premium, do you think the underlying stock price increased or decreased? Explain.

3. **Options versus Futures** Describe the general differences between a call option and a futures contract.

4. **Call Options on Futures** Describe a call option on interest rate futures. How does it differ from purchasing a futures contract?

5. **Change in Stock Option Premiums** Explain how and why the option premiums may change in response to a surprise announcement that the Fed will in-

crease interest rates even if stock prices are not affected.

6. **Managing in Financial Markets: Hedging with Stock Options** As a stock portfolio manager, you have investments in many U.S. stocks and plan to hold these stocks over a long-term period. However, you are concerned that the stock market may experience a temporary decline over the next three months and that your stock portfolio will probably decline by about the same degree as the market. You are aware that options on S&P 500 index futures are available. The following options on S&P 500 index futures are available and have an expiration date about three months from now:

Strike Price	Call Premium	Put Premium
1372	40	24
1428	24	40

The options on S&P 500 index futures are priced at $250 times the quoted premium. Currently, the S&P 500 index level is 1400. The strike price of 1372 represents a 2 percent decline from the prevailing index level, and the strike price of 1428 represents an increase of 2 percent above the prevailing index level.

  a. Assume that you want to take an options position to hedge your entire portfolio, which is currently valued at about $700,000. How many index option contracts should you take a position in to hedge your entire portfolio?

  b. Assume that you want to create a hedge so that your portfolio will lose no more than 2 percent from its present value. How can you take a position in options on index futures to achieve this goal? What is the cost to you as a result of creating this hedge?

  c. Given your expectations of a weak stock market over the next three months, how can you generate some fees from the sale of options on S&P 500 index futures to help cover the cost of purchasing options?

7. **Selling Options** Under what conditions would speculators sell a call option? What is the risk to speculators who sell put options?

8. **Put Options on Futures** Describe a put option on interest rate futures. How does it differ from selling a futures contract?

9. **Speculating with Call Options** How are call options used by speculators? Describe the conditions in which their strategy would backfire. What is the maximum loss that could occur for a purchaser of a call option?

10. **Speculating with Stock Options** The stock price of Garner stock is $40. There is a call option on Garner stock that is at the money, with a premium of $2.00. There is a put option on Garner stock that is at the money, with a premium of $1.80. Why would investors consider writing this call option and this put option? Why would some investors consider buying this call option and this put option?

11. **Factors Affecting Put Option Premiums** Identify the factors affecting the premium paid on a put option. Describe how each factor affects the size of the premium.

12. **Interpreting Financial News** Interpret the following comments made by Wall Street analysts and portfolio managers:

  a. "Our firm took a hit because we wrote put options on stocks just before the stock market crash."

  b. "Before hedging our stock portfolio with options on index futures, we search for the index that is most conducive."

  c. "We prefer to use covered call writing to hedge our stock portfolios."

13. **Hedging with Put Options** Why would a financial institution holding ABC stock consider buying a put option on this stock rather than simply selling the stock?

14. **Hedging Interest Rate Risk** Assume a savings institution has a large amount of fixed-rate mortgages and obtains most of its funds from short-term deposits. How could it use options on financial futures to hedge its exposure to interest rate movements? Would futures or options on futures be more appropriate if the institution is concerned that interest rates will decline, causing a large number of mortgage prepayments?

15. **Factors Affecting Call Option Premiums** Identify the factors affecting the premium paid on a call option. Describe how each factor affects the size of the premium.

16. **Leverage of Options** How can financial institutions with stock portfolios use stock options when they expect stock prices to rise substantially but do not yet have sufficient funds to purchase more stock?

17. **Speculating with Put Options** How are put options used by speculators? Describe the conditions in which their strategy would backfire. What is the maximum loss that could occur for a purchaser of a put option?

PROBLEMS

1. **Covered Call Strategy** Coral Inc. has purchased shares of stock M at $28 per share. Coral will sell the stock in six months. It considers using a strategy of covered call writing to partially hedge its position in this stock. The exercise price is $32, the expiration date is six months, and the premium on the call option is $2.50. Complete the following table:

Possible Price of Stock M in 6 Months	Profit or Loss Per Share If a Covered Call Strategy Is Used
$25	
28	
33	
36	

2. **Writing Call Options** A call option on Illinois stock specifies an exercise price of $38. Today the stock's price is $40. The premium on the call option is $5. Assume the option will not be exercised until maturity, if at all. Complete the following table:

Assumed Stock Price at the Time the Call Option Is About to Expire	Net Profit or Loss Per Share to Be Earned by the Writer (Seller) of the Call Option
$37	
39	
41	
43	
45	
48	

3. **Writing Put Options** A put option on Indiana stock specifies an exercise price of $23. Today the stock's price is $24. The premium on the put option is $3. Assume the option will not be exercised until maturity, if at all. Complete the following table:

Assumed Stock Price at the Time the Put Option Is About to Expire	Net Profit or Loss Per Share to Be Earned by the Writer (or Seller) of the Put Option
$20	
21	
22	
23	
24	
25	
26	

4. **Purchasing Call Options** A call option on Michigan stock specifies an exercise price of $55. Today the stock's price is $54 per share. The premium on the call option is $3. Assume the option will not be exercised until maturity, if at all. Complete the following table for a speculator who purchases the call option:

Assumed Stock Price at the Time the Call Option Is About to Expire	Net Profit or Loss Per Share to Be Earned by the Speculator
$50	
52	
54	
56	
58	
60	
62	

5. **Hedging with Bond Futures** Smart Savings Bank desired to hedge its interest rate risk. It considered two possibilities: (1) sell Treasury bond futures at a price of 94–00, or (2) purchase a put option on Treasury bond futures. At the time, the price of

Treasury bond futures was 95–00. The face value of Treasury bond futures was $100,000. The put option premium was 2–00, and the exercise price was 94–00. Just before the option expired, the Treasury bond futures price was 91–00, and Smart Savings Bank would have exercised the put option at that time, if at all. This is also the time when it would have offset its futures position, if it had sold futures. Determine the net gain to Smart Savings Bank if it had sold Treasury bond futures versus if it had purchased a put option on Treasury bond futures. Which alternative would have been more favorable, based on the situation that occurred?

6. **Purchasing Put Options** A put option on Iowa stock specifies an exercise price of $71. Today the stock's price is $68. The premium on the put option is $8. Assume the option will not be exercised until maturity, if at all. Complete the following table for a speculator who purchases the put option (and currently does not own the stock):

Assumed Stock Price at the Time the Put Option Is About to Expire	Net Profit or Loss Per Share to Be Earned by the Speculator
$60	
64	
68	
70	
72	
74	
76	

7. **Call Options on Futures** DePaul Insurance Company purchased a call option on an S&P 500 futures contract. The option premium is quoted as $6. The exercise price is 1430. Assume the index on the futures contract becomes 1440. Should DePaul exercise the call option or let it expire? What is the net gain or loss to DePaul after accounting for the premium paid for the option?

8. **Covered Call Strategy**
   a. Evanston Insurance Inc. has purchased shares of stock E at $50 per share. It will sell the stock in six months. It considers using a strategy of covered call writing to partially hedge its position in this stock. The exercise price is $53, the expiration date is six months, and the premium on the call option is $2. Complete the following table:

Possible Price of Stock E in 6 Months	Profit or Loss Per Share If a Covered Call Strategy Is Used	Profit or Loss Per Share If a Covered Call Strategy Is Not Used
$47		
50		
52		
55		
57		
60		

   b. Assume that each of the six stock prices in the first column in the table has an equal probability of occurring. Compare the probability distribution of the profits (or losses) per share when using covered call writing versus not using it. Would you recommend covered call writing in this situation? Explain.

9. **Call Options on Futures** Wisconsin Inc. purchased a call option on Treasury bond futures at a premium of 2–00. The exercise price is 92–08. If the price of the Treasury bond futures rises to 93–08, should Wisconsin exercise the call option or let it expire? What is Wisconsin's net gain or loss after accounting for the premium paid on the option?

10. **Put Options on Futures** Purdue Savings and Loan Association purchased a put option on Treasury bond futures with a September delivery date and an exercise price of 91–16. The put option has a premium of 1–32. Assume that the price of the Treasury bond futures decreases to 88–16. Should Purdue exercise the option or let it expire? What is Purdue's net gain or loss after accounting for the premium paid on the option?

FLOW OF FUNDS EXERCISE

Hedging with Options Contracts

Carson Company would like to acquire Vinnet Inc., a publicly traded firm in the same industry. Vinnet's stock price is currently much lower than the prices of other firms in the industry because it is inefficiently managed. Carson believes that it could restructure Vinnet's operations and improve its performance. It is about to contact Vinnet to determine whether Vinnet will agree to an acquisition. Carson is somewhat concerned that investors may learn of its plans and buy Vinnet in anticipation that Carson will need to pay a high premium (perhaps a 30 percent premium above the prevailing stock price) in order to complete the acquisition. Carson decides to call a bank about its risk,

as the bank has a brokerage subsidiary that can help it hedge with stock options.

a. How can Carson use stock options to reduce its exposure to this risk? Are there any limitations to this strategy, given that Carson will ultimately have to buy most or all of the Vinnet stock?

b. Describe the maximum possible loss that may be directly incurred by Carson as a result of engaging in this strategy.

c. Explain the results of the strategy you offered in the previous question if Vinnet plans to avoid the acquisition attempt by Carson.

EXERCISE

Assessing Stock Option Information

Use *The Wall Street Journal* to obtain recent stock options data for a particular stock in which you are interested. Complete the following table (use the same expiration month for all quoted premiums):

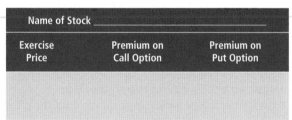

Explain the relationship between the option's exercise price and (1) the call option premium and (2) the put option premium.

Obtain recent stock options data for a particular stock in which you are interested. Use a recent issue of *The Wall Street Journal* to complete the following table (use the same exercise price for all quoted premiums):

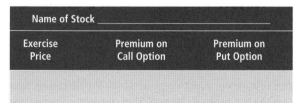

Explain the relationship between the option's time to maturity and (1) the call option premium and (2) the put option premium.

Obtain recent stock options data for a particular stock in which you are interested. Using *The Wall Street Journal*, complete the following table:

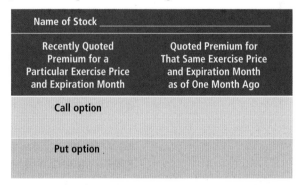

Explain why the call option premium increased or decreased. Determine the percentage change in the premium. Do the same for the put option premium.

Option Valuation

The Binomial Pricing Model

The binomial option-pricing model was originally developed by William F. Sharpe. An advantage of the model is that it can be used to price both European-style and American-style options with or without dividends. European options are put or call options that can be exercised only at maturity; American options can be exercised at any time prior to maturity.

Assumptions of the Binomial Pricing Model

The following are the main assumptions of the binomial pricing model:

1. The continuous random walk underlying the Black-Scholes model can be modeled by a discrete random walk with the following properties:

    ■ The asset price changes only at discrete (noninfinitesimal) time steps.
    ■ At each time step, the asset price may move either up or down; thus, there are only two returns, and these two returns are the same for all time steps.
    ■ The probabilities of moving up and down are known.

2. The world is risk-neutral. This allows the assumption that investors' risk preferences are irrelevant and that investors are risk-neutral. Furthermore, the return from the underlying asset is the risk-free interest rate.

Using the Binomial Pricing Model to Price Call Options

The following is an example of how the binomial pricing model can be employed to price a call option (that is, to determine a call option premium). To use the model, we need information for three securities: the underlying stock, a risk-free security, and the stock option.

Assume that the price of Gem Corporation stock today is $100. Furthermore, it is estimated that Gem stock will be selling for either $150 or $70 in one year. That is, the

stock is expected to either rise by 50 percent or fall by 30 percent. Also assume that the annual risk-free interest rate on a one-year Treasury bill is 10 percent, continuously compounded. Assume that a T-bill currently sells for $100. Since interest is continuously compounded, the T-bill will pay interest of $100 \times (e^{.10} - 1)$, or $10.52.

Currently, a call option on Gem stock is available with an exercise price of $100 and an expiration date one year from now. Since the call option is an option to buy Gem stock, the option will have a value of $50 if the stock price is $150 in one year. Conversely, the call option will have a value of $0 if the stock price is $70. Our objective is to value this call option using the binomial pricing model.

The first step in applying the model to this call option is to recognize that three investments are involved: the stock, a risk-free security, and the call option. Using the information given above, we have the following payoff matrix in one year:

Security	Price If Stock Is Worth $150 in One Year	Price If Stock Is Worth $70 in One Year	Current Price
Gem stock	$150.00	$70.00	$100.00
Treasury bill	110.52	110.52	100.00
Call option	50.00	0.00	?

The objective of the binomial pricing model is thus to determine the current price of the call option. The key to understanding the valuation of the call option using the binomial pricing model is that the option's value must be based on a combination of the value of the stock and the T-bill. If this were not the case, arbitrage opportunities would result. Consequently, in either the up or the down state, the payoff of a portfolio of N_s shares of Gem stock and N_b T-bills must be equal to the value of the call option in that state. Using the payoff matrix above, we thus get a system of two equations:

$$150N_s + 110.52N_b = 50$$

$$70N_s + 110.52N_b = 0$$

Since we are dealing with two linear equations with two unknowns, we can easily solve for the two variables by substitution. Doing so gives the following values for the number of shares and the number of T-bills in the investor's *replicating* portfolio:

$$N_s = 0.625$$

$$N_b = -0.3959$$

In other words, the payoffs of the call option on Gem stock can be replicated by borrowing $39.59 at the risk-free rate and buying 0.625 shares of Gem stock for $62.50 (since one share currently sells for $100). Since the payoff of this replicating portfolio is the same as that for the call, the cost to the investor must be the value of the call. In this case, since $39.59 of the outlay of $62.50 is financed by borrowing, the outlay to the investor is $62.50 − $39.59 = $22.91. Thus, the call option premium must be $22.91.

In equation form, the value of the call option (V) can thus be written as

$$V_0 = N_s P_s + N_b P_b$$

The computation of the N's can be simplified somewhat. More specifically,

$$N_s = h = \frac{P_{ou} - P_{od}}{P_{su} - P_{sd}}$$

where

P_{ou} = value of the option in the up state

P_{od} = value of the option in the down state

P_{su} = price of Gem stock in the up state

P_{sd} = price of Gem stock in the down state

This is also referred to as the *hedge ratio*.

The amount borrowed (BOR) in the example above is equal to the product of the number of risk-free securities in the replicating portfolio and the price of the risk-free security:

$$N_b P_b = BOR = PV(hP_{sd} - P_{od})$$

where

PV = present value of a continuously compounded sum

h = hedge ratio

Thus, the value of the call option can be expressed more simply as

$$V_0 = hP_s + BOR$$

To illustrate why the relationships discussed so far should hold, assume for the moment that a call option on Gem stock is selling for a premium of $25 (that is, the call option is overpriced). In this case, investors are presented with an arbitrage opportunity to make an instantaneous, riskless profit. More specifically, investors could write a call, buy the stock, and borrow at the risk-free rate. Now assume the call option on Gem stock is selling for a premium of only $20 (that is, the call option is underpriced). Using arbitrage, investors would buy a call, sell the stock short, and invest at the risk-free rate.

Using the Binomial Pricing Model to Price Put Options

Continuing with the example of Gem Corporation, the only item that changes in the payoff matrix when the option is a put option (that is, an option to sell Gem stock) is the value of the option at expiration in the up and down states. Specifically, if Gem stock is worth $150 in one year, the put option will be worthless; if Gem stock is worth only $70 in one year, the put option will be worth $30. Since the value of the risk-free security is contingent only on the T-bill interest rate, it will be unaffected by the fact that we are now dealing with a put option.

The hedge ratio and the amount borrowed can now be easily determined using the formulas introduced previously. Specifically, the hedge ratio is

$$h = \frac{0 - 30}{150 - 70} = -0.375$$

The amount borrowed is

$$BOR = PV[-0.375(70) - 30] = \frac{-56.25}{e^{RT}} = -50.90$$

Thus, to replicate the put option, the investor would sell short 0.375 Gem shares and lend $50.90 at the risk-free rate. Thus, the net amount the investor must put up is $50.90 − $37.50 = $13.40. Accordingly, this is the fair value of the put.

Put-Call Parity

With some mathematical manipulation, the following relationship can be derived between the prices of puts and calls (with the same exercise price and time to expiration):

$$P_p = P_c + \frac{E}{e^{RT}} - P_s$$

where

P_p = price of a put option

P_c = price of a call option

E = exercise price of the option

e^{RT} = present value operator for a continuously compounded sum, discounted at interest rate R for T years

P_s = price of the stock

Using the example of Gem Corporation,

$$P_p = \$22.91 + \frac{\$100}{e^{.1}} - \$100 = \$13.39$$

The Black-Scholes Option-Pricing Model for Call Options

In 1973, Black and Scholes devised an option-pricing model that motivated further research on option valuation that continues to this day.

Assumptions of the Black-Scholes Option-Pricing Model

The following are some of the key assumptions underlying the Black-Scholes option-pricing model:

1. The risk-free rate is known and constant over the life of the option.
2. The probability distribution of stock prices is lognormal.
3. The variability of a stock's return is constant.
4. The option is to be exercised only at maturity, if at all.
5. There are no transaction costs involved in trading options.
6. Tax rates are similar for all participants who trade options.
7. The stock of concern does not pay cash dividends.

The Black-Scholes Partial Differential Equation

The Black-Scholes option-pricing model was one of the first to introduce the concept of a *riskless hedge*. Assume that an amount Π is invested in a risk-free asset. Thus, the investor would see a return of $r\Pi dt$ over a time interval dt. If an appropriately selected portfolio, with a current value of Π consisting of a company's stock and an offsetting position in an option on that stock, returns more than $r\Pi dt$ over a time interval dt, an investor could conduct arbitrage by borrowing at the risk-free rate and investing in the portfolio. Conversely, if the portfolio returns less than $r\Pi dt$, the investor would short the portfolio and invest in the risk-free asset. In either case, the arbitrageur would make

a riskless, no-cost, instantaneous profit. Thus, the return on the portfolio and on the riskless asset must be more or less equal.

Using this argument, Black and Scholes developed what has become known as the *Black-Scholes partial differential equation:*

$$\frac{\partial V}{\partial t} + \frac{1}{2}\sigma^2 S^2 \frac{\partial^2 V}{\partial S^2} + rS\frac{\partial V}{\partial S} - rV = 0$$

where
$$V = \text{value of an option}$$
$$S = \text{price of the underlying stock}$$
$$r = \text{risk-free rate of return}$$
$$t = \text{a measure of time}$$
$$\sigma^2 = \text{variance of the underlying stock's price}$$
$$\partial \text{ and } \partial^2 = \text{first- and second-order partial derivatives}$$

The Black-Scholes Option-Pricing Model for European Call Options

In order to price an option, the partial differential equation must be solved for V, the value of the option. Assuming that the risk-free interest rate and stock price volatility are constant, solving the Black-Scholes partial differential equation results in the familiar Black-Scholes formula for European call options:

$$V = SN(d_1) - Ee^{-rT}N(d_2)$$

where
$$V = \text{value of the call option}$$
$$S = \text{stock price}$$
$$N(.) = \text{cumulative distribution function for a standardized normal random variable}$$
$$E = \text{exercise price of the call option}$$
$$e = \text{base } e \text{ antilog or } 2.7183$$
$$r = \text{risk-free rate of return for one year assuming continuous compounding}$$
$$T = \text{time remaining to maturity of the call option, expressed as a fraction of a year}$$

The terms $N(d_1)$ and $N(d_2)$ deserve further elaboration. N represents a cumulative probability for a unit normal variable, where

$$d_1 = \frac{\ln(S/E) + \left(r + \frac{1}{2}\sigma^2\right)(T)}{\sigma\sqrt{T}}$$

and

$$d_2 = \frac{\ln(S/E) + \left(r - \frac{1}{2}\sigma^2\right)(T)}{\sigma\sqrt{T}}$$

$$= d_1 - \sigma\sqrt{T}$$

where ln(*S/E*) represents the natural logarithm and σ represents the standard deviation of the continuously compounded rate of return on the underlying stock.

Using the Black-Scholes Option-Pricing Model to Price a European Call Option

To illustrate how the Black-Scholes equation can be used to price a call option, assume you observe a call option on MPB Corporation stock expiring in six months with an exercise price of $70. Thus, $T = .50$ and $E = \$70$. Furthermore, the current price of MPB stock is $72, and the stock has a standard deviation of 0.10. Moreover, the annual risk-free rate is 7 percent.

Solving for d_1 and d_2, we get

$$d_1 = \frac{\ln(72/70) + [0.07 + 0.5(0.10)^2](0.5)}{0.10\sqrt{0.5}} = 0.9287$$

$$d_2 = 0.9287 - 0.10\sqrt{0.50} = 0.8580$$

Using a table that identifies the area under the standard normal distribution function (see Exhibit 14A.1), the cumulative probability can be determined. Because d_1 is 0.9287, the cumulative probability from zero to 0.9287 is about 0.3235 (from Exhibit 14A.1, using linear interpolation). Because the cumulative probability for a unit normal variable from minus infinity to zero is 0.50, the cumulative probability from minus infinity to 0.9287 is 0.50 + 0.3235 = 0.8235.

For d_2, the cumulative probability from zero to 0.8580 is 0.3045. Therefore, the cumulative probability from minus infinity to 0.8580 is 0.50 + 0.3042 = 0.8042.

Now that $N(d_1)$ and $N(d_2)$ have been estimated, the call option value can be estimated:

$$V_c = (\$72 \times 0.8235) - \left(\frac{\$70}{e^{0.07 \times 0.50}} \times 0.8045\right) = \$4.91$$

Thus, a call option on MPB stock should sell for a premium of $4.91.

Put-Call Parity

Using the Black-Scholes option-pricing model, the same relationship exists between the price of a call and that of a put as in the binomial option-pricing model. Thus, we have

$$P_p = P_c + \frac{E}{e^{RT}} - P_s$$

Deriving the Implied Volatility

In the example of deriving the value of a call option, an estimate of the stock's standard deviation was used. In some cases, investors want to derive the market's implied volatility rather than a valuation of the call option. The volatility is referred to as "implied" under these circumstances because it is not directly observable in the market. The implied volatility can be derived with some software packages by inputting values for the other variables (prevailing stock price, exercise price, option's time to expiration, and interest rate) in the call option-pricing model and also inputting the market premium of the call

EXHIBIT 14A.1 Cumulative Probabilities of the Standard Normal Distribution Function

d	0.00	0.01	0.02	0.03	0.04	0.05	0.06	0.07	0.08	0.09
0.0	0.0000	0.0040	0.0080	0.0120	0.0160	0.0199	0.0239	0.0279	0.0319	0.0359
0.1	0.0398	0.0438	0.0478	0.0517	0.0557	0.0596	0.0636	0.0675	0.0714	0.0753
0.2	0.0793	0.0832	0.0871	0.0910	0.0948	0.0987	0.1026	0.1064	0.1103	0.1141
0.3	0.1179	0.1217	0.1255	0.1293	0.1331	0.1368	0.1406	0.1443	0.1480	0.1517
0.4	0.1554	0.1591	0.1628	0.1664	0.1700	0.1736	0.1772	0.1808	0.1844	0.1879
0.5	0.1915	0.1950	0.1985	0.2019	0.2054	0.2088	0.2123	0.2157	0.2190	0.2224
0.6	0.2257	0.2291	0.2324	0.2357	0.2389	0.2422	0.2454	0.2486	0.2517	0.2549
0.7	0.2580	0.2611	0.2642	0.2673	0.2704	0.2734	0.2764	0.2794	0.2823	0.2852
0.8	0.2881	0.2910	0.2939	0.2967	0.2995	0.3023	0.3051	0.3078	0.3106	0.3133
0.9	0.3159	0.3186	0.3213	0.3238	0.3264	0.3289	0.3315	0.3340	0.3365	0.3389
1.0	0.3413	0.3438	0.3461	0.3485	0.3508	0.3531	0.3554	0.3577	0.3599	0.3621
1.1	0.3643	0.3665	0.3686	0.3708	0.3729	0.3749	0.3770	0.3790	0.3810	0.3830
1.2	0.3849	0.3869	0.3888	0.3907	0.3925	0.3944	0.3962	0.3980	0.3997	0.4015
1.3	0.4032	0.4049	0.4066	0.4082	0.4099	0.4115	0.4131	0.4147	0.4162	0.4177
1.4	0.4192	0.4207	0.4222	0.4236	0.4251	0.4265	0.4279	0.4292	0.4306	0.4319
1.5	0.4332	0.4345	0.4357	0.4370	0.4382	0.4394	0.4406	0.4418	0.4429	0.4441
1.6	0.4452	0.4463	0.4474	0.4484	0.4495	0.4505	0.4515	0.4525	0.4535	0.4545
1.7	0.4554	0.4564	0.4573	0.4582	0.4591	0.4599	0.4608	0.4616	0.4625	0.4633
1.8	0.4641	0.4649	0.4656	0.4664	0.4671	0.4678	0.4686	0.4693	0.4699	0.4706
1.9	0.4713	0.4719	0.4726	0.4732	0.4738	0.4744	0.4750	0.4756	0.4761	0.4767
2.0	0.4773	0.4778	0.4783	0.4788	0.4793	0.4798	0.4803	0.4808	0.4812	0.4817
2.1	0.4821	0.4826	0.4830	0.4834	0.4838	0.4842	0.4846	0.4850	0.4854	0.4857
2.2	0.4861	0.4866	0.4868	0.4871	0.4875	0.4878	0.4881	0.4884	0.4887	0.4890
2.3	0.4893	0.4896	0.4898	0.4901	0.4904	0.4906	0.4909	0.4911	0.4913	0.4916
2.4	0.4918	0.4920	0.4922	0.4925	0.4927	0.4929	0.4931	0.4932	0.4934	0.4936
2.5	0.4938	0.4940	0.4941	0.4943	0.4945	0.4946	0.4948	0.4949	0.4951	0.4952
2.6	0.4953	0.4955	0.4956	0.4957	0.4959	0.4960	0.4961	0.4962	0.4963	0.4964
2.7	0.4965	0.4966	0.4967	0.4968	0.4969	0.4970	0.4971	0.4972	0.4973	0.4974
2.8	0.4974	0.4975	0.4976	0.4977	0.4977	0.4978	0.4979	0.4979	0.4980	0.4981
2.9	0.4981	0.4982	0.4982	0.4982	0.4984	0.4984	0.4985	0.4985	0.4986	0.4986
3.0	0.4987	0.4987	0.4987	0.4988	0.4988	0.4989	0.4989	0.4989	0.4990	0.4990

option. Instead of deriving a value for the call option premium, the prevailing market premium of the call option is used along with these other variables to derive the implied volatility. The software package will also show how the stock's implied volatility is affected for different values of the call option premium. If the market premium of the call option increases and other variables have not changed, this reflects an increase in the implied volatility. This relationship can be verified by plugging in a slightly higher market premium in the software program and checking how the implied volatility changes in response to a higher premium. The point is that investors can detect changes in the implied volatility of a stock by monitoring how the stock's call option premium changes over short intervals of time.

American versus European Options

American Call Options

An American call option is an option to purchase stock that can be exercised at any time prior to maturity. However, the original Black-Scholes model was developed to price European call options, which are options to purchase stock that can be exercised only at maturity. Naturally, European puts could be directly derived using the put-call parity relationship. Consequently, the question is whether the Black-Scholes equation can be used to price American call options.

In general, early exercise of a call may be justified only if the asset makes a cash payment such as a dividend on a stock. If there are no dividends during the life of the option, early exercise would be equivalent to buying something earlier than you need it and then giving up the right to decide later whether you really wanted it. If, however, it is possible to save a little money doing so, early purchase/exercise can sometimes be justified. Early exercise is not appropriate every time there is a dividend, but if early exercise is justified, it should occur just before the stock goes ex-dividend. This minimizes the amount of time value given up and still results in receiving the dividend. Thus, if there are no dividends on the underlying stock, the Black-Scholes model can be used to price American call options. If the underlying stock pays dividends, however, the Black-Scholes model may not be directly applicable. Conversely, the binomial option-pricing model can be used to price American call options that pay dividends.

American Put Options

Suppose you purchase a European put option. If the value of the underlying asset goes to zero, then the option has reached its maximum value. It allows you to sell a worthless asset for the exercise price. Since the option is European, however, it cannot be exercised prior to maturity. Its value will simply be the present value of the exercise price, and, of course, this value will gradually rise by the time value of money until expiration, at which time the option will be exercised. Clearly, this is a situation where you would wish the option were American, and if it were, you would exercise it as soon as the asset value goes to zero.

The example above indicates that there would be a demand for an option that allowed early exercise. It is not necessary, however, for the asset price to go to zero. The European put price must be at least the present value of the exercise price minus the asset price. Clearly, the present value of the exercise price minus the asset price is less than the exercise price minus the asset price, which is the amount that could be claimed if

the put could be exercised early. Thus, an American put will sell for more than the European put, and the Black-Scholes option-pricing model cannot be used to price an American put option. There is a point where the right to exercise early is at its maximum value, and at that point the American put would be exercised. Finding that point is difficult, but to do so is to unlock the mystery of pricing the American put.

The only surefire way to price the American put correctly is to use a numerical procedure such as the binomial model. The procedure is akin to partitioning a two-dimensional space of time and the asset price into finer points and solving either a difference or a differential equation at each time point. The process starts at expiration and successively works its way back to the present by using the solution at the preceding step. Thus, a closed-form solution does not exist. American puts can be viewed as an infinite series of compound options (that is, an option on an option). At each point in time, the holder of the put has the right to decide whether to exercise it or not. The decision not to exercise the put is tantamount to a decision to exercise the compound option and obtain a position in a new compound option, which can be exercised an instant later. This proceeds on to the expiration day. This logic can lead to an intuitive but complex mathematical formula that contains an infinite number of terms. Thus, the holders of American puts face an infinite series of early exercise decisions. Only at an instant before the asset goes ex-dividend do the holders know that they should wait to exercise. This is because they know the asset will fall in value an instant later so they might as well wait an instant and benefit from the decline in value.

CHAPTER 15

Interest Rate Derivative Markets

M any firms have inflow and outflow payments that are not equally sensitive to interest rate patterns. Consequently, they are exposed to interest rate risk. Interest rate swap contracts have been established to reduce these risks. Interest rate swap markets facilitate the trading of interest rate swap contracts.

The specific objectives of this chapter are to:

- describe the types of interest rate swaps that are available,
- explain the risks of interest rate swaps,
- identify other interest rate derivative instruments that are commonly used, and
- describe how the interest rate swap markets have become globalized.

Background

An **interest rate swap** is an arrangement whereby one party exchanges one set of interest payments for another. In the most common arrangement, fixed-rate interest payments are exchanged for floating-rate interest payments over time. The provisions of an interest rate swap include the following:

- The notional principal value to which the interest rates are applied to determine the interest payments involved.
- The fixed interest rate.
- The formula and type of index used to determine the floating rate.
- The frequency of payments, such as every six months or every year.
- The lifetime of the swap.

For example, a swap arrangement may involve an exchange of 11 percent fixed-rate payments for floating payments at the prevailing one-year Treasury bill rate plus 1 percent, based on $30 million of notional principal, at the end of each of the next seven years. Other money market rates are sometimes used instead of the T-bill rate to index the interest rate.

Although each participant in the swap agreement owes the other participant at each payment date, the amounts owed are typically netted out so that only the net payment is made. If a firm owes 11 percent of $30 million (the notional principal) but is supposed to receive 10 percent of $30 million on a given payment date, it will send a net payment of 1 percent of the $30 million, or $300,000.

The market for swaps is facilitated by over-the-counter trading rather than trading on an organized exchange. Given the uniqueness of the provisions in each swap arrangement, swaps are less standardized than other derivative instruments such as futures or options. Thus, a telecommunications network is more appropriate than an exchange to work out specific provisions of swaps.

Interest rate swaps became more popular in the early 1980s when corporations were experiencing the effects of large fluctuations in interest rates. Although some manufacturing companies were exposed to interest rate movements, financial institutions were exposed to a greater degree and became the primary users of interest rate swaps. By the mid-1980s, the volume of interest rate swaps amounted to hundreds of billions of dollars. Initially, only those institutions wishing to swap payments on amounts of $10 million or more engaged in interest rate swaps. In recent years, however, swaps have been conducted on smaller amounts as well.

Financial institutions such as savings institutions and commercial banks in the United States traditionally had more interest rate-sensitive liabilities than assets and therefore were adversely affected by increasing interest rates. Conversely, some financial institutions in other countries (such as some commercial banks in Europe) had access to long-term fixed-rate funding but used funds primarily for floating-rate loans. These institutions were adversely affected by declining interest rates.

By engaging in an interest rate swap, both types of financial institutions could reduce their exposure to interest rate risk. Specifically, a U.S. financial institution could send fixed-rate interest payments to a European financial institution in exchange for floating-rate payments. This type of arrangement is illustrated in Exhibit 15.1. In the event of rising interest rates, the U.S. financial institution receives higher interest payments from the floating-rate portion of the swap agreement, which helps to offset the rising cost of obtaining deposits. In the event of declining interest rates, the European financial institution provides lower interest payments in the swap arrangement, which helps to offset the lower interest payments received on its floating-rate loans.

In our example, the U.S. financial institution forgoes the potential benefits from a decline in interest rates, while the European financial institution forgoes the potential benefits from an increase in interest rates. The interest rate swap enables each institution

EXHIBIT 15.1   Illustration of an Interest Rate Swap

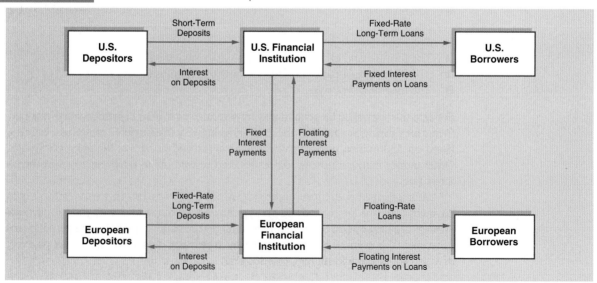

to offset any gains or losses that result specifically from interest rate movements. Consequently, as interest rate swaps reduce interest rate risk, they can also reduce potential returns. Most financial institutions that anticipate that interest rates will move in a favorable direction do not hedge their positions. Interest rate swaps are primarily used by financial institutions that would be adversely affected by the expected movement in interest rates.

A primary reason for the popularity of interest rate swaps is the existence of market imperfections. If the parties involved in a swap could easily access funds from various markets without having to pay a premium, they would not need to engage in swaps. Using our previous example, a U.S. financial institution could access long-term funds directly from the European market, while the European institution could access short-term funds directly from the U.S. depositors. However, a lack of information about foreign institutions and convenience encourages individual depositors to place deposits locally. Consequently, swaps are necessary for some financial institutions to obtain the maturities or rate sensitivities on funds that they desire.

Interest rate swaps are sometimes used by financial institutions and other firms for speculative purposes. For example, a firm may engage in a swap to benefit from its expectations that interest rates will rise, even if its other operations are not exposed to interest rate movements. When the swap is used for speculating rather than for hedging, any loss on the swap positions will not be offset by gains from other operations. Gibson Greetings Inc. incurred a loss of almost $17 million in 1994 as a result of positions in interest rate swaps. Procter & Gamble incurred a loss of about $157 million in 1994 as a result of positions in interest rate swaps. Procter & Gamble then claimed that Bankers Trust (a commercial bank that served as an intermediary and an adviser on interest rate swaps) did not properly advise it about the risk of its swap positions.

In the same year, Orange County, California, lost more than $2 billion as a result of positions in interest rate swaps and other derivative securities. It was positioned to generate large gains if interest rates declined. Interest rates increased instead, however, and the treasurer of the county took more positions to make up for those losses. He continued to take positions in anticipation that interest rates would decline, but the rates kept on rising throughout 1994. By December 1994, the treasurer resigned and Orange County announced that it would be filing for bankruptcy.

Although these cases received substantial attention from the media, interest rate swaps and other derivative securities can be used to reduce a firm's risk. These cases encouraged firms to more closely monitor the actions of their managers who take derivative positions to ensure that those positions are aligned with the firm's goals.

Financial Institutions Participation

Financial institutions participate in the swap markets in various ways, as summarized in Exhibit 15.2. Financial institutions such as commercial banks, savings institutions, insurance companies, and pension funds that are exposed to interest rate movements commonly engage in swaps to reduce interest rate risk.

A second way to participate in the swap market is by acting as an intermediary. Some commercial banks and securities firms serve in this capacity by matching up firms and facilitating the swap arrangement. Financial institutions that serve as intermediaries for swaps charge fees for their services. They may even provide credit guarantees (for a fee) to each party in the event that the counterparty does not fulfill its obligation. Under these circumstances, the parties engaged in swap agreements assess the creditworthiness of the intermediary that is backing the swap obligations. For this reason, participants in the swap market prefer intermediaries that have a high credit rating.

EXHIBIT 15.2 Participation of Financial Institutions in Swap Markets

Financial Institution	Participation in Swap Markets
Commercial banks	• Engage in swaps to reduce interest rate risk. • Serve as an intermediary by matching up two parties in a swap. • Serve as a dealer by taking the counterparty position to accommodate a party that desires to engage in a swap.
Savings and loan associations and savings banks	• Engage in swaps to reduce interest rate risk.
Finance companies	• Engage in swaps to reduce interest rate risk.
Securities firms	• Serve as an intermediary by matching up two parties in a swap. • Serve as a dealer by taking the counterparty position to accommodate a party that desires to engage in a swap.
Insurance companies	• Engage in swaps to reduce interest rate risk.
Pension funds	• Engage in swaps to reduce interest rate risk.

A third way to participate is by acting as a dealer in swaps. The financial institution takes the counterparty position in order to serve a client. In such a case, the financial institution may be exposing itself to interest rate risk unless it has recently taken the opposite position as a counterparty for another swap agreement.

Interest Rate Swap Types

In response to firms' diverse needs, a variety of interest rate swaps have been created. The following are some of the more commonly used swaps:

- Plain vanilla swaps
- Forward swaps
- Callable swaps
- Putable swaps
- Extendable swaps
- Zero-coupon-for-floating swaps
- Rate-capped swaps
- Equity swaps

Some types of interest rate swaps are more effective than others at offsetting any unfavorable effects of interest rate movements on the U.S. institution. However, those swaps also offset any favorable effects to a greater degree. Other types of interest rate swaps do not provide as effective a hedge but allow the institution more flexibility to benefit from favorable interest rate movements.

Plain Vanilla Swaps

In a **plain vanilla swap,** sometimes referred to as a fixed-for-floating swap, fixed-rate payments are periodically exchanged for floating-rate payments. The earlier example of the U.S. and European institutions involved this type of swap.

Consider the exchange of payments under different interest rate scenarios in Exhibit 15.3 when using a plain vanilla swap. Although infinite possible interest rate scenarios exist, only two scenarios are considered: (1) a consistent rise in market interest rates and (2) a consistent decline in market interest rates.

EXHIBIT 15.3   Illustration of a Plain Vanilla (Fixed-for-Floating) Swap

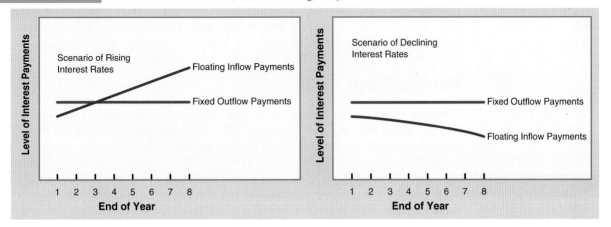

ILLUSTRATION

The Bank of Orlando has negotiated a plain vanilla swap in which it will exchange fixed payments of 9 percent for floating payments equal to LIBOR plus 1 percent at the end of each of the next five years. LIBOR is the London Interbank Offer Rate, or the interest rate charged on loans between European banks. The LIBOR varies among currencies; for swap examples involving U.S. firms, the LIBOR on U.S. dollars would normally be used. Assume the notional principal is $100 million.

Two scenarios for LIBOR are shown in Exhibit 15.4. The first scenario (in the top panel of Exhibit 15.4) reflects rising U.S. interest rates, which cause LIBOR to increase. The second scenario (in the lower panel) reflects declining U.S. interest rates, which

EXHIBIT 15.4   Possible Effects of a Plain Vanilla Swap Agreement (Fixed Rate of 9 Percent in Exchange for Floating Rate of LIBOR + 1 Percent)

	Year				
Scenario I	1	2	3	4	5
LIBOR	7.0%	7.5%	8.5%	9.5%	10.0%
Floating rate received	8.0%	8.5%	9.5%	10.5%	11.0%
Fixed rate paid	9.0%	9.0%	9.0%	9.0%	9.0%
Swap differential	−1.0%	−0.5%	+0.5%	+1.5%	+2.0%
Net dollar amount received based on notional value of $100 million	−$1,000,000	−$500,000	+$500,000	+$1,500,000	+$2,000,000
	Year				
Scenario II	1	2	3	4	5
LIBOR	6.5%	6.0%	5.0%	4.5%	4.0%
Floating rate received	7.5%	7.0%	6.0%	5.5%	5.0%
Fixed rate paid	9.0%	9.0%	9.0%	9.0%	9.0%
Swap differential	−1.5%	−2.0%	−3.0%	−3.5%	−4.0%
Net dollar amount received based on notional value of $100 million	−$1,500,000	−$2,000,000	−$3,000,000	−$3,500,000	−$4,000,000

cause LIBOR to decrease. The swap differential derived for each scenario represents the floating interest rate received minus the fixed interest rate paid. The net dollar amount to be transferred as a result of the swap is determined by multiplying the swap differential by the notional principal.

Forward Swaps

A **forward swap** involves an exchange of interest payments that does not begin until a specified future point in time. It is useful for financial institutions or other firms that expect to be exposed to interest rate risk at a future point in time.

ILLUSTRATION Detroit Bank is currently insulated against interest rate risk. Three years from now, it plans to increase its proportion of fixed-rate loans (in response to consumer demand for these loans) and reduce its proportion of floating-rate loans. To prevent the adverse effects of rising interest rates after that point in time, Detroit Bank may want to engage in interest rate swaps. It can immediately arrange for a forward swap that will begin three years from now. The forward swap allows Detroit Bank to lock in the terms of the arrangement today, even though the swap period is delayed (see Exhibit 15.5).

Although Detroit Bank could have waited before arranging for a swap, it may prefer a forward swap to lock in the terms of the swap arrangement at the prevailing interest rates. If it expects interest rates to be higher three years from now than they are today, and waits until then to negotiate a swap arrangement, the fixed interest rate specified in the arrangement will likely be higher. A forward interest rate swap may allow Detroit Bank to negotiate a fixed rate today that is less than the expected fixed rate on a swap negotiated in the future. Because Detroit Bank will be exchanging fixed payments for floating-rate payments, it wants to minimize the fixed rate used for the swap agreement.

The fixed rate negotiated on a forward swap will not necessarily be the same as the fixed rate negotiated on a swap that begins immediately. The pricing conditions on any swap are based on expected interest rates over the swap lifetime.

Like any interest rate swap, forward swaps involve two parties. Our example of a forward swap involves a U.S. institution that expects interest rates to rise and wants to immediately lock in the fixed rate that it will pay when the swap period begins. The party that takes the opposite position in the forward swap will likely be a firm that will be ad-

EXHIBIT 15.5   Illustration of a Forward Swap

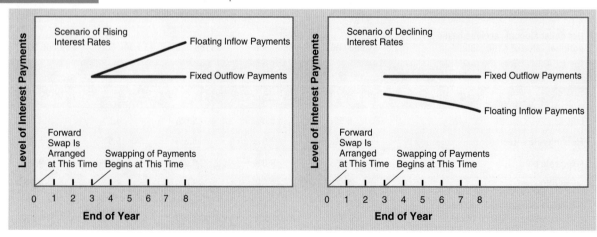

versely affected by declining interest rates and expects interest rates to decline. This firm would prefer to lock in the prevailing fixed rate, because that rate is expected to be higher than the applicable fixed rate when the swap period begins. Because this institution will be receiving the fixed interest payments, it wishes to maximize the fixed rate specified in the swap arrangement.

Callable Swaps

Another use of interest rate swaps is through **swap options** (or **swaptions**). A **callable swap** provides the party making the fixed payments with the right to terminate the swap prior to its maturity. It allows the fixed-rate payer to avoid exchanging future interest payments if it desires.

ILLUSTRATION Reconsider the U.S. institution that wanted to swap fixed interest payments for floating interest payments to reduce any adverse effects of rising interest rates. If interest rates decline, the interest rate swap arrangement offsets the potential favorable effects on this institution. A callable swap allows the institution to terminate the swap in the event that interest rates decline (see Exhibit 15.6).

The disadvantage of a callable swap is that the party given the right to terminate the swap pays a premium that is reflected in a higher fixed interest rate than the party would pay without the call feature. The party may also incur a termination fee in the event that it exercises its right to terminate the swap arrangement.

Putable Swaps

A **putable swap** provides the party making the floating-rate payments with a right to terminate the swap. To illustrate, reconsider the European institution that wanted to exchange floating-rate payments for fixed-rate payments to reduce the adverse effects of declining interest rates. If interest rates rise, the interest rate swap arrangement offsets the potential favorable effects on the financial institution. A putable swap allows the in-

EXHIBIT 15.6   Illustration of a Callable Swap

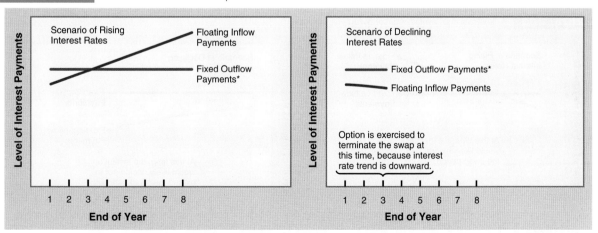

*Note that the fixed outflow payments in a callable swap are slightly higher than those of a plain vanilla swap because the payer of fixed outflow payments incurs the cost for the option to terminate the swap before it matures.

EXHIBIT 15.7   Illustration of a Putable Swap

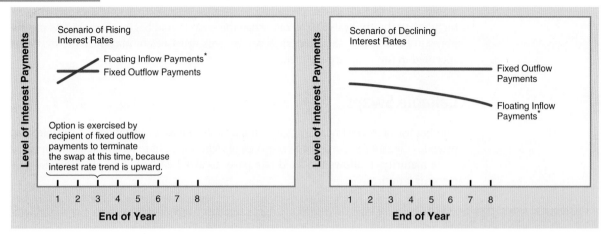

*Note that the floating inflow payments in a putable swap are slightly higher than those of a plain vanilla swap because the payer of the floating inflow payments incurs the cost for the option to terminate the swap before it matures.

stitution to terminate the swap in the event that interest rates rise (see Exhibit 15.7). As with callable swaps, the party given the right to terminate the swap pays a premium. For putable swaps, the premium is reflected in a higher floating rate than would be paid without the put feature. The party may also incur a termination fee in the event that it exercises its right to terminate the swap arrangement.

Extendable Swaps

An **extendable swap** contains a feature that allows the fixed-for-floating party to extend the swap period.

ILLUSTRATION   Cleveland Bank negotiates a fixed-for-floating swap for eight years. Assume that interest rates increase over this time period as expected. If Cleveland Bank believes interest rates will continue to rise, it may prefer to extend the swap period (see Exhibit 15.8). Although it could create a new swap, the terms would reflect the current economic con-

EXHIBIT 15.8   Illustration of an Extendable Swap

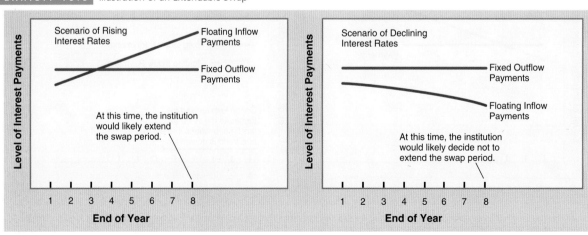

ditions. A new swap would typically involve an exchange of fixed payments at the prevailing higher interest rate for floating payments. Cleveland Bank would prefer to extend the previous swap agreement that calls for fixed payments at the lower interest rate that existed at the time the swap was created. It has additional flexibility because of the extendable feature.

The terms of an extendable swap reflect a price paid for the extendability feature. That is, the interest rates specified in a swap agreement allowing an extension are not as favorable for Cleveland Bank as they would have been without the feature. In addition, if Cleveland Bank does extend the swap period, it may have to pay an extra fee.

Zero-Coupon-for-Floating Swaps

Another special type of interest rate swap is the **zero-coupon-for-floating swap.** The fixed-rate payer makes a single payment at the maturity date of the swap agreement, while the floating-rate payer makes periodic payments throughout the swap period. For example, consider a financial institution that primarily attracts short-term deposits and currently has large holdings of zero-coupon bonds that it purchased several years ago. At the time it purchased the bonds, it expected interest rates to decline. Now it has become concerned that interest rates will rise over time, which will not only increase its cost of funds but also reduce the market value of the bonds. This financial institution can request a swap period that matches the maturity of its bond holdings. If interest rates rise over the period of concern, the institution will benefit from the swap arrangement, thereby offsetting any adverse effects on the institution's cost of funds. The other party in this type of transaction might be a firm that expects interest rates to decline (see Exhibit 15.9). Such a firm would be willing to provide floating-rate payments based on this expectation, because the payments will decline over time, while the single payment to be received at the end of the swap period is fixed.

Rate-Capped Swaps

A **rate-capped swap** involves the exchange of fixed-rate payments for floating-rate payments that are capped.

EXHIBIT 15.9   Illustration of a Zero-Coupon-for-Floating Swap

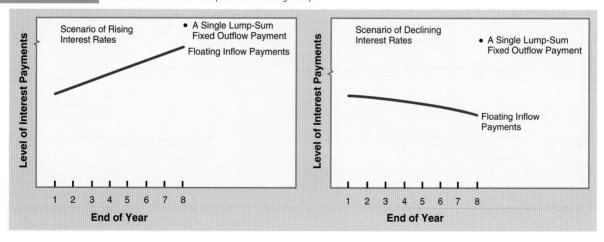

ILLUSTRATION

Reconsider the example in which the Bank of Orlando arranges to swap fixed payments for floating payments. The counterparty may want to limit its possible payments by setting a cap or ceiling on the interest rate it must pay. The floating-rate payer pays an up-front fee to the fixed-rate payer for this feature.

In this case, the size of the potential floating payments to be received by the Bank of Orlando would now be limited by the cap, which may reduce the effectiveness of the swap in hedging its interest rate risk. If interest rates rise above the cap, the floating payments received will not move in tandem with the interest the Bank of Orlando will pay depositors for funds (see Exhibit 15.10). However, the Bank of Orlando might believe that interest rates will not exceed a specified level and would therefore be willing to allow a cap. Moreover, the Bank of Orlando would receive an up-front fee from the counterparty for allowing this cap.

Equity Swaps

An **equity swap** involves the exchange of interest payments for payments linked to the degree of change in a stock index. For example, using an equity swap arrangement, a company could swap a fixed interest rate of 7 percent in exchange for the rate of appreciation on the S&P 500 index each year over a four-year period. If the stock index appreciates by 9 percent over the year, the differential is 2 percent (9 percent received minus 7 percent paid), which will be multiplied by the notional principal to determine the dollar amount received. If the stock index appreciates by less than 7 percent, the company will have to make a net payment. This type of swap arrangement may be appropriate for portfolio managers of insurance companies or pension funds that are managing stocks and bonds. The swap would enhance their investment performance in bullish stock market periods without requiring the managers to change their existing allocation of stocks and bonds.

Other Types of Swaps

A variety of other swaps are also available, and additional types will be created to accommodate firms' future needs.

EXHIBIT 15.10   Illustration of a Rate-Capped Swap

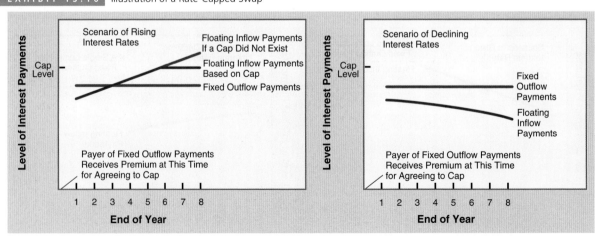

Use of Swaps to Accommodate Financing Preferences Some interest ra
are combined with other financial transactions such as the issuance of bonds. Corp
borrowers may be able to borrow at a more attractive interest rate when using floating
rate debt than when using fixed-rate debt. Yet, if they want to make fixed payments on
their debt, they can swap fixed-rate payments for floating-rate payments and use the
floating-rate payments received to cover their coupon payments. Alternatively, some
corporations may prefer to borrow at a floating rate but find it advantageous to borrow
at a fixed rate. These corporations can issue fixed-rate bonds and then swap floating-rate
payments in exchange for fixed-rate payments.

ILLUSTRATION

Quality Company is a highly rated firm that prefers to borrow at a variable rate.
Risky Company is a low-rated firm that prefers to borrow at a fixed rate. These com-
panies would pay the following rates when issuing either variable-rate or fixed-rate
Eurobonds:

	Fixed-Rate Bond	Variable-Rate Bond
Quality Company	9%	LIBOR+½%
Risky Company	10½%	LIBOR+1%

Based on the information given, Quality Company has a comparative advantage
when issuing either fixed-rate or variable-rate bonds, but its advantage is greater when
issuing fixed-rate bonds. Quality Company could issue fixed-rate bonds while Risky
Company issues variable-rate bonds. Quality could then provide variable-rate payments
to Risky in exchange for fixed-rate payments.

Assume that Quality negotiated with Risky to provide variable-rate payments at
LIBOR plus ½ percent in exchange for fixed-rate payments of 9½ percent. This interest
rate swap is shown in Exhibit 15.11. Quality Company benefits, because its fixed-rate
payments received on the swap exceed the payments owed to bondholders by ½ percent.
Its variable-rate payments to Risky Company are the same as what it would have paid if it
had issued variable-rate bonds. Risky is receiving LIBOR plus ½ percent on the swap,
which is ½ percent less than what it must pay on its variable-rate bonds. Yet, it is making
fixed payments of 9½ percent, which is 1 percent less than it would have paid if it had issued fixed-rate bonds. Overall, it saves ½ percent per year on financing costs.

EXHIBIT 15.11

Illustration of an Interest
Rate Swap to Reconfigure
Bond Payments

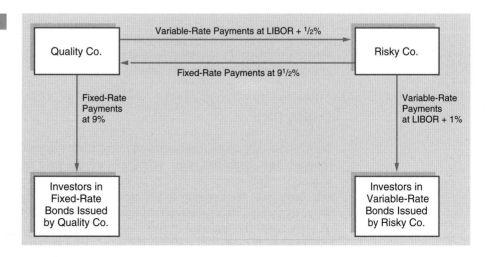

Two limitations of the swap just described are worth mentioning. First, the process of searching for a suitable swap candidate and negotiating the swap terms entails a cost in time and resources. Second, each swap participant faces the risk that the counterparty could default on payments. For this reason, financial intermediaries may match up participants and sometimes assume the credit (default) risk involved (for a fee).

Tax Advantage Swaps Some swaps have recently been used by firms for tax purposes.

Columbus Inc. has expiring tax loss carryforwards from previous years. To utilize the carryforwards before they expire, it may engage in a swap that calls for receipt of a large up-front payment with somewhat less favorable terms over time. Columbus may realize an immediate gain on the swap, with possible losses in future years. The tax loss carryforwards from previous years can be applied to offset any taxes on the immediate gain from the swap. Any future losses realized from future payments due to the swap agreement may be used to offset future gains from other operations.

Meanwhile, Ann Arbor Inc. expects future losses but will realize large gains from operations in this year. It can take a position opposite to that of Columbus. That is, Ann Arbor will arrange for a swap in which it makes an immediate large payment and receives somewhat favorable terms on future payments. This year the firm will incur a tax loss on the swap, which can be used to offset some of its gains from other operations to reduce its tax liability.

Interest Rate Swaps: Risks

Several types of risk must be considered when engaging in interest rate swaps. Three of the more common types of risks are basis risk, credit risk, and sovereign risk.

Basis Risk

The interest rate of the index used for an interest rate swap will not necessarily move perfectly in tandem with the floating-rate instruments of the parties involved in the swap. For example, the index used on a swap may rise by 0.7 percent over a particular period, while the cost of deposits to a U.S. financial institution rises by 1.0 percent over the same period. The net effect is that the higher interest rate payments received from the swap agreement do not fully offset the increase in the cost of funds. This so-called **basis risk** prevents the interest rate swap from completely eliminating the financial institution's exposure to interest rate risk.

Credit Risk

There is risk that a firm involved in an interest rate swap will not meet its payment obligations. This credit risk is not overwhelming, however, for the following reasons. As soon as the firm recognizes that it has not received the interest payments it is owed, it will discontinue its payments to the other party. The potential loss is a set of net payments that would have been received (based on the differential in swap rates) over time. In some cases, the financial intermediary that matched up the two parties incurs the credit risk by providing a guarantee (for a fee). If so, the parties engaged in the swap do

not need to be concerned with the credit risk, assuming that the financial intermediary will be able to cover any guarantees promised.

Concerns about a Swap Credit Crisis The willingness of large banks and securities firms to provide guarantees has increased the popularity of interest rate swaps, but it has also raised concerns that widespread adverse effects might occur if any of these intermediaries cannot meet their obligations. If a large bank that has taken numerous swap positions and guaranteed many other swap positions fails, there could be several defaults on swap payments. Such an event could cause cash flow problems for other swap participants and force them to default on some payment obligations they have on swaps or other financial agreements. Given the global integration of the swap network, defaults by a single large financial intermediary could be transmitted throughout the world.

Because of such concerns, various regulators have considered methods of reducing credit risk in the market. For example, bank regulators have considered forcing banks to maintain more capital if they provide numerous guarantees on swap payments. Other proposals include creating a regulatory agency that would oversee the swap market and minimize credit risk and requiring more complete disclosure of swap positions and guarantees created by financial intermediaries. Given the large growth in swaps, the concerns about credit risk in the market will continue to receive much attention.

Sovereign Risk

Sovereign risk reflects potential adverse effects resulting from a country's political conditions. Various political conditions could prevent the counterparty from meeting its obligation in the swap agreement. For example, the local government might take over the counterparty and then decide not to meet its payment obligations. Alternatively, the government might impose foreign exchange controls that prohibit the counterparty from making its payments.

Sovereign risk differs from credit risk because it is dependent on the financial status of the government rather than the counterparty itself. A counterparty could have very low credit risk but conceivably be perceived as having high sovereign risk because of its government. It does not have control over some restrictions that are imposed by its government.

Pricing Interest Rate Swaps

The setting of specific interest rates for an interest rate swap is referred to as pricing the swap. The pricing is influenced by several factors, including prevailing market interest rates, availability of counterparties, and credit and sovereign risk.

Prevailing Market Interest Rates

The fixed interest rate specified in a swap is influenced by supply and demand conditions for funds with the appropriate maturity. For example, a plain vanilla (fixed-for-floating) interest rate swap structured when interest rates are very high would have specified a much higher fixed interest rate than one structured in 2004 when interest rates were low. In general, the interest rates specified in a swap agreement reflect the prevailing interest rates at the time of the agreement.

Availability of Counterparties

Swap pricing is also determined by the availability of counterparties. When numerous counterparties are available for a particular desired swap, a party may be able to negotiate a more attractive deal. For example, consider a U.S. financial institution that wants a fixed-for-floating swap. If several European institutions are willing to serve as the counterparty, the U.S. institution may be able to negotiate a slightly lower fixed rate.

The availability of counterparties can change in response to economic conditions. For example, in a period when interest rates are expected to rise, many institutions will want a fixed-for-floating swap, but few institutions will be willing to serve as the counterparty. The fixed rate specified on interest rate swaps will be higher under these conditions than in a period when many financial institutions expect interest rates to decline.

Credit and Sovereign Risk

A party involved in an interest rate swap must assess the probability of default by the counterparty. For example, a firm that desires a fixed-for-floating swap will likely require a lower fixed rate applied to its outflow payments if the credit risk or sovereign risk of the counterparty is high. If a well-respected financial intermediary guarantees payments by the counterparty, however, the fixed rate will be higher.

Factors Affecting the Performance of Interest Rate Swaps

As Exhibit 15.12 shows, the performance of an interest rate swap is affected by several underlying forces; the most important are the forces that influence interest rate movements. The impact of the underlying forces on the performance of an interest rate swap depends on the party's swap position. For example, to the extent that strong economic growth can increase interest rates, it will be beneficial for a party that is swapping fixed-rate payments for floating-rate payments, but it will adversely affect a party that is swapping floating-rate payments for fixed-rate payments.

The diagram in Exhibit 15.12 can be adjusted to fit any currency. For an interest rate swap involving an interest rate benchmark denominated in a foreign currency, the economic conditions of that country are the primary forces that determine interest rate movements in that currency and therefore the performance of the interest rate swap.

Indicators Monitored by Participants in the Swaps Market

Since the performance of a particular interest rate swap position is normally influenced by future interest rate movements, participants in the interest rate swap market closely monitor indicators that may affect these movements. Among the more closely watched indicators are indicators of economic growth (employment, gross domestic product), indicators of inflation (consumer price index, producer price index), and indicators of government borrowing (budget deficit, expected volume of funds borrowed at upcoming Treasury bond auctions).

Interest rate swaps use a variety of proxies (such as LIBOR or a T-bill rate) for the benchmark rate from which a floating-rate payment is determined in each period. These benchmarks tend to move together, however, because they are similarly affected by the economic factors just described.

Framework for Explaining
Net Payments Resulting
from an Interest Rate Swap

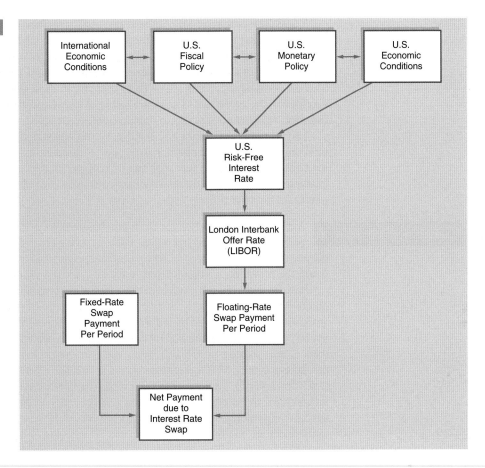

Interest Rate Caps, Floors, and Collars

In addition to the more traditional forms of interest rate swaps, three other interest rate derivative instruments are commonly used:

- Interest rate caps
- Interest rate floors
- Interest rate collars

These instruments are normally classified separately from interest rate swaps, but they do result in interest payments between participants. Each of these instruments can be used by financial institutions to capitalize on expected interest rate movements or to hedge their interest rate risk.

Interest Rate Caps

An **interest rate cap** offers payments in periods when a specified interest rate index exceeds a specified ceiling (cap) interest rate. The payments are based on the amount by which the interest rate exceeds the ceiling, multiplied by the notional principal specified in the agreement. A fee is paid up-front to purchase an interest rate cap, and the lifetime of a cap commonly ranges between three and eight years.

The typical purchaser of an interest rate cap is a financial institution that is adversely affected by rising interest rates. If interest rates rise, the payments received from the interest rate cap agreement will help offset any adverse effects.

The seller of an interest rate cap receives the fee paid up-front and is obligated to provide periodic payments when the prevailing interest rates exceed the ceiling rate specified in the agreement. The typical seller of an interest rate cap is a financial institution that expects interest rates to remain stable or decline.

Large commercial banks and securities firms serve as dealers for interest rate caps, in which they act as the counterparty on the transaction. They also serve as brokers, matching up participants that wish to purchase or sell interest rate caps. They may even guarantee (for a fee) the interest payments that are to be paid to the purchaser of the interest rate cap over time.

ILLUSTRATION   Assume that Buffalo Savings Bank purchases a five-year cap for a fee of 4 percent of notional principal valued at $60 million (so the fee is $2.4 million), with an interest rate ceiling of 10 percent. The agreement specifies LIBOR as the index used to represent the prevailing market interest rate.

Assume that LIBOR moved over the next five years as shown in Exhibit 15.13. Based on the movements in LIBOR, Buffalo Savings Bank received payments in three of the five years. The amount received by Buffalo in any year is based on the percentage points above the 10 percent ceiling multiplied by the notional principal. For example, in Year 1 the payment is zero because LIBOR was below the ceiling rate. In Year 2, however, LIBOR exceeded the ceiling by 1 percentage point, so Buffalo received a payment of $600,000 (1%×$60 million). To the extent that Buffalo's performance is adversely affected by high interest rates, the interest rate cap creates a partial hedge by providing payments to Buffalo that are proportionately related to the interest rate level. The seller of the interest rate cap in this example had the opposite payments of those shown for Buffalo in Exhibit 15.13.

Interest rate caps can be devised to meet various risk-return profiles. For example, Buffalo Savings Bank could have purchased an interest rate cap with a ceiling rate of 9 percent to generate payments whenever interest rates exceeded that ceiling. The bank would have had to pay a higher up-front fee for this interest rate cap, however.

Interest Rate Floors

An **interest rate floor** offers payments in periods when a specified interest rate index falls below a specified floor rate. The payments are based on the amount by which the interest rate falls below the floor rate, multiplied by the notional principal specified in the

EXHIBIT 15.13   Illustration of an Interest Rate Cap

		End of Year:				
	0	1	2	3	4	5
LIBOR		6%	11%	13%	12%	7%
Interest rate ceiling		10%	10%	10%	10%	10%
LIBOR's percent above the ceiling		0%	1%	3%	2%	0%
Payments received (based on $60 million of notional principal)		$0	$600,000	$1,800,000	$1,200,000	$0
Fee paid	$2,400,000					

agreement. A fee is paid up-front to purchase an interest rate floor, and the lifetime of the floor commonly ranges between three and eight years. The interest rate floor can be used to hedge against lower interest rates in the same manner that the interest rate cap hedges against higher interest rates. Any financial institution that purchases an interest rate floor will receive payments if interest rates decline below the floor, which will help offset any adverse interest rate effects.

The seller of an interest rate floor receives the fee paid up-front and is obligated to provide periodic payments when the interest rate on a specified money market instrument falls below the floor rate specified in the agreement. The typical seller of an interest rate floor is a financial institution that expects interest rates to remain stable or rise. Large commercial banks or securities firms serve as dealers and/or brokers of interest rate floors, just as they do for interest rate swaps or caps.

ILLUSTRATION Assume that Toland Finance Company purchases a five-year interest rate floor for a fee of 4 percent of notional principal valued at $60 million (so the fee is $2.4 million), with an interest rate floor of 8 percent. The agreement specifies LIBOR as the index used to represent the prevailing interest rate.

Assume that LIBOR moved over the next five years as shown in Exhibit 15.14. Based on the movements in LIBOR, Toland received payments in two of the five years. The dollar amount received by Toland in any year is based on the percentage points below the 8 percent floor multiplied by the notional principal. For example, in Year 1, LIBOR was 2 percentage points below the interest rate floor, so Toland received a payment of $1,200,000 (2% × $60 million). The seller of the interest rate floor in this example had the opposite payments of those shown for Toland in Exhibit 15.14.

Interest Rate Collars

An **interest rate collar** involves the purchase of an interest rate cap and the simultaneous sale of an interest rate floor. In its simplest form, the fee received up-front from selling the interest rate floor to one party can be used to pay the fee for purchasing the interest rate cap from another party. Any financial institution that desires to hedge against the possibility of rising interest rates can purchase an interest rate collar. The hedge results from the interest rate cap, which will generate payments to the institution if interest rates rise above the interest rate ceiling.

Because the collar also involves the sale of an interest rate floor, the financial institution is obligated to make payments if interest rates decline below the floor. Yet, if interest rates rise as expected, the rates will remain above the floor, so the financial institution will not have to make payments.

EXHIBIT 15.14 Illustration of an Interest Rate Floor

		End of Year:				
	0	1	2	3	4	5
LIBOR		6%	11%	13%	12%	7%
Interest rate floor		8%	8%	8%	8%	8%
LIBOR's percent below the floor		2%	0%	0%	0%	1%
Payments received (based on $60 million of notional principal)		$1,200,000	$0	$0	$0	$600,000
Fee paid	$2,400,000					

EXHIBIT 15.15 Illustration of an Interest Rate Collar (Combined Purchase of Interest Rate Cap and Sale of Interest Rate Floor)

		End of Year:				
	0	1	2	3	4	5
Purchase of interest rate cap:						
LIBOR		6%	11%	13%	12%	7%
Interest rate ceiling		10%	10%	10%	10%	10%
LIBOR's percent above the ceiling		0%	1%	3%	2%	0%
Payments received		$0	$600,000	$1,800,000	$1,200,000	$0
Fee paid	$2,400,000					
Sale of interest rate floor:						
Interest rate floor		8%	8%	8%	8%	8%
LIBOR's percent below the floor		2%	0%	0%	0%	1%
Payments made		$1,200,000	$0	$0	$0	$600,000
Fee received	$2,400,000					
Fee received minus fee paid	$0					
Payments received minus payments made		−$1,200,000	+$600,000	+$1,800,000	+$1,200,000	−$600,000

ILLUSTRATION Assume that Pittsburgh Bank's performance is inversely related to interest rates. It anticipates that interest rates will rise over the next several years and decides to hedge its interest rate risk by purchasing a five-year interest rate collar, with LIBOR as the index used to represent the prevailing interest rate. The interest rate cap specifies a fee of 4 percent of notional principal valued at $60 million (so the fee is $2.4 million), with an interest rate ceiling of 10 percent. The interest rate floor specifies a fee of 4 percent of notional principal valued at $60 million and an interest rate floor of 8 percent.

Assume that LIBOR moved over the next five years as shown in Exhibit 15.15. Based on the movements in LIBOR, the payments received from purchasing the interest rate cap and the payments made from selling the interest rate floor are derived separately over each of the five years. Because the fee received from selling the interest rate floor was equal to the fee paid for the interest rate cap, the initial fees offset. The net payments received by Pittsburgh Bank as a result of purchasing the collar are equal to the payments received from the interest rate cap minus the payments made as a result of the interest rate floor. In the years when interest rates were relatively high, the net payments received by Pittsburgh Bank were positive.

As this example illustrates, when interest rates are high, the collar can generate payments, which may offset the adverse effects of the high interest rates on the bank's normal operations. Although the net payments were negative in those years when interest rates were low, the performance of the bank's normal operations should have been strong. Like many other hedging strategies, the interest rate collar reduces the sensitivity of the financial institution's performance to interest rate movements.

Swap Market Globalization

GLBALASPECTS The market for interest rate swaps is not restricted to the United States. As mentioned earlier, European financial institutions commonly have the opposite exposure to interest rate risk and therefore take swap positions counter to the positions desired by U.S. financial institutions. Manufacturing corporations from various countries that are exposed to interest rate risk also engage in interest rate swaps.

Interest rate swaps are executed in various countries and are denominated in many different currencies. Dollar-denominated interest rate swaps account for about half the value of all interest rate swaps outstanding.

Given that swap participants are from various countries, the banks and securities firms that serve as intermediaries have a globalized network of subsidiaries. In this way, they can link participants from various countries. One obvious barrier to the global swap market is the lack of information about participants based in other countries. Thus, concerns about credit risk may discourage some participants from engaging in swaps. This barrier is reduced when international banks and securities firms that serve as intermediaries are willing to back the payments that are supposed to occur under the provisions of the swap agreement.

Currency Swaps

A **currency swap** is an arrangement whereby currencies are exchanged at specified exchange rates and at specified intervals. It is essentially a combination of currency futures contracts, although most futures contracts are not available for periods in the distant future. Currency swaps are commonly used by firms to hedge their exposure to exchange rate fluctuations.

ILLUSTRATION Springfield Company is a U.S. firm that expects to receive 2 million British pounds (£) in each of the next four years. It may want to lock in the exchange rate at which it can sell British pounds over the next four years. A currency swap will specify the exchange rate at which the £2 million can be exchanged in each year. Assume the exchange rate specified by a swap is $1.70 (the spot exchange rate at the time of the swap arrangement), so Springfield will receive $3.4 million (£2 million×$1.70 per £) in each of the four years. Conversely, if the firm does not engage in a currency swap, the dollar amount received will depend on the spot exchange rate at the time the pounds are converted to dollars.

The impact of the currency swap is illustrated in Exhibit 15.16. This exhibit also shows the payments that would have been received under two alternative scenarios if the

EXHIBIT 15.16

Impact of Currency Swaps

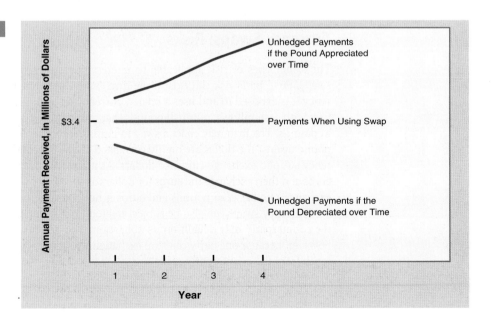

currency swap had not been arranged. Note that the payments received from the swap would have been less favorable than the unhedged strategy if the pound appreciated against the dollar over that period. However, the payments received from the swap would have been more favorable than the unhedged strategy if the pound depreciated against the dollar over that period. The currency swap arrangement reduces the firm's exposure to changes in the pound's value.

The large commercial banks that serve as financial intermediaries sometimes take positions. That is, they may agree to swap currencies with a firm rather than simply search for a suitable swap candidate.

Like interest rate swaps, currency swaps are available in several variations. Some currency swap arrangements allow one of the parties an option to terminate the contract. That party incurs a premium for the option, which is either charged up-front or reflected in the exchange rates specified in the swap arrangement.

Using Currency Swaps to Hedge Bond Payments Although currency swaps are commonly used to hedge payments on international trade, they may also be used in conjunction with bond issues to hedge foreign cash flows.

ILLUSTRATION Philly Company, a U.S. firm, wants to issue a bond denominated in euros (the currency now used in several European countries) because it could make payments with euro inflows to be generated from ongoing operations. Philly, however, is not well known to investors who would consider purchasing euro-denominated bonds. Another firm, Windy Company, wants to issue dollar-denominated bonds because its inflow payments are mostly in dollars, but Windy is not well known to the investors who would purchase these bonds. If Philly is known in the dollar-denominated market and Windy is known in the euro-denominated market, the following transactions are appropriate. Philly can issue dollar-denominated bonds, while Windy issues euro-denominated bonds. Philly can exchange euros for dollars to make its bond payments. Windy will receive euros in exchange for dollars to make its bond payments. This currency swap is illustrated in Exhibit 15.17.

Currency Swaps: Risks

The same types of risk applicable to interest rate swaps may also apply to currency swaps. First, basis risk can exist if the firm cannot obtain a currency swap on the currency it is exposed to and uses a related currency instead. For example, consider a U.S. firm with cash inflows in British pounds that cannot find a counterparty to enact a swap in pounds. The firm may enact a swap in euros because movements in the euro and the pound against the dollar are highly correlated. To be specific, the firm will enact a currency swap to exchange euros for dollars. As it receives pounds, it will convert them to euros and then exchange the euros for dollars as specified by the swap arrangement. The exchange rate between pounds and euros is not constant, however, so basis risk exists.

Currency swaps can also be subject to credit risk, which reflects the possibility that the counterparty may default on its obligation. The potential loss is somewhat limited, however, because one party can stop exchanging its currency if it no longer receives currency from the counterparty.

A third type of risk is sovereign risk, which reflects the possibility that a country may restrict the convertibility of a particular currency. In this case, a party involved in a swap

EXHIBIT 15.17

Illustration of a Currency
Swap

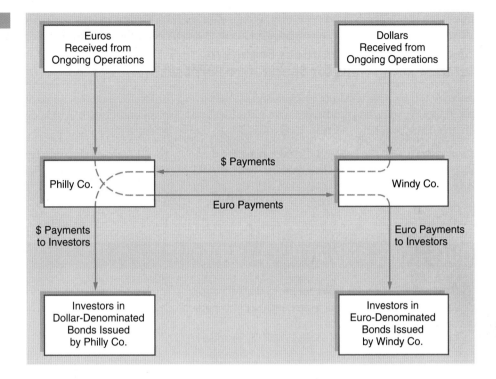

EXHIBIT 15.17

Illustration of a Currency
Swap

arrangement may not be able to fulfill its obligation because its government prohibits the
local currency from being converted to another currency. This scenario is less likely in
countries that encourage free trade of goods and securities across borders.

SUMMARY

■ Various types of interest rate swaps are used to reduce interest rate risk. Some of the more popular
types of interest rate swaps are plain vanilla swaps,
forward swaps, callable swaps, putable swaps, extendable swaps, rate-capped swaps, and equity
swaps. Each type of swap accommodates a particular need of financial institutions or other firms that
are exposed to interest rate risk.

■ When engaging in interest rate swaps, the participants can be exposed to basis risk, credit risk, and
sovereign risk. Basis risk prevents the interest rate
swap from completely eliminating the swap user's
exposure to interest rate risk. Credit risk reflects the
possibility that the counterparty on a swap agreement may not meet its payment obligations. Sovereign risk reflects the possibility that political conditions could prevent the counterparty in a swap
agreement from meeting its payment obligations.

■ In addition to the traditional forms of interest rate
swaps, three other interest rate derivative instruments are commonly used to hedge interest rate risk:
interest rate caps, interest rate floors, and interest rate
collars. Interest rate caps offer payments when a
specified interest rate index exceeds the interest rate
ceiling (cap) and therefore can hedge against rising
interest rates. Interest rate floors offer payments when
a specified interest rate index falls below a specified
interest rate floor; they can be used to hedge against
declining interest rates. An interest rate collar involves the purchase of an interest rate cap and the simultaneous sale of an interest rate floor and is used to
hedge against rising interest rates.

■ The interest rate swap market has become globalized in the sense that financial institutions from various countries participate. Interest rate swaps are
available in a variety of currencies.

POINT COUNTER-POINT

Should Financial Institutions Engage in Interest Rate Swaps for Speculative Purposes?

Point Yes. They have expertise in forecasting future interest rate movements and can generate gains for their shareholders by taking speculative positions.

Counter-Point No. They should use their main business to generate gains for their shareholders. They should serve as intermediaries for swap transactions only in order to generate transaction fees or should take a position only if it is to hedge their exposure to interest rate risk.

Who Is Correct? Use your favorite search engine to learn more about this issue. Offer your own opinion on this issue.

QUESTIONS AND APPLICATIONS

1. **Interpreting Financial News** Interpret the following comments made by Wall Street analysts and portfolio managers:
   a. "The swaps market is another Wall Street–developed house of cards."
   b. "As a dealer in interest rate swaps, our bank takes various steps to limit our exposure."
   c. "The regulation of commercial banks, securities firms, and other financial institutions that participate in the swaps market could create a regulatory war."

2. **Equity Swap** Explain how an equity swap could allow Marathon Insurance Company to capitalize on expectations of a strong stock market performance over the next year without altering its existing portfolio mix of stocks and bonds.

3. **Basis Risk** Comiskey Savings provides fixed-rate mortgages of various maturities, depending on what customers want. It obtains most of its funds from issuing certificates of deposit with maturities ranging from one month to five years. Comiskey has decided to engage in a fixed-for-floating swap to hedge its interest rate risk. Is Comiskey exposed to basis risk?

4. **Internet Exercise** Go to http://www.economagic.com/fedbog.htm.
   a. Review the recent annualized rate for a short-term security such as the 1-year Treasury rate versus a long-term security such as the 10-year Treasury rate. Based on this information, do you think that the market expects interest rates to rise over time? Explain.

   b. Assume that you could borrow at the short-term Treasury rate, and needed long-term funds. Based on the existing interest rates, would you consider engaging in a swap of a floating rate in exchange for a fixed rate? Explain.

5. **Sovereign Risk** Give an example of how sovereign risk is related to currency swaps.

6. **Hedging with Interest Rate Swaps** Bowling Green Savings & Loan uses short-term deposits to fund fixed-rate mortgages. Explain how Bowling Green can use interest rate swaps to hedge its interest rate risk.

7. **Hedging with Swaps** Chelsea Finance Company receives floating inflow payments from its provision of floating-rate loans. Its outflow payments are fixed because of its recent issuance of long-term bonds. Chelsea is somewhat concerned that interest rates will decline in the future. Yet, it does not want to hedge its interest rate risk because it believes interest rates may increase. Recommend a solution to Chelsea's dilemma.

8. **Managing in Financial Markets: Assessing the Effects of an Interest Rate Collar** As a manager of a commercial bank, you just purchased a three-year interest rate collar, with LIBOR as the interest rate index. The interest rate cap specifies a fee of 2 percent of notional principal valued at $100 million and an interest rate ceiling of 9 percent. The interest rate floor specifies a fee of 3 percent of notional principal valued at $100 million and an interest rate floor of 7 percent. Assume that LIBOR is expected to be 6 percent, 10 percent, and 11 percent, respectively, at the end of each of the next three years.

a. Determine the net fees paid, and also determine the expected *net* payments to be received as a result of purchasing the interest rate collar.

b. Assuming you are very confident that interest rates will rise, should you consider purchasing a callable swap instead of the collar? Explain.

c. Explain the conditions in which your purchase of an interest rate collar could backfire.

9. **Use of Currency Swaps** Explain why some companies that issue bonds engage in currency swaps. Why do they not simply issue bonds in the currency that they would prefer to use for making payments?

10. **Swap Options** Explain the advantage of a swap option to a financial institution that wants to swap fixed payments for floating payments.

11. **Currency Swaps** Markus Company purchases supplies from France once a year. Would Markus be favorably affected if it establishes a currency swap arrangement and the dollar strengthens? What if it establishes a currency swap arrangement and the dollar generally weakens?

12. **Decision to Hedge with Interest Rate Swaps** Explain the types of cash flow characteristics that would cause a firm to hedge interest rate risk by swapping floating-rate payments for fixed payments. Why would some firms avoid the use of interest rate swaps, even when they are highly exposed to interest rate risk?

13. **Rate-Capped Swaps** Bull and Finch Company wants a fixed-for-floating swap. It expects interest rates to rise far above the fixed rate that it would have to pay and to remain very high until the swap maturity date. Should it consider negotiating for a rate-capped swap with the cap set at two percentage points above the fixed rate? Explain.

14. **Fixed-for-Floating Swaps** North Pier Company entered into a two-year swap agreement, which would provide fixed-rate payments for floating-rate payments. Over the next two years, interest rates declined. Based on these conditions, did North Pier Company benefit from the swap?

15. **Role of Securities Firms in Swap Market** Describe the possible roles of securities firms in the swap market.

16. **Callable Swaps** Back Bay Insurance Company negotiated a callable swap involving fixed payments in exchange for floating payments. Assume that interest rates decline consistently up until the swap maturity date. Do you think Back Bay might terminate the swap prior to maturity? Explain.

17. **Swap Network** Explain how the failure of a large commercial bank could cause a worldwide swap credit crisis.

18. **Fixed-for-Floating Swaps** Shea Savings negotiates a fixed-for-floating swap with a reputable firm in South America that has an exceptional credit rating. Shea is very confident that there will not be a default on inflow payments because of the very low credit risk of the South American firm. Do you agree? Explain.

19. **Forward Swaps** Rider Company negotiates a forward swap to begin two years from now, in which it will swap fixed payments for floating-rate payments. What will be the effect on Rider if interest rates rise substantially over the next two years? That is, would Rider have been better off by using a forward swap than by simply waiting two years before negotiating the swap? Explain.

20. **Use of Interest Rate Swaps** Explain why some companies that issue bonds engage in interest rate swaps in financial markets. Why do they not simply issue bonds that require the type of payments (fixed or variable) that they prefer to make?

21. **Basis Risk** Explain basis risk as it relates to a currency swap.

PROBLEMS

1. **Interest Rate Floors** Iowa City Bank purchases a three-year interest rate floor for a fee of 2 percent of notional principal valued at $80 million, with an interest rate floor of 6 percent and LIBOR representing the interest rate index. The bank expects LIBOR to be 6 percent, 5 percent, and 4 percent, respectively, at the end of each of the next three years.

a. Determine the initial fee paid, and also determine the expected payments to be received by Iowa City if LIBOR moves as forecasted.

b. Determine the dollar amounts to be received (or paid) by the seller of the interest rate floor based on the forecasts of LIBOR assumed above.

2. **Vanilla Swaps** Cleveland Insurance Company has just negotiated a three-year plain vanilla swap in which it will exchange fixed payments of 8 percent for floating payments of LIBOR plus 1 percent. The notional principal is $50 million. LIBOR is expected to be 7 percent, 9 percent, and 10 percent, respectively, at the end of each of the next three years.

   a. Determine the net dollar amount to be received (or paid) by Cleveland each year.

   b. Determine the dollar amount to be received (or paid) by the counterparty on this interest rate swap each year based on the forecasts of LIBOR assumed above.

3. **Interest Rate Caps** Northbrook Bank purchases a four-year cap for a fee of 3 percent of notional principal valued at $100 million, with an interest rate ceiling of 9 percent and LIBOR as the index representing the market interest rate. Assume that LIBOR is expected to be 8 percent, 10 percent, 12 percent, and 13 percent, respectively, at the end of each of the next four years.

   a. Determine the initial fee paid, and also determine the expected payments to be received by Northbrook if LIBOR moves as forecasted.

   b. Determine the dollar amount to be received (or paid) by the seller of the interest rate cap based on the forecasts of LIBOR assumed above.

FLOW OF FUNDS EXERCISE

Hedging with Interest Rate Derivatives

Recall that if the economy continues to be strong, Carson Company may need to increase its production capacity by about 50 percent over the next few years to satisfy demand. It would need financing to expand and accommodate the increase in production. Recall that the yield curve is currently upward sloping. Also recall that Carson is concerned about a possible slowing of the economy because of potential Fed actions to reduce inflation. Carson currently relies mostly on commercial loans with floating interest rates for its debt financing. It has contacted Blazo Bank about the use of interest rate derivatives to hedge the risk.

a. How could Carson use interest rate swaps to reduce the exposure of its cost of debt to interest rate movements?

b. What is a possible disadvantage of Carson using the interest rate swap hedge as opposed to no hedge?

c. How could Carson use an interest rate cap to reduce the exposure of its cost of debt to interest rate movements?

d. What is a possible disadvantage of Carson using the interest cap hedge as opposed to no hedge?

e. Explain the tradeoff from using an interest rate swap versus an interest rate cap.

WSJ EXERCISE

Impact of Interest Rates on a Swap Arrangement

Use a recent issue of *The Wall Street Journal* to determine how short-term interest rates have changed over the last year. The three-month Treasury bill rate at the present time and one year ago appears in the part called "Interest" in the "Markets Diary" section. Explain whether the interest rate movement would have had a favorable impact on a firm that initiated a fixed-for-floating swap agreement one year ago.

CHAPTER 16

Foreign Exchange Derivative Markets

n recent years, various derivative instruments have been created to manage or capitalize on exchange rate movements. These so-called **foreign exchange derivatives** (or "forex" derivatives) include forward contracts, currency futures contracts, currency swaps, and currency options. Foreign exchange derivatives account for about half of the daily foreign exchange transaction volume.

The potential benefits from using foreign exchange derivatives are dependent on the expected exchange rate movements. Thus, it is necessary to understand why exchange rates change over time before exploring the use of foreign exchange derivatives.

The specific objectives of this chapter are to:

- explain how various factors affect exchange rates,
- explain how to forecast exchange rates,
- explain how to speculate,
- describe foreign exchange rate derivatives, and
- explain international arbitrage.

Foreign Exchange Markets

As international trade and investing have increased over time, so has the need to exchange currencies. Foreign exchange markets consist of a global telecommunications network among the large commercial banks that serve as financial intermediaries for such exchange. These banks are located in New York, Tokyo, Hong Kong, Singapore, Frankfurt, Zurich, and London. Foreign exchange transactions at these banks have been increasing over time.

At any point in time, the price at which banks will buy a currency (bid price) is slightly lower than the price at which they will sell it (ask price). Like markets for other commodities and securities, the market for foreign currencies is more efficient because of financial intermediaries (commercial banks). Otherwise, individual buyers and sellers of currency would be unable to identify counterparties to accommodate their needs.

Institutional Use of Foreign Exchange Markets

Exhibit 16.1 summarizes the ways financial institutions utilize the foreign exchange market and foreign exchange derivatives. The degree of international investment by financial institutions is influenced by potential return, risk, and government regulations.

EXHIBIT 16.1 Institutional Use of Foreign Exchange Markets

Type of Financial Institution	Uses of Foreign Exchange Markets
Commercial banks	• Serve as financial intermediaries in the foreign exchange market by buying or selling currencies to accommodate customers. • Speculate on foreign currency movements by taking long positions in some currencies and short positions in others. • Provide forward contracts to customers. • Some commercial banks offer currency options to customers; unlike the standardized currency options traded on an exchange, these options can be tailored to a customer's specific needs.
International mutual funds	• Use foreign exchange markets to exchange currencies when reconstructing their portfolios. • Use foreign exchange derivatives to hedge a portion of their exposure.
Brokerage firms and investment banking firms	• Some brokerage firms and investment banking firms engage in foreign security transactions for their customers or for their own accounts.
Insurance companies	• Use foreign exchange markets when exchanging currencies for their international operations. • Use foreign exchange markets when purchasing foreign securities for their investment portfolios or when selling foreign securities. • Use foreign exchange derivatives to hedge a portion of their exposure.
Pension funds	• Require foreign exchange of currencies when investing in foreign securities for their stock or bond portfolios. • Use foreign exchange derivatives to hedge a portion of their exposure.

Commercial banks use international lending as their primary form of international investing. Mutual funds, pension funds, and insurance companies purchase foreign securities. In recent years, technology has reduced information costs and other transaction costs associated with purchasing foreign securities, prompting an increase in institutional purchases of foreign securities. Consequently, financial institutions are increasing their use of the foreign exchange markets to exchange currencies. They are also increasing their use of foreign exchange derivatives to hedge their investments in foreign securities.

Exchange Rate Quotations

http://www.bloomberg.com
Spot rates of currencies and cross-exchange rates among currencies.

The "Using *The Wall Street Journal*" box on page 463 shows the approximate foreign exchange rates of the major currencies on August 10, 2004. These exchange rates are listed in any major newspaper on a daily basis. Directly across from the currency name (in the second column) is the **spot exchange rate** for immediate delivery. The exchange rates in this column define the value of a foreign currency in terms of U.S. dollars. The exchange rates in the fourth column are expressed as the number of units per dollar. According to the foreign exchange table, the British (see U.K.) pound's value is $1.8397, which means that .5436 pound equals $1. Each exchange rate in the fourth column is simply the reciprocal of what is shown in the second column.

For widely used currencies, **forward rates** are available and are listed just below the respective spot rates. The forward rates indicate the rate at which a currency can be exchanged in the future.

Cross-Exchange Rates Most exchange rate quotation tables express currencies relative to the dollar. In some instances, however, the exchange rate between two non-dollar currencies is needed.

USING THE WALL STREET JOURNAL

Foreign Exchange Rate Quotations

Foreign exchange rate quotations are provided in *The Wall Street Journal* as shown here. The name of each currency appears in the first column, the value of the currency (in dollars) on the previous day is shown in the second column, and the value of the currency (in dollars) two days ago is shown in the third column. The fourth and fifth columns also disclose the quotations for the previous day and two days ago, but express the value of the currency as number of units per dollar. Thus, the fourth column is the reciprocal of the second column, and the fifth column is the reciprocal of the third column. For four commonly traded currencies, the 30-day, 90-day, and 180-day forward rates are disclosed.

Exchange Rates

August 9, 2004

The foreign exchange mid-range rates below apply to trading among banks in amounts of $1 million and more, as quoted at 4 p.m. Eastern time by Reuters and other sources. Retail transactions provide fewer units of foreign currency per dollar.

Country	U.S. $ EQUIVALENT Mon	U.S. $ EQUIVALENT Fri	CURRENCY PER U.S. $ Mon	CURRENCY PER U.S. $ Fri
Argentina (Peso)-y	.3311	.3265	3.0202	3.0628
Australia (Dollar)	.7157	.7140	1.3972	1.4006
Bahrain (Dinar)	2.6525	2.6525	.3770	.3770
Brazil (Real)	.3288	.3298	3.0414	3.0321
Canada (Dollar)	.7589	.7619	1.3177	1.3125
1-month forward	.7586	.7616	1.3182	1.3130
3-months forward	.7581	.7610	1.3191	1.3141
6-months forward	.7574	.7604	1.3203	1.3151
Chile (Peso)	.001567	.001564	638.16	639.39
China (Renminbi)	.1208	.1208	8.2781	8.2781
Colombia (Peso)	.0003852	.0003848	2596.05	2598.75
Czech. Rep. (Koruna)				
Commercial rate	.03901	.03892	25.635	25.694
Denmark (Krone)	.1650	.1653	6.0606	6.0496
Ecuador (US Dollar)	1.0000	1.0000	1.0000	1.0000
Egypt (Pound)-y	.1609	.1617	6.2150	6.1851
Hong Kong (Dollar)	.1282	.1283	7.8003	7.7942
Hungary (Forint)	.004981	.004967	200.76	201.33
India (Rupee)	.02157	.02161	46.361	46.275
Indonesia (Rupiah)	.0001090	.0001090	9174	9174
Israel (Shekel)	.2209	.2207	4.5269	4.5310

Country	U.S. $ EQUIVALENT Mon	U.S. $ EQUIVALENT Fri	CURRENCY PER U.S. $ Mon	CURRENCY PER U.S. $ Fri
Japan (Yen)	.009041	.009058	110.61	110.40
1-month forward	.009054	.009071	110.45	110.24
3-months forward	.009080	.009097	110.13	109.93
6-months forward	.009129	.009143	109.54	109.37
Jordan (Dinar)	1.4104	1.4104	.7090	.7090
Kuwait (Dinar)	3.3921	3.3921	.2948	.2948
Lebanon (Pound)	.0006603	.0006605	1514.46	1514.00
Malaysia (Ringgit)-b	.2632	.2632	3.7994	3.7994
Malta (Lira)	2.8798	2.8831	.3472	.3468
Mexico (Peso)				
Floating rate	.0877	.0877	11.4064	11.3999
New Zealand (Dollar)	.6528	.6526	1.5319	1.5323
Norway (Krone)	.1479	.1472	6.7613	6.7935
Pakistan (Rupee)	.01698	.01705	58.893	58.651
Peru (new Sol)	.2932	.2934	3.4106	3.4083
Philippines (Peso)	.01794	.01795	55.741	55.710
Poland (Zloty)	.2805	.2799	3.5651	3.5727
Russia (Ruble)-a	.03420	.03425	29.240	29.197
Saudi Arabia (Riyal)	.2667	.2667	3.7495	3.7495
Singapore (Dollar)	.5827	.5821	1.7161	1.7179
Slovak Rep. (Koruna)	.03074	.03075	32.531	32.520
South Africa (Rand)	.1641	.1635	6.0938	6.1162
South Korea (Won)	.0008647	.0008639	1156.47	1157.54
Sweden (Krona)	.1336	.1337	7.4850	7.4794
Switzerland (Franc)	.7976	.7999	1.2538	1.2502
1-month forward	.7985	.8007	1.2523	1.2489
3-months forward	.8000	.8022	1.2500	1.2466
6-months forward	.8027	.8048	1.2458	1.2425
Taiwan (Dollar)	.02939	.02934	34.025	34.083
Thailand (Baht)	.02415	.02418	41.408	41.357
Turkey (Lira)	.00000069	.00000069	1449275	1449275
U.K. (Pound)	1.8397	1.8410	.5436	.5432
1-month forward	1.8343	1.8359	.5452	.5447
3-months forward	1.8247	1.8261	.5480	.5476
6-months forward	1.8111	1.8123	.5522	.5518
United Arab (Dirham)	.2723	.2722	3.6724	3.6738
Uruguay (Peso)				
Financial	.03420	.03420	29.240	29.240
Venezuela (Bolivar)	.000521	.000521	1919.39	1919.39
SDR	1.4701	1.4578	.6802	.6860
Euro	1.2271	1.2289	.8149	.8137

Special Drawing Rights (SDR) are based on exchange rates for the U.S., British, and Japanese currencies. Source: International Monetary Fund.

a-Russian Central Bank rate. b-Government rate. y-Floating rate.

ILLUSTRATION

If a Canadian firm needs Mexican pesos to buy Mexican goods, it is concerned about the value of the Mexican peso relative to the Canadian dollar. This type of rate is known as a cross-exchange rate because it reflects the amount of one foreign currency per unit of another foreign currency. Cross-exchange rates can be easily determined with the use of foreign exchange quotations. The general formula follows:

Value of 1 unit of Currency A in units of Currency B =
Value of Currency A in $/Value of Currency B in $

If the peso is worth $.07, and the Canadian dollar (C$) is worth $.70, the value of the peso in Canadian dollars is calculated as follows:

Value of peso in C$ = Value of peso in $/Value of C$ in $ = $.07/$.70 = .10

Thus, a Mexican peso is worth C$.10. The exchange rate can also be expressed as the number of pesos equal to one Canadian dollar. This figure can be computed by taking the reciprocal: .70/.07 = 10.0, which indicates that a Canadian dollar is worth about 10.0 pesos according to the information provided.

Exchange Rate System Types

From 1944 to 1971, the exchange rate at which one currency could be exchanged for another was maintained by governments within 1 percent of a specified rate. This period was known as the **Bretton Woods era,** because the agreement establishing the system was negotiated at the Bretton Woods Conference. The manner by which governments were able to control exchange rates is discussed later in the chapter.

By 1971 the U.S. dollar was clearly overvalued. That is, its value was maintained only by central bank intervention. In 1971, an agreement among all major countries (known as the **Smithsonian Agreement**) allowed for devaluation of the dollar. In addition, the Smithsonian Agreement called for a widening of the boundaries from 1 percent to $2\frac{1}{4}$ percent around each currency's set value. Governments intervened in the foreign exchange market whenever exchange rates threatened to wander outside the boundaries.

In 1973, the boundaries were eliminated. Since then, the exchange rates of major currencies have been floating without any government-imposed boundaries. Governments may still intervene in the foreign exchange market to influence the market value of their currency, however. A system with no boundaries in which exchange rates are market determined but are still subject to government intervention is called a **dirty float.** This can be distinguished from a **freely floating system,** in which the foreign exchange market is totally free from government intervention. Governments continue to intervene in the foreign exchange market from time to time.

Pegged Exchange Rate Systems Even when most exchange rates float, some currencies may be pegged to another currency or a unit of account and maintained within specified boundaries. For example, until 1999 many European currencies were part of the so-called exchange rate mechanism (ERM), which meant that they were pegged to a multicurrency unit of account known as the European Currency Unit (ECU). Because these currencies were pegged to the same unit of account, they were essentially pegged to each other; therefore the interest rates in these countries were forced to move in tandem. Governments intervened to ensure that the exchange rates between these currencies were maintained within the established boundaries. In 1999, most of the currencies participating in the ERM were converted to a single European currency (the euro), thereby eliminating the need for central banks to ensure exchange rate stability between European currencies.

Some other countries still use a pegged exchange rate system. Hong Kong has tied the value of its currency (the Hong Kong dollar) to the U.S. dollar (HK$7.8=$1) since 1983. In 2000, El Salvador set its currency (the colón) to be valued at 8.75 per dollar.

A country that pegs its currency does not have complete control over its local interest rates because they must be aligned with the interest rates of the currency to which its currency is tied. For example, if Hong Kong lowers its interest rates to stimulate its economy, its interest rates will be lower than U.S. interest rates. Investors based in Hong Kong will then be enticed to exchange Hong Kong dollars for U.S. dollars and invest in the United States where interest rates are higher. Since the Hong Kong dollar is tied to the U.S. dollar, the investors will be able to exchange their investment proceeds back to Hong Kong dollars at the end of the investment period without concern about exchange rate risk because the exchange rate is fixed.

As the example illustrates, Hong Kong no longer has control of its interest rates, as it is subject to movements in U.S. interest rates. Nevertheless, a country may view such an arrangement as advantageous because its interest rates (and therefore its economic conditions) might be much more volatile if they were not tied to the U.S. interest rates. Hong Kong's interest rate is typically equal to the U.S. interest rate plus a premium for risk. For example, when the Hong Kong government borrows funds, its interest rate is equal to the U.S. Treasury rate plus a small risk premium. As the U.S. Treasury rate changes, so does Hong Kong's interest rate.

In addition, because the Hong Kong dollar's value is fixed relative to the U.S. dollar, its value moves in tandem with the U.S. dollar against other currencies, including other Asian currencies. Thus, if the Japanese yen depreciates against the U.S. dollar, it will also depreciate against the Hong Kong dollar.

One concern about pegging a currency is that its value may change dramatically when the controls are removed. Many governments have imposed exchange controls to prevent their exchange rate from fluctuating, but when the controls were removed, the exchange rate abruptly adjusted to a new market-determined level. For example, on the day in October 1994 that the Russian authorities allowed the Russian ruble to fluctuate, the ruble depreciated by 27 percent against the dollar. On August 26, 1998, when Russia let its ruble float, the ruble declined against most major currencies by more than 50 percent. On January 13, 1999, when Brazil let its currency (the real) float, the real declined by 8 percent. When Argentina discontinued its peg to the U.S. dollar in January 2002, the peso's value declined by more than 50 percent over the next two months.

Factors Affecting Exchange Rates

The value of a currency adjusts to changes in demand and supply conditions, moving toward equilibrium. In equilibrium, there is no excess or deficiency of that currency.

ILLUSTRATION A large increase in the U.S. demand for European goods and securities will result in an increased demand for euros. Because the demand for euros will then exceed the supply of euros for sale, the market-makers (commercial banks) will experience a shortage of euros and will respond by increasing the quoted price of euros. Therefore, the euro will **appreciate,** or increase in value.

Conversely, if European corporations begin to purchase more U.S. goods and European investors purchase more U.S. securities, the opposite forces will occur. There will be an increased sale of euros in exchange for dollars, causing a surplus of euros in the market. The value of the euro will therefore **depreciate,** or decline, until it once again achieves equilibrium.

In reality, both the demand for euros and the supply of euros for sale can change simultaneously. The adjustment in the exchange rate will depend on the direction and magnitude of these changes.

Supply of and demand for a currency are influenced by a variety of factors, including (1) differential inflation rates, (2) differential interest rates, and (3) government intervention. These factors are discussed in the following subsections.

Differential Inflation Rates

Begin with an equilibrium situation and consider what will happen to the U.S. demand for euros and the supply of euros for sale if U.S. inflation suddenly becomes much higher

than European inflation. The U.S. demand for European goods will increase, reflecting an increased U.S. demand for euros. In addition, the supply of euros to be sold for dollars will decline as the European desire for U.S. goods decreases. Both forces will place upward pressure on the value of the euro.

Under the reverse situation, where European inflation suddenly becomes much higher than U.S. inflation, the U.S. demand for euros will decrease, while the supply of euros for sale increases, placing downward pressure on the value of the euro.

A well-known theory about the relationship between inflation and exchange rates, **purchasing power parity (PPP),** suggests that the exchange rate will, on average, change by a percentage that reflects the inflation differential between the two countries of concern.

ILLUSTRATION   Assume an initial equilibrium situation where the British pound's spot rate is $1.60, U.S. inflation is 3 percent, and British inflation is also 3 percent. If U.S. inflation suddenly increases to 5 percent, the British pound will appreciate against the dollar by approximately 2 percent according to PPP. The rationale is that as a result of the higher U.S. prices, U.S. demand for British goods will increase, placing upward pressure on the pound's value. Once the pound appreciates by 2 percent, the purchasing power of U.S. consumers will be the same whether they purchase U.S. goods or British goods. Although the prices of the U.S. goods will have risen by a higher percentage, the British goods will then be just as expensive to U.S. consumers because of the pound's appreciation. Thus, a new equilibrium exchange rate results from the change in U.S. inflation.

In reality, exchange rates do not always change as suggested by the PPP theory. Other factors that influence exchange rates (discussed next) can distort the PPP relationship. Thus, all these factors must be considered when assessing why an exchange rate has changed. Furthermore, forecasts of future exchange rates must account for the potential direction and magnitude of changes in all factors that affect exchange rates.

Differential Interest Rates

Interest rate movements affect exchange rates by influencing the capital flows between countries.

ILLUSTRATION   Assume U.S. interest rates suddenly become much higher than European interest rates. The demand by U.S. investors for European interest-bearing securities decreases, as these securities become less attractive. In addition, the supply of euros to be sold in exchange for dollars increases as European investors increase their purchases of U.S. interest-bearing securities. Both forces put downward pressure on the euro's value.

Under the reverse situation, opposite forces occur, resulting in upward pressure on the euro's value. In general, the currency of the country with a higher increase (or smaller decrease) in interest rates is expected to appreciate, other factors held constant.

Central Bank Intervention

Central banks commonly consider adjusting a currency's value to influence economic conditions. For example, the U.S. central bank may wish to weaken the dollar to increase demand for U.S. exports, which can stimulate the economy. However, a weaker dollar can also cause U.S. inflation by reducing foreign competition (by raising the prices of

foreign goods to U.S. consumers). Alternatively, the U.S. central bank may prefer to strengthen the dollar to intensify foreign competition, which can reduce U.S. inflation.

Direct Intervention A country's government can intervene in the foreign exchange market to affect a currency's value. Direct intervention occurs when a country's central bank (such as the Federal Reserve Bank for the United States or the European Central Bank for European countries that use the euro) sells some of its currency reserves for a different currency.

ILLUSTRATION Assume that the Federal Reserve and the European Central Bank desire to strengthen the value of the euro against the dollar. They use dollar reserves to purchase euros in the foreign exchange market. In essence, they dump dollars in the foreign exchange market and increase the demand for euros.

Central bank intervention can be overwhelmed by market forces, however, and therefore may not always succeed in reversing exchange rate movements. In fact, the efforts of the Fed and the European Central Bank to boost the value of the euro in 2000 were not successful. Nevertheless, central bank intervention may significantly affect the foreign exchange markets in two ways. First, it may slow the momentum of adverse exchange rate movements. Second, it may cause commercial banks and other corporations to reassess their foreign exchange strategies if they believe the central banks will continue intervention.

Indirect Intervention

The Fed can affect the dollar's value indirectly by influencing the factors that determine its value. For example, the Fed can attempt to lower interest rates by increasing the U.S. money supply (assuming that inflationary expectations are not affected). Lower U.S. interest rates tend to discourage foreign investors from investing in U.S. securities, thereby putting downward pressure on the value of the dollar. Or to boost the dollar's value, the Fed can attempt to increase interest rates by reducing the U.S. money supply. It has commonly used this strategy along with direct intervention in the foreign exchange market.

When countries experience substantial net outflows of funds (which put severe downward pressure on their currency), they commonly use indirect intervention by raising interest rates to discourage excessive outflows of funds and therefore limit any downward pressure on the value of their currency. This adversely affects local borrowers (government agencies, corporations, and consumers), however, and may weaken the economy.

Indirect Intervention during the Peso Crisis In 1994, Mexico experienced a large balance of trade deficit, perhaps because the peso was stronger than it should have been and encouraged Mexican firms and consumers to buy an excessive amount of imports. By December 1994, there was substantial downward pressure on the peso. On December 20, 1994, Mexico's central bank devalued the peso by about 13 percent. Mexico's stock prices plummeted, as many foreign investors sold their shares and withdrew their funds from Mexico in anticipation of further devaluation in the peso. On December 22, the central bank allowed the peso to float freely, and it declined by 15 percent. This was the beginning of the so-called Mexican peso crisis. The central bank increased interest rates as a form of indirect intervention to discourage foreign investors from withdrawing

their investments in Mexico's debt securities. The higher interest rates increased the cost of borrowing for Mexican firms and consumers, thereby slowing economic growth.

Indirect Intervention during the Asian Crisis In the fall of 1997, many Asian countries experienced weak economies, and their banks suffered from substantial defaults on loans. Concerned about their investments, investors began to withdraw their funds from these countries. Some countries (such as Thailand and Malaysia) increased their interest rates as a form of indirect intervention to encourage investors to leave their funds in Asia. However, the higher interest rates increased the cost of borrowing for firms that had borrowed funds there, making it more difficult for them to repay their loans. In addition, the high interest rates discouraged new borrowing by firms and weakened the economies (see Appendix 16A for a more comprehensive discussion of the Asian crisis).

During the Asian crisis, investors also withdrew funds from Brazil and reinvested them in other countries, causing major capital outflows and putting extreme downward pressure on the currency (the real). At the end of October, the central bank of Brazil responded by doubling its interest rates from about 20 percent to about 40 percent. This action discouraged investors from pulling funds out of Brazil because they could now earn twice the interest from investing in some securities there. Although the bank's action was successful in defending the real, it reduced economic growth because the cost of borrowing funds was too high for many firms.

Indirect Intervention during the Russian Crisis A similar situation occurred in Russia in May 1998. Over the previous four months, the Russian currency (the ruble) had consistently declined, and stock market prices had declined by more than 50 percent. Since the lack of confidence in Russia's currency and stocks could cause massive outflows of funds, the Russian central bank attempted to prevent further outflows by tripling interest rates (from about 50 percent to 150 percent). The ruble was temporarily stabilized, but stock prices continued to decline as investors were concerned that the high interest rates would reduce economic growth.

Foreign Exchange Controls

Some governments attempt to use foreign exchange controls (such as restrictions on the exchange of the currency) as a form of indirect intervention to maintain the exchange rate of their currency. When there is severe pressure, however, they tend to let the currency float temporarily toward its market-determined level and set new bands around that level. For example, during the mid-1990s, Venezuela imposed foreign exchange controls on its currency (the bolivar). In April 1996, Venezuela removed its controls on foreign exchange, and the bolivar declined by 42 percent the next day. This result suggests that the market-determined exchange rate of the bolivar was substantially lower than the exchange rate artificially set by the government.

Exchange Rate Movements

The foreign exchange market has received much attention in recent years because of the degree to which currency movements can affect a firm's performance or a country's economic conditions. Exhibit 16.2 shows the trend in various foreign currency values over time. Since the exhibit indicates that although exchange rate movements vary, they tend

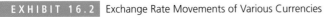

EXHIBIT 16.2 Exchange Rate Movements of Various Currencies

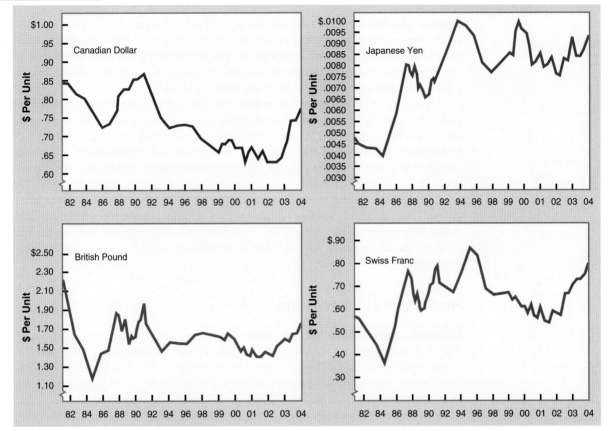

to be in the same direction over a period. In particular, the British pound and Swiss franc values are positively correlated.

Forecasting Exchange Rates

Market participants who use foreign exchange derivatives tend to take positions based on their expectations of future exchange rates. For example, U.S. portfolio managers may take positions in foreign exchange derivatives to hedge the exposure of their British stocks, if they anticipate a decline in the value of the British pound. Speculators may take positions in foreign exchange derivatives to benefit from the expectation that the Japanese yen will strengthen. Thus, the initial task is to develop a forecast of specific exchange rates. Although there are various techniques for forecasting, no specific technique stands out. Most techniques have had limited success in forecasting future exchange rates. Most forecasting techniques can be classified as one of the following:

■ Technical forecasting
■ Fundamental forecasting
■ Market-based forecasting
■ Mixed forecasting

Technical Forecasting

Technical forecasting involves the use of historical exchange rate data to predict future values. For example, the fact that a given currency has increased in value over four consecutive days may provide an indication of how the currency will move tomorrow. In some cases, a more complex statistical analysis is applied. For example, a computer program can be developed to detect particular historical trends.

There are also several **time-series models** that examine moving averages and thus allow a forecaster to develop some rule, such as, "The currency tends to decline in value after a rise in moving average over three consecutive periods." Normally, consultants who use such a method will not disclose their particular rule for forecasting. If they did, their potential clients might apply the rules themselves rather than pay for the consultant's advice.

Technical forecasting of exchange rates is similar to technical forecasting of stock prices. If the pattern of currency values over time appears random, then technical forecasting is not appropriate. Unless historical trends in exchange rate movements can be identified, examination of past movements will not be useful for indicating future movements.

Fundamental Forecasting

Fundamental forecasting is based on fundamental relationships between economic variables and exchange rates. Given current values of these variables along with their historical impact on a currency's value, corporations can develop exchange rate projections. For example, high inflation in a given country can lead to depreciation in its currency. Of course, all other factors that may influence exchange rates should also be considered.

A forecast may arise simply from a subjective assessment of the degree to which general movements in economic variables in one country are expected to affect exchange rates. From a statistical perspective, a forecast would be based on quantitatively measured impacts of factors on exchange rates.

Market-Based Forecasting

Market-based forecasting, the process of developing forecasts from market indicators, is usually based on either (1) the spot rate or (2) the forward rate.

Use of the Spot Rate   To clarify why the spot rate can serve as a market-based forecast, assume the British pound is expected to appreciate against the dollar in the very near future. This will encourage speculators to buy the pound with U.S. dollars today in anticipation of its appreciation, and these purchases could force the pound's value up immediately. Conversely, if the pound is expected to depreciate against the dollar, speculators will sell off pounds now, hoping to purchase them back at a lower price after they decline in value. Such action could force the pound to depreciate immediately. Thus, the current value of the pound should reflect the expectation of the pound's value in the very near future. Corporations can use the spot rate to forecast, since it represents the market's expectation of the spot rate in the near future.

Use of the Forward Rate   The forward rate can serve as a forecast of the future spot rate, because speculators would take positions if there was a large discrepancy between the forward rate and expectations of the future spot rate.

ILLUSTRATION   The 30-day forward rate of the British pound is $1.40, and the general expectation of speculators is that the future spot rate of the pound will be $1.45 in 30 days. Since speculators expect the future spot rate to be $1.45, and the prevailing forward rate is $1.40, they might buy pounds 30 days forward at $1.40 and then sell them when received (in 30 days) at the spot rate existing then. If their forecast is correct, they will earn $.05 ($1.45 − $1.40) per pound. If a large number of speculators implement this strategy, the substantial forward purchases of pounds will cause the forward rate to increase until this speculative demand stops. Perhaps this speculative demand will terminate when the forward rate reaches $1.45, since at this rate, no profits will be expected by implementing the strategy. The forward rate should move toward the market's general expectation of the future spot rate. In this sense, the forward rate serves as a market-based forecast because it reflects the market's expectation of the spot rate at the end of the forward horizon (30 days from now in this example).

Mixed Forecasting

Because no single forecasting technique has been found to be consistently superior to the others, some multinational corporations (MNCs) use a combination of forecasting techniques. This method is referred to as **mixed forecasting.** Various forecasts for a particular currency value are developed using several forecasting techniques. Each of the techniques used is assigned a weight so that the weights total 100 percent; the techniques thought to be more reliable are assigned higher weights. The actual forecast of the currency by the MNC will be a weighted average of the various forecasts developed.

Forecasting Exchange Rate Volatility

Foreign exchange market participants forecast not only future exchange rates but also exchange rate volatility in future periods. One reason they forecast exchange rate volatility is that they recognize how difficult it is to accurately forecast the exchange rates. If they can forecast the volatility, they can determine the potential range surrounding their forecast. This enables them to develop best case and worst case scenarios along with their point estimate forecast for a particular currency.

The first step in forecasting exchange rate volatility is to determine the relevant period of concern. For example, if a firm is forecasting the value of the Canadian dollar (C$) each day over the next quarter, it may attempt to also forecast the standard deviation of daily exchange rate movements over this quarter. This information can be used along with the point estimate forecast of the Canadian dollar for each day to derive confidence intervals around each forecast.

Numerous methods can be used to forecast the volatility of exchange rate movements for a future period. First, the volatility of historical exchange rate movements can be used as a forecast of the future. In our example, the standard deviation of daily exchange rate movements in the Canadian dollar during the previous month could be used as an estimate of the standard deviation of daily exchange rate movements in the Canadian dollar during the upcoming month.

A second method for forecasting exchange rate volatility is to use a time series of volatility patterns in previous periods. In our example, the standard deviation of daily exchange rate movements in the Canadian dollar could be determined for each of the last several months. Then, a time-series trend of these standard deviation levels could be used to form an estimate for the standard deviation of daily movements in the Canadian

dollar over the next month. This method differs from the first method in that it uses information beyond that contained in the previous month.

ILLUSTRATION

A forecast may be based on a weighting scheme such as 50 percent times the standard deviation in the last month, plus 30 percent times the standard deviation in the month before that, plus 20 percent times the standard deviation in the month before that. This scheme places more weight on the most recent data to derive the forecast, but allows data from the last three months to influence the forecast.

Normally, the weights and the number of previous periods (lags) that achieved the most accuracy (lowest forecast error) over previous periods are used when applying this method. Various economic and political factors can cause exchange rate volatility to change abruptly, however, so even sophisticated time-series models do not necessarily generate accurate forecasts of exchange rate volatility.

A third method for forecasting exchange rate volatility is to derive the exchange rate's implied standard deviation (ISD) from the currency option-pricing model. The premium to be paid on a call option for a currency is dependent on factors such as the relationship between the spot exchange rate and the exercise (strike) price of the option, the number of days until the expiration date of the option, and the anticipated volatility of the currency's exchange rate movements. There is a formula for estimating the call option premium based on various factors. The actual values of each of these factors is known, except for the anticipated volatility, and it can be derived by plugging in the option premium paid by investors for that specific currency option. In our example, the foreign exchange market participant would consider a call option on Canadian dollars that has 30 days to expiration (since the firm wishes to forecast volatility over a 30-day period). This measurement represents the anticipated volatility of the Canadian dollar over a 30-day period by investors who are trading currency options. Market participants may use this measurement as their own forecast of the Canadian dollar's volatility.

Exhibit 16.3 compares implied volatilities of several currencies based on one-year options as of January 30, 2004. Notice that the Canadian dollar has a lower implied volatility than the other currencies. This suggests that the Canadian dollar is expected to be less

EXHIBIT 16.3

Implied Volatilities of Foreign Currencies

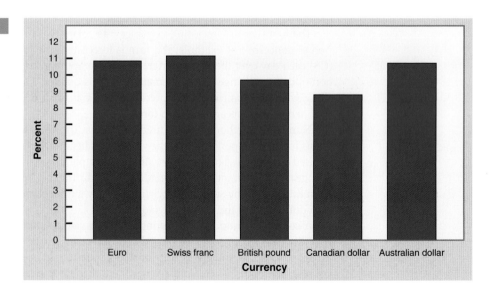

volatile than the other currencies and is consistent with historical exchange rate movements that substantiate the stability of the Canadian dollar. The website http://www.ny.frb.org provides updated estimates of implied volatilities for many currencies.

Speculation in Foreign Exchange Markets

Many commercial banks take positions in currencies to capitalize on expected exchange rate movements.

ILLUSTRATION Zona Bank expects the New Zealand dollar (NZ$) to depreciate against the U.S. dollar and plans to take a *short* position in NZ$ and a *long* position in dollars. That is, Zona Bank will first borrow NZ$ from another bank, then exchange the NZ$ for dollars to provide a short-term dollar loan to a bank that needs dollars. When the loan period is over, it will receive dollars back with interest, convert them back to NZ$, and pay off its debt in NZ$ with interest. If the dollar has strengthened over this period, the bank will receive more NZ$ per dollar than the number of NZ$ needed to purchase each dollar in the first place. Assume the following information:

- Interest rate on borrowed NZ$ is 6 percent annualized.
- Interest rate on dollars loaned out is 7 percent annualized.
- Spot rate is NZ$2 per dollar (one NZ$ = $.50).
- Expected spot rate in six days is 2.05 NZ$ per dollar.
- Zona Bank can borrow NZ$20 million.

The following steps can be taken to determine the profit from "shorting" NZ$ and "going long" on dollars:

1. Borrow NZ$20 million and convert to $10 million (at $.50 per NZ$).
2. Invest the $10 million for one week at 7 percent annualized or (.11667 percent over six days), which will generate $10,011,667.
3. After six days, convert the $10,011,667 into NZ$ at the spot rate that exists at that time. Based on the expected rate of NZ$2.05 per dollar, the dollars will convert to NZ$20,523,917.
4. Pay back the loan of NZ$20 million plus interest of 6 percent annualized (.1 percent over six days), which equals NZ$20,020,000.

The result is that Zona Bank earns NZ$503,917 profit over a six-day period. Although the potential profits are attractive, the speculative performance will depend on the uncertain future spot rate at the time the short and long positions are closed out.

Foreign Exchange Derivatives

Foreign exchange derivatives can be used to speculate on future exchange rate movements or to hedge anticipated cash inflows or outflows in a given foreign currency. As foreign security markets have become more accessible, institutional investors have increased their international investments, which has increased their exposure to exchange rate risk. Some institutional investors use foreign exchange derivatives to hedge their exposure. The most popular foreign exchange derivatives are forward contracts, currency futures contracts, currency swaps, and currency options contracts.

Forward Contracts

Forward contracts are contracts typically negotiated with a commercial bank that allow the purchase or sale of a specified amount of a particular foreign currency at a specified exchange rate on a specified future date. A **forward market** facilitates the trading of forward contracts. This market is not in one visible place, but is essentially a telecommunications network through which large commercial banks match participants who wish to buy a currency forward with other participants who wish to sell a currency forward.

Many of the commercial banks that offer foreign exchange on a spot basis also offer forward transactions for the widely traded currencies. By enabling a corporation to lock in the price to be paid for a foreign currency, forward purchases can hedge the corporation's risk that the currency's value may appreciate over time.

ILLUSTRATION   St. Louis Insurance Company plans to invest about $20 million in Mexican stocks two months from now. Because the Mexican stocks are denominated in pesos, the amount of stock that can be purchased is dependent on the peso's value at the time of the purchase. If St. Louis Insurance Company is concerned that the peso will appreciate by the time of the purchase, it can buy pesos forward to lock in the exchange rate.

A corporation receiving payments denominated in a particular foreign currency in the future can lock in the price at which the currency can be sold by selling that currency forward.

ILLUSTRATION   The pension fund manager of Gonzaga Inc. plans to liquidate the fund's holdings of British stocks in six months, but anticipates that the British pound will depreciate by that time. The pension fund manager can insulate the future transaction from exchange rate risk by negotiating a forward contract to sell British pounds six months forward. In this way, the British pounds received when the stocks are liquidated can be converted to dollars at the exchange rate specified in the forward contract.

The large banks that accommodate requests for forward contracts are buying forward from some firms and selling forward to others for a given date. They profit from the difference between the bid price at which they buy a currency forward and the slightly higher ask price at which they sell that currency forward. If a bank's forward purchase and sale contracts do not even out for a given date, the bank is exposed to exchange rate risk.

ILLUSTRATION   Nebraska Bank has contracts committed to selling C$100 million and purchasing C$150 million 90 days from now. It will receive C$50 million more than it sells. An increase in the Canadian dollar's value 90 days from now will be advantageous, but if the Canadian dollar depreciates, the bank will be adversely affected by its exposure to the exchange rate risk.

The forward rate of a currency will sometimes exceed the existing spot rate, thereby exhibiting a premium. At other times, it will be below the spot rate, exhibiting a discount. Forward contracts are sometimes referred to in terms of their percentage premium or discount rather than their actual rate. For example, assume that the spot rate (S) of the Canadian dollar is $.70 while the 180-day ($n=180$) forward rate ($FR$) is $.71. The forward rate premium (p) would be

Currency Futures Quotations

Currency futures quotations are provided in *The Wall Street Journal* as shown here. The futures quotations are segmented by currency, shown in bold. The settlement month is listed in the left column. For each settlement month of each currency, the opening futures price (second column), high price (third column), low price (fourth column), and closing price (fifth column) are disclosed. The change in the futures price from the previous day is disclosed in the sixth column. The lifetime high price (seventh column) and lifetime low price (eighth column) for each futures contract are also provided, as well as the open interest (number of existing contracts not offset).

Currency Futures

Japanese Yen (CME)-¥12,500,000; $ per ¥

Sept	.9065	.9092	.9028	.9057	−.0011	.9705	.8575	100,139
Dec	.9068	.9121	.9068	.9099	−.0011	.9740	.8800	10,571

Est vol 12,964; vol Fri 33,566; open int 110,723, −1,772.

Canadian Dollar (CME)-CAD 100,000; $ per CAD

Sept	.7623	.7625	.7580	.7591	−.0025	.7815	.6505	72,953
Dec	.7610	.7612	.7574	.7584	−.0025	.7800	.6940	4,808
Mr05	.7576	.7582	.7576	.7579	−.0025	.7775	.7150	791
June	.7570	.7570	.7570	.7574	−.0025	.7760	.7150	567

Est vol 12,183; vol Fri 19,916; open int 79,172, +3,634.

British Pound (CME)-£62,500; $ per £

Sept	1.8360	1.8387	1.8320	1.8353	.0002	1.8712	1.6330	69,169
Dec	1.8215	1.8226	1.8160	1.8205	.0002	1.8648	1.6850	510

Est vol 8,290; vol Fri 25,982; open int 69,686, −1,418.

Swiss Franc (CME)-CHF 125,000; $ per CHF

Sept	.8006	.8010	.7963	.7988	−.0012	.8209	.7110	38,318
Dec	.7995	.8028	.7992	.8013	−.0012	.8260	.7264	164

Est vol 9,389; vol Fri 27,005; open int 38,547, −2,579.

Australian Dollar (CME)-AUD 100,000; $ per AUD

Sept	.7110	.7154	.7094	.7141	.0031	.7780	.5756	30,258
Dec	.7085	.7095	.7078	.7077	.0031	.7705	.6150	277

Est vol 4,242; vol Fri 9,905; open int 30,629, +536.

Mexican Peso (CME)-MXN 500,000; $ per MXN

Aug	...	...	...	.08772	...	.08760	.08730	400
Sept	.08730	.08760	.08700	.08722	...	.08935	.08370	55,909
Dec	.08625	.08625	.08600	.08592	...	.08855	.08270	1,365

Est vol 8,912; vol Fri 15,536; open int 58,242, +6,695.

$$ p = \frac{FR - S}{S} \times \frac{360}{n} $$

$$ = \frac{\$.71 - \$.70}{\$.70} \times \frac{360}{180} $$

$$ = 2.86\% $$

This premium simply reflects the percentage by which the forward rate exceeds the spot rate on an annualized basis.

Currency Futures Contracts

An alternative to the forward contract is a currency futures contract, which is a standardized contract that specifies an amount of a particular currency to be exchanged on a specified date and at a specified exchange rate. A firm can purchase a futures contract to hedge payables in a foreign currency by locking in the price at which it could purchase that specific currency at a particular point in time. To hedge receivables denominated in a foreign currency, it could sell futures, thereby locking in the price at which it could sell that currency. A futures contract represents a standard number of units. Currency futures contracts also have specific maturity (or "settlement") dates from which the firm must choose.

Futures contracts differ from forward contracts in that they are standardized, whereas forward contracts can specify whatever amount and maturity date the firm

desires. Forward contracts have this flexibility because they are negotiated with commercial banks rather than on a trading floor.

Currency Swaps

A currency swap is an agreement that allows one currency to be periodically swapped for another at specified exchange rates. It essentially represents a series of forward contracts. Commercial banks facilitate currency swaps by serving as the intermediary that links two parties with opposite needs. Alternatively, commercial banks may be willing to take the position counter to that desired by a particular party. In such a case, they expose themselves to exchange rate risk unless the position they have assumed will offset existing exposure.

Currency Options Contracts

Another instrument used for hedging is the currency option. Its primary advantage over forward and futures contracts is that it provides a right rather than an obligation to purchase or sell a particular currency at a specified price within a given period.

A currency call option provides the right to purchase a particular currency at a specified price (called the exercise price) within a specified period. This type of option can be used to hedge future cash payments denominated in a foreign currency. If the spot rate remains below the exercise price, the option will not be exercised, because the firm could purchase the foreign currency at a lower cost in the spot market. A fee (or a premium) must be paid for options, however, so there is a cost to hedging with options, even if the options are not exercised.

A put option provides the right to sell a particular currency at a specified price (exercise price) within a specified period. If the spot rate remains above the exercise price, the option will not be exercised, because the firm could sell the foreign currency at a higher price in the spot market. Conversely, if the spot rate is below the exercise price at the time the foreign currency is received, the firm can exercise its put option.

When deciding whether to use forward, futures, or options contracts for hedging, a firm should consider the following characteristics of each contract. First, if the firm requires a tailor-made hedge that cannot be matched by existing futures contracts, a forward contract may be preferred. Otherwise, forward and futures contracts should generate somewhat similar results.

The choice of either an obligation type of contract (forward or futures) or an options contract depends on the expected trend of the spot rate. If the currency denominating payables appreciates, the firm will benefit more from a futures or forward contract than from a call option contract. The call option contract requires an up-front fee, but it is a wiser choice when the firm is less certain of the future direction of a currency. The call option can hedge the firm against possible appreciation but still allow the firm to ignore the contract and use the spot market if the currency depreciates. Put options may be preferred over futures or forward contracts for hedging receivables when future currency movements are very uncertain, because the firm has the flexibility to let the options expire if the currencies strengthen.

Conditional Currency Options Some currency options are structured with a conditional premium, meaning that the premium is conditioned on the actual movement in the currency's value over the period of concern.

WSJ USING THE WALL STREET JOURNAL

Foreign Exchange Derivatives

The Wall Street Journal provides the following information related to foreign exchange derivatives on a daily basis:

- Forward rates for different currencies.
- Price quotations on currency futures contracts for different currencies.
- Cross-exchange rates, or the exchange rates between non-U.S. currencies.
- A section called "Foreign Exchange" that provides reasons for recent exchange rate movements and suggests how exchange rates may change in the future.
- Price quotations on options on currency futures. For each currency, several different exercise (or strike) prices are available. Each row represents a particular exercise price. The volume of contracts traded and the premium per unit for currency call options and currency put options are disclosed for various expiration dates.

Source: Republished with permission of Dow Jones & Company, Inc., from The Wall Street Journal, September 28, 2004; permission conveyed through the Copyright Clearance Center, Inc.

Currency

Japanese Yen (CME)
12,500,000 yen; cents per 100 yen

Price	Oct	Nov	Dec	Oct	Nov	Dec
8900	0.00	0.00	2.02	0.19	0.53	0.82
8950	0.00	0.00	1.72	0.33	0.72	1.02
9000	0.72	1.14	1.44	0.52	0.94	1.24
9050	0.48	0.91	1.22	0.78	1.21	1.52
9100	0.31	0.72	1.02	1.11	1.52	1.82
9150	0.20	0.57	0.84	1.50	1.87	2.13

Est vol 594 Fr 190 calls 314 puts
Op int Fri 19,094 calls 13,959 puts

Canadian Dollar (CME)
100,000 Can.$; cents per Can.$

Price	Oct	Nov	Dec	Oct	Nov	Dec
7750	1.10	0.00	1.59	0.13	0.41	0.62
7800	0.72	1.06	1.29	0.25	0.59	0.82
7850	0.42	0.00	1.03	0.45	0.00	0.00
7900	0.23	0.57	0.81	0.00	0.00	0.00
7950	0.00	0.00	0.63	0.00	0.00	0.00
8000	0.05	0.00	0.48	0.00	0.00	0.00

Est vol 598 Fr 966 calls 358 puts
Op int Fri 6,384 calls 5,610 puts

British Pound (CME)
62,500 pounds; cents per pound

Price	Oct	Nov	Dec	Oct	Nov	Dec
1780	2.11	2.82	3.39	0.42	1.13	1.71
1790	1.41	2.22	2.83	0.72	1.53	2.14
1800	0.85	1.70	2.33	1.16	0.00	2.64
1810	0.50	1.30	1.90	1.81	0.00	3.20
1820	0.27	0.98	1.53	2.58	0.00	3.83
1830	0.17	0.00	1.22	0.00	0.00	0.00

Est vol 166 Fr 62 calls 156 puts
Op int Fri 3,955 calls 3,491 puts

Swiss Franc (CME)
125,000 francs; cents per franc

Price	Oct	Nov	Dec	Oct	Nov	Dec
7850	1.20	0.00	1.90	0.22	0.60	0.92
7900	0.83	1.27	1.61	0.35	0.79	1.13
7950	0.55	1.00	1.35	0.57	1.02	1.37
8000	0.35	0.78	1.13	0.87	0.00	1.65
8050	0.00	0.00	0.93	0.00	0.00	1.95
8100	0.13	0.45	0.76	1.65	0.00	2.27

Est vol 423 Fr 113 calls 4 puts
Op int Fri 2,375 calls 936 puts

Euro Fx (CME)
125,000 euros; cents per euro

Price	Oct	Nov	Dec	Oct	Nov	Dec
12200	1.27	1.87	2.35	0.42	1.02	1.50
12250	0.95	1.59	2.08	0.60	1.24	1.73
12300	0.69	1.33	1.83	0.84	1.48	1.98
12350	0.49	1.11	1.60	1.14	1.76	2.25
12400	0.33	0.91	1.41	1.48	2.06	2.56
12450	0.23	0.74	1.23	0.00	0.00	2.87

Est vol 2,029 Fr 817 calls 1,220 puts
Op int Fri 46,967 calls 25,743 puts

ILLUSTRATION

Canyon Company, a U.S.-based MNC, needs to sell British pounds that it will receive in 60 days. Assume it can negotiate a traditional currency put option on pounds in which the exercise price is $1.70 and the premium is $.02 per unit.

Alternatively, Canyon can negotiate with a commercial bank to obtain a conditional currency option that has an exercise price of $1.70 and a so-called trigger of $1.74. If the pound's value falls below the exercise price by the expiration date, Canyon will exercise the option, receiving $1.70 per pound, and does not need to pay a premium for the option. If the pound's value is between the exercise price ($1.70) and the trigger ($1.74), the option will not be exercised, and Canyon will not need to pay a premium. If the pound's value exceeds the trigger of $1.74, Canyon will pay a premium of $.04 per unit. Notice that this premium may be higher than the premium Canyon would pay if it purchases a basic put option. Canyon may not mind this outcome, however, because it will be receiving a high dollar amount from converting its pound receivables in the spot market.

Canyon must determine whether the potential advantage of the conditional option (avoiding the payment of a premium under some conditions) outweighs the potential disadvantage (paying a higher premium than the premium for a traditional put option on British pounds). The potential advantage and disadvantage are illustrated in Exhibit 16.4. At exchange rates below or equal to the trigger level ($1.74), the conditional option will result in a larger payment to Canyon by the amount of the premium that would have been paid for the basic option. Conversely, at exchange rates above the

EXHIBIT 16.4

Comparison of Conditional and Basic Currency Options

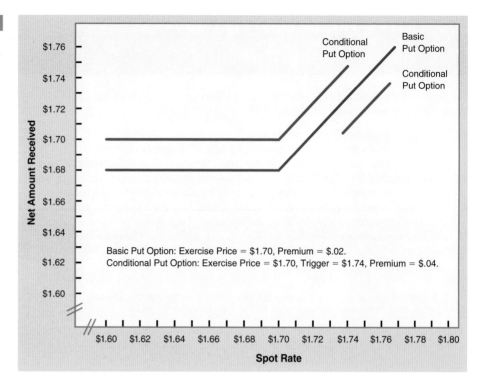

trigger level, the conditional option results in a lower payment to Canyon, as its premium of $.04 exceeds the premium of $.02 per unit paid on a basic option. The choice of a basic option versus a conditional option is dependent on the firm's expectations of the currency's exchange rate over the period of concern. If Canyon is very confident that the pound's value will not exceed $1.74, it will prefer the conditional currency option.

Conditional currency options are also available for U.S. firms that need to purchase a foreign currency in the near future. For example, a conditional call option on the pound may specify an exercise price of $1.70 and a trigger of $1.67. If the pound's value remains above the trigger of the call option, a premium will not have to be paid for the call option. However, if the pound's value falls below the trigger, a large premium (such as $.04 per unit) will be required. Some conditional options require a premium if the trigger is reached anytime up until the expiration date; others require a premium only if the exchange rate is beyond the trigger as of the expiration date.

Using Foreign Exchange Derivatives to Speculate

The forward, currency futures, and currency options markets may be used for speculating as well as for hedging. A speculator who expects the Singapore dollar to appreciate could consider any of these strategies:

1. Purchase Singapore dollars forward; when they are received, sell them in the spot market.
2. Purchase futures contracts on Singapore dollars; when the Singapore dollars are received, sell them in the spot market.

3. Purchase call options on Singapore dollars; at some point before the expiration date, when the spot rate exceeds the exercise price, exercise the call option and then sell the Singapore dollars received in the spot market.

Conversely, a speculator who expects the Singapore dollar to depreciate could consider any of these strategies:

1. Sell Singapore dollars forward and then purchase them in the spot market just before fulfilling the forward obligation.
2. Sell futures contracts on Singapore dollars; purchase Singapore dollars in the spot market just before fulfilling the futures obligation.
3. Purchase put options on Singapore dollars; at some point before the expiration date, when the spot rate is less than the exercise price, purchase Singapore dollars in the spot market and then exercise the put option.

Speculating with Currency Futures As an example of speculating with currency futures, consider the following information:

- Spot rate of British pound is $1.56 per pound.
- Price of futures contract is $1.57 per pound.
- Expectation of pound's spot rate as of settlement date of the futures contract is $1.63 per pound.

Given that the future spot rate is expected to be higher than the futures price, you could buy currency futures. You would receive pounds on the settlement date for $1.57. If your expectations are correct, you would then sell the pounds for $.06 more per unit than you paid for them.

The risk of your speculative strategy is that the pound may decline rather than increase in value. If it declines to $1.55 by the settlement date, you would have sold the pounds for $.02 less per unit than you paid.

To account for uncertainty, speculators may develop a probability distribution for the future spot rate:

Future Spot Rate of British Pound	Probability
$1.50	10%
1.59	20
1.63	50
1.66	20

This probability distribution suggests that four outcomes are possible. For each possible outcome, the anticipated gain or loss can be determined:

Possible Outcome for Future Spot Rate	Probability	Gain or Loss Per Unit
$1.50	10%	−$.07
1.59	20	.02
1.63	50	.06
1.66	20	.09

This analysis measures the probability and potential magnitude of a loss from the speculative strategy.

EXHIBIT 16.5

Estimating Speculative
Gains from Options Using
a Probability Distribution

(1) Possible Outcome for Future Spot Rate	(2) Probability	(3) Will the Option Be Exercised Based on This Outcome?	(4) Gain Per Unit from Exercising Option	(5) Premium Paid Per Unit for the Option	(6) Net Gain or Loss Per Unit
$1.50	10%	No	–	$.03	−$.03
1.59	20	Yes	$.02	.03	−.01
1.63	50	Yes	.06	.03	.03
1.66	20	Yes	.09	.03	.06

Speculating with Currency Options Consider the information from the previous example and assume that a British call option is available with an exercise price of $1.57 and a premium of $.03 per unit. Recall that your best guess of the future spot rate was $1.63. If your guess is correct, you will earn $.06 per unit on the difference between what you paid (the exercise price of $1.57) and the price for which you could sell a pound ($1.63). After the premium paid for the option ($.03 per unit) is deducted, the net gain is $.03 per unit.

The risk of purchasing this option is that the pound's value might decline over time. If so, you will be unable to exercise the option, and your loss will be the premium paid for it. To assess the risk involved, a probability distribution can be developed. In Exhibit 16.5, the probability distribution from the previous example is applied here. The distribution of net gains from the strategy is shown in the sixth column.

Speculators should always compare the potential gains from currency options and currency futures contracts to determine which type of contract (if any) to trade. It is possible for two speculators to have similar expectations about potential gains from both types of contracts, yet prefer different types of contracts because they have different degrees of risk aversion.

International Arbitrage

Exchange rates in the foreign exchange market are market determined. If they become misaligned, various forms of arbitrage will occur, forcing realignment. Common examples of international arbitrage follow.

Locational Arbitrage

Locational arbitrage is the act of capitalizing on a discrepancy between the spot exchange rate at two different locations by purchasing the currency where it is priced low and selling it where it is priced high.

ILLUSTRATION The exchange rates of the European euro quoted by two banks differ, as shown in Exhibit 16.6. The ask quote is higher than the bid quote to reflect the transaction costs charged by each bank. Because Baltimore Bank is asking $1.046 for euros and Sacramento Bank is willing to pay (bid) $1.050 for euros, an institution could execute locational arbitrage. That is, it could achieve a risk-free return without tying funds up

	Bid Rate on Euros	Ask Rate on Euros
Sacramento Bank	$1.050	$1.056
Baltimore Bank	$1.042	$1.046

EXHIBIT 16.6
Bank Quotes Used for Locational Arbitrage Example

for any length of time by buying euros at one location (Baltimore Bank) and simultaneously selling them at the other location (Sacramento Bank).

As locational arbitrage is executed, Baltimore Bank will begin to raise its ask price on euros in response to the strong demand. In addition, Sacramento Bank will begin to lower its bid price in response to the excess supply of euros it has recently received. Once Baltimore's ask price is at least as high as Sacramento's bid price, locational arbitrage will no longer be possible. Because some financial institutions (particularly the foreign exchange departments of commercial banks) watch for locational arbitrage opportunities, any discrepancy in exchange rates among locations should quickly be alleviated.

Covered Interest Arbitrage

The coexistence of international money markets and forward markets forces a special relationship between a forward rate premium and the interest rate differential of two countries, known as **interest rate parity.** The equation for interest rate parity can be written as

$$p = \frac{(1 + i_h)}{(1 + i_f)} - 1$$

where
p = forward premium of foreign currency
i_h = home country interest rate
i_f = foreign interest rate

ILLUSTRATION The spot rate of the New Zealand dollar is $.50, the one-year U.S. interest rate is 9 percent, and the one-year New Zealand interest rate is 6 percent. Under conditions of interest rate parity, the forward premium of the New Zealand dollar will be

$$p = \frac{(1 + 9\%)}{(1 + 6\%)} - 1$$
$$\approx 2.8\%$$

This means that the forward rate of the New Zealand dollar will be about $.514, to reflect a 2.8 percent premium above the spot rate.

A review of the equation for interest rate parity suggests that if the interest rate is lower in the foreign country than in the home country, the forward rate of the foreign currency will exhibit a premium. In the opposite situation, the forward rate will exhibit a discount.

Interest rate parity suggests that the forward rate premium (or discount) should be about equal to the differential in interest rates between the countries of concern. If the

relationship does not hold, market forces should occur that will restore the relationship. The act of capitalizing on the discrepancy between the forward rate premium and the interest rate differential is called **covered interest arbitrage.**

ILLUSTRATION

The spot rate and the one-year forward rate of the Canadian dollar are $.80. The Canadian interest rate is 10 percent, while the U.S. interest rate is 8 percent. U.S. investors can take advantage of the higher Canadian interest rate without being exposed to exchange rate risk by executing covered interest arbitrage. Specifically, they will exchange U.S. dollars for Canadian dollars and invest at the rate of 10 percent. They will simultaneously sell Canadian dollars one year forward. Because they are able to purchase and sell Canadian dollars for the same price, their return is the 10 percent interest earned on their investment.

As the U.S. investors demand Canadian dollars in the spot market while selling Canadian dollars forward, they place upward pressure on the spot rate and downward pressure on the one-year forward rate of the Canadian dollar. Thus, the Canadian dollar's forward rate will exhibit a discount. Once the discount becomes large enough, the interest rate advantage in Canada will be offset. What U.S. investors gain on the higher Canadian interest rate is offset by having to buy Canadian dollars at a higher (spot) rate than the selling (forward) rate. Consequently, covered interest arbitrage will no longer generate a return that is any higher for U.S. investors than an alternative investment in the United States. Once the forward discount (or premium) offsets the interest rate differential in this manner, interest rate parity exists.

The interest rate parity equation determines the forward discount that the Canadian dollar must exhibit to offset the interest rate differential:

$$p = \frac{(1 + i_h)}{(1 + i_f)} - 1$$
$$= \frac{(1 + 8\%)}{(1 + 10\%)} - 1$$
$$\approx -1.82\%$$

If the forward rate is lower than the spot rate by 1.82 percent, the interest rate is offset, and covered interest arbitrage would yield a return to U.S. investors similar to the U.S. interest rate.

The existence of interest rate parity prevents investors from earning higher returns from covered interest arbitrage than can be earned in the United States. Nevertheless, international investing may still be feasible if the investing firm does not simultaneously cover in the forward market. Of course, failure to do so usually exposes the firm to exchange rate risk; if the currency denominating the investment depreciates over the investment horizon, the return on the investment is reduced.

Explaining Price Movements of Foreign Exchange Derivatives

Exhibit 16.7 illustrates the underlying forces that cause changes in the spot exchange rate and the forward exchange rate of any particular currency against the dollar. Since

EXHIBIT 16.7 Framework for Pricing Forward and Currency Futures Rates

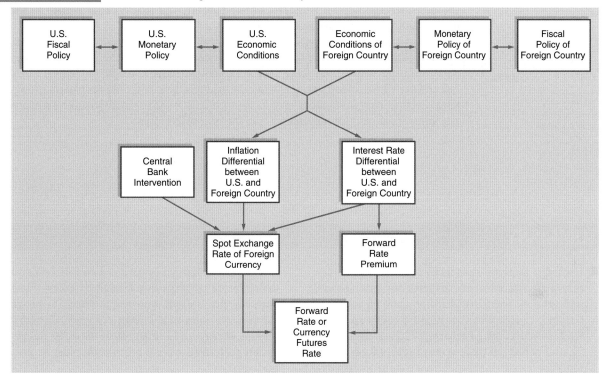

currency futures are typically priced similar to forward contracts, the exhibit can also be used to explain changes in currency futures prices over time. Given the influence of movements in the spot rate on the corresponding forward rate of a currency, the underlying forces that affect spot rate movements also affect the forward rate. However, the forward rate is also affected by changes in its premium, which are directly influenced by the change in the interest rate differential.

Indicators of Foreign Exchange Derivative Prices

The participants who use foreign exchange derivatives to speculate or hedge continuously forecast the direction and degree of movement in various currencies. Because of the influence of the spot rate on the forward rate or currency futures, they monitor indicators that may signal a change in economic conditions that will affect the supply of and demand for a particular currency and therefore affect the spot rate. To anticipate a given foreign currency's value against the dollar, they monitor indicators reflecting inflation in the foreign country and the United States so that they can anticipate possible changes in the trade patterns between the two countries. They may also monitor indicators that signal possible changes in interest rates, such as economic growth indicators (employment level, gross domestic product, retail sales level), inflation indicators, and indicators of the volume of government borrowing (budget deficit level) for the United States and the foreign country. This information can be used to anticipate changes in the interest rates of each country, which can be used to forecast how future flows of funds

between the two countries will change. The flows of funds can shift abruptly between countries in response to interest rate movements and can have a major impact on the corresponding exchange rate.

The manner in which participants in the forward or futures market use the indicators is dependent on the time to maturity of the contracts they are considering trading. Short-term speculators may focus on indicators that signal possible foreign exchange rate and derivative price movements over the next few days; corporations planning long-term direct foreign investment may focus on indicators that signal possible exchange rate and derivative price movements over the next several years.

SUMMARY

- Exchange rates are influenced by differential inflation rates, differential interest rates, and central bank intervention. There is upward pressure on a foreign currency's value when its home country has relatively low inflation or relatively high interest rates. Central banks can place upward pressure on a currency by purchasing that currency in the foreign exchange market (by exchanging other currencies held in reserve for that currency). Alternatively, they can place downward pressure on a currency by selling that currency in the foreign exchange market in exchange for other currencies.

- Exchange rates can be forecasted using technical, fundamental, and market-based methods. Each method has its own advantages and limitations.

- Speculators can invest in currencies that they expect to appreciate. Conversely, they can take a short position by borrowing currencies that they expect will depreciate. The borrowed funds are converted into a different currency and invested.

- Foreign exchange derivatives include forward contracts, currency futures contracts, currency swaps, and currency options contracts. Forward contracts can be purchased to hedge future payables or sold to hedge future receivables in a foreign currency. Currency futures contracts can be used in a manner similar to forward contracts to hedge payables or receivables in a foreign currency. Currency swaps can be used to lock in the exchange rate of a foreign currency to be received or purchased at a future point

in time. Currency call options can be purchased to hedge future payables in a foreign currency, while currency put options can be purchased to hedge future receivables in a foreign currency. Currency options offer more flexibility than the other foreign exchange derivatives, but a premium must be paid for them.

Foreign exchange derivatives can also be used to speculate on expected exchange rate movements. When speculators expect a foreign currency to appreciate, they can lock in the exchange rate at which they may purchase that currency by purchasing forward contracts, futures contracts, or call options on that currency. When speculators expect a currency to depreciate, they can lock in the exchange rate at which they may sell that currency by selling forward contracts or futures contracts on that currency. They could also purchase put options on that currency.

- International arbitrage ensures that foreign exchange market prices are set properly. If exchange rates vary among the banks that serve the foreign exchange market, locational arbitrage will be possible. Foreign exchange market participants will purchase a currency at the bank with a low quote and sell it to another bank where the quote is higher. If the interest rate differential is not offset by the forward rate premium (as suggested by interest rate parity), covered interest arbitrage will be possible. This involves investing in a foreign currency and simultaneously selling the currency forward. Arbitrage will occur until interest rate parity is restored.

POINT COUNTER-POINT

Do Financial Institutions Need to Consider Foreign Exchange Market Conditions when Making Domestic Security Market Decisions?

Point No. If there is no exchange of currencies, there is no need to monitor the foreign exchange market.

Counter-Point Yes. Foreign exchange market conditions can affect an economy or an industry and therefore affect the valuation of securities. In addition, the valua-

tion of a firm can be affected by currency movements because of its international business.

Who Is Correct? Use your favorite search engine to learn more about this issue. Offer your own opinion on this issue.

QUESTIONS AND APPLICATIONS

1. **Interaction of Capital Flows and Yield Curve** Assume a horizontal yield curve exists. How do you think the yield curve would be affected if foreign investors in short-term securities and long-term securities suddenly anticipate that the value of the dollar will strengthen? (You may find it helpful to refer back to the discussion of the yield curve in Chapter 3.)

2. **Bank Speculation** When would a commercial bank take a short position in a foreign currency? A long position?

3. **Impact of Inflation** Assume that Mexico suddenly experiences high and unexpected inflation. How could this affect the value of the Mexican peso according to purchasing power parity (PPP) theory?

4. **Exchange Rate Systems** Explain the exchange rate system that existed during the 1950s and 1960s. How did the Smithsonian Agreement in 1971 revise it? How does today's exchange rate system differ?

5. **Internet Exercise** Use the website http://www.oanda.com to assess exchange rates.
   a. What is the most recent value of the Australian dollar in U.S. dollars? For large transactions, how many British pounds does a dollar buy? What is the most recent value of the Hong Kong dollar in U.S. dollars? Do you notice anything unusual about this value over time? What could explain an exchange rate trend such as this?

6. **Risk from Speculating** Seattle Bank was long in Australian dollars and short in Canadian dollars. Ex-

plain a possible future scenario that could adversely affect the bank's performance.

7. **Impact of Quotas** Assume that European countries impose a quota on goods imported from the United States, and the United States does not plan to retaliate. How could this affect the value of the euro? Explain.

8. **Interpreting Financial News** Interpret the following statements made by Wall Street analysts and portfolio managers:
   a. "Our use of currency futures has completely changed our risk-return profile."
   b. "Our use of currency options resulted in an upgrade in our credit rating."
   c. "Our strategy to use forward contracts to hedge backfired on us."

9. **Dirty Float** Explain the difference between a freely floating system and a dirty float. Which type is more representative of the United States?

10. **Impact of Economic Conditions** Assume that Switzerland has a very strong economy, placing upward pressure on both inflation and interest rates. Explain how these conditions could place pressure on the value of the Swiss franc, and determine whether the franc's value will rise or fall.

11. **Managing in Financial Markets: Using Forex Derivatives for Hedging** You are the manager of a stock portfolio for a financial institution, and about 20 percent of the stock portfolio that you manage is in British

stocks. You expect the British stock market to perform well over the next year, and plan to sell the stocks one year from now (and will convert the British pounds received to dollars at that time). However, you are concerned that the British pound may depreciate against the dollar over the next year.

a. Explain how you could use a forward contract to hedge the exchange rate risk associated with your position in British stocks.

b. If interest rate parity exists, does this limit the effectiveness of a forward rate as a hedge?

c. Explain how you could use an options contract to hedge the exchange rate risk associated with your position in stocks.

d. Assume that although you are concerned about the potential decline in the pound's value, you also believe that the pound could appreciate against the dollar over the next year. You would like to benefit from the potential appreciation but also wish to hedge against the possible depreciation. Should you use a forward contract or options contracts to hedge your position? Explain.

12. **Impact of a Weak Dollar** How does a weak dollar affect U.S. inflation? Explain.

13. **Impact of Capital Flows** Assume that stocks in Great Britain become very attractive to U.S. investors. How could this affect the value of the British pound? Explain.

14. **Central Bank Intervention** The Bank of Japan desires to decrease the value of the Japanese yen against the dollar. How could it use direct intervention to do this?

15. **Speculating with Foreign Exchange Derivatives** Explain how foreign exchange derivatives could be used by U.S. speculators to speculate on the expected appreciation of the Japanese yen.

PROBLEMS

1. **Currency Futures** Using the following information, determine the probability distribution of per unit gains from selling Mexican peso futures:
   - Spot rate of peso is $.10.
   - Price of peso futures per unit is $.102.
   - Your expectation of the peso spot rate at maturity of the futures contract is:

Possible Outcome for Future Spot Rate	Probability
$.09	10%
.095	70
.11	20

2. **Interest Rate Parity** Determine how the forward rate premium would be affected if the foreign interest rate is higher, holding the U.S. interest rate constant, under conditions of interest rate parity.

3. **Bank Speculation** Assume the following information:

	Interbank Interest Rate	Spot Rate	Expected Spot Rate in 5 Days
Canadian dollars	6%	$ .80	$ .79
British pounds	7%	1.50	1.52

Based on this information, explain how Minnesota Bank can speculate by taking a short position in one currency and a long position in the other. What will be the gain if expectations come true, assuming that the bank can borrow one million units of either currency?

4. **Covered Interest Arbitrage** Assume the following information:
   - British pound spot rate = $1.58
   - British pound one-year forward rate = $1.58
   - British one-year interest rate = 11%
   - U.S. one-year interest rate = 9%

   Explain how U.S. investors could use covered interest arbitrage to lock in a higher yield than 9 percent. What would be their yield? Explain how the spot and forward rates of the pound would change as covered interest arbitrage occurs.

5. **Impact of Exchange Rates on Bond Payments** Assume that a U.S. firm issues three-year notes in New Zealand with a par value of 60 million New Zealand dollars and a 6 percent annual coupon rate, priced at par. The forecasted exchange rate of the New Zealand dollar is $.50 at the end of Year 1, $.53 at the end of Year 2, and $.57 at the end of Year 3. Estimate the dollar cash flows needed to cover these payments.

6. **Covered Interest Arbitrage** Assume the following information:
   - Mexican one-year interest rate = 15%
   - U.S. one-year interest rate = 11%

   If interest rate parity exists, what would be the forward premium or discount on the Mexican peso's forward rate? Would covered interest arbitrage be more profitable to U.S. investors than investing at home? Explain.

7. **Locational Arbitrage** Assume the following exchange rate quotes on British pounds:

	Bid	Ask
Orleans Bank	$1.46	$1.47
Kansas Bank	1.48	1.49

   Explain how locational arbitrage would occur. Also explain why this arbitrage will realign the exchange rates.

8. **Currency Call Options** Using the following information, determine the probability distribution of net gains per unit from purchasing a call option on British pounds:
   - Spot rate of British pound is $1.45.
   - Premium on British pound option is $.04 per unit.
   - Exercise price of a British pound option is $1.46.
   - Your expectation of the British pound spot rate prior to the expiration of the option is:

Possible Outcome for Future Spot Rate	Probability
$1.48	30%
1.49	40
1.52	30

FLOW OF FUNDS EXERCISE

Hedging with Foreign Exchange Derivatives

Carson Company expects that it will receive a large order from the government of Spain. If the order occurs, Carson will be paid about 3 million euros. All of Carson's expenses are in dollars. Carson would like to hedge this position. Carson has contacted a bank with brokerage subsidiaries that can help it hedge with foreign exchange derivatives.

a. How could Carson use currency futures to hedge its position?
b. What is the risk of hedging with currency futures?
c. How could Carson use currency options to hedge its position?
d. Explain the advantage and disadvantage to Carson of using currency options instead of currency futures.

WSJ EXERCISE

Assessing Exchange Rate Movements

Use a recent issue of *The Wall Street Journal* to determine how a particular currency's value has changed against the dollar over the past six months. The part called "U.S. Dollar" within the "Markets Diary" section shows the general trend in the value of the dollar over the last several months.

Impact of the Asian Crisis on Foreign Exchange Markets and Other Financial Markets

The Asian crisis provides an excellent example of the linkages between the foreign exchange markets and all of the major financial markets. During the crisis, problems in the foreign exchange markets caused abrupt price movements in securities in all markets. In fact, the high degree of integration among financial markets today makes each financial market susceptible to events in any other financial market.

Crisis in Thailand

Until July 1997, Thailand was one of the world's fastest growing economies. In fact, Thailand was the fastest growing country over the 1985–1994 period. Thai consumers spent freely, which resulted in lower savings than in other Southeast Asian countries. The high level of spending and low level of saving put upward pressure on prices of real estate and products and on the local interest rate. Normally, countries with high inflation tend to have a weak currency because of forces from purchasing power parity. Prior to July 1997, however, Thailand's currency (the baht) was linked to the dollar; this link made Thailand an attractive site for foreign investors, because they could earn a high interest rate on invested funds while being protected (until the crisis) from a large depreciation in the baht.

Flow of Funds Situation

The large inflow of funds made Thailand highly susceptible to a massive outflow of funds if the foreign investors ever lost confidence in the Thai economy. Given the large amount of risky loans and the potential for a massive outflow of funds, Thailand was sometimes described as a house of cards, waiting to collapse.

Export Competition

During the first half of 1997, the dollar strengthened against the Japanese yen and European currencies. Since the baht was linked to the dollar over this period, the baht strengthened against the yen and European currencies as well, and Thailand's products became more expensive to various importers.

Pressure on the Thai Baht

The baht experienced downward pressure in July 1997 when some foreign investors recognized its potential weakness. The outflow of funds expedited the currency's weakening as foreign investors exchanged their baht for their home currencies. The baht's value relative to the dollar was pressured by the large sales of baht in exchange for dollars. On July 2, 1997, the baht was detached from its link to the dollar. Thailand's central bank attempted to maintain the baht's value by intervention. Specifically, it swapped its baht reserves for dollar reserves at other central banks and then used its dollar reserves to purchase the baht in the foreign exchange market (the swap agreement required Thailand to reverse this transaction by exchanging dollars for baht at a future date). The bank hoped that its intervention would offset the sales of baht by foreign investors in the foreign exchange market, but its efforts were overwhelmed by market forces. The supply of baht for sale exceeded the demand for baht in the foreign exchange market, which caused the government to surrender in its effort to defend the baht's value. In July 1997, the value of the baht plummeted, declining by more than 20 percent against the dollar over a five-week period.

Rescue Package for Thailand

On August 5, 1997, the International Monetary Fund (IMF) and several countries agreed to provide Thailand with a $16 billion rescue package. Japan and the IMF each contributed $4 billion, and other countries provided the rest. This was the second largest bailout plan for a single country (Mexico received $50 billion in 1995). In return for the monetary support, Thailand agreed to reduce its budget deficit, prevent inflation from rising above 9 percent, raise its value-added tax from 7 to 10 percent, and clean up the financial statements of its banks, which had many undisclosed bad loans.

Spread of the Crisis throughout Southeast Asia

The crisis in Thailand proved contagious to other countries in Southeast Asia. The Southeast Asian economies are somewhat integrated because of their trade contacts. The crisis weakened Thailand's economy and therefore reduced Thai demand for products from the other countries of Southeast Asia. As the demand for the other countries' products declined, so did their national incomes and their own demand for products from other Southeast Asian countries.

The other Southeast Asian countries were similar to Thailand in that they had relatively high interest rates, and their governments tended to stabilize their currency. Consequently, these countries had also attracted a large amount of foreign investment, but the foreign investors now realized that the other countries were vulnerable as well. These investors began to withdraw funds from these countries.

Impact of the Asian Crisis on South Korea

South Korea also experienced financial problems, as many of its corporations were unable to repay their loans. On December 3, 1997, the IMF agreed to a $55 million rescue

package for South Korea. The World Bank and the Asian Development Bank joined with the IMF to provide a standby credit line of $35 billion. In exchange for the funding, South Korea agreed to reduce its economic growth and to impose restrictions on its conglomerates to prevent excessive borrowing. These measures led to some bankruptcies and unemployment, because the banks could no longer automatically provide loans to all conglomerates that needed funds unless the funding was economically justified.

Impact of the Asian Crisis on Japan

Japan was also affected by the Asian crisis for several reasons. It exports products throughout Southeast Asia, and many of its corporations have subsidiaries in other Asian countries and were therefore affected by the local economic conditions. Many of Japan's corporations experienced financial distress and could not repay their loans.

During the spring of 1998, the Japanese yen continued to weaken against the dollar. The yen's decline placed more pressure on other Asian currencies, because the Asian countries wanted to gain a competitive advantage in exporting to the United States as a result of their weak currencies. In April 1998, the Bank of Japan used more than $20 billion to purchase yen in the foreign exchange market. This effort to boost the yen's value was unsuccessful.

Effects on Asian Currencies

In July and August of 1997, the values of the Malaysian ringgit, Singapore dollar, Philippine peso, Taiwan dollar, and Indonesian rupiah also declined. The Philippine peso was devalued in July. Malaysia initially attempted to maintain the ringgit's value within a narrow band, but then surrendered and let the ringgit float to its market-determined level.

In August 1997, Bank Indonesia (the central bank) used more than $500 million in direct intervention to purchase rupiah in the foreign exchange market in an attempt to boost the currency's value. By mid-August, however, the bank gave up on its effort to maintain the rupiah's value within a band and let the rupiah float to its natural level. This decision to let the rupiah float may have been influenced by the failure of Thailand's costly efforts to maintain the baht. The market forces were too strong and could not be offset by direct intervention. In the spring of 1998, the IMF provided Indonesia with a rescue package worth about $43 billion.

Impact of the Asian Crisis on Hong Kong

On October 23, 1997, prices on the Hong Kong stock market declined by 10.2 percent on average; considering the three previous trading days as well, the cumulative four-day effect was a decline of 23.3 percent. The decline was primarily attributed to speculation that Hong Kong's currency might be devalued and that it could experience financial problems similar to those of the Southeast Asian countries. The decline of almost one-fourth in the market value of Hong Kong companies over a four-day period demonstrated the perceived exposure of Hong Kong to the crisis.

Hong Kong maintained its pegged exchange rate system during this period, as its dollar was tied to the U.S. dollar. Nevertheless, it had to increase interest rates to discourage investors from transferring their funds out of the country.

Impact of the Asian Crisis on China

Ironically, China did not experience the adverse economic effects of the crisis because its growth in the years prior to the crisis was not as strong as that of the countries in Southeast Asia. The Chinese government had more control over economic conditions than other Asian governments because it still owned most real estate and controlled most of the banks that provided credit to support growth. Thus, China experienced fewer bankruptcies as a result of the crisis. In addition, the government was able to maintain the value of the Chinese currency (the yuan) against the dollar, which limited speculative flows of funds out of China. Although interest rates increased during the crisis, they remained relatively low. This allowed Chinese firms to obtain funding at a reasonable cost and enabled them to continue to meet their interest payments.

Nevertheless, concerns about China mounted because it relies heavily on exports to stimulate its economy and was now at a competitive disadvantage relative to the Southeast Asian countries whose currencies had depreciated. Thus, importers from the United States and Europe shifted some of their purchases to countries where the currencies had weakened substantially. In addition, the decline in the other Asian currencies against the Chinese yuan encouraged Chinese consumers to purchase imports rather than locally manufactured products.

Impact of the Asian Crisis on Russia

During the crisis, investors also lost confidence in the value of the Russian ruble and began to transfer funds out of Russia. In response to the downward pressure these outflows placed on the ruble, the central bank of Russia engaged in direct intervention, using dollars to purchase rubles in the foreign exchange market. It also used indirect intervention, raising interest rates to make them more attractive to investors and discourage additional outflows.

In July 1998, the IMF organized a loan package (with some help from Japan and the World Bank) worth $22.6 billion to Russia. The package required that Russia boost its tax revenue, reduce its budget deficit, and create a more capitalist environment for its businesses.

During August 1998, Russia's central bank frequently intervened to prevent the ruble from declining substantially. On August 26, however, it gave up its fight to defend the ruble's value, and market forces caused the ruble to decline by more than 50 percent against most currencies on that day. This led to fears of a new crisis, and the next day (called "Bloody Thursday") paranoia swept stock markets around the world. Some stock markets (including the U.S. markets) experienced declines of more than 4 percent.

Impact of the Asian Crisis on Latin American Countries

The Asian crisis also affected Latin American countries. Countries such as Chile, Mexico, and Venezuela were adversely affected because they export to Asia and demand for their products declined due to the weak Asian economies. In addition, the Latin American countries lost business as other importers switched to Asian products because the substantial depreciation of the Asian currencies had made those goods cheaper than those of Latin America.

The adverse effects on Latin American countries placed pressure on Latin American currency values, as there was concern that speculative outflows of funds would weaken

these currencies in the same way that Asian currencies had weakened. In particular, Brazil's currency (the real) came under pressure in late October 1997. Some speculators believed that because most Asian countries had failed to maintain their currencies within bands, Brazil, too, would be unable to stabilize its currency.

In a form of direct intervention, the central bank of Brazil used about $7 billion of reserves to purchase real in the foreign exchange market and protect the currency from depreciation. The bank also used indirect intervention by raising short-term interest rates. This encouraged foreign investment in Brazil's short-term securities to capitalize on the high interest rates and also encouraged local investors to invest locally rather than in foreign markets. The increase in interest rates signaled that the bank was serious about maintaining the stability of the real. This type of intervention is costly, however, because it increases the cost of borrowing for households, corporations, and government agencies and thus can reduce economic growth. If Brazil's currency had weakened, the speculative forces might have spread to the other Latin American currencies as well.

The Asian crisis also caused bond ratings of many large corporations and government agencies in Latin America to be downgraded. For example, in November 1997, when top-grade government-backed bonds in South Korea were reduced to junk-level status in the international credit markets, rumors that banks were dumping Asian bonds created fears that all emerging-market debt would be dumped in the bond markets. Furthermore, there was concern that many banks experiencing financial problems (because their loans were not being repaid) would sell bond holdings in the secondary market to raise funds. Consequently, prices of bonds issued in emerging markets, including those of Latin American countries, declined.

Impact of the Asian Crisis on Europe

During the Asian crisis, European countries were experiencing strong economic growth. Nevertheless, many European firms were adversely affected by the crisis. Like firms in Latin America, some firms in Europe experienced reduced demand for their exports to Asia. In addition, they lost some exporting business to Asian exporters as a result of the weakened Asian currencies that reduced Asian prices from an importer's perspective.

Impact of the Asian Crisis on the United States

The effects of the Asian crisis were even felt in the United States. Stock values of U.S. firms such as IBM, Motorola, Hewlett-Packard, and Nike that conducted much business in Asia were adversely affected. Many U.S. engineering and construction firms were adversely affected as Asian countries curtailed their plans to improve infrastructure. Stock values of U.S. exporters to those countries were adversely affected because of the decline in spending by Asian consumers and corporations and because the weakening of the Asian currencies made U.S. products more expensive.

Lessons from the Asian Crisis

The Asian crisis demonstrated that financial markets can be exposed to the financial problems of other countries, as explained next.

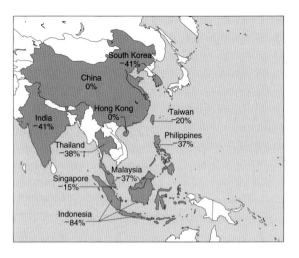

Exposure to Effects on Exchange Rates

The Asian crisis demonstrated that currencies are susceptible to depreciation in response to a lack of confidence in central banks' ability to stabilize their local currencies. If investors and firms had believed that the central banks could prevent the free fall in currency values, they would not have transferred their funds to other countries. This would have removed the downward pressure on the currency values.

Exhibit 16A.1 shows how exchange rates of some Asian currencies changed against the U.S. dollar within one year of the crisis (from June 1997 to June 1998). In particular, the currencies of Indonesia, Malaysia, South Korea, and Thailand declined substantially.

Exposure to Effects on Interest Rates

The Asian crisis also demonstrated how much interest rates could be affected by the flow of funds out of countries. Exhibit 16A.2 illustrates how interest rates changed from June 1997 (just before the crisis) to June 1998 for various Asian countries. The increases in

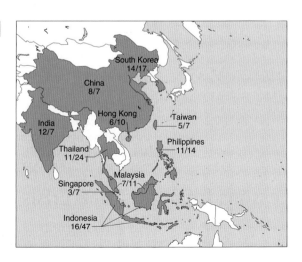

interest rates can be attributed to the indirect interventions intended to prevent the local currencies from depreciating further, or to the massive outflows of funds, or to both of these conditions. In particular, interest rates in Indonesia, Malaysia, and Thailand increased substantially from their precrisis levels. Countries whose local currencies experienced more depreciation had higher upward adjustments. Since the substantial increases in interest rates (which tend to reduce economic growth) may have been caused by the outflows of funds, they may be indirectly due to the lack of confidence of investors and firms in the ability of the Asian central banks to stabilize their local currencies.

Exposure to Effects on Security Prices

Exhibit 16A.3 provides a summary of how the Asian crisis affected financial market prices in Thailand. The exhibit is equally applicable to the other Asian countries that experienced financial distress during the crisis. For clarity, bonds, bank loans, and money market instruments are combined and simply referred to as debt securities in the exhibit.

 The initial conditions that instigated the crisis in Thailand were a weak economy, heavy reliance on foreign funding to finance growth, and excessive credit problems. These conditions scared investors and encouraged them to sell their investments and withdraw their funds from Thailand. The prices of debt securities issued in Thailand are primarily driven by the required rate of return by investors who may purchase debt

EXHIBIT 16A.3 How the Asian Crisis Affected Thailand's Security Prices

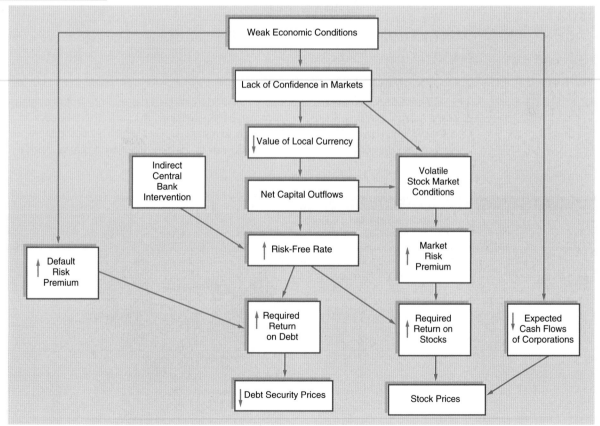

securities, which is influenced by the local risk-free rate and the default risk premium. During the crisis, Thailand experienced higher interest rates because of the speculative outflows by investors, which reduced the supply of funds available, and because of the central bank's efforts to boost interest rates. The default risk premium increased because of the weak economic conditions and the increased market awareness of the credit problems experienced by many local firms. In fact, the rescue package provided by the IMF may even have increased the default risk premium because the IMF required that the local banks increase credit standards, which may have made it more difficult for firms in Thailand to obtain funding and pushed them one step closer to bankruptcy. Since the risk-free rate increased and the default risk premium increased, the required rate of return on Thailand's debt securities increased, and prices of debt securities decreased.

Stock prices in Thailand are dependent on the expected cash flows of the firms that issued the stocks and the required rate of return by investors who may invest in them. The expected cash flows for firms in Thailand were reduced because of the weak economy and the limited amount of credit that was being extended. In addition, the increase in interest rates was expected to reduce borrowing because higher rates increase the cost of financing projects and therefore were expected to have an additional adverse effect on economic growth and expected cash flows. The required return on Thailand stocks is generally dependent on the risk-free rate and the stock market risk premium. The risk-free rate had risen as explained earlier, while the stock market risk premium increased because of the increased awareness of poor economic conditions and more uncertainty. Thus, both factors caused a higher required return on stocks. The combination of expectations of reduced cash flows and a higher required rate of return on stocks caused the prices of Thailand stocks to plummet.

The weakness of the stock and debt security markets reduced the wealth of local investors and had an additional adverse effect on the economy. The linkages between the economy, the currency, the stock markets, and the debt markets in Thailand created a cycle of adverse effects, further reducing the confidence of consumers, firms, and investors with every adverse effect.

Exhibit 16A.4 summarizes how the Asian crisis affected the security prices of many other Asian countries. In these countries, as in Thailand, the lack of confidence in a country's financial markets caused foreign investors to flee, which placed downward pressure on the currency's value. The outflow of funds combined with central bank in-

EXHIBIT 16A.4

How Stock Market Levels Changed during the Asian Crisis

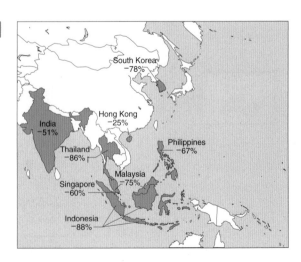

tervention placed upward pressure on interest rates, which increased the required return on investments. In addition, the weak economic conditions and high degree of uncertainty raised the risk premium on investments. Furthermore, the weak economic conditions resulted in lower cash flows for corporations.

Exposure to Capital Flight

Many other Asian countries also experienced weak economies and credit problems and relied heavily on foreign investment to finance growth. Thus, these countries were exposed to the same type of speculative outflows as Thailand. The crisis in Thailand soon infected them.

Some Latin American countries also had weak economies and credit problems, and their currencies were subject to potential depreciation. This scared foreign investors and caused some speculative outflows of funds from these countries as well. Consequently, these countries also experienced an increase in interest rates, which adversely affected the stock and debt security markets.

The impact of the Asian crisis on prices in stock and debt security markets does not imply that every adverse situation will adversely affect all markets simultaneously. It is unusual for an event to cause higher interest rates, default risk premiums, and market risk premiums in one country and simultaneously affect other countries. Nevertheless, an obvious lesson from the Asian crisis is that when countries rely on funding (investments) from foreign investors to support their growth, they are susceptible to the massive withdrawal of that funding if adverse conditions within the country scare investors. Any countries that are exposed to an abrupt outflow of funds are exposed to a potential abrupt increase in interest rates, which can harm stock markets and debt security markets and reduce economic growth.

Degree of Global Integration

The Asian crisis also demonstrated how integrated country economies are, especially during a crisis. Just as the U.S. and European economies can affect emerging markets, they are susceptible to conditions in emerging markets. Even if a central bank can withstand the pressure on its currency that is caused by conditions in other countries, it is not necessarily able to insulate its economy from other countries that are experiencing financial problems.

DISCUSSION QUESTIONS

The following discussion questions related to the Asian crisis illustrate how the foreign exchange market conditions are integrated with the other financial markets around the world. Thus, participants in any of these markets must understand the dynamics of the foreign exchange market. These questions can be used in several ways. They may serve as an assignment on a day that the professor is unable to attend class. They are especially useful for group exercises. The class could be divided into small groups; each group will assess all of the issues and determine a solution. Each group should have a spokesperson. For each issue, one group will be randomly selected and asked to present their solution; then other students not in that group may suggest alternative answers if they feel that the solution can be improved. Some of the issues have no perfect solution, which allows for students to present different points of view.

1. Was the depreciation of the Asian currencies during the Asian crisis due to trade flows or capital flows? Why might the degree of movement over a short period depend on whether the reason is trade flows or capital flows?

2. Why do you think the Indonesian rupiah was more exposed to an abrupt decline in value than the Japanese yen during the Asian crisis (even if the economies of Indonesia and Japan experienced the same degree of weakness)?

3. During the Asian crisis, direct intervention did not prevent depreciation of currencies. Offer your explanation for why the interventions did not work.

4. During the Asian crisis, some local firms in Asia borrowed dollars rather than local currency to support local operations. Why did they borrow dollars when they really needed their local currency to support operations? Why did this strategy backfire?

5. The Asian crisis showed that a currency crisis could affect interest rates. Why did the crisis place upward pressure on interest rates in Asian countries? Why did it place downward pressure on U.S. interest rates?

6. If high interest rates reflect high expected inflation, how would expectations of Asian exchange rates change after interest rates in Asia increased? Why? Is the underlying reason logical?

7. During the Asian crisis, why did the discount on the forward rate of Asian currencies change? Do you think it increased or decreased? Why?

8. During the Asian crisis, the Hong Kong stock market declined substantially over a four-day period due to concerns in the foreign exchange market. Why would stock prices decline due to concerns in the foreign exchange market? Why would some countries be more susceptible to this type of situation than others?

9. On August 26, 1998, when Russia decided to let the ruble float freely, the ruble declined by 50 percent. On the following day, "Bloody Thursday," stock markets around the world (including the U.S. markets) declined by more than 4 percent. Why do you think the decline in the ruble had such a global impact on stock prices? Was the markets' reaction rational? Would the effect have been different if the ruble's plunge had occurred at an earlier time, such as four years earlier? Why?

10. Normally, a weak local currency is expected to stimulate the local economy. Yet, it appears that the weak currencies of Asia adversely affected their economies. Why do you think the weakening of the currencies did not initially improve the countries' economies during the crisis?

11. During the Asian crisis, Hong Kong and China successfully intervened (by raising their interest rates) to protect their local currencies from depreciating. Yet, these countries were also adversely affected by the Asian crisis. Why do you think the actions to protect the values of their currencies affected their economies? Why do you think the weakness of other Asian currencies against the dollar and the stability of the Hong Kong and Chinese currencies against the dollar adversely affected their economies?

12. Why do you think the values of bonds issued by Asian governments declined during the crisis? Why do you think the values of Latin American bonds declined in response to the crisis?

13. Why do you think the depreciation of the Asian currencies adversely affected U.S. firms? (There are at least three reasons, each related to a different type of exposure of some U.S. firms to exchange rate risk.)

14. During the Asian crisis, the currencies of many Asian countries declined even though their respective governments attempted to intervene with direct intervention or by raising interest rates. Given that the abrupt depreciation of currencies was attributed to an abrupt outflow of funds in the financial markets, what alternative action by the Asian governments might have been more successful in preventing a substantial decline in their currency's value? Are there any possible adverse effects of your proposed solution?

Currency Option Pricing

Understanding what drives the premiums paid for currency options makes it easier to recognize the various factors that must be monitored when anticipating future movements in currency option premiums. Since participants in the currency options market typically take positions based on their expectations of how the premiums will change over time, they can benefit from understanding how options are priced.

Boundary Conditions

The first step in pricing currency options is to recognize boundary conditions that force the option premium to be within lower and upper bounds.

Lower Bounds

The call option premium (C) has a lower bound of at least zero or the spread between the underlying spot exchange rate (S) and the exercise price (X), whichever is greater, as shown here:

$$C \geq \text{MAX}(0, S - X)$$

This floor is enforced by arbitrage restrictions. For example, assume that the premium on a British pound call option is $.01, while the spot rate of the pound is $1.62 and the exercise price is $1.60. In this example, the spread ($S - X$) exceeds the call premium, which would allow for arbitrage. One could purchase the call option for $.01 per unit, immediately exercise the option at $1.60 per pound, and then sell the pounds in the spot market for $1.62 per unit. This would generate an immediate profit of $.01 per unit. Arbitrage would continue until the market forces realigned the spread ($S - X$) to be less than or equal to the call premium.

The put option premium (P) has a lower bound of zero or the spread between the exercise price (X) and the underlying spot exchange rate (S), whichever is greater, as shown next:

$$P \geq \text{MAX}(0, X - S)$$

This floor is also enforced by arbitrage restrictions. For example, assume that the premium on a British pound put option is $.02, while the spot rate of the pound is $1.60 and the exercise price is $1.63. One could purchase the pound put option for $.02 per unit, purchase pounds in the spot market at $1.60, and immediately exercise the option by selling the pounds at $1.63 per unit. This would generate an immediate profit of $.01

per unit. Arbitrage would continue until the market forces realigned the spread $(X - S)$ to be less than or equal to the put premium.

Upper Bounds

The upper bound for a call option premium is equal to the spot exchange rate (S), as shown:

$$C \leq S$$

If the call option premium ever exceeds the spot exchange rate, one could engage in arbitrage by selling call options for a higher price per unit than the cost of purchasing the underlying currency. Even if those call options were exercised, one could provide the currency that was purchased earlier (the call option was covered). The arbitrage profit in this example would be the difference between the amount received when selling (which is the premium) and the cost of purchasing the currency in the spot market. Arbitrage would occur until the call option's premium was less than or equal to the spot rate.

The upper bound for a put option is equal to the option's exercise price (X), as shown here:

$$P \leq X$$

If the put option premium ever exceeds the exercise price, one could engage in arbitrage by selling put options. Even if the put options were exercised, the proceeds received from selling the put options would exceed the price paid (which is the exercise price) at the time of exercise.

Given these boundaries that are enforced by arbitrage, option premiums lie within these boundaries.

Application of Pricing Models

Although boundary conditions can be used to determine the possible range for a currency option's premium, they do not precisely indicate the appropriate premium for the option. However, pricing models have been developed to price currency options. Based on information about an option (such as the exercise price and time to maturity) and about the currency (such as its spot rate, standard deviation, and interest rate), pricing models can derive the premium on a currency option. The currency option pricing model of Biger and Hull (1983) is

$$C = e^{-R_f^* T} S \cdot N(d_1) - e^{-R_f T} X \cdot N(d_1 - \sigma \sqrt{T})$$

where $d_1 = \{[ln(S/X) + (R_f - R_f^* + (\sigma^2/2))T]/\sigma\sqrt{T}\}$

C = price of the currency call option

S = underlying spot exchange rate

X = exercise price

R_f = U.S. riskless rate of interest

R_f^* = foreign riskless rate of interest

σ = instantaneous standard deviation of the return on a holding of foreign currency

T = time to option maturity expressed as a fraction of a year

$N(.)$ = standard normal cumulative distribution function

This equation is based on the stock option pricing model (OPM) when allowing for continuous dividends. Since the interest gained on holding a foreign security (R_f^*) is equivalent to a continuously paid dividend on a stock share, this version of the OPM holds completely. The key transformation in adapting the stock OPM to value currency options is the substitution of exchange rates for stock prices. Thus, the percentage change of exchange rates is assumed to follow a diffusion process with constant mean and variance.

Bodurtha and Courtadon (1987)[1] have tested the predictive ability of the currency option pricing model. They computed pricing errors from the model using 3,326 call options. The model's average percentage pricing error for call options was −6.90 percent, which is smaller than the corresponding error reported for the dividend-adjusted Black-Scholes stock OPM. Hence, the currency option pricing model has been more accurate than the counterpart stock OPM.

The model developed by Biger and Hull is sometimes referred to as the European model because it does not account for early exercise.[2] Unlike American currency options, European currency options do not allow for early exercise (before the expiration date). The extra flexibility of American currency options may justify a higher premium than on European currency options with similar characteristics. However, there is not a closed-form model for pricing American currency options. Although various techniques are used to price American currency options, the European model is commonly applied to price American currency options because it can be just as accurate. Bodurtha and Courtadon (1987) found that the application of an American currency option pricing model does not improve predictive accuracy. Their average percentage pricing error was −7.07 percent for all sample call options when using the American model.

Given all other parameters, the currency option pricing model can be used to impute the standard deviation σ. This implied parameter represents the option's market assessment of currency volatility over the life of the option.

Pricing Currency Put Options According to Put-Call Parity

Given the premium of a European call option (C), the premium for a European put option (P) on the same currency and same exercise price (X) can be derived from put-call parity as follows:

$$P = C + Xe^{-R_f T} - Se^{-R_f^* T}$$

where R_f is the riskless rate of interest, R_f^* is the foreign rate of interest, and T is the option's time to maturity expressed as a fraction of the year. If the actual put option premium is less than is suggested by the put-call parity equation just shown, arbitrage can be conducted. Specifically, one could (1) buy the put option, (2) sell the call option, and (3) buy the underlying currency. The purchases would be financed with the proceeds from selling the call option and from borrowing at the rate R_f. Meanwhile, the foreign currency that was purchased can be deposited to earn the foreign rate R_f^*. Regardless of the scenario for the path of the currency's exchange rate movement over the life of the option, the arbitrage will result in a profit. First, if the exchange rate is equal to the exercise price such that each option expires worthless, the foreign currency can be converted in the spot market to dollars, and this amount will exceed the amount required to repay the loan. Second, if the foreign currency appreciates and therefore exceeds the

[1] James N. Bodurtha, Jr., and George R. Courtadon, "Efficiency Tests of the Foreign Currency Options Market," *Journal of Finance* (March 1987): 151–161.
[2] Nahum Biger and John Hull, "The Valuation of Currency Options," *Financial Management* (Spring 1983): 24–28.

exercise price, there will be a loss from the call option being exercised. Although the put option would expire, the foreign currency would be converted in the spot market to dollars, and this amount will exceed the amount required to repay the loan and the amount of the loss on the call option. Third, if the foreign currency depreciates and therefore is below the exercise price, the amount received from selling the put option plus the amount received from converting the foreign currency to dollars will exceed the amount required to repay the loan. Since the arbitrage generates a profit under any exchange rate scenario, it will force an adjustment in the option premiums so that put-call parity is no longer violated.

If the actual put option premium is more than is suggested by put-call parity, arbitrage would again be possible. The arbitrage strategy would be the reverse of that used when the actual put option premium is less than suggested by put-call parity (as just described). The arbitrage would force an adjustment in option premiums so that put-call parity is no longer violated. The arbitrage that can be applied when there is a violation of put-call parity on American currency options differs slightly from the arbitrage applicable to European currency options. Nevertheless, the concept still holds that the premium of a currency put option can be determined according to the premium of a call option on the same currency and the same exercise price.

Part V Integrative Problem

Choosing among Derivative Securities

This problem requires an understanding of futures contracts (Chapter 13), options markets (Chapter 14), interest rate swap markets (Chapter 15), and foreign exchange derivative markets (Chapter 16). It also requires an understanding of how economic conditions affect interest rates and security prices.

Assume that the United States just experienced a mild recession. As a result, interest rates have declined to their lowest levels in a decade. The U.S. interest rates appear to be influenced more by changes in the demand for funds than by changes in the supply of U.S. savings, because the savings rate does not change much regardless of economic conditions. The yield curve is currently flat. The federal budget deficit has improved lately and is not expected to rise substantially.

The federal government recently decided to reduce personal tax rates significantly for all tax brackets as well as corporate tax rates. The U.S. dollar has just recently weakened. Economies of other countries were somewhat stagnant but have improved in the past quarter. Your assignment is to recommend how various financial institutions should respond to the preceding information.

Questions

1 A savings institution holds 50 percent of its assets as long-term fixed-rate mortgages. Virtually all of its funds are in the form of short-term deposits. Which of the following strategies would be most appropriate for this institution?

- Use a fixed-for-floating swap.
- Use a swap of floating payments for fixed payments.
- Use a put option on interest rate futures contracts.
- Remain unhedged.

Defend your recommendation.

2 An insurance company maintains a large portfolio of U.S. stocks. Which of the following would be most appropriate?

- Sell stock index futures contracts.
- Remain unhedged.

Defend your recommendation.

3 A pension fund maintains a large bond portfolio of U.S. bonds. Which of the following would be most appropriate?

- Sell bond index futures.
- Buy bond index futures.
- Remain unhedged.

Defend your recommendation.

4   An international mutual fund sponsored by a U.S. securities firm consists of bonds evenly allocated across the United States and the United Kingdom. One of the portfolio managers has decided to hedge all the assets by selling futures on a popular U.S. bond index. The manager has stated that because the fund concentrates only on risk-free Treasury bonds, the only concern is interest rate risk. Assuming that interest rate risk is the only risk of concern, will the hedge described above be effective? Why? Is there any other risk that deserves to be considered? If so, how would you hedge that risk?

PART VI

Commercial Banking

The chapters in Part VI focus on commercial banking. Chapter 17 identifies the common sources and uses of funds for commercial banks, and Chapter 18 describes the regulations imposed on sources and uses of funds and other banking operations. Chapter 19 explains how banks manage their sources and uses of funds to deal with risk. Chapter 20 explains how commercial bank performance can be measured and monitored to assess previous managerial policies.

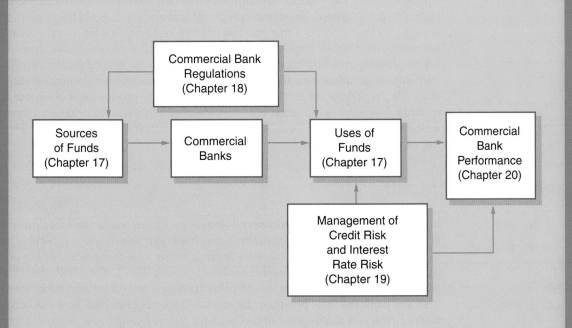

CHAPTER 17

Commercial Bank Operations

M easured by total assets, commercial banks are the most important type of financial intermediary. Like other financial intermediaries, they perform a critical function of facilitating the flow of funds from surplus units to deficit units.

The specific objectives of this chapter are to:

- describe the most common sources of funds for commercial banks,

- explain the most common uses of funds for commercial banks, and

- describe typical off-balance sheet activities for commercial banks.

Commercial Banks as Financial Intermediaries

Up to this point, the text has focused on the role and functions of financial markets. From this point forward, the emphasis is on the role and functions of financial institutions. Recall from Chapter 1 that financial institutions commonly serve as the financial intermediaries between surplus units and deficit units. Commercial banks represent a key financial intermediary because they serve all types of surplus and deficit units. They offer deposit accounts with the size and maturity characteristics desired by surplus units. They repackage the funds received from deposits to provide loans of the size and maturity desired by deficit units. They have the ability to assess the creditworthiness of deficit units that apply for loans, so that they can limit their exposure to credit (default) risk on the loans they provide.

Bank Market Structure

In 1985, more than 14,000 banks were located in the United States. Since then, the market structure has changed dramatically. Banks have been consolidating for several reasons. One reason is that interstate banking regulations were changed in 1994 to allow banks more freedom to acquire other banks across state lines. Consequently, banks in a particular region are now subject to competition not only from other local banks but also from any bank that may penetrate that market. This has prompted banks to become more efficient as a means of survival. They have pursued growth as a means of capitalizing on economies of scale (lower average costs for larger scales of operations) and enhanced efficiency. Acquisitions have been a convenient method to grow quickly.

EXHIBIT 17.1   Consolidation among Commercial Banks over Time

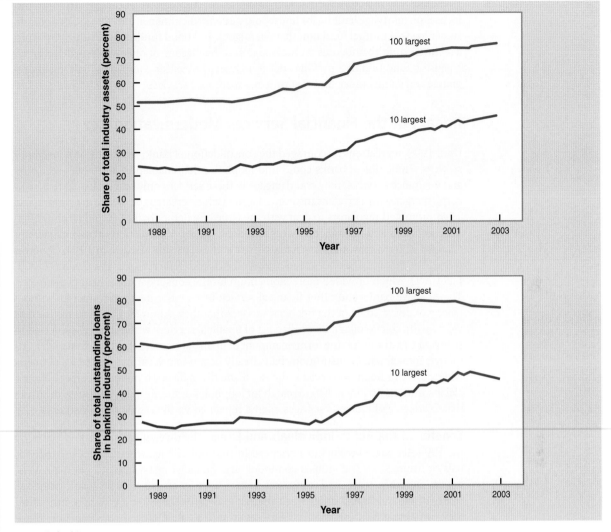

Source: Federal Reserve

As a result of this trend, there are only about half as many banks today as there were in 1985, and consolidation is still occurring. Exhibit 17.1 shows how the banking industry has become more concentrated. The top graph in the exhibit shows how the largest banks have substantially increased their market share over time. The largest 100 banks now account for about 75 percent of all bank assets versus about 50 percent in 1985. The lower graph in the exhibit shows how the largest banks have increased their market share of total commercial and industrial loans.

Bank Participation in Financial Conglomerates

Commercial banks have expanded not only by acquiring other banks but also by acquiring other types of financial service firms. They have also diversified their services by creating new subsidiaries (or units) that perform additional services or by merging with other types of financial institutions. The result has been the creation of financial conglomerates,

composed of various units offering specialized services. For example, a financial conglomerate may include a bank unit that focuses on commercial lending, a thrift unit that focuses on mortgage lending for households, a consumer finance unit that focuses on consumer loans, a mutual fund unit that offers stock and bond funds to individual investors, a securities unit that focuses on brokerage and the placement of newly issued securities, a pension fund unit that provides portfolio management for companies' retirement programs, and an insurance unit that provides insurance services.

Impact of the Financial Services Modernization Act

Until 1999, regulations discouraged the consolidation of bank, securities, and insurance services. Thus, unless banks could find loopholes that enabled them to offer securities and insurance services, they could engage in these services only to a limited extent. Citicorp's merger with Traveler's Insurance Group (which created the new firm Citigroup) in 1998 prompted regulators to deal with the issue of whether banks should be allowed to offer securities and insurance services to a larger degree. If regulations had remained unchanged, Citigroup would have had to divest some of its subsidiaries. In 1999, Congress passed the Financial Services Modernization Act (also referred to as the Gramm-Leach-Bliley Act), which provided more momentum for the consolidation of financial services. The Act gave banks and other financial service firms more freedom to merge, without having to divest some of the financial services that they acquired. Financial institutions were finally able to offer a diversified set of financial services without being subjected to stringent constraints on the form or amount of financial services that they could offer. Although some financial institutions had already begun to use various loopholes to offer a wide variety of financial services, the Act made diversification more convenient. Financial institutions no longer had to search for loopholes or monitor their business to ensure that the degree of financial services offered remained within regulatory constraints.

Benefits of the Act to Individuals and Firms The diversification made possible by the 1999 Act offers benefits to a financial institution's clients, whether they are individuals or firms. Since individuals commonly use financial institutions to place deposits, obtain mortgage loans and consumer loans (such as an automobile loan), purchase shares of mutual funds, order stock transactions (brokerage), and purchase insurance, they can obtain all their financial services from a single financial conglomerate. Since firms commonly use financial institutions to maintain a business checking account, obtain loans, issue stocks or bonds, have their pension fund managed, and purchase insurance services, they can receive all of their financial services from a single financial conglomerate. Some financial conglomerates can provide virtually every financial service that individuals or firms might desire. Other financial conglomerates specialize in the services desired by a particular type of client, such as individuals or large firms.

Benefits of the Act to Financial Institutions Diversification also offers benefits to financial institutions. By offering more diversified services, financial institutions can reduce their reliance on the demand for any single service that they offer. This diversification may result in less risk for the institution's consolidated business, assuming that the new services are not subject to a much higher degree of risk than its traditional services. A recent annual report of Bank of America summarized this concept:

> 66 *To further diversify risk, Bank of America continues to diversify its revenue stream—complementing the deposit and lending base by increasing income from value-added fee-based services our customers want.* 99

The individual units of a financial conglomerate may generate some new business simply because they are part of the conglomerate and offer convenience to clients who already rely on its other services. Each financial unit's list of existing clients represents a potential source of new clients for the other financial units to pursue.

The operations, management, and regulation of a financial conglomerate vary with the types of services offered. Therefore, the different types of financial services (such as banking, securities, and insurance) are discussed in separate chapters. This chapter on commercial bank operations applies to both independent commercial banks and commercial bank units that are part of a financial conglomerate.

Whether they are independent or part of a financial conglomerate, commercial banks play an important role in facilitating the flow of funds through financial markets. They serve individuals by offering various types of deposit accounts and financial services. They channel funds to corporations by providing commercial loans. Their primary operations can be most easily identified by reviewing their main sources of funds, their main uses of funds, and the off-balance sheet activities that they provide, as explained in this chapter.

Bank Sources of Funds

http://

http://www.fdic.gov
Statistics on bank sources
and uses of funds.

To understand how any financial institution (or subsidiary of the institution) obtains funds and uses funds, its balance sheet can be reviewed. Its reported liabilities and equity indicate its sources of funds, while its reported assets indicate its uses of funds. The major sources of commercial bank funds are summarized as follows:

Deposit Accounts
1. Transaction deposits
2. Savings deposits
3. Time deposits
4. Money market deposit accounts

Borrowed Funds
1. Federal funds purchased (borrowed)
2. Borrowing from the Federal Reserve banks
3. Repurchase agreements
4. Eurodollar borrowings

Long-Term Sources of Funds
1. Bonds issued by the bank
2. Bank capital

Each source of funds is briefly described in the following subsections.

Transaction Deposits

A **demand deposit account,** or checking account, is offered to customers who desire to write checks against their account. A conventional demand deposit account requires a small minimum balance and pays no interest. From the bank's perspective, demand deposit accounts are classified as transaction accounts that provide a source of funds that can be used until withdrawn by customers (as checks are written).

Another type of transaction deposit is the **negotiable order of withdrawal (NOW) account,** which provides checking services as well as interest. Since 1981, commercial

banks and other depository institutions throughout the entire country have been allowed to offer these accounts. Because NOW accounts at most financial institutions require a larger minimum balance than some consumers are willing to maintain in a transaction account, traditional demand deposit accounts are still popular.

Electronic Transactions Some transactions originating from transaction accounts have become much more efficient as a result of electronic banking. About two-thirds of all employees in the United States have direct deposit accounts, which allow their paychecks to be directly deposited to their transaction account (or other accounts). Most Social Security recipients have their checks directly deposited to their bank accounts. Computer banking enables bank customers to view their bank accounts online, pay bills, make credit card payments, order more checks, and transfer funds between accounts.

More than 60 percent of bank customers can use automated teller machines (ATMs) to make withdrawals from their transaction accounts, add deposits, check account balances, and transfer funds. ATMs are available around the world and enable customers to access cash in foreign currency. The customer's account balance is then reduced by an amount that reflects the prevailing exchange rate. In essence, customers can obtain foreign currencies at any time and generally at a more favorable exchange rate than if they used the retail foreign exchange shops that are located in many countries.

Debit cards allow bank customers to use a card to make purchases and have their bank account debited to reflect the amount spent. Banks also allow preauthorized debits, in which specific periodic payments are automatically transferred from a customer's bank account to a particular recipient. Preauthorized debits are commonly used to cover monthly utility bills, car loan payments, and mortgage payments.

Savings Deposits

The traditional savings account is the passbook savings account, which does not permit check writing. Until 1986, Regulation Q restricted the interest rate banks could offer on passbook savings. The idea was to prevent excessive competition that could cause bank failures, but in actuality, the ceilings prevented commercial banks from competing for funds during periods of higher interest rates. In 1986, Regulation Q was eliminated. Passbook savings accounts continue to attract savers with a small amount of funds, as such accounts often have no required minimum balance. Although legally customers are required to provide a 30-day written notice to withdraw funds, most banks will allow withdrawals from these accounts on a moment's notice.

Another type of savings account is the **automatic transfer service (ATS)** account, created in November 1978. It allows customers to maintain an interest-bearing savings account that automatically transfers funds to their checking account when checks are written. Only the amount of funds needed is transferred to the checking account. Thus, the ATS provides interest and check-writing ability to customers. Some ATS accounts were eliminated when NOW accounts were established.

Time Deposits

Time deposits are deposits that cannot be withdrawn until a specified maturity date. Although savings deposits are sometimes classified as time deposits because of the legal 30-day notice described above, they are treated separately here because the 30-day no-

tice normally is not enforced. The two most common types of time deposits are certificates of deposit (CDs) and negotiable certificates of deposit.

Certificates of Deposit A common type of time deposit known as a retail **certificate of deposit** (or retail **CD**) requires a specified minimum amount of funds to be deposited for a specified period of time. Banks offer a wide variety of CDs to satisfy depositors' needs. Annualized interest rates offered on CDs vary among banks, and even among maturity types at a single bank. There is no organized secondary market for retail CDs. Depositors must leave their funds in the bank until the specified maturity, or they will normally forgo a portion of their interest as a penalty.

CD rates are easily accessible on numerous websites. For example, Bank-Rate (http://www.bankrate.com) and Bank CD-Rate Scanner (http://www.bankcd.com) identify banks that are paying the highest rates on CDs at any point in time. Because of easy access to CD rate information online, many depositors invest in CDs at banks far away to earn a higher rate than that offered by local banks. Some banks allow depositors to invest in CDs online by providing a credit card number.

The interest rates on retail CDs have historically been fixed. In recent years, however, more exotic retail CDs have been offered. There are **bull-market CDs** that reward depositors if the market performs well and **bear-market CDs** that reward depositors if the market performs poorly. These new types of retail CDs typically require a minimum deposit of $1,000 to $5,000. Like more conventional CDs, they qualify for deposit insurance (assuming that the depository institution of concern is insured).

In recent years, some financial institutions have begun to offer CDs with a callable feature (referred to as **callable CDs**). That is, they can be called by the financial institution, forcing an earlier maturity. For example, a bank could issue a callable CD with a five-year maturity, callable after two years. In two years, the financial instituion will likely call the CD if it can obtain funds at a lower rate over the following three years than the rate paid on that CD. Depositors who invest in callable CDs earn a slightly higher interest rate, which compensates them for the risk that the CD may be called.

Negotiable Certificates of Deposit Another type of time deposit is the **negotiable CD (NCD),** offered by some large banks to corporations. NCDs are similar to retail CDs in that they require a specified maturity date and require a minimum deposit. Their maturities are typically short term, and their minimum deposit requirement is $100,000. A secondary market for NCDs does exist.

The level of large time deposits is much more volatile than that of small time deposits, because investors with large sums of money frequently shift their funds to wherever they can earn higher rates. Small investors do not have as many options as large investors and are less likely to shift in and out of small time deposits.

Money Market Deposit Accounts

Money market deposit accounts (MMDAs) were created by a provision of the Garn–St Germain Act of December 1982. They differ from conventional time deposits in that they do not specify a maturity. MMDAs are more liquid than retail CDs from the depositor's point of view. Because banks prefer to know how long they will have the use of a depositor's funds, they normally pay a higher interest rate on CDs. MMDAs differ from NOW accounts in that they provide limited check-writing ability (they allow only

a limited number of transactions per month), require a larger minimum balance, and offer a higher yield.

The remaining sources of funds to be described are of a nondepository nature. Such sources are necessary when a bank temporarily needs more funds than are being deposited. Some banks use nondepository funds as a permanent source of funds.

Federal Funds Purchased

The federal funds market allows depository institutions to accommodate the short-term liquidity needs of other financial institutions. Federal funds purchased (or borrowed) represent a liability to the borrowing bank and an asset to the lending bank that sells them. Loans in the federal funds market are typically for one to seven days. Such loans can be rolled over so that a series of one-day loans can take place. The intent of federal funds transactions is to correct short-term fund imbalances experienced by banks. A bank may act as a lender of federal funds on one day and as a borrower shortly thereafter, as its fund balance changes on a daily basis.

The interest rate charged in the federal funds market is called the **federal funds rate.** Like other market interest rates, it moves in reaction to changes in demand or supply or both. If many banks have excess funds and few banks are short of funds, the federal funds rate will be low. Conversely, a high demand by many banks to borrow federal funds relative to a small supply of excess funds available at other banks will result in a higher federal funds rate. Whatever rate exists will typically be the same for all banks borrowing in the federal funds market, although a financially troubled bank may have to pay a higher rate to obtain federal funds (to compensate for its higher risk). The federal funds rate is quoted in multiples of one-sixteenth, on an annualized basis (using a 360-day year). The federal funds rate is generally between .25 percent and 1.00 percent above the Treasury bill rate. The difference increases when the perceived risk of banks increases.

The federal funds market is typically most active on Wednesday, because that is the final day of each particular settlement period for which each bank must maintain a specified volume of reserves required by the Fed. Banks that were short of required reserves on average over the period must compensate with additional required reserves before the settlement period ends. Large banks frequently need temporary funds and therefore are common borrowers in the federal funds market.

Borrowing from Federal Reserve Banks

Another temporary source of funds for banks is the Federal Reserve System, which serves as the U.S. central bank. Along with other bank regulators, the Federal Reserve district banks regulate certain activities of banks. They also provide short-term loans to banks (as well as to some other depository institutions). This form of borrowing by banks is often referred to as borrowing at the discount window. The interest rate charged on these loans is known as the **discount rate.**

As of January 2003, the discount rate was to be set at a level above the federal funds rate at any point in time. This was intended to ensure that banks rely on the federal funds market for normal short-term financing, and use the discount window as a last resort.

Loans from the discount window are short term, commonly from one day to a few weeks. To ensure that the need for funds is justified, banks that wish to borrow at the discount window must first obtain the Fed's approval. Like the federal funds market, the discount window is mainly used to resolve a temporary shortage of funds. If a bank

needs more permanent sources of funds, it will develop a strategy to increase its level of deposits.

The discount window is intended to be a source of funds for banks that experience unanticipated shortages of reserves. Frequent borrowing to offset reserve shortages implies that the bank has a permanent rather than a temporary need for funds and should therefore satisfy this need with a more permanent source of funds. The Fed may disapprove of continuous borrowing by a bank unless there are extenuating circumstances, such as that the bank was experiencing financial problems and could not obtain temporary financing from other financial institutions.

Repurchase Agreements

A **repurchase agreement (repo)** represents the sale of securities by one party to another with an agreement to repurchase the securities at a specified date and price. Banks often use a repo as a source of funds when they expect to need funds for just a few days. The bank simply sells some of its government securities (such as Treasury bills) to a corporation with a temporary excess of funds and buys those securities back shortly thereafter. The government securities involved in the repo transaction serve as collateral for the corporation providing funds to the bank.

Repurchase agreement transactions occur through a telecommunications network connecting large banks, other corporations, government securities dealers, and federal funds brokers. The federal funds brokers match up firms or dealers that need funds (wish to sell and later repurchase their securities) with those that have excess funds (are willing to purchase securities now and sell them back on a specified date). Transactions are typically in blocks of $1 million. Like the federal funds rate, the yield on repurchase agreements is quoted in multiples of one-sixteenth on an annualized basis (using a 360-day year). The yield on repurchase agreements is slightly less than the federal funds rate at any given point in time, because the funds loaned out are backed by collateral and are therefore less risky.

Eurodollar Borrowings

If a U.S. bank is in need of short-term funds, it may borrow dollars from those banks outside the United States that accept dollar-denominated deposits, or **Eurodollars.** Some of these so-called Eurobanks are foreign banks or foreign branches of U.S. banks that participate in the Eurodollar market by accepting large short-term deposits and making short-term loans in dollars. Because U.S. dollars are widely used as an international medium of exchange, the Eurodollar market is very active. Some large U.S. banks commonly obtain short-term funds from Eurodollar deposits.

Bonds Issued by Banks

Like other corporations, banks own some fixed assets such as land, buildings, and equipment. These assets often have an expected life of 20 years or more and are usually financed with long-term sources of funds, such as through the issuance of bonds. Common purchasers of such bonds are households and various financial institutions, including life insurance companies and pension funds. Banks do not finance with bonds as much as most other corporations, because they have fewer fixed assets than corporations

that use industrial equipment and machinery for production. Therefore, banks have less need for long-term funds.

Bank Capital

Bank capital generally represents funds attained through the issuance of stock or through retaining earnings. With either form, the bank has no obligation to pay out funds in the future. This distinguishes bank capital from all the other sources of funds, which represent a future obligation by the bank to pay out funds. Bank capital as defined here represents the equity or net worth of the bank. Capital can be classified as primary or secondary. Primary capital results from issuing common or preferred stock or retaining earnings, while secondary capital results from issuing subordinated notes and bonds.

A bank's capital must be sufficient to absorb operating losses in the event that expenses or losses exceed revenues, regardless of the reason for the losses. Although long-term bonds are sometimes considered to be secondary capital, they are a liability to the bank and therefore do not appropriately cushion against operating losses.

The issuance of new stock dilutes the ownership of the bank because the proportion of the bank owned by existing shareholders decreases. In addition, the bank's reported earnings per share are reduced when additional shares of stock are issued, unless earnings increase by a greater proportion than the increase in outstanding shares. For these reasons, banks generally attempt to avoid issuing new stock unless absolutely necessary.

Bank regulators are concerned that banks may maintain a lower level of capital than they should and have therefore imposed capital requirements on them. Because capital can absorb losses, a higher level of capital is thought to enhance a bank's safety and may increase the public's confidence in the banking system. In 1981, regulators imposed a minimum primary capital requirement of 5.5 percent of total assets and a minimum total capital requirement of 6 percent of total assets. Because of regulatory pressure, banks have increased their capital ratios in recent years.

In 1988, regulators imposed new risk-based capital requirements that were completely phased in by 1992. Under this system, the required level of capital for each bank is dependent on its risk. Assets with low risk are assigned relatively low weights, and assets with high risk are assigned high weights. The capital level is set as a percentage of the risk-weighted assets. Therefore, riskier banks are subject to higher capital requirements. The same risk-based capital guidelines have been imposed in several other industrialized countries. Additional details are provided in the next chapter.

Summary of Bank Sources of Funds

Because banks cannot completely control the amount of deposits they receive, they may experience a shortage of funds. For this reason, the nondepository sources of funds are useful. To support the acquisition of fixed assets, long-term funds are obtained by issuing long-term bonds, issuing stock, or retaining a sufficient amount of earnings.

Exhibit 17.2 shows the distribution of fund sources. Transaction and savings deposits make up 54 percent of all bank liabilities. The distribution of bank sources of funds is influenced by bank size. Smaller banks rely more heavily on savings deposits than larger banks do because small banks concentrate on household savings and therefore on small deposits. Much of this differential is made up in large time deposits (such as NCDs) for very large banks. In addition, the larger banks rely more on short-term borrowings than do small banks. The impact of the differences in composition of fund sources on bank performance is discussed in Chapter 20.

EXHIBIT 17.2

Bank Sources of Funds (as a
Proportion of Total
Liabilities)

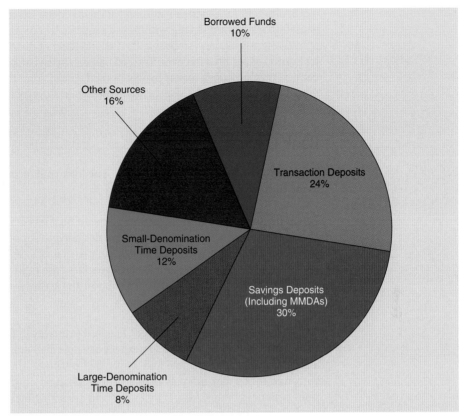

Source: Federal Reserve, 2004

Uses of Funds by Banks

Having identified the main sources of funds, bank uses of funds can be discussed. The
more common uses of funds by banks include the following:

- Cash
- Bank loans
- Investment in securities
- Federal funds sold (loaned out)
- Repurchase agreements
- Eurodollar loans
- Fixed assets

Cash

Banks must hold some cash as reserves to meet the reserve requirements enforced by the
Federal Reserve. Banks also hold cash to maintain some liquidity and accommodate any
withdrawal requests by depositors. Because banks do not earn income from cash, they
hold only as much cash as is necessary to maintain a sufficient degree of liquidity. They
can tap various sources for temporary funds and therefore are not overly concerned with
maintaining excess reserves.

Banks hold cash in their vaults and at their Federal Reserve district bank. Vault cash is useful for accommodating withdrawal requests by customers or for qualifying as required reserves, while cash held at the Federal Reserve district banks represents the major portion of required reserves. The Fed mandates that banks maintain required reserves because they provide a means by which the Fed can control the money supply. The required reserves of each bank depend on the composition of its deposits.

Bank Loans

The main use of bank funds is for loans. The loan amount and maturity can be tailored to the borrower's needs.

Types of Business Loans A common type of business loan is the **working capital loan** (sometimes called a self-liquidating loan), designed to support ongoing business operations. There is a lag between the time when a firm needs cash to purchase raw materials used in production and the time when it receives cash inflows from the sales of finished products. A working capital loan can support the business until sufficient cash inflows are generated. These loans are typically short term, but they may be needed by businesses on a frequent basis.

Banks also offer **term loans,** which are used primarily to finance the purchase of fixed assets such as machinery. With a term loan, a specified amount of funds is loaned out, for a specified period of time and a specified purpose. The assets purchased with the borrowed funds may serve as partial or full collateral on the loan. Maturities on term loans commonly range from 2 to 5 years and are sometimes as long as 10 years.

Because term loans are long term, the loan agreement may specify conditions by which the borrower must abide. These conditions, often referred to as **protective covenants,** may specify a maximum level of dividends that the borrower can pay to shareholders per year, require bank approval on some of the borrowing firm's major decisions (such as mergers), and limit the additional debt that the firm can accumulate. Term loans can be amortized so that the borrower makes fixed periodic payments over the life of the loan. Alternatively, the bank can periodically request interest payments, with the loan principal to be paid off in one lump sum (called a **balloon payment**) at a specified date in the future. This is known as a **bullet loan.** Several combinations of these payment methods are also possible. For example, a portion of the loan may be amortized over the life of the loan, while the remaining portion is covered with a balloon payment.

As an alternative to providing a term loan, the bank may consider purchasing the assets and leasing them to the firm in need. This method, known as a **direct lease loan,** may be especially appropriate when the firm wishes to avoid adding more debt to its balance sheet. Because the bank is the owner of the assets, it can depreciate them over time for tax purposes.

A more flexible financing arrangement is the **informal line of credit,** which allows the business to borrow up to a specified amount within a specified period of time. This is useful for firms that may experience a sudden need for funds but do not know precisely when. The interest rate charged on any borrowed funds is typically adjustable in accordance with prevailing market rates. Banks are not legally obligated to provide funds to the business, but they usually honor the arrangement to avoid harming their reputation.

An alternative to the informal line of credit is the **revolving credit loan,** which obligates the bank to offer up to some specified maximum amount of funds over a specified period of time (typically less than five years). Because the bank is committed to provide

EXHIBIT 17.3 Prime Rate over Time

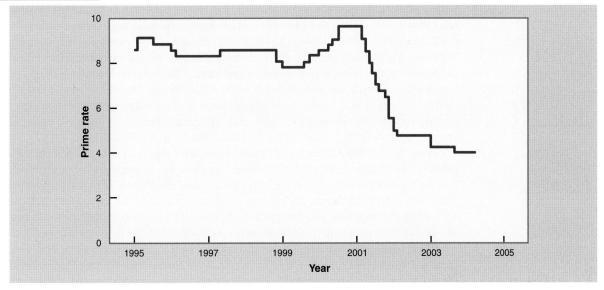

Source: Federal Reserve

funds when requested, it normally charges businesses a commitment fee (of about one-half of 1 percent) on any unused funds.

The interest rate charged by banks on loans to their most creditworthy customers is known as the **prime rate.** Banks periodically revise the prime rate in response to changes in market interest rates, which reflect changes in the bank's cost of funds. Thus, the prime rate moves in tandem with the Treasury bill rate. The prime rate in recent years is shown in Exhibit 17.3. Notice that it increased in the late 1990s when interest rates were rising. Then, in 2001, it declined in response to the weak economy as the demand for loanable funds decreased and the Fed took actions to reduce the federal funds rate. Thus, the prime rate tends to adjust in response to changes in other interest rates that influence the bank's cost of funds. When economic conditions are weak, however, the spread between the prime rate and the bank's cost of funds tends to widen because banks require a higher premium to compensate for credit risk.

Loan Participations Some large corporations wish to borrow a larger amount of funds than any individual bank is willing to provide. To accommodate a corporation, several banks may be willing to pool their available funds in what is referred to as a **loan partic-ipation.** Loan participations can take various forms, but in the most common form, one of the banks serves as the lead bank by arranging for the documentation, disbursement, and payment structure of the loan. The main role of the other banks is to supply funds that are channeled to the borrower by the lead bank. The borrower may not even real-ize that much of the funds have been provided by other banks. As interest payments are received, the lead bank passes the payments on to the other participants in proportion to the original loan amounts they provided. The lead bank receives fees for servicing the loan in addition to its share of interest payments.

The lead bank is expected to ensure that the borrower repays the loan. Normally, however, the lead bank is not required to guarantee the interest payments. Thus, all par-ticipating banks are exposed to credit (default) risk.

Loans Supporting Leveraged Buyouts Some commercial banks finance leveraged buyouts (LBOs). The loan amount provided by a single bank to support an LBO is usually between $15 million and $40 million. The exposure of some large commercial banks to LBO loans exceeds $1 billion. An attractive feature of LBO financing is the relatively high loan rate that can be charged. In addition, some fee income can be generated from the administrative services performed by commercial banks when financing LBOs.

In a sense, financing part of an LBO is no different than financing other privately held businesses. These businesses are highly leveraged and experience cash flow pressure during periods where sales are lower than normal. Their high degree of financial leverage causes cash outflows to be somewhat sensitive to business cycles.

Firms request LBO financing because they perceive that the market value of certain publicly held shares is too low. It is desirable that these firms have access to equity funds because it can serve as a cushion under poor economic conditions. Although these firms prefer not to go public again during such conditions, they are at least capable of doing so. Banks financing these firms can, as a condition of the loan, require that the firms reissue stock if they experience cash flow problems.

Many firms involved in LBOs are diversified conglomerates that will be split into various divisions and sold. This may enable banks to spread their lending base by lending to divisions that have been sold. Businesses may be separated if the sum of the parts appears to be worth more than the whole. A conglomerate could absorb the failure of a single division, however, whereas if the division is independent, its failure is absorbed by its creditors.

A commercial bank's risk may rise as it increases its financing of LBOs. Banks that reduce their more conservative assets to finance LBOs incur a higher degree of risk. Many LBOs were financed with junk bonds, which suggests a high degree of risk. Thus, banks could be incurring the same risk as if they had purchased junk bonds. With LBO financing, however, the bank-borrower relationship may allow for more personalized guidance of firms experiencing financial problems. In addition, banks may have first claim to the firm's assets if the firm fails. Thus, these bank loans are considered to be less risky.

Some banks originate the loans designed for LBOs and then sell them to other financial institutions, such as insurance companies, pension funds, and foreign banks. In this way, they can generate fee income by servicing the loans while avoiding the credit risk associated with the loans.

Bank regulators now monitor the amount of bank financing provided to corporate borrowers that have a relatively high degree of financial leverage. These loans, known as **highly leveraged transactions (HLTs),** are defined by the Federal Reserve as credit that results in a debt-to-asset ratio of at least 75 percent. In other words, the level of debt is at least three times the level of equity. About 60 percent of HLT funds are used to finance LBOs, while some of the funds are used to repurchase only a portion of the outstanding stock. HLTs are usually originated by a large commercial bank, which provides 10 to 20 percent of the financing itself. Other financial institutions participate by providing the remaining 80 to 90 percent of the funds needed.

Collateral Requirements on Business Loans Commercial banks are increasingly accepting intangible assets (such as patents, brand names, and licenses to franchises and distributorships) as collateral for commercial loans. This change is especially important to service-oriented companies that do not have tangible assets.

Lender Liability on Business Loans In recent years, businesses that previously obtained loans from banks are filing lawsuits, claiming that the banks terminated further

EXHIBIT 17.4 Volume of Business Loans Provided by Commercial Banks

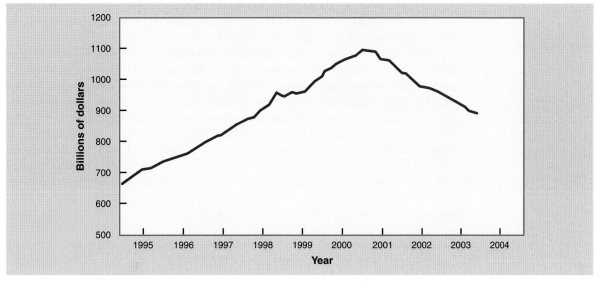

Source: Federal Reserve

financing without sufficient notice. These so-called lender liability suits have been prevalent in the farming industry. Some farmers have claimed that banks encouraged them to borrow and then refused to provide the additional financing necessary to make their projects successful. As a result, the farmers lost the land and equipment used as collateral. Lender liability lawsuits have also been filed by companies in other industries, including the grocery, clothing, and oil industries.

Volume of Business Loans Exhibit 17.4 shows the volume of business loans provided by commercial banks over time. Notice how the volume increased consistently during the 1990s but declined in the 2001–2003 period. The decline is directly attributed to weak economic conditions, which resulted in a lower aggregate demand for products and services provided by firms. Consequently, firms reduced their demand for loans. When commercial banks experience a lower demand for business loans, they attempt to use more funds for other purposes.

http://

http://www.fdic.gov
Information about bank
loan and deposit volume.

Types of Consumer Loans Commercial banks provide **installment loans** to individuals to finance purchases of cars and household products. These loans require the borrowers to make periodic payments over time.

Banks also provide credit cards to consumers who qualify, enabling them to purchase various goods without having to reapply for credit on each purchase. Credit card holders are assigned a maximum limit, based on their income and employment record, and a fixed annual fee may be charged. This service often involves an agreement with VISA or MasterCard. If consumers pay off the balance each month, they normally are not charged interest. Bank rates on credit card balances are sometimes about double the rate charged on business loans. State regulators can impose **usury laws** that restrict the maximum rate of interest charged by banks, and these laws may be applied to credit card loans as well. A federal law requires that banks abide by the usury laws of the state where they are located rather than the state where the consumer lives.

Assessing the applicant's creditworthiness is much easier for consumer loans than for corporate loans. An individual's cash flow is typically simpler and more predictable than a firm's cash flow. In addition, the average loan amount to an individual is relatively small, warranting a less detailed credit analysis.

Since the interest rate on credit card loans and personal loans is typically much higher than the cost of funds, many commercial banks have pursued these types of loans as a means of increasing their earnings. The most common method of increasing such loans is to use more lenient guidelines when assessing the creditworthiness of potential customers. However, there is an obvious tradeoff between the potential return and exposure to credit risk. Recently, many commercial banks experienced an increase in defaults on credit card loans and other personal loans. Some commercial banks responded by increasing their standards for extending credit card loans and personal loans. This resulted in a reduced allocation of funds to credit card loans, which also reduced the potential returns of the bank. As economic conditions change, commercial banks continue to reassess the allocation of funds toward credit card loans versus other less risky uses of funds.

Real Estate Loans Banks also provide real estate loans. For residential real estate loans, the maturity on a mortgage is typically 15 to 30 years, although shorter-term mortgages with a balloon payment are also common. The loan is backed by the residence purchased. Banks also provide some commercial real estate loans to finance commercial development.

Investment in Securities

Banks purchase Treasury securities as well as securities issued by agencies of the federal government. Government agency securities can be sold in the secondary market, but the market is not as active as it is for Treasury securities. Furthermore, government agency securities are not a direct obligation of the federal government. Therefore, credit risk exists, although it is normally thought to be very low. Banks that are willing to accept the slight possibility of credit risk and less liquidity from investing in government agency securities can earn a higher return than on Treasury securities with a similar maturity.

Federal agency securities are commonly issued by federal agencies, such as the Federal Home Loan Mortgage Corporation (called Freddie Mac) and the Federal National Mortgage Association (called Fannie Mae). Funds received by the agencies issuing these securities are used to purchase mortgages from various financial institutions. Such securities have maturities that can range from one month to 25 years. Unlike interest income from Treasury securities, interest income from federal agency securities is subject to state and local income taxes.

Banks also purchase corporate and municipal securities. Although corporate bonds are subject to credit risk, they offer a higher return than Treasury or government agency securities. Municipal bonds exhibit some degree of risk but can also provide an attractive return to banks, especially when their after-tax return is considered. The interest income earned from municipal securities is exempt from federal taxation. Banks purchase only **investment-grade securities,** which are rated as "medium quality" or higher by rating agencies.

Bank Investment in Securities over Time In general, banks hold securities that offer a lower expected return than the loans that the banks provide. However, these securities also tend to offer more liquidity and are subject to a lower risk of default than the loans. During periods of economic growth, the demand for loans by qualified borrow-

EXHIBIT 17.5 Bank Investment in Securities over Time

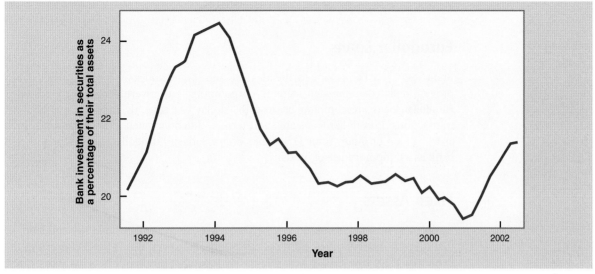

Source: Federal Reserve

ers increases, and banks tend to sell some of their security holdings so that they can provide more loans. They can increase their expected return by accommodating the loan demand, and the risk of default on the loans is relatively low. With favorable economic conditions, the borrowers are likely to have sufficient income to repay their loans.

When the economy weakens, business inventories increase, and firms are unwilling to expand. The demand for loans declines, and banks are unable to provide as many loans to qualified borrowers. Consequently, the banks increase their purchases of securities. Exhibit 17.5 shows the level of banks' investment in securities over time. In the late 1990s when economic growth was strong, banks used a relatively high proportion of their funds to accommodate the large demand for loans and therefore reduced their holdings of securities. In 2002 when the economy was weak, banks reduced their loans and increased their investment in securities.

Federal Funds Sold

Some banks often lend funds to other banks in the federal funds market. The funds sold, or lent out, will be returned at the time specified in the loan agreement, with interest. The loan period is typically very short, such as a day or a few days. Small banks are common providers of funds in the federal funds market. If the transaction is executed by a broker, the borrower's cost on a federal funds loan is slightly higher than the lender's return, because the broker matching up the two parties charges a transaction fee.

Repurchase Agreements

Recall that from the borrower's perspective, a repurchase agreement (repo) transaction involves repurchasing the securities it had previously sold. From a lender's perspective, the repo represents a sale of securities that it had previously purchased. Banks can act as the lender (on a repo) by purchasing a corporation's holdings of Treasury securities

and selling them back at a later date. This provides short-term funds to the corporation, and the bank's loan is backed by these securities.

Eurodollar Loans

Branches of U.S. banks located outside the United States and some foreign-owned banks provide dollar-denominated loans to corporations and governments. These so-called **Eurodollar loans** are common because the dollar is frequently used for international transactions. Eurodollar loans are short term and denominated in large amounts, such as $1 million or more. Some U.S. banks even establish Eurodollar deposits at a foreign bank as a temporary use of funds.

Fixed Assets

Banks must maintain some amount of fixed assets, such as office buildings and land, so that they can conduct their business operations. However, this is not a concern to the bank managers who decide how day-to-day incoming funds will be used. They direct these funds into the other types of assets already identified.

Summary of Bank Uses of Funds

The distribution of bank uses of funds is illustrated in Exhibit 17.6. Loans of all types make up about 59 percent of bank assets, while securities account for about 22 percent of bank assets. The distribution of assets for an individual bank varies with the type of bank. For example, smaller banks tend to have a relatively large amount of household

EXHIBIT 17.6 Bank Uses of Funds (as a Proportion of Total Assets)

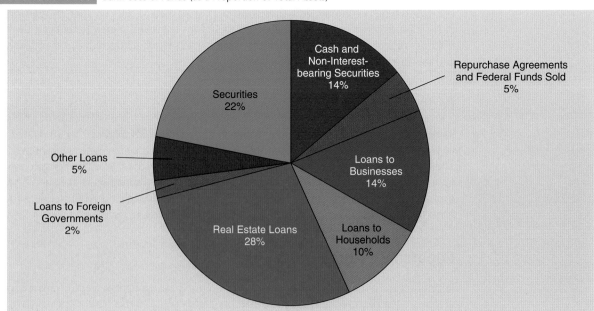

Source: Federal Reserve, 2004

EXHIBIT 17.7

Common Balance Sheet
Items for Commercial Banks

Assets	Liabilities and Stockholders' Equity
Cash	Demand deposits
Loans	Savings deposits
Securities	Time deposits
Federal funds sold (loaned out)	Money market deposit accounts
Repurchase agreements	Federal funds purchased (borrowed)
Eurodollar loans	Other short-term funds borrowed
Fixed assets	Long-term debt Stockholders' equity

loans and government securities; larger banks have a higher level of business loans (including loans to foreign firms).

The distribution of bank uses of funds indicates how commercial banks operate. In recent years, however, banks have begun to provide numerous services that are not indicated on their balance sheet. As explained earlier, these services differ distinctly from banks' traditional operations that focused mostly on the investment of deposited funds.

The desire by commercial banks to offer nonbanking services escalated in the early 1990s, when very low interest rates caused depositors to withdraw deposits and invest the proceeds in stocks and bonds. Many banks attempted to retain the business of those depositors by having their subsidiaries offer discount brokerage services or mutual fund services. Thus, even though the funds were withdrawn from the banking operations, they were commonly reinvested in the bank's subsidiaries.

Exhibit 17.7 shows the common balance sheet items for commercial banks and thus summarizes the main sources of bank funds (bank liabilities and stockholders' equity) and uses of bank funds (bank assets).

Impact of the September 11 Crisis Commercial banks in the United States experienced an unusual dilemma as a result of the terrorist attack on September 11, 2001. Households in the United States shifted funds to short-term money market securities such as bank CDs to avoid risk. Consequently, commercial banks experienced substantial inflows of funds, but the banks had only limited uses for the funds because many businesses did not plan to expand at that time and therefore did not need to borrow. Some businesses that did want to borrow did not qualify because of their questionable financial condition. Banks were especially cautious because they were already experiencing an increase in problem (potential default) loans as a result of the weak economy. Therefore, the banks had more money available than they could use for lending. Many banks increased their investments in securities because the demand for loanable funds had weakened. Although these investments would not earn as high a return as bank lending, they would limit the bank's exposure to any further weakness in the economy.

Off-Balance Sheet Activities

Banks commonly engage in off-balance sheet activities, which generate fee income without requiring an investment of funds. However, these activities do create a contingent obligation for banks. Accounting standards require that these activities be recognized as

assets or liabilities and reported at fair market value. The following are some of the more popular off-balance sheet activities:

- Loan commitments
- Standby letters of credit
- Forward contracts
- Swap contracts

Loan Commitments

A **loan commitment** is an obligation by a bank to provide a specified loan amount to a particular firm upon the firm's request. The interest rate and purpose of the loan may also be specified. The bank charges a fee for offering the commitment.

One type of loan commitment is a **note issuance facility (NIF),** in which the bank agrees to purchase the commercial paper of a firm if the firm cannot place its paper in the market at an acceptable interest rate. Although banks earn fees for their commitments, they could experience illiquidity if numerous firms request their loans at the same time.

Standby Letters of Credit

A **standby letter of credit (SLC)** backs a customer's obligation to a third party. If the customer does not meet its obligation, the bank will. The third party may require that the customer obtain an SLC to complete a business transaction. For example, consider a municipality that wants to issue bonds. To ensure that the bonds are easily placed, a bank could provide an SLC that guarantees payment of interest and principal. In essence, the bank uses its credit rating to enhance the perceived safety of the bonds. In return for the guarantee, the bank charges a fee to the municipality. The bank should be willing to provide SLCs only if the fee received compensates for the possibility that the municipality will default on its obligation.

Forward Contracts

A forward contract is an agreement between a customer and a bank to exchange one currency for another on a particular future date at a specified exchange rate. Banks engage in forward contracts with customers that desire to hedge their exchange rate risk. For example, a U.S. bank may agree to purchase 5 million euros in one year from a firm for $1.10 per euro. The bank may simultaneously find another firm that wishes to exchange 5 million euros for dollars in one year. The bank can serve as an intermediary and accommodate both requests, earning a transaction fee for its services. However, it is exposed to the possibility that one of the parties will default on its obligation.

Swap Contracts

Banks also serve as intermediaries for interest rate swaps, whereby two parties agree to periodically exchange interest payments on a specified notional amount of principal. Once again, the bank receives a transaction fee for its services. If it guarantees payments to both parties, it is exposed to the possibility that one of the parties will default on its

obligation. In that event, the bank must assume the role of that party and fulfill the obligation to the other party.

Some banks facilitate currency swaps (for a fee) by finding parties with opposite future currency needs and executing a swap agreement. Currency swaps are somewhat similar to forward contracts, except that they are usually for more distant future dates.

International Banking

 GL BALASPECTS Until historical barriers against interstate banking were largely removed in 1994, some U.S. commercial banks were better able to achieve growth by penetrating foreign markets than by expanding at home. It is somewhat ironic that New York banks historically had branches in Taiwan and Hong Kong but not in New Jersey or Connecticut. Even though interstate expansion within the United States is easier now, many U.S. banks are also expanding internationally to improve their prospects for growth and to diversify so that their business will not be dependent on a single economy.

The most common way for U.S. commercial banks to expand internationally is by establishing branches, full-service banking offices that can compete directly with other banks located in a particular area. Before establishing foreign branches, a U.S. bank must obtain the approval of the Federal Reserve Board. Among the factors considered by the Fed are the bank's financial condition and experience in international business. Commercial banks may also consider establishing agencies, which can provide loans but cannot accept deposits or provide trust services.

Global Competition in Foreign Countries

U.S. banks have recently established foreign subsidiaries wherever they expect more foreign expansion by U.S. firms, such as in Southeast Asia and Eastern Europe. Recently, expansion has also been focused on Latin America. As a result of the North American Free Trade Agreement (NAFTA), U.S. banks have expanded their business in Mexico to help finance the establishment of subsidiaries by U.S-based corporations. The banks offer banker's acceptances, foreign exchange services, credit card services, and other household services in Mexico.

As an example of the diversity in international banking services, consider the case of Citigroup. Some of the key services offered by Citigroup to firms around the world include foreign exchange transactions, forecasting, risk management, cross-border trade finance, acquisition finance, cash management services, and local currency funding. Citigroup serves not only large multinational corporations, such as Coca-Cola, Dow Chemical, IBM, and Sony, but also small firms that need international banking services. By spreading itself across the world, Citigroup can typically handle the banking needs of all of a multinational corporation's subsidiaries.

Expansion by Non-U.S. Banks in the United States

While U.S. banks have expanded into non-U.S. markets, non-U.S. banks have also entered U.S. markets. Initially, they entered primarily to serve non-U.S. corporations that set up subsidiaries in the United States. Because this is still their primary function, they concentrate on corporate rather than consumer services.

Japanese banks in particular have a very significant presence in the United States. A major reason for their growth is that they offer very competitive corporate loans. They also have been known to provide letters of credit for lower fees than those charged by U.S. banks. They also have a relatively low cost of capital, which allows them to take on ventures that might not be feasible for U.S. banks. Furthermore, the high Japanese savings rate allows for substantial growth in deposits in Japan, which may then be channeled to support operations in the United States.

In addition to establishing full-service branches, since 1913 non-U.S. banks have established **Edge Act corporations** in the United States to specialize in international banking and foreign financial transactions. These corporations can accept deposits and provide loans, as long as these functions are specifically related to international transactions.

Impact of the Euro on Global Competition

The inception of the euro has stimulated increased bank expansion throughout Europe. The use of a single currency in 12 European countries simplifies transactions because the majority of a bank's transactions between those countries are now denominated in euros. Use of the euro also reduces exposure to exchange rate risk, as banks can accept deposits in euros and use euros to lend funds or invest in securities. The use of a single currency throughout many European countries may also encourage firms to engage in a bond or stock offering to support their European business, as the euro can be used to support most of that business. Commercial banks can serve as intermediaries by underwriting and placing the debt or the equity issued by firms.

Given the potential advantages of a single currency, U.S. banks and European banks are expanding throughout Europe by acquiring existing banks. The single currency makes it easier to achieve economies of scale and enables banks' internal reporting systems to be more efficient. As banks expand and capitalize on economies of scale, the global competition has become more intense. Furthermore, the euro enables businesses in Europe to more easily compare the prices of services offered by banks based in different European countries. This also forces banks to be more competitive.

SUMMARY

- The most common sources of commercial bank funds are deposit accounts, borrowed funds, and long-term sources of funds. The common types of deposit accounts are transaction deposits, savings deposits, time deposits, and money market deposit accounts. These accounts vary in terms of liquidity (for the depositor) and the interest rates offered.

  Commercial banks can solve temporary deficiencies in funds by borrowing from other banks (federal funds market), from the Federal Reserve, or from other sources by issuing short-term securities such as repurchase agreements. When banks need long-term funds to support expansion, they may use retained earnings, issue new stock, or issue new bonds.

- The most common uses of funds by commercial banks are bank loans and investment in securities. Banks can use excess funds by providing loans to other banks or by purchasing short-term securities.

- Banks engage in off-balance sheet activities such as loan commitments, standby letters of credit, forward contracts, and swap contracts. These types of activities generate fees for commercial banks. However, they also reflect commitments by the banks, which can expose them to more risk.

POINT COUNTER-POINT

Should Banks Engage in Other Financial Services Besides Banking?

Point No. Banks should focus on what they do best.

Counter-Point Yes. Banks should increase their value by engaging in other services. They can appeal to customers who want to have all their financial services provided by one financial institution.

Who Is Correct? Use your favorite search engine to learn more about this issue. Offer your own opinion on this issue.

QUESTIONS AND APPLICATIONS

1. **Bank Capital** Explain the dilemma faced by banks when determining the optimal amount of capital to hold. A bank's capital is less than 10 percent of its assets. How do you think this percentage would compare to that of manufacturing corporations? How would you explain this difference?

2. **Money Market Deposit Accounts** How does the money market deposit account differ from other bank sources of funds?

3. **Repurchase Agreements** How does the yield on a repurchase agreement differ from a loan in the federal funds market? Why?

4. **Interpreting Financial News** Interpret the following comments made by Wall Street analysts and portfolio managers:
   a. "Lower interest rates may reduce the size of banks."
   b. "Banks are at a regulatory disadvantage when competing with other financial institutions for funds."
   c. "If the demand for loans rises substantially, interest rates will adjust to ensure that commercial banks can accommodate the demand."

5. **Bank Balance Sheet** Create a balance sheet for a typical bank, showing its main liabilities (sources of funds) and assets (uses of funds).

6 **Borrowing at the Discount Window** Describe the process of "borrowing at the discount window." What rate is charged, and who sets it? Why do banks commonly borrow in the federal funds market rather than through the discount window?

7. **International Banking** Explain the operations of foreign branches of U.S. banks.

8. **Managing in Financial Markets: Managing Sources and Uses of Funds** As a consultant, you have been asked to assess a bank's sources and uses of funds and to offer recommendations on how it can restructure its sources and uses of funds to improve its performance. This bank has traditionally focused on attracting funds by offering certificates of deposit (CDs). It offers checking accounts and money market deposit accounts (MMDAs), but it has not advertised these accounts because it has obtained an adequate amount of funds from the CDs. It pays about 3 percentage points more on its CDs than on its MMDAs, but the bank prefers to know the precise length of time it can use the deposited funds. (The CDs have a specified maturity while the MMDAs do not.) Its cost of funds has historically been higher than that of most banks, but it has not been concerned because its earnings have been relatively high. The bank's use of funds has historically focused on local real estate loans to build shopping malls and apartment complexes. The real estate loans have provided a very high return over the last several years. However, the demand for real estate in the local area has slowed.
   a. Should the bank continue to focus on attracting funds by offering CDs, or should it push its other types of deposits?
   b. Should the bank continue to focus on real estate loans? If the bank reduces its real estate loans, where should the funds be allocated?
   c. How will the potential return on the bank's uses of funds be affected by your restructuring of the asset portfolio? How will the cost of funds be affected by your restructuring of the bank's liabilities?

9. **Bank Sources of Funds** What are four major sources of funds for banks? What alternatives does a bank have if it needs temporary funds? What is the most common reason that banks issue bonds?

10. **Federal Funds** Define federal funds, federal funds market, and federal funds rate. Who sets the federal funds rate? Why is the federal funds market more active on Wednesday?

11. **HLTs** Would you expect a bank to charge a higher rate on a term loan or a highly leveraged transaction (HLT) loan? Why?

12. **Internet Exercise** Assess commercial bank interest rates, using the website http://www.chase.com. Under individuals, choose "Savings."

   a. What is the interest rate currently offered on Chase's Select Banking Money Market account? What is the minimum deposit necessary to avoid any fees on this account? What is the annual percentage rate on a 12-month CD? Why do you think this rate differs from the yield on the money market account?

13. **Bank Use of Funds** Why do banks invest in securities, even though loans typically generate a higher return? How does a bank decide the appropriate percentage of funds that should be allocated to each type of asset? Explain.

14. **CDs** Compare and contrast the retail CD and the negotiable CD.

15. **Bullet Loan** Explain the advantage of a bullet loan.

16. **Federal Funds Market** Explain the use of the federal funds market in facilitating bank operations.

FLOW OF FUNDS EXERCISE

Services Provided by Financial Conglomerates

Carson Company is attempting to compare the services offered by different banks, as it would like to have all services provided by one bank.

a. Explain the different types of services provided by a financial conglomerate that may allow Carson Company to obtain funds or to hedge its risk.

b. Review the services that you listed in the previous question. What services could provide financing to Carson Company? What services could hedge Carson's exposure to risk?

Electronic Funds Transfer

Electronic funds transfer (EFT) has facilitated the flow of funds among businesses, households, governments, and financial institutions. The more common forms of electronic funds transfer include automated teller machine (ATM) transfers, direct deposits or withdrawals of funds, and transfers initiated by telephone.

Banking Transactions

Electronic funds transfer has reduced the cost of accepting deposits. Banks have developed shared ATM networks to attract deposits without having to construct facilities or hire and train employees. Furthermore, economies of scale are achieved, as the main cost of the networks is fixed.

Another area of banking affected by EFT is the automated clearinghouse, a payment mechanism by which institutions transfer funds electronically, substituting for payments by check. The automated clearinghouse not only reduces the costs involved in transporting paper but also reduces the float involved with check processing, thereby reducing delays in crediting and debiting accounts.

Government Transactions

Through EFT, Social Security payments and federal income tax refunds made by the government can be directly deposited to individuals' accounts. This eliminates much paperwork related to the processing and printing of each check. Government accounting procedures are also more efficient because of direct depositing.

Household Transactions

EFT offers convenience, security, and privacy. Consumers can avoid bank lines and the inconvenience of lost checks. They also have access to funds on days when the bank is closed. Furthermore, they can use the automated clearinghouse to receive direct deposit of Social Security checks, income tax refunds, and payroll checks. Consumers can use EFT to make payments as well. For example, funds can be deducted directly from their bank accounts to make payments on automobile loans, home mortgages, or even insurance premiums.

Business Transactions

EFT is very useful to businesses for point-of-sale transactions in which funds are instantaneously transferred from the purchaser's account to the seller's account. This reduces the number of transactions by check, credit card, and cash, allowing each retail outlet to reduce its transaction costs. Moreover, the risks involved in accepting checks are eliminated. Because cash need not be handled inside the business, point-of-sale transactions protect against dishonest employees. In addition, a retail business's bookkeeping is simplified. Accounting for sales is easier when an exact record of each sale takes place on a point-of-sale terminal. Because of the lower costs associated with handling sales and less risk of embezzlement, retail firms may pass part of their cost savings on to consumers. Therefore, EFT can benefit various sectors at the same time.

Businesses that receive large volumes of cash receipts (such as utilities) use EFT for collection to reduce the processing tasks. Other types of businesses use EFT to direct deposit salaries and pension contributions into bank accounts. Again, time and money are saved on the processing. Businesses can also use EFT to consolidate their cash at various bank accounts into a single account at the end of the day.

International Transactions

International trade often requires payments to corresponding banks, and these payments are made more quickly and efficiently by using the EFT system. It is likely that this system will also be more frequently used to handle tourism and business travel transactions.

Clearing and Settlement of Payments

During the course of a normal day, more than $1 trillion in large-dollar (wholesale) wire transfer payments is exchanged among depository institutions. The EFT system allows for a more efficient transfer of these funds. In a typical transfer, a firm instructs its depository institution to make payment to another firm by wiring funds from its account to the other firm's account. The depository institution that wired the funds sends the relevant information (name of firms providing and receiving payment and name of depository institution where funds were wired) to the network clearinghouse. This clearinghouse debits the account of the institution that wired the funds and credits the account at the institution receiving the funds.

The settlement of the payment occurs when the clearinghouse notifies the receiving institution that the account is credited. The Federal Reserve System provides settlement services through its system, known as the Fedwire, in which fund transfers occur through reserve accounts of depository institutions at the 12 regional Federal Reserve banks. Many financial institutions have computers linked to the Fedwire so that they can conduct transactions for their corporate customers.

An alternative settlement facility, known as the Clearinghouse Interbank Payments System (CHIPS), is composed of a group of depository institutions that provide settlement services. Payment transfers served by CHIPS are confirmed at the end of the day, when the clearinghouse determines which account balances represent net credit and net debit positions for the day.

CHAPTER 18

Bank Regulation

B ank regulations are designed to prevent commercial banks from becoming too risky and thus maintain public confidence in the financial system.

The specific objectives of this chapter are to:

■ describe the key regulations imposed on commercial banks,

■ explain how regulators monitor banks, and

■ describe the main provisions of the Federal Deposit Insurance Corporation Improvement Act (FDICIA).

Background

http://

http://www.federalreserve.gov Detailed descriptions of bank regulations from the Federal Reserve Bank of New York.

The banking industry has experienced substantial changes in recent years. The industry has become more competitive due to deregulation. Today, banks have much flexibility on the services they offer, the locations where they operate, and the rates they pay depositors for deposits. Although generally viewed as favorable, this flexibility is creating intense competition among banks and even between banks and other financial institutions that now offer bank services.

Banks have recognized the potential benefits from economies of scale and economies of scope. Many banks have expanded across the country by opening new branches or making acquisitions in an attempt to use their resources efficiently. Others have diversified across services to capitalize on economies of scope. Many banks have expanded beyond their traditional banking business and now offer other financial services. Bank regulators have attempted to manage the speed of integration between banks and other financial service firms.

Bank regulation is needed to protect customers who supply funds to the banking system. By preventing bank runs that might occur if customers became concerned about the safety of their deposits, regulation ensures a safer banking environment. Regulators also attempt to enhance the safety of the banking system by overseeing individual banks. The regulators do not attempt to manage individual banks, but do impose some discipline so that banks assuming more risk are forced to create their own form of protection against the possibility that they will default. That is, regulators are shifting more of the burden of risk assessment to the individual banks themselves. This chapter explains the regulatory structure and the key regulatory events that have had the greatest impact on commercial banking operations.

Regulatory Structure

http://www.federalreserve
.gov/banknreg.htm Key
bank regulations from the
website of the Board of
Governors of the Federal
Reserve System.

The regulatory structure of the banking system in the United States is dramatically different from that of other countries. It is often referred to as a **dual banking system** because it includes both a federal and a state regulatory system. There are more than 6,000 separately owned commercial banks in the United States, supervised by three federal agencies and 50 state agencies. The regulatory structure in other countries is much simpler.

A charter from either a state or the federal government is required to open a commercial bank in the United States. A bank that obtains a state charter is referred to as a state bank; a bank that obtains a federal charter is known as a national bank. The federal charter is issued by the Comptroller of the Currency. An application for a bank charter must be submitted to the proper supervisory agency, should provide evidence of the need for a new bank, and should disclose how the bank will be operated. Regulators determine if the bank satisfies general guidelines to qualify for the charter.

State banks may decide whether they wish to be members of the Federal Reserve System (the Fed). The Fed provides a variety of services for commercial banks and controls the amount of funds within the banking system. About 35 percent of all banks are members of the Federal Reserve. These banks are generally larger than the norm; their combined deposits make up about 70 percent of all bank deposits.

Before 1980 nonmember banks were subject to reserve requirements enforced by their respective states. Because the Fed's requirements were generally more restrictive than state requirements, Fed members were forced to hold a much greater percentage of their funds as non-interest-bearing reserves. Consequently, many member banks decided to withdraw from membership. Today, both member and nonmember banks can borrow from the Fed, and both are subject to the Fed's reserve requirements. The advantages and disadvantages of being a Fed member bank are less significant than they once were.

Regulatory Overlap

National banks are regulated by the Comptroller of the Currency, while state banks are regulated by their respective state agency. Banks that are insured by the Federal Deposit Insurance Corporation (FDIC) are also regulated by the FDIC. Because all national banks must be members of the Federal Reserve and all Fed member banks must hold FDIC insurance, national banks are regulated by the Comptroller of the Currency, the Fed, and the FDIC. State banks are regulated by their respective state agency, the Fed (if they are Fed members), and the FDIC. The Comptroller of the Currency is responsible for conducting periodic evaluations of national banks, the Fed holds the same responsibility for state-chartered banks that are members of the Fed, and the FDIC is responsible for state-chartered banks that are not members of the Fed.

Because of the regulatory overlap, it has often been argued that a single regulatory agency should be assigned the role of regulating all commercial banks and savings institutions. The momentum for consolidation increased in 1989, when the Financial Institutions Reform, Recovery, and Enforcement Act (FIRREA) was passed. One of the provisions of FIRREA allows commercial banks to acquire either healthy or failing savings and loan associations (S&Ls). Prior to the Act, banks could not acquire S&Ls. With the merging of commercial banks and S&Ls resulting from the Act, there is even more rationale for a single regulatory agency that would oversee both industries.

Bank Ownership Regulation

Commercial banks can be either independently owned or owned by a holding company. Although some multibank holding companies (owning more than one bank) exist, one-bank holding companies (BHCs) are more common. More banks are owned by holding companies than are owned independently. The popularity of the holding company structure stems from 1970, when amendments to the Bank Holding Company Act of 1956 were enacted, allowing BHCs to participate in various nonbanking activities, such as leasing, mortgage banking, and data processing. As a result, BHCs have greater potential for product diversification.

Deregulation Act of 1980

For many years, discussions by Congress, the regulatory agencies, and depository institutions focused on reducing bank regulations. In 1980, the Depository Institutions Deregulation and Monetary Control Act (DIDMCA) was enacted to achieve these objectives. The Act contained a wide variety of provisions, but the main ones can be divided into two categories: (1) those intended to deregulate the banking (and other depository institutions) industry and (2) those intended to improve monetary control. Because this section focuses on deregulation, only the first category is discussed here.

The DIDMCA was a major force in deregulating the banking industry and increasing competition among banks. Its main deregulatory provisions are as follows:

- The interest rate ceilings (enforced by Regulation Q) on time and savings deposits of depository institutions were phased out, allowing banks to make their own decisions on what interest rates to offer for time and savings deposits.
- All depository institutions were allowed to offer NOW accounts. Because NOW accounts normally require a higher minimum balance, they are not suitable for all consumers; however, their ability to pay interest has attracted those who can afford the minimum balance.
- Depository institutions were allowed more flexibility to engage in various types of lending. For example, savings and loan associations were allowed to offer a limited amount of commercial and consumer loans. Consequently, competition among depository institutions for consumer and commercial loans increased, and the asset mix of different depository institutions has become more similar over time.
- In an effort to improve efficiency in the banking system, the DIDMCA required that the Fed explicitly charge for its services and offer them to any depository institutions that desired them.

Beyond these deregulatory provisions, the DIDMCA called for an increase in the maximum deposit insurance level from $40,000 to $100,000 per depositor at each given bank to reduce the chances of deposit runs.

The DIDMCA has had a significant impact on the banking industry, most importantly by increasing competition among depository institutions. In addition, there has been a shift from conventional demand deposits to NOW accounts. Consumers have also shifted funds from conventional passbook savings accounts to various types of CDs that pay market interest rates.

Garn-St Germain Act

Banks and other depository institutions were further deregulated in 1982 as a result of the Garn-St Germain Act. The Act came at a time when some depository institutions (especially savings and loan associations) were experiencing severe financial problems. One of its more important provisions permitted depository institutions to offer money market deposit accounts (MMDAs), which have no minimum maturity and no interest ceiling. These accounts allow a maximum of six transactions per month (three by check). They are very similar to the traditional accounts offered by **money market mutual funds** (whose main function is to sell shares and pool the funds to purchase short-term securities that offer market-determined rates). Because MMDAs offer savers similar benefits, they allow depository institutions to compete against money market funds in attracting savers' funds.

A second key deregulatory provision of the Garn-St Germain Act permitted depository institutions to acquire failing institutions across geographic boundaries. The intent was to reduce the number of failures that require liquidation, as the chances of finding a potential acquirer for a failing institution are improved when geographic barriers are removed. Also, competition was expected to increase, as depository institutions previously barred from entering specific geographic areas could do so by acquiring failing institutions.

Although the proper degree of deregulation is disputed, consumers appear to have benefited from these deregulatory moves. They now have a greater variety of financial services from which to choose, and the pricing of services is controlled by intense competition.

Deposit Insurance Regulation

Federal deposit insurance has existed since the creation of the FDIC in 1933 as a response to the bank runs that occurred in the late 1920s and early 1930s. During the Great Depression period of 1930–1932, about 5,100 banks failed, representing more than 20 percent of the existing banks at that time. The initial wave of failures caused depositors to withdraw their deposits from other banks, fearing that failures would spread. Their actions actually caused more banks to fail. If deposit insurance had been available, depositors might not have removed their deposits, and some bank failures might have been avoided.

The FDIC preserves public confidence in the U.S. financial system by providing deposit insurance to commercial banks and savings institutions. The FDIC is managed by a board of five directors, who are appointed by the president. Its headquarters is in Washington, D.C., but it has six regional offices and other field offices throughout the country. Today, the FDIC's insurance funds are responsible for insuring deposits of more than $3 trillion.

The specified amount of deposits per person insured by the FDIC has increased from $2,500 in 1933 to $100,000 today. The insured deposits make up 80 percent of all commercial bank balances, as very large deposit accounts are insured only up to the $100,000 limit. Deposits in foreign branches of U.S. banks are not insured by the FDIC, however. Federal deposit insurance continues to be instrumental in preventing bank runs. Depositors are not so quick to remove their deposits because of a rumor about a

bank or the banking system when they realize that their deposits are insured by the federal government.

The pool of funds used to cover insured depositors is now referred to as the **Bank Insurance Fund.** This fund is entirely supported by annual insurance premiums paid by commercial banks. The annual premium ranges from 23¢ to 31¢ per $100 of deposits, depending on the specific bank's financial condition. In 2003, only three banks insured by the fund failed, and their total assets were $1.1 billion. As of 2004, the fund's balance was about $34 billion.

Until 1991, the riskier banks obtained insurance for their depositors at the same rate as safer banks. Because the riskiest banks were more likely to fail, they were being indirectly subsidized by safer banks. This so-called **moral hazard problem** grew in the late 1980s and early 1990s, as the number of bank failures increased. The FDIC's insurance fund was reduced as a result of the expenses incurred in closing many banks. This prompted bank regulators and Congress to search for a way to discourage banks from taking excessive risk and to replenish the Bank Insurance Fund. As a result of the Federal Deposit Insurance Corporation Improvement Act (FDICIA) of 1991, risk-based deposit insurance premiums were phased in. Consequently, bank insurance premiums are now aligned with the risk of banks, thereby reducing the moral hazard problem.

Capital Regulation

Banks are also subject to capital requirements, which force them to maintain a minimum amount of capital (or equity) as a percentage of total assets. This regulation has been the focus of numerous controversies. In general, banks would prefer to maintain a low amount of capital to boost their return on equity ratio, whereas regulators have argued that banks need a sufficient amount of capital to absorb potential operating losses. In this way, the number of bank failures may be reduced, enhancing depositors' confidence in the banking system.

Minimum capital requirements were imposed on U.S. banks in 1981 by three different regulatory agencies. In 1985, the requirements were made uniform across agencies. Nevertheless, there were still two discrepancies. First, all banks with more than $150 million in assets were subject to the same requirements, even though some banks were taking much more risk than others. Second, banks outside the United States were subject to their respective country's capital requirements. This created an unequal global playing field, because banks with lower capital requirements had a competitive advantage. These banks could achieve an acceptable return on equity with smaller profit margins because of their lower capital level. Thus, they could gain market share by underpricing their competitors that were subject to higher capital requirements.

Basel Accord

In the Basel Accord in 1988, the central banks of 12 major countries agreed to uniform capital requirements. This accord was facilitated by the Bank for International Settlements (BIS), which is based in Basel, Switzerland. The BIS was established in 1930 to facilitate international monetary cooperation among countries. In the 1980s, it focused on facilitating solutions to the international debt problems. It played a major role in drafting the accord and in more recent efforts to refine it.

EXHIBIT 18.1   Trend of Tier 1 and Tier 2 Capital over Time at U.S. Banks

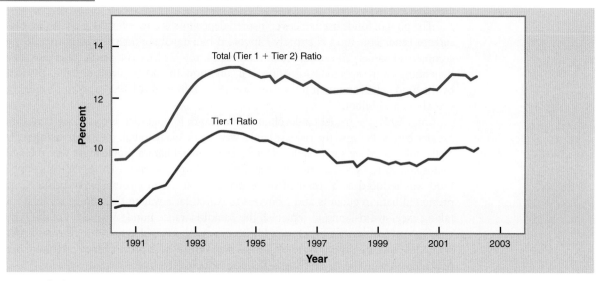

Source: Federal Reserve

A key change made by the Basel Accord was to base the capital requirements on a bank's risk level. Thus, it forced banks with greater risk to maintain a higher level of capital and thereby discouraged banks from excessive exposure to credit risk. The capital requirements were phased in so that banks deficient in capital would have time to build their capital base. By the end of 1992, banks were required to have a capital ratio of at least 8 percent of risk-weighted assets, with a minimum Tier 1 capital ratio of 4 percent. Tier 1 capital consists mostly of shareholders' equity, retained earnings, and preferred stock, while Tier 2 capital includes loan loss reserves (up to a specified maximum) and subordinated debt.

Assets are weighted according to risk. Very safe assets such as cash are assigned a zero weight, while very risky assets are assigned a 100 percent weight. Because the required capital is set as a percentage of risk-weighted assets, riskier banks are subject to more stringent capital requirements.

In 1996, the Basel Accord was amended so that other factors that affect bank risk are also considered. The amendment mandates that a bank's capital level also account for its sensitivity to market conditions, such as stock prices, interest rates, and exchange rates.

The trend of the average Tier 1 and Tier 2 capital levels among banks is shown in Exhibit 18.1. Notice the abrupt increase in Tier 1 capital levels in the early 1990s, a change that is directly attributed to the Basel Accord. Since 1993, the Tier 1 and Tier 2 capital levels have been somewhat stable.

Basel II Accord

In recent years, banking regulators who form the so-called Basel Committee have been working on a new accord (called Basel II) that will refine the risk measures and increase the transparency of a bank's risk to its customers. The goal is to properly account for a

bank's risk so that the bank's capital requirements are in line with its corresponding risk. This is a major challenge because different banks may have different risk levels even though they all have the same composition of corporate loans, household mortgage loans, and other types of loans. Risk levels could differ if, for example, some banks required better collateral to back their loans. In addition, some banks may take positions in derivative securities that can reduce their credit risk, while other banks may have positions in derivative securities that increase their credit risk. The Basel II Accord is attempting to account for such differences among banks.

Specifically, the Basel II Accord has three major parts:

1. Revise the measurement of credit risk.
2. Explicitly account for operational risk.
3. Require more disclosure for market participants.

Revised Measures of Credit Risk Banks can continue to use the traditional standardized approach to calculating credit risk, in which they categorize their assets and assign risk weights to the categories. To improve the calculation, however, the categories are being refined to account for possible differences in risk levels of loans within a category.

ILLUSTRATION As a result of Basel II, a bank's loans that are past due will be assigned a weight of 150 percent. This adjustment inflates the size of these assets for the purpose of determining minimum capital requirements, so that banks with more loans that are past due will be forced to maintain a higher level of capital (other things being equal).

An alternative method of calculating credit risk, called the internal ratings-based (IRB) approach, would also be available. A bank would provide summary statistics about its loans to the Basel Committee, which would apply preexisting formulas to the statistics to determine the required capital level for that bank.

Accounting for Operational Risk The Basel Committee defines operational risk as the risk of losses resulting from inadequate or failed internal processes or systems. The Basel Accord did not explicitly account for this type of risk. The Basel Committee wants to encourage banks to improve their techniques for controlling operational risk because doing so could reduce failures in the banking system. By imposing higher capital requirements on banks with higher levels of operational risk, Basel II would provide an incentive for banks to reduce their operational risk. Initially, banks will be allowed to use their own methods for assessing their exposure to operational risk. The Basel Committee suggests that a bank's average annual income over the last three years may serve as an indicator. The annual income represents the size of bank's operations and thus may reflect the degree of the bank's operational risk. However, the Basel Committee plans to develop a more sophisticated process to assess operational risk over time.

Public Disclosure of Risk Indicators The Basel Committee plans to require banks to provide more information to existing and prospective shareholders about their exposure to different types of risk. Whereas the other provisions of Basel II focus on ensuring that a bank's capital requirements are based on its risk, this provision would increase the information available about a bank's risk. By making banks' risk more transparent to investors, this provision may cause banks to use more conservative management.

Using the Value-at-Risk Method to Determine Capital Requirements

Under the 1996 amendment to the Basel Accord, the capital requirements on large banks that have substantial trading businesses (such as interest rate derivatives, foreign exchange derivatives, and underwriting services) were adjusted to incorporate their own internal measurements of general market risk, which reflects exposure to movements in market forces such as interest rates, stock prices, and exchange rates. The capital requirements imposed to cover general market risk are based on the bank's own assessment of risk when applying a value-at-risk (VAR) model. Recall that participants in the stock market commonly use this model to assess the risk of a stock portfolio. It is used in a somewhat similar manner to assess the risk of a bank.

The VAR model can be applied in various ways to determine capital requirements. In general, a bank defines the VAR as the estimated potential loss from its trading businesses that could result from adverse movements in market prices. Banks typically use a 99 percent confidence level, meaning that there is a 99 percent chance that the loss on a given day will be more favorable than the VAR estimate. When applied to a daily time horizon, the actual loss from a bank's trading businesses should not exceed the VAR estimated loss on more than 1 out of every 100 days. Banks estimate the VAR by assessing the probability of specific adverse market events (such as an abrupt change in interest rates) and the possible sensitivity in response to those events. Banks with a higher maximum loss based on a 99 percent confidence interval are subject to higher capital requirements.

This focus on daily price movements forces banks to continuously monitor their trading positions so that they are immediately aware of any losses. Many banks now have access to the market values of their trading businesses at the end of every day. If banks used a longer-term horizon (such as a month), larger losses might build up before being recognized.

Testing the Validity of a Bank's VAR   The validity of a bank's estimated VAR is assessed with backtests in which the actual daily trading gains or losses are compared to the estimated VAR over a particular period. If the VAR is estimated properly, only 1 percent of the actual daily trading days should show results that are worse than the estimated VAR. In reality, banks may not be very concerned if all their trading results exceed their estimated VAR, because this suggests that their risk may have been overestimated for that period. However, they would be concerned (as would regulators) if the actual results from the trading businesses were frequently worse than the estimated VAR.

Related Stress Tests   Some banks supplement the VAR estimate with stress tests.

ILLUSTRATION   Georgia Bank wants to estimate the loss that would occur in response to an extreme adverse market event. First, it identifies an extreme event that could occur, such as an increase in interest rates on one day that is 10 standard deviations from the mean daily change in interest rates. The mean and standard deviation of daily interest rate movements may be based on a recent historical period, such as the last 300 days. Georgia Bank then uses this scenario along with the typical sensitivity of its trading businesses to such a scenario to estimate the loss on its trading businesses as a result. It may then repeat this exercise based on a scenario of a decline in the market value of stocks that is 10 standard deviations from the mean daily change in stock prices. It may even

estimate the possible losses in its trading businesses from an adverse scenario in which interest rates increase and stock prices decline substantially on a given day.

Operations Regulation

Bank regulations govern many operations of commercial banks, including loans, investment in securities, the provision of securities services, and the provision of insurance services.

Loans Regulation

As a result of concern about the popularity of highly leveraged loans (for supporting leveraged buyouts and other activities), bank regulators monitor the amount of highly leveraged transactions (HLTs). HLTs are commonly defined as loan transactions in which the borrower's liabilities are valued at more than 75 percent of total assets.

Regulators also monitor a bank's exposure to debt of foreign countries. Because banks are required by regulators to report significant exposure to foreign debt, investors and creditors have access to more detailed information about the composition of bank loan portfolios.

Banks are restricted to a maximum loan amount of 15 percent of their capital to any single borrower (up to 25 percent if the loan is adequately collateralized). This forces them to diversify their loans to a degree.

Banks are also regulated to ensure that they attempt to accommodate the credit needs of the communities in which they operate. The Community Reinvestment Act (CRA) of 1977 (revised in 1995) requires that banks meet the credit needs of qualified borrowers in their community, even those with low or moderate incomes. The CRA is not intended to force banks to make high-risk loans but rather to ensure that lower-income (and qualified) borrowers receive the loans that they request. Each bank's performance in this regard is evaluated periodically by its respective regulator.

Investment in Securities Regulation

Banks are not allowed to use borrowed or deposited funds to purchase common stock, although they can manage stock portfolios through trust accounts that are owned by individuals. Banks can invest only in bonds that are investment-grade quality (as measured by a Baa rating or higher by Moody's or a BBB rating or higher by Standard & Poor's). These regulations are intended to prevent banks from taking excessive risks.

Securities Services Regulation

The Banking Act of 1933 (better known as the Glass-Steagall Act) separated banking and securities activities. The Act was prompted by problems during 1929 when some banks sold some of their poor-quality securities to their trust accounts established for individuals. Some banks also engaged in insider trading, buying or selling corporate securities based on confidential information provided by firms that had requested loans. The Glass-Steagall Act prevented any firm that accepted deposits from underwriting stocks

and bonds of corporations. Banks could underwrite general obligation bonds of states and municipalities or purchase and sell securities for their trust accounts. In addition, they could hold investment-grade corporate bonds within their asset portfolio. In this case, the bank was acting as a creditor and not as a shareholder.

The separation of securities activities from banking activities was intended to prevent potential conflicts of interest. For example, the belief was that if a bank was allowed to underwrite securities, it might advise its corporate customers to purchase these securities and could threaten to cut off future loans if the customers did not oblige. Furthermore, it might provide loans to customers with the understanding that a portion of the funds would be used to purchase securities underwritten by the bank.

Banks suggested, however, that any potential conflicts of interest could be prevented by regulators. Furthermore, banks argued that if they could engage in securities activities, they might have easier access to marketing, technological, and managerial resources and could reduce the prices of securities-related services to consumers. In addition, banks could become financial supermarkets, providing securities activities as well as normal banking services. This would be an added convenience to customers. Finally, the increased competition could force all firms providing securities activities to be more efficient.

Deregulation of Underwriting Services In 1989, the Federal Reserve approved debt underwriting applications for some banks, contingent on two requirements. First, banks had to have sufficient capital to support the subsidiary that would perform the underwriting. Second, they had to be audited to ensure that their management was capable of underwriting debt. The Fed imposed a ceiling on revenues from corporate debt underwriting. The approval set a precedent for applications, and several other banks were also allowed to underwrite corporate debt offerings.

By underwriting corporate debt offerings, banks can boost their fee income without significantly increasing their asset size. Although growth in loans automatically causes the amount of required capital to increase, underwritings can generate cash flow without an increase in required capital.

Banks that underwrite corporate debt may also establish better advisory relationships with corporations, which could result in more business in the mergers and acquisitions area. When seeking acquisition advice, corporations may be more likely to consider commercial banks that underwrite the debt needed to finance the acquisitions. Furthermore, underwriting is a new service offered by banks, which can provide diversification benefits.

Some commercial banks, such as J.P. Morgan Chase, have become major participants in the business of underwriting bonds. However, the investment banks still conduct most stock underwriting transactions.

http://
http://www.federalreserve
.gov/banknreg.htm Links
to regulations of securities
services offered by banks.

The Financial Services Modernization Act In 1999, Congress passed the Financial Services Modernization Act (also called the Gramm-Leach-Bliley Act), which essentially repealed the Glass-Steagall Act. The 1999 Act allows affiliations between banks, securities firms, and insurance companies. It also allows bank holding companies to engage in any financial activity through their ownership of subsidiaries. Consequently, a single holding company can engage in traditional banking activities, securities trading, underwriting, and insurance. The Act also requires that the holding company be well managed and have sufficient capital in order to expand its financial services. The Securities and Exchange Commission (SEC) regulates any securities products that are created, but the bank subsidiaries that offer the securities products are regulated by bank regulators.

Although many commercial banks had previously pursued securities services, the 1999 Act increased the degree to which banks can offer these services. Furthermore, it allowed securities firms and insurance companies to acquire banks. Under the Act, commercial banks must have a strong rating in community lending (meaning that they have been willing to actively provide loans in lower-income communities) in order to pursue additional expansion in securities and other nonbank activities.

Now that banks have more freedom to pursue securities and insurance activities and securities and insurance companies can more easily acquire banks, more consolidation among banks, securities firms, and insurance companies is occurring. Although this trend began earlier, the 1999 Act has enabled financial institutions to engage in consolidation without having to sell off specific subsidiaries because of barriers prohibiting them from combining all financial services under a single ownership.

Deregulation of Brokerage Services Even before the Financial Services Modernization Act, banks had been allowed to offer discount brokerage services. In the late 1990s, some banks acquired financial services firms that offered full-service brokerage services. The most notable example was Citicorp's 1998 merger with Traveler's Insurance Group, which had previously acquired the securities firms Salomon Brothers and Smith Barney. Thus, the merger between Citicorp and Traveler's to create Citigroup combined commercial banking and full-service brokerage. Citigroup was initially informed by regulators that it might have to divest some of its brokerage and other securities operations. Passage of the Financial Services Modernization Act in the following year, however, enabled Citigroup to retain all of its units.

Deregulation of Mutual Fund Services In June 1986, the Fed ruled that brokerage subsidiaries of bank holding companies could sell mutual funds. In addition, some banks have arranged with financial service firms to establish a mutual fund to be used almost exclusively by bank customers. In this arrangement, often referred to as a private label fund, the bank cannot sell shares of the fund but can make its customers aware of its availability.

Insurance Services Regulation

As with securities services, banks have been eager to offer insurance services. The arguments for and against bank involvement in insurance are quite similar to those regarding bank involvement in securities. Banks could increase competition in the insurance industry, as they would be able to offer services at a lower cost. In addition, they could offer their customers the convenience of one-stop shopping (especially if the bank could also offer securities services).

Before the late 1990s, banks were involved in insurance in various limited ways. Banks that had participated in insurance activities before 1971 were allowed to continue to do so. In addition, some banks leased space in their buildings to insurance companies in exchange for a payment equal to a percentage of the insurance company's sales. Banks also engaged in cooperative agreements with insurance companies; the banks would sell insurance to their customers, but the insurance company served as the insurer. The bank received a fee for generating business for the insurance company.

In 1995, the Supreme Court ruled that national banks could sell annuities. With an annuity, customers pay a premium in exchange for a future stream of annual payments. Since annuities had previously been sold only by insurance companies, the decision provided another way for banks to penetrate the insurance industry.

In 1998, regulators allowed the merger between Citicorp and Traveler's Insurance Group, which essentially paved the way for the consolidation of bank and insurance services. Passage of the Financial Services Modernization Act in the following year confirmed that banks and insurance companies could merge and consolidate their operations. These events encouraged banks and insurance companies to pursue mergers as a means of offering a full set of financial services.

Off-Balance Sheet Transactions Regulation

Banks offer a variety of off-balance sheet commitments. For example, banks provide letters of credit to back commercial paper issued by corporations. They also act as the intermediary on interest rate swaps and usually guarantee payments over the specified period in the event that one of the parties defaults on its payments.

Various off-balance sheet transactions have become popular because they provide fee income. That is, banks charge a fee for guaranteeing against the default of another party and for facilitating transactions between parties. Nevertheless, off-balance sheet transactions also expose the banks to risk. If, during a severe economic downturn, many corporations should default on their commercial paper or on payments specified by interest rate swap agreements, the banks that provided guarantees would incur large losses.

Bank exposure to off-balance sheet activities has become a major concern of regulators. Banks could be riskier than their balance sheets indicate because of these transactions. The risk-based capital requirements are higher for banks that conduct more off-balance sheet activities. In this way, regulators discourage banks from excessive off-balance sheet activities.

Regulating the Accounting Process

Publicly traded banks, like other publicly traded companies, are required to provide financial statements that indicate their recent financial position and performance. In the 2001–2002 period, the accounting scandals at Enron, WorldCom, and some other firms caused a lack of confidence in the financial information disclosed by firms. Investors are less willing to invest in firms whose earnings may be exaggerated. The Sarbanes-Oxley Act was enacted in 2002 to make corporate managers, board members, and auditors more accountable for the accuracy of the financial statements that their respective firms provide. Although publicly traded banks were not the cause of the accounting scandals, they must also follow the guidelines specified in the Sarbanes-Oxley Act. Meeting the guidelines is causing banks to incur higher expenses to ensure that they have a proper reporting process. Nevertheless, investors may have more confidence in the financial statements now that there is greater accountability that could discourage fraudulent accounting. Although privately held banks are not directly subject to the Sarbanes-Oxley guidelines, bank regulators have asked these banks to review their accounting processes and ensure that their disclosure of financial information is accurate and complete.

Interstate Expansion Regulation

The McFadden Act of 1927 prevented banks from establishing branches across state lines, regardless of their intrastate branching status. The Douglas Amendment to the

Bank Holding Company Act of 1956 complemented the McFadden Act by preventing interstate acquisitions of banks by bank holding companies.

Because banks were historically restricted from crossing state lines, no single bank could control the entire market for bank deposits. Thus, geographic restrictions effectively limited the concentration of any bank in the lending business. Similarly, because banks had limited deposit-accepting capabilities, no single bank could control the entire loan market. Furthermore, geographic restrictions discouraged banks from offering consumer loans or small business loans outside their boundaries. The cost of providing such services long distance did not allow these banks to be competitive with local banks. For large commercial loans, however, the amount of the loan transaction overshadowed the cost of long-distance servicing. Thus, the market for large commercial loans was nationwide, even with geographic restrictions on branching.

In recent years, there has been great momentum toward interstate banking. By 1994, most states had approved nationwide interstate banking. Some of these states require a reciprocal arrangement; that is, they allow acquisitions by out-of-state banks if those banks are located in states that also permit out-of-state acquisitions. Other states do not require a reciprocal arrangement. Some states allow acquisitions on a reciprocal basis only by banks located in a specified region.

Interstate Banking Act

Until 1994, most interstate expansion was achieved through bank acquisitions. In September 1994, however, federal guidelines were revised as Congress passed a banking bill that removed interstate branching restrictions. This bill, known as the Reigle-Neal Interstate Banking and Branching Efficiency Act of 1994, eliminated most restrictions on interstate bank mergers and allowed commercial banks to open branches nationwide. Shortly after the Act was passed, many interstate banks consolidated their operations so that their branches reported to the main holding company, rather than to state subsidiaries.

Banks became more efficient as a result of the Act because they were no longer required to maintain separate banking companies in each state to report to bank regulators. Previously, commercial banks operating in multiple states had to establish separate corporations in each state, with separate boards of directors. Banks with operations across several states reduced their costs as a result of the Act. In particular, reporting costs of banks were reduced over time. Furthermore, banks reduced their costs as a result of consolidating their operations. The reduction in the operating costs was even more pronounced than the reduction in reporting costs.

Bank customers have benefited not only because of lower costs to banks, but also because of convenience. Customer bank accounts are no longer restricted to a particular state. Customers can make deposits or withdraw funds from their accounts even when they are outside their home state. In fact, customers can now deposit checks or obtain a loan in any state where their bank has a branch.

One benefit of nationwide interstate banking is that it allows banks to grow and reduce operating costs per unit of output as output increases. This is commonly referred to as **economies of scale.** Interstate banking has also allowed banks in stagnant markets to penetrate markets where economic conditions are more favorable. In addition, banks in all markets have been pressured to become more efficient as a result of the increased competition.

How Regulators Monitor Banks

Bank regulators typically conduct an on-site examination of each commercial bank at least once a year. During the examination, regulators assess the bank's compliance with existing regulations and its financial condition. In addition to on-site examinations, regulators periodically monitor commercial banks with computerized monitoring systems, based on data provided by the banks on a quarterly basis.

Regulators monitor banks to detect any serious deficiencies that might develop so that they can correct the deficiencies before the bank fails. The more failures they can prevent, the more confidence the public will have in the banking industry. The evaluation approach described here is used by the FDIC, the Federal Reserve, and the Comptroller of the Currency.

The single most common cause of bank failure is poor management. Unfortunately, no reliable measure of poor management exists. Therefore, the regulators rate banks on the basis of six characteristics, which together comprise the CAMELS ratings, so named for the acronym that identifies the six characteristics:

- Capital adequacy
- Asset quality
- Management
- Earnings
- Liquidity
- Sensitivity

More details about the CAMELS ratings are provided at http://www.fdic.gov.

Capital Adequacy

Because adequate bank capital is thought to reduce a bank's risk, regulators determine the **capital ratio** (typically defined as capital divided by assets). Regulators have become increasingly concerned that some banks do not hold enough capital and have increased capital requirements. If banks hold more capital, they can more easily absorb potential losses and are more likely to survive. Banks with higher capital ratios are therefore assigned a higher capital adequacy rating. Even a bank with a relatively high level of capital could fail, however, if the other components of its balance sheet have not been properly managed. Thus, regulators must evaluate other characteristics of banks in addition to capital adequacy.

Asset Quality

Each bank makes its own decisions as to how deposited funds should be allocated, and these decisions determine its level of credit (default) risk. Regulators therefore evaluate the quality of the bank's assets, including its loans and its securities.

ILLUSTRATION

The Fed considers the 5 Cs to assess the quality of the loans extended by a bank it is examining:

- Capacity—the borrower's ability to pay.
- Collateral—the quality of the assets that back the loan.
- Condition—the circumstances that led to the need for funds.

- Capital—the difference between the value of the borrower's assets and its liabilities.
- Character—the borrower's willingness to repay loans, as measured by its payment history on the loan and credit report.

From an assessment of a sample of Skyler Bank's loans, the Fed determines that the borrowers have excessive debt, minimal collateral, and low capital levels. Thus, the Fed concludes that Skyler Bank's asset quality is weak.

Rating an asset portfolio can be difficult, however, as the following example illustrates.

ILLUSTRATION A bank currently has 1,000 loans outstanding to firms in a variety of industries. Each loan has specific provisions as to how it is secured (if at all) by the borrower's assets; some of the loans have short-term maturities, while others are for longer terms. Imagine the task of assigning a rating to this bank's asset quality. Even if all the bank's loan recipients are current on their loan repayment schedules, this does not guarantee that the bank's asset quality deserves a high rating. The economic conditions existing during the period of prompt loan repayment may not persist in the future. Thus, an appropriate examination of the bank's asset portfolio should incorporate the portfolio's exposure to potential events (such as a recession). The reason for the regulatory examination is not to grade past performance, but to detect any problem that could cause the bank to fail in the future.

Because of the difficulty in assigning a rating to a bank's asset portfolio, it is possible that some banks will be rated lower or higher than they deserve.

Management

Each of the characteristics examined relates to the bank's management. In addition, regulators specifically rate the bank's management according to administrative skills, ability to comply with existing regulations, and ability to cope with a changing environment. They also assess the bank's internal control systems, which may indicate how well the bank's management would detect its own financial problems. This evaluation is clearly subjective.

Earnings

Although the CAMELS ratings are mostly concerned with risk, earnings are very important. Banks fail when their earnings become consistently negative. A profitability ratio commonly used to evaluate banks is **return on assets (ROA),** defined as earnings after taxes divided by assets. In addition to assessing a bank's earnings over time, it is also useful to compare the bank's earnings with industry earnings. This allows for an evaluation of the bank relative to its competitors. In addition, regulators are concerned about how a bank's earnings would change if economic conditions change.

Liquidity

Some banks commonly obtain funds from some outside sources (such as the discount window or the federal funds market), but regulators would prefer that banks not consistently rely on these sources. Such banks are more likely to experience a liquidity crisis whereby they are forced to borrow excessive amounts of funds from outside

sources. If existing depositors sense that the bank is experiencing a liquidity problem, they may withdraw their funds, compounding the problem.

Sensitivity

Bank earnings and valuations are exposed to financial market conditions, such as interest rates, stock market conditions, and exchange rates. Consequently, regulators assess the degree to which a bank might be exposed to adverse financial market conditions. Two banks could be rated similarly in terms of recent earnings, liquidity, and other characteristics, and yet one bank may be much more sensitive than the other to financial market conditions. Regulators began to explicitly consider banks' sensitivity to financial market conditions in 1996 and added this characteristic to what were previously referred to as the CAMEL ratings. In particular, regulators place much emphasis on a bank's sensitivity to interest rate movements. Many banks have liabilities that are repriced more frequently than their assets and are therefore adversely affected by rising interest rates. Banks that are more sensitive to rising interest rates are more likely to experience financial problems.

Rating Bank Characteristics

Each of the CAMELS characteristics is rated on a 1-to-5 scale, with 1 indicating outstanding and 5 very poor. A composite rating is determined as the mean rating of the six characteristics. Banks with a composite rating of 4.0 or higher are considered to be problem banks. They are closely monitored, because their risk level is perceived as very high.

Exhibit 18.2 shows the number of problem banks over time. During the strong economy in the late 1990s, the number of problem banks was relatively low. However, the number increased in the 2001–2002 period when economic conditions deteriorated.

Limitations of a Rating System The rating system described here is essentially a screening device. Because there are so many banks, regulators do not have the resources

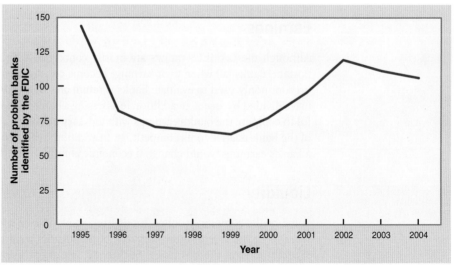

Source: FDIC.

to closely monitor each bank on a frequent basis. The rating system identifies what are believed to be problem banks. Over time, some problem banks improve and are removed from the "problem list," while others may deteriorate further and ultimately fail. Still other banks are added to the problem list.

Although examinations by regulators may help detect problems experienced by some banks in time to save them, many problems still go unnoticed, and by the time they are detected, it may be too late to find a remedy. Because financial ratios measure current or past performance rather than future performance, they do not always detect problems in time to correct them. Thus, although an analysis of financial ratios can be useful, the task of assessing a bank is as much an art as it is a science. Subjective opinion must complement objective measurements to provide the best possible evaluation of a bank.

Any system used to detect financial problems may err in one of two ways. It may classify a bank as safe when in fact it is failing or as very risky when in fact it is safe. The first type of mistake is more costly, because some failing banks are not identified in time to help them. To avoid this mistake, bank regulators could lower their benchmark composite rating. However, if they did, many more banks would be on the problem list requiring close supervision, and regulators would have to spread their limited resources too thin.

Corrective Action by Regulators

When a bank is classified as a problem bank, regulators thoroughly investigate the cause of its deterioration. Corrective action is often necessary. Regulators may examine such banks frequently and thoroughly and discuss with bank management possible remedies to cure the key problems. For example, regulators may request that a bank boost its capital level or delay its plans to expand. They can require that additional financial information be periodically updated to allow continued monitoring. They have the authority to remove particular officers and directors of a problem bank if doing so would enhance the bank's performance. They even have the authority to take legal action against a problem bank if the bank does not comply with their suggested remedies. Such a drastic measure is rare, however, and would not solve the existing problems of the bank.

Although reducing the number of bank failures may increase the public's confidence in the safety of the banking system, a possible tradeoff is involved. If regulators reduce bank failures by imposing regulations that reduce competition, bank efficiency will be reduced. Perhaps the ideal compromise is for regulators to allow fierce competition but to detect financial problems of banks in time to cure them. In this way, the number of failures within such a competitive environment would be minimized, and efficiency would be achieved without reducing the public's confidence in the banking system.

Funding the Closure of Failing Banks

The FDIC is responsible for the closure of failing banks. It must decide whether to liquidate the failed bank's assets or to facilitate the acquisition of that bank by another bank. When liquidating a failed bank, the FDIC draws from its Bank Insurance Fund to reimburse insured depositors. Although the FDIC insures deposits of commercial banks and savings and loan associations, its Bank Insurance Fund is specifically targeted to commercial banks. After reimbursing depositors of the failed bank, the FDIC attempts to sell any marketable assets (such as securities and some loans) of the failed bank. The cost to the FDIC of closing a failed bank is the difference between the reimbursement to depositors and the proceeds received from selling the failed bank's assets.

An alternative solution is for the FDIC to provide some financial support to facilitate another bank's acquisition of the failed bank. The acquiring bank recognizes that the market value of the failed bank's assets is less than its liabilities. Nevertheless, the potential acquirer may consider acquiring the failed bank if it is given sufficient funds by the FDIC. The FDIC may be willing to provide funding if doing so would be less costly than liquidating the failed bank. Whether a failing bank is liquidated or acquired by another bank, it loses its identity.

On November 27, 1991, Congress passed the Federal Deposit Insurance Corporation Improvement Act (FDICIA), which was intended to penalize banks that engage in high-risk activities and also to reduce the regulatory costs of closing troubled banks. The more significant provisions of this act were as follows:

1. Regulators were required to act more quickly in forcing banks with inadequate capital to correct the deficiencies. Regulators classify a bank's capital position in one of five categories, ranging from well capitalized to critically undercapitalized. Three of the five categories reflect some deficiency in capital. Any banks that are classified in one of these three categories must meet specific requirements to boost their capital. This provision of the FDICIA forces banks with inadequate capital to correct their deficiencies. Consequently, the regulatory costs of closing the banks that ultimately fail should be reduced. At the time these categories were developed, less than 2 percent of all banks were classified in one of the three categories that call for specific corrective action.

2. Regulators were required to close troubled banks more quickly, rather than provide financial support to such banks over extended periods of time. This provision was intended to minimize the losses that may otherwise accumulate if troubled banks are allowed to remain open.

3. Deposits exceeding the insured limit ($100,000) are not to be covered when a bank fails. This provision forces large depositors to consider the risk of a bank before depositing funds there. Because the larger banks typically obtain more funds in the form of large deposits, they are affected to a greater degree by this provision. In the past, larger banks were perceived to be protected from failure because so many uninsured depositors were exposed. Because these banks are no longer protected, their ability to obtain large deposits is now more closely linked to their financial condition. Banks with excessive risk have to pay higher interest rates (due to a higher risk premium) on large deposits.

4. Deposit insurance premiums were to be based on the risk of banks, rather than on the traditional fixed rate. Thus, riskier banks incur higher deposit insurance premiums. The risk-based deposit insurance premiums charged to financial institutions are based on a regulatory rating and the financial institution's capital level. The lower the financial institution's rating and the lower the capital level, the higher the annual deposit insurance premium that it must pay.

5. The FDIC was granted the right to borrow $30 billion from the Treasury to cover bank failures and an additional $45 billion to finance working capital needs (from the time the FDIC reimburses depositors until it is able to liquidate the assets). The extra funding gives the FDIC more flexibility in the event that its Bank Insurance Fund is depleted, so that it can continue to operate effectively. Without such flexibility, the FDIC could be forced to let troubled banks remain open, if its funding was not adequate to finance the bank closings. Thus, the costs of closing these banks later on would likely be higher. In fact, another objective of the FDICIA was to increase the Bank Insurance Fund within 15 years to at least 1.5 percent of all insured deposits.

Some additional provisions of the FDICIA complement those just described. The Act requires more complete disclosure by commercial banks, which is intended to help regulators detect financial problems at an early stage. This provision can reduce bank losses and may allow some banks to resolve problems before it is too late. Another provision limits the amount of loans that can be provided by the Fed to undercapitalized institutions. This complements other provisions that enforce capital standards. The FDICIA also requires that regulators enforce standards on real estate loans. This provision is intended to prevent institutions from excessive exposure to the real estate market.

In general, the provisions of the FDICIA attempt to tie a bank's operating costs to its risk level. This is a distinct change from the previous system, which did not link some costs (such as interest paid on large deposits and insurance premiums) to the bank's risk. Because the FDICIA provisions link costs with risks, banks may be discouraged from taking excessive risks. Thus, fewer banks may fail, thereby reducing the costs incurred by the FDIC (and ultimately the taxpayers). Furthermore, the provisions on capital deficiencies and quicker closings of troubled banks can reduce the costs to the FDIC of closing troubled banks.

The "Too-Big-to-Fail" Issue

Some troubled banks have received preferential treatment from bank regulators. The most obvious example is Continental Illinois Bank, which was rescued by the federal government in 1984. Continental Illinois Bank had experienced serious loan default problems in 1983 and 1984. As of May 1984, its depositors with more than the $100,000 insurable limit began to withdraw their funds. Roughly 75 percent of the time deposits at Continental were in accounts containing more than $100,000. The bank's concentration of large accounts was primarily due to its limited ability to obtain additional deposit funds by expanding geographically (because it was subject to unit-banking restrictions). Thus, Continental emphasized large CDs, which were marketed worldwide. Continental normally relied on new deposits to cover any withdrawal requests by old depositors. In May 1984, though, cash inflows (new deposits) were not sufficient to cover cash outflows (deposit withdrawals). To temporarily correct the cash deficiency, Continental borrowed heavily from the Federal Reserve System through the discount window.

Shareholders also recognized Continental's financial problems. Exhibit 18.3 compares the stock price index movements of Continental to those of other money center banks and the S&P 500. The indexes were designed to be equal as of October 1983. In less than a year, Continental's index declined by more than 80 percent, while the money center bank index and the S&P 500 index had only minor declines.

Continental's problems intensified as the remaining depositors began to withdraw their funds. This is a common scenario when a bank fails. In contrast to most other situations, however, the bank regulators intervened. During the massive deposit withdrawals in May 1984, the FDIC announced that it would guarantee *all* deposits (and nondeposit liabilities) of Continental, even those beyond the normal $100,000 limit. This was an attempt to prevent further deposit withdrawals until some arrangements could be made to rescue Continental. In July 1984, the FDIC arranged for a rescue plan whereby it would support Continental by purchasing some of its existing loan commitments and providing capital, with the total support amounting to more than $5 billion. As Continental's performance improved over time, the FDIC received income from selling loans it had assumed, thereby reducing the net cost of the rescue.

EXHIBIT 18.3
Impact of Continental's
Liquidity Crisis on Its Stock
Price

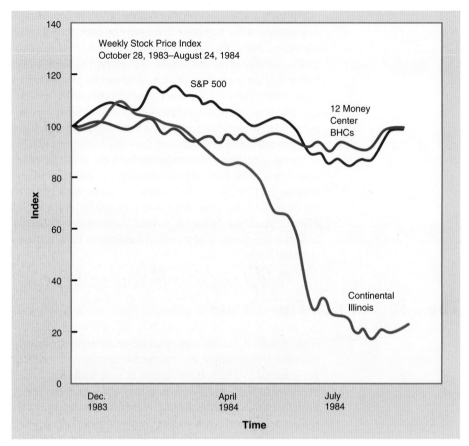

Source: *FRBSF Weekly Letter,* August 31, 1984.

During this same time period, other troubled banks were failing without any rescue attempt from the federal government. The reason for the Continental rescue plan was that, as one of the largest banks in the country, Continental's failure could have reduced public confidence in the banking system. Also, the rescue effort was less expensive to the FDIC than dealing with Continental's failure. But even if the direct costs to the FDIC had been higher, the potential indirect costs (such as the possible chain reaction of deposit withdrawals at other large banks) of letting the bank fail could have been too great to risk. Regardless of the reason for the FDIC's rescue, the fact remains that Continental Illinois Bank was rescued, while troubled smaller banks were not. This has important implications for the banking industry, identified in the following arguments for and against a government rescue.

Argument for Government Rescue

If the federal government had not intervened and Continental had failed and been liquidated, only depositors with less than $100,000 would have been assured full reimbursement. Then depositors with more than $100,000 at other banks could have become more concerned about their risk, and other large banks that were also experiencing serious loan

default problems would have been likely candidates for runs on their deposit accounts. Even if other large banks were financially sound, a false rumor could have heightened depositors' worries and caused a run on deposits.

To examine whether depositors may have become more concerned about large banks because of one large bank's problems, the spread between the rates on large three-month CDs and those on three-month Treasury bills can be compared during the period of Continental's crisis. The larger the spread, the larger the risk premium required by depositors. The risk premium hovered around 40 to 60 basis points in 1983 and early 1984. In May 1984, when Continental's problems became widely publicized, the risk premiums of CDs of other large banks increased to more than 100 basis points (1 percent), reaching about 190 basis points (1.90 percent) by July. The jump in the spread was likely due to the rumors about Continental. This illustrates how problems at a single large bank could reduce depositors' confidence in all large banks. Therefore, the possibility of a domino effect due to a single large bank's failure seems realistic and supports the FDIC's move to rescue Continental.

Argument against Government Rescue

A federal government bailout can be expensive. In January 1987, Continental Illinois Bank stated that the FDIC would recover as little as $1.1 billion of the $2.81 billion of troubled loans that it had assumed in 1984, depleting the FDIC's reserve fund.

When the federal government rescues a large bank, it sends a message to the banking industry that large banks will not be allowed to fail. Consequently, large banks may take excessive risks without concern about failure. If a large bank's risky ventures (such as loans to very risky borrowers) pay off, the return will be high. If they do not pay off, the federal government will bail the bank out. This argument has also been used in regard to international debt. On several occasions, large banks with risky loans to less developed countries (LDCs) have been aided by U.S. government financial support of the LDCs (increasing the chance that the LDCs would repay the U.S. banks). If large banks can be sure that they will be rescued, their shareholders will benefit because they face limited downside risk. The value of the stock can decline only so far during a crisis before government intervention will relieve investors' concerns and push the stock price back up. Meanwhile, smaller banks are at a disadvantage because the downside risk to their shareholders is much greater. The federal government is unlikely to rescue the smaller banks if they fail.

Just as deregulation can enhance efficiency, government intervention could reduce efficiency. Large banks would not need to improve their operations to survive because they could count on the government to bail them out. If medium-sized banks feel that they are treated unfairly relative to large banks, they may establish the long-term goal of becoming large enough that the FDIC will also consider them too big to be allowed to fail. With the loosening of restrictions on interstate banking, banks have greater potential for growth, but growing just to be backed by the federal government may conflict with the optimal size to maximize efficiency. Of course, efficiency would no longer be as critical for banks that have the support of the federal government.

Proposals for Government Rescue

There may never be complete agreement as to whether the federal government should have bailed out Continental. The critical question is how the federal government should

react in the future if another large bank is failing. An ideal solution would prevent a run on deposits of other large banks, yet not reward a poorly performing bank with a bailout. One possible solution would be for regulators such as the Federal Reserve and the FDIC to play a greater role in assessing bank financial conditions over time. In this way, they might be able to recognize problems before they become too severe. But there is no guarantee that increased regulatory reviews would have prevented Continental's financial problems. Bankers might suggest that regulators cannot contribute anything beyond what they already know. Thus, the role of a regulator should be more of a police officer (watching for illegal operations) than a consultant. In addition, increased regulatory reviews would result in an additional cost to the federal government.

Global Bank Regulations

Although the division of regulatory power between the central bank and other regulators varies among countries, each country has a system for monitoring and regulating commercial banks. Most countries also maintain different guidelines for deposit insurance. Differences in regulatory restrictions can allow some banks a competitive advantage in a global banking environment.

Canada's banks tend to be subject to fewer banking regulations than U.S. banks. For instance, Canadian banks can expand throughout Canada, allowing the larger Canadian banks to control much of the market share. Historically, Canadian banks were not as restricted in investment banking activities as U.S. banks and therefore control much of the Canadian securities industry. Recently, Canadian banks have begun to enter the insurance industry.

European banks have had much more freedom than U.S. banks in offering investment banking services such as underwriting corporate securities. In fact, many European branches of U.S. banks provided investment banking services in Europe that were not allowed in the United States. European banks have penetrated the insurance industry in recent years by acquiring numerous insurance companies. Many European banks are allowed to invest in stocks.

Japanese commercial banks have some flexibility to provide investment banking services, but not as much as European banks. Perhaps the most obvious difference between Japanese and U.S. bank regulations is that Japanese banks are allowed to use depositor funds to invest in stocks of corporations. Thus, Japanese banks are not only creditors of firms, but are also their shareholders.

Uniform Global Regulations

The standardization of some regulations around the world has contributed to the globalization of markets and other financial services. Three of the more significant regulatory events allowing for a more competitive global playing field are (1) the International Banking Act, which placed U.S. and foreign banks operating in the United States under the same set of rules; (2) the Single European Act, which placed all European banks operating in many European countries under the same set of rules; and (3) the uniform capital adequacy guidelines, which forced banks of 12 industrialized nations to abide by the same minimum capital constraints. A discussion of each of these key events follows.

Uniform Regulations for Banks Operating in the United States A key act related to international banking was the International Banking Act (IBA) of 1978, which was designed to impose similar regulations across domestic and foreign banks doing business in the United States. Prior to the Act, foreign banks had more flexibility to cross state lines in the United States than U.S.-based banks had. The IBA required foreign banks to identify one state as their home state so that they would be regulated like other U.S.-based banks residing in that state.

Uniform Regulations across Europe One of the most significant events affecting international banking markets has been the Single European Act of 1987, which was phased in throughout many European countries. The following are some of the more relevant provisions of the Act for the banking industry:

■ Capital can flow freely throughout the participating countries.
■ Banks can offer a wide variety of lending, leasing, and securities activities in the participating countries.
■ Regulations regarding competition, mergers, and taxes are similar throughout these countries.
■ A bank established in any participating European country has the right to expand into any or all of the other participating countries.

As a result of the Single European Act, a common market has been established for many European countries. One of the key objectives of the Act is to facilitate the free flow of capital across countries in order to enhance financial market efficiency. To this end, the Act eliminated capital controls imposed by individual European countries on services such as deposit taking, lending, leasing, portfolio management advice, and credit references.

As a result, European banks have begun to consolidate across countries. Efficiency in the European banking markets is increasing as banks can more easily cross countries without concern about country-specific regulations that prevailed in the past.

Another key provision of the Act is that banks can enter Europe and receive the same banking powers as other banks there. Similar provisions apply to non-U.S. banks that enter the United States.

Even some European savings institutions have been affected by the more uniform regulations. Savings institutions throughout the participating countries are now evolving into full-service institutions, expanding into services such as insurance, brokerage, and mutual fund management.

The inception of a single currency (the euro) in 1999 has expedited the integration among participating European countries. With one currency, consolidation of financial services among countries is easier.

Uniform Capital Adequacy Guidelines around the World Before 1988, capital standards imposed on banks varied across countries, which allowed some banks to have a comparative global advantage over others. The Based Accord (discussed earlier) resulted in more uniform capital requirements among countries. Even with uniform capital requirements across countries, some analysts still contend that some banks are at a competitive disadvantage because they are subject to different accounting and tax provisions. Nevertheless, the uniform capital requirements represent significant progress toward a more level global field.

SUMMARY

- Banks are regulated on the deposit insurance that they must maintain, the disclosure of their loan composition, the bonds that they are allowed to purchase, the minimum capital level they must maintain, the locations where they can operate, and the services that they can offer. Although capital requirements have become more stringent, regulations on where banks can operate and what services they can offer have been loosened. Most regulations are intended to enhance the safety and soundness of the banking system, without hampering efficiency.

- Bank regulators monitor banks by focusing on six criteria: capital, asset quality, management, earnings, liquidity, and sensitivity to financial market conditions. The regulators assign ratings to these criteria to determine whether corrective action is necessary.

- In 1991, Congress passed the Federal Deposit Insurance Corporation Improvement Act (FDICIA), which gave regulators the power to act quickly in taking corrective action. Specifically, regulators could force banks with inadequate capital to boost capital levels. Regulators were also required to close troubled banks more quickly.

POINT COUNTER-POINT

Should Regulators Intervene to Take Over Weak Banks?

Point Yes. Intervention could turn a bank around before weak management results in failures. Bank failures require funding from the FDIC to reimburse depositors up to the deposit insurance limit. This cost could be avoided if the bank's problems are corrected before it fails.

Counter-Point No. Regulators will not necessarily manage banks any better. Also, this would lead to excessive

government intervention each time a bank experienced problems. Banks would use a very conservative management approach to avoid intervention, but this approach would not necessarily appeal to their shareholders who want high returns on their investment.

Who Is Correct? Use your favorite search engine to learn more about this issue. Offer your own opinion on this issue.

QUESTIONS AND APPLICATIONS

1. **Interpreting Financial News** Interpret the following comments made by Wall Street analysts and portfolio managers:
   a. "The FDIC recently subsidized a buyer for a failing bank, which had different effects on FDIC costs than if the FDIC closed the bank."
   b. "Bank of America has pursued the acquisitions of many failed banks because it sees potential benefits."
   c. "By allowing a failing bank time to resolve its financial problems, the FDIC imposes an additional tax on taxpayers."

2. **DIDMCA** Describe the main provisions of the DIDMCA that relate to deregulation.

3. **FDIC Insurance** What led to the establishment of FDIC insurance?

4. **CAMELS Ratings** Explain how the CAMELS ratings are used.

5. **Internet Exercise** Browse the most recent Quarterly Banking Profile at http://www.fdic.gov/bank/analytical/index.html. Locate information on the total deposits and income of banks with deposit insurance and on the number of bank failures. Check historical

data from earlier quarters and compare with the current data.

6. **HLTs** Describe highly leveraged transactions (HLTs), and explain why a bank's exposure to HLTs is closely monitored by regulators.

7. **Regulating Bank Failures** Why are bank regulators more concerned about a large bank failure than a small bank failure, aside from the difference in direct cost to the FDIC?

8. **FIRREA** Explain how the Financial Institutions Reform, Recovery, and Enforcement Act (FIRREA) has resulted in increasing integration between the commercial banking industry and the savings institution industry.

9. **IBA** What was the purpose of the International Banking Act (IBA)?

10. **Managing in Financial Markets: Effect of Bank Strategies on Bank Ratings** A bank has asked you to assess various strategies it is considering and explain how they could affect its regulatory review. Regulatory reviews include an assessment of capital, asset quality, management, earnings, liquidity, and sensitivity to financial market conditions. Many types of strategies can result in more favorable regulatory reviews based on some criteria but less favorable reviews based on other criteria. The bank is planning to issue more stock, retain more of its earnings, increase its holdings of Treasury securities, and reduce its business loans. The bank has historically been rated favorably by regulators, but believes that these strategies will result in an even more favorable regulatory assessment.
    a. Which regulatory criteria will be affected by the bank's strategies? How?
    b. Do you believe that the strategies planned by the bank will satisfy shareholders? Is it possible for the bank to use strategies that would satisfy both regulators and shareholders? Explain.

    c. Do you believe that the strategies planned by the bank will satisfy the bank's managers? Explain.

11. **Regulation of Bank Sources and Uses of Funds** How are bank's balance sheet decisions regulated?

12. **Glass-Steagall Act** Briefly describe the Glass-Steagall Act. Then explain how the related regulations have changed.

13. **Moral Hazard** Explain the "moral hazard" problem as it relates to deposit insurance.

14. **Single European Act** Explain how the Single European Act affected international banking.

15. **Regulatory Acts about Interstate Banking** Briefly describe the McFadden Act of 1927, the Douglas Amendment to the Bank Holding Company Act of 1956, and the Riegle-Neal Interstate Banking Act of 1994.

16. **Bank Underwriting** Why might banks be even more interested in underwriting corporate debt issues since the higher capital requirements were imposed on them?

17. **Uniform Capital Requirements** Explain how the uniform capital requirements in 1988 created a more equal global playing field. Explain how the uniform capital requirements can discourage banks from taking excessive risk.

18. **Contagion Effects** How can the financial problems of one large bank affect the market's risk evaluation of other large banks?

19. **Off-Balance Sheet Activities** Provide examples of off-balance sheet activities. Why are regulators concerned about them?

20. **Financial Services Modernization Act** Describe the Financial Services Modernization Act of 1999. Explain how it affected commercial bank operations and changed the competitive landscape among financial institutions.

21. **Economies of Scale** How do economies of scale in banking relate to the issue of interstate banking?

FLOW OF FUNDS EXERCISE

Impact of Regulation and Deregulation on Financial Services

Carson Company relies heavily on commercial banks for funding and for some other services.

a. Explain how the services provided by a commercial bank (just the banking, not the nonbank, services) to Carson may be limited due to bank regulation.

b. Explain the types of nonbank services that Carson Company can receive from the subsidiaries of a commercial bank as a result of recent deregulation.

c. How might Carson Company be affected by the deregulation that allows subsidiaries of a commercial bank to offer nonbank services?

 ## EXERCISE

Impact of Bank Regulations

Using a recent issue of *The Wall Street Journal*, summarize an article that discussed a particular commercial bank regulation that has recently been passed or is currently being considered by regulators. (You may wish to use *The Wall Street Journal Index* in the library to identify a specific article on a commercial banking regulation or bill.) Would this regulation have a favorable or unfavorable impact on commercial banks? Explain.

Bank Management

The performance of any commercial bank depends on the management of the bank's assets, liabilities, and capital. Increased competition has made efficient management essential for survival.

The specific objectives of this chapter are to:

- describe the underlying goal of bank management,
- explain how banks manage liquidity,
- explain how banks manage interest rate risk,
- explain how banks manage credit risk, and
- explain how banks manage capital.

Bank Management

The underlying goal behind the managerial policies of a bank is to maximize the wealth of the bank's shareholders. Thus, bank managers should make decisions that maximize the price of the bank's stock.

In some cases, managers are tempted to make decisions that are in their own best interests rather than shareholder interests. For example, decisions that result in growth may be intended to increase employee salaries, as larger banks tend to provide more employee compensation. In addition, the compensation to a bank's loan officers may be tied to loan volume, which encourages a loan department to extend loans without concern about risk. As these examples suggest, banks can incur agency costs, or costs resulting from managers maximizing their own wealth instead of shareholder wealth. To prevent agency problems, some banks provide stock as compensation to managers. These managers may be more likely to maximize shareholder wealth because they are shareholders as well. Also, if managerial decisions conflict with the goal of maximizing shareholder wealth, the share price will not achieve its maximum. Therefore, the bank may become a takeover target, as other banks perceive it as undervalued, with the potential to improve under their own management. In this way, managers can be disciplined to maximize shareholder wealth.

Board of Directors

A bank's board of directors oversees the operations of the bank and attempts to ensure that managerial decisions are in the best interests of the shareholders. Bank boards tend

to have more directors and a higher percentage of outside directors than boards of other types of firms. Some of the more important functions of bank directors are to

- Determine a compensation system for the bank's executives.
- Ensure proper disclosure of the bank's financial condition and performance to investors.
- Oversee growth strategies such as acquisitions.
- Oversee policies for changing the capital structure, including decisions to raise capital or to engage in stock repurchases.
- Assess the bank's performance and ensure that corrective action is taken if the performance is weak due to poor management.

Bank directors are liable if they do not fulfill their duties. In the mid-1980s, several banks failed because of inappropriate lending. For example, some banks engaged in various forms of insider lending in which employees were given loans at favorable interest rates. These loans were clearly not intended to serve shareholder interests. The Federal Deposit Insurance Corporation (FDIC) filed numerous lawsuits against bank directors for being negligent in their oversight of bank lending behavior. In recent years, shareholders have taken the initiative and filed lawsuits against bank directors who were negligent in monitoring management decisions.

Managing Liquidity

Banks can experience illiquidity when cash outflows (due to deposit withdrawals, loans, etc.) exceed cash inflows (new deposits, loan repayments, etc.). They can resolve any cash deficiency either by creating additional liabilities or by selling assets. Banks have access to various forms of borrowing, such as the federal funds market or the discount window. They also maintain some assets that can readily be sold in the secondary market. The decision on how to obtain funds depends on the situation. If the need for funds is temporary, an increase in short-term liabilities (from the federal funds market or the discount window) may be appropriate. However, if the need is permanent, a policy for increasing deposits or selling liquid assets may be appropriate.

Because some assets are more marketable than others in the secondary market, the bank's asset composition can affect its degree of liquidity. At an extreme, banks could ensure sufficient liquidity by using most of their funds to purchase Treasury securities. However, they must also be concerned with achieving a reasonable return on their assets, which often conflicts with the liquidity objective. Although Treasury securities are liquid, their yield is low relative to bank loans or investments in other securities. Recent research has shown that high-performance banks are able to maintain relatively low (but sufficient) liquidity. Banks should maintain the level of liquid assets that will satisfy their liquidity needs but use their remaining funds to satisfy their other objectives. As the secondary market for loans has become active, banks are more able to satisfy their liquidity needs with a higher proportion of loans while striving for higher profitability.

Use of Securitization to Boost Liquidity

The ability to securitize assets such as automobile and mortgage loans can enhance a bank's liquidity position. The process of securitization commonly involves the sale of assets by the bank to a trustee, who issues securities that are collateralized by the assets. The bank may still service the loans, but it passes through the interest and principal pay-

ments received to the investors who purchased the securities. Banks are more liquid as a result of securitization because they effectively convert future cash flows into immediate cash. In most cases, the process includes a guarantor who, for a fee, guarantees future payments to investors who purchased the securities. The loans that collateralize the securities normally exceed the amount of the securities issued or are backed by an additional guarantee from the bank that sells the loans.

Managing Interest Rate Risk

The performance of a bank is highly influenced by the interest payments earned on its assets relative to the interest paid on its liabilities (deposits). The difference between interest payments received versus interest paid is measured by the **net interest margin:**

$$\text{Net interest margin} = \frac{\text{Interest revenues} - \text{Interest expenses}}{\text{Assets}}$$

In some cases, net interest margin is defined to include only the earning assets, excluding any assets that do not generate a return to the bank (such as required reserves). Because the rate sensitivity of a bank's liabilities normally does not perfectly match that of the assets, the net interest margin changes over time. The change depends on whether bank assets are more or less rate sensitive than bank liabilities, the degree of difference in rate sensitivity, and the direction of interest rate movements.

The composition of a bank's balance sheet will determine how its profitability is influenced by interest rate fluctuations. If a bank expects interest rates to consistently decrease over time, it will consider allocating most of its funds to rate-insensitive assets, such as long-term and medium-term loans (all with fixed rates) as well as long-term securities. These assets will continue to provide the same periodic yield. As interest rates decline, the bank's cost of funds will decrease, and its overall return will increase.

If a bank expects interest rates to consistently increase over time, it will consider allocating most of its funds to rate-sensitive assets such as short-term commercial and consumer loans, long-term loans with floating interest rates, and short-term securities. The short-term instruments will mature soon, so reinvestment will be at a higher rate if interest rates increase. The longer-term instruments will continue to exist, so the bank will benefit from increasing interest rates only if it uses floating rates.

During a period of rising interest rates, a bank's net interest margin will likely decrease if its liabilities are more rate sensitive than its assets, as illustrated in Exhibit 19.1. Under the opposite scenario, where market interest rates are declining over time, rates

EXHIBIT 19.1
Impact of Increasing Interest Rates on a Bank's Net Interest Margin (If the Bank's Liabilities Are More Rate Sensitive Than Its Assets)

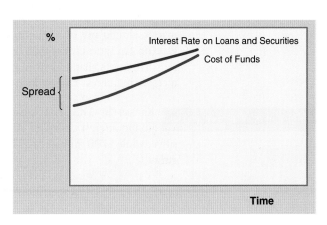

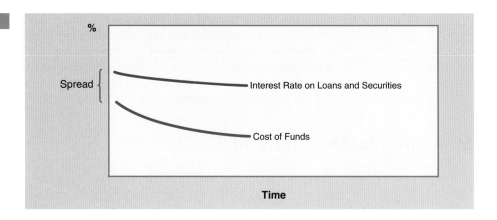

offered on new bank deposits, as well as those earned on new bank loans, will be affected by the decline in interest rates. The deposit rates will typically be more sensitive if their turnover is quicker, as illustrated in Exhibit 19.2.

To manage interest rate risk, a bank measures the risk and then uses its asessment of future interest rates to decide whether and how to hedge the risk. Methods of assessing the risk are described next, followed by a discussion of the hedging decision and methods of reducing interest rate risk.

Methods Used to Assess Interest Rate Risk

No method of measuring interest rate risk is perfect, so commercial banks use a variety of methods to assess their exposure to interest rate movements. The following are the most common methods of measuring interest rate risk:

- Gap analysis
- Duration analysis
- Regression analysis

Gap Analysis Banks can attempt to determine their interest rate risk by monitoring their **gap** over time, defined here as

$$Gap = \text{Rate-sensitive assets} - \text{Rate-sensitive liabilities}$$

An alternative formula is the **gap ratio,** which is measured as the volume of rate-sensitive assets divided by rate-sensitive liabilities. A gap of zero (or gap ratio of 1.00) indicates that rate-sensitive assets equal rate-sensitive liabilities, so the net interest margin should not be significantly influenced by interest rate fluctuations. A negative gap (or gap ratio of less than 1.00) indicates that rate-sensitive liabilities exceed rate-sensitive assets. Banks with a negative gap are typically concerned about a potential increase in interest rates, which could reduce their net interest margin.

ILLUSTRATION   Kansas City (K.C.) Bank had interest revenues of $80 million last year and $35 million in interest expenses. About $400 million of its $1 billion in assets are rate sensitive, while $700 million of its liabilities are rate sensitive. K.C. Bank's net interest margin is

$$\text{Net interest margin} = (\$80,000,000 - \$35,000,000)/\$1,000,000,000$$
$$= .045, \text{ or } 4.5\%$$

CHAPTER 19 • BANK MANAGEMENT

K.C. Bank's gap is

$$\text{Gap} = \$400,000,000 - \$700,000,000$$
$$= -\$300,000,000$$

K.C. Bank's gap ratio is

$$\text{Gap ratio} = \$400,000,000/\$700,000,000$$
$$= .5714, \text{ or } 57.14\%$$

Based on the gap analysis of K.C. Bank, an increase in market interest rates would cause its net interest margin to decline from its recent level of 4.5 percent. Conversely, a decrease in interest rates would cause its net interest margin to increase above 4.5 percent.

Many banks classify interest-sensitive assets and liabilities into various categories based on the time of repricing. Then the bank can determine the gap in each category so that its exposure to interest rate risk can be assessed.

ILLUSTRATION Deacon Bank compares the interest rate sensitivity of its assets versus its liabilities as shown in Exhibit 19.3. It has a negative gap in the less-than-1-month maturity range, the 3- to 6-month range, and the 6- to 12-month range. Thus, the bank may hedge this gap if it believes that interest rates are rising.

Although the gap as described here is an easy method for measuring a bank's interest rate risk, it has limitations. Banks must decide how to classify their liabilities and assets as rate sensitive versus rate insensitive. For example, should a Treasury security

EXHIBIT 19.3

Interest-Sensitive Assets and Liabilities: Illustration of the Gap Measured for Various Maturity Ranges for Deacon Bank

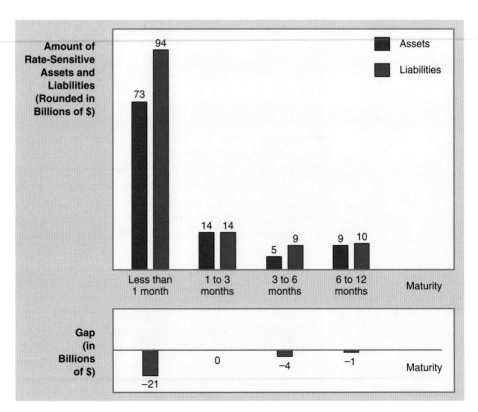

with a year to maturity be classified as rate sensitive or rate insensitive? How short must a maturity be to qualify for the rate-sensitive classification?

Each bank may have its own classification system, because there is no perfect measurement of the gap. Whatever system is used, there is a possibility that the measurement will be misinterpreted.

ILLUSTRATION

Spencer Bank obtains much of its funds by issuing CDs with seven-day and one-month maturities as well as money market deposit accounts (MMDAs). Assume that it typically uses these funds to provide loans with a floating rate, adjusted once per year. These sources of funds and uses of funds will likely be classified as rate sensitive. Thus, the gap will be close to zero, implying that the bank is not exposed to interest rate risk. Yet, there is a difference in the *degree* of rate sensitivity between the bank's sources and uses of funds. The rates paid by the bank on its sources of funds will change more frequently than the rates earned on its uses of funds. Thus, Spencer Bank's net interest margin would likely be reduced during periods of rising interest rates. This exposure would not be detected by the gap measurement.

Duration Measurement An alternative approach to assessing interest rate risk is to measure duration. Some assets or liabilities are more rate sensitive than others, even if the frequency of adjustment and the maturity are the same. A 10-year zero-coupon bond is more sensitive to interest rate fluctuations than a 10-year bond that pays coupon payments. Thus, the market value of assets in a bank that has invested in zero-coupon bonds will be very susceptible to interest rate movements. The duration measurement can capture these different degrees of sensitivity. In recent years, banks and other financial institutions have used the concept of **duration** to measure the sensitivity of their assets to interest rate movements. There are various measurements for an asset's duration; one of the more common is

$$\text{DUR} = \frac{\sum_{t=1}^{n} \dfrac{C_t(t)}{(1 + k)^t}}{\sum_{t=1}^{n} \dfrac{C_t}{(1 + k)^t}}$$

where C_t represents the interest or principal payments of the asset, t is the time at which the payments are provided, and k is the required rate of return on the asset, which reflects the asset's yield to maturity. The duration of each type of bank asset can be determined, and the duration of the asset portfolio is the weighted average (based on the relative proportion invested in each asset) of the durations of the individual assets.

The duration of each type of bank liability can also be estimated; the duration of the portfolio is estimated as the weighted average of the durations of the liabilities. The bank can then estimate its **duration gap,** which is commonly measured as the difference between the weighted duration of the bank's assets and the weighted duration of its liabilities, adjusted for the firm's asset size:

$$\text{DURGAP} = \frac{(\text{DURAS} \times \text{AS})}{\text{AS}} - \frac{(\text{DURLIAB} \times \text{LIAB})}{\text{AS}}$$

$$= \text{DURAS} - [\text{DURLIAB} \times (\text{LIAB/AS})]$$

where DURAS is the average duration of the bank's assets, DURLIAB is the weighted average of the bank's liabilities, AS represents the market value of the assets, and LIAB represents the market value of the liabilities. A duration gap of zero suggests that the bank's value should be insensitive to interest rate movements, meaning that the bank is not ex-

posed to interest rate risk. For most banks, the average duration of assets exceeds the average duration of liabilities, so the duration gap is positive. This implies that the market value of the bank's assets is more sensitive to interest rate movements than the value of its liabilities because the asset durations are higher on average. Thus, if interest rates rise, banks with positive duration gaps will be adversely affected. Conversely, if interest rates decline, banks with positive duration gaps will benefit. The larger the duration gap, the more sensitive the bank should be to interest rate movements.

Other things being equal, assets with shorter maturities have shorter durations; also, assets that generate more frequent coupon payments have shorter durations than those that generate less frequent payments. Banks and other financial institutions concerned with interest rate risk use duration to compare the rate sensitivity of their entire asset and liability portfolios. Because duration is especially critical for a savings institution's operations, a numerical example showing the measurement of the duration of a savings institution's entire asset and liability portfolio is provided in Chapter 21.

Although duration is a valuable technique for comparing the rate sensitivity of various securities, its capabilities are limited when applied to assets that can be terminated on a moment's notice. For example, consider a bank that offers a fixed-rate five-year loan that can be paid off early without penalty. If the loan is not paid off early, it is perceived as rate insensitive. Yet, there is the possibility that the loan will be terminated anytime over the five-year period. In this case, the bank would reinvest the funds at a rate dependent on market rates at that time. Thus, the funds used to provide the loan *can* be sensitive to interest rate movements, but the degree of sensitivity depends on when the loan is paid off. In general, loan prepayments are more common when market rates decline, because borrowers refinance by obtaining lower-rate loans to pay off existing loans. The point here is that the possibility of prepayment makes it impossible to perfectly match the rate sensitivity of assets and liabilities.

Regression Analysis Gap analysis and duration analysis are based on the bank's balance sheet composition. Alternatively, a bank can assess interest rate risk by simply determining how performance has historically been influenced by interest rate movements. To do this, a proxy must be identified for bank performance and for prevailing interest rates, and a model that can estimate the relationship between the proxies must be chosen. A common proxy for performance is return on assets, return on equity, or the percentage change in stock price. To determine how performance is affected by interest rates, regression analysis can be applied to historical data. For example, using an interest rate proxy called i, the S&P 500 stock index as the market and the bank's stock return (R) as the performance proxy, the following regression model could be used:

$$R = B_0 + B_1 R_m + B_2 i + \mu$$

where R_m is the return on the market, B_0, B_1, and B_2 are regression coefficients, and μ is an error term. The regression coefficient B_2 in this model can also be called the interest rate coefficient, because it measures the sensitivity of the bank's performance to interest rate movements. A positive (negative) coefficient suggests that performance is favorably (adversely) affected by rising interest rates. If the interest rate coefficient is not significantly different from zero, this suggests that the bank's stock returns are insulated from interest rate movements.

Models similar to that just described have been tested for the portfolio of all publicly traded banks to determine whether bank stock levels are affected by interest rate movements. The vast majority of this research has found that bank stock levels are inversely related to interest rate movements (the B_2 coefficient is negative and significant). These results can be attributed to the common imbalance between a bank's rate-sensitive

liabilities and its assets. Because banks tend to have a negative gap (their liabilities are more rate sensitive than their assets), rising interest rates reduce bank performance. These results are generalized for the banking industry and do not apply to every bank.

Because a bank's assets and liabilities are replaced over time, exposure to interest rate risk must be continually reassessed. As exposure changes, the reaction of bank performance to a particular interest rate pattern will change.

When a bank uses regression analysis to determine its sensitivity to interest rate movements, it may combine this analysis with the so-called value-at-risk (VAR) method to determine how its market value would change in response to specific interest rate movements. The VAR method can be applied by combining a probability distribution of interest rate movements with the interest rate coefficient (measured from the regression analysis) to determine a maximum expected loss due to adverse interest rate movements. For example, if the bank determines from applying the regression model to monthly data that its interest rate regression coefficient is −2.4, this implies that for a 1 percentage point increase in interest rates, the value of the bank would decline by 2.4 percent. Assume that the bank determines at the 99 percent confidence level that the change in the interest rate should be no worse than an increase of 2.0 percent. For a 2 percentage point increase, the value of the bank is expected to decline by 4.8 percent (computed as 2.0 percent multiplied by the regression coefficient of −2.4). Thus, the maximum expected loss due to interest rate movements (based on a 99 percent confidence level) is a 4.8 percent loss in market value.

Determining Whether to Hedge Interest Rate Risk

A bank can consider its measurement of its interest rate risk along with its forecast of interest rate movements to determine whether it should consider hedging its risk. The general conclusions resulting from a bank's analysis of its interest rate risk are presented in Exhibit 19.4. This exhibit shows the three methods that are commonly used by banks to measure their interest rate risk. Since none of these measures is perfect for all situations, some banks measure interest rate risk using all three methods. Other banks prefer just one of the methods. The use of any method along with an interest rate forecast can help a bank determine whether it should consider hedging its interest rate risk.

In general, the three methods should lead to a similar conclusion. If a bank has a negative gap, its average asset duration is probably larger than its liability duration (positive duration gap), and its past performance level is probably inversely related to interest rate movements. If the bank recently revised the composition of its assets or liabilities, however, it may wish to focus on the gap or the duration gap, as regression analysis is based on a historical relationship that may no longer exist. Banks use their analysis of gap along with their forecast of interest rates to make their hedging decision. The specific methods of hedging interest rate risk are described next.

Methods to Reduce Interest Rate Risk

Banks have monitored interest rate risk since the late 1970s, as interest rate movements have been very volatile. Interest rate risk can be reduced by

- Maturity matching
- Using floating-rate loans
- Using interest rate futures contracts
- Using interest rate swaps
- Using interest rate caps

EXHIBIT 19.4

Framework for Managing
Interest Rate Risk

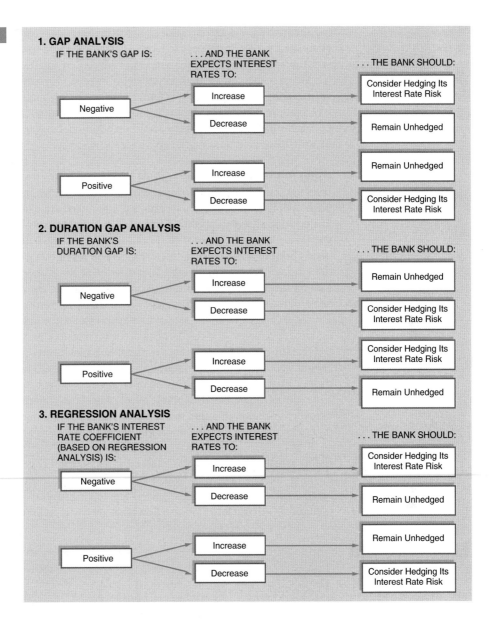

Maturity Matching One obvious method of reducing interest rate risk is to match each deposit's maturity with an asset of the same maturity. For example, if the bank receives funds for a one-year CD, it could provide a one-year loan or invest in a security with a one-year maturity. Although this strategy would avoid interest rate risk, it cannot be implemented effectively. Banks receive a large volume of short-term deposits and would not be able to match up maturities on deposits with the longer loan maturities. Borrowers rarely request funds for a period as short as one month or even six months. In addition, the deposit amounts are typically small relative to the loan amounts. A bank would have difficulty combining deposits with a particular maturity to accommodate a loan request with the same maturity.

Using Floating-Rate Loans An alternative solution is to use floating-rate loans, which allow banks to support long-term assets with short-term deposits without overly expos-

ing themselves to interest rate risk. Floating-rate loans cannot, however, completely eliminate the risk. If the cost of funds is changing more frequently than the rate on assets, the bank's net interest margin is still affected by interest rate fluctuations.

When banks reduce their exposure to interest rate risk by replacing long-term securities with more floating-rate commercial loans, they increase their exposure to credit risk, because the commercial loans provided by banks typically have a higher frequency of default than the securities they hold. In addition, bank liquidity risk would increase, because loans are not as marketable as securities.

Using Interest Rate Futures Contracts   Large banks frequently use interest rate futures and other types of derivative instruments to hedge interest rate risk. A common method of reducing interest rate risk is to use interest rate futures contracts, which lock in the price at which specified financial instruments can be purchased or sold on a specified future settlement date. Recall that the sale of a futures contract on Treasury bonds prior to an increase in interest rates will result in a gain, because an identical futures contract can be purchased later at a lower price once interest rates rise. Thus, a gain on the Treasury bond futures contracts can offset the adverse effects of higher interest rates on a bank's performance. The size of the bank's position in Treasury bond futures is dependent on the size of its asset portfolio, the degree of its exposure to interest rate movements, and its forecasts of future interest rate movements.

Exhibit 19.5 illustrates how the use of financial futures contracts can reduce the uncertainty about a bank's net interest margin. The sale of CD futures, for example, reduces the potential adverse effect of rising interest rates on the bank's interest expenses. Yet, it also reduces the potential favorable effect of declining interest rates on the bank's interest expenses. Assuming that the bank initially had more rate-sensitive liabilities, its use of futures would reduce the impact of interest rates on its net interest margin.

Using Interest Rate Swaps   Commercial banks can hedge interest rate risk by engaging in an interest rate swap, which is an arrangement to exchange periodic cash flows based on specified interest rates. A fixed-for-floating swap allows one party to periodically exchange fixed cash flows for cash flows that are based on prevailing market interest rates.

EXHIBIT 19.5

Effect of Financial Futures on the Expected Spread of Banks That Have More Rate-Sensitive Liabilities Than Assets

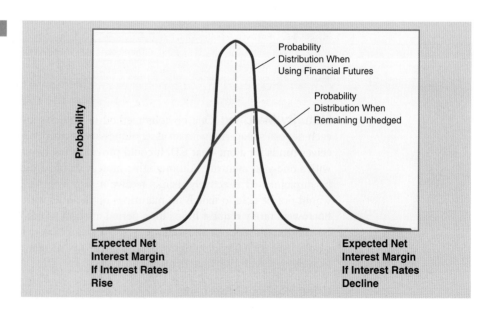

A bank whose liabilities are more rate sensitive than its assets can swap payments with a fixed interest rate in exchange for payments with a variable interest rate over a specified period of time. If interest rates rise, the bank benefits because the payments to be received from the swap will increase while its outflow payments are fixed. This can offset the adverse impact of rising interest rates on the bank's net interest margin. In the 2002–2004 period, interest rates were unusually low, causing banks to take swap positions that protected against a possible increase in interest rates.

An interest rate swap requires another party that is willing to provide variable-rate payments in exchange for fixed-rate payments. Financial institutions that have more rate-sensitive assets than liabilities may be willing to assume such a position, because they could reduce their exposure to interest rate movements in this manner. A financial intermediary is typically needed to match up the two parties that desire an interest rate swap. Some investment banking firms and large commercial banks serve in this role.

ILLUSTRATION   Assume that Denver Bank (DB) has large holdings of 11 percent fixed-rate loans. Because its sources of funds are mostly interest rate sensitive, DB desires to swap fixed-rate payments in exchange for variable-rate payments. It informs Colorado Bank of its situation, because it knows that this bank commonly engages in swap transactions. Colorado Bank searches for a client and finds that Brit Eurobank desires to swap variable-rate dollar payments in exchange for fixed dollar payments. Colorado Bank then develops the swap arrangement illustrated in Exhibit 19.6. DB will swap fixed-rate payments in exchange for variable-rate payments based on the London Interbank Offer Rate (LIBOR, the rate charged on loans between Eurobanks). Because the variable-rate payments will fluctuate with market conditions, DB's payments received will vary over time. The length of the swap period and the notional amount (the amount to which the interest rates are applied to determine the payments) can be structured to the participants' desires. Colorado Bank, the financial intermediary conducting the swap, charges a fee, such as .1 percent of the notional amount per year. Some financial intermediaries for swaps may act as the counterparty and exchange the payments desired, rather than just match up two parties.

Now assume that the fixed payments to be paid are based on a fixed rate of 9 percent. Also assume that LIBOR is initially 6 percent, and that DB's cost of funds is equal to LIBOR. Exhibit 19.7 shows how DB's spread is affected by various possible interest rates when unhedged versus when hedged with an interest rate swap. If LIBOR remains at 6 percent, DB's spread would be 5 percent if unhedged and only 3 percent when using a swap. However, if LIBOR increases beyond 9 percent, the spread when using the swap exceeds the unhedged spread because the higher cost of funds causes a lower unhedged spread. The swap arrangement would provide DB with increased payments that offset the higher cost of funds. The advantage of a swap is that it can lock in the spread to be earned on existing assets, or at least reduce the possible variability of the spread.

EXHIBIT 19.6

Illustration of an Interest Rate Swap

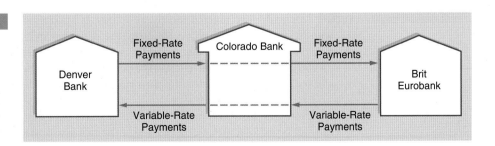

EXHIBIT 19.7   Comparison of Denver Bank's Spread: Unhedged versus Hedged

	Possible LIBOR Rates in the Future					
Unhedged Strategy	**7%**	**8%**	**9%**	**10%**	**11%**	**12%**
Average rate on existing mortgages	11%	11%	11%	11%	11%	11%
Average cost of deposits	6	7	8	9	10	11
Spread	5	4	3	2	1	0
Hedging with an Interest Rate Swap						
Fixed interest rate earned on fixed-rate mortgages	11	11	11	11	11	11
Fixed interest rate owed on swap arrangement	9	9	9	9	9	9
Spread on fixed-rate payments	2	2	2	2	2	2
Variable interest rate earned on swap arrangement	7	8	9	10	11	12
Variable interest rate owed on deposits	6	7	8	9	10	11
Spread on variable-rate payments	1	1	1	1	1	1
Combined total spread when using the swap	3	3	3	3	3	3

When interest rates decrease, a bank's outflow payments would exceed inflow payments on a swap. However, the spread between the interest rates received on existing fixed-rate loans and those paid on deposits should increase, offsetting the net outflow from the swap. During periods of declining interest rates, fixed-rate loans are often prepaid, which could result in a net outflow from the swap without any offsetting effect.

Using Interest Rate Caps   An alternative method of hedging interest rate risk is an interest rate cap, an agreement (for a fee) to receive payments when the interest rate of a particular security or index rises above a specified level during a specified time period. Various financial intermediaries (such as commercial banks and brokerage firms) offer interest rate caps. During periods of rising interest rates, the cap provides compensation, which can offset the reduction in the spread during such periods.

International Interest Rate Risk

When a bank has foreign currency balances, the strategy of matching the overall interest rate sensitivity of assets to that of liabilities will not automatically achieve a low degree of interest rate risk.

ILLUSTRATION   California Bank has deposits denominated mostly in euros, while its floating-rate loans are denominated mostly in dollars. It matches its average deposit maturity with its average loan maturity. However, the difference in currency denominations creates interest rate risk. The deposit and loan rates are dependent on the interest rate movements of the respective currencies. The performance of California Bank will be adversely affected if the interest rate on the euro increases and the U.S. interest rate decreases.

Even though a bank matches the mix of currencies in its assets and its liabilities, it can still be exposed to interest rate risk if the rate sensitivities differ between assets and liabilities for each currency.

Oklahoma Bank uses its dollar deposits to make dollar loans and its euro deposits to make euro loans. It has short-term dollar deposits and uses the funds to make long-term dollar loans. It also has medium- and long-term fixed-rate deposits in euros and uses those funds to make euro loans with adjustable rates. An increase in U.S. rates will reduce the spread on Oklahoma Bank's dollar loans versus deposits, because the dollar liabilities are more rate sensitive than the dollar assets. In addition, a decline in interest rates on the euro will decrease the spread on the euro loans versus deposits, because the euro assets are more rate sensitive than the euro liabilities. Thus, exposure to interest rate risk can be minimized only if the rate sensitivities of assets and liabilities are matched for each currency.

Managing Credit Risk

Most of a bank's funds are used either to make loans or to purchase debt securities. For either use of funds, the bank is acting as a creditor and is subject to credit (default) risk, or the possibility that credit provided by the bank will not be repaid. The types of loans provided and the securities purchased will determine the overall credit risk of the asset portfolio. A bank can also be exposed to credit risk if it serves as a guarantor on interest rate swaps and other derivative contracts in which it is the intermediary.

Tradeoff between Credit Risk and Expected Return

If a bank wants to minimize credit risk, it can use most of its funds to purchase Treasury securities, which are virtually free of credit risk. However, these securities may not generate a much higher yield than the average overall cost of obtaining funds. In fact, some bank sources of funds can be more costly to banks than the yield earned on Treasury securities.

At the other extreme, a bank concerned with maximizing its return could use most of its funds for consumer and small business loans. Such an asset portfolio would be subject to a high degree of credit risk, however. If economic conditions deteriorate, a relatively large amount of high-risk loans may default.

Ideally, a bank will manage its assets so as to simultaneously maximize return on assets and minimize credit risk. But, obviously, both objectives cannot be achieved simultaneously. The return on any bank asset depends on the risk involved. Because riskier assets offer higher returns, a bank's strategy to increase its return on assets will typically entail an increase in the overall credit risk of its asset portfolio.

Because a bank cannot simultaneously maximize return and minimize credit risk, it must compromise. That is, it will select some assets that generate high returns but are subject to a relatively high degree of credit risk and also some assets that are very safe but offer a lower rate of return. This way the bank attempts to earn a *reasonable* return on its overall asset portfolio and maintain credit risk at a *tolerable* level. What return level is reasonable? What level of credit risk is tolerable? There is no consensus on the answers. The actual degree of importance attached to a high return versus low credit risk is dependent on the risk-return preferences of a bank's shareholders and managers.

How the Loan Allocation Decision Affects Return and Risk A bank must develop a plan for allocating funds across different types of loans. The loan composition has a major influence on the bank's expected return and its exposure to credit risk. The top of Exhibit 19.8 compares the returns among types of bank loans, while the bottom of the

EXHIBIT 19.8 Return and Risk Tradeoff among Types of Loans

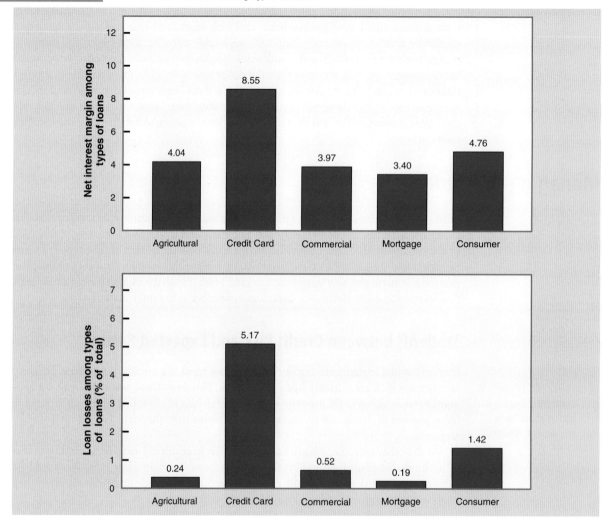

* Source: FDIC, 2004.

exhibit compares risk among types of bank loans. Of the loan types in the top of Exhibit 19.8, credit cards offer the highest net interest margin above the bank's cost of funds. Consumer loans provide the next highest interest margin above the bank's cost of funds. Thus, if banks focus on credit card or consumer loans, they will earn a very high rate of return if all of these loans are repaid fully and on time.

In reality, however, credit card and consumer loans experience more defaults than other types of loans. The bottom of Exhibit 19.8 compares loan loss levels (in proportion to loan value) among banks with different specializations. Notice how high the loan loss level is for banks that specialize in credit card loans. Banks that pursue the high potential returns associated with credit card loans must accept a high degree of credit risk.

Despite the risk, many banks have increased their credit card business in recent years. This is a typical example of increasing credit risk in an attempt to increase return. Many banks have also adopted more lenient credit standards in order to generate a greater amount of credit card business. Consequently, more undeserving consumers have ob-

tained credit cards, and the delinquency rate has increased. For those banks that were too lenient, the wide spread between the return on credit card loans and the cost of funds has been offset by a high level of bad debt (default) expenses.

Changes in Expected Return and Risk Over time, economic conditions change, causing the potential return and risk of assets to change. Banks adjust their asset portfolios accordingly. They tend to provide a larger than normal volume of loans during an economic upswing.

Banks generally reduce loans and increase their purchases of low-risk securities when the economy is weak, as it was in 2001. Following the September 11, 2001 attack, the U.S. economy was expected to weaken further. Businesses reduced their plans for expansion and reduced their demand for loanable funds. Banks had more funds than they needed to provide loans and therefore increased their allocation of high-quality (low-risk) loans and securities. In 2003, when economic conditions began to improve, banks were willing to extend loans subject to more risk. These loans not only provide a higher return, but are less likely to experience default problems under favorable economic conditions.

Measuring Credit Risk

An important part of managing credit risk is to measure it. This requires a credit assessment of loan applicants. Banks employ credit analysts who review the financial information of corporations applying for loans and evaluate their creditworthiness. The evaluation should indicate the probability that a firm can meet its loan payments so that the bank can decide whether to grant the loan.

Determining the Collateral When a bank assesses a request for credit, it must decide whether to require collateral that can back the loan in the event that the borrower is unable to repay it. For example, a loan extended to a firm that needs machinery may specify that the machinery serve as collateral. When a bank serves as an intermediary and a guarantor on derivative contracts, it commonly attempts to require collateral such as securities owned by the client.

Determining the Loan Rate If the bank decides to grant the loan, it can then use its evaluation of the firm to determine the appropriate interest rate. Loan applicants deserving of a loan may be rated on a basis of 1 to 5 (1 being the highest quality), reflecting their degree of credit risk. The rating dictates the premium to be added to the base rate. For example, a rating of 5 may dictate a 2 percent premium above the prime rate, while a rating of 3 may dictate a 1 percent premium. Given the current prime rate along with a rating of the potential borrower, the loan rate can be determined.

Some loans to high-quality (low-risk) customers are commonly offered at rates below the prime rate. This does not necessarily mean that banks have reduced their spread. It may instead imply that the banks have redefined the prime rate to represent the appropriate loan rate for borrowers with a moderate risk rating. Thus, a discount would be attached to the prime rate when determining the loan rate for borrowers with a superior rating.

Diversifying Credit Risk

Although all consumer and commercial loans exhibit some credit risk, banks can use several methods to manage this risk. Banks should diversify their loans to ensure that

their customers are not dependent on a common source of income. For example, a bank in a small farming town that provides consumer loans to farmers and commercial loans to farm equipment manufacturers is highly susceptible to credit risk. If the farmers experience a bad growing season because of poor weather conditions, they may be unable to repay their consumer loans. Furthermore, the farm equipment manufacturers would simultaneously experience a drop in sales and may be unable to repay their commercial loans.

This example is one of obvious mismanagement of the loan portfolio. In some cases, the mismanagement may not be so obvious. For example, consider a bank in a city that provides most of its commercial loans to firms in that city and has diversified its loans across various industries to avoid the problem just described. Assume that this city is the home of a large naval base. If, for some reason, the naval personnel employed at that base are sent out to sea, the city's firms may not be able to generate sufficient business to repay their loans. This example illustrates how corporate borrowers from different industries but from the same geographic region can be similarly affected by a particular event.

Applying Portfolio Theory to Loan Portfolios The benefits of proper loan diversification can be recognized when applying portfolio theory to a bank's asset portfolio. The risk of an asset portfolio is sometimes measured as the variability in the portfolio's returns, as this proxy indicates the degree of uncertainty about the portfolio returns. The variance of an asset portfolio's returns can be written as

$$\sigma_p^2 = \sum_{i=1}^{n} \sum_{j=1}^{n} w_i w_j \text{COV}(R_i, R_j)$$

for a portfolio of n assets, where w_i and w_j represent the proportion of funds allocated to the ith and jth assets, respectively, and $\text{COV}(R_i, R_j)$ represents the covariance between returns of the ith and jth assets. The covariance measures the degree to which the asset returns covary, or move in tandem. Because the covariance of any pair of asset returns is equal to the correlation coefficient between those asset returns (ρ_{ij}) times the standard deviation of each asset's returns (σ_i, σ_j), the portfolio variance can be rewritten as

$$\sigma_p^2 = \sum_{i=1}^{n} \sum_{j=1}^{n} w_i w_j \rho_{ij} \sigma_i \sigma_j$$

From this equation, the portfolio variance is positively related to the correlations between asset returns. If a bank's loans are driven by one particular economic factor (such as industry conditions in a particular region), the returns on the loans will be highly correlated. Thus, the returns of most loans will be high (few loan defaults) under favorable conditions but poor (many loan defaults) under unfavorable conditions.

Industry Diversification of Loans When a bank's loans are too heavily concentrated in a specific industry, it should attempt to expand its loans into other industries. In this way, if one particular industry experiences weakness (which will lead to loan defaults by firms in that industry), loans provided to other industries will be insulated from that industry's conditions.

The effectiveness of diversifying loans across industries is limited when economic conditions are weak, however. The level of nonperforming loans (loans not repaid on time) was about three times higher during the weak economy in 2001 and 2002 than in the 1998–1999 period when the U.S. economy was very strong. Thus, even banks that diversified their loans across many industries were susceptible to loan repayment problems in the 2001–2002 period. Banks cannot completely stop extending loans at the

EXHIBIT 19.9   Correlations of Production Levels across Federal Reserve Districts

District	\multicolumn{11}{c}{District}										
	2	3	4	5	6	7	8	9	10	11	12
1	.812	.634	.436	.426	.288	.318	.372	.055	−.220	−.312	.133
2		.881	.615	.789	.675	.515	.620	.337	.113	.099	.197
3			.886	.961	.886	.819	.892	.707	.483	.454	.528
4				.873	.797	.975	.960	.851	.633	.607	.821
5					.961	.823	.916	.782	.646	.648	.570
6						.742	.888	.796	.762	.749	.503
7							.945	.850	.622	.629	.847
8								.857	.705	.699	.751
9									.870	.805	.768
10										.937	.640
11											.622

Note: The variable measured is the deviation in the gross product per capita from the trend over the 1963–1986 period. A high correlation implies that the production level in the two districts is either above the norm or below the norm simultaneously. Each district is a Federal Reserve district.
Source: *New England Economic Review* (May–June 1990): 14.

first sign of a slow economy. Furthermore, many of their loans were initiated when the economy was stronger.

Geographic Diversification of Loans   To reduce exposure to a particular region, the bank may provide loans whose credit risk levels (and therefore returns) are not highly dependent on the regional market. It may consider providing loans outside its main region.

The possible benefits from geographic loan diversification can be seen by reviewing the correlations of regional production levels in Exhibit 19.9. A correlation coefficient between production levels was estimated for 12 different districts in the United States. The districts are numbered from 1 (in the Northeast) to 12 (the Far West), moving east to west. Notice that the correlations are generally high for any two districts next to each other (such as the correlation between Districts 1 and 2 = .812). This suggests that the production levels move closely in tandem. Thus, a bank that diversifies its loans within these two districts achieves only limited benefits, because any adverse conditions that cause high default rates could occur in both districts simultaneously. Conversely, production levels in districts that are far away from each other tend to have low correlations. Review the correlations between District 1 and other districts to confirm this.

Because the production level is a measure of economic conditions, it appears that the diversification of loans across districts throughout the United States could achieve significant risk reduction in the loan portfolio. Even if one or two districts experience financial problems in a particular period, the bank's exposure to debt of firms in those regions would be limited when using a broad diversification policy.

International Diversification of Loans   Many banks reduce their exposure to U.S. economic conditions by diversifying their loan portfolio internationally. They use a country risk assessment system to assess country characteristics that may influence the ability of a government or corporation to repay its debt. In particular, the country risk

assessment focuses on a country's financial and political conditions. Banks tend to focus on countries to which they have assigned a high country risk rating. Once a bank establishes a branch in a foreign country, however, it is committed to international loans in that country. After extending loans, a bank cannot recall them just because country conditions have deteriorated.

Lending to national governments is normally viewed as a conservative strategy, and diversification of loans across countries can reduce exposure to any one country. However, the international debt crisis in the early 1980s demonstrated that this strategy can be risky. During that crisis, several less developed countries (LDCs) could not repay the loans that they had obtained from U.S. banks. Many of these countries were simultaneously experiencing severe economic problems that were due in part to a worldwide recession in 1982. Consequently, the global demand for LDC exports declined substantially, and the LDC's income was not sufficient to repay the loans.

The Asian crisis in 1997 provided another lesson to banks about the limited benefits of international loan diversification. The Asian economies were growing rapidly in the mid-1990s, and banks aggressively attempted to increase their loans throughout Asia. They approved loans to Asian firms without much analysis, assuming that the Asian economies would continue to grow. When the economies of Thailand, Indonesia, and Malaysia weakened in 1997, many firms could not repay their loans. Because the Asian economies are integrated, the problems spread to other countries such as South Korea and Japan. Banks in Europe and the United States that had a strong presence in Asia incurred major losses.

The international debt crisis and the Asian crisis illustrate that the international diversification of loans among countries does not always prevent the possibility of several simultaneous defaulted loans. The crises were largely attributed to the similar economic cycles of these countries. If all borrowers around the world are similarly affected by specific events, international diversification of loans is not a viable solution.

In reality, diversifying loans across countries can often reduce the loan portfolio's exposure to any single economy or event. If diversification across geographic regions means that the bank must accept loan applicants with very high risk, however, the bank is defeating its purpose.

Selling Loans Banks can eliminate loans that are causing excessive risk to their loan portfolios by selling them in the secondary market. Most loan sales enable the bank originating the loan to continue servicing the loan by collecting payments and monitoring the borrower's collateral. However, the bank that originated the loan is no longer funding the loan, and the loan is therefore removed from the bank's assets. Bank loans are commonly purchased by other banks and some other financial institutions, such as pension funds and insurance companies, and some mutual funds.

Revising the Loan Portfolio in Response to Economic Conditions Banks continuously assess both the overall composition of their loan portfolios and the economic environment. As economic conditions change, so does the risk of a bank's loan portfolio. A bank is typically more willing to extend loans during strong economic conditions, since businesses are more likely to meet their loan payments under those conditions. During weak economic conditions, the bank is more cautious and reduces the amount of new loans that are extended to businesses. Under these conditions, the bank typically increases the credit it extends to the Treasury by purchasing more Treasury securities. Nevertheless, its loan portfolio may still be heavily exposed to economic conditions because some of the businesses that have already borrowed may be unable to repay their loans.

Managing Market Risk

From a bank management perspective, market risk results from changes in the value of securities due to changes in financial market conditions such as interest rate movements, exchange rate movements, and equity prices. As banks pursue new services related to the trading of securities, they have become much more susceptible to market risk. For example, some banks now provide loans to special partnerships called hedge funds, which use the borrowed funds to invest in stocks or derivative securities. Thus, these loans may not be repaid if the prices of the stocks or derivative securities held by the hedge funds decline substantially.

The increase in banks' exposure to market risk is also attributed to their increased participation in the trading of derivative contracts. Many banks now serve as intermediaries between firms that take positions in derivative securities and will be exchanging payments in the future. For some of these transactions, a bank serves as a guarantor to one of the parties if the counterparty in the transaction does not fulfill its payment obligation. If derivative security prices change abruptly and cause several parties involved in these transactions to default, a bank that served as a guarantor will suffer major losses. Furthermore, banks that purchase debt securities issued in developing countries are subject to abrupt losses as a result of abrupt swings in the economic or currency conditions in those countries.

The need to monitor the positions of banks with substantial trading businesses was reinforced by the shocking $488 million loss reported by Bankers Trust (now part of Deutsche Bank) in October 1998. The loss was attributed to markdowns on Russian and Latin American debt securities held by Bankers Trust, adverse currency movements, and a reduction in its securities underwriting business. If Bankers Trust had had a system that monitored the market values of its positions on a daily basis, it might have been able to reduce its losses.

Measuring Market Risk

Banks commonly measure their exposure to market risk by applying the value-at-risk (VAR) method, which involves determining the largest possible loss that would occur as a result of changes in market prices based on a specified percent confidence level. To estimate this loss, the bank first determines an adverse scenario (such as a 9 percent decline in stock prices or a 30 percent decline in derivative security prices) for market prices that has a 1 percent chance of occurring. Then it estimates the impact of that scenario on its positions, based on the sensitivity of the values of its positions to the scenario. All of the losses that would occur from existing positions are summed to determine the estimated total loss to the bank under this scenario. This estimate reflects the largest possible loss at the 99 percent confidence level, as there is only a 1-in-100 chance that such an unfavorable scenario would occur. By determining its exposure to market risk, the bank can ensure that it has sufficient capital to cushion against the adverse effects of such an event.

Bank Revisions of Market Risk Measurements Banks continually revise their estimate of market risk in response to changes in their investment and credit positions and to changes in market conditions. When market prices become more volatile, banks recognize that market prices could change to a greater degree and typically increase their estimate of their potential losses due to market conditions. For example, in the fall of 1998, market conditions across countries were unusually volatile due to the Russian

debt default. There was more uncertainty about exchange rates, interest rates, and equity prices. Many banks recognized that their market risk had increased (even if their existing investment and credit positions had not changed), and reestimated their potential loss due to market risk by adjusting the potential magnitude of foreign exchange, interest rate, and equity price movements.

How J.P. Morgan Assesses Market Risk Banks commonly disclose their estimate of market risk and their method of measuring it in their annual report. For example, J.P. Morgan & Co. (part of J.P. Morgan Chase, one of the largest U.S. banks) uses a 95 percent confidence level to determine the maximum expected one-day loss in its investments and credit instruments due to changes in interest rates, foreign exchange rates, equity prices, and commodity prices. If its measure of market risk is $35 million, under normal market conditions (95 percent of the time), market price movements should result in a one-day loss on its positions of no more than $35 million.

Diversification effects are considered because any potential adverse effects would not be expected to occur simultaneously for all types of market prices. For example, some of J.P. Morgan's investment positions might be adversely affected by adverse interest rate movements, but some of its other positions would not be adversely affected by foreign exchange prices as long as no unusual movement in foreign exchange prices occurred at the same time as the unusual interest rate movement.

Relationship between a Bank's Market Risk and Interest Rate Risk A bank's market risk is partially dependent on its exposure to interest rate risk. Banks give special attention to interest rate risk, however, because it is commonly the most important component of market risk. Moreover, many banks assess interest rate risk by itself when evaluating their positions over a longer time horizon. For example, a bank might assess interest rate risk by itself over the next year using the methods described earlier in the chapter. In this case, the bank might use the assessment to alter the maturities on the deposits it attempts to obtain or on its uses of funds. Conversely, banks' assessment of market risk tends to be focused on a shorter-term horizon, such as the next month. Nevertheless, they may still use their assessment of market risk to alter their operations, as explained next.

Methods Used to Reduce Market Risk

If a bank determines that its exposure to market risk is excessive, it can reduce its involvement in the activities that cause the high exposure. For example, it could reduce the amount of transactions in which it serves as guarantor for its clients or reduce its investment in foreign debt securities that are subject to adverse events in a specific region. Alternatively, it could attempt to take some trading positions to offset some of its exposure to market risk. It could also sell some of its securities that are heavily exposed to market risk.

Operating Risk

Operating risk is the risk resulting from a bank's general business operations. Banks are subject to risk related to information (sorting, processing, transmitting through technology), execution of transactions, damaged relationships with clients, legal issues (lawsuits by employees and customers), and regulatory issues (increased costs due to new

compliance requirements or penalties due to lack of compliance). Although these forms of risk are not closely related to the financial forms of risk discussed so far, they should at least be recognized since they can affect a bank's value.

Managing Risk of International Operations

http://

http://www.risknews.net
Links to risk-related information in international banking.

Banks that are engaged in international banking face additional types of risk.

Exchange Rate Risk

When a bank providing a loan requires that the borrower repay in the currency denominating the loan, it may be able to avoid exchange rate risk. However, some international loans contain a clause that allows repayment in a foreign currency, thus allowing the borrower to avoid exchange rate risk.

In many cases, banks convert available funds (from recent deposits) to whatever currency corporations want to borrow. Thus, they create an asset denominated in that currency, while the liability (deposits) is denominated in a different currency. If the liability currency appreciates against the asset currency, the bank's profit margin is reduced.

All large banks are exposed to exchange rate risk to some degree. They can attempt to hedge this risk in various ways.

ILLUSTRATION Cameron Bank, a U.S. bank, converts dollar deposits into a British pound (£) loan for a British corporation, which will pay £50,000 in interest per year. Cameron Bank may attempt to engage in forward contracts to sell £50,000 forward for each date when it will receive those interest payments. That is, it will search for corporations that wish to purchase £50,000 on the dates of concern.

In reality, a large bank will not hedge every individual transaction, but will instead net out the exposure and be concerned only with net exposure. Large banks enter into several international transactions on any given day. Some reflect future cash inflows in a particular currency, while others reflect cash outflows in that currency. The bank's exposure to exchange rate risk is determined by the net cash flow in each currency.

Settlement Risk

International banks that engage in large currency transactions are exposed not only to exchange rate risk as a result of their different currency positions, but also to settlement risk, or the risk of a loss due to settling their transactions. For example, a bank may send its currency to another bank as part of a transaction agreement, but it may not receive any currency from the other bank if that bank defaults before sending its payment. The best-known case of a bank that did not meet its settlement obligation is Herstatt, a German bank that failed in 1974. Before Herstatt failed, it had received payments on transactions with U.S. banks. It was closed before it sent its payments, resulting in an estimated $200 million in losses to those U.S. banks.

The failure of a single large bank could create more losses if other banks were relying on receivables from the failed bank to make future payables of their own. Consequently, there is concern about systemic risk, or the risk that many participants will be unable to meet their obligations because they did not receive payments on obligations due to them.

Given that the average currency trade between banks is $10 million and that more than $1 billion per day is traded in the foreign currency markets, central banks around the world are assessing methods of ensuring that a bank settlement problem does not ripple through the foreign exchange market.

Bank Capital Management

Like other corporations, banks must determine the level of capital that they should maintain. Bank operations are distinctly different from other types of firms because the majority of their assets (such as loans and security holdings) generate more predictable cash flows. Thus, banks can use a much higher degree of financial leverage than other types of firms. The FDIC, which insures depositors, bears most of the risk in the event of failure. Depositors who are fully insured normally do not penalize banks for taking excessive risk, which could encourage some banks to use a high degree of financial leverage.

Banks must also consider the minimum capital ratio required by regulators. This minimum could possibly force a bank to maintain more capital than it believes is optimal. To please shareholders, banks typically attempt to maintain only the amount of capital that is sufficient to support bank operations. If a bank has too much capital as a result of issuing excessive amounts of stock, each shareholder will receive a smaller proportion of any distributed earnings.

A common measure of the return to the shareholders is the **return on equity (ROE),** measured as

$$\text{ROE} = \frac{\text{Net profit after taxes}}{\text{Equity}}$$

The term *equity* represents the bank's capital. The return on equity can be broken down as follows:

$$\text{ROE} = \text{Return on assets (ROA)} \times \text{Leverage measure}$$

$$\frac{\text{Net profit after taxes}}{\text{Equity}} = \frac{\text{Net profit after taxes}}{\text{Assets}} \times \frac{\text{Assets}}{\text{Equity}}$$

The ratio (assets/equity) is sometimes called the **leverage measure,** because leverage reflects the volume of assets a firm supports with equity. The greater the leverage measure, the greater the amount of assets per dollar's worth of equity. The above breakdown of ROE is useful because it can demonstrate how excessive capital can lower a bank's ROE.

ILLUSTRATION   Consider two banks called Hilev and Lolev, each of which has a return on assets (ROA) of 1 percent. Hilev Bank has a leverage measure of 15, while Lolev Bank has a leverage measure of 10. The ROE for each bank is determined as follows:

$$\text{ROE} = \text{ROA} \times \text{Leverage measure}$$

$$\text{ROE for Hilev Bank} = 1\% \times 15$$

$$= 15\%$$

$$\text{ROE for Lolev Bank} = 1\% \times 10$$

$$= 10\%$$

Even though each bank's assets are generating a 1 percent ROA, the ROE of Hilev Bank is much higher, because Hilev Bank is supporting its assets with a smaller proportion of capital.

Bank regulators require banks to hold a minimum amount of capital, because capital can be used to absorb losses. Banks, however, generally prefer to hold a relatively low amount of capital for the reasons just expressed.

Because required capital is specified as a proportion of loans (and some other assets), banks can reduce the required level of capital by selling some of their loans in the secondary market. They can still service the loans to generate fee income but would be subject to a lower capital constraint as a result of removing loans from their asset portfolio.

If banks are holding an excessive amount of capital, they can reduce it by distributing a high percentage of their earnings to shareholders (as dividends). Thus, capital management is related to the bank's dividend policy.

A growing bank may need more capital to support construction of new buildings, Internet services, office equipment, and so forth. It will therefore need to retain a larger proportion of its earnings than a bank that has no plans for future growth. If the growing bank prefers to provide existing shareholders with a sizable dividend, it will then have to obtain the necessary capital by issuing new stock. This strategy allows the bank to distribute dividends but dilutes the proportional ownership of the bank. An obvious tradeoff exists here. The solution is not so obvious. A bank in need of capital must assess the tradeoff involved and follow a policy that it believes will maximize the wealth of shareholders.

Management Based on Forecasts

Some banks position themselves to significantly benefit from an expected change in the economy. Exhibit 19.10 provides possible policy decisions for four different forecasts and suggests how a bank might react to each. This exhibit is simplified in that it does not consider future economic growth and interest rate movements simultaneously. Furthermore, it does not consider other economic forecasts that banks would also consider.

EXHIBIT 19.10   Bank Management of Liabilities and Assets Based on Economic Forecasts

Economic Forecast by the Banks	Appropriate Adjustment to Liability Structure Based on the Forecast	Appropriate Adjustment to Asset Structure Based on the Forecast	General Assessment of Bank's Adjusted Balance Sheet Structure
1. Strong economy		Concentrate more heavily on loans; reduce holdings of low-risk securities.	Increased potential for stronger earnings; increased exposure of bank earnings to credit risk.
2. Weak economy		Concentrate more heavily on risk-free securities and low-risk loans; reduce holdings of risky loans.	Reduced credit risk; reduced potential for stronger earnings if the economy does not weaken.
3. Increasing interest rates	Attempt to attract CDs with long-term maturities.	Apply floating interest rates to loans whenever possible; avoid long-term securities.	Reduced interest rate risk; reduced potential for stronger earnings if interest rates decrease.
4. Decreasing interest rates	Attempt to attract CDs with short-term maturities.	Apply fixed interest rates to loans whenever possible; concentrate on long-term securities or loans.	Increased potential for stronger earnings; increased interest rate risk.

Nevertheless, it illustrates the type of risk-return tradeoff constantly faced by bank managers. For example, if managers expect a strong economy, they can boost earnings by shifting into relatively risky loans and securities that pay a high return. If the economy is strong as expected, only a small percentage of the loans and securities will default, and the bank's strategy will result in improved earnings. However, if the bank's forecast turns out to be wrong, its revised asset portfolio will be more susceptible to a weak economy. The bank could be severely damaged during a weak economy, because several borrowers are likely to default on their loans and securities.

An inaccurate forecast of the economy will have less effect on more conservative banks that maintain a sizable portion of very safe loans and securities. If the economy strengthens as predicted, however, these banks also will not benefit as much as the bank that assumed more risk. The degree to which a bank is willing to revise its balance sheet structure in accordance with economic forecasts depends on its confidence in those forecasts and its willingness to incur risk.

Because the first two forecasts shown in Exhibit 19.10 are on economic growth, they relate to credit risk. The last two forecasts are on interest rates and therefore relate to interest rate risk. Banks cannot completely adjust their balance sheet structure in accordance with economic forecasts. For example, they cannot implement a policy of accepting only long-term CDs just because they believe interest rates will rise. Yet, they could attract a greater than normal amount of long-term CDs by offering an attractive interest rate on long-term CDs and advertising this rate to potential depositors.

The bank's balance sheet management will affect its performance (as measured from its income statement) in the following ways. First, its liability structure will influence its interest and noninterest expenses on the income statement. If it obtains a relatively large portion of its funds from conventional demand deposits, interest expenses should be relatively low, while its noninterest expenses (due to check clearing, processing, etc.) should be relatively high. A bank's asset structure can also affect expenses. If a bank maintains a relatively large portion of commercial loans, its noninterest expenses should be high because of the labor cost of assessing the borrower's credit along with loan-processing costs. Yet, banks with the heaviest concentration in commercial loans expect their additional interest revenues to more than offset the additional noninterest expenses incurred. Their strategy will pay off only if they can avoid a sizable number of defaulted loans. Of course, this is the risk they must take in striving for a high return.

Ideally, banks would use an aggressive approach when they can capitalize on favorable economic conditions but insulate themselves during adverse economic conditions. Because economic conditions cannot always be accurately forecasted for several years in advance, even well-managed banks will experience defaults on loans. This is a cost of doing business. Banks attempt to use proper diversification so that a domino effect of defaulted loans will not occur within their loan portfolio. Similarly, interest rate movements cannot always be accurately forecasted. Thus, banks should not be overly aggressive in attempting to capitalize on interest rate forecasts. They should assess the sensitivity of their future performance to each possible interest rate scenario that could occur to ensure that their balance sheet is structured to survive any possible scenario.

Bank Restructuring

Bank operations change in response to changing regulations and economic conditions and to managerial policies designed to hedge various forms of risk. For example, in recent years banks have expanded across state lines, diversified their asset portfolios, boosted their capital ratios, and expanded their operations into services such as insurance, bro-

http://

http://www.fdic.gov
Statistical overview of how
banks have performed in
recent years.

kerage, underwriting of securities, and sales of mutual funds. Large changes in bank operations typically require restructuring, which normally must be assessed and approved by the bank's executives and board of directors.

Decisions to restructure are complex because of their effects on customers, shareholders, and employees. A strategic plan to satisfy customers and shareholders will not necessarily satisfy the majority of employees. During the early 1990s, many banks downsized their operations because their business had declined in response to poor economic conditions. Downsizing forced consolidation of some divisions and layoffs as well. Although downsizing may be unavoidable in some periods, the plan for restructuring should consider the potential effects on employee morale.

Bank Acquisitions

A common form of bank restructuring is growth through acquisitions of other banks. Growth can be achieved more quickly with acquisitions than by establishing new branches.

Bank acquisitions offer several potential advantages. First, some banks may be able to achieve economies of scale by acquiring other banks. If the costs of some operations are mostly fixed, an increase in the size of those operations should create efficiencies because the costs in proportion to total assets decline. A related advantage is that bank acquisitions can remove redundant operations. For example, if branches of the acquiring bank are right next to branches of the target bank, some of these branches can be closed without a loss of convenience to customers.

Bank acquisitions can also achieve diversification benefits as the acquirer can offer loans in some new industries. Furthermore, an acquiring bank may have some managerial advantages over a target, which should allow the acquirer to improve the target's performance after the acquisition.

Along with the potential advantages, some potential disadvantages are associated with bank acquisitions. First, some acquisitions are motivated by highly optimistic projections of the cost efficiencies that will result from combining the operations of the target and acquirer. Thus, an acquirer may pay an excessive price for the target bank. Second, the reorganization of operations after an acquisition can lead to significant employee morale problems and high employee turnover.

Are Bank Acquisitions Worthwhile?   Numerous studies have assessed the stock price reaction of banks that acquire other banks. If investors believe that the acquiring bank will benefit from the acquisition, the stock price should rise in response to the acquisition announcement. Most of the studies have found that the acquiring bank's stock price either does not change or reacts negatively. These results suggest that the market does not expect the acquisition to be favorable. One possible explanation is that the acquiring bank will never achieve the expected efficiencies that motivated the acquisition. Second, personnel clashes among the units to be merged could result in high turnover and low morale. Third, the acquiring bank may simply be paying too much for the target bank.

Integrated Bank Management

Bank management of assets, liabilities, and capital is integrated. A bank's asset growth can be achieved only if it obtains the necessary funds. Furthermore, growth may require an investment in fixed assets (such as additional offices) that will require an accumulation of

bank capital. Integration of asset, liability, and capital management ensures that all policies will be consistent with a cohesive set of economic forecasts. An integrated management approach is necessary to manage liquidity risk, interest rate risk, and credit risk.

Example

Assume that you are hired as a consultant by Atlanta Bank to evaluate its favorable and unfavorable aspects. Atlanta Bank's balance sheet is shown in Exhibit 19.11. A bank's balance sheet can best be evaluated by converting the actual dollar amounts of balance sheet components to a percentage of assets. This conversion enables the bank to be compared with its competitors. Exhibit 19.12 shows each balance sheet component as a percentage of total assets for Atlanta Bank (derived from Exhibit 19.11). To the right of each bank percentage is the assumed industry average percentage for a sample of banks with

EXHIBIT 19.11

Balance Sheet of Atlanta
Bank (in Millions of Dollars)

Assets			Liabilities and Capital		
Required reserves		$ 400	Demand deposits		$ 500
Commercial loans			NOW accounts		1,200
Floating-rate	3,000		MMDAs		2,000
Fixed-rate	1,100		CDs		
Total		4,100	Short-term	1,500	
Consumer loans		2,500	From 1 to 5 yrs.	4,000	
Mortgages			Total		5,500
Floating-rate	500		Long-term bonds		200
Fixed-rate	None		CAPITAL		600
Total		500			
Treasury securities					
Short-term	1,000				
Long-term	None				
Total		1,000			
Corporate securities					
High-rated	None				
Moderate-rated	1,000				
Total		1,000			
Municipal securities					
High-rated	None				
Moderate-rated	None				
Total		None			
Fixed assets		500			_____
TOTAL ASSETS		$10,000	TOTAL LIABILITIES and CAPITAL		$10,000

EXHIBIT 19.12

Comparative Balance Sheet of Atlanta Bank

Assets			Liabilities and Capital		
	Percentage of Assets for Atlanta Bank	Average Percentage for Industry		Percentage of Total for Atlanta Bank	Average Percentage for Industry
Required reserves	4%	4%	**Demand deposits**	5%	17%
Commercial loans			**NOW accounts**	12	10
Floating-rate	30	20	MMDAs	20	20
Fixed-rate	11	11	CD		
Total	41	31	Short-term	15	35
Consumer loans	25	20	From 1 to 5 yrs.	40	10
Mortgages			Long-term bonds	2	2
Floating-rate	5	7	CAPITAL	6	6
Fixed-rate	0	3			
Total	5	10			
Treasury securities					
Short-term	10	7			
Long-term	0	8			
Total	10	15			
Corporate securities					
High-rated	0	5			
Moderate-rated	10	5			
Total	10	10			
Municipal securities					
High-rated	0	3			
Moderate-rated	0	2			
Total	0	5			
Fixed assets	5	5		—	—
TOTAL ASSETS	100%	100%	**TOTAL LIABILITIES and CAPITAL**	100%	100%

a similar amount of assets. For example, the bank's required reserves are 4 percent of assets (the same as the industry average), its floating-rate commercial loans are 30 percent of assets (versus an industry average of 20 percent), and so on. The same type of comparison is provided for liabilities and capital on the right side of the exhibit. A comparative analysis relative to the industry can indicate the management style of Atlanta Bank.

It is possible to evaluate the potential level of interest revenues, interest expenses, noninterest revenues, and noninterest expenses for Atlanta Bank relative to the industry. Furthermore, it is possible to assess the bank's exposure to credit risk and interest rate risk as compared to the industry.

EXHIBIT 19.13 Evaluation of Atlanta Bank Based on Its Balance Sheet

	Main Influential Components	Evaluation of Atlanta Bank Relative to Industry
Interest expenses	All liabilities except demand deposits.	Higher than industry average because it concentrates more on high-rate deposits than the norm.
Noninterest expenses	Loan volume and checkable deposit volume.	Questionable; its checkable deposit volume is less than the norm, but its loan volume is greater than the norm.
Interest revenues	Volume and composition of loans and securities.	Potentially higher than industry average because its assets are generally riskier than the norm.
Exposure to credit risk	Volume and composition of loans and securities.	Higher concentration of loans than industry average; it has a greater percentage of risky assets than the norm.
Exposure to interest rate risk	Maturities on liabilities and assets; use of floating-rate loans.	Lower than the industry average; it has more medium-term liabilities, fewer assets with very long maturities, and more floating-rate loans.

A summary of Atlanta Bank based on the information in Exhibit 19.12 is provided in Exhibit 19.13. Although its interest expenses are expected to be above the industry average, so are its interest revenues. Thus, it is difficult to determine whether Atlanta Bank's net interest margin will be above or below the industry average. Because it is more heavily concentrated in risky loans and securities, its credit risk is higher than that of the average bank; yet, its interest rate risk is less because of its relatively high concentration of medium-term CDs and floating-rate loans. A gap measurement of Atlanta Bank can be conducted by first identifying the rate-sensitive liabilities and assets, as follows:

Rate-Sensitive Assets	Amount (in Millions)	Rate-Sensitive Liabilities	Amount (in Millions)
Floating-rate loans	$3,000	NOW accounts	$1,200
Floating-rate mortgages	500	MMDAs	2,000
Short-term Treasury securities	1,000	Short-term CDs	1,500
	$4,500		$4,700

$$\text{Gap} = \$4,500 \text{ million} - \$4,700 \text{ million}$$
$$= -\$200 \text{ million}$$

$$\text{Gap ratio} = \frac{\$4,500 \text{ million}}{\$4,700 \text{ million}}$$
$$= .957$$

The gap measurements suggest somewhat similar rate sensitivity on both sides of the balance sheet.

The future performance of Atlanta Bank relative to the industry depends on future economic conditions. If interest rates rise, it will be more insulated than other banks. If interest rates fall, other banks will likely benefit to a greater degree. Under conditions of a strong economy, Atlanta Bank would likely benefit more than other banks because of its aggressive lending approach. Conversely, an economic slowdown could cause more loan defaults, and Atlanta Bank would be more susceptible to possible defaults than other banks. This could be confirmed only if more details were provided (such as a more comprehensive breakdown of the balance sheet).

SUMMARY

- The underlying goal of bank management is to maximize the wealth of the bank's shareholders, which implies maximizing the price of the bank's stock.

- Banks manage liquidity by maintaining some liquid assets such as short-term securities and ensuring easy access to funds (through the federal funds market or the discount window).

- Banks measure their sensitivity to interest rate movements to assess their exposure to interest rate risk. Common methods of measuring interest rate risk include gap analysis and duration analysis. Some banks use regression analysis to determine the sensitivity of their earnings or stock returns to interest rate movements.

   Banks can reduce their interest rate risk by matching maturities of their assets and liabilities or by using floating-rate loans to create more rate sensitivity in their assets. Alternatively, they may use in-

terest rate futures contracts or interest rate swaps instead. If they are adversely affected by rising interest rates, they could sell financial futures contracts or engage in a swap of fixed-rate payments for floating-rate payments.

- Banks manage credit risk by carefully assessing the borrowers who apply for loans. They also diversify their loans across borrowers of different regions and industries so that the loan portfolio is not heavily susceptible to financial problems in any single region or industry.

- Banks attempt to maintain sufficient capital to satisfy regulatory constraints. However, they generally prefer to avoid holding excessive capital because a high level of capital can reduce their return on equity. If banks need to raise capital, they can attempt to retain more earnings (reduce dividends) or issue new stock.

POINT COUNTER-POINT

Can Bank Failures Be Avoided?

Point No. Banks are in the business of providing credit. When economic conditions deteriorate, there will be loan defaults and some banks will not be able to survive.

Counter-Point Yes. If banks focus on providing loans to creditworthy borrowers, most loans will not default even during recessionary periods.

Who Is Correct? Use your favorite search engine to learn more about this issue. Offer your own opinion on this issue.

QUESTIONS AND APPLICATIONS

1. **Commercial Borrowing** Do all commercial borrowers receive the same interest rate on loans?

2. **Managing Exchange Rate Risk** Explain how banks become exposed to exchange rate risk.

3. **Bank Exposure to Interest Rate Movements** According to this chapter, have banks been able to insulate themselves against interest rate movements? Explain.

4. **Integrating Asset and Liability Management** What is accomplished when a bank integrates its liability management with its asset management?

5. **Managing Interest Rate Risk** Assume that a bank expects to attract most of its funds through short-term CDs and would prefer to use most of its funds to provide long-term loans. How could it follow this strategy and still reduce interest rate risk?

6. **Gap Management** What is a bank's gap, and what does it attempt to determine? Interpret a negative gap. What are some limitations of measuring a bank's gap?

7. **Managing Interest Rate Risk** If a bank expects interest rates to decrease over time, how might it alter the rate sensitivity of its assets and liabilities?

8. **Bank Management Dilemma** Can a bank simultaneously maximize return and minimize default risk? If not, what can it do instead?

9. **Interpreting Financial News** Interpret the following comments made by Wall Street analysts and portfolio managers:

   a. "Bank D's biggest mistake was that it did not recognize that its forecasts of a strong local real estate market and declining interest rates could be wrong."

   b. "Banks still need some degree of interest rate risk to be profitable."

   c. "Bank X used interest rate swaps so that its spread is no longer exposed to interest rate movements. However, its loan volume and therefore its profits are still exposed to interest rate movements."

10. **Managing Interest Rate Risk** If a bank is very uncertain about future interest rates, how might it insulate its future performance from future interest rate movements?

11. **Managing Interest Rate Risk** If a bank has more rate-sensitive liabilities than rate-sensitive assets, what will happen to its net interest margin during a period of rising interest rates? During a period of declining interest rates?

12. **Bank Exposure to Interest Rate Risk** Oregon Bank has branches overseas that concentrate in short-term deposits in dollars and floating-rate loans in British pounds. Because it maintains rate-sensitive assets and liabilities of equal amounts, it believes it has essentially eliminated its interest rate risk. Do you agree? Explain.

13. **Managing in Financial Markets: Hedging with Interest Rate Swaps** As a manager of Stetson Bank, you are responsible for hedging Stetson's interest rate risk. Stetson has forecasted its cost of funds as follows:

Year	Cost of Funds
1	6%
2	5%
3	7%
4	9%
5	7%

It expects to earn an average rate of 11 percent on some assets that charge a fixed interest rate over the next five years. It considers engaging in an interest rate swap in which it would swap fixed payments of 10 percent in exchange for variable-rate payments of LIBOR + 1 percent. Assume LIBOR is expected to be consistently 1 percent above Stetson's cost of funds.

   a. Determine the spread that would be earned each year if Stetson uses an interest rate swap to hedge all of its interest rate risk. Would you recommend that Stetson use an interest rate swap?

   b. Although Stetson has forecasted its cost of funds, it recognizes that its forecasts may be inaccurate. Offer a method that Stetson can use to assess the potential results from using an interest rate swap while accounting for the uncertainty surrounding future interest rates.

   c. The reason for Stetson's interest rate risk is that it uses some of its funds to make fixed-rate loans, as some borrowers prefer fixed rates. An alternative method of hedging interest rate risk is to use adjustable-rate loans. Would you recommend that Stetson use only adjustable-rate loans to hedge its interest rate risk? Explain.

14. **Net Interest Margin** What is the formula for the net interest margin? Explain why it is closely monitored by banks.

15. **Managing Interest Rate Risk** Dakota Bank has a branch overseas with the following balance sheet characteristics: 50 percent of the liabilities are rate sensitive and denominated in Swiss francs; the remaining 50 percent of liabilities are rate insensitive and are denominated in dollars. With regard to assets, 50 percent are rate sensitive and are denominated in dollars; the remaining 50 percent of assets are rate insensitive and are denominated in Swiss francs.

   a. Is the performance of this branch susceptible to interest rate movements? Explain.

   b. Assume that Dakota Bank plans to replace its short-term deposits denominated in U.S. dollars with short-term deposits denominated in Swiss francs, because Swiss interest rates are currently lower than U.S. interest rates. The asset composition would not change. This strategy is intended to widen the spread between the rate earned on assets and the rate paid on liabilities. Offer your insight on how this strategy could backfire.

   c. One consultant has suggested to Dakota Bank that it could avoid exchange rate risk by making loans in whatever currencies it receives

as deposits. In this way, it will not have to exchange one currency for another. Offer your insight on whether there are any disadvantages to this strategy.

16. **Rate Sensitivity** List some rate-sensitive assets and some rate-insensitive assets of banks.

17. **Floating-Rate Loans** Does the use of floating-rate loans eliminate interest rate risk? Explain.

18. **Measuring Interest Rate Risk** Why do loans that can be prepaid on a moment's notice complicate the bank's assessment of interest rate risk?

19. **Liquidity** Given the liquidity advantage of holding Treasury bills, why do banks hold only a relatively small portion of their assets as T-bills?

20. **Bank Exposure to Economic Conditions** As economic conditions change, how do banks adjust their asset portfolio?

21. **Internet Exercise** Assess the services offered by an Internet bank, using the website http://www.netbank .com.
    a. Describe the types of online services offered by the bank. Do you think an Internet bank such as this offers higher or lower interest rates than a "regular" commercial bank? Why or why not?

22. **Illiquidity** How do banks resolve illiquidity problems?

23. **Asian Crisis** Explain why bank decision making is sometimes blamed for the Asian crisis.

24. **Bank Loan Diversification** In what two ways should a bank diversify its loans? Why? Is international diversification of loans a viable solution to credit risk? Defend your answer.

25. **Bank Dividend Policy** Why might a bank retain some excess earnings rather than distribute them as dividends?

26. **Duration** How do banks use duration analysis?

PROBLEMS

1. **Managing Risk** Use the balance sheet for San Diego Bank in Exhibit A on page 588 and the industry norms in Exhibit B on page 589 to answer the following questions:
   a. Estimate the gap and the gap ratio and determine how San Diego Bank would be affected by an increase in interest rates over time.
   b. Assess San Diego's credit risk. Does it appear high or low relative to the industry? Would San Diego Bank perform better or worse than other banks during a recession?
   c. For any type of bank risk that appears to be higher than the industry, explain how the balance sheet could be restructured to reduce the risk.

2. **Net Interest Margin** Suppose a bank earns $201 million in interest revenue but pays $156 million in interest expense. It also has $800 million in earning assets. What is its net interest margin?

3. **Calculating Return on Assets** If a bank earns $169 million net profit after tax and has $17 billion invested in assets, what is its return on assets?

4. **Measuring Risk** Montana Bank wants to determine the sensitivity of its stock returns to interest rate movements, based on the following information:

Quarter	Return on Montana Stock	Return on Market	Interest Rate
1	2%	3%	6.0%
2	2	2	7.5
3	−1	−2	9.0
4	0	−1	8.2
5	2	1	7.3
6	−3	−4	8.1
7	1	5	7.4
8	0	1	9.1
9	−2	0	8.2
10	1	−1	7.1
11	3	3	6.4
12	6	4	5.5

Use a regression model in which Montana's stock return is dependent on the stock market return and the interest rate. Determine the relationship between the interest rate and Montana's stock return by assessing the regression coefficient applied to the in-

EXHIBIT A

Balance Sheet for San Diego Bank (in Millions of Dollars)

Assets			Liabilities and Capital		
Required reserves		$ 800	Demand deposits		$ 800
Commercial loans			NOW accounts		2,500
Floating-rate	None		MMDAs		6,000
Fixed-rate	7,000		CDs		
Total		7,000	Short-term	9,000	
Consumer loans		5,000	From 1 to 5 yrs.	None	
Mortgages			Total		9,000
Floating-rate	None		Federal funds	500	
Fixed-rate	2,000		Long-term bonds		400
Total		2,000	CAPITAL		800
Treasury securities					
Short-term	None				
Long-term	1,000				
Total		1,000			
Long-term corporate securities					
High-rated	None				
Moderate-rated	2,000				
Total		2,000			
Long-term municipal securities					
High-rated	None				
Moderate-rated	1,700				
Total		1,700			
Fixed assets		500			
TOTAL ASSETS		$20,000	TOTAL LIABILITIES and CAPITAL		$20,000

terest rate. Is the sign of the coefficient positive or negative? What does it suggest about the bank's exposure to interest rate risk? Should Montana Bank be concerned about rising or declining interest rate movements in the future?

5. **Calculating Return on Equity** If a bank earns $75 million net profits after tax and has $7.5 billion invested in assets and $600 million equity investment, what is its return on equity?

FLOW OF FUNDS EXERCISE

Managing Credit Risk

Recall that Carson Company relies heavily on commercial banks for loans. When the company was first established with equity funding from its owners, Carson Company could easily obtain debt financing, as the financing was backed by some of the firm's assets. However, as Carson expanded, it continually relied on

EXHIBIT B
Industry Norms in
Percentage Terms

Assets		Liabilities and Capital	
Required reserves	4%	Demand deposits	17%
Commercial loans		NOW accounts	10
Floating-rate	20	MMDAs	20
Fixed-rate	11	CDs	
Total	31	Short-term	35
Consumer loans	20	From 1 to 5 yrs.	10
Mortgages		Total	45
Floating-rate	7	Long-term bonds	2
Fixed-rate	3	CAPITAL	6
Total	10		
Treasury securities			
Short-term	7		
Long-term	8		
Total	15		
Long-term corporate securities			
High-rated	5		
Moderate-rated	5		
Total	10		
Long-term municipal securities			
High-rated	3		
Moderate-rated	2		
Total	5		
Fixed assets	5		—
TOTAL ASSETS	**100%**	**TOTAL LIABILITIES and CAPITAL**	**100%**

extra debt financing, which increased its ratio of debt to equity. Some banks were unwilling to provide more debt financing because of the risk that Carson would not be able to repay additional loans. A few banks were still willing to provide funding, but they required an extra premium to compensate for the risk.

a. Explain the difference in the willingness of banks to provide loans to Carson Company. Why is there a difference between banks when they are assessing the same information about a firm that wants to borrow funds?

b. Consider the flow of funds for a publicly traded bank that is a key lender to Carson Company. This bank received equity funding from shareholders, which it uses to establish its business. It channels bank deposit funds, which are insured by the FDIC, to provide loans to Carson Company and other firms. The depositors have no idea how the bank uses their funds, as their deposits are insured. Yet, the FDIC is not preventing the bank from making risky loans. So who is monitoring the bank? Do you think the bank is taking more risk than its shareholders desire? How does the FDIC discourage the bank from taking too much risk? Why might the bank ignore the FDIC's efforts to discourage excessive risk taking?

WSJ EXERCISE
Bank Management Strategies

Summarize an article in *The Wall Street Journal* that discussed a recent change in managerial strategy by a particular commercial bank. (You may wish to use *The Wall Street Journal Index* in the library to identify an article on a commercial bank's change in strategy.) Describe the change in managerial strategy. How will the bank's balance sheet be affected by this change? How will the bank's potential return and risk be affected? What reason does the article give for the bank's decision to change its strategy?

Stock Price Reaction to Bank Policies

Bank managers attempt to implement policies that enhance the bank's stock performance. They can assess the market's reaction to previous policies implemented by various banks by performing an event study. A favorable reaction suggests that the market anticipates that the policy will improve the bank's performance over time. An unfavorable reaction implies that the policy is expected to reduce the bank's performance. When there is no market reaction, the policy is expected to have no impact on the bank's performance. A brief explanation of using the event study methodology follows.

Consider a bank policy to cut dividends. A possible hypothesis is that the market will view a dividend cut favorably because it expects the bank to reinvest an amount equal to the reduced dividends in a manner that will generate high returns in the future. However, an alternative hypothesis is that a dividend cut signals that the bank is expecting poor performance in the future and cannot afford its current dividend payment schedule. To determine how bank share prices are affected, a sample of banks that cut dividends must first be identified. Then the announcement date of each bank's dividend cut must be determined. The announcement date is more important than the actual date when the dividends are cut, because investors will likely react immediately to the announcement if they react at all.

Daily stock returns for each bank in the sample are compiled for a period before their respective announcement dates (sometimes weekly observations are used instead). This so-called estimation period is used to estimate the bank's beta with the following model:

$$R_{j,t} = B_0 + B_1 R_{m,t} + \mu_t$$

where

$R_{j,t}$ = bank's return over day t

$R_{m,t}$ = market return over day t

B_0 = intercept

B_1 = estimated beta of the bank

μ_t = error term

The length of the estimation period is somewhat subjective, but for our example, assume that it begins 120 days before the announcement date and ends 20 days before the

announcement date. Then the expected return of each bank is determined over the so-called examination period, based on the regression coefficients and the actual values of the market return.

For our example, assume that the examination period is on the date of the announcement and the day after. The expected return for each observation over this period represents the return on the bank's stock that should have occurred in the absence of any abnormal reaction by the market. By comparing the actual return to the bank's expected return, one can determine whether any abnormal return ($AR_{j,t}$) occurred for the bank during day t:

$$AR_{j,t} = R_{j,t} - E(R_{j,t})$$
$$R_{j,t} = R_{j,t} - (B_0 + B_1 R_{m,t})$$

The abnormal returns (sometimes called residuals) are estimated for each observation over the examination period. Positive abnormal returns suggest that the actual return is more than it would have been in the absence of any market reaction and therefore that the market reacted favorably. A negative abnormal return implies that the actual return was less than it would have been in the absence of any market reaction and therefore that the market reacted unfavorably.

In some cases, an abnormal return will occur before the announcement date, which suggests that the market anticipated the news before it was officially announced. Because the examination period usually contains some days before the announcement date, it is possible to detect such an anticipated reaction.

The market reaction to a single bank's policy normally is not considered to be sufficient for drawing implications about the industry as a whole. For this reason, the procedure described here is replicated for each bank that had a similar announcement. For each day within the examination period, the abnormal returns (or residuals) are consolidated among all banks to estimate an average residual for the portfolio ($AR_{p,t}$):

$$AR_{p,t} = \sum_{j=1}^{n} AR_{j,t}/n$$

for all n banks that were examined. The average residual is estimated over each day of the examination period, with specific emphasis around the announcement date. The average residuals, starting on the first day of the examination period, are accumulated over each successive day to determine cumulative average residuals. Because the average residuals for any given observation could differ from zero by chance, they are tested to determine whether they are statistically significant (different from zero). This test provides greater reliability about any implications that are drawn from the analysis.

The analysis described here (or some adaptation of it) has been used to assess the market reaction to a variety of bank managerial policies, such as bank recapitalization plans and the formation of holding companies. It has also been used to assess market reaction to regulatory events, such as the elimination of deposit rate ceilings and intrastate banking regulations. It has even been used to assess market reaction to the international debt crisis of the early 1980s. The analysis has also been applied to events affecting other financial institutions, such as brokerage firms, savings institutions, and insurance companies.

CHAPTER 20

Bank Performance

A commercial bank's performance is examined for various reasons. Bank regulators identify banks that are experiencing severe problems so that they can be remedied. Shareholders need to determine whether they should buy or sell the stock of various banks. Investment analysts must be able to advise prospective investors on which banks to select for investment. Commercial banks also evaluate their own performance over time to determine the outcomes of previous management decisions so that changes can be made where appropriate. Without persistent monitoring of performance, existing problems can remain unnoticed and lead to financial failure in the future.

The specific objectives of this chapter are to:

■ identify the factors that affect the valuation of a commercial bank,

■ compare the performance of banks in different size classifications over recent years, and

■ explain how to evaluate the performance of banks based on financial statement data.

Commercial Bank Valuation

Commercial banks (or commercial bank units that are part of a financial conglomerate) are commonly valued by their managers as part of their efforts to monitor performance over time and to determine the proper mix of services that will maximize the value of the bank. Banks may also be valued by other financial institutions that are considering an acquisition. An understanding of commercial bank valuation is useful because it identifies the factors that determine a commercial bank's value. The value of a commercial bank can be modeled as the present value of its future cash flows:

$$V = \sum_{t=1}^{n} \frac{E(CF_t)}{(1 + k)^t}$$

where $E(CF_t)$ represents the expected cash flow to be generated in period t, and k represents the required rate of return by investors who invest in the commercial bank. Thus, the value of a commercial bank should change in response to changes in its expected cash flows in the future and to changes in the required rate of return by investors:

$$\Delta V = f[\Delta E(CF), \Delta k]$$
$$\qquad\qquad + \qquad -$$

Factors That Affect Cash Flows

The change in a commercial bank's expected cash flows may be modeled as

$$\Delta E(CF) = f(\Delta ECON, \Delta R_f, \Delta INDUS, \Delta MANAB)$$
$$+ \quad - \quad ? \quad +$$

where ECON represents economic growth, R_f represents the risk-free interest rate, INDUS represents prevailing bank industry conditions (including regulations and competition), and MANAB represents the commercial bank's management abilities.

Change in Economic Growth Economic growth can enhance a commercial bank's cash flows by increasing the household or business demand for loans. During periods of strong economic growth, loan demand tends to be higher, allowing commercial banks to provide more loans. Since loans tend to generate better returns to commercial banks than investment in Treasury securities or other securities, expected cash flows should be higher. Another reason cash flows may be higher is that fewer loan defaults normally occur during periods of strong economic growth.

Furthermore, the demand for other financial services provided by commercial banks tends to be higher during periods of strong economic growth. For example, brokerage, insurance, and financial planning services typically receive more business when economic growth is strong, because households have relatively high levels of disposable income.

Change in the Risk-Free Interest Rate Interest rate movements may be inversely related to a commercial bank's cash flows. If the risk-free interest rate decreases, other market rates may decline in the same direction, which may result in a stronger demand for the commercial bank's loans. Second, commercial banks heavily rely on short-term deposits as a source of funds, and the rates paid on these deposits are typically revised in accordance with other interest rate movements. Banks' uses of funds (such as loans), are normally also sensitive to interest rate movements, but to a smaller degree. Therefore, when interest rates fall, the depository institution's cost of obtaining funds declines more than the decline in the interest earned on its loans and investments. Conversely, an increase in interest rates could reduce a commercial bank's expected cash flows because the interest paid on deposits may increase to a greater degree than the interest earned on loans and investments.

Change in Industry Conditions One of the most important industry characteristics that can affect a commercial bank's cash flows is regulation. If regulators reduce the constraints imposed on commercial banks, banks' expected cash flows should increase. For example, when regulators eliminated certain geographic constraints, commercial banks were able to expand across new regions in the United States. As regulators reduced constraints on the types of businesses that commercial banks could pursue, the banks were able to expand by offering other financial services (such as brokerage and insurance services).

Another important industry characteristic that can affect a bank's cash flows is technological innovation, which can improve efficiencies and therefore enhance cash flows. The level of competition is an additional industry characteristic that can affect cash flows, because a high level of competition may reduce the bank's volume of business or reduce the prices it can charge for its services. As regulation has been reduced, competition has intensified. While some commercial banks benefit, other banks may lose some of their market share.

Change in Management Abilities Of the four characteristics that commonly affect the cash flows, the only one in which the bank has control is management skills. It cannot dictate economic growth, interest rate movements, or regulations, but it can select its managers and its organizational structure. The managers can attempt to make internal decisions that will capitalize on the external forces (economic growth, interest rates, regulatory constraints) that the bank cannot control.

As the management skills of a commercial bank improve, so should its expected cash flows. For example, skillful managers will recognize how to revise the composition of the bank's assets and liabilities to capitalize on existing economic or regulatory conditions. They can capitalize on economies of scale by expanding specific types of businesses and by offering a diversified set of services that accommodate specific customers. They may restructure operations and use technology in a manner that can reduce expenses. They may also use derivative securities to alter the bank's potential return and risk. Thus, even if the other external forces are unchanged, a commercial bank's expected cash flows (and therefore value) can change in response to a change in its management skills.

Factors That Affect Required Rates of Return by Investors

The required rate of return by investors who invest in a commercial bank can be modeled as

$$\Delta k = f(\overset{+}{\Delta R_f}, \overset{+}{\Delta RP})$$

where R_f represents a change in the risk-free interest rate, and RP represents the risk premium of the bank.

Change in the Risk-Free Rate When the risk-free rate increases, so does the return required by investors. Recall that the risk-free rate of interest is driven by inflationary expectations (INF), economic growth (ECON), the money supply (MS), and the budget deficit (DEF):

$$\Delta R_f = f(\overset{+}{\Delta INF}, \overset{+}{\Delta ECON}, \overset{-}{\Delta MS}, \overset{+}{\Delta DEF})$$

High inflation, economic growth, and a high budget deficit place upward pressure on interest rates, while money supply growth places downward pressure on interest rates (assuming it does not cause inflation).

Change in the Risk Premium If the risk premium on a commercial bank rises, so will the required rate of return by investors who invest in the bank. The risk premium can change in response to changes in economic growth, industry conditions, or management abilities:

$$\Delta RP = f(\overset{-}{\Delta ECON}, \overset{?}{\Delta INDUS}, \overset{-}{\Delta MANAB})$$

High economic growth results in less risk for a commercial bank because its loans and investments in debt securities are less likely to default.

Bank industry characteristics such as regulatory constraints, technological innovations, and the level of competition can affect the risk premium on banks. Regulatory constraints may include a minimum level of capital required of banks. The most prominent regulatory change in recent years has been the reduction in constraints on services, which has allowed commercial banks to diversify their offerings to reduce risk. Conversely, this

EXHIBIT 20.1
Framework for Valuing a
Commercial Bank

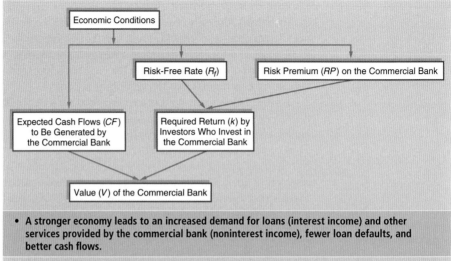

- A stronger economy leads to an increased demand for loans (interest income) and other services provided by the commercial bank (noninterest income), fewer loan defaults, and better cash flows.

- A lower risk-free rate can enhance the valuation of bank assets that do not have an adjustable interest rate, such as some consumer and mortgage loans. It can also increase the valuations of bonds. Commercial banks that have a higher proportion of these types of assets will benefit more from a decline in the risk-free rate and will be adversely affected to a greater degree by an increase in the risk-free rate.

- The valuation is also influenced by industry conditions and the commercial bank's management (not shown in the diagram). These factors affect the risk premium (and therefore the required return by investors) and the expected cash flows to be generated by the commercial bank.

change may allow commercial banks to engage in some services that are riskier than their traditional services and to pursue some services that they cannot provide efficiently. Thus, the reduction in regulatory constraints could increase the risk premium required by investors.

An improvement in management skills may reduce the perceived risk of a commercial bank. To the extent that more skillful managers allocate funds to assets that exhibit less risk, they may reduce the risk premium required by investors who invest in the bank.

Exhibit 20.1 provides a framework for valuing a commercial bank, based on the preceding discussion. In general, the valuation is favorably affected by economic growth, lower interest rates, a reduction in regulatory constraints (assuming the bank focuses on services that it can provide efficiently), and an improvement in the bank's management abilities.

The sensitivity of a commercial bank's value to economic and regulatory conditions is dependent on its own characteristics. For example, the value of a commercial bank that focuses on offering securities services (such as underwriting or full-service brokerage) will be more sensitive to bank regulations that restrict or limit these services than will the value of a commercial bank that focuses on traditional lending. However, it may be less sensitive to general economic conditions that could affect the demand for loans.

Impact of the September 11 Crisis on Commercial Bank Values

Valuations of commercial banks declined following the attack on the United States on September 11, 2001. The expected cash flows to commercial banks declined because economic conditions weakened and the volume of bank loans declined. In addition, more existing loans were expected to default because of the weak economic conditions.

Although short-term interest rates declined, the long-term risk-free rate did not change significantly. Nevertheless, the increased uncertainty surrounding the future cash flows of commercial banks resulted in a higher risk premium required by investors. Consequently, the required rate of return to invest in bank stocks increased. The reduced cash flows and the higher required rate of return by investors are the primary reasons for the decline in bank values after September 11.

Bank Performance Evaluation

http://

http://www.fdic.gov
Information about the performance of commercial banks.

Exhibit 20.2 summarizes the performance of all U.S.-chartered insured commercial banks during particular years. Each characteristic in the first column is measured as a percentage of assets to control for growth when assessing the changes in each characteristic over time. Exhibit 20.2 serves as a useful reference point for assessing each of the performance proxies discussed throughout this chapter. Bank performance is shown over time to illustrate how performance can be affected by changes in economic conditions. In particular, the United States experienced recessions in 1982, the early 1990s, and the early 2000s, and banks were adversely affected in those periods. In addition, the international debt crisis of the early 1980s had a major impact on the largest banks with loans to less developed countries, and the Asian crisis affected banks that lent to Asian countries in the 1997–1998 period. The following discussion examines the characteristics in the first column of Exhibit 20.2 in the order listed; these income statement items are also the key income and expense items that affect a bank's performance.

Interest Income and Expenses

Gross interest income (in Row 1 of Exhibit 20.2) is interest income generated from all assets. It is affected by market rates and the composition of assets held by banks. As a percentage of assets for all banks in aggregate, it was highest in the early 1980s, when

EXHIBIT 20.2 Performance Summary of All Insured Commercial Banks (1982–2003)

Item	1982	1986	1988	1992	1995	1998	2001	2002	2003
1. Gross interest income	11.36%	8.38%	8.95%	7.47%	7.30%	6.65%	6.40%	5.30%	4.66%
2. Gross interest expenses	8.07	5.10	5.42	3.57	3.58	3.29	2.98	1.80	1.32
3. Net interest income	3.28	3.28	3.53	3.90	3.72	3.36	3.42	3.50	3.32
4. Noninterest income	.96	1.40	1.47	1.95	2.02	2.27	2.51	2.53	2.57
5. Loan loss provision	.40	.77	.54	.77	.30	.41	.68	.68	.47
6. Noninterest expenses	2.93	3.22	3.33	3.87	3.64	3.57	3.56	3.46	3.42
7. Securities gains (losses)	−.06	.14	.01	.12	.01	.06	.07	.10	.08
8. Income before tax	.85	.82	1.14	1.33	1.81	1.66	1.77	1.98	2.08
9. Taxes	.14	.19	.36	.42	.63	.59	.59	.65	.67
10. Net income	.71	.64	.84	.91	1.18	1.13	1.17	1.33	1.41
11. Cash dividends provided	.31	.33	.44	.42	.75	.76	.87	1.01	1.08
12. Retained earnings	.40	.31	.40	.49	.43	.37	.30	.31	.33

Source: *Federal Reserve*.

EXHIBIT 20.3 Comparison of Gross Interest Income among Bank Classes

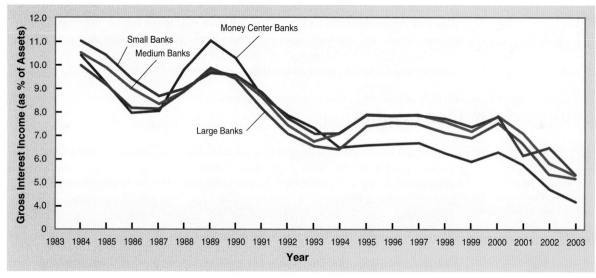

Source: *Federal Reserve.*

interest rates were at their peak. It was lowest in the early 2000s when interest rates were very low.

A comparison of gross interest income levels among four bank size classifications is shown in Exhibit 20.3. The size classifications range from "small" banks (with assets of less than $300 million) to "money center" banks, which are the 10 largest banks that serve money centers such as New York and San Francisco. In recent years, the gross interest income of small and medium banks has typically been higher than that of other banks. They have been able to charge higher interest rates on their loans than large banks or money center banks because they face less competition on loans to small local businesses. Money center banks and large banks tend to provide more loans to larger firms, which have various options available to obtain funds.

Gross interest expenses (in Row 2) represent interest paid on deposits and on other borrowed funds (from the federal funds market, discount window, etc.). These expenses are affected by market rates and the composition of the bank's liabilities. Since NOW accounts and money market deposit accounts (MMDAs) have become popular, banks are attracting a smaller percentage of funds through traditional non-interest-bearing demand deposit accounts. In addition, low interest rate passbook savings accounts are drawing fewer funds because of the alternative CDs available. A large percentage of banks' sources of funds have market-determined interest rates. Gross interest expenses were lower in the 1990s and early 2000s than in the early 1980s for all banks in general because of a decline in market interest rates.

A comparison of gross interest expenses among the four bank size classes is presented in Exhibit 20.4. Until the late 1990s, the interest expense of money center banks was consistently above that of other banks because money center banks obtain a greater percentage of their deposits on a wholesale (large-denomination) basis. In recent years, however, gross interest expenses have been similar among banks.

Net interest income (in Row 3) is the difference between gross interest income and interest expenses and is measured as a percentage of assets. This measure is commonly referred to as net interest margin. As Exhibit 20.2 shows, gross interest income and gross

EXHIBIT 20.4 Comparison of Gross Interest Expenses among Bank Classes

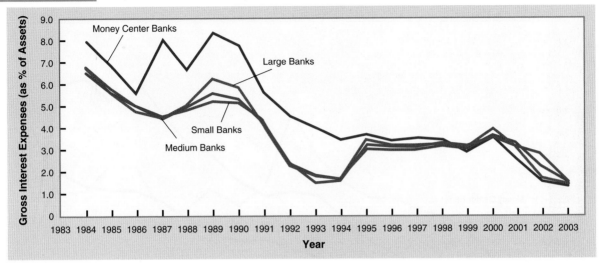

Source: *Federal Reserve.*

interest expenses have been similarly affected by interest rate movements; therefore, the net interest margin of all banks in aggregate has remained somewhat stable.

Banks that heavily emphasize credit card loans have a higher net interest margin because they earn high interest income. However, they tend to incur larger loan losses due to defaults by credit card holders.

Exhibit 20.5 shows that the net interest margin is typically highest for the small banks and lowest for the money center banks. These results are primarily attributed to the small banks' relatively high gross interest income.

Noninterest Income and Expenses

Noninterest income (in Row 4) results from fees charged on services provided, such as lockbox services, banker's acceptances, cashier's checks, and foreign exchange transactions. It has consistently risen over time for all banks in aggregate, as banks are offering

EXHIBIT 20.5 Comparison of Net Interest Margin among Bank Classes

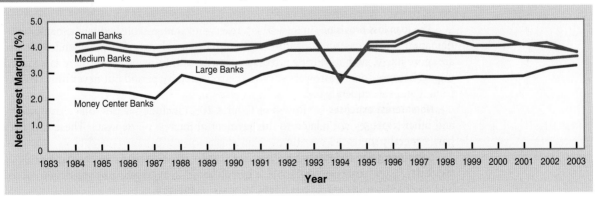

Source: *Federal Reserve.*

EXHIBIT 20.6   Comparison of Noninterest Income among Bank Classes

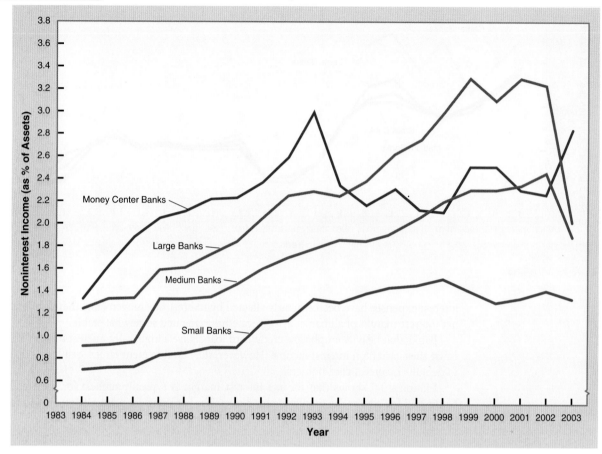

Source: *Federal Reserve*.

more fee-based services than in the past. As banks continue to offer new services (such as insurance or securities services), noninterest income will increase over time.

Exhibit 20.6 shows that noninterest income is usually higher for money center, large, and medium banks than for small banks. This difference occurs because the larger banks provide more services for which they can charge fees.

The **loan loss provision** (in Row 5) is a reserve account established by the bank in anticipation of loan losses in the future. It should increase during periods when loan losses are more likely, such as during a recessionary period. In many cases, there is a lagged impact because some borrowers survive the recessionary period but never fully recover from it and subsequently fail.

Noninterest expenses (in Row 6 of Exhibit 20.2) include salaries, office equipment, and other expenses not related to the payment of interest on deposits. These expenses have generally increased over time.

Securities gains and losses (in Row 7 of Exhibit 20.2) result from the bank's sale of securities. They have been negligible, when all banks in aggregate are considered. An individual bank's gains and losses might be more significant.

EXHIBIT 20.7 Overview of the Key Components Affecting the ROA (for Banks in Aggregate)

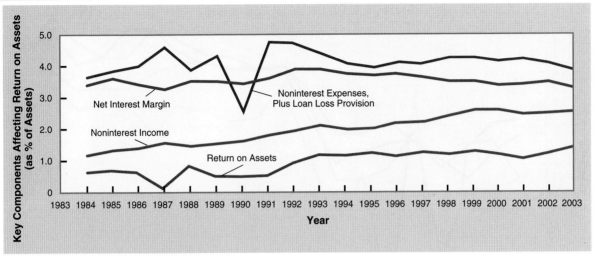

Source: *Federal Reserve.*

Income before tax (in Row 8 of Exhibit 20.2) is obtained by summing net interest income, noninterest income, and securities gains and subtracting from this sum the provision for loan losses and noninterest expenses. This income figure decreased during the early 1980s, primarily because of an increase in noninterest expenses and the provision for loan losses. In the 1990s and early 2000s, bank income was enhanced by the increase in noninterest income.

Net Income

The key income statement item, according to many analysts, is **net income** (in Row 10 of Exhibit 20.2), which accounts for any taxes paid.

Return on Assets The net income figure shown in Exhibit 20.2 is measured as a percentage of assets and therefore represents the **return on assets (ROA).** Fluctuations in the ROA for banks in aggregate can be explained by assessing changes in its components, as shown in Exhibit 20.7. Although the net interest margin has been somewhat stable, noninterest income has risen over time. The ROA was low in 1987, because of the high level of loan loss reserves, but has been unusually high in recent years because of the increase in noninterest income.

Exhibit 20.8 shows that the ROA for medium and large banks has been relatively high recently, largely because of low loan losses and higher noninterest income. The increase in noninterest income is attributed to bank efforts to pursue nonbanking activities (such as brokerage and insurance).

Any individual bank's ROA depends on the bank's policy decisions as well as uncontrollable factors relating to the economy and government regulations, as shown in Exhibit 20.9. Gross interest income and expenses are affected by the sources and uses of bank funds and the movements in market interest rates.

EXHIBIT 20.8   Comparison of Return on Assets (ROA) among Bank Classes

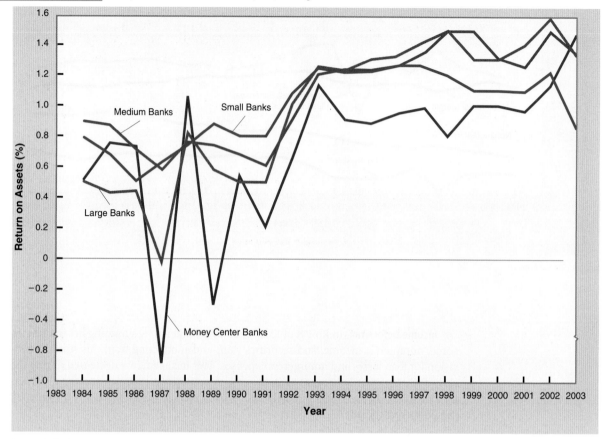

Source: *Federal Reserve.*

Noninterest income is earned on a variety of services, including many new services being offered by banks since some regulatory restrictions were eliminated. Noninterest expenses are partially dependent on personnel costs associated with the credit assessment of loan applications, which in turn are affected by the bank's asset composition (proportion of funds allocated to loans). Noninterest expenses also depend on the liability composition because small deposits are more time-consuming to handle than large deposits. Banks offering more nontraditional services will incur higher noninterest expenses, although they expect to offset the higher costs with higher noninterest income. Loan losses depend on the composition of assets (proportion of loans versus securities), the quality of these assets, and the economy. The return on assets is influenced by all previously mentioned income statement items and therefore by all policies and other factors that affect those items.

The performance characteristics of money center banks differ from small banks because of the differences in their balance sheet composition. For instance, small banks obtain a greater percentage of their funds from traditional demand deposits (at zero percent interest) and small savings accounts (at a relatively low interest rate), while money center banks obtain much of their funds from large deposits at a market-determined interest rate. Thus, the net interest margin for money center banks is typically lower than

EXHIBIT 20.9 Influence of Bank Policies and Other Factors on a Bank's Income Statement

Income Statement Item as a Percentage of Assets	Bank Policy Decisions Affecting the Income Statement Item	Uncontrollable Factors Affecting the Income Statement Item
(1) Gross interest income	• Composition of assets • Quality of assets • Maturity and rate sensitivity of assets • Loan pricing policy	• Economic conditions • Market interest rate movements
(2) Gross interest expenses	• Composition of liabilities • Maturities and rate sensitivity of liabilities	• Market interest rate movements
(3) Net interest income = (1) − (2)		
(4) Noninterest income	• Service charges • Nontraditional activities	• Regulatory provisions
(5) Noninterest expenses	• Composition of assets • Composition of liabilities • Nontraditional activities • Efficiency of personnel • Costs of office space and equipment • Marketing costs • Other costs	• Inflation
(6) Loan losses	• Composition of assets • Quality of assets • Collection department capabilities	• Economic conditions • Market interest rate movements
(7) Pretax return on assets = (3) + (4) − (5) − (6)		
(8) Taxes	• Tax planning	• Tax laws
(9) After-tax return on assets = (7) − (8)		
(10) Financial leverage, measured here as (assets/equity)	• Capital structure policies	• Capital structure regulations
(11) Return on equity = (9) × (10)		

for smaller banks. Consequently, their ROA will likely be lower, unless their noninterest income as a percentage of assets is significantly higher.

Return on Equity An alternative measure of overall bank performance is **return on equity (ROE).** A bank's ROE is affected by the same income statement items that affect ROA as well as by the bank's degree of financial leverage, as follows:

$$\text{ROE} = \text{ROA} \times \text{Leverage measure}$$

$$\frac{\text{Net income}}{\text{Equity capital}} = \frac{\text{Net income}}{\text{Total assets}} \times \frac{\text{Total assets}}{\text{Equity capital}}$$

The leverage measure is simply the inverse of the capital ratio (when only equity counts as capital). The higher the capital ratio, the lower the leverage measure and the lower the degree of financial leverage.

Exhibit 20.10 shows that in recent years money center banks have experienced a lower ROE than large banks and often a lower ROE than medium banks. This is primarily

EXHIBIT 20.10   Comparison of Return on Equity (ROE) among Bank Classes

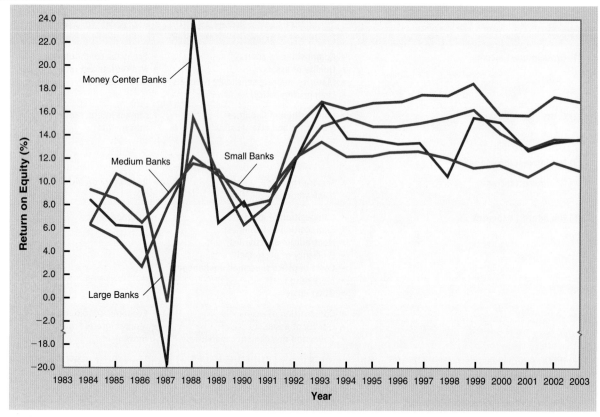

Source: *Federal Reserve.*

attributed to the money center banks' relatively low ROA and to the relatively high level of capital (a low degree of financial leverage) that they maintain.

Evaluating Bank Risk

In assessing bank performance, risk should not be ignored. However, no consensus measurement exists that would allow for comparison of various types of risk (such as loan default risk and liquidity risk) among all banks.

Some analysts measure a firm's risk by its beta, which is the degree of sensitivity of its stock returns to the returns of the stock market as a whole. Beta is normally measured by the following regression model:

$$R_{j,t} = B_0 + B_1 R_{m,t} + \mu_t$$

where $R_{j,t}$ = stock return for the firm of concern in period t

$R_{m,t}$ = return on a stock market index (such as the S&P 500 index) in period t

B_0 = intercept

B_1 = slope coefficient

μ_t = error term

The regression model is applied to historical data (usually on a quarterly basis). The regression coefficients B_0 and B_1 are estimated by the regression analysis. The coefficient B_1 is an estimate of beta, because it measures the sensitivity of R_j to R_m. Banks whose stock returns are less vulnerable to economic conditions have relatively low betas. The stock returns of a bank with very conservative management are likely to be less sensitive to stock market movements.

Although the beta reflects sensitivity to market conditions, it ignores any firm-specific characteristics. That is, the beta measures systematic risk but ignores unsystematic risk. A bank's beta will not necessarily remain constant from one period to another. If the bank adopts more aggressive policies, its beta will likely increase. Its performance and therefore its stock price will become more volatile, because the sensitivity of the bank's stock returns to economic conditions will increase. A higher beta can work for or against the bank, depending on future economic conditions.

Evaluating Bank Performance

Up to this point, the discussion has mostly focused on the performance of the overall industry and of banks of different sizes. Although this information can be beneficial, analysts often need to evaluate an individual bank's performance, in which case financial statements are used. The income and expenses shown earlier in Exhibit 20.2 can serve as an industry benchmark for evaluating a bank's performance.

Examining Return on Assets (ROA)

The ROA will usually reveal when a bank's performance is not up to par, but it does not indicate the reason for poor performance. Its components must be evaluated separately. Exhibit 20.11 identifies the factors that affect bank performance as measured by the ROA and ROE. If a bank's ROA is less than desired, the bank is possibly incurring excessive interest expenses. Banks typically know what deposit rate is necessary to attract deposits and therefore are not likely to pay excessive interest. Yet, if all a bank's sources of funds require a market-determined rate, the bank will face relatively high interest expenses. A relatively low ROA could also be due to low interest received on loans and securities because the bank has been overly conservative with its funds or was locked into fixed rates prior to an increase in market interest rates. High interest expenses and/or low interest revenues (on a relative basis) will reduce the net interest margin and therefore reduce the ROA.

EXHIBIT 20.11

Breakdown of Performance Measures

Measures of Bank Performance	Financial Characteristics Influencing Performance	Bank Decisions Affecting Financial Characteristics
(1) Return on assets (ROA)	Net interest margin	Deposit rate decisions Loan rate decisions Loan losses
	Noninterest revenues Noninterest expenses	Bank services offered Overhead requirements Efficiency Advertising
	Loan losses	Risk level of loans provided
(2) Return on equity (ROE)	ROA Leverage measure	See above Capital structure decision

A relatively low ROA may also result from insufficient noninterest income. Some banks have made a much greater effort than others to offer services that generate fee (noninterest) income. Because a bank's net interest margin is somewhat dictated by interest rate trends and balance sheet composition, many banks attempt to focus on noninterest income to boost their ROA.

A bank's ROA can also be damaged by heavy loan losses. Yet, if the bank is too conservative in attempting to avoid loan losses, its net interest margin will be low (because of the low interest rates received from very safe loans and investments). Because of the obvious tradeoff here, banks generally attempt to shift their risk-return preferences according to economic conditions. They may increase their concentration of relatively risky loans during periods of prosperity when they may improve their net interest margin without incurring excessive loan losses. Conversely, they may increase their concentration of relatively low-risk (and low-return) investments when economic conditions are less favorable.

Banks with relatively low ROAs often incur excessive noninterest expenses, such as overhead and advertising expenses. Any waste of resources due to inefficiencies can lead to relatively high noninterest expenses.

Example

Consider the information shown in Exhibit 20.12 for Bank of America and the industry. Because of differences in accounting procedures, the information may not be perfectly comparable. The industry data are based on the class of money center banks. The comparison in Exhibit 20.12 can at least identify some general reasons for the financial problems experienced by Bank of America in the 1980s and for its strong performance in the 1990s and early 2000s. Bank of America's income before tax was generally below the in-

EXHIBIT 20.12 Evaluation of Bank of America*

	1983 BA	1983 Industry	1987 BA	1987 Industry	1990 BA	1990 Industry	1993 BA	1993 Industry	1995 BA	1995 Industry
Net interest margin	3.30%	2.40%	3.28%	2.06%	3.85%	3.31%	3.98%	3.16%	3.64%	2.68%
Noninterest income	1.27	1.12	2.04	2.50	1.93	1.84	2.28	2.99	1.96	2.16
Loan loss provision	.62	.36	1.97	2.16	.84	1.17	.43	.64	.19	.11
Noninterest expenses	3.35	2.34	4.24	3.18	3.64	3.47	4.00	4.13	3.44	3.32
Income before tax	.60	.84	(0.89)	(.70)	1.30	.54	1.83	1.50	1.97	1.44

	1998 BA	1998 Industry	2000 BA	2000 Industry	2001 BA	2001 Industry	2002 BA	2002 Industry	2003 BA	2003 Industry
Net interest margin	2.96%	2.73%	2.87%	2.78%	3.31%	2.87%	3.26%	3.13%	2.80%	3.20%
Noninterest income	1.97	2.15	2.25	2.51	2.24	2.23	2.04	2.32	2.14	2.82
Loan loss provision	.47	.31	.39	.35	.69	.59	.56	.73	.37	.52
Noninterest expenses	3.32	3.47	2.81	3.30	3.33	4.24	2.79	4.14	2.63	3.41
Income before tax	1.30	1.10	1.83	1.60	1.63	.97	1.95	1.12	2.07	2.18

*All variables are measured as a percentage of assets. The industry net income before tax also accounts for securities gains and losses.
Sources: Bank of America's Annual Reports; and *Federal Reserve Bulletin,* various issues.

dustry norm in the 1980s. A comparison with the industry figures indicates that Bank of America's net interest margin was generally higher than the norm in the 1980s, but so were its noninterest expenses. Since 1990, Bank of America has performed relatively well, primarily because of its relatively high net interest margin, its relatively low non-interest expenses (since 1995), and its relatively low loan loss provision in some years. Exhibit 20.13 provides a separate comparison of each variable to the industry norm over time to confirm the conclusions drawn.

EXHIBIT 20.13 Comparison of Bank of America Expenses and Income to the Industry

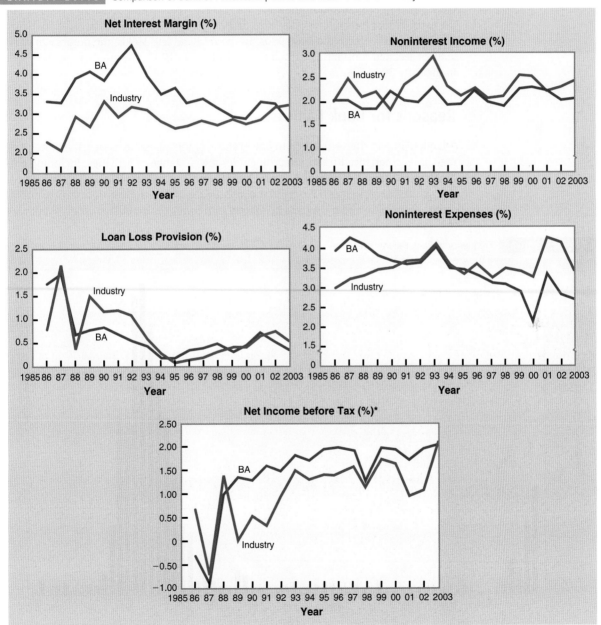

*The low net income before tax for Bank of America in 1998 was primarily due to restructuring expenses following large acquisitions.

Any particular bank will perform a more thorough evaluation of itself than that shown here. For example, Bank of America's annual reports provided a comprehensive explanation for its strong performance in recent years, along with a discussion of how it planned to improve its performance over time.

Bank Failures

The extreme consequence of poor performance is failure. Exhibit 20.14 shows the frequency of bank failures over time. From 1940 to 1980, there were usually fewer than 20 bank failures per year. But in the late 1980s, there were about 200 failures per year. In the early 1990s, the number of failures declined, but was still much larger than in any previous period except the late 1980s. In the mid and late 1990s, the number of bank failures declined substantially, reaching a low of one in 1997. The number remained low in the early 2000s.

Reasons for Bank Failure

A bank failure is often attributed to one or more of the following causes. First, the bank may have experienced fraud. Fraud includes a wide range of activities, including embezzlement of funds. Second, a high percentage of loan defaults can lead to failure. Although banks recognize the potential consequence of a high loan default percentage, some continue to fail for this reason anyway. A thorough examination of any bank may

EXHIBIT 20.14 Frequency of Bank Failures over Time

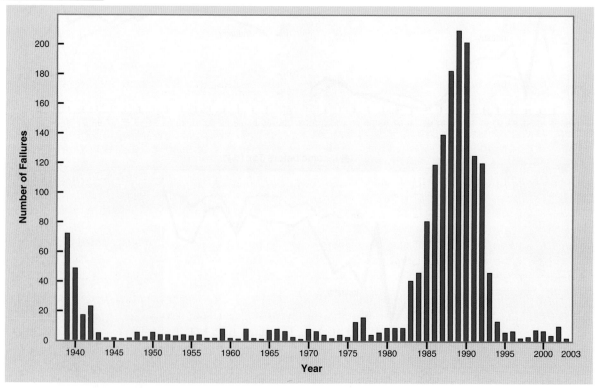

Source: *New England Economic Review* (July–August 1987): 38, updated by author.

show a general emphasis toward a specific industry such as oil, shipbuilding, aerospace, agriculture, or national defense systems that makes it vulnerable to a slowdown in that industry (or a related one). Moreover, no matter how well a bank diversifies its loans, its loan portfolio is still susceptible to a recessionary cycle.

A third reason for bank failure is a liquidity crisis. If a rumor that a particular bank might fail begins to circulate, depositors may withdraw funds from that bank, even though the bank is insured by the FDIC. The panic can even occur when the rumor is not justified. Under these conditions, a bank may be unable to attract a sufficient amount of new deposits, and its existing deposit accounts will subside. Once deposit withdrawals begin, it is difficult to stop the momentum.

A fourth reason for bank failures is increased competition. Deregulation has made the banking industry more competitive. When banks offer more competitive rates on deposits and loans, the result is a reduced net interest margin, and possibly failure if the margin is not large enough to cover other noninterest expenses and loan losses.

The Office of the Comptroller of the Currency reviewed 162 national banks that failed since 1979 and found the following common characteristics among many of these banks:

- 81 percent of the banks did not have a loan policy or did not closely follow their loan policy.
- 59 percent of the banks did not use an adequate system for identifying problem loans.
- 63 percent did not adequately monitor key bank officers or departments.
- 57 percent of the banks allowed one individual to make major corporate decisions.

Because all of these characteristics are controllable, it appears that many banks failed because of inadequate management, not because of the environment.

SUMMARY

- A bank's value is dependent on its expected future cash flows and the required rate of return by investors who invest in the bank. The bank's expected cash flows are influenced by economic growth, interest rate movements, regulatory constraints, and the abilities of the bank's managers. The required rate of return by investors who invest in the bank is influenced by the prevailing interest rate (which is affected by other economic conditions) and the risk premium (which is affected by economic growth, regulatory constraints, and the management abilities of the bank). In general, the value of commercial banks is favorably affected by strong economic growth, declining interest rates, and strong management abilities.

- A bank's performance can be evaluated by comparing its income statement items (as a percentage of total assets) to a control group of other banks with a similar size classification. The return on assets (ROA) of the bank may be compared to the control group's mean ROA. Any difference in ROA between the bank and the control group is typically because of differences in net interest margin, loan loss reserves, noninterest income, or noninterest expenses.

If the bank's net interest margin is relatively low, it either is relying too heavily on deposits with higher interest rates or is not earning adequate interest on its loans. If the bank is forced to boost loan loss reserves, this suggests that its loan portfolio may be too risky. If its noninterest income is relatively low, the bank is not providing enough services that generate fee income. If the bank's noninterest expenses are relatively high, its cost of operations is excessive. There may be other specific details that make the assessment more complex, but the key problems of a bank can usually be detected with the approach described here.

- A common measure of a bank's overall performance is its return on assets (ROA). The ROA has consistently been lower for money center banks than other banks. Their relatively low ROA is attributed to lower net interest income (relatively high interest expenses due to the heavy reliance on large deposits for funds). Loan losses have also been higher for

money center banks than other banks. Conversely, large and medium banks have had a relatively high ROA, because of their relatively high net interest margin and low level of loan loss reserves.

Money center banks have generated more noninterest income than the other banks, but this did not completely offset the relatively poor performance on the items just described.

POINT COUNTER-POINT

Does a Bank's Income Statement Clearly Indicate the Bank's Performance?

Point Yes. The bank's income statement can be partitioned to determine its performance and the underlying reasons for its performance.

Counter-Point No. The bank's income statement can be manipulated because the bank may not fully recognize

loan losses (will not write off loans that are likely to default) until a future period.

Who Is Correct? Use your favorite search engine to learn more about this issue. Offer your own opinion on this issue.

QUESTIONS AND APPLICATIONS

1. **Managing in Financial Markets: Forecasting Bank Performance** As a manager of Hawaii Bank, you anticipate the following:
   - Loan loss reserves at end of year = 1 percent of assets
   - Gross interest income over the next year = 9 percent of assets
   - Noninterest expenses over the next year = 3 percent of assets
   - Noninterest income over the next year = 1 percent of assets
   - Gross interest expenses over the next year = 5 percent of assets
   - Tax rate on income = 30 percent
   - Capital ratio (capital/assets) at end of year = 5 percent

   a. Forecast Hawaii Bank's net interest margin.
   b. Forecast Hawaii Bank's earnings before taxes as a percentage of assets.
   c. Forecast Hawaii Bank's earnings after taxes as a percentage of assets.
   d. Forecast Hawaii Bank's return on equity.
   e. Hawaii Bank is considering a shift in its asset structure to reduce its concentration of Treasury bonds and increase its volume of loans to small businesses. Identify each income statement item that would be affected by this strategy, and explain whether the forecast for that item would increase or decrease.

2. **Bank Betas** What does the beta of a bank indicate?

3. **Bank Failures** Provide some reasons for bank failures.

4. **Interest Income** How can gross interest income rise, while the net interest margin remains somewhat stable for a particular bank?

5. **Evaluating a Bank's Performance** When evaluating a bank, what are some of the key aspects to review?

6. **Impact of Deregulation** How did deregulation affect gross interest expenses (as a percentage of assets)?

7. **Interpreting Financial News** Interpret the following comments made by Wall Street analysts and portfolio managers:
   a. "The three most important factors that determine a local bank's bad debt level are the bank's location, location, and location."
   b. "Bank A's profitability was enhanced by its limited use of capital."
   c. "A low beta is not always desirable. Our bank's beta has been too low, given the market conditions. We will restructure operations in a manner to increase the beta."

8. **Net Interest Income** Suppose a bank generates net interest income as a percentage of assets of 1.50 percent. Based on past experience, would the bank experience a loss or a gain? Explain.

9. **Internet Exercise** Go to http://www.suntrust.com. Click on "Investor Relations" and then on "Annual Re-

ports." Use the income statement to determine Sun-Trust's performance. Describe SunTrust's performance in recent years.

10. **Noninterest Income** What has been the trend in non-interest income in recent years? Explain.

11. **Bank Income Statement** Assume that SUNY Bank plans to liquidate Treasury security holdings and use the proceeds for small business loans. Explain how this strategy will affect the different income statement items. Also identify any income statement items where the effects of this strategy are more difficult to estimate.

12. **Loan Loss Provisions** Explain why loan loss provisions of most banks could increase in a particular period.

13. **Net Interest Margin** How could a bank generate higher income before tax (as a percentage of assets) when its net interest margin has decreased?

14. **Analysis of a Bank's ROA** What are some of the more common reasons for a bank to experience a low ROA?

15. **Net Interest Margin** Why have large money center banks' net interest margins typically been lower than those of smaller banks?

PROBLEM

1. **Assessing Bank Performance** Select a bank whose income statement data are available. Using recent income statement information about the commercial bank, assess its performance. How does the performance of this bank compare to the performance of other banks? Is its return on equity higher or lower than the ROE of other banks as reported in this chapter? What is the main reason why its ROE is different from the norm? (Is it due to its interest expenses? Its noninterest income?)

FLOW OF FUNDS EXERCISE

How the Flow of Funds Affects Bank Performance

In recent years, Carson Company has requested the services listed below from Blazo Financial, a financial conglomerate. These transactions have created a flow of funds between Carson Company and Blazo.

a. Classify each service according to how Blazo benefits from the service.
   ■ Advising on possible targets that Carson may acquire
   ■ Futures contract transactions
   ■ Options contract transactions
   ■ Interest rate derivative transactions

   ■ Loans
   ■ Line of credit
   ■ Purchase of short-term CDs
   ■ Checking account

b. Explain why Blazo's performance from providing these services to Carson Company and other firms will decline if economic growth is reduced.

c. Given the potential impact of slow economic growth on a bank's performance, do you think that commercial banks would prefer that the Fed use a tight-money policy or a loose-money policy?

WSJ EXERCISE

Assessing Bank Performance

Using a recent issue of *The Wall Street Journal*, summarize an article that discussed the recent performance of a particular commercial bank. Does the article suggest that the bank's performance was better or worse than the norm? What is the reason given for the performance?

Part VI Integrative Problem

Forecasting Bank Performance

This problem requires an understanding of banks' sources and uses of funds (Chapter 17), bank management (Chapter 19), and bank performance (Chapter 20). It also requires the use of spreadsheet software such as Microsoft Excel. The data provided can be input onto a spreadsheet to more easily complete the necessary computations. A conceptual understanding of commercial banking is needed to interpret the computations.

As an analyst of a medium-sized commercial bank, you have been asked to forecast next year's performance. In June you were provided with information about the sources and uses of funds for the upcoming year. The bank's sources of funds for the upcoming year are as follows:

Source of Funds	Dollar Amount (in Millions)	Interest Rate to Be Offered
Demand deposits	$5,000	0%
Time deposits	2,000	6%
1-year NCDs	3,000	T-bill rate+1%
5-year NCDs	2,500	1-year NCD rate+1%

The bank also has $1 billion in capital.

The bank's uses of funds for the upcoming year are as follows:

Use of Funds	Dollar Amount (in Millions)	Interest Rate	Loan Loss Percentage
Loans to small businesses	$4,000	T-bill rate+6%	2%
Loans to large businesses	2,000	T-bill rate+4%	1
Consumer loans	3,000	T-bill rate+7%	4
Treasury bills	1,000	T-bill rate	0
Treasury bonds	1,500	T-bill rate+2%	0
Corporate bonds	1,100	Treasury bond rate+2%	0

The bank also has $900 million in fixed assets. The interest rates on loans to small and large businesses are tied to the T-bill rate and will change at the beginning of each new year. The forecasted Treasury bond rate is tied to the future T-bill rate, based on the expectation that an upward-sloping yield curve will exist at the beginning of next year. The corporate bond rate is tied to the Treasury bond rate, allowing for a risk premium of 2 percent. Consumer loans will be provided at the beginning of next year, and interest rates will be fixed over the lifetime of the loan. The remaining time to maturity on all assets except T-bills exceeds three years. As the one-year T-bills mature, the funds are to be reinvested in new one-year T-bills (all T-bills are to be purchased at the beginning of the year). The bank's loan loss percentage reflects the percentage of bad loans. Assume

that no interest will be received on these loans. In addition, assume that this percentage of loans will be accounted for as loan loss reserves (assume that they should be subtracted when determining before-tax income).

The bank has forecasted its noninterest revenues to be $200 million and its noninterest expenses to be $740 million. A tax rate of 34 percent can be applied to the before-tax income in order to estimate after-tax income. The bank has developed the following probability distribution for the one-year T-bill rate that will exist as of the beginning of next year:

Possible T-Bill Rate	Probability
8%	30%
9	50
10	20

Questions

1   Using the information provided, determine the probability distribution of return on assets (ROA) for next year by completing the following table:

Interest Rate Scenario (Possible T-Bill Rate)	Forecasted ROA	Probability
8%		
9		
10		

2   Will the bank's ROA next year be higher or lower if market interest rates are higher? (Use the T-bill rate as a proxy for market interest rates.) Why? The information provided did not assume any required reserves. Explain how including required reserves would affect the forecasted interest revenue, ROA, and ROE.

3   The bank is considering a strategy of attempting to attract an extra $1 billion as one-year NCDs to replace $1 billion of five-year NCDs. Develop the probability distribution of ROA based on this strategy:

Interest Rate Scenario	Forecasted ROA Based on the Strategy of Increasing One-Year NCDs	Probability
8%		
9		
10		

4   Is the bank's ROA likely to be higher next year if it uses the strategy of attracting more one-year NCDs?

5   What would be an obvious concern about a strategy of using more one-year NCDs and fewer five-year NCDs beyond the next year?

6 The bank is considering a strategy of using $1 billion to offer additional loans to small businesses instead of purchasing T-bills. Using all the original assumptions provided, determine the probability distribution of ROA (assume that noninterest expenses would not be affected by this change in strategy).

Interest Rate Scenario (Possible T-Bill Rate)	Forecasted ROA if an Extra $1 Billion Is Used for Loans to Small Businesses	Probability
8%		
9		
10		

7 Would the bank's ROA likely be higher or lower over the next year if it allocates the extra funds to small business loans?

8 What is the obvious risk of such a strategy beyond the next year?

9 The strategy of attracting more one-year NCDs could affect noninterest expenses and revenues. How would noninterest expenses be affected by the strategy? How would noninterest revenues be affected by the strategy?

10 Now assume that the bank is considering a strategy of increasing its consumer loans by $1 billion instead of using the funds for loans to small businesses. Using this information along with all the original assumptions provided, determine the probability distribution of ROA.

Interest Rate Scenario (Possible T-Bill Rate)	Possible ROA if an Extra $1 Billion Is Used for Consumer Loans	Probability
8%		
9		
10		

11 Other than possible changes in the economy that may affect credit risk, what key factor will determine whether this strategy is beneficial beyond one year?

12 Now assume that the bank wants to determine how its forecasted return on equity (ROE) next year would be affected if it boosts its capital from $1 billion to $1.2 billion. (The extra capital would not be used to increase interest or noninterest revenues.) Using all the original assumptions provided, complete the following table:

Interest Rate Scenario (Possible T-Bill Rate)	Forecasted ROE if Capital = $1 Billion	Forecasted ROE if Capital = $1.2 Billion	Probability
8%			
9			
10			

Briefly state how the ROE will be affected if the capital level is increased.

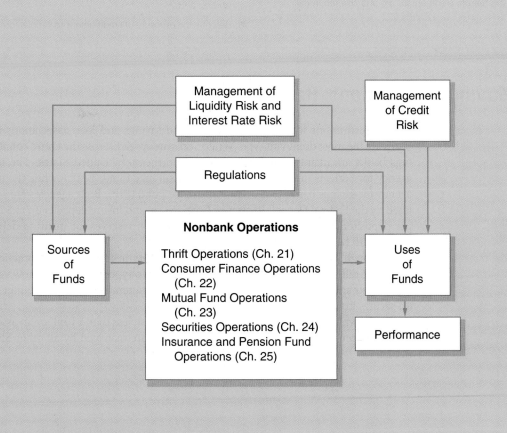

PART VII

Nonbank Operations

The chapters in Part VII cover the key nonbank operations. Each chapter is devoted to a particular type of operation, with a focus on sources of funds, uses of funds, regulations, management, and recent performance. Some of the institutions discussed are independent, others are units (subsidiaries) of financial conglomerates. Each financial institution's interactions with other institutions and its participation in financial markets are also emphasized in these chapters.

CHAPTER 21

Thrift Operations

The term *thrift institution* (or *savings institution*) is normally used to refer to a depository institution that specializes in mortgage lending. They were created to accept deposits and channel the funds for mortgage loans. Some thrift operations are independent financial institutions, while others are units (subsidiaries) of financial conglomerates. Sometimes credit unions are also considered to be thrift institutions. For this reason, credit unions are also covered in this chapter.

The specific objectives of this chapter are to:

■ identify the key sources and uses of funds for savings institutions,

■ describe the exposure of savings institutions to various types of risk,

■ explain the valuation of a savings institution,

■ describe the savings institution crisis and the actions taken to resolve the crisis,

■ describe the main sources and uses of funds for credit unions, and

■ describe the exposure of credit unions to various forms of risk.

U.S. Savings Institutions: Background

Savings institutions include savings banks and savings and loan associations (S&Ls). S&Ls are the most dominant type. While S&Ls are spread across the entire country, savings banks are mainly concentrated in the northeastern United States. The insuring agency for S&Ls is the Savings Association Insurance Fund (SAIF), while the insuring agency for savings banks is the Bank Insurance Fund (BIF). Both agencies are administered by the Federal Deposit Insurance Corporation and insure deposits up to $100,000 per depositor. In 2004, the SAIF had $12 billion in reserves for insuring depositors, and the BIF had $34 billion in reserves.

Although savings banks have had more flexibility in their investing practices than S&Ls, the difference has narrowed over time. The two types of thrifts are now very similar in their sources and uses of funds. Therefore, the remainder of the chapter focuses on savings institutions, abbreviated as SIs.

As shown in Exhibit 21.1, most SIs are small, with less than $1 billion in assets. The largest 10 percent of SIs manage more assets than are managed by all other SIs in the industry.

EXHIBIT 21.1
Structure of the Savings
Institution Industry

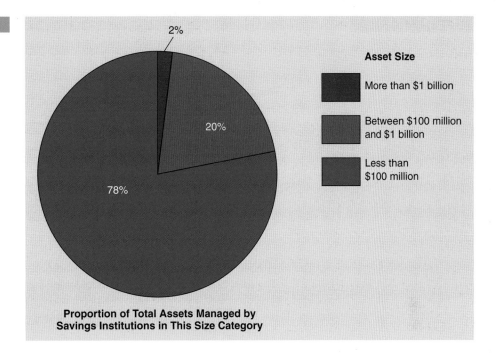

**Proportion of Total Assets Managed by
Savings Institutions in This Size Category**

Ownership

Savings institutions are classified as either stock owned or **mutual** (owned by depositors). Although most SIs are mutual, many SIs have shifted their ownership structure from depositors to shareholders through what is known as a **mutual-to-stock conversion.** This conversion allows SIs to obtain additional capital by issuing stock.

Beyond having the capability to boost capital, stock-owned institutions also provide their owners with greater potential to benefit from their performance. The dividends and/or stock price of a high-performance institution can grow, thereby providing direct benefits to the shareholders. Conversely, the owners (depositors) of a mutual institution do not benefit directly from high performance. Although they have a pro rata claim to the mutual SI's net worth while they maintain deposits there, their claim is eliminated once they close their account.

Because of the difference in owner control, stock-owned institutions are more susceptible to unfriendly takeovers. It is virtually impossible for another firm to take control of a mutual institution, because management generally holds all voting rights. From the owners' perspectives, the stock-owned institution may seem more desirable because the owners may have more influence on managerial decisions.

When a mutual SI is involved in an acquisition, it first converts to a stock-owned SI. If it is the acquiring firm, it then arranges to purchase the existing stock of the institution to be acquired. Conversely, if it is to be acquired, its stock is purchased by the acquiring institution. This process is often referred to as a **merger-conversion.**

Some SIs have been acquired by commercial banks that wanted to diversify their operations. Even after such an acquisition, the SI may still maintain its operations, but under the ownership of the commercial bank. Consolidation and acquisitions have caused the number of mutual and stock savings institutions to decline consistently over the years, as shown in Exhibit 21.2. There are only about half as many SIs today as in 1994.

EXHIBIT 21.2

Number of Mutual and
Stock Savings Institutions
over Time

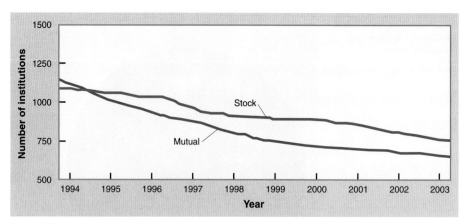

Source: FDIC.

The total assets of mutual and stock savings institutions over time are shown in Exhibit 21.3. The total assets of mutual SIs have remained steady, while the total assets of stock SIs have increased by more than 60 percent since 1994. Thus, consolidation among SIs has resulted in a smaller number of institutions, even though the total assets of SIs in aggregate have increased.

Regulation of Savings Institutions

Savings institutions are regulated at both the state and federal levels. All federally chartered SIs are regulated by the Office of Thrift Supervision (OTS). State-chartered SIs are subject to some oversight by the state that has chartered them, but the states have no authority over federally chartered institutions. Supervision can also vary according to whether the SI is mutual or stock owned.

Regulatory Assessment of Savings Institutions Regulators conduct periodic on-site examinations to ensure that SIs have the minimum level of capital required and maintain their exposure to risk within a tolerable range. SIs are monitored using the CAMELS rating in a manner similar to commercial banks. They are assessed according

EXHIBIT 21.3

Assets of Mutual and Stock
Savings Institutions over
Time

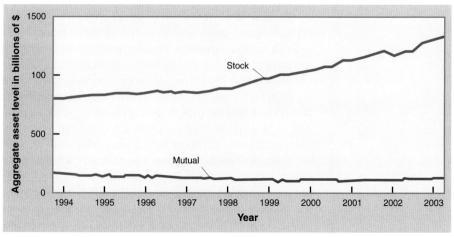

Source: FDIC.

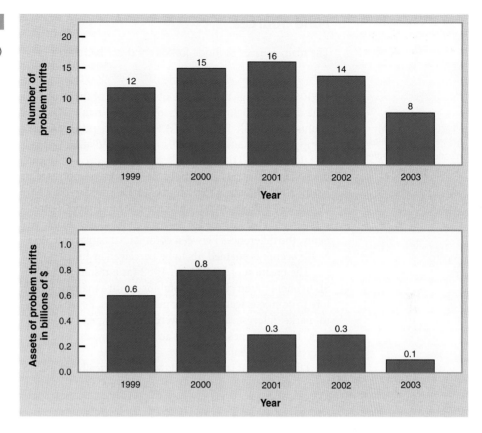

to their capital adequacy, asset quality, management, earnings, liquidity, and sensitivity to market conditions. If an SI receives a composite CAMELS rating of 4 or higher, it is classified as a "problem" and receives close attention. It may be subject to corrective action by the Office of Thrift Supervision. Exhibit 21.4 shows the number of problem thrifts and their aggregate asset level in recent years. In general, the number and aggregate asset level of "problem" SIs have been low in recent years. During the weak economy in 2001–2002, there was not a pronounced increase in problem SIs.

Deregulation of Services In recent years, SIs have been granted more flexibility to diversify the products and services they provide. They can offer products that historically were offered only by real estate, insurance, or brokerage firms. For example, some SIs serve as limited agents for registered brokerage firms and are therefore able to offer their customers access to discount brokerage services. In some joint ventures, an SI allows a registered broker to offer services on its premises. By offering discount brokerage service and other nontraditional services, an SI can attract customers searching for a one-stop shop.

Funds Sources and Uses

Like commercial banks, SIs serve as valuable financial intermediaries. However, their sources and uses of funds are different from those of commercial banks, so their management also differs from that of commercial banks.

Fund Sources

The main sources of funds for SIs are described next.

Deposits Savings institutions obtain most of their funds from a variety of savings and time deposits, including passbook savings, retail CDs, and money market deposit accounts (MMDAs). Before 1978 SIs focused primarily on passbook savings accounts. During the early and mid-1970s, disintermediation was common because market interest rates exceeded the passbook savings rate. Because disintermediation reduced the volume of savings at SIs, it reduced the amount of mortgage financing available.

In 1981 SIs across the country were allowed to offer NOW accounts as a result of the Depository Institution Deregulation and Monetary Control Act (DIDMCA) of 1980. This was a major change because they were previously unable to offer checking services. Suddenly, the differences between commercial banks and SIs were not so obvious to savers. NOW accounts enabled SIs to be perceived as full-service financial institutions.

The creation of MMDAs in 1982 (as a result of the Garn–St Germain Act) allowed SIs to offer limited checking combined with a market-determined interest rate and therefore to compete against money market funds. Because these new accounts offered close-to-market interest rates, they were a more expensive source of funds than passbook savings. The new types of deposit accounts also increased the sensitivity of SIs' liabilities to interest rate movements.

Like commercial banks, SIs were historically unable to offer a rate above a regulatory ceiling on deposits. In 1978 regulations were loosened, allowing them to offer limited types of retail CDs with rates tied to Treasury bills. With the wider variety of retail CDs allowed in the late 1970s and early 1980s and the introduction of MMDAs in 1982, the ceiling rate on passbook savings was no longer as relevant. By 1986, all deposits were free from ceiling rates.

Borrowed Funds When SIs are unable to attract sufficient deposits, they can borrow on a short-term basis from three sources. First, they can borrow from other depository institutions that have excess funds in the federal funds market. The interest rate on funds borrowed in this market is referred to as the federal funds rate.

Second, SIs can borrow at the Federal Reserve's discount window. The interest rate on funds borrowed from the Fed is referred to as the discount rate.

Third, SIs can borrow through a repurchase agreement (repo). With a repo, an institution sells government securities, with a commitment to repurchase those securities shortly thereafter. This essentially reflects a short-term loan to the institution that initially sold the securities until the time when it buys the securities back.

Capital The **capital** (or net worth) of an SI is primarily composed of retained earnings and funds obtained from issuing stock. During periods when SIs are performing well, capital is boosted by additional retained earnings. Capital is commonly used to support ongoing or expanding operations.

Savings institutions are required to maintain a minimum level of capital to cushion against potential losses that could occur and thus help to avoid possible failure. During the 1980s, many SIs experienced losses, and their capital levels were reduced. Concerned about the erosion of capital, regulatory agencies tightened requirements.

Fund Uses

The main uses of funds for SIs are

- Cash
- Mortgages
- Mortgage-backed securities
- Other securities
- Consumer and commercial loans
- Other uses

Cash Savings institutions maintain cash to satisfy reserve requirements enforced by the Federal Reserve System and to accommodate withdrawal requests of depositors. In addition, some SIs hold correspondent cash balances at other financial institutions in return for various services.

Mortgages Mortgages are the primary asset of SIs. They typically have long-term maturities and can usually be prepaid by borrowers. About 90 percent of the mortgages originated are for homes or multifamily dwellings, while 10 percent are for commercial properties. The volume of mortgage loans originated by SIs in recent years is shown in Exhibit 21.5. The dramatic increase in mortgage originations in 2003 substantially enhanced the overall performance of SIs. This increase is attributed to the strengthening of the economy in 2003, while mortgage rates remained at very low levels.

Mortgages can be sold in the secondary market, although their market value changes in response to interest rate movements, so they are subject to interest rate risk as well as credit (default) risk. To protect against interest rate risk, SIs use a variety of techniques, discussed later in the chapter. To protect against credit risk, the real estate represented by the mortgage serves as collateral.

Mortgage-Backed Securities To obtain funds, SIs commonly issue securities that are backed by mortgages. Other SIs with available funds can purchase these securities. The seller may continue to service the mortgages, but it passes on the periodic payments to the purchaser, retaining a small amount as a service fee. The cash flows to these holders

EXHIBIT 21.5

Mortgage Originations by SIs over Time

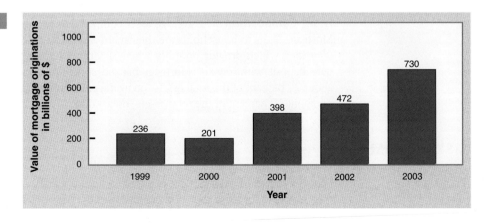

of mortgage-backed securities will not necessarily be even over time because the mortgages can be prepaid before their stated maturity.

Other Securities   All SIs invest in securities such as Treasury bonds and corporate bonds. Because savings banks are not as heavily concentrated in mortgage loans and mortgage-backed securities, they hold a greater percentage of securities than S&Ls. These securities provide liquidity, as they can quickly be sold in the secondary market if funds are needed. Savings banks are also able to invest in some other types of securities.

Thrifts have also invested in junk bonds. The proportion of funds invested in junk bonds varied substantially among SIs, as some states imposed limits on this type of investment. As a result of the savings institution crisis, regulators prohibited additional investment in junk bonds in 1989.

Consumer and Commercial Loans   Many SIs are attempting to increase their consumer loans and commercial loans. As a result of the DIDMCA and the Garn–St Germain Act, the lending guidelines for federally chartered SIs were loosened, and many state-chartered SIs were also granted more lending flexibility by their respective states. Specifically, federally chartered SIs are allowed to invest up to 30 percent of their assets in nonmortgage loans and securities. A maximum 10 percent of assets can be used to provide non-real estate commercial loans.

Savings institutions have taken advantage of the deregulatory acts by providing corporate and consumer loans with maturities typically ranging between one and four years. Because consumer and corporate loan maturities closely match their liability maturities, SIs that reduce their mortgage loan concentration in favor of more corporate and consumer loans reduce their exposure to interest rate risk. However, offering these loans results in some noninterest costs. The increased emphasis on corporate and consumer loans can increase an SI's overall degree of credit risk. The loss rate on mortgage loans has been significantly lower than the loss rate on credit card loans.

Despite their moves into corporate and consumer lending, SIs' participation in these fields is still limited by regulators. Thus, mortgages and mortgage-backed securities continue to be their primary assets.

Other Uses of Funds   Savings institutions can provide temporary financing to other institutions through the use of repurchase agreements. In addition, they can lend funds on a short-term basis through the federal funds market. Both methods allow them to efficiently use funds that they will have available for only a short period of time.

Asset Composition   The average asset composition for SIs is shown in Exhibit 21.6. Mortgage loans to households are their main asset. The second most important asset is securities, which provide liquidity when SIs do not have adequate funds to accommodate deposit withdrawals. Mortgage-backed securities and other securities represent about 20 percent of the total assets, on average. Commercial and consumer loans make up about 10 percent of the total assets, on average.

Risk Exposure

Like commercial banks, SIs are exposed to liquidity risk, credit risk, and interest rate risk. However, because their sources and uses of funds differ from those of banks, their exposure to risk varies as well.

EXHIBIT 21.6

Comparison of Assets
among Savings Institutions

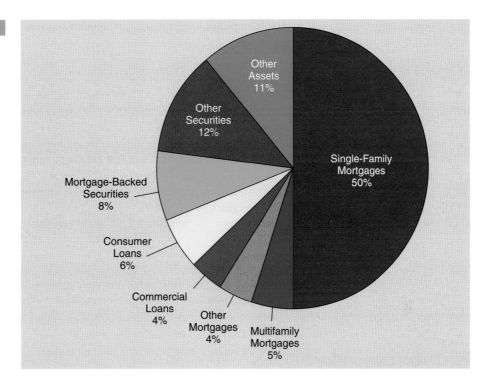

Liquidity Risk

Since SIs commonly use short-term liabilities to finance long-term assets, they depend on additional deposits to accommodate withdrawal requests. If new deposits are not sufficient to cover withdrawal requests, these institutions can experience liquidity problems. To remedy this situation, they can obtain funds through repurchase agreements or borrow funds in the federal funds market. These sources of funds will resolve only a short-term shortage, however. They will not be appropriate if a longer-term liquidity problem exists.

An alternative way to remedy a problem of insufficient liquidity is to sell assets in exchange for cash. Savings institutions can sell their Treasury securities or even some of their mortgages in the secondary market. Although the sale of assets can boost liquidity, it also reduces the institution's size and possibly its earnings. Therefore, minor liquidity deficiencies are typically resolved by increasing liabilities rather than selling assets.

Credit Risk

Because mortgages represent the primary asset, they are the main reason for credit risk at SIs. Although Federal Housing Authority (FHA) and Veterans Administration (VA) mortgages originated by SIs are insured against credit risk, conventional mortgages are not. Private insurance can normally be obtained for conventional mortgages, but SIs often incur the risk themselves rather than pay for the insurance. If they perform adequate credit analysis on their potential borrowers and geographically diversify their mortgage loans, they should be able to maintain a low degree of credit risk.

Many SIs were adversely affected by the weak economy in 2001–2002. Layoffs increased, and the expected income of households was subject to more uncertainty. Since

SIs rely on households for most of their income from loans, their exposure to credit risk increased.

Interest Rate Risk

The exposure of SIs to interest rate risk received much attention during the 1980s when interest rates increased substantially. At that time, they had a heavy concentration of fixed-rate mortgages, while their liabilities were mostly rate sensitive. Thus, the spread between their interest revenue and interest expenses narrowed when interest rates increased. The spread even became negative in the early 1980s because rates on deposits increased beyond the fixed interest rates charged on mortgages that the SIs had originated in previous years.

In contrast, many SIs benefitted from their exposure to interest rate risk in the 2001–2002 period. Interest rates declined in response to the weak economy, and the spread increased.

Measurement of Interest Rate Risk SIs commonly measure the gap between their rate-sensitive assets and their rate-sensitive liabilities in order to determine their exposure to interest rate risk. However, the gap measurement is dependent on the criteria used to classify an asset or liabilitity as rate sensitive.

ILLUSTRATION Siesta Savings Institution was recently created. It obtains most of its funds from two-year CDs and offers 30-year fixed-rate mortgages. It defines its assets and liabilities as rate sensitive if they are repriced within a year or less. Most of Siesta's liabilities are initially considered to be rate insensitve because their rate will not be affected within the year. Its assets are also considered to be rate insensitive because their rate will not be affected within the year. Thus, Siesta's gap is close to zero because its rate-sensitive assets and liabilities are close to zero, which implies that the institution is not exposed to interest rate risk. Nevertheless, Siesta will be adversely affected by an increase in interest rates because its interest expenses would rise over time while the rate on its mortgage loans is fixed for a long-term period. Thus, the gap measurement is not an accurate indicator of Siesta's exposure to interest rate risk.

Given the limitations of the gap measurement, some SIs measure the duration of their respective assets and liabilities to determine the imbalance in sensitivity of interest revenue versus expenses to interest rate movements. An example follows.

ILLUSTRATION Tucson Savings Institution (TSI) desires to measure the duration of its assets and liabilities. It first needs to classify each balance sheet component into various maturity categories, as shown in Exhibit 21.7. The rates on most adjustable-rate mortgages are adjusted every year, which is why the amounts under the longer-term categories show zero. The average duration for each category is provided below the dollar amount. Some fixed-rate mortgages are classified in the earlier term categories, because they are maturing or will be sold soon. The duration of .91 for adjustable-rate mortgages is a weighted average of their durations, computed as $(7,000/27,000).30 + (15,000/27,000).80 + (4,000/27,000)1.9 + (1,000/27,000)2.9$.

The durations for fixed-rate mortgages and investment securities were computed in a similar manner. The duration for total assets of 2.76 years was computed as a weighted average of the individual assets: $(27,000/61,000).91 + (20,000/61,000)5.32 + (14,000/61,000)2.65 = 2.76$.

EXHIBIT 21.7 Duration Schedule for Tucson Savings Institution (Dollar Amounts Are in Thousands)

Assets	Less Than 6 Months	6 Months to 1 Year	1–3 Years	3–5 Years	5–10 Years	10–20 Years	Over 20 Years	Total
Adjustable-rate mortgages								
Amount ($)	$7,000	$15,000	$4,000	$1,000	$0	$0	$0	$27,000
Average duration (yr)	.30	.80	1.90	2.90	0	0	0	.91
Fixed-rate mortgages								
Amount ($)	500	500	1,000	1,000	2,000	10,000	5,000	20,000
Average duration (yr)	.25	.60	1.80	2.60	4.30	5.50	7.60	5.32
Investment securities								
Amount ($)	2,000	3,000	4,000	2,000	1,000	0	2,000	14,000
Average duration (yr)	.20	.70	1.70	3.20	5.30	0	8.05	2.65
Total amount ($)	$9,500	$18,500	$9,000	$4,000	$3,000	$10,000	$7,000	$61,000

Asset duration = 2.76

Liabilities								
Fixed-maturity deposits								
Amount ($)	$14,000	$9,000	$2,000	$1,000	$0	$0	$0	$26,000
Duration (yr)	.30	.60	1.80	2.80	0	0	0	.62
NOW accounts								
Amount ($)	4,000	0	0	0	0	0	0	4,000
Duration (yr)	.40	0	0	0	0	0	0	.40
MMDAs								
Amount ($)	15,000	0	0	0	0	0	0	15,000
Duration (yr)	.20	0	0	0	0	0	0	.20
Passbook accounts								
Amount ($)	13,000	0	0	0	0	0	0	13,000
Duration (yr)	.40	0	0	0	0	0	0	.40
Total amount ($)	$46,000	$9,000	$2,000	$1,000	$0	$0	$0	$58,000

Liability duration = .45

A similar procedure was used to estimate the duration of liabilities. NOW accounts and passbook savings have no specified maturity, but their rate is adjusted less frequently than the rate on MMDAs, which is why MMDAs have a shorter duration. The total liability duration is about .45. TSI's total asset duration is more than six times its liability duration. Thus, its future performance is highly exposed to interest rate movements. Its market value would decrease substantially in response to an increase in interest rates. TSI can reduce its exposure to interest rate risk by reducing the proportion of its assets in the long-duration categories.

Financial institutions use computer programs to estimate their asset and liability duration and apply sensitivity analysis to proposed balance sheet adjustments. For example, TSI could determine how its asset and liability duration would change if it engaged in a promotional effort to issue five-year deposits and used the funds to offer adjustable-rate mortgages.

Managing Interest Rate Risk

Savings institutions can use a variety of methods to manage their interest rate risk, including the following:

- ■ Adjustable-rate mortgages
- ■ Interest rate futures contracts
- ■ Interest rate swaps

Adjustable-Rate Mortgages (ARMs)

The interest rates on adjustable-rate mortgages (ARMs) are tied to market-determined rates such as the one-year Treasury bill rate and are periodically adjusted in accordance with the formula stated in the ARM contract. A variety of formulas are used. ARMs enable SIs to maintain a more stable spread between interest revenue and interest expenses.

Although ARMs reduce the adverse impact of rising interest rates, they also reduce the favorable impact of declining interest rates. Suppose an SI that obtains most of its funds from short-term deposits uses the funds to provide fixed-rate mortgages. If interest rates decline and the SI does not hedge its exposure to interest rate risk, the spread will increase. If the SI uses ARMs as a hedging strategy, however, the interest on loans will decrease during a period of declining rates, so the spread will not widen.

During the 1970s, ARMs helped SIs perform better but exposed consumers to interest rate risk. Although ARMs typically have a maximum cap limiting the increase in interest rates (such as 2 percent per year and 5 percent over the loan life), the impact on household mortgage payments is still significant. Because some homeowners prefer fixed-rate mortgages, most SIs continue to offer them and therefore incur interest rate risk. Thus, additional strategies besides the use of ARMs are necessary to reduce this risk.

Interest Rate Futures Contracts

An interest rate futures contract allows for the purchase of a specific amount of a particular debt security for a specified price at a future point in time. Sellers of futures contracts are obligated to sell the securities for the contract price at the stated future point in time.

Some SIs use Treasury bond futures contracts because the cash flow characteristics of Treasury bonds resemble those of fixed-rate mortgages. Like mortgages, Treasury bonds offer fixed periodic payments, so their market value moves inversely to interest rate fluctuations. Savings institutions that sell futures contracts on these securities can effectively hedge their fixed-rate mortgages. If interest rates rise, the market value of the securities represented by the futures contract will decrease. The SIs will benefit from the difference between the market value at which they can purchase these securities in the future and the futures price at which they will sell the securities. This can offset the reduced spread between their interest revenue and interest expenses during the period of rising interest rates.

Although the concept of using interest rate futures to guard against interest rate risk is simple, the actual application is more complex. It is difficult to perfectly offset the potential reduction in the spread with a futures position.

Interest Rate Swaps

Another strategy for reducing interest rate risk is the interest rate swap, which allows an SI to swap fixed-rate payments (an outflow) for variable-rate payments (an inflow). The fixed-rate outflow payments can be matched against the fixed-rate mortgages held so that a certain spread can be achieved. In addition, the variable-rate inflows due to the swap can be matched against the variable cost of funds. In a rising rate environment, the institution's fixed-rate outflow payments from the swap agreement remain fixed, while the variable-rate inflow payments due to the swap increase. This favorable result can partially offset the normally unfavorable impact of rising interest rates on an SI's spread. However, an interest rate swap also reduces the favorable impact of declining interest rates. Inflow interest payments decrease, while the outflow interest payments remain the same during a period of declining rates.

Conclusions about Interest Rate Risk

Many SIs have used the strategies just described to reduce their interest rate risk. Although these strategies are useful, it is virtually impossible to completely eliminate the risk. One reason for this is the potential prepayment of mortgages. Homeowners often pay off their mortgages before maturity without much advance notice to the SI. Consequently, SIs do not really know the actual maturity of the mortgages they hold and cannot perfectly match the interest rate sensitivity of their assets and liabilities.

Savings Institution Valuation

Savings institutions (or SI operating units that are part of a financial conglomerate) are commonly valued by their managers to monitor progress over time or by other financial institutions that are considering an acquisition. The value of an SI can be modeled as the present value of its future cash flows. Thus, the value of an SI should change in response to changes in its expected cash flows in the future and to changes in the required rate by investors:

$$\Delta V = f[\Delta E(CF), \Delta k]$$
$$+ \quad -$$

Factors That Affect Cash Flows

The change in an SI's expected cash flows may be modeled as

$$\Delta E(CF) = f(\Delta ECON, \Delta R_f, \Delta INDUS, \Delta MANAB)$$
$$+ \quad - \quad ? \quad +$$

where ECON represents economic growth, R_f represents the risk-free interest rate, INDUS represents the industry conditions to which SIs are exposed, and MANAB represents the SI's management abilities.

Economic Growth Economic growth can enhance an SI's cash flows by increasing household demand for consumer loans or mortgage loans, thereby allowing the SI to provide more loans. In addition, loan defaults are normally reduced in periods of strong economic growth. Furthermore, the demand for other financial services (such as real estate and insurance services) provided by SIs tends to be higher during periods of strong economic growth when households have relatively high levels of disposable income.

Change in the Risk-Free Interest Rate An SI's cash flows may be inversely related to interest rate movements. First, if the risk-free interest rate decreases, other market rates may also decline, and the result may be a stronger demand for the SI's loans. Second, SIs rely heavily on short-term deposits as a source of funds, and the rates paid on these deposits are typically revised in accordance with other interest rate movements. Savings institutions' assets (such as consumer loans and mortgage loans) commonly have fixed rates, so interest income does not adjust to interest rate movements until those assets reach maturity or are sold. Therefore, when interest rates fall, an SI's cost of obtaining funds declines more than the decline in the interest earned on its loans and investments. An increase in interest rates can reduce the SI's expected cash flows because the interest paid on deposits may increase more than the interest earned on loans and investments.

Change in Industry Conditions Savings institutions are exposed to industry conditions such as regulatory constraints, technology, and competition. If regulatory constraints are reduced, the expected cash flows of some SIs should increase. For example, when regulators reduced constraints on the services that could be offered, SIs were able to provide more services for their customers. At the same time, however, a reduction in regulations can cause some of the less efficient SIs to lose market share and therefore experience a reduction in cash flows.

Change in Management Abilities An SI has control over the composition of its managers and its organizational structure. Its managers attempt to make internal decisions that will capitalize on the external forces (economic growth, interest rates, regulatory constraints) that the institution cannot control. Thus, the management skills of an SI influence its expected cash flows. For example, skillful managers will recognize whether to increase the funds allocated to fixed-rate mortgages based on expectations of future interest rates. They can capitalize on regulatory changes by offering a diversified set of services that accommodate specific customers. They can use technology in a manner that reduces expenses. They may also use derivative securities to alter the potential return and the exposure of the SI to interest rate movements.

Factors That Affect the Required Rate of Return by Investors

The required rate of return by investors who invest in an SI can be modeled as

$$\Delta k = f(\overset{+}{\Delta R_f}, \overset{+}{\Delta RP})$$

where ΔR_f represents a change in the risk-free interest rate, and ΔRP represents a change in the risk premium.

Change in the Risk-Free Rate An increase in the risk-free rate results in a higher return required by investors. Recall that the risk-free rate of interest is driven by inflation-

ary expectations (INF), economic growth (ECON), the money supply (MS), and the budget deficit (DEF):

$$\Delta R_f = f(\Delta INF, \Delta ECON, \Delta MS, \Delta DEF)$$
$$\quad\quad + \quad\quad + \quad\quad - \quad\quad +$$

High inflation, economic growth, and a high budget deficit place upward pressure on interest rates, while money supply growth places downward pressure on interest rates (assuming it does not cause inflation). Thus, a substantial increase in inflation or in the budget deficit typically results in lower valuations of SIs.

Change in the Risk Premium If the risk premium on an SI rises, so will the required rate of return by investors who invest in the SI. The risk premium can change in response to changes in economic growth, regulatory constraints, or management abilities.

$$\Delta RP = f(\Delta ECON, \Delta INDUS, \Delta MANAB)$$
$$\quad\quad\quad - \quad\quad\quad ? \quad\quad\quad -$$

High economic growth results in less risk for an SI because its consumer loans, mortgage loans, and investments in debt securities are less likely to default. The effect of industry conditions on SIs can be mixed. A reduction in regulatory constraints on services can reduce the risk of SIs as they diversify their offerings, or it can increase their risk if they engage in some services that are riskier than their traditional services. An improvement in management skills may reduce the perceived risk of the SIs and therefore reduce the risk premium.

Exhibit 21.8 provides a framework for valuing an SI, based on the preceding discussion. In general, the value of an SI is favorably affected by strong economic growth,

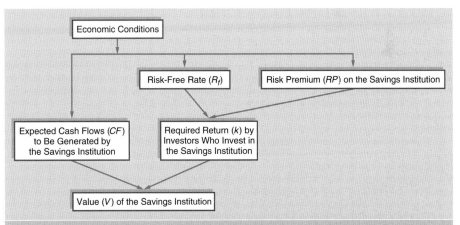

- A stronger economy leads to an increase in the demand for loans (interest income) and other services (noninterest income), fewer loan defaults, and therefore better cash flows for the savings institution.

- A lower risk-free rate leads to a lower cost of deposits obtained and more favorable valuations of the mortgages held by the savings institution.

- The valuation is also influenced by industry conditions and the saving institution's management (not shown in the diagram). These factors affect the risk premium (and therefore the required return by investors) and the expected cash flows to be generated by the savings institution. In particular, regulatory changes can affect the level of competition and therefore affect the savings institution's cash flows and risk premium.

EXHIBIT 21.9 Interaction between Savings Institutions and Other Financial Institutions

Type of Financial Institution	Interaction with Savings Institutions
Commercial banks	• Savings institutions compete with commercial banks in attracting deposits, providing consumer loans, and providing commercial loans. • Some savings institutions and commercial banks have merged in recent years. • Some savings institutions sell mortgages to commercial banks.
Finance companies	• Savings institutions compete with finance companies in providing consumer and commercial loans.
Money market mutual funds	• Savings institutions compete with money market mutual funds in attracting short-term deposits of investors.
Investment companies and brokerage firms	• Savings institutions often contact investment companies to engage in interest rate swaps and interest rate caps. • Savings institutions have made agreements with brokerage firms to indirectly offer brokerage services to their customers.
Insurance companies	• Mortgages sold by savings institutions in the secondary market are sometimes purchased by insurance companies.

a reduction in interest rates, and high-quality management. The sensitivity of an SI's value to these conditions depends on its own characteristics. For example, the value of an SI that emphasizes real estate and insurance services will be more sensitive to regulations that restrict or limit the offering of these services than will the value of an SI that focuses on traditional mortgage lending. The latter institution may be more sensitive to interest rate movements.

Interaction with Other Financial Institutions

Savings institutions interact with various types of financial institutions, as summarized in Exhibit 21.9. They compete with commercial banks and money market mutual funds to obtain funds as well as with commercial banks and finance companies in lending funds. Their hedging of interest rate risk is facilitated by investment companies that act as financial intermediaries for interest rate swaps and caps. Their ability to sell mortgages in the secondary market is enhanced by insurance companies that purchase them.

Many SIs have other financial institutions as subsidiaries that provide a variety of services, including consumer finance, trust company, mortgage banking, discount brokerage, and insurance.

Financial Market Participation

Savings institutions commonly participate in various financial markets, as summarized in Exhibit 21.10. Mortgage markets provide a source of funds to SIs that desire to issue mortgage-backed securities or sell their mortgages in the secondary market. Bond markets serve as a use of funds for SIs with excess funds and as a source of funds for SIs that issue new bonds in the primary market or sell bond holdings in the secondary market. Futures markets and options markets have enabled SIs to reduce interest rate risk that results from their investment in mortgages and bonds.

EXHIBIT 21.10   Participation of Savings Institutions in Financial Markets

Financial Market	Participation by Savings Institutions
Money markets	• Savings institutions compete with other depository institutions for short-term deposits. • Some savings institutions issue commercial paper.
Mortgage markets	• Savings institutions sell mortgages in the secondary market and issue mortgage-backed securities.
Bond markets	• Savings institutions purchase bonds for their investment portfolios. • Savings institutions issue bonds to obtain long-term funds.
Futures markets	• Some savings institutions hedge against interest rate movements by taking positions in interest rate futures.
Options markets	• Some savings institutions hedge against interest rate movements by purchasing put options on interest rate futures.
Swap markets	• Some savings institutions hedge against interest rate movements by engaging in interest rate swaps.

Savings Institution Performance

http://
http://www.fdic.gov
Information about the
performance of savings
institutions.

Changes in the general performance of SIs can be assessed by reviewing income statement items as a percentage of total assets in aggregate, as shown in Exhibit 21.11. Earnings before taxes are estimated as a percentage of total assets in the bottom row and provide a general measure of the performance of SIs in aggregate. The change in earnings before taxes over time can be explained by the income statement items shown in this table.

The difference between interest income and interest expenses has fluctuated in recent years, resulting in variable net interest income for SIs. Other income statement items have improved, however. The loan loss provision has declined slightly since 2001 in response to a lower level of anticipated loan losses. Noninterest income has increased as SIs offer more services that generate fees. Noninterest expenses have also increased slightly as a result of this increase in services.

Exhibit 21.12 shows the trend of the key factors from financial statements that can explain the changes in performance of SIs over time. The increase in noninterest income in recent years is evident in the exhibit.

EXHIBIT 21.11

Income Statement Items as a Percentage of Total Assets for Savings Institutions in Aggregate

		2001	2002	2003
	Interest income	6.32%	5.32%	4.67%
−	Total interest expense	3.42	2.26	1.78
=	Net interest income	2.90	3.06	2.89
−	Loan loss provision	.27	.29	.21
+	Noninterest income	1.38	1.45	1.74
−	Noninterest expense	2.37	2.35	2.43
=	Earnings before tax	1.64	1.87	1.99

Source: Office of Thrift Supervision.

EXHIBIT 21.12

Key Components That
Influence the Performance
of Savings Institutions
(Measured as a
Percentage of Total
Assets)

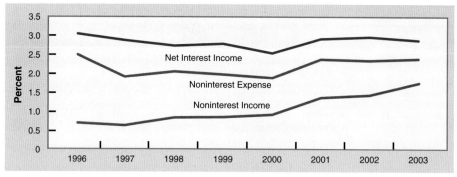

Source: Office of Thrift Supervision.

Performance of Savings Institutions versus Commercial Banks

The factors just discussed are also commonly used to assess the performance of commercial banks over time, but the relative importance of the measures differs because SIs and commercial banks have a different focus. First, loan loss provisions are typically much lower for SIs than for commercial banks because SIs experience fewer defaults on their (mostly mortgage) loans than commercial banks experience on their (mostly commercial) loans. Second, SIs earn substantially less noninterest income than commercial banks earn because the banks tend to offer more services that generate fee income. Third, noninterest expenses are lower for SIs than for commercial banks because SIs' operations are normally less complex. Credit analysis is normally easier for mortgage applications than for business loan applications. Also, since commercial banks normally provide more services that generate fee income, they incur higher expenses when offering these extra services.

Savings Institution Crisis

During the late 1980s, numerous SIs throughout the United States became insolvent and ultimately failed. To prevent further failures and restore confidence, Congress enacted the Financial Institutions Reform, Recovery, and Enforcement Act (FIRREA) in 1989. The underlying problems that precipitated the savings institution crisis are described here. The main provisions of the bailout plan are explained, followed by a discussion of the impact of the bailout on SIs and other financial institutions.

Reasons for Failure

The main reasons for the proliferation of SI failures were

■ An increase in interest expenses
■ Losses on loans and securities
■ Fraud
■ Illiquidity

Increase in Interest Expenses In the late 1980s, interest rates increased. Those SIs that had provided long-term mortgages were adversely affected, because the interest

they earned on assets remained constant while the interest they paid on liabilities increased. Consequently, the net interest income declined. In some cases, the interest paid on liabilities was higher than the interest the SIs earned on the mortgages they held.

Losses on Loans and Securities The crisis was precipitated by unpaid loans. Many loan defaults occurred in the Southwest, where economies were devastated by a decline in oil prices. Layoffs in the oil industry resulted, causing a decline in income. Real estate prices dropped so dramatically that foreclosures on bad real estate loans did not serve as adequate collateral. Although some housing loans defaulted, the major loan losses were in commercial real estate, such as office complexes. Savings institutions were forced to assume real estate holdings that were sometimes worth less than half the loan amount originally provided.

Savings institutions also experienced losses on their junk bond holdings. For example, Columbia S&L had purchased $4 billion worth of junk bonds. The value of these bonds declined by $1.5 billion as a result of numerous defaults.

Fraud Many SIs experienced financial problems because of various fraudulent activities. In one of the most common types of fraud, managers used depositors' funds for purchases of personal assets, including yachts, artwork, and automobile dealerships.

Illiquidity Many SIs experienced a cash flow deficiency as a result of loan losses, as the inflows from loan repayments were not sufficient to cover depositor withdrawals. Consequently, they were forced to offer higher interest rates on deposits to attract more funds. As depositors became aware of the S&L crisis, they began to withdraw their savings from SIs, which exacerbated the illiquidity problem. Normally, the threat of deposit runs is mitigated by deposit insurance. Depositors were aware, however, that the insuring agency (the Federal Savings and Loan Insurance Corporation, FSLIC) was already experiencing its own liquidity problems, as it provided subsidies to financial institutions willing to acquire failing SIs. By April 1988, the net worth of the FSLIC was estimated to be negative $11.6 billion. Media attention about the FSLIC's liquidity problems led to further depositor withdrawals, causing greater liquidity problems for the SIs.

Provisions of the FIRREA

In February 1989, the White House proposed a bill that was ultimately enacted by Congress as the Financial Institutions Reform, Recovery, and Enforcement Act (FIRREA); it was signed by President George Bush on August 9, 1989. The following is a summary of some of the Act's more relevant provisions:

- The FSLIC was terminated. A new insurance agency for SIs, called the Savings Association Insurance Fund (SAIF), was formed.
- As of January 1990, SIs were required to have $1.50 in tangible capital per $100 of deposits, or a 1.5 percent ratio. The ratio was to increase over time.
- The Federal Home Loan Bank Board (FHLBB), which historically regulated SIs, was replaced by the Office of Thrift Supervision (OTS). The Resolution Trust Corporation was created to deal with insolvent SIs.
- The penalties for officers of SIs and other financial institutions convicted of fraud were increased.
- Savings institutions were required to use 70 percent of their assets for housing loans, up from 60 percent.

- ■ Savings institutions were prohibited from holding some risky investments, including junk bonds, in the future. Those SIs holding junk bonds were required to divest them over time.
- ■ Commercial banks were allowed to purchase both failing and healthy SIs.

Creation of the RTC

The Resolution Trust Corporation (RTC) was formed to deal with insolvent SIs until it was closed at the end of 1995. The RTC liquidated SI assets and reimbursed depositors or sold the SI to another financial institution. The order in which SIs were processed was based on their size, health, and sales potential. Those that were more costly to maintain were typically dealt with first. The RTC executed acquisitions or liquidations of the insolvent SIs.

The most popular method for handling failures was the deposit transfer, in which deposits of the failed SIs were transferred to an acquiring firm for a fee (called a premium). With this method, the acquiring firm did not assume the low-quality assets of the failed SI. During its life, the RTC either liquidated or found a buyer for 747 insolvent SIs. It recovered $394 billion from liquidating assets and another $2.4 billion from legal settlements.

Impact of the Bailout

Beyond restoring confidence in the SI industry, the provisions of the FIRREA had significant ramifications for risk/return tendencies of SIs in the future.

Stronger Capital Positions As a result of the FIRREA, many SIs are now required to maintain a higher minimum level of capital. Some SIs have boosted their capital by issuing stock. Others have sold assets, because a given level of capital with a smaller book value of assets results in a higher capital ratio. Other SIs have searched for an acquirer, such as another SI or a commercial bank.

Higher Asset Quality In addition to boosting capital, SIs have been forced to maintain more conservative asset portfolios. The provisions requiring a higher minimum investment in home mortgages and the liquidation of junk bonds reflect not only less risk but also less potential return. Some SIs have converted to commercial banks so that they have more flexibility.

More Consolidation The FIRREA allows commercial banks and other financial institutions to purchase failing *or* healthy SIs. Some commercial banks have been enticed by the low share prices of SIs relative to their earning power. Under proper management, the acquired SIs have improved their performance significantly.

Some healthy SIs have acquired failing SIs for the same reason. They perceive the failing SIs as undervalued. The deposit bases of these failing SIs were sound, but the loan portfolios needed to be modified.

Performance since the FIRREA

Since the FIRREA was enacted, SIs have generally performed well based on the various criteria illustrated in Exhibit 21.13. The mean return on assets (ROA) for SIs (see the

EXHIBIT 21.13
Performance of Savings
Institutions since the FIRREA

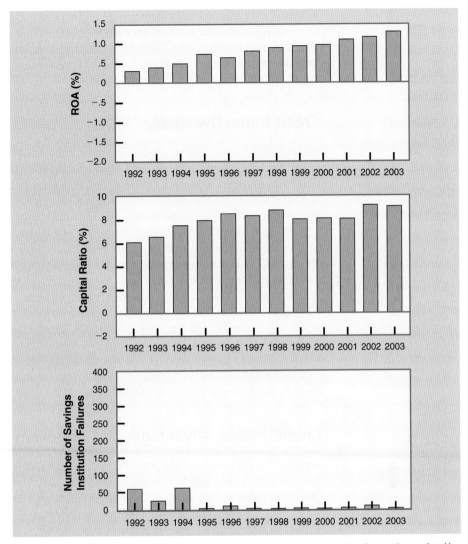

Source: Regulatory Financial Reports, *Financial Industry Trends,* 1993, and Resolution Trust Corporation; updated by author.

http://
http://www.ots.treas.gov
Review of performance of
savings institutions overall.

first graph) was negative in 1989 and 1990, but it became positive in 1991 and has increased since then. The capital ratio (the second graph) has increased substantially since 1989. The number of SI failures (the third graph) has declined from 355 in 1990 to less than 12 in each of the last several years.

Credit Union: Background

Credit unions (CUs) are nonprofit organizations composed of members with a common bond, such as an affiliation with a particular labor union, church, university, or even residential area. About 20 million people are members of a CU. A qualified person can typically become a member of a CU by depositing $5 or more into an account. Credit unions serve as intermediaries for their members. They accept deposits from members

who have excess funds and channel most of the funds to those members who want to finance the purchase of a car or other assets.

There are about 10,200 CUs in the United States. Although the number of CUs now exceeds the number of commercial banks, the total assets of CUs are less than one-tenth the amount of total assets in commercial banks.

Credit Union Ownership

Because CUs do not issue stock, they are technically owned by the depositors. The deposits are called shares, and interest paid on the deposits is called a dividend. Because CUs are nonprofit organizations, their income is not taxed. Like savings institutions and commercial banks, CUs can be federally or state chartered. If the state does not offer a charter, a federal charter is necessary.

Although a few CUs (such as the Navy Federal CU) have assets of more than $1 billion, most are very small. Federally chartered CUs are growing at a faster rate than state-chartered CUs, and their total assets are now significantly larger than the aggregate assets of state-chartered CUs.

Because CUs are owned by members, their objective is to satisfy those members. CUs offer interest on share deposits to members who invest funds. In addition, they provide loans to members who are in need of funds. Thus, as mentioned earlier, they act as intermediaries by repackaging deposits from member savers and providing them as loans to member borrowers. If CUs accumulate earnings, they can use the earnings to either offer higher rates on deposits or reduce rates on loans. Growth can allow CUs to be more diversified and more efficient if economies of scale exist.

Credit Unions: Advantages and Disadvantages

http://www.corningcu.org
Information about services related to financial planning that are provided by CUs.

Because CUs are nonprofit and therefore are not taxed, they can offer attractive rates to their member savers and borrowers. In addition, their noninterest expenses are relatively low, because their labor, office, and furniture are often donated or provided at a very low cost through the affiliation of their members.

Some characteristics of CUs can be unfavorable. Their volunteer labor may not have the incentive to manage operations efficiently. In addition, the common bond requirement for membership restricts a given CU from growing beyond the potential size of that particular affiliation. The common bond also limits the ability of CUs to diversify. This is especially true when all members are employees of a particular institution. If that institution lays off a number of workers, many members may simultaneously experience financial problems and withdraw their share deposits or default on their loans. This could cause the CU to become illiquid at a time when more members need loans to survive the layoff.

Even when the common bond does not represent a particular employer, many CUs are unable to diversify geographically because all members live in the same area. Thus, an economic slowdown in this area would have an adverse impact on most members. Furthermore, CUs cannot diversify among various products the way that commercial banks and savings institutions do. They are created to serve the members and therefore concentrate heavily on providing loans to members. Finally, in the event that CUs do need funds, they are unable to issue stock because they are owned by depositors rather than shareholders.

http://www.ncua.gov
Provides financial data for any federally chartered CU.

To try to overcome some of these disadvantages as well as to better diversify their services and take greater advantage of economies of scale, CUs increasingly have been

merging. Consequently, some CUs now draw their members from a number of employers, organizations, and other affiliations. CUs are also trying to diversify their products by offering traveler's checks, money orders, and life insurance to their members.

Credit Union Fund Sources and Uses

Credit unions obtain funds from their members and channel these funds to other members.

Funds Sources

Credit unions obtain most of their funds from share deposits by members. The typical deposit is similar to a passbook savings account deposit at commercial banks or savings institutions, as it has no specified maturity and is insured up to $100,000. CUs also offer share certificates, which provide higher rates than share deposits but require a minimum amount (such as $500) and a specified maturity. The share certificates offered by CUs compete against the retail CDs offered by commercial banks and savings institutions. The proportion of funds obtained through regular share deposits is relatively large compared to the counterpart passbook accounts offered by other depository institutions. This characteristic allows CUs to obtain much of their funds at a relatively low cost.

In addition to share deposits and certificates, most CUs also offer checkable accounts called share drafts, which became more popular in the early 1990s. These accounts can pay interest and allow an unlimited amount of checks to be written. They normally require a minimum balance to be maintained. Share drafts offered by CUs compete against the NOW accounts and MMDAs offered by commercial banks and savings institutions.

If a CU needs funds temporarily, it can borrow from other CUs or from the **Central Liquidity Facility (CLF).** The CLF acts as a lender for CUs in a manner similar to the Federal Reserve's discount window. The loans are commonly used to accommodate seasonal funding and specialized needs or to boost the liquidity of troubled CUs.

Like other depository institutions, CUs maintain capital. Their primary source of capital is retained earnings. In recent years, CUs have boosted their capital, which helps cushion against any future loan losses. Given that CUs tend to use conservative management, their capital ratio is relatively high compared with other depository institutions.

Funds Uses

Credit unions use the majority of their funds for loans to members. These loans finance automobiles, home improvements, and other personal expenses. They are typically secured and carry maturities of five years or less. Some CUs offer long-term mortgage loans, but many prefer to avoid assets with long maturities. In addition to providing loans, CUs purchase government and agency securities to maintain adequate liquidity.

Credit Union Exposure to Risk

Like other depository institutions, CUs are exposed to liquidity risk, credit risk, and interest rate risk. Their balance sheet structure differs from that of other institutions, however, so their exposure to each type of risk also differs.

Liquidity Risk

If a CU experiences an unanticipated wave of withdrawals without an offsetting amount of new deposits, it could become illiquid. It can borrow from the Central Liquidity Facility to resolve temporary liquidity problems, but if the shortage of funds is expected to continue, the CU must search for a more permanent cure. Other depository institutions have greater ability to boost deposit levels because they can tap various markets. Although some depository institutions attract deposits from international investors, the potential market for a CU's depositors is much more localized. Because the market is restricted to those consumers who qualify as members, CUs have less ability to quickly generate additional deposits.

Credit Risk

Because CUs concentrate on personal loans to their members, their exposure to credit (default) risk is primarily derived from those loans. Most of their loans are secured, which reduces the loss to CUs in the event of default. Poor economic conditions can have a significant impact on loan defaults. Some CUs will perform much better than others because of more favorable economic conditions in their area. However, even during favorable economic periods, CUs with very lenient loan policies could experience losses. A common concern is that CUs may not conduct a thorough credit analysis of loan applicants; the loans provided by CUs are consumer oriented, however, so an elaborate credit analysis is not required.

Interest Rate Risk

The majority of maturities on consumer loans offered by CUs are short term, causing their asset portfolios to be rate sensitive. Because their sources of funds are also generally rate sensitive, movements in interest revenues and interest expenses of CUs are highly correlated. Therefore, the spread between interest revenues and interest expenses remains somewhat stable over time, regardless of how interest rates change.

Credit Union Regulation

http://
http://www.ncua.gov
Background on the NCUA.

Federal CUs are supervised and regulated by the National Credit Union Administration (NCUA), which is composed of three board members, one of whom chairs the board.

The NCUA employs a staff of examiners to monitor CUs. The examiners conduct assessments of all federally chartered CUs as well as any state-chartered CUs applying for federal insurance. Each CU completes a semiannual call report that provides financial information. From this information, the NCUA examiners derive financial ratios that measure the financial condition of the CU. The ratios are then compared to an industry norm to detect any significant deviations. Then a summary of the CU, called a Financial Performance Report, is completed to identify any potential problems that deserve special attention in the future.

As part of the assessment, the examiners classify each CU into a specific risk category, ranging from Code 1 (low risk) to Code 5 (high risk). This is intended to serve as an early warning system so that CUs that are experiencing problems or are in potential danger can

be closely monitored in the future. The criteria used to assess risk are capital adequacy, asset quality, management, earnings, liquidity, and sensitivity to market conditions. This CAMELS system has been used since 1987 and is very similar to the Federal Deposit Insurance Corporation (FDIC) system for tracking the commercial banks it insures. In 1999, the NCUA implemented a Corporate Risk Information System (CRIS), which provides a more detailed analysis of each CU's risk. In addition, CUs are required to maintain a capital ratio of 8 percent of risk-weighted assets.

Regulating State-Chartered Credit Unions

State-chartered CUs are regulated by their respective states. The degree to which CUs can offer various products and services is influenced by the type of charter and by their location. In addition to services and rates, loans offered by CUs to officers and directors of CUs also carry certain limitations.

Credit Union Insurance

About 90 percent of CUs are insured by the National Credit Union Share Insurance Fund (NCUSIF), which is administered by the NCUA. The CUs typically pay an annual insurance premium of one-twelfth of 1 percent of share deposits. A supplemental premium is added if necessary. Some states require their CUs to be federally insured; others allow insurance to be offered by alternative insurance agencies.

The NCUSIF was created in 1970, without any contributing start-up capital from the U.S. Treasury and Federal Reserve. All federally chartered CUs are required to obtain insurance from the NCUSIF. State-chartered CUs are eligible for NCUSIF insurance only if they meet various guidelines. The maximum insurance per depositor is $100,000.

The NCUSIF sets aside a portion of its funds as reserves to cover expenses resulting from CU failures each year. Given the low number of failures, the reserves have been more than adequate to cover these expenses.

SUMMARY

- The main sources of funds for SIs are deposits and borrowed funds. The main uses of funds for SIs are mortgages, mortgage-backed securities, and other securities.

- Savings institutions are exposed to credit risk as a result of their heavy concentration in mortgages, mortgage-backed securities, and other securities. They attempt to diversify their investments to reduce credit risk.

Savings institutions are highly susceptible to interest rate risk, because their asset portfolios are typically less rate sensitive than their liability portfolios. They can reduce their interest rate risk by using interest rate futures contracts or interest rate swaps.

- The valuation of an SI is a function of its expected cash flows and the required return by its investors. The expected cash flows are influenced by economic

growth, interest rate movements, regulatory constraints, and the abilities of the institution's managers. The required rate of return is influenced by the prevailing risk-free rate and the risk premium. The risk premium is lower when economic conditions are strong. A reduction in regulatory constraints can reduce the risk premium by allowing the SI to diversify its services, but may increase the risk premium if the institution pursues services that it cannot provide efficiently.

- In the late 1980s, many SIs experienced heavy losses from loan defaults, adverse interest rate movements, and fraud. These adverse effects led to the SI crisis. In 1989, the FIRREA was passed to resolve the crisis. Specifically, the FIRREA boosted capital requirements, increased penalties for fraud, and prohibited SIs from purchasing junk bonds. It also created the Resolution Trust Corporation to liquidate assets of failed SIs.

- Credit unions obtain most of their funds from share deposits by members. If they experience a cash deficiency, they can borrow from other CUs or from the Central Liquidity Facility (CLF). They use the majority of their funds for personal loans to members.

- Credit unions are exposed to liquidity risk because they could experience an unanticipated wave of deposit withdrawals. They are also exposed to credit risk as a result of personal loans to members.

  Because the personal loans offered by CUs are short term, they are rate sensitive like the liabilities. Thus, the interest rate risk of CUs is typically less than that of other depository institutions.

POINT COUNTER-POINT

Can All Savings Institutions Avoid Failure?

Point Yes. If savings institutions use conservative management by focusing on adjustable-rate mortgages with limited default risk, they can limit their risk and avoid failure.

Counter-Point No. Some savings institutions will be crowded out of the market for high-quality adjustable-rate mortgages and will have to take some risk. There are too many savings institutions, and some that have weaker management will inevitably fail.

Who Is Correct? Use your favorite search engine to learn more about this issue. Offer your own opinion on this issue.

QUESTIONS AND APPLICATIONS

1. **Managing in Financial Markets: Hedging Interest Rate Risk** As a consultant to Boca Savings & Loan Association, you notice that a large portion of 15-year fixed-rate mortgages are financed with funds from short-term deposits. You believe the yield curve is useful in indicating the market's anticipation of future interest rates and that the yield curve is primarily determined by interest rate expectations. At the present time, Boca has not hedged its interest rate risk. Assume that a steep upward-sloping yield curve currently exists.
   a. Boca asks you to assess its exposure to interest rate risk. Describe how Boca will be affected by rising interest rates and by a decline in interest rates.
   b. Given the information about the yield curve, would you advise Boca to hedge its exposure to interest rate risk? Explain.
   c. Explain why your advice to Boca may possibly backfire.

2. **Regulation of SIs** What criteria are used by regulators to examine a thrift institution?

3. **Exposure to Interest Rate Risk** The following table discloses the interest rate sensitivity of two SIs (dollar amounts are in millions).

	Interest Sensitivity Period			
	Within 1 Year	From 1 to 5 Years	From 5 to 10 Years	Over 10 Years
Lawrence S&L				
Interest-earning assets	$ 8,000	$3,000	$7,000	$3,000
Interest-bearing liabilities	11,000	6,000	2,000	1,000
Manhattan S&L				
Interest-earning assets	1,000	1,000	4,000	3,000
Interest-bearing liabilities	2,000	2,000	1,000	1,000

Based on this information only, which institution's stock price would likely be affected more by a given change in interest rates? Justify your opinion.

4. **Liquidity and Credit Risk** Describe the liquidity and credit risk of savings institutions, and discuss how each is managed.

5. **SI Crisis** What were some of the more obvious reasons for the SI crisis?

6. **Interpreting Financial News** Interpret the following comments made by Wall Street analysts and portfolio managers:
   a. "Deposit insurance actually fueled the SI crisis because it allowed SIs to grow."
   b. "Thrifts are no longer so sensitive to interest rate movements, even if their asset and liability compositions have not changed."
   c. "Because of the FIRREA, another SI crisis is unlikely."

7. **SI Sources and Uses of Funds** Explain in general terms how savings institutions differ from commercial banks with respect to their sources of funds and uses of funds. Discuss each source of funds for savings institutions. Identify and discuss the main uses of funds for savings institutions.

8. **DIDMCA** What effect did the Depository Institution Deregulation and Monetary Control Act (DIDMCA) of 1980 and the Garn–St Germain Act of 1982 have on savings institutions?

9. **Internet Exercise** Assess the recent performance of SIs using the website http://www2.fdic.gov/qbp. Click on "Quarterly Banking Profile," then on "Savings Institutions" and "View Report."

a. Summarize the general performance of SIs in the most recent quarter.

10. **Use of Interest Rate Swaps** Explain how savings institutions could use interest rate swaps to reduce interest rate risk. Will savings institutions that use swaps perform better or worse than those that were unhedged during a period of declining interest rates? Explain.

11. **Regulation of Credit Unions** Who regulates CUs? What are the regulators' powers? Where do credit unions obtain deposit insurance?

12. **Offering More Diversified Services** Discuss the entrance of savings institutions into consumer and commercial lending. What are the potential risks and rewards of this strategy? Discuss the conflict between diversification and specialization of savings institutions.

13. **Risk of Credit Unions** Explain how credit union exposure to liquidity risk differs from that of other financial institutions. Explain why credit unions are more insulated from interest rate risk than some other financial institutions.

14. **Use of Financial Futures** Explain how savings institutions could use interest rate futures to reduce interest rate risk.

15. **FIRREA** Explain how the Financial Institutions Reform, Recovery, and Enforcement Act (FIRREA) reduced the perceived risk of savings institutions.

16. **Ownership of SIs** What are the alternative forms of ownership of a savings institution?

17. **Hedging Interest Rate Movements** If market interest rates are expected to decline over time, will a savings institution with rate-sensitive liabilities and a large amount of fixed-rate mortgages perform best by (a) using an interest rate swap, (b) selling financial futures, or (c) remaining unhedged? Explain.

18. **ARMs** What is an adjustable-rate mortgage (ARM)? Discuss potential advantages such mortgages offer a savings institution.

19. **Sources of Credit Union Funds** Describe the main source of funds for credit unions. Why might the average cost of funds to credit unions be relatively stable even when market interest rates are volatile?

20. **MMDAs** How did the creation of money market deposit accounts influence a savings institution's overall cost of funds?

21. **Advantages and Disadvantages of Credit Unions** Identify some advantages of credit unions. Identify disadvantages of credit unions that relate to their common bond requirement.

22. **Background on Credit Unions** Who are the owners of credit unions? Explain the tax status of credit unions and the reason for that status. What is the typical size range of credit unions? Give reasons for that range.

FLOW OF FUNDS EXERCISE

Market Participation by Savings Institutions

Rimsa Savings is a savings institution that provided Carson Company with a mortgage for its office building. Rimsa recently offered to refinance the mortgage if Carson Company would prefer a fixed-rate loan rather than an adjustable-rate loan.

a. Explain the interaction between Carson Company and Rimsa Savings.

b. Why is Rimsa willing to allow Carson Company to transfer its interest rate risk to Rimsa? (Recall that there is an upward-sloping yield curve.)

c. If Rimsa maintains the mortgage on the office building purchased by Carson Company, who is the ultimate source of the money that was provided for the office building? If Rimsa sells the mortgage in the secondary market to a pension fund, who is the source that is essentially financing the office building? Why would a pension fund be willing to purchase this mortgage in the secondary market?

 # EXERCISE

Assessing Performance of Savings Institutions

Using a recent issue of *The Wall Street Journal*, summarize an article that discussed the recent performance of a particular SI. Does the article suggest that the SI's performance was better or worse than the norm? What reason is given for the unusual level of performance?

CHAPTER 22

Consumer Finance Operations

Finance companies provide short- and intermediate-term credit to consumers and small businesses. Although other financial institutions provide this service, only finance companies specialize in it. Many finance companies operate with a single office, while others have hundreds of offices across the country and even in foreign countries. Consumer finance operations can be conducted by an independent finance company or a unit (subsidiary) of a financial conglomerate.

The specific objectives of this chapter are to:

■ identify the main sources and uses of finance company funds,

■ describe how finance companies are exposed to various forms of risk,

■ identify the factors that determine the values of finance companies, and

■ explain how finance companies interact with other financial institutions.

Finance Company Types

Until recently, most finance companies could be classified as one of two types. **Consumer finance companies** concentrated on providing direct loans to consumers, while **sales finance companies** concentrated on purchasing credit contracts from retailers and dealers. The differences in business resulted in a distinctly different balance sheet structure. Consumer finance companies provided smaller loans and operated with more offices. Their main source of funds was long-term loans. Sales finance companies provided larger loans and obtained most of their funds by selling commercial paper.

Recently, so-called commercial finance companies have been created to provide loans to firms that cannot obtain financing from commercial banks. Commercial finance companies commonly pursue small firms, with annual sales between $1 million and $20 million.

Finance companies have diversified their sources and uses of funds in recent years. Thus, it is difficult to classify most finance companies as a particular type today.

Finance Company Fund Sources

The main sources of funds for finance companies are

- Loans from banks
- Commercial paper
- Deposits
- Bonds
- Capital

Loans from Banks

Finance companies commonly borrow from commercial banks and can consistently renew the loans over time. For this reason, bank loans can provide a continual source of funds, although some finance companies use bank loans mainly to accommodate seasonal swings in their business.

Commercial Paper

Although commercial paper is available only for short-term financing, finance companies can continually roll over their issues to create a permanent source of funds. Only the most well-known finance companies have traditionally been able to issue commercial paper to attract funds, because unsecured commercial paper exposes investors to the risk of default. In the past, small or medium-sized finance companies had difficulty placing unsecured commercial paper. In recent years, as secured commercial paper has become popular, more finance companies have access to funds through this market.

The best-known finance companies can issue commercial paper through direct placement, thereby avoiding a transaction fee and lowering their cost of funds. Most companies, however, utilize the services of a commercial paper dealer.

Deposits

Under certain conditions, some states allow finance companies to attract funds by offering customer deposits similar to those of the depository institutions discussed in previous chapters. Although deposits have not been a major source of funds for finance companies, they may become more widely used where legal.

Bonds

Finance companies in need of long-term funds can issue bonds. The decision to issue bonds versus some alternative short-term financing depends on the company's balance sheet structure and its expectations about future interest rates. When the company's assets are less interest rate sensitive than its liabilities and when interest rates are expected to increase, bonds can provide long-term financing at a rate that is completely insulated from rising market rates. If the finance company is confident that interest rates will rise, it might consider using the funds obtained from bonds to offer loans with variable interest rates. Conversely, when interest rates decline, finance companies may use more long-term debt to lock in the cost of funds over an extended period of time.

Capital

Finance companies can build their capital base by retaining earnings or by issuing stock. Like other financial institutions, finance companies maintain a low level of capital as a percentage of total assets. Recently, several finance companies engaged in initial public offerings of stock so that they could expand their businesses.

Finance Company Fund Uses

Finance companies use funds for

- Consumer loans
- Business loans and leasing
- Real estate loans

Each use of funds is described in turn.

Consumer Loans

Finance companies extend consumer loans in the form of personal loans. One of the most popular types is the automobile loan offered by a finance company that is owned by a car manufacturer. For example, General Motors Acceptance Corporation (GMAC) finances purchases of automobiles built by General Motors. Ford Motor Company and DaimlerChrysler also have their own finance companies. Subsidiaries of automobile manufacturers may offer unusually low rates to increase automobile sales.

In addition to offering automobile loans, finance companies offer personal loans for home improvement, mobile homes, and a variety of other personal expenses. Personal loans are often secured by a co-signer or by real property. The maturities on personal loans are typically less than five years.

Some finance companies also offer credit card loans through a particular retailer. For example, a retail store may sell products to customers on credit and then sell the credit contract to a finance company. Customers make payments to the finance company under the terms negotiated with the retail store. The finance company is responsible for the initial credit approval and for processing the credit card payments. The retailer can benefit from the finance company's credit allowance through increased sales; the finance company benefits by obtaining increased business. Finance companies increase their customer base in this way and are accessible for additional financing for those customers who prove to be creditworthy. The specific arrangement between a finance company and retailer can vary.

As a related form of consumer credit, some finance companies offer consumers a credit card that can be used at a variety of retail stores.

ILLUSTRATION Bencharge Credit Services offers the Bencharge card, which is accepted at many stores. Its credit card business is a useful way to attract consumer loan applicants. In addition, borrowers with charge cards tend to meet their loan payments so that they can continue to use their cards.

The main competition in the consumer loan market comes from commercial banks and credit unions. Finance companies have consistently provided more credit to

consumers than credit unions have, but they are a distant second to commercial banks. Savings institutions have recently entered this market and are now also considered a major competitor.

Business Loans and Leasing

In addition to consumer loans, finance companies also provide business (commercial) loans. Companies commonly obtain these loans from the time they purchase raw materials until cash is generated from sales of the finished goods. Such loans are short term but may be renewed, as many companies permanently need financing to support their cash cycle. Business loans are often backed by inventory or accounts receivable.

Some finance companies provide loans to support leveraged buyouts (LBOs). These loans are generally riskier than other business loans but offer a higher expected return. In 2001, some highly leveraged firms experienced financial problems, and exposure to LBO loans received more attention.

Finance companies commonly act as **factors** for accounts receivable; that is, they purchase a firm's receivables at a discount and are responsible for processing and collecting the balances of these accounts. The finance company incurs any losses due to bad debt. Factoring reduces a business's processing costs and also provides short-term financing, as the business receives cash from the finance company earlier than it would have obtained funds from collecting the receivables.

Leasing   Another way finance companies provide financing is by leasing. They purchase machinery or equipment and then lease it to businesses that prefer to avoid the additional debt on their balance sheet that purchases would require. Avoiding debt can be important to a business that is already close to its debt capacity and is concerned that additional debt will adversely affect its credit rating.

Real Estate Loans

Finance companies offer real estate loans in the form of mortgages on commercial real estate and second mortgages on residential real estate. The offering of second mortgages has become increasingly popular over time. These mortgages are typically secured and historically have a relatively low default rate.

Finance Company Regulation

When finance companies are acting as bank holding companies or are subsidiaries of bank holding companies, they are federally regulated. Otherwise they are regulated by the state. They are subject to a loan ceiling, which sets a maximum limit on the size of the loans they can make. They are also subject to ceiling interest rates on loans provided and to a maximum length on the loan maturity. These regulations are imposed by states, and they vary among the states. Because ceiling rates are now sufficiently above market rates, they normally do not interfere with the rate-setting decisions of finance companies.

Finance companies are subject to state regulations on intrastate business. If a finance company wishes to set up a new branch, it must convince regulators that the branch would serve the needs of the people in that location.

Finance Company Risks

Finance companies, like other financial institutions, are exposed to three types of risks:

- Liquidity risk
- Interest rate risk
- Credit risk

Because finance companies' characteristics differ from those of other financial institutions, their degree of exposure to each type of risk differs as well.

Liquidity Risk

Finance companies generally do not hold assets that could be easily sold in the secondary market. Thus, if they are in need of funds, they have to borrow. However, their balance sheet structure does not call for much liquidity. Virtually all of their funds are from borrowings rather than deposits anyway. Consequently, they are not susceptible to unexpected deposit withdrawals. Overall, the liquidity risk of finance companies is less than that of other financial institutions.

Interest Rate Risk

Both liability and asset maturities of finance companies are short or intermediate term. Therefore, they are not as susceptible to increasing interest rates as are savings institutions. Finance companies can still be adversely affected, however, because their assets are typically not as rate sensitive as their liabilities. They can shorten their average asset life or make greater use of adjustable rates if they wish to reduce their interest rate risk.

Credit Risk

Because the majority of a finance company's funds are allocated as loans to consumers and businesses, credit risk is a major concern. Customers who borrow from finance companies usually exhibit a moderate degree of risk. The loan delinquency rate of finance companies is typically higher than that of other lending financial institutions. However, this higher default level may be more than offset by the higher average rate charged on loans. Because their loans entail both relatively high returns and high risk, the performance of finance companies can be quite sensitive to prevailing economic conditions.

Impact of the September 11 Crisis The September 11, 2001 attack on the United States caused businesses to cut their expansion plans and reduce their need for loans. Thus, finance companies had fewer qualified borrowers to whom they could lend funds. In addition, the generally weak economy in 2001–2002 caused the number of problem loans provided by finance companies to increase.

Captive Finance Subsidiaries

A **captive finance subsidiary (CFS)** is a wholly owned subsidiary whose primary purpose is to finance sales of the parent company's products and services, provide wholesale

financing to distributors of the parent company's products, and purchase receivables of the parent company. The actual business practices of a CFS typically include various types of financing apart from just the parent company business. When a captive is formed, the captive and the parent company draw up an operating agreement containing specific stipulations, such as the type of receivables that qualify for sale to the captive and specific services to be provided by the parent.

The motive for creating a CFS can be easily understood by considering the automobile industry. Historically, automobile manufacturers were unable to finance dealers' inventories and so had to demand cash from each dealer. Many dealers were unable to sell cars on an installment basis because they needed cash immediately. Banks were the primary source of capital to dealers. However, banks viewed automobiles as luxury items not suitable for bank financing and were not willing to buy the installment plans created from automobile sales. For this reason, the automobile manufacturers became involved in financing.

The number of CFSs grew most rapidly between 1946 and 1960 as a result of liberalized credit policies and a need to finance growing inventories. By 1960 more than 100 captive finance subsidiaries existed.

There are several advantages to maintaining a CFS. A CFS can be used to finance distributor or dealer inventories until a sale occurs, making production less cyclical for the manufacturer. It can serve as an effective marketing tool by providing retail financing. It can also be used to finance products leased to others.

Advantages of Captive Finance Subsidiaries

A CFS allows a corporation to clearly separate its manufacturing and retailing activities from its financing activities. Therefore, analysis of each segment of the parent company is less expensive and easier. Also, when lending to a CFS rather than a division of the parent company, the lender need be less concerned with the claims of others. Unlike commercial banks, a CFS has no reserve requirements and no legal prohibitions on how it obtains funds or uses funds. Furthermore, a firm with a CFS can gain a competitive advantage because sale items such as automobiles and housing may depend on the financing arrangements available.

CFSs have diversified their financing activities to include more than just the parent company's product installment plans. General Electric Credit Corporation (GECC) has been the most innovative of all the CFSs. Its financing includes industrial and equipment sales, consumer installment credit, and second mortgage loans on private residences.

Valuing Finance Companies

Finance companies (or consumer finance units that are part of a financial conglomerate) are commonly valued by their managers to monitor progress over time or by other financial institutions that are considering an acquisition. The value of a finance company can be modeled as the present value of its future cash flows. Thus, the value of a finance company should change in response to changes in its expected cash flows in the future and to changes in the required rate of return by investors:

$$\Delta V = f\,[\,\Delta E(CF),\ \Delta k\,]$$
$$+ \qquad -$$

Factors That Affect Cash Flows

The change in a finace company's expected cash flows may be modeled as

$$\Delta E(CF) = f(\Delta ECON, \Delta R_f, \Delta INDUS, \Delta MANAB)$$
$$\quad\quad + \quad\quad - \quad\quad ? \quad\quad +$$

where ECON represents economic growth, R_f represents the risk-free interest rate, INDUS represents industry conditions (such as regulatory constraints), and MANAB represents the finance company's management abilities.

Economic Growth Economic growth can enhance a finance company's cash flows by increasing household demand for consumer loans, thereby allowing the finance company to provide more loans. In addition, loan defaults are normally reduced in periods of strong growth. The valuation of finance companies can be very sensitive to economic conditions because they commonly offer relatively risky loans; thus, loan repayments are sensitive to economic conditions.

Change in the Risk-Free Interest Rates A finance company's cash flows may be inversely related to interest rate movements. If the risk-free interest rate decreases, other market rates may also decline, and as a result, there may be stronger demand for the finance company's loans. Second, finance companies rely heavily on short-term funds, and the rates paid on these funds are typically revised in accordance with other interest rate movements. Finance companies' assets (such as consumer loans) commonly have fixed rates, so interest income does not adjust to interest rate movements until those assets reach maturity. Therefore, when interest rates fall, the finance company's cost of obtaining funds declines more than the decline in the interest earned on its loans and investments. An increase in interest rates could reduce the finance company's expected cash flows because the interest paid on its sources of funds increases, while the interest earned on its existing loans and investments does not.

Change in Industry Conditions Industry conditions include regulatory constraints, technology, and competition within the industry. Some finance companies may be valued higher if state regulators give them the opportunity to generate economies of scale by expanding throughout the state. However, this would result in more competition, causing some finance companies to gain at the expense of others.

Change in Management Abilities A finance company has control over the composition of its managers and its organizational structure. Its managers attempt to make internal decisions that will capitalize on the external forces (economic growth, interest rates, regulatory constraints) that the institution cannot control. Thus, the management skills of a finance company can influence its expected cash flows. In particular, finance companies need skilled managers to analyze the creditworthiness of potential borrowers and assess how future economic conditions may affect their ability to repay their loans. Finance company managers may also be able to capitalize on technology by advertising to consumers and accepting loan applications over the Internet.

Factors That Affect the Required Rate of Return by Investors

The required rate of return by investors who invest in a finance company can be modeled as

$$\Delta k = f(\Delta R_f, \Delta RP)$$
$$\quad\quad + \quad +$$

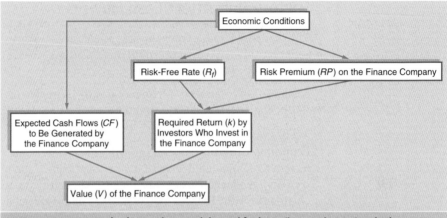

- A stronger economy leads to an increased demand for loans (interest income) and other services provided by the finance company (noninterest income), fewer loan defaults, and better cash flows. The economic conditions are especially important for finance companies because the risk of default on loans tends to be higher for them. A weak economy could result in major loan losses.

- The valuation is also influenced by industry conditions and the finance company's management (not shown in the diagram). These factors affect the risk premium (and therefore the required return by investors) and the expected cash flows to be generated by the finance company.

where ΔR_f represents a change in the risk-free interest rate, and ΔRP represents a change in the risk premium.

The risk-free interest rate is normally expected to be positively related to inflation, economic growth, and the budget deficit level, but inversely related to money supply growth (assuming it does not cause inflation). The risk premium on a finance company is inversely related to economic growth because there is less uncertainty about loan repayments when economic conditions are strong. The risk premium is also inversely related to the company's management skills, as more skillful managers may be able to focus on financial services that reduce the finance company's exposure to risk.

Exhibit 22.1 provides a framework for valuing a finance company, based on the preceding discussion. In general, the value of a finance company is favorably affected by strong economic growth, a reduction in interest rates, and skilled management. The sensitivity of a finance company's value to these conditions depends on its own characteristics. The higher the risk tolerance reflected in the loans provided by a finance company, the more sensitive its valuation to changes in economic growth (and therefore in the ability of borrowers to repay their loans).

Interaction with Other Financial Institutions

Finance companies and their subsidiaries often interact with other financial institutions, as summarized in Exhibit 22.2. Because of their concentration in consumer lending, finance companies are more closely related to commercial banks, savings institutions, and credit unions. However, those finance companies with subsidiaries that specialize in other financial services compete with insurance companies and pension plans.

Because finance companies compete with savings institutions in providing consumer loans, they are able to increase their market share when savings institutions experience financial problems. Furthermore, some finance companies (such as House-

EXHIBIT 22.2 Interaction between Finance Companies and Other Financial Institutions

Type of Financial Institution	Interaction with Finance Companies
Commercial banks and savings institutions (SIs)	• Finance companies compete with banks and SIs for consumer loan business (including credit cards), commercial loans, and leasing. • Finance companies obtain loans from commercial banks. • Finance companies have acquired some commercial banks. • Some finance companies are subsidiaries of commercial banks.
Credit unions	• Finance companies compete with credit unions for consumer loan business.
Investment banking firms	• Finance companies issue bonds that are underwritten by investment banking firms.
Pension funds	• Insurance subsidiaries of finance companies manage pension plans of corporations and therefore compete with pension funds.
Insurance companies	• Insurance subsidiaries of finance companies compete directly with other insurance companies.

hold International Inc.) have acquired savings institutions. Before being acquired by the British-based conglomerate HSBC Holdings in 2003, Household International Inc. acquired numerous branches of depository institutions across the country in an effort to diversify its services. Like many other finance companies, Household became a diversified financial services company.

Financial Market Participation

Finance companies utilize various financial markets to manage their operations, as summarized in Exhibit 22.3. For their core business, finance companies use financial markets mainly to obtain funds. However, the subsidiaries of finance companies often utilize financial markets to invest funds or to hedge investment portfolios against interest rate risk or market risk. They may even diversify their financial services in foreign countries. As large finance companies expand internationally, they are better able to use the international bond and commercial paper markets as a source of funds.

EXHIBIT 22.3 Participation of Finance Companies in Financial Markets

Type of Financial Market	Participation by Finance Companies
Money markets	• Finance companies obtain funds by issuing commercial paper.
Bond markets	• Finance companies issue bonds as a method of obtaining long-term funds. • Subsidiaries of finance companies commonly purchase corporate and Treasury bonds.
Mortgage markets	• Finance companies purchase real estate and also provide loans to real estate investors. • Subsidiaries of finance companies commonly purchase mortgages.
Stock markets	• Finance companies issue stock to establish a capital base. • Subsidiaries of finance companies commonly purchase stocks.
Futures markets	• Subsidiaries of finance companies that offer insurance-related services sometimes use futures contracts to reduce the sensitivity of their bond portfolio to interest rate movements and also may trade stock index futures to reduce the sensitivity of their stock portfolio to stock market movements.
Options markets	• Subsidiaries of finance companies that offer insurance-related services sometimes use options contracts to protect against temporary declines in particular stock holdings.
Swap markets	• Finance companies may engage in interest rate swaps to hedge their exposure to interest rate risk.

Some finance companies have recently acquired insurance companies to enter the insurance business. They have also acquired commercial banks located in various states. In addition, the larger finance companies have diversified into a variety of nonfinancial businesses as well.

Multinational Finance Companies

 **GL BALASPECTS** Some finance companies are large multinational corporations with subsidiaries in several countries. For example, the consumer finance division of Household International has more than 1,000 offices in the United States, Canada, Germany, and the United Kingdom. U.S.-based finance companies penetrate foreign countries to enter new markets and to reduce their exposure to U.S. economic conditions.

SUMMARY

■ The main sources of finance company funds are loans from banks, sales of commercial paper, bonds, and capital. The main uses of finance company funds are consumer loans, business loans, leasing, and real estate loans.

■ Finance companies are exposed to credit risk as a result of their consumer loans, business loans, and real estate loans. They are also exposed to liquidity risk, because their assets are not very marketable in the secondary market. They may also be exposed to interest rate risk.

■ Finance companies are valued as the present value of their expected cash flows. Their valuation is highly dependent on economic conditions, since there are more requests for loans by qualified borrowers when economic conditions are favorable. In addition, the amount of loan defaults is normally lower when the economy is strong.

■ Finance companies compete with depository institutions (such as commercial banks, savings institutions, and credit unions) that provide loans to consumers and businesses. Many finance companies have insurance subsidiaries that compete directly with other insurance subsidiaries.

POINT COUNTER-POINT

Will Finance Companies Be Replaced by Banks?

Point Yes. Commercial banks specialize in loans and can provide the services that are provided by finance companies. The two types of financial institutions will ultimately merge into one.

Counter-Point No. Finance companies tend to target a different market for loans than commercial banks.

Thus, commercial banks will not replace finance companies because they do not serve that market.

Who Is Correct? Use your favorite search engine to learn more about this issue. Offer your own opinion on this issue.

QUESTIONS AND APPLICATIONS

1. **Types of Finance Companies** What was the historical difference between so-called consumer finance companies and sales finance companies?

2. **Exposure to Credit Risk** Explain how the default risk of finance companies differs from that of other lending financial institutions.

3. **Managing in Financial Markets: Managing a Finance Company** As a manager of a finance company, you are attempting to increase the spread between the rate earned on your assets and the rate paid on your liabilities.
   a. Assume that you expect interest rates to decline over time. Should you issue bonds or commercial paper in order to obtain funds?
   b. If you expect interest rates to decline, will you benefit more from providing medium-term fixed-rate loans to consumers or floating-rate loans to businesses?
   c. Why would you still maintain some balance between medium-term fixed-rate loans and floating-rate loans to businesses, even if you anticipate that one type of loan will be more profitable under a cycle of declining interest rates?

4. **Interpreting Financial News** Interpret the following comments made by Wall Street analysts and portfolio managers:
   a. "During a credit crunch, finance companies tend to generate a large amount of business."
   b. "Some finance companies took a huge hit as a result of the last recession because they opened their wallets too wide before the recession occurred."
   c. "During periods of strong economic growth, finance companies generate unusually high returns without any hint of excessive risk; but their returns are at the mercy of the economy."

5. **Exposure to Interest Rate Risk** Is the cost of funds obtained by finance companies very sensitive to market interest rate movements? Explain.

6. **Exposure to Interest Rate Risk** Explain how the interest rate risk of finance companies differs from that of savings institutions.

7. **Internet Exercise** Go to http://www.gmaccf.com.
   a. Describe the services offered by GMAC Commercial Finance.

8. **Issuance of Commercial Paper** How are small and medium-sized finance companies able to issue commercial paper? Why do some well-known finance companies directly place their commercial paper?

9. **Finance Company Affiliations** Explain why some finance companies are associated with automobile manufacturers. Why do some of these finance companies offer below-market rates on loans?

10. **Regulation of Finance Companies** Explain how finance companies are regulated.

11. **Credit Card Services** Explain how finance companies benefit from offering consumers a credit card.

12. **Uses of Funds** Describe the major uses of funds by finance companies.

13. **Leasing Services** Explain how finance companies provide financing through leasing.

14. **Liquidity Position** Explain how the liquidity position of finance companies differs from that of depository institutions such as commercial banks.

FLOW OF FUNDS EXERCISE

How Finance Companies Facilitate the Flow of Funds

Carson Company has sometimes relied on debt financing from Fente Finance Company. Fente has been willing to lend money even when most commercial banks were not. Fente obtains funding from issuing commercial paper and focuses mostly on channeling the funds to borrowers.

a. Explain how finance companies are unique by comparing Fente's net interest income, noninterest income, noninterest expenses, and loan losses to those of commercial banks.

b. Explain why Fente performs better than commercial banks in some periods.

c. Describe the flow of funds channeled through finance companies to firms such as Carson Company. What is the original source of the money that is channeled to firms or households that borrow from finance companies?

WSJ EXERCISE
Finance Company Performance

Using a recent issue of *The Wall Street Journal*, summarize an article that discussed the recent performance of a particular finance company. Does the article suggest that the finance company's performance was better or worse than the norm? What was the reason for the unusual level of performance?

CHAPTER 23

Mutual Fund Operations

A **mutual fund** is an investment company that sells shares and uses the proceeds to manage a portfolio of securities. Mutual funds have grown substantially in recent years, and they serve as major suppliers of funds in financial markets.

The specific objectives of this chapter are to:

- explain how characteristics vary among mutual funds,
- describe the various types of stock and bond mutual funds, and
- describe the characteristics of money market funds.

Mutual Fund Background

http://

http://www.bloomberg.com
Information on mutual fund
performance.

Mutual funds serve as a key financial intermediary. They pool investments by individual investors and use the funds to accommodate financing needs of governments and corporations in the primary markets. They also frequently invest in securities in the secondary market.

Mutual funds provide an important service not only for corporations and governments that need funds, but also for individual investors who wish to invest funds. Small investors are unable to diversify their investments because of their limited funds. Mutual funds offer a way for these investors to diversify. Some mutual funds have holdings of 50 or more securities, and the minimum investment may be only $250 to $2,500. Small investors could not afford to create such a diversified portfolio on their own. Moreover, the mutual fund uses experienced portfolio managers, so investors do not have to manage the portfolio themselves. Some mutual funds also offer liquidity because they are willing to repurchase an investor's shares upon request. They also offer various services, such as 24-hour telephone or Internet access to account information, money transfers between different funds operated by the same firm, consolidated account statements, check-writing privileges on some types of funds, and tax information.

A mutual fund hires portfolio managers to invest in a portfolio of securities that satisfies the desires of investors. Like other portfolio managers, the managers of mutual funds analyze economic and industry trends and forecasts and assess the potential impact of various conditions on companies. They adjust the composition of their portfolio in response to changing economic conditions.

Because of their diversification, management expertise, and liquidity, mutual funds have grown at a rapid pace. The growth of mutual funds is illustrated in Exhibit 23.1.

655

Growth in Mutual Funds

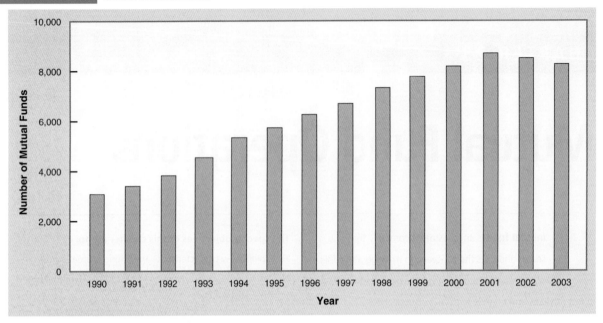

Note: The number shown here includes money market funds.
Source: *2004 Mutual Fund Fact Book.*

Today, there are more than 8,000 different mutual funds; in the last two decades, total mutual fund assets have increased by more than 23 times. More than 88 million households now own shares of one or more mutual funds.

Fund Types

Funds are classified as open-end, closed-end, exchange traded, and hedge funds.

Open-End Funds **Open-end funds** are open to investment from investors at any time. Investors can purchase shares directly from the open-end fund at any time. In addition, investors can sell (redeem) their shares back to the open-end fund at any time. Thus, the number of shares of an open-end fund is always changing. When the fund receives additional investment, it invests in additional securities. It maintains some cash on hand in case redemptions exceed investments on a given day. If there are substantial redemptions, the fund will have to sell some of its securities to obtain sufficient funds to accommodate the redemptions. There are many different categories of open-end mutual funds, allowing investors to invest in a fund that fits their particular investment objective. Investors can select from thousands of open-end mutual funds to meet their particular return and risk profile. Although closed-end and exchange traded funds are described next, the focus of this chapter is on open-end mutual funds. When the term *mutual fund* is used, it normally refers to the open-end type just described.

Closed-End Funds **Closed-end funds** do not repurchase (redeem) the shares they sell. Instead, investors must sell the shares on a stock exchange just like corporate stock. The number of outstanding shares sold by a closed-end investment company usually remains constant and is equal to the number of shares originally issued.

USING THE WALL STREET JOURNAL

WSJ Closed-End Fund Quotations

Quotations of closed-end funds are published in *The Wall Street Journal* as shown here. For each fund, the symbol (SYM), dividend per share (DIV), closing price (LAST), and change in price from the previous day (CHG) are disclosed. The return on each closed-end fund over the last year is provided in the last column.

CLOSED-END FUNDS

STOCK (SYM)	DIV	LAST	NET CHG
◆NuvInsDivAdv NVG	.93a	14.14	−0.04
◆NuvFL Muni NWF	.86	13.89	0.05
◆NuvMA Muni NGX	.86a	14.95	...
◆NuvNY InsDivAdv NKO	.89a	14.04	...
◆NuvNY Muni NRK	.87	13.60	−0.17
◆NuvMuni NEA	.93a	14.10	−0.01
◆NuvMD NFM	.94	15.55	−0.05
◆NuvMD Fd2 NZR	.88a	15	0.02
NuvMD Fd3 NWI	.79	13.83	0.03
◆NuvMA NMB	.93a	15.33	−0.27
◆NuvMI NZW	.89	14.72	−0.04
◆NuvMO Prm NOM	.88	16.98	−0.01
NuvMuniIncoOpp NMZ n	1.07	14.55	0.06
◆NuvNJ NXJ	.94	14.51	−0.06
◆NuvNJ Fd2 NUJ	.92a	14.39	−0.04
◆NuvNY Fd2 NXK	.95a	14.48	−0.01
◆NuvNC NRB	.92a	15.90	...
◆NuvNC Fd2 NNO	.86a	15.32	−0.09
◆NuvNC Fd3 NII	.80a	14.53	0.04
◆NuvOH NXI	.97a	15.16	−0.05
◆NuvOH Fd2 NBJ	.92	15.03	−0.01
◆NuvOH Fd3 NVJ	.88a	14.50	0.13
◆NuvPA Fd2 NVY	.92a	14.55	−0.07
◆NuveenRlEst JRS	1.38a	17.52	0.14
◆NuvVA NGB	.94	16.45	0.15
◆NuvVA Fd2 NNB	.89a	15.55	0.13
◆PachldrHi PHF	.90	9.19	0.09
PutnmCA Inv PCA	.74	13.20	...
PutnmNYInv PMN	.68	11.62	−0.04
RMR HospFd RHR n	.50e	18.02	−0.08
RMR RlEstFd RMR n	1.20	13.10	0.07
ReavesUtilFd UTG n	1.16	17.24	0.14
S&P GblEquty BQY n	.19p	13.85	...
◆ScudderRE II SRO n	1.20	14.21	0.06
◆ScudderRE SRQ	1.44	18.98	0.12
◆ThaiCapFd TF	.06p	6.60	−0.12
! Tuxis TUX		6.90	−0.10
◆VnKmAdvII VKI	.96	14.16	0.01
◆VnKmCA VKC	.60a	9.40	0.13
◆VnKmOHInc VOV	.89	14.90	−0.20
◆VnKmSelect VKL	.78	12.47	0.15

STOCK (SYM)	DIV	LAST	NET CHG
◆BlkRkDurInco Tr BLW	1.50	18.99	0.07
◆BlkRkKMT Tr BPK	.78	14.72	−0.08
◆BlkRkMuni20 BKK n	.94	14.66	−0.09
◆BlkRkMuniBd Tr BBK	1.04	14.35	0.03
◆BlkRkMunilnco Tr BFK	.97	13.70	...
◆BlkRkMTT Tr BMN	.48	10.67	−0.03
◆BlkRkNJ MI Tr BNJ	.90	13.96	−0.04
◆BlkRkNY Tr BLN	.75a	16.07	−0.04
◆BlkRkNY MT Tr BLH	.74	14.81	−0.04
◆BlkRkNY Muni BQH	.93	13.63	0.08
◆BlkRkNY MI Tr BNY	.90	13.67	0.07
◆BlkRkPfOppTr BPP	2.00	23.60	−0.07
◆BlkRkStrBd Tr BHD	1.56	15.99	0.01
BlkRkStrDivAch BDT n	.23p	13.15	−0.08
◆BlkRkStrMuni Tr BSD	.96	14.10	0.01
◆BlueChipVal BLU	.55e	5.96	0.01
BoulderGro BIF	.03m	6.14	0.01
BouldrTotR BTF		16.23	0.08
BrazilEqty BZL	.38e	6.10	0.25
◆BrazilFd BZF	.63e	23.80	0.46
CignaHiInco HIS	.28a	2.77	0.02
CignaInv IIS	.92	16.41	0.06
CalamosConvFd CHY	1.46	15.90	−0.09
Calamos CHI	1.80a	19.73	0.03
CalamosStrat CSQ n	.22e	13.17	0.18
CapIncoStratFd CII n	.30p	17	−0.04
CntlEurRus Fd CEE	.22e	20.37	−0.11
ChrtwlDvdInco CWF	1.00	9.54	0.09
ChileFd CH	.45e	12.29	0.09
ChinaFund CHN	1.78e	26.47	0.37
CitigrpInvLnFd TLI	.66	14.50	−0.03
◆ChnStrAdvInco RLF	1.44	18.10	0.14
◆ChnStrPrInco RPF	1.44	18.26	−0.03
◆ChnStrQuInco RQI	1.38	17.31	−0.01
◆ChnStrPfInco RNP	2.10	24.10	−0.07
◆ChnStrUtilFd RTU n	1.26	16.70	0.01
◆ChnStrSelUtil UTF n	1.02	17.24	0.01
◆ChnStrTR RFI	1.02a	17.48	0.02
◆ColonlHiInco CXE	.48	6.25	0.01
◆ColonlIntmk CMK	.65a	8.35	...
◆ColonialIntr CIF	.29	3.35	−0.01

STOCK (SYM)	DIV	LAST	NET CHG
◆HnckJ PtPremII PDT	.78a	11.02	0.13
◆HnckJ PtSel DIV	1.08	14.35	−0.05
◆HnckJ PfdInco HPI	2.16a	24.34	−0.06
◆HnckJ PfdInco II HPF	2.16a	24.58	−0.03
◆HnckJ PfdInco III HPS	2.16	23.59	0.10
HnckJ TxAdv HTD n	1.16	16.60	−0.22
HrtfrdIncoFd HSF	.55	7.43	−0.01
HatterasSec HAT	.78	12.81	0.07
HiIncoFd HIO	.60	6.81	0.02
HiYldFd HYI	.51a	5.92	0.07
HiYldPlsFd HYP	.42	4.40	0.02
Hyperion05 HTO	.12	9.58	−0.01
Hyperion HSM	1.30	13.86	...
HyperionFd HTR	.90	9.88	−0.01
IndiaFd IFN	.13e	21.60	0.60
◆ING Prime PPR	.42e	7.97	−0.02
InsrdMuniFd PIF	.78	13.22	−0.05
InvGrdMuni PPM	.90	14.02	0.11
JF China fd JFC		10.70	0.09
◆JapanEquity JEQ		5.91	0.08
JapanSmlCap JOF	.12	8.40	...
KoreaEqty KEF		4.51	0.09
◆KoreaFd KF	.30e	17.75	0.55
LatAmDiscv LDF	.27e	12.85	0.20
LatAmEq LAQ	.14e	14.85	0.32
LazrdGblInFd LGI nx	.33e	16.60	0.14
◆LibtyASE USA	1.09e	8.46	0.10
◆LibtyASG ASG	.79e	5.90	...
◆LncInNtlSec LNV	.68	12.40	0.05
◆LncInNtlInco LND	1.83e	12.79	−0.05
MFS Charter MCR	.54	8.64	0.01
MFS GvMkTr MGF	.32	6.52	...
MFS Intermd MIN	.36	6.52	−0.01
MFS MultInco MMT	.39	6.11	−0.04
MFS MuniTr MFM	.55	7.69	0.02
MFS SpcVal MFV	1.00e	11.16	−0.01
MacqFstTrGlbl MFD n	.30p	17.46	0.08
MdsnClymrCvrd MCN n		15.01	0.01
MalaysaFd MF	.11e	4.98	0.11
MgdHiInc MHY	.60	6.59	...
MgdHiYldPI HYF	.66f	5.64	0.01

There are about 500 closed-end funds. Approximately 75 percent of the closed-end funds invest mainly in bonds or other debt securities, while the other 25 percent focus on stocks. The total market value of closed-end funds is less than $200 billion, versus a total market value of more than $5 trillion for open-end funds focused on stocks and bonds. Thus, the asset size of open-end funds that focus on stocks and bonds is more than 40 times the asset size of closed-end funds.

Exchange Traded Funds As explained in Chapter 8, **exchange traded funds (ETFs)** are designed to mimic particular stock indexes and are traded on a stock exchange just like stocks. They differ from open-end funds in that their shares are traded on an exchange, and their share price changes throughout the day. Also unlike an open-end fund, an ETF has a fixed number of shares. ETFs differ from most open-end and closed-end funds in that they are not actively managed. The management goal of an ETF is to mimic an index so that the share price of the ETF moves in line with that index. ETFs

have become very popular in recent years because they are an efficient way for investors to invest in a particular stock index. Since ETFs are not actively managed, they normally do not have capital gains and losses that must be distributed to shareholders.

One disadvantage of ETFs is that each purchase of additional shares must be done through the exchange where they are traded. Investors incur a brokerage fee from purchasing the shares just as if they had purchased shares of a stock. This cost is especially important to investors who plan to frequently add to their investment in a particular ETF.

Hedge Funds   **Hedge funds** sell shares to wealthy individuals and financial institutions and use the proceeds to invest in securities. They differ from an open-end mutual fund in several ways. First, they require a much larger initial investment (such as $1 million), whereas mutual funds typically allow a minimum investment in the range of $1,000 to $2,500. Second, many hedge funds are not "open" in the sense that they may not always accept additional investments or accommodate redemption requests unless advance notice is provided. Third, hedge funds have been unregulated, although they are now subject to some regulation. They provide very limited information to prospective investors. Fourth, hedge funds invest in a wide variety of investments to achieve high returns. Consequently, they tend to take more risk than mutual funds.

Comparison to Depository Institutions

Mutual funds are like depository institutions in that they repackage the proceeds received from individuals to make various types of investments. Nevertheless, investing in mutual funds is distinctly different from depositing money in a depository institution in that it represents partial ownership, whereas deposits represent a form of credit. Thus, the investors share the gains or losses generated by the mutual fund, while depositors simply receive interest on their deposits. Individual investors view mutual funds as an alternative to depository institutions. In fact, much of the money invested in mutual funds in the 1990s came from depository institutions. When interest rates decline, many individuals withdraw their deposits and invest in mutual funds.

Regulation and Taxation

Mutual funds must adhere to a variety of federal regulations. They must register with the Securities and Exchange Commission (SEC) and provide interested investors with a prospectus that discloses details about the components of the fund and the risks involved. Mutual funds are also regulated by state laws, many of which attempt to ensure that investors fully understand the fund.

Since July 1993, mutual funds have been required to disclose in the prospectus the names of their portfolio managers and the length of time that they have been employed by the fund in that position. Many investors regard this information as relevant because the performance of a mutual fund is highly dependent on its portfolio managers.

Mutual funds must also disclose their performance record over the past 10 years in comparison to a broad market index. They must also state in the prospectus how their performance was affected by market conditions.

If a mutual fund distributes at least 90 percent of its taxable income to shareholders, it is exempt from taxes on dividends, interest, and capital gains distributed to shareholders. The shareholders are, of course, subject to taxation on these forms of income.

Information Contained in a Prospectus

A mutual fund prospectus contains the following information:

1. The minimum amount of investment required.
2. The investment objective of the mutual fund.
3. The return on the fund over the past year, the past three years, and the past five years.
4. The exposure of the mutual fund to various types of risk.
5. The services (such as check writing, ability to transfer money by telephone, etc.) offered by the mutual fund.
6. The fees incurred by the mutual fund (such as management fees) that are passed on to the investors.

Estimating Net Asset Values

The **net asset value (NAV)** of a mutual fund indicates the value per share. It is estimated each day by first determining the market value of all securities comprising the mutual fund (any cash is also accounted for). Any interest or dividends accrued from the mutual fund are added to the market value. Then any expenses are subtracted, and the amount is divided by the number of shares of the fund outstanding.

ILLUSTRATION Newark Mutual Fund has 20 million shares issued to its investors. It used the proceeds to buy stock of 55 different firms. A partial list of its stock holdings is shown below:

Name of Stock	Number of Shares	Prevailing Share Price	Market Value
Aztec Co.	10,000	$40	$ 400,000
Caldero Inc.	20,000	30	600,000
⋮	⋮	⋮	⋮
Zurkin, Inc.	8,000	70	560,000
Total market value of shares today			$500,020,000
+ Interest and dividends received today			+10,000
− Expenses incurred today			−30,000
= Market value of fund			=$500,000,000

$$\text{Net asset value} = \text{Market value of fund/number of shares}$$
$$= \$500{,}000{,}000/20{,}000{,}000$$
$$= \$25 \text{ per share}$$

The SEC monitors the reporting of the NAV by mutual funds. When a mutual fund pays its shareholders dividends, its NAV declines by the per-share amount of the dividend payout.

Shareholder Distributions

Mutual funds can generate returns to their shareholders in three ways. First, they can pass on any earned income (from dividends or coupon payments) as dividend payments to the

shareholders. Second, they distribute the capital gains resulting from the sale of securities within the fund. A third type of return to shareholders is through mutual fund share price appreciation. As the market value of a fund's security holdings increases, the fund's NAV increases, and the shareholders benefit when they sell their mutual fund shares.

Although investors in a mutual fund directly benefit from any returns generated by the fund, they are also directly affected if the portfolio generates losses. Because they own the shares of the fund, there is no other group of shareholders to whom the fund must be accountable. This differs from commercial banks and stock-owned savings institutions, which obtain their deposits from one group of investors and sell shares of stock to another.

Mutual Fund Classifications

Mutual funds are commonly classified as stock (or equity) mutual funds, bond mutual funds, or money market mutual funds, depending on the types of securities in which they invest. The distribution of investments in these three classes of mutual funds is shown in Exhibit 23.2. Stock funds are dominant when measured by the market value of total assets among mutual funds. Many investment companies offer a family of many different mutual funds so that they can accommodate the diverse preferences of investors. With one phone call, an investor can normally transfer from one mutual fund to another within the same family.

Shareholder Expenses

Mutual funds pass on their expenses to their shareholders. The expenses include compensation to the portfolio managers and other employees, research support and investment advice, record-keeping and clerical fees, and marketing fees. Some mutual funds

EXHIBIT 23.2

Distribution of Investment in Mutual Funds

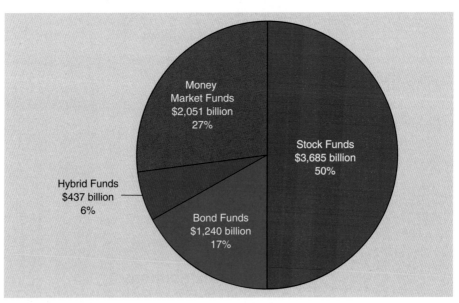

Source: *2004 Mutual Fund Fact Book*.

have recently increased their focus on marketing, but marketing does not necessarily enable a mutual fund to achieve high performance relative to the market or other mutual funds. In fact, marketing expenses increase the expenses that are passed on to the mutual fund's shareholders.

Expenses can be compared among mutual funds by measuring the expense ratio, which is equal to the annual expenses per share divided by the fund's NAV. An expense ratio of 2 percent in a given year means that shareholders incur annual expenses reflecting 2 percent of the value of the fund. Many mutual funds have an expense ratio between 1 and 2 percent. A high expense ratio can have a major impact on the growth of an investment in a mutual fund over time.

ILLUSTRATION

Consider two mutual funds, each of which generates a return on its portfolio of 9.2 percent per year, ignoring expenses. One mutual fund has an expense ratio of 3.2 percent, so its actual return to shareholders is 6 percent per year. The other mutual fund has an expense ratio of 0.2 percent per year (some mutual funds have expense ratios at this level), so its actual return to shareholders is 9 percent per year. Assume you have $10,000 to invest. Exhibit 23.3 compares the accumulated value of your shares over time between the two mutual funds. After five years, the value of the mutual fund with the low expense ratio is about 20 percent higher than the value of the mutual fund with the high expense ratio. After 10 years, its value is about 40 percent more than the value of the mutual fund with the high expense ratio. After 20 years, its value is about 87 percent more. Even though both mutual funds had the same return on investment when ignoring expenses, the returns to shareholders after expenses are very different because of the difference in expenses charged.

Thus, the higher the expense ratio, the lower the return for a given level of portfolio performance. Mutual funds with lower expense ratios tend to outperform others that have a similar investment objective. That is, funds with higher expenses are generally unable to generate higher returns that could offset those expenses. Since expenses can vary substantially among mutual funds, investors should review the annual expenses of any fund before making an investment.

EXHIBIT 23.3

How the Accumulated Value Can Be Affected by Expenses (Assume Initial Investment of $10,000 and a Return before Expenses of 9.2%)

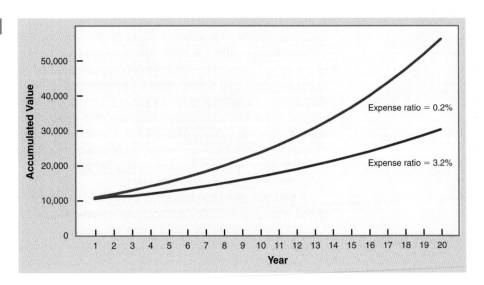

Sales Load

Mutual funds can also be classified as either **load,** meaning that there is a sales charge, or **no-load,** meaning that the funds are promoted strictly by the mutual fund of concern. Load funds are promoted by registered representatives of brokerage firms, who earn a sales charge typically ranging between 3 percent and 8.5 percent. Investors in a load fund pay this charge through the difference between the bid and ask prices of the load fund. Loads, commissions, and bid-asked spreads are not included in the expense ratio of a mutual fund.

Some investors may feel that the sales charge is worthwhile, because the brokerage firm helps determine the type of fund that is appropriate for them. Other investors who feel capable of making their own investment decisions often prefer to invest in no-load funds. Some no-load mutual funds can be purchased through a discount broker for a relatively low fee (such as 1 to 2 percent), although investors receive no advice from the discount broker.

ILLUSTRATION As an example of the potential advantage of no-load funds, consider separate $10,000 investments in no-load and load funds. Assuming an 8.5 percent load fee, the actual investment in the load fund is $9,150. If the value of both funds grows by 10 percent per year, the investment in the no-load fund will be worth $2,204 more than the investment in the load fund after 10 years.

In recent years, some small no-load funds have become load funds because they could not attract investors without a large budget for national advertising. As a load fund, they will be recommended by various brokers and financial planners, who will earn a commission on any shares sold.

Types of Loads. Mutual funds charge different types of loads: front-end loads, back-end loads, and level loads.

A **front-end load** is paid only once, at the time you invest money in a mutual fund. The legal limit on front-end loads is 8.5 percent, but most funds charge 5.75 percent or less. Mutual funds with a front-end load often offer discounts like breakpoints, right of accumulation, letters of intent, or free transfers. Breakpoints are basically volume discounts, which means that the percentage load becomes smaller as you invest more. Such discounts often start at $25,000. Many funds waive their loads entirely for investments of more than $1 million. A right of accumulation is a discount based on the total amount of money you invest in the fund family (as opposed to just the individual fund). Letters of intent are often used for investors who invest only a small amount today but commit themselves to additional purchases over the next year. With this setup, the investor is entitled to the breakpoint discount today even though he or she has not yet invested enough money to actually qualify for it. Of course, if the investor fails to invest the additional funds, the fund will retroactively collect the higher fee from the account. Free transfers allow investors to move money between funds with no additional load, provided the money stays in the same family.

A **back-end load** (also known as a rear-load or reverse load) is a withdrawal fee assessed when you withdraw money from the mutual fund. Back-end loads are often between 5 and 6 percent for the first year but decline by a certain percentage each subsequent year. Some mutual funds have features that can minimize the back-end load. For example, some funds permit investors to withdraw dividends and capital gains at any time without a charge. Other funds allow a certain percentage withdrawal of the invest-

ment each year without incurring a load. Also, many funds allow for free transfers within the fund family without incurring additional charges.

12b-1 Fees

In 1980, the SEC allowed mutual funds to charge shareholders a distribution fee, also called a 12b-1 fee in reference to SEC rule 12b-1. In some cases, funds have used the proceeds from 12b-1 fees to pay commissions to brokers whose clients invested in the fund. In essence, the fee substituted for the load (sales charge) that was directly charged to investors in load funds. A fund that states that it does not charge a sales load may charge shareholders 12b-1 fees and use the proceeds to pay commissions to brokers. Some shareholders who believed that they were not incurring a cost on a no-load fund did pay a commission indirectly through the 12b-1 fees. The fees are generally included in a fund's expense ratio as part of its marketing expenses. These fees are controversial because many mutual funds do not clarify how they use the money received from the fees. Because of the controversy, the SEC is assessing whether the rule on 12b-1 fees should be eliminated or changed to ensure more complete disclosure of information by mutual funds.

Corporate Control by Mutual Funds

Large mutual funds can exert some control over the management of firms because they commonly are a firm's largest shareholders. For example, Fidelity is the largest shareholder of more than 700 firms in which it owns stock. Portfolio managers of many mutual funds serve on the board of directors of various firms. Even when a fund's managers do not serve on a firm's board, the firm may still attempt to satisfy them so that they do not sell their holdings of the firm's stock. To illustrate the importance of mutual funds, Fidelity typically accounts for at least 5 percent of all the trading on the New York Stock Exchange on a given day. Fidelity is commonly one of the first institutional investors to be asked whether it wants to invest in a firm's new offerings of stock. Fidelity has more than 200 analysts who assess the financial condition of firms. Many firms discuss any major policy changes with analysts and portfolio managers of mutual funds to convince them that the changes should have a favorable effect on performance over time. In this way, a firm may discourage the funds from selling their holdings of the firm's stock and may even persuade them to purchase more.

Stock Mutual Fund Categories

Because investors have various objectives, no single portfolio can satisfy everyone. Consequently, a variety of stock mutual funds have been created. The more popular categories include

- Growth funds
- Capital appreciation funds
- Growth and income funds
- International and global funds
- Specialty funds
- Index funds
- Multifund funds

Growth Funds

For investors who desire a high return and are willing to accept a moderate degree of risk, **growth funds** are appropriate. These funds are typically composed of stocks of companies that have not fully matured and are expected to grow at a higher than average rate in the future. The primary objective of a growth fund is to generate an increase in investment value, with less concern about the generation of steady income. Growth funds may entail different degrees of risk. Some concentrate on companies that have existed for several years but are still experiencing growth, while others concentrate on relatively young companies.

Capital Appreciation Funds

Also known as aggressive growth funds, **capital appreciation funds** are composed of stocks that have potential for very high growth but may also be unproven. These funds are suited to investors who are willing to risk a possible loss in value. As the economy changes, portfolio managers of capital appreciation funds constantly revise the portfolio composition to take full advantage of their expectations. They sometimes even use borrowed money to support their portfolios, thereby using leverage to increase their potential return and risk.

Growth and Income Funds

Some investors are looking for potential for capital appreciation along with some stability in income. For these investors, a **growth and income fund,** which contains a unique combination of growth stocks, high-dividend stocks, and fixed-income bonds, may be most appropriate.

International and Global Funds

In recent years, awareness of foreign securities has been increasing. Investors historically avoided foreign securities because of the high information and transaction costs associated with purchasing them and monitoring their performance. International mutual funds were created to enable investors to invest in foreign securities without incurring these excessive costs.

The returns on international stock mutual funds are affected not only by foreign companies' stock prices but also by the movements of the currencies that denominate these stocks. As a foreign currency's value strengthens against the U.S. dollar, the value of the foreign stock as measured in U.S. dollars increases. Thus, U.S. investors can benefit not only from higher stock prices but also from a strengthened foreign currency (against the dollar). Of course, they can also be adversely affected if the foreign currencies denominating the stocks depreciate.

An alternative to an international mutual fund is a global mutual fund, which includes some U.S. stocks in its portfolio. International and global mutual funds have historically included stocks from several different countries to limit the portfolio's exposure to economic conditions in any single foreign economy.

In recent years some new international mutual funds have been designed to fully benefit from a particular emerging country or continent. Although the potential return from such a strategy is greater, so is the risk, because the entire portfolio value is sensitive to a single economy. For investors who prefer minimum transaction costs, mutual

USING THE WALL STREET JOURNAL

Mutual Fund Prices and Performance

Mutual fund quotations like those shown here are provided in *The Wall Street Journal*. The bold letters indicate the sponsoring firms that offer the mutual funds; the types of funds offered by each firm are listed just below its name. The fund's net asset value is disclosed in the second column, and the change in this value from the previous day is shown in the third column. The year-to-date return on the fund is disclosed in the fourth column, and the 3-year return of the fund is disclosed in the fifth column.

FUND	NAV	NET CHG	YTD %RET	3-YR %RET
NYTF B t	11.65	...	2.3	4.7
PacGrB p	12.26	-0.07	2.0	13.7
SmMdSpVal t	13.25	-0.10	6.0	NS
SP500B p	11.61	-0.07	-0.6	2.9
SpcValB p	17.60	-0.17	2.4	10.2
SpGroB t	14.18	-0.17	1.7	0.4
StratB t	16.46	-0.09	1.0	3.4
ToRtnB t	13.79	-0.10	-0.4	1.1
TotMktB p	9.12	-0.07	-0.1	4.7
TxESecB p	11.99	...	2.8	5.3
USGvtB t	9.26	0.01	3.3	4.7
UtilB	12.02	-0.01	7.5	0.3
ValAdB t	33.18	-0.25	1.2	9.6
Value p	11.70	-0.04	5.4	4.4
Morgan Stanley Fds C				
500InxC p	11.61	-0.07	-0.6	3.0
AmOppC p	20.38	-0.12	-4.1	-2.3
DivGtC p	36.77	-0.24	-1.0	3.6
Morgan Stanley Fds D				
500InxD	12.14	-0.07	0.2	4.0
AmOppD	22.17	-0.13	-3.4	-1.3
CapOpptD	13.58	-0.07	7.0	4.0
DevGrD	19.92	-0.14	5.8	9.9
DivGtD	36.83	-0.24	-0.3	4.6
GlbDivD	12.34	-0.05	1.5	9.7
GrowthD	11.60	-0.07	-4.1	0.4
HiYldD	1.81	...	6.0	7.5
IntlD	8.82	-0.04	0.9	6.7
IntValD	11.83	-0.03	2.7	11.3
SpcValD	18.86	-0.18	3.2	11.3
TaxExD	11.94	0.01	3.3	5.9
USGvtD	9.25	0.01	3.4	5.0
ValAdD	33.76	-0.25	1.9	10.7
Morgan Stanley Inst				
ActIntl	9.60	-0.05	0.8	7.7
Balanced	10.83	-0.04	0.8	3.9
CorPlusFxdIncAdv	11.72	0.01	3.6	5.6
CorPlusFxdIncInv	11.73	0.01	3.6	5.7
CorPlusFxdInInst	11.73	0.01	3.7	5.9
EmMkt	16.20	-0.10	4.4	25.5
EqGrA	15.12	-0.08	-3.9	0.3
EqGrB p	14.90	-0.08	-4.2	0.0
Equity	10.26	-0.06	2.9	3.6
HiYld	5.59	...	5.8	8.0
IntlEq	19.66	-0.05	3.1	12.3
IntlEqB p	19.51	-0.05	3.0	12.0
IntlFxdInc	11.14	...	0.4	12.3
IntlSmCapA	22.86	-0.02	12.6	19.5
InvGrdFxdIncInst	11.62	0.01	3.8	5.9
LtdDur	10.50	...	1.0	3.0
MCapGr	18.24	-0.12	6.0	8.0
MCapGrAdv p	17.84	-0.12	5.7	7.8
Muni	12.67	-0.02	2.1	5.2
SmCoGrA	11.07	-0.13	2.4	145

FUND	NAV	NET CHG	YTD %RET	3-YR %RET
HiYldMuBd p	21.24	...	8.3	9.0
IntDMunBd p	9.27	...	4.1	4.7
InsMnB p	11.15	...	3.4	5.6
KYMunBd p	11.24	...	3.9	6.0
LargeCapV p	22.98	-0.12	0.8	2.9
LtdMnBd p	10.92	...	2.3	4.2
MlMunBd p	11.83	...	4.5	5.9
MOMunBd p	11.16	...	4.0	5.7
NCMunBd p	10.69	...	3.4	5.8
NYMunBd p	10.97	0.01	3.8	6.0
OHMunBd p	11.60	0.01	3.9	6.0
TNMunBd p	11.54	0.01	3.9	6.1
VAMunBd p	10.99	0.01	4.2	5.8
Nuveen Cl B				
HYMunBd p	21.22	...	7.7	8.2
GrowthB p	18.21	-0.10	-4.8	-3.4
Nuveen Cl C				
HYMunBd t	21.23	...	7.8	8.4
LtdMuBd p	10.89	...	2.1	3.8
Nuveen Cl R				
CAMunBd	10.46	...	4.8	5.6
CAInsM	11.02	...	3.3	5.4
InsMnB	11.12	...	3.5	5.8
IntDMunBd	9.29	0.01	4.3	4.9
NYMunBd	10.99	...	3.9	6.2
NYInsM	10.91	0.01	4.0	6.5
OHMunBd	11.59	0.01	4.0	6.2
Oak Associates Funds				
PinOakAgg	17.46	-0.28	-11.5	-0.1
RedOakTec	6.00	-0.07	-12.2	-1.2
WhiteOakG	30.11	-0.40	-14.4	-0.1
Oak Value	28.02	-0.24	-1.6	5.1
Oakmark Funds Cl I				
Eqtylnc r	22.95	-0.09	4.2	11.3
Global r	19.44	-0.09	0.8	23.0
IntlSmCp r	17.93	-0.03	11.6	25.0
Oakmark r	38.55	-0.25	2.7	7.8
OakmrkInt r	18.70	-0.08	3.8	15.8
Select r	31.01	-0.19	1.3	8.1
SmCap r	16.53	...	-5.5	8.5
Oberweis Funds				
EmergGr	23.61	-0.28	-12.7	12.6
Old Westbury Fds				
Intl p	NA	...	NA	NA
LgCapEq p	NA	...	NA	NA
MidCapEq p	NA	...	NA	NA
OlsteinAdv p	16.91	-0.23	-0.3	13.0
OlsteinAlt t	16.24	-0.22	-0.8	12.2
One Group Cl A				
Balanced p	12.47	-0.04	...	3.4
Bond	11.06	0.02	3.9	5.7
DivMidCap	17.98	-0.15	0.6	8.8
DivrsEq p	11.26	-0.06	-2.1	1.6
EqIndx p	25.28	-0.15	...	3.9

FUND	NAV	NET CHG	YTD %RET	3-YR %RET
LrgCpGr	18.70	-0.18	-3.1	0.1
LrgCp20	14.13	-0.15	-4.8	-0.4
MidCp	17.37	-0.15	1.1	10.5
HeltReit	11.74	-0.03	14.4	20.3
SelGrwth	19.31	-0.27	-8.0	-2.0
TechCom	9.68	-0.12	-10.5	-6.1
PIMCO Fds Admin MMS				
CapAppAd p	15.76	-0.13	-0.8	1.5
MdCpAd p	20.48	-0.14	1.9	5.1
Renais p	23.23	-0.24	0.1	14.1
PIMCO Fds Admin PIMS				
HiYldAd p	9.74	0.01	4.9	9.9
LDurAd p	10.28	0.01	1.7	3.9
LTrmGvt p	11.31	0.03	7.0	8.7
RealRetAd p	11.58	0.05	5.9	9.7
ShortTrmAd p	10.05	...	1.0	2.2
StockPIAd p	10.55	-0.05	0.1	5.2
TotRtAd p	10.95	0.01	3.8	6.3
TRII Ad p	10.55	0.02	3.8	5.8
PIMCO Fds Instl MMS				
CapApp	16.07	-0.13	-0.6	1.6
EmgComps	21.81	-0.29	-3.5	18.0
MdCp	20.84	-0.15	2.1	5.4
SmCpVl	27.50	-0.21	7.5	19.2
Value	16.85	-0.07	6.4	11.7
RCM GlobTechI	29.19	-0.21	-5.2	11.2
RCM LGwth	11.50	-0.08	-3.8	-0.9
RCM MidCap	2.33	-0.04	-2.1	4.5
PIMCO Fds Instl PIMS				
AllAsset	12.71	0.02	6.3	NS
CommodtyRR	15.49	0.16	17.1	NS
DivInc	10.87	0.01	5.1	NS
EmMktsBd	10.77	...	6.1	22.0
FrgnBd	10.54	0.01	3.6	5.4
GlblBd	10.31	...	1.7	12.0
GlblBdII	10.05	0.01	3.7	6.1
HiYld	9.74	0.01	5.1	10.2
LowDur	10.28	0.01	1.9	4.2
LowDurII	9.85	...	1.7	3.4
LTUSG	11.31	0.03	7.2	8.9
ModDur	10.51	0.01	3.4	6.2
MuniBd	10.22	...	1.8	5.1
RealRet	12.10	0.06	8.0	NS
RealRtnI	11.58	0.05	6.1	9.9
RERRStg r	11.70	0.04	16.8	NS
ShDuMuInc	10.08	-0.01	0.5	2.3
ShortT	10.05	...	1.2	2.5
StksPLS	9.26	-0.05	0.3	5.6
TotRt	10.95	0.01	4.0	6.6
TRII	10.55	0.02	4.0	6.0
TRIII	9.69	0.01	4.2	6.9
PIMCO Funds Instl				
LowDurIII p	10.13	0.01	1.8	4.2

funds have begun to offer index funds. Each of these funds is intended to mirror a stock index of a particular country or group of countries. For example, Vanguard offers a fund representing a European stock index and a Pacific Basin stock index. Because these mutual funds simply attempt to mirror an existing stock index, they avoid the advisory and transaction costs that are common to other mutual funds. International funds are discussed further at the end of this chapter.

Specialty Funds

Some mutual funds, called **specialty funds,** focus on a group of companies sharing a particular characteristic. For example, there are industry-specific funds such as energy, banking, and high-tech funds. Some funds include only stocks of firms that are likely takeover targets. Other mutual funds specialize in options or other commodities, such

as precious metals. There are even mutual funds that invest only in socially conscious firms. The risk of specialty funds varies with the particular characteristics of each fund.

Some specialty funds focus their investment on Internet companies. Internet funds performed extremely well in the late 1990s when stock prices of Internet companies surged, but poorly in the 2000–2002 period. Investors who want to invest in technology but do not have any insight about specific companies commonly invest in these mutual funds.

Index Funds

Some mutual funds are designed to simply match the performance of an existing stock index. For example, Vanguard offers an **index fund** that is designed to match the S&P 500 index. Index funds are composed of stocks that, in aggregate, are expected to move in line with a specific index. They contain many of the same stocks contained in the corresponding index and tend to have very low expenses because they require little portfolio management and execute a relatively small number of transactions.

Investors who are satisfied with matching the performance of a specific index tend to prefer index funds. Investors who rely on mutual fund managers to outperform specific indexes are less interested in index funds. Index funds are becoming increasingly popular as investors recognize that most mutual fund managers do not consistently outperform indexes.

Multifund Funds

In recent years, **multifund mutual funds** have been created. A multifund mutual fund's portfolio managers invest in a portfolio of different mutual funds. A multifund mutual fund achieves even more diversification than a typical mutual fund, because it contains several mutual funds. However, investors incur two types of management expenses: (1) the expenses of managing each individual mutual fund and (2) the expenses of managing the multifund mutual fund.

Bond Mutual Fund Categories

Investors in bonds are primarily concerned about interest rate risk, credit (default) risk, and tax implications. Thus, most bond funds can be classified according to either their maturities (which affect interest rate risk) or the type of bond issuers (which affects credit risk and taxes incurred).

Income Funds

For investors who are mainly concerned with stability of income rather than capital appreciation, **income funds** are appropriate. These funds are usually composed of bonds that offer periodic coupon payments and vary in exposure to risk. Income funds composed of only corporate bonds are susceptible to credit risk, while those composed of only Treasury bonds are not. A third type of income fund contains bonds backed by government agencies, such as the Government National Mortgage Association (GNMA, or Ginnie Mae). These funds are normally perceived to be less risky than a fund containing corporate bonds. Those income funds exhibiting more credit risk will offer a higher potential return, other things being equal.

The market values of even medium-term income funds are quite volatile over time because of their sensitivity to interest rate movements. Thus, income funds are best suited for investors who rely on the fund for periodic income and plan to maintain the fund over a long period of time.

Tax-Free Funds

Investors in high tax brackets have historically purchased municipal bonds as a way to avoid taxes. Because these bonds are susceptible to default, a diversified portfolio is desirable. Mutual funds containing municipal bonds allow investors in high tax brackets with even small amounts of funds to avoid taxes while maintaining a low degree of credit risk.

High-Yield (Junk) Bond Funds

Investors desiring high returns and willing to incur high risk may wish to consider bond portfolios with at least two-thirds of the bonds rated below Baa by Moody's or BBB by Standard & Poor's. These portfolios are sometimes referred to as **high-yield (or junk bond) funds.** Typically, the bonds were issued by highly leveraged firms. The issuing firm's ability to repay the bonds is very sensitive to economic conditions.

International and Global Bond Funds

 International bond funds contain bonds issued by corporations or governments based in other countries. Global bond funds differ from international bond funds in that they contain U.S. as well as foreign bonds. Global funds may be more appropriate for investors who want a fund that includes U.S. bonds within a diversified portfolio, whereas investors in international bond funds may already have a sufficient investment in U.S. bonds and prefer a fund that focuses entirely on foreign bonds. International and global bond funds provide U.S. investors with an easy way to invest in foreign bonds. However, these funds are subject to risk. Like bond funds containing U.S. bonds, these funds are subject to credit risk, based on the financial position of the corporations or governments that issued the bonds. They are also subject to interest rate risk, as the bond prices are inversely related to the interest rate movements in the currency denominating each bond. These funds are also subject to exchange rate risk, as the NAV of the funds is determined by translating the foreign bond holdings to dollars. Thus, when the foreign currency denominating the bonds weakens, the translated dollar value of those bonds will decrease.

Maturity Classifications

Since the interest rate sensitivity of bonds is dependent on the maturity, bond funds are commonly segmented according to the maturities of the bonds they contain. Intermediate-term bond funds invest in bonds with 5 to 10 years remaining until maturity. Long-term bond funds typically contain bonds with 15 to 30 years until maturity. The bonds in these funds normally have a higher yield to maturity and are more sensitive to interest rate movements than the bonds in intermediate-term funds. For a given type of bond fund classification (such as municipal or tax-free), various alternatives with different maturity characteristics are available, so investors can select a fund with the desired exposure to interest rate risk.

The variety of bond funds available can satisfy investors who desire combinations of the features described here. For example, investors who are concerned about interest rate

risk and credit risk could invest in bond funds that focus on Treasury bonds with inter-mediate terms to maturity. Investors who expect interest rates to decline but are concerned about credit risk could invest in a long-term Treasury bond fund. Investors who expect interest rates to decline and are not concerned about credit risk may invest in high-yield bond funds. Investors who wish to avoid federal taxes on interest income and are concerned about interest rate risk may consider short-term municipal bond funds.

Asset Allocation Funds

Asset allocation funds contain a variety of investments (such as stocks, bonds, and money market securities). The portfolio managers adjust the compositions of these funds in response to expectations. For example, a given asset allocation fund will tend to concentrate more heavily on bonds if interest rates are expected to decline; it will focus on stocks if a strong stock market is expected. These funds may even concentrate on international securities if the portfolio managers forecast favorable economic conditions in foreign countries.

Mutual Fund Growth and Size

Exhibit 23.4 shows how the number of mutual funds has grown over time. The number of stock and bond funds is substantially larger than it was during the 1980s. The popu-

EXHIBIT 23.4
Growth in the Number of
Stock Funds and Bond
Funds

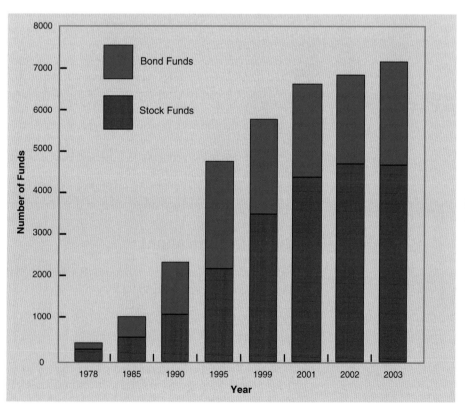

Source: *2004 Mutual Fund Fact Book.*

larity of stock funds is mainly due to the stock market boom periods that occurred during the 1990s, along with the relatively low returns offered by alternative short-term securities. The relative growth of investment in stock mutual funds versus bond mutual funds is illustrated in Exhibit 23.5, based on asset size. In the 1980s, investment in bond funds exceeded that of stock funds, but by the mid-1990s, investment in stock funds was higher, as investors substantially increased their investment in stock funds in response to unusually high returns in the stock market.

Growth funds, income funds, international and global funds, and long-term municipal bond funds are the most popular types of funds. Growth and income funds are the most popular when measured according to total assets. Although mutual funds originally targeted more conservative investors, new kinds of funds have recently been created to accommodate all types of investors. Exhibit 23.6 shows the composition of all mutual fund assets in aggregate. Common stocks are clearly the dominant asset maintained by mutual funds.

EXHIBIT 23.5

Investment in Bond and Stock Mutual Funds

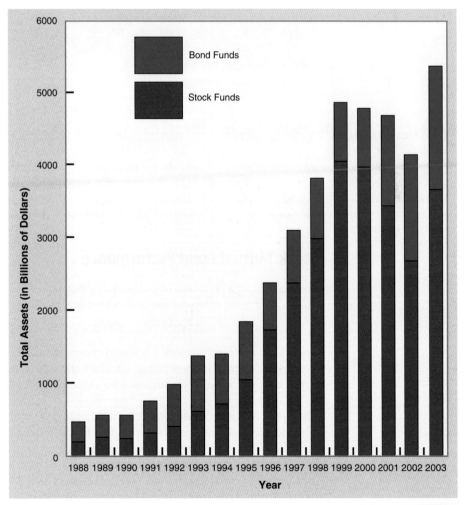

Source: *2004 Mutual Fund Fact Book.*

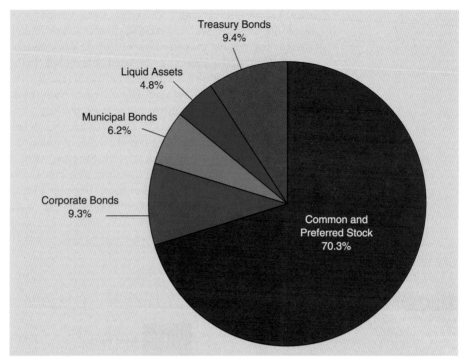

Source: *2004 Mutual Fund Fact Book.*

Mutual Fund Performance

Investors in mutual funds closely monitor the performance of these funds. They also monitor the performance of other mutual funds in which they may invest in the future. In addition, portfolio managers of a mutual fund closely monitor its performance, as their compensation is typically influenced by the performance level.

Stock Mutual Fund Performance

The change in the performance (measured by risk-adjusted returns) of an open-end mutual fund focusing on stocks can be modeled as

$$\Delta\text{PERF} = f(\Delta\text{MKT}, \Delta\text{SECTOR}, \Delta\text{MANAB})$$

where MKT represents general stock market conditions, SECTOR represents conditions in the specific sector (if there is one) on which the mutual fund is focused, and MANAB represents the abilities of the mutual fund's management.

Change in Market Conditions A mutual fund's performance is usually closely related to market conditions. In fact, some mutual funds (index funds) attempt to resemble a particular stock market index. During the late 1990s, most mutual funds focusing on U.S. stocks experienced high performance because the U.S. market experienced high performance. Conversely, mutual funds focusing on Asian stocks experienced weak performance in the late 1990s because the Asian markets experienced weak performance. In the 2001–2002 period, weak economic conditions caused a major decline in stock

prices, and most stock mutual funds performed poorly. However, in the 2003–2004 period, mutual funds performed well as economic conditions improved.

The attack on the United States on September 11, 2001, further weakened economic conditions and caused stock prices to continue their decline. Stock valuations were weak because expected cash flows of firms had been reduced and were subject to much uncertainty. Since most stocks were adversely affected by the crisis, most mutual funds were adversely affected as well. Mutual funds that had a high concentration of travel services stocks or insurance stocks experienced larger declines in their prices. Even international mutual funds were adversely affected because stocks of most countries experienced a decline in price immediately after September 11.

To measure the sensitivity of a mutual fund's exposure to market conditions, investors estimate its beta. A mutual fund's beta is estimated in the same manner as a stock's beta. Mutual funds with high betas are more sensitive to market conditions and therefore have more potential to benefit from favorable market conditions. If unfavorable market conditions occur, however, they are subject to a more pronounced decline in NAV.

Change in Sector Conditions The performance of a stock mutual fund focused on a specific sector is influenced by market conditions in that sector. Mutual funds focusing on small stocks had higher returns in the early 1990s, while mutual funds focusing on large stocks had higher returns in the late 1990s. When economic conditions weakened in 2001, small stocks typically performed worse, which resulted in very poor performance of growth funds.

In the late 1990s, many mutual funds that focused on U.S. technology stocks experienced very high performance because most technology companies performed well during this period. In 2001, these funds generally performed poorly because most stocks in the technology sector experienced weak performance during this year.

Change in Management Abilities In addition to market and sector conditions, a mutual fund's performance may also be affected by the abilities of its managers. Mutual funds in the same sector can have different performance levels because of differences in management abilities. If the portfolio managers of one mutual fund in the sector can select stocks that generate higher returns, that fund should generate higher returns. Also important is a mutual fund's operating efficiency, which affects the expenses incurred by the fund and therefore affects its value. A fund that is managed efficiently such that its expenses are low may be able to achieve higher returns for its shareholders even if its portfolio performance is about the same as other mutual funds in the same sector.

Closed-End Stock Fund Performance

The performance of closed-end stock funds is essentially driven by the same factors that influence open-end (mutual) stock funds. In addition, however, the performance of closed-end stock funds is affected by a change in their premium or discount.

When the demand for a particular closed-end mutual fund is strong, the market price may be higher than its NAV; the fund is thus priced at a premium. When a closed-end fund's market price per share is less than the NAV per share, the fund is priced at a discount.

Some closed-end funds, especially those focusing on securities of a foreign country, can have large premiums or discounts relative to their NAVs. If a fund's premium increases relative to its NAV (or if its discount is reduced), the return to the fund's shareholders is

increased. The main reason for a change in the discount or premium is a shift in the demand for shares of the fund. For example, when large stock markets are priced relatively high, more investors from those markets seek investments in smaller, foreign markets where prices of securities are lower. Investing in individual stocks in those markets can be difficult, however, because the respective governments may impose restrictions. In that case, investing in a closed-end fund representing foreign markets is an easier approach than investing in those countries, and investors' demand for those funds increases. Given the fixed supply of closed-end fund shares, a strong demand for those shares by investors can push the market price of the shares high above the NAV.

Some research has documented high returns from investing in closed-end funds that are priced at a large discount from their NAV, which suggests that closed-end funds with large discounts in price are undervalued. Applying this strategy will not always generate high risk-adjusted returns, however, because the market price of some closed-end funds with large discounts continues to decline over time (their discount becomes larger).

Bond Mutual Fund Performance

The change in the performance of an open-end mutual fund focusing on bonds can be modeled as

$$\Delta\text{PERF} = f(\Delta R_f, \Delta RP, \text{CLASS}, \Delta\text{MANAB})$$

where R_f represents the risk-free rate, RP represents the risk premium, CLASS represents the classification of the bond fund, and MANAB represents the abilities of the fund's managers.

Change in the Risk-Free Rate The prices of bonds tend to be inversely related to changes in the risk-free interest rate. In periods when the risk-free interest rate declines substantially, the required rate of return by bondholders declines, and most bond funds perform well. Those bond funds that are focused on bonds with longer maturities are more exposed to changes in the risk-free rate.

Change in the Risk Premium The prices of bonds tend to decline in response to an increase in the risk premiums required by investors who purchase bonds. When economic conditions deteriorate, the risk premium required by bondholders usually increases, which results in a higher required rate of return (assuming no change in the risk-free rate) and lower prices on risky bonds. In periods when risk premiums increase, prices of risky bonds tend to decrease, and bond mutual funds focusing on risky bonds perform poorly.

Change in Management Abilities The performance levels of bond mutual funds in a specific bond classification can vary due to differences in the abilities of the funds' managers. If the portfolio managers of one bond fund in that classification can select bonds that generate higher returns, that bond fund should generate higher returns. Also important is a bond fund's operating efficiency, which affects the expenses incurred by the fund and therefore affects the fund's value. A bond fund that is managed efficiently such that its expenses are low may be able to achieve higher returns for its shareholders even if its portfolio performance is about the same as other bond mutual funds in the same classification.

Closed-End Bond Fund Performance

The performance levels of closed-end bond funds are driven by the same factors that influence open-end (mutual) bond funds. In addition, though, the performance of closed-end bond funds is affected by a change in their premium or discount. If demand for a closed-end fund's shares is abnormally high or low, its discount or premium relative to its NAV may adjust, thereby affecting the fund's performance. Closed-end bond funds that focus on bonds in a foreign country are most susceptible to an abrupt shift in the premium or discount. Thus, the performance levels of those closed-end bond funds are most likely to be affected by shifts in the premium or discount.

Performance from Diversifying among Mutual Funds

The performance of any given mutual fund may be primarily driven by a single economic factor. For example, the performance of growth stock funds may be highly dependent on the stock market's performance (market risk). The performance of any bond mutual fund is highly dependent on interest rate movements (interest rate risk). The performance of any international mutual fund is influenced by the dollar's value (exchange rate risk). When all securities in a given mutual fund are similarly influenced by an underlying economic factor, the fund does not achieve full diversification benefits. For this reason, some investors diversify among different types of mutual funds so that only a portion of their entire investment is susceptible to a particular type of risk.

Diversification among types of mutual funds can substantially reduce the volatility of returns on the overall investment. The proportion of the entire investment allocated to each type of mutual fund may be based on the forecasts for the underlying factors that affect each fund's value. To achieve full diversification benefits, constraints can be imposed on the maximum proportion allocated to any one type of mutual fund.

Research on Stock Mutual Fund Performance

A variety of studies have attempted to assess mutual fund performance over time. Measuring mutual fund performance solely by return is not a valid test, because the return will likely be highly dependent on the performance of the stock and bond markets during the period of concern. An alternative measure of performance is to compare the mutual fund return to the return of some market index (such as the Dow Jones Industrial Average or the S&P 500 index).

Most studies that assess mutual fund performance find that mutual funds do not outperform the market, especially when accounting for the type of securities that each fund invests in. A study by Malkiel[1] found that mutual funds tend to underperform the market, even when the expenses incurred from owning mutual funds are ignored.

To appropriately evaluate a mutual fund's performance, risk should also be considered. Even when returns are adjusted to account for risk, mutual funds have, on the average, failed to outperform the market. These results may seem surprising, because the funds are managed by experienced portfolio managers. Yet, many individual stock purchase decisions are also ultimately derived from the so-called expert advice of investment

[1] Burton G. Malkiel, "Returns from Investing in Mutual Funds 1971 to 1991," *Journal of Finance* (June 1995): 549–572.

companies that instruct their brokers on what securities to recommend. In addition, advocates of market efficiency suggest that beyond insider information, market prices should already reflect any good or bad characteristics of each stock, making it difficult to construct a portfolio whose risk-adjusted returns will consistently outperform the market. Even if mutual funds do not outperform the market, they can still be attractive to investors who wish to diversify and who prefer that a portfolio manager make their investment decisions.

Research on Bond Mutual Fund Performance

A study by Blake, Elton, and Gruber[2] assessed the performance of bond mutual funds. One of the objectives was to determine whether mutual fund managers make better investment decisions than other investors in the bond market. The researchers found that, in general, bond mutual funds underperformed bond indexes. Their general results remain, regardless of the models used for comparing performance. They also determined that bond mutual funds with higher expense ratios generated lower returns. Thus, they recommended that investors select bond mutual funds that have lower expense ratios. Given their results, the authors suggest the creation of additional bond index funds, because these funds can provide bond diversification for small investors without requiring large management fees. Overall, bond mutual funds may still appeal to investors, but investors should recognize that the managers of these funds have not been able to outperform the market. This conclusion is only a generalization, as some bond mutual funds have experienced very high performance.

The authors also assessed whether past performance of bond mutual funds served as an accurate predictor of future performance. They found no conclusive evidence that the past performance of bond mutual funds can serve as a valuable predictor of future performance.

Mutual Fund Scandals

In 2003, mutual funds received unfavorable publicity because some of the funds were allowing their large clients to buy or sell the fund's shares after the stock exchange's 4 P.M. closing but at the 4 P.M. prices. Thus, if favorable news about the market occurred after 4 P.M., the clients could buy fund shares at a price that was less than what was appropriate. This late trading, as it is called, is distinctly different from night trading (or after-hours trading) in the stock market where trades occur at prevailing market prices. Late trading of mutual funds involves engaging in a trade on prices that are "stale" or no longer appropriate. It is a clear violation of laws established by the SEC in 1968. Other shareholders of the mutual fund who were not able to trade on the inside information are adversely affected by these actions. The scandal was a major blow to mutual funds because they were commonly viewed as a safe way to diversify among firms and avoid exposure to possible scandals such as accounting irregularities that could affect a firm's stock price. Although many mutual funds were completely innocent, it was difficult for investors to identify the funds that had violated the rules.

---

[2] Christopher R. Blake, Edwin J. Elton, and Martin J. Gruber, "The Performance of Bond Funds," *Journal of Business* (July 1993): 371–403.

As soon as this problem was publicized, the SEC began to investigate mutual funds and fined some of them heavily. The SEC was concerned that investors might come to mistrust all mutual funds (even those that were innocent) and withdraw their investments; massive redemptions could adversely affect the values of the securities that the funds invest in. Consequently, the SEC and other agencies of the federal government took steps to restore investor confidence in mutual funds including prosecuting managers of mutual funds who violated the rules.

Mutual Fund Governance

A mutual fund is usually run by an investment company, whose owners are different from the shareholders in the mutual funds. In fact, some managers employed by mutual funds invest their money in the investment company rather than in the mutual funds that they manage. Thus, the investment company may have an incentive to charge high fees to the shareholders of the mutual fund. The expenses charged to the fund represent income generated by the investment company. Although valid expenses are incurred in running a mutual fund, the expenses charged by some investment companies may be excessive. Many mutual funds have grown substantially over time and should be able to capitalize on economies of scale. Nevertheless, their expense ratios have generally increased over time. Competition is expected to ensure that mutual funds will charge shareholders only reasonable expenses, but many investors are not aware of the expenses that they are charged.

Mutual funds, like corporations, are subject to some forms of governance that are intended to ensure that the managers are serving the shareholders. Each mutual fund has a board of directors who are supposed to represent the fund's shareholders. The effectiveness of the boards is questionable, however. The SEC requires that a majority of the directors of a mutual fund board be independent (not employed by the fund). However, an employee of the company can retire and qualify as an independent board member just two years later. In addition, the average annual compensation paid to the board members of large mutual funds exceeds $100,000. Thus, some board members may be willing to avoid confrontation with management if doing so enables them to keep their positions. This same criticism is also leveled at boards of publicly traded companies. Another problem is that board members of a mutual fund family commonly oversee all funds in the entire family. Consequently, they may concentrate on general issues that are not particular to any one fund and spend a relatively small amount of time on any individual fund within the family.

Mutual funds also have a compliance officer who is supposed to ensure that the fund's operations are in line with the fund's objective and guidelines for trading rules. Until recently, however, some compliance officers reported to the investment company instead of the mutual fund's board of directors. As a result of the recent scandals, more compliance officers are now reporting to the board.

Money Market Funds

Money market mutual funds, sometimes called money market funds (MMFs), are portfolios of money market (short-term) instruments constructed and managed by investment companies. The portfolio is divided into shares that are sold to individual investors. Because investors can participate in some MMFs with as little as $1,000, they

are able to invest in money market instruments that they could not afford on their own. Most MMFs allow check-writing privileges, although there may be restrictions on the number of checks written per month or on the minimum amount of the check.

MMFs send periodic account statements to their shareholders to update them on any changes in their balance. They also send shareholders periodic updates on any changes in the asset portfolio composition, providing a breakdown of the names of securities and amounts held in the MMF portfolio.

Because the sponsoring investment company is willing to purchase MMFs back at any time, investors can liquidate their investment whenever they desire. In most years, additional sales exceed redemptions, allowing the companies to build their MMF portfolios by purchasing more securities. When redemptions exceed sales, the company accommodates the amount of excessive redemptions by selling some of the assets contained in the MMF portfolios.

Exhibit 23.7 illustrates the growth in assets of MMFs over time. As investors increase their investment in MMFs, the asset level increases. When economic conditions are weak, the investment in money market funds tends to increase, as investors become more concerned about the risk of stocks and bonds.

MMFs can be distinguished from one another and from other mutual funds by the composition, maturity, and risk of their assets. Each of these characteristics is described next.

Asset Composition of Money Market Funds

Exhibit 23.8 shows the composition of money market fund assets in aggregate. Commercial paper dominates, but repurchase agreements and Treasury securities are also popular. This composition reflects the importance of each type of asset for MMFs overall and does not represent the typical composition of any particular MMF. Each MMF is usually more concentrated in whatever assets reflect its objective. During recessionary periods, the proportion of Treasury bills in MMFs normally increases, and the proportion of the more risky money market securities decreases.

Money Market Fund Maturity

Exhibit 23.9 shows the average maturity of MMFs over time. The average maturity is determined by individual asset maturities, weighted according to their relative value. In the mid-1970s, the average maturity was relatively long. As interest rates increased, yields of MMFs were slower to adjust, as the rates on existing assets were fixed. Those MMFs with shorter asset maturities were able to capitalize more quickly on higher interest rates. By the late 1970s, the average maturity on MMFs had declined to less than half of what it was during the mid-1970s. Thus, most MMFs were in a position to fully benefit from the very high short-term interest rates in 1981. During the 1980s, the average maturity of money market fund assets was about 40 days. The average maturity has generally increased since then.

Money Market Fund Risk

From an investor's perspective, MMFs usually have a low level of credit risk. There may be some concern that an economic downturn could cause frequent defaults on

EXHIBIT 23.7   Growth in Money Market Funds

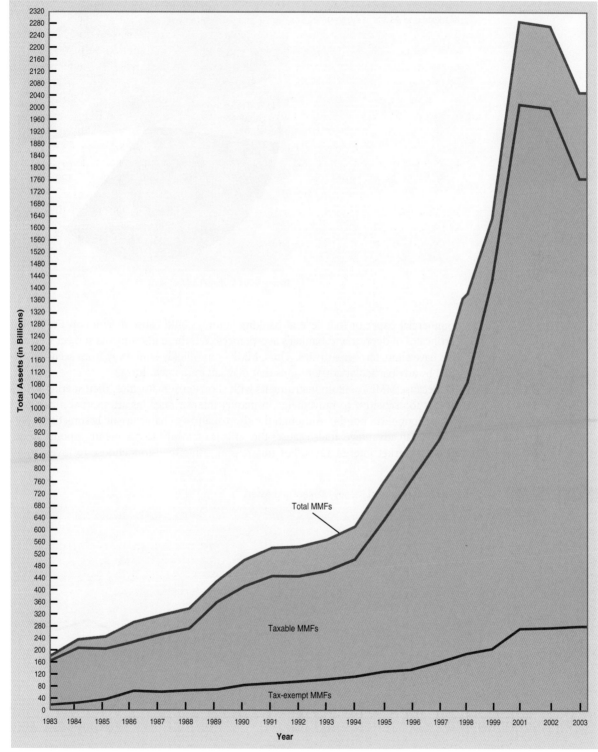

Source: *2004 Mutual Fund Fact Book*.

EXHIBIT 23.8

Composition of Taxable Money
Market Fund Assets in Aggregate

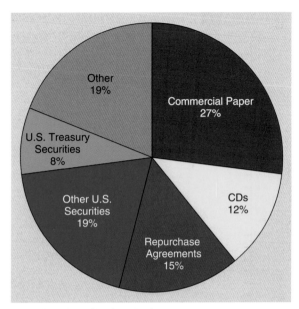

Source: *2004 Mutual Fund Fact Book.*

commercial paper or that several banking failures could cause defaults on Eurodollar certificates of deposit and banker's acceptances. Yet, these instruments subject to credit risk have short-term maturities. Thus, MMFs can quickly shift away from securities issued by any particular corporations that may fail in the near future.

Because MMFs contain instruments with short-term maturities, their market values are not too sensitive to movements in market interest rates (as are mutual funds containing long-term bonds). Although the short-maturity characteristic is sometimes perceived as an advantage, it also causes the returns on MMFs to decline in response to decreasing market interest rates. For this reason, some investors choose to invest in an

EXHIBIT 23.9   Weighted Average Maturity of Money Market Fund Assets

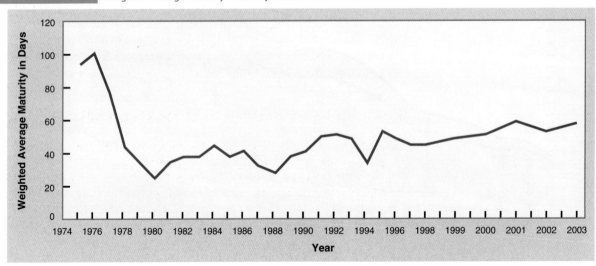

Source: *2004 Mutual Fund Fact Book.*

MMF offered by an investment company that also offers a bond mutual fund. During periods when interest rates are expected to decline, a portion of the investor's funds can be transferred from the MMF to the bond mutual fund upon the investor's request.

The expected returns on MMFs are low relative to bonds or stocks because of the following factors. First, the credit risk of MMFs is normally perceived to be lower than that of corporate bonds. Second, MMFs have less interest rate risk than bond funds. Third, they consistently generate positive returns over time, whereas bond and stock funds can experience negative returns. Because MMFs are normally characterized as having relatively low risk and low expected returns, they are popular among investors who need a conservative investment medium. Furthermore, they provide liquidity with their check-writing privileges.

Money Market Fund Management

The role of MMF portfolio managers is to maintain an asset portfolio that satisfies the underlying objective of a fund. If the managers expect a stronger economy, they may replace maturing risk-free securities (Treasury bills) with more commercial paper or CDs. The return on these instruments will be higher but will not overexpose the fund to credit risk. For some MMFs there is very little flexibility in the composition. For example, some MMFs may as a rule maintain a high percentage of their investment in T-bills to assure investors that they will continue to refrain from risky securities.

Even if managers are unable to change the asset composition of MMFs, they can still influence performance by changing the maturities of the securities in which they invest. For example, if managers expect interest rates to increase in the future, they should use funds generated from maturing securities to purchase new securities with shorter maturities. The greater the degree to which a manager adjusts the average maturity of an MMF to capitalize on interest rate expectations, the greater the reward or penalty. If the expectation turns out to be correct, the MMF will yield relatively high returns, and vice versa.

Although individual investors and institutions do not manage the portfolio composition or maturity of an MMF, they have a variety of MMFs from which to choose. If they expect a strong economy, they may prefer an MMF that contains securities with some risk that offer higher returns than T-bills. If they expect interest rates to increase, they could invest in MMFs with a short average maturity. They are in a sense managing their investment by choosing an MMF with the characteristics they prefer. Some investment companies offer several MMFs, allowing investors to switch from one fund to another based on their expectations of economic conditions.

Regulation and Taxation of Money Market Funds

As a result of the Securities Act of 1933, sponsoring companies must provide full information on any MMFs they offer. In addition, they must provide potential investors with a current prospectus that describes the fund's investment policies and objectives. The Investment Company Act of 1940 contains numerous restrictions that prevent a conflict of interest by the fund's managers.

Earnings generated by an MMF are generally passed on to the fund's shareholders in the form of interest payments or converted into additional shares. If the fund distributes at least 90 percent of its income to its shareholders, the fund itself is exempt from federal taxation. This tax rule is designed to avoid double taxation. Although the fund can

Money Market Fund Quotations

Money market fund quotations are provided every Thursday in *The Wall Street Journal,* as shown here. The name of each fund is in the first column. The average term to maturity of the assets contained in each fund is disclosed in the second column. Note that the range varies among funds, but most funds have an average maturity of less than 100 days. The annualized yield for each fund over the last seven days is provided in the third column. These yields are normally comparable to yields on Treasury bills, commercial paper, and other money market securities. The asset level of each fund is disclosed in the fourth column (in millions of dollars). Some MMFs have more than $3 billion in assets.

MONEY MARKET MUTUAL FUNDS

FUND	AVG. MAT.	7 DAY YIELD	ASSETS	FUND	AVG. MAT.	7 DAY YIELD	ASSETS	FUND	AVG. MAT.	7 DAY YIELD	ASSETS	FUND	AVG. MAT.	7 DAY YIELD	ASSETS
DryGvt	22	.47	273	FinSqTrsy	26	1.05	1456	HuntgtnMMT	29	.51	367	ML CMAMn	62	.87	10203
DryInG	18	.29	25	FinSq TOF	26	1.14	4183	HuntgtnUST	30	.53	460	MerLyGv	46	1.17	5695
DryInst	49	.85	480	FinSq MMF	42	1.27	9980	ING AeltusMMA	49	.78	127	MerLITr	43	1.06	1258
DryfLA	33	.68	4854	FITPrMonMktl	28	1.16	58	ING AeltusMMI	49	.78	79	MerLyIn	54	1.26	10882
DryMM	74	.61	309	FstAmGvObD	39	.81	789	INGBrokCsh	45	.48	316	MerLyRdy	61	.81	4596
DryResR	23	.88	191	FstAmGvObY	39	.96	1712	INGLexingt a	49	.60	...	MerLyRet	61	.89	4572
DryWld	52	.60	887	FstAmTrObD	31	.76	4601	ING MM B	42	...	20	ML CMATr	62	.62	589
DryfGenTrPrA	21	.19	24	FstAmGvObA p	39	.66	167	IFT CashRes	43	.52	188	MerLyUSA	50	.57	136
DryInstGv	30	1.03	207	FstAmPrObA	45	.69	1566	InstDlyIncA	47	1.00	60	ML US Tr	58	.56	54
DryInstPrm1	27	1.06	502	FstAmPrObY	45	.99	5008	InstDlyIncB	47	1.27	298	MerLyPremInsti	52	1.30	42719
DryInstUST1	30	1.01	386	FstAmPrObD	45	.84	858	InstDlyTreaA	32	.87	195	MerLyRetII p	61	.69	159
DryUSTR	29	.78	75	FstAmTrObA p	31	.61	1138	InstDlyTreaB	32	1.12	528	MerrCshIns	58	1.00	25
EtradeMMPr	60	1.05	101	FstAmTrObY	31	.91	3721	InvGvtCshInst	45	1.21	92	MerriCashInv	58	.90	649
EV MM	25	...	86	FirstCshRsvl	51	1.17	31	InvGvtCshMgd	45	.99	234	MerrCshPrm	58	1.25	2917
EatVCsh	25	.58	92	FirstCshRsvC	51	.92	208	InvCshTrGv	45	1.17	177	MerrCshRes	58	1.15	44
EdwJones IS	41	.56	7693	FtInvCs	76	.71	171	InvGvtMF	28	.56	42	MerrTreasInv	34	.58	275
ElfunMM	51	1.16	331	First Muni I	26	.83	67	InvescoMMR	26	1.27	896	MerrTrsPlInv	1	.81	184
EnterpriseA p	50	.85	340	First USGv	57	1.16	125	InvCshTrTrs	27	1.08	9	MerrTrsPrm	34	.93	47
EnterpriseB p	50	.85	38	FlexInst	48	1.19	34	InvFLMuniCsh p	29	.13	23	MerrTrsPlPr	1	1.16	70
EquiTrust MM	34	.39	19	FlexFd	48	1.05	168	InvNJMuniCsh p	26	.10	30	MerrUSGvInv	63	.90	848
EtradeMM p	60	.42	1279	FrnkIFT	43	1.01	3683	IvyMnyA	55	.55	42	MerPrimPrm	39	1.26	542
EurekaPrimeA	15	.58	146	FrkMnyC	43	.16	82	IvyMnyA	61	.60	5	MidasDollarRs	47	.12	...
EurekaPrimeT	15	.83	42	FrkFdl bf	37	.52	112	JHanUS	39	.50	55	MilestnTOInst	22	1.18	783
EurekaTreaOblA	1	.59	76	FremntMM	63	.98	578	JPMUSGvInst	44	1.20	1897	MilestnTOInv	22	.93	290
EurekaUSTrOblT	1	.84	10	FrkMny	43	.73	1600	JPMorg100 Agcy	57	1.02	812	MonrcDACISS	26	.97	24
EvSelUSTrIS	49	.68	241	FstAmGvObZ	39	1.21	387	JPMorgan100	57	.68	2076	MonarDAGOB	15	1.03	20

avoid federal taxes on its income, shareholders are subject to taxes on the income they receive, regardless of whether it is in the form of interest payments or additional shares.

Hedge Funds

As explained earlier in this chapter, hedge funds sell shares to wealthy individuals and financial institutions (such as pension funds) and use the proceeds to invest in securities. They have historically been unregulated, although they are not allowed to advertise. Most hedge funds are organized as limited partnerships. Many hedge funds consider only individuals who have a net worth of $1 million or more. Some hedge funds allow investors to withdraw their investments, but require advance notice of 30 days or

more. There are at least 7,000 hedge funds, with a combined market value of about $1 trillion. The investment strategies used by hedge funds include investing in derivative securities, selling stocks short, and using borrowed funds along with equity investments by investors to magnify returns on investment. Consequently, hedge funds strive for high returns, but also have a very high degree of risk. The performance of hedge funds is not publicized. Although some hedge funds have performed well, many have failed.

Hedge Fund Fees

Hedge funds charge a management fee of between 1 and 2 percent of the investment per year. In addition, they charge an incentive fee that is based on the return of the fund. The typical incentive fee is 20 percent of the return.

ILLUSTRATION Consider a hedge fund that charges a management fee of 2 percent and an incentive fee of 20 percent of the annual return. In the most recent year, the fund earned a return of 15 percent. The investors in this fund would have paid an incentive fee of 3 percent (computed as 20 percent of the 15 percent return) along with a 2 percent management fee, or a total fee of 5 percent of their total investment. Considering that some index mutual funds have a very small management fee and no incentive fee, this hedge fund would have been a better investment only if its performance exceeded that of index funds by about 5 percent in that year.

Regulation

Hedge funds were not regulated until 2004, which allowed anyone who was capable of obtaining funds from investors to start one. In 2004, the Securities and Exchange Commission required that hedge funds register (starting in 2006). In fact, some individuals who have been charged with fraud when trading securities overseen by the SEC have become managers of hedge funds.

Financial Problems Experienced by Long-Term Capital Management

One of the best-known hedge funds was Long-Term Capital Management (LTCM), which was managed by a group of partners who had a very strong track record in the field of finance. In fact, two of its partners, Robert Merton and Myron Scholes (co-creator of the Black-Scholes pricing model for options), received the Nobel Prize in economics. LTCM was created in 1994 and earned relatively high returns in the mid-1990s, which caused more wealthy investors and financial institutions to invest in the fund.

LTCM relied heavily on quantitative models to identify pricing discrepancies in financial markets. For example, if the prices of two stocks that had historically moved together suddenly diverged, LTCM would consider purchasing the stock that had experienced the relatively weak price movement, while simultaneously selling short the stock that had experienced the relatively strong price movement. LTCM expected to benefit if the stock prices converged in the future. More commonly, LTCM applied this strategy to other securities by complementing an investment in one security with a short position in a derivatives contract representing the other security.

LTCM relied heavily on financial leverage to boost its returns. At times, it had about $30 in debt for every dollar of equity investment. By 1998, LTCM had about $5 billion in equity and $125 billion in debt to support its $130 billion portfolio, a ratio of $25 of debt for every dollar of equity. The overall leverage was actually higher than this because derivative positions magnify returns beyond the level of the underlying securities. From May to July of 1998, LTCM experienced losses of about 16 percent due to volatile market movements. In August 1998, Russia defaulted on some of its bonds, which aroused general concern about bond credit risk throughout the world. The prices of existing corporate bonds declined, as the risk premiums (reflected in the required rate of return of investors) on bonds increased. At the time, LTCM had investments in relatively risky bonds and short positions in AAA-rated bonds because it expected the spread between the yields to decline. The Russian bond default caused the risk premiums of the riskier bonds to increase much more than those of the AAA-rated bonds. Consequently, LTCM experienced a major loss. In August alone, it lost more than $2 billion or about 40 percent of its total capital; after accounting for the loss, its existing debt of $125 billion was about 50 times its remaining equity. On September 23, 1998, the Federal Reserve Bank of New York organized a rescue of LTCM by 14 large commercial banks and securities firms. These firms provided a capital infusion of $3.6 billion, which gave them a 90 percent stake in LTCM. The rescue plan was intended to prevent a default by LTCM on all of its positions, which could have caused the counterparties of those positions to lose billions of dollars. In addition, LTCM would have defaulted on some of its loans at a time when the debt markets had just recently been shaken by the Russian bond default; thus, a default by LTCM would have added to a potential international debt crisis. Asian countries were still suffering from the Asian crisis, and additional market paranoia would have resulted in more capital flows out of countries where funds were needed. Nevertheless, some critics suggest that LTCM was given preferential treatment because it was too big to fail.

As a result of the LTCM situation, regulators of several countries are considering ways to increase the regulation of hedge funds. For example, they may force commercial banks and other financial institutions that lend to hedge funds to retain a higher capital ratio on those loans.

Real Estate Investment Trusts (REITs)

A **real estate investment trust (REIT)** (pronounced "reet") is a closed-end mutual fund that invests in real estate or mortgages. Like other mutual funds, REITs allow small investors to participate with a low minimum investment. The funds are pooled to invest in mortgages and in commercial real estate. REITs generate income for shareholders by passing through rents on real estate or interest payments on mortgages. Most existing REITs can be sold on stock exchanges, which allows investors to sell them at any time. The composition of a REIT is determined by its portfolio manager, who is presumed to have expertise in real estate investments. In the early and mid-1970s, many of the mortgages held by REITs defaulted. Consequently, investors' interest in REITs declined. However, REITs have grown substantially since that time. Although the price of a REIT is somewhat influenced by its portfolio composition, it is basically determined by supply and demand. Even if the portfolio has performed well in the past, the REIT's share value may be low if investors are unwilling to invest in it.

REITs can be classified as **equity REITs,** which invest directly in properties, or **mortgage REITs,** which invest in mortgage and construction loans. A third type of REIT, called a hybrid, invests in both properties and mortgages.

Equity REITs are sometimes purchased to hedge against inflation, as rents tend to rise and property values rise with inflation. Their performance varies according to the perceived future value of the real estate held in each portfolio. REITs that have concentrated in potential high-growth properties are expected to generate a higher return than those with a more nationally diversified portfolio. However, they are also susceptible to more risk if the specific locations experience slow growth.

Because mortgage REITs essentially represent a fixed-income portfolio, their market value will be influenced by interest rate movements. As interest rates rise, the market value of mortgages declines, and therefore the demand for mortgage REITs declines. If interest rates are expected to decrease, mortgage REITs become more attractive.

Interaction with Other Financial Institutions

Mutual funds interact with various financial institutions, as described in Exhibit 23.10. They serve as an investment alternative for portfolio managers of financial institutions such as insurance companies and pension funds.

Some mutual funds are subsidiaries of commercial banks. At least 100 commercial banks such as Citigroup and Bank of America now offer mutual funds. This provides them with a means of retaining customer funds when customers wish to switch from bank deposits to stock or bond mutual funds. Since many customers periodically switch their savings between bank deposits and stocks (or bonds), commercial banks may be able to attract more funds in their mutual funds as they lose deposits, and vice versa. Their mutual funds also attract funds from investors who are not bank customers.

As interest rates declined in the 1990s and early 2000s, and investors withdrew deposits from commercial banks, they frequently invested the proceeds in mutual funds

EXHIBIT 23.10   Interaction between Mutual Funds and Other Financial Institutions

Type of Financial Institution	Interaction with Mutual Funds
Commercial banks and savings institutions (SIs)	• Money market mutual funds invest in certificates of deposit at banks and SIs and in commercial paper issued by bank holding companies. • Some commercial banks (such as Citigroup and J.P. Morgan Chase) have investment company subsidiaries that offer mutual funds. • Some stock and bond mutual funds invest in securities issued by banks and SIs.
Finance companies	• Some money market mutual funds invest in commercial paper issued by finance companies. • Some stock and bond mutual funds invest in stocks and bonds issued by finance companies.
Securities firms	• Mutual funds hire securities firms to execute security transactions for them. • Some mutual funds own a discount brokerage subsidiary that competes with other securities firms for brokerage services.
Insurance companies	• Some stock mutual funds invest in stocks issued by insurance companies. • Some insurance companies (such as Kemper) have investment company subsidiaries that offer mutual funds. • Some insurance companies invest in mutual funds.
Pension funds	• Pension fund portfolio managers invest in mutual funds.

EXHIBIT 23.11   How Mutual Funds Utilize Financial Markets

Type of Market	How Mutual Funds Use That Market
Money markets	• Money market mutual funds invest in various money market instruments, such as Treasury bills, commercial paper, banker's acceptances, and certificates of deposit.
Bond markets	• Some bond mutual funds invest mostly in bonds issued by the U.S. Treasury or a government agency. Others invest in bonds issued by municipalities or firms. • Foreign bonds are sometimes included in a bond mutual fund portfolio.
Mortgage markets	• Some bond mutual funds invest in bonds issued by the Government National Mortgage Association (GNMA, or "Ginnie Mae"), which uses the proceeds to purchase mortgages that were originated by some financial institutions.
Stock markets	• Numerous stock mutual funds include stocks with various degrees of risk and potential return.
Futures markets	• Some bond mutual funds periodically attempt to hedge against interest rate risk by taking positions in interest rate futures contracts.
Options markets	• Some stock mutual funds periodically hedge specific stocks by taking positions in stock options. • Some mutual funds take positions in stock options for speculative purposes.
Swap markets	• Some bond mutual funds engage in interest rate swaps to hedge interest rate risk.

sold by subsidiaries of the banks. Some of these subsidiaries are conveniently located on the first floor of the bank, near the area where customers withdraw deposits.

Use of Financial Markets

Each type of mutual fund uses a particular financial market, as described in Exhibit 23.11. Because the main function of mutual funds is to invest, all securities markets are commonly used. The futures and options markets are also utilized to hedge against interest rate risk or market risk. Some specialized mutual funds sponsored by Morgan Stanley, Merrill Lynch, and other securities firms take speculative positions in futures contracts.

Globalization through Mutual Funds

 GL BALASPECTS   International and global mutual funds have facilitated international capital flows and therefore have helped create a global securities market. They can reduce the excessive transaction costs that might be incurred by small investors who attempt to invest in foreign securities on their own. They also increase the degree of integration among stock markets. As international markets become more accessible, the volume of U.S. investment in foreign securities will become more sensitive to events and financial market conditions in those countries.

Mutual funds are popular not only in the United States but in other countries as well. The types of investment companies that sponsor mutual funds vary across countries. Insurance companies are the most common sponsor of mutual funds in the United Kingdom, while banks dominate in France, Germany, and Italy.

European countries have recently agreed to allow their respective mutual fund shares to be sold across their borders. The shares are under the supervision of their home country but are subject to marketing rules of the countries where they are being

marketed. This deregulatory step in Europe may provide the momentum for other countries to do the same.

As a result of the North American Free Trade Agreement (NAFTA), qualified companies are allowed to sell mutual fund shares in Mexico. Consequently, many U.S. companies that commonly sponsor mutual funds, such as securities firms, commercial banks, and insurance companies, are generating new business in Mexico.

SUMMARY

- Mutual funds can be characterized as open-end funds (which are willing to repurchase their shares upon demand) or as closed-end funds (which do not repurchase the shares they sell). Mutual funds can also be characterized as load funds (which impose a sales charge) versus no-load funds (which do not impose a sales charge).

- The more common types of mutual funds include capital appreciation funds, growth and income funds, income funds, tax-free funds, high-yield funds, international funds, global funds, asset allocation funds, and specialty funds.

- Money market funds invest in short-term securities, such as commercial paper, repurchase agreements, CDs, and Treasury bills. The expected returns on MMFs are relatively low, but the risk levels are also low.

POINT COUNTER-POINT

Should Mutual Funds Be Subject to More Regulation?

Point No. Mutual funds can be monitored by their shareholders (just like many firms), and the shareholders can enforce governance.

Counter-Point Yes. Mutual funds need to be governed by regulators, because they are accountable for such a large amount of money. Without regulation, there could be massive withdrawals from mutual funds when unethical behavior by managers of mutual funds is publicized.

Who Is Correct? Use your favorite search engine to learn more about this issue. Offer your own opinion on this issue.

QUESTIONS AND APPLICATIONS

1. **Risk of Money Market Funds** Explain the relative risk of the various types of securities in which a money market fund may invest.

2. **Load versus No-Load Mutual Funds** Explain the difference between load and no-load mutual funds.

3. **Tax Effects on Mutual Funds** Explain how the income generated by a mutual fund is taxed when it distributes at least 90 percent of its taxable income to shareholders.

4. **Tax Effects on Money Market Funds** Explain how the income generated by a money market fund is taxed if it distributes at least 90 percent of its income to shareholders.

5. **Exposure to Exchange Rate Movements** Explain how changing foreign currency values can affect the performance of international mutual funds.

6. **Managing in Financial Markets: Investing in Mutual Funds** As an individual investor, you are attempting

to invest in a well-diversified portfolio of mutual funds so that you will be somewhat insulated from any type of economic shock that may occur.

a. An investment adviser recommends that you buy four different U.S. growth stock funds. Since these funds contain over 400 different U.S. stocks, the adviser says that you will be well insulated from any economic shocks. Do you agree? Explain.

b. A second investment adviser recommends that you invest in four different mutual funds that are focused on different countries in Europe. The adviser says that you will be completely insulated from U.S. economic conditions and that your portfolio will therefore have low risk. Do you agree? Explain.

c. A third investment adviser recommends that you avoid exposure to the stock markets by investing your money in four different U.S. bond funds. The adviser says that because bonds make fixed payments, these bond funds have very low risk. Do you agree? Explain.

7. **Mutual Fund Services** Explain why mutual funds are attractive to small investors. How can mutual funds generate returns to their shareholders?

8. **Interpreting Financial News** Interpret the following comments made by Wall Street analysts and portfolio managers:

a. "Just because a mutual fund earned a 20 percent return in one year, that does not mean that investors should rush into it. The fund's performance must be market adjusted."

b. "An international mutual fund's performance is subject to conditions beyond the fund manager's control."

c. "Small mutual funds will need to merge to compete with the major players in terms of efficiency."

9. **REITs** Explain the difference between equity REITs and mortgage REITs. Which type would likely be a better hedge against high inflation? Why?

10. **Fund Selection** Describe the ideal mutual fund for investors who wish to generate tax-free income and also maintain a low degree of interest rate risk.

11. **Internet Exercise** Assess today's mutual fund performance, using the website http://www.bloomberg.com/markets/. Click on "Funds."

a. What is the best-performing mutual fund today in terms of the yield-to-date (YTD)? What is the net asset value (NAV) of this fund, and what is its YTD? Now find the top 25 mutual funds in terms of five-year returns by clicking on the "5 YR" button. What is the best-performing fund in the United States today based on its most recent five-year performance? What is the five-year return on this fund, and what is its YTD this year? Do you think mutual fund rankings change frequently? Why or why not?

12. **Risk of Treasury Bond Funds** Support or refute the following statement: Investors can avoid all types of risk by purchasing a mutual fund that contains only Treasury bonds.

13. **Components of Mutual Funds** Considering all stock and bond mutual funds in aggregate, what type of security is dominant?

14. **Open- versus Closed-End Funds** How do open-end mutual funds differ from closed-end mutual funds?

15. **Performance** According to research, have mutual funds outperformed the market? Explain. Would mutual funds be attractive to some investors even if they are not expected to outperform the market? Explain.

16. **Use of Funds** Like mutual funds, commercial banks and stock-owned savings institutions sell shares; yet, proceeds received by mutual funds are used in a different way. Explain.

17. **Diversification among Mutual Funds** Explain why diversification across different types of mutual funds is highly recommended.

18. **Money Market Funds** How do money market funds differ from other types of mutual funds in terms of how they use the money invested by shareholders? Which security do money market funds invest in most often? How can a money market fund accommodate shareholders who wish to sell their shares when the amount of proceeds received from selling new shares is less than the amount needed?

19. **Risk of Mutual Funds** Is the value of a money market fund or a bond fund more susceptible to increasing interest rates? Explain.

FLOW OF FUNDS EXERCISE

How Mutual Funds Facilitate the Flow of Funds

Carson Company is considering a private placement of bonds with Venus Mutual Fund.

a. Explain the interaction between Carson and Venus. How would Venus serve Carson's needs, and how would Carson serve the needs of Venus?

b. Why does Carson interact with Venus Mutual Fund instead of trying to obtain the funds directly from individuals who invested in Venus Mutual Fund?

c. Would Venus Mutual Fund serve as a better monitor of Carson Company than the individuals who provided money to the mutual fund? Explain.

 EXERCISE

Performance of Mutual Funds

Using an issue of *The Wall Street Journal*, summarize an article that discussed the recent performance of a specific mutual fund. Has this mutual fund's perfor- mance been better or worse than the norm? What reason is given for the particular level of performance?

CHAPTER 24

Securities Operations

Securities firms serve as important intermediaries by helping governments and firms raise funds. They also facilitate the transactions involving debt and equity securities that are desired by investors. Some securities firms are independent, while others are units of a financial conglomerate. Securities firms offer a variety of services, most of which can be classified as investment banking or brokerage.

The specific objectives of this chapter are to:

■ describe the key functions of investment banking,

■ describe the key functions of the brokerage business,

■ explain the exposure of securities to risk, and

■ identify the factors that affect the valuation of securities firms.

Investment Banking Services

http://

http://finance.yahoo.com
Search engine for
information about any
publicly traded stocks
in the United States.

One of the main functions of investment banking firms (IBFs) is raising capital for corporations. These firms originate, structure, and place securities in the capital markets to raise funds for corporations. Their role is primarily as an intermediary rather than as a lender or investor. Therefore, their compensation for raising funds is typically in the form of fees.

How IBFs Facilitate New Stock Offerings

An IBF acts as an intermediary between a corporation issuing securities and investors by providing the following services:

■ Origination
■ Underwriting
■ Distribution
■ Advising

Origination When a corporation decides to publicly issue additional stock, it may contact an IBF. The IBF can recommend the appropriate amount of stock to issue, because it can anticipate the amount of stock the market can likely absorb without causing a reduction in the stock price.

Next, the IBF will evaluate the corporation's financial condition to determine the appropriate price for the newly issued stock. If the firm has issued stock to the public

before, the price should be the same as the market price on its outstanding stock. If not, the firm's financial characteristics will be compared with other similar firms in the same industry that have stock outstanding to help determine the price at which the stock should be sold.

The issuing corporation then registers with the Securities and Exchange Commission (SEC). All information relevant to the security, as well as the agreement between the issuer and the IBF, must be provided in the **registration statement,** which is intended to ensure that accurate information is disclosed by the issuing corporation. Some publicly placed securities do not require registration if the issue is very small or sold entirely within a particular state. SEC approval does not guarantee the quality or safety of the securities to be issued; it simply acknowledges that a firm is disclosing accurate information about itself. Included in the required registration information is the **prospectus,** which discloses relevant financial data on the firm and provisions applicable to the security. The prospectus can be issued only after the registration is approved, which typically takes 20 to 40 days.

The IBF along with the issuing firm may meet with institutional investors who may be interested in the offering. They engage in a road show in which they travel to various cities where they meet with institutional investors to discuss the plans for using the funds that will be obtained from the offering.

http://www.sec.gov/edgar.shtml Identifies upcoming IPOs and the securities firms that are involved in the underwriting process.

Underwriting The original IBF may form an **underwriting syndicate** by asking other IBFs to underwrite a portion of the stock. Each participating IBF shares in the underwriting fees charged to the issuer. The original IBF hopes that the other IBFs invited into the syndicate will someday return the favor when they are the original underwriters and need participation from other IBFs. A syndicate may include just a few IBFs for a relatively small stock issue or include as many as 50 or more for a large issue. Some of the more well-known IBFs for underwriting include Merrill Lynch, Goldman Sachs, Morgan Stanley, and Salomon Smith Barney (a division of Citigroup).

The term *underwrite* is sometimes wrongly interpreted to mean that the underwriting syndicate guarantees the price at which shares will be sold. However, stock offerings are normally based on a **best-efforts agreement,** whereby the IBF does not guarantee a price to the issuing corporation. In such a case, the issuing corporation bears the risk because it does not receive a guaranteed price from the IBF on the stock to be issued.

When IBFs facilitate initial public offerings (IPOs), they attempt to price the stock high enough to satisfy the issuing firm. The higher the average price at which the shares are issued, the greater the proceeds received by the issuing firm. If the IBFs price the stock too high, however, they will not be able to place the entire issue. The reputation of the underwriting syndicate is at stake when it attempts to place the stock of the issuing firm. It knows that other corporations that may issue stock in the future will monitor its ability to place the stock.

IBFs must also attempt to satisfy the institutional investors that may invest in the IPO. The higher the price institutional investors pay for the stock being issued, the lower the return they earn on their investment when they sell the stock. Underwriting syndicates recognize that other institutional investors monitor stock prices after offerings to determine whether the initial offer price charged by the syndicate was appropriate. If the institutional investors do not earn reasonable returns on their investment, they may not invest in future IPOs. Since IBFs rely on institutional investors when placing shares of newly issued stock, they want to maintain a good relationship with them.

Research documents that IBFs tend to underprice IPOs. That is, institutional investors that invest at the offer price earn high returns on average if they retain the investment for a short-term period, such as three months or less. Much of the return oc-

curs within the first few days after the IPO. Consequently, the returns to investors who purchase the shares shortly after the IPO are generally poor.

Distribution of Stock Once all agreements between the issuing firm, the originating IBF, and other participating IBFs are complete and the registration is approved by the SEC, the stock may be sold. The prospectus is distributed to all potential purchasers of the stock, and the issue is advertised to the public. In some cases, the issue sells within hours. If the issue does not sell as expected, the underwriting syndicate will likely have to reduce the price to complete the sale. The demand for the stock is somewhat influenced by the sales force involved in selling the stock. Some IBFs participating in a syndicate have brokerage subsidiaries that can sell stock on a retail level. Others may specialize in underwriting but still utilize a group of brokerage firms to sell the newly issued stock. The brokers earn a commission on the amount they sell but do not guarantee a specific amount of sales.

When a corporation publicly places stock, it incurs two types of **flotation costs,** or costs of placing the securities. First, there are fees paid to the underwriters who place the stock with investors. Second, **issue costs** from issuing stock include printing, legal, registration, and accounting expenses. Because these issue costs are not significantly affected by the size of the issue, flotation costs as a percentage of the value of securities issued are lower for larger issues.

Advising The IBF acts as an adviser throughout the origination stage. Even after the stock is issued, the IBF may continue to provide advice on the timing, amount, and terms of future financing. Included with this advice would be recommendations on the appropriate type of financing (bonds, stocks, or long-term commercial loans).

Private Placements of Stocks IBFs are also hired to facilitate private placements of stock. With a **private placement** (or direct placement), an entire stock offering may be placed with a small set of institutional investors and not offered to the general public. Under the SEC's Rule 144A, firms may engage in private placements of stock without filing the extensive registration statement that is required for public placements. Consequently, the issuing firm's costs of reporting are lower than with a public placement. In addition, the underwriting services are more manageable because an underwriting syndicate may not be necessary.

Institutional investors that are willing to hold the stock for a long period of time are prime candidates for participating in a private placement. Since all the stock is held by a small set of institutional investors, there will not be an established secondary market for the stock. Thus, the institutional investors may expect a higher return on the stock to compensate for the lack of liquidity.

How IBFs Facilitate New Bond Offerings

An IBF's role in placing bonds is somewhat similar to its role in placing stock. The four main services of an IBF in placing bonds are explained in turn.

Origination The IBF may suggest a maximum amount of bonds that should be issued, based on the issuer's characteristics. If the issuer already has a high level of outstanding debt, the bonds may not be well received by the market, because the issuer's ability to meet the debt payments will be questionable. Consequently, the bonds will need to offer a relatively high yield, which will increase the cost of borrowing to the issuer.

Next, the coupon rate, the maturity, and other provisions are decided, based on the characteristics of the issuing firm. The asking price on the bonds is determined by evaluating market prices of existing bonds that are similar in their degree of risk, term to maturity, and other provisions.

Issuers of bonds must register with the SEC. The registration statement contains information about the bonds to be issued, states the agreement between the IBF and the issuer, and also includes a prospectus with financial information about the issuer.

Underwriting Bonds Some issuers of bonds, particularly public utilities, may solicit competitive bids on the price of bonds from various IBFs so that they can select the IBF with the highest bid. IBFs provide several services to the issuer, however, so price is not the only consideration. Corporations typically select an IBF based on reputation rather than competitive bids.

Underwriting spreads on newly issued bonds are normally lower than on newly issued stock, because bonds can often be placed in large blocks to financial institutions. Conversely, a stock issue must be segmented into smaller pieces and is more difficult to sell.

As with stocks, the IBF may organize an underwriting syndicate of IBFs to participate in placing the bonds. Each IBF assumes a portion of the risk. Of course, the potential income earned by the original IBF is reduced, too. If the IBF is uncomfortable guaranteeing a price to the issuer, it may offer only a best-efforts agreement.

Distribution of Bonds Upon SEC approval of registration, a prospectus is distributed to all potential purchasers of the bonds, and the issue is advertised to the public. The asking price on the bonds is normally set at a level that will ensure a sale of the entire issue. The flotation costs generally range from 0.5 percent to 3 percent of the value of the bonds issued, which can be significantly lower than the flotation costs of issuing common or preferred stock.

Advising As with a stock placement, an IBF that places bonds for issuers may serve as an adviser to the issuer even after the placement is completed. Most issuers of bonds will need to raise long-term funds in the future and will consider the IBF's advice on the type of securities to issue at that time.

Private Placements of Bonds If an issuing corporation knows of a potential purchaser for its entire issue, it may be able to sell its securities directly without offering the bonds to the general public (or using the underwriting services of an IBF). This private placement avoids the underwriting fee. Corporations have been increasingly using private placements. Potential purchasers of securities that are large enough to buy an entire issue include insurance companies, commercial banks, pension funds, and mutual funds. Securities can even be privately placed with two or more of these institutions. Private placements of bonds are more common than private placements of stocks.

The price paid for privately placed securities is determined by negotiations between the issuing corporation and the purchaser. Although the IBF is not needed here for underwriting, it may advise the issuing corporation on the appropriate terms of the securities and identify potential purchasers.

Unlike the standardized provisions of a publicly placed issue, the provisions of a privately placed issue can be tailored to the desires of the purchaser. A possible disadvantage of a private placement is that the demand may not be as strong as for a publicly placed issue, because only a fraction of the market is targeted. This could force a lower price for the bonds, resulting in a higher cost of financing for the issuing firm.

How IBFs Facilitate Leveraged Buyouts

Investment banking firms facilitate leveraged buyouts (LBOs) in three ways. First, they assess the market value of the firm (or division) of concern so that the participants planning to purchase the firm do not pay more than the firm's value. Second, they arrange financing, which involves raising funds and purchasing any common stock outstanding that is held by the public. Finally, they may be retained in an advisory capacity.

A client may not be able to afford an LBO because of constraints on the amount of funds it can borrow. The IBF may therefore consider purchasing a portion of the firm's assets, thereby providing the client with some financial support. It will either try to sell these assets immediately or hold them for some time. In the latter case, the IBF may finance the purchase by issuing bonds. Its return on this deal is based on the difference between the net cash inflows generated by the assets and the cash outflows resulting from the bond issue. Some IBFs have generated substantial returns on such deals by selling the assets later at a much higher price than the purchase price. Nevertheless, such transactions may pose a significant risk to an IBF. First, there is no guarantee that the assets will sell at a premium. Second, an IBF's financing with bonds normally occurs with a lag. The IBF initially borrows short term until the bonds are issued. If interest rates rise prior to the issue date, the cost of long-term financing may be much higher than the IBF had anticipated. If the IBF engages in more LBO financing activity, its holdings of other assets will increase, and its overall performance will be more susceptible to economic downturns. However, the potential fee income and returns on asset holdings may more than offset this risk.

Merrill Lynch has designed a mutual fund that finances LBOs. Investments in the mutual fund are used mostly to purchase junk bonds of firms that went private. In addition to purchasing junk bonds, the mutual fund provides **bridge loans** that offer firms temporary financing until junk bonds can be issued. The fund also invests in the equity of some firms.

How IBFs Facilitate Arbitrage

Some IBFs also facilitate **arbitrage activity,** which in the securities industry involves purchasing undervalued shares and reselling them at a higher price. The IBFs work closely with **arbitrage firms** (which specialize in arbitrage) by searching for undervalued firms and raising funds for the arbitrage firms. It is sometimes difficult to distinguish between arbitrage and an LBO because both activities involve an attempt to purchase an undervalued firm, mostly with borrowed funds. LBOs, however, are commonly executed by management or other employees, who may plan to maintain ownership of the firm. Sometimes arbitrage activity is referred to as a hostile LBO.

In a common form of arbitrage, a firm is acquired, and then its individual divisions are sold off. This **asset stripping,** as it is called, is motivated by the perception that the sum of the parts is sometimes greater than the whole.

IBFs generate fee income from advising arbitrage firms and also receive a commission on the bonds issued to support the arbitrage activity. They also receive fees from divestitures of divisions. When the fund raising is not expected to be complete before the acquisition is initiated, IBFs provide bridge loans. Because the acquisitions are largely financed with borrowed funds, arbitrage firms essentially pay off their debts with the target's cash flow.

When hostile (uninvited) takeovers became popular, some IBFs offered advice on takeover defense maneuvers. Sometimes these IBFs found themselves simultaneously

financing some hostile takeovers, while advising other firms on how to defend against hostile takeovers. Some arbitrage firms take positions in targets, just to benefit from the expected takeover by another group.

Some attempts at arbitrage fail because target firms are successful at defending against a takeover. However, such defenses are usually expensive. One common defense is for the target firm to buy back the shares held by the arbitrage firm. The arbitrage firm may only be willing to sell the shares back at a premium, however, so to repurchase the shares, the target may require massive financing, which can even lower its credit rating.

History of Arbitrage Activity Sometimes arbitrage firms have accumulated shares of targets with the expectation that the targets would be willing to buy their shares back at a premium. With this tactic, known as **greenmail,** the arbitrage firms did not anticipate completing the takeover but still profited from the difference between their selling and buying prices on the shares. Some IBFs helped to finance greenmail. The final result of greenmail is that the target is not acquired but incurs a large expense of buying back the stock held by the arbitrage firm. Thus, even though the target has been singled out as being undervalued (possibly as a result of inefficient management), it is still run by the same management.

Arbitrage activity has been criticized because it often results in excessive financial leverage and risk for corporations. In addition, the restructuring of divisions after acquisitions results in corporate layoffs. Because some IBFs facilitate arbitrage activity, they are criticized as well. Yet, arbitrage helps remove managerial inefficiencies. If a firm is not efficiently managed, it should become a target so that an acquirer can restructure the firm and enable it to reach its full potential. In addition, shareholders of a target firm can benefit from arbitrage activity because the share price generally rises as the arbitrage firm purchases shares.

How IBFs Facilitate Corporate Restructuring

Another critical function of IBFs is providing advice on corporate restructuring. A key component of the advisory function is the valuation of a business. IBFs assess the potential value of target firms so that they can advise corporations on whether to merge and on the appropriate price to offer. The valuation process is also used for advising on potential divestitures and on LBOs. IBFs not only assist with valuations but also help firms with the process of implementing a merger, acquisition, or divestiture.

Advising on Corporate Restructuring Many IBFs have expertise at assessing how corporate restructuring could change the valuation of a business. They assess potential synergies that might result from combining two businesses. In some cases, they view the sum of the two parts as being worth less than the whole. Thus, the combination of two businesses may be worth more than the sum of the values of the businesses if they remain separate. Consequently, one of the businesses may be able to realize benefits from the acquisition of the other, even after considering the premium above the target's market value that it will likely have to pay.

In some situations, IBFs may suggest that the sum of the parts of a particular business will be worth more than the whole if their ownership is separated. In this case, the IBF may suggest that the firm engage in a carve-out and sell one of its units to new shareholders through an IPO. The proceeds of the IPO go to the parent firm. The parent benefits if the funds raised exceed the present value of the future cash flows that the unit would generate if it was retained. Although estimating the future cash flows of a unit can be difficult, IBFs normally have experience in such valuations.

Alternatively, an IBF may advise the firm to spin off a unit by creating new shares representing the unit and distributing them to existing shareholders. Consequently, the firm's old shares no longer represent ownership of the unit, so their price will decline. Together, however, the sum of the values of both the old and the new shares may exceed the value of the firm's shares before the spin-off. The separation of a subsidiary from its parent may also reduce asymmetric information problems between managers and investors. Because the unit is now valued separately, monitoring its performance is easier than it was when the unit was just one component of a firm with many different businesses. In addition, now that the unit has a market value, its managers can be compensated with stocks or stock options to align their compensation directly with the unit's value.

Financing Mergers and Acquisitions Many mergers and acquisitions require outside financing, and IBFs that are able to raise large amounts of funds in the capital markets are more likely to be chosen as advisers for mergers and acquisitions. In recent years, IBFs have loaned their own funds to companies involved in a merger or acquisition. In some cases, they have even provided equity financing, whereby they become part owner of the acquired firms.

Exhibit 24.1 illustrates how IBFs participate in an acquisition. Note how many different functions the IBFs may perform for the acquiring firms, all of which generate fees or interest. The IBFs can help finance an acquisition by (1) providing loans to the

EXHIBIT 24.1 Participation of Investment Banking Firms in an Acquisition

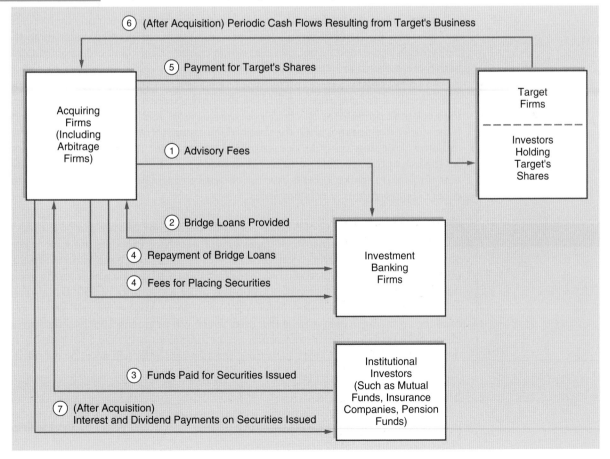

acquirer, (2) underwriting bonds or stock for the acquirer, and (3) investing their own equity in the acquirer's purchase of the target.

Brokerage Services

http://

http://www.ml.com
Information on securities firm performance.

Customer requests for brokerage firms to execute securities transactions can usually be classified as one of the following:

- Market orders
- Limit orders
- Short selling

Market Orders

Requests by customers to purchase or sell securities at the market price existing when the order reaches the exchange floor are called **market orders.** In most cases, the actual transaction will occur within a few minutes from the time of the customer's request, assuming that the request is made while the markets are open.

Limit Orders

Requests by customers to purchase or sell securities at a specified price or better are called **limit orders.** An exchange's specialists are responsible for monitoring limit orders and executing the transactions in accordance with the limits specified. Some limit orders are canceled if they are not executed within one day. Other limit orders remain until they are executed or canceled by the customer.

A **stop-loss order** is a more specific type of limit order. With a stop-loss order, the investor specifies a selling price that is below the current market price of the stock. When the stock price drops to the specified level, the stop-loss order becomes a market order. If the stock price does not reach the specified minimum, the stop-loss order will not be executed. If the stop-loss order does become a market order, then the investor may not get the exact price specified in the stop-loss order, since the stock price may fluctuate until the time the market order is executed. Investors generally place stop-loss orders to either (1) protect gains or (2) limit losses.

ILLUSTRATION Paul bought 100 shares of Bostner Corporation stock one year ago at a price of $50 per share. Today, Bostner stock trades for $60 per share. Paul does not want to liquidate his position, however, because he believes Bostner stock has additional upside potential. Nonetheless, Paul would like to realize at least a 10 percent gain from the stock transaction. Consequently, he places a stop-loss order with a price of $55. If the stock price drops to $55, the stop-loss order will convert to a market order, and he will receive the prevailing market price at that time, which will be around $55. If Paul receives exactly $55, his gain from the transaction will be 100 shares × ($55 − $50) = $500. If the price of Bostner stock keeps increasing, the stop-loss order will never be executed.

Short Selling

Investors can speculate on expectations of a decline in securities prices by **short selling,** or selling securities that they do not own.

ILLUSTRATION   Jason, an investor, anticipates that the price of IBM stock will decline, so he requests a short sale of IBM stock from a broker. The broker borrows the stock from an inventory of stocks held on margin (from other accounts) and sells it for Jason. He is required to deposit funds that reflect the market value of the stock. At some point in the future, Jason will request a purchase of the stock and repay the broker for the stock borrowed. If the stock price has declined by the time Jason requests the purchase, the short-sale strategy will generate a positive return.

Short-sellers are required to reimburse the owners of the stock for any missed dividends.

Another specific type of order often used in short sales is the **stop-buy order.** With a stop-buy order, the investor specifies a purchase price that is above the current market price. When the stock price rises to the specified level, the stop-buy order becomes a market order. If the stock price does not reach the specified maximum, the stop-buy order will not be executed. In a sense, a stop-buy order is very similar to a stop-loss order, except that it is used to protect gains (or limit losses) resulting from a short sale.

ILLUSTRATION   A year ago, Mary sold short 200 shares of Patronum Corporation stock for $70 per share. Patronum's stock currently trades for $80 a share. Consequently, Mary currently has an unrealized loss on the short sale, but she still believes that Patronum stock will drop below $70 in the near future. Nonetheless, Mary is unwilling to accept a loss of more than $15 per share on the transaction. Consequently, she places a stop-buy order with a specified purchase price of $85 per share. If Patronum stock increases to $85 per share, the stop-buy order will become a market order, and Mary will pay approximately $85 per share. This purchase will cover her short position. In that case, Mary's loss from the short sale will be 200 shares $\times$ ($70 − $85) = −$3,000. If Patronum stock does not increase to $85 per share, the stop-buy order will never be executed.

Full-Service versus Discount Brokerage Services

Brokerage firms can be classified by the services they provide. **Full-service brokerage firms** provide information and personalized advice and execute orders. Conversely, **discount brokerage firms** only execute orders upon request and do not provide advice. They are often unable to maintain a long-term relationship with clients, because they provide a service difficult to differentiate from competitors. Their required minimum opening balance is typically in the range of $1,000 to $3,000. Most discount brokers offer some degree of research on stocks on a website exclusively for their clients.

Although discount brokers still concentrate on executing stock transactions, they have expanded their services to include precious metals, options, and municipal bonds. Some also offer credit cards, cash management accounts, 24-hour phone service, and research reports. Many discount brokerage firms are owned by large commercial banks, which were historically prohibited from offering full-service brokerage services.

Online Orders

Many investors now place orders online rather than calling brokers. Brokerage firms have reduced their costs by implementing online order systems because the online format is less expensive than having brokers receive the orders by phone. Online trading has become very competitive, however, with numerous brokerage firms fighting for market share. Consequently, the prices charged for online orders are very low. The fee

for an online order to trade 100 shares of stock is typically $25 or less for investors who have an established account with the brokerage firm.

Income Sources

Since securities firms provide a wide variety of services (as described earlier in this chapter), their income comes from many sources. The main income sources for a securities firm are identified in Exhibit 24.2 and categorized under investment banking services, brokerage services, or investing its own funds.

Each source of income shown is broadly defined and covers a variety of functions. For example, the management fees for managing an investor's account may be for managing an individual's account or a firm's pension fund. In addition, some securities firms manage mutual funds and receive annual management fees from managing the fund's securities portfolio. The trading commissions may come from trades of stocks, bonds, and various derivative securities. The profits generated from investing its own funds come from many sources. The firm can invest its own funds in shares and may also receive an allotment of shares when it serves as the underwriter of an IPO. It may establish a division that focuses on speculating on futures or options.

Income Allocation among Securities Firms

The proportion of income derived from each source in any particular year varies among securities firms. When IPOs are hot, some securities firms that offer investment banking generate significant income from underwriting fees. When there is more acquisition activity, securities firms that offer advisory services for corporate restructuring generate

EXHIBIT 24.2

Sources of Income for a Securities Firm

Investment Banking Services	
Underwriting	Fees from underwriting stock offerings by firms or underwriting bond offerings by firms and government agencies
Advising	Fees for providing advice to firms about: • Identifying potential targets • Valuing targets • Identifying potential acquirers • Protecting against takeovers
Restructuring	Fees for facilitating: • Mergers • Divestitures • Carve-outs • Spin-offs
Brokerage Services	
Management fees	Fees for managing an individual's or a firm's securities portfolio
Trading commissions	Fees for executing securities trades requested by individuals or firms in the secondary market
Margin interest	Interest charged to investors who buy securities on margin
Investing Its Own Funds	
Investing	Profits from investing in securities

much of their income from advisory fees. When market conditions are favorable, the trading volume tends to increase, and securities firms will generate more income from trading commissions.

Some securities firms such as Goldman Sachs and Salomon Smith Barney emphasize investment banking and therefore generate a higher proportion of income from underwriting and advising fees. Conversely, Charles Schwab emphasizes brokerage and therefore generates a higher proportion of income from trading commissions.

Many securities firms attempt to diversify their services so that they can capitalize on economies of scale and also so that they can reduce their exposure if the demand for any particular service is weak. However, the demand is highly correlated across services. When market conditions are weak, the volume of IPOs, secondary market trades, and acquisitions is usually low. Thus, securities firms will likely perform poorly under these conditions.

Impact of the September 11 Crisis on Revenue Sources   The attack on the United States on September 11, 2001, had a major impact on the main revenue sources of securities firms. First, trading profits declined because stock prices declined abruptly. Second, the attack led to more uncertainty about economic prospects for an economy that was already weak. Consequently, some firms that were planning to go public withdrew their plans. In addition, some publicly traded firms that had planned a secondary offering canceled their plans. The decline in stock offerings reduced the underwriting business of securities firms. Third, the volume of acquisitions declined, as many firms did not want to make large acquisitions in an environment filled with so much uncertainty. The decline in acquisitions led to a decline in the advising fees earned by securities firms.

Securities Firm Regulation

Securities firms are subject to a wide variety of regulation. The SEC plays a key role in regulation by enforcing financial disclosure laws that attempt to ensure that investors who buy or sell securities have access to financial information. These laws give the SEC the power to require publicly traded companies to provide sufficient financial information to existing or prospective investors.

Stock exchanges and the Nasdaq market are expected to prevent unfair or illegal practices, ensure orderly trading, and address customer complaints. Stock exchanges have regulatory divisions, while the Nasdaq market is regulated by the National Association of Securities Dealers (NASD). Both the exchanges and the NASD have surveillance departments that monitor trading patterns and behavior by specialists, market-makers, and floor traders. They also have enforcement divisions that investigate possible violations and can take disciplinary actions. They can take legal actions as well and sometimes work with the SEC to correct cases of market trading abuse. While the SEC tends to establish general guidelines that can affect trading on security exchanges, the day-to-day regulation of exchange trading is the responsibility of the exchange.

Regulation of trading behavior is necessary to ensure that investors who place orders are properly accommodated. This can establish credibility within the systems used to execute securities transactions. However, the exchanges have been criticized for primarily reacting to abuses only after they been publicized by the media. Consequently, some investors question whether their trades are properly accommodated.

In addition to the SEC, NASD, and exchanges, the Federal Reserve Board has some regulatory influence because it determines the credit limits (margin requirements) on

securities purchased. The Securities Investor Protection Corporation (SIPC) offers insurance on cash and securities deposited at brokerage firms and can liquidate failing brokerage firms. The insurance limit is $500,000, including $100,000 against claims on cash. All brokers that are registered with the SEC are assessed premiums by the SIPC, which are used to maintain its insurance fund. In addition to its insurance fund, the SIPC has a $500 million revolving line of credit with a group of banks and can borrow up to $1 billion from the SEC. Because the SIPC boosts investor confidence in the securities industry, economic efficiency is increased, and market concerns are less likely to cause a run on deposits of cash and securities at securities firms.

Several regulatory events that were mentioned in previous chapters had a direct or indirect effect on securities firms. Here is a summary of recent regulatory events that are related to securities firms.

Financial Services Modernization Act

In the 1990s, financial institutions focusing on different types of financial services found numerous loopholes in regulations. To clarify the situation, Congress enacted the Financial Services Modernization Act of 1999, which allowed banking, securities activities, and insurance to be consolidated. As a result, financial institutions no longer need to search for loopholes. Specifically, the act provides for a special holding company structure that enables a financial holding company to own subsidiaries that focus on various financial services. Firms that adopt this structure are regulated by the Federal Reserve. Capital requirements for the bank subsidiaries are imposed by bank regulators. Capital requirements for the insurance subsidiaries are subject to state insurance regulators. Many securities firms that had already expanded into other financial services through loopholes have not created financial holding companies, however, because they do not want to be subject to regulation by the Federal Reserve.

The Financial Services Modernization Act resulted in the creation of more financial conglomerates that include securities firms. One of the key benefits to securities firms in a financial conglomerate is cross-listing. When individuals use brokerage services of a securities firm, that firm may steer them to do their banking with the affiliated commercial bank or to obtain a mortgage with the affiliated savings institution. When firms use investment banking services of a securities firm, that firm may steer them to do their banking with the affiliated commercial bank. The other types of financial institutions that form the conglomerate can reciprocate by steering their customers toward the securities firm. Thus, the bundling of financial services can generate more business for each type of financial institution that is part of the financial conglomerate. However, just as a financial conglomerate can increase market share by pulling business away from other financial institutions, it may lose market share when other financial conglomerates use their bundling of financial services to attract customers.

Regulation FD

Recall that in October 2000, the SEC enacted Regulation Fair Disclosure (FD), which requires that firms disclose any significant information simultaneously to all market participants. This rule was partially intended to prevent firms from leaking information to analysts. Before Regulation FD, sometimes a firm's chief financial officer would leak information to an analyst about the firm's earnings or other relevant financial details. Some

analysts capitalized on the information by disclosing it to their key clients. These analysts also implicitly rewarded the firm that provided the inside information by assigning a high rating to its stock. Small investors were left out of the loop and were at a competitive disadvantage.

As a result of Regulation FD, firms more frequently provide their information in the form of news releases or conference calls rather than leaking it to a few analysts. Thus, analysts no longer have inside information, as all market participants receive the information at the same time. To the extent that Regulation FD has limited leaks to analysts, it may have limited their performance and credibility. Since analysts are commonly employees of securities firms, the securities firms have been affected as well. Those analysts who relied on inside information when providing their insight to clients have lost their competitive advantage, while analysts who relied on their own analysis rather than information leaks have gained a competitive edge.

Rules Regarding Analyst Compensation and Ratings

In the 2001–2002 period, the process by which analysts rated stocks was widely criticized. Firms recognize that the demand for their stock may be partially dictated by the rating assigned by an analyst. When they need underwriting or advisory services from a securities firm, they are more likely to hire a securities firm whose analysts rate their stock highly. Security firms also recognize that they are more likely to attract business from a firm if they give its stock a high rating, regardless of their real opinion of the stock. In fact, some analysts were spending much of their time generating new business, and their compensation was sometimes aligned with the business they brought to the securities firm. Consequently, analysts were tempted to inflate the ratings they assigned to stocks, and the investors who relied on the ratings to make investment decisions were misled.

In 2002, in an attempt to prevent the obvious conflict of interest, the SEC implemented new rules, as summarized here.

- If a securities firm underwrites an IPO, its analysts cannot promote the stock for the first 40 days after the IPO. Thus, the price of the stock should be driven by factors other than hype provided by the underwriter's analysts in the first 40 days.
- An analyst's compensation cannot be directly aligned with the amount of business that the analyst brings to the securities firm.
- Analysts cannot be supervised by the investment banking department within the securities firm. This rule is intended to prevent the investment bankers from pressuring the analysts to provide high rankings of firms in order to attract more underwriting business from those firms.
- An analyst's rating must also divulge any recent investment banking business provided by the securities firm that assigned the rating.

Rules Preventing IPO Market Abuses

In the 2001–2003 period, various abuses in the IPO market were highly publicized.

- Some securities firms that served as underwriters on IPOs allocated shares to corporate executives who were considering an IPO for their own firm. Some critics viewed this process, referred to as spinning, as an implicit bribe to obtain the future business of the firm.

- Some securities firms that served as underwriters of IPOs encouraged institutional investors to place bids above the offer price on the first day that the shares traded as a condition for being allowed to participate in the next IPO. They also charged excessive commissions to investors in some cases when the demand for the IPO shares was well in excess of the supply.

The SEC investigated cases of abuse and imposed fines on some securities firms. In addition, it enacted rules to prevent such abuses from occurring in the future.

Repeal of the Trade-Through Rule

As explained in Chapter 8, specialists serve the New York Stock Exchange by matching up buyers and sellers of a stock and can also take a position in the stock. As a result of the trade-through rule, specialists were sometimes able to jump ahead of other orders (called penny-jumping), thereby preventing other investors from having their orders executed. In 2004, the SEC ruled that investors could circumvent the trade-through rule to avoid penny-jumping by specialists. Consequently, investors may have a better chance to have their trades executed.

Mutual Fund Disclosure

As explained in Chapter 23, mutual funds received bad publicity in 2003 because some funds were allowing their large clients to buy or sell the fund's shares after the 4 P.M. closing but at the 4 P.M. price. This so-called late trading enables investors to trade on prices that are "stale" or no longer appropriate. Thus, the late trader can obtain shares at a price below the prevailing market price, at the expense of the other shareholders of the fund. Late trading is a violation of regulations established by the SEC in 1968. Some of these mutual funds were managed by securities firms, so the publicity and the subsequent actions taken by the SEC affected these firms. The publicity made investors more aware of the limited governance over mutual funds.

The SEC imposed heavy fines on those mutual funds that were found guilty of late trading. It also began to work on new regulations that would require more disclosure of the fees that the funds charge their shareholders and better governance by their boards of directors.

Securities Firm Risks

The operations conducted by securities firms create exposure to market risk, interest rate risk, credit risk, and exchange rate risk, as explained next.

Market Risk

Securities firms offer many services that are linked to stock market conditions. When stock prices are rising, there is normally a greater volume of stock offerings and secondary market transactions. Because securities firms typically are needed to facilitate these transactions, they benefit from a bullish stock market. Those securities firms that sponsor mutual funds typically benefit from the large investment in mutual funds during a bullish market.

Some securities firms take equity positions in the stocks they underwrite (especially the IPOs). They also commonly take a partial equity interest in target firms acquired by their client firms. These firms tend to benefit from a bullish stock market. Acquisitions tend to be more numerous during favorable stock market conditions. Given their participation in advising and financing acquisitions, securities firms can generate more business under these conditions.

When the stock market is depressed, stock transactions tend to decline, causing a reduction in business for securities firms. Although securities firms have diversified into different services, the demand for many of these services is tied to stock market conditions. Thus, the performance of most securities firms is highly sensitive to the stock market cycles.

Interest Rate Risk

The performance of securities firms can be sensitive to interest rate movements for the following reasons. First, the market values of bonds held as investments by securities firms increase as interest rates decline. Second, lower interest rates can encourage investors to withdraw deposits from depository institutions and invest in the stock market, thereby increasing stock transactions. Thus, the performance of some securities firms is inversely related to interest rate movements.

Credit Risk

Many securities firms offer bridge loans and other types of credit to corporations. The securities firms are subject to the possibility that these corporations will default on their loans. The probability of default tends to increase during periods when economic conditions deteriorate.

Exchange Rate Risk

GLBALASPECTS   Many securities firms have operations in foreign countries. The earnings remitted by foreign subsidiaries are reduced when the foreign currencies weaken against the parent firm's home currency. In addition, the market values of securities maintained as investments and denominated in foreign currencies decline as the currencies weaken against the parent firm's home currency.

Securities Firm Valuation

Securities firms (or securities operating units that are part of a financial conglomerate) are commonly valued by their managers to monitor progress over time or by other financial institutions that are considering an acquisition. The value of a securities firm can be modeled as the present value of its future cash flows. Thus, the value of a securities firm should change in response to changes in its expected cash flows in the future and to changes in the required rate of return by investors:

$$\Delta V = f[\underset{+}{\Delta E(CF)}, \underset{-}{\Delta k}]$$

Factors That Affect Cash Flows

The change in a securities firm's expected cash flows may be modeled as

$$\Delta E(CF) = f(\underset{+}{\Delta ECON}, \underset{-}{\Delta R_f}, \underset{?}{\Delta INDUS}, \underset{+}{\Delta MANAB})$$

where ECON represents economic growth, R_f represents the risk-free interest rate, INDUS represents industry conditions, and MANAB represents the abilities of the securities firm's management.

Economic Growth Economic growth can enhance a securities firm's cash flows because it increases the level of income of firms and households and can increase the demand for the firm's services. Specifically, the volume of brokerage activity tends to increase when households have more income, and corporations are more likely to hire securities firms to help them raise funds for expansion when economic conditions are favorable. During periods of strong economic growth, debt securities maintained by securities firms are less likely to default. In addition, equity security investments by securities firms should perform well because the firms represented by these securities should generate relatively high cash flows.

Change in the Risk-Free Interest Rate Some of a securities firm's assets (such as bonds) are adversely affected by rising interest rates, so the valuation of a security firm may be inversely related to interest rate movements.

Change in Industry Conditions Securities firms can be affected by industry conditions, including regulations, technology, and competition. For example, regulatory constraints can restrict firms from offering specific banking services or set the margin limits for investors. If regulators reduce the regulatory constraints, the expected cash flows of a securities firm should increase. Loosening of regulations to allow other financial institutions to offer securities services reduces the expected cash flows of securities firms.

Change in Management Abilities A securities firm has control over the composition of its managers and its organizational structure. Its managers can attempt to make internal decisions that will capitalize on the external forces (economic growth, interest rates, regulatory constraints) that the firm cannot control. Thus, the management skills of a securities firm can influence its expected cash flows. In particular, securities firms need skillful management to create new financial services that may complement the brokerage services they already offer to individuals. Skillful management is also needed to create new products (such as specialized derivative instruments) that will be used by firms.

Factors That Affect the Required Rate of Return by Investors

The required rate of return by investors who invest in a securities firm can be modeled as

$$\Delta k = f(\underset{+}{\Delta R_f}, \underset{+}{\Delta RP})$$

where ΔR_f represents a change in the risk-free interest rate, and ΔRP represents a change in the risk premium. The risk-free interest rate is normally expected to be positively related to inflation, economic growth, and the budget deficit level, but inversely related to money supply growth (assuming it does not cause inflation). The risk premium on a se-

EXHIBIT 24.3

Framework for Valuing a
Securities Firm

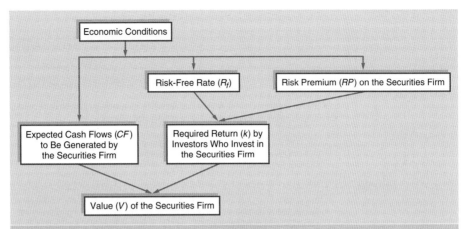

- A stronger economy leads to more securities transactions (brokerage fee income), an increase
  in security offerings and other services provided by the securities firm, and therefore better
  cash flows.

- A lower risk-free rate enhances the valuations of bonds held by securities firms. It also may encourage some corporations to pursue bond offerings while interest rates are low and therefore
  may create more business for the securities firm.

- The valuation is also influenced by industry conditions and the securities firm's management
  (not shown in the diagram). These factors affect the risk premium (and therefore the required
  return by investors) and the expected cash flows to be generated by the securities firm. In
  particular, regulations that affect the degree of competition for securities services affect the
  risk premium and cash flows generated by the securities firm.

curities firm is inversely related to economic growth and the company's management
skills. Industry conditions such as regulatory constraints may discourage securities
firms from taking excessive risk. However, the removal of regulatory barriers to entry in
the securities industry may increase the risk of securities firms.

Exhibit 24.3 provides a framework for valuing a securities firm, based on the preceding discussion. In general, the value of a securities firm is favorably affected by strong
economic growth, a reduction in interest rates, and strong management capabilities.

Interaction with Other Financial Institutions

Securities firms commonly interact with various types of financial institutions as summarized in Exhibit 24.4. They offer investment advice and execute security transactions
for financial institutions that maintain security portfolios. They also compete against
those financial institutions that have brokerage subsidiaries. Furthermore, they compete
with some commercial banks that have recently been allowed to underwrite securities
and sponsor mutual funds. Because securities firms commonly offer banking and insurance services, and many insurance companies and commercial banks offer securities services, it is sometimes difficult to distinguish among financial institutions. Some savings
institutions that experienced financial problems have been acquired by securities firms
and operate as wholly owned subsidiaries.

As mentioned earlier, in 1999 the Financial Services Modernization Act was passed.
The act created a more competitive environment for securities firms by allowing

EXHIBIT 24.4 Interaction between Securities Firms and Other Financial Institutions

Type of Financial Institution	Interaction with Securities Firms
Commercial banks and savings institutions	• Securities firms compete with those commercial banks and savings institutions that provide brokerage services. • Those commercial banks that underwrite commercial paper or provide advice on mergers and acquisitions compete directly with securities firms.
Mutual funds	• Securities firms execute trades for mutual funds. • Some mutual funds are organized by securities firms. • Mutual funds purchase newly issued securities that are underwritten by securities firms.
Insurance companies	• Securities firms advise portfolio managers of insurance companies on what securities to buy or sell. • Securities firms execute securities transactions for insurance companies. • Securities firms advise portfolio managers of insurance companies on how to hedge against interest rate risk and market risk. • Securities firms underwrite stocks and bonds that are purchased by insurance companies. • Securities firms compete with some insurance companies in the sales of some mutual funds to investors. • Securities firms obtain financing on LBOs from insurance companies. • Some securities firms have acquired or have merged with insurance companies in order to offer more diversified services.
Pension funds	• Securities firms advise pension fund portfolio managers on securities to purchase or sell. • Securities firms execute securities transactions for pension funds. • Securities firms advise pension fund portfolio managers on how to hedge against interest rate risk and market risk. • Pension funds purchase newly issued securities that are underwritten by securities firms.

commercial banks, securities firms, and insurance companies to merge. It removed limitations on the degree to which banks could offer securities services, which resulted in more intense competition from the banks. Some banks acquired securities services and attempted to market these new services to their existing customer base. In the most prominent example of a bank expanding into securities services, Citicorp merged with Traveler's Insurance Company, creating the financial conglomerate named Citigroup. Since Traveler's Insurance Group already owned Salomon Smith Barney, the merger was a massive consolidation of banking, securities, and insurance services. This merger occurred in 1998, the year before the passage of the Financial Services Modernization Act. Nevertheless, the act was still critical, because it allowed Citigroup to retain its banking, securities, and insurance services. The act not only created more competition among securities firms, but also made the offerings of securities services more efficient. Many individual and corporate customers need banking, securities, and insurance services and may prefer the convenience of obtaining all services from one financial institution.

Financial Market Participation

Securities firms participate in all types of financial markets as summarized in Exhibit 24.5. Their investment banking divisions participate in the primary markets by placing newly issued securities, while the brokerage divisions concentrate mostly on executing secondary market transactions for investors. Both the investment banking and brokerage divisions serve as advisers to financial market participants.

EXHIBIT 24.5 Participation of Securities Firms in Financial Markets

Type of Financial Market	Participation by Securities Firms
Money markets	• Some securities firms, such as Merrill Lynch, have created money market mutual funds, which invest in money market securities. • Securities firms underwrite commercial paper and purchase short-term securities for their own investment portfolios.
Bond markets	• Securities firms underwrite bonds in the primary market, advise clients on bonds to purchase or sell, and serve as brokers for bond transactions in the secondary market. • Some bond mutual funds have been created by securities firms. • Securities firms facilitate mergers, acquisitions, and LBOs by placing bonds for their clients. • Securities firms purchase bonds for their own investment portfolios.
Mortgage markets	• Securities firms underwrite securities that are backed by mortgages for various financial institutions.
Stock markets	• Securities firms underwrite stocks in the primary market, advise clients on what stocks to purchase or sell, and serve as brokers for stock transactions in the secondary market. • Securities firms purchase stocks for their own investment portfolios.
Futures markets	• Securities firms advise large financial institutions on how to hedge their portfolios with financial futures contracts. • Securities firms serve as brokers for financial futures transactions.
Options markets	• Securities firms advise large financial institutions on how to hedge portfolios with options contracts. • Securities firms serve as brokers for options transactions.
Swap markets	• Some securities firms engage in interest rate swaps to reduce their exposure to interest rate risk. • Many securities firms serve as financial intermediaries in swap markets.

Competition between Securities Firms and Commercial Banks

Commercial banks can compete against securities firms by offering discount brokerage services at substantially lower fees than full-service fees. Of course, they still must compete with discount brokerage firms. They can offer such discount services by either acquiring a discount brokerage firm or creating a subsidiary to perform the services. If they opt for the latter course, they face the up-front costs of organizing the operations and training new personnel. In addition, an initial promotional effort is necessary, whereas in an acquisition, the bank can continue to use the acquired firm's name and reputation for the brokerage business.

Still another method is to purchase brokerage services from a registered brokerage firm. In this case, the bank simply acts as an intermediary between customers and the brokerage firm. It normally receives the transactions and communicates the information to the brokerage firm, which executes the transaction. It may even provide customers with a toll-free number that is answered with the name of the bank so that customers will believe the brokerage operation is run by the bank. In this arrangement, the bank promotes the service and receives a portion of the commissions generated; the portion is determined by the work (regarding custodial services, mailing periodic statements, etc.) for which the bank is responsible.

The Glass-Steagall Act of 1933 separated the functions of commercial banks and investment banking firms, allowing commercial banks to underwrite general obligation municipal bonds but generally prohibiting them from other securities activities. In 1999, the Glass-Steagall Act was repealed as a result of the Financial Services Modernization Act. Since 1987, commercial banks have been allowed to underwrite commercial paper.

They not only offer advice on mergers and acquisitions and on private placements of securities, but also serve as intermediaries for interest rate swaps and currency swaps. In recent years, commercial banks have become major underwriters of corporate securities. In these ways, they compete directly with securities firms.

Recently, some securities firms have provided loans to businesses. For example, Merrill Lynch has begun to originate large loans to businesses. Since it has expertise in assessing the financial condition of firms when it issues stocks or bonds for them, it can utilize this expertise to assess the creditworthiness of firms to which it can provide loans. It typically sells the loans that it originates to other financial institutions, so its main role is as the originator of the loans rather than the actual source of funds.

Securities Firm Globalization

 GL BALASPECTS

Since 1986 many securities firms have increased their presence in foreign countries. In October 1986, the so-called Big Bang allowed for deregulation in the United Kingdom. With the commission structure competitive instead of fixed, British securities firms recognized that they would have to rely more on other services, as commission income would be reduced by competitive forces. Commercial banks from the United States have established investment banking subsidiaries overseas, where regulations do not attempt to separate banking and securities activities.

Most large securities firms have established a presence in foreign markets. For example, Morgan Stanley has offices in Frankfurt, London, Melbourne, Sydney, Tokyo, and Zurich. Merrill Lynch has more than 500 offices spread across the United States and numerous other countries. Becoming internationalized can give securities firms several possible advantages. First, their international presence allows them to place securities in various markets for corporations or governments. Second, some corporations that are heavily involved with international mergers and acquisitions prefer advice from securities firms that have subsidiaries in all potential markets. Third, institutional investors that invest in foreign securities prefer securities firms that can easily handle such transactions.

Growth in International Joint Ventures

In recent years, securities firms have expanded their international business by engaging in joint ventures with foreign securities firms. In this way, they penetrate foreign markets but have a limited stake in each project. Many securities firms have also increased their global presence by facilitating privatizations of firms in foreign markets such as Latin America and Eastern Europe.

Growth in International Securities Transactions

The growth in international securities transactions has created more business for the larger securities firms. For example, many stock offerings are now conducted across numerous countries, as some corporations attempt to achieve global name recognition. In addition, an international stock offering can avoid the downward pressure on the stock's price that might occur if the entire issue is sold in the domestic country. Large securities firms facilitate international stock offerings by creating an international syndicate to place the securities in various countries. Those securities firms that have established a global presence receive most of the requests for international stock offerings.

Growth in Latin America As a result of the North American Free Trade Agreement (NAFTA), U.S. securities firms have increased their business in Mexico and other Latin American countries. Securities firms have facilitated the increased trading of stocks, bonds, and other securities between the United States and Mexico. They are also facilitating mergers between firms from both countries.

Growth in Japan The Japanese government now allows foreign securities firms to enter its markets. Merrill Lynch, Goldman Sachs, and other U.S. and non-U.S. securities firms have acquired seats on the Tokyo Stock Exchange. Nevertheless, there are still explicit and implicit barriers to entry or at least limits on the degree of penetration by non-Japanese firms. Some securities firms complain that restrictions are excessive or vague. Although Japanese securities firms enter other financial markets, non-Japanese securities firms account for a tiny fraction of transactions on the Tokyo Stock Exchange.

SUMMARY

- Investment banking firms help corporations raise capital, provide advice on mergers and acquisitions, and may even help finance acquisitions. Some IBFs commonly acquire firms and frequently restructure them.

- Investment banking firms facilitate new issues of stock by advising on how much stock the firm can issue, determining the appropriate price for the stock, underwriting the stock, and distributing the stock. IBFs facilitate new issues of bonds in a somewhat similar manner.

- Brokerage firms can execute securities transactions for their clients by accommodating market orders, limit orders, and short-selling requests. Full-service brokerage firms provide information and advice and execute the securities transactions desired by their clients. Discount brokers tend to focus exclu-

sively on executing security transactions for their clients.

- Securities firms are exposed to market risk, because their volume of business is larger when stock market conditions are stronger. They are subject to interest rate risk because their underwriting business is sensitive to interest rate movements. They also hold some long-term financial assets whose values decline in response to higher interest rates. Securities firms are also subject to credit risk, since they commonly provide loans to some of their business clients.

- The value of a securities firm is affected by any factors that can affect its future cash flows or the required rate of return by investors. The value is enhanced when economic conditions are strong, because the demand for the firm's services increases when economic conditions are strong.

POINT COUNTER-POINT

Should Analysts Be Separated from Investment Banks to Prevent Conflicts of Interest?

Point No. Investment banks are known for their ability to analyze companies and value them. Investors may be more comfortable when analysts work within the investment banks, because they have access to substantial information.

Counter-Point Yes. Analysts have a conflict of interest, because they may be unwilling to offer negative views

about a company that is a client of their investment bank.

Who Is Correct? Use your favorite search engine to learn more about this issue. Offer your own opinion on this issue.

QUESTIONS AND APPLICATIONS

1. **Valuation Discrepancy** A division of Spence Inc. has experienced a major decline in sales. Assume the corporation prefers not to lay off any employees as a general policy. It is often suggested that this division may become a primary target for arbitrage firms. Given that the value of a division is the sum of its discounted cash flows, explain why the value of this division to an arbitrage firm may exceed its value to Spence Inc.

2. **Interpreting Financial News** Interpret the following comments made by Wall Street analysts and portfolio managers:
   a. "The stock prices of most securities firms took a hit because of the recent increase in interest rates."
   b. "Now that commercial banks are allowed more freedom to offer securities services, there may be a shakeout in the underwriting arena."
   c. "Chaos in the securities markets can be good for some securities firms."

3. **Regulation of Securities Activities** Explain the role of the SEC, the NASD, and the stock exchanges in regulating the securities industry.

4. **Sensitivity to Stock Market Conditions** Most securities firms experience poor profit performance after periods in which the stock market performs poorly. Given what you know about securities firms, offer some possible reasons for these reduced profits.

5. **Internet Exercise** Go to http://www.ml.com.
   a. Using this website, describe the different types of financial services offered by Merrill Lynch.

6. **Origination Process** Describe the origination process for corporations that are about to issue new stock.

7. **Arbitrage Activities** Explain how some investment banking firms (IBFs) facilitate arbitrage activity in the securities industry.

8. **Managing in Financial Markets: Assessing the Operations of Securities Firms** As a consultant, you are assessing the operations of a securities firm.

   a. The securities firm relies heavily on full-service brokerage commissions. Do you think the firm's heavy reliance on these commissions is risky? Explain.
   b. If this firm attempts to enter the underwriting business, would it be an easy transition?
   c. In recent years, the stock market volume has increased substantially, and this securities firm has performed very well. In the future, however, many institutional and individual investors may invest in indexes rather than in individual stocks. How would this affect the securities firm?

9. **Access to Inside Information** Why do IBFs typically have some inside information that could affect future stock prices of other firms?

10. **SIPC** What is the purpose of the SIPC?

11. **Greenmail** How have some arbitrage firms attempted to benefit from greenmail tactics?

12. **Underwriting Function** Describe the underwriting function of an investment bank.

13. **Flotation Costs** Describe the flotation costs incurred by a corporation that issues stock. Compare flotation costs of issuing bonds versus stock.

14. **Investment Banking Services** How do investment banks facilitate leveraged buyouts? Why are investment banks that are more capable of raising funds in the capital markets preferred by corporations that need advice on proposed acquisitions?

15. **International Expansion** Explain why securities firms from the United States have expanded into foreign markets.

16. **Asset Stripping** What is asset stripping?

17. **Best-Efforts Agreement** What is a best-efforts agreement?

18. **Direct Placement** Describe a direct placement of bonds. What is an advantage of a private placement? What is a disadvantage?

FLOW OF FUNDS EXERCISE

How Investment Banking Facilitates the Flow of Funds

Recall that Carson Company has periodically borrowed funds, but contemplates a stock or bond offering so that it can expand by acquiring some other businesses. It has contacted Kelly Investment Company, an investment bank.

a. Explain how Kelly Investment Company can serve Carson and how it will serve other clients as well when it serves Carson. Also explain how Carson Company can serve Kelly Investment Company.

b. In a securities offering, Kelly Investment Company would like to do a good job for its clients, which include both the issuer and institutional investors. Explain Kelly's dilemma.

c. The issuing firm in an IPO hopes that there will be strong demand for its shares at the offer price, which will ensure that it receives a reasonable amount of proceeds from its offering. In some previous IPOs, the share price by the end of the first day was more than 80 percent above the offer price at the beginning of the day. This reflects a very strong demand relative to the price at the end of the

day. In fact, it probably suggests that the IPO was fully subscribed at the offer price and that some institutional investors who purchased the stock at the offer price flipped their shares near the end of the first day to individual investors who were willing to pay the market price. Do you think that the issuing firm would be pleased that its stock price increased by more than 80 percent on the first day? Explain. Who really benefits from the increase in price on the first day?

d. Continuing the previous question, assume that the stock price drifts back down to near the original offer price over the next three weeks (even though the general stock market conditions were stable over this period) and then moves in tandem with the market over the next several years. Based on this information, do you think the offer price was appropriate? If so, how can you explain the unusually high one-day return on the stock? Who benefited from this stock price behavior, and who was adversely affected?

WSJ EXERCISE

Performance of Securities Firms

Using a recent issue of *The Wall Street Journal,* summarize an article that discussed the recent performance of a particular securities firm. Does the article suggest that

the securities firm's performance was better or worse than the norm? What reason is given for the particular level of performance?

CHAPTER 25

Insurance and Pension Fund Operations

nsurance companies and pension funds were created to provide insurance and retirement funding for individuals, firms,
and government agencies. They serve financial markets by
supplying funds to a variety of financial and nonfinancial corporations as well as government agencies. Some insurance and
pension operations are independent companies, while others
are units (or subsidiaries) of financial conglomerates.

The specific objectives of this chapter are to:

- describe the main uses of insurance company funds,
- explain the exposure of insurance companies to various forms of risk,
- identify the factors that affect the value of insurance companies,
- describe the common types of private pension plans, and
- explain how pension funds are managed.

Background

http://

http://www.insure.com
Information about more
than 200 insurance
companies.

Insurance companies provide various forms of insurance and investment services to individuals and charge a fee (called a premium) for this financial service. In general, the
insurance provides a payment to the insured (or a named beneficiary) under conditions
specified by the insurance policy contract. These conditions typically result in expenses
or lost income, so the insurance is a means of financial protection. It reduces the potential financial damage incurred by individuals or firms due to specified conditions.

Common types of insurance offered by insurance companies include life insurance,
property and casualty insurance, health insurance, and business insurance. Many insurance companies offer multiple types of insurance.

An individual's decision to purchase insurance may be influenced by the likelihood
of the conditions that would result in receiving an insurance payment. Individuals who
are more exposed to specific conditions that cause financial damage will purchase insurance against those conditions. Consequently, the insurance industry faces a type of
adverse selection problem. Furthermore, insurance can cause the insured to take more
risks because they are protected. This is known as the moral hazard problem in the insurance industry.

Insurance companies employ underwriters to calculate the risk of specific insurance
policies. The companies decide what types of policies to offer based on the potential
level of claims to be paid on those policies and the premiums that they can charge.

Insurance Premium Determinants

The premium charged by an insurance company for each insurance policy is based on the probability of the condition under which the company will have to provide a payment and the potential size of the payment. The premium may also be influenced by the degree of competition within the industry for the specific type of insurance offered. Insurance companies can estimate the present value of a payment that they will have to make for a specific insurance policy. The premium charged for that insurance is influenced by the present value of the expected payment. The premium will also contain a markup to cover overhead expenses and to provide a profit beyond expenses.

Furthermore, the insurance premium is higher when there is more uncertainty about the size of the payment that may ultimately have to be made. Insurance companies recognize that the timing of the payout of any particular policy may be difficult to predict, but are more concerned with the total flow of payments in any particular period. That is, if they have 20,000 policies, they may not know which policies will require payment this month, but may be able to predict the typical amount of payments per month.

Insurance companies tend to charge lower premiums when they provide services to all employees of a corporation through group plans. The lower premium represents a form of quantity discount in return for being selected to provide a particular type of insurance to all employees.

Insurance Company Investments

Insurance companies invest the insurance premiums and fees received from other services until the funds are needed to pay insurance claims. In some cases, the claims occur several years after the premiums are received. Thus, the performance of insurance companies is partially dependent on the return on the invested funds. Their investment decisions balance the goals of return, liquidity, and risk. They want to generate a high rate of return while maintaining risk at a tolerable level. They need to maintain sufficient liquidity so that they can easily access funds to accommodate claims by policyholders. Those insurance companies whose claims are less predictable need to maintain more liquidity.

Life Insurance Operations

Since life insurance companies are a dominant force in the insurance industry, they will receive more attention in this chapter. In aggregate, they generate more than $100 billion in premiums each year and serve as key financial intermediaries by investing their funds in financial markets.

Life insurance companies compensate (provide benefits to) the beneficiary of a policy upon the policyholder's death. They charge policyholders a premium that should reflect the probability of making a payment to the beneficiary as well as the size and timing of the payment. Despite the difficulty of forecasting the life expectancy of a given individual, life insurance companies have historically forecasted with reasonable accuracy the benefits they will have to provide beneficiaries. Because they hold a large portfolio of policies, these companies use actuarial tables and mortality figures to forecast the percentage of policies that will require compensation over a given period, based on characteristics such as the age distribution of policyholders.

Life insurance companies also commonly offer employees of a corporation a **group life policy.** This service has become quite popular and has generated a large volume of

business in recent years. Group policies can be provided at a low cost because of the high volume. Group life coverage now makes up about 40 percent of total life coverage, compared to only 26 percent of total life insurance coverage in 1974.

Ownership

There are about 2,000 life insurance companies, classified as having either stock or mutual ownership. A stock-owned company is owned by its shareholders, while a mutual life insurance company is owned by its policyholders. About 95 percent of U.S. life insurance companies are stock owned, and in recent years some mutual life insurance companies have converted to become stock owned. As in the savings institutions industry, a primary reason for the conversions is to gain access to capital by issuing stock. The mutual companies are relatively large and account for more than 46 percent of the total assets of all life insurance companies.

Life Insurance Types

http://

http://www.bloomberg.com
Click on "Insurance Center." Provides quotes on any type of insurance.

Some of the more common types of life insurance policies are described here.

Whole Life Insurance From the perspective of the insured policyholders, **whole life insurance** protects them until death or as long as the premiums are promptly paid. In addition, whole life policies provide a form of savings to policyholders. They build a cash value that the policyholder is entitled to even if the policy is canceled.

From the perspective of the life insurance company, whole life policies generate periodic (typically, quarterly or semiannual) premiums that can be invested until the policyholder's death, when benefits are paid to the beneficiary. The amount of benefits is typically fixed.

Term Insurance **Term insurance** is temporary, providing insurance only over a specified term, and does not build a cash value for policyholders. The premiums paid represent only insurance, not savings. Term insurance, however, is significantly less expensive than whole life insurance. Policyholders must compare the cash value of whole life insurance to their additional costs to determine whether it is preferable to term insurance. Those who prefer to invest their savings themselves will likely opt for term insurance.

People who need more insurance now than later may choose decreasing term insurance, in which the benefits paid to the beneficiary decrease over time. Families with mortgages commonly select this form of insurance. As time passes, the mortgage balance decreases, and the family is more capable of surviving without the breadwinner's earnings. Thus, less compensation is needed in later years.

Variable Life Insurance Under **variable life insurance,** the benefits awarded by the life insurance company to a beneficiary vary with the assets backing the policy. Until 1984, the premium payments on variable life insurance were constant over time. Since 1984, flexible-premium variable life insurance has been available, allowing flexibility on the size and timing of payments.

Universal Life Insurance **Universal life insurance** combines the features of term and whole life insurance. It specifies a period of time over which the policy will exist but also builds a cash value for the policyholder over time. Interest is accumulated from the cash

EXHIBIT 25.1

Distribution of U.S. Life Insurance
Company Income

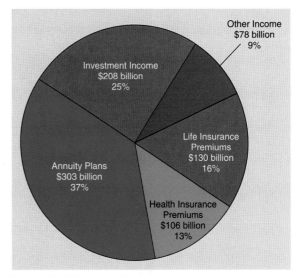

Source: *2004 Life Insurance Fact Book.*

value until the policyholder uses those funds. Universal life insurance allows flexibility
on the size and timing of the premiums, too. The growth in a policy's cash value is dependent on the pace of the premiums. The premium payment is divided into two por-
tions. The first is used to pay the death benefit identified in the policy and to cover any
administrative expenses. The second is used for investments and reflects savings for the
policyholder. The Internal Revenue Service prohibits the value of these savings from exceeding the policy's death benefits.

Fund Sources

Life insurance companies obtain much of their funds from premiums, as shown in Exhibit 25.1. Total premiums (life plus health insurance) represent about 29 percent of total income. The most important source of funds, however, is the provision of **annuity
plans,** which offer a predetermined amount of retirement income to individuals. Annuity plans have become very popular and now generate proportionately more income to
insurance companies than in previous years. More information about the annuities provided by numerous life insurance companies can be found at http://www.annuity.com. The
third largest source of funds is investment income, which results from the investment of
funds received from premium payments.

Capital Insurance companies build capital by retaining earnings or issuing new stock.
They use capital as a means of financing investment in fixed assets, such as buildings,
and as a cushion against operating losses. Since a relatively large amount of capital can
enhance safety, insurance companies are required to maintain adequate capital. Insurance companies are required to maintain a larger amount of capital when they are exposed to a higher degree of risk. Their risk can be measured by assessing the risk of their
assets (as some assets are more exposed to losses than others) and their exposure to the
types of insurance they provide.

Insurance companies maintain an adequate capital level not only to cushion potential losses, but also to reassure their customers. When customers purchase insurance,

EXHIBIT 25.2

Assets of U.S. Life Insurance
Companies

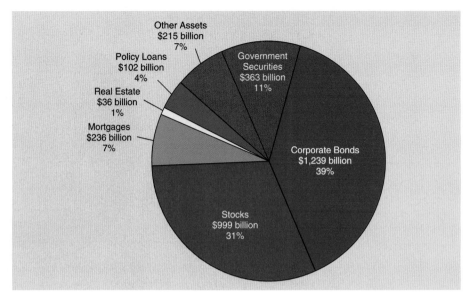

Source: *2004 Life Insurance Fact Book*.

the benefits are received at a future point in time. The customers are more comfortable purchasing insurance from an insurance company that has an adequate capital level and is therefore likely to be in existence at the time the benefits are to be provided.

Fund Uses

The uses of funds by life insurance companies strongly influence their performance. Life insurance companies are major institutional investors. Exhibit 25.2, which shows the assets of life insurance companies, indicates how funds have been used. The main assets are described in the following subsections.

Government Securities Life insurance companies invest in U.S. Treasury securities, state and local government bonds, and foreign bonds. They maintain investments in U.S. Treasury securities because of their safety and liquidity, but also invest in bonds issued by foreign governments in an attempt to enhance profits.

Corporate Securities Corporate bonds are the most popular asset of life insurance companies. Companies usually hold a mix of medium- and long-term bonds for cash management and liquidity needs. Although corporate bonds provide a higher yield than government securities, they have a higher degree of credit (default) risk. Some insurance companies focus on high-grade corporate bonds, while others invest a portion of their funds in junk bonds.

Because life insurance companies expect to maintain a portion of their long-term securities until maturity, this portion can be somewhat illiquid. Thus, they have the flexibility to obtain some high-yielding, directly placed securities where they can directly negotiate the provisions. Because such nonstandard securities are less liquid, life insurance companies balance their asset portfolios with other more liquid securities. A minor portion of corporate securities are foreign. The foreign holdings typically represent in-

dustrialized countries and are therefore considered to have low credit risk. Of course, the market values of these foreign bonds are still susceptible to interest rate and currency fluctuations.

Mortgages Life insurance companies hold all types of mortgages, including one to four family, multifamily, commercial, and farm related. These mortgages are typically originated by another financial institution and then sold to insurance companies in the secondary market. The mortgages are still serviced by the originating financial institution. Commercial mortgages make up more than 90 percent of the total mortgages held by life insurance companies. They help to finance shopping centers and office buildings.

Real Estate Although life insurance companies finance real estate by purchasing mortgages, their return is limited to the mortgage payments, as they are simply acting as a creditor. In an attempt to achieve higher returns, they sometimes purchase real estate and lease it for commercial purposes. The ownership of real estate offers them the opportunity to generate very high returns but also exposes them to greater risk. Real estate values can be volatile over time and can have a significant effect on the market value of a life insurance company's asset portfolio.

Policy Loans Life insurance companies lend a small portion of their funds to whole life policyholders (called policy loans). Whole life policyholders can borrow up to their policy's cash value, at a guaranteed rate of interest as stated in their policy over a specified period of time. Other sources of funds for individuals typically do not guarantee an interest rate at which they can borrow. For this reason, policyholders tend to borrow more from life insurance companies during periods of rising interest rates, when alternative forms of borrowing would be more expensive.

Asset Management of Life Insurance Companies

Because life insurance companies tend to receive premiums from policyholders for several years before paying out benefits to a beneficiary, their performance can be significantly affected by their asset portfolio management. Like other financial institutions, they adjust their asset portfolios to counter changes in the factors that affect their risk. If they expect a downturn in the economy, they may reduce their holdings of corporate stocks and real estate. If they expect higher interest rates, they may reduce their holdings of fixed-rate bonds and mortgages.

To cope with the existing forms of risk, life insurance companies attempt to balance their portfolios so that any adverse movements in the market value of some assets will be offset by favorable movements in others. For example, under the presumption that interest rates will move in tandem with inflation, life insurance companies can use real estate holdings to partially offset the potential adverse effect of inflation on bonds. When higher inflation causes higher interest rates, the market value of existing bonds decreases, whereas the market values of real estate holdings tend to increase with inflation. Conversely, an environment of low or decreasing inflation may cause real estate values to stagnate but have a favorable impact on the market value of bonds and mortgages (because interest rates would likely decline). Although such a strategy may be useful, it is much easier to implement on paper than in practice. Because real estate values can fluctuate to a great degree, life insurance companies allocate only a limited amount of funds to real estate. In addition, real estate is less liquid than most other assets.

Many insurance companies are diversifying into other businesses by offering a wide variety of financial products. Such a strategy not only provides diversification but also enables these companies to offer packages of products to policyholders who desire to cover all these needs at once.

Overall, life insurance companies want to earn a reasonable return while maintaining their risk at a tolerable level. The degree to which they avoid or accept the various forms of risk depends on their degree of risk aversion. Companies that accept a greater amount of risk in their asset portfolios are likely to generate a higher return. If market conditions move in an unexpected manner, however, they will be more severely damaged than companies that employed a more conservative approach.

Property and Casualty Insurance Operations

Property and casualty (PC) insurance protects against fire, theft, liability, and other events that result in economic or noneconomic damage. Property insurance protects businesses and individuals from the impact of financial risks associated with the ownership of property, such as buildings, automobiles, and other assets. Casualty insurance protects policyholders from potential liabilities for harm to others as a result of product failure or accidents. PC insurance companies charge policyholders a premium that should reflect the probability of a payout to the insured and the potential magnitude of the payout.

There are about 3,800 individual PC companies. The largest providers of PC insurance are State Farm Insurance Group, Allstate Insurance Group, Farmers Insurance Group, and Nationwide Insurance Enterprise. No single company controls more than 10 percent of the PC insurance market. Although there are more PC companies than life insurance companies, the PC insurance business in aggregate is only about one-fourth as large as the life insurance business in aggregate (based on assets held). Nevertheless, the PC insurance business generates about the same amount of insurance premiums as the life insurance business. Many insurance companies now diversify their business, offering both life and PC insurance.

PC and life insurance have very different characteristics. First, PC policies often last one year or less, as opposed to the long-term or even permanent life insurance policies. Second, PC insurance encompasses a wide variety of activities, ranging from auto insurance to business liability insurance. Life insurance is more focused. Third, forecasting the amount of future compensation to be paid is more difficult for PC insurance than for life insurance. PC compensation depends on a variety of factors, including inflation, trends in terrorism, and the generosity of courts in lawsuits. Because of the greater uncertainty, PC insurance companies need to maintain more liquid asset portfolios. Earnings can be quite volatile over time, as the premiums charged may be based on highly overestimated or underestimated compensation.

Cash Flow Underwriting

A unique aspect of the PC insurance industry is its cyclical nature. As interest rates rise, companies tend to lower their rates so as to write more policies and acquire more premium dollars to invest. They are hoping losses will hold off long enough to make the cheaper premiums profitable through increased investment income. As interest rates decline, the price of insurance rises to offset decreased investment income. This method of

EXHIBIT 25.3

EXHIBIT 25.3

Uses of Funds by Property and Casualty Insurance Companies

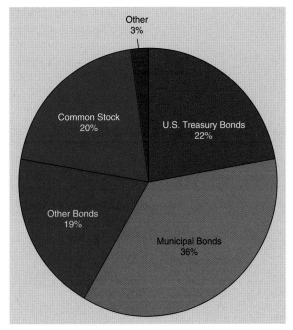

Source: Federal Reserve.

adapting prices to interest rates is called **cash flow underwriting.** It can backfire for companies that focus on what they can earn in the short run and ignore what they will pay out later. A company that does not accurately predict the timing of the cycle can experience inadequate reserves and a drain on cash.

Uses of Funds

The primary uses of funds for PC insurance companies are illustrated in Exhibit 25.3. Municipal bonds dominate, followed by Treasury bonds, and then by common stock. The amount of common stock holdings has been more volatile than that of the other components. The most obvious difference in the asset structure of PC companies relative to life insurance companies is the much higher concentration of government bonds.

Property and Casualty Reinsurance

PC companies commonly obtain **reinsurance,** which effectively allocates a portion of their return and risk to other insurance companies. It is similar to a commercial bank's acting as the lending agent by allowing other banks to participate in the loan. A particular PC insurance company may agree to insure a corporation but spread the risk by inviting other insurance companies to participate. Reinsurance allows a company to write larger policies, because a portion of the risk involved will be assumed by other companies.

The number of companies willing to offer reinsurance has declined significantly because of generous court awards and the difficulty of assessing the amount of potential claims. Reinsurance policies are often described in the insurance industry as "having

long tails," which means that the probability distribution of possible returns on reinsurance is widely dispersed. Although many companies still offer reinsurance, their premiums have increased substantially in recent years. If the desire to offer reinsurance continues to decline, the primary insurers will be less able to "sell off" a portion of the risk they assume when writing policies. Consequently, they will be pressured to more closely evaluate the risk of the policies they write.

Health Care Insurance Operations

Insurance companies provide various types of health care insurance, including coverage for hospital stays, visits to physicians, and surgical procedures. They serve as intermediaries between the health care providers and the recipients of health care. Since the cost of health care is so high, individuals seek health care insurance as a form of protection against conditions that cause them to incur large health care expenses.

Health Care Plan Types

Insurance companies provide two types of health care plans: managed health care plans and indemnity plans. The primary difference between the two types of plans is that individuals who are insured by a managed care plan may choose only specified health care providers (hospitals and physicians) who participate in the plan. Individuals who are insured under an indemnity plan can usually choose any provider of health care services. The payment systems of the two types of plans are also distinctly different. The premiums for managed health care plans are generally lower, and payment is typically made directly to the provider. In contrast, indemnity plans reimburse insured individuals for the health care expenses they incur.

Managed Health Care Plans

Managed health care plans can be classified as health maintenance organizations (HMOs) or preferred provider organizations (PPOs).

Health Maintenance Organizations HMOs usually require individuals to choose a primary care physician (PCP). The PCP is the "gatekeeper" for that individual's health care. Before patients insured under an HMO can see a specialist, they must first see a PCP to obtain a referral for the specialist.

Preferred Provider Organizations PPOs usually allow insured individuals to see any physician without a referral. However, PPO insurance premiums are higher than HMO insurance premiums.

Future Health Care Insurance

Health care expenses have risen dramatically in recent years, and some insurance companies underestimated the payouts they would have to make to cover the expenses specified by their policies. Consequently, some insurance companies that provide health care insurance have incurred major losses and have increased the premiums they charge

for health care insurance. Because of the high cost of health care, many politicians argue that the entire U.S. health care system needs to be reformed. Thus, the status of health care insurance and reimbursement could change if reform occurs.

Business Insurance

Insurance companies provide a wide variety of insurance policies that protect businesses from many types of risk. Some forms of business insurance overlap with property and casualty insurance. Property insurance protects a firm against the risk associated with ownership of property, such as buildings and other assets. It can provide insurance against property damage by fire or theft. Liability insurance can protect a firm against potential liability for harm to others as a result of product failure or a wide range of other conditions. This is a key type of insurance for businesses, because of the increasing number of lawsuits filed by customers who claim that they suffered physical or emotional distress as a result of products produced by businesses.

Liability insurance can also protect a business against potential liability for claims by its employees. For example, a business may be subject to a lawsuit by an employee who is hurt on the job. Employment liability insurance also covers claims of wrongful termination and sexual harassment.

Some other forms of business insurance are separate from property and casualty insurance. Key employee insurance provides a financial payout if specified employees of a business become disabled or die. The insurance is intended to enable the business to replace the skills of the key employees so that the business can continue. Business interruption insurance protects against losses due to a temporary closing of the business. Credit line insurance covers debt payments owed to a creditor if a borrower dies. Fidelity bond insurance covers losses due to dishonest employees. Marine insurance covers losses due to damage during transport. Malpractice insurance protects business professionals from losses due to lawsuits by dissatisfied customers. Surety bond insurance covers losses due to a contract not being fulfilled. Umbrella liability insurance provides additional coverage beyond that provided by the other existing insurance policies.

Insurance Company Regulation

http://

http://www.naic.org Links to information about insurance regulations.

The insurance industry is highly regulated by state agencies (called commissioners in some states). Each state attempts to make sure that insurance companies are providing adequate services, and the state also approves the rates insurers may charge. Insurance company agents must be licensed. In addition, the forms used for policies are state approved to avoid misleading wording.

State regulators also evaluate the asset portfolios of insurance companies to ensure that investments are reasonably safe and that adequate reserves are maintained to protect policyholders. For example, some states have limited investment in junk bonds to no more than 20 percent of total assets.

The National Association of Insurance Commissioners (NAIC) facilitates cooperation among the various state agencies whenever an insurance issue is a national concern. It attempts to maintain a degree of uniformity in common reporting issues. It also conducts research on insurance issues and participates in legislative discussions.

The Insurance Regulatory Information System (IRIS) has been developed by a committee of state insurance agencies to assist in each state's regulatory duties. The IRIS

compiles financial statements, lists of insurers, and other relevant information pertaining to the insurance industry. In addition, it assesses the companies' respective financial statements by calculating 11 ratios that are then evaluated by NAIC regulators to monitor the financial health of a company. The NAIC provides all state insurance departments with IRIS assessment results that can be used as a basis for comparison when evaluating the financial health of any company. The regulatory duties of state agencies often require a comparison of the financial ratios of a particular insurance company to the industry norm. Use of the industry norm facilitates the evaluation.

Assessment System

The regulatory system is designed to detect any problems in time to search for a remedy before the company deteriorates further. The more commonly used financial ratios assess a variety of relevant characteristics, including the following:

- The ability of the company to absorb either losses or a decline in the market value of its investments
- Return on investment
- Relative size of operating expenses
- Liquidity of the asset portfolio

Regulators monitor these characteristics to ensure that insurance companies do not become overly exposed to credit risk, interest rate risk, and liquidity risk.

Capital Regulation

Since 1994, insurance companies have been required to report a risk-based capital ratio to insurance regulators. The ratio was created by the NAIC and is intended to force those insurance companies with a higher exposure to insurance claims, potential losses on assets, and interest rate risk to hold a higher level of capital. The application of risk-based capital ratios not only discourages insurance companies from excessive exposure to risk, but also forces companies that take high risks to back their business with a large amount of capital. Consequently, there is less likelihood of failures in the insurance industry.

Risk Exposure

The major types of risk faced by insurance companies are interest rate risk, credit risk, market risk, and liquidity risk.

Interest Rate Risk

Because insurance companies carry a large amount of fixed-rate long-term securities, the market value of their asset portfolios can be very sensitive to interest rate fluctuations. When interest rates increase, insurance companies are unable to fully capitalize on these rates, because much of their funds are tied up in long-term bonds.

Insurance companies have been reducing their average maturity on securities. In addition, they have been investing in long-term assets that offer floating rates, such as com-

mercial mortgages. Both strategies reduce the impact of interest rate movements on the market value of their assets.

As insurance companies have become more aware of their exposure to interest rate risk and more knowledgeable about techniques to hedge the risk, they are increasingly utilizing futures contracts and interest rate swaps to manage their exposure.

Credit Risk

The corporate bonds, mortgages, state and local government securities, and real estate holdings in insurance companies' asset portfolios are subject to credit risk. To deal with this risk, some insurance companies typically invest only in securities assigned a high credit rating. They also diversify among securities issuers so that the repayment problems experienced by any single issuer will have only a minor impact on the overall portfolio. Other insurance companies, however, have invested heavily in risky assets, such as junk bonds.

Market Risk

A related risk to insurance companies is market risk. A good example of market risk was the October 1987 stock market crash, which significantly reduced the market value of stock holdings of insurance companies. The value of the stock portfolios managed by insurance companies also declined in 2001–2002, when the weak economy caused stock prices to weaken. The real estate holdings of insurance companies may also be adversely affected by an economic downturn. Some insurance companies became insolvent in the early 1990s as a result of losses on real estate investments.

Liquidity Risk

An additional risk to insurance companies is liquidity risk. A high frequency of claims at a single point in time could force a company to liquidate assets at a time when the market value is low, thereby depressing its performance. Claims due to death are not likely to occur simultaneously, however. Life insurance companies can therefore reduce their exposure to this risk by diversifying the age distribution of their customer base. If the customer base becomes unbalanced and is heavily concentrated in the older age group, life insurance companies should increase their proportion of liquid assets to prepare for a higher frequency of claims.

Valuing Insurance Companies

Insurance companies (or insurance company units that are part of a financial conglomerate) are commonly valued by their managers to monitor progress over time or by other financial institutions that are considering an acquisition. The value of an insurance company can be modeled as the present value of its future cash flows. Thus, the value of an insurance company should change in response to changes in its expected cash flows in the future and to changes in the required rate of return by investors:

$$\Delta V = f[\Delta E(CF), \Delta k]$$
$$\qquad\qquad +\qquad -$$

Factors That Affect Cash Flows

The change in an insurance company's expected cash flows may be modeled as

$$\Delta E(CF) = f(\Delta PAYOUT, \Delta ECON, \Delta R_f, \Delta INDUS, \Delta MANAB)$$
$$\qquad\qquad - \qquad + \qquad - \qquad ? \qquad +$$

where PAYOUT represents insurance payouts to beneficiaries, ECON represents economic growth, R_f represents the risk-free interest rate, INDUS represents industry conditions, and MANAB represents the abilities of the insurance company's management.

Change in Payouts The payouts on insurance claims are somewhat stable for most life insurance companies with a diversified set of customers. In contrast, the payouts on property and casualty claims can be volatile for PC companies. The September 11, 2001, attack on the United States serves as an example of how a single event can cause billions of dollars worth of liabilities.

Change in Economic Conditions Economic growth can enhance an insurance company's cash flows because it increases the level of income of firms and households and can increase the demand for the company's services. During periods of strong economic growth, debt securities maintained by insurance companies are less likely to default. In addition, equity securities maintained by insurance companies should perform well because the firms represented by these securities should generate relatively high cash flows.

Change in the Risk-Free Interest Rate Some of an insurance company's assets (such as bonds) are adversely affected by rising interest rates. Thus, the valuation of an insurance company may be inversely related to interest rate movements.

Change in Industry Conditions Insurance companies are subject to industry conditions, including regulatory constraints, technology, and competition within the industry. For example, they now compete against various financial institutions when offering some services. As regulators have reduced barriers, competition within the insurance industry has become more intense.

Change in Management Abilities An insurance company has control over the composition of its managers and its organizational structure. Its managers can attempt to make internal decisions that will capitalize on the external forces (economic growth, interest rates, regulatory constraints) that the company cannot control. Thus, the management skills of an insurance company can influence its expected cash flows. In particular, skillful management is needed to determine the likelihood of events that will necessitate quick and massive payouts to policyholders. Managers must be able to estimate the present value of cash inflows from insurance premiums and the present value of future cash outflows resulting from payouts to policyholders. This analysis determines the types of insurance offered by the company and the size of the premiums charged on insurance. Insurance company managers must also be capable of analyzing the creditworthiness of firms issuing the bonds that they may purchase.

Factors That Affect the Required Rate of Return by Investors

The required rate of return by investors who invest in an insurance company can be modeled as

$$\Delta k = f(\Delta R_f, \Delta RP)$$
$$\qquad\quad +\quad\;\; +$$

where ΔR_f represents a change in the risk-free interest rate, and ΔRP represents a change in the risk premium.

The risk-free interest rate is normally expected to be positively related to inflation, economic growth, and the budget deficit level, but inversely related to money supply growth (assuming it does not cause inflation). The risk premium on an insurance company is inversely related to economic growth and the company's management skills. It can also be affected by industry conditions, such as regulatory constraints. Some constraints (such as capital constraints) discourage insurance companies from taking excessive risk; other constraints, such as those on the services that can be offered, may increase risk because they limit the degree of diversification. The risk premium on PC companies can also change in response to the degree of expected terrorism.

Exhibit 25.4 provides a framework for valuing an insurance company, based on the preceding discussion. In general, the value of an insurance company is favorably affected by strong economic growth, a reduction in interest rates, and strong management capabilities. The sensitivity of an insurance company's value to these conditions is dependent

EXHIBIT 25.4

A Framework for Valuing
an Insurance Company

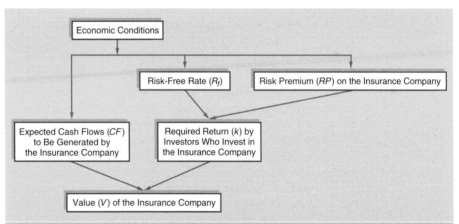

- A stronger economy leads to more services being provided by insurance companies and better cash flows. It may also enhance stock valuations and therefore can enhance the valuations of stocks held by the insurance company.

- A lower risk-free rate results in more favorable valuations of the bonds held by the insurance company.

- The valuation of an insurance company is also influenced by industry conditions and the firm's management (not shown in the diagram). These factors affect the risk premium (and therefore the required return by investors) and the expected cash flows to be generated by the insurance company. In particular, property and casualty companies are exposed to court rulings that result in large damages awards paid by insurance, while health insurance companies are exposed to regulations regarding reimbursement for health care services.

on its own characteristics. The higher the risk tolerance reflected in the types of insurance offered, the more sensitive the company's valuation to events (such as catastrophes) that could trigger massive payouts to policyholders.

Performance Evaluation

Some of the more common indicators of an insurance company's performance are available in investment service publications such as *Value Line*. A time-series assessment of the dollar amount of life insurance and/or PC insurance premiums indicates the growth in the company's insurance business. A time-series analysis of investment income can be used to assess the performance of the company's portfolio managers. However, the dollar amount of investment income is affected by several factors that are not under the control of portfolio managers, such as the amount of funds received as premiums that can be invested in securities and market interest rates. In addition, a relatively low level of investment income may result from a high concentration in stocks that pay low or no dividends rather than from poor performance.

Because insurance companies have unique characteristics, the financial ratios of other financial institutions are generally not applicable. Liquidity of an insurance company can be measured using the following ratio:

$$\text{Liquidity ratio} = \frac{\text{Invested assets}}{\text{Loss reserves and unearned premium reserves}}$$

The higher the ratio, the more liquid the company. This ratio can be evaluated by comparing it to the industry average.

The profitability of insurance companies is often assessed using the return on net worth (or policyholders' surplus) as a ratio, as follows:

$$\text{Return on net worth} = \frac{\text{Net profit}}{\text{Policyholders' surplus}}$$

Net profit consists of underwriting profits, investment income, and realized capital gains. Changes in this ratio over time should be compared to changes in the industry norms, as the norm is quite volatile over time. The return on net worth tends to be quite volatile for PC insurance companies because of the volatility in their claims.

Although the net profit reflects all income sources and therefore provides only a general measure of profitability, various financial ratios can be used to focus on a specific source of income. For example, underwriting gains or losses are measured by the net underwriting margin:

$$\text{Net underwriting margin} = \frac{\text{Premium income} - \text{Policy expenses}}{\text{Total assets}}$$

When policy expenses exceed premium income, the net underwriting margin is negative. Yet, as long as other sources of income can offset such a loss, net profit will still be positive.

Interaction with Other Financial Institutions

Insurance companies interact with financial institutions in several ways, as summarized in Exhibit 25.5. They compete in one form or another with all types of financial institu-

EXHIBIT 25.5 Interaction between Insurance Companies and Other Financial Institutions

Type of Financial Institution	Interaction with Insurance Companies
Commercial banks and savings institutions (SIs)	• Insurance companies compete with banks and SIs to finance leveraged buyouts. • Insurance companies sometimes compete with banks and SIs by offering CDs. • Insurance companies sometimes compete with banks by offering an account on which checks can be written. • Insurance companies merge with banks in order to offer various banking services. • Insurance companies face increased competition for insurance-related services as banks and SIs attempt to offer such services. • Insurance companies commonly purchase loans that were originated by banks.
Finance companies	• Insurance companies are sometimes acquired by finance companies and maintained as subsidiaries.
Securities firms	• Insurance companies compete directly with securities firms by offering mutual funds.
Brokerage firms	• Insurance companies compete directly with brokerage firms by offering securities-related services. • Insurance companies compete directly with brokerage firms that offer insurance-related services; many brokerage firms now offer a wide variety of insurance-related services and plan to increase their offerings in the future.
Investment banking firms	• Insurance companies compete with investment companies to finance leveraged buyouts. • Insurance companies commonly purchase stocks and bonds issued by corporations that were underwritten by investment banking firms. • Insurance companies issue stock that is underwritten by investment banking firms.
Pension funds	• Insurance companies offer to manage pension plans for corporations.

tions. As time passes, their penetration into nontraditional markets will likely increase. In addition, as other financial institutions increase their offerings of insurance-related services, differences between insurance companies and other financial institutions are diminishing. For example, some insurance companies offer certificates of deposit to investors, thereby competing directly with commercial banks for these offerings. In addition, some insurance companies offer a cash management account on which checks can be written. Those insurance companies that have merged with brokerage firms offer a wide variety of securities-related services. Several insurance companies offer mutual funds to investors. Some state insurance regulators have allowed commercial banks to underwrite and sell insurance, which will result in more intense competition in the insurance industry.

In 1999, Congress passed the Financial Services Modernization Act, which created a more competitive environment for insurance companies. Commercial banks, securities firms, and insurance companies were allowed to merge, thereby making it easier for banks to offer a complete set of financial services. By removing the constraints on the insurance services that banks could offer, the act was expected to enable them to offer insurance services more efficiently. Some banks acquired insurance companies, which then marketed their insurance services under the bank's brand name to the bank's existing customer base. The momentum toward consolidation began in 1998 when Citicorp merged with Traveler's Insurance Company, resulting in the financial conglomerate named Citigroup. In the following year, the Financial Services Modernization Act was passed, thereby allowing Citigroup to retain its banking, securities, and insurance services. Since the act clarified the rules on offering insurance services, financial institutions no longer had to search for loopholes that would allow them to offer some types of insurance services.

EXHIBIT 25.6 Participation of Insurance Companies in Financial Markets

Financial Market	Participation by Insurance Companies
Money markets	• Insurance companies maintain a portion of their funds in money market securities, such as Treasury bills and commercial paper, to maintain adequate liquidity.
Bond markets	• Some life insurance company assets and PC insurance company assets are allocated to corporate bond portfolios. • Insurance companies frequently purchase bonds that are directly placed, and they are less likely to liquidate these bonds before maturity. • Insurance companies also purchase Treasury bonds for their safety and liquidity. • Some U.S. insurance companies purchase foreign bonds, primarily issued by Canadian firms.
Mortgage markets	• Life insurance companies have, in aggregate, allocated some of their assets to a mortgage portfolio. They hold mostly conventional mortgages, as only a small percentage of their mortgages are federally insured. Although PC companies also hold mortgages, their mortgage portfolio represents a smaller percentage of total assets.
Stock markets	• Life insurance companies have, in aggregate, allocated a portion of their assets to a stock portfolio; PC companies have also allocated a portion of their assets to a stock portfolio. Foreign stocks are often included in their stock portfolios.
Futures markets	• Some insurance companies sell futures contracts on bonds or a bond market index to hedge their bond and mortgage portfolios against interest rate risk. • Some insurance companies take positions in stock market index futures to hedge their stock portfolios against market risk.
Options markets	• Some insurance companies purchase call options on particular stocks that they plan to purchase in the near future. • Some insurance companies also purchase put options or write call options on stocks they own that may experience a temporary decline in price.
Swap markets	• Insurance companies commonly engage in interest rate swaps to hedge the exposure of their bond and mortgage portfolios to interest rate risk.

Financial Market Participation

The manner in which insurance companies use their funds indicates their form of participation in the various financial markets. Insurance companies are common participants in the stock, bond, and mortgage markets because their asset portfolios are concentrated in these securities. They also use the money markets to purchase short-term securities for liquidity purposes. Although their participation in money markets is less than in capital markets, they have recently increased their holdings of money market instruments such as Treasury bills and commercial paper. Some insurance companies use futures and options markets to hedge the impact of interest rates on bonds and mortgages and to hedge against anticipated movements in stock prices. Insurance companies generally participate in the futures, options, and swap markets for risk reduction rather than speculation. Exhibit 25.6 summarizes the manner in which life insurance companies participate in financial markets.

Multinational Insurance Companies

 GL BALASPECTS Some life insurance companies are multinational corporations with subsidiaries and joint ventures in several countries. By expanding their international business, insurance companies may reduce their exposure to the U.S. economy. However, they must comply with

foreign regulations regarding services offered in foreign countries. The differences in regulations among countries increase the information costs of entering foreign markets.

Many U.S. insurance companies have recently established insurance subsidiaries in less developed countries that are underinsured. For example, less than 3 percent of the people in Mexico have life or home insurance, and less than 25 percent have automobile insurance. The lack of a developed insurance market offers much potential to U.S. insurance companies. In addition, the economic growth in Mexico resulting from the North American Free Trade Agreement (NAFTA) has created more demand for commercial insurance.

Pension Fund Background

Pension plans provide a savings plan for employees that can be used for retirement. They receive premiums from the employer and/or the employee. In aggregate, most of the contributions come from the employer.

Public Pension Funds

Public pension funds can be either state, local, or federal. The best-known government pension fund is Social Security. In addition to that system, all government employees and almost half of all nongovernment employees participate in other pension funds.

Many public pension plans are funded on a pay-as-you-go basis. Thus, existing employee and employer contributors are essentially supporting previous employees. At some point, this strategy could cause the future benefits owed to outweigh contributions to such an extent that the pension fund would be unable to fulfill its promises or would have to obtain more contributions to do so.

Private Pension Plans

Private pension plans are created by private agencies, including industrial, labor, service, nonprofit, charitable, and educational organizations. Some pension funds are so large that they are major investors in corporate securities.

Defined-Benefit Plan Private pension funds can be classified by the way contributions are received and benefits are paid. With a **defined-benefit plan,** contributions are dictated by the benefits that will eventually be provided. When the value of pension assets exceeds the current and future benefits owed to employees, companies respond by reducing future contributions. Alternatively, they may distribute the surplus amount to the firm's shareholders rather than the employees. Thus, the management of the pension fund can have a direct impact on shareholders.

Defined-Contribution Plan In contrast, a **defined-contribution plan** provides benefits that are determined by the accumulated contributions and the fund's investment performance. Some firms match a portion of the contribution made by their employees. With this type of plan, a firm knows with certainty the amount of funds to contribute, whereas that amount is undetermined in a defined-benefit plan. However, a defined-contribution plan provides uncertain benefits to the participants. Firms commonly hire an investment company to manage the pension portfolios of employees.

Defined-contribution plans outnumber defined-benefit plans, but defined-benefit plans have more participants and a greater aggregate value of assets. New plans allow employees more flexibility to choose what they want. In recent years, defined-benefit plans have commonly been replaced by defined-contribution plans. Employees can often decide the pace of their contributions and how their contributions will be invested. Common investment alternatives include stocks, investment-grade bonds, real estate, and money market securities. Communications from the benefits coordinator to the employees have become much more important, because employees now have more influence on their pension plan contributions and the investment approach used to invest the premiums.

Underfunded Pensions

The future pension obligations of a defined-benefit plan are uncertain because the obligations are stated in terms of fixed payments to retirees. These payments are dependent on salary levels, retirement ages, and life expectancies. Even if future payment obligations can be accurately predicted, the amount the plan needs today will be uncertain because of the uncertain rate of return on today's investments. The higher the future return on the plan's investments, the fewer the funds that must be invested today to satisfy future payments.

In the early 1990s, many defined-benefit plans used optimistic projections of the rate of return to be earned on their investments, which created the appearance that their existing investments were adequate to cover future payment obligations. This allowed the corporations to reduce their contributions (an expense) to the plan and thereby increase their earnings. However, when projected rates of return on the pension funds were overestimated, the pension funds became underfunded, or inadequate to cover future payment obligations.

Some pension funds have recently made investments that offer high potential returns in order to justify their high projected rates of return. These investments, which include real estate, junk bonds, and international securities, also carry a high degree of risk. Thus, it is possible that some pension plans could be heavily underfunded if these investments perform poorly.

When pension funds become underfunded because of a rate of return projection that turns out to be too optimistic, corporations are forced to replenish their underfunded pension funds. To illustrate the impact, consider the case of General Motors, which recognized that its projected rate of return of 8.6 percent was overly optimistic. It reduced the projected rate of return to 7.6 percent, which caused the pension fund to be underfunded by about $5 billion. Some corporations are placing new stock in their pension fund portfolios. In this way, they are contributing to their pension funds without using up their cash.

Pension Regulations

http://

http://www.eric.org
Information about pension guidelines.

The regulation of pension funds varies with the type of plan. All plans must comply with the set of Internal Revenue Service tax rules that apply to pension fund income. For defined-contribution plans, the sponsoring firm's main responsibility is its contributions to the fund.

Defined-contribution plans are also subject to guidelines specified by the Employee Retirement Income Security Act (ERISA) of 1974 (also called the Pension Reform Act)

and its 1989 revisions. This act requires that a pension fund choose one of two vesting schedule options:

1. One hundred percent vesting after five years of service.
2. Graded vesting, with 20 percent vesting in the third year, 40 percent in the fourth, 60 percent in the fifth, 80 percent in the sixth, and 100 percent in the seventh year.

ERISA also requires that any contributions be invested in a prudent manner, meaning that pension funds should concentrate their investments in high-grade securities. Although this was implicitly expected before, ERISA made this so-called fiduciary responsibility (monitored by the U.S. Department of Labor) explicit to encourage portfolio managers to serve the interests of the employees rather than themselves. Pension plans can face legal ramifications if they do not comply.

In addition, ERISA allows employees changing employers to transfer any vested amount into the pension plan of their new employer or to invest it in an Individual Retirement Account (IRA). With either alternative, taxes on the vested amount are still deferred until retirement when the funds become available.

The Pension Benefit Guaranty Corporation

In addition, ERISA established the Pension Benefit Guaranty Corporation (PBGC) to provide insurance on pension plans. This federally chartered agency guarantees that participants of defined-benefit pension plans will receive their benefits upon retirement. If the pension fund is incapable of fully providing the benefits promised, the PBGC will make up the difference. The PBGC does not receive government support. It is financed by annual premiums, income from assets acquired from terminated pension plans, and income generated by investments. It also receives employer-liability payments when an employer terminates its pension plan.

About 40 million Americans, or one-third of the workforce, have pension plans insured by the PBGC. As a wholly owned independent government agency, it differs from other federal regulatory agencies in that it has no regulatory powers.

The PBGC monitors pension plans periodically to determine whether they can adequately provide the benefits they have guaranteed. If a plan is judged inadequate, it is terminated, and the PBGC (or a PBGC appointee) takes control as the fund manager. The PBGC has a claim on part of a firm's net worth if it is needed to support the underfunded pension assets.

The PBGC's funding requirements depend on all the pension funds it monitors. Because the market values of these funds are similarly susceptible to economic conditions, funding requirements are volatile over time. A poor economic environment will depress stock prices and simultaneously reduce the asset values of most pension funds.

When companies experience problems, they often cut their pension contributions to the minimum funding level established by ERISA. In a sense, the funding of pensions becomes a financing source for firms experiencing cash flow problems. Nevertheless, the benefits the firm is obligated to pay out continue to accumulate (on defined-benefit plans).

Pension Fund Management

Regardless of the manner in which premiums are contributed, the premiums received must be managed (invested) until needed to pay benefits. Private pension portfolios are

http://www.pensionfunds
.com/ News related to
pension funds.

dominated by common stock. Public pension portfolios are somewhat evenly invested in corporate bonds, stock, and other credit instruments.

Pension fund management can be classified according to the strategy used to manage the portfolio. With a **matched funding** strategy, investment decisions are made with the objective of generating cash flows that match planned outflow payments. An alternative strategy is **projective funding,** which offers managers more flexibility in constructing a pension portfolio that can benefit from expected market and interest rate movements. Some pension funds segment their portfolios, with part used for matched funding and the rest for projective funding.

An informal method of matched funding is to invest in long-term bonds to fund long-term liabilities and intermediate bonds to fund intermediate liabilities. The appeal of matching is the assurance that future liabilities are covered regardless of market movements. Matching limits the manager's discretion, however, because it allows only investments that match future payouts. For example, portfolio managers required to use matched funding would need to avoid callable bonds, because these bonds could potentially be retired before maturity. This requirement precludes consideration of many high-yield bonds. In addition, each liability payout may require a separate investment to which it can be perfectly matched; this would require several small investments and increase the pension fund's transaction costs.

Pension funds that are willing to accept market returns on bonds can purchase bond index portfolios that have been created by investment companies. The bond index portfolio may include investment-grade corporate bonds, Treasury bonds, and U.S. government agency bonds. It does not include the entire set of these bonds but includes enough of them to mirror market performance. Investing in a market portfolio is a passive approach that does not require any analysis of individual bonds. Some pension funds are not willing to accept a totally passive approach, so they compromise by using only a portion of their funds to purchase a bond market portfolio.

Equity portfolio indexes that mirror the stock market are also available for passive portfolio managers. These index funds have become popular over time, as they avoid transaction costs associated with frequent purchases and sales of individual stocks.

Management of Insured versus Trust Portfolios

Some pension plans are managed by life insurance companies. Contributions to such plans, called **insured plans,** are often used to purchase annuity policies so that the life insurance companies can provide benefits to employees upon retirement.

As an alternative, some pension funds are managed by the trust departments of financial institutions, such as commercial banks. The trust department invests the contributions and pays benefits to employees upon retirement. Although the day-to-day investment decisions of the trust department are controlled by the managing institution, the corporation owning the pension normally specifies general guidelines that the institution should follow. These guidelines might include

- The percentage of the portfolio that should be used for stocks or bonds
- A desired minimum rate of return on the overall portfolio
- The maximum amount to be invested in real estate
- The minimum acceptable quality ratings for bonds
- The maximum amount to be invested in any one industry
- The average maturity of bonds held in the portfolio
- The maximum amount to be invested in options
- The minimum size of companies in which to invest

There is a significant difference in the asset composition of pension portfolios managed by life insurance companies and those managed by trust departments. Assets managed by insurance companies are designed to create annuities, whereas the assets managed by a trust department still belong to the corporation. The insurance company becomes the legal owner of the assets and is allowed to maintain only a small portion of its assets as equities. Therefore insurance companies concentrate on bonds and mortgages. Conversely, the pension portfolios managed by trusts concentrate on stocks.

Pension portfolios managed by trusts offer potentially higher returns than insured plans and also have a higher degree of risk. The average return of trust plans is much more volatile over time.

Portfolio Risk Management

Pension fund portfolio managers are very concerned about interest rate risk. If they hold long-term, fixed-rate bonds, the market value of their portfolio will decrease during periods when interest rates increase. They may periodically hedge against interest rate movements by selling bond futures contracts.

Many portfolio managers periodically sell futures contracts on stock indexes to hedge against market downturns. Portfolio managers of pension funds can obtain various types of insurance to limit the risk of the portfolio. For example, a policy could insure beyond a specified decline (such as 10 percent) in the asset value of a pension fund. This insurance allows managers to use more aggressive investment strategies. The cost of the insurance depends on the provisions of the contract and the length of time the portfolio is to be insured.

The pension funds of some companies, such as Lockheed Martin, simply concentrate investment in stocks and bonds and do not employ immunization techniques (to hedge the portfolio against risk). Lockheed Martin has generally focused on highly liquid investments so that the proportion of stocks and bonds within the portfolio can be revised in response to market conditions.

Pension Funds: Corporate Control

Pension funds in aggregate hold a substantial portion of the common stock outstanding in the United States. These funds are increasingly using their ownership as a means of influencing policies of the corporations whose stock they own. In particular, the California Pension Employees Retirement System (CALPERS) and the New York State Government Retirement Fund have taken active roles in questioning specific policies and suggesting changes to the board of directors at some corporations. Corporate managers consider the requests of pension funds because of the large stake the pension funds have in the corporations. As pension funds exert some corporate control to ensure that the managers and board members serve the best interests of shareholders, they can benefit because of their position as large shareholders.

Pension Fund Performance

Pension funds commonly maintain a portfolio of stocks and a portfolio of bonds. Since pension funds focus on investing pension contributions until payments are provided, the performance of the investments is critical to the pension fund's success.

Determinants of a Pension Fund's Stock Portfolio Performance

The change in the performance (measured by risk-adjusted returns) of a pension fund's portfolio focusing on stocks can be modeled as

$$\Delta \text{PERF} = f(\Delta \text{MKT}, \Delta \text{MANAB})$$

where MKT represents general stock market conditions, and MANAB represents the abilities of the pension fund's management.

Change in Market Conditions The stock portfolio's performance is usually closely related to market conditions. Most pension funds' stock portfolios performed well in the late 1990s when stock market conditions were very favorable. However, they performed poorly when the economy weakened in the 2000–2002 period.

Change in Management Abilities Stock portfolio performance can vary among pension funds in a particular time period because of differences in management abilities. The composition of the stocks in a pension fund's portfolio is determined by the fund's portfolio managers. In addition, a pension fund's operating efficiency affects the expenses the fund incurs and therefore affects its performance. A fund that is managed efficiently such that its expenses are low may be able to achieve higher returns even if its portfolio performance is about the same as the performance of other pension funds' portfolios.

Determinants of a Pension Fund's Bond Portfolio Performance

The change in the performance of a pension fund's bond portfolio can be modeled as

$$\Delta \text{PERF} = f(\Delta R_f, \Delta RP, \Delta \text{MANAB})$$

where R_f represents the risk-free rate, RP represents the risk premium, and MANAB represents the abilities of the portfolio managers.

Impact of Change in the Risk-Free Rate The prices of bonds tend to be inversely related to changes in the risk-free interest rate. In periods when the risk-free interest rate declines substantially, the required rate of return by bondholders declines, and most bond portfolios managed by pension funds perform well.

Impact of Change in the Risk Premium The prices of bonds tend to be inversely related to changes in the risk premiums required by investors who purchase bonds. When economic conditions deteriorate, the risk premium required by bondholders usually increases, which results in a higher required rate of return (assuming no change in the risk-free rate) and lower prices on risky bonds. In periods when risk premiums increase, bond portfolios of pension funds that contain a high proportion of risky bonds perform poorly.

Impact of Management Abilities The performance levels of bond portfolios can vary due to differences in management abilities. If a pension fund's portfolio managers can effectively adjust the bond portfolio in response to accurate forecasts of changes in interest rates or shifts in bond risk premiums, that fund's bond portfolio should experience relatively high performance. In addition, a pension fund's operating efficiency af-

fects the expenses it incurs. If a bond portfolio is managed efficiently such that its expenses are low, it may be able to achieve relatively high returns even if its investments perform the same as those of other pension funds.

Performance Evaluation

If a manager has the flexibility to adjust the relative proportion of stocks versus bonds, the portfolio performance should be compared to a benchmark representing a passive strategy. For example, assume that the general long-run plan is a balance of 60 percent bonds and 40 percent stocks. Also assume that management has decided to create a more bond-intensive portfolio in anticipation of lower interest rates. The risk-adjusted returns on this actively managed portfolio could be compared to a benchmark portfolio composed of 60 percent bond index plus 40 percent stock index.

Any difference between the performance of the pension portfolio and the benchmark portfolio would result from (1) the manager's shift in the relative proportion of bonds versus stocks and (2) the composition of bonds and stocks within the respective portfolios. A pension portfolio could conceivably have stocks that outperform the stock index and bonds that outperform the bond index yet be outperformed by the benchmark portfolio when the shift in the relative bond/stock proportion backfires. In this example, a period of rising interest rates could cause the pension portfolio to be outperformed by the benchmark portfolio.

In many cases, the performances of stocks and bonds in a pension fund are evaluated separately. Stock portfolio risk is usually measured by the portfolio's beta, or the sensitivity to movements in a stock index (such as the S&P 500). Bond portfolio risk can be measured by the bond portfolio's sensitivity to a bond index or to a particular proxy for interest rates.

Performance of Pension Portfolio Managers

Many pension funds hire several portfolio managers to manage the assets. The general objective of portfolio managers is to make investments that will earn a large enough return to adequately meet future payment obligations. Some research has found that managed pension portfolios perform no better than market indexes. Based on these results, pension funds might consider investing in indexed mutual funds, which would perform as well as the market without requiring the pension plan to incur expenses for portfolio management.

Pension Fund Participation in Financial Markets

Various financial institutions and markets participate in the management of a pension fund. First, the sponsor corporation decides on a trust pension fund through a commercial bank's trust department or an insured pension fund through an insurance company. The financial institution that is delegated the task of managing the pension fund then receives periodic contributions and invests them. Many investments in the stock, bond, and mortgage markets require the brokerage services of securities firms. Managers of pension funds instruct securities firms on the type and amount of investment instruments to purchase. In some cases, the financial institutions may bypass brokerage firms by purchasing a directly placed new issue of bonds or stocks by a corporation. The premiums contributed to pension funds are ultimately used to provide financing for

EXHIBIT 25.7 Interaction between Pension Funds and Other Financial Institutions

Type of Financial Institution	Interaction with Pension Funds
Commercial banks	• Commercial banks sometimes manage pension funds. • Pension funds commonly purchase commercial loans that are sold by commercial banks in the secondary market.
Insurance companies	• Insurance companies sometimes create annuities for pension funds.
Mutual funds	• Some pension funds invest in various mutual funds, which allows them to achieve diversification without incurring excessive transaction costs.
Brokerage firms and investment banking firms	• Brokerage firms normally execute securities transactions for pension funds. • Brokerage firms offer investment advice to pension portfolio managers. • Investment banking firms commonly act as advisers on leveraged buyouts in which pension funds participate. • Investment banking firms underwrite newly issued stocks and bonds that are purchased by pension funds.

corporations and governments that issue securities. Exhibit 25.7 summarizes the interaction between pension funds and other financial institutions.

Because pension fund portfolios are normally dominated by stocks and bonds, the participation of pension fund managers in the stock and bond markets is obvious. Pension fund managers also participate in money and mortgage markets to fill out the remainder of their respective portfolios. They sometimes utilize the futures and options markets as well in order to partially insulate their portfolio performance from interest rate and/or stock market movements. Exhibit 25.8 summarizes how pension fund managers participate in various financial markets.

EXHIBIT 25.8   Participation of Pension Funds in Financial Markets

Financial Market	Participation by Pension Funds
Money markets	• Pension fund managers maintain a small proportion of liquid money market securities that can be liquidated when they wish to increase investment in stocks, bonds, or other alternatives.
Bond markets	• At least 25 percent of a pension fund portfolio is typically allocated to bonds. Portfolios of defined-benefit plans usually have a higher concentration of bonds than defined-contribution plans. Pension fund managers frequently conduct transactions in the bond market.
Mortgage markets	• Pension portfolios frequently contain some mortgages, although the relative proportion is low compared with bonds and stocks.
Stock markets	• At least 30 percent of a pension fund portfolio is typically allocated to stocks. In general, defined-contribution plans usually have a higher concentration of stocks than defined-benefit plans.
Futures markets	• Some pension funds use futures contracts on debt securities and on bond indexes to hedge the exposure of their bond holdings to interest rate risk. In addition, some pension funds use futures on stock indexes to hedge against market risk. Other pension funds use futures contracts for speculative purposes.
Options markets	• Some pension funds use stock options to hedge against movements of particular stocks. They may also use options on futures contracts to secure downside protection against bond price movements.
Swap markets	• Pension funds commonly engage in interest rate swaps to hedge the exposure of their bond and mortgage portfolios to interest rate risk.

SUMMARY

- The main uses of life insurance company funds are as investments in government securities, corporate securities, mortgages, and real estate. Property and casualty insurance companies focus on similar types of assets, but maintain a higher concentration in government securities.

- Insurance companies are exposed to interest rate risk, as they tend to maintain large bond portfolios whose values decline when interest rates rise. They are also exposed to credit risk and market risk, as a result of their investments in corporate debt securities, mortgages, stocks, and real estate.

- The value of an insurance company is based on its expected cash flows and the required rate of return by investors. The payouts of claims are somewhat predictable for life insurance firms, so they tend to

have stable cash flows. In contrast, the payouts of claims for property and casualty insurance firms are subject to much uncertainty.

- Pension funds provide a savings plan for retirement. For defined-benefit pension plans, the contributions are dictated by the benefits that are specified. For defined-contribution pension plans, the benefits are determined by the accumulated contributions and the returns on the pension fund investments.

- Pension funds can use a matched funding strategy, in which investment decisions are made with the objective of generating cash flows that match planned outflow payments. Alternatively, pension funds can use a projective funding strategy, which attempts to capitalize on expected market or interest rate movements.

POINT COUNTER-POINT

Should Defined-Contribution Pension Funds Be Actively Managed?

Point Yes. Pension funds should be actively managed so that the funds can benefit from market timing by the pension fund managers. Higher returns will lead to a greater accumulation of retirement benefits.

Counter-Point No. Active management of a pension fund results in expenses, which reduce the return on the investment portfolio. A passive approach can be used, in which the funds contributed to the pension

plan are automatically invested in a mutual fund or an exchange traded fund that fits the investment objectives of the employees. This approach can avoid the fees associated with active management.

Who Is Correct? Use your favorite search engine to learn more about this issue. Offer your own opinion on this issue.

QUESTIONS AND APPLICATIONS

1. **Managing Interest Rates** Why are life insurance equity values sensitive to interest rate movements? What are two strategies that reduce the impact of changing interest rates on the market value of life insurance companies' assets?

2. **PC Insurance** What purpose do property and casualty (PC) insurance companies serve? Explain how the characteristics of PC insurance and life insurance differ.

3. **Managing in Financial Markets: Assessing Insurance Company Operations** As a consultant to an insurance

company, you have been asked to assess the asset composition of the company.

   a. The insurance company has recently sold a large amount of bonds and invested the proceeds in real estate. Its logic was that this would reduce the exposure of the assets to interest rate risk. Do you agree? Explain.

   b. This insurance company currently has a small amount of stock. The company expects that it will need to liquidate some of its assets soon to make payments to beneficiaries. Should it

shift its bond holdings (with short terms remaining until maturity) into stock in order to strive for a higher rate of return before it needs to liquidate this investment?

c. The insurance company maintains a higher proportion of junk bonds than most other insurance companies. In recent years, junk bonds have performed very well during a period of strong economic growth, as the yields paid by junk bonds have been well above those of high-quality corporate bonds. There have been very few defaults over this period. Consequently, the insurance company has proposed that it invest more heavily in junk bonds, as it believes that the concerns about junk bonds are unjustified. Do you agree? Explain.

4. **Life Insurance** How is whole life insurance a form of savings to policyholders?

5. **Internet Exercise** Obtain a life insurance quotation online, using the website http://www.eterm.com.
a. Fill in information about you (or a family member or friend) and obtain a quotation for a $1 million life insurance policy. What are the monthly and annual premiums for the various term lengths? Next, leaving all other information unchanged, change your gender. Are the premiums the same or different? Do you think insurance premiums are higher or lower for insurance companies operating entirely through the Internet?

6. **Guidelines for a Trust** What type of general guidelines may be specified for a trust that is managing a pension fund?

7. **ERISA** Explain how ERISA affects employees who frequently change employers.

8. **Managing Credit Risk and Liquidity Risk** How do insurance companies manage credit risk and liquidity risk?

9. **Interpreting Financial News** Interpret the following comments made by Wall Street analysts and portfolio managers:
a. "Insurance company stocks may benefit from the recent decline in interest rates."
b. "Insurance company portfolio managers may serve as shareholder activists to implicitly control a corporation's actions."
c. "If a life insurance company wants a portfolio manager to generate sufficient cash to meet expected payments to beneficiaries, it cannot ex-

pect the manager to achieve relatively high returns for the portfolio."

10. **Assets of Life Insurance Companies** What are the main assets of life insurance companies? Identify the main categories. What is the main use of funds by life insurance companies?

11. **Whole Life versus Term Insurance** How do whole life and term insurance differ from the perspective of insurance companies? From the perspective of the policyholders?

12. **Private versus Public Pension Funds** Explain the general difference between the portfolio composition of private pension funds versus public pension funds.

13. **Financing the Real Estate Market** How do insurance companies finance the real estate market?

14. **Liquidity Risk** Discuss the liquidity risk experienced by life insurance and property and casualty (PC) insurance companies.

15. **Pension Agency Problems** The objective of the pension fund manager for McCanna Inc. is not the same as the objective of McCanna's employees participating in the pension plan. Why?

16. **Universal Life Insurance** Identify the characteristics of universal life insurance.

17. **Exposure to Interest Rate Risk** How can pension funds reduce their exposure to interest rate risk?

18. **Policy Loans** What is a policy loan? When is it popular? Why?

19. **Cash Flow Underwriting** Explain the concept of cash flow underwriting.

20. **PBGC** What is the main purpose of the Pension Benefit Guarantee Corporation (PBGC)?

21. **Group Plan.** Explain group plan life insurance.

22. **Impact of Inflation on Assets** Explain how a life insurance company's asset portfolio may be affected by inflation.

23. **Management of Pension Portfolios** Explain the general difference in the composition of pension portfolios managed by trusts versus those managed by insurance companies. Explain why this difference occurs.

24. **Reinsurance** What is reinsurance?

25. **Defined-Benefit versus Defined-Contribution Plan** Describe a defined-benefit pension plan. Describe a defined-contribution plan, and explain how it differs from a defined-benefit plan.

26. **NAIC** What is the NAIC and what is its purpose?

FLOW OF FUNDS EXERCISE

How Insurance Companies Facilitate the Flow of Funds

Carson Company is considering a private placement of equity with Secura Insurance Company.

a. Explain the interaction between Carson Company and Secura. How will Secura serve Carson's needs, and how will Carson serve Secura's needs?

b. Why does Carson interact with Secura Insurance Company instead of trying to obtain the funds directly from individuals who pay premiums to Secura?

c. Who will benefit if the stock purchased by Secura performs well—Secura's shareholders or Secura's policyholders who purchased term life insurance and property insurance? Is it worthwhile for Secura to closely monitor Carson Company's management? Explain.

WSJ EXERCISE

Insurance Company Performance

Using an issue of *The Wall Street Journal,* summarize an article that discussed the recent performance of a particular insurance company. Does the article suggest that the insurance company's performance was better or worse than the norm? What reason is given for the particular level of performance?

Part VII Integrative Problem

Assessing the Influence of Economic Conditions across a Financial Conglomerate's Units

This problem requires an understanding of the operations and asset compositions of savings institutions (Chapter 21), finance companies (Chapter 22), mutual funds (Chapter 23), securities firms (Chapter 24), and insurance companies (Chapter 25).

A diversified financial conglomerate has five units (subsidiaries). One unit conducts thrift operations; the second unit conducts consumer finance operations; the third, mutual fund operations; the fourth, securities operations; and the fifth, insurance operations. As a financial analyst for the conglomerate's holding company, you have been asked to assess all of the units and indicate how each unit will be affected as economic conditions change and which units will be affected the most.

In the past few months, all economic indicators have been signaling the possibility of a recession. Stock prices have already declined as the demand for stocks has decreased significantly. It appears that the pessimistic outlook will last for at least a few months. Economic conditions are already somewhat stagnant and are expected to deteriorate further in future months. During that time, firms will not consider mergers, new stock issues, or new bond issues.

An economist at your financial conglomerate believes that individual investors will overreact to the pessimistic outlook. Once stock prices are low enough, some firms will acquire target firms whose stock appears to be undervalued. In addition, some firms will buy back some of their own stock once they believe it is undervalued. Although these activities have not yet occurred, the economist believes it is only a matter of time.

Questions

1. Your strategy is to identify the units that will be less adversely affected by the recession. You believe that the units' different characteristics will cause some of them to be affected more than others.

2. Currently, each unit employs economists who develop forecasts for interest rates and other economic conditions. When assessing potential economic effects on each unit, what are the disadvantages of this approach versus having just one economist at the holding company provide forecasts?

Comprehensive Project

One of the best ways to clearly understand the key concepts explained in this text is to apply them directly to actual situations. This comprehensive project enables you to apply numerous concepts regarding financial markets and institutions discussed throughout the text to actual situations. The tasks in this project can be categorized as follows:

Part I.   Applying "Financial Markets" concepts
Part II. Applying "Financial Institutions" concepts
Part III. Measuring Stock Performance

At the beginning of the school term, you should complete two tasks. First, compile the information on financial markets needed to fill in the blank spaces in steps (a) through (j) in Part I. This information will be needed when applying "Financial Markets" concepts in the questions that follow (Part I of the project). Second, obtain the information on financial institutions identified at the beginning of Part II below. This information will be needed when applying the "Financial Institutions" concepts in the questions that follow (Part II of the project).

Part I. Applying "Financial Markets" Concepts

The exercises on Financial Markets concepts require you to measure the change in the yields and values of securities over the school term and explain why the values changed. In doing so, you will apply the concepts in the chapters on financial markets to actual situations.

At the beginning of the school term and near the end of the term, use an issue of *The Wall Street Journal (WSJ)* or various financial websites to obtain the information requested here. Your professor will identify the dates to use as the beginning and end of the term. The dates will allow you sufficient time to assess the changes in the yields and values of securities so that you can answer the questions. Your professor will explain the specific format of the assignment, such as whether any parts are excluded or whether students should work in teams. Your professor will also indicate whether the answers will be handed in, presented to the class, or both. A commonly used format is to divide the project into parts and assign a team of students to present their answers to one specific part. Each student will be a member of one of the teams. All students may still be required to hand in answers to all parts of the project, even though their team's presentation focuses on only one part.

	Beginning of Term	End of Term

a. Use the Markets Diary section in the *WSJ* to record the:

S&P 500 (stock) index level: _____ _____

Nasdaq Composite (stock) index level: _____ _____

DJ World: _____ _____

b. Use the Money Rates section in the *WSJ* to record the:

Prime rate: _____ _____

Discount rate: _____ _____

Federal funds rate: _____ _____

Commercial paper rate (90 days): _____ _____

Certificate of deposit rate (3-month): _____ _____

Treasury bill rate (13 weeks): _____ _____

Treasury bill rate (26 weeks): _____ _____

c. Use the Interest Rates and Bonds table in the *WSJ* to record the:

Treasury long-term bond yield: _____ _____

DJ Corporate bond yield: _____ _____

Corporate (Master) bond yield: _____ _____

High-yield corporate bond yield: _____ _____

Tax-exempt (7–12 yr) bond yield: _____ _____

d. Use the Stock Exchange Quotations to record the stock price and dividend of one stock from each stock exchange in which you would like to invest:

New York Stock Exchange: Stock price: _____ _____

Name of firm _____ Dividend: _____ _____

American Stock Exchange: Stock price: _____ _____

Name of firm _____ Dividend: _____ _____

Nasdaq Market: Stock price: _____ _____

Name of firm _____ Dividend: _____ _____

e. Use the Futures Prices table in the *WSJ* to record the recent ("settle") price of:

Treasury bond futures with the first settlement
   date beyond your school term: _____ _____

	Beginning of Term	End of Term
S&P 500 index futures with the first settlement date beyond your school term:	_____	_____
British pound futures with the first settlement date beyond your school term:	_____	_____

f. **Use the Listed Options Quotations table in the *WSJ* to select a call option on a firm where you expect the stock price to increase (select the option with the first expiration month beyond the end of the school term):**

Name of firm: _____

Expiration month: _____

Strike price: _____

	Beginning of Term	End of Term
Stock price:	_____	_____
Option premium:	_____	_____

g. **Use the Listed Options Quotations table in the *WSJ* to select a put option on a firm where you expect the stock price to decrease (select the option with the first expiration month beyond the end of the school term):**

Name of firm: _____

Expiration month: _____

Strike price: _____

	Beginning of Term	End of Term
Stock price:	_____	_____
Option premium:	_____	_____

h. **Use the Currency Trading table in the *WSJ* to record exchange rates:**

	Beginning of Term	End of Term
Exchange rate of the British pound (in $):	_____	_____
Exchange rate of the Japanese yen (in $):	_____	_____
Exchange rate of the Mexican peso (in $):	_____	_____

i. **Use Currency Option data (if available) to select a call option on a foreign currency that you expect will strengthen against the dollar (select the option with the first expiration month beyond the end of the school term):**

Currency: _____

Expiration month: _____

Strike price: _____

	Beginning of Term	End of Term
Currency's existing value (from the Currency Trading table in the *WSJ*):	_____	_____
Option premium:	_____	_____

	Beginning of Term	End of Term

   j. Use currency options data (if available) to select a put option on a foreign currency that you expect will weaken against the dollar (select the option with the first expiration month beyond the end of the school term):

Currency: _____

Expiration month: _____

Strike price: _____

Currency's existing value (from the Currency
   Trading table in the *WSJ*):   _____   _____

Option premium: _____   _____

1. **Explaining changes in interest rates (from Chapter 2)**
    a. Compare the 13-week Treasury bill rate (which is a proxy for short-term interest rates) at the end of the school term to the rate that existed at the beginning of the school term.
    b. Recall that Chapter 2 offered reasons why interest rates change over time. Apply the concepts in that chapter to explain why you think that interest rates have changed over the school term.

2. **Comparing yields among securities (from Chapter 3)**
    a. What is the difference between the yield on corporate high-quality bonds and the yield on Treasury bonds as of the end of the school term?
    b. Apply the concepts discussed in Chapter 3 to explain why this premium exists.
    c. What is the difference between the yield on long-term Treasury bonds and the yield on long-term municipal bonds as of the end of the school term?
    d. Apply the concepts discussed in Chapter 3 to explain why this difference exists.

3. **Assessing the forecasting ability of the yield curve (from Chapter 3)**
    a. What was the difference between the 26-week T-bill yield and the 13-week T-bill yield at the beginning of the school term?
    b. Does this imply that the yield curve had an upward or downward slope at that time?
    c. Assuming that this slope can be primarily attributed to expectations theory, did the direction of the slope indicate that the market expected higher or lower interest rates in the future?
    d. Did interest rates move in that direction over the school term?

4. **Explaining shifts in the yield curve over time (from Chapter 3)**
    a. What was the difference between the long-term Treasury bond yield and the 13-week T-bill yield at the beginning of the school term?
    b. What is the difference between the long-term Treasury bond yield and the 13-week T-bill yield at the end of the school term?
    c. Given your answers to the two previous questions, describe how the yield curve changed over the school term. Explain the changes in expectations about future interest rates that are implied by the shift in the yield curve over the school term.

5. **The Fed's influence on interest rates (from Chapter 5)**
    a. Did the Fed change the federal funds rate over the school term?
    b. Do you think the movements in interest rates over the school term were caused by the Fed's monetary policy? Explain.

6. **Explaining stock price movements (from Chapter 7)**
   a. Determine the return on the stock market over your school term, based on the percentage change in the S&P 500 index level over the term. Annualize this return by multiplying the return times $(12/m)$, where m is the number of months in your school term. Apply concepts discussed in Chapter 7 to explain why the market return was high or low over your school term.
   b. Repeat the previous question for smaller stocks by using the Nasdaq Composite instead of the S&P 500 index. What was the annualized return on the Nasdaq Composite over your school term?
   c. Explain why the return on the Nasdaq Composite was high or low over your school term.
   d. Determine the return over the school term on the stock in which you chose to invest. The return is $(P_t - P_{t-1} + D)/P_{t-1}$, where P_t is the stock price as of the end of the school term, P_{t-1} is the stock price at the beginning of the school term, and D is the dividend paid over the school term. In most cases, one quarterly dividend is paid over a school term, which is one-fourth of the annual dividend amount per share shown in stock quotation tables.
   e. What was your return over the school term on the stock you selected from the New York Stock Exchange? What was your return over the school term on the stock you selected from the American Stock Exchange? What was your return over the school term on the stock you selected from the Nasdaq market? Apply the concepts discussed in Chapter 7 to explain why you think these three stocks experienced different returns over the school term.

7. **Measuring and explaining premiums on money market securities (from Chapter 9)**
   a. What is the difference between the yield on 90-day commercial paper and the yield on 13-week T-bills as of the end of the school term? Apply the concepts discussed in Chapter 9 to explain why this premium exists.
   b. Compare the premium on the 90-day commercial paper yield (relative to the 13-week T-bill yield) that exists at the end of the school term to the premium that existed at the beginning of the term. Apply the concepts discussed in Chapter 9 to explain why the premium may have changed over the school term.

8. **Explaining bond premiums and price movements (from Chapter 11)**
   a. What is the difference between the yield on high-yield corporate bonds and the yield on high-quality corporate bonds as of the end of the school term? Apply the concepts discussed in Chapter 11 to explain why this premium exists.
   b. Compare the long-term Treasury bond yield at the end of the school term to the long-term Treasury bond yield that existed at the beginning of the school term. Given the direction of this change, did prices of long-term bonds rise or fall over the school term?
   c. Compare the change in the yields of Treasury, municipal, and corporate bonds over the school term. Did the yields of all three types of securities move in the same direction and by about the same degree? Apply the concepts discussed in Chapter 11 to explain why yields of different types of bonds move together.
   d. Compare the premium on high-yield corporate bonds (relative to Treasury bonds) at the beginning of the school term to the premium that existed at the end of the school term. Did the premium increase or decrease? Apply the concepts discussed in Chapter 11 to explain why this premium changed over the school term.

9. **Explaining mortgage rates (from Chapter 12)**
   a. Compare the rate paid by a homeowner on a 30-year mortgage to the rate (yield) paid by the Treasury on long-term Treasury bonds as of the end of the school term. Explain the difference.
   b. Compare the 30-year mortgage rate at the end of the school term to the 30-year mortgage rate that existed at the beginning of the school term. What do you think is the primary reason for the change in the 30-year mortgage rates over the school term?

10. **Measuring and explaining futures price movements (from Chapter 13)**
    a. Assume that you purchased an S&P 500 futures contract at the beginning of the school term, with the first settlement date beyond the end of the school term. Also assume that you sold an S&P 500 futures contract with this same settlement date at the end of the school term. Given that this contract has a value of the futures price times $250, determine the difference between the dollar value of the contract you sold and the dollar amount of the contract that you purchased.
    b. Assume that you invested an initial margin of 20 percent of the amount that you would owe to purchase the S&P 500 index at the settlement date. Measure your return from taking a position in the S&P 500 index futures as follows. Take the difference determined in the previous question (which represents the dollar amount of the gain on the futures position), and divide it by the amount you originally invested (the amount you originally invested is 20 percent of the dollar value of the futures contract that you purchased).
    c. The return that you just derived in the previous question is not annualized. To annualize your return, multiply it by $(12/m)$, where m is the number of months in your school term.
    d. Apply the concepts discussed in Chapter 13 to explain why your return on your S&P 500 index futures position was low or high over the school term.
    e. Assume that you purchased a Treasury bond futures contract at the beginning of the school term with the first settlement date beyond the end of the school term. Also assume that you sold this same type of futures contract at the end of the school term. Recall that Treasury bond futures contracts are priced relative to a $100,000 face value, and the fractions are in thirty-seconds. What was the dollar value of the futures contract at the beginning of the school term when you purchased it?
    f. What was the dollar value of the Treasury bond futures contract at the end of the school term when you sold it?
    g. What was the difference between the dollar value of the Treasury bond futures contract when you sold it and the value when you purchased it?
    h. Assume that you invested an initial margin of 20 percent of the amount that you would owe to purchase the Treasury bonds at settlement date. Your investment is equal to 20 percent of the dollar value of the Treasury bond futures contract as of the time you purchased the futures. Determine the return on your futures position, which is the difference you derived in the previous question as a percentage of your investment.
    i. The return that you just derived in the previous question is not annualized. To annualize your return, multiply your return times $(12/m)$, where m is the number of months in your school term.
    j. Apply the concepts discussed in Chapter 13 to explain why the return on your Treasury bond futures position was low or high.

11. **Measuring and explaining option price movements (from Chapter 14)**
    a. Assume that you purchased a call option (representing 100 shares) on the specific stock that you identified in Part I (f) of this project. What was your return from purchasing this option? [Your return can be measured as $(\text{Prem}_t - \text{Prem}_{t-1})/\text{Prem}_{t-1}$, where Prem_{t-1} represents the premium paid at the beginning of the school term and Prem_t represents the premium at which the same option can be sold at the end of the school term.] If the premium for this option is not quoted at the end of the school term, measure the return as if you exercised the call option at the end of the school term (assuming that it is feasible to exercise the option at that time). That is, the return is based on purchasing the stock at the option's strike price and then selling the stock at its market price at the end of the school term.
    b. Annualize the return on your option by multiplying the return you derived in the previous question by $(12/m)$, where m represents the number of months in your school term.
    c. Compare the return on your call option to the return that you would have earned if you simply invested in the stock itself. Notice how the magnitude of the return on the call option is much larger than the magnitude of the return on the stock itself. That is, the gains are larger and the losses are larger when investing in call options on a stock instead of the stock itself.
    d. Assume that you purchased a put option (representing 100 shares) on the specific stock that you identified in Part I (g) of this project. What was your return from purchasing this option? [Your return can be measured as $(\text{Prem}_t - \text{Prem}_{t-1})/\text{Prem}_{t-1}$, where Prem_{t-1} represents the premium paid at the beginning of the school term and Prem_t represents the premium at which the same option can be sold at the end of the school term.] If the premium for this option is not quoted at the end of the school term, measure the return as if you exercised the put option at the end of the school term (assuming that it is feasible to exercise the option at that time). That is, the return is based on purchasing the stock at its market price and then selling the stock at the option's strike price at the end of the school term.

12. **Determining swap payments (from Chapter 15)**
    a. Assume that at the beginning of the school term, you engaged in a fixed-for-floating rate swap in which you agreed to pay 6 percent in exchange for the prevailing 26-week T-bill rate that exists at the end of the school term. Assume that your swap agreement specifies the end of the school term as the only time at which a swap will occur, and that the notional amount is $10 million. Determine the amount that you owe on the swap, the amount you are owed on the swap, and the difference. Did you gain or lose as a result of the swap?

13. **Measuring and explaining exchange rate movements (from Chapter 16)**
    a. Determine the percentage change in the value of the British pound over the school term. Did the pound appreciate or depreciate against the dollar?
    b. Determine the percentage change in the value of the Japanese yen over the school term. Did the yen appreciate or depreciate against the dollar?
    c. Determine the percentage change in the value of the Mexican peso over the school term. Did the peso appreciate or depreciate against the dollar?
    d. Determine the per unit gain or loss if you had purchased British pound futures at the beginning of the term and sold British pound futures at the end of the term.
    e. Given that a single futures contract on British pounds represents 62,500 pounds, determine the dollar amount of your gain or loss.

Part II. Applying "Financial Institutions" Concepts

Obtain an annual report of (1) a commercial bank, (2) a savings and loan association, (3) an investment bank, and (4) an insurance company. The annual reports will allow you to relate the theory in specific related chapters to the particular financial institution of concern. The exercises in Part II of the Comprehensive Project require the use of these annual reports. The annual reports can be obtained by calling the Shareholder Services department for each financial institution, or they may be available online. Also, order a prospectus of a specific mutual fund in which you are interested. The prospectus can be obtained from the specific investment company that sponsors the mutual fund, or it may be available online.

1. **Commercial bank operations (from Chapter 17)**
    For the commercial bank that you selected at the beginning of the term, use its annual report or any other related information to answer the following questions:
    a. Identify the types of deposits that the commercial bank uses to obtain most of its funds.
    b. Identify the main uses of funds by the bank.
    c. Summarize any statements made by the commercial bank in its annual report about how recent or potential regulations will affect its performance.
    d. Does it appear that the bank is attempting to enter the securities industry by offering securities services? If so, explain how.
    e. Does it appear that the bank is attempting to enter the insurance industry by offering insurance services? If so, explain how.

2. **Commercial bank management (from Chapter 19)**
    For the commercial bank that you selected at the beginning of the term, use its annual report or any other related information to answer the following questions:
    a. Assess the bank's balance sheet as well as any comments in its annual report about the gap between its rate-sensitive assets and its rate-sensitive liabilities. Does it appear that the bank has a positive gap or a negative gap?
    b. Does the bank use any methods to reduce its gap and therefore reduce its exposure to interest rate risk?
    c. Summarize any statements made by the bank in its annual report about how it attempts to limit its exposure to credit risk on the loans it provides.

3. **Commercial bank performance (from Chapter 20)**
    For the commercial bank that you selected at the beginning of the term, use its annual report or any other related information to answer the following questions:
    a. Determine the bank's interest income as a percentage of its total assets.
    b. Determine the bank's interest expenses as a percentage of its total assets.
    c. Determine the bank's net interest margin.
    d. Determine the bank's noninterest income as a percentage of its total assets.
    e. Determine the bank's noninterest expenses (do not include the addition to loan loss reserves here) as a percentage of total assets.
    f. Determine the bank's addition to loan loss reserves as a percentage of its total assets.
    g. Determine the bank's return on assets.
    h. Determine the bank's return on equity.
    i. Identify the bank's income statement items described previously that would be affected if interest rates rise in the next year, and explain how they would be affected.

j. Identify the bank's income statement items described previously that would be affected if U.S. economic conditions deteriorate, and explain how they would be affected.

4. **Savings institutions (from Chapter 21)**

For the savings institution that you selected at the beginning of the term, use its annual report or any other related information to answer the following questions:

a. Identify the types of deposits that the savings institution uses to obtain most of its funds.

b. Identify the main uses of funds by the savings institution.

c. Summarize any statements made by the savings institution in its annual report about how recent or potential regulations will affect its performance.

d. Assess the savings institution's balance sheet as well as any comments in its annual report about the gap between its rate-sensitive assets and its rate-sensitive liabilities. Does it appear that the savings institution has a positive gap or a negative gap?

e. Does the savings institution use any methods to reduce its gap and therefore reduce its exposure to interest rate risk?

f. Summarize any statements made by the savings institution in its annual report about how it attempts to limit its exposure to credit risk on the loans it provides.

g. Determine the savings institution's interest income as a percentage of its total assets.

h. Determine the savings institution's interest expenses as a percentage of its total assets.

i. Determine the savings institution's noninterest income as a percentage of its total assets.

j. Determine the savings institution's noninterest expenses (do not include the addition to loan loss reserves here) as a percentage of total assets.

k. Determine the savings institution's addition to loan loss reserves as a percentage of its total assets.

l. Determine the savings institution's return on assets.

m. Determine the savings institution's return on equity.

n. Identify the savings institution's income statement items described previously that would be affected if interest rates rise in the next year, and explain how they would be affected.

o. Identify the savings institution's income statement items described previously that would be affected if the U.S. economic conditions deteriorate, and explain how they would be affected.

5. **Mutual funds (from Chapter 23)**

For the mutual fund that you selected at the beginning of the term, use its prospectus or any other related information to answer the following questions:

a. What is the investment objective of this mutual fund? Do you consider this mutual fund to have low risk, moderate risk, or high risk?

b. What was the return on the mutual fund last year? What was the average annual return over the last three years?

c. What is a key economic factor that influences the return on this mutual fund? (That is, are the fund's returns highly influenced by U.S. stock market conditions? By U.S. interest rates? By foreign stock market conditions? By foreign interest rates?)

d. Must any fees be paid when buying or selling this mutual fund?

e. What was the expense ratio for this mutual fund over the last year? Does this ratio seem high to you?

6. **Investment banks (from Chapter 24)**

   For the investment bank that you selected at the beginning of the term, use its annual report or any other related information to answer the following questions:

   a. What are the main types of business conducted by the investment bank?

   b. Summarize any statements made by the investment bank in its annual report about how it may be affected by existing or potential regulations.

   c. Describe the recent performance of the investment bank, and explain why the performance has been favorable or unfavorable.

7. **Insurance companies (from Chapter 25)**

   For the insurance company that you selected at the beginning of the term, use its annual report or any other related information to answer the following questions:

   a. How does the insurance company allocate its funds? (That is, what is its asset composition?)

   b. Is the insurance company exposed to interest rate risk? Explain.

   c. Does the insurance company use any techniques to hedge its exposure to interest rate risk?

   d. Summarize any statements made by the insurance company in its annual report about how it may be affected by existing or potential regulations.

   e. Describe the recent performance of the insurance company (using any key financial ratios that measure its income). Explain why its recent performance was strong or weak.

Part III. Measuring Stock Performance

This part of the project enables you to analyze the risk and return characteristics of one particular stock that you own or would like to purchase. You should input your data on the electronic spreadsheet. Perform the following tasks:

a. Obtain stock price data at the end of each of the last 16 quarters, and fill in that information in Column 1 of your electronic spreadsheet. Historical stock price data are available in the *Daily Stock Price Guide* (in many libraries) and may also be available online. Your professor may offer some suggestions on where to obtain this information.

b. Obtain the data on dividend per share for this firm for each of the last 16 quarters, and input that information in Column 2 of your electronic spreadsheet. When you obtain dividend data, recognize that it is often listed on an annual basis. In this case, divide the annual dividend by 4 to obtain the quarterly dividend.

c. Use "compute" statements to derive the quarterly return on your stock in Column 3 of your electronic spreadsheet. The return on the stock during any quarter is computed as follows. First, compute the stock price at the end of that quarter minus the stock price at the end of the previous quarter, then add the quarterly dividend, and then divide by the stock price at the end of the previous quarter.

d. Input the S&P 500 stock index level as of the end of each of the 16 quarters in Column 4 of your electronic spreadsheet.

e. Use "compute" statements to derive the quarterly stock market return in Column 5, which is equal to the percentage change in the S&P 500 index level from the previous quarter.

f. Using the tools in an electronic package, run a regression analysis in which your quarterly stock return (Column 3) represents the dependent variable, and the stock

market return (Column 5) represents the independent variable. This analysis can be easily run by Excel or Lotus.

g. Based on your regression results, what is the relationship between the market return and your stock's return? (The slope coefficient represents the estimate of your firm's beta, which is a measure of its systematic risk.)

h. Based on your regression results, does it appear that there is a significant relationship between the market return and your stock's return? (The t-statistic for the slope coefficient can be assessed to determine whether there is a significant relationship.)

i. Based on your regression results, what proportion of the variation in the stock's returns can be explained by movements (returns) in the stock market overall? (The R-SQUARED statistic measures the proportion of variation in the dependent variable that is explained by the independent variable in a regression model like the one described previously.) Does it appear that the stock's return is driven mainly by stock market movements or by other factors that are not captured in the regression model?

j. What is the standard deviation of your stock's quarterly returns over the 16-quarter period? (You can easily compute the standard deviation of your column of stock return data by using a compute statement; the exact compute statement varies with the software package that is used.) What is the standard deviation of the quarterly stock market returns (as measured by quarterly returns on the S&P 500 index) over the 16-quarter period? Is your stock more volatile than the stock market in general? If so, why do you think it is more volatile than the market?

k. Assume that the average risk-free rate per quarter over the 16-quarter period is 1.5 percent. Determine the Sharpe index for your stock. (The Sharpe index is equal to your stock's average quarterly return minus the average risk-free rate, divided by the standard deviation of your stock's returns.) Determine the Treynor index for your stock. (The Treynor index is equal to your stock's average quarterly return minus the average risk-free rate, divided by the estimated beta of your stock.)

Using Excel for Statistical Analysis

Financial market participants commonly conduct statistical analysis for analyzing data. This appendix explains some of the more commonly used statistical techniques.

Regression Analysis

Various software packages are available to run regression analysis. The Excel package is recommended because of its simplicity. The following example illustrates the ease with which regression analysis can be run.

Assume that a financial institution wishes to measure the relationship between the change in the interest rate in a given period (Δi_t) and the change in the inflation rate in the previous period (ΔI_{t-1}); that is, the financial institution wishes to assess the lagged impact of inflation on interest rates. Assume that the data over the last 20 periods are as follows:

Column A Period	Column B Δi_t	Column C ΔINF_{t-1}
1	.50%	.90%
2	.65	.75
3	−.70	−1.20
4	.50	.30
5	.40	.60
6	−.30	−.20
7	.60	.85
8	.75	.45
9	.10	−.05
10	1.10	1.35
11	.90	1.10
12	−.65	−.80
13	−.20	−.35

Column A Period	Column B Δi_t	Column C ΔINF_{t-1}
14	.40	.55
15	.30	.40
16	.60	.75
17	−.05	−.10
18	1.30	1.50
19	−.55	−.70
20	.15	.25

Assume the firm applies the following regression model to the data:

$$\Delta i_t = b_0 + b_1 \Delta INF_{t-1} + \mu$$

where

Δi_t = change in the interest rate in period t

ΔINF_{t-1} = change in the inflation rate in period $t - 1$ (the previous period)

b_0 and b_1 = regression coefficients to be estimated by regression analysis

μ = error term

Regression Analysis Using Excel

In our example, Δi_t is the dependent variable, and ΔINF_{t-1} is the independent variable. The first step is to input the two columns of data that were provided earlier (Columns B and C) into a file using Excel. Then you can perform regression analysis as follows. Click the *Tools* menu and then click *Data Analysis*. If *Data Analysis* does not appear on your *Tools* menu, select *Add Ins*. Select *Analysis Toolpak* and click *OK*. You should now be able to choose *Data Analysis* from your *Tools* menu. Once you click *Data Analysis*, you are presented with a new menu in which you should select *Regression*. Select *Input Y Range* and identify the range of the dependent variable ($B$1:$B$20 in our example). Then select *Input X Range* and identify the range of the independent variable ($C$1:CC20 in our example). Click *OK*, and within a few seconds, the regression analysis will be complete. For our example, the output is as follows:

Summary Output	
Multiple R	0.96884081
R-SQUARE	0.93865251
Adjusted R-SQUARE	0.93524431
Standard Error	0.1432744
Observations	20

ANOVA

	df	SS	MS	F	Significance F
Regression	1	5.653504056	5.653504	275.4105	2.34847E-12
Residual	18	0.369495944	0.020528		
Total	19	6.023			

	Coefficients	Standard Error	t Stat	P-value	Lower 95%	Upper 95%
Intercept	0.0494173	0.035164424	1.405321	0.176951	−0.024460473	0.123295
X Variable 1	0.75774079	0.045659421	16.5955	2.35E-12	0.661813835	0.853668

The estimate of the so-called slope coefficient is about .76, which suggests that every 1 percent change in the inflation rate is associated with a .76 percent change (in the same direction) in the interest rate. The t-statistic is 16.6, which suggests that there is a significant relationship between Δi_t and ΔINF_{t-1}. The R-SQUARED statistic suggests that about 94 percent of the variation in Δi_t is explained by ΔINF_{t-1}. The correlation between Δi_t and ΔINF_{t-1} can also be measured by the correlation coefficient, which is the square root of the R-SQUARED statistic.

If you had more than one independent variable (multiple regression), you should place the independent variables next to each other in the file. Then, for the X-RANGE, identify this block of data. The output for the regression model will display the coefficient and standard error for each of the independent variables. The t-statistic can be estimated for each independent variable to test for significance. For multiple regression, the R-SQUARED statistic represents the percentage of variation in the dependent variable explained by the model as a whole.

Using Regression Analysis to Forecast

The regression results can be used to forecast future values of the dependent variable. In our example, the historical relationship between Δi_t and ΔINF_{t-1} can be expressed as

$$\Delta i_t = b_0 + b_1(\Delta INF_{t-1})$$

Assume that last period's change in inflation (ΔINF_{t-1}) was 1 percent. Given the estimated coefficients derived from regression analysis, the forecast for this period's Δi_t is

$$\Delta i_t = 0494\% + .7577(1\%)$$

$$= 8071$$

There are some obvious limitations that should be recognized when using regression analysis to forecast. First, if other variables that influence the dependent variable are not included in the model, the coefficients derived from the model may be improperly estimated. This can cause inaccurate forecasts. Second, some relationships are contemporaneous rather than lagged, which means that last period's value for ΔINF could not be used. Instead, a forecast would have to be derived for ΔINF, to use as input for forecasting Δi_t. If the forecast for ΔINF is poor, the forecast for Δi_t will likely be poor even if the regression model is properly specified.

Glossary

A

adjustable-rate mortgage (ARM)
Mortgage that requires payments that adjust periodically according to market interest rates.

American depository receipts (ADRs)
Certificates representing ownership of foreign stocks.

amortization schedule Schedule developed from the maturity and interest rate on a mortgage to determine monthly payments broken down into principal and interest.

annuity Even stream of payments over a given period of time.

annuity plans Plans provided by insurance companies that offer a predetermined amount of retirement income to individuals.

appreciate Increase in the value of a foreign currency.

arbitrage activity In the securities industry, the purchasing of undervalued shares and the resale of these shares for a higher profit.

arbitrage firms (arbitrageurs) Securities firms that capitalize on discrepancies between prices of index futures and stocks.

arbitrage pricing theory (APT) Theory on the pricing of assets, which suggests that stock prices may be driven by a set of factors in addition to the market.

ask price Price at which a broker is willing to sell a specific security.

ask quote Price at which a seller is willing to sell.

asset stripping A strategy of acquiring a firm, breaking it into divisions, segmenting the divisions, and then selling them separately.

at the money Refers to an option in which the prevailing price of the underlying security is equal to the exercise price.

automatic transfer service (ATS) Savings account that allows funds to be transferred to a checking account as checks are written.

B

balloon-payment mortgage Mortgage that requires payments for a three-to five-year period; at the end of the period, full payment of the principal is required.

banker's acceptance Agreement in which a commercial bank accepts responsibility for a future payment; it is commonly used for international trade transactions.

bank holding company (BHC) Company that owns a commercial bank.

Bank Insurance Fund Reserve fund used by the FDIC to close failing banks; the fund is supported with deposit insurance premiums paid by commercial banks.

basis Difference between the price movement of a futures contract and the price movement of the underlying security.

basis risk As applied to interest rate swaps, risk that the index used for an interest rate swap does not move perfectly in tandem with the floating-rate instrument specified in a swap arrangement. As applied to financial futures, risk that the futures prices do not move perfectly in tandem with the assets that are hedged.

bearer bonds Bonds that require the owner to clip coupons attached to the bonds and send them to the issuer to receive coupon payments.

best-efforts agreement Arrangement in which the investment banking firm does not guarantee a price on securities to be issued by a corporation, but states only that it will give its best effort to sell the securities at a reasonable price.

beta Sensitivity of an asset's returns to market returns; measured as the covariance between asset returns and market returns divided by the variance of market returns.

bid quote Price a purchaser is willing to pay for a specific security.

big bang Deregulatory event in London in 1986 that allowed investment firms trading in the United States and Japan to trade in London and eliminated the fixed commission structure on securities transactions.

Board of Governors Composed of seven individual members appointed by the president of the United States; also called the Federal Reserve Board. The board helps regulate commercial banks and control monetary policy.

Bond Buyer Index Index based on 40 actively traded general obligation and revenue bonds.

bond price elasticity Sensitivity of bond prices to changes in the required rate of return.

bonds Debt obligations with long-term maturities issued by governments or corporations.

Brady Plan Plan endorsed as a means of mitigating the international debt crisis. The plan was based on voluntary bank actions to either forgive a portion of LDC loans or provide additional loans. The specifics of the plan were negotiated with each country separately.

Bretton Woods era Period from 1944 to 1971, when exchange rates were fixed (maintained within 1 percent of a specified rate).

bridge loans Funds provided as temporary financing until other sources of long-term funds can be obtained; commonly provided by securities firms to firms experiencing leveraged buyouts.

broker One who executes securities transactions between two parties.

bullet loan Loan structured so that interest payments and the loan principal are to be paid off in one lump sum at a specified future date.

C

call option Contract that grants the owner the right to purchase a speci-

fied financial instrument for a specified price within a specified period of time.

call premium Difference between a bond's call price and its par value.

call provision (call feature) Provision that allows the initial issuer of bonds to buy back the bonds at a specified price.

callable swap (or swaption) Swap of fixed-rate payments for floating-rate payments, whereby the party making the fixed payments has the right to terminate the swap prior to maturity.

CAMEL ratings Characteristics used to rate bank risk.

capital As related to banks, capital is mainly composed of retained earnings and proceeds received from issuing stock.

capital appreciation funds Mutual funds composed of stocks of firms that have potential for very high growth, but may be unproven.

capital asset pricing model (CAPM) Theory that suggests the return of an asset is influenced by the risk-free rate, the market return, and the covariance between asset returns and market returns.

capital markets Financial markets that facilitate the flow of long-term funds.

capital market securities Long-term securities, such as bonds, whose maturities are more than one year.

capital ratio Ratio of capital to assets.

captive finance subsidiary (CFS) Wholly owned subsidiary of a finance company whose primary purpose is to finance sales of the parent company's products and purchase receivables of the parent company.

cash flow underwriting Method by which insurance companies adapt insurance premiums to interest rates.

Central Liquidity Facility (CLF) Facility that acts as a lender for credit

unions to accommodate seasonal funding and specialized needs or to boost liquidity.

certificate of deposit (CD) Deposit offered by depository institutions that specifies a maturity, a deposit amount, and an interest rate.

chattel mortgage bond Bond that is secured by personal property.

circuit breakers Used to temporarily halt the trading of some securities or contracts on an exchange.

closed-end investment funds Mutual funds that do not repurchase the shares they sell.

collateralized mortgage obligations (CMOs) Represent securities that are backed by mortgages; segmented into classes (or tranches) that dictate the timing of the payments.

commercial paper Short-term securities (usually unsecured) issued by well-known creditworthy firms.

commission brokers (floor brokers) Brokers who execute orders for their customers.

common stock Certificate representing partial ownership of a corporation.

Competitive Banking Equality Act Act passed in 1987 that prohibits commercial banks from creating nonbank banks and from offering new insurance, real estate, and securities underwriting services.

consumer finance companies Finance companies that concentrate on direct loans to consumers.

contagion effects Adverse effects of a single firm that become contagious throughout the industry.

convertibility clause Provision that allows investors to convert a bond into a specified number of common stock shares.

convertible bonds Bonds that can be converted into a specified number of the firm's common stock.

corporate bonds Bonds issued by corporations in need of long-term funds.

covered call Sale of a call option to partially cover against the possible decline in the price of a stock that is being held.

covered interest arbitrage Act of capitalizing on higher foreign interest rates while covering the position with a simultaneous forward sale.

credit crunch A period during which banks are less willing to extend credit; normally results from an increased probability that some borrowers will default on loans.

credit risk The risk of loss that will occur when a counterparty defaults on a contract.

cross-hedging The use of a futures contract on one financial instrument to hedge a financial institution's position in a different financial instrument.

crowding-out effect Phenomenon that occurs when insufficient loanable funds are available for potential borrowers, such as corporations and individuals, as a result of excessive borrowing by the Treasury, because limited loanable funds are available to satisfy all borrowers, interest rates rise in response to the increased demand for funds, which crowds some potential borrowers out of the market.

currency call option Contract that grants the owner the right to purchase a specified currency for a specified price, within a specified period of time.

currency futures contract Standardized contract that specifies an amount of a particular currency to be exchanged on a specified date and at a specified exchange rate.

currency put option Contract that grants the owner the right to sell a specified currency for a specified price, within a specified period of time.

currency swap An agreement that allows the periodic swap of one currency for another at specified exchange rates; it essentially represents a series of forward contracts.

D

day traders Traders of financial futures contracts who close out their contracts on the same day that they initiate them.

dealers Securities firms that make a market in specific securities by adjusting their inventories.

debentures Bonds that are backed only by the general credit of the issuing firm.

debt-equity swap An exchange of debt for an equity interest in the debtor's assets.

debt securities Securities that represent credit provided to the initial issuer by the purchaser.

default risk Credit risk; risk that loans provided or securities purchased will default, cutting off principal and/or interest payments.

defensive open market operations Implemented to offset the impact of other market conditions that affect the level of funds.

deficit units Individual, corporate, or government units that need to borrow funds.

defined-benefit plan Pension plan in which contributions are dictated by the benefits that will eventually be provided.

defined-contribution plan Pension plan in which benefits are determined by the accumulated contributions and on the fund's investment performance.

demand deposit account Deposit account that offers checking services.

demand-pull inflation Inflation caused by excess demand for goods.

Depository Institutions Deregulation and Monetary Control Act (DIDMCA) Act that deregulated some aspects of the depository institutions industry, such as removing the ceiling interest rates on deposits and allowing NOW accounts nationwide.

deposit transfer Procedure of handling failures of savings institutions; the deposits of a failing institution are transferred to a healthy depository institution for a fee.

depreciate Decrease in the value of a foreign currency.

derivative instruments Instruments created from a previously existing security.

derivative markets Markets that allow for the buying or selling of derivative securities.

derivatives Financial contracts whose values are derived from the values of underlying assets.

direct lease loan Act of purchasing assets and then leasing the assets to a firm.

dirty float System whereby exchange rates are market determined without boundaries, but subject to government intervention.

discount bonds Bonds that sell below their par value.

discount brokerage firms Brokerage firms that focus on executing transactions.

discount rate Interest rate charged on loans provided by the Federal Reserve to depository institutions.

disintermediation Process in which savers transfer funds from intermediaries to alternative investments with market-determined rates.

Dow Jones Industrial Index Index of stocks representing 20 large firms.

dual banking system Regulatory framework of the banking system, composed of federal and state regulators.

duration Measurement of the life of a bond on a present value basis.

duration gap Difference between the average duration of a bank's assets versus its liabilities.

dynamic asset allocation Switching between risky and low-risk investment positions over time in response to changing expectations.

dynamic open market operations Implemented to increase or decrease the level of funds.

E

economies of scale Reduction in average cost per unit as the level of output increases.

Edge Act corporations Corporations established by banks to specialize in international banking and foreign financial transactions.

effective yield Yield on foreign money market securities adjusted for the exchange rate.

Employee Retirement Income Security Act (ERISA) Act that provided three vesting schedule options from which a pension fund could choose. It also stipulated that pension contributions be invested in a prudent manner and that employees can transfer any vested pension amounts to new employers as they switch employers.

employee stock ownership plans (ESOPs) Plans to offer periodic contributions of a corporation's stock to participating employees; ESOPs have been used as a means of preventing a takeover.

equity REIT REIT (real estate investment trust) that invests directly in properties.

equity securities Securities such as common stock and preferred stock that represent ownership in a business.

equity swap Swap arrangement involving the exchange of interest payments for payments linked to the degree of change in a stock index.

Eurobanks Foreign banks or foreign branches of U.S. banks that participate in the Eurodollar market by accepting deposits and making loans denominated in dollars and other foreign currencies.

Euro-commercial paper (Euro-CP) Securities issued in Europe without the backing of a bank syndicate.

Eurocredit market Market in which banks provide medium-term loans in foreign currencies.

Eurocurrency market Market made up of several banks that accept large deposits and provide short-term loans in foreign currencies.

Eurodollar certificate of deposit Large U.S. dollar deposits in non-U.S. banks.

Eurodollar floating-rate CDs (FRCDs) Eurodollar CDs with floating interest rates that adjust periodically to the LIBOR.

Eurodollar loans Short-term loans denominated in dollars provided to corporations and governments by branches of U.S. banks located outside the United States and some foreign-owned banks.

Eurodollar market Market in Europe in which dollars are deposited and loaned for short time periods.

Eurodollars Large dollar-denominated deposits accepted by banks outside the United States.

Euronotes Notes issued in European markets in bearer form, with short-term maturities.

European Currency Unit (ECU) Multicurrency unit of account, composed of several European currencies, that is used to price some internationally traded goods and securities.

event risk An increase in the perceived risk of default on bonds resulting from the restructuring of debt or an acquisition.

ex ante real interest rate Real interest rate that is anticipated (equal to the nominal interest rate minus the expected inflation rate).

exchange rate mechanism (ERM) Arrangement in which many European currency values were pegged to the European Currency Unit (within boundaries), which linked the exchange rates between these currencies.

exchange rate risk Risk that currency values will change in a manner that adversely affects future cash flows.

exercise price (or strike price) Price at which the instrument underlying an option contract can be purchased (in the case of a call option) or sold (in the case of a put option).

ex post real interest rate Real interest rate that occurred in a previous period (nominal interest rate minus the inflation rate in that period).

extendable swap Swap of fixed payments for floating payments that contains an extendable feature allowing the party making fixed payments to extend the swap period if desired.

F

factor Firm that purchases accounts receivable at a discount and is responsible for processing and collecting on the balances of these accounts; finance companies commonly have subsidiaries that serve as factors.

Federal Deposit Insurance Corporation (FDIC) Federal agency that insures the deposits of commercial banks.

federal funds rate Interest rate charged on loans between depository institutions.

Federal National Mortgage Association (FNMA) Issues mortgage-backed securities and uses the funds to purchase mortgages.

Federal Open Market Committee (FOMC) Composed of the seven members of the Board of Governors plus the presidents of five Federal Reserve district banks. The main role of the FOMC is to control monetary policy.

Federal Reserve Central bank of the United States.

Federal Reserve district bank A regional government bank that facilitates operations within the banking system by clearing checks, replacing old currency, providing loans to banks, and conducting research; there are 12 Federal Reserve district banks.

financial futures contract Standardized agreement to deliver or receive a specified amount of a specified financial instrument at a specified price and date.

Financial Institutions Reform, Recovery, and Enforcement Act (FIRREA) Act intended to enhance the safety of savings institutions; prevented savings institutions from investing in junk bonds, increased capital requirements, and increased the penalties for fraud.

financial market Market in which financial assets (or securities) such as stocks and bonds are traded.

first mortgage bond Bond that has first claim on specified assets as collateral.

Fisher effect Positive relationship between interest rates and expected inflation.

fixed-rate mortgage Mortgage that requires payments based on a fixed interest rate.

floor brokers Individuals who facilitate the trading of stocks on the New York and American Stock Exchanges by executing transactions for their clients.

floor traders (locals) Members of a futures exchange who trade futures contracts for their own account.

flotation costs Costs of placing securities.

flow-of-funds accounts Reports on the amount of funds channeled to and from various sectors.

foreign exchange derivatives Instruments created to lock in a foreign exchange transaction, such as forward contracts, futures contracts, currency swaps, and currency options contracts.

forward contract Contract typically negotiated with a commercial bank that allows a customer to purchase or sell a specified amount of a particular foreign currency at a specified exchange rate on a specified future date.

forward market Market that facilitates the trading of forward contracts; commercial banks serve as intermediaries in the market by matching up participants who wish to buy a currency forward with other participants who wish to sell the currency forward.

forward rate In the context of term structure of interest rates, the market's forecast of the future interest rate. In the context of foreign exchange, the exchange rate at which a specified currency can be purchased or sold for a specified future point in time.

forward swap Involves an exchange of interest payments that does not begin until a specified future point in time.

freely floating system System whereby exchange rates are market determined, without any government intervention.

full-service brokerage firms Brokerage firms that provide complete information and advice about securities, in addition to executing transactions.

fundamental forecasting Is based on fundamental relationships between economic variables and exchange rates.

futures contract Standardized contract allowing one to purchase or sell a specified amount of a specified instrument (such as a security or currency) for a specified price and at a specified future point in time.

G

gap Defined as rate-sensitive assets minus rate-sensitive liabilities.

gap ratio Measured as the value of rate-sensitive assets divided by the value of rate-sensitive liabilities.

Garn-St Germain Act Act passed in 1982 that allowed for the creation of money market deposit accounts (MMDAs), loosened lending guidelines for federally chartered savings institutions, and allowed failing depository institutions to be acquired by other depository institutions outside the state.

general obligation bonds Bonds that provide payments that are supported by the municipal government's ability to tax.

Glass-Steagall Act Act in 1933 that separated commercial banking and investment banking activities; largely repealed in 1999.

global crowding out Situation in which excessive government borrowing in one country can cause higher interest rates in other countries.

global junk bonds Low-quality bonds issued globally by governments and corporations.

golden parachute Provisions that allow specific employees to receive specified compensation if they are terminated from their positions.

Government National Mortgage Association (Gnma) Agency that guarantees the timely payment of principal and interest to investors who purchase securities backed by mortgages.

graduated-payment mortgage (GPM) Mortgage that allows borrowers to initially make small payments on the mortgage; the payments are increased on a graduated basis.

greenmail The accumulation of shares of a target, followed by sale of the shares back to the target; the target purchases the shares back (at a premium) to remove the threat of a takeover.

gross interest expense Interest paid on deposits and on other borrowed funds.

gross interest income Interest income generated from all assets.

group life policy Policy provided to a group of policyholders with some common bond.

growing-equity mortgage Mortgage where the initial monthly payments are low and increase over time.

growth funds Mutual funds containing stocks of firms that are expected to grow at a higher than average rate; for investors who are willing to accept a moderate degree of risk.

H

health maintenance organizations (HMOs) Intermediaries between purchasers and providers of health care.

hedgers Participants in financial futures markets who take positions in contracts to reduce their exposure to risk.

high-yield funds Mutual funds composed of bonds that offer high yields (junk bonds) and have a relatively high degree of credit risk.

highly leveraged transactions (HLTs) Credit provided that results in a debt-to-asset ratio of at least 75 percent.

I

IMF Funding Bill Bill passed to provide funding to LDCs experiencing problems in repaying their debt.

immunize The act of insulating a security portfolio from interest rate movements.

impact lag Lag time between when a policy is implemented by the government and the time when the policy has an effect on the economy.

imperfect markets Markets in which buyers and sellers of securities do not have full access to information and cannot always break down securities to the precise size they desire.

implementation lag Lag time between when the government recognizes a problem and the time when it implements a policy to resolve the problem.

income funds Mutual funds composed of bonds that offer periodic coupon payments.

indenture Legal document specifying the rights and obligations of both the issuing firm and the bondholders.

index arbitrage Act of capitalizing on discrepancies between prices of index futures and stocks.

informal line of credit Financing arrangement that allows a business to borrow up to a specified amount within a specified period of time.

initial margin A margin deposit established by a customer with a brokerage firm before a transaction can be executed.

initial public offering (IPO) A first-time offering of shares by a specific firm to the public.

installment loans Loans to individuals to finance purchases of cars and household products.

insured plans Pension plans that are used to purchase annuity policies so that the life insurance companies can provide benefits to employees upon retirement.

interest-inelastic Insensitive to interest rates.

interest rate cap Arrangement that offers a party interest payments in periods when the interest rate on a specific money market instrument exceeds a specified ceiling rate; the payments are based on the amount by which the interest rate exceeds the ceiling as applied to the notional principal specified in the agreement.

interest rate collar The purchase of an interest rate cap and the simultaneous sale of an interest rate floor.

interest rate floor Agreement in which one party offers an interest rate payment in periods when the interest rate on a specified money market instrument is below a specified floor rate.

interest rate futures Financial futures contracts on debt securities such as Treasury bills, notes, or bonds.

interest rate parity Theory that suggests the forward discount (or premium) is dependent on the interest rate differential between the two countries of concern.

interest rate risk Risk that an asset will decline in value in response to interest rate movements.

interest rate swap Arrangement whereby one party exchanges one set of interest payments for another.

international mutual fund Portfolio of international stocks created and managed by a financial institution; individuals can invest in international stocks by purchasing shares of an international mutual fund.

in the money Describes a call option whose premium is above the exercise price or a put option whose premium is below the exercise price.

investment-grade bonds Bonds that are rated Baa or better by Moody's and BBB or better by Standard and Poor's.

investment-grade securities Securities that are rated as "medium" quality or higher by rating agencies.

issue costs Cost of issuing stock, including printing, legal registration, and accounting expenses.

J

junk bonds Corporate bonds that are perceived to have a high degree of risk.

junk commercial paper Low-rated commercial paper.

K

Keynesian theory Theory that suggests how the government can improve economic conditions; as related to monetary policy, the theory explains how the money supply can be adjusted to affect interest rates and the economy.

L

letter of credit (L/C) Guarantee by a bank on the financial obligations of a firm that owes payment (usually an importer).

leveraged buyout (LBO) A buyout of a firm that is financed mostly with debt.

leverage measure Measure of financial leverage; defined as assets divided by equity.

limit orders Requests by customers to purchase or sell securities at a specified price or better.

liquidity Ability to sell assets easily without loss of value.

liquidity preference theory Theory used to explain how changes in the money supply affect interest rates.

liquidity premium theory Theory that suggests the yield to maturity is higher for illiquid securities, other things being equal.

liquidity risk Potential price distortions due to a lack of liquidity.

load funds Mutual funds that have a sales charge imposed by brokerage firms that sell the funds.

loan commitment Obligation by a bank to provide a specified loan amount to a particular firm upon the firm's request.

loan loss provision A reserve account established by a bank in anticipation of loan losses in the future.

loan participation Arrangement in which several banks pool funds to provide a loan to a corporation.

loanable funds theory Theory that suggests the market interest rate is determined by the factors that control the supply and demand for loanable funds.

locational arbitrage Arbitrage intended to capitalize on a price (such as foreign exchange rate quote) discrepancy between two locations.

London Interbank Offer Rate (LIBOR) Interest rate charged on interbank loans.

long hedge The purchase of financial futures contracts to hedge against a possible decrease in interest rates.

long-term equity anticipations (LEAPs) Stock options with relatively long-term expiration dates.

low-coupon bonds Bonds that pay low coupon payments; most of the expected return to investors is attributed to the large discount in the bond's price.

M

M1 Definition of the money supply; composed of currency held by the public plus checking accounts.

M2 Definition of the money supply; composed of M1 plus savings accounts, small time deposits, MMDAs, and some other items.

M3 Definition of the money supply; composed of M2 plus large time deposits and other items.

maintenance margin A margin requirement that reduces the risk that participants will later default on their obligations.

margin call Call from a broker to participants in futures contracts (or other investments) informing them that they must increase their margin.

margin requirements The proportion of invested funds that can be borrowed versus paid in cash; set by the Federal Reserve.

market-based forecasting Process of developing forecasts from market indicators.

market-makers Individuals who facilitate the trading of stocks on the Nasdaq by standing ready to buy or sell specific stocks in response to customer orders made through a telecommunications network.

market microstructure Process by which securities are traded.

market orders Requests by customers to purchase or sell securities at the market price existing when the order reaches the exchange floor.

market risk Risk that the stock market experiences lower prices in response to adverse economic conditions or pessimistic expectations.

matched funding Strategy in which investment decisions are made with the objective of matching planned outflow payments.

McFadden Act of 1927 Act preventing all banks from establishing branches across state lines.

merger-conversion Procedure used in acquisitions whereby a mutual S&L converts to a stock-owned S&L before either acquiring or being acquired by another firm.

mixed forecasting The use of a combination of forecasting techniques, resulting in a weighted average of the various forecasts developed.

modern quantity theory of money Theory that suggests an increase in the quantity of money leads to a

predictable increase in the value of goods produced.

Monetarists Economists who advocate a stable low growth in the money supply.

monetizing the debt Action of the Fed to increase the money supply to offset any increased demand for funds resulting from a larger budget deficit.

money markets Financial markets that facilitate the flow of short-term funds.

money market deposit account (MMDA) Deposit account that pays interest and allows limited checking and does not specify a maturity.

money market mutual funds Mutual funds that concentrate their investment in money market securities.

money market securities Short-term securities, such as Treasury bills or certificates of deposit, whose maturities are one year or less.

moral hazard problem Refers to the deposit insurance pricing system that existed until the early 1990s; insurance premiums per $100 of deposits were similar across all commercial banks. This system caused an indirect subsidy from safer banks to risky banks and encouraged banks to take excessive risk.

mortgage-backed securities Securities backed by mortgages that are commonly sold and purchased by savings institutions.

mortgage pass-through securities Securities issued by a financial institution and backed by a group of mortgages. The mortgage interest and principal are sent to the financial institution, which then transfers the payments to the owners of the mortgage-backed securities after deducting a service fee.

mortgage REIT REIT (real estate investment trust) that invests in mortgage and construction loans.

Municipal Bond Index (MBI) futures Futures contract allowing for the future purchase or sale of municipal bonds at a specified price.

municipal bonds Debt securities issued by state and local governments, which can usually be classified as either general obligation bonds or revenue bonds.

mutual fund An investment company that sells shares representing an interest in a portfolio of securities.

mutual S&Ls S&Ls that are owned by depositors.

mutual-to-stock conversion Procedure by savings institutions to shift the ownership structure from depositors to shareholders.

N

National Association of Insurance Commissioners (NAIC) Agency that facilitates cooperation among the various state agencies when an insurance issue is a concern.

National Association of Securities Dealers (NASD) Regulator of the securities industry.

National Association of Securities Dealers Automatic Quotations (Nasdaq) A service for the over-the-counter market that reports immediate price quotations for many of the stocks.

National Credit Union Administration (NCUA) Regulator of credit unions; the NCUA participates in the creation of new CUs, examines the financial condition of CUs, and supervises any liquidations or mergers.

National Credit Union Share Insurance Fund (NCUSIF) Agency that insures deposits at credit unions.

negotiable certificate of deposit (NCD) Deposit account with a minimum deposit of $100,000 that requires a specified maturity; there is a secondary market for these deposits.

net asset value (NAV) Financial characteristic used to describe a mutual fund's value per share; estimated as the market value of the securities comprising the mutual fund, plus any accrued interest or dividends, minus any expenses. This value is divided by the number of shares outstanding.

net exposure In the context of futures markets, the difference between asset and liability positions.

net interest margin Estimated as interest revenues minus interest expenses, divided by assets.

noise traders Uninformed investors whose buy and sell positions push the stock price away from its fundamental value.

noise trading Theory used to explain that stock prices may deviate from their fundamental values as a result of the buy and sell positions of uninformed investors (called "noise traders"); a market correction may not eliminate the discrepancy if the informed traders are unwilling to capitalize on the discrepancy (because of uncertainty surrounding the stock's fundamental value).

no-load funds Mutual funds that do not have a sales charge, meaning that they are not promoted by brokerage firms.

noninterest expenses Expenses that are unrelated to interest payments on deposits or borrowed funds, such as salaries and office equipment.

noninterest income Income resulting from fees charged or services provided.

note issuance facility (NIF) Commitment in which a bank agrees to purchase the commercial paper of a firm if the firm cannot place its paper in the market at an acceptable interest rate.

notional principal Value to which interest rates from interest rate swaps are applied to determine the interest payments involved.

NOW (negotiable order of withdrawal) accounts Deposit accounts that allow unlimited checking and pay interest.

O

open-end investment funds Mutual funds that are willing to repurchase the shares they sell from investors at any time.

Open Market Desk Division of the New York Fed district bank that is responsible for conducting open market operations.

open market operations The Fed's buying and selling of government securities (through the Trading Desk).

operational risk The risk of losses as a result of inadequate management or controls.

option premium Price paid for an option contract.

organized exchange Visible marketplace for secondary market transactions.

origination Decisions by a firm (with the help of a securities firm) on how much stock or bonds to issue, the type of stock (or bonds) to be issued, and the price at which the stock (or bonds) should be sold.

out of the money Describes a call option whose premium is below the exercise price or a put option whose premium is above the exercise price.

over-the-counter (OTC) market Market used to facilitate transactions of securities not listed on organized exchanges.

P

participation certificates (PCs) Certificates sold by the Federal Home Loan Mortgage Association; the proceeds are used to purchase conventional mortgages from financial institutions.

Pension Benefit Guaranty Corporation (PBGC) Established as a result of the ERISA to provide insurance on pension plans.

perfect markets Markets in which all information about any securities for sale would be freely and continuously available to investors. Furthermore, all securities for sale could be broken down into any size desired by investors, and transaction costs would be nonexistent.

Phillips curve Represents the relationship between unemployment and inflation.

plain vanilla swap Involves the periodic exchange of fixed-rate payments for floating-rate payments.

policy directive Statement provided by the FOMC to the Trading Desk regarding the target money supply range.

portfolio insurance Program trading combined with the trading of stock index futures to hedge against market movements.

position traders Traders of financial futures contracts who maintain their futures positions for relatively long periods (such as weeks or months) before closing them out.

preemptive rights Priority given to a particular group of people to purchase newly issued stock, before other investors are given the opportunity to purchase the stock.

preferred habitat theory Theory that suggests that although investors and borrowers may normally concentrate on a particular natural maturity market, certain events may cause them to wander from it.

preferred stock Certificate representing partial ownership of a corporation, without significant voting rights; it provides owners dividends, but normally does not provide a share of the firm's profits.

prepayment risk The possibility that the assets to be hedged may be prepaid earlier than their designated maturity.

present value interest factor (PVIF) Factor that represents the present value of $1 for a specified period and interest (discount) rate.

present value interest factor of an annuity (PVIFA) Factor that represents the present value of a stream of $1 payments for a specified number of periods and a specified interest (discount) rate.

primary market Market where securities are initially issued.

prime rate Interest rate charged on loans by banks to their most credit-worthy customers.

private placement Process in which a corporation sells new securities directly without using underwriting services.

privatization Process of converting government ownership of businesses to private ownership.

program trading The simultaneous buying and selling of a portfolio of at least 15 different stocks valued at more than $1 million.

projective funding Strategy that offers pension fund managers some flexibility in constructing a pension portfolio that can benefit from expected market and interest rate movements.

prospectus A pamphlet that discloses relevant financial data on the firm and provisions applicable to the security.

protective covenants Restrictions enforced by a bond indenture that protect the bondholders from an increase in risk; such restrictions may include limits on the dividends paid, the salaries paid, and the additional debt the firm can issue.

purchasing power parity (PPP) Theory that suggests exchange rates adjust, on average, by a percentage that reflects the inflation differential between the two countries of concern.

pure expectations theory Theory suggesting that the shape of the yield curve is determined solely by interest rates.

put option Contract that grants the owner the right to sell a specified financial instrument for a specified price within a specified period of time.

putable swap Swap of fixed-rate payments for floating rate payments whereby the party making floating-rate payments has the right to terminate the swap.

R

rate-capped swap Swap arrangement involving fixed-rate payments for floating-rate payments, whereby the floating payments are capped.

real estate investment trust (REIT) Closed-end mutual fund that invests in real estate or mortgages.

real estate mortgage conduit (REMIC) Allows financial institutions to sell mortgage assets and issue mortgage-backed securities.

real interest rate Nominal interest rate adjusted for inflation.

recognition lag Lag time between when a problem arises and when it is recognized by the government.

registered bonds Require the issuer to maintain records of who owns the bonds and automatically send coupon payments to the owners.

registration statement Statement of relevant financial information disclosed by a corporation issuing securities, which is intended to ensure that accurate information is disclosed by the issuing corporation.

Regulation Q Bank regulation that limited the interest rate banks could pay on deposits.

reinsurance Manner by which insurance companies can allocate a portion of their return and risk to other insurance companies, which share in insuring large policies.

repurchase agreement (repo) Agreement in which a bank (or some other firm) sells some of its government security holdings, with a commitment to purchase those securities back at a later date. This agreement essentially reflects a loan from the time the firm sold the securities until the securities are repurchased.

reserve requirement ratio Percentage of deposits that commercial banks must maintain as required reserves. This ratio is sometimes used by the Fed as a monetary policy tool.

Resolution Trust Corporation (RTC) Agency created in 1989 to help bail out failing savings institutions. The RTC liquidated an institution's assets and reimbursed depositors or sold the savings institution to another depository institution.

retail certificate of deposit (retail CD) Deposit requiring a specific minimum amount of funds to be deposited for a specified period of time.

return on assets (ROA) Defined as net income divided by assets.

return on equity (ROE) Defined as net income divided by equity.

revenue bonds Bonds that provide payments that are supported by the revenue generated by the project.

reverse leveraged buyout (reverse LBO) Process of issuing new stock after engaging in a leveraged buyout and improving the firm's performance.

reverse repo The purchase of securities by one party from another with an agreement to sell them in the future.

revolving credit loan Financing arrangement that obligates the bank to loan some specified maximum amount of funds over a specified period of time.

S

S&P 500 Index Futures Futures contract allowing for the future purchase or sale of the S&P 500 index at a specified price.

sales finance companies Finance companies that concentrate on purchasing credit contracts from retailers and dealers.

Savings Association Insurance Fund (SAIF) Insuring agency for S&Ls as of 1989.

secondary market Market where securities are resold.

secondary stock offering A new stock offering by a firm that already has stock outstanding.

Securities and Exchange Commission (SEC) Agency that regulates the issuance of securities disclosure rules for issuers, the exchanges, and participating brokerage firms.

Securities Exchange Act of 1933 Intended to ensure complete disclosure of relevant information on publicly offered securities and prevent fraudulent practices in selling these securities.

Securities Exchange Act of 1934 Intended to ensure complete disclosure of relevant information on securities traded in secondary markets.

securities gains and losses Bank accounting term that reflects the gains or losses generated from the sale of securities.

Securities Investor Protection Corporation (SIPC) Offers insurance on cash and securities deposited at brokerage firms.

securitization Pooling and repackaging of loans into securities, which are sold to investors.

segmented markets theory Theory that suggests investors and borrowers choose securities with maturities that satisfy their forecasted cash needs.

semistrong-form efficiency Security prices reflect all public information, including announcements by firms, economic news or events, and political news or events.

shared-appreciation mortgage Mortgage that allows a home purchaser to pay a below-market interest rate; in return, the lender shares in the appreciation of the home price.

shareholder activism Actions taken by shareholders to correct a firm's deficiencies so that the stock price may improve.

Sharpe index Measure of risk-adjusted return; defined as the asset's excess mean return beyond the mean risk-free risk, divided by the standard deviation of returns of the asset of concern.

shelf-registration Registration with the SEC in advance of public placement of securities.

short hedge The sale of financial futures contracts to hedge against a possible increase in interest rates.

short selling The sale of securities that are borrowed, with the intent of buying those securities to repay what was borrowed.

Single European Act of 1987 Act that called for a reduction in barriers between European countries. This allowed for easier trade and capital flows throughout Europe.

sinking-fund provision Requirement that the firm retire a specific amount of the bond issue each year.

Smithsonian Agreement Agreement among major countries to devalue the dollar against some currencies and widen the boundaries around each exchange rate from 1 percent to 2.25 percent.

sovereign risk As applied to swaps, risk that a country's political conditions could prevent one party in the swap from receiving payments due.

specialists Individuals who facilitate the trading of stocks on the New York and American Stock Exchanges by taking positions in specific stocks; they stand ready to buy or sell these stocks on the trading floor.

speculators Those who take positions to benefit from future price movements.

spot exchange rate Present exchange rate.

spread Used to represent the difference between bid and ask quotes. This term is also sometimes used to reflect the difference between the average interest rate earned on assets and the average interest rate paid on liabilities.

Standard & Poor's 500 index Index of stocks of 500 large firms.

standby letter of credit Agreement that backs a customer's financial obligation.

stock index futures Financial futures contracts on stock indexes.

stock index option Provides the right to trade a specified stock index at

a specified price by a specified expiration date.

stop-loss order Order of a sale of a specific security when the price reaches a specified minimum.

strike price (exercise price) Price at which an option can be exercised.

stripped securities Securities that are stripped of their coupon payments to create two separate types of securities: (1) a principal-only part that pays a future lump sum, and (2) an interest-only part that pays coupon payments, but no principal.

strips program Program created by the Treasury in which it exchanges stripped securities for Treasury securities.

strong-form efficiency Security prices fully reflect all information, including private (insider) information.

subordinated debentures Debentures that have claims against the firm's assets that are junior to the claims of both mortgage bonds and regular debentures.

surplus units Individual, business, or government units that have excess funds that can be invested.

swap options (swaptions) Options on interest rate swaps.

systematic risk Risk that is attributable to market movements and cannot be diversified away.

T

T-bill discount Percentage by which the price paid for a Treasury bill is less than the par value.

technical analysis Method of forecasting future stock prices with the use of historical stock price patterns.

technical forecasting Involves the use of historical exchange rate data to predict future values.

term insurance Temporary insurance over a specified term; the policy does not build a cash value.

term loan Business loan used to finance the purchase of fixed assets.

term structure of interest rates Relationship between the term remaining until maturity and the annualized yield of Treasury securities.

theory of rational expectations Suggests that the public accounts for all existing information when forming its expectations; as applied to monetary policy, it implies that historical effects of money supply growth will be considered when forecasting the effects of prevailing money supply growth.

time-series model Examines moving averages and allows forecasters to develop rules.

Trading Desk Located at the New York Federal Reserve district bank, it is used to carry out orders from the FOMC about open market operations.

Treasury bills Securities issued by the Treasury that have maturities of one year or less.

Treynor index Measure of risk-adjusted return; defined as the asset's excess mean return beyond the mean risk-free rate, divided by the beta of the asset of concern.

trustee Appointed to represent the bondholders in all matters concerning the bond issue.

U

underwrite Act of guaranteeing a specific price to the initial issuer of securities.

underwriting spread Difference between the price at which an investment banking firm expects to sell securities and the price it is willing to pay the issuing firm.

underwriting syndicate Group of investment banking firms that are required to underwrite a portion of a corporation's newly issued securities.

universal life insurance Combines the features of term and whole life insurance. It specifies a period of time over which the policy will exist but also builds a cash value for policyholders over time.

usury laws Laws that enforce a maximum interest rate that can be imposed on loans to households.

V

variable life insurance Insurance in which benefits awarded by the life insurance company to a beneficiary vary with the assets backing the policy.

variable-rate bonds Bonds whose coupon rates adjust to market interest rates over time.

W

weak-form efficiency Theory that suggests that security prices reflect all market-related data, such as historical security price movements and volume of securities traded.

whole life insurance Insurance that protects the insured policyholders until death or as long as premiums are promptly paid; the policy builds a cash value that the policyholder is entitled to even if the policy is canceled.

working capital loan Business loan designed to support ongoing operations, typically for a short-term period.

writer The seller of an option contract.

Y

yield curve Curve depicting the relationship between the term remaining until maturity and the annualized yield of Treasury securities.

yield to maturity Discount rate at which the present value of future payments would equal the security's current price.

Z

zero-coupon bonds Bonds that have no coupon payments.

zero-coupon-for-floating swap Swap arrangement calling for one party to swap a lump-sum payment at maturity in exchange for periodic floating-rate payments.

Index

12b-1 fee, 663
52-week price range, 146

A

Abnormal return, 190, 192, 193, 592
ABS. See Automated Bond System
Accounts receivable, 27, 244, 646
Adjustable-rate mortgage, 334–336, 348, 624, 625, 626
Adjusted dividend discount model, 171–172
ADR. See American depository receipt
Advisory committee, 81, 84, 85
After-tax yield, 48, 49, 52
Agency cost, 159
Agency problem, 154
Aggregate demand for loanable funds, 28–29
Aggregate supply of loanable funds, 30, 31
AICPA. See American Institute of Certified Public Accountants
Allstate Insurance Group, 718
Amazon.com, 136
America Online, 136
American currency option, 501
American depository receipt, 160, 162, 163, 164
American Institute of Certified Public Accountants, 212
American Stock Exchange, 141, 143, 144, 218, 220, 226, 282, 394
American-style option, 394, 428
Ameritrade, 215
Amex. See American Stock Exchange
Amortization schedule, 337

Analyst, 179–181, 192, 197, 210, 231, 232, 593, 701
Analyst rating service, 180–181
Announcement date, 592
Annuity, 297
Annuity plan, 715, 736
Antitakeover amendment, 159
Apple Computer, 144
Arbitrage, 377, 381, 429, 430, 431, 500, 502, 693–694
Arbitrage firm, 693, 694, 695
Arbitrage pricing model, 172, 174
Arbitrage restriction, 499
Arbitrageur, 381
Archipelago Exchange, 226
ARM. See Adjustable-rate mortgage
Arthur Andersen, 210
Asian crisis, 21, 122–123, 197, 468, 489–497, 574, 597, 682
Asian Development Bank, 491
Ask quote, 15, 213, 221, 222, 223, 224, 225, 251, 269, 270, 395, 461, 480, 662
Asset allocation fund, 668, 685
Asset quality, 544–545, 554, 619, 634, 639
Asset stripping, 693
Asymmetric information, 9, 279, 695
ATM. See Automated teller machine
ATS. See Automatic transfer service
Audit committee, 154
Automated Bond System, 282
Automated teller machine, 510
Automatic transfer service, 510

B

B/A. See Banker's acceptance
Back-end load, 662

Bad debt expense, 571
Balance of trade deficit, 467
Balloon-payment mortgage, 337, 516
Bank failure, 608–609
Bank for International Settlements, 535
Bank holding company, 85, 245, 253, 254, 533, 540, 541, 646, 683
Bank Holding Company Act, 533, 543
Bank Insurance Fund, 535, 547, 548, 616
Bank of America, 211, 606–608
Bank of Canada, 97
Bank of England, 402
Bank of Japan, 97
Bank of New York, 219
Bank regulation, 80
Banker's acceptance, 4, 240, 251–253, 254, 259, 263, 599, 678
Bankers Trust, 575
Banking Act of 1933, 539, 540, 707
Banking Committee, 212
Banking syndicate, 262
Barbell strategy, 312
Barclays Bank, 220
Barings PLC, 401
Basel Accord, 535–536, 538, 553
Basel Committee, 536, 537
Basel II Accord, 536–537
Basis, 371
Basis risk, 384, 448, 456, 457
Bearer bond, 267, 289
Bear-market CD, 511
Before-tax yield, 48, 49, 71
Beige Book, 85
BellSouth, 278
Beneficiary, 712, 713, 714
Best-efforts agreement, 690, 692

Beta, 172, 173, 174, 179, 181, 182–183, 185, 187–189, 197, 591, 604, 605, 671
Bid quote, 15, 213, 221, 222, 223, 224, 225, 251, 269, 270, 395, 461, 480, 662
Bid-ask spread, 15, 224–225, 282, 364, 662
Big Bang, 708
Binomial pricing model, 428–431, 433, 435
BIS. See Bank for International Settlements
Black Monday, 228
Black-Scholes option-pricing model, 431–435
Black-Scholes partial differential equation, 431–432
Bloody Thursday, 196, 492
BNP Paribus, 210
Board of directors, 131, 205, 209, 557–558, 581
Board of Governors, 81, 83, 84, 85, 89, 90, 97, 532
Boeing, 278
Bond Buyer Index, 374
Bond convexity, 311–312
Bond dealer, 269, 270, 276
Bond index futures, 373–375
Bond market, 117, 239, 267–290, 651, 684, 707, 728, 736
Bond mutual fund, 117, 290, 386, 389, 420, 658, 660, 668, 669, 674, 679, 683, 684
Bond price elasticity, 306–308
Bond rating, 46, 304–305
Bookbuilding, 132
Boundary conditions, 499–500
Bretton Woods era, 463
Bridge loan, 693, 695
Broker, 15, 17, 20, 139, 143, 163, 217, 223, 224, 226, 234, 269, 383, 394, 395,